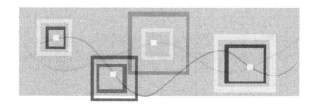

FOUNDATIONS OF BEHAVIORAL RESEARCH

FOURTH EDITION

FRED N. KERLINGER

HOWARD B. LEE
CALIFORNIA STATE UNIVERSITY, NORTHRIDGE

Harcourt College Publishers

A Harcourt Higher Learning Company

A Division of Harcourt College Publishers

Fort Worth   Philadelphia   San Diego   New York   Orlando   Austin   San Antonio
Toronto   Montreal   London   Sydney   Tokyo

To Betty, Paul, and Steven

Fred N. Kerlinger

To Dandan and the memory of Robert, Jean, Yunfen and Edward

Howard B. Lee

Publisher	Earl McPeek
Executive Editor	Carol Wada
Associate Acquisitions Editor	Lisa Hensley
Developmental Editor	Janie Pierce-Bratcher
Project Editor	Claudia Gravier
Art Director	David A. Day
Production Manager	Andrea Archer

ISBN: 0-15-507897-6
Library of Congress Catalog Card Number: 99-61157

Address for Domestic Orders
Harcourt College Publishers, 6277 Sea Harbor Drive, Orlando, FL 32887-6777
800-782-4479

Address for International Orders
International Customer Service
Harcourt, Inc., 6277 Sea Harbor Drive, Orlando, FL 32887-6777
407-345-3800
(fax) 407-345-4060
(e-mail) hbintl@harcourt.com

Address for Editorial Correspondence
Harcourt College Publishers, 301 Commerce Street, Suite 3700, Fort Worth, TX 76102

Web Site Address
http://www.harcourtcollege.com

Harcourt College Publishers will provide complimentary supplements or supplement packages to those adopters qualified under our adoption policy. Please contact your sales representative to learn how you qualify. If as an adopter or potential user you receive supplements you do not need, please return them to your sales representative or send them to: Attn: Returns Department, Troy Warehouse, 465 South Lincoln Drive, Troy, MO 63379.

Printed in the United States of America

1 2 3 4 5 6 7 8 751 9 8 7 6 5 4
Harcourt College Publishers

Preface to the Third Edition

Some activities command more interest, devotion, and enthusiasm than do others. So it seems to be with science and with art. Why this is so is an interesting and significant psychological question to which there is no unequivocal answer. All that seems to be clear is that once we become immersed in scientific research or artistic expression we devote most of our thoughts, energies, and emotions to these activities. It seems a far cry from science to art. But in one respect at least they are similar: we make passionate commitments to them.[1]

This is a book on scientific behavioral research. Above everything else, it aims to convey the exciting quality of research in general, and in the behavioral sciences and education in particular. A large portion of the book is focused on abstract conceptual and technical matters, but behind the discussion is the conviction that research is a deeply absorbing and vitally interesting business.

It may seem strange in a book on research that I talk about interest, enthusiasm, and passionate commitment. Shouldn't we be objective? Shouldn't we develop a hardheaded attitude toward psychological, sociological, and educational phenomena? Yes, of course. But more important is somehow to catch the essential quality of the excitement of discovery that comes from research well done. Then the difficulties and frustrations of the research enterprise, while they never vanish, are much less significant. What I am trying to say is that strong subjective involvement is a powerful motivator for acquiring an objective approach to the study of phenomena. It is doubtful that any significant work is ever done without great personal involvement. It is doubtful that students can learn much about science, research design, and research methods without considerable personal involvement. Thus I would encourage students to discuss, argue, debate, and even fight about research. Take a stand. Be opinionated. Later try to soften the opinionation into intelligent conviction and controlled emotional commitment.

The writing of this book has been strongly influenced by the book's major purpose: to help students understand the fundamental nature of the scientific approach to problem solution. Technical and methodological problems have been considered at length. One cannot understand any complex human activity, especially scientific research activity, without some technological and methodological competence. But technical competence is empty without an understanding of the basic intent and nature of scientific research: the controlled and objective study of the relations among phenomena. All else is subordinate to this. Thus the book, as its name indicates, strongly emphasizes the *fundamentals* or *foundations* of behavioral research.

To accomplish the major purpose indicated above, the book has four distinctive general features. First, it is a treatise on scientific research; it is limited to what is generally accepted as the scientific approach. It does not discuss historical research, legal research, library research, philosophical inquiry, and so on.[2] It emphasizes, in short, understanding scientific research problem solutions.

---

[1]The term "passionate commitment" is Polanyi's. M. Polanyi, *Personal Knowledge*. Chicago: University of Chicago Press, 1958.
[2]Historical inquiry and methodological research are briefly discussed in Appendix A.

Second, the student is led to grasp the intimate and often difficult relations between a research problem and the design and methodology of its solution. While methodological problems are treated at length, the book is not a "methods" book. Stress is always on the research problem, the design of research, and relation between the two. The student is encouraged to think relationally and structurally.

Third, the content of much of the book is tied together with the notions of set, relation, and variance. These ideas, together with those of probability theory, statistics, and measurement, are used to integrate the diverse content of research activity into a unified and coherent whole.

Fourth, a good bit of the book's discussion is slanted toward psychological, sociological, and educational research problems. It seemed to me that a foundation research book was needed in education. But there is little scientific research in education that is uniquely educational; for the most part it is behavioral research, research basically psychological and sociological in nature. In sum, while this is a book on the intellectual and technical foundations of scientific behavioral research in general, it emphasizes psychological, sociological, and educational problems and examples, while not ignoring other behavioral disciplines.

.   .   .

Some word of the book's level and audience is in order. The book is a behavioral science text intended for graduated students who have elementary backgrounds in psychology, statistics, and measurement. While many terms and ideas used in educational and psychological problems are defined, some familiarity with terms like intelligence, aptitude, socioeconomics status, authoritarianism, and the like is assumed. All technical terms are defined, though many students will probably need instructor help with some of them.

As usual, statistical terms and ideas may hinder the student's progress. While it is possible to study the book and master its contents without statistical background, the student who has had an elementary statistics course will probably find the going easier. Suggestions are given in Part Four to help the student conquer certain statistical difficulties.

Foundations of Behavioral Research can be used in courses of either one or two semesters. When used in one-semester courses, it should be selectively studied. Although individual instructors will, of course, make their own selection decisions, the following parts and chapters are suggested for a single-semester course: Parts 1 and 2 and Chapters 8–12, 17, 19, 23, and 25–29. (Chapters 25, 26, and 27 can also be omitted.) For a two-semester course, all or most of the chapters may well be studied. Whatever selection is made, it should be borne in mind that later discussions often presuppose understanding of earlier discussions.

To aid students study and understanding and to help surmount some of the inherent difficulties of the subject, several devices have been used. One, many topics have been discussed at length. If a choice had to be made between repetition and possible lack of student understanding, material was repeated, though in different words with different examples. Two, many examples from actual research as well as many hypothetical examples have been used. The student who reads the book through will have been exposed to a large number and a wide variety of problems, hypotheses, designs, and data and to many actual research studies in the social sciences and education.

Three, an important feature of the book is the frequent use of simple numerical examples in which the numbers are only those between 0 and 9. The fundamental ideas of statistics, measurement, and design can be conveyed as well with small numbers as with large numbers, without the additional burden of tedious arithmetic computations. It is suggested that the reader work through each example at least once. Intelligent handling of data is indispensable to understanding research design and methodology.

Four, most chapters have study suggestions that include readings as well as problems designed to help integrate and consolidate the material presented in the chapters. Many of them arose from practical use with graduated students. Answers to most of the computational problems have been given immediately after the problems. An answer, if checked against a supplied answer and found to be correct, reassures students about computational details. They should not have to waste time wondering about the right answers. Understanding the procedures is what is important and not the calculations as such.

· · ·

All books are cooperative enterprises. Though one person may undertake the actual writing, he is dependent on many others for ideas, criticism, and support. Among the many persons who contributed to this book, I am most indebted to those mentioned below. I here express my sincere thanks to them.

Three individuals read the entire original manuscript of the first edition and made many valuable and constructive suggestions for improvement: Professors T. Newcomb, D. Harris, and J. Nunnally. Professor Newcomb also furnished the early prodding and encouragement needed to get the book going. Professor Harris contributed from his wide research experience insights whose worth cannot be weighed. The late Professor Nunnally's trenchant and penetrating analysis was invaluable, especially with a number of difficult technical matters.

I am grateful to the many teachers and students who have corresponded with me about aspects of the book (especially the errors). All suggested corrections and changes have been given careful consideration. I owe a large debt in the writing of both revisions to my colleague and friend, Professor E. Pedhazur, and to Professor E. Page. They have ferreted out weaknesses and made many suggestions for improvement. I also want to express my gratitude to my former colleagues of the Psychology Laboratory, University of Amsterdam, who pointed out errors and ambiguities in the text, some of which I have been able to correct.

· · ·

The price a family pays for an author's book is high. Its members put up with his obsession and his unpredictable writing ups and downs. I express my gratitude and indebtedness to my wife and sons by dedication the book to them. I must say more than this, however. My wife has had to cope with two overseas moves and one transcontinental move, two retirements, and innumerable logistical and temperamental problems. To express thanks and gratitude in the face of this extraordinary example of coping seems pale and inadequate. Nevertheless, I here express both.

Fred N. Kerlinger
Eugene, Oregon
June 1985

Preface to the Fourth Edition

I first read *Foundations of Behavioral Research* when I was a first year graduate student, and I was impressed with the lucid explanations of topics that I had previously classified as complex. It later served as an invaluable reference book, one of those books which I would always consult first when encountering a logical or design problem.

Professor Kerlinger's death raised the possibility that his significant contributions to the field might be forgotten and this valuable tool allowed to go out of print. I am grateful to Kerlinger's estate and the publisher to have the opportunity to revise such a fine text. Without knowing what Kerlinger would have written for this edition, I hope that my efforts have enhanced his classic work and will inspire future generations of students to do research properly. Following this prologue is Kerlinger's preface from the third edition; he so well described his intent and purpose for this text, that I felt it only appropriate that his words and rationale remain.

In keeping with Kerlinger's original intent, the fourth edition was written to continue the emphasis on the *fundamentals* or *foundations* of research. As a comprehensive text in research methodology, *Foundations of Behavioral Research* would be applicable for use in advanced undergraduate and first year graduate courses in psychology, education, sociology, political science, and health sciences. It is intended as a broad treatment of research problems that arise in these areas.

Major changes to this edition include the following: (a) the development of an instructor's manual which contains essay and multiple choice questions; (b) the replacement of approximately 75% of the older references with newer studies; (c) the addition of several pedagogical features, such as a brief outline at the beginning of each chapter and a chapter summary at the end of each chapter; and (d) the addition of current topics of importance to today's researchers, with some regrettable but necessary elimination of other topics.

The most significant advancement in research methodology since the publication of the third edition is the widespread availability of computer technology. In the fourth edition, this availability is reflected in the treatment of computer applications within individual chapters, as well as in the addition of several topics made possible by these advances. In the previous edition, Kerlinger discussed the use of computers in behavioral and social science research in an appendix. That appendix has been removed in favor of integrating computer applications into the appropriate chapters, using SPSS for most examples and more specialized tools (EQS and ILOG) where necessary.

Several new chapters and appendices have been included in the fourth edition, including the following:

- A new chapter (Chapter 17) focuses on ethical issues in research.
- Chapter 22 (Quasi-Experimental Design) is an expansion and update of Kerlinger's original material on "compromise research designs."
- Appendix A provides a useful introduction to APA style in writing research reports.
- Appendix B consists of common statistical tables, making the book more complete as a reference tool.

In addition to the new chapters and appendices, the fourth edition also boasts a large number of new topics and revisions:

- Chapter 7 (Probability) includes a discussion of Bayes' Theorem and Keynes' probability notion.
- Chapter 8 (Sampling and Randomness) now includes discussion of alternative sampling procedures.
- Chapter 10 (The Analysis of Frequencies) addresses the use of the current term "crosstabs," as well as information about computing odds ratios.
- Chapter 12 (Testing Hypotheses and the Standard Error) introduces the five steps of hypothesis testing and added variation of computer approach to the Monte Carlo method.
- Chapter 15 (Analysis of Variance: Correlated Groups) classifies all ANOVA designs into five major types of models.
- Chapter 20 (General Designs of Research) presents material on matching pairs of participants.
- Chapters 20 and 21 were combined into one chapter entitled "Research Design Applications: Randomized Groups and Correlated Groups."
- Chapter 24 (Laboratory Experiments, Field Experiments, and Field Studies) notes the addition of information about qualitative research.
- Chapter 25 (Survey Research) provides additional information on meta-analysis.
- Chapters 26–28 (Foundations of Measurement, Reliability, Validity) includes the addition of discussions on specific reliability coefficients such as the Kuder-Richardson and coefficient alpha and examines Taylor-Russell tables in the discussion of validity issues.
- Chapter 29 (Interviews and Interview Schedules) addresses focus groups as a method of interviewing.
- Chapter 33 (Multiple Regression, Analysis of Variance, and Other Multivariate Methods) provides a more detailed treatment of discriminant function analysis, logistic regression, ridge regression and canonical correlation.
- Chapter 34 (Factor Analysis) includes new material on confirmatory factor analysis.
- Chapter 35 (Analysis of Covariance Structures) sees the substitution of EQS system for LISREL system for studying covariance structures.

With so much new material, it was necessary to abridge or eliminate other information where appropriate. The former chapters 31 and 33 (covering projective methods, content analysis, and q-methodology) were eliminated, and presentation of several other topics was streamlined.

Acknowledgments

First, I would like to extend my appreciation to the following reviewers whose suggestions guided my writing of this text: Kay Coleman, Boston University; Andrew L. Comrey, University of California, Los Angeles;. Joan E. Haase, University of Arizona; Robert Harrison, Boston University; Timothy Z. Keith, Alfred University; Robert Leve, University of

Harford; J. Robert Newman, California State University, Long Beach; Virginia Norris, South Dakota State University; Steven Philipp, University of West Florida; Janice Podolski, Rush University; James Stiff, University of Kansas; Ellen Susman, Metropolitan State College of Denver; Elizabeth M. Timberlake, The Catholic University of America; Richard Williams, University of Miami; and Shapard Wolf, Arizona State University.

I also wish to thank the many people who have been a tremendous influence on me. It is their influence on me that enabled me to make my contribution to this book: Dr. Andrew L. Comrey at UCLA, Morton P. Friedman, James E. Bruno, Peter M. Bentler, Robert E. Dear, William F. Prokasy, James B. MacQueen, Augusto Britton-delRio, Robert L. Docter, and Rodney Skager (my most influential professors during my graduate school days). Dr. Comrey was and is still my mentor and friend. I relied heavily on his teachings and philosophy when writing my contributions to this book. I am also indebted to my friends, Steven G. Little, Hofstra University; Daniel H. Tingstrom, University of Southern Mississippi; Frank M. Gresham, University of California, Riverside; Mary Lynn Brecht, UCLA; Yuri and Nellie Koral, ANNY; and Stanley Sue, University of California at Davis. I thank Dr. Charles W. Simon for introducing to me the notion of megafactor experimental designs—I am sorry I could not have devoted more space in this volume to his ideas. I thank my former students Maria L. Cook, Dorothy Scattone, Joyce Nakamoto and Karen Siegel for their contributions to this book. I also thank John Mills, John Priebe, Elaine Nagano, Michael Posen, Simone Berman and Dr. Ward Jenssen for educating me on marketing research. Thanks also go out to Dr. Alan Norton, Dr. Abdul Abukurah and Ms. Paula Phipps for saving my vision and health. I apologize for not mentioning by name all of the other fine students who have worked with me. Several colleagues at the California State University, Northridge (Edward E. Sampson, Richard Smith, Roy Griffiths, Irv Streimer, Leta Chow and Ronald Doctor) and elsewhere (Mehrdad Jalalighjar, Rahim A. Munshi, Richard Gorsuch, Timothy Keith, Susan Cochran, Vickie Mays, Wendell Jeffreys and Eric Holman) stimulated my thinking about many issues and topics. In addition, the book could not have been written without the approval of Professor Kerlinger's widow, Betty, who allowed me to update and make changes to her husband's classic work in research methods. I also want to acknowledge and thank those unsung people that work at Harcourt College Publishers in Fort Worth, TX for making this fourth edition a reality: Dr. Lisa Hensley, Janie Pierce-Bratcher, Claudia Gravier, Andrea Archer, and David Day. A special note of appreciation goes to Harcourt Representative Bill Brisick, who initially approached me about revising this book. I especially thank my wife, Dandan and her mother, Yunfen, father, Ming Dong, and brothers, Bin, Cheng and Bo for their love, encouragement and support. I also want to thank my brother, Steven for putting up with me all these years and his dog LingLing for pleasant distractions.

Thanks to the Personnel Committee in the College of Social and Behavioral Sciences at CSUN and the Department Chairperson, Joyce Brotsky for granting me a one-semester sabbatical leave during the revision of this book.

Howard B. Lee
Northridge, California
May 1999

Contents

PART ONE
THE LANGUAGE AND APPROACH OF SCIENCE

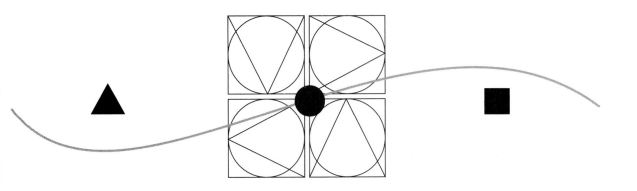

Chapter 1
SCIENCE AND THE SCIENTIFIC APPROACH

Chapter 2
PROBLEMS AND HYPOTHESES

Chapter 3
CONSTRUCTS, VARIABLES, AND DEFINITIONS

1

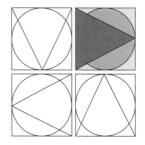

SCIENCE AND
THE SCIENTIFIC APPROACH

To understand any complex human activity one must grasp the language and approach of the individuals who pursue it. So it is with understanding science and scientific research. One must know and understand, at least in part, scientific language and the scientific approach to problem-solving.

One of the most confusing things to the student of science is the special way scientists use ordinary words and, to complicate matters, they even invent new words. There are good reasons for this specialized use of language, which will become evident later. For now, suffice it to say that we must understand and learn the language of social scientists. When investigators tell us about their independent and dependent variables, we must know what they mean. When they tell us that they have randomized their experimental procedures, we must not only know what they mean— we must understand why they do as they do.

Similarly, the scientist's approach to problems must be clearly understood. It is not so much that this approach is different from the layperson's. It *is* different, of course, but it is neither strange nor esoteric. This is quite the contrary. When understood, it will seem natural and almost inevitable what the scientist does. Indeed, we will probably wonder why much more human thinking and problem-solving are not consciously structured along such lines.

The purpose of chapters 1 and 2 of this book is to help the student learn and understand the language and approach of science and research. In these chapters many of the basic constructs of the social, behavioral, and educational scientist will be studied. In some cases it will not be possible to give complete and satisfactory definitions due to lack of background at this early point in the reader's development. In such cases an attempt will be made to formulate and use reasonably accurate first approximations and to progress to more satisfactory definitions. Let us begin our study by considering how the scientist approaches problems and how this approach differs from what might be called a common-sense approach.

Science and Common Sense

Whitehead (1911/1992, p. 157) at the beginning of the twentieth century pointed out that in creative thought common sense is a poor master. "Its sole criterion for judgment is that the new ideas shall look like the old ones." This is well said. Common sense may often be a bad master for the evaluation of knowledge. But how are science and common sense alike and how are they different? From one viewpoint, science and common sense are alike. This view would say that science is a systematic and controlled extension of common sense. James Bryant Conant (1951) states that common sense is a series of concepts and conceptual schemes[1] satisfactory for the practical uses of humanity. However, these concepts and conceptual schemes may be seriously misleading in modern science—and particularly in psychology and education. To many educators in the 1800s, it was common sense to use punishment as a basic tool of pedagogy. However, in the mid-1900s evidence emerged to show that this older commonsense view of motivation may be quite erroneous. Reward appears to be more effective than punishment in aiding learning. However, recent findings suggest that different forms of punishment are useful in classroom learning (Marlow, et al., 1997; Tingstrom, et al., 1997). Science and common sense differ sharply in five ways. These disagreements revolve around the words *systematic* and *controlled*.

---

[1] A *concept* is a word that expresses an abstraction formed by generalization from particulars. "Aggression" is a concept, an abstraction that expresses a number of particular actions having the similar characteristic of harming people or objects. A *conceptual scheme* is a set of concepts interrelated by hypothetical and theoretical propositions. A *construct* is a concept with the additional meaning of having been created or appropriated for special scientific purposes. "Mass," "energy," "hostility," "introversion," and "achievement" are constructs. They might more accurately be called "constructed types" or "constructed classes"; classes or sets of objects or events bound together by the possession of common characteristics defined by the scientist. The term "variable" will be defined in a later chapter. For now let it represent a symbol or name of a characteristic that takes on different numerical values.

First, the uses of conceptual schemes and theoretical structures are strikingly different. The common person may use "theories" and concepts, but usually does so in a loose fashion. This person often blandly accepts fanciful explanations of natural and human phenomena. An illness, for instance, may be thought to be a punishment for sinfulness (Klonoff & Landrine, 1994). Jolliness is due to being overweight. Scientists, on the other hand, systematically build theoretical structures, test them for internal consistency, and put aspects of them to empirical test. Further, they realize that the concepts they use are man-made terms that may or may not exhibit a close relationship to reality.

Second, scientists systematically and empirically test their theories and hypotheses. Non-scientists test "hypotheses," too, but they test them in a selective fashion. They often "select" evidence simply because it is consistent with the hypotheses. Take the stereotype: Asians are science and math oriented. If people believe this, they can easily "verify" their beliefs by noting that many Asians are engineers and scientists (see Tang, 1993). Exceptions to the stereotype are not perceived: the non-science Asian or the mathematically challenged Asian. Sophisticated social and behavioral scientists knowing this "selection tendency" to be a common psychological phenomenon, carefully guard their research against their own preconceptions and predilections and against selective support of hypotheses. For one thing, they are not content with armchair or fiat exploration of relations; they must test the relations in the laboratory or in the field. They are not content, for example, with the presumed relationships between methods of teaching and achievement, between intelligence and creativity, between values and administrative decisions. They insist on systematic, controlled, and empirical testing of these relations.

A third difference lies in the notion of control. In scientific research, control means several things. For the present, let it mean that the scientist tries to systematically rule out variables that are possible "causes" of the effects under study other than the variables hypothesized to be the "causes." Laypeople seldom bother to control their explanations of observed phenomena systematically. They ordinarily make little effort to control extraneous sources of influence. They tend to accept those explanations that are in accord with their preconceptions and biases. If they believe that slum conditions produce delinquency, they tend to disregard delinquency in nonslum neighborhoods. The scientist, on the other hand, seeks out and "controls" delinquency incidence in different kinds of neighborhoods. The difference, of course, is profound.

Another difference between science and common sense is perhaps not so defined. It was said earlier that the scientist is constantly preoccupied with relationships among phenomena. The layperson also does this by using common sense for explanations of phenomena. But the scientist consciously and systematically pursues relationships. The layperson's preoccupation with relationships is loose, unsystematic, and uncontrolled. The layperson often seizes, for example, on the fortuitous occurrence of two phenomena and immediately links them indissolubly as cause and effect.

Take the relation tested in the classic study done many years ago by Hurlock (1925). In more recent terminology, this relation may be expressed: Positive reinforcement (reward) produces greater increments of learning than does punishment. The relation is between reinforcement (or reward and punishment) and learning.

Educators and parents of the nineteenth century often assumed that punishment was the more effective agent in learning. Educators and parents of the present often assume that positive reinforcement (reward) is more effective. Both may say that their viewpoint is "only common sense." It is obvious, they may say, that if you reward (or punish) a child, he or she will learn better. The scientist, on the other hand, while personally espousing one or the other or neither of these viewpoints, would probably insist on systematic and controlled testing of both (and other) relationships, as Hurlock did. Using the scientific method, Hurlock found incentive to be substantially related to arithmetic achievement. The group receiving praise scored higher than the reproofed or ignored groups.

A final difference between common sense and science lies in different explanations of observed phenomena. The scientist, when attempting to explain the relations among observed phenomena, carefully rules out what have been called "metaphysical explanations." A metaphysical explanation is simply a proposition that cannot be tested. To say, for example, that people are poor and starving because God wills it, or that it is wrong to be authoritarian, is to talk metaphysically.

None of these propositions can be tested; thus they are metaphysical. As such, science is not concerned with them. This does not mean that scientists would necessarily spurn such statements, say they are not true, or claim they are meaningless. It simply means that *as scientists* they are not concerned with them. In short, science is concerned with things that can be publicly observed and tested. If propositions or questions do not contain implications for such public observation and testing, they are not scientific propositions or questions.

Four Methods of Knowing

Charles Sanders Peirce as reported in Buchler (1955) said that there are four general ways of knowing or, as he put it, fixing belief. In the ensuing discussion, the authors are taking some liberties with Peirce's original formulation in an attempt to clarify the ideas and to make them more germane to the present discussion. The first is the *method of tenacity*. Here people hold firmly to the truth, the truth that they know to be true because they hold firmly to it, because they have always known it to be true. Frequent repetition of such "truths" seems to enhance their validity. People often cling to their beliefs in the face of clearly conflicting facts. And they will also infer "new" knowledge from propositions that may be false.

A second method of knowing or fixing belief is the *method of authority*. This is the method of established belief. If the Bible says it, it is so. If a noted physicist says there is a God, it is so. If an idea has the weight of tradition and public sanction behind it, it is so. As Peirce points out, this method is superior to the method of tenacity because human progress, although slow, can be achieved using this method. Actually, life could not go on without the method of authority. Dawes (1994) states that as individuals, we cannot know everything. We accept the authority of the U.S. Food and Drug Administration in determining that what we eat and drink is safe. Dawes states that the completely open mind that questions all authority does not exist. We must take a large body of facts and information on the basis of authority. Thus, it should not be concluded that the method of authority is unsound; it is unsound only under certain circumstances.

The *a priori method* is the third way of knowing or fixing belief. Graziano and Raulin (1993) call it the *method of intuition*. It rests its case for superiority on the assumption that the propositions accepted by the "a priorist" are self-evident. Note that a priori propositions "agree with reason" and not necessarily with experience. The idea seems to be that people, through free communication and intercourse, can reach the truth because their natural inclinations tend toward truth. The difficulty with this position lies in the expression "agree with reason." Whose reason? Suppose two honest and well-meaning individuals, using rational processes, reach different conclusions. Who is right? Is it a matter of taste, as Peirce puts it? If something is self-evident to many people—for instance, that learning difficult subjects trains the mind and builds moral character, that American education is inferior to Asian and European education—does this mean it is so? According to the a priori method, it does—it just "stands to reason."

The fourth method is the *method of science*. Peirce says:

> To satisfy our doubts, . . . therefore, it is necessary that a method should be found by which our beliefs may be determined by nothing human, but by some external permanency—by something upon which our thinking has no effect. . . . The method must be such that the ultimate conclusion of every man shall be the same. Such is the method of science. Its fundamental hypothesis . . . is this: "There are real things, whose characters are entirely independent of our opinions about them . . ." (Buchler, 1955, p. 18).

The scientific approach has a characteristic that no other method of attaining knowledge has: self-correction. There are built-in checks all along the way to scientific knowledge. These checks are so conceived and used that they control and verify scientific activities and conclusions to the end of attaining dependable knowledge. Even if a hypothesis seems to be supported in an experiment, the scientist will test alternative plausible hypotheses that, if also supported, may cast doubt on the first hypothesis. Scientists do not accept statements as true, even though evidence may at first look promising. They insist on testing them. They also insist that any testing procedure be open to *public* scrutiny. One interpretation of scientific method is that there is no one specific scientific method. Rather, there are a number of methods that scientists can and do use, but it probably can be said that there is one scientific approach.

As Peirce says, the checks used in scientific research are anchored as much as possible in reality lying outside the scientist's personal beliefs, perceptions, biases, values, attitudes, and emotions. Perhaps the best single word to express this is *objectivity*. Objectivity is agreement among "expert" judges on what is observed or what is to be done or has been done in research (see Kerlinger, 1979 for a discussion of objectivity, its meaning and its controversial character). According to Sampson (1991, p. 12) objectivity "refers to those statements about the world that we currently can justify and defend using the standards of argument and proof employed within the community to which we belong—for example, the community of scientists." But, as we shall see later, the scientific approach involves more than both of these statements. The point is that more dependable knowledge is attained because science ultimately appeals to evidence: propositions are subjected to empirical testing. An objection may be raised: Theory, which scientists use and exalt, comes from people, the scientists themselves. But, as Polanyi (1958/1974, p. 4) points out, "A theory is something other than myself." Thus a theory helps the scientist to attain greater objectivity. In short, scientists systematically and consciously use the self-corrective aspect of the scientific approach.

Science and Its Functions

What is science? This question is not easy to answer. Indeed, no definition of science will be directly attempted. We shall instead talk about notions and views of science and then try to explain the functions of science.

Science is a misunderstood word. There seem to be three popular stereotypes that impede understanding of scientific activity. One is the white coat–stethoscope–laboratory stereotype. Scientists are perceived as individuals who work with facts in laboratories. They use complicated equipment, do innumerable experiments, and pile up facts for the ultimate purpose of improving the lot of humanity. Thus, while somewhat unimaginative grubbers after facts, they are redeemed by noble motives. You can believe them when, for example, they tell you that such-and-such toothpaste is good for you or that you, should not smoke cigarettes.

The second stereotype of scientists is that they are brilliant individuals who think, spin complex theories, and spend their time in ivory towers aloof from the world and its problems. They are impractical theorists, even though their thinking and theories occasionally lead to results of practical significance, like atomic energy.

The third stereotype erroneously equates science with engineering and technology: the building of bridges, the improvement of automobiles and missiles, the automation of industry, the invention of teaching machines. The scientist's job, in this stereotype, is to work at the improvement of inventions and artifacts. The scientist is perceived to be some sort of highly skilled engineer working to make life smooth and efficient.

These stereotypical notions impede student understanding of science, the activities and thinking of the scientist, and scientific research in general. In short, they make the student's task harder than it would otherwise be. Thus they should be cleared away to make room for more adequate notions.

There are two broad views of science: the static and the dynamic. According to Conant (1951, pp. 23–27) the *static view,* the view that seems to influence most laypeople and students, is that science is an activity that contributes systematized information to the world. The scientist's job is to discover new facts and to add them to the already existing body of information. Science is even conceived to be a body of facts. In this view, science is also a way of explaining observed phenomena. The emphasis, then, is on the *present state of knowledge* and *adding to it* and on the present set of laws, theories, hypotheses, and principles.

The *dynamic view*, on the other hand, regards science more as an activity, what scientists do. The present state of knowledge is important, of course. But it is important mainly because it is a base for further scientific theory and research. This has been called a *heuristic view*. The word *heuristic*, meaning "serving to discover or reveal," now has the connotation of self-discovery. A heuristic method of teaching, for instance, emphasizes students' discovering things for themselves. The heuristic view in science emphasizes theory and interconnected conceptual schemata that are fruitful for further research. A heuristic emphasis is a discovery emphasis.

It is the heuristic aspect of science that distinguishes it in good part from engineering and technology. On the basis of a heuristic hunch, the scientist takes a risky leap. As Polanyi (1958/1974, p. 123) says, "It is the plunge by which we gain a foothold at another shore of reality. On such plunges the scientist has to stake bit by bit his entire professional life." Michel (1991, p. 23) adds "anyone who fears being mistaken and for this reason studies a 'safe' or 'certain' scientific method, should never enter upon any scientific enquiry." Heuristic may also be called problem-solving, but the emphasis is on imaginative and not routine problem-solving. The heuristic view in science stresses problem-solving rather than facts and bodies of information. Alleged established facts and bodies of information are important to the heuristic scientist because they help lead to further theory, further discovery, and further investigation.

Still avoiding a direct definition of science—but certainly implying one—we now look at the function of science. Here we find two distinct views. The practical person, generally the non-scientist, thinks of science as a discipline or activity aimed at improving things, at making progress. Some scientists, too, take this position. The function of science, in this view is to make discoveries, to learn facts, to advance knowledge in order to improve things. Branches of science that are clearly of this genre receive wide and strong support. Witness the continuing generous support of medical and meteorological research. The criteria of practicality and "payoff" are preeminent in this view, especially in educational research (see Kerlinger, 1977; Bruno, 1972).

A very different view of the function of science is well expressed by Braithwaite (1953/1996, p. 1):

> The function of science . . . is to establish general laws covering the behaviors of the empirical events or objects with which the science in question is concerned, and thereby to enable us to connect together our knowledge of the separately known events, and to make reliable predictions of events as yet unknown.

The connection between this view of the function of science and the dynamic–heuristic view discussed earlier is obvious, except that an important element is added: the establishment of general laws—or theory, if you will. If we are to understand modern behavioral research and its strengths and weaknesses, we must

▣ TABLE 1.1 *Sampson's Two Views of the Science of Social Psychology*

	Traditional (Quantitative)	Nontraditional (Sociohistorical) (Qualitative)
Primary Goal	Describing the reality of human social interactions and functions.	Describing the variety of human social experience and activity through social and historical information and the roles they play in human life.
Philosophical Position	Reality can be discovered independently by nonpositioned observers. Reality can be grasped without occupying any particular biasing standpoint.	Reality can be discovered only from some standpoint; thus, the observer is always a positioned observer.
Metaphoric Statement	Science can be perceived to be like a mirror. It is designed to reflect things as they really are.	Science is perceived to be a storyteller. It gives different or personal accounts and versions of reality.
Methodological Considerations	Methods created and used to control or eliminate factors that would weaken the researcher's ability to discover the true shape of reality.	The researcher's understanding of reality is shaped by broad social and historical factors. The methods can yield a richer and deeper understanding of reality based on encountering the diverse accounts used by people in making sense of their lives.

explore the elements of Braithwaite's statement. We do so by considering the aims of science, scientific explanation, and the role and importance of theory.

Sampson (1991) discusses two opposing views of science. There is the conventional or traditional perspective and then there is the sociohistorical perspective. The conventional view perceives science as a mirror of nature or a windowpane of clear glass that presents nature without bias or distortion. The goal here is to describe with the highest degree of accuracy what the world really looks like. Here Sampson states that science is an objective referee. Its job is to "resolve disagreements and distinguish what is true and correct from what is not." When the conventional view of science is unable to resolve the dispute, it only means that there is insufficient data or information to do so. Conventionalists, however, feel it is only a matter of time before the truth is apparent.

The sociohistorical view sees science as a story. The scientists are storytellers. Here the idea is that reality can only be discovered by the stories that can be told about it. Here, this approach is unlike the traditional–conventional view in that there is no neutral arbitrator. Every story will be flavored by the storyteller's orientation. As a result there is no single true story. The author's interpretation of Sampson's table comparing these two is shown in Table 1.1.

Even though Sampson gives these two views of science in light of social psychology, his presentation has applicability in all areas of the behavioral sciences.

The Aims of Science, Scientific Explanation, and Theory

The basic aim of science is theory. Perhaps less cryptically, the basic aim of science is to explain natural phenomena. Such explanations are called "theories." Instead of trying to explain each and every separate behavior of children, the scientific psychologist seeks general explanations that encompass and link together many differing behaviors. Rather than try to explain children's methods of solving arithmetic problems, for example, the scientist seeks general explanations of all kinds of problem-solving. It might be called a general theory of problem-solving.

This discussion of the basic aim of science as theory may seem strange to the student who has probably been inculcated with the notion that human activities have to pay off in practical ways. If we said that the aim of science is the betterment of humanity, most readers would quickly read the words and accept them. But the *basic* aim of science is *not* the betterment of humanity. It is theory. Unfortunately, this sweeping and really complex statement is not easily understood. Still, we must try to grasp it because it is important. More on this point is given in Chapter 16 of Kerlinger (1979).

Other aims of science that have been stated are: explanation, understanding, prediction, and control. If we accept theory as the ultimate aim of science, however, explanation and understanding become subaims of the ultimate aim. This is because of the definition and nature of theory: *A theory is a set of interrelated constructs (concepts), definitions, and propositions that present a systematic view of phenomena by specifying relations among variables, with the purpose of explaining and predicting the phenomena.*

This definition says three things: (1) a theory is a set of propositions consisting of defined and interrelated constructs, (2) a theory sets out the interrelations among a set of variables (constructs), and in so doing, presents a systematic view of the phenomena described by the variables, and (3) a theory explains phenomena; it does so by specifying which variables are related to which variables and how they are related, thus enabling the researcher to predict from certain variables to certain other variables. One might, for example, have a theory of school failure. One's variables might be intelligence, verbal and numerical aptitudes, anxiety, social class membership, nutrition, and achievement motivation. The phenomenon to be explained, of course, is school failure or, perhaps more accurately, school achievement. That is, school failure could be perceived as being at one end of the school achievement continuum with school success being at the other end. School failure is explained by specified relations between each of the seven variables and school failure, or by combinations of the seven variables and school failure. The scientist, successfully using this set of constructs, then "understands" school failure. He or she is able to "explain" and, to some extent at least, "predict" it.

It is obvious that explanation and prediction can be subsumed under theory. The very nature of a theory lies in its explanation of observed phenomena. Take reinforcement theory, for example. A simple proposition flowing from this theory is: If a response is rewarded (reinforced) when it occurs, it will tend to be repeated. The psychological scientist who first formulated some such proposition did so as an explanation of the observed repetitious occurrences of responses. Why did they occur and reoccur with dependable regularity? Because they were rewarded. Although this is an explanation, it may not be a satisfactory explanation to many people. Someone else may ask why reward increases the likelihood of a response's occurrence. A full-blown theory would have the explanation. Today, however, there is no really satisfactory answer. All we can say is that, with a high degree of probability, the reinforcement of a response makes the response more likely to occur and reoccur (see Nisbett & Ross, 1980). In other words, the propositions of a theory, the statements of relations, constitute the explanation, as far as that theory is concerned, of observed natural phenomena.

On prediction and control, it can be said that scientists do not really have to be concerned with explanation and understanding. Only prediction and control are necessary. Proponents of this point of view may say that the adequacy of a theory is its predictive power. If by using the theory we are able to predict successfully, then the theory is confirmed and this is enough. We need not necessarily look for further underlying explanations. Since we can predict reliably, we can control because control is deducible from prediction.

The prediction view of science has validity. But as far as this book is concerned, prediction is considered to be an aspect of theory. By its very nature, a theory predicts; that is, when from the primitive propositions of a theory we deduce more complex ones, we are in essence "predicting." When we explain observed phenomena, we are always stating a relation between, say, class A and class B. Scientific explanation inheres in specifying the relations between one class of empirical events and another, under certain conditions. We say: If A, then B, A and B referring to classes of objects or events.[2] But this is prediction, prediction from A to B. Thus a theoretical explanation implies prediction. And we come back to the idea that theory is the ultimate aim of science. All else flows from theory.

---

[2] Statements of the form "If p, then q," called *conditional statements* in logic, are the core of scientific inquiry. They and the concepts or variables that go into them are the central ingredient of theories. The logical foundation of scientific inquiry that underlies much of the reasoning in this book is outlined in Kerlinger (1977).

There is no intention here to discredit or denigrate research that is not specifically and consciously theory-oriented. Much valuable social scientific and educational research is preoccupied with the shorter-range goal of finding specific relations; that is, merely to discover a relation is part of science. The ultimately most usable and satisfying relations, however, are those that are the most generalized, those that are tied to other relations in a theory.

The notion of generality is important. Theories, because they are general, apply to many phenomena and to many people in many places. A specific relation, of course, is less widely applicable. If, for example, one finds that test anxiety is related to test performance. This finding, though interesting and important, is less widely applicable and less understood than finding a relation in a network of interrelated variables that are parts of a theory. Modest, limited, and specific research aims, then, are good. Theoretical research aims are better because, among other reasons, they are more general and can be applied to a wide range of situations. Additionally, when both a simple and a complex theory exist and both account for the facts equally well, the simple explanation is preferred (Occam's Razor). Hence, in the discussion of generalizability, a good theory is also parsimonious. However, a number of incorrect theories concerning mental illness persist because of this parsimony feature. Some still believe that individuals are possessed with demons. Such an explanation is simple when compared to psychological and/or medical explanations.

Theories are tentative explanations. Each theory is evaluated empirically to determine how well it predicts new findings. Theories can be used to guide a research plan by generating testable hypotheses and to organize facts obtained from the testing of these hypotheses. A good theory is one that cannot fit all observations. One should be able to find an occurrence that would contradict it. Blondlot's theory of N-rays is an example of a poor theory. Blondlot claimed that all matter emitted N-rays (Weber, 1973). Although N-rays were later demonstrated to be nonexistent, Barber (1976) reported that nearly 100 papers were published in a single year on N-rays in France. Blondlot even developed elaborate equipment for the viewing of N-rays. Scientists claiming they saw N-rays only added support to Blondlot's theory and findings. However, when a person did not see N-rays, Blondlot claimed that the person's eyes were not sensitive enough or the person did not set up the instrument correctly. No possible outcome was taken as evidence against the theory. In more recent times, another faulty theory that took over 75 years to debunk concerned the origin of peptic ulcers. In 1910 Schwartz (as reported in Blaser, 1996) claimed that he had firmly established the cause of ulcers. He stated that peptic ulcers were due to stomach acids. In the years that followed, medical researchers devoted their time and energies toward treating ulcers by developing medications to either neutralize or block the acids. These treatments were never totally successful and were expensive. However, in 1985, J. Robin Warren and Barry Marshall (as reported in Blaser, 1996) discovered that the helioc bacter pylori was the real cause of stomach ulcers. Almost all cases of this type of ulcer were successfully treated with antibiotics, and for a considerably lower cost. For seventy-five years no possible outcome was taken as evidence against this stress-acid theory of ulcers.

Scientific Research: A Definition

It is easier to define scientific research than it is to define science. It would not be easy, however, to get scientists and researchers to agree on such a definition. Even so, we attempt one here: *Scientific research is systematic, controlled, empirical, amoral, public, and critical investigation of natural phenomena. It is guided by theory and hypotheses about the presumed relations among such phenomena.* This definition requires little explanation since it consists mostly of a condensed and formalized statement of much that was said earlier or that will soon be said. Two points need emphasis, however.

First, when we say that scientific research is systematic and controlled, we mean, in effect, that scientific investigation is so ordered that investigators can have critical confidence in research outcomes. As we shall see later, scientific research observations are tightly disciplined. Moreover, among the many alternative explanations of a phenomenon, all but one are systematically ruled out. One can thus have greater confidence that a tested relation is as it is than if one had not controlled the observations and ruled out alternative possibilities. In some instances a cause-and-effect relationship can be established.

Second, scientific investigation is empirical. If the scientist believes something is so, that belief must somehow or other be put to an outside independent test. Subjective belief, in other words, must be checked against objective reality. Scientists must always subject their notions to the court of empirical inquiry and test. Scientists are hypercritical of the results of their own and others' research. Every scientist writing a research report has other scientists reading what is being written while he or she writes it. Though it is easy to err, to exaggerate, to overgeneralize, when writing up one's own work, it is not easy to escape the feeling of scientific eyes constantly peering over one's shoulder.

In science there is peer review. This means that others of equal training and knowledge are called upon to evaluate another scientist's work before it is published in scientific journals. There are both positive and negative points concerning this. It is through peer review that fraudulent studies have been exposed. The essay written by R. W. Wood (1973) on his experiences with Professor Blondlot of France concerning the nonexistence of N-rays gives a clear demonstration of peer review. Peer review works well for science and promotes quality research. The system, however, is not perfect. There are occasions when peer review has worked against science. This is documented throughout history with people such as Kepler, Galileo, Copernicus, Jenner, and Semelweiss. The ideas of these individuals were not popular with their peers. More recently in psychology, the works of John Garcia on the biological constraints on learning went contrary to his peers. Garcia managed to publish his findings in a journal (*Bulletin of the Psychonomic Society*) that did not have peer review. Others who read Garcia's work and replicated it found Garcia's work to be valuable. In the large majority of cases, peer review of science is beneficial.

Third, knowledge obtained scientifically is not subject to moral evaluation. The results are neither considered "bad" nor "good," but in terms of validity and reliability. The scientific method is, however, subject to issues of morality; that is, scientists are held responsible for the methods used in obtaining scientific knowledge. In psychology, codes of ethics are enforced to protect those under study. Science is a co-operative venture. Scientific information is available to all, and the scientific method is well-known and available to all who choose to use it.

The Scientific Approach

The scientific approach is a special systematized form of all-reflective thinking and inquiry. Dewey (1933/1991), in his influential *How We Think*, outlined a general paradigm of inquiry. The present discussion of the scientific approach is based largely on Dewey's analysis.

Problem – Obstacle – Idea

Scientists may experience obstacles to understanding, a vague unrest about observed and unobserved phenomena, a curiosity as to why something is as it is. The first and most important step is to get the idea out in the open, to express the problem in some reasonably manageable form. Rarely or never will the problem spring full-blown at this stage. The scientist must struggle with it, try it out, and live with it. Dewey (1933/1991, p. 108) says, "There is a troubled, perplexed, trying situation, where the difficulty is, as it were, spread throughout the entire situation, infecting it as a whole." Sooner or later, explicitly or implicitly, the scientist states the problem, even if the expression of it is inchoate and tentative. Here the scientist intellectualizes, as Dewey (p. 109) puts it, "what at first is merely *an emotional* quality of the whole situation." (Italics added.) In some respects, this is the most difficult and important part of the whole process. Without some sort of statement of the problem, the scientist can rarely go further and expect the work to be fruitful. With some researchers, the idea may come from speaking to a colleague or observing a curious phenomenon. The idea here is that the problem usually begins with vague and/or unscientific thoughts or unsystematic hunches. It then goes through a series of refinement steps.

Hypothesis

After intellectualizing the problem, referring to past experiences for possible solutions, observing relevant phenomena, the scientist may formulate a hypothesis. A hypothesis is a conjectural statement, a tentative proposition about the relation between two or more phenomena or variables. Our scientist will say, "If such-and-such occurs, then so-and-so results."

Reasoning – Deduction

This step or activity is frequently overlooked or underemphasized. It is perhaps the most important part of Dewey's analysis of reflective thinking. The scientist deduces the consequences of the hypothesis he or she has formulated. Conant (1951), in talking about the rise of modern science, says that the new element added in the seventeenth century was the use of deductive reasoning. Here is where experience, knowledge, and perspicacity are important.

Often the scientist, when deducing the consequences of a formulated hypothesis, will arrive at a problem quite different from the original one. On the other hand, deductions may lead to the belief that the problem cannot be solved with present technical tools. For example, before modern statistics were developed, certain behavioral research problems were insoluble. It was difficult, if not impossible, to test two or three interdependent hypotheses simultaneously. It was next to impossible to test the interactive effect of variables. We now have reason to believe that certain problems are insoluble unless they are tackled in a multivariate manner. An example of this is teaching methods and their relationship to achievement and other variables. It is likely that teaching methods, per se, do not differ much if we study only their simple effects. Teaching methods work differently under different conditions, with different teachers, and with different pupils. It is said that the methods "interact" with the conditions and characteristics of teachers and of pupils. Simon (1987) stated another example of this: A research study on pilot training proposed by Williams and Adelson in 1954 could not be carried out using traditional experimental research methods. The study proposed to examine thirty-four variables and their influence on pilot training. Using traditional research methods, the number of variables under study was too overwhelming. Over twenty years later, Simon (1976) and Simon and Roscoe (1984) demonstrate how such studies could be effectively undertaken using economical megafactor designs. An example may help us understand this reasoning–deduction step.

Suppose an investigator becomes intrigued with aggressive behavior. The investigator wonders why people are often aggressive in situations where aggressiveness may be inappropriate. Personal observation leads to the notion that aggressive behavior seems to occur when people have experienced difficulties of one kind or another. (Note the vagueness of the problem here.) After thinking for some time, reading the literature for clues, and making further observations, the hypothesis is formulated: Frustration leads to aggression. *Frustration* is defined as prevention from reaching a goal and *aggression* as behavior characterized by physical or verbal attack on other persons or objects.

What follows from this is a statement like: If frustration leads to aggression, then we should find a great deal of aggression among children who are in schools that are restrictive, schools that do not permit children much freedom and self-expression. Similarly, in difficult social situations assuming such situations are frustrating, we should expect more aggression than is "usual." Reasoning further, if we give experimental subjects interesting problems to solve and then prevent them from solving them, we can predict some kind of aggressive behavior. In a nutshell, this process of moving from a broader picture to a more specific one is called *deductive reasoning*.

Reasoning may, as indicated above, change the problem. We may realize that the initial problem was only a special case of a broader, more fundamental and important problem. We may, for example, start with a narrower hypothesis: Restrictive school situations lead to negativism in children. Then we can generalize the problem to the form: Frustration leads to aggression. While this is a different form of thinking from that discussed earlier, it is important because of what could almost be called its heuristic quality. Reasoning can help lead to wider, more basic, and thus more significant problems, as well as provide operational (testable) implications of the original hypothesis. This type of reasoning is called *inductive reasoning*. It starts from particular facts and moves to a general statement or hypothesis. If one is not careful, this method could lead to faulty reasoning due to the method's natural tendency to exclude data that do not fit the hypothesis. The inductive reasoning method is inclined to look for supporting data rather than refuting evidence.

Consider the classical study by Peter Wason (Wason & Johnson-Laird, 1972) that has been a topic of much interest (Hoch, 1986; Klayman & Ha, 1987). In this study, students were asked to discover a rule the experimenter had in mind that generated a sequence of numbers. One example was to generate a rule for the following sequence of numbers: "3, 5, 7." Students were told that they could ask about other sequences and would receive feedback on each sequence proposed as to whether it fit or did not fit the rule the experimenter had in mind. When the students felt confident, they could put forth the rule. Some students offered "9, 11, 13," and were told that this sequence fit the rule. They then followed with "15, 17, 19," and again were told that this sequence fit. The students then offered as their answer: "The rule is three consecutive odd numbers," but were told that this was *not* the rule. Others that would be offered after some more proposed sequences are "increasing numbers in increments of two," or "odd numbers in increments of two." In each of these, they are told that it is not the rule that the experimenter was thinking of. The actual rule in mind was "any three increasing positive numbers." Had the students proposed the sequences "8, 9, 10" or "1, 15, 4500" they would have been told that these also fit the rule. Where the students made their error was in testing only the cases that fitted their first proposed sequence that confirmed their hypothesis.

Although oversimplified, the Wason study demonstrated what could happen in actual scientific investigations. A scientist could easily be locked into repeating the same type of experiment that always supported the hypothesis.

Observation – Test – Experiment

It should be clear by now that the observation–test–experiment phase is only part of the scientific enterprise. If the problem has been well stated, the hypothesis or hypotheses adequately formulated, and the implications of the hypotheses carefully deduced, this step is almost automatically assuming that the investigator is technically competent.

The essence of testing a hypothesis is to test the *relation* expressed by the hypothesis. We do not test variables, as such; we test the relation between the variables. Observation, testing, and experimentation are for one large purpose: putting the problem relation to empirical test. To test without knowing—at least fairly well—*what* and *why* one is testing is to blunder. Simply to state a vague problem, like "How does Open Education affect learning?" and then to test pupils in schools presumed to differ in "openness"; or to ask: "What are the effects of cognitive dissonance?" and then, after experimental manipulations to create dissonance, to search for presumed effects, could only lead to questionable information. Similarly, to say one is going to study attribution processes without really knowing why one is doing it, or without stating relations between variables, is research nonsense.

Another point about testing hypotheses is that we usually do not test hypotheses directly. As indicated in the previous step on reasoning, we test deduced implications of hypotheses. Our test hypothesis may be: "Subjects told to suppress unwanted thoughts will be more preoccupied with them than subjects who are given a distraction." This was deduced from a broader and more general hypothesis: "Greater efforts to suppress an idea leads to greater preoccupation with the idea." We do not test "suppression of ideas" or "preoccupation," we test the relation between them—in this case the relation between suppression of unwanted thoughts and the level of preoccupation (see Wegner, Schneider, Carter, & White, 1987; Wegner, 1989).

Dewey emphasized that the temporal sequence of reflective thinking or inquiry is not fixed. We can repeat and reemphasize what he says in our own framework. The steps of the scientific approach are not neatly fixed. The first step is not neatly completed before the second step begins. Further, we may test before adequately deducing the implications of the hypothesis. The hypothesis itself may seem to need elaboration or refinement as a result of deducing implications from it. Hypotheses and their expression will often be found inadequate when implications are deduced from them. A frequent difficulty occurs when a hypothesis is so vague that one deduction is as good as another; that is, the hypothesis may not yield to precise testing.

Feedback to the problem, the hypotheses, and, finally, the theory of the results of research is highly important. Learning theorists and researchers, for example, have frequently altered their theories and research as a result of experimental findings (see Malone, 1991; Schunk, 1996; Hergenhahn, 1996). Theorists and researchers have been studying the effects of early environment and training on later development. Kagan and Zentner (1996) reviewed the results of 70 studies concerned with the relation between early life experiences and psychopathology in adulthood. They found that juvenile delinquency could be predicted by the amount of impulsivity detected at preschool age. Lynch, Short and Chua (1995) found that musical processing was influenced by the perceptual stimulation an infant experienced at age 6 months to 1 year. These and other research have yielded varied evidence converging on this extremely important theoretical and practical problem. Part of the essential core of scientific research is the constant effort to replicate and check findings, to correct theory on the basis of empirical evidence, and to find better explanations of natural phenomena. One can even go so far as to say that science has a cyclic aspect. A researcher finds, say, that *A* is related to *B* in such-and-such a way. Then more research is conducted to determine under what other conditions *A* is similarly related to *B*. Other researchers challenge this theory and research, offering explanations and evidence of their own. The original researcher, it is hoped, alters his or her work in the light of new data. The process never ends.

Let us summarize the so-called scientific approach to inquiry. First, there is doubt, a barrier, an indeterminate situation crying out to be made determinant. The scientist experiences vague doubts, emotional disturbance, and inchoate ideas. There is a struggle to formulate the problem, even if inadequately. The scientist then studies the literature, scans his or her own experience and the experiences of others. Often the researcher simply has to wait for an inventive mind leap. Maybe it will occur; maybe not. With the problem formulated, with the basic question or questions properly asked, the rest is much easier. The hypothesis is then constructed, after which its empirical implications are deduced. In this process the original problem and, of course, the original hypothesis, may be changed. It may be broadened or narrowed. It may even be abandoned. Last, but not finally, the relation expressed by the hypothesis is tested by observation and experimentation. On the basis of the research evidence, the hypothesis is supported or rejected. This information is then fed back to the original problem, and the problem is kept or altered, as dictated by the evidence. Dewey pointed out that one phase of the process may be expanded and be of great importance, another may be skimped, and there may be fewer or more steps involved. Research is rarely an orderly business. Indeed, it is much more disorderly than the above discussion may imply. Order and disorder, however, are not of primary importance. What *is* important is the controlled rationality of scientific research as a process of reflective inquiry, the interdependent nature of the parts of the process, and the paramount importance of the problem and its statement.

CHAPTER SUMMARY

1. To understand complex human behavior, one must understand the scientific language and approach.
2. Science is a systematic and controlled extension of common sense. There are five differences between science and common sense:
   a. Science uses conceptual schemes and theoretical structures,
   b. Science systematically and empirically tests theories and hypotheses,
   c. Science attempts to control possible extraneous causes,
   d. Science pursues relations consciously and systematically,
   e. Science rules out metaphysical (untestable) explanations.
3. Peirce's Four Methods of Knowing
   a. method of tenacity—influenced by established past beliefs;
   b. method of authority—influenced by the weight of tradition or public sanction;
   c. a priori method (also known as the method of intuition)—natural inclination toward the truth;
   d. method of science—self-correcting; notions are testable and objective.
4. The stereotype of science has hindered understanding of science by the public.
5. Views, functions of science
   a. Static view sees science contributing scientific information to world; science adds to the body of information and present state of knowledge.

    b. Dynamic view is concerned with the activity of science (what scientists do). With this comes the heuristic view of science. This is one of self-discovery. Science takes risks and solves problems.

6. The aims of science are:
   a. develop theory and explain natural phenomenon,
   b. promote understanding and develop predictions.
7. A theory has three characteristics:
   a. set of properties consisting of defined and interrelated constructs,
   b. systematically sets the interrelations among a set of variables,
   c. explains phenomenon.
8. Scientific research is a systematic, controlled, empirical, and critical investigation of natural phenomenon. It is guided by theory and hypotheses about presumed relations among such phenomenon. It is also public and amoral.
9. The scientific approach according to Dewey is made up of the following:
   a. Problem–Obstacle–Idea—formulate the research problem or question to be solved
   b. Hypothesis—formulate a conjectural statement about the relationship between phenomena or variables
   c. Reasoning–Deduction—scientist deduces the consequences of the hypothesis. This can lead to a more significant problem and provide ideas on how the hypothesis can be tested in observable terms.
   d. Observation–Test–Experiment—This is the data collection and analysis phase. The results of the research conducted are related back to the problem.

STUDY SUGGESTIONS

Some of the content of this chapter is highly controversial. The views expressed are accepted by some thinkers and rejected by others. Readers can enhance understanding of science and its purpose, the relationship between science and technology, and the differences between basic and applied research, by selective reading of the literature. Such reading can be the basis for class discussions. Extended treatment of the controversial aspects of science, especially behavioral science, is given in the first author's book, *Behavioral Research: A Conceptual Approach* (New York: Holt, Rinehart and Winston, 1979, chaps. 1, 15, and 16). Many fine articles on science and research have been published in science journals and philosophy of science books. Here are some of them. Also included is a special report in *Scientific American*. All are pertinent to this chapter's substance.

Barinaga, M. (1993). Philosophy of science: Feminists find gender everywhere in science. *Science* 260: 392-393. Discusses the difficulty of separating cultural views of women and science. Talks about science as a predominantly male field.

Hausheer, J., & Harris, J. (1994). In search of a brief definition of science. *The Physics Teacher* 32(5): 318. Mentions that any definition of science must include guidelines for evaluating theory and hypotheses as either science or nonscience.

Holton, G. (1996). The controversy over the end of science. *Scientific American* 273(10): 191. This article is concerned with the development of two camps of thought: the linearists and the cyclists. The linearists take a more conventional perspective of science; the cyclists see science as degenerating within itself.

Horgan, J. (1994). Anti-omniscience: An eclectic gang of thinkers pushes at knowledge's limits. *Scientific American* 271: 20-22. Discusses the limits of science.

Horgan, J. (1997). *The end of science*. New York: Broadway Books.

Miller, J. A. (1994). Postmodern attitude toward science. *Bioscience* 41(6): 395. Discuses the reasons some educators and scholars in the humanities have adopted a hostile attitude toward science.

Scientific American. Science versus antiscience. (Special report). January 1997, 96-101. Presents three different antiscience movements: creationist, feminist, and media.

Smith, B. (1995). Formal ontology, common sense and cognitive science. *International Journal of Human-Computer Studies* 43(5-6): 641-667. An article examining common sense and cognitive science.

Timpane, J. (1995). How to convince a reluctant scientist. *Scientific American* 272: 104. This article warns that too much originality in science would lead to non-acceptance and difficulty of understanding. It also discusses how scientific acceptance is governed by both old and new data and the reputation of the scientist.

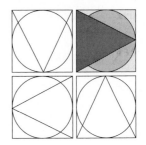

PROBLEMS AND HYPOTHESES

Many people believe that science is basically a fact-gathering activity. It is not. As M. R. Cohen (1956/1997, p. 148) says:

> There is . . . no genuine progress in scientific insight through the Baconian method of accumulating empirical facts without hypotheses or anticipation of nature. Without some guiding idea we do not know what facts to gather . . . we cannot determine what is relevant and what is irrelevant.

The scientifically uninformed person often has the idea that the scientist is a highly objective individual who gathers data without preconceived ideas. Poincare (1952/1996, p. 143) pointed out how wrong this idea is: "It is often said that experiments should be made without preconceived ideas. That is impossible. Not only would it make every experiment fruitless, but even if we wished to do so, it could not be done."

Problems

It is not always possible for a researcher to formulate the problem simply, clearly, and completely. The researcher may often have only a rather general, diffuse, even confused notion of the problem. This is in the nature of the complexity of scientific research. It may even take an investigator years of exploration, thought, and research before he or she can state the questions clearly. Nevertheless, adequate statement of the research problem is one of the most important parts of research. The difficulty of stating a research problem satisfactorily at a given time should not cause one to lose sight of the ultimate desirability and necessity of doing so.

Bearing this difficulty in mind, a fundamental principle can be stated: If one wants to solve a problem, one must generally know what the problem is. It can be said that a large part of the solution lies in knowing what it is one is trying to do. Another part lies in knowing what a problem is and especially what a scientific problem is.

What is a good problem statement? Although research problems differ greatly and there is no one "right" way to state a problem, certain characteristics of problems and problem statements can be learned and used to good advantage. To start, let us take two or three examples of published research problems and study their characteristics. First, take the problem of the study by Hurlock (1925)[1] mentioned in Chapter 1: What are the effects on pupil performance of different types of incentives? Note that the problem is stated in question form. Here, the simplest way is the best way. Also note that the problem states a relation between variables, in this case between the variables *incentives* and *pupil performance* (achievement). (*Variable* will be defined formally in Chapter 3. For now, *variable* is used as the name of a phenomenon, or a construct, that takes a set of different numerical values.)

A *problem*, then, is an interrogative sentence or statement that asks: What relationship exists between two or more variables? The answer is what is being sought in the research. A problem in most cases will have two or more variables. In the Hurlock example, the problem statement relates incentive to pupil performance. Another problem, studied in an influential experiment by Bahrick (1984, 1992), is associated with the age-old questions: How much of what you are now studying will you remember ten years from now? How much of it will you remember fifty years from today? How much will you remember later if you never use it? Formally, Bahrick asks: Does semantic memory involve separate processes? One variable is the amount of time since the material was first learned, a second would be the quality of original learning, and the other variable is remembering (or forgetting). Still another problem, by Little, Sterling, and Tingstrom (1996), is quite different: Do geographic

---

[1] When citing problems and hypotheses from the literature, we have not always used the authors' words verbatim. In fact, the statements of many of the problems are ours and not those of the cited authors. Some authors use only problem statements; some use only hypotheses; others use both.

and racial cues influence attribution (perceived blame)? One variable is geographical cues, a second would be racial information, and the third is attribution.

Not all research problems contain two or more clear variables. For example, in experimental psychology, the research focus is often on psychological processes like memory and categorization. In her justifiably well-known and influential study of perceptual categories, Rosch (1973) in effect asked the question: Are there nonarbitrary ("natural") categories of color and form? Although the relationship between two or more variables is not apparent in this problem statement, in the actual research the categories were related to learning. Toward the end of this book we will see that factor analytical research problems also lack the relationship form discussed above. In most behavioral research problems, however, the relations among two or more variables are studied, and we will therefore emphasize such relation statements.

Criteria of Problems and Problem Statements

There are three criteria of good problems and problem statements. One, the problem should express a relation between two or more variables. It asks, in effect, questions like: Is *A* related to *B*? How are *A* and *B* related to *C*? How is *A* related to *B* under conditions *C* and *D*? The exceptions to this dictum occur mostly in taxonomic or methodological research.

Two, the problem should be stated clearly and unambiguously in question form. Instead of saying, for instance, "The problem is . . ." or "The purpose of this study is . . . ," ask a question. Questions have the virtue of posing problems directly. The purpose of a study is not necessarily the same as the problem of a study. The purpose of the Hurlock study, for instance, was to throw light on the use of incentives in school situations. The problem was the question about the relation between incentives and performance. Again, the simplest way is the best way: ask a question.

The third criterion is often difficult to satisfy. It demands that the problem and the problem statement must *imply* possibilities of empirical testing. A problem that does not contain implications for testing its stated relation(s) is not a scientific problem. This means not only that an actual relation is stated, but also that the variables of the relation can somehow be measured. Many interesting and important questions are not scientific questions simply because they are not amenable to testing. Certain philosophic and theological questions, while perhaps important to the individuals who consider them, cannot be tested empirically and are thus of no interest to the scientist as a scientist. The epistemological question, "How do we know?" is such a question. Education has many interesting but nonscientific questions, such as, "Does democratic education improve the learning of youngsters?" "Are group processes good for children?" These questions can be labeled metaphysical in the sense that they are, at least as stated, beyond empirical testing possibilities. The key difficulties are that some of them are not relations, and most of their constructs are very difficult or impossible to define so that they can be measured.

Hypotheses

A *hypothesis* is a conjectural statement of the relation between two or more variables. Hypotheses are always in declarative sentence form, and they relate—either generally or specifically—variables to variables. There are two criteria for "good" hypotheses and hypothesis statements. They are the same as two of those for problems and problem statements. (1) Hypotheses are statements about the relations between variables. (2) Hypotheses carry clear implications for testing the stated relations. These criteria mean, then, that hypothesis statements contain two or more variables that are measurable or potentially measurable and that they specify how the variables are related.

Let us take three hypotheses from the literature and apply the criteria to them. The first hypothesis from a study by Wegner, et al. (1987) seems to defy common sense: The greater the suppression of unwanted thoughts, the greater the preoccupation with those unwanted thoughts (suppress now; obsess later). Here a relation is stated between one variable, suppression of an idea or thought, and another variable, preoccupation or obsession. Since the two variables are readily defined and measured, implications for testing the hypothesis, too, are readily conceived. The criteria are satisfied. In the Wegner, et al. study, subjects were asked *not* to think about a "white bear." Each time they did think of the white bear, they would ring a bell. The number of bell rings indicated the level of preoccupation. A second hypothesis is from a study by Ayres and Hughes (1986). This study's hypothesis is unusual. It states a relation in the so-called null form: Levels of noise or music have no effect on visual functioning. The relation is stated clearly: one variable, loudness of sound (like music), is related to another variable, visual functioning, by the words "has no effect on." On the criterion of potential testability, however, we meet with difficulty. We are faced with the problem of defining "visual functioning" and "loudness" so they can be are measured. If we can solve this problem satisfactorily, then we definitely have a hypothesis. Ayres and Hughes did solve this by defining loudness as 107 decibels and visual functioning in terms of a score on a visual acuity task. And this hypothesis did lead to answering a question that people often ask: "Why do we turn down the volume of the car stereo when we are *looking* for a street address?" Ayres and Hughes found a definite drop in perceptual functioning when the level of music was at 107 decibels.

The third hypothesis represents a numerous and important class. Here the relation is indirect, concealed, as it were. It customarily comes in the form of a statement that groups *A* and *B* will differ on some characteristic. For example: Women more often than men believe they should lose weight even though their weight is well within normal bounds (Fallon & Rozin, 1985). That is, women differ from men in terms of their perceived body shape. Note that this statement is one step removed from the actual hypothesis, which may be stated: Perceived body shape is in part a function of gender. If the latter statements were the hypothesis stated, then the first might be called a subhypothesis or a specific prediction based on the original hypothesis.

Let us consider another hypothesis of this type but removed one step further. Individuals having the same or similar characteristics will hold similar attitudes toward cognitive objects significantly related to their occupational role (Saal & Moore, 1993). (*Cognitive objects* are defined as a concrete or abstract thing perceived and "known" by individuals. People, groups, job or grade promotion, the government, and education are examples.) The relation in this case is, of course, between personal characteristics and attitudes (toward a cognitive object related to the personal characteristic, for example, gender and attitudes toward others receiving a promotion). In order to test this hypothesis, it would be necessary to have at least two groups, each with a different characteristic, and then to compare the attitudes of the groups. For instance, as in the case of the Saal and Moore study, the comparison would be between men and women. They would be compared on their assessment of fairness toward a promotion given to a coworker of the opposite or same sex. In this example, the criteria are satisfied.

The Importance of Problems and Hypotheses

There is little doubt that hypotheses are important and indispensable tools of scientific research. There are three main reasons for this belief. The first reason is that they are, so to speak, the working instruments of theory. Hypotheses can be deduced from theory and from other hypotheses. If, for instance, we are working on a theory of aggression, we are presumably looking for causes and effects of aggressive behavior. We might have observed cases of aggressive behavior occurring after frustrating circumstances. The theory, then, might include the proposition: Frustration produces aggression (Berkowitz, 1983; Dill & Anderson, 1995; Dollard, Doob, Miller, Mowrer, & Sears, 1939). From this broad hypothesis we may deduce more specific hypotheses, such as: To prevent children from reaching desired goals (frustration) will result in their fighting each other (aggression); if children are deprived of parental love (frustration), they will react in part with aggressive behavior.

The second reason is that hypotheses can be tested and shown to be probably true or probably false. Isolated facts are not tested, as we said before; only relations are tested. Since hypotheses are relational propositions, this is probably the main reason why they are used in scientific inquiry. They are, in essence, predictions of the form, "If *A*, then *B*," which we set up to test the relation between *A* and *B*. We let the facts have a chance to establish the probable truth or falsity of the hypothesis.

Reason three is that hypotheses are powerful tools for the advancement of knowledge because they enable scientists to get outside themselves. Although constructed by humans, hypotheses exist, can be tested, and can be shown to be probably correct or incorrect apart from a person's values and opinions (biases). This is critical: there would be no science in any complete sense without hypotheses.

Just as important as hypotheses are the problems behind the hypotheses. As Dewey (1938/1982, pp. 105-107) has pointed out, research usually starts with a problem. He states that there is first an indeterminant situation in which ideas are vague, doubts are raised, and the thinker is perplexed. Dewey further points out that the problem is not enunciated; indeed, cannot be enunciated until one has experienced such an indeterminant situation.

The indeterminancy, however, must ultimately be removed. Although it is true, as stated earlier, that a researcher may often have only a general and diffuse notion of the problem, sooner or later he or she has to have a fairly clear idea of just what the problem is. Even though this statement seems self-evident, one of the most difficult things to do is to state one's research problem clearly and completely. In other words, one must know what one is trying to find out. When this is finally known, the problem is a long way toward solution.

Virtues of Problems and Hypotheses

Problems and hypotheses, then, have important virtues: (1) they direct investigation (The relations expressed in the hypotheses tell the investigator what to do); (2) problems and hypotheses, because they are ordinarily generalized relational statements, enable the researcher to deduce specific empirical manifestations implied by the problems and hypotheses. We may say, following Guida and Ludlow (1989): If it is indeed true that children in one type of culture (Chile) have higher test anxiety than children of another type of culture (white Americans), then it follows that children in the Chilean culture should do more poorly in academics than children in the American culture. The Chilean children also should perhaps have a lower self-esteem or more external locus-of-control when it comes to school and academics.

There are important differences between problems and hypotheses. Hypotheses, if properly stated, can be tested. A given hypothesis may be too broad to be tested directly, yet if it is a "good" hypothesis, then other testable hypotheses can be deduced from it. Facts or variables are not tested as such. The relations stated by the hypotheses are tested. And a problem cannot be solved scientifically unless it is reduced to its hypothesis form because a problem is a question, usually broad in nature, and not directly testable. One does not test questions: Does the presence or absence of another person in a public restroom alter personal hygiene (Pedersen, Keithly, & Brady, 1986)? Do group counseling sessions reduce the level of psychiatric morbidity in police officers (Doctor, Cutris, & Issacs, 1994)? Perhaps, one tests one or more hypotheses implied by these questions. For example, to study the latter problem, one may hypothesize that police officers who attend stress-reduction counseling sessions will use fewer sick days than those police officers who did not attend counseling sessions. The hypothesis in the former problem could state that the presence of a person in a public restroom will cause the other person to wash his or her hands.

Problems and hypotheses advance scientific knowledge by helping an investigator confirm or disconfirm theory. Suppose a psychological investigator gives a number of subjects three or four tests, among which is a test for anxiety related to an arithmetic test. Routinely computing the intercorrelations between the three or four tests, one finds that the correlation between anxiety and arithmetic is negative. One therefore concludes that the greater the anxiety the lower the arithmetic score. But it is quite conceivable that the relation is fortuitous or even spurious. If, however, the investigator had hypothesized the relation on the basis of theory, he or she could have greater confidence in the results. Investigators who do not hypothesize relations in advance do not, in short, give the facts a chance to prove or disprove anything. The words *prove* and *disprove* are not to be taken here in their literal sense. A hypothesis is never really proved or disproved. To be more accurate we should probably say something like: The weight of evidence is on the side of the hypothesis, or the weight of the evidence casts doubt on the hypothesis. Braithwaite (1953/1996 , p. 14) says:

> Thus the empirical evidence of its instance never proves the hypothesis: in suitable cases we may say that *it establishes* (italics added) the hypothesis, meaning by this that the evidence makes it reasonable to accept the hypothesis; but it never *proves* the hypothesis in the sense that the hypothesis is a logical consequence of the evidence.

This use of the hypothesis is similar to playing a game of chance. The rules of the game are set up and bets are made in advance. One cannot change the rules after an outcome, neither can one change one's bets after placing them. One cannot throw the dice first and then bet. That would not be "fair." Similarly, if one gathers data first and then selects a datum and comes to a conclusion on the basis of the datum, one has violated the rules of the scientific game. The game is not "fair" because the investigator can easily capitalize on, say, two significant relations out of five tested. What usually happens to the other three is that they are forgotten. In a "fair" game, every throw of the dice is counted, in the sense that one either wins or does not win on the basis of the outcome of each throw.

Hypotheses direct inquiry. As Darwin pointed out over a hundred years ago, observations have to be for or against some view if they are to be of any use. Hypotheses incorporate aspects of the theory under test in testable or near-testable form. Earlier, an example of reinforcement theory was given in which testable hypotheses were deduced from the general problem. The importance of recognizing this function of hypotheses may be shown by going through the back door and using a theory that is very difficult, or perhaps impossible, to test. Freud's theory of anxiety includes the construct of repression. By repression, Freud meant the forcing of unacceptable ideas deep into the unconscious. In order to test the Freudian theory of anxiety it is necessary to deduce relations suggested by the theory. These deductions will, of course, have to include the repression notion, which includes the construct of the unconscious. Hypotheses can be formulated using these constructs; in order to test the theory, they have to be so formulated. But testing them is another, more difficult matter because of the extreme difficulty of defining terms such as "repression" and "unconscious" so that they can be measured. To the present, no one has succeeded in defining these two constructs without seriously departing from the original Freudian meaning and usage. Hypotheses, then, are important bridges between theory and empirical inquiry.

Problems, Values, and Definitions

To clarify further the nature of problems and hypotheses, two or three common errors will now be discussed. First, scientific problems are not moral and ethical questions: Are punitive disciplinary measures bad for children? Should an organization's leadership be democratic? What is the best way to teach college students? To ask these questions is to ask value and judgmental questions that science cannot answer. Many so-called hypotheses are not hypotheses at all. For instance: The small-group method of teaching is better than the lecture method. This is a value statement; it is an article of faith and not a hypothesis. If it were possible to state a relation between the variables, and if it were possible to define the variables so as to permit testing the relation, then we might have a hypothesis. But there is no way to test value questions scientifically.

A quick and relatively easy way to detect value questions and statements is to look for words such as *should, ought, better than* (instead of *greater than*). Also, one can look for similar words that indicate cultural or personal judgments or preferences (biases). Value statements, however, are tricky. While a "should" statement is obviously a value statement, certain other kinds of statements are not so obvious. Take the statement: Authoritarian methods of teaching lead to poor learning. Here there is a relation. But the statement fails as a scientific hypothesis because it uses two value expressions or words, "authoritarian methods of teaching" and "poor learning," neither of which can be defined for measurement purposes without deleting the words *authoritarian* and *poor*.[2]

Other kinds of statements that are not hypotheses, or are poor ones, are frequently formulated, especially in education. Consider, for instance: The core curriculum is an enriching experience. Another statement type, used too frequently, is vague generalization: Reading skills can be identified in the second grade; The goal of the unique individual is self-realization; Prejudice is related to certain personality traits.

Another common defect of problem statements often occurs in doctoral theses: the listing of methodological points or "problems" as subproblems. These methodological points have two characteristics that make them easy to detect: (1) they are not substantive problems that spring from the basic problem; and (2) they relate to techniques or methods of sampling, measuring, or analyzing. They are usually not in question form but rather contain such words as *test, determine, measure*. "To *determine* the reliability of the instruments used in this research," "To *test* the significance of the differences between the means," or "To *assign* pupils at random to the experimental groups" are examples of this mistaken notion of problems and subproblems.

---

[2] An almost classic case of the use of the word *authoritarian* is the statement sometimes heard among educators: The lecture method is authoritarian. This seems to mean that the speaker does not like the lecture method and is telling us that it is bad. Similarly, one of the most effective ways to criticize a teacher is to say that teacher is authoritarian.

Generality and Specificity of Problems and Hypotheses

One difficulty that a researcher usually encounters, and that almost all students working on a thesis find annoying, is the generality and specificity of problems and hypotheses. If the problem is too general, it is also too vague to be tested. Thus, it is scientifically useless, even though it may be interesting to read. Problems and hypotheses that are too general or too vague are common. For example: Creativity is a function of the self-actualization of the individual; Democratic education enhances social learning and citizenship; Authoritarianism in the college classroom inhibits the creative imagination of students. These are interesting problems but, in their present form, are worse than useless scientifically because they cannot be tested and because they give one the spurious assurance that they are hypotheses that can "someday" be tested.

Terms such as "creativity," "self-actualization," "democracy," "authoritarianism," and the like have, at the present time at least, no adequate empirical referents.[3] It is quite true that we can define *creativity*, say, in a limited way by specifying one or two creativity tests. This may be a legitimate procedure. Still, in so doing, we run the risk of getting far away from the original term and its meaning. This is particularly true when we speak of artistic creativity. We are, of course, often willing to accept the risk in order to be able to investigate important problems. Yet a term like "democracy" is almost hopeless to define. Even when we do define it, we often find we have destroyed its original meaning. An outstanding exception to this statement is Bollen's (1980) definition and measurement of "democracy." We will examine both in subsequent chapters.

The other extreme is too great specificity. Every student has heard that it is necessary to narrow down problems to workable size. This is true. But, unfortunately, we can also narrow the problem out of existence. In general, the more specific the problem or hypothesis, the clearer is its testing implications. But triviality may be the price we pay. Researchers cannot handle problems that are too broad because they tend to be too vague for adequate research operations. On the other hand, in their zeal to cut down the problems to workable size or to find a workable problem, they may cut the life out of it. They may make it trivial or inconsequential. A thesis, for instance, on the simple relation between the speed of reading and size of type, while important and maybe even interesting, is too thin by itself for a doctoral study. The doctoral student would need to expand on the topic by also recommending a comparison between genders and considering variables such as culture and family

---

[3] Although many studies of authoritarianism have been done with considerable success, it is doubtful that we know what authoritarianism in the classroom means. For instance, an action of a teacher that is authoritarian in one classroom may not be authoritarian in another classroom. The alleged democratic behavior exhibited by one teacher may even be called authoritarian if exhibited by another teacher. Such elasticity is not the stuff of science.

background. The researcher could possibly expand the study to look at levels of illumination and font types. Too great specificity is perhaps a worse danger than too great generality. The researcher may be able to answer the specific question but will not be able to generalize the finding to other situations or groups of people. At any rate, some kind of compromise must be made between generality and specificity. The ability to make such compromises effectively is a function partly of experience and partly of critical study of research problems.

Here are a few examples contrasting research problems stated as too general or too specific:

1. Too General: There are gender differences in game playing.
   Too Specific: Tommy's score will be 10 points higher than Carol's on Tetris Professional Gold.
   About Right: Video game playing will result in a higher transfer of learning for boys than girls.
2. Too General: People can read large-size letters faster than small-size letters.
   Too Specific: Seniors at Duarte High School can read 24-point fonts faster than 12-point fonts.
   About Right: A comparison of three different font sizes and visual acuity on reading speed and comprehension.

The Multivariable Nature of Behavorial Research and Problems

Until now the discussion of problems and hypotheses has been limited to two variables, x and y. We must hasten to correct any impression that such problems and hypotheses are the norm in behavioral research. Researchers in psychology, sociology, education, and other behavioral sciences have become keenly aware of the multivariable nature of behavioral research. Instead of saying: If p, then q, it is often more appropriate to say: If $p_1, p_2, \ldots, p_k$, then q; or: If p then q, under conditions r, s, and t.

An example may clarify the point. Instead of simply stating the hypothesis: If frustration, then aggression, it is more realistic to recognize the multivariable nature of the determinants and influences of aggression. This can be done by saying, for example: If high intelligence, middle class, male, and frustrated, then aggression. Or: If frustration, then aggression, under the conditions of high intelligence, middle class, and male. Instead of one x, we now have four xs. Although one phenomenon may be the most important in determining or influencing another phenomenon, it is unlikely that most of the phenomena of interest to behavioral scientists are determined simply. It is much more likely that they are determined multiply. It is much more likely that aggression is the result of several influences working in complex ways. Moreover, aggression itself has multiple aspects., There are after all, different kinds of aggression.

Problems and hypotheses thus have to reflect the multivariable complexity of psychological, sociological, and educational reality. We will talk of one x and one y, especially in the early part of the book. However, it *must* be understood that behavioral research, which used to be almost exclusively univariate in its approach, has become more and more multivariable. We have purposely used the word "multivariable" instead of "multivariate" for an important reason. Traditionally, "multivariate" studies are those that have more than one y variable and one or more x variables. When we speak of one y and more than one x variable, we use the more appropriate term "multivariable" to make the distinction. For now, we will use "univariate" to indicate one x and one y. "Univariate," strictly speaking, also applies to y. We will soon encounter multivariate conceptions and problems. And later parts of the book will be especially concerned with a multivariate approach and emphasis. For a clear explanation on the differences between *multivariable* and *multivariate* (see Kleinbaum, Kupper, Muller, & Nizam, 1997).

Concluding Remarks: The Special Power of Hypotheses

One sometimes hears that hypotheses are unnecessary in research. Some feel that they restrict the investigative imagination unnecessarily, and that the job of science and scientific investigation is to discover new things and not to belabor the obvious. Some feel that hypotheses are obsolete. Such statements are quite misleading. They misconstrue the purpose of hypotheses.

It can almost be said that the hypothesis is one of the most powerful tools yet invented to achieve dependable knowledge. We observe a phenomenon. We speculate on possible causes. Naturally, our culture has answers to account for most phenomena—many correct, many incorrect, many a mixture of fact and superstition, many pure superstition. It is the business of scientists to doubt most explanations of phenomena. Such doubts are systemic. Scientists insist on subjecting explanations of phenomena to controlled empirical testing. In order to do this, they formulate the explanations into theories and hypotheses. In fact, the explanations are hypotheses. Scientists simply discipline the business by writing systematic and testable hypotheses. If an explanation cannot be formulated into a testable hypothesis, it can be considered to be a metaphysical explanation and thus not amenable to scientific investigation. As such, it is dismissed by scientists as being of no interest.

The power of hypotheses go further than this, however. A hypothesis is a prediction. It says that if x occurs, y will also occur; that is, y is predicted from x. If, then, x is made to occur (vary), and it is observed that y also occurs (varies concomitantly), then the hypothesis is confirmed. This is more powerful evidence than simply observing, without prediction, the covarying of x and y. It is more powerful in the betting-game sense discussed earlier. The scientist makes a bet that x leads to y. If, in an experiment, x does lead to y, then one has won the bet. A person cannot just enter the game at any point and pick a perhaps fortuitous common occurrence of x and y. Games are not played this way (at least in our culture). This person must play according to the rules, and the rules in science are made to minimize error and fallibility. Hypotheses are part of the rules of the science game.

Even when hypotheses are not confirmed, they have power. Even when y does not covary with x, knowledge is still advanced. Negative findings are sometimes as important as positive ones, since they reduce the total universe of ignorance and sometimes point up fruitful further hypotheses and lines of investigation. *But the scientist cannot tell positive from negative evidence unless he or she uses hypotheses.* It is, of course, possible to conduct research without hypotheses, particularly in exploratory investigations. But it is hard to conceive modern science in all its rigorous and disciplined fertility without the guiding light and power of hypotheses.

CHAPTER SUMMARY

1. Formulating the research problem is not an easy task. The researcher starts with a general, diffused, and vague notion and then gradually refines it. Research problems differ greatly and there is no one right way to state the problem.

2. Three criteria of a good problem and problem statement
   a. The problem should be expressed as a relationship between two or more variables.
   b. The problem should be put in the form of a question.
   c. The problem statement should imply the possibilities of empirical testing.

3. A hypothesis is a conjectural statement of the relationship between two or more variables. It is put in the form of a declarative statement. A criteria for a good hypothesis is the same as (a) and (b) in criteria of a good problem.

4. Importance of problems and hypotheses
   a. It is a working instrument of science and a specific working statement of theory
   b. Hypotheses can be tested and be predictive
   c. Advance knowledge

5. Virtues of problems and hypotheses
   a. Direct investigation and inquiry
   b. Enable the researcher to deduce specific empirical manifestations
   c. Serve as the bridge between theory and empirical inquiry.

6. Scientific problems are not moral or ethical questions. Science cannot answer value or judgmental questions.

7. Detection of value questions: Look for words such as *better than*, *should*, or *ought*.
8. Another common defect of problem statements is the listing of methodological points as subproblems.
   a. They are not substantive problems that come directly from the basic problem
   b. They relate to techniques or methods of sampling, measuring, or analyzing; not in question form.
9. On problems, there is a need to compromise between being too general and too specific. The ability to do this comes with experience.
10. Problems and hypotheses need to reflect the multivariate complexity of behavioral science reality.
11. The hypothesis is one of the most powerful tools invented to achieve dependable knowledge. It has the power of prediction. A negative finding for a hypothesis can serve to eliminate one possible explanation and open other hypotheses and lines of investigation.

STUDY SUGGESTIONS

1. Use the following variable names to write research problems and hypotheses: frustration, academic achievement, intelligence, verbal ability, race, social class (socioeconomic status), sex, reinforcement, teaching methods, occupational choice, conservatism, education, income, authority, need for achievement, group cohesiveness, obedience, social prestige, permissiveness.
2. Ten problems from the research literature are given below. Study them carefully, choose two or three, and construct hypotheses based on them.
   a. Do children of different ethnic groups have different levels of test anxiety (Guida & Ludlow, 1989)?
   b. Do cooperative social · tuations lead to higher levels of intrinsic motivation? (Hom, Berger, Duncan, Miller, & Belvin, 1994)?
   c. Are affective responses influenced by people's facial activity (Strack, Martin & Stepper, 1988)?
   d. Will jurors follow prohibitive judicial instructions and information (Shaw & Skolnick, 1995)?
   e. What are the positive effects of using alternating pressure pads to prevent pressure sores in homebound hospice patients (Stoneberg, Pitcock, & Myton, 1986)?
   f. What are the effects of early Pavlovian conditioning on later Pavlovian conditioning (Lariviere & Spear, 1996)?
   g. Does the efficacy of encoding information into long-term memory depend on the novelty of the information (Tulving & Kroll, 1995)?

   h. What is the effect of alcohol consumption on the likelihood of condom use during causal sex (MacDonald, Zanna, & Fong, 1996)?

   i. Are there gender differences in predicting retirement decisions (Talaga & Beehr, 1995)?

   j. Is the Good Behavior Game a viable intervention strategy for children in a classroom that require behavior change procedures (Tingstrom, 1994)?

3. Ten hypotheses are given below. Discuss possibilities of testing them. Then read two or three of the studies to learn how the authors tested them.

   a. Job applicants who claim a great deal of experience at nonexistent tasks overstate their ability on real tasks (Anderson, Warner, & Spencer, 1984).

   b. In social situations, men misread women's intended friendliness as a sign of sexual interest (Saal, Johnson, & Weber, 1989).

   c. The greater the team success, the greater the attribution of each team member toward one's ability and luck (Chambers & Abrami, 1991).

   d. Increasing interest in a task will increase compliance (Rind, 1997).

   e. Extracts from men's perspiration can affect women's menstrual cycles (Cutler, Preti, Kreiger, & Huggins, 1986).

   f. Physically attractive people are viewed as having higher intelligence than nonattractive people (Moran & McCullers, 1984).

   g. One can receive help from a stranger if that stranger is similar to oneself, or if the request is made at a certain distance (Glick, DeMorest, & Hotze, 1988).

   h. Cigarette smoking (nicotine) improves mental performance (Spilich, June, & Remer, 1992).

   i. People stowing valuable items in unusual locations will have better memory of that location than stowing valuable items in usual locations (Winograd & Soloway, 1986).

   j. Gay men with symptomatic HIV disease are significantly more distressed than gay men whose HIV status is unknown (Cochran and Mays, 1994).

4. Multivariate (for now, more than two dependent variables) problems and hypotheses have become common in behavioral research. To give the student a preliminary feeling for such problems, we here append several of them. Try to imagine how you would do research to study them.

   a. Do men and women differ in their perceptions of their genitals, sexual enjoyment, oral sex and masturbation (Reinholtz & Muehlenhard, 1995)?

   b. Are youthful smokers more extroverted whereas older smokers are more depressed and withdrawn (Stein, Newcomb, & Bentler, 1996)?

   c. How much do teacher's ratings of social skills for popular students differ from rejected students (Frentz, Gresham, & Elliot, 1991; Stuart, Gresham, & Elliot, 1991)?

d. Do counselor–client matching on ethnicity, gender, and language influence treatment outcomes of school-aged children (Hall, Kaplan, & Lee, 1994)?

e. Are there any differences in the cognitive and functional abilities of Alzheimer's patients who reside at a special care unit versus those residing at a traditional care unit (Swanson, Maas, & Buckwalter, 1994)?

f. Do hyperactive children with attention deficit differ from nonhyperactive children with attention deficit on reading, spelling, and written language achievement (Elbert, 1993)?

g. Will perceivers see women who prefer the courtesy title of Ms. as being higher on instrumental qualities and lower on expressiveness qualities than women who prefer traditional courtesy titles (Dion & Cota, 1991)?

h. Will an empowering style of leadership increase team member satisfaction and will perceptions of team efficacy increase effectiveness (Kumpfer, Turner, Hopkins, & Librett, 1993)?

i. How do ethnicity, gender, and socioeconomic background influence psychosis proneness: perceptual aberration, magical ideation, and schizotypal personality (Porch, Ross, Hanks, & Whitman, 1995)?

j. Does stimulus exposure have two effects, one cognitive and one affective, which in turn affect liking, familiarity, and recognition confidence and accuracy (Zajonc, 1980)?

The last two problems and studies are quite complex because the stated relations are complex. The other problems and studies, though also complex, have only one phenomenon presumably affected by other phenomena, whereas the last two problems have several phenomena influencing two or more other phenomena. Readers should not be discouraged if they find these problems a bit difficult. By the end of the book they should appear interesting and natural.

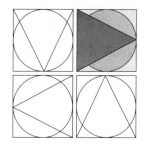

CONSTRUCTS, VARIABLES, AND DEFINITIONS

Scientists operate on two levels: theory–hypothesis–construct and observation. More accurately, they shuttle back and forth between these levels. A psychological scientist may say, "Early deprivation produces learning deficiency." This statement is a hypothesis consisting of two concepts, "early deprivation" and "learning deficiency," joined by a relation word, *produces*. It is on the theory–hypothesis–construct level. Whenever scientists utter relational statements and use concepts, or constructs as we shall call them, they are operating at this level.

Scientists must also operate at the level of observation. They must gather data to test hypotheses. To do this, they must somehow get from the construct level to the observation level. They cannot simply make observations of "early deprivation" and "learning deficiency." They must define these constructs so that observations are possible. The problem studied in this chapter is how to examine and clarify the

39

nature of scientific concepts or constructs. This chapter will also examine and clarify the way in which behavioral scientists get from the construct level to the observation level, how they shuttle from one to the other.

Concepts and Constructs

The terms "concept" and "construct" have similar meanings, yet there is an important distinction. A *concept* expresses an abstraction formed by generalization from particulars. "Weight" is a concept. It expresses numerous observations of things that are "more or less" and "heavy or light." "Mass," "energy," and "force" are concepts used by physical scientists. They are, of course, much more abstract than concepts such as "weight," "height," and "length."

A concept of more interest to readers of this book is "achievement." It is an abstraction formed from the observation of certain behaviors of children. These behaviors are associated with the mastery or "learning" of school tasks—reading words, doing arithmetic problems, drawing pictures, and so on. The various observed behaviors are put together and expressed in a word. "Achievement," "intelligence," "aggressiveness," "conformity," and "honesty" are all concepts used to express varieties of human behavior.

A *construct* is a concept. It has the added meaning, however, of having been deliberately and consciously invented or adopted for a special scientific purpose. "Intelligence" is a concept, an abstraction from the observation of presumably intelligent and nonintelligent behaviors. But as a scientific construct, "intelligence" means both more and less than it may mean as a concept. It means that scientists consciously and systematically use it in two ways: (1) it enters into theoretical schemes and is related in various ways to other constructs (we may say, for example, that school achievement is in part a function of intelligence and motivation) and (2) "intelligence" is so defined and specified that it can be observed and measured (we can make observations of the intelligence of children by administering an intelligence test, or by asking teachers to tell us the relative degrees of intelligence of their pupils).

Variables

Scientists somewhat loosely call the constructs or properties they study "variables." Some examples of important variables in sociology, psychology, political science, and education are: gender, income, education, social class, organizational productivity, occupational mobility, level of aspiration, verbal aptitude, anxiety, religious affiliation, political preference, political development (of nations), task orientation, racial and ethnic prejudices, conformity, recall memory, recognition memory, and achievement. It can be said that a variable is a property that takes on different values. Putting it redundantly, a variable is something that varies. While this way of speaking gives us an intuitive notion of what variables are, we need a more general and yet more precise definition.

A *variable* is a symbol to which numerals or values are assigned. For instance, x is a variable: it is a *symbol* to which we assign numerical values. The variable x may take on any justifiable set of values, for example, scores on an intelligence test or an attitude scale. In the case of intelligence we assign to x a set of numerical values yielded by the procedure designated in a specified test of intelligence. This set of values ranges from low to high, from, say, 50 to 150.

A variable, x, however, may have only two values. If gender is the construct under study, then x can be assigned 1 and 0, where 1 represents one of the genders and 0 the other. It is still a variable. Other examples of two-valued variables are in–out, correct–incorrect, old–young, citizen–noncitizen, middle class–working class, teacher–nonteacher, Republican–Democrat, and so on. Such variables are called *dichotomies*, dichotomous, or binary variables.

Some of the variables used in behavioral research are true dichotomies; that is, they are characterized by the presence or absence of a property: male–female, home–homeless, employed–unemployed. Some variables are *polytomies*. A good example is religious preference: Protestant, Catholic, Muslim, Jew, Buddhist, Other. Such dichotomies and polytomies have been called "qualitative variables." The nature of this designation will be discussed later. Most variables, however, are theoretically capable of taking on continuous values. It has been common practice in behavioral research to convert continuous variables to dichotomies or polytomies. For example, intelligence, a continuous variable, has been broken down into high and low intelligence, or into high, medium, and low intelligence. Variables such as anxiety, introversion, and authoritarianism have been treated similarly. While it is not possible to convert a truly dichotomous variable such as gender to a continuous variable, it is always possible to convert a continuous variable to a dichotomy or a polytomy. As we will see later, such conversion can serve a useful conceptual purpose, but is poor practice in the analysis of data because it discards information.

Constitutive and Operational Definitions of Constructs and Variables

The distinction made earlier between "concept" and "construct" leads naturally to another important distinction between kinds of definitions of constructs and variables. Words or constructs can be defined in two general ways. First, we can define a word by using other words, which is what a dictionary does. We can define *intelligence* by saying it is "operating intellect," "mental acuity," or "the ability to think abstractly." Such definitions use other concepts or conceptual expressions in lieu of the expression or word being defined. Second, we can define a word by assigning expressed or implied actions or behaviors. Defining *intelligence* this way requires that we specify which behaviors of children are "intelligent" and what behaviors are "not intelligent." We may say that a seven-year-old child who successfully reads a story is "intelligent." If the child cannot read the story, we may say the child is "not intelligent." In different words, this kind of definition can be called a *behavioral* or *observational* definition. Both "other word" and "observational" definitions are used constantly in everyday living.

There is a disturbing looseness about this discussion. Although scientists use the types of definitions just described they do so in a more precise manner. We express this usage by defining and explaining Margenau's (1950/1977) distinction between constitutive and operational definitions. A *constitutive* definition defines a construct using other constructs. For instance, we can define *weight* by saying that it is the "heaviness" of objects. Or we can define *anxiety* as "subjectified fear." In both cases we have substituted one concept for another. Some of the constructs of a scientific theory may be defined constitutively. Torgerson (1958/1985), borrowing from Margenau, says that all constructs, in order to be useful scientifically, must possess constitutive meaning. This means that they must be capable of being used in theories.

An *operational* definition assigns meaning to a construct or a variable by specifying the activities or "operations" necessary to measure it and evaluate the measurement. Alternatively, an operational definition is a specification of the activities of the researcher in measuring a variable or in manipulating it. An operational definition is a sort of manual of instructions to the investigator. It says, in effect, "Do such-and-such in so-and-so a manner." In short, it defines or gives meaning to a variable by spelling out what the investigator must do to measure it and evaluate that measurement.

Michel (1990) gives an excellent historical account on how operational definitions became popular in the social and behavioral sciences. Michel cites P. W. Bridgeman, a Nobel laureate, for creating the operational definition in 1927. Bridgeman as quoted in Michel (1990, p. 15) states: "In general we mean by any concept nothing more than a set of operations; *the concept is synonymous with the corresponding set of operations.*" Each different operation would define a different concept.

A well-known, if extreme, example of an operational definition is: Intelligence (anxiety, achievement, and so forth) is scores on X intelligence test, or intelligence is what X intelligence test measures. Also high scores indicate a greater level of intelligence than low scores. This definition tells us what to do to measure intelligence. It says nothing about how well intelligence is measured by the specified instrument. (Presumably the adequacy of the test was ascertained prior to the investigator's use of it.) In this usage, an operational definition is an equation where we say, "Let intelligence equal the scores on X test of intelligence and high scores indicate a higher degree of intelligence than low scores." We also seem to be saying, "The meaning of intelligence (in this research) is expressed by the scores on X intelligence test."

There are, in general, two kinds of operational definitions: (1) *measured*, and (2) *experimental*. The definition given above is more closely tied to measured than to experimental definitions. A *measured* operational definition describes how a variable will be measured. For example, achievement may be defined by a standardized achievement test, by a teacher-made achievement test, or by grades. Doctor, Cutris, and Isaacs (1994), studying the effects of stress counseling on police officers, operationally defined psychiatric morbidity as scores on the General Health Questionnaire and the number of sick-leave days taken. Higher scores and large number of days indicated elevated levels of morbidity. Little, Sterling, and Tingstrom (1996) studied the effects of race and geographic origin on attribution. Attribution was operationally defined as a score on the Attributional Style Questionnaire. A study may include the variable *consideration*. It can be defined operationally by listing behaviors of children that are presumably considerate behaviors and then requiring teachers to rate the children on a five-point scale. Such behaviors might be when children say to each other, "I'm sorry," or "Excuse me." Or when one child yields a toy to another on request (but not on threat of aggression), or when one child helps another with a school task. It can also be defined as counting the number of considerate behaviors. The greater the number, the higher the level of consideration.

An *experimental* operational definition spells out the details (operations) of the investigator's manipulation of a variable. Reinforcement can be operationally defined by giving the details of how subjects are to be reinforced (rewarded) and not reinforced (not rewarded) for specified behaviors. Hom, Berger, Duncan, Miller, and Belvin (1994) operationally defined reinforcement experimentally. In this study, children were assigned to one of four groups. Two of the groups received a cooperative reward condition while the other two groups received an individualistic reward condition. Bahrick (1984) defines long-term memory in terms of at least two processes when it comes to the retention of academically oriented information. One process, called "permastore," selectively chooses some information to be stored permanently and is highly resistant to decay (forgetting). The other process appears to select certain apparently less-significant information, and hence appears less resistant to forgetting. This definition contains clear implications for experimental manipulation. Strack, Martin, and Stepper (1988) operationally defined smiling as the activation of the muscles associated with the human smile. This was done by having a person hold a pen in his or her mouth in a certain way. This was unobtrusive in that the participants in the study were not asked to pose with a smiling face. Other examples of both kinds of operational definitions will be given later.

Scientific investigators must eventually face the necessity of measuring the variables of the relations they are studying. Sometimes measurement is easy, sometimes difficult. To measure gender or social class is easy; to measure creativity, conservatism, or organizational effectiveness is difficult. The importance of operational definitions cannot be overemphasized. They are indispensable ingredients of scientific research because they enable researchers to measure variables and because they are bridges between the theory–hypothesis–construct level and the level of observation. There can be no scientific research without observations, and observations are impossible without clear and specific instructions on what and how to observe. Operational definitions are such instructions.

Although indispensable, operational definitions yield only limited meanings of constructs. No operational definition can ever express the rich and diverse aspects of some variables, such as human prejudice. This means that the variables measured by scientists are always limited and specific in meaning. The "creativity" studied by psychologists is not necessarily the "creativity" referred to by artists, though there will of course be common elements. A person who thinks of a creative solution for a math problem may show little creativity as a poet (Barron & Harrington, 1981). Some psychologists have operationally defined creativity as performance on the Torrance Test of Creative Thinking (Torrance, 1982). Children who score high on this test are more likely to make creative achievements as adults.

Some scientists claim that such limited operational meanings are the only meanings that "mean" anything, that all other definitions are metaphysical nonsense. They say that discussions of anxiety are metaphysical nonsense, unless adequate operational definitions of anxiety are available and used. This view is extreme, though it has healthy aspects. To insist that every term we use in scientific discourse be operationally defined would be too narrowing, too restrictive, and, as we shall see, scientifically unsound. Northrop (1947/1983, p. 130) says, for example, "The importance of operational definitions is that they make verification possible and enrich meaning. They do not, however, exhaust scientific meaning." Margenau (1950/1977, p. 232) makes the same point in his extended discussion of scientific constructs.

Despite the dangers of extreme operationalism, it can be safely said that operationalism has been and still is a healthy influence. As Skinner (1945, p. 274) puts it,

> The operational attitude, in spite of its shortcomings, is a good thing in any science, but especially in psychology, because of the presence there of a vast vocabulary of ancient and nonscientific origin.

When the terms used in education are considered, clearly education, too, has a vast vocabulary of ancient and nonscientific terms. Consider these: the whole child, horizontal and vertical enrichment, meeting the needs of the learner, core curriculum, emotional adjustment, and curricular enrichment. This is also true in the field of geriatric nursing. Here nurses deal with such terms as the aging process, self-image, attention span, and unilateral neglect (Eliopoulos, 1993; Smeltzer & Bare, 1992).

◉ **FIGURE 3.1**

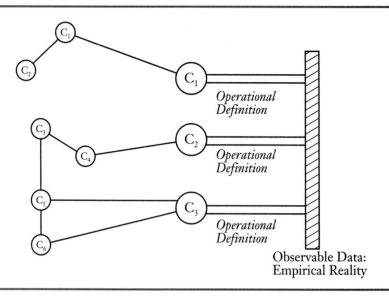

To clarify constitutive and operational definitions (as well as theory) look at Figure 3.1, which has been adapted after Margenau (1950/1977) and Torgerson (1958/1985). The diagram is intended to illustrate a well-developed theory. The single lines represent theoretical connections or relations between constructs. These constructs, labeled with lowercase letters, are defined constitutively; that is, c_4 is somehow defined by c_3, or vice versa. The double lines represent operational definitions. The constructs are directly linked to observable data; they are indispensable links to empirical reality. However, not all constructs in a scientific theory are defined operationally. Indeed, it is a rather thin theory that has all its constructs so defined.

Let us build a "small theory" of underachievement to illustrate these notions. Suppose an investigator believes that underachievement is in part a function of pupils' self-concepts. The investigator believes that pupils who perceive themselves as inadequate and have negative self-perceptions, also tend to achieve less than their potential capacity and aptitude indicate they should achieve. It follows that ego-needs (which we will not define here) and motivation for achievement (call this nach, or need for achievement) are tied to underachievement. Naturally, the investigator is also aware of the relation between aptitude and intelligence and achievement in general. A diagram to illustrate this "theory" might look like Figure 3.2.

▣ **FIGURE 3.2**

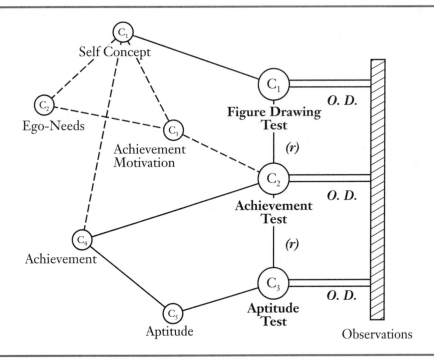

The investigator has *no direct* measure of self-concept, but assumes that inferences can be drawn about an individual's self-concept from a figure drawing test. Self-concept is operationally defined, then, as certain responses to the figure drawing test. This is probably the most common method of measuring psychological (and educational) constructs. The heavy single line between c_1 and C_1 indicates the relatively direct nature of the presumed relation between self-concept and the test. (The double line between C_1 and the level of observation indicates an operational definition, as it did in Figure 3.1.)

Similarly, the construct achievement (c_4) is operationally defined as the discrepancy between measured achievement (C_2) and measured aptitude (c_5). In this model the investigator has no direct measure of achievement motivation, no operational definition of it. In another study an investigator may specifically hypothesize a relationship between achievement and achievement motivation, in which case he or she will try to define achievement motivation operationally.

A single solid line between concepts, for example, the one between the construct achievement (c_4) and achievement test (C_2), indicates a relatively well-established relation between postulated achievement and what standard achievement tests measure. The single solid lines between C_1 and C_2 and between C_2 and C_3 indicate obtained relations between the test scores of these measures. (The lines between C_1 and C_2 and between C_2 and C_3 are labeled (r) for "relation," or "coefficient of correlation.")

The broken single lines indicate postulated relations between constructs that are not relatively well established. A good example of this is the postulated relation between self-concept and achievement motivation. One of the aims of science is to make these broken lines solid lines by bridging the operational definition–measurement gap. In this case, it is quite conceivable that both self-concept and achievement motivation can be operationally defined and directly measured.

In essence, this is the way a behavioral scientist operates. The scientist shuttles back and forth between the level of construct and the level of observation. This is done by operationally defining the variables of the theory that are amenable to such definition. Then the relations are estimated between the operationally-defined and measured variables. From these estimated relations the scientist draws inferences as to the relations between the constructs. In the above example, the behavioral scientist calculates the relation between C_1 (figure drawing test) and C_2 (achievement test). If the relation is established on this observational level, the scientist infers that a relation exists between c_1 (self-concept) and c_4 (achievement).

Types of Variables

Independent and Dependent Variables

With definitional background behind us, we return to variables. Variables can be classified in several ways. In this book three kinds of variables are very important and will be emphasized: (1) independent and dependent variables, (2) active and attribute variables, and (3) continuous and categorical variables.

The most useful way to categorize variables is either as independent or dependent. This categorization is highly useful because of its general applicability, simplicity, and special importance, both in conceptualizing and designing research and in communicating the results of research. An *independent variable* is the *presumed* cause of the *dependent variable*, the *presumed* effect. The independent variable is the antecedent; the dependent is the consequent. Since one of the goals of science is to uncover relations between different phenomena, looking at the relation between independent and dependent variables accomplishes this. It is the independent variable that is assumed to influence the dependent variable. In some studies, the independent variable "causes" changes in the dependent variable. When we say: If A, then B, we have the conditional conjunction of an independent variable (A) and a dependent variable (B).

The terms "independent variable" and "dependent variable" come from mathematics, where X is the independent and Y the dependent variable. This is probably the best way to think of independent and dependent variables because there is no need to use the touchy word *cause* and related words, and because use of such symbols applies to most research situations. There is no theoretical restriction on numbers of Xs and Ys. When we later consider multivariate thinking and analysis, we will deal with several independent and dependent variables.

In experiments the independent variable is the variable manipulated by the experimenter. Changes in the values or levels of the independent variable produce changes in the dependent variable. When educational investigators studied the effects of differing teaching methods on math test performance, they varied the method of teaching. In one condition they may have "lecture only," in the other it might be "lecture plus video." Teaching method is the independent variable. The outcome variable, test score on mathematics, is the dependent variable.

The assignment of participants to different groups based on the existence of some characteristic is an example of where the researcher was not able to manipulate the independent variable. The values of the independent variable in this situation preexist. The participant either has the characteristic or not. Here, there is no possibility of experimental manipulation, but the variable is considered to "logically" have some effect on a dependent variable. Subject characteristic variables make up most of these types of independent variables. One of the more common independent variables of this kind is gender (female and male). So, if a researcher wanted to determine if females and males differ on math skills, a math test would be given to representatives of both groups, and the test scores then compared. The math test would be the dependent variable. A general rule is that when the researcher manipulates a variable or assigns participants to groups according to some characteristic, that variable is the independent variable. Table 3.1 gives a comparison between the two types of independent variable and their relation to the dependent variable. The independent variable must have at least two levels or values. Notice in Table 3.1 that both situations have two levels for the independent variable.

TABLE 3.1 *Relation of Manipulated and Nonmanipulated Independent Variables to the Dependent Variable*

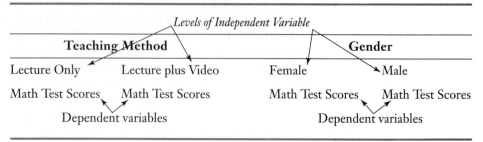

The dependent variable is of course the variable predicted *to*, whereas the independent variable is predicted *from*. The dependent variable, Y, is the presumed effect, which varies concomitantly with changes or variations in the independent variable, X. It is the variable that is observed for variation as a presumed result of variation in the independent variable. The dependent variable is the outcome measure that the researcher uses to determine if changes in the independent variable had an effect. In predicting from X to Y, we can take any value of X we wish, whereas the value of Y we predict to is "dependent on" the value of X we have selected. The dependent variable is ordinarily the condition we are trying to explain. The most common dependent variable in education, for instance, is "achievement" or "learning." We want to account for or explain achievement. In so doing we have a large number of possible Xs or independent variables from which to choose.

When the relation between intelligence and school achievement is studied, intelligence is the independent and achievement is the dependent variable. (Is it conceivable that it might be the other way around?) Other independent variables that can be studied in relation to the dependent variable achievement, are social class, methods of teaching, personality types, types of motivation (reward and punishment), attitudes toward school, class atmosphere, and so on. When the presumed determinants of delinquency are studied, such determinants as slum conditions, broken homes, lack of parental love, and the like, are independent variables and, naturally, delinquency (more accurately, delinquent behavior) is the dependent variable. In the frustration–aggression hypothesis, frustration is the independent variable and aggression the dependent variable. Sometimes a phenomenon is studied by itself, and either an independent or a dependent variable is implied. This is the case when teacher behaviors and characteristics are studied. The usual implied dependent variable is achievement or child behavior. Teacher behavior can of course be a dependent variable. Consider an example in nursing science. When cognitive and functional measures of Alzheimer's patients are compared between traditional nursing homes and special care units (SCU), the independent variable is the place of care. The dependent variables are the cognitive and functional measures (Swanson, Maas, & Buckwalter, 1994).

The relation between an independent variable and a dependent variable can perhaps be more clearly understood if we lay out two axes at right angles to each other. One axis represents the independent variable and the other represents the dependent variable. (When two axes are at right angles to each other, they are called *orthogonal* axes.) Following mathematical custom, x, the independent variable, is the horizontal axis and y, the dependent variable, is the vertical axis (x is called the *abscissa* and y the *ordinate*). The values for x are laid out on the x-axis, and y values on the y-axis.

A very common and useful way to "see" and interpret a relation is to plot the pairs of xy values, using the x and y axes as a frame of reference. In a study of child development, let us suppose that we have two sets of measures. The x measures chronological age and the y measures reading age. *Reading age* is a so-called growth age. Seriatim measurements of individuals' growths—in height, weight, intelligence, and so forth—are expressed as the average chronological age at which they appear in the standard population.

x: Chronological Age (in Months)	y: Reading Age (in Months)
72	48
84	62
96	69
108	71
120	100
132	112

These measures are plotted in Figure 3.3.

The relation between chronological age (CA) and reading age (RA) can now be "seen" and roughly approximated. Note that there is a pronounced tendency (as might be expected) for more advanced CA to be associated with higher RA, medium CA with medium RA, and less advanced CA with lower RA. In other words, the relation between the independent and dependent variables, in this case between CA and RA, can be seen from a graph such as shown in Figure 3.3. A straight line has been drawn in to "show" the relation. It is a rough average of all the points of the plot. Note that if one has knowledge of independent variable measures and a relation such as that shown in Figure 3.3, one can predict—with considerable accuracy—the dependent variable measures. Plots like this can, of course, be used with any independent and dependent variable measures.

The student should be alert to the possibility of a variable being an independent variable in one study and a dependent variable in another, or even both in the same study. An example is job satisfaction. A majority of the studies involving job satisfaction use it as a dependent variable. Day and Schoenrade (1997) show the effect of sexual orientation on work attitudes. One of these work attitudes is job satisfaction.

⊡ FIGURE 3.3

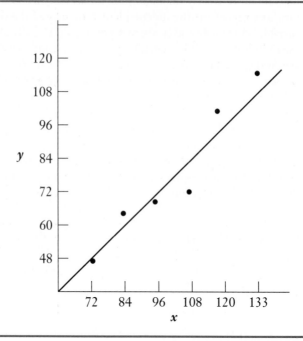

Likewise, Hodson (1989) studies gender differences in job satisfaction. Scott, Moore, and Miceli (1997) find job satisfaction linked to the behavior patterns of workaholics. There are studies where job satisfaction is used as an independent variable. Meiksins and Watson (1989) show how much job satisfaction influences the professional autonomy of engineers. Studies by Somers (1996); Francis-Felsen, Coward, Hogan, and Duncan (1996); and Hutchinson and Turner (1988) examined job satisfaction's effect on nursing personnel turnover.

Another example is anxiety. Anxiety has been studied as an independent variable affecting the dependent variable achievement. Oldani (1997) found mother's anxiety during pregnancy influenced the achievement (measured as success in the music industry) of the offspring. Capaldi, Crosby, and Stoolmiller (1996) used the anxiety levels of teenage boys to predict the timing of their first sexual intercourse. Onwuegbuzie and Seaman (1995) studied the effects of test anxiety on test performance in a statistics course. Anxiety can also be readily conceived and used as a dependent variable. For example, it could be used to study the difference between types of culture, socioeconomic status and gender (see Guida & Ludlow, 1989; Murphy, Olivier, Monson, & Sobol, 1991). In other words, the independent and dependent variable classification is really a classification of uses of variables rather than a distinction between different kinds of variables.

Active and Attribute Variables

A classification that will be useful later in our study of research design is based on the distinction between experimental and measured variables. It is important when planning and executing research to distinguish between these two types of variables. Manipulated variables will be called *active* variables; measured variables will be called *attribute* variables. For example, Colwell, Foreman, and Trotter (1993) compared two methods of treating pressure ulcers of bedridden patients. The dependent variables were efficacy and cost effectiveness. The two treatment methods were moist gauze dressing and hydrocolloid wafer dressing. The researchers had control over who got which type of treatment. As such, the treatment or independent variable was an active or manipulated variable.

Any variable that is manipulated, then, is an active variable. "Manipulation" means, essentially, doing different things to different groups of subjects, as we will see clearly in a later chapter where we discuss in depth the differences between experimental and nonexperimental research. When a researcher does one thing to one group (for example, positively reinforces a certain kind of behavior), and does something else to another group, or has the two groups follow different instructions, this is manipulation. When one uses different methods of teaching, or rewards the subjects of one group and punishes those of another, or creates anxiety through worrisome instructions, one is *actively* manipulating the variables methods, reinforcement, and anxiety.

Another related classification, used mainly by psychologists, is *stimulus* and *response* variables. A *stimulus variable* is any condition or manipulation by the experimenter of the environment that evokes a response in an organism. A *response variable* is any kind of behavior of the organism. The assumption is made that for any kind of behavior there is always a stimulus. Thus the organism's behavior is a response. This classification is reflected in the well-known equation: $R = f(O, S)$, which is read: "Responses are a function of the organism and stimuli," or "Response variables are a function of organismic variables and stimulus variables."

Variables that cannot be manipulated are *attribute variables* or *subject-characteristic* variables. It is impossible, or at least difficult, to manipulate many variables. All human characteristic variables such as intelligence, aptitude, gender, socioeconomic status, conservatism, field dependence, need for achievement, and attitudes are attribute variables. Subjects come to our studies with these variables (attributes) ready-made or preexisting. Early environment, heredity, and other circumstances have made individuals what they are. Such variables are also called *organismic* variables. Any property of an individual, any characteristic or attribute, is an organismic variable. It is part of the organism, so to speak. In other words, organismic variables are those characteristics that individuals have in varying degrees when they come to the research situation. The term *individual differences* implies organismic variables. One of the more common attribute variables in the social and behavioral sciences is gender: female–male. Studies designed to compare gender differences involve an attribute variable. Take, for example, the study by de Weerth and Kalma (1993). These researchers compared females to males on their response to spousal or partner infidelity. The attribute variable here is gender. Gender is *not* a manipulated variable. There are studies where a test score or a collection of test scores were used to divide a group of people into two or more groups. In this case the group differences are reflected in an attribute variable. For example, the study by Hart, Forth, and Hare (1990) administered a psychopathology test to male prison inmates. Based on their scores, inmates were assigned to one of three groups: low, medium, and high. They were then compared on their score on a battery of neuropsychological tests. The level of psychopathology preexists and is not manipulated by the researcher. If an inmate scored high, he was placed in the high group. Hence psychopathology is an attribute variable in this study. There are some studies where the independent variable could have been manipulated; however, for logistical or legal reasons, they were not. An example of where the independent variable could have been manipulated but was not is the study by Swanson, Maas, and Buckwalter (1994). These researchers compared different care facilities' effect on cognitive and functional measures of Alzheimer's patients. The attribute variable was the type of facility. The researchers were not allowed to place patients into the two different care facilities (traditional nursing home versus special care unit). The researchers were forced to study the subjects after they had been assigned to a care facility. Hence the independent variable can be thought of as a nonmanipulated variable. The researchers inherited intact groups.

The word *attribute*, moreover, is accurate enough when used with inanimate objects or referents. However, organizations, institutions, groups, populations, homes, and geographical areas also have attributes—*active attributes*. Organizations are variably productive; institutions become outmoded; groups differ in cohesiveness; geographical areas vary widely in resources.

This active attribute distinction is general, flexible, and useful. We will see that some variables are by their very nature always attributes, but other variables that are attributes can also be active. This latter characteristic makes it possible to investigate the "same" relations in differing ways. Again, using the variable anxiety example, we can measure the anxiety of subjects. Anxiety is in this case obviously an attribute variable. However, we can also manipulate anxiety by inducing different degrees of anxiety. For example, telling the subjects of one experimental group that the task they are about to do is difficult, that their intelligence is being measured, and that their futures depend on the scores they get. The subjects of another experimental group are told to do their best but to relax. They are told the outcome is unimportant and will have no influence on their futures. Actually, we cannot assume that the measured (attribute) and the manipulated (active) "anxieties" are the same. We may assume that both are "anxiety" in a broad sense, but they are certainly not the same.

Continuous and Categorical Variables

A distinction especially useful in the planning of research and the analysis of data between continuous and categorical variables has already been introduced. Its later importance, however, justifies more extended consideration.

A *continuous* variable is capable of taking on an ordered set of values within a certain range. This definition means, first, that the values of a continuous variable reflect at least a rank order, a larger value of the variable meaning more of the property in question than a smaller value. The values yielded by a scale to measure dependency, for instance, express differing amounts of dependency from high through medium to low. Second, continuous measures in actual use are contained in a range, and each individual obtains a "score" within that range. A scale to measure dependency may have the range 1 through 7. Most scales in use in the behavioral sciences also have a third characteristic: there is a theoretically infinite set of values within the range. (Rank-order scales are somewhat different; they will be discussed later in the book.) That is, a particular individual's score may be 4.72 rather than simply 4 or 5.

Categorical variables, as we will call them, belong to a kind of measurement called nominal (explained in Chapter 25). In nominal measurement, there are two or more subsets of the set of objects being measured. Individuals are categorized by their possession of the characteristic that defines any subset. "To categorize" means to assign an object to a subclass (or subset) of a class (or set) on the basis of the object's having or not having the characteristic that defines the subset. The individual being categorized either has the defining property or does not have it; it is an all-or-none kind of thing. The simplest examples are dichotomous categorical variables: female–male, Republican–Democrat, right–wrong. Polytomies—variables with more than two subsets or partitions—are fairly common, especially in sociology and economics: religious preference, education (usually), nationality, occupational choice, and so on.

Categorical variables and nominal measurement have simple requirements: all the members of a subset are considered the same and all are assigned the same name (nominal) and the same numeral. If the variable is religious preference, for instance, all Protestants are the same, all Catholics are the same, and all "others" are the same. If an individual is a Catholic (operationally defined in a suitable way), that person is assigned to the category "Catholic" and also assigned a "1" in that category. In brief, that person is counted as a "Catholic." Categorical variables are "democratic." There is no rank order, or greater than and less than, among the categories, and all members of a category are assigned the same value.

The expression "qualitative variables" has sometimes been applied to categorical variables, especially to dichotomies, probably in contrast to "quantitative variables" (our continuous variables). Such usage reflects a somewhat distorted notion of what variables are. They are always quantifiable, or they are not variables. If x has only two subsets and can take on only two values (1 and 0), these are still values, and the variable varies. If x is a polytomy, like political affiliation, we quantify again by assigning integer values to individuals. If an individual, say, is a Democrat, then put that person in the Democrat subset. That individual is assigned a 1. All individuals in the Democrat subset would be assigned a value of 1. It is extremely important to understand this because, for one thing, it is the basis of quantifying many variables, even experimental treatments, for complex analysis. In multiple regression analysis, as we will see later, all variables—continuous and categorical—are entered as variables into the analysis. Earlier, the example of gender was given, 1 being assigned to one gender and 0 to the other. We set up a column of 1s and 0s just as we would set up a column of dependency scores. The column of 1s and 0s is the quantification of the variable gender. There is no mystery here. Such variables have been called "dummy variables." Since they are highly useful and powerful, even indispensable in modern research data analysis, they need to be understood clearly. A deeper explanation of this can be found in Kerlinger and Pedhazur (1973) and Chapter 34 of this book. The method is easily extended to polytomies. A *polytomy* is a division of the members of a group into three or more subdivisions.

Constructs, Observables, and Latent Variables

In much of the previous discussion of this chapter it has been implied, though not explicitly stated, that there is a sharp difference between constructs and observed variables. Moreover, we can say that constructs are nonobservables; and variables, when operationally defined, are observables. This distinction is important because, if we are not always keenly aware of the level of discourse we are on when talking about variables, we can hardly be clear about what we are doing.

An important and fruitful expression, which we will encounter and use extensively later in this book, is "latent variable." A latent variable is an unobserved "entity" presumed to underlie observed variables. The best-known example of an important latent variable is "intelligence." We can say that three ability tests—verbal, numerical, and spatial—are positively and substantially related. This means, for the most part, that people high on one tend to be high on the others; similarly, persons low on one tend to be low on the others. We believe that something is common to the three tests or observed variables, and name this something "intelligence." It is a latent variable.

We have encountered many examples of latent variables in previous pages: achievement, creativity, social class, job satisfaction, religious preference, and so on. Indeed, whenever we utter the names of phenomena on which people or objects vary, we are talking about latent variables. In science, our real interest is more in the relations among latent variables than it is in the relations among observed variables, because we seek to explain phenomena and their relations. When we enunciate a theory, we enunciate in part systematic relations among latent variables. We are not too interested in the relation between observed frustrated behaviors and observed aggressive behaviors, for example, though we must of course work with them at the empirical level. We are really interested in the relation between the latent variable frustration and the latent variable aggression.

We must be cautious, however, when dealing with nonobservables. Scientists, using such terms as "hostility," "anxiety," and "learning," are aware that they are talking about invented constructs. The "reality" of these constructs is inferred from behavior. If they want to study the effects of different kinds of motivation, they must know that "motivation" is a latent variable, a construct invented to account for presumably "motivated" behavior. They must know that its "reality" is only postulated. They can only judge that youngsters are motivated or not motivated by observing their behaviors. Still, in order to study motivation, they must measure or manipulate it. But they cannot measure it directly because it is, in short, an "in-the-head" variable, an unobservable entity, a latent variable. The construct was invented for "something" *presumed to be* inside individuals, "something" prompting them to behave in such-and-such a manner. This means that researchers must always measure presumed indicators of motivation and not motivation itself. They must, in different words, always measure some kind of behavior, be it marks on paper, spoken words, or meaningful gestures, and then draw inferences about presumed characteristics—or latent variables.

Other terms have been used to express more or less the same ideas. For example, Tolman (1951 pp. 115–129.) calls constructs intervening variables. *Intervening variable* is a term invented to account for internal, unobservable psychological processes that in turn account for behavior. An intervening variable is an "in-the-head" variable. It cannot be seen, heard, or touched. It is inferred from behavior. "Hostility" is inferred from presumably hostile or aggressive acts. "Anxiety" is inferred from test scores, skin responses, heartbeat, and certain experimental manipulations. Another term is "hypothetical construct." Since this expression means much the same as latent variable with somewhat less generality, we need not pause over it. We should mention, however, that "latent variable" appears to be a more general and applicable expression than "intervening variable" and "hypothetical construct," because it can be used for virtually any phenomena that presumably influence or are influenced by other phenomena. In other words, "latent variable" can be used with psychological, sociological, and other phenomena. "Latent variable" seems to be the preferable term because of its generality. Also, because it is now possible, in the analysis of covariance structures approach, to assess the effects of latent variables on each other and on so-called manifest or observed variables. This rather abstract discussion will later be made more concrete and, it is hoped, meaningful. We will then see that the idea of latent variables and the relations between them is an extremely important, fruit-ful, and useful one, that is helping to change fundamental approaches to research problems.

Examples of Variations and Operational Definitions

A number of constructs and operational definitions have already been given. To illustrate and clarify the preceding discussion, especially where the distinction was made between experimental and measured variables and between constructs and operationally defined variables, several examples of constructs or variables and operational definitions are given below. If a definition is experimental, it is labeled (E); if it is measured, it is labeled (M).

Operational definitions differ in degree of specificity. Some are quite closely tied to observations. "Test" definitions, like "intelligence is defined as a score on X intelligence test," are very specific. A definition like "frustration is prevention from reaching a goal" is more general and requires further specification to be measurable.

Social Class ". . . two or more orders of people who are believed to be, and are accordingly ranked by the members of a community, in socially superior and inferior positions" (M) (Warner & Lunt, 1941, p. 82). To be operational, this definition has to be specified by questions aimed at people's beliefs about other people's positions. This is a subjective definition of social class. Social class, or social status, is also defined more objectively by using such indices as occupation, income, and education, or by combinations of such indices. For example, ". . . we converted information about the education, occupation and income of the parents of the NLSY youths into an index of socioeconomic status (SES) in which the highest scores indicate advanced education, affluence and prestigious occupations. Lowest scores indicate poverty, meager education and the most menial jobs" (M) (Herrnstein & Murray, 1996, p. 131).

Achievement (School, Arithmetic, and Spelling) Achievement is customarily defined operationally by citing a standardized test of achievement (for example, Iowa Tests of Basic Skills, Elementary or the Achievement Test of the Kaufman Assessment Battery for Children [K-ABC]), by grade-point averages, or by teacher judgments. "Student achievement was measured by the combined test scores of reading and mathematics" (M) (Peng & Wright, 1994). Occasionally, achievement is in the form of a performance test. Silverman (1993) examined students on two skills in volleyball: the serve test and the forearm passing test. In the serve test, students received a score between 0 and 4 depending on where the served ball dropped. The forearm passing test involved bouncing the ball off of one's forearm. The criteria used was to count the number of times a student could pass the ball above an 8-foot line against the wall within a 1-minute period (M). Also used in some educational studies is an operational definition of the concept *student achievement perception*. Here, students are asked to evaluate themselves. The question used by Shoffner (1990) was "What kind of student do you think you are?" The response choices available were "A student," "B student," and "C student" (M).

Achievement (Academic Performance) "As a result, grades for all students in all sections were obtained and used to determine the section-rank for each student participating in the study. Section percentile rank was computed for each of these students and was used as the dependent measure of achievement in the final data analysis" (M) (Strom, Hocevar, & Zimmer, 1990).

Intrinsic Motivation is defined operationally by Hom, Berger, et al. (1994) as "The cumulative amount of time that each student played with the pattern blocks with the reward system absent" (M).

Popularity. Popularity is often defined operationally by the number of sociometric choices an individual receives from other individuals (in his or her class, play group, and so on). Individuals are asked: "With whom would you like to work?" "With whom would you like to play?" and the like. Each individual is required to choose one, two, or more individuals from his or her group on the basis of such criterion questions (M).

Task Involvement ". . . each child's behavior during a lesson was coded every 6 sec. as being appropriately involved, or deviant. The task involvement scores for a lesson was the percentage of 6-sec. units in which the children were coded as appropriately involved" (M) (Kounin & Doyle, 1975).

Reinforcement. Reinforcement definitions come in a number of forms. Most involve, in one way or another, the principle of reward. However, both positive and negative reinforcement may be used. Specific experimental definitions of "reinforcement" follow.

In the second 10 minutes, every opinion statement S made was recorded by E and reinforced. For two groups, E agreed with every opinion statement by saying: "Yes, you're right," "That's so," or the like, or by nodding and smiling affirmation if he could not interrupt (E).

> . . . the model and the child were administered alternately 12 different sets of story items. . . . To each of the 12 items, the model consistently expressed judgmental responses in opposition to the child's moral orientation . . . and the experimenter reinforced the model's behavior with verbal approval responses such as "Very good," "That's fine," and "That's good." The child was similarly reinforced whenever he adopted the model's class of moral judgments in response to his own set of items [this is called "social reinforcement"] (E) (Bandura & MacDonald, 1994).

The teacher gives verbal praise each time the child exhibits the target behavior. The target behaviors are attending to instruction, schoolwork, and responding aloud. The recording is done every 15 seconds (E) (Martens, Hiralall, & Bradley, 1997).

Attitudes Toward AIDS is defined by an 18-item scale. Each item consisted of a Likert-type format reflecting different attitudes toward AIDS patients. Some sample items are: "People with AIDS should not be permitted to use public toilets," and "There should be mandatory testing of all Americans for AIDS" (M) (Lester, 1989).

Borderline Personality is defined by Comrey (1993) as having low scores on three scales of the Comrey Personality Scales. The three scales are: Trust versus Defensiveness, Social Conformity versus Rebelliousness, and Emotional Stability versus Neuroticism.

Employee Delinquency is defined operationally as a combination of three variables. The variables are the number of chargeable accidents, the number of warning letters, and the number of suspensions (M) (Hogan & Hogan, 1989).

Religiosity is defined as a score on the Francis Scale of Attitudes toward Christianity. This scale consists of 24 items. Each item has a Likert-type response scale. Sample items include: "Saying my prayers helps me a lot," and "God helps me to lead a better life" (M) (Gillings & Joseph, 1996). Religiosity should not be confused with religious preference. Here religiosity refers to the strength of devotion to one's chosen religion.

Self-esteem is a manipulated independent variable in the study by Steele, Spencer, and Lynch (1993). Here subjects are given a self-esteem test, but when they are given feedback, the information on the official-looking feedback report is bogus. Subjects of the same measured level of self-esteem are divided into three feedback groups: positive, negative, and none. In the positive feedback condition (positive self-esteem), subjects are described with statements such as "clear thinking." Those in the negative group (negative self-esteem) are given adjectives like "passive in action." The "no feedback" group are told that their personality profiles (self-esteem) were not ready due to a backlog in scoring and interpretation (E). Most studies on self-esteem use a measured operational definition. In the above example, Steele, Spencer, and Lynch also used the Janis-Field Feelings of Inadequacy Self-esteem Scale (M). In another example, Luhtanen and Crocker (1992) define collective self-esteem as a score on a scale containing 16 Likert-type items. These items ask respondents to think about a variety of social groups and membership such as gender, religion, race, and ethnicity (M).

Race is usually a measured variable. However, in a study by Annis and Corenblum (1986), 83 Canadian Indian kindergartners and first graders were asked questions on racial preferences and self-identity by either a white or Indian experimenter (E). The interest here was on whether or not the race of the experimenter influenced responses.

Loneliness. One definition of this is a score on the UCLA Loneliness Scale. This scale includes items such as "No one really knows me well," or "I lack companionship." There is also the Loneliness Deprivation Scale that has items such as "I experience a sense of emptiness," or "There is no one who shows a particular interest in me" (M) (Oshagan & Allen, 1992).

Halo. There have been many operational definitions of the halo effect. Balzer and Sulsky (1992) found and summarized 108 definitions that fit into six categories. One of the definitions states that halo is ". . . the average within-rate variance or standard deviation of ratings." Another would be "comparing obtained ratings with true ratings provided by expert raters" (M).

Memory: Recall and Recognition ". . . recall is to ask the participant to recite what he or she remembers of the items shown him or her, giving a point for each item that matches one on the stimulus list (M) (Norman, 1976, p. 97). "The recognition test consisted of 62 sentences presented to all subjects . . . subjects were instructed to rate each sentence on their degree of confidence that the sentence had been presented in the acquisition set" (M) (Richter & Seay, 1987).

Social Skills. These can be operationally defined as a score on the Social Skills Rating Scale (Gresham & Elliot, 1990). There is the possibility of input from the student, parent and teacher. Social behaviors are rated in terms of frequency of occurrence and also on the level of importance. Some social skill items include: "Gets along with people who are different [teacher]," "Volunteers to help family members with tasks [parent]," and "I politely question rules that may be unfair [student]" (M).

Ingratiation. One of many impression management techniques (see Orpen, 1996; Gordon, 1996). Ingratiation is defined operationally as a score on the Kumar and Beyerlein (1991) Scale. This scale consisted of 25 Likert-type items and designed to measure the frequency that subordinates, in a superior–subordinate relationship, use ingratiatory tactics (M). Strutton, Pelton, and Lumpkin (1995) modified the Kumar–Beyerlein scale. Instead of measuring ingratiation between and employee and employer–supervisor, it measured ingratiation behavior between a salesperson and a customer (M).

Feminism. This is defined by a score on the Attitudes toward Women Questionnaire. This instrument consists of 18 statements to which the respondent registers agreement on a 5-point scale. Items include: "Men have held power for too long"; "Beauty contests are degrading to women"; "Children of working mothers are bound to suffer" (Wilson & Reading, 1989).

Values. "Rank the ten goals in the order of their importance to you. (1) financial success; (2) being liked; (3) success in family life; (4) being intellectually capable; (5) living by religious principles; (6) helping others; (7) being normal, well-adjusted; (8) cooperating with others; (9) doing a thorough job; (10) occupational success" (M) (Newcomb, 1978).

Democracy (Political Democracy) "The index [of political democracy] consists of three indicators of popular sovereignty and three of political liberties. The three measures of popular sovereignty are: (1) fairness of elections, (2) effective executive selection, and (3) legislative selection. The indicators of political liberties are: (4) freedom of the press, (5) freedom of group opposition, and (6) government sanctions" (M). Bollen (1979) gives operational details of the six social indicators in an appendix (pp. 585–586). This is a particularly good example of the operational definition of a complex concept. Moreover, it is an excellent description of the ingredients of democracy.

The benefits of operational thinking have been great. Indeed, operationalism has been and is one of the most significant and important movements of our times. Extreme operationalism, of course, can be dangerous because it clouds recognition of the importance of constructs and constitutive definitions in behavioral science, and because it can also restrict research to trivial problems. There can be little doubt, however, that it is a healthy influence. It is the indispensable key to achieving objectivity (without which there is no science), because its demand that observations must be public and replicable helps to put research activities outside of and apart from researchers and their predilections. And, as Underwood (1957, p. 53) has said in his classical text on psychological research:

> I would say that operational thinking makes better scientists. The operationist is forced to remove the fuzz from his empirical concepts . . . operationism facilitates communication among scientists because the meaning of concepts so defined is not easily subject to misinterpretation.

CHAPTER SUMMARY

1. A *concept* is an expression of an abstraction formed from generalization of particulars, for example, weight. This expression is from observations of certain behaviors or actions.
2. A *construct* is a concept that has been formulated so that it can be used in science. It is used in theoretical schemes. It is defined so that it can be observed and measured.
3. A *variable* is defined as a property that can take on different values. It is a symbol to which values are assigned.
4. Constructs and words can be defined by
   a. other words or concepts,
   b. description of an implicit or explicit action or behavior.

5. A *constitutive definition* is where constructs are defined by other constructs.
6. An *operational definition* is where meaning is assigned by specifying the activities or operations necessary to measure and evaluate the construct. Operational definitions can give only limited meaning of constructs. They cannot completely describe a construct or variable. There are two types of operational definitions:
    a. measured—tells us how the variable or construct will be scaled.
    b. experimental—lays out the details of how the variable (construct) is manipulated by the experimenter.
7. Types of variables
    a. The *independent* variable is varied and has a presumed cause on another variable, the dependent variable. In an experiment, it is the manipulated variable. It is the variable under the control of the experimenter. In a nonexperimental study, it is the variable that has a logical effect on the dependent variable.
    b. The *dependent* variable's effect alters concomitantly with changes or variations in the independent variable.
    c. An *active* variable is manipulated. Manipulation means that the experimenter has control over how the values change.
    d. An *attributive* variable is measured and cannot be manipulated. A variable that cannot be manipulated is one where the experimenter has no control over the values of the variable.
    e. A *continuous* variable is capable of taking on an ordered set of values within a certain range. Between two values there are an infinite number of other values. These variables reflect at least a rank order.
    f. *Categorical* variables belong to a kind of measurement where objects are assigned to a subclass or subset. The subclasses are distinct and nonoverlapping. All objects put into the same category are considered to have the same characteristic(s).
    g. *Latent* variables are unobservable entities. They are assumed to underlie observed variables.
    h. *Intervening* variables are constructs that account for internal unobservable psychological processes that account for behavior. It cannot be seen but is inferred from behavior.

STUDY SUGGESTIONS

1. Write operational definitions for five or six of the following constructs. When possible, write two such definitions: an experimental and a measured definition.

reinforcement	punitiveness
achievement	reading ability

underachievement	needs
leadership	interests
transfer of training	delinquency
level of aspiration	need for affiliation
organizational conflict	conformity
political preference	marital satisfaction

Some of these concepts or variables—for example, needs and transfer of training—may be difficult to define operationally. Why?

2. Can any of the variables in 1, above, be both independent and dependent variables? Which ones?

3. It is instructive and broadening for specialists to read outside their fields. This is particularly true for students of behavioral research. It is suggested that the student of a particular field read two or three research studies in one of the best journals of another field. If you are in psychology, read a sociology journal, for example, the *American Sociological Review*. If you are in education or sociology, read a psychology journal, for example, the *Journal of Personality and Social Psychology* or the *Journal of Experimental Psychology*. Students not in education can sample the *Journal of Educational Psychology* or the *American Educational Research Journal*. As you read, jot down the names of the variables and compare them to the variables in your own field. Are they primarily active or attribute variables? Note, for instance, that psychology's variables are more "active" than sociology's. What implications do the variables of a field have for its research?

4. Reading the following articles is useful in learning and developing operational definitions.

Kinnier, R. T. (1995). A reconceptualization of values clarification: Values conflict resolution. *Journal of Counseling and Development, 74(1)*, 18–24.

Lego, S. (1988). Multiple disorder: An interpersonal approach to etiology, treatment and nursing care. *Archives of Psychiatric Nursing, 2(4)*, 231–235.

Lobel, M. (1994). Conceptualizations, measurement, and effects of prenatal maternal stress on birth outcomes. *Journal of Behavioral Medicine, 17(3)*, 225–272.

Navathe, P. D., & Singh, B. (1994). An operational definition for spatial disorientation. *Aviation, Space & Environmental Medicine, 65(12)*, 1153–1155.

Sun, K. (1995). The definition of race. *American Psychologist, 50(1)*, 43–44.

Talaga, J. A., & Beehr, T. A. (1995). Are there gender differences in predicting retirement decisions? *Journal of Applied Psychology, 80(1)*, 16–28.

Woods, D. W., Miltenberger, R. G., & Flach, A. D. (1996). Habits, tics, and stuttering: Prevalence and relation to anxiety an somatic awareness. *Behavior Modification, 20(2)*, 216–225.

PART TWO
SETS, RELATIONS, AND VARIANCE

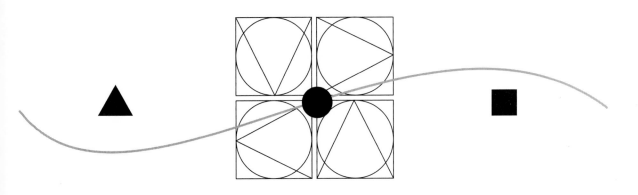

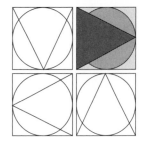

CHAPTER 4

SETS

- SUBSETS
- SET OPERATIONS
- SET DIAGRAMS
- THE UNIVERSAL AND EMPTY SETS: SET NEGATION
- SET OPERATIONS WITH MORE THAN TWO SETS
- PARTITIONS AND CROSS PARTITIONS
- LEVELS OF DISCOURSE

The concept of "set" is one of the most powerful and useful of mathematical ideas for understanding the methodological aspects of research. Sets and their elements are the primitive materials under which mathematics operates. Even if we are unaware of it, sets and set theory are foundations of our descriptive, logical, and analytical thinking and operating. They are the basis of virtually all else in this book. They are the foundations upon which we erect the complexities of numerical, categorical, and statistical analysis, even though we do not always make the set basis of our thinking and work explicit. For example, set theory provides an unambiguous definition of relations. It helps one to approach and understand probability and sampling, and is first cousin to logic. It also helps one understand the highly important subject of categories and categorizing the objects of the world. Moreover, set thinking can even help one to understand that difficult problem of human communication: confusion caused by mixing levels of discourse.

Science works basically with group, class, or set concepts. When scientists discuss individual events or objects, they do so by considering such objects as members of sets of objects. But this is true of human discourse in general. We say "goose," but the word *goose* is meaningless without the concept of a goose-like group called "geese." When we talk about a child and the child's problems, we inevitably must talk of the groups, classes, or sets of objects to which the child belongs. This would include a seven-year-old (first set), second grade (second set), bright (third set), and healthy (fourth set), boy (fifth set).

According to Farlow (1988) and Smith (1992), a *set* is a well-defined collection of objects. A set is well defined when there is no doubt as to whether a given object does or does not belong to the set. Terms like class, school, family, flock, and group indicate sets. There are two ways to define a set: (1) by listing all the members of the set, and (2) by giving a rule for determining whether objects do or do not belong to the set. Call (1) a "list" definition and (2) a "rule" definition. In research, the rule definition is usually used, although there are cases where all members of a set are actually or imaginatively listed. For example, suppose we study the relation between voting behavior and political preference. *Political preference* can be defined as being a registered Republican or Democrat. We then have a large set of all people with political preferences with two smaller subsets: the subset of Republicans and the subset of Democrats. This is a rule definition of sets. Of course, we might list all registered Democrats and all registered Republicans to define the two subsets, but this is often difficult if not impossible. Besides, it is unnecessary. The rule is usually sufficient. Such a rule might be: A Republican is any person who is registered with the Republican Party. Another such rule might be: A Republican is any person who says he or she is a Republican.

Subsets

A *subset* of a set is a set that results from selecting sets from an original set. Each subset of a set is part of the original set. More succinctly and accurately, the set B is a subset of a set A whenever all the elements of B are elements of A (Kershner & Wilcox, 1974). We designate sets by capital letters: A, B, K, L, X, Y, and so forth. If B is a subset of A we write $B \subset A$, which means "B is a subset of A," "B is contained in A," or "All members of B are also members of A."

Whenever a population is sampled, the resulting samples are subsets of the population. Suppose an investigator samples four eleventh-grade classes out of all the eleventh-grade classes in a large high school. The four classes form a subset of the population of all the eleventh-grade classes. Each of the four classes of the sample can also be considered a subset of the four classes—and also of the total population of classes. All the students of the four classes can be broken down into two subsets: boys and girls. Whenever a researcher breaks down or partitions a population or a sample into two or more groups, subsets are created using a "rule" or criterion to do so. Examples are numerous: religious preferences into Protestant, Catholic, Jew; intelligence into high and low; and so on. Even experimental conditions can be so viewed. The classic experimental–control group idea is a set–subset idea. Individuals are put into the experimental group; this is a subset of the whole sample. All other individuals used in the experiment (the control-group individuals) also form a subset.

Set Operations

There are two basic set operations: *intersection* and *union*. An operation is simply "a doing-something-to." In arithmetic we add, subtract, multiply, and divide. We "intersect" and "union" sets. We also "negate" them. When dealing with sets, there are logical operators involved. For intersection the logical operator is "and." For union, the proper logical operator is "or." For negation, the operator is "not." For more on logical operators see Udolf (1973).

Intersection is the overlapping of two or more sets; it is the elements shared in common by the two or more sets. The symbol for intersection is ∩ (read "intersection" or "cap"). The intersection of the sets A and B is written $A ∩ B$, and $A ∩ B$ is itself a set. More precisely, it is the set that contains those elements of A and B that belong *to both A* and B. Intersection is also written $A \cdot B$, or simply AB.

Let $A = \{0, 1, 2, 3\}$; let $B = \{2, 3, 4, 5\}$. (Note that braces "{ }" are used to symbolize sets.) Then $A ∩ B = \{2, 3\}$. This is shown in Figure 4.1. $A ∩ B$, or $\{2, 3\}$, is a new set composed of the members *common to* both sets. Note that A ∩ B also indicates the *relation* between the sets—the elements shared in common by A and B.

The *union* of two sets is written $A ∪ B$. $A ∪ B$ is a set that contains all the members of A and all the members of B. Mathematicians define $A ∪ B$ as a set that contains those elements that belong either to A or to B, or to both. In other words, we "add" the elements of A to those of B to form the new set $A ∪ B$. Take the example in Figure 4.1. A included 0, 1, 2, and 3; B included 2, 3, 4, and 5. $A ∪ B = \{0, 1, 2, 3, 4, 5\}$. The union of A and B in Figure 4.1 is indicated by the whole area of the two circles. Note that we do not count the members of $A ∩ B$ $\{2, 3\}$, twice.

Examples of union in research would be putting males and females together, $M ∪ F$, or Republican and Democrats together, $R ∪ D$. Let A be all the children of the elementary schools, and B be all the children of the secondary schools of X school district. Then $A ∪ B$ is the set of all the school children in the district.

◫ **FIGURE 4.1**

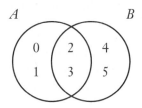

The Universal and Empty Sets; Set Negation

The *universal set*, labeled U, is the set of all elements under discussion. It can be called the *universe of discourse* or *level of discourse*. (It is much like the terms *population* and *universe* in sampling theory.) This means that we limit our discussion to the fixed set of elements — all of them — from this fixed class, U. If we were to study determinants of achievement in the elementary school, for example, we might define U as all pupils in grades 1 through 6. We can define U, alternatively, as the scores on an achievement test of these same pupils. Subsets of U, perhaps to be studied separately, might be the scores of Grade 1 pupils, the scores of Grade 2 pupils, and so on.

U can be large or small. Returning to the example of Figure 4.1, $A = \{0, 1, 2, 3\}$ and $B = \{2, 3, 4, 5\}$. If $A \cup B = U$, then $U = \{0, 1, 2, 3, 4, 5\}$. Here U is quite small. Let $A = \{Jane, Mary, Phyllis, Betty\}$, and $B = \{Tom, John, Paul\}$. If these individuals are all we are talking about, then $U = \{Jane, Mary, Phyllis, Betty, Tom, John, Paul\}$. And, of course, $U = A \cup B$. This is another example of a small U. In research Us are more often large. If we sample the schools of a large county, then U is all the schools in the county, a rather large U. U might also be all the children or all the teachers in these schools, a still larger U.

In research, it is important to know the U one is studying. Ambiguity in the definition of U can lead to erroneous conclusions. It is known, for example, that social classes differ in incidences of neurosis and psychosis (Murphy, Olivier, Monson, & Sobol, 1991). If we were studying presumed determinants of mental illness and used only middle-class persons as subjects, our conclusions would of course be limited to the middle class. It is easy to generalize to all people but such generalizations can be grossly in error. In such a case we have generalized to all people, U, when in fact we have studied our relations only in U_1, middle class. It is quite possible, perhaps even likely, that the relations are different in U_2, working class.

The *empty set* is the set with no members in it. We label it E. It can also be called the *null* set. Though it may seem peculiar to the student that we bother with sets with no members, the notion is quite useful, even indispensable. With it we can convey certain ideas economically and unambiguously. To indicate that there is no relation between two sets of data for example, we can write the set equation $A \cap B = E$, which simply says that the intersection of the sets A and B is empty, meaning that no member of A is a member of B, and vice versa.

Let $A = \{1, 2, 3\}$; let $B = \{4, 5, 6\}$. Then $A \cap B = E$. Clearly there are no members common to A and B. The set of possibilities of the Democratic and Republican presidential candidates both winning the national election is empty (E). The set of occurrences of rain without clouds is empty (E). The empty set, then, is another way of expressing the falsity of propositions. In this case we can say that the statement "Rain without clouds" is false. In set language this can be expressed $P \cap Q = E$, where P equals the set of all occurrences of rain, Q equals the set of all occurrences of clouds, and $\sim Q$ equals the set of all occurrences of no clouds.

The *negation* or *complement* of the set A is written $\sim A$. It means all members of U not in A. If we let A equal all men, when U equals all human beings, then $\sim A$ equals all women (not-men). Simple dichotomization seems to be a fundamental basis of

⊡ FIGURE 4.2

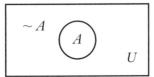

human thinking. Categorization is necessary in order to think: one must, at the most elementary level, separate objects into those belonging to a certain set and those not belonging to that set. We must distinguish between human and not-human, me and not-me, early and not-early, good and not-good.

If $U = \{0, 1, 2, 3, 4\}$, and $A = \{0, 1\}$, then $\sim A = \{2, 3, 4\}$. A and $\sim A$ are of course subsets of U. An important property of sets and their negation is expressed in the set equation: $A \cup \sim A = U$. Note, too, that $A \cap \sim A = E$.

Set Diagrams

We now pull together and illustrate the basic set ideas already presented by diagramming them. Sets can be depicted using various figures, but rectangles and circles are ordinarily used. They have been adapted from a system invented by John Venn, a nineteenth-century logician. In this book rectangles, circles, and ovals will be used. Look at Figure 4.2 where U is represented by the rectangle. All members of the universe under discussion are in U. All members of U not in A form another subset of U: $\sim$A. Note, again, that $A \cup \sim A = U$. Note, too, that $A \cap \sim A = E$; that is, there are no members common to both A and $\sim A$.

Next we depict, (Figure 4.3) two sets, A and B, both subsets of U. From the diagram it can be seen that $A \cap B = E$. We adopt a convention: when we wish to indicate a set or a subset, we shade it either horizontally, vertically, or diagonally. The set $A \cup B$ has been shaded in Figure 4.3.

⊡ FIGURE 4.3

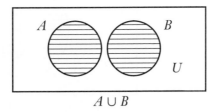

$A \cup B$

■ FIGURE 4.4

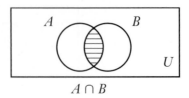

$A \cap B$

Intersection, probably the most important set notion from the point of view of this book, is indicated by the shaded portion in Figure 4.4. The situation can be expressed by the equation $A \cap B \neq$. E; the intersection of the sets A and B is *not* empty.

When two sets, A and B, are equal, they have the same set elements or members. The Venn diagram would show two congruent circles in U. In effect, only one circle would show. When $A = B$, then $A \cap B = A \cup B = A = B$.

We diagram $A \subset B$; A is a subset of B, in Figure 4.5. B has been shaded horizontally, A vertically. Note that $A \cup B = B$ (whole shaded area) and $A \cap B = A$ (area shaded both horizontally and vertically). All members of A are also in B, or all *a*s are also *b*s, if we let a equal any member of A and b equal any member of B.

Set Operations with More Than Two Sets

Set operations are not limited to two subsets of U. Let A, B, and C be three subsets of U. Suppose the intersection of these three subsets of U is not empty, as shown in Figure 4.6. The triply hatched area shows $A \cap B \cap C$. There are four intersections, each hatched differently: $A \cap B, A \cap C, B \cap C$, and $A \cap B \cap C$.

■ FIGURE 4.5

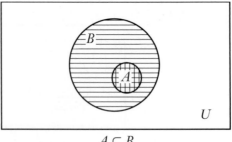

$A \subset B$

■ FIGURE 4.6

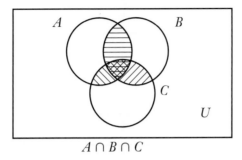

$A \cap B \cap C$

Although four or more sets can be diagrammed, such diagrams become cumbersome and not easy to draw and inspect. There is no reason, however, why the intersection and union operations cannot be applied symbolically to four or more sets.

Partitions and Cross Partitions

Our discussion of sets has been abstract and perhaps a bit dull. We leave the discussion by examining an aspect of set theory of great importance for clarifying principles of categorization, analysis, and research design: partitioning. U can be broken down (partitioned) into subsets that do not intersect and that exhaust all of U. When this is done the process is called *partitioning*. Formally stated, partitioning breaks down a universal set into subsets that are *disjoint* and *exhaustive* of the universal set.

Let U be a universe, and let A and B be subsets of U that are partitions. We label subsets of A: $A_1, A_2 \ldots, A_k$ and of B: $B_1, B_2 \ldots, B_m$. Partitions are usually set off by square brackets, whereas sets and subsets are set off by curled brackets or braces. Now, $[A_1 A_2]$ and $[B_1 B_2]$, for example, are partitions if:

$$A_1 \cup A_2 = U \text{ and } A_1 \cap A_2 = E$$
$$B_1 \cup B_2 = U \text{ and } B_1 \cap B_2 = E$$

Diagrams make this clearer. The partitioning of U (represented by a rectangle) separately into the subsets A_1 and A_2 and into B_1 and B_2, is shown in Figure 4.7. Both partitionings have been performed on the same U. We have met examples of such partitions: male–female, middle class–working class, high income–low income, Democrat–Republican, pass–fail, approve–disapprove, and so on. Some of these are true dichotomies; some are not.

It is possible to put the two partitions together into a cross partition. A *cross partition* is a new partitioning that arises from successively partitioning the same set U by forming all subsets of the form $A \cap B$. In other words, perform the A partitioning,

◙ **FIGURE 4.7**

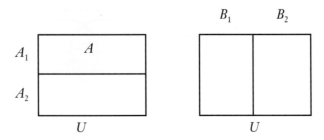

then the B partitioning on the same U, or the same square. This is shown in Figure 4.8. Each cell of the partitioning is an intersection of the subsets of A and B. We shall find in a later chapter that such cross-partitioning is very important in research design and in the analysis of data.

Anticipating later developments, we give a research example of a cross partition. Such examples are called crossbreaks or crosstabs. *Crossbreaks* or crosstabs provide the most elementary way to show a relation between two variables. The example is from Miller and Swanson's (1960) study of child-rearing practices. One of the tables they use is a crosstab in which the variables are social class (middle class and working class) and weaning (early and late). The data converted to percentages are given in Table 4.1. The cell frequencies reported by Miller and Swanson are given in the lower-right corner of each cell. Evidently, there is a relation between social class and weaning, middle-class mothers show a tendency to wean their children earlier than working-class mothers do. The two conditions of disjointness and exhaustiveness are satisfied. The intersection of any two cells is empty, for example, $(A_1 \cap B_1)$ $(A_1 \cap B_2) \cap (A_2 \cap B_1) \cap (A_2 \cap B_2) = E$. And the cells exhaust all the cases: $(A_1 \cap B_1)$ $\cup (A_1 \cap B_2) \cup (A_2 \cap B_1) \cup (A_2 \cap B_2) = U$.

Partitioning, of course, extends beyond two partitions. Instead of dichotomies, we can have polytomies; instead of success–failure, for instance, we can have

◙ **FIGURE 4.8**

		B	
		B_1	B_2
A	A_1	$A_1 \cap B_1$	$A_1 \cap B_2$
	A_2	$A_2 \cap B_1$	$A_2 \cap B_2$

⊡ TABLE 4.1 *Crossbreak Table: Relation between Social Class and Weaning (Miller & Swanson Study)*

		Weaning	
		Early (B_1)	*Late* (B_2)
Social Class	*Middle Class* (A_1)	60% (33)	40% (22)
	Working Class (A_2)	35% (17)	65% (31)

success–partial success–failure. Theoretically, a variable can be partitioned into any number of subsets, though there are usually practical limitations. There is no theoretical limitation, either, on the number of variables in a cross partition, but practical considerations usually limit the number to three or four. The study by Foster, Dingman, Muscolino, and Jankowski (1996) demonstrates how one variable is partitioned into three categories. Their research is concerned with job-hiring decisions. In this study, participants served as human resource managers. Each participant is given three résumés to review. The name on the résumé determined the sex of the candidate. Participants are to recommend one applicant for the advertised position. The researchers developed two different packages. In one package, a male candidate is the most qualified and the woman is less qualified. The second package is the reverse of the first. The most qualified person is a woman candidate with the male candidate being least qualified. There is also a third résumé from a person whose sex cannot be determined. The table Foster et al. report is a crossbreak in which the variables are gender of reviewer-decisionmaker (women and men) and résumé type (highly qualified male, lesser qualified male, highly qualified female, lesser qualified female, highly qualified unknown sex, lesser qualified unknown sex). These data, converted to percentages, are given in Table 4.2. The frequencies reported by Foster et al. are given in the lower-right corner of each cell. The data presented shows a relation between gender of reviewer and gender of candidate. Women reviewers (decisionmakers) tend to select women candidates when making hiring recommendations. Men reviewers (decisionmakers) tend to select male candidates even when the woman candidate is superior in qualification. In a later chapter we will extend the partitioning of variables.

▣ **TABLE 4.2** *Crossbreak Table: Relation between Gender of Reviewer and Qualification of the Job Applicant (Foster et al. Study)*

Gender of Reviewer	Résumé A Highly Qualified	Résumé B Less Qualified	Résumé C Less Qualified
[**Package 1**]	Jill	Sidney	George
Female	50%　(12)	33%　(8)	17%　(4)
Male	41%　(7)	24%　(4)	35%　(6)
[**Package 2**]	Andrew	Pat	Jennifer
Female	45%　(9)	5%　(1)	50%　(10)
Male	53%　(10)	26%　(5)	21%　(4)

Levels of Discourse

When we talk about anything we talk about it in a context or frame of reference. The expressions, context and frame of reference are closely related to U, the universe of discourse. The universe of discourse must be able to include any objects we talk about. If we go to another U (another level of discourse), the new level will not include all the objects. Indeed, it may not include any of the objects. If we are talking about people, for instance, we do not—or perhaps we should say "should not"—start talking about birds and their habits unless we somehow relate birds and their habits to people, and make it clear that this is what we are doing. There are two levels of discourse or universes (Us) of discourse here: people and birds. When discussing the democratic implications of segregation, we should not abruptly shift to religious preference unless, of course, we somehow relate the latter to the former. If we do relate the latter to the former, we lose our original universe of discourse, or cannot assign the objects of the one level (perhaps religion) to the other level (the education of African American children).

To color the picture differently, let's change our level of discourse to music and judging and understanding different genres of music. One of the great difficulties in listening to modern music is that the classical system of rules our ears have learned is not suited to the music of composers like Bartók, Schöenberg, or Ives. One has less difficulty with Bartók and much more difficulty with Schöenberg and Ives because Bartók maintains more of the classical bases than do Schöenberg and Ives. Take Ives's "Concord Sonata," a truly great work. At first hearing one is bewildered by the seeming cacophony and lack of structure. After a number of hearings, however, one begins to suspend classical judgmental frames of reference and to hear the beauty, meaning, and structure of the work. Ives's universe of musical discourse is simply quite different from the classical universe of discourse, and it is extremely difficult for one to shift from the classical U to Ives's U. Some people are unable or even unwilling to make the shift. They find Ives's music strange, even repugnant. They are unable to shake the classical aesthetic and judgmental level of discourse to make the shift.[1]

In research, we must be careful not to mix or shift our levels of discourse, or to do so only knowingly and consciously. Set-thinking helps us avoid such mixing and shifting. As an extreme example, suppose an investigator decided to study the toilet training, authoritarianism, musical aptitude, creativity, intelligence, reading achievement, and general scholastic achievement of ninth-grade youngsters. While it is conceivable that some sort of relations can be teased out of this array of variables, it is more conceivable that it is an intellectual mess. At any rate, remember sets. Ask yourself: "Do the objects I am discussing or am about to discuss belong to the set or sets of my present discussion?" If so, then you are on one level of discourse. If not, then another level of discourse, another set, or set of sets, is entering the discussion. If this occurs without your knowing it, the result is confusion. In short, ask: "What are U and the subsets of U?"

Research requires precise definitions of universal sets. *Precise* means to give a clear rule that tells you when an object is or is not a member of U. Similarly, it defines subsets of U and the subsets of the subsets of U. If the objects of U are people, then you cannot have a subset with objects that are not people. (Although you might have a set A of people and the set $\sim A$ of not-people, this logically amounts to U being people. "Not-people" is in this case a subset of "people," by definition or convention.)

The set idea is fundamental in human thinking. This is because all or most thinking probably depends on putting things into categories and labeling the categories (see Ross & Murphy, 1996; Smith, 1995). What we do is to group together classes of objects—things, people, events, phenomena in general—and name these classes. Such names are then concepts, labels that we no longer need to learn anew and that we can use for efficient thinking.

Set theory is also a general and widely applicable tool of conceptual and analytical thinking. Its most important applications pertinent to research methodology are probably to the study of relations, logic, sampling, probability, measurement, and data analysis (see Curtis, 1985; Hays, 1994). But sets can be applied to other areas and problems that are not considered technical in the sense, say, that probability and measurement are. The use of sets and Venn diagrams are not in abundance in the behavioral sciences. Well-known researchers throughout the years have employed sets and Venn diagrams in their research. Piaget (1957), for example, has used set algebra to help explain the thinking of children (see also Piaget, Garcia, Davidson, & Easley,

---

[1] We do not want to imply that it is necessarily desirable to make the shift, neither do we want to imply that all modern music, even all of Ives's music is great or good music. We are merely trying to illustrate the generality and applicability of the ideas of sets and levels of discourse.

回 FIGURE 4.9

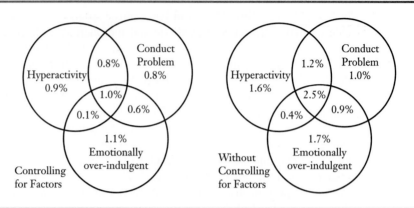

1991). Lewin's (1935) classical work in gestalt psychology used sets and Venn diagrams to describe the interaction between people and their environment as well as within themselves. More recently, Kubat (1993) has applied sets to studies of concept learning. Sheridan (1997) has used the Venn diagram to depict her conceptual framework for conjoint behavioral consultation in school psychology. Sheridan states that the problem identification, problem analysis, plan implementation, and plan evaluation for a child's behavior can be explained as an intersection of that child's home system, school system and support system. Dayton (1976) uses a Venn diagram to explain how a creative individual confronts his or her inner preconscious mind and the outer world. Trites and Laprade (1983) use Venn diagrams to depict a contingency analysis graphically. This analysis involves a composite of factor scores in the study of hyperactivity and conduct disorder in children (see Figure 4.9).

Bolman (1995) discusses the role and need of behavioral science knowledge in medical education and practice. In doing so, he uses a Venn diagram to show what he means by "biopsychosocial forces." This is the intersection of the biological sciences (anatomy, physiology) with psychology (feelings, self, goals) and sociology and anthropology (culture, family, ethics). The combination of these three factors is in Bolman's term "clinical reality." Lane (1986) is a strong proponent of teaching children conditional reasoning (logical thinking) using Venn diagrams and set theory. Lane conducted a number of studies comparing different instructional material used in teaching logical thinking. In each study, Venn diagrams (the set theory approach) were found to be superior over other methods in terms of immediate performance, retention, and transfer of learning. Figure 4.10 presents a sample used by Lane in comparing Venn diagrams to Cartesian Logic Board. The concept or rule card under study is "If it is yellow, then it is a circle." Later in this book, measurement will be defined using a single set-theoretic equation. In addition, basic principles of sampling, analysis, and of research design will be clarified with sets and set theory. Unfortunately, most social scientists and educators are still not aware of the generality,

◙ FIGURE 4.10

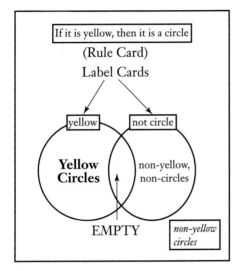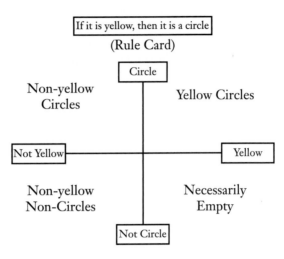

power, and flexibility of set thinking. It can be safely predicted, however, that researchers in the social sciences and education will find set thinking and theory increasingly useful in the conceptualization of theoretical and research problems.

CHAPTER SUMMARY

1. Sets are useful in understanding research methods. It is the foundation of descriptive, logical, and analytical thinking and processing. It is the basis of numerical, categorical, and statistical analysis.
2. A set is a well-defined collection of objects or elements. Two ways of defining a set:
   a. list all members of a set
   b. give a rule for determining whether objects do or do not belong to the set
3. Subsets are parts of the original set. If the entire set is the population, then subsets are samples of the population.
4. Set operations include intersection and union.
   a. Intersection is the elements that are common in two or more sets or subsets; the symbol is ∩.
   b. Union is the combination of nonredundant elements from two or more sets or subsets; the symbol is ∪.

5. The universal set, U, is defined as all elements under consideration. It is sometimes referred to as the population. The empty set, E, is the set that contains no members or elements. It is also called the *null* set.
6. Negation set is symbolized by "~". Placing this symbol in front of a set tells us that it contains members in the universal set, U, that are not contained in the set. For example ~A says this set contains all the elements in U that is *not in A*.
7. A partition is one that breaks U into subsets such that when the subsets are combined, U is reformed. Also, another requirement of a partition is that no elements of one subset overlap the elements in the other subsets.
8. Cross partition is the combination of two or more different partitions. Cross-breaks or contingency tables are examples of a cross partition that show the relationship between two variables.

STUDY SUGGESTIONS

1. Draw two overlaping circles, enclosed in a rectangle. Label the following parts: the universal set U, the subsets A and B, the intersection of A and B, and the union of A and B.
   a. If you were working on a research problem involving fifth-grade children, what part of the diagram would indicate the children from which you might draw samples?
   b. What might the sets A and B represent?
   c. What meaning might the intersection of A and B have?
   d. How would you have to change the diagram to represent the empty set? Under which conditions would such a diagram have research meaning?
2. Consider the following cross partition:

	Republican (B_1)	Democrat (B_2)
Male (A_1)		
Female (A_2)		

What is the meaning of the following sets; that is, what would we call any object in the sets?
   a. $(A_1 \cap B_1)$; $(A_2 \cap B_2)$
   b. A_1; B_1
   c. $(A_1 \cap B_1) \cup (A_1 \cap B_2) \cup (A_2 \cap B_1) \cup (A_2 \cap B_2)$
   d. $(A_1 \cap B_1) \cup (A_2 \cap B_1)$
3. Create a cross partition using the variables socioeconomic status and voting preference (Democrat and Republican). Can a sample of American individuals

be unambiguously assigned to the cells of the cross partition? Are the cells exhaustive? Are they disjoint? Why are these two conditions necessary?

4. Under which conditions will the following set equation be true? [Note: $n(A)$ represents the number of objects in the set A.]

$$n(A \cup B) = n(A) + n(B)$$

5. Suppose a researcher in sociology wants to do a study of the influence of race on occupational status. How can this researcher conceptualize the problem in set terms?

6. How are sets related to variables? Can we talk about the partitioning of variables? Is it meaningful to talk about subsets and variables? Explain.

7. Let A = {Opus 101, Opus 106, Opus 109, Opus 110, Opus 111}, which is the set of Beethoven's last five piano sonatas. This is a list definition. Here is a rule definition:

$$A = \{a | a \text{ is one of the last five Beethoven sonatas}\}$$

(The sign "|" is read "given") Under which conditions are rule definitions better than list definitions?

Intelligence	Achievement
136	55
125	57
118	42
110	48
100	42
97	35
90	32

Consider the two sets as one set of pairs. Then this set is a relation. If we graph the two sets of scores on X and Y axes, as we did in Chapter 3 (Figure 3.3), the relation becomes easier to "see." This has been done in Figure 5.1. Each point is defined by two scores. For example, the point farthest to the right is defined by (136, 55), and the point farthest to the left is (90, 32). Graphs like Figure 5.1 are highly useful and succinct ways to express relations. One sees at a glance, for instance, that higher values of X are accompanied by higher values of Y, and lower values of X by lower values of Y. As we will see in a later chapter, it is also possible to draw a line through

■ **FIGURE 5.1**

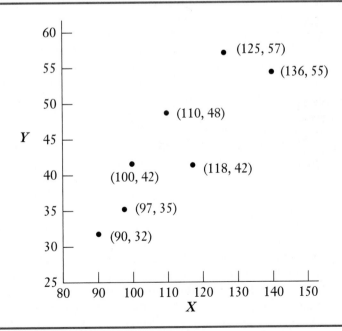

the plotted points of Figure 5.1, from lower left to upper right. (The reader should try this.) This line, called a *regression line*, expresses the relation between X and Y, between intelligence and achievement, but it also succinctly gives us considerably more information about the relation: namely its direction and magnitude.

We are now ready to define "relation" formally: *A relation is a set of ordered pairs.* Any relation is a set, a certain kind of set: a set of ordered pairs. An *ordered pair* is two objects, or a set of two elements, in which there is a fixed order for the objects to appear. Actually, we speak of ordered pairs, which means (as indicated earlier) that the members of *each pair* always appear in a certain order. If the members of the sets, A and B are paired, then we must specify whether the members of A or the members of B come first in each pair. If we define the relation of marriage, for example, we specify the set of ordered pairs with, say, husbands always placed first in each pair. In other words, the pair (*a, b*) is not the same as the pair (*b, a*). Ordered pairs are enclosed thusly: ( ). A set of ordered pairs is indicated: {(*a, k*), (*b, l*), (*c, m*)}.

We have fortunately left the previous ambiguity of the dictionary definition behind. The definition of relations as sets of ordered pairs, though it may seem a bit strange and even curious to the reader, is unambiguous and general. Moreover, the scientist, like the mathematician, can work with it.

When discussing relations, there are two special types of sets that play an important role. One set is called the *domain* and the other is called the *range*. Instead of formally defining these immediately, it may be clearer if we consider an example: Say we let A be the set of all men and B the set of all women. Let's also say we want to define the relation "married to." We can do this by forming the appropriate intersection of A and B (i.e., $A \cap B$) so that every ordered pair in the intersection would consist of married couples (shown in Figure 5.2). The intersection consists of the married couples. Given this example, the domain in this relation are the men who are married. The range would be all of the women who are married. Hence the domain would be that set of men who are in the intersection, $A \cap B$ and the range would be that set of women who are in the intersection. The domain is {John, Don, Rob, Warren, Bob, Dick, and Carl}. The range is {Carol, Debbi, Dawn, Elaine, Jean, Ramona, and Enid}. Note that the domain of the relation is always a subset of A and the range of the relation is always a subset of B.

Formally, if we let RL represent the relation, *a* be elements of the set A, and *b* be the elements of set B, then the domain of RL is the set of all things *a* such that, for some *b*, the ordered pair, (*a, b*) is in RL. The range (it is also known as the counterdomain) of the relation RL is the set of all things *b* such that, for some *x*, the ordered pair (*a, b*) is in RL.

Defining the domain and range in a relation is important because they play a key role in defining a *function*. Hays (1994) considers the function as one of the most important concepts in mathematics and science. Functions and relations are very similar. A function can be thought of as a special kind of relation. A relation is a function when each element of the domain is paired with one and only one member of the range. Most people think of a function in numerical terms, but this is not necessarily so. In American society, for example, the relation of being a husband is a function since that man has at most one wife at any given time. However, the relation of being

▣ FIGURE 5.2

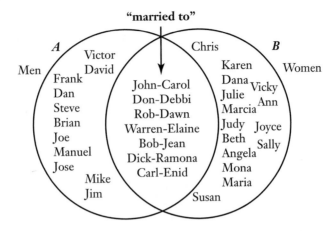

a mother is not a function since that person could be the mother of several different children. If we look at it very carefully, the relation of being a mother's daughter is a function since that child can have only one biological mother. Hence, a function is a set of ordered pairs in which no two distinct or different pairs have the same element.

Determining Relations in Research

Although we have avoided ambiguity with our definition of relations, we have not cleared up the definitional and especially the practical problem of "determining" relations. There is another way to define a relation that may help us. Let A and B be sets. If we pair each individual member of A with every member of B, we obtain *all the possible pairs* between the two sets. This is called the *Cartesian product* of the two sets and is labeled $A \times B$. A relation is then defined as a subset of $A \times B$; that is, any subset of ordered pairs drawn from $A \times B$ is a relation. (see Kershner & Wilcox, 1974, for an excellent discussion of relations).

To illustrate this idea simply, let set $A = \{a_1, a_2, a_3\}$ and set $B = \{b_1, b_2, b_3\}$.[1] Then the Cartesian product, $A \times B$, can be diagrammed as in Figure 5.3. That is, we generate nine ordered pairs: $(a_1, b_1), (a_1, b_2), \ldots, (a_3, b_3)$. With large sets, of course, there would be many pairs, in fact mn pairs, where m and n are the numbers of elements in A and B, respectively.

---

[1] The subscript integers merely label and distinguish individual members of sets. They do not imply order. Note, too, that there does not have to be equal numbers of members in the two sets.

◙ FIGURE 5.3

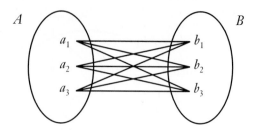

This is not very interesting—at least in the present context. What do we do to determine or "discover" a relation? Empirically, we determine which elements of A "go with" which elements of B according to some criterion. Obviously, there are many subsets of pairs of $A \times B$, most of which do not "make sense" or do not interest us. Kershner and Wilcox (1974) say that a relation is "a method for distinguishing some ordered pairs from others; it is a scheme for singling out certain pairs from all of them." According to this way of viewing relations, the relation of "marriage" is a method or procedure for distinguishing married couples from all possible pairings of men and women. In this way we can even think of religion as a relation. Let $A = \{a_1, a_2, \ldots , a_n\}$ be the set of all people in the United States, and let B equal {Catholic, Protestant, Jew, and so forth} be the set of religions. If we order pairs, in this case each person with a religion, then we have the "relation" of religion, or perhaps more accurately, "religious affiliation." Lest the student be too disturbed by the perhaps jarring sensation of defining a relation as a subset of $A \times B$, we add, again, that many of the possible subsets of ordered pairs of $A \times B$, naturally, will make no sense. Perhaps the main point to be made is that our definition of relation is unambiguous and completely general. No matter what sets of ordered pairs we choose, it is a relation. It is up to us to decide whether or not the sets we pick make scientific sense according to the dictates of the problems to which we are seeking answers.

The reader may wonder why so much trouble has been taken to define relations. The answer is simple: Almost all science pursues and studies relations. There is literally no empirical way to "know" anything except through its relations to other things, as indicated earlier. If, like Behling and Williams (1991), our interests are in the perception of intelligence and expectations of scholastic achievement, we have to relate perception and expectation to other variables. To explain a phenomenon like perception of intelligence, we must "discover" its determinants—the relations it has with other pertinent variables. Behling and Williams "explained" teachers' perceptions of intelligence and expectation of scholastic achievement toward students by relating it to the type of clothing and style worn by high school students. Behling and Williams found that the style of dress influences the perceptions of both teachers and peers. Obviously, if relations are fundamental in science, then we must know clearly what they are, as well as how to study them. The definition of "relation" has been neglected in behavioral research. It seems to be a concept whose meaning is assumed to be known by everyone. It is also confused with "relationship," which is a connection of some kind between people, or between people and groups, like a mother–child relationship. *It is not the same as a relation.*

Rules of Correspondence and Mapping

Any objects—people, numbers, gambling outcomes, points in space, symbols, and so on—can be members of sets and can be related in the ordered-pair sense. It is said that the members of one set are *mapped* onto the members of another set by using of a rule of correspondence. A *rule of correspondence* is a prescription or a formula that tells us how to map the objects of one set onto the objects of another. It tells us, in brief, how the correspondence between set members is achieved. Study Figure 5.4, which shows the relation between the names of five individuals and the symbols 1 and 0, which represent male (1) and female (0). We have here a mapping of sex (1 and 0) onto the names. This is, of course, a relation, each name having either 1 or 0, male or female, assigned to it.

In a relation the two sets whose "objects" are being related are called the *domain* and the *range*, or D and R. D is the set of first elements, and R the set of second elements. In Figure 5.4, we assigned 1 to male and 0 to female. To each member of the domain the appropriate member of the range is assigned. D = {Jane, Arthur, Michael, Alberta, Ruth}, and R = {0, 1}. The rule of correspondence says: If the object of D is female assign a "0," if male assign a "1."

In other words, objects, especially numbers, are assigned to other objects—persons, places, numbers, and so on—according to rules. The process is highly varied in its applications but simple in its conception. Instead of thinking of all the different ways of expressing relations separately, we realize that they are all sets of ordered

■ **FIGURE 5.4**

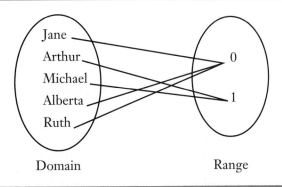

Domain   Range

pairs and that the objects of one set are simply mapped onto the objects of another set. All the varied ways of expressing relations—as mappings, correspondences, equations, sets of points, tables, or statistical indices—can be reduced to sets of ordered pairs.

Some Ways to Study Relations

Relations can be and are expressed in various ways. In the previous discussion, some of these were illustrated. One way is to simply list and pair the members of sets, as in Figures 5.3 and 5.4. Actually, this method is not often used in the research literature. We now examine more useful ways.

Graphs

A *graph* is a drawing in which the two members of each ordered pair of a relation are plotted on two axes, X and Y (or any appropriate designation). Figure 5.1 is a graph of the ordered pairs of the fictitious intelligence and achievement scores given earlier. We can see from that graph that the ordered pairs tend to "go together": high values of Y go with high values of X, and low values of Y go with low values of X.

A more interesting set of ordered pairs is graphed in Figure 5.5. The numbers used to make the graph are from a fascinating study by Miller and DiCara (1968), in which seven rats were "trained" to secrete urine. (Since urine secretion is an autonomic function, it is normally beyond control and thus training and learning.) The "Before" or X axis of the graph indicates values of urine secretion before the training; the "After" or Y axis indicates values after the training. We will use these same data in another context later in the book (at that time the study will be described in more detail), no further details are given here. The relation between the two sets of urine secretion values is pronounced. Again, high values before training are accompanied by high values after training, and similarly with low values. The graph and the relation it expresses reflect individual differences in urine secretion. The full meaning of this statement will be made clear when we later describe the statistical analysis of these data.

Tables

Perhaps the most common way to present data to show relations is in tables. The variables of the relations presented are usually given at the top and the sides of the table and the data in the table itself. The statistical data are most often means, frequencies, and percentages. Consider Table 5.1, which is a summary presentation of the frequency data presented by Freedman, Wallington, and Bless (1967). These researchers tested the notion that compliance is related to guilt: the greater the feeling of guilt, the greater the compliance with demands. The experimenters induced half

■ FIGURE 5.5

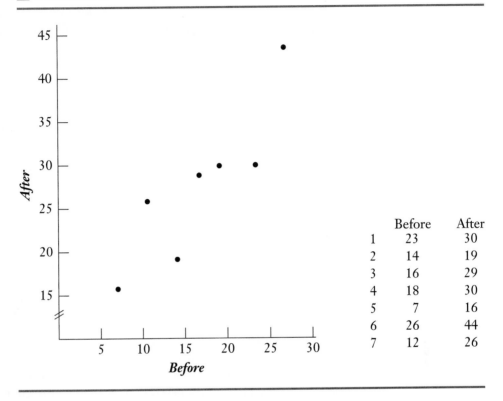

	Before	After
1	23	30
2	14	19
3	16	29
4	18	30
5	7	16
6	26	44
7	12	26

their subjects to lie; they assumed that lying would engender guilt (apparently it did). The Guilt or Lie variable is labeled at the top of the table. This is the independent variable, of course. The dependent variable was compliance to demands made of all subjects. This variable is labeled at the side of the table. The data in the cells of the table are frequencies; that is, the numbers of subjects who fell into the subsets or sub-categories. Of the 31 subjects induced to lie, 20 complied with the demands of the experimenter; 11 did not comply with the demands. Of the 31 subjects who were not induced to lie, 11 complied and 20 did not comply. The data are consistent with the hypothesis. In a later chapter we will study in detail how to analyze and interpret frequency data and tables of this kind.

The point of Table 5.1 is that a relation and the evidence on the nature of the relation are expressed in the table. In this case the tabled data are in frequency form. (A frequency is the number of members of sets and subsets. A percentage is a rate or proportion per hundred. It is computed by multiplying 100 times the ratio of a subset to a set, or a subset to another subset.) The table itself is a cross partition, often called a crossbreak or crosstab, in which one variable of the relation is set up against another variable of the relation. The two variable labels appear on the top and side of the table, as indicated earlier. The direction and magnitude of the relation itself is

回 **TABLE 5.1** *Frequency Results of Experiment to Study Relation Between Guilt and Compliance (Freedman, Wallington, & Bless study).*

	Lie (Guilt)	Not Lie (No Guilt)
Comply	20	11
Not-Comply	11	20
	31	31

expressed by the relative sizes of the frequencies in the cells of the table. In Table 5.1 many more of the subjects (20 of 31) induced to lie complied than did the subjects not induced to lie (11 of 31).

A more complicated example is given in Table 5.2. This is a summary presentation of the frequency data of a study by Mays and Arrington (1984). These researchers tested the notion that the violation of territoriality or spatial boundaries is related to demographic characteristics. Persons with low status characteristics (race or gender) more often tend to have their space violated. The experimenters created 10 conditions to represent 10 dyadic configurations. These dyads were produced by crossing two levels of race (white American and African American) with two levels of sex (female and male); for example, "African American female with white American male." Confederates meeting the proper demographic specifications for each of 10 conditions stood at a comfortable conversation distance and engaged in a casual discussion. Two hidden observers recorded the path taken by approximately 210 oncomers in each condition. They noted their tendency to walk through (thus penetrating dyadic boundaries) or to pass around it. Also recorded were the oncomer's ethnicity and gender. The independent variable is the dyadic configurations. The dependent variable is the penetration of the dyadic boundary or nonpenetration (pass around it). Although Mays and Arrington considered many variables in the study, for the example here, we will use only the dyadic combination of sex (male–male, female–female, female–male). The combinations are labeled at the top of Table 5.2 and the dependent variable is labeled at the side of the table. The table shows both the frequencies and the percentages.

回 **TABLE 5.2** *Frequency and Percentage Results of Experiment to Study Relation between Sexual Dyads and Space Violation (Mays & Arrington study).*

	Male–Male	Female–Female	Female–Male	
Around	650 (30)	600 (28)	898 (42)	2148 (86)
Through	106 (33)	119 (37)	98 (30)	323 (14)
	756 (31)	719 (29)	996 (40)	2471

The total percentages for male–male and female–female combinations were very similar (31% versus 29%). Also, the percentages of pass arounds for male and female dyads were very similar (30% versus 28%). However, the table shows that there is a tendency to pass around the female–male combination dyad (42%). One can speculate from this that there is greater respect for the shared space of a different sex combination than a same sex combination. Mays and Arrington give credence to this notion by pointing out the percentages given in the violation or "through" data (second row of Table 5.2). In terms of percentages, the female dyads shared space is more often violated than male (37% versus 33%). For the different sex combination (female–male), the space is less invaded than are the others (30%). In a later chapter we will study in detail how to analyze and interpret frequency (percentage) data and tables of this kind.

Table 5.2 shows the nature of the relation table form. In this, case the tabled data are in frequency and percentage form. Using the percentages in Table 5.2 for a simple visual analysis is easier than using the pure frequencies. With percentages in Table 5.2 the maximum value is 100 and the minimum value is 0. In Table 5.2 there are more invaders of the female–female dyad (119 of 323 or 37%) than of the male–male dyad (106 of 323 or 33%).

A different kind of table presents means, arithmetic averages, in the body of the table. The means express the dependent variable. If there is only one independent variable, its categories are labeled at the top of the table. If there are two or more independent variables, their categories can be presented in various ways at the top and sides of tables, as we will see in later chapters. An example is given in Table 5.3, which is the simplest form such a table can take. Hyatt and Tingstrom (1993) studied the effect of behavioral jargon usage on the perception of teachers toward two behavioral interventions: reinforcement and punishment. The findings from past research on the effect of jargon on teachers were equivocal. In this study, teachers were given a hypothetical student with a behavioral problem. Teachers were then presented descriptions of two types of interventions. The description either contained behavioral jargon such as "operantly conditioned and incompatible appropriate behavior" or a nonjargon description with words such as "rewarded for sitting correctly." Teachers receiving the behavioral jargon can be considered as being in the experimental group and teachers receiving nonjargon descriptions can be considered as being in the control group. All teachers' perceptions were measured by the Treatment Evaluation Inventory (also referred to as the TEI). This measure allows the teachers to rate the interventions in terms of their perceived acceptability, suitability, fairness, and effectiveness. Scores ranged from 15 to 105. High scores indicated greater acceptability. As can be seen in Table 5.3, the experimental group mean is larger than the control group mean. Is the difference between the means "large" or "small"? We will see later how to assess the size and meaning of such differences. At present, we are only interested in why the table expresses a relation.

In tables of this kind a relation is always expressed or implied. Tables as simple as this are rarely used in the literature. It saves space merely to mention the two means in the text of a report. Moreover, there can be more than two means compared. The principle is the same, however; the means "express" the dependent variable, and the

◻ **TABLE 5.3** *Means of Jargon and Nonjargon Groups (Hyatt & Tingstrom study).*[a]

Experimental (Jargon)	Control (No Jargon)
79.38	73.68

[a]The means were calculated from the Treatment Evaluation Inventory.

differences among them express the presumed effect of the independent variable. In the present case there are two variables being related: jargon and perception. The rubric "Experimental–Control" expresses the jargon that was received by the experimental group but not by the control group. This is the independent variable. The two means in the table express the teachers' perception of the intervention methods as measured by the TEI. This is the dependent variable. If the means differ sufficiently, then it can be assumed that behavioral jargon had an effect on teachers' perception or acceptability.

Tables of means are extremely important in behavioral research, especially in experimental research. There can be two, three, or more independent variables, and they can express the separate and combined effects of these variables on a dependent variable, or even on two or more dependent variables. The central point is that relations are always studied, even though it is not always easy to conceptualize and to state the relations.

Graphs and Correlation

Although we briefly examined relations and graphs earlier, it will be profitable to pursue this important topic further. Suppose we have two sets of scores of the same individuals on two tests, X and Y:

X	Y
1	1
2	1
2	2
3	3

The two sets form a set of ordered pairs. This set is, of course, a relation. It can also be written, letting R stand for relation, $R = \{(1,1), (2,1), (2,2), (3,3)\}$. It is plotted in the graph of Figure 5.6.

We can often get a rough idea of the direction and degree of a relation by inspecting the list of ordered pairs, but such a method is imprecise. Graphs, such as those of Figure 5.1 and Figure 5.6 tell us more. It can more easily be "seen" that Y

🔲 FIGURE 5.6

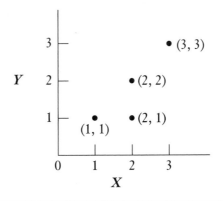

values "go along" with X values. Higher values of Y accompany higher values of X, and lower values of Y accompany lower values of X. In this case, the relation—or correlation, as it is also called—is positive. (If we had the equation, $R = \{(1,3), (2,1), (2,2), (3,1)\}$, the relation would be negative. The student should plot these values and note their direction and meaning.) If the equation were $R = \{(1,2), (2,1), (2,2), (3,2)\}$, the relation would be null or zero. This is plotted in Figure 5.7. It can be seen that Y values do not "go along" with X values in any systematic way. This does not mean that there is "no" relation. There is always a relation—by definition—since there is a set of ordered pairs. It is commonly said, however, that there is "no" relation. It is more accurate to say that the relation is null or zero.

🔲 FIGURE 5.7

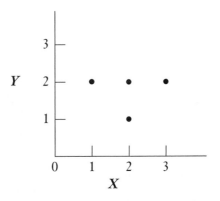

▣ **TABLE 5.4** *Three Sets of Ordered Pairs Showing Different Directions and Degrees of Correlation.*

(I) $r = 1.00$		(II) $r = -1.00$		(III) $r = 0$	
X	Y	X	Y	X	Y
1	1	1	5	1	2
2	2	2	4	2	5
3	3	3	3	3	3
4	4	4	2	4	1
5	5	5	1	5	4

Social scientists commonly calculate indices of relation, usually called coefficients of correlation, between sets of ordered pairs in order to obtain more precise estimates of the direction and degree of relations. If one such index, the product–moment coefficient of correlation, or r, is calculated for the ordered pairs of Figure 5.6, $r = .85$ is obtained. For the pairs of $R = \{(1,3), (2,1), (2,2), (3,1)\}$, the relation we said was negative, $r = -.85$. For the pairs of Figure 5.7, the set of pairs showed a null or zero relation, $r = 0$.[2]

Product–moment and related coefficients of correlation, then, are based on the concomitant variation of the members of sets of ordered pairs. If they *covary*—vary together high values with high values, medium values with medium values, and low values with low values, or high values with low values, and so on—it is said that there is a positive or negative relation as the case may be. If they do not covary, it is said there is "no" relation. The most useful of such indices range from $+1.00$ through 0 to 1.00. A $+1.00$ indicates a perfect positive relation, -1.00 a perfect negative relation, and 0 no discernible relation (or zero relation). Some indices range only from 0 to $+1.00$. Other indices may take on other values.

Most coefficients of relation tell us how similar the rank orders of two sets of measures are. Table 5.4 presents three examples to illustrate this going together of rank orders. The coefficients of correlation are given with each of the sets of ordered pairs. *I* is obvious: the rank orders of the *X* and *Y* scores of *I* go together perfectly. So do the *X* and *Y* scores of *II*, but in the opposite direction. In *III*, no relation between the rank orders can be discerned. In *I* and *II*, one can predict perfectly the value of *Y* given the value of *X*, but in *III* one cannot predict values of *Y* from knowledge of *X*. Coefficients of correlation are rarely 1.00 or 0. Ordinarily, they take on intermediate values.

---

[2] Methods of calculating these rs and other coefficients of correlation are discussed in statistics texts. These texts also discuss at greater length than is possible in this book the interpretation of correlation coefficients.

Research Examples

To put some flesh on the rather abstract bones of our discussion of relations, let's look at two interesting examples of relations and correlation. Russell, Fujino, Sue, Cheung, and Snowden (1996) examined the effects of therapist–client ethnic match in the assessment of mental health functioning. These researchers used a large data set of adult clients seen in outpatient services of a large metropolitan mental health facility. From these data, the researchers extracted out four ethnic groups for the study. They were Asian Americans, African Americans, Mexican Americans, and white Americans. The Global Assessment Scale (GAS) obtained at the time of admission was used as the measure of mental health functioning. GAS scores were assigned to the client by the therapist appointed to oversee their case. High scores indicated good general functioning whereas low scores indicated severe impairment.

Russell, et al. examined the GAS scores for those clients who were matched ethnically to a therapist (i.e., Asian American therapist with Asian American client; African American therapist with African American client, etc.) against the GAS scores of those clients who were not matched ethnically to a therapist. Figure 5.8 shows the relationship between therapist–client match and non-match and GAS scores. Note here that the relation is presented in the form of a graph that is different from what we have seen previously. This style of graphing is called *histogram* or *bar chart*. The graph shows consistently that GAS scores were higher (better mental health) when the therapists were matched ethnically to the clients than when the therapists were not matched ethnically to the clients. This says the therapist perceived the client to have a higher level of mental health functioning when the client

▣ **FIGURE 5.8**

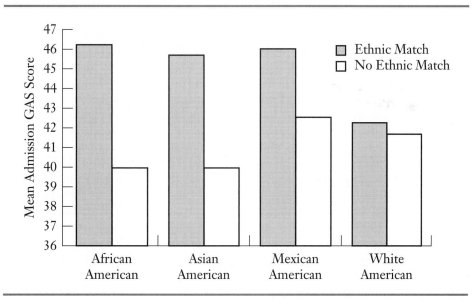

▣ **TABLE 5.5**   *The Relation between Religious Affiliation and Output of Scholarly Doctorates in the United States, Hardy Study*

Religious Type	Productivity Rating
Liberal, secularized Protestants, and Jews	High productivity
Moderately liberal, dissent, antitraditional Protestants	Above average productivity
Traditional Protestant	Fair productivity
Fundamentalist, conservative Protestant	Low productivity
Catholic	Very low productivity

was of the same ethnicity than when the client was of a different ethnicity. Also, for ethnic minorities, the matched therapist–clients had a higher GAS score than did white Americans. However, for nonmatched clients, the GAS scores were the highest for Mexican Americans and lowest for African Americans and Asian Americans. The greatest discrepancy between matched and nonmatched GAS scores were with the ethnic minority groups.

Our second example is not quantitative, though quantity is implied and it would not be difficult to quantify the variables. Hardy (1974) studied, among other things, the relation between religious affiliation and doctoral productivity. Which religious groups produce the most scholarly doctorates and which the least? (Hardy was really studying values and their influence on scholarship.) The results are given in Table 5.5. They need little comment. It is apparent that the relation is strong: the more liberal a religious group the higher the production of doctoral degrees. The ordered pairs of religious groups and their productivity ratings are easily seen.

Our last example is a study by Little (1997). It is a variant of the Hardy study presented above. Unlike Hardy's study, Little's study involves a high level of quantification. Little (1997) studied the relation between degree-granting universities and scholarly productivity in the field of school psychology. The question asked was: Which university's graduate education produces the most scholarly graduates? The answer to the question is important because it will give information that goes beyond the results from previous research. Previous research was primarily based on the current institutional affiliation of the authors and gives no information concerning where those people were educated. Little's study provides that information by presenting data as to where the authors received their terminal degree. Little states that this measure may be a better measure of the quality of graduate education programs in school psychology. A partial reproduction of the total results is given in Table 5.6. Little shows that a majority of graduate programs are in the United States with a concentration in the Midwest, Southeast and East Coast regions of the United States. Among the data reported by Little is one set of ordered pairs between university and productivity. Little in this study finds a number of discrepancies between his findings and those published by *US News & World Report* (1995) on America's best

■ TABLE 5.6 *The Relation between Graduate Education and Scholarship in School Psychology from 1987 to 1995 (Little study)*

Rank	University	Number of Graduates	Weighted Total
1	Georgia	19	65.98
2	Indiana	10	52.48
3	Minnesota	13	40.88
4	Texas	12	38.61
5	Wisconsin	11	27.92
6	Columbia	10	27.60
7	California, Berkeley	7	27.24
8	South Carolina	4	22.39
9	Oregon	5	21.48
10	Ball State	7	20.32
11	Ohio State	7	19.56
12	Kent State	5	19.36
13	Nebraska	8	18.31
14	Arizona State	2	16.28
15	Utah	5	15.90
16	Temple	5	15.88
17	Indiana State	4	15.61
18	Illinois	2	13.43
19	Southern Mississippi	7	13.36
20	Connecticut	4	12.75
21	Michigan State	5	12.38
22	Pittsburgh	1	11.97
23	Cincinnati	5	11.91
24	Pennsylvania	3	11.03
25	Penn State	4	10.09

graduate programs in school psychology. Little's results were based on empirical data gathered over the six major journals publishing school psychology research. *US News & World Report* based its rankings on the reputation of the university.

Multivariate Relations and Regression

In our discussion of relations we may have given the impression that scientists and researchers are always preoccupied with the relations between two variables. When, for instance, we talked about the relations between ethnic match and mental health, jargon and perception, graduate institution and production of scholarly works, we perhaps erroneously conveyed the idea that scientists are preoccupied with studying only two-variable relations. This is not so. Indeed, much research has been two-variable research, but in the behavioral sciences this has changed dramatically. The preoccupation of behavioral researchers is today more likely to be with multiple relations. While modern researchers know that the relation between intelligence and achievement is substantial and positive, they also know that there are many determinants of both achievement and intelligence. They know, for instance, that social class has a substantial influence on both variables. They also believe, though the evidence is conflicting, that self-esteem affects both intelligence and achievement. Moreover, methodologists have developed powerful analytical approaches and methods to handle what we will call multivariate problems. Let us look briefly at the logic and substance of such problems.

Some Logic of Multivariate Inquiry

The hidden structure of our argument up to now has been epitomized by the expression "If p, then q": "If intelligence, then achievement," "If lower status, then violation of space," "If this type of dressing style, then this perception of intelligence." These are of course implied relations. But they go further: they also imply direction—from independent variables to dependent variables. They can all be conceptualized as "*If p, then q*" statements. In logic, "*If p, then q*" is called a conditional statement, and it is possible to conceptualize most research problems and study the structure of scientific arguments using conditional and related statements (Kerlinger, 1969). But the relations of behavioral research are more complex than simple "If p, then q" statements. Contemporary researchers are more likely to say "If p, then q, under conditions r and t." This conditional statement can be written: $p \rightarrow q|r$, t, which is read as in the preceding sentence ("|" means "under conditions," or "given"). Or, somewhat simpler, we can write: $(p_1, p_2, p_3) \rightarrow q$ which means "If p_1 and p_2 and p_3, then q." More concretely, this means that the variables p_1 and p_2 and p_3 influence the variable q in certain ways. We might say, for instance, that intelligence, social class, and self-esteem affect school achievement in such-and-such ways.

The simplest way to show the relations graphically is with so-called path diagrams. A path diagram for the above statement is given in Figure 5.9. In this diagram—in which we use x_1, x_2, and x_3 for the independent variables and y for the

◎ FIGURE 5.9

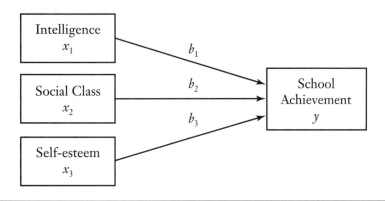

dependent variable specifies, in effect that the three independent variables all directly affect the dependent variable. This is what is called a straightforward multiple regression problem (see below), in which k (=3) independent variables mutually influence a dependent variable. This approach, too, has changed dramatically in the past decade. Researchers are now apt to talk about and test both direct and indirect influences. An alternative model and path analytic diagram is given in Figure 5.10. Here Intelligence and Self-esteem influence School Achievement directly, but Social Class does not. Instead, it influences School Achievement indirectly *through* Intelligence and Self-esteem, which is quite a different concept.

◎ FIGURE 5.10

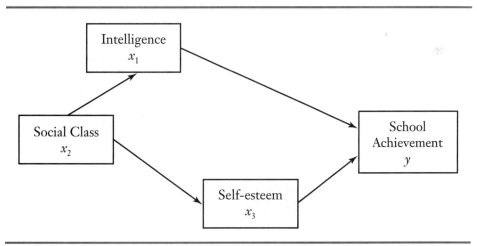

Multiple Relations and Regression

The research situation depicted in Figure 5.9 is a multiple regression problem: k (=3) independent variables mutually and simultaneously influence a dependent variable. Later in the book we will show how such a problem is solved. (The method is technically complex but conceptually simple, but it will give us little trouble.) For now, the problem is one of first finding the relation between the three independent variables, taken simultaneously, and the dependent variable. The second concerns determining how much each independent variable, x_1, x_2, and x_3, influences the dependent variable, y. Although now much more complex, the problem is still a relation, a set of ordered pairs.

What the method does essentially—and beautifully—is to find the best possible combination of x_1 x_2, and x_3, given y and the relations among the four variables, so that the correlation between the three-variable combination and y is a maximum. In the problem shown in Figure 5.9, multiple regression finds those values of b_1, b_2, and b_3 that will make the correlation between x_1, x_2, and x_3, taken together; and y as high as possible. (The student of mathematics will recognize this as a calculus problem.) The b weights, called regression weights or coefficients, are then used with the three variables in predicting the dependent variable, y. The method in effect creates a new variable which is a combination of x_1 x_2, and x_3. Call this variable y'. Then the multiple correlation is between y, the observed dependent variable, and y', the dependent variable predicted from knowledge of x_1, x_2, and x_3.

The alert reader will have seen that relations and correlations are symmetric: it often doesn't matter much which variable is independent and which dependent. In regression analysis, however, it does make a difference; regression is asymmetric. We say, If x, then y, or: If x_1, x_2, and x_3, then y. Many authors talk about "causal analysis," especially when talking about problems such as those given in Figure 5.9 and Figure 5.10. We prefer to avoid the words *cause* and *causal* because they are exceedingly sticky ideas—for instance, what is a cause?—and because their use is not necessary. Comrey and Lee (1992, p. 338) state "causal inferences cannot be made with any certainty. The best that can be said is that the data are consistent with the proposed causal inference . . ." Hence, we can adequately operate with conditional statements, though not always easily. [3]

Regression, in other words, deals with relations, but the traffic is mostly one-way from independent to dependent variables. To further anticipate a later discussion, let's look at a regression equation:

$$Y = a + b_1X_1 + b_2X_2$$

---

[3] The language is saturated with words that imply cause, for example, "influence" and "depend upon." Yet we will avoid causal expressions as much as possible, if for no other reason than that it is never possible to say unambiguously that one thing causes another. More pragmatically, we don't need the word or concept of "cause"; conditional statements of the if p, then q kind are sufficient for scientific purposes.

If we ignore the *a*—it is not important for the argument—we see that *Y* is the sum of X_1 and X_2, each weighted by its *b*. When we solve the equation for the *b*s (and of course the *a*) we use them to produce a score *Y'* for each person in the sample. *Y* and *Y'* (keep in mind that *Y* and *Y'* represent values for each person in the sample) are then a set of ordered pairs and thus a relation. The correlation between them is merely an ordinary correlation coefficient, *r*. But it is labeled *R* and is called the multiple coefficient of correlation, or the coefficient of multiple correlation. Later, we will examine the use and interpretation of multiple regression, the coefficient of multiple correlation, and regression weights in greater detail and with actual research examples. At that time, the student's natural bewilderment with the presumed mysteries of multivariate thinking should be dissipated and replaced by admiration and perhaps a bit of awe and excitement at these engaging and very powerful ideas and methods.

CHAPTER SUMMARY

1. Relations are the essence of knowledge. Almost all science pursues and studies relations.
2. Relations in science are between classes or sets of objects.
3. Relations can be expressed as sets of ordered pairs.
4. Ordered pairs are sets of elements with a fixed order of appearance.
5. There are two special sets: domain and range from a relation.
6. A special type of relation is a function. Function connects elements of the domain and the range.
7. Members of one set are mapped to members of the other set using a rule of correspondence
8. The rule of correspondence is a prescription or formula that shows how to map the objects.
9. Ways of studying relations
   a. graphs (two-dimensional plots)
   b. tables
   c. graphs and correlation (here the correlation is a statistical/numerical value)
10. Multiple regression is a statistical method that relates one dependent variable to a linear combination of one or more independent variables. This procedure can even tell a researcher how much each independent variable explains or relates to the dependent variable.

STUDY SUGGESTIONS

1. Discussions of relations appear to be confined to mathematics texts. The best discussion we have found, albeit abstract and somewhat difficult, is found in Kershner and Wilcox (1974).

2. Six examples of relations are given below. Assume that the first-named set is the domain and the second the range. Why are all of these relations?
   a. Book pages and page numbers
   b. Chapter numbers and pages of a book
   c. Population table headings or categories and population figures in a census report
   d. A class of third-grade children and their scores on a standardized achievement test
   e. $Y = 2x$
   f. $Y = a + b_1X_1 + b_2X_2$

3. An educational investigator has studied the relation between anxiety and school achievement. Express the relation in set language.

4. Suppose you wish to study the relations among the following variables: intelligence, socioeconomic status, need for achievement, and school achievement. Set up two alternative models that "explain" school achievement. Draw path diagrams of the two models.

5. Determine which of the following relations are functions:
   a. $(\neq Q, R\neq, \neq S, T\neq)$
   b. $(\neq w, j\neq, \neq k, l\neq, \neq p, q\neq)$
   c. $(\neq a, b\neq, \neq 102, 103\neq, \neq a, c\neq)$
   d. Given $A = \{a, b, c\}$ and $B = \{4, 5, T\}$ is the Cartesian cross-product $A \times B$ a function? Explain why or why not.

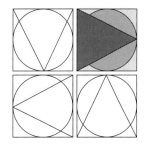

CHAPTER 6

VARIANCE AND COVARIANCE

To study scientific problems and answer scientific questions, we must study differences among phenomena. In Chapter 5, we examined relations among variables; in a sense, we were studying similarities. Now we concentrate on differences because without differences and without variation, there is no technical way to determine the relations among variables. If we want to study the relation between race and achievement, for instance, we are helpless if we have only achievement measures of white American children. We must have achievement measures of children of more than one race. In short, race must vary; it must have variance. It is necessary to explore the variance notion analytically and in some depth. To do so adequately, it is also necessary to skim some of the cream off the milk of statistics.

Studying sets of numbers as they are is unwieldy. It is usually necessary to reduce the sets in two ways: (1) by calculating averages or measures of central tendency, and (2) by calculating measures of variability. The measure of central tendency used in this book is the mean. The measure of variability most used is the *variance*. Both kinds of measures epitomize sets of scores, but in different ways. They are both "summaries" of whole sets of scores, summaries that express two important facets of the sets of scores: (1) their central or average tendency, and (2) their variability. Solving research problems without these measures is extremely difficult. We begin our study of variance, then, with some simple computations.

Calculation of Means and Variances

Take the set of numbers $X = \{1, 2, 3, 4, 5\}$. The mean is defined:

$$M = \frac{\Sigma X}{n} \tag{6.1}$$

n equals the number of cases in the set of scores; Σ means "the sum of" or "add them up" and X represents any one of the scores (each score is an X). The formula then, says, "Add the scores and divide by the number of cases in the set." Thus:

$$M = \frac{1 + 2 + 3 + 4 + 5}{5} = \frac{15}{5} = 3$$

The mean of the set X is 3. In this book, "M" will be used to represent the mean. Other symbols that are commonly used are $\overline{X}$ and μ.

Calculating the variance, while not as simple as calculating the mean, is still simple. The formula is:

$$V = \frac{\Sigma x^2}{n} \tag{6.2}$$

where V means variance; n and Σ are the same as in Equation 6.1. Σx^2 is called the sum-of-squares (it needs some explanation). The scores are listed in a column:

X	x	x^2
1	-2	4
2	-1	1
3	0	0
4	1	1
5	2	4

ΣX:	15	
M:	3	
Σx^2:		10

In this calculation x is a deviation from the mean. It is defined:

$$x = X - M \qquad (6.3)$$

Thus, to obtain x, simply subtract from X the mean of all the scores. For example, when $X = 1$, $x = 1 - 3 = -2$; when $X = 4$, $x = 4 - 3 = 1$; and so on. This has been done above in the table. Equation 6.2, however, says to square each x. This has also been done above. (Remember, that the square of a negative number is always positive.) In other words, Σx^2 tells us to subtract the mean from each score to get x, square each x to get x^2, and then add up the x^2s. Finally, the average of the x^2s is taken by dividing Σx^2 by n, the number of cases. Σx^2, the *sum-of-squares*, is a very important statistic that we will use often.

The variance, in the present case, is

$$V = \frac{(-2)^2 + (-1)^2 + (0)^2 + (1)^2 + (2)^2}{5} = \frac{4 + 1 + 0 + 1 + 4}{5} = \frac{10}{5} = 2$$

"V" will be used for variance in this book. Other symbols commonly used are σ^2 and s^2. The former is a so-called population value; the latter is a sample value. N is used to represent the total number of cases in a total sample or in a population. ("Sample" and "population" will be defined in a later chapter.) n is used for a subsample or subset of U of a total sample. Appropriate subscripts will be added and explained as necessary. For example, if we wish to indicate the number of elements in a set A, a subset of U, we can write n_A or n_a. Similarly we attach subscripts to x, V, and so on. When double subscripts are used, such as r_{xy}, the meaning will usually be obvious.

The variance is also called the *mean square* (when calculated in a slightly different way). It is called this because it is obviously the mean of the x^2s. Clearly, it is not difficult to calculate the mean and the variance.[1]

The question is: Why calculate the mean and the variance? The rationale for calculating the mean is explained easily. The mean expresses the general level, the center of gravity, of a set of measures. It is a good representative of the level of a group's characteristics or performance. It also has certain desirable statistical properties, and is the most ubiquitous statistic of the behavioral sciences. In much behavioral research, for example, means of different experimental groups are compared to study relations, as pointed out in Chapter 5. We may be testing the relation between organizational climates and productivity, for instance. We may have used three kinds of climates and be interested in the question of which climate has the greatest effect on productivity. In such cases, means are customarily compared. For instance, of three groups, each operating under one of three climates, A_1, A_2, and A_3, which has the greatest mean on, say, a measure of productivity?

---

[1] The method of calculating the variance used in this chapter differs from the methods ordinarily used. In fact, the method given above is impracticable in most situations. Our purpose is not to learn statistics, as such. Rather, we are pursuing basic ideas. Methods of computation, examples, and demonstrations have been constructed to aid this pursuit of basic ideas.

The rationale for computing and using the variance in research is more difficult to explain. In the usual case of ordinary scores, the variance is a measure of the dispersion of the set of scores: It tells us how much the scores are spread out. If a group of pupils is very heterogeneous in reading achievement, then the variance of their reading scores will be large compared to the variance of a group that is homogeneous in reading achievement. The variance, then, is a measure of the spread of the scores; it describes the extent to which the scores differ from each other. For descriptive purposes, the square root of the variance is ordinarily used. It is called the *standard deviation*. Certain mathematical properties, however, make the variance more useful in research. It is suggested that the student supplement this topic of study with the appropriate sections of an elementary statistics text (see Comrey & Lee, 1995). It is not possible in this book to discuss all the facets of meaning and interpretation of means, variances, and standard deviations. The remainder of this chapter and later parts of this book will explore other aspects of the use of the variance statistic.

Kinds of Variance

Variances come in a number of forms. When you read the research and technical literature, you will frequently come across the term, sometimes with a qualifying adjective, sometimes not. To understand the literature, it is necessary to have a good idea of the characteristics and purposes of these different variances. And to design and do research, one must have a rather thorough understanding of the variance concept as well as considerable mastery of statistical variance notions and manipulations.

Population and Sample Variances

The *population variance* is the variance of U, a universe or population of measures. Greek symbols are usually used to represent population parameters or measures. For the population variance, the symbol σ^2 (sigma squared) is used. The symbol σ is used for the population standard deviation. The population mean is μ (mu). If all the measures of a defined universal set, U, are known, then the variance is known. More likely, however, all the measures of U are not available. In such cases, the variance is estimated by calculating the variance of one or more samples of U. A good deal of statistical energy goes into this important activity. A question may arise: How variable is the intelligence of the citizens of the United States? This is a U or population question. If there were a complete list of all the millions of people in the United States—and also a complete list of intelligence test scores of these people—the variance could be simply, if wearily, computed. No such list exists. So samples, representative samples, of Americans are tested and means and variances computed. The samples are used to estimate the mean and variance of the entire population. These estimated values are called statistics (in the population they are called parameters). The sample mean is denoted by the symbol M and the sample variance is denoted by SD^2 or s^2. A number of statistics textbooks use the $\overline{X}$ (X-bar) to represent the sample mean.

Sampling variance is the variance of statistics computed from samples. The means of four random samples drawn from a population will differ. If the sampling is random and the samples large enough, the means should not vary too much; that is, the *variance of the means* should be relatively small.[2]

Systematic Variance

Perhaps the most general way to classify variance is as systematic variance and *error variance*. *Systematic variance* is the variation in measures due to some known or unknown influences that "cause" the scores to lean in one direction more than another. Any natural or man-made influences that cause events to happen in a certain predictable way are systematic influences. The achievement test scores of children in a wealthy suburban school will tend to be systematically higher than scores of the children in a city slum area school. Adept teaching may systematically influence the achievement of children, as compared to the achievement of children who are ineptly taught.

There are many causes of systematic variance. Scientists seek to separate those in which they are interested from those in which they are not interested. They also attempt to separate random variance from systematic variance. Indeed, research may narrowly and technically be defined as the controlled study of variances.

Between-Groups (Experimental) Variance

One important type of systematic variance in research is between-groups or experimental variance. *Between-groups* or *experimental variance*, as the name indicates, is the variance that reflects systematic differences between *groups* of measures. The variance discussed previously as score variance reflects the differences between individuals in a group. We can say, for instance, that, on the basis of present evidence and current tests, the variance in intelligence of a random sample of 11-year-old children is about 225 points. (This is obtained by squaring the standard deviation reported in a test manual. The standard deviation of the California Test of Mental Maturity for 11-year-old children, for instance, is about 15, and $15^2 = 225$.) This figure is a statistic that tells us how much the individuals differ from each other. Between-groups

---

[2]Unfortunately, in much actual research only one sample is usually available—and this one sample is frequently small. We can, however, estimate the sampling variance of the means by using what is called the *standard variance of the mean*. (The term "standard error of the mean" is usually used. The standard error of the mean is the square root of the standard variance of the mean.) The formula is $V_M = V_S / n_S$ where V_M is the standard variance of the mean, V_S the variance of the sample, and n_S, the size of the sample. Note an important conclusion that can be reached from this equation: If the size of the sample is increased, V_M is decreased. In other words, to be more confident that the sample is close to the population mean, make n large. Conversely, the smaller the sample, the riskier the estimate (see Study Suggestions 5 and 6).

variance, on the other hand, is the variance due to the differences between *groups* of individuals. If the achievement of northern region and southern region children in comparable schools is measured, there would be differences between the northern and southern groups. Groups as well as individuals differ or vary, and it is possible and appropriate to calculate the variance between these groups.

Between-groups variance and experimental variance are fundamentally the same. Both arise from differences between groups. Between-groups variance is a term that covers all cases of systematic differences between groups, experimental and nonexperimental. Experimental variance is usually associated with the variance engendered by active manipulation of independent variables by experimenters.

Here is an example of between-groups variance—in this case experimental variance. Suppose an investigator tests the relative efficacies of three different kinds of reinforcement on learning. After reinforcing the three groups of subjects differentially, the experimenter calculates the means of the groups. Suppose they are 30, 23, and 19. The mean of the three means is 24, and we calculate the variance *between the means* or *between the groups:*

	X	x	x^2
	30	6	36
	23	−1	1
	19	−5	25
ΣX:	72		
M:	24		
Σx^2:			62

$$V_b = \frac{62}{3} = 20.67$$

In the experiment just described, presumably the different methods of reinforcement tend to "bias" the scores one way or another. This is, of course, the experimenter's purpose. The goal of Method A is to increase all the learning scores of an experimental group. The experimenter may believe that Method B will have no effect on learning, and that Method C will have a depressing effect. If the experimenter is correct, the scores under Method A should all tend to go up, whereas under Method C they should all tend to go down. Thus, the scores of the groups, as wholes—and, of course, their means—differ systematically. Reinforcement is an *active* variable. It is a variable deliberately manipulated by the experimenter with the conscious intent to "bias" the scores differentially. Prokasy (1987), for example, helps solidify this point by summarizing the number of variations of reinforcement within the Pavlovian paradigm in the study of skeletal responses. Thus any experimenter-manipulated variables are intimately associated with systematic variance. When Camel, Withers, and Greenough (1986) gave their experimental group of rats different degrees of early experience—environmental (enriched experiences such as a large cage with other rats and opportunities for exploration), and the control group a condition of reduced experience (isolation, kept in individual cages)—they were deliberately attempting to build systematic variance into their outcome measures (pattern and number of dendrite branching [dendrites are the branching structures of a neuron].) The basic idea behind the famous "classical design" of scientific research in which experimental and control groups are used is that, through careful control and manipulation, the experimental group's outcome measures (also called "criterion measures") are made to vary systematically, to all go up or down together, while the control group's measures are ordinarily held at the same level. The variance, of course, is between the two groups, that is, the two groups are made to differ. For example, Braud and Braud (1972) manipulated experimental groups in a most unusual way. They trained the rats of an experimental group to choose the larger of two circles in a choice task; the control group rats received no training. Extracts from the brains of the animals of both groups were injected into the brains of two new groups of rats. Speaking statistically, they were attempting to increase the between-groups variance and they succeeded: the new "experimental group" animals exceeded the new "control group" animals in choosing the larger circle in the same choice task!

This is clear and easy to see in experiments. In research that is not experimental, in research where already existing differences between groups are studied, it is not always so clear and easy to see that one is studying between-groups variance. But the idea is the same. The principle may be stated in a somewhat different way: The greater the differences between groups, the more an independent variable (or variables) can be presumed to have operated. If there is little difference between groups, then the presumption must be that an independent variable or variables have *not* operated. In other words, their effects are too weak to be noticed, or else different influences have canceled each other out. We judge the effects of independent variables that have been manipulated or that have worked in the past, then, by between-groups variance. Whether the independent variables have or have not been manipulated, the principle is the same.

To illustrate the principle, we use the well-studied problem of the effect of anxiety on school achievement. It is possible to manipulate anxiety by having two experimental groups and inducing anxiety in one and not in the other. This can be achieved by giving each group the same test with differing instructions. We tell the members of one group that their grades depend wholly on the test. We tell the members of the other group that the test does not matter particularly, that its outcome will not affect grades. On the other hand, the relation between anxiety and achievement may also be studied by comparing groups of individuals on whom it can be assumed that different environmental and psychological circumstances have acted to produce anxiety. (Of course, the experimentally induced anxiety and the already existing anxiety—the stimulus variable and the organismic variable, are not assumed to be the same.) A study to test the hypothesis that different environmental and psychological circumstances act to produce different levels of test anxiety was done by Guida and Ludlow (1989). These investigators hypothesized that students in the United States culture would show a lower level of test anxiety than students from the Chilean culture. Using the language of this chapter, the investigators hypothesized a larger between-groups variance than could be expected by chance because of the difference between

Chilean and American environmental, educational, and psychological conditions. (The hypothesis was supported. Chilean students exhibited a higher level of test anxiety than students from the United States. However, when considering only the lower socioeconomic groups of each culture, the United States students had higher test anxiety than the Chilean students.)

Error Variance

Error variance is the fluctuation or varying of measures that is unaccounted for. The fluctuations of the measurements in the dependent variable in a research study where all participants were treated equally is considered error variance. Some of these fluctuations are due to chance. In this case, error variance is random variance. It is the variation in measures due to the usually small and self-compensating fluctuations of measures—now here, now there; now up, now down. The sampling variance discussed earlier in the chapter, for example, is random or error variance.

To digress briefly, it is necessary in this chapter and the next to use the notion of "random" or "randomness." Ideas of randomness and randomization will be discussed in considerably more detail in Chapter 8. For the present, however, *randomness* means that there is no known way of correctly describing or explaining events and their outcomes in language. In different words, random events cannot be predicted. A random sample is a subset of a universe. Its members are so drawn that each member of the universe has an equal chance of being selected. This is another way of saying that if members are randomly selected, there is no way to predict which member will be selected on any one selection—other things being equal.

However, one should not think that random variance is the only possible source of error variance. Error variance can also consist of other components as pointed out by Barber (1976). What gets "pooled" into the term called error variance can include measurement errors within the measuring instrument, procedural errors by the researcher, misrecording of responses, and the researcher's outcome expectancy. It is possible that "equal" subjects differ on the dependent variable because one may be experiencing a different physiological and psychological functioning at the time the measurements were taken.

Returning to our main discussion, it can be said that error variance is the variance in measurements due to ignorance. Imagine a great dictionary in which everything in the world—every occurrence, every event, every little thing, every great thing—is given in complete detail. To understand any event that has occurred, that is now occurring, or that will occur, all one needs do is to look it up in the dictionary. With this dictionary there are obviously no random or chance occurrences. Everything is accounted for. In brief, there is no error variance; all is systematic variance. Unfortunately (or more likely, fortunately), we do not have such a dictionary. Many events and occurrences cannot be explained. Much variance eludes identification and control. This is error variance as long as identification and control eludes us.

While seemingly strange and even a bit bizarre, this mode of reasoning is useful, provided we remember that some of the error variance of today may not be the error variance of tomorrow. Suppose that we conduct an experiment on teaching problem-solving in which we assign pupils to three groups at random. After we finish the experiment, we study the differences between the three groups to see if the teaching has had an effect. We know that the scores and the means of the groups will always show minor fluctuations, now plus a point or two or three, now minus a point or two or three, which can probably never be controlled. Something or other makes the scores and the means fluctuate in this fashion. According to the view under discussion, they do not fluctuate for just any reason; there is probably no "absolute randomness." Assuming determinism, there must be some cause (or causes) for the fluctuations. True, we can learn some of them and possibly control them. When we do this, however, we have systematic variance.

We discover, for example, that gender "causes" the scores to fluctuate, since males and females are mixed in the experimental groups. (We are, of course, talking figuratively here. Obviously, gender does not make scores fluctuate.) So we do the experiment and control gender by using, say, only males. The scores still fluctuate, though to a somewhat lesser degree. We remove another presumed cause of the perturbations: intelligence. The scores still fluctuate, though to a still lesser extent. We continue to remove such sources of variance. We are controlling systematic variance and also identifying and controlling more and more unknown variance gradually.

Now note that before we controlled or removed these systematic variances, before we "knew" about them, we would have to label each such variance as "error variance"—partly through ignorance and partly through inability to control or do anything about such variance. We could go on and on doing this and there will still be variance left over. Finally we give in; we "know" no more; we have done all we can. There will still be variance. A practical definition of error variance, then, would be: *Error variance* is the variance left over in a set of measures after all known sources of systematic variance have been removed from the measures. This is so important that it deserves a numerical example.

An Example of Systematic and Error Variance

Suppose we are interested in knowing whether politeness in the wording of instructions for a task affects memory of the polite words. Call "politeness" and "impoliteness" the variable A partitioned into A_1 and A_2 (this idea is from Holtgraves, 1997). Students are assigned at random to two groups. Treatments A_1 and A_2 are assigned at random to the two groups. In this experiment, students of A_1 receive instructions that are worded impolitely, such as, "You must write out the full name for each state you remember." Students of A_2, on the other hand, receive instructions that are of the same meaning as those received by A_1 students but the wording of the instructions is in a polite form: "It would help if you write out the full name for each state you recall." After reading the instructions, subjects are given a distracter task. This task involves recalling the 50 states of the United States. The students are subsequently given a recognition memory test. This test is used to determine the overall memory of the polite words. The scores are as follows:

	A_1	A_2
	3	6
	5	5
	1	7
	4	8
	2	4
M	3	6

The means are different; they vary. There is between-groups variance. Taking the difference between the means at face value—later we will be more precise—we may conclude that vagueness in lecturing had an effect. Calculating the between-groups variance just as we did earlier, we get:

		x	x^2
	3	1.5	2.25
	6	1.5	2.25
M:	4.5		
Σx^2:			4.50

$$V_b = \frac{4.5}{2} = 2.25$$

In other words, we calculate the between-groups variance just as we earlier calculated the variance of the five scores 1, 2, 3, 4, and 5. We simply treat the two means as though they were individual scores, and go ahead with an ordinary variance calculation. The between-groups variance, V_b, is, then, 2.25. An appropriate statistical test would show that the difference between the means of the two groups is what is called a "statistically significant" difference. (The meaning of this will be taken up in another chapter.)[3] Evidently, using polite words in instructions helped increase the memory scores of the students.

---

[3] The method of computation used here is not what would be used to test statistical significance. It is used here purely as a pedagogical device. Note, too, that the small numbers of cases in the examples given and the small size of the numbers are used only for simplicity of demonstration. Actual research data, of course, are usually more complex, and many more cases are needed. In actual analysis of variance the correct expression for the between sum-of-squares is: $SS_b = n\Sigma x_b^2$. For pedagogical simplicity, however, we retain Σx_b^2, later replacing it with SS_b.

If we put the 10 scores in a column and calculate the variance we get:

X	x	x²
3	−1.5	2.25
5	.5	.25
1	−3.5	12.25
4	−.5	.25
2	−2.5	6.25
6	1.5	2.25
5	.5	.25
7	2.5	6.25
8	3.5	12.25
4	−.5	.25

M: 4.5

Σx^2: 42.50

$$V_t = \frac{42.5}{10} = 4.25$$

This is the total variance, $V_t \cdot V_t = 4.25$ contains all sources of variation in the scores. We already know that one of these is the between-groups variance, $V_b = 2.25$. Let us calculate still another variance. We do this by calculating the variance of A_1 alone and the variance of A_2 alone and then averaging the two:

A_1	x	x²	A_2	x	x²
3	0	0	6	0	0
5	2	4	5	−1	1
1	−2	4	7	1	1
4	1	1	8	2	4
2	−1	1	4	−2	4

ΣX: 15   30

M: 3   6

Σx^2: 10   10

$$V_{A_1} = \frac{10}{5} = 2 \qquad V_{A_2} = \frac{10}{5} = 2$$

The variance of A_1 is 2, and the variance of A_2 is 2. The average is 2. Since each of these variances was calculated *separately* and then averaged, we call the average variance calculated from them the "within-groups variance." We label this variance V_w meaning within variance, or within-groups variance. Thus $V_w = 2$. *This variance is unaffected by the difference between the two means.* This is easily demonstrated by subtracting a constant of 3 from the scores of A_2. This makes the mean of A_2 equal to

◉ FIGURE 6.1

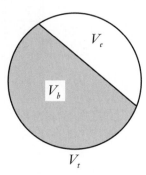

3. Then, if the variance of A_2 is calculated, it will be the same as before: 2. Obviously, the within-groups variance will be the same: 2.

Now write an equation: $V_t = V_b + V_w$. This equation says that the total variance is made up of the variance between the groups and the variance within the groups. But is it? Substitute the numerical values: $4.25 = 2.25 + 2.00$. Our method works— it shows us, too, that these variances are additive (as calculated).

The variance ideas under discussion can perhaps be clarified with a diagram. In Figure 6.1, a circle is broken up into two parts. Let the area of the total circle represent the total variance of the 10 scores, or V_t. The larger shaded portion represents the between-groups variance, or V_b. The smaller unshaded portion represents the error variance, or V_w or V_e. From the diagram one can see that $V_t = V_b + V_e$. (Note the similarity to set thinking and the operation of union.)

A measure of all sources of variance is represented by V_t and a measure of the between-groups variance (or a measure of the effect of the experimental treatment) by V_b. But what is V_w, the within-groups variance? Since, of the total variance, we have accounted for a known source of variance via the between-groups variance, we assume that the variance remaining is due to chance or random factors. We call this *error variance*. But, you may say, surely there must be other sources of variance? How about individual differences in intelligence, gender, and so on? Since we assigned the students to the experimental groups at random, assume that these sources of variance are equally, or approximately equally, distributed between A_1 and A_2. And because of the random assignment we cannot isolate and identify any other sources of variance. We call this remaining variance *error variance*, knowing full well that there are probably other sources of variance but assuming, and hoping our assumption is correct, that they have been equally distributed between the two groups.

A Subtractive Demonstration: Removing Between-Groups Variance from Total Variance

Let us demonstrate this another way by removing from the original set of scores the between-groups variance, using a simple subtractive procedure. First, let each of the means of A_1 and A_2 be equal to the total mean; we remove the between-groups variance. The total mean is 4.5. (See above where the mean of all 10 scores was calculated.) Second, adjust each individual score of A_1 and A_2 by subtracting or adding, as the case may be, an appropriate constant. Since the mean of A_1 is 3, we add $4.5 - 3 = 1.5$ to each of the A_1 scores. The mean of A_2 is 6, and $6 - 4.5 = 1.5$ is the constant to be *subtracted* from each of the A_2 scores.

Study the "corrected" scores and compare them with the original scores. Note that they naturally vary less than they did before. We removed the between-groups variance, a sizable portion of the total variance. The variance that remains is that portion of the total variance due, presumably, to chance. We calculate the variance of the "corrected" scores of A_1, A_2, and the total, and note these surprising results:

Correction:	$+1.5$	-1.5
	A_1	A_2
	$3 + 1.5 = 4.5$	$5 - 1.5 = 3.5$
	$5 + 1.5 = 6.5$	$5 - 1.5 = 3.5$
	$1 + 1.5 = 2.5$	$7 - 1.5 = 5.5$
	$4 + 1.5 = 5.5$	$8 - 1.5 = 6.5$
	$2 + 1.5 = 3.5$	$4 - 1.5 = 2.5$
ΣX:	22.5	22.5
M:	4.5	4.5

	A_1	x	x^2	A_2	x	x^2
	4.5	0	0	4.5	0	0
	6.5	2	4	3.5	-1	1
	2.5	-2	4	5.5	1	1
	5.5	1	1	6.5	2	4
	3.5	-1	1	2.5	-2	4
ΣX:	22.5			22.5		
M:	4.5			4.5		
Σx^2:			10			10

$$V_{A_1} = \frac{10}{5} = 2 \qquad V_{A_2} = \frac{10}{5} = 2$$

The within-groups variance is the same as before. It is unaffected by the correction operation. Obviously, the between-groups variance is now zero. What about the total variance, V_t? Calculating it, we obtain $\Sigma x_t^2 = 20$, and $V_t = 20 \div 10 = 2$. Thus the within-groups variance is now equal to the total variance. The reader should study this example carefully until he or she has a firm grasp of what has happened and *why*.

Although the previous example is perhaps sufficient to make the essential points, it may solidify the student's understanding of these basic variance ideas if we extend the example by putting in and pulling out another source of variance. The reader may recall that we knew that the within-groups variance contained variation due to individual differences. Now assume that, instead of assigning the students to the two groups randomly, we had matched them on intelligence—and intelligence is related to the dependent variable. That is, we put pair members with approximately equal intelligence test scores into the two groups. The outcome of the experiment might be:

	A_1	A_2
	3	6
	1	5
	4	7
	2	4
	5	8
M:	3	6

Note carefully that the only difference between this setup and the previous one is that the matching has caused the scores to covary. The A_1 and A_2 measures now have nearly the same rank order. In fact, the coefficient of correlation between the two sets of scores is 0.90. We have here another source of variance: that due to individual differences in intelligence which is reflected in the rank order of the pairs of criterion measures. (The precise relation between the rank order and matching ideas and their effects on variance will be taken up in another chapter. The student should take it on faith for the present that matching produces systematic variance.)

This variance can be calculated and extracted as before, except that there is an additional operation. First, equalize the A_1 and A_2 means and "correct" the scores as before. This yields:

Correction:	+1.5	−1.5
	4.5	4.5
	2.5	3.5
	5.5	5.5
	3.5	2.5
	6.5	6.5
M:	4.5	4.5

Second, by equalizing the rows (making each row mean equal to 4.5 and "correcting" the row scores accordingly) we find the following data:

Correction	A_1	A_2	Original Means	Corrected Means
0	4.5 + 0 = 4.5	4.5 + 0 = 4.5	4.5	4.5
+1.5	2.5 + 1.5 = 4.0	3.5 + 1.5 = 5.0	3.0	4.5
−1.0	5.5 − 1.0 = 4.5	5.5 − 1.0 = 4.5	5.5	4.5
+1.5	3.5 + 1.5 = 5.0	2.5 + 1.5 = 4.0	3.0	4.5
−2.0	6.5 − 2.0 = 4.5	6.5 − 2.0 = 4.5	6.5	4.5
M	4.5	4.5	4.5	4.5

The doubly corrected measures now show very little variance. The variance of the 10 doubly corrected scores is 0.10, very small indeed. There is, of course, no between-groups (columns) or between-individuals (rows) variance left in the measures. After double correction, all of the total variance is error variance. (As we will see later, when the variances of both columns and rows are extracted like this — although with a quicker and more efficient method — there is no within-groups variance.)

A Recap of Removing Between-Group Variance from Total Variance

This has been a long operation. A brief recapitulation of the main points may be useful. Any set of measures has a total variance. If the measures from which this variance is calculated have been derived from the responses of human beings, then there will always be at least two sources of variance. One will be due to systematic sources of variation like individual differences of the subjects whose characteristics or accomplishments have been measured and differences between the groups or subgroups involved in research. The other will be due to chance or random error, fluctuations of measures that cannot currently be accounted for. Sources of systematic variance tend to make scores lean in one direction or another. This is of course reflected in differences in means. If gender is a systematic source of variance in a study of school achievement, for instance, then the gender variable will tend to act in a manner such that the achievement scores of females will tend to be higher than those of males. Sources of random error, on the other hand, tend to make measures fluctuate now this way, now that way. Random errors, in other words, are self-compensating; they tend to balance (or cancel) each other out.

In any experiment or study, the independent variable (or variables) is a source of systematic variance — at least it should be. The researcher "wants" the experimental groups to differ systematically and usually seeks to maximize such variance while controlling or minimizing other sources of variance, both systematic and error. The experimental example given above illustrates the additional idea that these variances are additive, and because of this additive property, it is possible to analyze a set of scores into systematic and error variances.

Components of Variance

The discussion so far may have convinced the student that any total variance has "components of variance." The case just considered, however, included one experimental component due to the difference between A_1 and A_2, one component due to individual differences, and a third component due to random error. We now study the case of two components of systematic experimental variance. To do this, we synthesize the experimental measures, creating them from *known* variance components. In other words, we go backwards. We start from "known" sources of variance because there will be no error variance in the synthesized scores.

We have a variable X that has three values. Let $X = \{0, 1, 2\}$. We also have another variable Y, which has three values. Let $Y = \{0, 2, 4\}$. X and Y, then, are *known* sources of variance. We assume an ideal experimental situation where there are two independent variables acting *in concert* to produce effects on a dependent variable, Z. That is, each score of X operates with each score of Y to produce a dependent variable score Z. For example, the X score, 0, has no influence. The X score, 1, operates with Y as follows: $\{(1 + 0), (1 + 2), (1 + 4)\}$. Similarly, the X score, 2, operates with Y: $\{(2 + 0), (2 + 2), \text{and} (2 + 4)\}$. All this is easier to see if we generate Z in clear view.

The set of scores in the 3×3 matrix (a matrix is any rectangular set or table of numbers) is the set of Z scores. The purpose of this example will be lost unless the reader remembers that in practice we do not know the X and Y scores; we only know the Z scores. In actual experimental situations we manipulate or set up X and Y and can only hope they are effective. They may not be. In other words, the sets $X = \{0, 1, 2\}$ and $Y = \{0, 2, 4\}$ can never be known like this. The best we can do is to estimate their influence by estimating the amount of variance in Z due to X and to Y.

	Y					Z		
	0	2	4			0	2	4
X 0	0 + 0	0 + 2	0 + 4		0	0	2	4
1	1 + 0	1 + 2	1 + 4	=	1	1	3	5
2	2 + 0	2 + 2	2 + 4		2	2	4	6

The sets X and Y have the following variances:

X	x	x^2
0	−1	1
1	0	0
2	1	1

ΣX: 3
M: 1
Σx^2: 2

Y	y	y^2
0	−2	4
2	0	0
4	2	4

ΣY: 6
M: 2
Σy^2: 8

$$V_x = \frac{2}{3} = .67 \qquad V_y = \frac{8}{3} = 2.67$$

The set Z has variance as follows:

Z	z	z^2
0	−3	9
2	−1	1
4	1	1
1	−2	4
3	0	0
5	2	4
2	−1	1
4	1	1
6	3	9

ΣZ: 27

M: 3

Σz^2:   30

$$V_z = \frac{30}{9} = 3.33$$

Now $.67 + 2.67 = 3.34$, or $V_z = V_x, + V_y$, within errors of rounding.

This example illustrates that, under certain conditions, variances operate additively to produce the experimental measures we analyze. While the example is "pure" and therefore unrealistic, it is not unreasonable. It is possible to think of X and Y as independent variables; they might be level of aspiration and pupil attitudes. And Z might be verbal achievement, a dependent variable. That real scores do not behave exactly this way does not alter the idea. They behave approximately this way. We plan research to make this principle as true as possible, and analyze data as though it were true. And it works!

Covariance

Covariance is really nothing new. Recall, in an earlier discussion of sets and correlation that we talked about the relation between two or more variables being analogous to the intersection of sets. Let X be {0, 1, 2, 3}, a set of attitude measures for four children. Let Y be {1, 2, 3, 4}, a set of achievement measures of the same children, but not in the same order. Let R be a set of ordered pairs of the elements of X and Y, the rule of pairing being: Each individual's attitude and achievement measures are paired, with the attitude measure placed first. Assume that this yields R = {(0, 2), (1, 1), (2, 3), (3, 4)}. By our previous definition of relation, this set of ordered pairs is a relation, in this case the relation between X and Y. The results of the calculations of the variance of X and the variance of Y are:

X	x	x^2	Y	y	y^2
0	−1.5	2.25	2	−.5	.25
1	−.5	.25	1	−1.5	2.25
2	.5	.25	3	.5	.25
3	1.5	2.25	4	1.5	2.25

ΣX: 6   10
M: 1.5   2.5
Σx^2:   5   5

$$V_x = \frac{5}{4} = 1.25 \qquad V_y = \frac{5}{4} = 1.25$$

We now set ourselves a problem. (Note carefully in what follows that we are going to work with deviations from the mean, *x*s and *y*s, and not with the original raw scores.) We have calculated the variances of X and Y above by using the *x*s and *y*s; that is, the deviations from the respective means of X and Y. If we can calculate the variance of any set of scores, is it not possible to calculate the relation *between* any two sets of scores in a similar way? Is it conceivable that we can calculate the variance of the two sets simultaneously? And if we do so, will this be a measure of the variance of the two sets together? Will this variance also be a measure of the relation between the two sets?

What we want to do is to use some statistical operation analogous to the set operation of intersection, $X \cap Y$. To calculate the variance of X or of Y, we squared the deviations from the mean, the *x*s or the *y*s, and then added and averaged them. A natural answer to our problem is to perform an analogous operation on the *x*s and *y*s *together*. To calculate the variance of X, we first did this: $(x_1 \cdot x_1), \ldots, (x_4 \cdot x_4) = x_1^2, \ldots, x_4^2$. Why then not follow this through with both *x*s and *y*s, multiplying the ordered pairs like: $(x_1 \cdot y_1), \ldots, (x_4 \cdot y_4)$? Then, instead of writing Σx^2 or Σy^2, we write Σxy, as follows:

x	y	=	xy
−1.5	−.5	=	.75
−.5	−1.5	=	.75
.5	.5	=	.25
1.5	1.5	=	2.25

$$\Sigma xy = 4.00$$

$$V_{xy} = CoV_{xy} = \frac{4}{4} = 1.00$$

Let us give names to Σxy and V_{xy}. Σxy is called the *cross product*, or the sum of the cross products. V_{xy} is called the *covariance*. We will write it CoV with suitable subscripts. If we calculate the variance of these products—symbolized as V_{xy}, or CoV_{xy}—

we obtain 1.00, as indicated above. This 1.00, then, can be taken as an index of the relation between two sets. But it is an unsatisfactory index because its size fluctuates with the ranges and scales of different Xs and Ys; that is, it might be 1.00 in this case and 8.75 in another case, making case-to-case comparisons difficult and unwieldy. We need a measure that is comparable from problem to problem. Such a measure—an excellent one, too—is obtained simply by writing a fraction or ratio. It is the covariance, CoV_{xy}, divided by an average of the variances of X and Y. The average is usually in the form of a square root of the product of V_x and V_y. The whole formula for our index of relation, then, is

$$R = \frac{CoV_{xy}}{\sqrt{V_x \cdot V_y}}$$

This is one form of the well-known product-moment coefficient of correlation. Using it with our little problem, we obtain:

$$R = \frac{CoV_{xy}}{\sqrt{V_x \cdot V_y}} = \frac{1.00}{1.25} = .80$$

This index, usually written r, can range from $+1.00$ through 0 to -1.00, as we learned in Chapter 5. So we have another important source of variation in sets of scores, provided the set elements, the Xs and Ys, have been ordered into pairs after conversion into deviation scores. This variation is aptly called *covariance* and is a measure of the relation between the sets of scores.

It can be seen that the definition of relation as a set of ordered pairs leads to several ways to define the relation of the above example:

$$R = \{(x, y); x \text{ and } y \text{ are numbers, } x \text{ always coming first}\}$$
$$xRy = \text{the same as above or "}x\text{ is related to }y\text{"}$$

$$R = \{(0, 2), (1, 1), (2, 3), (3, 4)\}$$
$$R = \{(-1.5, -.5), (-.5, -1.5), (.5, .5), (1.5, 1.5)\}$$

$$R = \frac{CoV_{xy}}{\sqrt{V_x \cdot V_y}} = \frac{1.00}{1.25} = .80$$

Variance and covariance are concepts of the highest importance in research and in the analysis of research data. There are two main reasons. First, they summarize, so to speak, the variability of variables and the relations among variables. This is most easily seen when we realize that correlations are covariances that have been standardized to have values between -1 and $+1$. But the term also means the covarying of variables in general. In much or most of our research we literally pursue and study covariation of phenomena. Second, variance and covariance form the statistical backbone of multivariate analysis, as we will see toward the end of this book. Most discussions of the analysis of data are based on variances and covariances. Analysis of variance, for example, studies different sources of variance of observations, mostly in experiments, as indicated earlier. Factor analysis is in effect the study of covariances, one of whose major purposes is to isolate and identify common sources of variation. The contemporary ultimate in analysis, the most powerful and advanced multivariate approach yet devised, is called *analysis of covariance structures* because the system studies complex sets of relationships by analyzing the covariances among variables. Variances and covariances will obviously be the core of much of our discussion and preoccupation from this point on.

The Computer Addendum

One of the major problems textbook writers have today when introducing the use of computer programs is how quickly the material becomes dated. Within a period of one year or less some major producers of statistical computer software may have a few updates and changes to the software. These updates and changes will cause a mismatch between the software and what is written on how to use the software. For example, when the revision of this textbook began, one popular program, Statistical Package for the Social Sciences (SPSS) for Windows was at version 6.0. At the time of this writing, the current version is 8.0 with 9.0 soon to be released. Hence, to present any specific set of programming statements for such programs may quickly become unusable for students and researchers. So the goal is to present some general underlying characteristics within all statistical software programs that may have greater applicability to later and newer releases of the program. It is also important to choose a statistical program that will last the time period between revisions of the book (wishful thinking!). For example, in the third edition of this book published in 1986, the personal computer was still in its infancy. Other than some spreadsheet programs, there was little development in terms of programming languages and statistical software. Among the earliest, as far as desktop or personal computers were concerned, were SPSS-PC, STATA, NCSS, and Anderson-Bell STAT. Most of these were not competitive in terms of computing flexibility and power when compared to the statistical software available on large-scale (mainframe) computers. A number of specialized statistical programs were written by a large number of researchers who did not use large computers. Some of these programs were written in BASIC, FORTRAN, C, and COBOL.

However, today's researcher is "blessed" with very powerful and flexible statistical programs that can be used easily for data analysis purposes. From this chapter to the end of the book, we will mainly use SPSS for Windows to demonstrate statistical computing. Why? Well, in recent years, a number of competing software companies (including the second author's favorite one) have been acquired by SPSS, Inc. "Competing" software is still available, but the development that goes into them is suspect. Another reason is that SPSS is available at every major university. There are student versions of the program that students can purchase and install on their home computers. Despite the criticisms leveled at SPSS, they have (since their

◉ FIGURE 6.2

Untitled - SPSS Data Editor						
File Edit View Data Transform Statistics Graphs Utilities Windows Help						
	var	var	var	var	var	var
1						
2						
3						
4						
5						
6						
7						

conception) released very easy to use programs for researchers and students. Once some general ideas are made clear as to how one's data should be laid out and entered into the computer program, the request for certain statistical routines becomes very easy.

The discussion of SPSS in this book will deal with the Windows version available for the personal computer. The discussion is not necessarily valid for mainframe versions of the program or non-Windows version (such as DOS versions). This discussion will assume that the reader is using Windows 95 or better and that the reader is knowledgeable with Windows commands and functions. Knowledge on how to use a mouse (the pointing device) is imperative when dealing with Windows operations because all operations are performed by pointing with the mouse, and clicking on (highlighting) an object to select that object.

When executing the SPSS for Windows program, hereafter referred to as SPSS-WIN, the first screen to appear on the computer is a table for data entry. It looks something like that in Figure 6.2. This data entry table is in the form of a spreadsheet. The user will need to input the data into this spreadsheet. If the researcher has a previously created dataset acceptable for input to SPSSWIN, it can be used directly without the researcher reentering the data.

The general data format for nearly every statistical computer program is the data table where variables are the columns of the table and the observations (people, individuals) are the rows. If we had the following set of data, its entry into SPSSWIN would be easy.

	Variables		
	Age	Gender	Test Score
Person			
1	12	M	60
2	13	F	75
3	15	F	45
4	14	M	80
5	14	F	85
6	12	M	39
7	13	F	62

Your first step is to define the variables for SPSSWIN. Wherever you see the "var" label on the spreadsheet, you change them to reflect your variables. To do this, use the mouse and double-click on the cell in the spreadsheet labeled "var." When this action is performed, another screen appears that allows you to specify the variable name and attributes of that variable (e.g., numeric or character data). In the first column type (enter) "Age," then click the "OK" button (see Figure 6.3). Repeat this operation for each of your variables. For the variable "Gender" use a "1" for "F" and a "2" for "M." Next, enter the data from your data table. Each value occupies one cell of the spreadsheet. After you have entered all the data, your spreadsheet should look like that shown in Figure 6.4.

■ FIGURE 6.3

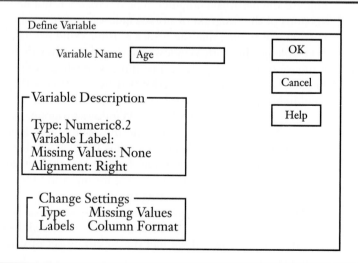

□ FIGURE 6.4

	Age	Gender	Score	var	var	var	
1	12	2	60				
2	13	1	75				
3	15	1	45				
4	14	2	80				
5	14	1	85				
6	12	2	39				
7	13	1	62				

Untitled - SPSS Data Editor
File Edit View Data Transform Statistics Graphs Utilities Windows Help

You can save this as a dataset by clicking "FILE" and selecting "SAVE." When you have done this, you will be asked for a dataset name. Your next step is to perform the statistical analysis. For this chapter we will do only descriptive statistics. This includes means and standard deviations. Figure 6.5 shows the SPSS screens that are

□ FIGURE 6.5

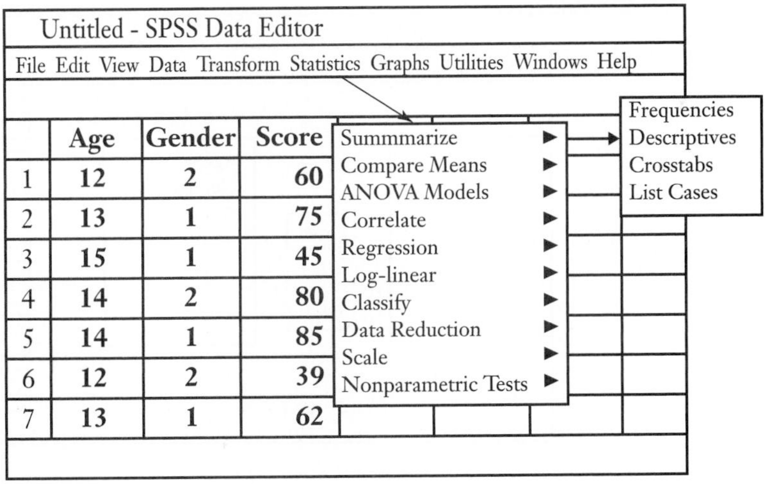

Untitled - SPSS Data Editor
File Edit View Data Transform Statistics Graphs Utilities Windows Help

	Age	Gender	Score
1	12	2	60
2	13	1	75
3	15	1	45
4	14	2	80
5	14	1	85
6	12	2	39
7	13	1	62

Summmarize ►
Compare Means ►
ANOVA Models ►
Correlate ►
Regression ►
Log-linear ►
Classify ►
Data Reduction ►
Scale ►
Nonparametric Tests ►

Frequencies
Descriptives
Crosstabs
List Cases

▣ FIGURE 6.6

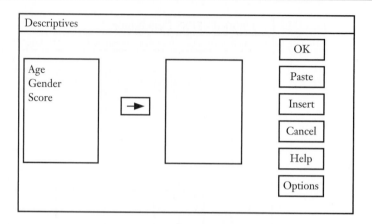

used. First click "Statistics"; that will produce a new menu. From this second menu choose "Sumarize." When you do this you get a third menu from which you choose (click on it) "Descriptives." Choosing "Descriptive" produces the "descriptive statistics" screen (window) shown in Figure 6.6. Your next action will be to move the variables from the left block to the right block. To accomplish this action, highlight the variable with your mouse and click on the right arrow button. This button is located between the two blocks. Descriptive statistics will be computed for those in the right

▣ FIGURE 6.7

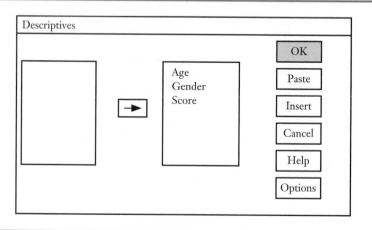

◙ FIGURE 6.8

	Age	Gender	Score	
				Summmmarize ►
1	12	2	60	Compare Means ►
				ANOVA Models ►
2	13	1	75	Correlate ► → Bivariate
3	15	1	45	Regression ►
				Log-linear ► Partial
4	14	2	80	Classify ►
5	14	1	85	Data Reduction ►
				Scale ►
6	12	2	39	Nonparametric Tests ►
7	13	1	62	

Untitled - SPSS Data Editor
File Edit View Data Transform Statistics Graphs Utilities Windows Help

block only. Variables that may be of little or no interest for the researcher can remain in the left block. Figure 6.7 shows the screen after the three variables have been moved to the right block. The purpose of this window is to allow the researcher to choose which variables should be used in the analysis. After this is done, select the "OK" button; the program will then perform all the necessary computations and display them on the SPSS Output screen.

The result of the analysis is shown below. After completion you can save the output to a file if you so desire. With SPSS for Windows, you can perform a number of different analyses on the same dataset.

Variable	Mean	Std Dev	Variance	Minimum	Maximum	N
Gender	1.43	.53	.29	1	2	7
Age	13.29	1.11	1.24	12.00	15.00	7
Score	63.71	17.43	303.90	39.00	85.00	7

If you want to compute the covariances between the variables, select "Correlate" from the menu. This will in turn produce a new menu from which you choose "Bivariate" (see Figure 6.8). To obtain the covariances, select the "options" button and put a check mark in the box requesting the display of covariances.

The computer output is as follows:

Variables		Cases	Cross-Prod Dev	Variance-Covar
Age	Gender	7	−1.8571	−.3095
Age	Score	7	28.5714	4.7619
Gender	Score	7	−12.1429	−2.0238

When other chapters cover computations, they will be based on the demonstration given here. The information here is fundamental and important in order to work efficiently with SPSS for Windows. However, this very brief introduction is not meant to serve as a substitute for the SPSS manuals that are available. The user of statistical computer software should realize that the computer only computes the statistics requested. It cannot interpret the output or know if logical errors have occurred.

Chapter Summary

1. Differences between measurements are needed in order to study the relations between variables.
2. A statistical measure used in studying differences is the variance.
3. The variance along with the mean is used to solve research problems.
4. Kinds of variance:
    a. The variability of a variable or characteristic in the universe or population is called the population variance.
    b. A subset of the universe is called a sample and that sample also has variability. That variability is referred to as sample variance.
    c. Since the statistic computed from sample to sample differs, this difference is referred to as sampling variance.
    d. Systematic variance is the variation that can be accounted for. It can be explained. Any natural or human-made influences that cause events to happen in a predictable way are systematic variance.
    e. One type of systematic variance is called between-groups variance. When there are differences between groups of subjects, and the cause of that difference is known, it is referred to as between-group variance.
    f. Another type of systematic variance is called experimental variance. Experimental variance is slightly more specific than between-groups variance in that it is associated with variance engendered by active manipulation of the independent variable.
    g. Error variance is the fluctuation or varying of measures in the dependent variable that cannot be directly explained by the variables under study. One part of error variance is due to chance. This is also known as random vari-

ance. The source of this fluctuation is generally unknown. Other possible sources for error variance include the procedure of the study, the measuring instrument and the researcher's outcome expectancy.

5. Variances can be broken down into components. In this case, the word *variance* is referred to as total variance. The partitioning of total variance into components of systematic and error variances plays an important role in statistical analyses of research data.

6. Covariance is the relationship between two or more variables:
   a. it is an unstandardized correlation coefficient;
   b. covariance and variance are the statistical foundations of multivariate statistics (to be presented in later chapters).

STUDY SUGGESTIONS

1. A social psychologist has done an experiment in which one group, A_1, was given a task to do in the presence of an audience, and another group, A_2, was given the same task to do without an audience. The scores of the two groups on the task, a measure of digital skill, were:

A_1	A_2
5	3
5	4
9	7
8	4
3	2

   a. Calculate the means and variances of A_1 and A_2, using the method described in the text.
   b. Calculate the between-groups variance, V_b, and the within-groups variance, V_w.
   c. Arrange all 10 scores in a column, and calculate the total variance, V_t.
   d. Substitute the calculated values obtained in (b) and (c) above, in the equation: $V_t = V_b + V_w$. Interpret the results.
   [Answers: (a) $V_{A_1} = 4.8$; $V_{A_2} = 2.8$; (b) $V_b = 1.0$; $V_w = 3.8$; (c) $V_t = 4.8$.]

2. To 1 above, add 2 to each of the scores of A_1, and calculate V_t, V_b, and V_w. Which of the variances changed? Which stayed the same? Why?
   [Answers: $V_t = 7.8$; $V_b = 4.0$; $V_w = 3.8$.]

3. To 1 above, equalize the means of A_1 and A_2, by adding a constant of 2 to each of the scores of A_2. Calculate V_t, V_b, and V_w. What is the main difference between these results and those of 1, above? Explain why.

4. Suppose a sociological researcher obtained measures of conservatism (A), attitude toward religion (B), and anti-Semitism (C) from 100 individuals. The correlations between the variables were: $r_{ab} = .70$; $r_{ac} = .40$; $r_{bc} = .30$. What do these correlations mean? [Hint: Square the rs before trying to interpret the relations. Also, think of ordered pairs.]

5. The purpose of this Study Suggestion and Study Suggestion 6 is to give the student an intuitive feeling for the variability of sample statistics, the relation between population and sample variances, and between-groups and error variances. Appendix C contains 40 sets of 100 random numbers 0 through 100, with calculated means, variances, and standard deviations. Draw 10 sets of 10 numbers each from 10 different places in the table.

   a. Calculate the mean, variance, and standard deviation of each of the 10 sets. Find the highest and lowest means and the highest and lowest variances. Do they differ much from each other? What value "should" the means be (50)? While doing this, save the 10 totals and calculate the mean of all 100 numbers. Do the 10 means differ much from the total mean? Do they differ much from the means reported in the table of means, variances, and standard deviations given after the random numbers?

   b. Count the odd and even numbers in each of the 10 sets. Are they what they "should be"? Count the odd and even numbers of the 100 numbers. Is the result "better" than the results of the 10 counts? Why should it be?

   c. Calculate the variance of the 10 means. This is, of course, the between-groups variance, V_b. Calculate the error variance, using the formula: $V_e = V_t - V_b$.

   d. Discuss the meaning of your results after reviewing the discussion in the text.

6. As early as possible in their study, students of research should start to understand and use the computer. Study Suggestion 5 can be better and less laboriously accomplished with the computer. It would be better, for example, to draw 20 samples of 100 numbers each. Why? In any case, students should learn how to perform simple statistical operations using existing computer facilities and programs at their institutions. All institutions own software programs for calculating means and standard deviations (variances can be obtained by squaring the standard deviations)[4] and for generating random numbers. If you can use your institution's facilities, use them for Study Suggestion 5, but increase the number of samples and their ns.

---

[4] There may be small discrepancies between your hand-calculated standard deviations and variances and those of the computer because existing programs and built-in routines of hand-held calculators usually use a formula with N minus 1 rather than N in the denominator of the formula. The discrepancies will be small, however, especially if N is large. (The reason for the different formulas will be explained later when we take up sampling and other matters.)

PART THREE
PROBABILITY, RANDOMNESS, AND SAMPLING

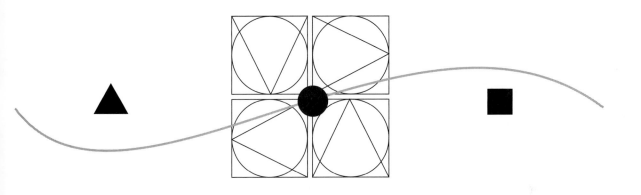

Chapter 7
PROBABILITY

Chapter 8
SAMPLING AND RANDOMNESS

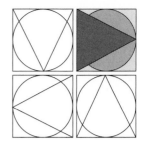

CHAPTER 7

PROBABILITY

Probability is an obvious and simple subject; it is a baffling and complex subject. It is a subject we know a great deal about; it is a subject we know nothing about. Kindergartners and philosophers can study probability. It is dull; it is interesting. Such contradictions are the stuff of probability.

Take the expression "laws of chance." The expression itself is seemingly contradictory. Chance or randomness, by definition, is the absence of law. If events can be explained lawfully, they are not random. Then why say "laws of chance"? The answer, too, is seemingly contradictory. It is possible to gain knowledge from ignorance if we view randomness as ignorance. This is because random events, in the aggregate, occur in lawful ways with monotonous regularity. From the disorder of randomness the scientist welds together the order of scientific prediction and control.

It is not easy to explain these disconcerting statements. Indeed, philosophers disagree on the answers. Fortunately, there is no disagreement on the empirical probabilistic events—or at least very little. Almost all scientists and philosophers agree that if two dice are thrown a number of times, there will probably be more 7s than 2s or 12s. They will also agree that certain events like finding a $100 bill or winning a sweepstakes are extremely unlikely.

Definition of Probability

What is probability? We ask this question and immediately strike a perplexing problem. Wang (1993), Brady and Lee (1989a), and Cowles (1989) have stated that historically there seems to be no agreement on the answer. This seems to be because there are two broad schools of thought: frequency and nonfrequency. Even among the frequency school, there are at least two definitions, among others, which seem irreconcilable: the *a priori* and the *a posteriori*. The a priori definition we owe to the controversial Pierre Laplace and the accomplished mathematician Augustus DeMorgan (Cowles, 1989). Here, the probability of an event is the number of favorable cases divided by the total number of (equally possible) cases, or $p = f \div (f + u)$, where p is probability, f the number of favorable cases, and u the number of unfavorable cases. The method of calculating probability implied by the definition is a priori in the sense that probability is given so that we can determine the probabilities of events before empirical investigation. People often make a number of statements concerning probabilities without any empirical data. It is rather a statement about one's state of mind. The Laplace–DeMorgan interpretation of probability is referred to as the classical definition. This definition is the basis of theoretical mathematical probability.

The *a posteriori*, or relative long-run frequency, definition is empirical in nature. It says that, in an actual series of tests, probability is the ratio of the number of times an event occurs to the total number of trials. With this definition, one approaches probability empirically by performing a series of tests, counting the number of times a certain kind of event happens, and then calculating the ratio. The result of the calculation is the probability of the certain kind of event. Frequency definitions have to be used when theoretical enumeration over classes of events is not possible. For example, to calculate longevity and horse race probabilities one has to use actuarial tables and calculate probabilities from past counts and calculations. A statement that a diamond cutter is 95% accurate indicates that out of every 100 diamonds this person has cut in the past, 95 of them were cut correctly.

Practically speaking (and for our purposes), the distinction between the a priori and a posteriori definition is not too vital. Following Margenau (1950/1977, p. 264), we put the two together by saying that the a priori approach supplies a constitutive definition of probability, whereas the a posteriori approach supplies an operational definition of probability. We need to use both approaches; we need to supplement one with the other.

The nonfrequency approach is attributed to John Maynard Keynes (1921/1979). Keynes was a world-class economist who wrote a number of important and often-cited publications. An entire economic theory is based on Keynes's contributions.

Those who engage in such research are called *Keynesians*. Keynes's contribution to probability and statistics is generally not mentioned in most textbooks on probability but yet is important for those doing behavioral science research (Brady & Lee, 1989a). In this approach, there are two values: (1) the probability value itself, and (2) the weight of evidence associated with it. The weight of evidence is subjective. It involves the perception of the decisionmaker toward the quality and amount of information surrounding the probability value that was obtained empirically. Essentially, Keynes states that decisionmakers are confronted with the probabilities of the events and also the amount and/or quality of information associated with it. The decisionmaker utilizes the information along with the probability in making a decision. Keynes defines a coefficient of weight and risk. This coefficient essentially places a weight on an empirical probability value. If the weight of evidence is strong, the probability is weighted more heavily. A weight closer to zero is assigned if the weight of evidence concerning that probability is weak. According to Brady and Lee (1989b, 1991), Keynes's approach explains some of the so-called paradoxes in decision making that frequency theory could not adequately explain. Bakan (1974) states that Keynes's theory of probability captures the essence of the process faced by clinical psychologists who deal with problems of relevancy. When conducting therapy, the psychologist hears, reads, and sees many clues and information. However, the psychologist selectively places some as being more relevant than others. Keynes's development has a greater reach of probabilistic explanations. Keynes's theory can be used to explain the outcome of a study by Rosenthal and Gaito reported in Bakan (1974). Here, psychology faculty holding a doctorate were asked to judge two different studies *A* and *B*. Studies *A* and *B* each had the same statistical test conducted and obtained the same *p* value. However, the sample size for study *A* was 10 and 100 for study *B*. Each faculty member was asked which study they would place the greater confidence or belief in. Most faculty members placed greater confidence in the results of study *B*. Keynes would explain this in light of the fact that these individuals gave a sample size of 100 as having more weight in their judgment than a sample size of 10.

In summary, the long-run relative frequency approach is the most prevalent in behavioral science research (Cowles, 1989). Most behavioral research scientists who rely on statistical manipulation of their data follow the long-run relative frequency school of thought. In almost all elementary statistics textbooks that cover probability, only the relative frequency approach and its effect on statistical methods is discussed.

Sample Space, Sample Points, and Events

To calculate the probability of any outcome, first determine the total number of possible outcomes. With a die the outcomes are 1, 2, 3, 4, 5, 6. Call this set *U*. *U* is the sample space, or universe of possible outcomes. The sample space includes all possible outcomes of an "experiment" that are of interest to the experimenter. The primary elements of *U* are called elements or sample points. Then let us write *U* = {1, 2, 3, 4, 5, 6}, and bring this chapter in line with the set reasoning and method of

◫ **TABLE 7.1** *Matrix of Possible Outcomes with Two Dice*

		Second Die					
		1	2	3	4	5	6
	1	2	3	4	5	6	7
	2	3	4	5	6	7	8
First Die	3	4	5	6	7	8	9
	4	5	6	7	8	9	10
	5	6	7	8	9	10	11
	6	7	8	9	10	11	12

chapters 4, 5, and 6. Letting x_j equal any sample point or element in U, we write $U = \{x_1, x_2, \ldots, x_n\}$. Examples of different Us are all possible outcomes of tossing two dice (see Table 7.1); all kindergarten children in such-and-such a school system; all eligible voters in X county.

Sometimes the determination of the sample space is easy; sometimes it is difficult. The problem is analogous to the definition of sets of Chapter 4. Sets can be defined by listing all the members of the set, and by giving a rule for the inclusion of elements in a set. In probability theory, both definitions are used. What is U in tossing two coins? We list all the possibilities: $U = \{(H, H), (H, T), (T, H), (T, T)\}$. This is a list definition of U. A rule definition—although we would not use it—might be: $U = \{x; x \text{ is all combinations of } H \text{ and } T\}$. In this case U is a Cartesian product. Let $A_1 = \{H_1, T_1\}$, the outcome of the first coin; let $A_2 = \{H_2, T_2\}$, the second coin. Recalling that a Cartesian product of two sets is the set of all ordered pairs whose first entry is an element of one set and whose second entry is an element of another set, we can diagram the generation of the Cartesian product of this case, $A_1 \times A_2$, as in Figure 7.1. Note that there are four lines connecting A_1 and A_2. Thus there are four possibilities: $\{(H_1, H_2), (H_1, T_2), (T_1, H_2), (T_1, T_2)\}$. This thinking and procedure can be used in defining many sample spaces of Us, although the actual procedure can be tedious.

With two dice, what is U? Think of the Cartesian product of two sets and you will probably have little trouble. Let A_1 be the outcomes or points of the first die: $\{1, 2, 3 \ 4, 5, 6\}$. Let A_2 be the outcomes or points of the second die. Then $U = A_1 \times A_2 = \{(1, 1), (1, 2), \ldots, (5, 6), (6, 6)\}$. We can diagram this as we diagrammed the coin example, but counting the lines is more difficult because there are too many of them. We can know the number of possible outcomes simply by $6 \times 6 = 36$, or in a formula: mn, where m is the number of possible outcomes of the first set, and n is the number of possible outcomes of the second set.

It is often possible to solve difficult probability problems by using trees. Trees define sample spaces, logical possibilities, with clarity and precision. A *tree* is a

◫ FIGURE 7.1

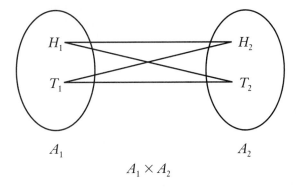

$$A_1 \times A_2$$

diagram that gives all possible alternatives or outcomes for combinations of sets by providing paths and set points. This definition is a bit unwieldy. Illustration is better. Take the coin example (we turn the tree on its side). Its tree is shown in Figure 7.2.

To determine the number of possible alternatives, count the number of alternatives or points at the "top" of the tree. In this case, there are four alternatives. To name the alternatives, read off, for each end point, the points that led to it. For example, the first alternative is (H_1, H_2). Obviously, three, four, or more coins can be used. The only trouble is that the procedure is tedious because of the large number of alternatives. The tree for three coins is illustrated in Figure 7.3. There are eight possible alternatives, outcomes, or sample points: $U = \{(H_1, H_2, H_3), (H_1, H_2, T_3), \ldots, (T_1, T_2, T_3)\}$ (the elements of this set are called *ordered triples*).

◫ FIGURE 7.2

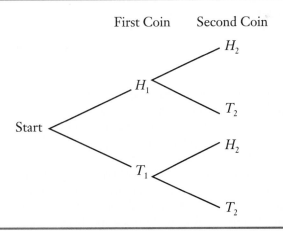

Sample points of a sample space may seem a bit confusing to the reader because two kinds of points have been discussed without differentiation. Another term and its use may help clear up this possible confusion. An event is a subset of U. Any element of a set is also a subset of the set. Recall that with set $A = \{a_1, a_2\}$, for example, both $\{a_1\}$ and $\{a_2\}$ are subsets of A, as well as $\{a_1, a_2\}$, and $\{\ \}$, the empty set. Identically, all the outcomes of Figure 7.2 and Figure 7.3, for example, (H_1, T_2), (T_1, H_2), and (T_1, H_2, T_3), are subsets of their respective Us. Therefore they are also by definition events. But in standard usage, events are more encompassing than points. All points are events (subsets), but not all events are points. Or, a point or outcome is a special kind of event, the simplest kind. Any time we state a proposition, we describe an event. We ask, for instance, "If two coins are thrown, what is the probability of getting two heads?" The "two heads" is an event. It so happens, in this case, that it is also a sample point. But suppose we asked, "What is the probability of getting at least one head?" "At least one head" is an event, but not a sample point because it includes, in this case, three sample points: (H_1, H_2), (H_1, T_2), and (T_1, H_2) (see Figure 7.2).

Determining Probabilities with Coins

Suppose we toss a newly minted coin three times. We write $p(H) = 1/2$ and $p(T) = 1/2$, meaning the probability of heads is 1/2, and similarly for tails. We assume, then, equiprobability. The sample space for three tosses of a coin (or one toss of three coins) is: $U = \{(H, H, H), (H, H, T), (H, T, H), (H, T, T), (T, H, H), (T, H, T), (T, T, H), (T, T, T)\}$. Note that if we pay no attention to the order of heads and tails, we obtain one case of 3 heads, one case of 3 tails, three cases of 2 heads and 1 tail, and three cases of 2 tails and 1 head. The probability of each of the eight outcomes is obviously 1/8. Thus the probability of 3 heads is 1/8, and the probability of 3 tails is 1/8. The probability of 2 heads and 1 tail, on the other hand, is 3/8, and similarly for the probability of 2 tails and 1 head.

The probabilities of all the points in the sample space must add up to 1.00. It also follows that probabilities are always positive. If we write a probability tree for the three-toss experiment, it looks like Figure 7.3. Each complete path of the tree (from the start to the third toss) is a sample point. All the paths comprise the sample space. The single path sections are labeled with the probabilities, in this case all are labeled 1/8. This leads naturally to the statement of a basic principle. If the outcomes at the different points in the tree (at the first, second, and third tosses) are independent of each other (that is, if one outcome does not influence another in any way), then the probability of any sample point (*HHH* perhaps) is the product of the probabilities of the separate outcomes. For example, the probability of 3 heads is $1/2 \times 1/2 \times 1/2 = 1/8$.

Another principle is: To obtain the probability of any event, add the probabilities of the sample points that comprise that event. For example, what is the probability of tossing 2 heads and 1 tail? We look at the paths in the tree that have 2 heads and 1 tail. There are three paths (they are checked in Figure 7.3). Thus, $1/8 + 1/8 + 1/8 =$

■ FIGURE 7.3

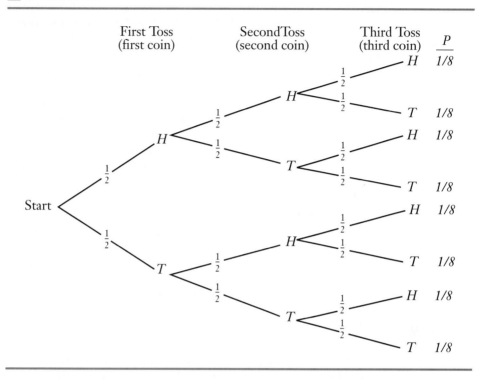

3/8. In set language, we find the subsets (events) of U and note their probabilities. The subset of U of the type "2 heads and 1 tail" are, from the tree or the previous definition of U, {(H, H, T), (H, T, H), (T, H, H)}. Call this the set or event A. Then $p(A_1) = 3/8$.

This procedure could be followed with a laborious experiment of 100 tosses. Instead, to get the theoretical expectations, merely multiply the number of tosses by the probability of any one of them, to arrive at the expected number of heads (or tails). This can be done because *all* the probabilities are the same. An important question to ask here is: In actual experiments in which 100 coins are tossed, will we get exactly 50 heads if we assume the coins are fair? No, not often; about eight times in 100 such experiments. This can be written $p = 8/100$ or .08. (Probabilities can be written in fractional or decimal forms, more usually in decimal form.)

An Experiment with Dice

We tossed two newly manufactured dice 72 times under carefully controlled conditions. If we add the number of spots on the two dice on all 72 throws, we obtain a set of sums from 2 to 12. Some of these outcomes (sums) will turn up more frequently than others simply because there are more ways for them to do so. For example, there is only one way for 2 or 12 to turn up: $1 + 1$ and $6 + 6$, but there are three ways for 4 to turn up: $1 + 3$, $3 + 1$, and $2 + 2$. If this is true, then the probabilities for getting different sums must be different. The game of craps is based on these differences in frequency expectations.

To solve the a priori probability problem, we must first define the sample space: $U = \{(1, 1), (1, 2), (1, 3), \ldots , (6, 4), (6, 5), (6, 6)\}$. That is, we pair each number of the first die with each number of the second die in turn (the Cartesian product again). This can easily be seen if we set up this procedure in a matrix (see Table 7.1). Suppose we want to know the probability of the event—a very important event too—"a 7 turns up." Simply count the number of 7s in the table. There are six of them nicely arrayed along the center diagonal. There are 36 sample points in U, obtained by some method of enumerating them as above, or by using the formula mn. This formula says: Multiply the number of possibilities of the first thing by the number of possibilities of the second thing. This method can be defined as follows. Say there are m ways of doing something, A. There are n ways of doing something else, B. Then, if the n ways of doing B are independent of the m ways of doing A, there are $m \times n$ ways of doing both A and B. This principle can be extended to more than two things. If, for example, there are three things, A, B, and C, where there are r ways of doing C, then the formula is mnr.

Applied to the dice problem, $mn = 6 \times 6 = 36$. Assuming equipossibility again, the probability of any single outcome is 1/36. The probability of a 12, for instance, is 1/36. The probability of a 4, however, is different. Since 4 occurs three times in the table above, we must add the probabilities for each of these elements of the sample space: $1/36 + 1/36 + 1/36 = 3/36$. Thus $p(4) = 3/36 = 1/12$. As we have seen, the probability of a 7 is $p(7) = 6/36 = 1/6$. The probability of an 8 is $p(8) = 5/36$. Note, too, that we can calculate the probabilities of combinations of events. Gamblers often bet on such combinations. For example, what is the probability of a 4 or a 10? In set language, this is a union question: $p(4 \cup 10)$. Count the number of 4s and 10s in the table. There are three 4s and three 10s. Thus $p(4 \cup 10) = 6/36$.

In Table 7.1, counting the probabilities of each kind of outcome, we lay out a table of expected frequencies (f_e) for 36 throws. Then double these frequencies to

■ **TABLE 7.2** *Expected and Obtained Frequencies of Sums of Two Dice Tossed 72 Times*

Sum of Dice	2	3	4	5	6	7	8	9	10	11	12
$f_e(36)$	1	2	3	4	5	6	5	4	3	2	1
$f_e(72)$	2	4	6	8	10	12	10	8	6	4	2
$f_o(72)$	4	2	6	6	10	15	7	11	6	4	1
Difference	2	2	0	2	0	3	3	3	0	0	1

get the expected (a priori) frequencies for 72 throws. We juxtapose against these expected frequencies the frequencies obtained (f_o) when two dice were actually thrown 72 times. The absolute differences between expected and obtained frequencies are then apparent (the results are laid out in Table 7.2). The discrepancies are not great. In fact, by actual statistical test, they do not differ significantly from chance expectation. The a priori method seems to have virtue.

Some Formal Theory

We have the sample space U, with subsets A, B, ... The elements of U (and of A, B, . . .) are a_i, b_i, . . . , that is, a_1, a_2, . . . , a_n and b_1, b_2, . . . , b_n, and so forth. A, B, and so forth, are events. Actually, although we have often talked about the probability of a single occurrence, we really mean the probability of a type of occurrence. When we talk about the probability of any single event of U, for instance, we can only do so because any particular member of U is conceived as representative of all of U. And, similarly, for the probabilities of subsets A, B, . . . , K of U. The probability of U is 1; the probability of E (the empty set), is 0. Or $p(U) = 1.00$; $p(E) = 0$. To determine the probability of any subset of U, a measure of the set must be assigned. In order to assign such a measure, we must assign a weight to each element of U and thus to each element of the subsets of U. A *weight* is defined by Kemeny, Snell, and Thompson (1974) as:

A weight is a positive number assigned to each element, x, in U, and written $w(x)$, such that the sum of all these weights, $\Sigma w(x)$, is equal to 1.

This is a function notion; w is called a weight function. It is a rule that assigns weights to elements of a set, U, in a way such that the sum of the weights is equal to 1; that is, $w_1 + w_2 + w_3 + \ldots + w_n = 1.00$, and $w_i = 1/n$. The weights are equal, assuming equiprobability; each weight is a fraction with 1 in the numerator and the number of cases, n, in the denominator. In the previous experiment of the tosses of a coin (Figure 7.3), the weights assigned to each element of U, U being *all* the outcomes are 1/8. The sum of all the weight functions, $w(x)$, is 1/8 + 1/8 . . . + 1/8 = 1. In probability theory, the sum of the elements of the sample space must always equal 1.

To get from weights to the measure of a set is easy: The measure of a set is the sum of the weights of the elements of the set.

$$\sum_{x\ in\ U} w(x) \quad \text{or} \quad \sum_{x\ in\ A} w(x)$$

(Note that the sum of the weights in a subset A of U does not have to equal 1. In fact, it is usually less than 1.)

We write $m(A)$, meaning "The measure of the set A." This simply says the sum of the weights of the elements in the set A.

Suppose we randomly sample children from the 400 children of the fourth grade of a school system. Then U is all 400 children. Each child is a sample point of U. Each child is an x in U. The probability of selecting any one child at random is 1/400. Let A equal the males in U, and B equal the females in U. There are 100 males and 300 females. Each male is assigned the weight 1/400, and each female is assigned the weight 1/400. Suppose we wish to sample 100 children all together. Our expectation is, then, 25 males and 75 females in the sample. The measure of the set A, $m(A)$, is the sum of the weights of all the elements in A. Since there are 100 males in U, we sum the 100 weights: $1/400 + 1/400 + \ldots + 1/400 = 100/400 = 1/4$, or

$$m(A) = \sum_{x\ in\ A} w(x) = \frac{1}{4}$$

Similarly,

$$m(B) = \sum_{x\ in\ B} w(x) = \frac{3}{4}$$

For set B (the females), we sum 300 weights, each of them being 1/400. In short, the sums of the weights are the probabilities. That is, the measure of a set is the probability of a member of the set being chosen. Thus, we can say that the probability that a member of the sample of 400 children will be a male is 1/4, and the probability that the selected member will be a female is 3/4. To determine the expected frequencies, multiply the sample size by these probabilities: $1/4 \times 100 = 25$ and $3/4 \times 100 = 75$.

Probability has three fundamental properties:

1. The measure of any set, as defined above, is greater than or equal to 0 and less than or equal to 1. In brief, probabilities (measures of sets) are either 0, 1, or in between.
2. The measure of a set, $m(A)$, equals 0 if, and only if, there are no members in A; that is, A is empty.
3. Let A and B be sets. If A and B are disjoint, that is, $A \cap B = E$, then: $m(A \cup B) = m(A) + m(B)$.

This equation says that when no members of A and B are shared in common, then the probability of either A or B or both is equal to the combined probabilities of A and B.

There is no need to give an example to illustrate (1). We have had several earlier. To illustrate (2), assume, in the boys–girls example, that we asked the probability of drawing a teacher in the sample. But U did not include teachers. Let C be the set of fourth-grade teachers. In this case, the set C is empty, and $m(C) = 0$. Use the same male–female students example to illustrate (3). Let A be the set of males, B the set of females. Then $m(A \cup B) = m(A) + m(B)$. But $m(A \cup B) = 1.00$ because they were the only subsets of U. And we learned that $m(A) = 1/4$ and $m(B) = 3/4$. The equation holds.

Compound Events and Their Probabilities

We said earlier that an event is a subset of U, but we need to elaborate this. An event is a set of possibilities; it is a possible set of events; it is an outcome of a probability "experiment." A compound event is the co-occurrence of two or more single (or compound) events. The two set operations of intersection and union—the operations of most interest to us—imply compound events. If we toss a coin and roll a die, the outcome is a compound event, and we can calculate the probability of such an event. More interesting, we might ask how certain demographic variables are related. One way to do this is to seek answers to such questions as: "What is the probability of detecting a drug user who chooses their specific days of drug usage without regard for drug testing strategy?" (see Borack, 1997) or, "What is the probability that two students in the same classroom have the same month and day of birth?" (see Nunnikhoven, 1992) or, "What is the probability that a graduate student will drop out of graduate school?" (see Cooke, Sims, & Peyrefitte, 1995).

Compound events are more interesting than single events—and more useful in research. Relations can be studied with them. To understand this, we first define and illustrate compound events and then examine certain counting problems and the ways in which counting is related to set theory and probability theory. It will be found that if the basic theory is understood, the application of probability theory to research problems is considerably facilitated. In addition, the interpretation of data becomes less subject to error.

Assume that a group of elementary schoolchildren has been studied, that there are 100 children altogether in the group: 60 fourth graders and 40 sixth graders. The numerical function is useful: it assigns to any set the number of members in the set. The number of members in A is $n(A)$. In this case $n(U) = 100$, $n(A) = 60$, and $n(B) = 40$, where A is the set of fourth graders and B the set of sixth graders, both subsets of U, the 100 elementary schoolchildren. If there is no overlap between two sets, $A \cap B = E$, then the following equation holds:

$$n(A \cup B) = n(A) + n(B) \tag{7.1}$$

Recall that earlier the frequency definition of probability was given as:

$$p = \frac{f}{f + u} \tag{7.2}$$

where f is the number of favorable cases, and u the number of unfavorable cases. The numerator is $n(f)$ and the denominator $n(U)$, the total number of possible cases. Similarly, we can divide through the terms of Equation 7.1 by $n(U)$:

$$\frac{n(A \cup B)}{n(U)} = \frac{n(A)}{n(U)} + \frac{n(B)}{n(U)} \tag{7.3}$$

This reduces to probabilities, analogously to Equation 7.2:

$$p(A \cup B) = p(A) + p(B) \tag{7.4}$$

Using the example of the 100 schoolchildren, and substituting values in Equation 7.3, we get

$$\frac{100}{100} = \frac{60}{100} + \frac{40}{100},$$

which yields for Equation 7.4:

$$1.00 = .60 + .40.$$

In many cases, two (or more) sets in which we are interested are not disjoint. Rather, they overlap. When this is so, then $A \cap B \neq E$, and it is not true that $n(A \cup B) = n(A) + n(B)$. Look at Figure 7.4. Here A and B are subsets of U; sample points are indicated by dots. The number of sample points in A is 8; the number in B is 6. There are two sample points in $A \cap B$. Thus the equation above does not hold. If we calculate all the points in $A \cup B$ with Equation 7.1, we get $8 + 6 = 14$ points; but there are only 12 points. This equation has to be altered to a more general equation that fits all cases:

$$n(A \cup B) = n(A) + n(B) - n(A \cap B) \tag{7.5}$$

It should be clear that the error when Equation 7.1 is used results from counting the two points of $A \cap B$ twice. Therefore, we subtract $n(A \cap B)$ once, which corrects the equation. It now fits any possibility. If, for example, $n(A \cap B) = E$, the empty set, Equation 7.5 reduces to Equation 7.1. Equation 7.1 is a special case of Equation 7.5. Calculating the number of sample points in $n(A \cap B)$ of Equation 7.4, then, we get: $n(A \cup B) = 8 + 6 - 2 = 12$. If we divide Equation 7.5 through by $n(U)$, as in (7.3):

$$p(A \cup B) = p(A) + p(B) - p(A \cap B) \tag{7.6}$$

◉ **FIGURE 7.4** *Variables Moved for Right Block for Analysis*

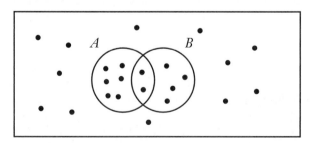

Substituting our number of dots or sample points, we find that

$$\frac{12}{24} = \frac{8}{24} + \frac{6}{24} - \frac{2}{24}$$

$$.50 = .33 + .25 - .08$$

In a random sample of U, then, the probabilities of an element being a member of A, B, $A \cap B$ and $A \cup B$, respectively, are .33, .25, .08, and .50.

Independence, Mutual Exclusiveness, and Exhaustiveness

Consider the following questions, variants of which must be asked by researchers. Does the occurrence of this event, A, preclude the possibility of the occurrence of this other event, B? Does the occurrence of event A have an influence on the occurrence of event B? Are the events A, B, and C related? When A has occurred does this influence the outcomes of B—and, perhaps, C? Do the events A, B, C, and D exhaust the possibilities? Or are there, perhaps, other possibilities E, F, and so on? Suppose, for instance, that a researcher is studying board of education decisions and their relation to political preference, religious preference, education, and other variables. In order to relate these variables to board decisions, the researcher has to have some method of classifying the decisions. One of the first questions to be asked is "Have I exhausted all possibilities in my classification system?" An additional question is "If a board makes one kind of decision does this preclude the possibility of making another kind of decision?" Perhaps the most important question the researcher can ask is, "If a board makes a particular decision, does this decision influence its action on any other decision?"

We have been talking about exhaustiveness, mutual exclusiveness, and independence. We now define these ideas in a more detailed manner and use them in probability examples. Their general applicability and importance will also become apparent in the chapters when we take up analysis of data.

Let A and B be subsets of U. We ask the questions: Are there any other subsets of U (other than the empty set)? Do A and B exhaust the sample space? Are all the sample points of the sample space U included in A or in B? A simple example is: Let $A = \{H, T\}$; let $B = \{1, 2, 3, 4, 5, 6\}$. If we toss a coin and throw a die together, what are the possibilities? Unless all the possibilities are exhausted, we cannot solve the probability problem. There are 12 possibilities (2×6). The sets A and B exhaust the sample space. (This is, of course, obvious, since A and B generated the sample space.) Now take a more realistic example. Suppose a researcher is studying religious preferences. The following system is set up to categorize individuals: (Protestants, Catholics, and Jews). Implicitly, U is set up so that U equals all people (with or without religious preferences) and subsets of U, A equals Protestants, B equals Catholics,

C equals Jews. The set question is: Does *A* ∪ *B* ∪ *C* = *U*? Are all religious preferences exhausted? How about Buddhists? Muslims? atheists?

Exhaustiveness, then, means that the subsets of *U* use up all the sample space, or *A* ∪ *B* ∪ . . . ∪ *K* = *U*, where *A*, *B*, . . . , *K* are subsets of *U*, the sample space. In probability language, this means: *p*(*A* ∪ *B* ∪ . . . ∪ *K*) = 1.00. Unless the sample space, *U*, is used up, so to speak, probabilities cannot be adequately calculated. For example, in the religious preference example, suppose we thought that *A* ∪ *B* ∪ *C* = *U*, but in fact there were a large number of individuals with no particular religious preference. So, really, *A* ∪ *B* ∪ *C* ∪ *D* = *U*, where *D* is the subset of individuals with no religious preference. The probabilities calculated on the assumption of this equation would be quite different from those based on the assumption of the earlier equation.

Two events, *A* and *B*, are *mutually exclusive* when they are disjoint, or when *A* ∩ *B* = *E*. That is, when the intersection of two (or more) sets is the empty set—or when two sets have no elements in common—the sets are said to be mutually exclusive. This is the same as saying, again in probability language, *p*(*A* ∩ *B*) = 0. It is more convenient for researchers when events are mutually exclusive because they can then add the probabilities of events. We state a principle in set and probability terms: If the events (sets) *A*, *B*, and *C* are mutually exclusive, then *p*(*A* ∪ *B* ∪ *C*) = *p*(*A*) + *p*(*B*) + *p*(*C*). This is the special case of the more general principle we discussed in the previous sections (see equations 7.1, 7.4, 7.5, and 7.6 and the accompanying discussion, above).

One of the chief purposes of research design is to set up conditions of independence of events so that conditions of dependence of events can be studied adequately. Two events, *A* and *B*, are statistically independent if the following equation holds:

$$p(A \cap B) = p(A) \cdot p(B) \tag{7.7}$$

which says that the probability of *A* and *B* both occurring is equal to the probability of *A* times the probability of *B*. Easy and clear examples of independent events are dice throws and coin tosses. If *A* is the event of a die throw and *B* is the event of a coin toss, and *p*(*A*) = 1/6 and *p*(*B*) = 1/2, then, if *p*(*A*) · *p*(*B*) = 1/6 · 1/2 = 1/12, *A* and *B* are independent. If we toss a coin 10 times, one toss has no influence on any other toss; the tosses are independent, and so are the throws of dice. Similarly, when we throw a die and toss a coin simultaneously, the events of throwing a die, *A*, and tossing a coin, *B*, are independent. The outcome of a die throw has no influence on the coin toss—and vice versa. Unfortunately, this neat model does not always apply in research situations.

The commonsense notion of the so-called law of averages is utterly erroneous, but it illustrates lack of understanding of independence nicely. It says that if there is a large number of occurrences of an event, then the chance of that event occurring on the next trial is smaller. Suppose a coin is being tossed. Heads has come up five times in a row. The commonsense notion of the "law of averages" would lead one to believe that there is a greater chance of getting tails on the next toss. Not so. The probability is still 1/2. Each toss is an independent event.

Suppose students in a college class are taking an examination. They are working under the usual conditions of no communication, no looking at each other's papers, and so forth. The responses of any student can be considered independent of the responses of any other student. Can the within-test responses to the items be considered independent? Suppose that the answer to one item later in the test is embedded in an item earlier in the test. The probability of getting the later item correct by chance, say, is 1/4. But the fact that the answer was given earlier can change this probability. With some students it might even become 1.00. What is important for the researcher to know is that independence is often difficult to achieve and that lack of independence when research operations assume independence can seriously affect the interpretation of data.

Suppose we rank order examination papers and then assign grades on the basis of these ranks. This is a perfectly legitimate and useful procedure. But it must be realized that the grades given by the rank-order method are not independent (if they ever could be). Take five such papers. After reading them one is ranked as the first (the best), the second next, and so on through the five papers. We assign the number "1" to the first, "2" to the second, "3" to the third, "4" to the fourth, and "5" to the fifth. After using up 1, we have only 2, 3, 4, and 5 left. After using up 2, only 3, 4, and 5 remain. When we assign 4, obviously we must assign 5 to the remaining examination. In short, the assignment of 5 was influenced by the assignment of 4—and also 1, 2, and 3. The assignment events are not independent. One may ask, "Does this matter?" Suppose we take the ranks, treat them as scores, and draw inferences about mean differences between groups, say between two classes. The statistical test used to do this is probably based on the coin–dice paradigm with its pristine independence. But we have not followed this model—one of its most important assumptions, independence, has been ignored.

When research events lack independence, statistical tests lack a certain validity. A χ^2 test, for example, assumes that the events (responses of individuals to an interview question), recorded in the cells of a crossbreak or crosstab table, are independent of each other. If the recorded events are not independent of each other, then the basis of the statistical test and the inferences drawn from it are corrupted.

Consider the research on the relations between perceived self-efficacy and behavior. Here, researchers attempt to show the congruency between self-efficacy judgments and actual behavior. In these studies, participants are usually administered self-efficacy scales that describe a set of well-defined tasks. Each participant is asked to judge whether he or she can accomplish each task. Perception and behavior are congruent when the participant perception matches actual performance, that is, "said she could do it and then she did it," and "said she could not do it and she in reality could not do it." Cervone (1987) reports that a large number of researchers doing work in this area have reported exceptionally high congruencies. A number of studies reported congruencies of 80–90%. Cervone states, however, that data obtained from self-efficacy scales are not independent because each individual participant contributes more than one observation to the analysis. Cervone (1987, p. 710) states "As in any area of research, one cannot assume that multiple observations of one subject are independent."

Kramer and Schmidhammer (1992) found similar problems of independence in animal behavior research. Some studies on animal and human behavior depend on frequency-type ethological data. This type of data usually counts the number of encounters between organisms (animal or human) or performance of a behavior. Kramer and Schmidhammer use the example of measuring frog behavior. To have independent observations of male frog behavior of vocalizing or not along a section of a lake shore, the researcher needs to ascertain that the absence or presence of vocalization of one frog does not have an effect on other frogs. Kramer and Schmidhammer observe that many patterns of behavior of interest to the ethologist tend to occur in clusters and are not independent. Kramer and Schmidhammer cite a number of studies that may have a potential independence problem.

One possible study is by Keane (1990). Keane's study examined the male preferences of estrous female white-footed mice. Keane recorded the number of encounters each estrous female mouse had with each male mouse. Encounters were classified as either aggressive (fighting, chasing) or amicable (grooming, smelling). The male mice's breeding origins were documented from the time of birth so that the experimenter knew how each female mouse was related to each male mouse. Keane wanted to know if the estrous female mouse preferred a related or unrelated male mouse. Keane found that the estrous female mouse exhibited more amicable behaviors and fewer aggressive behaviors toward first cousins than toward nonrelatives. Using Kramer and Schmidhammer points from their paper, Keane's study could be flawed in that the observations may not be independent. One female mouse may have had a special "dislike" for a nonrelative or a special "like" for a first cousin, and the frequency counts could be weighted in favor of that one pair of mice.

Along these lines, consider a dated but still important research study on the aggressive behavior of apes by Hebb and Thompson (1968). The problem was the relation between sex and aggression. Samples of the behavior of 30 adult chimpanzees were taken in an effort to study individual differences in ape temperament. Without going into detail, it can be said that one analysis of the observations showed that males and females displayed friendly behavior about equally often, but that males were more aggressive. Hebb and Thompson's data on this observation seem to say: "Watch out for males!" But, the authors point out, this is quite out of line with the experience of the apes' caretakers. Nineteen out of 20 cuts and scratches were inflicted by females! Then Hebb and Thompson pursued the interesting, if disconcerting idea of tabulating incidence of aggressive acts in two ways: when such were preceded by quasi-aggression; that is by warning of attack, and when aggressive acts were preceded by friendly behavior. The resulting incidences of behavior seem to indicate: "Watch out for female apes when they are friendly!" Males were the only ones to display quasi-aggressive acts before actual agressive acts (37 male acts, 0 female acts). However, only females acted aggressively after displaying friendly behavior (15 female acts, 0 male acts).

These data cannot be validly analyzed statistically, since the numbers indicate the frequency of kinds of acts. But all 37 acts by males may have been committed by only one or two of them. If one ape had committed all 37 acts, then it should be clear that the acts were not independent of each other. That ape might have had a bad temper, and bad tempers notoriously create lack of independence in animal and human acts.

The next example is hypothetical. Suppose a researcher decides to sample 100 board of education decisions. There is a variety of ways to do this. Many decisions can be sampled from a few boards, or many decisions can be sampled from many boards, or both. If the researcher wants to be assured of the independence of the decisions, then many decisions should be sampled from many boards of education. Theoretically, only one decision should be taken from each board. This gives some assurance of independence—at least as much as such assurance is possible. As soon as more than one decision is taken from the same board, however, the researcher must entertain the notion that decisions of the kind *A* may influence decisions of the kind *B*. Decision *A* may influence decision *B*, for example, because the board members may wish to appear consistent. Both decisions may involve expenditures for instructional equipment, and since the board adopted a liberal policy on *A* it must adopt a liberal policy on *B*.

Suppose an investigator calculated the probability of the difference between two means. In this example, the difference was due to chance. This probability was 5/100, or .05. This indicates that there were approximately five chances in 100 that the obtained result was due to chance. That is, if the experimental condition is repeated 100 times without the experimental manipulation, approximately five of those times could yield a mean difference as large as the one obtained with the experimental manipulation. Feeling shaky about the result—after all, there are five chances in 100 that the result could have been due to chance—the researcher carefully repeated the whole experiment. The same result is obtained (luck!). Having controlled everything carefully to be sure the two experiments were independent, the probability calculated for the two results were due to chance. This probability was approximately .02. Thus we see both the values of independence in experimentation and the importance of replication of results.[1]

Note, finally, that the formula for independence works two ways. (1) It tells us, the probability of both events occurring by chance, if events are independent and we know the probabilities of the separate events. If it is found that dice repeatedly show say 12s, then there is probably something wrong with the dice. If a gambler notes that another gambler seems always to win, the losing gambler will of course get suspicious. The chances of continually winning a fair game are small. It can happen, of course, but it is unlikely to happen. In research, it is unlikely that one would get two or three significant results by chance. Something beyond chance is probably

---

[1] The method of calculating these combined probabilities was proposed by Fisher and is described in Mosteller and Bush (1954). The astute student may wonder why the set principle applied to probability, $p(A \cap B) = p(A) \cdot p(B)$, is not applicable. That is, why not calculate $.05 \times .05 = .0025$? Mosteller and Bush explain this point. Since it is a rather difficult and moot point, we do not consider it in this book. All the reader need do is to remember that the probability of getting, say, a substantial difference between means in the same direction on repeated experiments is considerably smaller than getting such a difference once. Thus one can be more sure of one's data and conclusions, other things being equal.

operating—the independent variable, we hope. (2) The formula for independence can be turned around, so to speak. It can tell the researchers what to do in order to take advantage of the multiplicative probabilities. The researcher must, if it is at all possible, plan the research so that events are independent. That this is easier said than done will become quite evident before this book is finished.

Conditional Probability

In all research—and perhaps especially in social scientific and educational research—events are often not independent. Look at independence in another way. When two variables are related they are not independent. Our previous discussion of sets makes it clear. If $A \cap B = E$, then there is no relation (more accurately, a zero relation), or A and B are independent. If $A \cap B \neq E$, then there is a relation, or A and B are not independent. When events are not independent, scientists can sharpen their probabilistic inferences. The meaning of this statement can be explicated to some extent by studying conditional probability.

When events are not independent, the probability approach must be altered. Here is a simple example. What is the probability that, of any married couple picked at random, both mates are Republicans? First, assuming equiprobability and that everything else is equal, the sample space U (all the possibilities) is {*RR, RD, DR, DD*}, where the wife comes first in each possibility or sample point. Thus the probability that both husband and wife are Republicans is $p\{RR\} = 1/4$. But suppose we know that one of them is a Republican. What is the probability of both being Republicans now? U is reduced to {*RR, RD, DR*}. The knowledge that one is a Republican deletes the possibility *DD*, thus reducing the sample space. Therefore, $p(RR) = 1/3$. Suppose we have the further information that the wife is a Republican, what is the probability that both mates are Republicans? Now $U = \{RR, RD\}$. Thus $p(RR) = 1/2$. The new probabilities are, in this case, "conditional" on prior knowledge or facts.

Definition of Conditional Probability

Let A and B be events in the sample space, U, as usual. The conditional probability is denoted: $p(A|B)$, which is read, "The probability of A, given B." For example, we might say, "The probability that a husband and wife are both Republicans, given that the husband is a Republican," or, much more difficult to answer, though more interesting, "The probability of high effectiveness in college teaching, given the Ph.D degree." Of course, we can write $p(B|A)$, too. The formula for the conditional probability involving two events is:

$$p(A|B) = \frac{p(A \cap B)}{p(B)} \tag{7.8}$$

The formula takes an earlier notion of probability and alters it for the conditional probability situations. (Please note that the theory of conditional probability extends

TABLE 7.3 *Probability Matrix Showing Joint Probabilities of Two Independent Events*

		Second Toss		
		H_2	T_2	
First Toss	H_1	1/4	1/4	1/2
	T_1	1/4	1/4	1/2
		1/2	1/2	

to more than two events, but will not be discussed in this book.) Remember that in probability problems the denominator has to be the sample space. The formula above changes the denominator of the ratio and thus changes the sample space. The sample space has, through knowledge, been reduced from U to B. To demonstrate this point take two examples: one of independence or simple probability and one of dependence or conditional probability.

Toss a coin twice. The events are independent. What is the probability of getting heads on the second toss if heads appeared on the first toss? We already know: 1/2. Let us calculate the probability using Equation 7.8. First we write a probability matrix (see Table 7.3). For the probabilities of heads (H) and tails (T) on the first toss, read the marginal entries on the right side of the matrix. Similarly, for the probabilities of the second toss, they are on the bottom of the matrix. Thus $p(H_1) = 1/2$, $p(H_2) = 1/2$, and $p(H_1 \cap H_2) = 1/4$. Therefore,

$$p(H_2|H_1) = \frac{p(H_2 \cap H_1)}{p(H_1)} = \frac{\frac{1}{4}}{\frac{1}{2}} = \frac{1}{2}$$

The result agrees with our previous simpler reasoning. If we make the problem a bit more complex, however, perhaps the formula will become more useful. Suppose, somehow, that the probability of getting heads on the second toss was .60 instead of .50, and the events are still independent. Does this change the situation? The new situation is set up in Table 7.4. (The .30 in the cell $H_1 \cap H_2$ is calculated with the probabilities on the margins: .50 × .60 = .30. This is permissible since we know that the events are independent. If they are not independent, conditional probability problems cannot be solved without knowledge of at least one of the values.) The formula gives us:

$$p(H_2|H_1) = \frac{p(H_2 \cap H_1)}{p(H_1)} = \frac{.30}{.50} = .60$$

▣ TABLE 7.4 *Matrix of Joint Probabilities of Events*

		Second Toss		
		H_2	T_2	
First Toss	H_1	.30	.20	.50
	T_1	.30	.20	.50
		.60	.40	1.00

But this .60 is the same as the simple probability of H_2. When events are independent, we get the same results. That is, in this case: $p(H_2 \mid H_1) = p(H_2)$, and in the general case:

$$p(A \mid B) = p(A) \qquad (7.9)$$

We have another definition or condition of independence. If Equation 7.9 holds, the events are independent.

An Academic Example

There are more interesting examples of conditional probability than coins and other such chance devices. Take the baffling and frustrating problem of predicting the success of doctoral students in graduate school. Can the coin–dice models be used in such a complex situation? Yes, under certain conditions. Unfortunately, these conditions are difficult to arrange. There has been some limited success, however. Provided that we have certain empirical information, the model can be quite useful. Assume that the administrators of a graduate school are interested in predicting the success of their doctoral students. They are distressed by the poor performance of many of their graduates and want to set up a selection system. The school continues to admit all doctoral applicants as in the past, but for three years all incoming students take the Miller Analogies Test (MAT), a test that has been found to be fairly successful in predicting success in graduate school in a number of areas (e.g., psychology, education, economics). This test has also been used in evaluating personnel for high-level jobs in industry. An arbitrary cutoff point of a raw score of 65 is selected.

The school administration finds that 30% of all the candidates of the three-year period score 65 or above. Each is categorized as a Success (S) or Failure (F). The criterion is simple: Does he or she get the degree? If so, this is defined as Success. It is found that 40% of the total number succeed. To determine the relation between MAT score and Success or Failure, the administration, again using a cutoff point of 65, determines the proportions shown in Table 7.5. The MAT divides the successful group in half (.20 and .20), but sharply differentiates in the failure group (.10 and

▣ TABLE 7.5 *Joint Probabilities, Graduate School Problem*

	Success (S)	Failure (F)	
MAT ≥65	.20	.10	.30
MAT <65	.20	.50	.70
	.40	.60	1.00

.50). Now, the questions are asked: What is the probability of getting the doctoral degree if a candidate receives a MAT score of 65 or higher? What is the probability of a candidate's getting the degree if the MAT score is lower than 65? The computations are:

$$p(S \mid \geq 65) = \frac{p(S \cap \geq 65)}{p(\geq 65)} = \frac{.20}{.30} = .67$$

$$p(S \mid < 65) = \frac{p(S \cap < 65)}{p(< 65)} = \frac{.20}{.70} = .29$$

Clearly, it would seem that the MAT is a good predictor of success in the program.

Note carefully what happens in all these cases. When we write $p(A \mid B)$ instead of simply $p(A)$, in effect we reduce the sample space from U to B. Take the example just given. The probability of success without any other knowledge is a probability problem on the whole sample space U. This probability is .40. But given knowledge of MAT score, the sample space is reduced from U to a subset of $U \geq 65$. The actual number of occurrences of the success event, of course, does not change; the same number of persons succeed. But the probability fraction gets a new denominator. Put differently, the probability estimate is refined by knowledge of "pertinent" subsets of U. In this case, ≥ 65 and < 65 are "pertinent" subsets of U. By "pertinent" subsets we mean that the variable implied is related to the criterion variable, success and failure.

Maybe the following mode of looking at the problem will help. An area interpretation of the graduate student problem is diagrammed in Figure 7.5. The idea of a measure of a set is used here. Recall that a measure of a set or subset is the sum of the weights of the set or subset. The weights are assigned to the elements of the set or subset. Figure 7.5 is a square with 10 equal parts on each side. Each part is equal to 1/10 or .10. The area of the whole square is the sample space U, and the measure of U, $m(U)$, equals 1.00. This means that all the weights assigned to all the elements of the square add up to 1.00. The measures of the subsets have been inserted: $m(F) = .60$, $m(<65) = .70$, $m(S \cap \geq 65) = .20$. The measures of these subsets can be calculated by multiplying the lengths of their sides. For example, the area of the upper left

◙ FIGURE 7.5

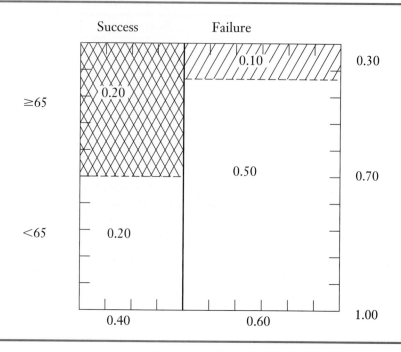

(doubly hatched) box is .5 ×.4 = .20. Recall that the probability of any set (or subset) is the measure of the set (or subset). So the probability of any of the boxes in Figure 7.5 is as indicated. We can find the probability of any two boxes by adding the measures of sets; for example, the probability of success is .20 + .20 = .40.

These measures (or probabilities) are defined on the whole area, or $U = 1.00$. The probability of success is equal to .40/1.00. We have knowledge of the students' performances on the MAT. The areas indicating the probabilities associated with ≥ 65 and < 65 are marked off by horizontal dashed lines. The simple probability of ≥ 65 is equal to .20 + .10 = .30, or .30/1.00. The whole shaded area on the top indicates this probability. The areas of the Success and Failure measures are indicated by the heavy lines separating them on the square.

Our conditional probability problem is: What is the probability of success, given knowledge of MAT scores, or given ≥ 65 (it could also be < 65, of course)? We have a new small sample space, indicated by the whole shaded area at the top of the square. In effect U has been reduced to this smaller space because we know the "truth" of the smaller space. Instead of letting this smaller space be equal to .30, we now let it be equal to 1.00. (You might say it becomes a new U.) Consequently, the measures of the boxes that constitute the new sample space must be recalculated. For instance, instead of calculating the probability of $p(≥ 65 \cap S) = .20$ because it is 2/10 of the area of the whole square, we must calculate, since we now know that the elements in the set ≥ 65 do have MAT scores greater than or equal to 65, the probability on the basis of the area of ≥ 65 (the whole shaded area at the top of the square). Having done this, we get .20/.30 = .67, [shaded area for success ÷ shaded area for success plus shaded area for failure] which is exactly what we got when we used Equation 7.8.

What happens is that additional knowledge makes U no longer relevant as the sample space. *All probability statements are relative to sample spaces.* The basic question, then, is that of adequately defining sample spaces. In the earlier problem of husbands and wives, we asked the question: What is the probability of both mates being Republican? The sample space was U = {*RR, RD, DR, DD*}. But when we add the knowledge that one of them is certainly a Republican and ask the same question, in effect we make the original U irrelevant to the problem. A new sample space, call it U', is required. Consequently, the probability that both are Republicans is different when we have more knowledge.

We can calculate other probabilities similarly. Suppose we wanted to know the probability of failure, given a MAT score less than 65. Look at Figure 7.5. The probability we want is the larger box on the right, labeled .50. Since we know that the score is < 65, we use this knowledge to set up a new sample space. The two lower boxes whose area equals .20 + .50 = .70 represent this sample space. Thus we calculate the new probability: .50/.70 = .71; the probability of failure to get the degree if one has a MAT score less than 65 is .71.

Bayes' Theorem: Revising Probabilities

No discussion of conditional probabilities would be complete without briefly mentioning Bayes' Theorem and its usefulness in applied behavioral science research. Through the manipulation of the conditional probability formula, the Reverend Thomas Bayes was able to develop a formula for computing special conditional probabilities. With Bayes' Theorem, one could update or revise current probabilities based on new information or data. This information can be used to realign uncertainty. A number of scientists and researchers advocate the use of Bayes' Theorem (see Wang, 1993).

Seldom are empirical data conclusive. For example, some very good students seeking admission to college will do poorly on a college entrance examination. Yet there will be some poor students who will score quite well on the entrance test. However, an unfavorable test result can increase the chances of rejecting a poor student and a favorable test result can increase the probability of selecting a good student. Likewise, in everyday life, we constantly adjust older likelihoods based on new information. Bayes' Theorem, expressed in formula form, is a numerical formula that shows how this can be done.

$$p(H_i|A) = \frac{p(H_i)p(A|H_i)}{\sum_{j=1}^{k} p(H_j)p(A|H_j)}$$

Example

Using data that currently exist, a researcher has determined that 10% of the population have an eating disorder. Such data are generally published and come from established sources. What this tells us is that without any additional information, if 100 people were chosen at random, 10 would have an eating disorder. If D is used to designate that a person has an eating disorder then $\sim D$ is used to indicate no eating disorder. Hence $p(D) = .10$ and $p(\sim D) = .90$. These are called "old" probabilities. Some psychologists refer to these as base rates. Using these probabilities by themselves may not lead to fruitful results.

To try to enhance one's ability for detecting eating disorders, a psychological test was developed. The test result, even though imperfect, is the new information and could help a practicing therapist in making a correct diagnosis. The researcher took individuals that were known to have an eating disorder and administered the test. Likewise, the test was given to a group that was known not to have an eating disorder. The number of people scoring positive on the test who in reality had the disorder can be expressed as a conditional probability $p(+|D)$. The number of people scoring negative on the test who in reality did not have the disorder can be written as $p(-|\sim D)$. These two conditional probabilities are referred to as correct classifications. Empirically, $p(+|D) = .91$ and $p(-|\sim D) = .95$. Hence, using known data, the test is able to detect 91% of those with the disorder and 95% of those without the disorder correctly. The number of people receiving a positive score but are in reality without the disorder is designated $p(+|\sim D)$ and called a false positive. The number of people receiving a negative score but who in reality have the disorder is written as $p(-|D)$ and called a false negative. These last two conditional probabilities give the level of imperfection of the test. It follows that $p(+|\sim D)$ is .05 and $p(-|D) = .09$. Now, using Bayes' Theorem, one can answer the following questions. What is the probability the person actually has the disorder if he or she scored negative: $p(D|-)$? What is the probability that the person has the disorder given that he or she scored positive on the test: $p(D|+)$? Hence in using the conditional probabilities, one can update the "old" probabilities. Using these numbers, the equation for Bayes' Theorem, we obtain:

$$p(D|+) = \frac{p(+|D)p(D)}{p(+|D)p(D) + p(+|\sim D)p(\sim D)} = \frac{.91(.10)}{.91(.10) + (.05)(.90)}$$

$$= \frac{.091}{.091 + .045} = \frac{.091}{.136} = 0.669 = 0.67$$

Similarly,

$$p(D|-) = \frac{p(-|D)p(D)}{p(-|D)p(D) + p(-|\sim D)p(\sim D)}$$

$$= \frac{.09(.10)}{.09(.10) + (.95)(.90)} = \frac{.009}{.009 + .855} = \frac{.009}{.864} = 0.01$$

Hence, with the use of the test, if a person gets a positive score, there is a 67% chance that person has an eating disorder. Using Bayes' Theorem, we have adjusted the probability that the person has an eating disorder from a probability of .10 to .67. There is a 1% chance a person who receives a negative score has an eating disorder.

Doscher and Bruno (1981) used Bayes' theorem in place of the usual formula to correct for guessing on exams. With Bayes' Theorem, probability distributions of true knowledge levels were developed. Given a student's actual test score, the calibration tables developed from Bayes' Theorem would give a probabilistic estimate of the true score. Bayes' Theorem was used to adjust test scores for guessing. Doscher and Bruno found that the Bayes' method was superior to the usual correction for guessing formula. These researchers found that for inner-city children the use of an unadjusted test score would usually overestimate the knowledge of the child. This could result in the child being placed in a learning situation where tasks are too difficult. They found that by using the usual correction for guessing formula, the adjustment was too great and would usually place the child in a learning situation with unchallenging tasks. Doscher and Bruno (1981, p. 488) say:

> An analytic procedure based on [Bayes' Theorem] allows the probabilistic estimation of true scores from an observed test score using prior information about the likely true score distribution and the guessing pattern specific to the population being studied.

Similar to Doscher and Bruno's study, Jones (1991) introduces the use of Bayes' Theorem in conjunction with counselor decisions. Jones advocates the Bayesian analysis since a probability statement is made about the person being measured instead of just giving a score and an interpretation. Jones' research using Bayes' Theorem was directed at selecting operators for employment on a rehabilitation program for the visually challenged. Jones lays out the steps a counselor on the program would take to utilize Bayes' Theorem. The counselor on the program would start with an examination of the agency's records and would locate the psychometric data on those candidates hired as operators. The counselor would also determine which ones were eventually classified as successful and unsuccessful. Jones labels these as the prior beliefs. The records also give the counselor the scores on the Cognitive Skills Test. The counselor then determines how many of the successful applicants had a mastery or above score. Likewise, the counselor is able to determine how many successful applicants had a below master score. Similar data would be obtained for those who were unsuccessful. Armed with this information the counselor can now go on to estimate (using Bayes' Theorem) the probability that a given person would be successful given that he or she has or does not have a mastery score on the test. Jones then goes on to show how to integrate personality profiles into the classification process.

The Bayesian framework permeates many areas of research. Many of the more advanced statistical methods such as confirmatory factor analysis, structural equation modeling, and discriminant analysis all rely on a Bayesian approach. The reader should read one or more of the following for more information. Estes (1991) gives some additional details not mentioned here on the use of Bayes' Theorem in criminal law cases. Smith, Penrod, Otto, and Park (1996) conducted an experiment to measure the behavior of jurors who are taught the use of Bayes' Theorem and probabilistic evidence in criminal law cases. Wang (1993) shows the superiority of Bayesian method over other methods in business forecasting. Bierman, Bonini, and Hausman (1991) give details on the use of Bayes' theorem in marketing and business research.

CHAPTER SUMMARY

1. Probability is not easy to define.
2. Three broad definitions:
    a. a priori involves the ability of people to give a probability estimate in the absence of empirical data.
    b. a posteriori is the most common definition used in statistics, based on long-run relative frequency.
    c. Keynes's weight-of-evidence involves two numbers for probability. One is subjective and based on the amount of information available.
3. Sample space is the total number of possible outcomes of an experiment. Any single outcome is called a sample point or element. An event is one or more elements arranged in some meaningful way or combination.
4. The probability of the sample space is 1.00. Sample points and events are less than 1.00. The sum of all the probabilities of elements is 1.00. Each sample point can be weighted. The sum of the weights used must total to 1.00.
5. Probability has three fundamental properties:
    a. The measure of any set, as defined above, is greater than or equal to 0 and less than or equal to 1. In brief, probabilities (measures of sets) are either 0, 1, or in between.
    b. The measure of a set, $m(A)$, equals 0 if and only if there are no members in A; that is, A is empty.
    c. Let A and B be sets. If A and B are disjoint—that is, $A \cap B = E$—then $m(A \cup B) = m(A) + m(B)$.
6. A compound event is the cooccurrence of two or more single (or compound) events.
7. Exhaustiveness refers to the partitioning of the sample space into subsets. These subsets when combined will cover the entire sample space.
8. If the intersection of two or more sets results in an empty set, these sets are called mutually exclusive.
9. Two events are considered independent if the probability of the two events both occurring is equal to the probability of one event multiplied by the probability of the other.

10. There are times when we want to compute the probability of an event after receiving additional information that may alter the sample space. This probability is called conditional probability.

11. Bayes' Theorem involves conditional probabilities. Bayes' probabilities are effective for revising probabilities using new or additional information.

STUDY SUGGESTIONS

1. Suppose that you are sampling ninth-grade youngsters for research purposes. There are 250 ninth graders in the school system: 130 boys and 120 girls.
   a. What is the probability of selecting any youngster?
   b. What is the probability of selecting a girl? a boy?
   c. What is the probability of selecting either a boy or a girl? How would you write this problem in set symbols? [Hint: Is it equivalent to set intersection or union?]
   d. Suppose you drew a sample of 100 boys and girls. You got 90 boys and 10 girls. What conclusions might you reach?
   [Answers: (a) 1/250; (b) 120/250, 130/250; (c) 1.]

2. Toss a coin and throw a die once. What is the probability of getting heads on the coin and a 6 on the die? Draw a tree to show all the possibilities. Label the branches of the tree with the appropriate weights or probabilities. Now answer some questions. What is the probability of getting:
   a. tails and either a 1, a 3, or a 6?
   b. heads and either a 2 or a 4?
   c. heads or tails and a 5?
   d. heads or tails and a 5 or a 6?
   [Answers: (a) 1/4; (b) 1/6; (c) 1/6; (d) 1/3.]

3. Toss a coin and roll a die 72 times. Write the results side by side on a ruled sheet as they occur. Check the obtained frequencies against the theoretically expected frequencies. Now check your answer to each of the questions in question 2. Do the obtained results come close to the expected results? (For example, suppose you calculated a certain probability for 2(a), above. Now count the number of times tails is paired with a 1, a 3, or a 6. Does the obtained fraction equal the expected fraction?)

4. Suppose that in Figure 7.6, there are 20 elements in U, of which four are in A, six in B, and two in $A \cap B$. If you randomly select one element, what is the probability
   a. that it will be in A?
   b. that it will be in B?
   c. that it will be in $A \cap B$?
   d. that it will either be in A or B? [Hint: Remember the equation: $p(A \cup B) = p(A) + p(B) - p(A \cap B)$.]
   e. that it will neither be in A nor in B?
   f. that it will be in B but not in A?
   [Answers: (a) 1/5; (b) 3/10; (c) 1/10; (d) 2/5; (e) 3/5; (f) 1/5.]

▣ **FIGURE 7.6**

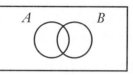

5. Using Figure 7.6, answer the following questions:
   a. Given *B*, what is the probability of *A*?
   b. Given *A*, what is the probability of *B*?
   [Answers: (a) 1/3; (b) 1/2.]

6. Consider Figure 7.7. There are 20 elements in *U*, 4 in *B*, and 8 in *A*. If an element of *U* is selected at random, what are the probabilities that the element will be in
   a. *A*?
   b. *B*?
   c. *A* ∩ *B*?
   d. *A* ∪ *B*?
   e. *U*?
   [Answers: (a) 2/5; (b) 1/5; (c) 1/5; (d) 2/5; (e)1.]

7. Using Figure 7.7, answer the following questions:
   a. Given *A* (knowing that a sampled element came from *A*), what is the probability of *B*?
   b. Given *B*, what is the probability of *A*?
   [Answers: (a) 1/2; (b) 1.]

8. Suppose you had a two-item, four-choice, multiple-choice test, with the four choices of each item labeled *a*, *b*, *c*, and *d*. The correct answers to the two items are *c* and *a*.
   a. Write out the sample space. (Draw a tree; see Figure 7.3.)
   b. What is the probability of any testee getting both items correct by guessing?
   c. What is the probability of getting at least one of the items correct by

▣ **FIGURE 7.7**

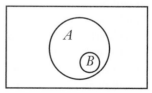

guessing? (Hint: This may be a bit troublesome. Draw the tree and think of the possibilities. Count them.)

   d. What is the probability of getting both items wrong by guessing?

   e. Given that a testee gets the first item correct, what is the probability of that person getting the second item correct by guessing?

   [Answers: (b) 1/16; (c) 7/16; (d) 9/16; (e) 1/4.]

9. Most of the discussion in the text has been based on the assumption of equiprobability. This assumption is often not justified, however. What is wrong with the following argument, for instance? The probability of one's dying tomorrow is one-half. Why? Because one will either die tomorrow or not die tomorrow. Since there are two possibilities, they each have a probability of occurrence of one-half. How would insurance companies fare with this reasoning? Suppose, now, that a political scientist studied the relation between religious and political preferences, and assumed that the probabilities that a Catholic was Democrat or Republican were equal. What would you think of his or her research results? Do these examples have implications for researchers knowing something of the phenomena they are studying? Explain.

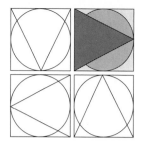

SAMPLING AND RANDOMNESS

Imagine the many situations in which we want to know something about people, about events, about things. To learn something about people, for instance, we take a few people whom we know—or do not know—and study them. After our "study," we reach certain conclusions, often about people in general. Some such method is behind much folk wisdom. Common sensical observations about people, their motives, and their behaviors derive, for the most part, from observations and experiences with relatively few people. We make such statements as: "People nowadays have no sense of moral values"; "Politicians are corrupt"; and "Public school pupils are not learning the three Rs." The basis for making such statements is simple. People, mostly through their limited experiences, come to certain conclusions about other people and about their environment. In order to come to such conclusions, they must *sample* their "experiences" of other people. Actually, they take relatively small samples of all possible experiences. The word *experiences* here has to be taken in a broad sense. It can mean direct experience with other people—for example, first-hand interaction with, say, Muslims or Asians. Or it can mean indirect experience: hearing about Muslims or Asians from friends, acquaintances, parents, and others. Whether experience is direct or indirect, however, does not concern us much at this point. Let us assume that all such experience is direct. An individual claims to "know" something about Asians and says "I 'know' they are clannish because I have

163

had direct experience with a number of Asians." Or, "Some of my best friends are Asians, and I know that . . ." The point is that this person's conclusions are based on a sample of Asians, or a sample of the behaviors of Asians, or both. This individual can never "know" all Asians, and must depend, in the last analysis, on samples. Indeed, most of the world's knowledge is based on samples, most often on inadequate samples.

Sampling, Random Sampling, and Representativeness

Sampling refers to taking a portion of a population or universe as representative of that population or universe. This definition does not say that the sample taken—or drawn, as researchers say—is representative. It says, rather, taking a portion of the population and *considering* it to be representative. When a school administrator visits certain classrooms in the school system "to get the feel of the system," that administrator is sampling classes from all the classes in the system. This person might assume that by visiting, say, eight to ten classes out of forty "at random," he or she will get a fair notion of the quality of teaching going on in the system. Another way would be to visit one teacher's class two or three times to sample teaching performance. By doing this, the administrator is now sampling behaviors, in this case teaching behaviors, from the universe of all possible behaviors of the teacher. Such sampling is necessary and legitimate. However, you can come up with some situations where the entire universe could be measured, so why bother with samples? Why not just measure every element of the universe? Take a census? A major reason is one of economics. The second author (HBL) worked in a marketing research department of a large grocery chain in southern California. This chain consisted of 100 stores. Research on customers and products occasionally took the form of a controlled store test. These studies were conducted in a real day-to-day grocery store operation. Perhaps one was interested in testing a new dog food. Certain stores would be chosen to receive the new product while another set of stores would not carry the new product. Secrecy is very important in such studies. If a competing manufacturer of dog food received information that a marketing test was being done at such-and-such store, they could contaminate the results. To conduct controlled store tests of cents-off coupons, or new products, or shelf allocation space, a research study could be conducted with two groups of 50 stores each. However, the labor and administrative costs alone would be prohibitive. It would make a lot more sense to use samples that are representative of the population. Choosing 10 stores in each group to conduct the research would reduce the costs of doing the study. Smaller studies are more manageable and controllable. A study using samples could be completed in a timely manner. In some disciplines, such as quality control and education (instructional evaluation), sampling is essential. In quality control there is a procedure called destructive testing. One way to determine whether a product meets specifications is to put it through an actual performance test. When the product is destroyed (fails), the product can be evaluated. In testing tires, for example, it would make little sense to destroy every tire just to determine if the manufacturer has adequate quality control. Likewise, a teacher who wants to determine if a child has learned the material will give an examination. It would be difficult to write an examination that covers every aspect of instruction and knowledge retention of the child.

Random sampling is that method of drawing a portion (or sample) of a population or universe so that each member of the population or universe has an equal chance of being selected. This definition has the virtue of being easily understood. Unfortunately, it is not entirely satisfactory because it is limited. A better definition is given by Kirk (1990, p. 8).

> The method of drawing samples from a population such that every possible sample of a particular size has an equal chance of being selected is called *random sampling*, and the resulting samples are *random samples*.

This definition is general and thus more satisfactory than the earlier definition.

Define a universe to be studied as all fourth-grade children in X school system. Suppose there are 200 such children. They comprise the population (or universe). We select one child at random from the population. His (or her) chance of being selected is 1/200, if the sampling procedure is random. Likewise, a number of other children are similarly selected. Let us assume that after selecting a child, that child (or a symbol assigned to the child) is returned to the population. Then the chance of selecting any second child is also 1/200. (If we do not return this child to the population, then the chance each of the remaining children has, of course, is 1/199. This is called *sampling without replacement*. When the sample elements are returned to the population after being drawn, the procedure is called *sampling with replacement*.)

Suppose from the population of the 200 fourth-grade children in X school system we decide to draw a random sample of 50 children. This means, if the sample is random, that all possible samples of 50 have the same probability of being selected—a very large number of possible samples. To make the ideas involved comprehensible, suppose a population consists of four children, *a*, *b*, *c*, and *d*, and we draw a random sample of two children. Then the list of all the possibilities, or the *sample space*, is: (*a*, *b*), (*a*, *c*), (*a*, *d*), (*b*, *c*), (*b*, *d*), (*c*, *d*). There are six possibilities. If the sample of two is drawn at random, then its probability is 1/6. Each of the pairs has the same probability of being drawn. This sort of reasoning is needed to solve many research problems, but we will usually confine ourselves to the simpler idea of sampling connected with the first definition. The first definition, then, is a special case of the second general definition—the special case in which $n = 1$.

Unfortunately, we can never be sure that a random sample is representative of the population from which it is drawn. Remember that any particular sample of size n has the same probability of being selected as any other sample of the same size. Thus a particular sample may not be representative at all. We should know what "representative" means. Ordinarily, *representative* means to be typical of a population; that is, to exemplify the characteristics of the population. From a research point of view, *representative* must be more precisely defined, though it is often difficult to be precise. We must ask: What characteristics are we talking about? So, in research, a *representative sample* means that the sample has approximately the characteristics of the population relevant to the research in question. If sex and socioeconomic class are variables (characteristics) relevant to the research, a representative sample will have approximately the same proportions of men and women and middle-class and working-class individuals as the population. When we draw a random sample, *we hope* that it will be representative. We hope that the relevant characteristics of the population will be present in the sample in approximately the same way they are present in the population. But we can never be sure. There is no guarantee.

What we rely on is the fact, as Stilson (1966) points out, that the characteristics typical of a population are those that are the most frequent and therefore most likely to be present in any particular random sample. When sampling is random, the sampling variability is predictable. We learned in Chapter 7, for example, that if we throw two dice a number of times, the probability of a 7 turning up is greater than that of a 12 turning up (see Table 7.1).

A sample drawn at random is unbiased in the sense that no member of the population has more chance of being selected than any other member. We have here a democracy in which all members are equal before the bar of selection. Rather than using coins or dice, let's use a research example. Suppose we have a population of 100 children. The children differ in intelligence, a variable relevant to our research. We want to know the mean intelligence score of the population, but for some reason we can only sample 30 of the 100 children. If we sample randomly, there are a large number of possible samples of 30 each. The samples have equal probabilities of being selected. The means of most of the samples will be relatively close to the mean of the population. A few will not be close. If the sampling has been random, the probability of selecting a sample with a mean close to the population mean is greater than the probability of selecting a sample with a mean not close to the population mean.

If we do not draw our sample at random, however, some factor or factors unknown to us may predispose us to select a biased sample. In this case, perhaps one of the samples with a mean not close to the population mean. The mean intelligence of this sample will then be a biased estimate of the population mean. If we knew the 100 children, we might unconsciously tend to select the more intelligent children. It is not so much that *we would* do so; it is that our method *allows* us to do so. Random methods of selection do not allow our own biases or any other systematic selection factors to operate. The procedure is objective, divorced from our own predilections and biases.

The reader may be experiencing a vague and disquieting sense of uneasiness. If we can't be sure that random samples are representative, how can we have confidence in our research results and their applicability to the populations from which we draw our samples? Why not select samples systematically so that they are representative? The answer is complex. First—and again—we cannot ever be sure. Second, random samples are more likely to include the characteristics typical of the population if the characteristics are frequent in the population. In actual research, we draw random samples whenever we can and hope and assume that the samples are representative. We learn to live with uncertainty. We try to reduce it whenever we can—just as we do in ordinary day-to-day living but more systematically and with considerable knowledge of and experience with random sampling and random outcomes. Fortunately, our lack of certainty does not impair our research functioning.

Randomness

The notion of randomness is at the core of modern probabilistic methods in the natural and behavioral sciences. But it is difficult to define *random*. The dictionary notion of haphazard, accidental, without aim or direction, does not help much. In fact, scientists are quite systematic about randomness; they carefully select random samples and plan random procedures.

The position can be taken that nothing happens at random, that for any event there is a cause. The only reason, this position might say, that one uses the word *random* is that human beings do not know enough. To omniscience nothing is random. Suppose an omniscient being has an omniscient newspaper. It is a gigantic newspaper in which every event down to the last detail—for tomorrow, the next day, and the next day, and on and on into indefinite time—is carefully inscribed (see Kemeny, 1959, p. 39). There is nothing unknown. And, of course, there is no randomness. Randomness is, as it were, ignorance, in this view.

Taking a cue from this argument, we define randomness in a backhand way. We say events are random if we cannot predict their outcomes. For instance, there is no known way to win a penny-tossing game. Whenever there is no system for playing a game that ensures our winning (or losing), then the events (outcomes of the game) are random. More formally put, *randomness* means that there is no known law, capable of being expressed in language that correctly describes or explains events and their outcomes. In different words, when events are random we cannot predict them individually. Strange to say, however, we can predict them quite successfully in the aggregate. That is, we can predict the outcomes of large numbers of events. We cannot predict whether a coin tossed will be heads or tails, but if we toss a fair coin 1,000 times, we can predict, with considerable accuracy, the total numbers of heads and tails.

An Example of Random Sampling

To give the reader a feeling for randomness and random samples, we will demonstrate using a table of random numbers. A table of random numbers contains numbers generated mechanically so that there is no discernible order or system in them. It was said above that if events are random they cannot be predicted. But now we are going to predict the *general nature* of the outcomes of our experiment. We select, from a table of random digits, ten samples of ten digits each. Since the numbers are random, each sample "should" be representative of the universe of digits. The universe can be variously defined. We simply define it as the complete set of digits in

◨ TABLE 8.1 *Ten Samples of Random Numbers*

	1	2	3	4	5	6	7	8	9	10	
	9	0	8	0	4	6	0	7	7	8	
	7	2	7	4	9	4	7	8	7	7	
	6	2	8	1	9	3	6	0	3	9	
	7	9	9	1	6	4	9	4	7	7	
	3	3	1	1	4	1	0	3	9	4	
	8	9	2	1	3	9	6	7	7	3	
	4	8	3	0	9	2	7	2	3	2	
	1	4	3	0	0	2	6	9	7	5	
	2	1	8	8	4	5	2	1	0	3	
	3	1	4	8	9	2	9	3	0	1	
Mean	5.0	3.9	5.3	2.4	5.7	3.8	5.2	4.4	5.0	4.9	Total Mean = 4.56

the Rand Corporation table of random digits.[1] We now draw samples from the table. The means of the ten samples will, of course, be different. However, they should fluctuate within a relatively narrow range, with most of them fairly close to the mean of all 100 numbers and to the theoretical mean of the whole population of random numbers. The number of even numbers in each sample of ten should approximately equal the number of odd numbers. There will be fluctuations, some perhaps extreme but most comparatively modest. The samples are given in Table 8.1.

The means of the samples are given below each sample. The mean of U, the theoretical mean of the whole population of Rand random numbers, {0, 1, 2, 3, 4, 5, 6, 7, 8, 9}, is 4.5. The mean of all 100 numbers, which can be considered a sample of U, is 4.56. This is, of course, very close to the mean of U. It can be seen that the means of the ten samples vary around 4.5, the lowest being 2.4 and the highest 5.7. Only two of these means differ from 4.5 by more than 1. A statistical test (later we will learn the rationale of such tests) shows that the ten means do not differ from each other significantly. (The expression "do not differ from each other significantly" means that the differences are no greater than the differences that would occur by

---

[1]The source of random numbers used was Rand Corporation (1955). This is a large and carefully constructed table of random numbers. These numbers were *not* computer generated. There are many other such tables, however, that are good enough for most practical purposes. Modern statistics texts have such tables. Appendix C at the end of this book contains 4,000 computer-generated random numbers.

chance.) And, by another statistical test, nine are "good" estimates of the population mean (4.5) and one (2.4) is not.

Changing the sampling problem, we can define the universe to consist of odd and even numbers. Let's assume that in the entire universe there is an equal number of both. In our sample of 100 numbers there should be approximately 50 odd and 50 even numbers. There are actually 54 odd and 46 even numbers. A statistical test shows that the deviation of 4 for odd and 4 for even does not depart significantly from chance expectation.[2]

Similarly, if we sample human beings, then the numbers of men and women in the samples should be approximately in proportion to the numbers of men and women in the population, if the sampling is random and the samples are large enough. If we measure the intelligence of a sample, and the mean intelligence score of the population is 100, then the mean of the sample should be close to 100. Of course, we must always bear in mind the possibility of selection of the deviant sample, the sample with a mean of say 80 or less or 120 or more. Deviant samples do occur, but they are less likely to occur. The reasoning is similar to that for coin-tossing demonstrations. If we toss a coin three times, it is less likely that three heads (H) or three tails (T) will turn up than it is that two heads and one tail or two tails and one head will turn up. This is because $U = \{HHH, HHT, HTH, HTT, THH, THT, TTH, TTT\}$. There is only one HHH point and one TTT point, while there are three points with two Hs and three with two Ts.

Randomization

Suppose an investigator wishes to test the hypothesis that counseling helps under-achievers. The test involves using two groups of underachievers: one to be counseled, one not to be counseled. Naturally, the wish is to have the two groups equal in other independent variables that may have a possible effect on achievement. One way this can be done is to assign the children to both groups at random by, say, tossing a coin for each child. The child is assigned to one group if the toss is heads and to the other group if the toss is tails. Note that if there were three experimental groups coin tossing would probably not be used. A six-sided die may be used. Outcomes of 1 or 2 would assign that child to Group 1. Outcomes of 3 and 4 would put the child in Group 2, and the outcomes 5 and 6 would designate the child to be in Group 3. Or a table of random numbers can be used to assign the children to groups. If an odd number turns up, assign a child to one group, and if an even number turns up, assign the child to the other group. The investigator can now assume that the groups are approximately equal in all possible independent variables. The larger the groups, the

---

[2] The nature of such statistical tests, as well as the reasoning behind them, will be explained in detail in Part Four. The student should not be too concerned if he or she does not completely grasp the statistical ideas expressed here. Indeed, one of the purposes of this chapter is to introduce some of the basic elements of such ideas.

safer the assumption. Just as there is no guarantee, however, of not drawing a deviant sample (as discussed earlier), there is no guarantee that the groups are equal or even approximately equal in all possible independent variables. Nevertheless, it can be said that the investigator has used randomization to equalize the groups, or, as it is said, to control influences on the dependent variable other than that of the manipulated independent variable. Although we will use the term "randomization," a number of researchers prefer to use the words *random assignment*. The procedure calls for assigning participants to experimental conditions on a random basis. While some believe that random assignment removes variation, in reality it only distributes it.

An "ideal" experiment is one in which all the factors or variables likely to affect the experimental outcome are controlled. If we knew all these factors in the first place, and *could* make efforts to control them in the second place, then we might have an ideal experiment. However, the sad case is that we can neither know all the pertinent variables, nor could we control them even if we did know them. Randomization, however, comes to our aid.

Randomization is the assignment to experimental treatments of members of a universe in a way such that, for any given assignment to a treatment, every member of the universe has an equal probability of being chosen for that assignment. The basic purpose of *random assignment*, as indicated earlier, is to apportion subjects (objects, groups) to treatments. Individuals with varying characteristics are spread approximately equally among the treatments so that variables that might affect the dependent variable, other than the experimental variables, have "equal" effects in the different treatments. There is no guarantee that this desirable state of affairs will be attained, but it is more likely to be attained with randomization than otherwise. Randomization also has a statistical rationale and purpose. If random assignment has been used, it is then possible to distinguish between systematic or experimental variance and error variance. Biasing variables are distributed to experimental groups according to chance. The tests of statistical significance (discussed later) logically depend on random assignment. These tests are used to determine whether the observed phenomenon is statistically different from chance. Without random assignment the significance tests lack logical foundation. The idea of randomization seems to have been discovered or invented by Sir Ronald Fisher (see Cowles, 1989). It was Fisher who virtually revolutionized statistical and experimental design thinking and methods, using random notions as part of his leverage. He has been referred to as "the father of analysis-of-variance." In any case, randomization and what can be called the principle of randomization is one of the great intellectual achievements of our time. It is not possible to overrate the importance of both the idea and the practical measures that come from it to improve experimentation and inference.

Randomization can perhaps be clarified in three ways: by stating the principle of randomization, by describing how one uses it in practice, and by demonstrating how it works with objects and numbers. The importance of the idea deserves all three.

The *principle of randomization* may be stated as the following. Since, in random procedures, every member of a population has an equal chance of being selected, members with certain distinguishing characteristics—male or female, high or low intelligence, conservative or liberal, and so on—will, if selected, probably be offset in the long run by the selection of other members of the population with counterbalancing quantities or qualities of the characteristics. We can say that this is a practical principle of what usually happens; we cannot say that it is a law of nature. It is simply a statement of what most often occurs when random procedures are used.

We say that subjects are assigned at random to experimental groups, and that experimental treatments are assigned at random to groups. For instance, in the example cited above of an experiment to test the effectiveness of counseling on achievement, subjects can be assigned to two groups at random by using random numbers or by tossing a coin. When the subjects have been so assigned, the groups can be randomly designated as experimental group and control group using a similar procedure. We will encounter a number of examples of randomization as we go along.

A Senatorial Randomization Demonstration

To show how, if not why, the principle of randomization works, we now set up a sampling and design experiment. We have a population of 100 members of the United States Senate from which we can sample. In this population (in 1993), there are 56 Democrats and 44 Republicans. We have selected two important votes: Issue 266, an amendment to prohibit higher grazing fees; and Issue 290, an amendment concerning funding for abortions. The data used in this example are from the 1993 *Congressional Quarterly*. These votes were important because each reflected presidential proposals. A nay vote on Issue 266 and a yea vote on Issue 290 indicates support of the President. Here we ignore their substance and treat the actual votes or, rather, the senators who cast the votes, as populations from which we sample.

Suppose we do an experiment using three groups of senators, with twenty in each group. The nature of the experiment is not relevant here. We want the three groups of senators to be approximately equal in all possible characteristics. Using a computer program written in BASIC (Microsoft's GWBASIC or QUICKBASIC program source is given at the end of the chapter) we generate approximate random numbers between 1 and 100. The first sixty numbers drawn with no repeated numbers (sampling without replacement), are recorded in groups of twenty each. Political party affiliation for Democrats (d) and Republicans (r) are noted with the senator's name. Also included are the senators' votes on the two issues, y equals yea and n equals nay. These data are listed in Table 8.2.

How "equal" are the groups? In the total population of 100 senators, 56 are Democrats and 44 are Republicans, or 56% and 44%. In the total sample of 60 there are 34 Democrats and 26 Republicans, or 57% for Democrats and 43% for Republicans. There is a difference of 1% from the expectation of 56% and 44%. The obtained and expected frequencies of Democrats in the three groups (I, II, and III) and the total sample are given in Table 8.3. The deviations from expectation are small. The three groups are not exactly "equal" in the sense that they have equal numbers of Republican and Democratic senators. The first group has 11 Democrats and nine Republicans, the second group has 10 Democrats and 10 Republicans, and

◉ **TABLE 8.2** *Senatorial Vote per Groups of n = 20 on Senate Issue 266 and Issue 290*

#	Name-party	266	290	#	Name-party	266	290	#	Name-party	266	290
73	hatfield-r	y	n	78	chafee-r	y	y	58	smith-r	y	n
27	coats-r	y	n	20	coverdell-r	y	n	95	byrd-d	n	n
54	kerrey-d	y	y	25	mosley-brown-d	n	y	83	matthews-d	y	n
93	murray-d	n	y	42	kerry-d	n	y	52	burns-r	y	n
6	mccain-r	y	n	68	dorgan-d	y	n	80	thurmond-r	y	n
26	simon-d	n	y	57	gregg-r	y	n	13	dodd-d	y	y
7	bumpers-d	n	y	11	campbell-d	y	y	88	hatch-r	y	n
81	daschle-d	n	y	31	dole-r	y	n	63	moynihan-d	y	y
76	specter-r	n	y	37	mitchell-d	n	y	89	leahy-d	n	y
38	cohen-r	n	y	30	grassley-r	y	n	75	wofford-d	n	y
32	kasselbaum-r	y	n	22	inouye-d	y	y	92	warner-r	y	n
44	riegel-d	n	y	99	simpson-r	y	n	91	robb-d	n	y
98	kohl-d	n	y	8	pryor-d	n	?	34	mcconnell-r	y	n
77	pell-d	n	y	4	stevens-r	y	n	96	rockefeller-d	n	y
61	bingaman-d	y	n	23	craig-r	y	n	28	lugar-r	y	n
16	roth-r	n	n	12	brown-r	y	n	43	levin-d	n	y
24	kempthorne-r	y	n	10	feinstein-d	y	y	59	bradley-d	n	y
100	wallop-r	y	n	87	bennett-r	y	n	69	glenn-d	n	y
15	biden-d	n	n	19	nunn-d	n	n	9	boxer-d	n	y
14	lieberman-d	n	y	45	wellstone-d	n	y	67	conrad-d	y	n

the third group has 13 Democrats and 7 Republicans. This not an "unusual" outcome that happens with random sampling. Later we will see that the discrepancies do not differ statistically.

Remember, we are demonstrating both random sampling and randomization, but especially randomization. We therefore ask whether or not the random assignment of senators to the three groups has resulted in "equalizing" the groups in all characteristics. We can never test all characteristics, of course; we can only test those available. In the present case, we have only political party affiliation, which we tested

🔲 **TABLE 8.3** *Obtained and Expected Frequencies of Political Party (Democrats) in Random Samples of 20 U.S. Senators[a]*

	Groups			Totals
	I	**II**	**III**	
Obtained	11	10	13	34
Expected[b]	11.2	11.2	11.2	33.6
Deviation	.2	1.2	1.8	.4

[a]Only the larger of the two expectations of the Republican–Democrat split, the Democrats (.56), is reported.
[b]The expected frequencies were calculated as follows: $20 \times .56 = 11.2$. Similarly, the total is calculated: $60 \times .56 = 33.6$.

above, and the votes on the two issues: prohibition to increase grazing fees (Issue 266), and prohibition of funds for certain types of abortions (Issue 290). How did the random assignment work with the two issues? The results are presented in Table 8.4. The original vote on Issue 266 of the 99 senators who voted was 59 yeas and 40 nays. These total votes yield expected yea frequencies in the total group of $59 \div 99 = .596$, or 60%. We therefore expect $20 \div .60 = 12$ in each experimental group. The original vote of the 99 senators who voted on Issue 290 was 40 yeas, or 40% ($40 \div 99 = .404$). The expected group yea frequencies, then, are: $20 \div .40 = 8$. The obtained and expected frequencies and the deviations from expectation for the three groups of 20 senators and for the total sample of 60 on Issue 266 and Issue 290 are given in Table 8.4.

🔲 **TABLE 8.4** *Obtained and Expected Frequencies on Yea Votes on Issue 266 and Issue 290 in Random Groups of Senators*

	Groups							
	I		*II*		*III*		*Total*	
	266	**290**	**266**	**290**	**266**	**290**	**266**	**290**
Obtained	9	10	13	9	11	9	33	28
Expected[a]	12	8	12	8	12	8	36	24
Deviation	3	2	1	1	1	1	3	4

[a]The expected frequencies were calculated for Group I, Issue 266, as follows: there were 59 yeas of a total of 99 votes or $59/99 = .60$; $20 \times .60 = 12$. For the total group, the calculation is: $60 \times .60 = 36$.

It appears that the deviations from chance expectation are all small. Evidently the three groups are approximately "equal" in the sense that the incidence of the votes on the two issues is approximately the same in each of the groups. The deviations from chance expectation of the yea votes (and, of course, nay votes) are small. So far as we can see, then, the randomization has been "successful." This demonstration can also be interpreted as a random sampling problem. We may ask, for example, whether or not the three samples of 20 each and the total sample of 60 are representative. Do they accurately reflect the characteristics of the population of 100 senators? For instance, do the samples reflect the proportions of Democrats and Republicans in the Senate? The proportions in the samples were .55 and .45 (I), .50 and .50 (II), .65 and .35 (III). The actual proportions are .56 and .44. Although there is a 1%, 6%, and 9% deviation in the samples, these deviations are within chance expectation. We can say, therefore, that the samples are representative insofar as political party membership is concerned. Similar reasoning applies to the samples and the votes on the two issues.

We can now do our experiment believing that the three groups are "equal." They may not be, of course, but the probabilities are in our favor. And as we have seen, the procedure usually works well. Our checking of the characteristics of the senators in the three groups showed that the groups were fairly "equal" in political preference and yea (and nay) votes on the two issues. Thus, we can have greater confidence that if the groups become unequal, the differences are probably due to our experimental manipulation and not to differences between the groups before we started.

However, no less an expert than Feller (1967, p. 29), writes:

> In sampling human populations the statistician encounters considerable and often unpredictable difficulties, and bitter experience has shown that it is difficult to obtain even a crude image of randomness.

Williams (1978) presents a number of examples where "randomization" does not work in practice. One such example that influenced the lives of a large number of men was the picking of military draft lottery numbers in 1970. Although it was never absolutely proven, the lottery numbers did not appear to be random. In this particular instance, the month and day of birth for all 366 days was each put into a capsule. The capsules went into a rotating drum. The drum was turned a number of times so that the capsules would be well mixed. The first capsule drawn had the highest draft priority, number 1. The second capsule drawn had the next highest, and so forth. The results showed that the dates for later months had a lower median than earlier months. Hence men with later birthdates were drafted earlier. If the drawings were completely random, the medians for each month should have been much more equal. The point to made here is that many statistical analyses are dependent on successful randomization. To have one in practice is not such an easy task.

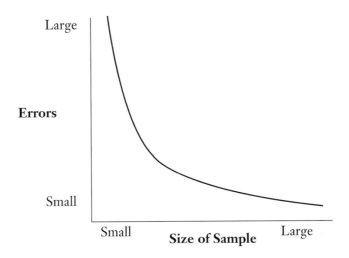

Sample Size

A rough-and-ready rule taught to beginning students of research is: Use as large a sample as possible. Whenever a mean, a percentage, or other statistic is calculated from a sample, a population value is being estimated. A question that must be asked is: How much error is likely to occur in statistics calculated from samples of differing sizes? The curve of Figure 8.1 roughly expresses the relations between sample size and error, error meaning deviation from population values. The curve says that the smaller the sample the larger the error, and the larger the sample the smaller the error.

Consider the following rather extreme example. Global Assessment Scale (hereafter referred to as GAS) admission score and total days in therapy of 3,166 Los Angeles County children seeking help at Los Angeles County Mental Health facilities from 1983 to 1988, were made available to the second author through the generosity of Dr. Stanley Sue. Dr. Sue is Professor of Psychology and Director of the National Research Center on Asian American Mental Health at the University of California, Davis. Dr. Sue granted the second author permission to use the data. The information contained in Table 8.5 and Table 8.6 was created from these data. We express our thanks and appreciation to Dr. Stanley Sue. The GAS is a score assigned by a therapist to each client based on psychological, social, and occupational functioning. The GAS score used here in our example is the GAS score the client received at the time of admission or first visit to the facility.

From this "population," ten samples of two children were randomly selected. The random selection of these samples and of others was done using the "sample"

回 **TABLE 8.5** *Samples (n = 2) of GAS and Total Days in Therapy Scores of 3,166 Children, Mean of the Samples, and Deviations of the Sample Means from the Population. (Sue data)*

GAS

Sample	1	2	3	4	5	6	7	8	9	10
	61	46	65	50	51	35	45	44	43	60
	60	50	35	55	55	50	41	47	50	55
Mean	60.5	48	50	52.5	53	42.5	43	45.4	46.5	57.5
Dev.	11.21	−1.29	.71	3.21	3.71	−6.79	−6.29	−3.79	−2.79	8.21

Total Mean (20) = 49.9
Population Mean (3,166) = 49.29

Total Days in Therapy

Sample	1	2	3	4	5	6	7	8	9	10
	92	9	172	0	3	141	28	189	28	17
	57	58	38	70	603	110	0	51	72	398
Mean	74.5	33.5	105	35	303	125.5	14	120	50	207.5
Dev.	−9.04	−50.04	21.46	−48.54	219.46	41.96	−69.54	36.46	−33.54	123.96

Total Mean (20) = 106.80
Population Mean (3,166) = 83.54

function in SPSS (Statistical Package for the Social Sciences [Norusis, 1992]). The sample means were computed by the "descriptive" routine in SPSS and are given in Table 8.5. The deviations of the means from the means of the population are also given in that table.

The GAS means range from 42.5 to 60.5, and the Total Days means range from 14 to 303. The two total means (calculated from the 20 GAS and the 20 Total Days scores) are 49.9 and 106.8. These small sample means vary considerably. The GAS and Total Days means of the population ($N = 3,166$) were 49.29 and 83.54. The deviations (Dev.) of the GAS means range a good deal: from −6.79 to 11.21. The Total Days deviations range from −69.54 to 219.46. With very small samples like these we cannot depend on any one mean to estimate the population value. However, we can depend more on the means calculated from all 20 scores, although both have an upward bias.

Four more random samples of 20 GAS and 20 Total Days scores were drawn from the population. The four GAS and the four Total Days means are given in Table 8.6. The deviations (Dev.) of each of the means of the samples of 20 from the population means are also given in the table, as well as the means of the sample of 80 and of the total population. The GAS deviations range from .06 to 1.31, and the

◙ **TABLE 8.6** *Means and Deviations from Population Means of Four GAS and Four Total Days Samples (n = 20), Total Sample (n = 80), and Population, (N = 3,166) (Sue data)*

	Samples (*n* = 20)				Total (*n* = 80)	Population (N = 3166)
GAS	49.35	48.9	49.85	50.6	49.68	49.29
Dev.	.06	.39	.56	1.31	.385	
Total-Days	69.4	109.95	89.55	103.45	93.08	83.54
Dev.	14.14	26.41	6.01	19.91	9.54	

Total Days deviations from 6.01 to 26.41. The mean of the 80 GAS scores is 49.68, and the mean of all 3,166 GAS scores is 49.29. The comparable Total Days means are 93.08 (*n* = 80) and 83.54 (*N* = 3,166). These means are quite clearly much better estimates of the population means.

We can now draw conclusions. First, statistics calculated from large samples are more accurate (other things being equal) than those calculated from small samples. A glance at the deviations of Table 8.5 and and Table 8.6 will show that the means of the samples of 20 deviated much less from the population mean than did the means of the samples of two. Moreover, the means from the sample of 80 deviated little from the population means (.39 and 9.54).

It should now be fairly clear why the research and sampling principle is: Use large samples.[3] Large samples are not advocated just because large numbers are good in and of themselves. They are advocated in order to give the principle of randomization, or simply randomness, a chance to "work," to speak somewhat anthropomorphically. With small samples, the probability of selecting deviant samples is greater than with large samples. For example, in one random sample of 20 senators drawn some years ago, the first 10 senators (of 20) drawn were all Democrats! Such a run of 10 Democrats is most unusual, *but it can and does happen!* Let's say we had chosen to do an experiment with only two groups of 10 each. One of the groups had 10 Democrats and the other had both Democrats and Republicans. The results could have been seriously biased, especially if the experiment had anything to do with political preference or social attitudes. With large groups, say 30 or more, there is less danger. Many psychology departments at major universities have a research requirement for students enrolled in an introductory psychology class. For such situations, it may be relatively easy to obtain large samples. However, for certain research studies (such as those found in human engineering or marketing research), the cost of recruiting participants is high. Remember the Williams and Adelson study discussed by Simon

---

[3] The situation is more complex than this simple statement indicates. Samples that are too large can lead to other problems; the reasons will be explained in a later chapter.

(1987) in Chapter 1. So the rule of getting large samples may not be appropriate for all research situations. In some studies, 30 or more elements, participants, or subjects may be too little. This is especially true in studies that are multivariate in nature. Comrey and Lee (1992), for example, state that samples of 50 or less give very inadequate reliability of correlation coefficients. Hence it may be more appropriate to obtain an approximation to the sample size needed. The statistical determination of sample size will be discussed in Chapter 12 for the various kinds of samples.

Kinds of Samples

The discussion of sampling has until now been confined to simple random sampling. The purpose is to help the student understand fundamental principles; thus the idea of simple random sampling is emphasized, which is behind much of the thinking and procedures of modern research. The student should realize, however, that simple random sampling is not the only kind of sampling used in behavioral research. Indeed, it is relatively uncommon, at least for describing characteristics of populations and the relations between such characteristics. It is, nevertheless, the model upon which all scientific sampling is based.

Other kinds of samples can be classified broadly into probability and nonprobability samples (and certain mixed forms). *Probability samples* use some form of random sampling in one or more of their stages. *Nonprobability samples* do not use random sampling; they thus lack the virtues being discussed, but are still often necessary and unavoidable. Their weakness can to some extent be mitigated by using knowledge, expertise, and care in selecting samples, and by replicating studies with different samples. It is important for the student to know that probability sampling is not necessarily superior to nonprobability sampling in all possible situations. Also, probability sampling does not guarantee more representative samples of the universe under study. In probability sampling the emphasis is placed on the method and the theory behind it. With nonprobability sampling the emphasis relies on the person doing the sampling, and that can bring with it an entirely new and complicated batch of concerns. The person doing the sampling must be knowledgeable of the population to be studied and the phenomena under study.

One form of nonprobability sampling is *quota sampling*. Here, the knowledge of the strata of the population—sex, race, region, and so on—is used to select sample members that are representative, "typical," and suitable for certain research purposes. A *strata* is the partitioning of the universe or population into two or more nonoverlapping (mutually exclusive) groups. A sample is taken from each partition. Quota sampling derives its name from the practice of assigning quotas, or proportions of kinds of people, to interviewers. Such sampling has been used a good deal in public opinion polls. To perform this sampling correctly, the researcher would need to have a very complete set of characteristics for the population. Next, the researcher must know the proportions for each quota. After knowing this, the next step is to collect the data. Since the proportions might be unequal from quota to quota, the sample elements are assigned a weight. Quota sampling is difficult to accomplish because it requires accurate information on the proportions for each quota, and such information is rarely available.

Another form of nonprobability sampling is *purposive sampling*, which is characterized by the use of judgment and a deliberate effort to obtain representative samples by including presumably typical areas or groups in the sample. Purposive sampling is used extensively in marketing research. To test the reaction of consumers to a new product, the researcher may distribute the new product to people who fit the researcher's notion of what the universe looks like. Political polls are another example where purposive sampling is used. On the basis of past voting results and existing political party registration, in a given region, the researcher purposively selects a group of voting precincts. The researcher feels that this selection will match the characteristics of the entire electorate. A very interesting presentation of how this information was used to help elect a U.S. Senator in California is given in Barkan and Bruno (1972).

So-called *accidental sampling*, the weakest form of sampling, is probably also the most frequently used. In effect, one takes available samples at hand—classes of seniors in a high school, sophomores in college, a convenient PTA, and the like. This practice is hard to defend. Yet, used with reasonable knowledge and care, it probably does not deserve the bad reputation it has. The most sensible advice seems to be: Avoid accidental samples unless you can get no others (random samples are usually expensive and in some situations, hard to come by). If you do use accidental samples, use extreme circumspection in analysis and interpretation of data.

Probability sampling includes a variety of forms. When we discussed simple random sampling, we were talking about one version of probability sampling. Some of the other common forms of probability sampling are stratified sampling, cluster sampling, two-stage cluster sampling, and systematic sampling. Other, more unconventional methods, include the Bayesian approach or the sequential approach. The superiority of one method of sampling over another is usually evaluated in terms of the amount of reduced variability in parameters estimated and in terms of cost. Cost is sometimes interpreted as the amount of labor in data collection and data analysis.

In *stratified sampling*, the population is first divided into strata such as men and women, African American and Mexican American, and the like. Then random samples are drawn from each strata. If the population consists of 52% women and 48% men, a stratified sample of 100 participants would consist of 52 women and 48 men. The 52 women would be chosen randomly from the available group of women and the 48 men would be selected randomly from the group of men. This is also called proportional allocation. When this procedure is performed correctly it is superior to simple random sampling. When compared to simple random sampling, stratified sampling usually reduces both the amount of variability and the cost of data collection and analyses. Stratified sampling capitalizes on the between-strata differences. Figure 8.2 conveys the basic idea of stratified sampling. Stratified sampling adds control to the sampling process by decreasing the amount of sampling error. This design is recommended when the population is composed of sets of dissimilar groups. Randomized stratified sampling allows one to study stratum differences. It allows special attention to certain groups that would otherwise be ignored because of their size.

▣ **FIGURE 8.2**

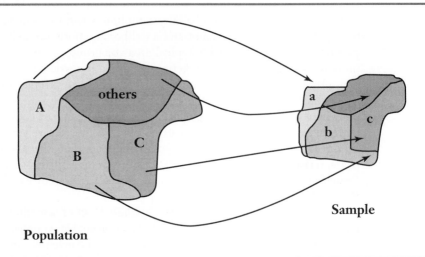

Stratified random sampling is often accomplished through proportional allocation procedures (PAP). When using such procedures, the sample's proportional partitioning resembles that of the population. The major advantage in using PAP is that it provides a "self-weighted" sample.

Cluster sampling, the most often used method in surveys, is the successive random sampling of units, or sets and subsets. A cluster can be defined as a group of things of the same kind. It is a set of sample elements held together by some common characteristic(s). In cluster sampling, the universe is partitioned into clusters. Then the clusters are sampled randomly. Each element in the chosen clusters is then measured. In sociological research, the investigator may use city blocks as clusters. City blocks are then chosen randomly and interviewers then talk to every family in each block selected. This type of cluster sampling is sometimes referred to as *area sampling*. If a researcher were to use simple random sampling or stratified random sampling, that person would need a complete list of families or households from which to sample. Such a list may be very difficult to obtain for a large city. Even with such a list, the sampling costs would be high because it would involve measuring households over a wide area of the city. Cluster sampling is most effective if a large number of smaller size clusters are used. In educational research, for example, school districts of a state or county can be used as clusters and a random sample of the school districts is taken. Every school within the school district would be measured. However, school districts may form too large of a cluster. In this case using schools as clusters may be better.

In *two-stage cluster sampling*, we begin with a cluster sampling as described above. Then, instead of measuring every element of the clusters chosen at random, we select a random sample of the elements and measure those elements. In the educational example given above, we would identify each school district as a cluster. We would then choose k school districts randomly. From these k school districts, instead of measuring every school in the chosen districts (as in regular cluster sampling), we would take another random sample of schools within each district. We would then measure only those schools chosen.

Another kind of probability sampling—if indeed, it can be called probability sampling—is *systematic sampling*. This method is a slight variation of simple random sampling. This method assumes that the universe or population consists of elements that are ordered in some way. If the population consists of N elements and we want to choose a sample of size n, we first need to form the ratio N/n. This ratio is rounded to a whole number, k, and then used as the sampling interval. Here the first sample element is randomly chosen from numbers 1 through k and subsequent elements are chosen at every kth interval. For example, if the element selected randomly from the elements 1 through 10 is 6, then the subsequent elements are 16, 26, 36, and so on. The representativeness of the sample chosen in this fashion is dependent upon the ordering of the N elements of the population.

The student who will pursue research further should, of course, know much more about these methods. The student is encouraged to consult one or more of the excellent references on the subject presented at the end of this chapter. Williams (1978) gives an interesting presentation and demonstration of each sampling method using artificial data.

Another related topic to randomness and sampling is randomization or permutation tests. We will discuss this topic again when we discuss the data analysis for quasi-experimental designs. The proponent of this method in psychology and the behavioral sciences has been Edgington (1980, 1996), who advocates the use of approximate randomization tests to handle statistical analyses of data from nonrandom samples and single subject research designs. We briefly discuss here how this procedure works. Take Edgington's example of the correlating the IQ scores of foster parents and their adopted children. If the sample was not randomly selected, the sample may be biased in favor of parents who want to have their IQ and the IQ of their adopted child measured. It is likely that some foster parents will lower their scores to match those of their adopted child intentionally. One way of handling nonrandom data like this is to first compute the correlation between the parents and child. Then one would randomly pair the parents' scores with the child's; that is, parent 1 may in a random pairing get matched up with the child from parent number 10. After such a random pairing, the correlation is again computed. If the researcher performs 100 such randomization pairings and computes the correlation each time, he or she can then compare the original correlation to the 100 created from random pairings. If the original correlation is the best (highest), the researcher will have a better idea that the correlation obtained may be credible. These randomizations or permutation tests have been quite useful in certain research and data analysis situations. They have been used to evaluate clusters obtained in a cluster analysis (see Lee & MacQueen, 1980), and have proposed as a solution to analyzing self-efficacy data that are not independent (see Cervone, 1987).

Randomness, randomization, and random sampling are among the great ideas of science, as indicated earlier. Although research can, of course, be performed without using ideas of randomness, it is difficult to conceive how it can have viability and validity, at least in most aspects of behavioral scientific research. Modern notions of research design, sampling, and inference, for example, are literally inconceivable without the idea of randomness. One of the most remarkable of paradoxes is that through randomness, or "disorder," we are able to achieve control over the often-obstreperous complexities of psychological sociological and educational phenomena. We impose order, in short, by exploiting the known behavior of sets of random events. One is perpetually awed by what can be called the structural beauty of probability, sampling, and design theory, and by its great usefulness in solving difficult problems of research design and planning and the analysis and interpretation of data.

Before leaving the subject, let's return to a view of randomness mentioned earlier. To an omniscient being, there is no randomness. By definition such a being would "know" the occurrence of any event with complete certainty. As Poincare (1952/1996) points out, to gamble with such a being would be a losing venture. Indeed, it would not be gambling. When a coin was tossed 10 times, he or she would predict heads and tails with complete certainty and accuracy. When dice were thrown, this being would know infallibly what the outcomes will be. Every number in a table of random numbers would be correctly predicted! And certainly this being would have no need for research and science. What we seem to be saying here is that randomness is a term for ignorance. If we, like the omniscient being, knew all the contributing causes of events, then there would be no randomness. The beauty of it, as indicated above, is that we use this "ignorance" and turn it to knowledge. How we do this should become more and more apparent as we go on with our study.

Some Books on Sampling

Babbie, E. R. (1990). *Survey research methods* (2nd ed.). Belmont, CA: Wadsworth.

Babbie, E. R. (1995). *The practice of social research* (7th ed.). Belmont, CA: Wadsworth.

Cowles, M. (1989). *Statistics in psychology: A historical perspective*. Hillsdale, NJ: Erlbaum.

Deming, W. E. (1966). *Some theory of sampling*. New York: Dover.

Deming, W. E. (1990). *Sampling design in business research*. New York: Wiley.

Kish, L. (1953). Selection of the sample. In Festinger, L., & Katz, D. (Eds.), *Research methods in the behavioral sciences*. New York: Holt, Rinehart and Winston, (pp. 175–239).

Kish, L. (1995). *Survey sampling*. New York: Wiley.

Snedecor, G., & Cochran, W. (1989). *Statistical Methods* (8th ed.). Ames, IA: Iowa State University Press.

Stephan, F., & McCarthy, P. (1974). *Sampling opinions*. Westport, CT: Greenwood Press.

Sudman, S. (1976). *Applied sampling*. New York: Academic Press.

Warwick, D., & Lininger, D. (1975). *The sample survey: Theory and practice*. New York: McGraw-Hill.

Williams, B. (1978). *A sampler on sampling*. New York: Wiley.

CHAPTER SUMMARY

1. Sampling refers to taking a portion of a population or universe as representative of that population or universe.
2. Studies using samples are economical, manageable, and controllable.
3. One of the more popular methods of sampling is random sampling.
4. Random sampling is that method of drawing a portion (or sample) of a population or universe so that each member of the population or universe has an equal chance of being selected.
5. A researcher defines the population or universe. A sample is a subset of the population.
6. We can never be sure that a random sampling is representative of the population.
7. With a random sampling, the probability of selecting a sample with a mean close to the population mean is greater than the probability of selecting a sample with a mean not close to the population mean.
8. Nonrandom sampling may be biased and the chances increase that the sample mean will not be close to the population mean.
9. We say events are random if we cannot predict their outcomes.
10. Random assignment is another term for randomization. This is where participants are assigned to research groups randomly. It is used to control unwanted variances.
11. There are two types of samples: nonprobability and probability.
12. Nonprobability samples do not use random assignment, whereas probability samples do use random sampling.
13. Simple random sampling, stratified random sampling, cluster sampling, and systematic sampling are four types of probability sampling.
14. Quota sampling, purposive sampling, and accidental sampling are three types of nonprobability sampling.

STUDY SUGGESTIONS

A variety of experiments with chance phenomena are recommended: games using coins, dice, cards, roulette wheels, and tables of random numbers. Such games, properly approached, can help one learn a great deal about fundamental notions of modern scientific research, statistics, probability, and, of course, randomness. Try the problems given in the suggestions below. Do not become discouraged by the seeming laboriousness of such exercises here and later on in the book. It is evidently necessary and, indeed, helpful occasionally to go through the routine involved in certain problems. After working the problems given, devise some of your own. If you can devise intelligent problems, you are probably well on your way to understanding.

1. From a table of random numbers draw 50 numbers, 0 through 9. (Use the random numbers of Appendix C, if you wish.) List them in columns of 10 each.

   a. Count the total number of odd numbers; count the total number of even numbers. What would you expect to get by chance? Compare the obtained totals with the expected totals.

   b. Count the total number of numbers 0, 1, 2, 3, 4. Similarly count 5, 6, 7, 8, 9. How many of the first group should you get? the second group? Compare what you do get to these chance expectations. Are you far off?

   c. Count the odd and even numbers in each group of 10. Count the two groups of numbers 0, 1, 2, 3, 4 and 5, 6, 7, 8, 9 in each group of 10. Do the totals differ greatly from chance expectations?

   d. Add the columns of the five groups of 10 numbers each. Divide each sum by 10. (Simply move the decimal point one place to the left.) What would you expect to get as the mean of each group if only chance were "operating"? What did you get? Add the five sums and divide by 50. Is this mean close to the chance expectation? [Hint: To obtain the chance expectation, remember the population limits.]

2. This is a class exercise and demonstration. Assign numbers arbitrarily to all the members of the class from 1 through N, N being the total number of members of the class. Take a table of random numbers and start with any page. Have a student wave a pencil in the air and blindly stab at the page of the table. Starting with the number the pencil indicates, choose n two-digit numbers between 1 and N (ignoring numbers greater than N and repeated numbers) by, say, going down columns (or any other specified way). n is the numerator of the fraction n/N, which is decided by the size of the class. If $N = 30$, for instance, let $n = 10$. Repeat the process twice on different pages of the random numbers table. You now have three equal groups (if N is not divisible by 3, drop one or two persons at random). Write the random numbers on the chalkboard in the three groups. Have each class member call out his or her height in inches. Write these values on the chalkboard separate from the numbers, but in the same three groups. Add the three sets of numbers in each of the sets on the chalkboard, the random numbers and the heights. Calculate the means of the six sets of numbers. Also calculate the means of the total sets.

   a. How close are the means in each of the sets of numbers? How close are the means of the groups to the mean of the total group?

   b. Count the number of men and women in each of the groups. Are the sexes spread fairly evenly among the three groups?

   c. Discuss this demonstration. What do you think is its meaning for research?

3. In Chapter 6, it was suggested that the student generate 20 sets of 100 random numbers between 0 and 100 and calculate means and variances. If you did this, use the numbers and statistics in this exercise. If you did not, use the numbers and statistics of Appendix C at the end of the book.

a. How close to the population mean are the means of the 20 samples? Are any of the means "deviant"? (You might judge this by calculating the standard deviation of the means and adding and subtracting two standard deviations to the total mean.)

b. On the basis of (a), above, and your judgment, are the samples "representative"? What does "representative" mean?

c. Pick out the third, fifth, and ninth group means. Suppose that 300 subjects had been assigned at random to the three groups and that these were scores on some measure of importance to a study you wanted to do. What do you think you can conclude from the three means?

4. Most published studies in the behavioral sciences and education have not used random samples, especially random samples of large populations. Occasionally, however, studies based on random samples are done. One such study is by Osgood, Wilson, O'Malley, Bachman, and Johnston (1996). This study is worth careful reading, even though its level of methodological sophistication puts a number of its details beyond your present grasp. Try not to be discouraged by this sophistication. Get what you can out of it, especially its sampling of a large population of young men. Later in the book we will return to the interesting problem pursued. At that time, perhaps the methodology will no longer appear so formidable. (In studying research, it is sometimes helpful to read beyond our present capacity—provided one doesn't do too much of it!)

Another study random samples from a large population is by Voekl (1995). In this study the researcher gives some detail about using a two-stage stratified random sampling plan to measure student's perception of school warmth.

5. Random assignment of subjects to experimental groups is much more common than random sampling of subjects. A particularly good, even excellent, example of research in which subjects were assigned at random to two experimental groups, is by Thompson (1980). Again, don't be daunted by the methodological details of this study. Get what you can out of it. Note at this time how the subjects were classified into aptitude groups and then assigned at random to experimental treatments. We will also return to this study later. At that time, you should be able to understand its purpose and design and be intrigued by its carefully controlled experimental pursuit of a difficult substantive educational problem: the comparative merits of so-called individualized mastery instruction and conventional lecture–discussion–recitation instruction.

6. Another noteworthy example of random assignment is done in a study by Glick, DeMorest, and Hotze (1988). This study is noteworthy because it takes place in a real setting outside the laboratories of the university. Also the participants are not necessarily university students. Participants in this study are people in a public eating area within a large indoor shopping mall. Participants were chosen and then assigned to one of six experimental conditions. This article is easy to read and the statistical analysis is not much beyond the level of elementary statistics.

7. Another interesting study that uses yet another variation of random sampling is by Moran and McCullers (1984). In this study, the researchers selected photographs from school yearbooks randomly. These photographs were then grouped randomly into 10 sets of 16 pictures. Students who were not familiar with the students in the photos were then asked to rate each person in the photo in terms of attractiveness.

Special Note. In some of the above study suggestions and in those of Chapter 6, instructions were given to draw numbers from tables of random numbers or to generate sets of random numbers using a computer. If you have a microcomputer or access to one, you may well prefer to generate the random numbers using the built-in random number generator (function) of the microcomputer. An outstanding and fun book to read and learn how to do this is Walter's (1999) "The Secret Guide to Computers." Walter shows you how to write a simple computer program using the BASIC language, the language common to most microcomputers. How "good" are the random numbers generated? ("How good?" means "How random?") Since they are produced in line with the best contemporary theory and practice, they should be satisfactory, although they may not meet the exacting requirements of some experts. In our experience, they are quite satisfactory, and we recommend their use to teachers and students. An alternative is the use of the Rand Corporation random numbers which are reproduced partially in the appendix of this book.

Computer Program Listing to Generate Table 8.2

```
10 DIM N(100),A$(100)
20 FOR I=1 TO 100: READ A$(I): N(I)=0
30 NEXT I
40 R=0: D=0
50 RANDOMIZE
60 I=1
70 X=RND
80 K=INT(X*100)
90 IF K=0 THEN K=100
100 IF N(K)=1 THEN 70
110 N(K)=1
120 PRINT K,A$(K)
140 Z$=RIGHT$(A$(K),1)
150 IF Z$="d" THEN D=D+1
160 IF Z$="r" THEN R=R+1
170 I=I+1
180 IF I>60 THEN 200
190 GOTO 70
200 FOR I=1 TO 100: PRINT N(I);: NEXT I
220 PRINT " ",D,R
```

```
230 DATA heflin-d,shelby-d,murkowski-r,stevens-r,deconcini-d
240 DATA mccain-r,bumpers-d,pryor-d,boxer-d,feinstein-d,campbell-d
250 DATA brown-r,dodd-d,lieberman-d,biden-d,roth-r,graham-d,mack-r
260 DATA nunn-d,coverdell-r,akaka-d,inouye-d,craig-r,kempthorne-r
270 DATA mosley-brown-d,simon-d,coats-r,lugar-r,harkin-d,grassley-r
280 DATA dole-r,kasselbaum-r,ford-d,mcconnell-r,breaux-d,johnston-d
290 DATA mitchell-d,cohen-r,mikulski-d,sarbanes-d,kennedy-d,kerry-d
300 DATA levin-d,riegel-d,wellstone-d,durenburger-r,cochran-r
310 DATA lott-r,bond-r,danforth-r,bacus-d,burns-r,exon-d,kerrey-d
320 DATA bryan-d,reid-d,gregg-r,smith-r,bradley-d,lautenberg-d
330 DATA bingaman-d,domenici-r,moynihan-d,damato-r,faircloth-r
340 DATA helms-r,conrad-d,dorgan-d,glenn-d,metzenbaum-d,boren-d
350 DATA nickles-r,hatfield-r,packwood-r,wofford-d,specter-r
360 DATA pell-d,chafee-r,hollings-d,thurmond-r,daschle-d,pressler-r
370 DATA matthews-d,sasser-d,gramm-r,hutchinson-r,bennett-r,hatch-r
380 DATA leahy-d,jeffords-r,robb-d,warner-r,murray-d,gorton-r
390 DATA byrd-d,rockefeller-d,feingold-d,kohl-d,simpson-r,wallop-r
400 END
```

PART FOUR
ANALYSIS, INTERPRETATION, STATISTICS, AND INFERENCE

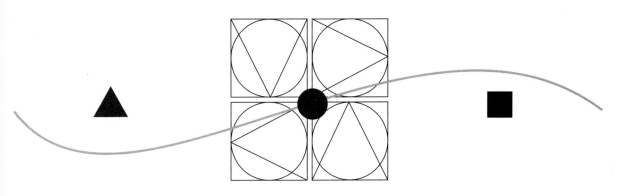

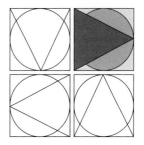

CHAPTER 9

PRINCIPLES OF ANALYSIS AND INTERPRETATION

■ FREQUENCIES AND CONTINUOUS MEASURES

■ RULES OF CATEGORIZATION

■ KINDS OF STATISTICAL ANALYSIS
    Frequency Distributions
    Graphs and Graphing
    Measures of Central Tendency and Variability
    Measures of Relations
    Analysis of Differences
    Analysis of Variance and Related Methods
    Profile Analysis
    Multivariate Analysis

■ INDICES

■ SOCIAL INDICATORS

■ THE INTERPRETATION OF RESEARCH DATA
    Adequacy of Research Designs, Methodology, Measurements, and Analysis
    Negative and Inconclusive Results
    Unhypothesized Relations and Unanticipated Findings
    Proof, Probability and Interpretation

The research analyst breaks down data into constituent parts to obtain answers to research questions and to test research hypotheses. The analysis of research data, however, does not in and of itself provide the answers to research questions. Interpretation of the data is necessary. To interpret is to explain, to find meaning. It is difficult or impossible to explain raw data; one must first analyze the data and then interpret the results of the analysis.

191

Data, as used in behavioral research, means research results from which inferences are drawn: usually numerical results, like scores of tests and statistics such as means, percentages, and correlation coefficients. The word is also used to represent the results of mathematical and statistical analysis; we will soon study such analysis and its results. Data can be more, however. Data can be information from newspaper and magazine articles, biographical materials, diaries, and so on—indeed, verbal materials in general. In different words, "data" is a general term with several meanings. Think also of research data as the results of systematic observation and analysis used to make inferences and arrive at conclusions. Scientists observe, assign symbols and numbers to the observations, and manipulate the symbols and numbers to put them into interpretable form. Then, from these data, they draw inferences concerning the relationships among the variables of research problems. (*Data* is usually a plural noun, and we will so use it in this book; the singular is the seldom-used *datum*.)

Analysis means the categorizing, ordering, manipulating, and summarizing of data to obtain answers to research questions. The purpose of analysis is to reduce data to intelligible and interpretable form so that the relationships of research problems can be studied and tested. A primary purpose of statistics, for example, is to manipulate and summarize numerical data and to compare the obtained results to chance expectations. A researcher hypothesizes that styles of leadership affect group–member participation in certain ways. The researcher plans an experiment, executes the plan, and gathers data from the subjects. Then, by ordering, breaking down, and manipulating the data an answer to the question "How do styles of leadership affect group–member participation?" will be determined. It should be apparent that this view of analysis infers that the categorizing, ordering, and summarizing of data should be planned early on in the research. A researcher should lay out analysis paradigms or models even when working on the problem and hypotheses. Only in this way can it be seen, even if only dimly, whether the data and its analysis can and will answer the research questions.

Interpretation takes the results of analysis, makes inferences pertinent to the research relations studied, and draws conclusions about these relations. The researcher who interprets research results searches them for their meaning and implications. This is achieved in two ways: (1) The relations *within* the research study and its data are interpreted. This is the narrower and more frequent use of the term *interpretation*. Here, interpretation and analysis are closely intertwined. One almost automatically interprets as one analyzes. That is, when one calculates, say, a coefficient of correlation, one almost immediately infers the existence of a relation. (2) The broader meaning of research data is sought. One compares the results and inferences drawn from the data to theory and other research results. One seeks the meaning and implications of research results within the study results, and their congruence or lack of congruence with the results of other researchers. More importantly, one compares results to the demands and expectations of theory.

An example that may illustrate these ideas is research on the nature and impact of self-disclosure on perception. The theory under consideration is interpersonalism. Interpersonalism states that one's goals, plans, and strategies provide a means for understanding people and certain interactions. It can involve the construction of mental models of action. On the basis of this general theoretical framework, Miller, Cooke, Tsang, and Morgan (1992) predicted that perceptions or judgments of attribution would be determined by the disclosure strategy a person decided to adopt. Miller et al. studied the difference between three types of disclosure: negative, positive, and boastful. Scenarios were developed with different methods of disclosure. Participants of the study were asked to describe their impression of the person in the scenario on five attribution dimensions. Each dimension was correlated with scenario type. The correlation (computed in the form of η^2[eta^2]) was very high. This is the analysis. The data have been delineated into a series of two sets of measure, which are then compared through a statistical procedure.[1]

The result of the analysis—a correlation coefficient—now has to be interpreted. What is its meaning? Specifically, what is its meaning within the study? What is its broader meaning in light of previous related research findings and interpretations? And what is its meaning as confirmation or lack of confirmation of theoretical prediction? If the "internal" prediction holds up, one then relates the finding to other research findings that may or may not be consistent with the present finding.

The correlation was substantial. Within the study, then, the correlation data are consistent with theoretical expectation. Interpersonalism theory states that different strategies of disclosure influence perceptions. Bragging is one strategy of disclosure; it should therefore influence perception. The specific inference is that the things you say about yourself influence what other people think about you. In certain situations, bragging about oneself serves a useful purpose. People will see you as confident and successful. Whereas, negative disclosures will tend to make people think you are socially sensitive but not successful. We measure at least two variables and correlate the measures. From the correlation coefficient we make an inferential leap to the hypothesis. Since it is substantial (as predicted), the hypothesis is supported. We then attempt to relate the finding to other research and theory.

Frequencies and Continuous Measures

Quantitative data come in two general forms: frequencies and continuous measures. Obviously, continuous measures are associated with continuous variables (see the discussion of continuous and categorical variables in Chapter 3). Although both kinds of variables and measures can be subsumed under the same measurement frame of reference, in practice it is necessary to distinguish them.

Frequencies are the numbers of objects in sets and subsets. Let U be the universal set with N objects. Then N is the *number* of objects in U. Let U be partitioned into

---

[1] The Miller, Cooke, Tsang, and Morgan (1992) study used more than a correlational analysis. They also performed both univariate and multivariate analyses of variance. η^2 measures the relation between the independent variable—disclosure; and the dependent variable(s)—attribution.

$A_1, A_2, \ldots, A_k$. Let $n_1, n_2, \ldots, n_k$ be the numbers of objects in $A_1, A_2, \ldots, A_k$. Then $n_1, n_2, \ldots, n_k$ are called frequencies.

It is helpful to look at this as a function. Let X be any set of objects with members $\{x_1, x_2, \ldots, x_k\}$. We wish to measure an attribute of the members of the set; call it M. Let $Y = \{0,1\}$. Let the measurement be described as a function: $f = \{(x, y)$; where x is a member of the set X, and y is either 1 or 0 depending on x's possessing or not possessing $M\}$. This is read: f, a function, or rule of correspondence, equals the set of ordered pairs (x, y) such that x is a member of X, y is 1 or 0, and so on. If x possesses M (determined in some empirical fashion), assign a 1. If x does not possess M, assign a 0. To find the frequency of objects with characteristic M, count the number of objects that have been assigned 1.

With continuous measures, the basic idea is the same. Only the rule of correspondence, f, and the numerals assigned to objects change. The rule of correspondence is more elaborate and the numerals are generally 0, 1, 2, . . . and fractions of these numerals. In other words, we write a measurement equation:

$$f = \{(x, y); x \text{ is an object, and } y = \text{any numeral}\}$$

which is the generalized form of the function. (This equation and the ideas behind it will be explained in detail in Chapter 25.) This digression is important because it helps us to see the basic similarity of frequency analysis and continuous measure analysis.

Rules of Categorization

The first step in any analysis is categorization. It was said earlier (Chapter 4) that partitioning is the foundation of analysis. We will now see why. *Categorization* is merely another word for partitioning—that is, a *category* is a partition or a subpartition. If a set of objects is categorized in some way, it is partitioned according to some rule. The rule tells us, in effect, how to assign set objects to partitions and subpartitions. If this is so, then the rules of partitioning we studied earlier apply to problems of categorization. We need only explain the rules, relate them to the basic purposes of analysis, and put them to work in practical analytic situations.

The five rules of categorization are as follows, of which (2) and (3) are the exhaustiveness and disjointness rules discussed in Chapter 4. Others, (4) and (5), can actually be deduced from the fundamental rules, (2) and (3). For practical reasons, we nevertheless list them as separate rules.

1. Categories are set up according to the research problem and purpose.
2. The categories are exhaustive.
3. The categories are mutually exclusive and independent.

4. Each category (variable) is derived from one classification principle.

5. Any categorization scheme must be on one level of discourse.

Rule 1 is the most important. If categorizations are not set up according to the demands of the research problem, then there can be no adequate answers to the research questions. We constantly ask: Does my analysis paradigm conform to the research problem? Suppose the research question asked was: What is the influence of television on the ability to process nonverbal communication of children? It has been said that too much television is bad for children; is this so? Whatever data are gathered and analyses done must bear on the research problem, which in this case is the relation between amount of television and understanding of nonverbal communication.

The simplest kind of analysis is frequency analysis. Feldman, Coats, and Spielman (1996), in their study on the amount of television viewing and understanding of nonverbal communication, selected a sample of children and determined the frequency of their TV viewing. They then measured each child's understanding of the strategic use of nonverbal emotional displays by the main character in a TV program. Feldman, Coats, and Spielman divided the children into three groups of TV viewing frequency: light, moderate and heavy. They then counted how many of these children were able to offer a complex or simple response to questions concerning the display of emotions by the main character in the TV program they viewed. The paradigm for the frequency analysis looked like this:

Level of Television Viewing

Display Rule Categorization	Light	Moderate	Heavy
Simple Complex		Frequency	

Since Feldman et al.'s data on the amount of TV viewing were measured on a continuous measure, they could have used this paradigm:

Display Rule Categorization

Simple	Complex
Amount of TV Viewing	

It is obvious that both paradigms bear directly on the problem: It is possible in both to test the relation between understanding and TV viewing, albeit in different ways. The authors chose the first method—and found that those children who watched TV less showed a higher level of understanding. In the light viewing group,

50% of the children gave complex and heterogeneous explanations. In the group of heavy viewers, 0% showed a high level of understanding. The second paradigm would undoubtedly have led to the same conclusion. The point is that an analytical paradigm is, in effect, another way to state a problem, a hypothesis, a relation. That one paradigm uses frequencies whereas another uses continuous measures in no way alters the relation tested. In other words, both modes of analysis are logically similar: they both test the same proposition but may differ in the data used, in statistical tests, and in sensitivity and power.

There are several things a researcher might do that would be irrelevant to the problem. If one, two, or three variables are included in the study with no theoretical or practical reason for doing so, then the analytic paradigm would be at least partly irrelevant to the problem. Suppose a researcher, in a study of the hypothesis that religious education enhances the moral character of children, collected achievement test data from public and parochial schoolchildren. This would probably have no bearing on the problem. The researcher is interested in the moral differences—not the achievement differences—between the two types of schools and between religious instruction and no religious instruction. Other variables may be brought into the picture that have little or no bearing on the problem; for example, differences in teacher experience and training or teacher–pupil ratios. If, on the other hand, the researcher thought that certain variables, like sex, family religious background, and perhaps personality variables, might interact with religious instruction to produce differences, then it might be justifiable to build such variables into the research problem and consequently into the analytic paradigm.[2]

Rule 2, on exhaustiveness, means that all subjects, all objects of U, must be used up. All individuals in the universe must be capable of being assigned to the cells of the analytic paradigm. With the example just considered, each child either goes to parochial school or to public school. If, somehow, the sampling had included children who attend private schools, then the rule would be violated because there would be a number of children who could not be fitted into the implied paradigm of the problem. (What would a frequency analysis paradigm look like? Conceive the dependent variable as honesty.) If, however, the research problem called for private school pupils, then the paradigm would have to be changed by adding the rubric "Private" to the rubrics "Parochial" and "Public."

The exhaustiveness criterion is not always easy to satisfy. With some categorical variables, there is no problem. If gender is one of the variables, any individual has to be either male or female. Suppose, however, that a variable under study was

---

[2]In Chapter 6, elementary consideration is given to frequency analysis with more than one independent variable. In later chapters there will be more detailed consideration of both frequency and continuous measure analysis with several independent variables. The reader should not now be concerned with complete understanding of examples like those given above. They will be clarified later.

religious preference and we set up, in a paradigm, Protestant–Catholic–Muslim. Now suppose some subjects were atheists or Buddhists. Clearly, the categorization scheme violates the exhaustiveness rule: some subjects would have no cells to which to be assigned. Depending upon numbers of cases and the research problem, we might add another rubric, "Others," to which we assign subjects who are neither Protestants, Catholics, nor Muslims. Another solution, especially when the number of Others is small, is to delete these subjects from the study. Still another solution is to place these other subjects, if it is possible to do so, under an already existing rubric. Examples of other variables where this problem is encountered are political preference, social class, and types of education.

Rule 3 is one that often causes research workers concern. To demand that the categories be mutually exclusive means, as we learned earlier, that each object of *U*, each research subject (actually the measure assigned to each subject), must be assigned to one cell and one cell only of an analytic paradigm. This is a function of operational definition. Definitions of variables must be clear and unambiguous so that it is unlikely for any subject to be assigned to more than one cell. If religious preference is the variable being defined, then the definition of membership in the subsets Protestant, Catholic, and Muslim must be clear and unambiguous. It may be "registered membership in a church," or be "born in the church." It may simply be the subject's identification of oneself as a Protestant, a Catholic, or a Muslim. Whatever the definition, it must enable the investigator to assign any subject to one *and only one* of the three cells.

The independence part of Rule 3 is often difficult to satisfy, especially with continuous measures—and sometimes with frequencies. *Independence* means that the assignment of one object to a cell in no way affects the assignment of any other object to that cell or to any other cell. Random assignment from an infinite or large universe, of course, satisfies the rule. Without random assignment, however, we run into problems. When assigning objects to cells on the basis of the object's possession of certain characteristics, the assignment of an object now may affect the assignment of another object later.

Rule 4, that each category (variable) be derived from one classificatory principle, is sometimes violated by the neophyte. If one has a firm grasp of partitioning, this error is easily avoided. The rule means that, in setting up an analytic design, each variable has to be treated separately because each variable is a separate dimension. One does *not* put two or more variables in one category or one dimension. If one were studying, for example, the relations between social class, sex, and drug addiction, one would not put social class and sex on one dimension.

Let us illustrate this with a study by Glick, DeMorest, and Hotze (1988). These researchers were studying the relations among group membership, personal space, and compliance to a request for help. In this study, confederates in the study either sought help from a person who was either similar or different in physical characteristics (group membership). Additionally, when asking for help, they were either at a near, medium, or far (personal space) distance from the subject. The person they approached either complied or did not comply with their request for help. In this study an error in Rule 4 stated above might look like this:

	In-group	Out-group	Near	Medium	Far
Complied					
			Frequencies		
Refused					

Clearly this paradigm violates the rule: it has one category derived from two variables. Each variable must have its own category. A correct paradigm might look like this:

	In-Group			*Out-Group*		
	Near	**Medium**	**Far**	**Near**	**Medium**	**Far**
Complied						
			Frequencies			
Refused						

Rule 5 is the hardest to explain because the term "level of discourse" is difficult to define. It was defined in an earlier chapter as a set that contains all the objects that enter into a discussion. If we use the expression "universe of discourse," we tie the idea to set ideas. When talking about U_1, do not bring in U_2 without good reason and without making it clear that you are doing so. For a discussion of levels of discourse and relevance, see Kerlinger (1969, pp. 1127–1144, especially p. 1131).

Research analysis usually measures the dependent variable: for example, take the problem of group membership, personal space, and compliance to a request for help. Group membership and personal space are the independent variables; compliance to a request for help is the dependent variable. The objects of analysis are the compliance measures. The independent variables and their categories are actually used to structure the dependent variable analysis. The universe of discourse, U, is the set of dependent variable measures. The independent variables can be perceived as the partitioning principles used to break down or partition the dependent variable measures. If we suddenly switch to another kind of dependent variable measure, then we may have switched levels or universes of discourse.

Kinds of Statistical Analysis

There are many kinds of statistical analysis and presentation that cannot be discussed in detail in this book. Later discussions of certain more advanced forms of statistical analysis have as their purpose basic understanding of statistics and statistical inference and the relation of statistics and statistical inference to research. Here, the major forms of statistical analysis are discussed briefly to give the reader an overview of the subject; they are discussed, however, only as they relate to research. It is assumed that the reader has already studied the simpler descriptive statistics. Those who have not can find good discussions in elementary textbooks (see Comrey & Lee, 1995; Kirk, 1990; Howell, 1997; Hays, 1994).

Frequency Distributions

Although frequency distributions are used primarily for descriptive purposes, they can also be used for other research purposes. For example, one can test whether two or more distributions are sufficiently similar to warrant merging them. Suppose one were studying the verbal learning of boys and girls in the sixth grade. After obtaining large numbers of verbal learning scores, one can compare and test the differences between the boy and girl distributions. If the test shows the distributions to be the same—and other criteria are satisfied—they can perhaps be combined for other analysis.

Observed distributions can also be compared to theoretical distributions. The best known such comparison is with the so-called *normal distribution*. It may be important to know that obtained distributions are normal in form or, if not normal, depart from normality in certain specifiable ways. Such analysis can be useful in other theoretical and applied work and research. In theoretical study of abilities it is important to know whether such abilities are in fact distributed normally. Since a number of human characteristics have been found to be normally distributed (see Anastasi, 1958)[3] researchers can ask significant questions about "new" characteristics being investigated.

Applied educational research can profit from careful study of distributions of intelligence, aptitude, and achievement scores. Is it conceivable that an innovative learning program can change the distributions of the achievement scores, say, of third and fourth graders? Can it be that massive early education programs can change the shape of distributions, as well as the general levels of scores?

Allport's (1947) study of social conformity showed that even a complex behavioral phenomenon like conformity can be studied profitably using distribution analysis. Allport was able to show that a number of social behaviors—stopping for red lights, parking violations, religious observances, and so on—were distributed in the form of a *J* curve, with most people conforming, but with predictable smaller numbers not conforming in differing degrees. Coren, Ward, and Enns (1994) present a number of different distributional shapes for certain human perceptions of physical stimuli based on Steven's psychophysics law.

Distributions have probably been too little used in the behavioral sciences and education. The study of relations and the testing of hypotheses are almost

---

[3] The student of research in education, psychology, and sociology should study Anastasi's outstanding contribution to our understanding of individual differences. Her book also contains many examples of distributions of empirical data.

automatically associated with correlations and comparisons of averages. The use of distributions is considered less often. Some research problems, however, can be solved better by using distribution analysis. Studies of pathology and other unusual conditions are perhaps best approached through a combination of distribution analysis and probabilistic notions.

Graphs and Graphing

One of the most powerful tools of analysis is the graph. A *graph* is a two-dimensional representation of a relation or relations. It pictorially exhibits sets of ordered pairs in a way no other method can. If a relation exists in a set of data, a graph will not only clearly show it, it will show its nature: positive, negative, linear, quadratic, and so on. While graphs have been used a good deal in the behavioral sciences, they, like distributions, have probably not been used enough. To be sure, there are objective ways of epitomizing and testing relations, such as correlation coefficients, comparison of means, and other statistical methods. However, none of these so vividly and uniquely describes a relation as a graph.

Look back at the graphs in Chapter 5 (Figures 5.1, 5.4, 5.5, and 5.6). Note how they convey the nature of the relations. Later we will use graphs in a more interesting way to show the nature of rather complex relations among variables. To give the student just a taste of the richness and interest of such analysis, we anticipate later discussion; in fact, we will attempt to teach a complex idea using graphs.

The three graphs of Figure 9.1 show three hypothetical relations between age, as an independent variable, and verbal achievement (labeled "achievement") as dependent variable, of middle-class children (A), and working-class children (B). One can call these growth graphs. The horizontal axis is the abscissa; it is used to indicate the independent variable, or X. The vertical axis is the ordinate; it is used to indicate the

▣ FIGURE 9.1

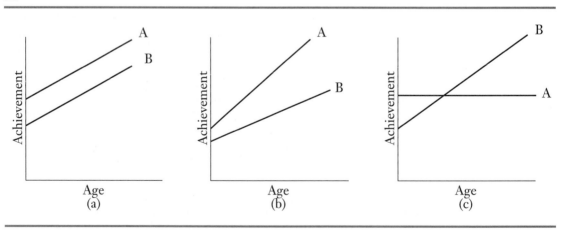

dependent variable, or *Y*. Graph (a) shows the same positive relation between age and achievement with both A and B samples. It also shows that the A children exceed the B children. Graph (b), however, shows that both relations are positive, but that as time goes on, the A children's achievement increases more than the B children's achievement. Graph (c) is more complex. It shows that the A children were superior to the B children at an early age and remained the same to a later age, but the B children, who started lower, advanced and continued to advance over time until they exceeded the A children. This sort of relation is unlikely with verbal achievement, but it can occur with other variables.

The phenomenon shown in graphs (b) and (c) is known as *interaction*. Briefly, it means that two (or more) variables interact in their "effect" on a dependent variable. In this case, age and group status interact in their relation to verbal achievement. Expressed differently, interaction means that the relation of an independent variable to a dependent variable differs in different groups, as in this case, or at different levels of another independent variable. The study by Behling and Williams (1991) gave results that could be plotted to look like graph (b). In this study, the researchers examined student and teacher perceptions of intelligence toward different styles of clothes on males and females. A graph of one style of dress is given in Figure 9.2. A graph similar to graph (c) can be constructed from the data given in Little, Sterling, and Tingstrom (1996). Their study involved the perception of northern and southern United States students toward a target person described as either a northern or southern person. Here, southern students gave similar semantic differential ratings to both northern and southern target persons. However, the northern students gave the northern target person much higher ratings than the southern target person. This is depicted in Figure 9.3. The notion of an interaction effect will be explained in detail and more accurately when we study analysis of variance and multiple regression analysis.

While means are one of the best ways to report complex data, complete reliance on them can be unfortunate. Most cases of significant mean differences between

■ **FIGURE 9.2**

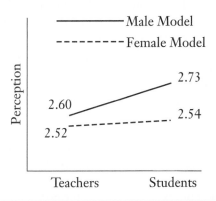

◼ FIGURE 9.3

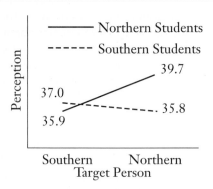

groups are also accompanied by considerable overlap of the distributions. Clear examples are given by Anastasi (1958) who points out the necessity of paying attention to overlapping and gives examples and graphs of sex distribution differences, among others. In short, students of research are advised to get into the habit, from the beginning of their study, of paying attention to and understanding distributions of variables and to graphing relations of variables.

Measures of Central Tendency and Variability

There is little doubt that measures of central tendency and variability are the most important tools of behavioral data analysis. Since much of this book will be preoccupied with such measures—indeed, a whole section is called "The Analysis of Variance"—here, we will only characterize averages and variances. The three main averages (or measures of central tendency) used in research—mean, median, and mode—are epitomes of the sets of measures from which they are calculated. Sets of measures are too vast and too complex to grasp and understand readily. They are "represented" or epitomized by measures of central tendency. They tell what sets of measures "are like" on average, but are also compared to test relations. Moreover, individual scores can be usefully compared to them to assess the status of the individual. We say, for instance, that individual A's score is such-and-such a distance above the mean.

While the mean is the most used average in research, and while it has desirable properties that justify its preeminent position, the median (the midmost measure of a set of measures) and the mode (the most frequent measure) can sometimes be useful in research. For instance, the median, in addition to being an important descriptive measure, can be used in tests of statistical significance where the mean is inappropriate (see Bradley, 1968). The study by Allman, Walker, Hart, Laprade, Noel, and Smith (1987), which compared the effectiveness and adverse effects of air-fluidized beds and conventional therapy for hospitalized patients with pressure sores, serves as a good example of the use of the median as the primary measure of central tendency. The mode is used mostly for descriptive purposes, but can be useful in research for studying characteristics of populations and relations. Suppose that a mathematical aptitude test was given to all incoming freshmen in a college that had just initiated open admissions, and that the distribution of scores was bimodal. Suppose, further, that only a mean was calculated, compared to means of previous years, and found to be considerably lower. The simple conclusion that the average mathematical aptitude of incoming freshmen was considerably lower than in previous years conceals the fact that because of the open admissions policy many freshmen were admitted whose backgrounds were deficient in mathematics. While this is an obvious example, deliberately chosen because it is obvious, it should be noted that obscuring important sources of differences can be more subtle. It often pays off in research, in other words, to calculate medians and modes as well as means.[4]

The principal measures of variability are the variance and the standard deviation. These have already been discussed and will be discussed further in later chapters. We therefore forego discussion of them here, except to say that research reports should always include variability measures. Means should almost never be reported without standard deviations (and Ns, the sizes of samples) because adequate interpretation of research by readers is virtually impossible without variability indices. Another measure of variability that has in recent years become more important is the *range:* the difference between the highest and lowest measures of a set of measures. It has become possible, especially with small samples (with N about 20 or 15 or less), to use the range in tests of statistical significance.

Measures of Relations

There are many useful measures of relations: the product–moment coefficient of correlation (r), the rank–order coefficient of correlation (*rho*), the correlation ratio (eta: η), the distance measure (D), the phi coefficient (ϕ), the coefficient of multiple correlation (R), and so on. Almost all coefficients of relation, no matter how different in derivation, appearance, calculation, and use, do essentially the same thing: express the extent to which the pairs of sets of ordered pairs vary concomitantly. In effect, they tell the researcher the magnitude and (usually) the direction of the relation. Some of them vary in value from -1.00 through 0 to $+1.00$, -1.00 and 1.00 indicating perfect negative and positive association, respectively, and 0 indicating no discernible relation.

Measures of relations are comparatively direct indices of relations in the sense that from them one has some direct idea of the degree of the covarying of the variables. The square of the product–moment coefficient of correlation, for example, is a direct estimate of the amount of the variance shared by the variables. One can say,

---

[4]Types of means and other measures of central tendency are exceptionally well discussed in Tate's (1955) old but very valuable book. He also gives a number of good examples of distributions and graphs of various kinds.

at least roughly, how high or low the relation is. This is in contrast to measures of statistical significance which say, in effect, that a relation is or is not "significant" at some specified level of significance. Ideally, any analysis of research data should include both kinds of indices: measures of the significance of a relation and measures of the magnitude of the relation.

Measures of relations, but especially product–moment coefficients of correlation, are unusual in that they themselves are subject to extensive and elaborate forms of analysis, mainly multiple regression analysis and factor analysis (covered in later chapters). They are thus extremely useful and powerful tools of the researcher.

Analysis of Differences

The analysis of differences, particularly the analysis of differences between means, occupies a rather large part of statistical analysis and inference. It is important to note two things about difference analysis. First, it is by no means confined to the differences between measures of central tendency. Almost any kind of difference—between frequencies, proportions percentages, ranges, correlations, and variances—can be so analyzed. Take variances. Suppose an educational psychologist ascertains whether or not a certain form of instruction has the effect of making pupils more heterogeneous in concept learning. The difference between the variances of groups taught by differing methods can be tested easily. Or one might want to know whether or not groups set up to be homogeneous are homogeneous on variables other than those used to form the groups (see Comrey & Lee, 1995, pp. 229–234; Mattson, 1986, Chapter 10).

The second point is more important. All analyses of differences are intended for the purpose of studying relations. Suppose one believes that altering the amount of narcissism will have an effect on interpersonal consequences. Carroll, Hoeningmann, Stovall, and Whitehead (1996) created three protocols with differing levels of narcissism—extreme, moderate, and none—and then measured the participants' attractiveness toward that person. These researchers' hypothesis was supported in that participants reported greater rejection of the person with extreme narcissism than with the other levels of narcissism. It is not really these differences that interest us, however. It is the relation of the study. It is the relation between the changing of levels of narcissism and the effect it has on how people perceive that person. Differences between means, then, really reflect the relation between the independent variable and the dependent variable. If there are no significant differences among means, the correlation between independent variable and dependent variable is zero. And, conversely, the greater the differences the higher the correlation, all other things being equal.

Take the experiment by Strack, Martin, and Stepper (1988) that studied the effect of people's facial activity on their affective responses. Here, the persons in the experimental group received instructions to hold pens in their mouths using only their teeth while looking at cartoons. The control group persons received instructions to hold pens with their lips while viewing the same stimuli. The experimental group gave a mean rating of 5.09 on a scale from 0 to 9 in terms of "funniness." The

◉ FIGURE 9.4

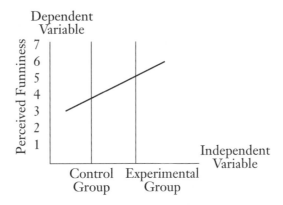

control group, however, gave a mean rating of 3.90. The difference is statistically significant, and we conclude from the significant difference that there is a relation between which facial muscles are used and not used and perceived funniness. In earlier chapters, relations between measured variables were plotted to show the nature of the relations. It is possible, too, to graph the present relation between the experimental (manipulated) independent variable and the measured dependent variable. This has been done in Figure 9.4, where the means have been plotted as indicated. While the plotting is more or less arbitrary—for instance, there are no real baseline units for the independent variable—the similarity to the earlier graphs is apparent and the basic idea of a relation is clear.

If the reader will always keep in mind that relations are sets of ordered pairs, the conceptual similarity of Figure 9.4 to earlier graphs will be evident. In the earlier graphs, each member of each pair was a score. In Figure 9.4, an ordered pair consists of an experimental treatment and a score. If we assign the value 1 to the experimental group and 0 to the control group, two ordered pairs might be: (1, 5.09), (0, 3.90).

Analysis of Variance and Related Methods

A sizable portion of this book will be devoted to analysis of variance and related methods, So there is little need to say much here. The reader need only put this important method of analysis in perspective. Analysis of variance is what its name implies—and more: a method of identifying, breaking down, and testing for statistical significance variances that come from different sources of variation. That is, a dependent variable has a total amount of variance, some of which is due to the experimental treatment, some to error, and some to other causes. Analysis of variance's role is to work with these different variances and sources of variance. Strictly speaking, analysis of variance is more appropriate for experimental than for nonexperimental data, even though its inventor, Fisher (1950), used it with both. We will consider it, then, a method for the analysis of data yielded by experiments in which randomization and manipulation of at least one independent variable have been used.

There is probably no better way to study research design than through an analysis of variance approach. Those proficient with the approach almost automatically think of alternative analysis of variance models when confronted with new research problems. Take the study by Rozin, Nemeroff, Wane, and Sherrod (1989) on the law of contagion. The law of contagion states that objects that have been in contact with one another, may continue to influence each other through the transfer of some of their properties. Rozin et al. constructed six objects (sweater, hamburger, apple, hairbrush [received], hairbrush [given], and a lock of hair) that have been in contact with four different people (friend, lover, dislike, unsavory). The four different people were considered as four levels of the categorical variable: source. Participants were asked to rate each object on a scale from −100 to +100, where −100 was "the most unpleasant thing you can imagine" and +100 was "the most pleasant thing you can imagine." Zero was the neutral point. Rozin et al. (1989) analyzed the data with a simple one-way analysis of variance for each object using the source (different people

▣ FIGURE 9.5

(a)

Source (people in contact with the object)

Friend	Lover	Dislike	Unsavory
	Pleasantness Ratings		

(b)

Source (people in contact with the object)

Objects	Friend	Lover	Dislike	Unsavory
Sweater				
Hamburger				
Apple				
Hairbrush (received)		Pleasantness Ratings		
Hairbrush (given)				
Lock of hair				

◨ FIGURE 9.6

(a)

Emergency Care Providers

Physicians	Nurses	Prehospital
Staphylococcal bacteria count		

(b)

Emergency Care Provider

Work Shift	Friend	Lover	Dislike
Day Night	Staphylococcal bacteria count		

who have been in contact with the object) as the independent variable. The analysis would look like the paradigm marked (a) of Figure 9.5. If the researchers used the objects as another independent variable, thinking the objects affect people's evaluations, then the paradigm will look like the one marked (b), which is a two-way analysis of variance. Clearly, analysis of variance is an important method of studying differences.

Similarly, a study by Jones, Hoerle, and Riekse (1995) compared the extent of the presence of staphylococcus bacteria on stethoscopes of emergency care providers. A one-way analysis of variance was used to make this comparison between physicians, nurses, and prehospital personnel. Here, the independent variable was the type of care provider, and the dependent variable was the amount of staphylococcal bacteria count. Figure 9.6 (a) gives the paradigm used in this study. If these researchers felt that there might be a difference between the providers working different shifts, the paradigm would resemble the one given in Figure 9.6 (b).

Profile Analysis

Profile analysis is basically the assessment of the similarities of the profiles of individuals or groups. A *profile* is a set of different measures of an individual or group, each of which is expressed in the same unit of measure. An individual's scores on a set of different tests constitute a profile, if all scores have been converted to a common measure system, like percentiles, ranks, and standard scores. Profiles have been used mostly for diagnostic purposes—for instance, the profiles of scores from test batteries are used to assess and advise high school pupils. But profile analysis is becoming increasingly important in psychological and sociological research, as we will see later when we study, among other things, Q methodology.

Profile analysis has special problems that require researchers' careful considerations. Similarity, for example, is not a general characteristic of persons; it is similarity only of specified characteristics or complexes of characteristics (see Cronbach & Gleser, 1953). Another difficulty lies in what information one is willing to sacrifice when calculating indices of profile similarity. When one uses the product–moment coefficient of correlation—which is a profile measure—one loses level; that is, differences between means are sacrificed. This is loss of *elevation*. Product–moment *r*s only take *shape* into account. Further, *scatter*—differences in variability of profiles—is lost in the calculation of certain other kinds of profile measures. In short, information can be and is lost. The student will find excellent help and guidance with profile analysis in Nunnally and Bernstein's (1993) book on psychometrics, though the treatment is not elementary.

Multivariate Analysis

Perhaps the most important forms of statistical analysis, especially at the present stage of development of the behavioral sciences, are multivariate analysis and factor analysis. *Multivariate analysis* is a general term used to categorize a family of analytical methods whose chief characteristic is the simultaneous analysis of *k* independent variables and *m* dependent variables. In this book we will not be excessively concerned about the terminology used with multivariate analysis. To some, multivariate analysis includes factor analysis and other forms of analysis, like multiple regression analysis. *Multivariate* to these individuals infers more than one independent variable or more than one dependent variable, or both. Others in the field use "multivariate analysis" only in the case of *both* multiple independent and multiple dependent variables. If an analysis includes, for instance, four independent variables and two dependent variables handled simultaneously, it is a multivariate analysis.

It can be argued that, of all methods of analysis, multivariate methods are the most powerful and appropriate for scientific behavioral research. The argument to support this statement is long and involved and would sidetrack us from our main pursuit. Basically, it rests on the idea that behavioral research problems are almost all multivariate in nature and cannot be solved with a bivariate (two-variable) approach—that is, an approach that considers only one independent and one dependent variable at a time. This has become strikingly clear in much educational research where, for instance, the determinants of learning and achievement are complex: intelligence, motivation, social class, instruction, school and class atmosphere and organization, and so on. Evidently, variables like these work with each other, sometimes against each other, mostly in unknown ways, to affect learning and achievement. In other words, to account for the complex psychological and sociological phenomena of education requires design and analytic tools that are capable of handling the complexity that manifests itself above all in multiplicity of independent and dependent variables. A similar argument can be given for psychological and sociological research.

This argument and the reality behind it impose a heavy burden on those individuals teaching and learning research approaches and methods. It is unrealistic and irresponsible to study and learn only an approach that is basically bivariate in conception. Multivariate methods, however, are like the behavioral reality they try to reflect: complex and difficult to understand. The pedagogical necessity, as far as this book is concerned, is to try to convey the fundamentals of research thinking, design, methods, and analysis mainly through a modified bivariate approach. We will extend this approach as much as possible to multivariate conceptions and methods, and hope that the student will pursue matters further after having received an adequate foundation.

Multiple regression, probably the single most useful form of the multivariate methods analyzes the common and separate influences of two or more independent variables on a dependent variable. This statement has limitations, especially about the separate contributions of independent variables that will be discussed in Chapter 33. The increased use of multiple regression as a behavioral science analytic tool was due for the most part to the high-speed digital computer. Ezekiel and Fox (1959) are two of the few authors whose books are available on multiple regression prior to heavy use of computers. Ezekiel and Fox actually summarized the number of studies that used multiple regression prior to the publication of their book in 1959. There weren't very many. Since the ready availability of computers and statistical software, the number of studies using multiple regression has increased exponentially. Erlich and Lee (1978) had a novel use for regression analysis. They used it on test scores for the purpose of assessing educational accountability. Griffiths, Bevil, O'Connor, and Wieland (1995) used regression to predict the level of competence on an anatomy and physiology exam. Among the predictor variables were grade-point-average and the type of college where the prerequisite anatomy and physiology courses were taken. The method has been used in hundreds of studies probably because of its flexibility, power, and general applicability to many different kinds of research problems. (It also has limitations!) We can hardly ignore it, then, in this book. Fortunately, it is not too difficult to understand and learn to use—given sufficient desire to do so.

Canonical correlation is a logical extension of multiple regression. Indeed, it is a multiple regression method. It adds more than one dependent variable to the multiple regression model. In other words, it handles the relations between sets of independent variables and sets of dependent variables. As such, it is a theoretically powerful method of analysis. It has limitations, however, that can restrict its usefulness: in the interpretation of the results it yields and in its limited ability to test theoretical models.

Discriminant analysis is also closely related to multiple regression. Its name indicates its purpose: to discriminate groups from one another on the basis of sets of measures. It is also useful in assigning individuals to groups on the basis of their scores on tests. While this explanation is not adequate, it is sufficient for now.

It is difficult at this stage to characterize, even at a superficial level, the technique known as *multivariate analysis of variance* because we have not yet covered analysis of variance. We will therefore postpone its discussion.

Factor analysis is essentially different in kind and purpose from other multivariate methods. Its fundamental purpose is to help a researcher discover and identify the unities or dimensions, called *factors*, behind many measures. We now know, for example, that behind many measures of ability and intelligence lay fewer general dimensions or factors. Verbal aptitude and mathematical aptitude are two of the best known such factors. Religious, economic, and educational factors have been found when measuring social attitudes.

The above-mentioned multivariate methods are "standard" in the sense that they are usually what is meant by "multivariate methods." There are, however, other multivariate methods of equal, even greater, importance. As said in the Preface, it is not possible in a book of this kind to give adequate and correct technical explanations of all multivariate methods. While enormously important, for example, analysis of covariance structures and log-linear models analysis may be far too complex and difficult to describe and explain adequately and completely. Similarly, multidimensional scaling and path analysis cannot be adequately presented. Then what are we to do? Some of these approaches and procedures are so powerful and important—indeed, they are revolutionizing behavioral research—that a book that ignores them will be sadly deficient. The solution to the problem was also outlined in the Preface. It is worth repeating. The most common and accessible approaches—analysis of variance, multiple regression, and factor analysis—will be presented in sufficient technical detail to enable a motivated and diligent student to at least use them and interpret their results. Certain other highly complex methods (like analysis of covariance structures and log-linear models) will be described and explained "conceptually." That is, their purpose and rationale will be explained, with generous citation and description of fictitious and actual research use. Such an approach will be used in later chapters with the following three methodologies.

Path analysis is a graphic method of studying the presumed direct and indirect influences of independent variables on each other and on dependent variables. It is a method, in other words, of portraying and testing "theories" (see Kerlinger & Pedhazur, 1973; Pedhazur, 1996). Perhaps its main virtue is that it requires researchers to make explicit the theoretical framework of research problems. To accomplish its goals, path analysis uses so-called causal or path diagrams and regression analysis. Readers can assuage a little of their curiosity by turning to Chapter 34 and examining one or two of the path analytic examples given there. Path analysis has been a useful conceptual framework for explaining the relations between variables. The person credited with the development of path analysis was Wright (1921). Wright's applications were in the field of genetics. Duncan (1966) and Blalock (1971) made Wright's work popular in the behavioral sciences. It is helpful to study path analysis because it makes understanding the analysis of covariance structure easier. In fact, path analysis is a part of analysis of covariance structures, as we will see in a later chapter.

Analysis of covariance structures—or causal modeling,[5] or structural equation models—is the ultimate approach to the analysis of complex data structures. It means, essentially, the analysis of the varying together of variables that are in a structure dictated by theory. For example, we can test the adequacy of theories of intelligence mentioned in earlier chapters by fitting the theories into the analysis of covariance structure framework and then testing how well they account for actual intelligence test data. The method—or rather, methodology—is an ingenious mathematical and statistical synthesis of factor analysis, multiple regression, path analysis, and psychological measurement into a single comprehensive system that can express and test complex theoretical formulations of research problems. This creation is usually attributed to Joreskog (1970) and his associates, although Bentler (1989) has been a strong proponent of the method, having created a different algorithm (EQS) to that of Joreskog's (LISREL).

Log-linear models are the ultimate multivariate method—or again, methodology—of analyzing frequency data. The above-mentioned multivariate methods are for the most part geared to analyzing data obtained from continuous measures: test scores, attitude and personality scale measures, measures of ecological variables, and the like. As we will see in the next chapter, however, behavioral research data are occasionally in the form of frequencies, mostly counts of individuals. Examples would include numbers of males and females, ethnic minority and nonethnic minority, teachers and nonteachers, middle- and working-class individuals, Catholics, Protestants, and Muslims. Log-linear analysis makes it possible to study complex combinations of such nominal variables and, like analysis of covariance structures, to test theories of the relations and influences of such variables on each other. We will briefly characterize the methodology in a later chapter, though space constraints and technical difficulties will force us to limit the discussion to the basic ideas involved. We will at least see, however, that, like analysis of covariance structures, it is one of the most powerful and important methodological developments in the latter part of the twentieth century.

Indices

Index can be defined in two related ways. First, an index is an observable phenomenon that is substituted for a less-observable phenomenon. A thermometer, for example, gives readings of numbers that represent degrees of temperature. The numerals on a speedometer indicate how many miles per hour a vehicle is traveling. Test scores indicate achievement levels, verbal aptitudes, degrees of anxiety, and so on.

A second, perhaps more useful definition to the researcher is: *an index is a number that is a composite of two or more numbers.* An investigator makes a series of

---

[5] The term "causal modeling" is no longer in vogue since it was pointed out by a number of prominent statisticians that analyses based on correlation in the social and behavioral sciences could not establish cause and effect.

observations, for example, and derives some single number from the measures of the observations to summarize the observations, to express them succinctly. By this definition, all sums and averages are indices: they include in a single measure more than one measure. But the definition also includes the idea of indices as composites of different measures. Coefficients of correlation are such indices. They combine different measures in a single measure or index.

There are indices of social-class status. For example, one can combine income, occupation, and place of residence to obtain a rather good index of social class. An index of cohesiveness can be obtained by asking members of a group whether or not they would like to remain part of the group. Their responses can be combined in a single number. In business and economics, the buying power of the American dollar varies over time. As such it is necessary to adjust other values in order to make meaningful comparisons. Take, for example, the comparison of the cost of an automobile in 1997 with the cost in 1950. One of the first steps is to determine the buying power of the U.S. dollar in 1997 with that of the buying power in 1950. The Bureau of Labor Statistics computes and publishes regularly the consumer price index (CPI). The CPI is viewed as a cost-of-living measure.

Indices are most important in research because they simplify comparisons. Indeed, they enable researchers to make comparisons that otherwise cannot be made or that can be made only with considerable difficulty. Raw data are usually too complex to be grasped and used in mathematical and statistical manipulations. They must be reduced to manageable form. The percentage is a good example. Percentages transform raw numbers into comparable form.

Indices generally take the form of quotients: one number is divided by another number. The most useful such indices range between 0 and 1.00 or between -1.00 through 0 to $+1.00$. This makes them independent of numbers of cases and aids comparison from sample to sample and study to study. (They are generally expressed in decimal form.) There are two forms of quotients: ratios and proportions. A third form, the percentage, is a variation of the proportion.

A *ratio* is a composite of two numbers that relates one number to the other in fractional or decimal form. Any fraction, any quotient, is a ratio. Either or both the numerator and denominator of a ratio can themselves be ratios. The chief purpose and utility of a ratio is relational: it permits the comparison of numbers. In order to do this, it is perhaps best to put the larger of the two numbers of the quotient in the denominator. This of course satisfies the condition mentioned above of having the ratio values range between 0 and 1.00, or between -1.00 through 0 to $+1.00$. This is not absolutely necessary, however. Let's say we wished to compare the ratio of male and female high school graduates to the ratio of male and female graduates of junior high school over several years. The ratio will sometimes be less than 1.00 and sometimes greater than 1.00, since it is possible that the preponderance of one sex over the other in one year may change in another year.

Sometimes ratios give more accurate information (in a sense) than the parts from which they are composed. If one were studying the relation between educational variables and tax rate, for instance, and used actual tax rates, an erroneous notion of the relation might be obtained. This is because tax rates on property are often misleading. Some communities with high *rates* actually have relatively low levels of taxation. The assessed valuation of property may be low. To avoid the discrepancies between one community and another, one can calculate, for each community, the ratio of assessed valuation to true valuation. Then an adjusted tax rate, a "true" tax rate, can be calculated by multiplying the tax rate in use by this fraction. This will yield a more accurate figure to use in calculations of relations between the tax rate and other variables. The odds-ratio is one type of index that is valuable when considering frequency data in contingency tables. We will examine this type of statistical index in greater detail when we discuss the analysis of frequency data and log-linear analysis.

A *proportion* is a fraction with the numerator one of two or more observed frequencies and the denominator the sum of the observed frequencies. The probability definition given earlier, $p = s/(s + f)$, where s equals number of successes and f equals number of failures, is a proportion. Take any two numbers, say 20 and 60. The ratio of the two numbers is $20/60 = .33$. (It could also be $60/20 = 3$.) If these two numbers were the observed frequencies of the presence and lack of presence of an attribute in a total sample, where $N = 60 + 20 = 80$, then a proportion would be: $20/(60 + 20) = .25$. Another proportion, of course, is $60/80 = .75$.

A *percentage* is simply a proportion multiplied by 100. With the above example, $20/80 \times 100 = 25\%$. The main purpose of proportions and percentages is to reduce different sets of numbers to comparable sets of numbers with a common base. Any set of frequencies can be transformed to proportions or percentages in order to facilitate statistical manipulation and interpretation.

A word of caution is in order. Because they are often a mixture of two fallible measures, indices can be dangerous. The old method of computing IQ is a good example. The numerator of the fraction is itself an index since MA, mental age, is a composite of a number of measures. A better example is the so-called Achievement Quotient: $AQ = 100 \times EA/MA$, where EA equals Educational Age, and MA equals Mental Age. Here, both the numerator and the denominator of the fraction are complex indices. Both are mixtures of measures of varying reliability. What is the meaning of the resulting index? How can we interpret it sensibly? It is hard to say. In short, while indices are indispensable aids to scientific analysis, they must be used with circumspection and care.

Social Indicators

Indicators, although closely related to indices—indeed, they are frequently indices as defined above—form a special class of variables. Variables like income, life expectancy, fertility, quality of life, educational level (of people), and environment can be called social indicators. It is evident that these are variables because statistics on them are usually calculated. Social indicators are both variables and statistics. Before continuing, it is necessary to mention that Bauer (1966) did the pioneering work on social indicators. Unfortunately, it is difficult to define "social indicators," and no formal attempt will be made here to do so. The article by Jaeger (1978) documents the difficulties in defining social indicators. Readers should know, however, that the idea of social indicators is important and is likely to become increasingly important in the future. Their use is expanding into all fields and will eventually be systematically studied from a scientific viewpoint, as well as from a "public" and social viewpoint.

In this book we are interested in social indicators as a class of sociological and psychological variables that in the future may be useful in developing and testing scientific theories of the relations among social and psychological phenomena. Certain social indicators are now used in so-called causal modeling studies of educational and occupational achievement. Duncan, Featherman, and Duncan (1972) use social class, parents' occupation, and earnings, to name a few. Psychological indicators, such as perceived quality of life, or "happiness," have also been used. An example of this can be found in Campbell, Converse, and Rodgers (1976). In general, however, there appears to have been little systematic methodological work done to categorize and study social indicators, their relations to each other, and their relations to other variables. Most of the work can be called demographic and narrowly pragmatic—in essence, descriptive. Nevertheless, the field, after problems of reliability and validity are addressed and perhaps solved, is richly promising. It should offer behavioral scientists more than such statistics as "51.2% of the population was female in 1996, or 54% of the population over age 18 had 9–12 years of education." Among some of the more promising studies are the ones by researchers Vickie Mays and Susan Cochran concerning risks of sexual practices. In one study by Cochran, DeLeeuw, and Mays (1995), the researchers used two statistical methods—homogeneity analysis and latent class analysis—to provide an optimal scaling of sexual behavior patterns. The use of these methods effectively reduces multiple indicators into a single score that can then be used as an outcome variable in human immunodeficiency virus (HIV)-related research. With such research, we can continue to look forward to factor analytical studies of indicators, analysis of covariance studies in which indicators are variables of the analyzed structures. We also look forward to an increasing general use of the idea of indicators in social and psychological research. One can easily see this in educational research where the achievement of children appears to be affected in complex ways by different kinds of variables, some of which are of the social indicator genre. One of the virtues of the social indicator movement is that these influences on achievement will be more consciously and systematically used in studying and testing theories of achievement.

The Interpretation of Research Data

Scientists, when evaluating research, can disagree on two broad fronts: data and the interpretation of data. Disagreements on data focus on problems such as the validity and reliability of measurement instruments, and the adequacy and inadequacy of research design, methods of observation, and analysis. Assuming competence, however, major disagreements ordinarily focus on the interpretation of data. Most psychologists, for example, will agree on the data of reinforcement experiments, but disagree vigorously on the interpretation of the data from the experiments. Such disagreements are in part a function of theory. In a book like this we cannot belabor interpretation from theoretical standpoints. We must content ourselves with a more limited objective: the clarification of some common precepts of the interpretation of data *within* a particular research study or series of studies.

Adequacy of Research Design, Methodology, Measurement, and Analysis

One of the major themes of this book is the appropriateness of methodology to the problem under investigation. The researcher usually has a choice of research designs, methods of observation, methods of measurement, and types of analysis. All of these must be congruent; they must fit together. One does not use, for example, an analysis appropriate to frequencies with, say, the continuous measures yielded by an attitude scale. Most important, the design, methods of observation, measurement, and statistical analysis must all be appropriate to the research problem.

Investigators must scrutinize the technical adequacy of methods, measurements, and statistics carefully. The adequacy of data interpretation depends on such scrutiny. A frequent source of interpretative weakness, for example, is neglect of measurement problems. It is urgently necessary to pay particular attention to the reliability and validity of the measures of variables, as we will see in later chapters. Even the best research organizations and individuals sometimes falter. For many years, for example, the measurement in sociology and psychology of the social attitudes commonly called "liberalism" and "conservatism" has been in question. For one thing, it has been assumed—even in the face of contrary evidence—that liberalism and conservatism form a single continuum. For another, social attitudes have been measured with far too few items. Even some highly respected and competent organizations, institutions, and individuals have made errors (Barber, 1976). It is not a grievous sin so to err. The real sin is in drawing sweeping conclusions as to the characteristics of people on the basis of measurements with questionable reliability and validity (see Dawes, 1994).

Simply to accept without question the reliability and validity of the measurements of variables, then, is a gross error. Researchers must be especially careful to question the validity of their measurements, since the whole interpretative framework can collapse on this one point alone. If a psychologist's problem includes the variable anxiety, for instance, and the statistical analysis shows a positive relation between anxiety and achievement, the investigator must ask himself or herself and the data whether the anxiety measured (or manipulated) is the type of anxiety germane to the problem. The researcher may, for example, have measured test anxiety when the problem variable was really general anxiety. Similarly, one must ask whether the chosen measure of achievement is valid for the research purpose. If the research problem demands application of principles but the measure of achievement is a standardized test that emphasizes factual knowledge, the interpretation of the data can be erroneous.

In other words, we face here the obvious, but too easily overlooked fact that adequacy of interpretation is dependent upon each link in the methodological chain, as well as on the appropriateness of each link to the research problem and the congruence of the links to each other. This is clearly seen when faced with negative or inconclusive results.

Negative and Inconclusive Results

Negative or inconclusive results are much harder to interpret than positive results. When results are positive, when the data support the hypotheses, one interprets the data along the lines of the theory and the reasoning behind the hypotheses. Although one carefully asks critical questions, upheld predictions are evidence for the validity of the reasoning behind the problem statement.

This is one of the great virtues of scientific prediction. When we predict something and plan and execute a scheme for testing the prediction, and things turn out as we said they would, then the adequacy of our reasoning and our execution seems supported. We are never completely sure, of course. The outcome, though predicted, may be as it is for reasons quite different from than those we fondly espouse. Still, the fact that the whole complex chain of theory, deduction from theory, design, methodology, measurement, and analysis has led to a predicted outcome is cogent evidence for the adequacy of the whole structure. We make a complex bet with the odds against us, so to speak. We then throw the research dice or spin the research wheel. If our predicted number comes up, the reasoning and the execution leading to the successful prediction would appear to be adequate. If we can repeat the feat, then the evidence of adequacy is even more convincing.

But now take the negative case. Why were the results negative? Why did the results not come out as predicted? Note that any weak link in a research chain can cause negative results. These can be due to any one, or several, or all of the following: incorrect theory and hypotheses, inappropriate or incorrect methodology, inadequate or poor measurement, and faulty analysis. Barber (1976) says that it could even be the result of incorrect wording. All must be carefully examined, scrutinized, and the negative results laid at the door of one, several, or all. If we can be fairly sure that the methodology, the measurement, and the analysis are adequate, then negative results can be definite contributions to scientific advancement. It is with such results that we have some confidence that our hypotheses are not correct.

Unhypothesized Relations and Unanticipated Findings

The testing of hypothesized relations is strongly emphasized in this book. This does not mean, however, that other relations in the data are not sought and tested. Quite the contrary. Practicing researchers are always keen to seek out and study relations in their data. The unpredicted relation may be an important key to a deeper understanding of the theory. It may throw light on aspects of the problem not anticipated when the problem was formulated. Therefore, researchers—while emphasizing hypothesized relations—should always be alert to unanticipated relations in their data.

Suppose we hypothesize that a homogeneous grouping of pupils will be beneficial to bright pupils but not beneficial to pupils of lesser ability. The hypothesis is upheld, say. But we note an apparent difference between suburban and rural areas. The relation seems stronger in the suburban areas and is reversed in some rural areas! We analyze the data using the suburban–rural variable. We find that homogeneous grouping seems to have a marked influence on bright children in the suburbs, but that it has little or no influence in rural areas. This would indeed be an important finding.

One of the strongest and best-supported of findings in modern psychology has been that positive reinforcement strengthens response tendencies (see Hergenhahn, 1996). For example, it has been believed that to enhance the learning of children their correct responses to problems should be positively reinforced. Unexpectedly, however, it has also been found that external motivation sometimes has deleterious effects. The work of Lepper, Greene, and Nisbett (1973) found that extrinsic positive reinforcement undermined children's intrinsic interest in a drawing activity, a result certainly not predictable from reinforcement theory.[6]

Unpredicted and unexpected findings must be treated with more suspicion than predicted and expected findings. Before being accepted, they should be substantiated in independent research in which they are specifically predicted and tested. Only when a relation is deliberately and systematically tested with the necessary controls built into the design can we have much faith in it. The unanticipated finding may be fortuitous or spurious.

Tukey (1977) developed methods for investigating one's data. The use of these methods is called *exploratory data analysis.* Tukey as well as Hoaglin, Mosteller, and Tukey (1985) have presented a number of easy-to-construct diagrams that summarize and describe the data. These diagrams can provide useful information to the researcher for further consideration. One of the more popular is the *stem-and-leaf diagram.* This diagram is similar to the histogram but has the advantage of not losing the original data. The stem-and-leaf method works best when the sample size is less than 100. The principle behind the stem-and-leaf method is that a stem and a leaf is used to represent each score or value. The stem is placed to the left of the vertical line and the leaf to the right of the vertical line.

Let's take, for example, the data presented in Table 9.1. The leaf for each score is the last digit and the stem is the remaining digits of a number. For example the number 81 from Table 9.1 would look like the following.

Stem	Leaf
8	1

Figure 9.7 shows what happens when we put it all together to form the final stem-and-leaf diagram. With this diagram we can get a good idea of what the

---

[6]Lepper et al.'s work as well as others on the intrinsic and extrinsic motivation is reviewed in Cameron and Pierce (1994, 1996).

◉ **TABLE 9.1** *Fictitious Data Used to Demonstrate the Stem-and-Leaf Method*
(N = 46)

81	54	91	74	88	78	90	77	88	90	69	94	74	76	96	50	93	93	70	77	58	60	75
53	81	73	66	86	81	64	77	56	71	71	56	53	83	85	70	71	76	80	87	62	57	73

distribution looks like. It gives a more detailed description of the data than do ordinary frequency distributions or histograms. The development of such methods can help researchers generate hypotheses to be tested.

Proof, Probability, and Interpretation

The interpretation of research data culminates in conditional probabilistic statements of the "If *p*, then *q*" kind. We enrich such statements by qualifying them in some such way as: If *p*, then *q*, under conditions *r*, *s*, and *t*. Ordinarily we eschew causal statements, because we are aware that they cannot be made without grave risk of error.

Perhaps of greater practical importance to the researcher interpreting data is the problem of proof. Let us flatly assert that nothing can be "proved" scientifically. All one can do is to bring evidence to bear that such-and-such a proposition is true. Proof is a deductive matter. Experimental methods of inquiry are not methods of proof, they are controlled methods of bringing evidence to bear on the probable truth or falsity of relational propositions. In short, no single scientific investigation ever proves anything. Thus the interpretation of the analysis of research data should never use the word *proof*.

Fortunately, for practical research purposes, it is not necessary to worry excessively about causality and proof. Evidence at satisfactory levels of probability is sufficient for scientific progress. Causality and proof were discussed in this chapter to sensitize the reader to the danger of loose usage of the terms. The understanding of

◉ **FIGURE 9.7**

Stem	Leaf
5	0 3 3 4 6 6 7 8
6	0 2 4 6 9
7	0 0 1 1 1 3 3 4 4 5 6 6 7 7 7 8
8	0 1 1 1 3 5 6 7 8 8
9	0 0 1 3 3 4 6

scientific reasoning, and practice and reasonable care in the interpretation of research data, while no guarantees of the validity of one's interpretations, are helpful guards against inadequate inference from data to conclusions.

CHAPTER SUMMARY

1. Analysis is the process of categorizing, ordering, manipulating, and summarizing data in order to answer research questions.
2. Purpose of analysis is to reduce data to interpretative form so that relations can be studied and tested.
3. Interpretation takes the results of analysis and makes inferences and discusses relations.
4. Data comes in the form of frequencies and continuous measures.
5. Categorization or partitioning is the first step of any analysis.
6. Kinds of statistical analyses:
   a. graphs
   b. measures of central tendency and variability
   c. measures of relations
   d. analysis of differences
   e. analysis of variance
   f. profile and multivariate analyses
7. Indices are used to simplify comparisons. Examples of indices are percentages, quotients, and ratios.
8. Data and interpretation of data are two areas where scientists disagree.
9. When interpreting research data, one needs to consider the technical adequacy of the research methodology, measurement process, and the statistics used.
10. Negative or inconclusive results are much harder to interpret than positive results.
11. In conducting a research study, unhypothesized relations and unanticipated findings may emerge.
12. Unpredicted and unexpected findings must be treated with more suspicion than predicted and expected findings.

STUDY SUGGESTIONS

1. Suppose you wish to study the relation between social class and test anxiety. What are the two main possibilities for analyzing the data (omitting the possibility of calculating a coefficient of correlation)? Set up two analytic structures.
2. Assume that you want to add sex as a variable to the problem above. Set up the two kinds of analytic paradigms.

3. Suppose an investigator has tested the effects of three methods of teaching reading on reading achievement. He had 30 subjects in each group and a reading achievement score for each subject. He also included gender as an independent variable: half the subjects were male and half were female. What does his analytic paradigm look like? What goes into the cells?

4. Study Figure 9.3. Do these analysis of variance designs or paradigms represent partitioning of variables? Why or why not? Why is partitioning important in setting up research designs and in analyzing data? Do the rules of categorization (and partitioning) have any effect on the interpretation of data? If so, what effects might they have? (Consider the effects of violations of the two basic partitioning rules.)

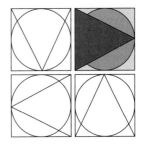

CHAPTER 10

THE ANALYSIS OF FREQUENCIES

- ■ DATA AND VARIABLE TERMINOLOGY
- ■ CROSSTABS: DEFINITIONS AND PURPOSE
- ■ SIMPLE CROSSTABS AND RULES FOR CROSSTAB CONSTRUCTION
- ■ CALCULATION OF PERCENTAGES
- ■ STATISTICAL SIGNIFICANCE AND THE χ^2 TEST
- ■ LEVELS OF STATISTICAL SIGNIFICANCE
- ■ TYPES OF CROSSTABS AND TABLES
    - One-Dimensional Tables
    - Two-Dimensional Tables
    - Two-Dimensional Tables, "True" Dichotomies, and Continuous Measures
    - Three- and k-Dimensional Tables
- ■ SPECIFICATION
- ■ CROSSTABS, RELATIONS, AND ORDERED PAIRS
    - The Odds Ratio
    - Multivariate Analysis of Frequency Data
    - Computer Addendum

So far, we have talked mostly *about* analysis. Now we learn how to *do* analysis. The simplest way to analyze data to study relations is by cross-partitioning frequencies. A cross partition, as we learned in Chapter 4, is a new partitioning of the set U by forming all subsets of the form $A \cap B$. That is, we form subsets of the form $A \cap B$ from the known subsets A and B of U. Examples were given in Chapter 4; more will be given shortly. The expression "cross partition" refers to an abstract process of set theory. Now, however, when the cross partition idea is applied to the analysis of frequencies to study relations between variables, we call the cross partitions *crosstabs*.

◱ **TABLE 10.1**   *Relation between Political Party Affiliation and Budget-Reconciliation Vote, U.S. Senate, 1995*

	Republican	Democrat	
Nay	1	46	47
	2%	100%	
Yea	52	0	52
	98%	0%	
	53	46	99

Source: Data from *Congressional Quarterly* (1996).

They are also sometimes called *crossbreaks*. The kind of analysis to be shown is called *contingency* analysis, or contingency table analysis.

Because we can no longer get along without statistics, we introduce a form of statistical analysis commonly associated with frequencies, the χ^2 (chi-square) test, and the idea of statistical "significance." This study of crosstabs and χ^2 should help ease us into statistics.

The political struggle between Republicans and Democrats is often shown dramatically by votes in the Congress. One of these important recent votes in the U.S. Senate was taken on the Fiscal 1996 Budget-Reconciliation bill. The Republican–Democrat struggle during the winter of 1995 centered on proposals to balance the budget by year 2002: Republicans being generally for these proposals and the Democrats, including President Clinton, being against. One of these proposals was to reduce spending on certain welfare services and reduce taxes. The bill was passed, 52 to 47. This was a defeat for the President. More interesting to us is how the Republican–Democrat vote turned out, which is given in Table 10.1. It is clear from the frequencies (in this case) that there is a strong relation between political party membership and vote on the budget bill: Democrats voted Nay and Republicans Yea.

◱ **TABLE 10.2**   *Vote of the U.S. Senate to Impose Penalties on Physicians Performing Certain Late-Term Abortions, 1995*

	Republican	Democrat	
Yea	45	9	54
	85%	20%	
Nay	8	36	44
	15%	80%	
	53	45	98

Not all frequency crosstabs are this clear. It is common practice, therefore, to calculate percentages. If we do so in a way to be described later, the percentages are those given in the lower right of each cell. We see the strength of the relation between political party membership and vote: 98% of the Republicans voted Yea, and 100% of the Democrats voted Nay.

Studies of similar votes at about the same time show the same general relation. For instance, the vote to impose penalties on physicians who perform certain late-term abortions is given in Table 10.2. The relation is again strong, though not as strong as in the Budget-Reconciliation vote (note the percentages). A "nay" vote on this bill supports the President's position.

Data and Variable Terminology

In Chapter 3 a distinction was made between active and attribute variables, the former meaning an experimental or manipulated variable and the latter a measured variable. The term "attribute" was used because it is general and can cover the properties of an object, animate or inanimate. Unfortunately, however, "attribute" has sometimes been used to mean what have been called categorical variables in this book. In this usage, for example, sex, race, religion, and similar categorical variables have been called attributes. They have also been called "qualitative variables." Both usages seem ill-advised. An attribute is any property of any object, whether the object is measured in an all-or-none way or with a set of continuous measures. We so use it in this book not to upset any conventional usage, if that were possible, but rather to clarify the distinction between experimental and measured variables.

What we have called categorical variables are also called, perhaps more accurately, "nominal variables." This is because they belong to what we will later learn is the level of measurement called "nominal." Since in this and later chapters we have to be quite clear about the difference between continuous and categorical variables, let us briefly anticipate a later discussion and define *measurement*. When the numbers or symbols assigned to objects have no number meaning beyond presence or absence of the property or attribute being measured, that measurement is called "nominal." A variable that is nominal is, of course, what we have been calling "categorical." To name something ("nominal") is to place it into a category ("categorical"). Some categorical data occur naturally like gender (female–male) or eye-color (blue, brown, grey, hazel). Other categorical data are created by categorizing data measured on a continuous scale.

All this is perhaps clarified by the following set equation, which is a general definition of measurement:

$$f = \{(x, y): x = \text{any object, and } y = \text{any numeral}\}$$

which is read: f is a rule of correspondence that is defined as a set of ordered pairs, (x, y), such that x is some object and y is some numeral assigned to x. This is a general definition that covers all cases of measurement. Obviously, y can be a set of continuous measures or simply the set $\{0, 1\}$. Categorical or nominal variables are those variables where $y = \{0, 1\}$, 0 and 1 being assigned on the basis of the object x either possessing or not possessing some defined property or attribute. Continuous variables are those variables where $y = \{0, 1, 2, \ldots, k\}$, or some numerical system where the numbers indicate more or less of the attribute in question. (It is mathematically difficult to define *continuous measures*, and the definition just given is not satisfactory. Nevertheless, the reader will know what is meant.)

The level of measurement of this chapter is mostly nominal. Even when continuous variables are used, they are converted to nominal variables. If this conversion results in categories that can be ordered in terms of "importance," "quantity," or similar hierarchical attributes, these data are called *ordinal*. One category can be thought of as possessing more of some attribute than the other categories. In general, the conversion of continuous data to nominal or ordinal should not be done because it throws away (discards) information (variance). Nevertheless, there are times when, in the judgment of the researcher, it is necessary or desirable to treat a continuous variable as a nominal variable. For example, it may be possible to measure a potentially continuous variable in only a crude way by, say, having an observer judge whether or not objects possess or do not possess an attribute. While there are degrees of aggressive behavior, it may only be possible to say that an individual did or did not exhibit aggressive behavior.

Crosstabs: Definitions and Purpose

A *crosstab* is a numerical tabular presentation of data, usually in frequency or percentage form, in which variables are cross partitioned. A common form of the crossbreak or crosstabulation is cross partitions used to study the relations between the variables. It is a common form of analysis that can be used with almost any kind of data. Its principal use, however, is with categorical or nominal data. Apart from its actual research use, the crosstab is a valuable pedagogical device. Its clarity and simplicity make it an effective tool for learning how to structure research problems and how to analyze data. Crosstabs are cross partitions, as indicated earlier. Therefore the partitioning rules and the set notions already learned can be applied to their analysis easily.

Crosstabs are also used in descriptive ways. The investigator may not be interested in relations. The interest may be only to describe a situation that exists. For instance, take the case where a table breaks social-class membership against possession of TV sets, refrigerators, and so on. This is a descriptive comparison rather than a variable crosstab, even though we might conceivably call possession of a TV set by some variable name. Our concern is exclusively with the analysis of data gathered to test or explore relations.

Crosstabs enable the researcher to determine the nature of the relations between variables, but also have other side purposes: They can be used to organize data in convenient form for statistical analysis. A statistical test is then applied to the data. Indices of association, too, are readily calculated.

Another purpose of crosstabs is to control variables. As we shall see later, crosstabs enable one to study and test a relation between two variables while controlling a third variable. In this way "spurious" relations can be unmasked and the relations between variables can be "specified"—that is, differences in degree of relation at different levels of a control variable can be determined.

Yet another purpose of crosstabs was alluded to above: their study and use sensitize the student and practicing researcher to the design and structure of research problems. There is something salutary about reducing a research problem to a crosstab. In fact, if you cannot write a diagrammatic paradigm of your research problem in either analysis of variance or crosstab form, then the problem is not clear in your mind, or you do not really have a research problem.

Simple Crosstabs and Rules for Crosstab Construction

The simplest form a crosstab can take is a 2-by-2 (or 2 × 2) table. Two examples were given above. A third example is given in Table 10.3. The data are from a study by Payette and Clarizio (1994). This study examined the influence of student characteristics on the misclassification of students as learning disabled (LD) or not. The student characteristics under study were Race, Gender, Intellectual and Achievement, and Grade-Level Status. Each student in the study was classified as eligible or ineligible for LD placement. Under the current guidelines mentioned by Payette and Clarizio, severe discrepancy was defined as underachievement. The tabled data are the number of male and female students who did not show severe discrepancy but were classified as eligible or ineligible. Payette and Clarizio found the number of males and females classified as eligible to be very close. However, females were more likely to be classified as "eligible" than males (.40 versus .21). Although we can get into a discussion about why this difference emerged, our main purpose here is to show how this table was set up.

▣ **TABLE 10.3** *Frequencies of Students Not Showing a Severe Discrepancy Under Current Guidelines by Gender and Eligibility Decision (Payette & Clarizio study)*[a]

	Gender			
Eligibility	Female		Male	
Eligible	17 (.40)		16 (.21)	33
Ineligible	26 (.60)		60 (.79)	86
	43		76	119

[a]The figures in the center of each cell are frequencies. The figures in parentheses of each cell are percentages calculated from Gender to Eligibility, for example, 17/43 = 40, and 60/76 = .79. The latter are written as proportions: multiply by 100 and the proportions become percentages. We follow this convention of writing proportions henceforth.

◉ **FIGURE 10.1**

	B_1	B_2
A_1	A_1B_1	A_1B_2
A_2	A_2B_1	A_2B_2

There appear to be no generally accepted rules on how to set up crosstabs. We know, however, that they are cross partitions and thus must follow the rules of partitioning or categorization discussed earlier. Those rules were (1) categories are set up according to the research hypotheses; (2) categories are independent and mutually exclusive; (3) categories are exhaustive; (4) each category is derived from one and only one classification principle; and (5) all categories are on one level of discourse. In studies where there is a clear-cut distinction between which variable is the independent variable and which is the dependent variable, we will report the levels of the independent variable in columns and the outcome responses of the dependent variable as rows in the contingency table.

A 2×2 crosstab, in variable symbols, is given in Figure 10.1. A_1 and A_2 are the partitions of the variable A; B_1 and B_2 are the partitions of the variable B. The cells A_1B_1, A_1B_2, A_2B_1, A_2B_2 are simply the intersections of the subsets of A and B: A_1B_1, A_1B_2, A_2B_1, A_2B_2. Any object in U, the universe of objects, can be categorized as A_1B_1, A_1B_2, A_2B_1, A_2B_2. If U is a sample of children, and B is Gender and A is Delinquency, then an A_1B_1 member is a delinquent male, whereas an A_2B_2 child is a nondelinquent

◉ **FIGURE 10.2**

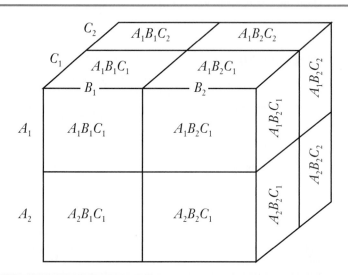

female. In Table 10.3, B would be Gender; A would be Eligibility; A_1 equals Eligibile; A_2 equals Ineligible; B_1 equals female; B_2 equals male. Then A_1B_1 is a female who is eligible for LD, and A_2B_2 is a male who is classified as ineligible. Larger tables $2 \times 3, 2 \times 4, 3 \times 2$, and so on, are merely extensions of this idea.

In the three-variable case, strictly speaking, a cube is necessary. Let there be three dichotomized (for simplicity) variables A, B, C. The actual situation would resemble that shown in Figure 10.2. Each cell is a cube with a triple label. All visible cubes have been properly labeled. If the variables A, B, and C were Sex, Social Class, and Delinquency, respectively, then, for example, an $A_2B_2C_1$, cell member might be a working-class female who is delinquent. Since handling cubes is cumbersome, we use a simpler system. The three-variable crosstab table can resemble that shown in Figure 10.3. We will return to three-variable crosstabs later.

Calculation of Percentages

Percentages are calculated from the independent variable to the dependent variable. In studies where it is not possible to label the variables as independent and dependent, the rule, of course, does not apply; but in most cases it does apply. In Table 10.1 and Table 10.2, the percentages were calculated from Republican and Democrat to Yea and Nay, for example., $51/52 = .98$ and $1/52 = .02$ in Table 10.1, and $9/45 = .20$ and $36/45 = .80$ in Table 10.2. In the three tables above, the convention used was to put independent variables at the top of the table and dependent variables on the side of the table. It could just as well have been the other way around, however. Indeed, when there are more than one independent variable, published contingency tables are frequently printed from the top down. In Figure 10.3, for example, B and C would be the independent variables and A the dependent variable.

Let's return to Table 10.3, the data from the Payette and Clarizio study. Does this table indicate a relation greater than chance expectation between gender and learning disability eligibility? Do the proportions in the four cells of the table depart significantly from the proportions to be expected by chance? If they do, we say that there is a relation between the variables. Suppose a statistical test has been performed and its result indicated a greater than chance departure of the proportions. (We will see how to perform such a test shortly.) We then say that there is a statistically significant relation between Gender and Learning Disability Eligibility.

◉ **FIGURE 10.3**

	B_1		B_2	
	C_1	C_2	C_1	C_2
A_1	$A_1B_1C_1$	$A_1B_1C_2$	$A_1B_2C_1$	$A_1B_2C_2$
A_2	$A_2B_1C_1$	$A_2B_1C_2$	$A_2B_2C_1$	$A_2B_2C_2$

But what is the nature of the relation? This is determined by study of the table, especially the percentages (proportions). The weightiest part of the relation seems to be the Eligible column: 40% of the females are eligible even though they did not show severe discrepancy whereas only 21% of the males were placed here. As a result, fewer females are considered ineligible when compared to males.

Crosstabs with frequencies can sometimes be interpreted without converting them to percentages, but it is usually advisable to convert them following the rule given above: calculate from the independent variable to the dependent variable one column (or row) at a time. To do this, first add the frequencies in the rows and in the columns and enter the resulting sums at the bottom and side of the table. In Table 10.3, these sums have been entered and are called "marginal frequencies," or "marginals." (Actually, to calculate the percentages, only the column sums of Table 10.3 need be calculated. Both row and column sums will be needed later.) In the relations of Table 10.1 and Table 10.2, the independent variable is clearly Political Party Affiliation and the dependent variable is Vote on the Issue. In Table 10.3, the independent variable is Gender and the dependent variable Eligibility. Sometimes, however, determining which variable is which is not so simple. At any rate, in all three tables we calculate the percentages down the columns, or from the independent variable (columns) to the dependent variable (rows).

To be sure we know what we are doing, let's calculate the percentages of Table 10.3. Take the rows separately: the Female row: $17 \div 43 = .40$, and $26 \div 43 = .60$. These are the proportions. Multiplying by 100 (by moving the decimal point two places to the right) yields, of course, 40% and 60%. Now the Male column: $16 \div 76 = .21$, and $60 \div 76 = .79$, or 21% and 79%. (Note that each column must total 1.00, or 100%.) The relation is now clear. The Females are (proportionally) more likely to be classified as eligible than males. Notice how the percentage crosstab highlights the relation, which was not clear in the frequencies because of unequal numbers of Females (43) and Males (76). In other words, the percentage calculation transforms both rows to a common base and enhances the comparison—and the relation.

The reader may suggest two things: (1) Why not calculate the percentages the other way: from the dependent variable to the independent variable? (2) Why not calculate the percentages over the whole table? There is nothing inherently wrong with either of these suggestions. In the first case, however, we would be asking the data a different question. In the second case, we would merely be transforming the frequency data to percentage or proportion data without changing the pattern of the frequencies.

The Payette–Clarizio problem is pointed toward the misclassification of children as eligible or ineligible for learning disability treatment. A hypothesis implied by the problem is: Decisionmakers are biased in their decisions about female children. This is a statement of the "If p, then q" kind: If female, then they are most likely eligible for learning disable considerations. There can be no doubt of the independent and dependent variables. Therefore the calculation of the percentages is determined since we must ask: Given the child is female, what proportion of them will be classified as eligible? The question is answered in the first column of Table 10.3: .40, or 40%. (The second column is, of course, also important in the overall relation.)

If percentages are calculated across the rows, it is tantamount to the hypothesis: If eligible for learning disabilities, then the gender is female. But we are not trying to account for Gender, gender is not the dependent variable. If we went ahead anyway and calculated the percentages, they would be misleading (see Study Suggestion 3). The theoretical rationale for the percentage calculation from the independent variable to the dependent variable is based on the consideration that percentages calculated in this way are conditional probabilities (see Chapter 7), whose correct statements are derived from the research problem. For example, for Table 10.1 we can say: "If Republican, then vote Nay," which is a conditional statement. In set and probability theory language, this is: the probability of B_1, a Nay vote, given A_1, Republican, or:

$$p(B_1|A_1) = \frac{p(A_1 \cap B_1)}{P(A_1)} = \frac{1/99}{53/99} = .02$$

and this is the conditional probability: the probability of B_1, given A_1. It is also the percentage in the A_1B_1 [Republican-Nay] cell of Table 10.1.

Statistical Significance and the χ^2 Test

We must now interrupt our study of crosstabs to learn a little about statistics and thus anticipate the work and study of the next chapter. While it is possible to discuss about crosstabs and how they are constructed without using statistics, it is not really possible to go into the analysis and interpretation of frequency data without using at least some statistics. So we examine one of the simplest and yet most useful of statistical tests, the χ^2 (chi-square) test.

Look at the frequencies of Table 10.3. Do they really express a relation between gender and learning disability eligibility? Or could they have happened by chance? Are they one pattern among many patterns of frequencies that one would get picking numbers from a table of random numbers, such selection being limited only by the given marginal frequencies? Such questions have to be asked of every set of frequency results obtained from samples. Until they are answered, there is little or no point in going further with data interpretation. If our results could have happened by chance, of what use is our effort to interpret them?

What does it mean to say that an obtained result is "statistically significant"— that it departs "significantly" from chance expectation? Suppose that we were to do an actual experiment 100 times (toss a coin 100 times). Each experiment is like a coin toss or a throw of the dice. The outcome of each experiment can be considered a sample point. The sample space, properly conceived, is an infinite number of such experiments or sample points. For convenience, we conceive of the 100 replications of the experiment as the sample space U. This is nothing new. It is what we did with the coins and the dice.

Take a simple example. A university administration is considering the wisdom of changing its marking system, but wants to know faculty attitudes toward the proposed change. The administration has found from past experience, that if most of the faculty do not approve a change, a new system can run into serious trouble. By means of a suitable procedure, 100 faculty members selected at random are questioned to discern their attitudes toward the proposed change. Sixty faculty members approve the change, and 40 disapprove. The administration now has to ask: Is this a "significant" majority? The administration reasons as follows: If the faculty members were completely indifferent, their responses would be like chance—now this way, now that way. The expected frequency on an indifference hypothesis would of course be 50/50, the result to be expected by chance.

To answer the question whether 60/40 differs significantly from indifference or chance, a χ^2 statistical test is performed. A table (Table 10.4) is set up to obtain the necessary terms for the calculation of χ^2. The term f_o represents "frequency obtained" and f_e represents "frequency expected." The function of statistical tests is to compare obtained results with those to be expected on the basis of chance. Here, then, we compare f_o with f_e. On the indifference or chance assumption, we write 50 and 50; but 60 and 40 were obtained. The difference is 10. Could a difference as large as 10 have occurred by chance? Another way to put the question is: If we performed the same experiment 100 times and only chance were operating—that is, the faculty members answered the questions indifferently or, in effect, randomly—how many times in the 100 could we expect to get a deviation as large as 60/40? If we tossed a coin 100 times, we know that sometimes we would get 60 heads and 40 tails and 40 heads and 60 tails. How many times would such a large discrepancy, if it is a large discrepancy, happen by chance? The χ^2 test is a convenient way to get an answer.

We now write a χ^2 formula:

$$\chi^2 = \Sigma \left[\frac{(f_o - f_e)^2}{f_e} \right]$$

which simply says: "Subtract each expected frequency, f_e, from the comparable obtained frequency, f_o, square this difference, divide the difference squared by the

🔲 **TABLE 10.4** *Calculation of χ^2: Faculty Approval and Disapproval of Proposed Change in Marking System*

	Approve	**Disapprove**
f_o	60	40
f_e	50	50
$f_o - f_e$	10	-10
$(f_o - f_e)^2$	100	100
$(f_o - f_e)^2/f_e$	100/50 = 2	100/50 = 2

expected frequency f_e, and then add up these quotients." This was done in Table 10.4. To make sure the reader knows what is happening, we write it out:

$$\chi^2 = \frac{(60 - 50)^2}{50} + \frac{(40 - 50)^2}{50} = \frac{100}{50} + \frac{100}{50} = 4$$

But what does $\chi^2 = 4$ mean? χ^2 is a measure of the departure of obtained frequencies from the frequencies expected by chance. Provided we have some way of knowing what the chance expectations are, and provided the observations are independent, we can always calculate χ^2. The larger the χ^2, the greater the obtained frequencies deviate from the expected chance frequencies. The value of χ^2 ranges from 0, which indicates no departure of obtained from expected frequencies via a large number of increasing values.

In addition to the formula above, it is necessary to know the *degrees of freedom* (*df*) of the problem, and to have a χ^2 table. Chi-square tables are found in almost any statistics text, together with instructions on how to use them. Table 10.5a gives an abbreviated χ^2 table. Explanations of degrees of freedom are also given in statistics textbooks (see Walker, 1951; Graziano & Raulin, 1993). We may say here that "degrees of freedom" defines the latitude of variation contained in a statistical problem. In the problem above, there is one degree of freedom because the total number of cases is fixed, 100, and because as soon as one of the frequencies is given, the other is immediately determined. That is, there are no degrees of freedom when two numbers must sum to 100, and one of them, say 40, is given. Once 40, or 45, or any other number is given, there are no more places to go. The remaining number has no freedom to vary.

■ TABLE 10.5a χ^2 *Distribution Probabilities*

df	.25 level	.10 level	.05 level	.01 level
1	1.32	2.71	3.84	6.63
2	2.77	4.61	5.99	9.21
3	4.11	6.25	7.81	11.3
4	5.39	7.78	9.49	13.3
5	6.63	9.24	11.1	15.1
6	7.84	10.6	12.6	16.8
7	9.04	12.0	14.1	18.5
8	10.2	13.4	15.5	20.1
9	11.4	14.7	16.9	21.7
10	12.5	16.0	18.3	23.2
11	13.7	17.3	19.7	24.7

◙ **TABLE 10.5b** *Frequencies and Corresponding* χ^2 [a]

Frequencies	χ^2
40/60	4.00
41/59	3.24
42/58	2.56
43/57	1.96
44/56	1.44
45/55	1.00
46/54	.64
47/53	.36
48/52	.16
49/51	.04
50/50	0

[a] The values of χ^2 for 51/49, . . . , 60/40 are, of course, the same as those in the table but in reverse order.

To understand more about what is going on here, suppose we calculate all the χ^2s for all possibilities: 40/60, 41/59, 42/58, . . . , 50/50, . . . , 60/40. Doing so, we get the set of values given in Table 10.5b. (When reading the table, it is helpful to conceive of the first frequency of each pair as "Heads," or "Agrees with," or "Male," or any other variable.) Only two of these χ^2s, the values of 4.00 associated with 40/60 and 60/40, are statistically significant. They are statistically significant because by checking the χ^2 table (Table 10.5a) for one degree of freedom we find an entry of 3.84 at what is called the .05 level of significance. All the other χ^2 values in Table 10.5b are less than 3.84. Take, for example, the χ^2 for 42/58, which is 2.56. If we consult the table, 2.56 falls between the values of χ^2 with probabilities of .10 and .25, or 2.71 and 1.32, respectively. This is actually a probability of about .14. In most cases, we do not need to bother finding out where it falls. All we need to do is to note that it does not make the .05 grade of 3.84. If it does not, we say that it is not statistically significant—at the .05 level. The reader may now ask: "What is the .05 level?" and "Why the .05 level?" "Why not .10 or even .15?" To answer these questions, we must digress a little.

Levels of Statistical Significance

The .05 level means that an obtained result that is significant at the .05 level could occur *by chance* no more than five times in 100 trials. With our responses to the administration's question of 60 Agrees and 40 Disagrees, we can say that a discrepancy as large as this *will happen by chance* about five times or less in 100 trials.

A level of statistical significance is to some extent chosen arbitrarily. Some have attributed this choice to Fisher (1950), but it is certainly not completely arbitrary. Another level of significance frequently used is the .01 level. The .05 and .01 levels correspond fairly well to two and three standard deviations from the mean of a normal probability distribution. (A normal probability distribution is the symmetric bell-shaped curve that the student has probably often seen. We discuss this later.)

Think back to the coin-tossing experiment when a coin was tossed 100 times. Heads turned up 52 times and tails 48 times (consult Table 10.5b, $\chi^2 = .16$, a result clearly not significant.) But suppose the coin had been tossed not one set of 100 tosses but 100 sets of 100 tosses, which would be tantamount to 100 experiments. From these 100 experiments we would get a variety of results: $58 \div 42$, $46 \div 54$, $51 \div 49$, and so on. About 95 or 96 of these experiments would yield heads within the bounds of 40 and 60. That is, only four or five of the experiments would yield less than 40 or greater than 60 heads. Similarly, if we perform an experiment and find a difference between two means which, after an appropriate statistical test, is at the .05 level of significance, then we have reason to believe that the obtained mean difference is not merely a chance difference. It *could* be a chance difference, however. If the experiment were done 100 times and there really are no real differences between the means, at most five of these 100 replications might show mean differences large enough to be considered "significant."

While this discussion may help to clarify the meaning of statistical significance, it does not yet answer all the questions asked before. The .05 level was originally chosen—and has persisted with researchers—because it is considered a reasonably good gamble. It is neither too high nor too low for most social scientific research. Many researchers prefer the .01 level of significance. This is quite a high level of certainty; indeed, it is "practical certainty." Some researchers say that the .10 level may sometimes be used. Still others say that 10 chances in 100 are too many, so that they are not willing to risk a decision with such odds. Others say that the .01 level, or 1 chance in 100, is too stringent, that "really" significant results may be discarded in this manner.

Should a certain level of significance be chosen and adhered to? This is a difficult question. The .05 and .01 levels have been advocated widely. There is a newer trend of thinking that advocates reporting the significance levels of all results. That is, if a result is significant at the .12 level, say, it should be reported accordingly. Some practitioners object to this practice. They say that one should make a bet and stick to it. Another school of thought advocates working with what are called "confidence intervals." Many investigators say that the results are not significant if they do not make the .05 or .01 grade. Rozeboom (1960) advocates the use of confidence intervals and the reporting of precise probability values of experimental outcomes. However, Brady (1988) states that such precision is generally meaningless in the social and behavioral sciences because of the inaccuracy of measurements. The basic idea is that, instead of categorically rejecting hypotheses if the .05 grade is not achieved, we say the probability is .95 that the unknown value falls between .30

and .50. Now, if the obtained empirical proportion is, say, .60, then this is evidence for the correctness of the investigator's substantive hypothesis or, in null hypothesis language, the null hypothesis is rejected. A convenient and excellent source of these and similar problems is Kirk (1972). This book by Kirk contains a number of important essays dealing with these issues. Cohen (1994), Simon (1976, 1987), and Simon and Roscoe (1984) have argued against using tests of significance. The issues here are deep and complex and cannot be adequately discussed here.

In this book the statistical "levels" approach will be used because it is simpler. For the student who does not plan to do any research, the matter is not serious. But it is emphasized that those who will engage in research should study other procedures, such as statistical estimation methods, confidence intervals, and exact probability methods. A statistically significant result does not imply personal or practical significance. Babbie (1990) has mentioned four important points concerning why he is against the use of significance tests in social science research. For one, he states that the assumptions underlying statistical tests are generally not met in certain types of social research studies. These assumptions center around the sampling methods used in research. Babbie also feels that there is a tendency for researchers to interpret a statistically significant test as a strength of association or substantive significance.

To illustrate the calculation and use of the χ^2 test with crosstabs, we now apply it to the frequency data of Table 10.1. The formula given previously is used, but with crosstab tables its application is more complicated than its use in Table 10.4. The main difference is the calculation of the expected frequencies. The necessary calcula-

▣ **TABLE 10.6** *Calculation of χ^2, Data of Table 10.1*

25.1616[a]		27.8384	
	1	52	53
	−24.1616[b]	24.1616	
21.8384		24.1616	
	46	0	46
	−24.1616	24.1616	
	47	52	99

[a] $f_e = (53 \times 47)/99 = 25.616$; $(53 \times 52)/99 = 27.8384$; and so on.
[b] $f_o - f_e = 1 - 25.1616 = -24.1616$; and so on.

$$\chi^2 = \Sigma \frac{(f_o - f_e)^2}{f_e}$$

$$= \frac{(1 - 25.1616)^2}{25.1616} + \frac{(52 - 27.8384)^2}{27.8384} + \frac{(46 - 21.8384)^2}{21.8384} + \frac{(0 - 24.1616)^2}{24.1616}$$

$$= 23.2013 + 20.9704 + 26.7319 + 24.1616 = 95.0653$$

tions are given in Table 10.6. The expected frequencies, f_e, are in the upper-left corner of each cell; they are calculated as shown in footnote a of the table. The obtained frequencies, f_o terms, are given in the right center of each cell. The $f_o - f_e$ terms, required by the formula, are given in the lower left corner of the cells. They are the same in all cells, except for sign. This will be true in 2×2 tables. The χ^2 formula simply requires squaring these differences, dividing the squares by the expected frequencies, and summing the results. These calculations are indicated below: $\chi^2 = 95.0653$, at one degree of freedom. (Why one degree of freedom?) Looking up the tabled χ^2 value, one degree of freedom at the .01 level, we read 6.635. Since our value exceeds this substantially, it can be said that χ^2 is statistically significant, the obtained results are probably not chance results, and the relation expressed in the table is a "real" one in the sense that it is probably not due to chance. Note that χ^2 needs a correction if N is small. The approximate rule is that the so-called correction for continuity is used—it consists merely of subtracting .5 from the absolute difference between f_o and f_e in the χ^2 formula *before* squaring—when *expected* frequencies are less than 5 in 2×2 tables. This correction is called the "Yates correction" (see Comrey & Lee, 1995).

χ^2, like other statistics that indicate statistical significance, tells us nothing about the magnitude of the relation. It is a test of the independence of the variables in the sense of independence discussed in Chapter 9. It is not, strictly speaking, a measure of association. One of the oldest problems of statistics is indexing the strength or magnitude of association or relation between categorical variables. Its complexity forbids discussion here. But we give one statistic that is easily applicable and can be used with any size contingency or crosstab table. It is Cramer's V, a measure of association based on the chi-square value. The formula is:

$$V = \sqrt{\frac{\chi^2}{N(k-1)}}$$

The value of k is determined from either the number of rows or the number of columns in the contingency table. Whichever is smaller, the number of rows or the number of columns, is used for the value of k. N is the total frequency. In this case it is 99, since only 99 senators voted. If we substitute the value of χ^2 calculated above and insert it, N, and k in the equation, we obtain:

$$V = \sqrt{\frac{95.0653}{99(1)}} = \sqrt{.9602} = .9799 \approx .98$$

which is an index of the strength of the relation.

Cramer's V is the generalization of the phi-coefficient (ϕ). In 2×2 tables, Cramer's V and (ϕ) phi are identical. Occasionally the coefficient of contingency, C, appears in the literature. The general consensus is that this value C is not as adequate as Cramer's V. For one, it is not really comparable across different sized contingency tables. For another, it can never reach the value of 1.00, which is the value of a perfect association. These same criticisms are not true for Cramer's V or (ϕ) phi. However, as pointed out by Comrey and Lee (1992), these measures of association, especially the phi coefficient are subject to other problems. Hays (1994) is a strong advocate of using measures of association along with tests of significance. Generally speaking, the best advice for handling categorical data is to calculate χ^2 (to determine statistical significance), calculate V, calculate the percentages as outlined earlier, and then interpret the data using all the information.

Types of Crosstabs and Tables

In general there are three types of tables: one-dimensional, two-dimensional, and k-dimensional. The number of variables determines the number of dimensions of a table: a one-dimensional table has one variable, a two-dimensional table has two variables, and so on. It makes no difference how many categories any single variable has; the number of variables always fixes the dimensions of a table. We have already considered the two-dimensional table where two variables—one independent and one dependent—are set against each other. It is often fruitful and necessary to consider more than two variables simultaneously. Theoretically, there is no limit to the number of variables that can be considered at one time. The only limitations are practical ones: insufficient sample size and difficulty of comprehension of the relations contained in a multidimensional table.

One-Dimensional Tables

There are two kinds of one-dimensional tables. One is a "true" one-dimensional table; it is of little interest to us because it does not express a relation. Such tables occur commonly in newspapers, government publications, magazines, and so forth. In reporting the number or proportion of males and females in San Francisco, the number of cars of different makes produced in 1992, the number of children in each of the grades of X school system, we have "true" one-dimensional tables. Only one variable is used in the table.

Social scientists sometimes choose to report their data in tables that look one-dimensional but are really two-dimensional. Consider a table reported by Walker and Andrade (1996). This study sampled school-aged children who participated in a replication of the 1956 Asch conformity study. In the Asch study, the participant was placed in a group of "confederates" of the experimenter who behaved as if they were also participants in the study. The task involved choosing one of three lines that was of the same length as the test line. On the key trial, a confederate purposely chose the incorrect line. The interest was then on whether or not the participant would now conform and choose the same incorrect line when the choice was supported by the other confederates. Table 10.7 shows the percentage of instances in each age group where the participant conformed. (In the original table, only the row of per-

◉ **TABLE 10.7** *Replication of the Asch Conformity Study (Walker & Andrade data)*

	Age Groups (years)				
	3–5	6–8	9–11	12–14	15–17
% conforming	85	42	38	9	0
% not conforming	15	58	62	91	100

centages on the top row was given.) The table looks one dimensional, but really expresses a relation between two variables: Age and Conformity.

The key point is that tables of this kind are not really one-dimensional. In Table 10.7, one of the variables, Conformity, is incompletely expressed. To make this clear, simply add another row of percentages beside those in the original table (this has been done in Table 10.7). This row can be labeled "Not Conforming." Now we have a complete two-dimensional table, and the relation becomes obvious. (Sometimes this cannot be done because data for "completing" the table are missing.)

As another example, consider the data presented in Table 10.8. The data were from a study by Child, Potter, and Levine (1946). In this study, the values expressed in third grade children's textbooks were content analyzed. Table 10.8 shows the percentages of instances in which rewards were given for various modes of acquisition. Like the Walker and Andrade study, only one response level was given. We have added the other response level into Table 10.8. It is the last row and the values are in parentheses.

Two-Dimensional Tables

Two-dimensional tables or crosstabs have two variables, each with two or more subclasses. The simplest form of a two-dimensional table, as we have seen, is called two-by-two, or simply 2 × 2. Two-dimensional tables are by no means limited to the 2 × 2 form. In fact, there is no logical limitation on the number of subclasses that each variable can possess. Let us look at a few examples of $m \times n$ tables.

◉ **TABLE 10.8** *Incomplete Data (presented in the Child, Potter, & Levine study)*

	Effort	Buying, Selling, Trading	Asking Wishing, Taking What Is Offered	Dominance, Aggression, Stealing, Trickery
% in which rewarded	93	80	68	41
(% in which not rewarded)	(7)	(20)	(32)	(59)

🔲 **TABLE 10.9** *Effect of Request Size on Donation Size (Doob & McLaughlin study)*[a]

	Request Size		
	No Specific Amount	**Smaller Request ($5, $10, $25)**	**Larger Request ($50, $100, $250)**
Donation Size			
<$30	52%	36%	44%
$30–$49	19%	38%	8%
$50–$74	21%	16%	29%
$75–$99	1%	1%	4%
$100	7%	8%	12%
>$100	0%	1%	3%

[a]$\chi^2 = 111.3$ $(p < .01)$; $V = .26$.

Doob and McLaughlin (1989) studied the relation between the Donate–Not Donate dimension and request size. Participants in this study were asked to make a monetary donation. The amount of money asked for was manipulated to examine its effect on whether people will donate or not donate. In their article they presented a table relating donation size and request size. They reported the 6 × 3 crosstab of Table 10.9. The results showed that donation size is related to request size. The obtained chi-square value was $\chi^2 = 111.3$, which is highly significant and $V = .26$, a medium relation. (The authors did not calculate a measure of association.) We see here a simple but effective method of testing the hypothesis and analyzing the data. The researchers found that larger requests were more effective. This study is also noteworthy in that it juxtaposes a continuous variable (donation amount) with an ordinal variable (amount requested). This table also illustrates a point that seems to confuse students; namely, that the *m* and *n* numbers of an *m* × *n* crosstab tell the number of subclasses or subcategories, and not the number of variables (*m* represents the number of categories of the first variable, and *n* the number of categories of the second variable).

Another example of a two-dimensional table that affords interesting data to study, is from Stouffer's (1955) classic study[1] on conformity and tolerance. Stouffer

---

[1]This book contains exhaustive crosstab analyses. It can almost be considered a text and model of how to analyze relations via crosstabs. Stouffer's untiring specifications of his data are especially valuable. For example, see Chapter 4 where Stouffer juxtaposes age, education, tolerance, and other variables.

▣ TABLE 10.10 *Relation between Education and Tolerance (Stouffer study)*

| Percentage of Distribution of Scores on Scale of Tolerance | Education | | | | |
	College Graduates	Some College	High School Graduates	Some High School	Grade School
Less tolerant	5	9	12	17	22
In between	29	38	46	54	62
More tolerant	66	53	42	29	16
N	308	319	768	576	792

studied the relation between tolerance, on the one hand, and several other sociological variables, on the other hand. One of the latter was Education. Stouffer sought an answer to the question: What is the relation between the amount of education and degree of tolerance? The crosstab given in Table 10.10 is instructive. A study of the table shows that a relation between the two variables exists: evidently the more education, the more tolerance.

Let's look briefly at a similar analysis of a different kind of research problem. Shaw, Borough, and Fink (1994) studied the relation between perceived sexual orientation and helping behavior. These researchers essentially asked: Is there a relation between receiving help and the sexual orientation of the person requesting help? Using the "wrong number technique" the researchers obtained a nonreactive measure of homophobia. Table 10.11 presents a partial finding. The main numbers in the cells are frequencies. Percentages (proportions) are given in the parentheses. It is evident from the percentages that people are more likely to help a person who is heterosexual than one who is homosexual. The χ^2 was 18.34 and was statistically significant at the $\alpha = .01$ level. Cramer's $V = .48$. However, it is interesting to note

▣ TABLE 10.11 *Relation between Perceived Sexual Orientation and Sex of Respondent (Shaw, Borough, & Fink study)*

| | Orientation of Caller | | Total Response |
	Heterosexual	Homosexual	
Help	32(80)	13(33)	45
No help	8(20)	27(67)	35
Total	40	40	80

that there is no significant relation between sex of the respondent and the perceived sexual orientation of the requester. The χ^2 was 0.33.

Two-Dimensional Tables, "True" Dichotomies, and Continuous Measures

Many two-dimensional tables report "true" nominal data, data of variables that are truly dichotomous: sex, alive–dead, and the like. Yet many such tables have one or both variables presumably continuous and artificially dichotomized or trichotomized. In their study of the self-esteem of African American children in the Baltimore public schools, Rosenberg and Simmons (1971) showed that African American self-esteem was not, as thought, lower than white American self-esteem. The independent variable, Race, is at the top of the table, and the dependent variable, Self-esteem, at the side. (Thus, the percentages are calculated down the columns.) Note, too, that a continuous variable, Self-esteem, has been converted into an ordinal variable.

Three- and *k*-Dimensional Tables

It is theoretically possible to crosstab any number of variables, but in practice the limit is three or four, more often three. The reasons for such limitation are obvious: very large *N*s are required and, more important, the interpretation of data becomes considerably more difficult. Another point to bear in mind is: Never use a complex analysis when a simpler one will accomplish the analytic job. Still, three- and four-dimensional tables can be useful and can supply indispensable information.

The analysis of three or more variables simultaneously has two main purposes. First, is to study the relations among three or more variables. Take a three-dimensional example, and call the variables *A*, *B*, and *C*. We can study the following relations: between *A* and *B*, between *A* and *C*, between *B* and *C*, and between *A*, *B*,

▣ **TABLE 10.12** *Relation of Self-esteem and Race, Baltimore Schoolchildren (Rosenberg & Simmons study)*

Self-esteem	Race	
	African American (%)	White American (%)
Low	19	37
Medium	35	30
High	46	33
	100	100
N	1213	682

and *C*. The second purpose is to control one variable while studying the relation between the other two variables. For instance, we can study the relation between *B* and *C* while controlling *A*. An important use of this notion is to help detect spurious relations. Another use is to "specify" a relation, to tell us when or under which conditions a relation is more or less pronounced.

Specification

Specification is a process of describing the conditions under which a relation does or does not exist, or exists to a greater or a lesser extent. An example will help to clarify this statement. We also take this opportunity to introduce *k*-dimensional contingency tables and multivariate analysis of frequency data.

Suppose you are an investigator interested in the hypothesis that Level of Aspiration is positively related to Success in College. Specifically, the hypothesis is that the higher the level of aspiration, the greater the probability of graduating. Suppose, further, that you had a relatively crude dichotomous measure of level of aspiration and measure of success in college. This measure would be whether the student graduated or not. The variables and categories, then, are Hi LA (high level of aspiration), Lo LA (low level of aspiration), SC (success in college), and NSC (not successful in college). Let's say you drew a random sample of 400 sophomores from a college and obtained level of aspiration measures from them. The 400 students are divided into halves on the basis of the level-of-aspiration measures. At the end of three years you categorized the students on the basis of having graduated or not. Suppose the results were those shown in Table 10.13.[2] There is evidently a relation between the variables: $\chi^2 = 64$, significant at the .001 level, and $V = .40$.

You show the results to a male colleague, a rather sour individual, who says they are questionable, that if social class were brought into the picture the relation might be quite different. He reasons that social class and level of aspiration are strongly

▣ **TABLE 10.13** *Relation between Level of Aspiration and School Achievement, Hypothetical Data*

	Hi LA	Lo LA	
SC	140	60	200
NSC	60	140	200
	200	200	(400)

---

[2] The marginal totals of Table 10.13 (and those of Table 10.14) have been made equal to simplify the discussion and to highlight certain points to be made here and later. This is of course unrealistic: frequency tables are rarely this obliging.

related, and that the original relation might hold for middle-class students, but not for working-class students. Fortunately, when you go back and review the collected data, you notice that you do have indices of social class for all the subjects. The results of using the three variable crosstab are shown in Table 10.14. Inspection of the data shows that the your colleague was correct. The relation between level of aspiration and success in college is considerably more pronounced in middle-class (MC) students than in working-class (WC) students.

The investigator can study the relations in more depth by calculating percentages separately for the middle-class and working-class sides of Table 10.14. In this case, since the frequencies in each row of the halves of the table total to 100, the frequencies are, in effect, percentages. It can be seen that the relation between level of aspiration and college success is stronger with middle-class students than it is with working-class students.

In the above analysis, the data were specified: it was shown, by introducing the social-class variable, that the relation between level of aspiration and success in college was stronger in one group (middle class) than in another group (working class). This is similar to the phenomenon of interaction discussed in Chapter 9, where we stated that interaction infers that an independent variable affects a dependent variable differently at different levels or facets of another independent variable. Strictly speaking, "interaction" is a term used in experimental research and analysis of variance, as we shall see in subsequent chapters. There is some question, therefore, whether the term can be applied in nonexperimental research and in the kind of analyses we are now examining. The position taken in this book is that interaction is a general phenomenon of great importance occuring in both experimental and nonexperimental research. The "validity" of interaction in nonexperimental research, however, is much harder to establish than in experimental research. Indeed, this is true of the "validity" of all relations in nonexperimental research, as we will see clearly detailed in Chapter 22 and Chapter 23. In sum, the specified relations of Table 10.13 can be viewed as interaction or simply as specification of relations. The main thing, of course, is that we understand what is going on: Relations are stronger, weaker, or even zero at differing levels of other independent variables. In the above

■ TABLE 10.14 *Relations among Level of Aspiration, Social Class, and School Achievement, Hypothetical Data*

| | MC | | WC | | |
	Hi LA	Lo LA	Hi LA	Lo LA	
SC	80	20	60	40	200
NSC	20	80	40	60	200
	100	100	100	100	(400)
		(200)		(200)	

example, the relation between level of aspiration and college success is different in the two social classes. With such multivariate statements, we are getting closer to the heart and spirit of scientific investigation, analysis, and interpretation.

Crosstabs, Relations, and Ordered Pairs

A relation is a set of ordered pairs. Two of the ways in which we can express a set of ordered pairs are (1) by listing the pairs, and (2) by graphing them. A coefficient of correlation is an index that expresses the magnitude of a relation. A crosstab expresses the ordered pairs in a table of frequencies.

To show how these ideas are related, take the fictitious data of Table 10.15. The relation studied is between state control of the economic system and political democracy. In a study of political democracy in modern countries, Bollen (1979) hypothesized that the greater the control of the economic system of a country, the lower its level of political democracy. Suppose that of a sample of 23 countries, we count 12 countries with low economic control (Low EC), and 11 countries with high economic control (High EC). We also count 13 countries with high political development (High PD) and 10 countries with low political development (Low PD). This gives us the marginal totals of a 2 × 2 crosstab. It does not tell us how many countries are in each of the cells, however.

We now count the number of Low EC countries that have High PD and the number of High EC countries that have Low PD. These counts are entered in the appropriate cells of the 2 × 2 crosstab of Table 10.15. We find that the cell frequencies depart significantly from chance expectation. There is thus a significant relation between state economic control and political development.

For 2 × 2 tables where the expected frequencies are small (<10), one should use the exact test of significance developed by Fisher (1950). Other alternatives would be to use Yates correction on a χ^2 test, or to use Finney's Tables (see Pearson & Hartley, 1954; Ferguson, 1971; Comrey & Lee, 1995).

So that we can see the ordered pairs clearly, let's change the variable notation. Let B_1 equal Low EC, B_2 equal High EC, A_1 equal Low PD, and A_2 equal High PD.

▣ **TABLE 10.15** *Relation between State Control of Economic System and Political Development, Fictitious Data*

	B_1 Low EC		B_2 High EC		
A_1 Low PD	(0, 0)	2	(0, 1)	8	10
A_2 High PD	(1, 0)	10	(1, 1)	3	13
	12		11		

◉ TABLE 10.16 *Ordered Pair Arrangement of the Data from Table 10.15*

Countries	A	B	Crosstab Intersections
1	1	0	
2	1	0	
3	1	0	
4	1	0	
5	1	0	A_2B_1
6	1	0	
7	1	0	
8	1	0	
9	1	0	
10	1	0	
11	1	1	
12	1	1	A_2B_2
13	1	1	
14	0	0	A_1B_1
15	0	0	
16	0	1	
17	0	1	
18	0	1	
19	0	1	A_1B_2
20	0	1	
21	0	1	
22	0	1	
23	0	1	

The *A* and *B* labels have been appropriately inserted in Table 10.15. Now, how do we set up the ordered pairs of the crosstab? We do so by assigning each of the 23 countries one of the following subset combinations: (1, 1), (0, 1), (1, 0), (0, 0) (see the designations in Table 10.15). In other words, A_1 and B_1 are assigned 0s, and A_2 and B_2 are assigned 1s. If a country has Low EC and High PD, then it is A_2B_1; consequently, the ordered pair assigned to it is (1, 0). The first 10 countries of Table 10.16 belong to the A_2B_1 category and are thus assigned (1, 0). Similarly, the remaining countries are assigned ordered pairs of numbers according to their subset membership. The full list of 23 ordered pairs is given in Table 10.16. The categories or crosstab (set) intersections have been indicated.

◫ FIGURE 10.4

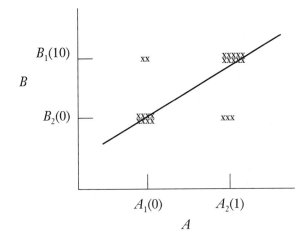

The relation is the set of ordered pairs of 1s and 0s. Table 10.16 is merely a different way of expressing the same relation shown in Table 10.15. We can calculate a coefficient of correlation for both tables. If, for example, we calculate a coefficient of correlation, a product-moment r of the Table 10.16 data, we obtain .56. (The product-moment r calculated with 1s and 0s is called a phi (ϕ) coefficient.)

Graph the relation. Let there be two axes, A and B, at right angles to each other, and let A and B represent the two variables contained in Table 10.15 and Table 10.16. We are interested in studying the relation between A and B. Figure 10.4 shows the graphed ordered pairs, and also shows a "relation" line running through the larger clusters of pairs. We ask: Where is the relation? Is there a set of ordered pairs that defines a significant relation between A and B? We have *paired* each country's score on A with that country's "score" on B and plotted the pairs on the A and B axes. Going back to the substance of the relation, we pair each individual country's "score" on economic control with its "score" on political development. In this manner we obtain a set of ordered pairs and this set is a relation. Our real question, however, is not: Is there a relation between A and B? but rather: What is the nature of the relation between A and B?

We can see from Figure 10.4 that the relation between A and B is fairly strong. This is determined by the ordered pairs: the pairs are mostly (A_1B_2) and (A_1B_2). There are comparatively few (A_1B_1) and (A_2B_2) pairs. Explicating in words, Low EC scores pair with High PD scores (1); and High EC scores pair with Low PD (0); with comparatively few exceptions (five cases out of 23). We cannot name this relation succinctly, as we can relations such as "marriage," "brotherhood," and the like. We might, however, call it "state economic control–political development," meaning that there is a relation of these variables in the ordered pair sense.

The Odds Ratio

A highly useful statistic that can be computed from 2×2 contingency tables is the odds ratio. This statistic is one of those that is difficult to define verbally, but easy to illustrate. By definition, it is the ratio of two odds. Odds are computed as the ratio of the probability that the event will occur to the probability that it will not occur. For example, take a deck of 52 playing cards; if we wanted to know the probability of drawing a queen, we would form the ratio

$$Prob(Queen) = \frac{4}{52} = \frac{1}{13} = 0.077$$

The probability of not drawing a queen is

$$Prob(Not\ Queen) = \frac{48}{52} = \frac{12}{13} = 0.923$$

The odds ratio of drawing a queen would be

$$Odds(Queen) = \frac{4/52}{48/52} = \frac{1}{12} = 0.083$$

If we use the data presented in Table 10.13, we can see how the odds ratio works and why it is useful in many situations. To remain consistent with the example above, we change the frequencies to probabilities or proportions. The table below reflects this.

	HiLA	LoLA
SC	.7	.3
NSC	.3	.7

The odds of success if the student is in the High Level of Aspiration group is

$$Odds(Success \mid High) = \frac{.7}{.3} = 2.33$$

This tells us that students in the high aspiration level group are 2.33 times more likely to be successful in college. The odds of success if the student is in the Low Level of Aspirations group is

$$\text{Odds}(Success \mid Low) = \frac{.3}{.7} \approx .43$$

One would interpret this as being a less than half a chance that a student in the low aspiration group will succeed in college. If we form the ratio between these two odds, we arrive at the odds ratio.

$$Odds\ Ratio = \frac{2.333}{0.429} = 5.444$$

The odds ratio tells us that students in the high aspirations group are 5.444 times more likely than the low aspiration group to succeed in college.

The odds ratio gives useful information. It helps in trying to explain what has happened. The Chi-square statistic is still the preferred method; however, it is unable to give the type of information that odds ratios can give. The concept behind the odds ratio is somewhat more difficult for students. However, learning about this statistic is important when dealing with categorical data. It is especially useful when one is considering multiway contingency tables or analyses using the logistic function. We will see more of this statistic when we get to Chapter 35. At that time we will also see a different Chi-square statistic. Howell (1997) presents an interesting example concerning the effectiveness of aspirin in lowering incidence of heart attack. The individual odds were very small; however, the odds ratio was quite large. A person in the no aspirin group is 1.83 times more likely to have a heart attack than the person who takes a low dosage of aspirin.

Multivariate Analysis of Frequency Data

Most of the above discussion was limited to two variables: an independent variable and a dependent variable. Many frequency data analyses, however, are of three and more variables. A fictitious example with three variables was given earlier in Table 10.14. While most three-variable cases can be analyzed and interpreted using percentages, study data with four or more variables are not so amenable to analysis and interpretation. Another approach is needed. Even with three variables another approach is often needed because the data are too complex and subtle for simple interpretation. With a two-variable crosstab there is only one relation: between *A* and *B*. With three variables, however, there are four relations of possible interest: *AB*, *AC*, *BC*, and *ABC*. The three two-variable crosstabs are the kind we have been studying. The one three-variable crosstab, *ABC*, is like that shown in Table 10.14, and in this case can be viewed most fruitfully as follows. Study of the relation between Level of Aspiration and Success in College in two samples: middle class and working class. That is, we study whether the relation between Level of Aspiration and College Success is the same in the middle class as it is in the working class. If it is the same, we have "established" an *invariance*. If it is different, however, we have an *interaction*: the relation is such-and-such in the middle class, but it is so-and-so in the working class.

Since the early 1970s remarkable changes in conceptualization of research problems and in data analysis have taken place. Some of the noted works that have contributed to the area of multi-way contingency tables with frequency data are Grizzle, Starmer, and Koch (1969); Bishop, Fienberg, and Holland (1976); Goodman (1971) and Clogg (1979). Before the development of multivariate analysis of both continuous measures and frequencies, analysis—and the conceptualization of analysis—was mostly bivariate. Investigators studied the relations between pairs of variables, as we have pretty much done in this chapter. While the idea of studying the operation of several variables simultaneously was well-known, the practical means of doing so had to wait for both the computer and a different way of thinking. Later in this book we will examine the nature of the computer and its important role in research. We will also give a more complete description on the multivariate analysis of frequency data. In the previous edition of this book, a brief discussion was introduced in this chapter concerning log-linear models for multiway frequency/contingency tables. Since that time the field has expanded enough to warrant a larger section, and will be presented in the chapters dealing with multivariate statistics.

Computer Addendum

Two-dimensional crosstabs can be performed using the SPSS computer program. There are two different setups that the user should be aware of. The first involves a dataset of raw values. An example of such a set of raw values is given in Table 10.16. With the raw data, we will need to instruct SPSS to process the data by first creating a contingency table followed by the analysis. The second setup is used when the researcher has already constructed the contingency table and needs only to obtain the statistical analysis for that table. Such a table is shown in Table 10.14 and Table 10.15.

To illustrate the first setup we will use the data given in Table 10.16. We will assume that the reader has read the computer addendum in Chapter 6 and knows how to navigate SPSS for Windows program. This would include knowing how to define the variables and how to enter the data into SPSS's data spreadsheet. Figure 10.5 shows the SPSS screen after the data have been entered and the proper statistical analysis is about to be selected. Note that Table 10.16 has 23 observations, but in Figure 10.5 we show only the first 14 cases due to space constraints. Also note the similarities between Table 10.16 and Figure 10.5 in terms of the data layout.

Next, select "Statistics" by clicking it, then from the next menu select "Crosstabs," arriving at the screen shown in Figure 10.6. This screen allows you to select which variable will be the row (dependent) variable in the contingency table and which will serve as the column (independent) variable. You will also need to click the "Statistics" button so that you can select the statistics you want to display in your output. To select the row variable, highlight the "a" variable in the left-most box and click the top arrow. This will effectively move the variable "a" to the "Row(s)" box. Next, highlight the "b" variable and click on the bottom arrow. When this is done, the "b" variable will be moved from the left box to the "Column(s)" box. Figure 10.7 will show the end result of those operations.

◙ **FIGURE 10.5**

Untitled - SPSS Data Editor

File Edit View Data Transform Statistics Graphs Utilities Windows Help

	a	**b**	Summmarize ►	Frequencies
1	1	0	Compare Means ►	Descriptives
2	1	0	ANOVA Models ►	Crosstabs
3	1	0	Correlate ►	List Cases
4	1	0	Regression ►	
5	1	0	Log-linear ►	
6	1	0	Classify ►	
7	1	0	Data Reduction ►	
8	1	0	Scale ►	
9	1	0	Nonparametric Tests ►	
10	1	0		
11	1	1		
12	1	1		
13	1	1		
14	0	0		

◙ **FIGURE 10.6**

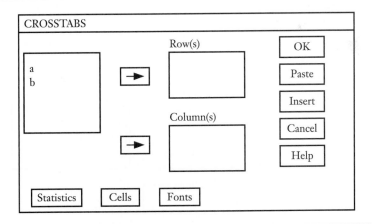

CROSSTABS

a
b

Row(s)

Column(s)

OK
Paste
Insert
Cancel
Help

Statistics   Cells   Fonts

◉ **FIGURE 10.7**

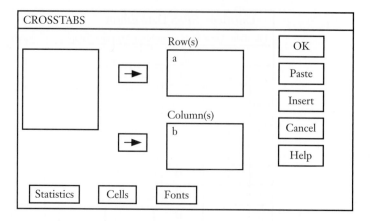

Next, click the "Statistics" button, which produces another screen. From this screen and for your purposes, select "chi-square" and the "Phi & Cramer's V" statistics. These are selected by clicking the box that is adjacent to these statistics. Once you have done that, click the "Continue" button. This will take you back to the previous screen, which was shown in Figure 10.7. Once you have that screen back, click "OK." You will then see SPSS switch to the Output Screen and display the results of your statistical analysis. These results are presented in Figure 10.9.

The second setup involves doing the analysis using only the contingency table instead of the raw data values. You would define the variables *A* and *B* in SPSS again. However, this time you would only enter the cell identifications. Remember, for Table 10.15, we gave Low PD–Low EC the subset combination (0, 0). We also gave such designation to the other cells of the contingency table; that is, Low PD–High

◉ **FIGURE 10.8**

CROSSTABS   Statistics

☒ chi-square   [Continue]

┌─── Nominal Data ───┐   ┌─── Original Data ───┐   [Cancel]
☐ Contingency Coefficient   ☐ Gamma
☒ Phi & Cramer's V   ☐ Somer's d   [Help]
☐ Lambda   ☐ Kendall's tau-b
☐ Uncertainty Coefficient   ☐ Kendall's tau-c

┌─── Nominal Interval ───┐   ☐ Kappa
☐ Eta   ☐ Risk

◙ FIGURE 10.9

		B	Low EC	High EC	
		Count	0	1	Row Totals
A					
Low PD	0		2	8	10 43.5
High PD	1		10	3	13 56.5
		Column Total	12 52.2	11 47.8	23

Chi-Square		Value	DF	Significance
Pearson		7.33963	1	.00675
Continuity Correction		5.23565	1	.02213
Phi	−.56490			
Cramer's V	.56490			

EC was (0, 1), High PD–Low EC was (1, 0), and High PD–High EC was (1, 1). Figure 10.10 shows the SPSS spreadsheet where this is done in the first two columns. Note that there is a column labeled "Count." In this column you would enter the frequency counts for each cell. For example, (0, 0) or Low PD–Low EC had a

◙ FIGURE 10.10

Untitled - SPSS Data Editor

File Edit View Data Transform Statistics Graphs Utilities Windows Help

	a	b	count	var	var	var	
1	0	0	2				
2	0	1	8				
3	1	0	10				
4	1	1	3				
5							

◙ FIGURE 10.11

Untitled - SPSS Data Editor						
File Edit View Data Transform Statistics Graphs Utilities Windows Help						
	a	**b**	**count**	Define Variables	**var**	
				Define Dates		
1	**0**	**0**	**3**	Templates		
2	**0**	**1**	**8**	Insert Variable		
				Insert Case		
3	**1**	**0**	**10**	Go To Case		
4	**1**	**1**	**2**	Sort Cases		
5				Merge Files ►		
				Aggregate		
				Split File		
				Select Cases		
				Weight Cases		

frequency of 2. Next to the (0, 0) designation on the spreadsheet, under the "Count" column, enter 2. For (0, 1) enter an 8, a 10 for (1, 0), and a 3 for (1, 1).

After entering the appropriate data into SPSS, you need to tell SPSS that you have a special setup. SPSS usually expects setup to be in the form shown in Figure 10.5. To inform SPSS, select "Data" from the top action bars. This brings you to another menu. From this menu, choose "Weight Cases" (see Figure 10.11).

Note that "Weight Cases" is in boldface type to indicate that you are going to choose that option. After choosing that option, you will get a new screen where you can instruct SPSS how to weight the cases. This screen is shown in Figure 10.12. Note in the left-most box that there are our three variables: "a," "b," and "count."

◙ FIGURE 10.12

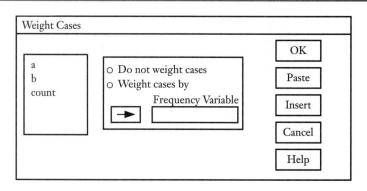

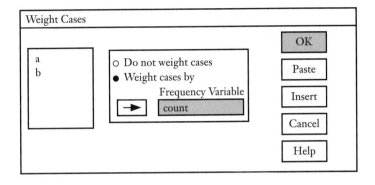

First, click the button labeled "Weight cases by" (see Figure 10.13). Then use your mouse and highlight the "count" variable in the left-most box. By clicking on the right arrow button in the panel, you will see the "count" variable moved from the left box into the right-most box. After this move is accomplished, click the "OK" button. This will return you to the SPSS spreadsheet.

To perform the statistical analysis, you need now to follow the steps outlined in the first setup. These are depicted in Figure 10.6, Figure 10.7, and Figure 10.8. The output should be identical to the one obtained using the first setup shown in Figure 10.9. The key to performing the contingency table analysis for this second setup lies in how the cells of the contingency were designated. If you had a 2 × 3 contingency table, the designation would be (0, 0), (0, 1), (0, 2), (1, 0), (1, 1), and (1, 2).

CHAPTER SUMMARY

1. Fundamentals on how to do analysis with cross-partition frequency data are introduced.
2. Cross partitions are called crosstabs, contingency analysis, or contingency table analysis.
3. Categorical variables are also called nominal variables.
4. Crosstabs are numerical tabular presentations of data.
5. Crosstabs can be used to determine the nature of relations between variables.
6. The simplest form of a crosstab is a 2-by-2 table or fourfold table.
7. The generally accepted rule on the set up of crosstab tables has the columns for levels of the independent variable and the rows for the outcomes of the dependent variable.
8. Percentages in crosstab tables are computed from the independent variable to the dependent variable.

9. The chi-square (χ^2) statistic is used to determine statistical significance in a crosstab.

10. Statistical significance is defined as having an empirical result that differs significantly from chance expectations.

11. The level of statistical significance is chosen arbitrarily; 0.05 and 0.01 are usually the accepted levels in the behavioral sciences.

12. If an observed result is significant at the 0.05 level, it says that the result could occur by chance in no more than five out of every 100 trials of the same experiment.

13. Cramer's V or the phi (ϕ) coefficient are measures of association between two variables in a crosstab. The phi coefficient is used in 2×2 tables. The Cramer's V is for larger tables.

14. Types of crosstab tables:
    a. one-dimensional
    b. two-dimensional
    c. three- and k-dimensional

15. Specification is a process of describing the conditions under which a relation does or does not exist.

16. Relation is a set of ordered pairs. Crosstabs express ordered pairs in a table of frequencies.

17. The analysis of multidimensional tables is also referred to as log-linear analysis. These tables are more complicated to analyze and require more complex computations.

STUDY SUGGESTIONS

1. Freedman, Wallington, and Bless (1967) present a classical study that tested the hypothesis that guilt leads to compliance. These researchers induced guilt in their experimental subjects by having them lie about a test they were to take. Control subjects were not made to lie. The subjects were then asked whether or not they would be willing the participate in an unrelated study (dependent variable: compliance). The authors report the following frequency table:

	Experimental (Lie)	Control (Not Lie)
Comply	20	11
Not Comply	11	20

Calculate χ^2, V, and percentages. Interpret the results. Is the hypothesis supported? Is the relation weak? moderate? strong?
(Answers: $\chi^2 = 5.23$ ($p < .05$); $V = .29$. Yes, the hypothesis is supported. The relation is weak to moderate.)

2. The *Congressional Quarterly* (1993) reported that on August 3, 1993, the U.S. Senate voted to authorize $1.5 billion for the National Service program. This

would provide people age 17 or older with $4,725 a year for up to two years in education awards for work in community service programs. The vote was as follows.

	Republican	Democrat
For	7	51
Against	37	4

Calculate χ^2, V, and percentages. Interpret the results.
(Answers: $\chi^2 = 59.45$; $V = .78$.)
3. Zavala, Barnett, Smedi, Istvan, and Matarazzo (1990) investigated the relation between cigarette, alcohol, and coffee use among U.S. Army personnel. One of their tables is partially reproduced below.

	Smokers	Ex-smokers	Nonsmoker
Coffee Consumption			
0 cups	24	12	66
1 to 2 cups	10	3	8
3+ cups	16	3	6

a. Examine the data carefully, then interpret the table.
b. Calculate percentages, first by columns and then by rows. Does the interpretation change? If so, how?
4. If possible, find a computer program that computes χ^2 (many are available commercially and some are available as shareware and can be downloaded from the Internet). Using that program, analyze the examples and the problems in this section. Check your answers.
5. Have occupations of women changed under the impact of the Equal Rights Movement? Here are data from a U.S. Census Report (in thousands). These data were obtained from the Web page of the U.S. Census Bureau: http://www.census.gov.

	1983		1995	
	Male	Female	Male	Female
Professional, Managerial, Administrative	13,943	9,649	18,365	16,953
Clerical, Sales, Service	11,068	20,198	13,320	24,097

(Note: The above figures were obtained by adding the categories Professional + Managerial + Administrative; Clerical + Sales + Service.)

a. Calculate percentages, being careful to calculate from the independent variables to the dependent variable, as usual.

b. Calculate χ^2 and V for 1983 and 1995 separately. (Use the above figures; i.e., neglect the fact that the figures indicate thousands. This affects χ^2 but not V.)

c. Interpret the results of your calculations. (Be circumspect. The method of adding the category numbers may have been biased or even incorrect.)

d. In **b**, above, you calculated χ^2 and V using the tabled frequencies as they are. Now do the same calculations using the numbers in the thousands (i.e., instead of 13,943, use 13,943,000). Note the enormous increase in χ^2 but V is the same. Here is a generalization: With very large numbers virtually everything is statistically significant. This is one reason for measures of association that remain unaffected by the magnitude of the numbers.

6. The following are data collected by Glick, DeMorest, and Hotze (1988) in their study concerning group membership, personal space, and request for a small favor. This study was described briefly in an earlier chapter. These researchers wanted to determine if the similarity of personal characteristics between a requester and a requestee will influence whether or not the requestee will comply with a request. Also of interest was whether the distance between the requester and the requestee had any influence on compliance.

Type of Confederate

	Out-Group			**In-Group**		
	Distance			Distance		
	Near	Medium	Far	Near	Medium	Far
Response to Request						
Complied	1	6	12	10	12	9
Refused	14	9	3	5	3	6

a. Calculate percentages and interpret. Consider each confederate type separately.

b. How does distance influence compliance? strongly? moderately? Is the relation the same with the in-group requester as it is with the out-group requester?

c. This study should be analyzed using multidimensional contingency tables. Explain why?

7. If you have available a current version of SPSS for Windows, try analyzing the data given in Study Suggestions 1, 2, and 3.

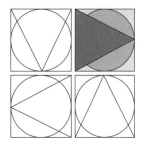

CHAPTER 11

STATISTICS:
PURPOSE, APPROACH, METHOD

- THE BASIC APPROACH
- DEFINITION AND PURPOSE OF STATISTICS
- BINOMIAL STATISTICS
- THE VARIANCE
- THE LAW OF LARGE NUMBERS
- THE NORMAL PROBABILITY CURVE AND THE STANDARD DEVIATION
- INTERPRETATION OF DATA USING THE NORMAL PROBABILITY CURVE—
  FREQUENCY DATA
- INTERPRETATION OF DATA USING THE NORMAL PROBABILITY CURVE—
  CONTINUOUS DATA

The Basic Approach

The basic principle behind the use of statistical tests of significance can be stated as: Compare obtained results to chance expectation. Another summation might be: Did you get what you would expect by chance? When a research study is done and statistical results have been obtained, they are checked against the results expected by chance. In Chapter 7 we met examples of checking empirical results of coin tossing and dice throwing against theoretical expectations. For example, if a die is thrown a large number of times, the expected proportion of occurrences of say 4, is one-sixth of the total number of throws. In Chapter 10 we learned that the rationale of the χ^2

test was the comparison of numbers of observed frequencies of events to the numbers of frequencies expected by chance. Indeed, the statistical ideas of Chapter 10 were presented before those of this chapter in part to give the student preliminary experience with obtained and expected results.

Two dice were thrown 72 times in a demonstration described in Chapter 7. Theoretically, 7 should turn up $1/6 \times 72 = 12$ times. However, Table 7.2 showed that 7 turned up 15 times in 72 throws rather than 12 times. We ask important questions: Does this obtained result differ significantly from the theoretically expected result? Does this obtained result differ from chance expectation enough to warrant a belief that something other than chance is at work? Can the obtained results be explained solely by chance?

Such questions are the essence of the statistical approach. Statisticians are skeptics. They do not believe in the "reality" of empirical results until they have applied statistical tests to them. They assume that results are chance results until shown to be otherwise. They are inveterate probabilists. The core of their approach to empirical data is to set up chance expectation as their hypothesis and to try to fit empirical data to the chance model. If the empirical data "fit" the chance model, then it is said that they are "not statistically significant." If they do not fit the chance model—if they depart "sufficiently" from the chance model—it is said that they are "statistically significant."

This and several succeeding chapters are devoted to the statistical approach to research problems. In this chapter we extend the discussion of Chapter 7 on probability to basic conceptions of the mean, variance, and standard deviation. The socalled law of large numbers and the normal probability curve are also explained and interpreted, and some idea is given of their potent use in statistics. In the next chapter we tackle the idea of statistical testing itself. These two chapters are the foundation.

Definition and Purpose of Statistics

Statistics is the theory and method of analyzing quantitative data obtained from samples of observations in order to study and compare sources of variance of phenomena, to help make decisions to accept or reject hypothesized relations between the phenomena, and to aid in drawing reliable inferences from empirical observations.

Four purposes of statistics are suggested in this definition. The first is the most common and most traditional: to reduce large quantities of data to manageable and understandable form. It is impossible to digest 100 scores, for instance, but if a mean and a standard deviation are calculated, a trained person can readily interpret the scores. The definition of *statistic* stems from this traditional usage and purpose of statistics. A statistic is a measure calculated from a sample. A statistic contrasts from a parameter, which is a population value. If, in U, a population or universe, we calculate the mean, this is a parameter. Now take a subset (sample) A of U. The mean of A is a statistic. For our purpose, parameters are of theoretical interest. They are not usually known. They are estimated with statistics. Thus we deal mostly with sample or subset statistics. These samples are usually conceived to be representative of U. Statistics, then, are epitomes or summaries of the samples—and often, presumably, of the populations—from which they are calculated. Means, medians, variances, standard deviations, percentiles, percentages, and so on, calculated from samples, are statistics.

A second purpose of statistics is to aid in the study of populations and samples. This use of statistics is so well-known that it will not be discussed here; besides, we studied something of populations and samples in earlier chapters.

A third purpose of statistics is to aid in decision making. If an educational psychologist needs to know which of three methods of instruction promotes the most learning with the least cost, statistics can be used to help gain this knowledge. This use of statistics is comparatively recent.

Although most decision situations are more complex, we use an example that is quite familiar by now. Let's say, for this example, that you are the decisionmaker/dice gambler. Your first task is to lay out the outcomes for dice throws. These are, of course, 2 through 12. You note the differing frequencies of the numbers. For example, 2 and 12 will probably occur much less often than 7 or 6. Next, you calculate the probabilities for the various outcomes. Finally, on the basis of how much money you can expect to make, you devise a betting system. You decide, for instance, that, since 7 has a probability of 1/6, you will require your opponent to give you odds of 5 to 1 instead of even money on the first throw. (We here take liberties with craps.) To make this whole thing a bit more dramatic, suppose that two players operate with different decisionmakers (this example was suggested by Bross, 1953). You are player A and propose the following game: A will win if 2, 3, or 4 turns up; your opponent B will win if 5, 6, or 7 turns up (outcomes 8 through 12 are to be disregarded). It is obvious that your decisionmaker is faulty. Your decisionmaker is based on the assumption that 2, 3, 4, 5, 6, and 7 are equiprobable. B should have a good time with this game.

The fourth and last purpose of statistics—to aid in making reliable inferences from observational data—is closely allied to, indeed, is part of, the purpose of helping to make decisions among hypotheses. An inference is a proposition or generalization derived by reasoning from other propositions, or from evidence. Generally speaking, an inference is a conclusion arrived at through reasoning. In statistics, a number of inferences may be drawn from tests of statistical hypotheses. We "conclude" that methods A and B really differ. We conclude from evidence, say, $r = .67$, that two variables are really related.

Statistical inferences have two characteristics. (1) The inferences are usually made from samples to populations. When we say that the variables A and B are related because the statistical evidence is $r = .67$, we are inferring that because $r = .67$ in this sample it is $r = .67$, or near .67, in the population from which the sample was drawn. (2) Inferences are used when investigators are not interested in the populations, or only interested secondarily in them. An educational investigator is studying the presumed effect of the relations between board of education members and chief educational administrators, on the one hand, and teacher morale, on the other. The hypothesis is that, when relations between boards and chief administrators are strained, teacher morale is lower than otherwise. The interest is only in testing this hypothesis in Y county. The investigator makes the study and obtains statistical results that support the hypothesis; for example, morale is lower in system A than in systems B and C. The researcher infers, from the statistical evidence of a difference between system A, on the one hand, and systems B and C on the other hand, that the initial hypothetical proposition is correct—in Y county. And it is possible for the investigator's interest to be limited strictly to Y county.

To summarize much of the above discussion, the purposes of statistics can be reduced to one major purpose: to aid in inference making. This is one of the basic purposes of research design, methodology, and statistics. Scientists want to draw inferences from data. The science of statistics, through its power to reduce data to manageable forms (statistics), and to study and analyze variances, enables scientists to attach probability estimates to the inferences they draw from data. Statistics says, in effect, "The inference you have drawn is correct at such-and-such a level of significance. You may act as though your hypothesis were true, remembering that there is such-and-such a probability that it is untrue." It should be reasonably clear why some contemporary statisticians call statistics the discipline of decision making under uncertainty. It should also be reasonably clear that, whether you know it or not, you are always drawing inferences, attaching probabilities to various outcomes or hypotheses, and making decisions on the basis of statistical reasoning. Statistics, using probability theory and mathematics, makes the process more systematic and objective.

Binomial Statistics

When things are counted, the number system used is simple and useful. Whenever objects are counted, they are counted on the basis of some criterion, some variable or attribute, in research language. Many examples have already been given: heads, tails, numbers on dice, sex, aggressive acts, political preference, and so on. If a person or a thing possesses the attribute, we say that person or thing is "counted in." When something is "counted in" because it possesses the attribute in question, it is assigned a 1. If it does not possess the attribute, it is assigned a 0. This is a binomial system.

Earlier, the mean was defined as $M = \Sigma X/n$. The variance is $V = \Sigma x^2/n$, where $x = X - M$ (each x is a deviation of the rawscore X from the mean). The standard deviation is $SD = \sqrt{V}$. Of course, these formulas work with any scores; here we use them only with 1s and 0s. And it is useful to alter the formula for the mean. The formula $\Sigma X/n$ is not general enough. It assumes that all scores are equiprobable. A more general formula, which can be used when equiprobability is not assumed, is

$$M = \Sigma[X \cdot w(X)] \tag{11.1}$$

where $w(X)$ is the weight assigned to an X; $w(X)$ simply means the probability each X has of occurring. The formula says: Multiply each X, each score, by its weight (probability), and then add them all up. Notice that if all Xs are equally probable, this formula is the same as $\Sigma X/n$.

The mean of the set {1, 2, 3, 4, 5,} is

$$M = \frac{1 + 2 + 3 + 4 + 5}{5} = \frac{15}{5} = 3$$

By Equation 11.1 it is, of course, the same, but its computation looks different:

$$M = 1 \cdot \frac{1}{5} + 2 \cdot \frac{1}{5} + 3 \cdot \frac{1}{5} + 4 \cdot \frac{1}{5} + 5 \cdot \frac{1}{5} = 3$$

Why the hair-splitting? We shall see with our next example. Let a coin be tossed. $U = \{H, T\}$. The mean number of heads is, by Equation 11.1,

$$M = 1 \cdot \frac{1}{2} + 0 \cdot \frac{1}{2} = \frac{1}{2}$$

Let two coins be tossed. $U = \{HH, HT, TH, TT\}$. The mean number of heads, or the expectation of heads, is

$$M = 2 \cdot \frac{1}{4} + 1 \cdot \frac{1}{4} + 1 \cdot \frac{1}{4} + 0 \cdot \frac{1}{4} = \frac{4}{4} = 1$$

This says that if two coins are tossed many times, the average number of heads per toss of the two coins is 1. If we sample one person from 30 men and 70 women, the mean of men is: $M = 3/10 \cdot 1 + 7/10 \cdot 0 = .3$. The mean for women is: $M = 3/10 \cdot 0 + 7/10 \cdot 1 = .7$. These are the means for one outcome. (This is a little like saying "an average of 2.5 children per family.")

What has been said in these examples is that the mean of any single experiment (a single coin toss, a sample of one person) is the probability of the occurrence of one of two possible outcomes (heads, a man). If the outcome occurs, it is assigned a 1 and, if it does not occur, 0. This is tantamount to saying: $p(1) = p$ and $p(0) = 1 - p$. In the one-toss experiment, let 1 be assigned if heads turns up and 0 if tails turns up. Then $p(1) = 1/2$ and $p(0) = 1 - 1/2 = 1/2$. In tossing a coin twice, let 1 be assigned to each head that occurs and 0 to each tail. We are interested in the outcome "heads." $U = \{HH, HT, TH, TT\}$. The mean is

$$M = \frac{1}{4} \cdot 2 + \frac{1}{4} \cdot 1 + \frac{1}{4} \cdot 1 + \frac{1}{4} \cdot 0 = 1$$

Can we arrive at the same result in an easier manner? Yes. Just add the means for each outcome. The mean of the outcome of one coin toss is 1/2. For two coin tosses it is $1/2 + 1/2 = 1$. To assign probabilities with one coin toss, we weight 1 (heads) with its probability and 0 (tails) with its probability. This gives $M = p \cdot 1 + (1 - p) \cdot 0 = p$. Take the men–women sampling problem. Let p equal the probability of a man being sampled on a single outcome and $1 - p = q$ equal the probability of a woman being sampled on a single outcome. Then $p = 3/10$ and $q = 7/10$. We are interested in the mean of a man being sampled. Since $M = p \cdot 1 + q \cdot 0 = p$, $M = 3/10 \cdot 1 + 7/10 \cdot 0 = 3/10 = p$, the mean is 3/10 and the probability is 3/10. Evidently, $M = p$, or the mean is equal to the probability.

How about a series of outcomes? We write S for the sum of n outcomes. One example, the tossing of two coins, was given above. Let us take the men–women sampling problem. The mean of a man's occurring is 3/10 and of a woman's occurring 7/10. We sample 10 persons. What is the mean number of men? Put differently, what is the expectation of men? If we sum the 10 means of the individual outcomes, we get the answer:

$$M(S_{10}) = M_1 + M_2 + \cdots + M_{10} \tag{11.2}$$

$$= 3/10 + 3/10 + \cdots + 3/10 = 30/10 = 3$$

In a sample of 10, we expect to get the answer: 3 men. The same result could have been obtained by $3/10 \cdot 10 = 3$, but $3/10 \cdot 10$ is pn, or

$$M(S_n) = pn \tag{11.3}$$

In n trials the mean number of occurrences of the outcome associated with p is pn.

The Variance

Recall that in Chapter 6 the variance was defined as $V = \Sigma x^2/n$. Of course it will be the same in this chapter, with a change in symbols (for the same reason given with the formula for the mean):

$$V = \Sigma[w(X)(X - M)^2] \tag{11.4}$$

To make clear what a variance—and a standard deviation—is in probability theory, we work two examples. Recall that in a binomial only two outcomes are possible: 1 and 0. Therefore X is equal to 1 or 0. We set up a table to help us calculate the variance of the heads outcome of a coin toss:

Outcome	X	$w(X) = p$	$(X-M)^2$	$(11/2)^2$
H	1	1/2	$(1 - 1/2)^2 = 1/4$	
T	0	1/2	$(0 - 1/2)^2 = 1/4$	

The variance is, then,

$$V = 1/2(1 - 1/2)^2 + 1/2(0 - 1/2)^2 = 1/2 \cdot 1/4 + 1/2 \cdot 1/4 = 1/4$$

The mean is 1/2 and the variance is 1/4. The standard deviation is the square root of the variance, or

$$\sqrt{1/4} = 1/2$$

The variance of an individual outcome, however, does not have much meaning. We really want the variance of the sum of a number of outcomes. If the outcomes are independent, the variance of the sum of the outcomes is the sum of the variances of the outcomes:

$$V(S_n) = V_1 + V_2 + \cdots + V_n \qquad (11.5)$$

For 10 coin tosses, the variance of heads is $V(H_{10}) = 10 \cdot 1/4 = 10/4 = 2.5$. Earlier we showed that $M(S_n) = np$. We now want a formula for the variance. That is, instead of Equation 11.5 we want a direct, simple formula. With a little algebraic manipulation we can arrive at such a formula:

$$V = p(1 - p) = pq \qquad (11.6)$$

This is the variance of one outcome. The variance of the number of times that an outcome occurs is, analogously to equations 11.2, 11.3, and 11.5, the sum of the individual outcome variances, or

$$V(S_n) = npq \qquad (11.7)$$

The standard deviation is

$$SD(S_n) = \sqrt{npq} \qquad (11.8)$$

Equations 11.3, 11.7, and 11.8 are important and useful. They can be applied in many statistical situations. Take two or three applications of the formula. First consider an example where out of 100 people sampled ($n = 100$), 60 agree with a political issue and 40 disagree. On the assumption of equiprobability, $p = 1/2$ and $q = 1/2$, $M(S_{100}) = np = 100 \cdot 1/2 = 50$, $V(S_{100}) = npq = 100 \cdot 1/2 \cdot 1/2 = 25$, and $SD(S_{100}) = \sqrt{25} = 5$. It was found that there were 60 Agrees. So, this is a deviation of two standard deviations from the mean of 50, $60 - 50 = 10$, and $10/5 = 2$. Second, take the coin-tossing experiment of the chapter on probability. In one experiment, 52 heads turned up in 100 tosses. The calculations are the same as those just given. Since there were 52 heads, the deviation from the mean, or expected frequency, is $52 - 50 = 2$. In standard deviation terms or units, this is $2/5 = .4$ standard deviation units from the mean. We now get back to one of the original questions asked: Are these differences "statistically significant"? We found, via χ^2, that the result of 60 Agrees was statistically significant and that the result of 52 heads was not statistically significant. Can we do the same thing with the present formula? Yes, we can. Further, the beauty of the present method is that it is applicable to all kinds of numbers, not just to binomial numbers. Before demonstrating this, however, we must study, if only briefly, the so-called law of large numbers and the properties of the standard deviation and the normal probability curve.

The Law of Large Numbers

The law of large numbers took Jacob Bernoulli (aka Jacques or James) twenty years to work out. In essence it is so simple that one wonders why he took so long to develop it. Bernoulli, who developed this law in 1713, called it the "golden theorem." It was renamed "The Law of Large Numbers" by Poisson in 1837. Newman (1988) gives an interesting and detailed account of the developments and controversies surrounding this theorem. Roughly, the law says that with an increase in the size of sample, n, there is a decrease in the probability that the observed value of an event, A, will deviate from the "true" value of A by no more than a fixed amount, k. Provided the members of the samples are drawn independently, the larger the sample the closer the "true" proportion value of the population is approached. Let's say a fair coin is tossed 100 times and the number of heads is recorded. Now let's say we toss the same coin 1,000 times and the number of heads is recorded. By the law of large numbers, there is a greater probability that the 1,000 tosses will have an outcome of 550 heads (a difference of 10 heads from the expectation of 500 heads), than the event of 100 coin tosses having an outcome of 60 heads (also a difference of 10 heads from an expectation of 50 heads). What this essentially says is that the errors are smaller with the 1,000 trial experiment than with the 100 trial experiment. The law is also a gateway to the testing of statistical hypotheses, as we shall see. It plays a particularly important role in Tchebysheff's Theorem. This theorem states that if we are given a number k that is greater than or equal to 1 and a set of n measurements, we are guaranteed (regardless of the shape of the distribution) that at least $(1 - 1/k^2)$ of the measurements will lie within k standard deviation units on either side of the mean.

Toss a coin 1, 10, 50, 100, 400, and 1,000 times. Let heads be the outcome in which we are interested. We calculate means, variances, standard deviations, and two new measures. The first of these new measures is the proportion of favorable outcomes, heads in this case, in the total sample. We call this measure H_n and define it as $H_n = S_n /n$. (Recall that S_n is the total number of times the favorable outcome occurs in n trials.) Then the fraction of time that the favorable outcome occurs is H_n. The mean of H_n is p, or $M(H_n) = p$. [This follows from Equation 11.3, where $M(S_n) = pn$, and since $H_n = S_n /n$, $M(H_n) = M(S_n)/n = np/n = p$.] In short, $M(H_n)$ equals the expected probability. The second measure is the variance of H_n. It is defined: $V(H_n) = pq/n$. The variance, $V(H_n)$, is a measure of the variability of the mean,

▣ TABLE 11.1 *Means, Variances, Standard Deviations, and Expected Probabilities of the Outcome Heads with Different Sample Sizes*[a]

n	$M(S_n) = np$	$V(S_n) = npq$	$SD(S_n)$	$M(H_n) = p$	$V(H_n) = pq/n$
1	1/2	.25	.50	1/2	1/4
10	5	2.50	1.58	1/2	1/40
50	25	12.50	3.54	1/2	1/200
100	50	25.00	5.00	1/2	1/400
400	200	100.00	10.00	1/2	1/1600
1000	500	250.00	15.81	1/2	1/4000

[a] See text for explanation of symbols in this table.

$M(H_n)$. Later more will be said about the square root of $V(H_n)$, called the standard error of the mean. The results of the calculation are given in Table 11.1.

Note that, although the means, variances, and standard deviations of the sums increase with the sizes of the samples, the $M(H_n)$s or ps remain the same. That is, the average number of heads, or $M(H_n)$, is always 1/2. But the variance of the average number of heads, $V(H_n)$, gets smaller and smaller as the sizes of the samples increase. Again, $V(H_n)$ is a measure of the variability of the averages. As Table 11.1 clearly indicates, the average number of outcomes should come closer and closer to the "true" value, in this case 1/2. (The student should ponder this example carefully before going further.)

The Normal Probability Curve and the Standard Deviation

The normal probability curve is the lovely bell-shaped curve encountered so often in statistics and psychology textbooks. Its importance stems from the fact that chance events in large numbers tend to distribute themselves in the form of the curve. The so-called theory of errors uses the curve. Many phenomena—physical and psychological—are considered to distribute themselves in approximately normal form. Height, intelligence, aptitude and achievement are three familiar examples. The means of samples distribute themselves normally. The reader should avoid the untested belief that all or even most phenomena are distributed normally. Whenever possible, data should be checked by appropriate methods, especially by plotting or graphing. Data are often subtle. Take aptitude, for example. In the whole population, aptitude may be normally distributed. But suppose we are studying whether the Graduate Record Examination (GRE) scores are predictive of success in graduate school. Reported correlations between success and GRE scores do not have a very high value (Morrison & Morrison, 1995). GRE scores are considered to be distributed normally. However, they are not for those who have been admitted to a top graduate school where scores on this test are taken seriously. Since only those with top scores are admitted, those with low scores are not. As a result, those with low scores generally do not get their level of success measured. Subsequently, they are not considered in the computation of the relation between GRE scores and success. A truncated distribution (no longer normal) leads to a low correlation value (Kirk, 1990; House, 1983). It is hard to conceive of modern statistics without this curve. Every statistics text has a table called the "table of the normal deviate," or "table of the normal curve."

The most important statistical reason for using the normal curve is to be able to interpret the probabilities of the statistics one calculates easily. If the data are, as is said, "normal" or approximately normal, one has a clear interpretation for what one does.

There are two types of graphs ordinarily used in behavioral research. In one of these, as we have seen, the values of a dependent variable are plotted against the values of an independent variable. The second major type of graph has a different purpose: to show the distribution of a single variable. On the horizontal axis, values are laid out similarly to the first type of graph. But on the vertical axis, frequencies or frequency intervals or probabilities are laid out.

We draw a normal curve and lay out two sets of values on the horizontal axis. In one set of values, we use intelligence test scores with a mean of 100 and a standard deviation of 16. Say we have a sample of 400 and the data (the scores) are in approximately normal form. (It is said that the data are "distributed normally.") The curve looks like that of Figure 11.1. Imagine a Y (vertical) axis with frequencies (or

◉ FIGURE 11.1

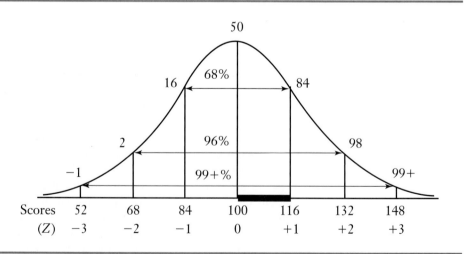

proportions) marked off on the axis. The major characteristics of normal curves are unimodality (one curve), symmetry (one side the same as the other), and certain mathematical properties. It is the mathematical properties that interest us because they allow us to draw statistical inferences of considerable power.

A standard deviation can be conceived as a length along the base line of the curve from the mean or middle of the baseline out to the right or left to the point where the curve inflects. It can also be visualized as a point on the baseline a certain distance from the mean. One standard deviation from the mean of this particular distribution is $100 + 16 = 116$. A heavy line in Figure 11.1 indicates the distance from 100 to 116. Similarly, one standard deviation below the mean is $100 - 16 = 84$. Two standard deviations are represented by $100 + (2)(16) = 132$ and $100 - (2)(16) = 68$. If one can be reasonably confident that one's data are distributed normally, then one can draw a curve like the one above, mark the mean, and lay out the standard deviations. This has also been done in Figure 11.1. The baseline has also been labeled in standard deviation units (labeled Z in the figure). That is, instead of scores of 100, 116, and 68, for instance, standard deviation scores can be used. They are 0, $+1$, -2, and so on; points between these marked points can be indicated. For example, one-half of a standard deviation above the mean, in raw scores, is $100 + (1/2)(16) = 108$. In standard deviation scores, it is $0 + .5 = .5$. These standard deviation scores are called standard scores or Z scores. Z scores range, in practical usage, from about -3 through 0 to about $+3$. To transform any raw score to a Z score, use the formula $Z = x/SD$, where $x = X - M$ and SD is the sample standard deviation. The xs are called deviation scores. Now we can divide the standard deviation into any x to convert the X (raw score) to a Z score. As an example, take $X = 120$. Then $Z = (120 - 100)/16 = 20/16 = 1.25$. That is, a raw score of 120 is equivalent to a Z score of 1.25. Or, it is one and one-quarter standard deviations above the mean.

If Z scores are used, and the total area under the curve is set equal to 1.00, the curve is said to be in standard form. This immediately suggests probability. Portions of the area of the curve are conceived as probabilities and interpreted as such. If the total area under the whole curve is equal to 1.00, then if a vertical line is drawn upward from the base line at the mean ($Z = 0$) to the top of the bell, the areas to the left and to the right of the vertical line are each equal to 1/2 or 50%. But vertical lines might be drawn elsewhere on the baseline, at one standard deviation above the mean ($Z = 1$) or two standard deviations below the mean ($Z = -2$). To interpret such points in area terms—and in probability terms—we must know the area properties of the curve.

The approximate percentages of the areas one, two, and three standard deviations above and below the mean have been indicated in Figure 11.1. For our purposes, it is not necessary to use the exact percentages. The area between $Z = -1$ and $Z = +1$ is approximately 68%. The area between $Z = -2$ and $Z = +2$ is approximately 96%. (The exact figure is .9544. We use .96 because it makes interpretation easier.) The area between $Z = -3$ and $Z = +3$ is 99+%. Similarly, all other possible baseline distances and their associated areas can be translated into percentages of the whole curve. An important point to remember is that, since the area of the whole curve is equal to 1.00, or 100%, and thus is equivalent to U in probability theory, the percentages of area can be interpreted as probabilities. In fact, the normal probability table entries are given as percentages of areas corresponding to Z scores.

These percentages pertain only to a normal distribution. If the shape of the distribution is non-normal these percentages do not apply. In order to find the percentages for a non-normal distribution, one can apply Tchebysheff's Theorem mentioned earlier. With this theorem, one is guaranteed 75% between $Z = -2$ and $Z = +2$ and 89.9% between $Z = -3$ and $Z = +3$.

Interpretation of Data Using the Normal Probability Curve – Frequency Data

We now inquire about the probabilities of events. To do this, we must first go back to tossing coins. Strictly speaking, the frequencies of heads and tails are discontinuous events, whereas the normal probability curve is continuous. But this need not worry us, since the approximations are close. It is possible to specify with great accuracy and considerable ease the probabilities that chance events will occur. Instead of calculating exact probabilities, as we did before, we can estimate probabilities from knowledge of the properties of the normal curve. This normal curve approximation of the binomial distribution is most useful and accurate when N is large and the value of p (the probability of one of the two events) is close to .5. Comrey and Lee (1995, pp. 186–187) show how much the approximation changes for different values of p and N.

Suppose we again, somewhat wearily perhaps, toss 100 coins. We found that the mean number of times heads will probably turn up is $M(S_{100}) = np = 100 \cdot 1/2 = 50$, and the standard deviation was

$$SD(S_{100}) = \sqrt{V(S_{100})} = \sqrt{npq} = \sqrt{100 \cdot 1/2 \cdot 1/2} = \sqrt{25} = 5$$

Using the percentages of the curve (probabilities), we can make probability statements. We can say, for example, that in 100 tosses the probability that heads will turn up between one standard deviation below the mean ($Z = -1$) and one standard deviation above the mean ($Z = +1$) is approximately .68. Roughly, then, there are about two out of three chances that the number of heads will be between 45 and 55 (50 $\pm$ 5). There is one chance in three, approximately, that the number of heads will be less than 45 or greater than 55. That is, $q = 1 - p = 1 - .68 = .32$.

Take two standard deviations above and below the mean. These points would be $50 - (2)(5) = 40$ and $50 + (2)(5) = 60$. Since we know that about 95–96% of the cases will probably fall into this band, that is, between $Z = -2$ and $Z = +2$, or between 40 and 60, we can say that the probability that the number of heads will not be less than 40 or greater than 60 is about .95 or .96. In other words, there are only about four or five chances in 100 that less than 40, or more than 60, heads will occur. It can happen, but it is unlikely.

If we want or need to be practically certain (as in certain kinds of medical or engineering research), we can go out to three standard deviations, $Z = -3$ and $Z = +3$, or perhaps somewhat less than three standard deviations. (The .01 level is about 2.58 standard deviations.) Three standard deviations say the numbers of heads is between 35 and 65. Since three standard deviations above and below the mean in Figure 11.1 take up more than 99% of the area of the curve, we can say that we are practically certain that the number of heads in 100 tosses of a fair coin will not be less than 35 or more than 65. The probability is greater than .99. If you tossed a coin 100 times and got, say, 68 heads, you might conclude that there was probably something wrong with the coin. Of course, 68 heads can occur, but it is extremely unlikely that they will with a fair coin.

The earlier Agree–Disagree problem is treated exactly the same as the coin problem above. The result of 60 Agrees and 40 Disagrees is unlikely to happen. There are only about four chances in 100 that 60 Agrees and 40 Disagrees will happen by chance. We knew this before from the χ^2 test and from the exact probability test. We now have a third way that is generally applicable to all kinds of data—provided the data are distributed normally or approximately so.

Interpretation of Data Using the Normal Probability Curve – Continuous Data

Suppose we have the mathematics test scores of a sample of 100 fifth-grade children. The mean of the scores is 70; the standard deviation is 10. From previous knowledge we know that the distribution of test scores on this test is approximately normal. Obviously we can interpret the data using the normal curve. Our interest is in the reliability of the mean. How much can we depend on this mean? With future samples of similar fifth-grade children, will we get the same mean? If the mean is undependable, that is, if it fluctuates widely from sample to sample, obviously any interpretation of the test scores of individual children is in jeopardy. A score of 75 might be average this time, but if the mean is unreliable this 75 might be, on a future testing, a superior score. In other words, we must have a dependable or reliable mean.

Imagine giving this same test to the same group of children again and again and again. Go further. Imagine giving the test under exactly the same conditions 100,000 times. Assume that all other things are equal: the children learn nothing new in all these repetitions; they do not get fatigued; environmental conditions remain the same; and so on.

If we calculate a mean and a standard deviation for each of the many times, we obtain a gigantic distribution of means (and standard deviations). What will this distribution be like? First, it will form a beautiful bell-shaped normal curve. Means have the property of falling nicely into the normal distribution, even when the original distributions from which they are calculated are not normal. This is because we assumed "other things equal" and thus have no source of mean fluctuations other than chance. The means will fluctuate, but the fluctuations will all be chance fluctuations. Most of these fluctuations will cluster around what we will call the "true" mean, the "true" value of the gigantic population of means. A few will be extreme values. If we repeated the 100 coin-tosses experiment many times, we would find that heads would cluster around what we know is the "true" value: 50. Some would be slightly higher, some slightly lower, a few considerably higher, a few considerably lower. In brief, the heads and the means will obey the same "law." Since we assumed that nothing else is operating, we must come to the conclusion that these fluctuations are due to chance. And chance errors, given enough of them, distribute themselves into a normal distribution. This is the theory called the *theory of errors*.

Continuing our story of the mean, if we had the data from the many administrations of the mathematics test to the same group, we could calculate a mean and a standard deviation. The mean so calculated would be close to the "true" mean. If we had an infinite number of means from an infinite number of test administrations and calculated the mean of the means, we would then obtain the "true" mean. This would be similar for the standard deviation of the means. Naturally, we cannot do this because we do not have an infinite or even a very large number of test administrations.

There is fortunately a simple way to solve the problem. It consists in accepting the mean calculated from the sample as the "true" mean and then estimating how accurate this acceptance (or assumption) is. To do this, a statistic known as the standard error of the mean is calculated. It is defined:

$$SE_M = \frac{\sigma_{pop}}{\sqrt{n}} \tag{11.9}$$

where the standard error of the mean is SE_M, the standard deviation of the population (σ is read "sigma"), σ_{pop}; and the number of cases in the sample, n.

There is a little snag here. We do not know or can know, the standard deviation of the population. Recall that we also did not know the mean of the population, but that we estimated it with the mean of the sample. Similarly, we estimate the standard deviation of the population with the standard deviation of the sample. Thus the formula to use is

$$SE_M = \frac{SD}{\sqrt{n}} \tag{11.10}$$

The mathematics test mean can now be studied for its reliability. We calculate:

$$SE_M = \frac{10}{\sqrt{100}} = \frac{10}{10} = 1$$

Again, imagine a large population of means of this test. If they are put into a distribution and the curve of the distribution plotted, the curve would look something like the curve shown in Figure 11.2. Keep firmly in mind: this is an imaginary distribution

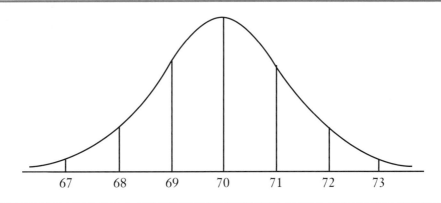

| | | | | | | |
|67|68|69|70|71|72|73|

of *means of samples;* it is *not* a distribution of scores. It is easy to see that the means of this distribution are not very variable. If we double the standard error of the mean we get 2. Subtract and add this to the mean of 70: 68 to 72. The probability is approximately .95 that the population ("true") mean lies within the interval 68 to 72; that is, approximately 5% of the time the means of random samples of this size will lie outside this interval.

If we do the same calculation for the intelligence test data of Figure 11.1, we obtain

$$SE_M = \frac{16}{\sqrt{400}} = \frac{16}{20} = .80$$

Three standard errors above and below the mean of 100 give the range 97.60 to 102.40, or we can say that the "true" mean very probably (less than 1% chance of being wrong) lies within the interval 98 to 102. Means are reliable—with fair-size samples. Even with relatively small samples, the mean is quite stable (see the intelligence test data in Chapter 8). Five samples of 20 intelligence scores each were drawn from a population of such scores with a mean of 95. The means of the five samples were calculated. Standard errors of the mean were calculated for the first two samples, and interpretations made. Then comparisons were made to the "true" value of 95. The mean of the first sample was 93.55 with a standard deviation of 12.22. $SE_M = 2.73$. The .05 level range of means was: 88.09 to 99.01. Obviously 95 falls within this range. The mean of the second sample was more deviant: 90.20. The standard deviation was 9.44. $SE_M = 2.11$. The .05 level range was 85.98 to 94.42. Our 95 does not fall in this range. The .01 level range is: 83.87 to 96.53. Now 95 is encompassed. This is not bad at all for samples of only 20. For samples of 50 or 100 it would be even better. The mean of the five means was 93.31; the standard deviation of these means was 2.73. Compare this to the standard errors calculated from the two samples: 2.73 and 2.11. A more convincing demonstration of the stability of means will be given in Chapter 12.

The standard error of the mean, then, is a standard deviation. It is a standard deviation of an infinite number of means. Only chance error makes the means fluctuate. Thus, the standard error of the mean—or the standard deviation of the means, if you like—is a measure of chance or error in its effect on one measure of central tendency.

A caution is in order. All the theory discussed here is based on the assumptions of random sampling and independence of observations. If these assumptions are violated, the reasoning, while not entirely invalidated, practically speaking, is open to question. Estimates of error may be biased to a greater or lesser extent. The trouble is we cannot tell how much a standard error is biased. A number of years ago Guilford and Fruchter (1977) gave interesting examples of the biases encountered when the assumptions are violated. With large numbers of Air Force pilots, they found that estimates of standard errors were sometimes considerably off. No one can give hard-and-fast rules. The best maxim probably is: If at all possible, use random sampling and keep observations independent. Simon (1987) would take issue with this rule.

If random sampling cannot be used, and there is doubt about the independence of observations, calculate the statistics and interpret them. But be circumspect about interpretations and conclusions. They may be in error. Because of such possibilities of error, it has been said that statistics are misleading, and even useless. Like any other method—consulting authority, using intuition, and the like—statistics can be misleading. But even when statistical measures are biased, they are usually less biased than authoritative and intuitive judgments. It is not that numbers lie; the numbers do not know what they are doing. It is the human beings using the numbers who may be informed or misinformed, biased or unbiased, knowledgeable or ignorant, intelligent or stupid. Treat numbers and statistics neither with too great respect nor too great contempt. Calculate statistics and act as though they were "true," but always maintain a certain reserve toward them, a willingness to disbelieve them if the evidence indicates such disbelief.

CHAPTER SUMMARY

1. The basic principle behind the use of statistical tests of significance is to compare obtained (observed, empirical) results to chance expectations.
2. Four purposes of statistics are to
   a. reduce data to manageable and understandable form;
   b. aid in the study of populations and samples;
   c. aid in decision making; and
   d. aid in making reliable inferences from samples to populations.
3. Binomial data consists of two admissible outcomes.
4. Under certain conditions, the normal curve can be used to approximate the binomial distribution.

5. The law of large numbers states that the larger the sample, the closer the sample value approaches the true (population) value.
6. Chance events tend to distribute themselves in the form of a normal curve.
7. Using the normal curve simplifies the interpretation of data analysis.
8. The normal curve has certain mathematical properties that make it attractive to use in statistical analysis and interpretation.
9. Standard scores, Z, are linear transformations (reexpressions) of raw scores.
10. Use of Z-scores enhances interpretability of data because they are expressed as "standard deviation units."
11. Z-scores from different distributions can be meaningfully compared to one another.
12. Converting normally distributed raw scores to Z-scores allows one to use the table for the normal curve to determine percentages, areas, and probabilities.

STUDY SUGGESTIONS

1. Statistics are used to summarize large sets of data. Give an example where statistics could be misleading when used to evaluate a single person, company, or group.
2. Explain how laypersons and statisticians differ in their concept of the word *error*.
3. What is the one major purpose of statistics?
4. When using the normal probability curve, approximately 0.68 of the area under the curve lies between 1 standard deviation of the mean. For ± 2 standard deviations it is 0.96. What would be the approximate percentages if the curve was not normal?
5. A friend tosses a coin 1,000 times and comes up with 505 heads and 495 tails. She claims the results support her notion that the coin is fair. However, we know that a fair coin should generate 500 heads. Let's say she is correct. How would one explain the difference of 5 heads (or tails)?
6. Distinguish between a parameter and a statistic.

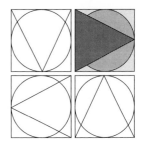

CHAPTER 12

TESTING HYPOTHESES AND THE STANDARD ERROR

The standard error,[1] as an estimate of chance fluctuation, is the measure against which the outcomes of experiments are checked. Is there a difference between the means of two experimental groups? If so, is the difference a "real" difference or merely a consequence of the many relatively small differences that could have arisen

---

[1]The term "error" here refers to the fluctuations found between different samples of the same size taken from the same population. It should not be construed as "mistakes."

by chance? To answer this question, the standard error of the differences between means is calculated and the obtained difference is compared to this standard error. If it is sufficiently greater than the standard error, it is said to be a "significant" difference. Similar reasoning can be applied to any statistic. There are thus many standard errors: of correlation coefficients, of differences between means, of means, of medians, of proportions, and so on. The purpose of this chapter is (1) to examine the general notion of the standard error, (2) to see how hypotheses are tested using the standard error, and (3) to see the important role they play in the estimation of sample size.

Examples: Differences Between Means

A particularly difficult problem in contemporary psychology centers on the question of whether behavior is controlled more by situational or environmental factors, or by dispositions of individuals. McGee and Snyder (1975), using a presumed difference between those individuals who salt their food before they taste it and those who taste their food before they salt it, hypothesized that those individuals who construe their behavior dispositionally salt their food before tasting it, whereas those individuals who construe their behavior situationally taste their food before salting it. They further reasoned that the former individuals would ascribe more traits to themselves than the latter individuals. They found that the former group, the "salters," ascribed a mean of 14.87 traits to themselves, whereas the latter group, the "tasters," ascribed a mean of 6.90 traits to themselves. The direction of the difference was as the authors predicted. Is the size of the difference between the means, 7.97, sufficient to warrant the authors' claim that their hypothesis was supported? A test of the statistical significance of this difference showed that it was highly significant. (This statement is a generalization of the original.)

A growing psychological problem where nearly 75% of the sufferers do not seek help is panic disorder. With increasing regulations imposed by health management organizations (HMOs) it is possible that even fewer individuals afflicted will seek treatment. The study by Gould and Clum (1995) provides data that seems extremely promising to partially alleviate this problem. Gould and Clum studied the benefit of a self-help program in treating panic disorder sufferers. In an extensive effort to recruit subjects for their study, they were able to form two groups of participants. Both groups consisted of panic disorder sufferers. One group received instructions and some counseling on self-help. Self-help involved reading the book *Coping with Panic.* The other group, labeled wait-list, received no treatment (they were told that they were on a waiting list for therapy). Each participant was measured over a 14-week period of time covering three major sections: pre-treatment, post-treatment, and follow-up. One of the measures was the number of panic attacks per week. Prior to treatment, the self-help group had a mean of 2.6 attacks per week, whereas the wait-list group reported a mean of 1.8 attacks. After treatment, the self-help group reported a mean of 0.9 (a mean change of −1.7) and the wait-list group reported a mean of 2.1 (mean change of +0.3). In the follow-up period, the self-help group reported a mean number of 0.5 attacks, whereas the wait-list group reported 2.5. The hypotheses of these researchers were supported. A test of the statistical significance of this difference showed that it was highly significant.

The point of these two examples in the present context is that the difference between means was tested for statistical significance with a standard error. The standard error in this case was the standard error of the difference between means. The difference in each study was found to be significant. The McGee and Snyder (1975) study tells us that those individuals who perceive behavior as influenced by individual traits tend to salt their food before tasting it, whereas those individuals whose perception is more environmentally oriented taste their food before salting it. In the Gould and Clum (1995) study, the self-help program is a more promising mode of treatment for panic disorder. While the wait-list experienced a nonsignificant change in terms of mean number of panic attacks, the self-help group showed great improvements. Gould and Clum (1995) used other dependent measures, such as Panic Symptoms and Coping with Panic Anxiety, and found a similar pattern of significance. Let us now look at an example in which the difference between means was not significant.

Gates and Taylor (1925) in a well-known early study of transfer of training, set up two matched groups of 16 pupils each. The experimental group was given practice in digit memory; the control was not. The mean gain of the experimental group right after the practice period was 2.00, the mean gain of the control group, was 0.67, a mean difference of 1.33. Four to five months later, the children of both groups were tested again. The mean score gain of the experimental group was 0.35; the mean score gain of the control group was 0.36. This finding was surprising because one would expect the experimental group to do better than the control group as it did earlier in the study. In this case, the control group's performance matched the performance of those in the experimental group. Statistical tests are hardly necessary with data like these.

Absolute and Relative Differences

Since differences between statistics—especially between means—are tested and reported a great deal in the literature, we must try to get some perspective on the absolute and relative sizes of such statistics. Although the discussion uses differences between means as examples, the same points apply to differences between proportions, correlation coefficients, and so on. In a study by Scattone and Saetermoe (1997) U.S.-born Asians were found to be more accepting of people with disabilities than foreign-born Asians. Using a social distance scale of 1 to 5, where 5 indicates higher acceptance, U.S.-born Asians had a mean of 4.17 while foreign-born Asians had a mean of 3.71. The mean difference was 0.46 and was statistically significant. Is such a small difference meaningful? Contrast this small difference to the mean difference between males and females on consumption of beer obtained by Zavela, Barrett, Smedi, Istvan, and Matarazzo (1990). Zavela and associates studied gender differences on the consumption of alcohol, cigarettes, and coffee. For the consumption of beer per month males had a mean of 18.68 and females had 9.14. The mean difference here was 9.54 and was statistically significant.

The problem here is actually two problems: one of absolute and relative size of differences and one of practical or "real" significance versus statistical significance. What appears to be a very small difference may, on close examination, not be so small. In a study by Evans, Turner, Ghee, and Getz (1990) on the relation between androgynous role and cigarette smoking, there was a mean difference of 0.164 between androgynous and non-androgynous subjects on smoking frequency. The difference of 0.164 is probably trivial even though statistically significant. The 0.164 was derived from a 7-point scale of smoking frequency, and is thus really small. Now, take an entirely different sort of example from an important study by Miller and DiCara (1968) on the instrumental conditioning of urine secretion. The means of a group of rats before and after training to secrete urine were 0.017 and 0.028, and the difference was highly statistically significant. But the difference was only 0.011. Is this too small to warrant serious consideration? But now the nature of the measures has to be considered. The small means of 0.017 and 0.028 were obtained from measures of urine secretion of rats. When one considers the size of rats' bladders and that instrumental conditioning (reward for secreting urine) produced the mean difference of 0.011, the meaning of the difference is dramatic: it is even quite large! (We will analyze the data in a later chapter and perhaps see this more clearly.)

One should ordinarily not be enthusiastic about mean differences like 0.20, 0.15, 0.08, and so on, but one has to be intelligent about it. Suppose that a very small difference is reported as statistically significant, and you think this ridiculous. But also suppose that it was the mean difference between the dendrite length of groups of rats under enriched and deprived experiences in the early days of their lives (Camel, Withers, & Greenough, 1986). To obtain any difference in dendrite branching in neurons due to experience is an outstanding achievement and, of course, an important scientific discovery.

Correlation Coefficients

Correlation coefficients are reported in large quantities in research journals. Questions as to the significance of the coefficients—and the "reality" of the relations they express must be asked. For example, to be statistically significant a coefficient of correlation calculated between 30 pairs of measures has to be approximately 0.31 at the 0.05 level and 0.42 at the 0.01 level. With 100 pairs of measures the problem is less acute (the law of large numbers again). To carry the 0.05 day, an r of 0.16 is sufficient; to carry the 0.01 day, an r of about 0.23 does it. If rs are less than these values, they are considered to be not significantly different from zero.

If one draws, say, 30 pairs of numbers from a table of random numbers and correlates them, theoretically the r should be near zero. Clearly, there should be near-zero relations between sets of random numbers, but occasionally sets of pairs can yield statistically significant and reasonably high rs *by chance*. At any rate, coefficients of correlation, as well as means and differences, have to be weighed in the balance for statistical significance by stacking them up against their standard errors. Fortunately, this is easy to do, since rs for different levels of significance and for different sizes of samples are given in tables in most statistics texts. Thus, with rs, it is not necessary to calculate and use the standard error of an r. The reasoning behind the tables has to be understood, however.

Of the thousands of correlation coefficients reported in the research literature, many are of low magnitude. How low is low? At what point is a correlation coefficient too low to warrant treating it seriously? Usually, r less than 0.10 cannot be taken too seriously: an r of 0.10 means that only 1% ($0.10^2 = 0.01$) of the variance of y is shared with x! If an r of 0.30, on the other hand, is statistically significant, it may be important because it may point to an important relation. The problem becomes more difficult with rs between 0.20 and 0.30. (And remember that with large Ns, rs between 0.20 and 0.30 are statistically significant.) To be sure, an r, of say 0.20 says that the two variables share only 4% of their variance. But an r of 0.26—7% of the variance shared—or even one of 0.20 may be important because it may provide a valuable lead for theory and subsequent research. The problem is complex. In basic research, low correlations—of course, they should be statistically significant—may enrich theory and research. It is in applied research where prediction is important. It is here where value judgments about low correlations and the trivial amounts of variance shared have grown. In basic research, however, the picture is more complicated. One conclusion is fairly sure: correlation coefficients, like other statistics, must be tested for statistical significance.

Hypothesis Testing: Substantive and Null Hypotheses

The main research purpose of inferential statistics is to test research hypotheses by testing statistical hypotheses. Broadly speaking, scientists use two types of hypotheses: substantive and statistical. A *substantive hypothesis* is the usual type of hypothesis discussed in Chapter 2, where a conjectural statement of the relation between two or more variables is expressed. For example, "The greater the cohesiveness of a group, the greater its influence on its members" is a substantive hypothesis posed by Schacter, Ellertson, McBride, and Gregory (1951). An investigator's theory dictates that this variable is related to that variable. The statement of the relation is a substantive hypothesis.

A substantive hypothesis itself, strictly speaking, is not testable. It must first be translated into operational terms. One very useful way to test substantive hypotheses is through statistical hypotheses. A *statistical hypothesis* is a conjectural statement, in statistical terms, of statistical relations deduced from the relations of the substantive hypothesis. This rather clumsy statement needs translation. A statistical hypothesis expresses an aspect of the original substantive hypothesis in quantitative and statistical terms: $\mu_A > \mu_B$, Mean A is greater than Mean B; $r > +0.20$, the coefficient of correlation is greater than +0.20; $\mu_A > \mu_B > \mu_C$, at the 0.01 level; χ^2 is significant at the 0.05 level; and so on. A statistical hypothesis is a prediction of how the statistics used in analyzing the quantitative data of a research problem will turn out. In our discussion of hypothesis testing we will use μ to indicate the population mean, and M for the sample mean. Statistical hypotheses are expressed in terms of population values. After collecting data, the computed mean from the sample will use M.

Statistical hypotheses must be tested against something, however. It is not possible to simply test a stand-alone statistical hypothesis. That is, we do not directly test the statistical proposition $\mu_A > \mu_B$ in and of itself. We test it *against* an alternative proposition. Naturally, there can be several alternatives to $\mu_A > \mu_B$. The alternative usually selected is the null hypothesis, which was invented by Sir Ronald Fisher. The *null hypothesis* is a statistical proposition that states, essentially, that there is no relation between the variables (of the problem). The null hypothesis says, "You're wrong, there is no relation; disprove me if you can." It says this in statistical terms such as $\mu_A = \mu_B$; or $\mu_A - \mu_B = 0$; $r_{xy} = 0$; χ^2 is not significant; t is not significant; and so on.

Researchers sometimes unwittingly use null hypotheses as substantive hypotheses. Instead of saying that one method of presenting textual materials has a greater effect on recall memory than another method, for instance, they may say that there is no difference between the two methods. This is poor practice because it in effect uses the statistical null hypothesis as a substantive hypothesis, and thus confuses the two kinds of hypotheses. Strictly speaking, any significant result, positive or negative, then, supports the hypothesis. But this is certainly not the intention. The intention is to bring statistical evidence to bear on the substantive hypothesis, for example, on $\mu_A > \mu_B$. If the result is statistically significant (μ_A μ_B, or the null hypothesis is rejected) $\mu_A > \mu_B$, then the substantive hypothesis is supported. Using the null hypothesis substantively loses the power of the substantive hypothesis, which amounts to the investigator making a specific nonchance prediction.

There is, of course, always the rather rare possibility that a null hypothesis is the substantive hypothesis. If, for example, an investigator seeks to show that two methods of teaching make no difference in achievement, then the null hypothesis is presumably appropriate. The trouble with this is that it places the investigator in a difficult position logically because it is extremely difficult—perhaps impossible—to demonstrate the empirical "validity" of a null hypothesis. After all, if the hypothesis $\mu_A = \mu_B$ is supported, it could well be one of the many chance results that are possible, rather than a meaningful nondifference! Good discussions of hypothesis testing are given in Giere (1979), chapters 6, 8, 11, and 12, especially Chapter 11.

Fisher (1950) says, "Every experiment may be said to exist only in order to give the facts a chance of disproving the null hypothesis." Aptly said, but what does it mean? Suppose you entertain a hypothesis to the effect that method A is superior to method B. If you solve the problems of defining what you mean by "superior" satisfactorily—setting up an experiment, and the like—you must now specify a statistical hypothesis. In this case, you might say $\mu_A > \mu_B$ (the mean of method A is, or will be greater than, the mean of method B on such-and-such a criterion measure). Assume that after the experiment the two means are 68 and 61, respectively. It would seem that your substantive hypothesis is upheld since $68 > 61$, or μ_A is greater than μ_B. As we have already learned, however, this is not enough, since this difference may be one of the many possible similar differences due to chance.

In effect, we set up what can be called the chance hypothesis: $\mu_A = \mu_B$, or $\mu_A - \mu_B = 0$. These are null hypotheses. What we do, then, is write hypotheses. First we write the statistical hypothesis that reflects the operational–experimental meaning of the substantive hypothesis. Then we write the null hypothesis against which we test the first type of hypothesis. Here are the two kinds of hypothesis suitably labeled:

$$H_o: \mu_A = \mu_B$$

$$H_1: \mu_A > \mu_B$$

H_1 represents "Hypothesis 1." There is often more than one such hypothesis. If that is so, they are labeled H_1, H_2, H_3, and so on. H_o represents "null hypothesis." Note that the null hypothesis could in this case have been written $H_o: \mu_A - \mu_B = 0$. This form shows where the null hypothesis got its name: the difference between μ_A and m_B is zero. But it is unwieldy in this form, especially when there are three or more means or other statistics being tested. $\mu_A = \mu_B$ is general and, of course, means the same as $\mu_A - \mu_B = 0$ and $\mu_B - \mu_A = 0$. Note that we can write quite easily $\mu_A = \mu_B = \mu_C = \ldots = \mu_N$.

Although as researchers we want to demonstrate that H_1 is true, it cannot be done in a direct way easily. Let's say our substantive hypothesis leads us to write the statistical hypothesis $H_1: \mu_A \neq \mu_B$. This hypothesis can be rewritten $H_1: \mu_A - \mu_B \neq 0$. In order to test this hypothesis directly, we would need to test an infinite number of values. That is, we would need to test each and every situation where $\mu_A - \mu_B$ is *not* equal to zero. In hypothesis testing, the procedure dictates that we test the null hypothesis. The null hypothesis is written as $H_o: \mu_A - \mu_B = 0$. Note that it points directly to a value, namely zero. What we need do is to gather enough empirical data to show that the null hypothesis is not tenable. In statistical terms, we would "reject H_o." Rejecting H_o would indicate to us that we have a significant result. Rejecting H_o leads us toward supporting H_1. Supporting H_1, in turn leads to support for our substantive hypothesis. If there are not enough empirical data to refute the null hypothesis, we would not be able to reject the null hypothesis. Statistically we would say "failed to reject H_o" or "do not reject H_o." Note that we do not "accept" H_o because the results were "not significant." Regardless of the results, it is only possible to "fail to reject" H_o or "reject" H_o; one can never "accept" H_o. To "accept" H_o would require repeating the study an infinite number of times, and getting exactly zero each time. On the other hand, we can "fail to reject" H_o because the results are not sufficiently different from what one would predict (under the assumption that H_o is true) to warrant the conclusion that it is false.

The status of H_o is akin to the defendant in a trial who is deemed to be "innocent" until proved "guilty." If the trial results in a verdict of "not guilty," this does not mean the defendant is "innocent." It merely means that guilt could not be demonstrated beyond a reasonable doubt. When the investigator fails to reject H_o it does not mean H_o is true, merely that H_o cannot be shown to be false beyond a "reasonable" doubt. Propst (1988) and Kenney (1985) give an interesting analogy of hypothesis testing within the criminal justice system.

The General Nature of a Standard Error

If this were the best of all possible research worlds, there would be no random error. And if there was no random error, there would be no need for statistical tests of significance. The word *significance* would in fact be meaningless. Any difference at all would be a "real" difference. But alas, such is never the case. There are always chance errors (and biased errors, too), and in behavioral research they often contribute substantially to the total variance. Standard errors are measures of this error, and are used, as has been said repeatedly, as a sort of yardstick against which experimental or "variable" variance is checked.

The *standard error* is the standard deviation of the sampling distribution of any given measure—the mean or the correlation coefficient, for instance. In most cases, population or universe values (parameters) cannot be known; they must be estimated from sample measures, usually from single samples.

Suppose we draw a random sample of 100 children from eighth-grade classes in such-and-such a school system. It is difficult or impossible, say, to measure the whole universe of eighth-grade children. We calculate the mean and the standard deviation from a test we give the children, and find these statistics to be $M = 110$; $SD = 10$. Important questions we must ask are: How accurate is this mean? or If we were to draw a large number of random samples of 100 eighth-grade pupils from this same population, will the means of these samples be 110 or near 110? And, if they are near 110, how near? What we do, in effect, is to set up a *hypothetical distribution of sample means*, all calculated from samples of 100 pupils, each drawn from the parent population of eighth-grade pupils. If we could calculate the mean of this population of means, or if we knew what it was, everything would be simple. But we do not know this value, and we are not able to know it, since the possibilities of drawing different samples are so numerous. The best we can do is *to estimate it with our sample value, or sample mean*. We simply say, in this case, "Let the sample mean equal the mean of the population mean"—and hope we are right. Then we must test our equation. We do this with the standard error.

A similar argument applies to the standard deviation of the whole population (of the original scores). We do not know and probably can never know it. But we can estimate it with the standard deviation calculated from our sample. Again, we say, in effect, "Let the standard deviation of the sample equal the standard deviation of the population." We know they are probably not the same value, but we also know, if the sampling has been random, that they are probably close.

In Chapter 11 the sample standard deviation was used as a substitute for the standard deviation of the population in the formula for the *standard error of the mean*:

$$SE_M = \frac{SD}{\sqrt{n}} \tag{12.1}$$

This is also called the *sampling error*. Just as the standard deviation is a measure of the dispersion of the original scores, the standard error of the mean is a measure of the dispersion of the distribution of sample means. It is *not* the standard deviation of the population of individual scores. It is *not* the same as testing every member of the population, and then calculating the mean and standard deviation of this population.

A Monte Carlo Demonstration

To give us material to work with, we now resort to the computer and what are called Monte Carlo methods. Monte Carlo methods are computer-assisted simulation methods designed to obtain solutions to mathematical, statistical, numerical, and even verbal problems, by using random procedures and samples of random numbers. Usually associated with mathematical problems whose solutions are intractable, Monte Carlo methods have been extended to "testing" the statistical characteristics of samples of large populations. For example, the consequences of violating the assumptions behind statistical tests of significance can be studied effectively by simulating statistical distributions with random numbers, and introducing violations of assumptions into the procedure to study the consequences. In the behavioral sciences, Monte Carlo procedures are usually empirical studies of statistical and other models, using the computer-generated random numbers to help simulate the random processes needed to study the models. In any case, we now use an elementary form of Monte Carlo to test a most important theorem of statistics, and to explore the variability of means and the use of the standard error of the mean. We also want to lay a foundation for understanding the computer in studying random processes.

The Procedure

A computer program is written to generate 4,000 random numbers evenly distributed between 0 and 100 (so that each number has an equal chance of being "drawn") in 40 sets of 100 numbers each, and to calculate various statistics with the numbers. Consider this set of 4,000 numbers a population, or U. The mean of U is 50.33 (by actual computer calculation) and the standard deviation is 29.17. We wish to estimate this mean from samples drawn randomly from U. Of course, in a real situation we would usually not know the mean of the population. One of the virtues of Monte Carlo procedures is that we can know what we ordinarily do not know.

Five of the 40 sets of 100 numbers are drawn at random. (The sets drawn are numbers 5, 7, 8, 16, and 36 [see Appendix C].) The means and standard deviations of the five sets were computed. So were the five standard errors of the mean. These statistics are reported in Table 12.1. We want to give an intuitive notion of what the standard error of the mean is and then show how it is used.

First, calculate the standard deviation (*SD*) of this sample of means. If we simply treat the five means (53.21, 49.64, 51.37, 49.02, and 55.51) as ordinary scores and calculate the mean of these means and the standard deviation of these five means, we obtain: $M_* = 51.75$; $SD_* = 2.38$. The mean of all 4,000 scores is 50.33. Each of the five means is a sample estimate of this population mean. Note that three of them,

◫ TABLE 12.1 *Means Standard Deviations, and Standard Errors of the Mean, Five Samples of 100 Random Numbers (0 through 100)*[a]

	Samples				
	1	2	3	4	5
N	53.21	49.64	51.37	49.02	55.51
SD	29.62	27.91	29.83	26.72	29.23
SE_M	2.96	2.79	2.98	2.67	2.92

[a] Population statistics: $M = 50.33$; $SD = 29.1653$; $N = 4,000$

49.64, 51.37, and 49.02, are rather close to the population mean; and two of them, 53.21 and 55.51, are farther away from it. So it seems that three of the samples provide good estimates of the population mean and two do not—or do they?

The standard deviation of 2.38 is *akin* to the standard error of the mean. (It is, of course, not the standard error of the mean, because it has been calculated from only five means.) Suppose only one sample—$M = 53.21$ and $SD = 29.62$—had been drawn, and this is the usual situation in research, and the standard error of the mean calculated:

$$SE_M = \frac{SD}{\sqrt{n}} = \frac{29.62}{\sqrt{100}} = 2.96$$

This value is an estimate of the standard deviation of the population *means* of many, many samples of 100 cases, each randomly drawn from the population. Our population has 40 groups and thus 40 means. (Of course, this is not many, many means.) The standard deviation of these means is actually 3.10. The SE_M calculated with the first sample, then, is close to this population value: 2.96 as an estimate of 3.10.

The five standard errors of the mean are given in the third data line of Table 12.1. They fluctuate very little—from 2.67 to 2.98—even though the means of the sets of 100 scores vary considerably. The standard deviation of 2.38 calculated from the five means is only a fair estimate of the standard deviation of the population of means. Yet it is an estimate. The interesting and important point is that the standard error of the mean, which is a "theoretical" estimate, calculated from the data of any one of the five groups, is an accurate estimate of the variability of the means of samples of the population.

To reinforce these ideas, let's now look at another Monte Carlo demonstration of much greater magnitude. The same computer program used to produce the 4,000 random numbers discussed above is now used to produce 15 more sets of 4,000 random numbers each, evenly distributed between 0 and 100. That is, a total of 80,000 random numbers, in 20 sets of 4,000 each, are generated. The theoretical mean, again, of numbers between 0 and 100 is 50. Consider each of the 20 sets as a sample of 4,000 numbers. The means of the 20 sets are given in Table 12.2.

▣ TABLE 12.2 *Means from 20 Sets of 4,000 Computer-Generated Random Numbers (0 through 100)*[a]

50.3322	49.9447	50.1615	50.0995
50.1170	49.5960	51.0585	51.1450
49.8200	49.3175	49.5822	50.6440
49.8227	49.9022	49.7505	49.8437
49.5875	50.6180	50.0990	49.3605

[a] Mean of means equals 50.0401; standard deviation of the means equals 0.4956; standard error of the mean, first sample equals 0.4611.

The 20 means cluster closely around 50: the lowest is 49.3175, the highest is 51.1450, and most are near 50. The mean of the 20 means is 50.0401, very close indeed to the theoretical expectation of 50. The standard deviation of the 20 means is 0.4956. The standard deviation of the first sample of 4,000 cases (see note a, Table 12.1) is 29.1653. If we use this standard deviation to calculate the standard error of the mean, we obtain:

$$SE_M = \frac{29.1653}{\sqrt{4000}} = .4611$$

Note that this estimate of the standard error of the mean is close to the calculated standard deviation of the 20 means. We would not go wrong using it to assess the variability of the means of samples of 4,000 random numbers. Clearly, means of large samples are highly stable statistics, and standard errors are good estimates of their variability.

Generalizations

Several generalizations of great usefulness in research can now be made. For example, means of samples are stable in the sense that they are much less variable than the measures from which they are calculated. This is, of course, true by definition. Variances, standard deviations, and standard errors of the mean are even more stable; they fluctuate within relatively narrow ranges. Even when the sample means of our example varied by as much as four or five points, the standard errors fluctuated by no more than a point and a half. This means that we can have considerable faith that estimates of sample means will be rather close to the mean of a population of such means. And the law of large numbers tells us that the larger the sample size, the closer to the population values the statistics will probably be.

A difficult question for researchers is: Do these generalizations always hold, especially with nonrandom samples? The validity of the generalizations depends on random sampling. If the sampling is not random, we cannot really know whether the generalizations hold. Nevertheless, we often have to act as though they do hold, even with nonrandom samples. Fortunately, if we are careful about studying our data to detect substantial sample idiosyncrasy, we can use the theory profitably. For example, samples can be checked for easily verified expectations. If one expects approximately equal numbers of males and females in a sample, or known proportions of young and old or Republican and Democrat, it is simple to count these numbers. There are experts who insist on random sampling as a condition of the validity of the theory—and they are correct to some degree. However, if the theory is forbidden to us with nonrandom samples, much use of statistics and the inferences that accompany statistics would have to be abandoned. The reality is that the statistics seem to work very well even with nonrandom samples, provided the researcher knows the limitations of such samples. The researcher needs to be even more careful with nonrandom samples than with random samples. Replication of nonrandom studies is a must.

The Central Limit Theorem

Before studying the actual use of the standard error of the mean, we should look briefly at an extremely important generalization about means: *If samples are drawn from a population at random, the means of the samples will tend to be normally distributed.* The larger the Ns, the more this is so. And the shape and kind of distribution of the original population makes no difference. That is, the population distribution does not have to be normally distributed (see Hays, 1994, pp. 251–254 for a good example on how the theorem works).

For example, the distribution of the 4,000 random numbers in Appendix C is rectangular, since the numbers are evenly distributed. If the central limit theorem is empirically valid, then the means of the 40 sets of 100 scores each should be approximately normally distributed. If so, this is a remarkable thing. And it is so, though one sample of 40 means is hardly sufficient to well demonstrate the trend. Therefore, three more populations of 4,000 different evenly distributed random numbers, partitioned into 40 subsets of 100 numbers each, are computer-generated.

The means for the $4 \times 40 = 160$ subsets of 100 numbers each were calculated and put into one distribution. A frequency polygon of the means is given in Figure 12.1. It can be seen that the 160 means look almost like the bell-shaped normal curve. Apparently the central limit theorem "works." And bear in mind that this distribution of means was obtained from rectangular distributions of numbers.

Why go to all this bother? Why is it important to show that distributions of means approximate normality? We work with means a great deal in data analysis, and if they are normally distributed then one can use the known properties of the normal curve to interpret obtained research data. Knowing that approximately 96% of the means will lie between two standard deviations (standard errors) above and below the mean is valuable information. It is valuable because an obtained result can be assessed against the known properties of the normal curve. In Chapter 11 we saw the use of the normal curve in interpreting means. We now turn to what is perhaps a more interesting use of the curve in assessing the differences between means.

■ FIGURE 12.1

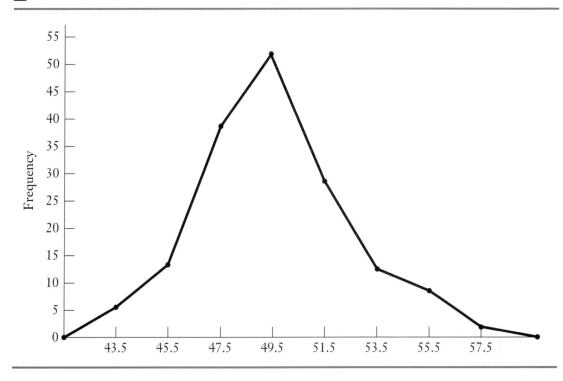

The Standard Error
of the Differences Between Means

One of the most frequent and useful strategies in research is to compare means of samples. From differences in means we infer effects of independent variables. Any linear combination of means is also governed by the central limit theorem. That is, differences in means will be normally distributed, given large enough samples. (A linear combination is any equation of the first degree, for example, $Y = M_1 - M_2$. $Y = M_1^2 - M_2$ is not linear.) We can therefore use the same theory with differences between means that we use with means.

Suppose we have assigned 200 subjects to two groups randomly, 100 to each group. We show a movie on intergroup relations to one group (Group A), for example, and no movie to the other group (Group B). Next, we give both groups an attitude measure. The mean score of Group A is 110, and the mean score of Group B is 100. Our problem is: Is the difference of 10 units a "real" difference, a statistically significant difference? Or is it a difference that could have arisen by chance —more than five times in 100, say, or some other amount—when no difference actually exists?

If we similarly create double samples of 100 each and calculate the differences between the means of these samples, and go through the same experimental procedure, will we consistently get this difference of 10? Again, we use the standard error to evaluate our differences, but this time we have a sampling *distribution of differences between means*. It is as if we took each $M_i - M_j$ and considered it as an X. Then the several differences between the means of the samples are considered as the Xs of a new distribution. At any rate, the standard deviation of this sampling distribution of differences *is akin* to the standard error. But this procedure is only for illustration, because we actually do not do this. Here, we again estimate the standard error from our first two groups, A and B, by using the formula:

$$SE_{M_A - M_B} = \sqrt{SE_{MA}^2 + SE_{MB}^2} \qquad (12.2)$$

where $SE_{M_A}^2$ and $SE_{M_B}^2$ are the standard errors squared, respectively, of Group A and Group B, as previously stated.

Suppose we do the experiment with five double groups; that is, 10 groups, two at a time. The five differences between the means are 10, 11, 12, 8, 9. The mean of these differences is 10; the standard deviation is 1.414. This 1.414 is again *akin* to the standard error of the sampling distribution of the differences between the means, in the same sense as the standard error of the mean in the earlier discussion. If we now calculate the standard error of the mean for each group (by making up standard deviations for the two groups, $SD_A = 8$ and $SD_B = 9$), we obtain:

$$SE_{M_A} = \frac{SD_A}{\sqrt{n_A}} = \frac{8}{\sqrt{100}} = .8, \qquad SE_{M_B} = \frac{SD_B}{\sqrt{n_B}} = \frac{9}{\sqrt{100}} = .9$$

Using Equation 12.2, we calculate the standard error of the differences between the means:

$$SE_{M_A - M_B} = \sqrt{SE_{MA}^2 + SE_{MB}^2} = \sqrt{(.8)^2 + (.9)^2} = \sqrt{.64 + .81} = \sqrt{1.45} = 1.20$$

What do we do with the resulting 1.20 now that we have it? If the scores of the two groups had been chosen from a table of random numbers and there were no experimental conditions, we would expect no difference between the means. But we have learned that there are always relatively small differences due to chance factors. These differences are random. *The standard error of the differences between the means is an estimate of the dispersion of these differences.* But it is a measure of these differences that is an estimate for the whole population of such differences. For instance, the standard error of the differences between the means is 1.20. This says that, by chance alone, the difference between M_A and M_B will fluctuate randomly around 10. That is, it may now be 10, then later be 10.2, or 9.8, and so on. Only rarely will the differences exceed, say, 13 or 7 (about three times the *SE*). Another way of putting it is to say that the standard error of 1.20 indicates the limits (if we multiply the 1.20 by the appropriate factor) beyond which sample differences between the means probably will not go.

What has all this to do with our experiment? It is precisely here that we evaluate the experimental results. The standard error of 1.20 estimates random fluctuations. Could $M_A - M_B = 10$ have arisen by chance, as a result of random fluctuations as just described? It should by now be halfway clear that this cannot be, except under very unusual circumstances. We evaluate this difference of 10 by comparing it to our estimate of random or chance fluctuations. *Is it one of them?* We make the comparison by means of the *t*-ratio, or *t*-test:

$$t = \frac{M_A - M_B}{SE_{M_A - M_B}} = \frac{110 - 100}{1.20} = \frac{10}{1.20} = 8.33$$

This tells us that our measured difference between M_A and M_B would be 8.33 standard deviations (error units) away from a hypothesized mean of zero (zero difference, no difference between the two means).

We would not have any difference, theoretically, if our subjects were well randomized and there had been no experimental manipulation. We would have, in effect, two distributions of random numbers from which we could expect only chance fluctuations. But here we have a comparatively huge difference of 10, compared to an insignificant 1.20 (our estimate of random deviations). Decidedly, something may be happening here besides chance. And this something is just what we are looking for. It is, presumably, the effect of the movie, or the effect of the experimental condition, other conditions having been sufficiently controlled, of course.

Look at Figure 12.2. It represents a *population of differences between* means with a mean of zero and a standard deviation of 1.20. (The mean is set at zero because we assume that the mean of all the mean differences is zero.) Where would the difference of 10 be placed on the baseline of the diagram? In order to answer this

■ **FIGURE 12.2**

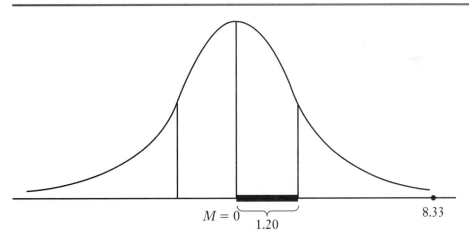

question, the 10 must first be converted into standard deviation (or standard error) units. (Recall standard scores from Chapter 11.) This is done by dividing by the standard deviation (standard error), which is 1.20: $10/1.2 = 8.33$. But this is what we got when we calculated the t-ratio. It is, then, simply the difference between M_A and M_B, 10, expressed in standard deviation (standard error) units. We can now put it on the baseline of the diagram. Look far to the right for the dot. Clearly the difference of 10 is a deviate. It is so far out, in fact, that it probably does not belong to the population in question. In short, the difference between M_A and M_B is statistically significant, so significant that it amounts to what Bernoulli called "moral certainty." Such a large difference, or deviation from chance expectation, can hardly be attributed solely to chance. The odds are actually greater than a billion to one. It can happen by chance. But it is hardly likely to happen. An important question is: How large a difference, or in the language of statistics, how far away from the hypothetical mean of zero must a deviation be to be significant? This question cannot be answered definitively in this book. In large samples, the 0.05 level is 1.96 standard deviations from the mean, and the 0.01 level is 2.58 standard deviations from the mean. But there are complications, especially with small samples. The student must, as usual, study a good statistics text. A simple rule is: 2 standard deviations (SEs) are significant (about the 0.05 level); 2.5 standard deviations are very significant (about the 0.01 level); and 3 standard deviations are highly significant (a little less than the 0.001 level).

Such is the standard error and its use. The standard errors of other statistics are used in the same way. A very important and useful tool; it is a basic instrument in contemporary research. Indeed, it would be difficult to imagine modern research methodology, and impossible to imagine modern statistics, without the standard error. As a key to statistical inference its importance cannot be overestimated. Much of statistical inference boils down to a family of fractions epitomized by the fraction:

$$\frac{\text{Statistic}}{\text{Standard Error of the Statistic}}$$

Statistical Inference

To *infer* is to derive a conclusion from premises or from evidence. To *infer statistically* is to derive probabilistic conclusions from probabilistic premises. We conclude probabilistically; that is, at a specified level of significance. We infer, probabilistically, if an experimental result deviates from chance expectation, if the null hypothesis is not "true," that a "real" influence is at work. If, in the methods experiment, $M_A > M_B$ and $M_A \neq M_B$, or H_1 is "true" and H_0 is not "true," we infer that method A is "superior" to method B, "superior" being specified in the sense defined in the experiment.

Another form of inference, discussed at length in the chapter on sampling, is that from a sample to a population. Since, for instance, 55% of a random sample of 2,000 people in the United States say they will vote for a certain presidential candidate, it is inferred that the whole population of the United States, if asked, will respond similarly. This is a rather big inference. One of the gravest dangers of research—or perhaps we should say of any human reasoning—is the inferential leap from sample data to population fact. Inferential leaps are constantly made in politics, economics, education, and other areas of large concern. If the government cuts spending, inflation will decrease, for example. If we use teaching machines, children will learn more. Scientists, too, make inferential leaps—often very large ones—with one important difference: The scientist is (or should be) aware of such leaps and that such leaps are always risky.

It can be said, in sum, that statistics enable scientists to test substantive hypotheses indirectly by enabling them to test statistical hypotheses directly (if it is at all possible to test anything directly). In this process, they use null hypotheses, hypotheses written by chance. They test the "truth" of substantive hypotheses by subjecting null hypotheses to statistical tests on the bases of probabilistic reasoning. They then make appropriate inferences. Indeed, the objective of all statistical tests is to test the justifiability of inferences. A reviewer of this chapter has questioned the message the chapter implies, namely that all statistical tests of hypotheses involve standard errors. This implication would be unfortunate. Indeed, as we shall see in later chapters, other means of assessing statistical significance are often used. For example, the nonparametric analysis of variance tests presented in Chapter 16 depend on ranking, and the complex tests of analysis of covariance structures of Chapter 37 depend on comparisons of covariances (correlations) and the comparison of latent structures with empirical data.

Testing Hypotheses and the Two Types of Errors

In a coin-tossing experiment, we can test the hypothesis that the coin is balanced or not balanced. These hypotheses are stated as follows:

$$H_o: p = 1/2$$

$$H_1: p \neq 1/2$$

where H_o equals the hypothesis to be tested, and p equals the true probability of a head. The hypothesis to be tested, H_o, states that p, the true probability of getting a head on any given trial, is 1/2. If it is true, the coin is indeed balanced. Of course, in practice the number of heads obtained with an unbiased coin cannot be guaranteed to be exactly 1/2 unless the coin is tossed an infinite number of times—an impossibility. For a fair coin, the obtained number of heads approaches 50% as the number of trials increase.

In a coin-tossing experiment where 12 out of 16 tosses are heads for the coin suspected of yielding too many heads, the probability for such an event can be obtained from using the binomial formula (see Comrey & Lee, 1995, Chapter 7) or by consulting a table of binomial value (see Beyer, 1971, p. 44). The probability or p value for the obtained result is 0.038. If we choose the 0.05 level of significance in advance, the result would be declared "significant" since $0.038 < 0.05$. It would not, however be significant if we had chosen the 0.01 level of significance, since $0.038 > 0.01$.

If we conduct another experiment with the same coin and it yields 15 heads in 19 tosses; the probability of this happening, if we assume the coin is fair, is 0.0096. In this case, the results are not only significant at the 0.05 level ($0.0096 < 0.05$), the results would also be significant at the 0.01 level ($0.0096 < 0.01$).

In the example where 12 heads are obtained in 16 tosses of a coin, the null hypothesis that the coin is fair is rejected. It is rejected because the probability of such an event occurring given that the coin is fair is 0.038, and this value is less than the tolerable amount of 0.05. Rejecting H_o, however, is an error if in fact the coin is fair. We call this error the *Type I error*. A fair coin might generate 12 or more heads in 16 tosses. The likelihood of that happening is 0.038, or 38 out of 1,000 repetitions of the same "16 toss" experiment. It is not shown beforehand whether this particular experiment is one of the 38, when a fair coin generated 12 heads in 16 tosses, or if the coin really is unfair. However, H_o is rejected with the awareness that an error might have been made, but the chances of that happening are less than 0.05. The conclusion of rejecting H_o on an average is correct more than 95% of the time. For the 1% level of significance, rejecting a true null hypothesis occurs an average of one time in every 100 experiments. For the 5% level, it occurs an average of five times in every 100 experiments. Hence, rejecting a true null hypothesis is a Type I error. The symbol used to represent the probability of a Type I error is the Greek letter α (alpha). The term "level of confidence" is often interchangeable with "level of significance" and "alpha level."

A second type of error, called a *Type II error*, is made when H_o is false, but the conclusion of the analysis is that H_o is true. That is, accepting a false null hypothesis is a Type II error. Generally, observing 8 heads in 16 tosses of a coin is evidence that the coin is fair. However, an unfair coin (one where the probability of heads is 0.25 instead of 0.5), can generate 8 heads in 16 tosses. The ease in doing so is not as high as for a fair coin, but an unfair coin can do it. The experiment can be repeated many times before a judgment is made. However, in some real world experiments, such as those found in human factors engineering studies, it is not financially feasible to repeat the experiment. Generally, one has only a single experimental result from which a decision is to be made. In the example above, if the coin is in fact unfair, but the conclusion of the experiment is that the coin is fair, a Type II error has been made. The Greek letter used to represent the probability of a Type II error is β (beta).

Most novice researchers tend to establish a very stringent Type I error criterion. By doing so, there is less likelihood of a Type I error. There is, however, a relationship between the Type I and Type II errors that needs to be considered before making the decision to make either error too stringent. If the probability of a Type I error is made smaller, the probability of a Type II error gets larger for a fixed sample size. Likewise, by reducing the probability of a Type II error, the probability of a Type I error increases. As a rule, in selecting a significance level one must decide which type of error is more important to avoid or minimize. To be certain that an event of some importance has been identified before reporting it, use a fairly stringent criterion of significance, such as 0.01. On the other hand, if there is greater concern not to miss something, use a less stringent level, such as 0.05. Table 12.3 and

■ FIGURE 12.3

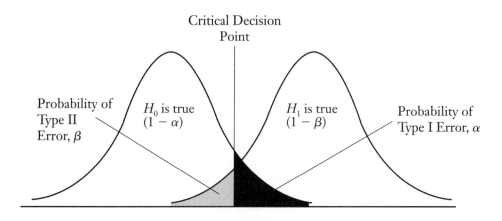

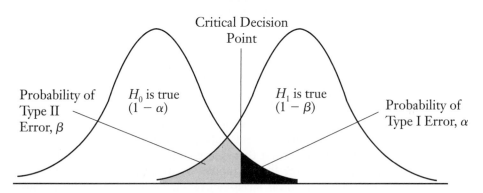

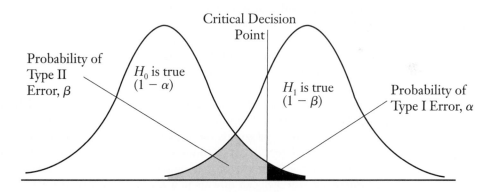

Figure 12.3 show the relationship between the Type I and Type II errors. Probst (1988) presents an absorbing discussion of the trade-off between Type I and Type II errors in some real-world situations.

▣ **TABLE 12.3** *Type I and Type II Decision Errors.*

		True State of Affairs	
		The null hypothesis is correct	**The experimental hypothesis is correct**
Our decision	Fail to reject H_o	Correct decision, $1 - \alpha$	Type II error, β
	Reject H_o	Type I error, α	Correct decision, $1 - \beta$

In examining Figure 12.3, the filled in area indicates the probability of a Type I error. The critical decision point is the point that divides the "H_o is true" distribution so 0.05 or 0.01 of the area lies to the right of the point. By setting the probability of a Type I error, the probability of a Type II error is set. By moving the critical decision point, the Type I error becomes smaller or larger, and in return, the Type II error becomes larger or smaller.

The size of the sample is related to both types of errors. With a fixed value of α and a fixed sample size n, the value of β is predetermined. If β is too large, it can be reduced by either raising the level of α for fixed n, or by increasing n for a fixed level of α. Although β is seldom determined in an experiment, researchers can be assured that it is reasonably small by collecting a large sample.

The power of a test concept arises from the Type II error, β. In fact, the power of a test is defined as $1 - \beta$. The power of a test is the probability of rejecting a false null hypothesis. A test that is termed to be more powerful than another is defined as a test that is more likely to discover significant differences than another. These tests with different power levels can be further compared with a power efficiency index, which usually ranges from 0.63 to 1.00. When a test has a power efficiency of 0.75 in comparison to another test, it indicates that the weaker test requires a sample size of 100 to achieve the same power level as the stronger test does with a sample size of 75. The *power of test* is usually not computed. Tables are available to estimate the power of a test. A more complete treatment of this material may be found in Cohen (1988). The notion of power is often used in the estimation of sample size. Several computer software programs for conducting power analysis are available. One of the more established and better-known is by Borenstein, Cohen, and Rothstein (1997), called "Power Precision!" Others are N & Nsurv, and PASS (Power Analysis and Sample Size). These programs are expensive and, at the time of this writing, only PASS is designed to run on Windows. The other two are DOS-based programs. Although Internet information gets outdated quickly, at the present time there is a site where a researcher can download a list and a review of software for computing power. The Web site address is http://www.interchg.ubc.ca/cacb/power/.[2] A DOS-

---

[2]This valuable information was provided by one of the anonymous reviewers of this textbook.

based power analysis program is available with the book by Woodward, Bonett, and Brecht (1990).

The Five Steps of Hypothesis Testing

After our discussion given in the previous sections, we are ready to put in place the five major steps used in hypothesis testing. Using our substantive hypothesis we can state it statistically. Even though we have referred to it as our statistical hypothesis, many statisticians refer to it as the research, or experimental or alternative hypothesis. Step 1 is to state this statistical hypothesis. It will generally be stated in terms of population values and it will contain either the not equal sign ($\neq$), the greater than sign ($>$), or the less than sign ($<$). For example, the statistical hypothesis could be $H_1: \mu_A > \mu_B$, or $\mu_A - \mu_B = 0$. Step 2 is to state the null hypothesis, H_o. This hypothesis will contain the equal to ($=$) sign. For example, it could be $H_0 : \mu_A = \mu_B$, or $\mu_A - \mu_B = 0$. Step 3 is to compute the test statistic using empirical data. The test statistic is usually some kind of standard score that expresses a difference in terms of standard error (deviation) units. Step 4 is the definition of a decision rule. The decision rule gives guidelines or a yardstick to evaluate the test statistic. The probability of a Type I error, namely α, enters into the determination of the critical value that is used in the rule. Finding the critical value also involves determinating (computing) the degrees of freedom and the use of a table of critical values. The decision rule tells us whether or not the null hypothesis should be rejected. Step 5 makes the leap of inference from the decision made in Step 4 back to the actual problem. It relates the statistical test results back to the substantive hypothesis. Table 12.4 gives a summary of these five steps.

Sample Size Determination

When starting a study a question arises as to how large of a sample should be taken. This question is important because we are interested in getting the best information for the lowest cost. For those researchers who conduct large surveys where the cost of data collection is expensive, sample size determination is critical. When a researcher applies for a research grant, determining the sample size as part of the research proposal is important because it tells how much the data collection process will cost in terms of time and labor. A sample size that is too large is a waste of resources. A sample that is too small is also a wasted effort since it will not be large enough to detect a significant effect (difference). How the samples are drawn and the size of the sample controls the total amount of relevant information contained in a sample. In Chapter 8 we discussed many sampling procedures. In this chapter, after the introduction of some statistics and in particular the standard error, we can observe how sample sizes are determined. It is the standard error with some algebraic manipulation and some additional information that makes sample size determination

▣ TABLE 12.4 *Summary of the Five Steps of Hypothesis Testing.*

Steps for hypothesis testing	Notes
1. Statement of the null hypothesis	$H_0: \mu_1 = \mu_2$ (note that the null hypothesis contains the $=$ sign)
2. Statement of the alternative hypothesis	$H_1: \mu_1 \neq \mu_2 (\mu_1 > \mu_2 \text{ or } \mu_1 < \mu_2)$
3. Computation of test statistic	Statistic can be z, t, F, χ^2. Computed from observed data.
4. Decision Rule	Uses α, df, and table to determine critical value.
5. Relate decision back to original problem	This is the inferential part.

possible. By increasing the sample size, the sampling distribution becomes narrower and the standard error becomes smaller. As a result, a large sample increases the likelihood of detecting a difference. However, too large of a sample will make a very small difference statistically significant, but not necessarily of practical significance. Although we will try to simplify the concepts and procedures involved, the process of determining sample sizes for research studies is not a trivial or easy process. In fact, Williams (1978) says it is one of the most difficult problems in applied statistics. The answer given by these methods is not entirely accurate and should only be used as a guideline for helping make intelligent decisions about the conduct of the study. Such usage is still an improvement over a number of rule-of-thumb methods that researchers use without justification. One such rule is the decision to select *n* number of participants based on a proportion of the population size. Although the second author of this book (HBL) has heard of such rules, he has yet to find such rules written anywhere with justification.

First, we shall introduce how to determine sample sizes for simple random samples. Here the researcher needs to have the actual value of the population standard deviation σ, or an estimate of it. Estimates can come from past data or studies. However, if this is unavailable, the researcher can use the range. This would require an estimate of the largest and smallest value in the measurements. Mendenhall and Beaver (1994) recommend dividing the range by 4 to obtain an estimate of σ. Williams (1978) recommends dividing the range by 6. Second, the researcher needs to specify the amount of precision (how close the sample mean is from the population [true] mean). Some refer to this as how much error the researcher is willing to tolerate between the sample mean and the true mean. The third ingredient is the amount of risk (in terms of probability) or certainty that is acceptable to the researcher. This is traditionally known as the probability of the Type I error, α.

The formula to estimate sample size for a simple random sample is

$$n = \frac{Z^2\sigma^2}{d^2}$$

$$(12.3)$$

where

Z^2 = standard score corresponding to the specified probability of risk. If the risk is 0.10 (i.e., α = .10), Z = 1.645. For a risk of 0.05, Z = 1.96 and for 0.01 the Z is 2.575.

σ = the standard deviation of the population.

d = specified deviation.

This is the desired accuracy of the sample mean. How close does the sample mean have to be to the true mean?

Example

A researcher is designing a study concerning college students. She will select two groups of students. She wants to determine the appropriate number of students she should sample for the study. The dependent variable in this study is grade point average. She feels she can tolerate a 0.2 deviation between the sample mean and the true mean. She is willing to take a risk of 0.05. And past research using grade point average has reported a standard deviation that is approximately 0.6.

For a risk of 0.05 probability, the corresponding Z-value is 1.96. The standard deviation is 0.6 and the deviation is 0.2. Using the formula given above, the required sample size is estimated to be:

$$n = \frac{1.96^2(0.6^2)}{.2^2} = \frac{3.842(.36)}{.04} = \frac{1.383}{.04} \approx 34.6 \approx 35$$

This is 35 subjects per group. So the researcher will need 70 subjects.

If sampling is from a finite population of size N, and the sampling is done without replacement, Williams (1978) suggests the following adjustment to the formula given above.

$$n' = \frac{n}{1 + n/N}$$

n' is the estimated sample size, n is the sample size estimated using formula 12.3, and N is the size of the population. Using the above example, if we had ascertained that the population size was $N = 1,000$, then n' would be

$$n' = \frac{70}{1 + 70/1000} = 65.421 \approx 66, \text{ or } 33 \text{ in each group.}$$

This method requires only knowledge of the populations' standard deviation or its estimate and α, the probability of a Type I error. Guilford and Fruchter (1978) present a method that also utilizes β, the probability of the Type II error. In specifying β, as mentioned previously, the power of the statistical test, $1 - \beta$ is also specified. Researchers who want to protect themselves on both α and β can use the formula given by Guilford and Fruchter to find a sample size that gives them the desired risks.

The formula is

$$n = \frac{(Z_\beta - Z_\alpha)^2 \sigma^2}{d^2}$$

where α = the standard deviation of the population

d = specified deviation. This is the desired accuracy of the sample mean, i.e., how close does the sample mean have to be to the true mean?

Z_α = distance from critical value to mean in H_o (in standard deviation units with appropriate sign).

Z_β = distance from critical value to mean in H_1 (in standard deviation units with appropriate sign).

To demonstrate how this formula works, we need to refer back to Figure 12.3, which shows the relation between α and β. By specifying both α and β along with the standard deviation, the sample size can be determined. Provided that the standard deviation was accurately measured, the number of data points collected from a research study would meet the specification set up by the α and β levels. With specific values of α and β, the two sampling distributions can be displaced in a way such that the appropriate critical value can be found. For example, if we set for our study $\alpha = 0.05$ and $\beta = 0.10$, the Z-values that would satisfy this would be -1.28 for the H_1 distribution and 1.645 for the H_o distribution. Figure 12.4 shows this $Z = -1.28$ would be the value that would cut off $\beta = 0.10$ on the "H_1 is true distribution." For that same point marked "critical value" in Figure 12.4, it would correspond to $Z = 1.645$ on the H_o is true distribution.

Using the data from the previous example, the estimated sample size would be

$$n = \frac{(-1.28 - 1.645)^2 (0.6^2)}{.2^2} = \frac{18.656(.36)}{.04} = \frac{6.716}{.04} = 167.9 = 168$$

This is 168 participants per group.

◫ FIGURE 12.4

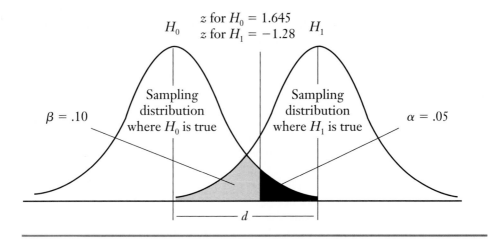

The procedure described above is for a one-tailed test. For a two-tailed test, only the Z_α will change. If the test is two-tailed, then instead of using all of α in the tail, we would use $\alpha/2$ instead. For the example given above, the appropriate Z-value for this would be 1.96.

Using essentially the same data for both examples have led to different values. Why is this so? Recall that the probability of a Type II error is not rejecting the null hypothesis when there is a true difference. With the Example, the use of 35 subjects per group would be necessary to reject the null hypothesis. It is not concerned with the possibility of missing any opportunities. Reworking this example with Guilford and Fruchter formula, β, the probability of the Type II is considered and it makes for a more sensitive test in terms of detecting a true difference. Hence, with an $n = 168$, we as researchers would not only have enough subjects to reject H_o at $\alpha = 0.05$, but also enough to give us a power $(1 - \beta)$ of 0.90.

CHAPTER SUMMARY

1. The standard error is the standard deviation of the sampling distribution of sample statistics.
2. Standard errors serve to evaluate
   a. difference between means
   b. difference between the sample correlation and zero.
3. Small differences can be statistically significant if the standard error is proportionally smaller.

4. Standard errors serve as a yardstick against which experimental variance is checked.
5. Monte Carlo is a method used to create simulated data for a number of situations where collecting actual data may be expensive or not feasible.
6. Monte Carlo can be used to show the behavior and meaning of the standard error.
7. The Central Limit Theorem is one of the most important theorems in statistics.
8. By the Central Limit Theorem, the sampling distribution of sample means is approximately normal in shape even though the distribution from which the samples were drawn was not normal.
9. A substantive hypothesis is a conjectural statement of relation between two variables.
10. Statistical hypotheses are restatements of substantive hypothesis into statistical terms.
11. Hypothesis tests involve the null and statistical hypotheses.
12. There are five basic steps of hypothesis testing.
13. The standard error is an important part in sample size determination.

STUDY SUGGESTIONS

1. Good references on statistics, fortunately, are plentiful. Ask your instructor for recommendations. The books mentioned below may be helpful. Choose one or two to supplement your study. In reading a statistics book, do not be discouraged if you do not completely understand everything you read. Indeed, sometimes you may be completely bewildered. As you acquire understanding of the language and methods of the statistician, most of the difficulties will disappear.

Comrey, A. L., & Lee, H. B. (1995). *Elementary statistics: A problem-solving approach* (3rd ed.). Dubuque, IA: Kendall-Hunt. A good book for the beginning student. The topics are organized in the form of 50 problems.
Freedman, D., Pisani, R., & Purves, R. (1997) *Statistics* (3rd ed.). New York: Norton. Accessible to the beginning student. Good discussions of interesting studies and problems. Applications oriented. Tries to avoid the use of symbols and statistical notation.
Glass, G., & Hopkins, (1996). *Statistical methods in education and psychology* (3rd ed.). Boston: Allyn & Bacon. A well-written book with good treatment of difficult concepts. Gives an interesting computer demonstration of the Central Limit Theorem.
Hays, W. L. (1994). *Statistics* (5th ed.). Fort Worth, TX: Harcourt Brace. Superb: thorough, authoritative, research-oriented—but not elementary. Its careful study should be a goal of serious students and researchers.

Kirk, R. E. (1990). *Statistics: An introduction* (3rd ed.). Fort Worth, TX: Holt, Rinehart and Winston. A well-written and informative treatment of statistics; a good reference for beginners.

Mattson, D. E. (1984). *Statistics: Difficult concepts, understandable explanations.* Oak Park, IL: Bolchazy-Carducci Publishers. Each chapter is broken down into lessons. A good treatment on public health data.

Natrella, M. G. (1966). *Experimental Statistics. National Bureau of Standards Handbook 91.* Washington, DC: U.S. Government Printing Office. A dated but well-presented book produced by the U.S. Government. Contains a set of charts that are useful in estimating sample sizes for a number of different statistical tests.

Snedecor, G., Cochran, W., & Cox, D. R. (1989). *Statistical method* (8th ed.). Ames: Iowa State University Press. Solid, authoritative, helpful, but not elementary. Excellent reference book.

2. The proportions of men and women voters in a certain county are 0.70 and 0.30, respectively. In one election district of 400 people, there are 300 men and 100 women. Can it be said that the district's proportions of men and women voters differ significantly from those of the county?
   [Answer: Yes. $\chi^2 = 4.76$. χ^2 table entry, 0.05 level, for $df = 1$ is 3.84.]

3. An investigator in the field of prejudice experimented with various methods of answering the prejudiced person's remarks about minority group members. The investigator assigned 32 subjects randomly to two groups with 16 in each group. With the first group method A is used. Method B is used on the second group. The means of the two groups on an attitude test, administered after the methods were used were A: 27, and B: 25. Each group had a standard deviation of 4. Do the two group means differ significantly?
   [Answer: No. $(27 - 25)/1.414 = 1.414$.]

4. The evenly distributed 4,000 random numbers discussed in the text and the statistics calculated from the random numbers are given in Appendix C at the end of the book. Use a table of random numbers—the 4,000 random numbers will do—and wave a pencil in the air with eyes closed and let it come to rest at any point in the table. Going down the columns from the place the table was entered, copy out 10 numbers in the range from 1 through 40. Let these be the numbers of 10 of the 40 groups. The means, variances, and standard deviations are given right after the table of 4,000 random numbers. Copy out the means of the groups selected randomly. Round the means; that is, 54.33 becomes 54, 47.87 becomes 48, and so on.
   a. Calculate the mean of the means, and compare it to the population mean of 50 (really 50.33). Did you come close?
   b. Calculate the standard deviation of the 10 means.
   c. Take the first group selected and calculate the standard error of the mean, using $N = 100$ and the reported standard deviation. Do the same for the fourth and ninth groups. Are the SE_Ms alike? Interpret the first SE_M. Compare the results of (b) and (c).

d. Calculate the differences between the first and sixth means and the fourth and tenth means. Test the two differences for statistical significance. Should they be statistically significant? Give the reason for your answer. Make up an experimental situation and imagine that the fourth and tenth means are your results. Interpret.

e. Discuss the central limit theorem in relation to (d), above.

5. For now, the variance and the standard deviation have been calculated with N in the denominator. In statistics books, the student will encounter the variance formula as: $V = \Sigma x^2/N$, or $V = \Sigma x^2/(N - 1)$. The first formula is used when only describing a sample or population. The second is used when estimating the variance of a population with the sample variance (or standard deviation). With N large, there is little practical difference. In later chapters, we will see that the denominators of variance estimates always have $N - 1$, $k - 1$, and so on. These are really degrees of freedom. Most computer programs use $N - 1$ to calculate standard deviations. Perhaps the best advice is to always use $N - 1$. Even when it is not appropriate, it will not make that much difference.

6. Statistics are not always viewed favorably. Marxists, for example, are not too sympathetic. (Why, do you suppose?) There is an interesting education study where a design with a control group was used. However no statistical tests of significance or measures of the magnitude of relations were used: See DeCorte and Verschaffel (1981). The student may find it interesting to read this study.

7. There has been much discussion in education about the presumed virtues of the "open" educational environment. In a study by Wright (1975) of the difference between "open" and "traditional" school environments, a number of interesting mean differences were reported. Among these mean differences, those in Word Meaning and Verbal Creativity (p. 453) were as follows:

	Word Meaning		Verbal Creativity	
	Traditional	*Open*	*Traditional*	*Open*
N	50	50	50	50
M	4.84	4.35	135.38	129.60
SD	1.19	.78	23.5	19.2

Calculate the two *t*-ratios and interpret the results. (Use Equation 12.1 and substitute in Equation 12.2.)
[Answers: Word Meaning: $t = 2.43$ (p , 0.05); Verbal Creativity: $t = 1.35$ (n.s.).]

8. Review the Scattone and Saetermoe (1997) study. Note that the authors did a *t*-test of the means. These means, however, reflect the independent variable. Analysis of data with *t*-tests and similar statistics is usually done on de-

pendent variable measures. Were the authors wrong? If so, why? Could a t-test of the dependent variable, or "disability" measures conceivably have been not significant? If so, what happens to the authors' hypothesis? (We ignore here other possible kinds of analysis.)

[Hint: What is predicted in problems of this kind? Think of hypotheses as "If p, then q" statements.]

9. A researcher is asked to conduct a study on intelligence test scores. A specific school district claims that the students are averaging a score of 90 on the test. She needs to obtain a sample of size n that is large enough in order to obtain a sample mean that will not differ from 90 by more than 2 points with 99% confidence. The district also reports a standard deviation of 10.2. How large should n be?

10. Using the data from Problem 9, if we know the district has 1,500 students, how large should n be?

PART FIVE

ANALYSIS OF VARIANCE

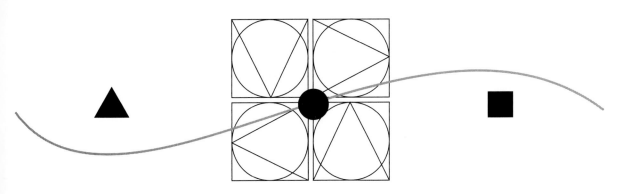

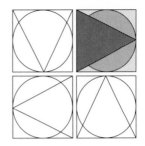

ANALYSIS OF VARIANCE: FOUNDATIONS

The analysis of variance is not merely a statistical method. It is an approach and a way of thinking. It is also one of the many expressions of what is known as the general linear model. This model is actually a linear equation—*linear* means that no terms of the equation have powers greater than 1—that expresses the sources of variance of a set of measures. In a form suitable for analysis of variance, it can be written:

$$y = b_0 x_0 + b_1 x_1 + b_2 x_2 + \cdots + b_k x_k + e$$

(Note that none of the xs has a power greater than 1; that is, there are no x^2s or x^3s.) If we conceive a score of one individual, y, as having one or more sources of variance, $x_1, x_2, \ldots$, then we can roughly grasp the idea of the model. The bs are weights that express the relative degrees of influence of the xs in accounting for y. e is error; it expresses the unknown factors that influence y along with, of course, ubiquitous random error. The equation is general: it fits most analytic situations in which we wish to explain the variation of a set of measures of a dependent variable, y. For analysis of variance models, the equation simplifies to one of several specific forms, which we need not now examine. The point is that dependent variable measures are conceived as having two or more components, and the task of analysis of variance is to determine the relative contributions of these components to the dependent variable variation. As we will see toward the end of the book, this is one of the goals of multiple regression, as well as of other analytic methods. We must try to make these abstractions concrete and understandable. However, for now, just bear this in mind: the total dependent variable variance of any statistical situation is broken down into component sources of variance.

In this chapter and in chapters 14 and 15 we explore the analysis of variance. The emphasis will be on the few fundamental and general notions that underlie the method. The chapters are not meant merely to teach analysis of variance and related methods as statistics; their intent is to convey the basic ideas of the methods in relation to research and research problems. To accomplish this pedagogical purpose, simple examples will be used. It makes little difference whether five scores or 500 scores are used, or if two or 20 variables are used. The fundamental ideas, the theoretical conceptions, are the same. In this chapter, *simple one-way analysis of variance* is discussed. The next two chapters consider so-called factorial analysis of variance and the analysis of variance of correlated groups or subjects. By then the student should have a good basis for the study of research design.

Variance Breakdown: A Simple Example

In Chapter 6, two sets of scores were analyzed in a variance fashion. The *total variance* of all the scores was broken down into a *between-groups variance* and a *within-groups variance*. We now pick up the theme of Chapter 6 by using, in altered form, the two-group example given there, and by correcting the method of calculation. Then we extend analysis of variance ideas considerably.

Suppose an investigator is interested in the relative efficacies of two methods A_1 and A_2. We use *methods* here and elsewhere because the word is general and easily grasped. Students can supply the substance of different methods of their own field. For example, in education, it might be methods of teaching; in psychology, methods of reinforcement or attention arousal; in political science, methods of participation in political processes. Ten students are selected as a sample. The sample is divided into two groups at random. Each group is assigned at random to the experimental treatments. After a suitable length of time, the learning of the students in both groups is measured using an achievement test. The results, together with certain computations, are given in Table 13.1.

⊡ **TABLE 13.1** *Two Sets of Hypothetical Experimental Data with Sums, Means, and Sums of Squares*

	A_1	x	x^2	A_2	x	x^2	
	4	0	0	3	0	0	
	5	1	1	1	−2	4	
	3	−1	1	5	2	4	
	2	−2	4	2	−1	1	
	6	2	4	4	1	1	
ΣX	20			15			$\Sigma X_t = 35$
M	4			3			$M_t = 3.5$
Σx^2			10			10	

Our job is to locate and calculate the different variances that make up the total variance. The total variance and the other variances are calculated as before, with an important difference. Instead of using N or n in the denominator of variance fractions, we use so-called degrees of freedom. Degrees of freedom are ordinarily defined as one case less than N or n; that is, $N − 1$ and $n − 1$. In the case of groups, instead of k (the number of groups), we use $k − 1$. While this method has a great advantage from a statistical point of view, from a mathematical–conceptual point of view it makes our job a bit more difficult. First, we do the computations, and then return to the difficulty.

To calculate the total variance, we use the formula:

$$V_t = \frac{\Sigma x^2}{N − 1} \qquad \textbf{(13.1)}$$

where (Σx^2 equals the sum-of-squares, as before, $x = X − M$, or deviation from the mean of any score, and N equals number of cases in the total sample. To calculate V_t, simply take all the scores, regardless of their grouping, and calculate the necessary terms of Equation 13.1, as in Table 13.2. Since $N − 1 = 10 − 1 = 9$, $V_t = 22.50/9 = 2.5$. Thus, if we arrange the data of Table 13.1 without regard to the two groups, $V_t = 2.5$.

There is variance between the groups, and this variance is due, presumably, to the experimental manipulation. That is, the experimenter did something to one group and something different to the other group. These different treatments should make the groups and their means different. They will have *between-groups variance*. Take the two means, treat them like any other scores (Xs), and calculate their variance (see Table 13.3).

⊡ TABLE 13.2 *Calculation of V_b from Table 13.1 Data*

	X	x	x^2
	4	.5	.25
	5	1.5	2.25
	3	−.5	.25
	2	−1.5	2.25
	6	2.5	6.25
	3	−.5	.25
	1	−2.5	6.25
	5	1.5	2.25
	2	−1.5	2.25
	4	.5	.25
Σx	35		
M	3.5		
Σx^2			22.50

There is a remaining source of variance left over: the ubiquitous random error. We saw in Chapter 6 that this could be obtained by calculating the variance *within* each group separately, and then averaging these separate variances. We do this using the figures given in Table 13.1. Each group has $\Sigma x^2 = 10$. Dividing each of these sums-of-squares by its degrees of freedom, we get:

$$\frac{\Sigma x^2_{A_1}}{n_{A_1} - 1} = \frac{10}{4} = 2.5$$

and

$$\frac{\Sigma x^2_{A_2}}{n_{A_2} - 1} = \frac{10}{4} = 2.5$$

The averaging yields, of course, 2.5. Therefore, the *within-groups* variance, V_w, is 2.5. Three variances have been calculated: $V_t = 2.5$, $V_b = .50$, $V_w = 2.5$. The theoretical equation given in Chapter 6 says that the total variance is made up of separate sources of variance: the between-groups and the within-groups variances. Logically, they should add up to the total variance. The theoretical equation is

$$V_t = V_b + V_w \tag{13.2}$$

■ TABLE 13.3 *Calculation of V_b from Table 13.1 Data*

	X	x	x^2
	4	.5	.25
	3	.5	.25
ΣX	7		
M	3.5		
Σx^2			.50

$$V_b = \frac{\Sigma x_b^2}{k-1} = \frac{.50}{2-1} = .50$$

Since 2.5 is not equal to 0.50 and 2.5, something must be wrong. The trouble is that degrees of freedom were used in the denominators of the variance formula instead of N, n, and k. Had N, n, and k been used, the relation of Equation 13.2 would have held (see Chapter 6). If N, n and k were used, the values would have been $V_t = 2.25$, $V_b = 0.25$ and $V_w = 2$.

The student may ask: Why not follow the N, n, and k procedure? And if you cannot follow it, why bother with all this? The answer is that the calculation of the variances with N, n, and k is mathematically correct but statistically "unsatisfactory." Another important aspect of the analysis of variance is the estimation of population values. It can be shown that using degrees of freedom in the denominators of the variance formula yields unbiased estimates of the population values, a matter of great statistical concern. The reason we bother going through the present procedure is to show the reader clearly the mathematical basis of the reasoning. One should remember, though, that variances, as used in the analysis of variance, are not necessarily additive.

Sums-of-squares, on the other hand, are always additive. (They are calculated from the scores and not divided by anything.) And sums-of-squares, of course, are also measures of variability. Except at the final stage of analysis of variance, sums-of-squares are calculated, studied, and analyzed. To convince ourselves of the additive property of sums-of-squares, note that the between-groups and the within-groups sums-of-squares add to the total sum-of-squares. If we multiply the between-groups sum-of-squares by n, the number of cases in each group:

$$\Sigma x_t^2 = n\Sigma x_b^2 + \Sigma x_w^2$$

or numerically, $22.50 = (5)(.50) + 20$.

The reasoning behind the expression $n\Sigma x_b^2$ in this equation is as follows. The definition of an unbiased estimate of the variance of the population of means is

$V_M = \Sigma x^2/(n-1)$. But from our reasoning on the standard error and the standard variance, we know that $V_M = SV_M = V/n$. Substituting in the first equation, we get $V/n = \Sigma x^2/(k-1)$, and thus $V = n\Sigma x^2/(k-1)$. It should be noted here that the expression, $n\Sigma x_b^2$, indicated in Chapter 6, is really the *between* sum-of-squares—and not Σx_b^2, as indicated in Chapter 6 and subsequent chapters. That is, instead of writing Σx_b^2, statisticians write ss_b, which is really $n\Sigma x_b^2$.

The *t*-Ratio Approach

Using the data from Table 13.1, we calculate several statistics for the A_1 and A_2 data separately: the variances, standard deviations, standard errors of the means, and standard variances of the means. The methods of analysis used in the first part of this chapter are not used in actual calculation because they are too cumbersome. They are used here only for pedagogical reasons. Unfortunately, the usual method of calculation tends to obscure the important relations and operations underlying the analysis of variance. These calculations are shown in Table 13.4. (Note that V is now calculated with $n-1$ instead of n.)

We now consider the central statistical idea behind the analysis of variance. The question the investigator has to ask himself or herself is: Do the means differ significantly? It is obvious that 4 does not equal 3, but the question has to be asked statistically. We know that if sets of random numbers are drawn, the means of the sets will not be equal. They should, however, not be too different; that is, they should differ only within the bounds of chance fluctuations. Thus the question becomes: Does 4 differ from 3 *significantly?* Again the null hypothesis is set up: H_o: $\mu_{A1} - \mu_{A2} = 0$, or $\mu_{A1} = \mu_{A2}$. The substantive hypothesis was: H_1: $\mu_{A1} > \mu_{A2}$. Which hypothesis does the evidence support? In different words, it is not simply a question of 4 being absolutely greater than 3; it is, rather, a question of whether 4 differs from 3 beyond the differences to be expected by chance.

▣ **TABLE 13.4** *Various Statistics Calculated from Table 13.1 Data*

	A_1	A_2
V:	$\dfrac{\Sigma x^2}{n-1} = \dfrac{10}{4} = 2.5$	$\dfrac{10}{4} = 2.5$
SD:	$\sqrt{2.5} = 1.58$	$\sqrt{2.5} = 1.58$
SE_M:	$\dfrac{SD}{\sqrt{n}} = \dfrac{1.58}{\sqrt{5}} = .705$	$\dfrac{1.58}{\sqrt{5}} = .705$
SV_M:	$\dfrac{V}{n} = \dfrac{2.5}{5} = .50$	$\dfrac{2.5}{5} = .50$

This question can be quickly answered using the methods of the last chapter. First, calculate the standard error of the differences between the means:

$$SE_{M_{A1} - M_{A2}} = \sqrt{SE_{M_{A1}}^2 + SE_{M_{A2}}^2}$$

$$= \sqrt{(.705)^2 + (.705)^2} = \sqrt{.994} = .997 = 1.00 \text{ (rounded)}.$$

Now, the *t*-ratio:

$$t = \frac{M_{A1} - M_{A2}}{SE_{M_{A1} - M_{A2}}} = \frac{4 - 3}{1.00} = \frac{1}{1} = 1$$

Since the difference being evaluated is no greater than the measure of error, it is obvious that it is not significant. The numerator and the denominator of the *t*-ratio are equal. The difference, $4 - 3 = 1$, is clearly one of the differences that could have occurred with random numbers. Remember that a "real" difference would be reflected in the *t*-ratio by a considerably larger numerator than denominator.

The Analysis of Variance Approach

In the analysis of variance, the approach is conceptually similar, although the method differs. The method is general: Differences of more than two groups can be tested for statistical significance, whereas the *t*-test applies to only two groups. (With two groups, as we shall see shortly, the results of the two methods are really identical.) The method of analysis of variance uses variances entirely, instead of using actual differences and standard errors, even though the actual difference–standard error reasoning is behind the method. Two variances are always pitted against each other. One variance, presumably due to the experimental (independent) variable or variables, is pitted against another variance, which is presumably due to error or randomness. To get a grip on this idea, go back to the problem.

We found that the between-groups variance was 0.50. We must now find a variance that is a reflection of error. This is the within-groups variance. After all, since we calculate the within-groups variance, essentially, by calculating the variance of each group separately and then averaging the two (or more) variances, this estimate of error is unaffected by the differences between the means. Thus, *if nothing else is causing the scores to vary*, it is reasonable to consider the within-groups variance as a measure of chance fluctuation. If this is so, then we can *stack up the variance due to the experimental effect, the between-groups variance, against this measure of chance error, the within-groups variance*. The only question is: How is the within-groups variance calculated?

Remember that the variance of a population of means can be estimated with the standard variance of the mean (the standard error squared). One way to obtain the within-groups variance is to calculate the standard variance of each of the groups and then average them for all of the groups. This should yield an estimate of error that can be used to evaluate the variance of the means of the groups. The reasoning here is basic. To evaluate the differences between the means, it is necessary to refer to a theoretical population of means that would be obtained from the random sampling of groups of scores like the groups of scores we have. In the present case we have two means from samples with five scores in each group. (It is well to remember that we might have three, four, or more means from three, four, or more groups. The reasoning is the same.) If participants were assigned to the groups at random, and nothing has operated—that is, there have been no experimental manipulations and no other systematic influences at work—then it is possible to estimate the variance of the means of the population of means with the standard variance of the means $(SE_M^2$, or $SV_M)$. Each group provides such an estimate. These estimates will vary to some extent among themselves. We can pool them by averaging to form an overall estimate of the variance of the population means.

Recall that the standard error of the mean formula was: $SE_M = SD/\sqrt{n}$. Simply square this expression to get the standard variance of the mean: $SE_M^2 = (SD)^2/n = SV_M = V/n$. The variances of each of the groups was 2.5. Calculating the standard variances, we obtain for each group: $SV_M = V/n = 2.50/5 = 0.50$. Averaging them obviously yields .50. Note carefully that each standard variance was calculated from each group *separately and then averaged*. Therefore, this average standard variance is uninfluenced by differences between the means, as noted earlier. The average standard variance, then, is a *within-groups variance*. It is an estimate of random errors.

But if random numbers had been used, the same reasoning applies to the between-groups variance, the variance calculated from the actual means. We calculated a variance from the means of 4 and 3: it was 0.50. If the numbers were random, estimating the variance of the population of means should be possible by calculating the variance of the obtained means.

Note carefully, however, that if any extraneous influence has been at work, if anything like experimental effects have operated, then the variance calculated from the obtained means will no longer be a good estimate of the population variance of means. If an experimental influence—or some influence other than chance—has operated, the effect may be to increase the variance of the obtained means. In a sense, this is the purpose of experimental manipulation: to increase the variance between means, to make the means different from each other. This is the crux of the analysis of variance matter. If an experimental manipulation has been influential, then it should show up in differences between means above and beyond the differences that arise by chance alone. And the between-groups variance should show the influence by becoming greater than expected by chance. Clearly we can use V_b then, as a measure of experimental influence. Equally clearly, as we showed above, we can use V_w, as a measure of chance variation. Therefore, we have almost reached the end of a rather long but profitable journey: We can evaluate the between-groups variance, V_b, with the within-groups variance, V_w. Or information, experimental information, can be weighed against error or chance.

It might be possible to evaluate V_b by subtracting V_w from it. In the analysis of variance, however, V_b is divided by V_w. The ratio so formed is called the *F*-ratio.

Snedecor named the *F*-ratio in honor of Ronald Fisher, the inventor of the analysis of variance. It was Snedecor who worked out the *F*-tables used to evaluate *F*-ratios. One calculates the *F*-ratio from observed data and checks the result against a value from the *F*-table. (The *F*-table with direction for its use can be found in any statistics text.) If the obtained *F*-ratio is as great or greater than the appropriate tabled entry, the differences that V_b reflect are statistically significant. In such a case the null hypothesis of no differences between the means is rejected at the chosen level of significance. In the present case:

$$F = \frac{V_b}{V_w} = \frac{.50}{.50} = 1$$

One obviously does not need the *F*-table to see that the *F*-ratio is not significant. Evidently the two means of 4 and 3 do not differ from each other significantly. In other words, of the many possible random samples of pairs of groups of five cases each, this particular case could easily be one of them. Had the difference been considerably greater, great enough to tip the *F*-ratio balance scale, then the conclusion would have been quite different, as we shall see. Note that the *t*-test and analysis of variance yielded the same result. With only two groups, or one degree of freedom $(k - 1)$, $F = t^2$, or $t = \sqrt{F}$. This equality shows that it does not matter, in the case of two groups, whether *t* or *F* is calculated. (But the analysis of variance is a bit easier to calculate than *t*, in most cases.) With three or more groups, however, the equality breaks down; *F* must always be calculated. Thus *F* is the general test of which *t* is a special case.

An Example of a Statistically Significant Difference

Suppose that the investigator had obtained quite different results. Say the means had been 6 and 3, rather than 4 and 3. We now take the above example and add a constant of 2 *to each* A_1 *score*. This operation, of course, merely restores the scores used in Chapter 6. It was said earlier that adding a constant, to a set of scores (or subtracting a constant) changes the mean by the constant, *but has no effect whatsoever on the* variance. The figures are given in Table 13.5.

It is important to note carefully that the Σx^2 values are the same as they were before, 10. Note, too, that the variances, *V*, are the same, 2.5. So are the standard variances, each being 0.50. As far as these statistics are concerned, then, there is no difference between this example and the previous example. But now we calculate the between-groups variance (Table 13.6). V_b is nine times greater than it was before: 4.50 versus 0.50. But V_w is exactly the same as it was before. This is an important point. To repeat: adding a constant to one set of scores—which is tantamount to an experimental manipulation, since one of the purposes of an experiment of this kind is to augment or diminish one set of measures (the experimental group measures), while the other set does not change (the control group measures)—has no effect on

◉ **TABLE 13.5** *Hypothetical Experimental Data for Two Groups: Table 13.1 Data Altered*

	A_1	x	x^2	A_2	x	x^2
	$4 + 2 = 6$	0	0	3	0	0
	$5 + 2 = 7$	1	1	1	−2	4
	$3 + 2 = 5$	−1	1	5	2	4
	$2 + 2 = 4$	−2	4	2	−1	1
	$6 + 2 = 8$	2	4	4	1	1
ΣX	30			15		
M	6			3		
ΣX^2			10			10

$$V: \quad \frac{10}{4} = 2.5 \qquad\qquad \frac{10}{4} = 2.5$$

$$SV: \quad \frac{V}{n} = \frac{2.5}{5} = .50 \qquad\qquad \frac{2.5}{5} = .50$$

the within-groups variance, whereas the between-groups variance changes drastically. Note that the *estimates* of V_b and V_w, are independent of each other. (If they are not, by the way, the rules and assumptions of F-test are violated.)

The F-ratio is $F = V_b/V_w = 4.50/.50 = 9$. Evidently, information is much greater than error. Does this mean that the difference $6 - 3 = 3$ is a statistically

◉ **TABLE 13.6** *Calculation of Between-Groups Variance Data from Table 13.5*

	X	x	x^2
	6	1.5	2.25
	3	−1.5	2.25
ΣX	9		
M	4.5		
Σx^2			4.50

$$V_b = \frac{\Sigma x_b^2}{k - 1} = \frac{4.50}{2 - 1} = 4.50$$

significant difference? If we check an *F*-table, we find that, in this case, an *F*-ratio of 5.32 or greater is significant at the 0.05 level. (The details of how to read an *F*-table are given later in this chapter.) To be significant at the 0.01 level, the *F*-ratio in this case would have to be 11.26 or greater. Our *F*-ratio is 9. It is greater than 5.32 but less than 11.26. It seems that the difference of 3 is a statistically significant difference at the 0.05 level. Therefore, $6 \neq 3$, and the null hypothesis is rejected.

Calculation of One-Way Analysis of Variance

In this computer age, a researcher interested in performing an analysis of variance would most likely have a computer and appropriate software for statistical analysis available. The use of a computer would be the first choice as far as computations are concerned. However, if you happen to be in a situation where you do not have a computer and are armed only with a hand calculator, doing the calculations for a one-way ANOVA via calculator is not difficult or complex. This section is given for those who feel they either need to know how a one-way ANOVA would be computed, or they would want to do one using a hand calculator.

Simple one-way analysis of variance is easier to do than the procedure outlined in the previous section. To show the method, the example just considered will be used. By now the reader should be able to follow the procedure without difficulty. Note that deviation scores (*x*'s) are not used at all. One can calculate entirely with raw scores. There will be certain differences in the variances. In the preceding examples, standard variances were used in order to show the underlying rationale of the analysis of variance. In the following method, however, although the same method is used, certain steps are omitted because it is possible to do the calculation in a much easier way.

The calculations of Table 13.7 can easily be followed. First, in the body of the table, note that the raw scores, the *X*s, are each squared. They are then added to yield the ΣX^2s at the bottom of the table (190 and 55). The purpose of doing this is to obtain $\Sigma X_t^2 = 245$ (190 + 55), at the right and bottom: read ΣX_t^2 as "The total sum of all the squared *X*s." The ΣXs and *M*s are calculated as usual (even though we do not really need the *M*s, except for later interpretation). Next, each group sum is squared and written $(\Sigma X)^2$. They are $(30)^2 = 900$ and $(15)^2 = 225$. (Be careful here. A frequent mistake is to confuse ΣX^2 and $(\Sigma X)^2$.) At the bottom right of the table proper, $(X_t, (\Sigma X_t)^2, M_t$ and ΣX_t^2 are entered. They are statistics of all the scores and are calculated in the same way as the individual group statistics.

Next, the calculations of the sums-of-squares (hereafter, *ss*). In the analysis of variance, mostly sums-of-squares are calculated and used. The variances or mean squares are reserved for the final analysis of variance table (at the bottom of Table 13.7). What we are after in this procedure are the total, the between and the within sums-of-squares, or ss_t, ss_b, and ss_w. First, the calculation of *C*, the correction term. Since we are using raw scores, and since we are aiming at sums-of-squares, which are the sums of the *deviations* squared, we must reduce the raw scores to deviation scores. To accomplish this, we subtract *C* from every calculation. This accomplishes the reduction: it changes, in effect, Xs to xs. The actual calculation of C is obvious. Here it is 202.50.

The total sum-of-squares, ss_t, is now calculated: 42.50. The between, or between-groups, or between-means, sum-of-squares is not as obvious. The sum of each group's scores is squared and then divided by the number of scores in the group. These averages are then added. From this sum C is subtracted. The result is the between-groups sum-of-squares, or ss_b. And this is all there is to the simple one-way analysis of variance. The within sum-of-squares, ss_w is calculated by subtraction. The following equation is important and should be remembered:

$$ss_t = ss_b + ss_w \qquad\qquad (13.3)$$

Almost all calculators that are priced around $10 today have built-in statistical function keys. There is generally one which allows the user to find the mean and another to find the standard deviation. In many cases, these calculators have a standard

◉ **TABLE 13.7** *Calculation of Analysis of Variance: Fictitious Data.*

	X_{A1}	X_{A1}^2	X_{A2}	X_{A2}^2	
	6	36	3	9	N = 10
	7	49	1	1	n = 5
	5	25	5	25	k = 2
	4	16	2	4	
	8	64	4	16	
ΣX:	30		15		$X_t = 45$
$(\Sigma X)^2$:	900		225		$(\Sigma X_t)^2 = 2025$
M	6		3		$M_t = 9$
ΣX^2		190		55	$\Sigma X_t^2 = 245$

$$C = \frac{(\Sigma X_t)^2}{N} = \frac{(45)^2}{10} = \frac{2025}{10} = 202.50$$

$$\text{Total } ss = \Sigma X_t^2 - C = 245 - 202.50 = 42.50$$

$$\text{Between } ss = \left[\frac{(\Sigma X_{A1})^2}{n_{A1}} + \frac{(\Sigma X_{A2})^2}{n_{A2}}\right] - C$$

$$= \left[\frac{(30)^2}{5} + \frac{(15)^2}{5}\right] - 202.50 = (180 + 45) - 202.50 = 22.50$$

Source	df	ss	MS	F
Between groups	k − 1 = 1	22.50	22.50	9.0(0.05)
Within groups	N − k = 8	20.00	2.50	
Total	N − 1 = 9	42.50		

deviation function for standard deviations computed using N and another using $N − 1$. Learning how to use these function buttons greatly simplifies computations and leads to fewer errors. Also, using these function keys will help in doing the computations for a one-way ANOVA. For example, the C term can be computed as $M^2 \times N$. This says that you can enter in all of your data, disregarding group membership and then get C by pressing the key for the mean, squaring it, and multiplying by the number of data points (scores). Likewise, you can get the total sum-of-squares ss_t by the formula $SD^2 \times (N)$ or $s_1^2 \times (N − 1)$. [Note: The lowercase s was computer using the degrees of freedom; i.e, N-1, instead of N.] This is done by pressing the key for the standard deviation, squaring it, and multiplying it by either N or $N − 1$. You would multiply by N if the function key you pressed was for the standard deviation computed using N. You would multiply by $N − 1$ if the key you pressed was for the standard deviation computed using $N − 1$. Hence, you can enter your data into the calculator one time and get C and ss_t through some simple key presses.

Recall Equation 13.2: $V_t = V_b + V_w$. Equation 13.3 is the same equation in the sums-of-squares form. Equation 13.2 cannot be used since, as was pointed out earlier, it is a theoretical formulation that only works exactly under the conditions specified. Equation 13.3 always works; that is, sums-of-squares in the analysis of variance are always additive. So, with a little algebraic manipulation we see that $ss_w = ss_t − ss_b$. To obtain the within sum-of-squares, in other words, simply subtract the between from the total sum-of-squares. In the table, $42.50 − 22.50 = 20$. (It is, of course, possible to calculate the within sum-of-squares directly.)

After completing the above calculation, we enter the degrees of freedom (df in the final table). Although formulas have been entered, they are not necessary to the operation. For the total degrees of freedom, simply take one less than the total number of participants used. If, for example, there were three experimental groups with 30 ss in each group, the total degrees of freedom are $N − 1 = 90 − 1 = 89$. The between-groups degrees of freedom are one less than the number of experimental groups. With three experimental groups, $k − 1 = 3 − 1 = 2$. With the example of Table 13.7, $k − 1 = 2 − 1 = 1$. The within-groups degrees of freedom, like the within-groups sum-of-squares, are obtained by subtraction. In this case, $9 − 1 = 8$. Next, divide the degrees of freedom into the sums-of-squares (ss/df) to obtain the between- and within-mean squares, labeled MS in the table. In the analysis of variance, the variances are called "mean squares." Finally, obtain the F-ratio by dividing the within or error variance or mean square into the between variance or mean square: $F = MS_b/MS_w = 22.50/2.50 = 9$. This final F-ratio (also called the variance

◉ TABLE 13.8 *Critical Values of F*

df for Within	df for between			
	1	**2**	**3**	**4**
1	161	200	216	225
	4,052	**4,999**	**5,403**	**5,625**
2	18.51	19.00	19.16	19.25
	98.49	**99.00**	**99.17**	**99.25**
3	10.13	9.55	9.28	9.12
	34.12	**30.82**	**29.46**	**28.71**
4	7.71	6.94	6.39	6.26
	21.20	**18.00**	**15.98**	**15.52**
5	6.61	5.14	4.76	4.53
	16.26	**10.92**	**9.78**	**9.15**
6	5.99	5.14	4.76	4.53
	13.74	**10.92**	**9.78**	**9.15**
7	5.59	4.74	4.35	4.12
	12.25	**9.55**	**8.45**	**7.85**
8	5.32	4.46	4.07	3.84
	11.26	**8.65**	**7.59**	**7.01**
9	5.12	4.26	3.86	3.63
	10.56	**8.02**	**6.99**	**6.42**
10	4.96	4.10	3.71	3.48
	10.04	**7.56**	**6.55**	**5.99**

ratio) is checked against appropriate entries in an *F*-table to determine its significance, as discussed previously.

An abbreviated *F*-Table is presented in Table 13.8. In order to use this table, we must first decide on a level of significance (either 0.05 or 0.01). Then we look along the top row to find the degrees of freedom for the between group variance. In our example it is $k - 1 = 1$. Next we look down the first column to find the degrees of freedom for the within-groups variance. It is $N - k = 8$. The value we seek (also called the critical value) is found by the intersection of the row and the column. When we do this we find two values: 5.32 and **11.26**. The boldfaced type is for $\alpha = 0.01$ and the text type is for $\alpha = 0.05$.

A Research Example

To illustrate the research use of one-way analysis of variance, data from an early experimental study by Hurlock (1925), mentioned earlier in this book, are given in Table 13.9. The data were not analyzed in this manner by Hurlock, the analysis of variance not being available at the time of the study. The first three lines in Table 13.9 were reported by Hurlock. All the other figures were calculated by the authors from these figures (see Addendum to chapter). Hurlock divided 106 fourth- and sixth-grade pupils into four groups, E_1, E_2, E_3, and C. Five forms of an addition test, A, B, C, D, and E, were used. Form A was administered to all the participants on the first day. For the next four days the experimental groups, E_1, E_2, and E_3, were given a different form of the test. Group C (the control group) was separated from the other groups and given different forms of the test on four separate days. The participants of Group C were told to work as usual. But each day before the tests were given, the E_1 group was brought to the front of the room and *praised* for its good work. Then the E_2 group was brought forward and *reproved* for its poor work. The members of the E_3 group were *ignored*. On the fifth day of the experiment, Form E was administered to all groups. Scores were the number of correct answers on this form of the test. Summary data are given in Table 13.9, together with the table of the final analysis of variance.

Since $F = 10.08$, which is significant at the 0.001 level, the null hypothesis of no differences between the means has to be rejected. Evidently the experimental manipulations were effective. There is not much difference between the Ignored and Control groups, an interesting finding. The Praised group has the largest mean, with the Reproved group mean in between the Praised group and the other two groups.

▣ **TABLE 13.9** *Summary Data and Analysis of Variance of Data (from Hurlock study)*

	E1: Praise	E2: Reprove	E3: Ignore	C: Control
n:	27	27	26	26
M:	20.22	14.19	12.38	11.35
SD:	7.68	6.78	6.06	4.21

Source	df	SS	MS	F
Between groups	3	1260.06	420.02	10.08(0.001)
Within groups	102	4249.29	41.66	
Total	105	5509.35		

The student can complete the interpretation of the data. After an analysis of variance of this kind, some investigators test pairs of means with *t*-tests. Unless specific differences between means, or groups of means, have been predicted before the analysis, this procedure is questionable. We take up this problem later in the chapter (see Study Suggestion 6).

Strength of Relations: Correlation and the Analysis of Variance

Tests of statistical significance like *t* and *F* unfortunately do not indicate the magnitude or strength of relations. A *t*-test of the difference between two means, if significant, simply tells the investigator that there is a relation. An *F*-test, similarly, if significant, simply states that a relation exists. The relation is inferred from the significant differences between two, three, or more means. A statistical test like *F* says in an indirect way that there is or is not a relation between the independent variable (or variables) and the dependent variable.

In contrast to tests of statistical significance like *t* and *F*, coefficients of correlation are relatively direct measures of relations. They have an easily "seen" and direct intuitive message, since the joining of two sets of scores more obviously seems like a relation. It follows our earlier definition of a relation as a set of ordered pairs. If, for example, $r = .90$, it is easy to see that the rank orders of the measures of two variables are very similar. But *t*- and *F*-ratios are one or two steps removed from the actual relation. An important research technical question, then, is how *t* and *F*, on the one hand, and measures like *r*, on the other, are related.

In an analysis of variance, the variable on the margins of the data table (methods of incentive in the Hurlock example) is the independent variable. The measures in the body of the table reflect the dependent variable (i.e., arithmetic achievement in the Hurlock example). The analysis of variance works with the relation between these two kinds of variables. If the independent variable has had an effect on the dependent variable, then this would upset the "equality" of the means of the experimental groups that would be expected if the numbers being analyzed were random numbers. The effect of a really influential independent variable is to make means unequal. We can say, then, that any relation that exists between the independent and dependent variables is reflected in the inequality of the means. The more unequal the means, the wider apart they are, the higher the relation, other things being equal.

If no relation exists between the independent variable and the dependent variable, then it is as though we had sets of random numbers and, consequently, random means. The differences between the means would only be chance fluctuations. An *F*-test would show them not to be significantly different. If a relation does exist, if there is a tie or bond between the independent and dependent variables, the imposition of *different* aspects of the independent variable, like different methods of instruction, should make the measures of the dependent variable vary accordingly. Method A_1 might make achievement scores go up, whereas method A_2 might make them go down

☐ TABLE 13.10 *Strong Relation between Methods of Instruction and Achievement*

Independent Variable (Methods of Instruction)	Dependent Variable (Achievement)	Means
Method A_1	10	9
	9	
	9	
	8	
Method A_2	7	7
	7	
	7	
	7	
Method A_3	5	4
	4	
	4	
	3	

or stay about the same. Note that we have the same phenomenon of concomitant variation that we did with the correlation coefficient. Take two extreme cases: a strong relation and a zero relation. We lay out a hypothetically strong relation between methods and achievement in Table 13.10. Note that the dependent variable scores vary directly with the independent variable methods: Method A_1 has high scores, method A_2 medium scores, and method A_3 low scores. The relation is also shown by comparing methods and the means of the dependent variable.

Compare the example of Table 13.10 with chance expectation. If there was no relation between methods and achievement, then the achievement means would not covary with methods. That is, the means would be nearly equal. In order to show this, we wrote the 12 achievement scores of Table 13.10 on separate slips of paper. These slips were mixed up thoroughly in a hat. All slips were then thrown on the floor. The slips were picked up four at a time, assigning the first four to A_1, the second four to A_2, and the third four to A_3. The results are shown in Table 13.11.

Now it is difficult, or impossible, to "see" a relation. The means differ, but not much. Certainly, the relation between methods and achievement scores (and means) is not nearly as clear as it was before. Still, we have to be sure. Analyses of variance of both sets of data were performed. The F-ratio of the data of Table 13.10 (strong relation) was 57.59, highly significant, whereas the F-ratio of the data of Table 13.11

▣ TABLE 13.11 *Zero Relation between Methods of Instruction and Achievement*

Independent Variable (Methods of Instruction)	Dependent Variable (Achievement)	Means
Method A_1	4	
	8	7.25
	10	
	7	
Method A_2	3	
	5	5.25
	4	
	9	
Method A_3	7	
	7	7.50
	7	
	9	

(low or zero relation) was 1.29, not significant. The statistical tests confirm our visual impressions. We now know that there is a relation between methods and achievement in Table 13.10 but not in Table 13.11.

The problem, however, is to show the relation between significance tests like the *F*-test and the correlation method. This can be done in several ways. We illustrate with two such ways, one graphical and one statistical. In Figure 13.1 the data from Table 13.10 and Table 13.11 have been plotted much as continuous X and Y measures in the usual correlation problem are plotted. In each case, the independent variable (Methods) is placed on the horizontal axis, and the dependent variable (Achievement) is on the vertical axis. To indicate the relation, lines have been drawn as near to the means as possible. A diagonal line making a 45-degree angle with the horizontal axis would indicate a strong relation. A horizontal line across the graph would indicate a zero relation. Note that the plotted scores of the data from Table 13.10 clearly indicate a strong relation: the height of the plotted scores (crosses) and the means (circles) varies with the method. The plot of the data from Table 13.11, even with a rearrangement of the methods for purposes of comparison, shows a weak relation or no relation.

Let us now look at the problem statistically. It is possible to calculate correlation coefficients with data of this kind. If one has done an analysis of variance, a simple

▣ FIGURE 13.1

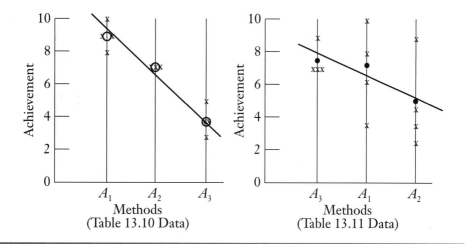

Methods
(Table 13.10 Data)   Methods
(Table 13.11 Data)

(but not entirely satisfactory) coefficient is yielded by the following formula:

$$\eta = \sqrt{\frac{ss_b}{ss_t}} \tag{13.4}$$

Of course ss_b and ss_t are the between-groups sum-of-squares and the total sum-of-squares, respectively. One simply takes these sums-of-squares from the analysis of variance table to calculate the coefficient. η, usually called the *correlation ratio*, is a general coefficient or index of relation often used with data that are not linear. (*Linear*, roughly speaking, means that, if two variables are plotted one against another, the plot tends to follow a straight line. This is another way of saying what was said in Chapter 12 about linear combinations.) Its values vary from 0 to 1.00. We are interested here only in its use with analysis of variance and in its power to tell us the magnitude of the relation between independent and dependent variables.

Recall that the means of the data from Table 13.1 were 3 and 4. They were not significantly different. Therefore there is no relation between the independent variable (methods) and the dependent variable (achievement). If an analysis of variance of the data from Table 13.1 is done using the method outlined in Table 13.7, then $ss_b = 2.50$ and $ss_t = 22.50$.

$$\eta = \sqrt{2.50/22.50} = \sqrt{.111} = 0.33$$

yields the correlation between methods and achievement. Since we know that the data are not significant ($F = 1$), η is not significant. In other words, $\eta = 0.33$ is here tantamount to a zero relation. Had there been no difference at all between the means, then, of course, $\eta = 0$. If $ss_b = ss_t$, then $\eta = 1.00$. This can happen only if all the scores of one group are the same, and all the scores of the other group are the same as, and yet different from, those of the first group. In practice this event is highly unlikely. For example, if the A_1 scores were 4, 4, 4, 4, 4, and the A_2 scores were 3, 3, 3, 3, 3, then

$$ss_e = ss_t = 2.5, \text{ and } \eta = \sqrt{2.5/2.5} = 1.$$

It is obvious that there is no within-groups variance. Again, this is extremely unlikely. Take the data from Table 13.7. The means are 6 and 3. They are significantly different, since $F = 9$. Calculate η:

$$\eta = \sqrt{\frac{ss_b}{ss_t}} = \sqrt{\frac{22.50}{42.50}} = \sqrt{.529} = 0.73$$

Note the substantial increase in η. And since F is significant, $\eta = 0.73$ is significant. There is a substantial relation between methods and achievement.

The Hurlock study is more interesting:

$$\eta = \sqrt{1260.06/5509.35} = \sqrt{.229} = 0.48,$$

which is of course significant. Other things being equal, incentive is substantially related to arithmetic achievement, as defined.

By now the student has sufficient background to interpret η^2 in variance terms. In Chapter 6, this was done for r, where it was explained that r^2 indicated the variance shared by two variables. η^2 can be given a similar interpretation. If η is squared, η^2 indicates, in essence, the variance shared by the independent and dependent variables. Perhaps more to the point, η^2 indicates the proportion of the variance of the dependent variable, say achievement, determined by the variance of the independent variable, methods, or incentives. For example, in the Hurlock example, $\eta^2 = (0.48)^2 = 0.23$, which indicates that 23% of the variance of the arithmetic addition scores is accounted for by the different modes of incentives used by Hurlock.

η^2 is an index of the proportion of variance accounted for in this sample. Another index, ω^2, omega squared, (see Hays, 1994) is an estimate of the strength of association between the independent variable and the population dependent variable. We recommend its use:

$$\omega^2 = \frac{ss_b - (k-1)MS_w}{ss_t + MS_w} \tag{13.5}$$

where k equals number of groups in the analysis of variance and the other terms are the sums-of-squares and mean squares defined earlier. η^2 is a conservative estimate of the strength of association or relation between the independent variable X and the dependent variable Y, or between the variable reflected by the experimental treatment and the dependent variable measure. Calculating ω^2 for the Hurlock example,

$$\omega^2 = \frac{1260.06 - (4 - 1)(41.66)}{5509.35 + 41.66} = 0.205$$

This is rather close to the value of η^2, 0.23. η^2 is comparable to ω^2 rather than to η. Both indices indicate the proportion of variance in a dependent variable due to the presumed influence of an independent variable. There are other indices available to report the amount of variance accounted for. In the first and second editions of this book, the intraclass correlation coefficient, *RI*, was recommended. *RI* however, is better suited for a different type of analysis of variance model than the one presented here (see Hays, 1994).

The formula for RI is:

$$RI = \frac{MS_b - MS_w}{MS_b + (n_j - 1)MS_w}$$

The relations between these measures, and their relative merits are not easy problems. Vaughan and Corballis (1969) discusses this problem. Simon (1987) highly encourages the use of these measures over significant tests. Simon points out that significant tests are prone to sample size influences. However, η^2 and ω^2 are not.

The point of the above discussion has been to bring out the similarity of conception of these and other indices of association or correlation. A more important discussion concerned the similarity of the principle and structure of analysis of variance and correlation methods. From a practical and applied standpoint, it should be emphasized that η^2, ω^2 and *RI*, or other measures of association should always be calculated and reported. It is not enough to report *F*-ratios and whether they are statistically significant. We must know how strong relations are. After all, with large enough *N*s, *F*- and *t*-ratios can almost always be statistically significant. While often sobering in their effect, especially when they are low, coefficients of association of independent and dependent variables are indispensable parts of research results.

Broadening the Structure:
Post Hoc Tests and Planned Comparisons

The approach used in this chapter and the next two chapters, while pedagogically useful, is too rigid. That is, the emphasis is on neat paradigms that have as their culmination the *F*-test and some measure of relation. Actual research, however, frequently does not fit into such nice shapes and thinking. Nevertheless, the basic analysis of variance notions can be used in a broader and freer way, with an expansion of the design and statistical possibilities. We examine such possibilities within the general framework of this chapter.

Post Hoc Tests

Suppose an experiment like Hurlock's has been done and the experimenter has the data from Table 13.9. The experimenter knows that the overall differences among the means are statistically significant. But the experimenter does not know which differences contribute to the significance. Can one simply test the differences between all pairs of means to tell which are significant? Yes and no, but generally no. Such tests are not independent and, with sufficient numbers of tests, one can be significant by chance. In short, such a "shotgun" procedure capitalizes on chance. Moreover, it is blind and what has been called "no-headed."

There are several ways to do post hoc tests, but we mention only one of them briefly. Zwick (1993), Edwards (1984), and Kirk (1995) give excellent descriptions of a number of different tests. The Scheffé test (see Scheffé, 1959), if used with discretion, is a general method that can be applied to all comparisons of means after an analysis of variance. If and only if the F-test is significant, one can test all the differences between means. One can test the combined mean of two or more groups against the mean of one other group; or one can select any combination of means against any other combination. Such a test with the ability to do so much is very useful. But we pay for the generality and usefulness: the test is quite conservative. To attain significance, differences have to be rather substantial. The Scheffé test is the most conservative test available for *multiple comparison tests.* Linton and Gallo (1975) shows the relation between the different tests and probability of a Type I error. The Scheffé test has the lowest probability of committing a Type I error yet has the lowest probability of detecting a difference when one exists (power). The main point is that post hoc comparisons and tests of means can be done mainly for exploratory and interpretative purposes. One examines his or her data in detail; one rummages for insights and clues.

Since it would take us too far afield, the mechanics of the Scheffé test are not given here (but see Study Suggestion 6 at the end of the chapter or Comrey and Lee, 1995, chapters 10 and 11). Suffice it to say that, when applied to the Hurlock data from Table 13.9, it shows that the Praised mean is significantly greater than the other three means and that none of the other differences are significant. This is important information because it points directly to the main source of the significance of the overall F-ratio: Praise versus Reproof, Ignoring, and Control. (However, the difference between an average of means 1 and 2 versus an average of means 3 and 4 is also statistically significant.) Although one can see this from the relative *sizes* of the means, the Scheffé test makes things precise—in a conservative way.

Planned Comparisons

While post hoc tests are important in actual research, especially for exploring one's data and for getting leads for future research, the method of planned comparisons is perhaps more important scientifically. Whenever hypotheses are formulated and systematically tested and empirical results support them, this is much more powerful evidence on the empirical validity of the hypotheses than when "interesting" (sometimes translated: "support my predilections") results are found *after* the data are obtained. This point was made in Chapter 2 where the power of hypotheses was explained.

In the analysis of variance, an overall F-test, if significant, simply indicates that there are significant differences somewhere in the data. Inspection of the means can tell one, though imprecisely, which differences are important. To test hypotheses, however, more or less controlled and precise statistical tests are needed. There is a large variety of possible comparisons in any set of data that one can test. But which ones? As usual, the research problem and the theory behind the problem should dictate the statistical tests. One designs research in part to test substantive hypotheses.

Suppose the reinforcement theory behind the Hurlock study said, in effect, that any kind of attention, positive or negative, will improve performance, and that positive reinforcement will improve it more than punishment. This would mean that E_1 and E_2 of Table 13.9, taken together or separately, will be significantly greater than E_3 and C taken together or separately. That is, both Praised (positive reinforcement) and Reproved (punishment) will be significantly greater than Ignored (no reinforcement) and Control (no reinforcement). In addition, the theory says that the effect of positive reinforcement is greater than the effect of punishment. Thus Praised will be significantly greater than Reproved. These implied tests can be written symbolically:

$$H_1:C_1 = \frac{M_1 + M_2}{2} > \frac{M_3 + M_4}{2}$$

$$H_2:C_2 = M_1 > M_2$$

where C_1 indicates the first comparison and C_2 the second. We have here the ingredients of a one-way analysis of variance, but the simple overall test and its democracy of means have been radically changed. That is, the plan and design of the research have changed under the impact of the theory and the research problem.

When the Scheffé test is used, the overall F-ratio must be significant because none of the Scheffé tests can be significant if the overall F is not significant. When planned comparisons are used, however, no overall F-test need be made. The focus is on the planned comparisons and the hypotheses. The number of comparisons and tests made are limited by the degrees of freedom. In the Hurlock example, there are three degrees of freedom for between groups ($k - 1$); therefore, three tests can be made. These tests have to be *orthogonal* to each other—that is, they must be independent. We keep the comparisons orthogonal by using what are called *orthogonal coefficients* or *contrasts*, which are weights to be attached to the means in the comparisons. The coefficients, in other words, specify the comparisons. The coefficients or weights for H_1 and H_2, above, are:

$$H_1: 1/2 \quad 1/2 \quad -1/2 \quad -1/2$$
$$H_2: \ \ 1 \quad \ -1 \quad \ \ \ 0 \quad \ \ \ \ 0$$

For comparisons to be orthogonal, two conditions must be met: the sum of each set of weights must equal 0, and the sum of the products of any two sets of weights must also be zero. It is obvious that both of the above sets sum to zero. Test the sum of the products: $(1/2)(1) + (1/2)(-1) + (-1/2)(0) + (-1/2)(0) = 0$. Thus the two sets of weights are orthogonal.

It is important to understand orthogonal weights, as well as the two conditions just given. The first set of weights simply represents: $(M_1 + M_2)/2 - (M_3 + M_4)/2$. The second set represents: $M_1 - M_2$. Now, suppose we also wanted to test the notion that the Ignored mean is greater than the Control mean. This is tested by: $M_3 - M_4$, and is coded: H_3: 0 0 1 -1. Henceforth, we will call these weight *vectors*. The values of the vector sum to zero. What about its sum of products with the other two vectors?

$$H_1 \times H_3: (1/2)(0) + (1/2)(0) + (-1/2)(1) + (-1/2)(-1) = 0$$

$$H_2 \times H_3: (1)(0) + (-1)(0) + (0)(1) + (0)(-1) = 0$$

The third vector is orthogonal to, or independent of, the other two vectors. The third comparison can be made. If these three comparisons are made, no other is possible because the available $k - 1 = 4 - 1 = 3$ degrees of freedom are used up.

Suppose, now, that instead of the H_3 above, we wanted to test the difference between the average of the first three means against the fourth mean. The coding is: 1/3 1/3 1/3 -1. This is tantamount to $(M_1 + M_2 + M_3)/3 + M_4$. Is the vector orthogonal to the first two? Calculate:

$$(1/2)(1/3) + (1/2)(1/3) + (-1/2)(1/3) + (-1/2)(-1)$$
$$= 1/6 + 1/6 - 1/6 + 1/2 = 4/6 = 2/3.$$

Since the sum of the products does not equal zero, it is not orthogonal to the first vector, and the comparison should not be made. The comparison implied by the vector would yield redundant information. In this case, the comparison using the third vector supplies information already given in part by the first vector.

The method of calculating the significance of the differences of planned comparisons need not be detailed. Besides, at this point we do not need the actual calculations. Our purpose, we hope, is a larger one: to show the flexibility and power of analysis of variance when properly conceived and understood. F-tests (or t-tests) are used with each comparison or, in this case, with each degree of freedom. The details of calculations can be found in Hays (1994) and other texts. The basic idea of planned comparisons is quite general, and we use it again when we study research design.

We have come a long, perhaps hard, way on the analysis-of-variance road. One may wonder why so much space has been devoted to the subject. There are several reasons. First, the analysis of variance has wide practical applicability. It takes many forms that are applicable in psychology, sociology, economics, political science, agriculture, biology, education, and other fields. It frees us from working with only one independent variable at a time and gives us a powerful lever for solving measurement problems. It increases the possibilities of making experiments exact and precise. It also permits us to test several hypotheses simultaneously, as well as to test hypotheses that cannot be tested in any other way, at least with precision. Thus its generality of application is great.

More germane to the purposes of this book, the analysis of variance gives us insight into modern research approaches and methods. It does this by focusing sharply and constantly on variance thinking, by making clear the close relation between research problems and statistical methods and inference, and by clarifying the structure, the architecture, of research design. It is also an important step in understanding contemporary multivariate conceptions of research because it is an expression of the general linear model.

The model of this chapter is simple and can be written:

$$y = a_o + A + e$$

where y is the dependent variable score of an individual, a_o is a term common to all individuals, for example, the general mean of y. A is the effect of the independent variable treatment, and e is error. The model of the next chapter will be slightly more complex and, before the book is finished, models will become much more complex. As we will see, the general linear model is flexible and generally applicable to many research problems and situations. Perhaps of more immediate weight to us, it can help us better understand the common threads and themes of different multivariate approaches and methods.

Computer Addendum

In this chapter we examined the t-ratio that was used to analyze the difference between two means and the one-way analysis of variance that can be used to analyze the difference between two or more group means. Technically we would refer to the groups as levels of the independent variable and the outcome measure as the dependent variable. Although such computations can be done by hand or with a hand calculator, it is sometimes more efficient to use a computer. We introduced in Chapter 6 and demonstrated how it can be used to analyze frequency data in Chapter 10. In this chapter we will show how one can use it to perform a t-test and a one-way ANOVA. It is expected that the reader has read and understood the computer material in Chapter 6 and Chapter 10 concerning the creation of the data table in SPSS.

t-Ratio or t-Test on SPSS

The data are taken from Table 13.1. Note that when dealing with group membership, it is expressed as a categorical variable. In this case, the independent variable,

◉ FIGURE 13.2 *Data Table for t-Test in SPSS*

	Group	Score				
1	1	4				
2	1	5				
3	1	3				
4	1	2				
5	1	6				
6	2	3				
7	2	1				
8	2	5				
9	2	2				
10	2	4				

File Edit View Data Transform Statistics Graphs Utilities Windows Help

◉ FIGURE 13.3 *Selecting the Appropriate Statistical Analysis in SPSS*

File Edit View Data Transform Statistics Graphs Utilities Windows Help

	Group	Score		Summarize ▶	Means
1	1	4		**Compare Means** ▶	One-Sample T-Test
2	1	5		ANOVA Models ▶	**Independent Samples T-Test**
3	1	3		Correlate ▶	Paired Samples T-Test
4	1	2		Regression ▶	One Way ANOVA
5	1	6		Log-linear ▶	
6	2	3		Classify ▶	
7	2	1		Data Reduction ▶	
8	2	5		Scale ▶	
9	2	2		Nonparametric Tests ▶	
10	2	4			

◉ FIGURE 13.4 *SPSS Screen for Specifying the Independent and Dependent Variables*

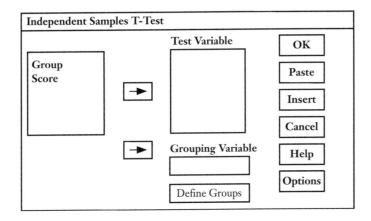

Group, is written as a variable with two levels. For A_1, Group $= 1$; for A_2, Group $= 2$. The second variable, Score is the dependent variable. SPSS and some other computer programs for statistical analyses expect the data to be entered into the program in such a manner. Figure 13.2 shows what the data table for SPSS should look like for this problem.

Using the mouse, point to and click on "Statistics." Another menu will appear listing the different analyses one can perform on the data. For your *t*-test, select "Compare Means." This selection in turn gives another menu from which you choose "Independent Samples T-Test." This is shown in Figure 13.3.

When "Independent Samples T-Test" is selected, you are given a new screen asking you to decide which variable listed in your data table should be specified as the independent variable and which should be the dependent variable. Figure 13.4 shows this panel without any changes made by the user. Using SPSS terminology, "Test Variable" refers to the dependent variables; "Grouping Variable" refers to the independent variables.

We can specify the dependent or test variable first by highlighting the "Score" variable in the left-most box and clicking on the arrow button associated with the Test Variable box. We will see the Score variable name move from the left-most box to the top right-most box when this happens. Next, highlight (select) the independent or "Grouping Variable." In our example it is named "Group." After highlighting it click on the arrow button associated with the "Grouping Variable" box, the variable name, Group will move from the left-most box to the Grouping Variable box. Figure 13.5 shows what this screen looks like after these operations.

Note that the Group variable has a set of parentheses surrounding two question marks. This tells you that you need to specify the levels of the independent variable.

◉ **FIGURE 13.5** *Screen after Specifying the Independent and Dependent Variables*

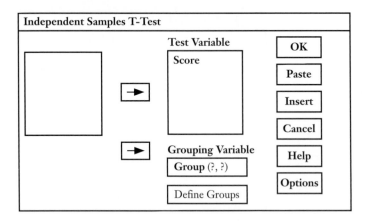

◉ **FIGURE 13.6** *Screen Used to Define Levels of the Independent Variable*

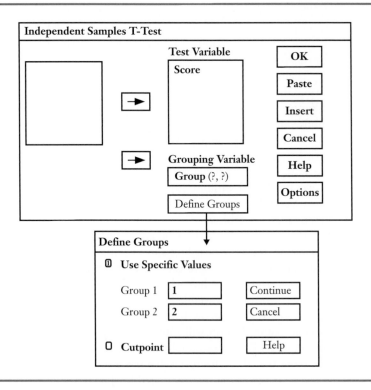

■ FIGURE 13.7 *Screen Showing Aftermath of Defining the Groups for the Independent Variable*

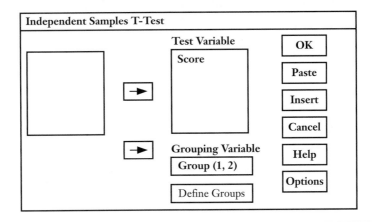

The values would correspond to the ones used in your original data table. For our example it would be 1 and 2. To tell SPSS this, click on the "Define Groups" button. When this is done, you get yet another panel screen that allows you to define the levels for the variable, Group. Figure 13.6 shows what this screen looks like. Note that we will enter "1" for Group 1 and "2" for Group 2. By clicking on the "Continue" button, you will return to the previous screen. However, the two question marks are gone and replaced by the specification "1, 2."

We need to digress here a bit before finishing SPSS and the *t*-test. Let's say we had more than two levels of the independent variable (i.e., say, three or more groups). The *t*-test can only compare two levels (groups) at a time. If we had three groups, we could do the *t*-test between groups 1 and 2, groups 1 and 3, or groups 2 and 3. In the screen displayed in Figure 13.6, we would specify Group 1 with an index of "1" and Group 2 with an index of "3" if we were interested in comparing groups 1 and 3. If we were interested in comparing groups 2 and 3, we would have specified a "2" for Group 1 and a "3" for Group 2 in the screen shown in Figure 13.6.

Figure 13.7 shows the screen after clicking on the "Continue" button shown in Figure 13.6. If we now click on the "OK" button, the statistical analysis requested will be performed on the data. The output from this analysis is given in the box below. Note that the *t*-value computed is the same as the one done by hand for the data in Table 13.1. SPSS also gives us the probability of a Type I error. In this case it is .347. It is larger than .05, so the difference between means is not statistically signifcant.

t-test for Independent Samples of GROUP

Variable	Number of Cases	Mean	SD	SE of Mean
SCORE				
GROUP 1	5	4.0000	1.581	.707
GROUP 2	5	3.0000	1.581	.707

Mean Difference = 1.0000
Levene's Test for Equality of Variances: F = .000 p = 1.000

t-test for Equality of Means

Variances	t-value	df	2-Tail Sig	SE of Diff	95% CI for Diff
Equal	1.00	8	.347	1.000	(−1.306, 3.306)
Unequal	1.00	8.00	.347	1.000	(−1.306, 3.306)

One-Way ANOVA on SPSS

Again, we are assuming that the reader has created the data table within SPSS and is about to select and perform a specific statistical analysis. Figure 13.8 shows the data

■ **FIGURE 13.8** *Data Table for One-Way ANOVA Example*

File Edit View Data Transform Statistics Graphs Utilities Windows Help

	Group	Score					
1	1	6					
2	1	7					
3	1	5					
4	1	4					
5	1	8					
6	2	3					
7	2	1					
8	2	5					
9	2	2					
10	2	4					

■ **FIGURE 13.9a** *SPSS Screen Used to Select Independent and Dependent Variables*

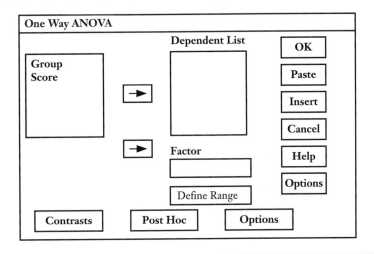

table to be used in SPSS. The data were taken from Table 13.7. Although there are only two groups, the procedure shown here would be very similar for more than two groups or more than two levels of the independent variable. We saw when we did the *t*-test, that having the mouse point to and click on "Statistics," gave us another menu listing the different analyses one can perform on the data. Figure 13.3 shows the menus.

■ **FIGURE 13.9b** *Screen Used for Specifying the Dependent and Independent Variables*

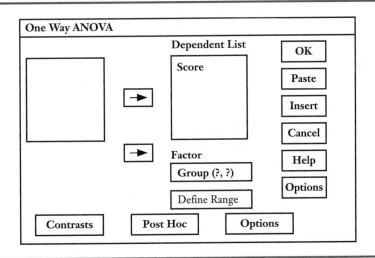

For a one-way ANOVA, choose "Compare Means." This selection gives a new menu from which you choose "One Way ANOVA." When you do this, you get a screen that asks you to specify which variable in your data table will be the independent variable(s) and the dependent variable(s). This screen is shown in Figure 13.8. As you did for the *t*-test, choose "Score" as the dependent variable and "Group" as the independent variable. Here, in SPSS terminology "Dependent List" is for the dependent variable and "Factor" is for the independent variable (see Figure 13.9a). Like the screens used in the *t*-test, highlight the "Score" variable name in the leftmost box and click on the arrow for the "Dependent List" box. This moves the variable name "Score" to the box associated with the Dependent List. Do likewise for the "Group" variable label—move it to the box associated with "Factor." When this is done, you will see that SPSS asks you to specify the range of values for the dependent variable. Figure 13.9a and Figure 13.9b show this. To define the factors (independent variables) click on the button labeled "Define Range." From this operation, another screen appears. This is shown in Figure 13.10. Enter the numbers "1" and "2" for the minimum and maximum values of the independent variable. If you had three groups which were specified in the data table as "1, 2, and 3," you would specify the minimum as 1 and the maximum as 3. SPSS expects a systematic ordering of the categories of the independent variable. Once you have finished defining the

▣ **FIGURE 13.10** *Screen Used to Define the Range of Values for the Independent Variable*

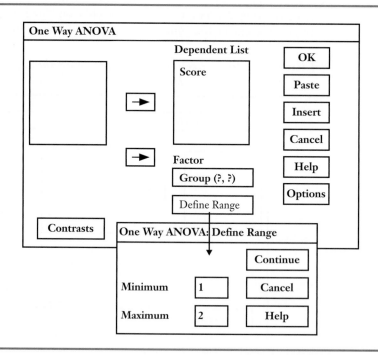

■ FIGURE 13.11 *One-Way ANOVA Screen after Defining the Range*

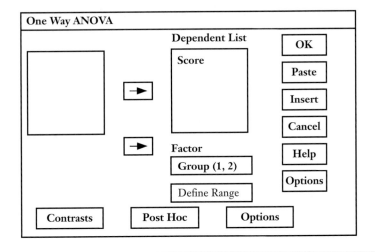

range, click on the "Continue" button. This action will return you to the One Way ANOVA screen with the range for the independent variable defined (shown in Figure 13.11). Now click the "OK" button and analysis will begin. Note that if we wanted post hoc multiple comparison tests we could do those by clicking on "Post Hoc" (see Figure 13.11) before telling SPSS to go ahead with the analysis. When "Post Hoc" is activated, a screen containing a list of the most used post hoc tests is presented. The user needs only to select the one wanted.

The results of the one-way ANOVA for the data are given in the box below. The results agree with those we had performed by hand. With SPSS, a table lookup for the critical value used to reject or not reject the null hypothesis is not necessary.

- - - - - *O N E W A Y* - - - - -

Variable SCORE
By Variable GROUP

Analysis of Variance

Source	D.F.	Sum of Squares	Mean Squares	F Ratio	F Prob.
Between Groups	1	22.5000	22.5000	9.0000	.0171
Within Groups	8	20.0000	2.5000		
Total	9	42.5000			

Addendum

Analysis of Variance Calculations with Means, Standard Deviations, and ns

It is sometimes useful to be able to do analysis of variance from means, standard deviations, and ns of groups rather than from raw scores. One method of doing so follows (the data from Table 13.7 are used to illustrate the method):

1. From the ns and Ms calculate the sums of the groups, ΣX_j. Add these to obtain ΣX_t. Calculate total N from the ns of the groups.

$$\Sigma X_t = \Sigma\,[M_j n_j] = (5)(6) + (5)(3) = 45;\ \ N = 5 + 5 = 10$$

2. Correction term: $(\Sigma X_t)^2/N = 45^2/10 = 202.50\ (C)$.
3. Calculate the within-groups sum-of-squares: the average of the sums-of-squares within the groups:

$$(1.5811^2)(4) + (1.5811^2)(4) = 19.9990 = 20 = ss_w$$

4. Calculate between sums-of-squares:

$$ss_b = \Sigma\,[n_j Mj^2] - C$$
$$ss_b = [(6^2)(5) + (3^2)(5)] - C = 225.00 - 202.50 = 22.50.$$

5. Set up analysis of variance table (as in Table 13.7), and calculate mean squares and F-ratio.

Special Note: This method assumes that the original standard deviations were calculated with $n - 1$. If they were calculated with n, alter step 3, above: $(1.4142^2)(5) + (1.4142^2)(5) = 20$. That is, change 4 to 5, or $n - 1$ to n.

CHAPTER SUMMARY

1. The variance of the dependent variable can be broken up into two or more components.
2. Components are called sources of variance.
3. The sources of variance serve as the basis for the statistical method known as analysis of variance or ANOVA.
4. In a one-way ANOVA, the sources are between-group and within-group variances.
5. A statistically significant difference is present when the between group variance exceed the within-group variance by a significant amount. An F-table is used to determine the critical value.

6. A demonstration is given with both fictitious data and real data on how to compute the appropriate values in an analysis of variance.
7. The strength of the relation between the independent and dependent variables is determined by either η^2 or ω^2. These measures are not sensitive to sample size and are interpreted like r^2.
8. When an *F*-test is significant and there are three or more groups (or levels of the independent variable), multiple comparison tests are needed to determine which means are statistically different.
9. The Scheffé test is presented as a multiple comparison test. Where there is no predetermined plan for comparisons, the tests are called *post hoc tests*.
10. Comparisons determined before conducting the test are called *planned comparisons*.
11. The material in this chapter introduces the concepts necessary for the next two chapters concerning the analysis of variance.

STUDY SUGGESTIONS

1. There are many good references on analysis of variance, varying in difficulty and clarity of explanation. Hays' (1994) discussion that includes the general linear model, is as usual excellent, but not easy. It is highly recommended for careful study. The following four books are very good indeed. All are staples of statistical diet. Some are also listed in the reference section because they were cited in the text.

Edwards, A. L. (1984). *Experimental design in psychological research* (5th ed.). Reading, MA: Addison-Wesley.
Hays, W. L. (1994). *Statistics* (5th ed.). Fort Worth, TX: Harcourt Brace.
Kirk, R. E. (1995). *Experimental designs: Procedures for the behavioral sciences.* Pacific Grove, CA: Brooks/Cole.
Woodward, J. A., Bonett, D. G., & Brecht, M. (1990). *Introduction to linear models and experimental design.* San Diego, CA: Harcourt Brace Jovanovich.

Some students may like to read an interesting history of analysis of variance, especially in psychology, followed by a history of the 0.05 level of statistical significance. For those students, the following are recommended:

Cowles, M. (1989). *Statistics in psychology: An historical perspective.* Hillsdale, NJ: Lawrence Erlbaum.
Rucci, A., & Tweny, R. (1980). Analysis of variance and the second discipline of scientific psychology: A historical account. *Psychological Bulletin, 87,* 166–184.

2. A university professor conducts an experiment to test the relative efficacies of three methods of instruction: A_1, Lecture; A_2, Large-Group Discussion; and A_3, Small-Group Discussion. From a universe of sophomores, 30 are selected at random and assigned randomly to three groups. The three methods are assigned randomly to the three groups. The students are tested for their achievement at the end of four months of the experiment. The scores for the three groups are given below.

Methods

A_1(Lecture)	A_2 (Large-Group Discussion)	A_3 (Small-Group Discussion)
4	5	3
7	6	5
9	3	1
6	8	4
9	3	4
6	2	5
5	5	7
7	6	3
7	7	5
10	5	3

Test the null hypothesis, using one-way analysis of variance and the 0.01 level of significance. Calculate η^2 and ω^2. Interpret the results. Draw a graph of the data similar to those in the text.
[Answers: $F = 7.16$ (.01); $\eta^2 = .35$; $\omega^2 = .29$]

3 From a table of random numbers—you can use those in Appendix C—draw three samples of 10 each of numbers 0 through 9.
   a. Make up a research study, with problem and hypotheses, and imagine that the three sets of numbers are your results.
   b. Do an analysis of variance of the three sets of numbers. Calculate η, η^2, and ω^2. Draw a graph of the results like those of Figure 13.1. Interpret the results both statistically and substantively.
   c. Add a constant of 2 to each of the scores of the group with the highest mean. Do the calculations and graph of (b), above, again. Interpret. What changes take place in the statistics? [Examine the sums-of-squares especially, taking careful note of the within groups variances (mean squares) of both examples.]

4. Take the scores of the highest and lowest groups in Study Suggestion 2, above (groups A_1 and A_3).

  a. Do an analysis of variance, and calculate the square root of F, $\sqrt{F}$. Now do a t-test as described in Chapter 12. Compare the t obtained with $\sqrt{F}$.

  b. Is it legitimate, after doing the analysis of variance of the three groups, to calculate the t-ratio as instructed and then to draw conclusions about the difference between the two methods? (Consult your instructor, if necessary. This point is difficult.)

  [Answers: (a) $F = 14.46$; $\sqrt{F} = 3.80$, $t = 3.80$; (c) $\eta^2 = .45$; $\omega^2 = .40$]

5. Aronson and Mills (1959) tested the interesting and perhaps humanly perverse hypothesis that individuals who undergo an unpleasant initiation to become members of a group have more liking for the group than do members who do not undergo such an initiation. Three groups of 21 young women each were subjected to three experimental conditions: (i) *severe condition*, in which the Ss were asked to read obscene words and vivid descriptions of sexual activity in order to become members of a group; (ii) *mild condition*, in which Ss read words related to sex but were not obscene; and (iii) *control condition*, in which Ss were not required to do anything to become members of the group. After a rather elaborate procedure, the Ss were asked to rate the discussion and the members of the group to which they then ostensibly belonged. The means and standard deviations of the total ratings are *severe:* $M = 195.3$, $SD = 31.9$; mild: $M = 171.1$, $SD = 34.0$; *control:* $M = 166.7$, $SD = 21.6$. Each n was 21.

  a. Do an analysis of variance of these data. Use the method outlined in the addendum to this chapter. Interpret the data. Is the hypothesis supported?

  b. Calculate ω^2. Is the relation strong? Would you expect the relation to be strong in an experiment of this find?

  [Answers: (a) $F = 5.39$ (.01); (b) $\omega^2 = .12$]

6. Use the Scheffé test to calculate the significance of all the differences between the three means of Study Suggestion 2, above. One way to do the Scheffe test is to calculate the standard error of the differences between two means with the following formula:

$$SE_{M_i - M_j} = \sqrt{MS_w\left(\frac{1}{n_i} + \frac{1}{N_j}\right)} \tag{13.6}$$

where MS_w equals within-groups mean square, and n_i and n_j are the numbers of cases in groups i and j. For the example, this is:

$$SE_{M_{A1} - M_{A2}} = \sqrt{(3.26)\left(\frac{1}{10} + \frac{1}{10}\right)} = .81$$

Then calculate the statistic S (for Scheffe):

$$S = \sqrt{(k - 1)F_{.05(k-1,m)}} \qquad (13.7)$$

where k equals number of groups in the analysis of variance, and the F term is the .05 level F-ratio obtained from an F-table at $k - 1$ ($3 - 1 = 2$) and $m = N - k = 30 - 3 = 27$ degrees of freedom. This is 3.35. Thus,

$$S = \sqrt{(3 - 1)(3.35)} = \sqrt{6.70} = 2.59.$$

The final step is to multiply the results of equations 13.6 and 13.7:

$$S \times SE_{M_i - M_j} = (2.59)(.81) = 2.10.$$

Any difference, to be statistically significant at the 0.05 level, must be as large or larger than 2.10. Now use the statistic in the example.

7. Studies using one-way analysis of variance are fewer than studies using other methods. From the following list of nine studies using one-way analysis of variance, select two for study. Pay particular attention to post hoc tests of the significance of the differences between means.

Gibson, R. L., & Hartshorne, T. S. (1996). Childhood sexual abuse and adult loneliness and network orientation. *Child Abuse & Neglect, 20,* 1087–1093.

Goldenberg, D., & Iwasiw, C. (1993). Professional socialization of nursing students as the outcome of a senior clinical preceptorship experience. *Nurse Education Today, 13,* 3–5.

Gupta, S. (1992). Season of birth in relation to personality and blood groups. *Personality and Individual Differences, 13,* 631–633.

Jamal, M., & Baba, V. V. (1992). Shiftwork and department-type related to job stress, work attitudes and behavioral intentions: A study of nurses. *Journal of Organizational Behavior, 13,* 449–464.

Kirsch, I., Mobayed, C. P., Council, J. R., & Kenny, D. A. (1992). Expert judgments of hypnosis from subjective state reports. *Journal of Abnormal Psychology, 101,* 657–662.

Silverstein, B. (1982). Cigarette smoking, nicotine addiction, and relaxation. *Journal of Personality and Social Psychology, 42,* 946–950.

Sonnenschein, S. (1986). Developing referential communication: Transfer across novel tasks. *Bulletin of the Psychonomic Society, 24,* 127–130.

Uddin, M. (1996). College women's sexuality in an era of AIDS. *Journal of American College Health, 44,* 252–261.

Wittrock, M. (1967). Replacement and nonreplacement strategies in children's problem solving. *Journal of Educational Psychology, 58,* 69–74

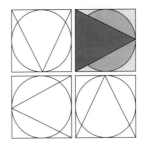

CHAPTER 14

FACTORIAL ANALYSIS OF VARIANCE

We now study the statistical and design approach that epitomizes the true beginning of the modern behavioral science research outlook. The idea of factorial design and factorial analysis of variance is one of the creative research ideas put forward in the past sixty or more years. Its influence on contemporary behavioral research, especially in psychology and education, has been great. It is no exaggeration to say that factorial designs are the most used of all experimental designs, and that factorial analysis of variance is used more in experimental psychological research than any other form of analysis. These are strong statements and require explanation. We devote this chapter to such explanation, together with description and explanation of the mechanics of factorial analysis of variance. Its importance and complexity will make it necessary to belabor aspects of the subject more than usual. This chapter, in other words, will be heavier than most. Readers should thus have patience, persistence, and forbearance. Believe that it is in a good cause. We begin with two instructive research examples.

Two Research Examples

Prejudice is a deep and subtle phenomenon. Once born it penetrates large parts of our thinking. It is an obvious truism that negative prejudice against minorities is a widespread and potent phenomenon. Is prejudice so pervasive and subtle that it can work the "other way"? Do people who believe themselves free of prejudice discriminate positively toward minorities? Is there such a thing, in other words, as "inverse prejudice"? Is some of the hiring of African Americans and women practiced by business firms and universities prompted by inverse prejudice—or is it merely good business? Such questions can, of course, be asked easily, although they are not answered so easily—at least not scientifically.

In an insightful and somewhat upsetting study, Dutton and Lake (1973) hypothesize that if people are threatened by the thought that they themselves might be prejudiced, they would act in a reverse discriminatory manner toward minority group members. They would discriminate, but favorably, in other words.

From a pool of 500 college students, 40 male and 40 female students, who had evaluated themselves as relatively unprejudiced on questionnaires administered before the experiment, were assigned to two experimental conditions: "Threat" and "Race," partitioned into high threat and low threat, and African American panhandler and White American panhandler. The design, then, was the simplest factorial design possible: a so-called two-by-two (2×2). It is given in Table 14.1, together with the means of the dependent variable, which was money (cents) given to a panhandler. Note that this 2×2 table looks like the 2×2 crosstabs (crossbreaks) discussed in Chapter 10. It is essentially different, however, and the student should clearly understand that difference: Crosstabs have frequencies or percentages in the table cells whereas factorial designs have measures of the dependent variable in the cells, usually means. The dependent variable is always one of the variables in the margins (outside) of the *crosstab*; in factorial designs, the dependent variable is always the measure inside the cells.

Dutton and Lake reasoned that reverse discrimination was likely to occur if participants who saw themselves as unprejudiced were led to suspect that they might actually be prejudiced. This suspicion would be a threat to self, and a subject experiencing this threat would, under appropriate conditions, act in a reverse discriminatory manner. High Threat participants were told that they had shown high emotional arousal—as presumably measured by galvanic skin response and pulse rate—to slides depicting interracial scenes. Low Threat participants were given no

▣ TABLE 14.1 *Factorial Design, 2 × 2, of Dutton and Lake Reverse Discrimination Experiment*[a]

	Threat		
Race	**High Threat**	**Low Threat**	
African American Panhandler	47.25	16.75	32.00
White American Panhandler	28.25	27.75	28.00
	37.75	22.25	

[a]Numbers in the cells are means, in cents, given to panhandlers. The original design included sex, but we omit this variable here.

such feedback to the slides. This experimental condition is given at the top of the design in Table 14.1.

The second experimental variable, "Race," was manipulated as follows. After the completion of the Threat variable manipulation, subjects were paid in quarters and then dismissed. On their way out of the laboratory, half the subjects were asked by an African American confederate, and half the subjects asked by a white American confederate the following question: "Can you spare some change for some food?" This second experimental variable, Race, is given in the side margin of Table 14.1, African American panhandler and White American panhandler. It was predicted that the High Threat subjects would give more money to the African American panhandler than to the White American panhandler, since it was assumed that the High Threat subjects would react against the idea that they were prejudiced, as suggested by the polygraph of the experimental condition, by giving more money to the African American panhandler. Low Threat subjects, since they had not been made to doubt their lack of prejudice, would not give money to the same extent. In other words, there would be a between-threat difference of money given to the African American panhandler, but no between-threat difference of money given to the White American panhandler. The predicted outcome is known as an *interaction*, a term we will explain later in considerable depth.

The data of Table 14.1, taken from the more extensive data reported by Dutton and Lake, seem to support the hypothesis. The means of High Threat versus Low Threat under the African American panhandler condition were 47.25 and 16.75 (cents), whereas the Threat means under the White American panhandler condition were 28.25 and 27.75. Statistical analysis indicated that the hypothesized outcomes were indeed as the authors indicated they would be. We try to bring out and emphasize the nature of the obtained data by the plot of the means given in Figure 14.1. The plotted points—indicated by the small black circles—are the means of Table 14.1. The horizontal axis is "Threat." Since there are only two "values," their placement on the line is almost arbitrary. The vertical axis is the amounts of money given to the panhandler.

▣ FIGURE 14.1

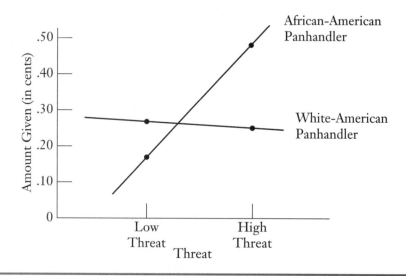

The relation is apparent: the African American panhandler is given more money under the High Threat condition than under the Low Threat condition, whereas there is virtually no difference in the two threat conditions with the White American panhandler. Evidently the interaction hypothesis is supported. Reverse discrimination was practiced, and we can perhaps say that inverse prejudice "exists."

In an interesting experimental study of the effects of two variables, Self-disclosure and Group Gender Composition, Elias (1989) found that both had an effect on group cohesiveness, commitment to task, and productivity. Elias assigned at random each of the 144 undergraduate college students (72 females and 72 males) to one of 36 groups. Each group was composed of four members. Of these 36 groups, 12 were males only, 12 were females only, and 12 were mixed (males and females). Six groups from each category (male, female, mixed) were then assigned randomly to either the experimental condition (Self-disclosure) or the control condition (No Self-disclosure). All groups completed a simple puzzle task as a measure of Productivity and questionnaires assessing Cohesiveness and Commitment to Task. The subjects were instructed to have no verbal communication between the group members. The subjects were told that they could give puzzle pieces to other members. In the Self-disclosure groups, group members participated in a group discussion after completing the first puzzle. The discussion centered on the facts and feelings that were relevant to the puzzle task. Self-disclosure cue cards were used to facilitate discussion. The control group received a videotape of nature scenes. Subjects in the control condition were instructed not to communicate with each other. After this, both groups participated in a second puzzle-solving task. The amount of time it took to complete the second puzzle served as the measure for Productivity. A questionnaire was used to measure Cohesiveness and Commitment to Task. The data showed that Self-disclosure intervention resulted in higher Cohesiveness, Commitment to Task, and Productivity. This is more readily understood by considering Table 14.2. One variable is group gender composition, which is partitioned into "Male," "Female," and "Mixed." The other variable, "Disclosure," was partitioned similarly into "Self-disclosure" and "Control." These were experimental conditions. The dependent variables are: Cohesiveness, Commitment to Task, and Productivity. In Cohesiveness and Commitment to Task, both independent variables had a statistically significant effect. Under both of these dependent variables, female participants reported higher group Cohesiveness and Commitment to Task than males or mixed groups. For Group Productivity, only Self-disclosure versus Control had a statistically significant effect.

▣ **TABLE 14.2** *Design and Results (Means) of the Elias Study: 2 × 3 Factorial.*[a]

Cohesiveness Disclosure	Group Gender Female	Male	Composition Mixed	
Self-disclosure	14.20	15.96	15.61	15.25
Control	15.92	19.08	17.75	17.58
	15.06	17.52	16.68	

Commitment to Task Disclosure	Group Gender Female	Male	Composition Mixed	
Self-disclosure	77.13	71.80	71.88	73.60
Control	72.08	65.50	68.88	68.68
	74.60	68.85	70.17	

Productivity Disclosure	Group Gender Female	Male	Composition Mixed	
Self-disclosure	149.17	71.17	143.67	121.00
Control	193.00	217.17	310.17	240.11
	171.09	144.17	226.92	

[a]Lower scores indicate greater cohesiveness.

The Nature of Factorial Analysis of Variance

In factorial analysis of variance two or more independent variables vary independently or interact with each other to produce variation in a dependent variable. *Factorial analysis of variance is the statistical method that analyzes the independent and interactive effects of two or more independent variables on a dependent variable.*

If there are two independent variables, as in the examples just discussed, the linear model is an extension of the linear model of the last chapter:

$$y = a_o + A + B + AB + e \tag{14.1}$$

where y, as usual, is a score of an individual on the dependent variable; a_o is the term common to all individuals, for example, the general mean A; is the effect of one independent variable; B is the effect of another independent variable; AB is the effect of both variables working together, or interacting; and e is error. In addition to the one effect, A, and error, e, in one-way analysis of variance, we now have a second effect, B, and a third "effect," the joint working or influence on y of A and B, or AB. There is no theoretical limit to the number of independent variables in factorial designs. Here is the model for three independent variables:

$$y = a_o + A + B + C + AB + AC + BC + ABC + e \tag{14.2}$$

Here, there are three independent variables, A, B, and C; the interactions between them, AB, AC, and BC; and the simultaneous interaction of all three, ABC. As complex as this model seems, there are many uses of it in the literature (we will give examples later). And we can add more independent variables. The only limitations are practical ones: how to handle so many variables at one time and how to interpret interactions, especially triple and quadruple ones. What we are after, however, are the basic ideas behind factorial designs and models.

One of the most significant and revolutionary developments in modern research design and statistics is the planning and analysis of the simultaneous operation and interaction of two or more variables. Scientists have long known that variables do not act independently. Rather, they often act in concert. The virtue of one method of teaching contrasted with another method of teaching depends on the teachers using the methods. The educational effect of a certain kind of teacher depends, to a large extent, on the kind of pupil being taught. An anxious teacher may be quite effective with anxious pupils but less effective with nonanxious pupils. Different methods of teaching in colleges and universities may depend on the intelligence and personality of both professors and students. In the Dutton and Lake (1973) study, the effect of Threat depended on the race of the panhandler (see Table 14.1 and Figure 14.1). In the Elias (1989) study, the interaction was different. There were no interactions on any of the analyses on the three dependent variables. The joint effect of the independent variables—Disclosure and Group Gender Composition—was cumulative; the effect was strongest when both were present (see Table 14.2).

Before the invention of analysis of variance and the designs suggested by the method, the traditional conduct of experimental research was to study the effect of one independent variable on one dependent variable. We are not implying, by the way, that this approach is wrong. It is simply limited. Nevertheless, many research questions can be adequately answered using this "one-to-one" approach. Many other research questions can be adequately answered only by considering multiple and interacting influences. Educational scientists knew that the study of the effects of different pedagogical methods and techniques on educational outcomes was in part a function of other variables, such as the intelligence of the students, the personality of the teachers, the social background of both the teacher and the students, and the general atmosphere of the class and the school. But many researchers believed that the most effective research method was to vary one independent variable while controlling, as best one could, other independent variables that might contribute to the variance of the dependent variable. Simon (1976; 1987) disagrees with this traditional approach and advocates economic multifactor designs. These designs, however, require careful planning and execution of the experiment but can yield useful information on a large number of variables.

In the studies summarized above, the conclusions go beyond the simple differences between effects or groups. It was possible to qualify the conclusions in important ways because the authors studied the simultaneous workings of the two independent variables. They were consequently able to talk about the *differential effect* of their variables. They could say, for example, that treatment A_1 is effective when coupled with level B_1, but not effective when alone or when coupled with level B_2, and that, perhaps, A_2 is effective only when coupled with B_1.

The implied logic behind this sort of research thinking can be better understood by returning to the conditional statements and thinking of an earlier chapter. Recall that a conditional statement takes the form "If p, then q," or "If p, then q, under conditions r and s." In logical notation: $p \rightarrow q$ and $p \rightarrow q \mid r,s$. Schematically, the conditional statement behind the one-way analysis of variable problems of Chapter 13 is the simple statement: If p, then q. In the Hurlock study, if certain incentives, then certain achievement. In the Aronson and Mills study (see Study Suggestion 5, Chapter 13), if severity of initiation, then liking for the group.

The conditional statements associated with the research problems of this chapter, however, are more complex and subtle: If p, then q, under conditions r and s, or $p \rightarrow q \mid r,s$, where "|" means "under condition(s)." In the Dutton and Lake (1973) study, this would be $p \rightarrow q > \mid r$; or If threat then reverse discrimination, under the condition that the target (the panhandler) is African American. While structurally similar, the "cumulative" logic of Elias (1989) is different: If p and r, then q; or If Self-disclosure and Group Gender Composition, then the greater the Cohesiveness and Commitment to Task, or in logical symbols: $(p \cap r) \rightarrow q$ (read: If p and r, then q). Here we cannot say "under the condition" because p and q (Self-disclosure and Group Gender Composition) are equal partners and combine to affect cohesiveness and commitment to task. In another study to be considered later in this chapter, Martin and Seneviratne (1997) make the statement: If Hungry then Precipitation of Headaches.

The Meaning of Interaction

Interaction is the working together of two or more independent variables in their influence on a dependent variable. More precisely, interaction means that the operation or influence of one independent variable on a dependent variable depends on the level of another independent variable. This is a rather clumsy way of saying what we said earlier in talking about conditional statements; for example, If *p*, then *q*, under condition *r*. In other words, interaction occurs when an independent variable has differing effects on a dependent variable at different levels of another independent variable.

The above definition of interaction encompasses two independent variables. This is called a first-order interaction. It is possible for three independent variables to interact in their influence on a dependent variable. This is a second-order interaction. Still higher order interactions are possible but interpreting those higher order interactions becomes difficult; unlike the first-order interactions we have shown here in a two-dimensional figure. Higher order interactions are difficult to visualize and graph. When we have a significant interaction effect, we know that there is a treatment difference. However, in order to determine exactly how the treatments differ, we would need to examine the levels of the other independent variables. In order to predict the result of treatment for a single individual, the prediction can only be made if that individual's status is known on all independent variables. Some textbook authors have gone as far as saying that higher order interaction effects are negligible. This may be true if the study is properly designed, but may not be true with all studies. In a brief survey of a number of intermediate and advanced statistics books used in graduate education, the discussion of interpreting higher order interaction effects is brief at best (see Hays, 1994; Kirk, 1995; Howell, 1997). However, the works of Daniel (1976) and Simon (1976) have discussed how to handle higher order interaction effects. Before we turn to the computational aspects, the reader should be aware that interaction can occur in the absence of any separate effects of the independent variables. (Interaction can also be absent when one or more independent variables have significant separate effects.) Separate independent variable effects are called *main effects*. We will now show this possibility using a fictitious example and then later using an example from published research.

A Simple Fictitious Example

As usual we take a simple, if unrealistic, example that highlights the basic problems and characteristics of factorial analysis of variance. Assume that an educational investigator is interested in the relative efficacy of two methods of teaching: A_1 and A_2. Call this variable Methods. The investigator believes that methods of teaching, in and of themselves, do not differ very much. They differ only when used with certain kinds of students, by certain kinds of teachers, in certain kinds of educational situations, and with certain kinds of motives. Studying all of these variables simultane-

■ FIGURE 14.2

		Methods	
		A_1	A_2
Motivations	B_1	A_1B_1	A_2B_1
	B_2	A_1B_2	A_2B_2

ously is a large order, though not necessarily impossible. So a decision is made to study Methods and Motivations, which gives two independent variables and one dependent variable. Call the dependent variable Achievement. (Some type of Achievement measure will be used, perhaps scores on a standardized test.)

The investigator conducts an experiment with eight sixth-grade children. (A real experiment would work with many more than eight children.) The eight children are assigned randomly to four groups, two per group. The investigator also assigns randomly methods A_1 and A_2 and motivations B_1 and B_2 to the four groups. Refer back to the earlier discussion on partitions of sets. Recall that we can partition and cross-partition sets of objects. The objects can be assigned to a partition or subpartition on the basis of the possession of certain characteristics. But they can also be assigned at random—and then presumably be "given" certain characteristics by the experimenter. In either case, the partitioning logic is the same. The experimenter will end up with four subpartitions: A_1B_1, A_1B_2, A_2B_1, and A_2B_2. The experimental paradigm is shown in Figure 14.2.

Each cell in the design is the intersection of two subsets. For instance, method A_1 combined with motivation B_2 is conceptually $A_1 \cap B_2$. Method A_2 combined with motivation B_2 is the intersection $A_2 \cap B_2$. In this design, we write only A_1B_2 and A_2B_2 for simplicity. Now, two children have been assigned at random to each of the four cells. This means that each child will get a combination of two experimental manipulations, and each pair of children will get a different combination.

Call A_1 Recitation, and A_2 No Recitation. Call B_1 Praise, and B_2 Blame. The children in cell A_1B_1, then, will be taught with recitation and will be praised for their work. The children in cell A_1B_2 will be taught with recitation but will be blamed for their work. And similarly for the other two cells. If the experimental procedures have been handled adequately, it is possible to conceive of the variables as being independent; that is, two separate experiments are actually being run with the same participants. One experiment manipulates Methods; the other, types of Motivations. The design of the experiment, in other words, makes it possible for the investigator to test *independently* the effects on a dependent variable, in this case, achievement, of (1) Methods and (2) Type of Motivation. To show this and other important facets of factorial designs, let us jump to the fictitious data of the experiment. These "data" are reported in Table 14.3, together with the necessary computations for a factorial analysis of variance. First, we calculate the sums-of-squares as we would for

■ **TABLE 14.3** *Data of Hypothetical Factorial Experiment with Analysis of Variance Calculations.*

	Methods	
Type of Motivation	A_1	A_2
B_1	8, 6	4, 2
B_2	8, 6	4, 2

		Methods		
Type of Motivation		A_1	A_2	
B_1	ΣX	14	6	$\Sigma X_{B_1} = 20$
	$(\Sigma X)^2$	196	36	$(\Sigma X_{B_1})^2 = 400$
	M	7	3	$M_{B_1} = \mathbf{5}$
B_2	ΣX	14	6	$\Sigma X_{B_2} = 20$
	$(\Sigma X)^2$	196	36	$(\Sigma X_{B_2})^2 = 400$
	M	7	3	$M_{B_2} = \mathbf{5}$
		$\Sigma X_{A_1} = 28$	$\Sigma X_{A_2} = 12$	$\Sigma X_t = 40$
		$(\Sigma X_{A_1})^2 = 784$	$(\Sigma X_{A_2})^2 = 144$	$(\Sigma X_t)^2 = 1600$
		$M_{A_1} = \mathbf{7}$	$M_{A_2} = \mathbf{3}$	$M_t = \mathbf{5}$
				$\Sigma X_t^2 = 240$

a simple one-way analysis of variance. There is, of course, a *total* sum-of-squares, calculated from all the scores, using C, the correction term:

$$C = \frac{(40)^2}{8} = \frac{1600}{8} = 200$$

or

$$C = M^2(N) = 5^2(8) = 200$$

$$\text{Total} = 240 - 200 = 40$$

or

$$\text{Total} = SD^2(N) = \left[\frac{240 - \dfrac{40^2}{8}}{8} \right](8) = 40$$

Since there are four groups, there is a sum-of-squares associated with the means of the four groups. Simply conceive of the four groups placed side by side as in one-way analysis of variance, and calculate the sum-of-squares as in the last chapter. Now, however, we call this the *between all groups* sum-of-squares to distinguish it from sums-of-squares to be calculated later.

$$\text{Between all groups} \; = \; \Sigma \frac{(\Sigma X)^2}{n_i} - C$$

$$\text{Between all groups} \; = \; \left(\frac{196}{2} + \frac{36}{2} + \frac{196}{2} + \frac{36}{2} \right) - 200 = 32$$

This sum-of-squares is a measure of the variability of all four group means. Therefore, if we subtract this quantity from the total sum-of-squares, we should obtain the sum-of-squares due to error, the random fluctuations of the scores within the cells (groups). This is familiar: it is the *within-groups* sum-of-squares:

$$\text{Within groups} = 40 - 32 = 8$$

To calculate the sum-of-squares for *methods*, proceed exactly as with one-way analysis of variance: treat the scores (Xs) and sums-of-scores (ΣXs) of the columns (Methods) as though there were no B_1 and B_2:

Methods

	A_1	A_2
	8	4
	6	2
	8	4
	6	2
ΣX	28	12

The calculation is:

$$\text{Between methods } (A_1, A_2) \; = \; \left(\frac{(28)^2}{4} + \frac{(12)^2}{4} \right) - 200$$

$$= \left(\frac{784}{4} + \frac{144}{4} \right) - 200 = 32.$$

Similarly, treat types of motivation (B_1 and B_2) as though there were no Methods:

Motivation		ΣX
B_1	8 6 4 2	20
B_2	8 6 4 2	20

The calculation of the between-types sum-of-squares is really not necessary. Since the sums (and the means) are the same, the between-types sum-of-squares is zero:

$$\text{Between types } (B_1, B_2) \; = \; \left[\frac{(20)^2}{4} + \frac{(20)^2}{4} \right] - 200 = 0$$

There is another possible source of variance, the variance due to the *interaction* of the two independent variables. The between-all-groups sum-of-squares comprises the variability due to the means of the four groups: 7, 3, 7, and 3. This sum-of-squares is 32. If this were not a contrived example, part of this sum-of-squares would be due to Methods, part to Type of Motivation, and a remaining part left over, *which is due to the joint action, or interaction,* of methods and types. In many cases it would be relatively small, no greater than chance expectation. In other cases, it would be large enough to be statistically significant; it would exceed chance expectation. In the present problem it is clearly zero, since the between-methods sum-of-squares was 32, and this is equal to the between-all groups sum-of-squares. To complete the computational cycle we calculate:

Interaction: methods $\times$ types = between all groups
　　　　　　　　− (between methods + between types) = 32 − (32 + 0) = 0

Note that in more complex factorial anlysis of variance the interactions are not so easy to compute. The reader should consult Hays (1994) or Kirk (1995) for more information. We are now in a position to set up the final analysis of variance table. We postpone this, however, until we perform a minor operation on these scores.

We use exactly the same scores, but rearrange them slightly: we reverse the scores A_1B_2 and A_2B_2. Since all the individual scores (Xs) are exactly the same, the total sum-of-squares must also be exactly the same. Further, the sums and sums-of-squares of B_1 and B_2 (types) must also be exactly the same. Table 14.4 shows just what was done, and its effect on the means of the four groups.

Study the numbers of Tables 14.3 and 14.4 and note the differences. To emphasize the differences, the means have been **boldfaced** in both tables. To make the differences still clearer, the means of both tables have been laid out in Table 14.5. The table on the left shows two variabilities: between all four means, and between A_1 and A_2 means. In the table on the right, there is only one variability, that between the four means. In both tables, the variability of the four means is the same, since they both have the same four means: 7, 3, 7, and 3. Obviously, there is no variability of the B means in both tables. There are two differences between the tables, then: the A means and the arrangement of the four means inside the squares. If we analyze the

▣ TABLE 14.4 *Data of Hypothetical Factorial Experiment of Table 14.3 with B_2 Figures Rearranged*

	Methods		
Type of Motivation	A_1	A_2	
B_1	8	4	
	6	2	
ΣX	14	6	$\Sigma X_{B_1} = 20$
M	7	3	$M_{B_1} = 5$
B_2	4	8	
	2	6	
ΣX	6	14	$\Sigma X_{B_2} = 20$
M	3	7	$M_{B_2} = 5$
ΣX_A	20	20	$\Sigma X_t = 40$
M_A	5	5	$M_t = 5$
			$\Sigma X_t^2 = 240$

sum-of-squares of the four means (the between-all-groups sums-of-squares), we find that B_1 and B_2 contribute nothing to it in both tables, since there is no variability with 5, 5, the means of B_1 and B_2. In the table on the right, the A_1 and A_2 means of 5 and 5 contribute no variability. In the table on the left, however, the A_1 and A_2 means differ considerably, 7 and 3, and thus contribute variance.

Assuming for the moment that the means of 7 and 3 differ significantly, we can say that Methods of the data of Table 14.3 had an effect irrespective of Type of Motivation. That is, $\mu_{A_1} \neq \mu_{A_2}$, or $\mu_{A_1} > \mu_{A_2}$. As far as this experiment is concerned, Methods differ significantly *no matter what the Type of Motivation*. And, obviously, Type of Motivation had no effect, since $\mu_{B_1} = \mu_{B_2}$. In Table 14.4, on the other hand, the situation is quite different. Neither Methods nor Type of Motivation had an effect *by themselves*. Yet there is variance. The problem is: What is the source of the variance? It is in the *interaction of the two variables*, the interaction of methods and types of motivation.

If we had performed an experiment and obtained data like those of Table 14.4, we could then come to the likely conclusion that there was an interaction between the two variables in their effect on the dependent variable. In this case, we would interpret the results as follows. Methods A_1 and A_2, operating in and of themselves, do not differ in their effect. Type of Motivation B_1 and B_2, in and of themselves, do not

▣ TABLE 14.5 *Means of the Data of Table 14.3 and Table 14.4.*

	Table 14.3 Means				Table 14.4 Means		
	A_1	A_2			A_1	A_2	
B_1	7	3	5	B_1	7	3	5
B_2	7	3	5	B_2	3	7	5
	7	3			5	5	

differ in their effect. When Methods and Type of Motivation are allowed to "work together," when they are permitted to interact, there are significant differences in their effect. Specifically, Method A_1 is superior to Method A_2 when combined with Type of Motivation B_1. When combined with Type of Motivation B_2, it is inferior to A_2. This interaction effect is indicated on the right-hand side of Table 14.5 by the crisscrossed arrows. Qualitatively interpreting the original methods, we find that Recitation seems to be superior to No Recitation under the condition of Praise, but that it is inferior to No Recitation under the condition of Blame (reproof).

It is instructive to note, before going further, that interaction can be studied and calculated by a subtractive procedure. In a 2×2 design, this procedure is simple. Subtract one mean from another in each row, and then calculate the variance of these differences. Take the fictitious means of Table 14.5. If we subtract the Table 14.3 means, we get $7 - 3 = 4$; $7 - 3 = 4$. Clearly the mean square is zero. Thus the interaction is zero. Follow the same procedure for the Table 14.4 means (right-hand side of the table): $7 - 3 = 4$; $3 - 7 = - 4$. If we now treat these two differences as we did means in the last chapter and calculate the sum-of-squares and the mean square, we will arrive at the interaction sum-of-squares and the mean square, 32 in each case. The reasoning behind this procedure is simple. If there were no interactions, we would expect the differences between row means to be approximately equal to each other and to the difference between the means at the bottom of the table, the methods means, in this case. Note that this is so for the Table 14.3 means: the bottom row difference is 4, and so are the differences of each of the rows. The row differences of Table 14.4, however, deviate from the difference between the bottom row (methods) means. They are 4 and $- 4$, whereas the bottom row difference is $5 - 5 = 0$. From this discussion and a little reflection, it can be seen that a significant interaction can be caused by one deviant row. For example, the means of the above example might be:

7	3	5
5	5	5
6	4	

⊡ **TABLE 14.6** *Final Analysis of Variance Tables: Data from Table 14.3 and Table 14.1*

Source	df	\<SS\>	ms	F	ss	ms	F
		Data from Table 14.3			*Data from Table 14.4*		
Between Methods							
(A_1, A_2)	1	32	32	16(.05)	0	0	
Between Types							
(B_1, B_2)	1	0	0		0	0	
Interaction:							
$A \times B$	1	0	0		32	32	16(.05)
Within Groups	4	8	2		8	2	
Totals	7	40			40		

Subtract the rows. $7 - 3 = 4$; $5 - 5 = 0$; and $6 - 4 = 2$. There is obviously some variance in these remainders.

It will be profitable to write the final analysis of variance tables in which the different variances and *F*-ratios are calculated. Table 14.6 gives the final analysis of variance tables for both examples. The between-all-groups sums-of-squares have not been included in the table. They are only useful for calculating the within-groups sums-of-squares. The degrees of freedom for the main effects (methods and types), and for between all groups, and within groups, are calculated in the same way as in one-way analysis of variance. This should become apparent upon studying the table. The interaction degrees of freedom is the product of the degrees of freedom of the main effects, that is, $1 \times 1 = 1$. If Methods had four groups, and Types three groups, the interaction degrees of freedom would have been $3 \times 2 = 6$.

The sum-of-squares and mean square, and the resulting *F*-ratio of 16 on the left-hand side of the table, indicate what we already know from the preceding discussion: Methods are significantly different (at the 0.05 level), and Type of Motivation and Interaction are not significant. The parallel figures of the right-hand side of the table indicate that only the interaction is significant.

Interaction: An Example

In the last chapter, it was said that if sampling was random the means of the *k* groups would be approximately equal. If, for example, there were four groups and the general mean M_t was 4.5, then it would be expected that each of the means would be approximately 4.5. Similarly, in factorial analysis of variance, if random samples of numbers are drawn for each of the cells, then the means of the cells should be approximately equal. If the general mean, M_t were 10, then the best expectation for any cell means in the factorial design would be 10. These means, of course, would very rarely be exactly 10. Indeed, some might be considerably far from 10. The fundamental statistical question is: Do they differ significantly from 10? The means of combinations of means, too, should hover around 10. For example, in a design like that of the previous example, the A_1 and A_2 means should be approximately 10, and the B_1 and B_2 means should be approximately 10. In addition, the means of each of the cells, A_1B_1, A_1B_2, A_2B_1, and A_2B_2, should hover around 10.

Using a table of random numbers, we drew 60 digits, 0 through 24, to fill the six cells of a factorial design. The resulting design has two levels or independent variables, A and B. A is subdivided into A_1, A_2 and A_3; B into B_1 and B_2. This is called a 3 × 2 factorial design. (The examples in Table 14.3 and Table 14.4 are 2 × 2 designs.)

For the following example, the data are fictitious. The example is based on an actual study by Pury and Mineka (1997). This study examines the effect of two independent variables on emotional reaction. One independent variable, Degree of Fear, is a nonmanipulated (attribute), the second independent variable is the type of visual stimuli. One might hypothesize that people with different levels of blood–injury fears would have a different emotional response to different types of stimuli. For the Fear variable, we would examine high and low levels. For the visual stimuli, we would use pictures of (1) minor injuries (such as cuts, bites, bruises), (2) flowers, and (3) rabbits. The dependent variable would be the combined ratings on three emotional dimensions. The design of the study is a 3 × 2 factorial design. Imagine the experiment to have been done with the results given in Table 14.7, which gives the design paradigm and the means of each cell, as well as the means of the two variables, A and B, and the general mean, M_t. These means were calculated from the 60 random numbers drawn in lots of 10 each and inserted in the cells.

We hardly need a test of statistical significance to know that these means do not differ significantly. Their total range is 10.4 to 13.6. The mean expectation, of course, is the mean of the numbers 0 through 24, 12.0. The closeness of the means to $M_t = 12.00$ is remarkable, even for random sampling. At any rate, if these were the results of an actual experiment, the experimenter would probably be most chagrined. Type of Visual Stimuli, Degree of Fear, and the interaction between them are all not significant.

Note how many different outcome possibilities other than chance there would be if one or both variables had been effective. The three means of Visual Stimuli (M_{A_1}, M_{A_2} and M_{A_3}) might have been significantly different, with the means of Fear (M_{B_1} and M_{B_2}) not significantly different. Or the Fear means might be significantly different, with the Visual means not significantly different; or both sets of means could be different; or both could turn out not to be different, with their interaction significant. The possibilities of *kinds* of differences and interactions are considerable, too, although it would take too many words and numbers to illustrate even a small number of them. If the student will juggle the numbers a bit, he or she can get considerable insight into both statistics and design possibilities. Since our present

▣ TABLE 14.7 *Two-Way Factorial Design: Means of Groups of Random Numbers 0 through 9*

Fear	A_1 Minor Injuries	A_2 Flowers	A_3 Rabbits	Fear Means
	Type of Visual Stimuli			
B_1 High	12.9	13.3	10.4	12.2
B_2 Low	10.5	11.5	13.6	11.9
Visual Means	11.7	12.4	12.0	$M_t = 12.03$

preoccupation is with interaction, let us alter the means to create a significant interaction. We increase the A_1B_1 mean by 2, decrease the A_1B_2 mean by 2, increase the A_3B_2 mean by 2, and decrease the A_3B_1 mean by 2. We let the A_2 means stand as they are, and alter the main effect means accordingly. The changes are shown in Table 14.8.

Table 14.8 should be studied carefully. Compare it to Table 14.7. Interaction has been produced by the arbitrary alterations. The cell means have been unbalanced, so to speak, while the marginal means (A_1, A_2, A_3, B_1, B_2) are almost undisturbed. The total mean remains unchanged at 12.03. The three A means are the same. (Why?) The two B means are changed very little. A factorial analysis of variance of the appropriately altered random numbers—which, of course, are no longer random—yields the final analysis of variance table given in Table 14.9.

Neither of the main effects (Fear and Visual Stimuli) is significant. That is, the means of A_1, A_2, and A_3 do not differ significantly from chance. Neither do the means of B_1 and B_2. The only significant F-ratio is that of interaction, which is significant at the 0.05 level. Evidently the alteration of the scores has had an effect. If

▣ TABLE 14.8 *Means from Table 14.7 Altered Systematically by Adding and Subtracting Constants*

Fear	A_1	A_2	A_3	Fear Means
	Type of Visual Stimuli			
B_1	12.9 + 2 = 14.9	13.3	10.4 − 2 = 8.4	12.2
B_2	10.5 − 2 = 8.5	11.5	13.6 + 2 = 15.6	11.9
Visual Means	11.7	12.4	12.0	12.03

▣ TABLE 14.9 *Final Analysis of Variance: Table of Altered Random Number Data*[a]

Source	df	ss	ms	F
Between All Groups	5	485.13		
Within Groups	54	2984.80	55.27	
Between Stimuli (A_1, A_2, A_3)	2	4.93	2.47	< 1.0 (n.s.)
Between Fears (B_1, B_2)	1	1.67	1.67	< 1.0 (n.s.)
Interaction: $A \times B$	2	478.53	239.27	4.33 (0.05)
Totals	59	3469.93		

[a]n.s. equals not significant.

we were interpreting the results, as given in Table 14.8 and Table 14.9, we would say that, in and of themselves, neither type of visual stimuli to the person nor the fear differs. The analysis found no differences between high and low fears, and no differences between the three visual stimuli. However, people with high levels of fear will perceive the rabbit with lower negative emotional responses than the low fear group. On the other hand, high fear people will perceive minor injuries as being more negative than will low fear people.

Kinds of Interaction

To now, we have said nothing about kinds of interaction of independent variables in their joint influence on a dependent variable. To leap to the core of the matter of interactions, let us lay out several sets of means to show the main possibilities. There are, of course, many possibilities, especially when one includes higher-order interactions. The six examples in Table 14.10 indicate the main possibilities with two independent variables. The first three setups show the three possibilities of significant main effects. They are so obvious that they need not be discussed. (There is, naturally, another possibility: neither *A* nor *B* is significant.)

When there is a significant interaction, on the other hand, the situation is not so obvious. The setups (*d*), (*e*), and (*f*) show three common possibilities. In (*d*), the means crisscross, as indicated by the arrows in the table. It can be said that *A* is effective in one direction at B_1, but is effective in the other direction at B_2. Or, $A_1 > A_2$ at B_1, but $A_1 < A_2$ at B_2. This sort of interaction with this crisscross pattern is called *disordinal* interaction (see below). In this chapter, the fictitious example of Table 14.4 was a disordinal interaction (see also Table 14.5). The fictitious example in Table 14.8, where interaction was deliberately induced by adding and subtracting constants, is another disordinal interaction.

▣ **TABLE 14.10** *Various Sets of Means Showing Different Kinds of Main Effects and Interaction.*

	A_1	A_2		A_1	A_2		A_1	A_2	
B_1	30	20	25	30	30	30	30	20	25
B_2	30	20	25	20	20	20	40	30	35
	30	20		25	25		35	25	

(a) *A* significant; *B* not significant; Interaction not significant	(b) *A* not significant; *B* significant; Interaction not significant	(c) *A* significant; *B* significant; Interaction not significant

	A_1	A_2		A_1	A_2		A_1	A_2	
B_1	30	20	25	30	20	25	20	20	20
B_2	20	30	25	20	20	20	30	20	25
	25	25		25	20		25	20	

(d) Interaction significant (disordinal)	(e) Interaction significant (ordinal)	(f) Interaction significant (ordinal)

The setups in (*e*) and (*f*), however, differ. Here one independent variable is effective at only one level of the other independent variable. In (*e*), $A_1 > A_2$ at B_1, but $A_1 = A_2$ at B_2. In (*f*), $A_1 = A_2$ at B_1, but $A_1 > A_2$ at B_2. The interpretation changes accordingly. In the case of (*e*), we would say that *A* is effective at B_1 level, but makes no difference at B_2 level. The case of (*f*) would take a similar interpretation. Such interactions are called *ordinal* interactions.

A simple way to study the interaction with a 2 × 2 setup (it is more complex with more complex models) is to subtract one entry from another in each row, as we did earlier. If this be done for (*a*), we get, for rows B_1 and B_2, 10 and 10. For (*b*), we get 0 and 0, and for (*c*), 10 and 10 again. When these two differences are equal, as in these cases, there is no interaction. But now try it with (*d*), (*e*), and (*f*). We get 10 and −10 for (*d*), 10 and 0 for (*e*), and 0 and 10 for (*f*). When these differences are significantly unequal, interaction is present. The student can interpret these differences as an exercise.

It is also possible—and often very profitable—to graph interactions, as we did earlier in Figure 14.1. Set up one independent variable by placing the experimental groups (A_1, A_2, and so on) at equal intervals on the horizontal axis and appropriate values of the dependent variable on the vertical axis. Then plot, against the horizontal axis group positions (A_1, A_2, and so on), the mean values in the table at the levels of the other independent variable (B_1, B_2, and so on). This method can quite easily be

▣ FIGURE 14.3

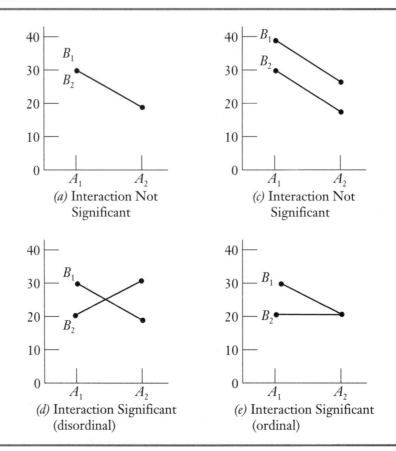

(a) Interaction Not
Significant

(c) Interaction Not
Significant

(d) Interaction Significant
(disordinal)

(e) Interaction Significant
(ordinal)

used with 2×3, 3×3, and other such designs. The plots of (a), (c), (d), and (e) are given in Figure 14.3.

We will discuss these graphs only briefly, since both graphs and graphing relations have already been discussed. In effect, we first ask if there is a relation between the main effects (independent variables) and the measures of the dependent variables. Each of these relations is plotted as in the preceding chapter, except that the relation between one independent variable and the dependent variable is plotted at both levels of the other independent variables; for instance, A is plotted against the dependent variable (vertical axis) at B_1 and B_2. The slope of the lines roughly indicates the extent of the relation. In each case, we have chosen to plot the relations using A_1 and A_2 on the horizontal axis. If the plotted line is horizontal, obviously there is no relation. There is no relation between A and the dependent variable at level B_2 in (e) of Figure 14.3, but there is a relation at level B_1. In (a), there is a relation between A and the dependent variable at both levels, B_1 and B_2. The same is true of (c). The nearer the line comes to being diagonal, the higher the relation. If the two lines make approximately the same angle in the same direction (that is, they are parallel), as in (*a*) and (*c*), the relation is approximately the same magnitude at each level. To the extent that the lines form different angles with the horizontal axis (are not parallel), there is interaction present.

If the graphs of Figure 14.3 were plotted from actual research data, we could interpret them as follows. Call the measures of the dependent variable (on the vertical axis) Y. In (*a*), A is related to Y regardless of B. It makes no difference what B is; A_1 and A_2 differ significantly. The interpretation of (*c*) is similar: A is related to Y at both levels of B. There is no interaction in either (*a*) or (*c*). In (*d*) and (*e*), however, the case is different. The graph of (*d*) shows interaction. A is related to Y, but the kind of relation depends on B. Under the B_1 condition, A_1 is greater than A_2. But under the B_2 condition A_2 is greater than A_1. The graph of (*e*) says that A is related to Y at level B_1 but not at level B_2; or A_1 is greater than A_2 at B_1 but at B_2 they are equal. (Note that it is possible to plot B on the horizontal axis. The interpretations would, however, differ accordingly.)

Notes of Caution

Interaction is not always a result of the "true" interaction of experimental treatments. There are, rather, three possible causes of a significant interaction. One is "true" interaction, the variance contributed by the interaction that "really" exists between two variables in their mutual effect on a third variable. Another is error. A significant interaction can happen by chance, just as the means of experimental groups can differ significantly by chance. A third possible cause of interaction is some extraneous, unwanted, uncontrolled effect operating at one level of an experiment but not at another. Such a cause of interaction is particularly to be watched for in nonexperimental uses of the analysis of variance; that is, in the analysis of variance of data gathered after independent variables have already operated. Suppose, for example, that the levels in an experiment on methods was schools. Extraneous factors in such a case can cause a significant interaction. Assume that the principal of one school, although he had consented to having the experiment run in his school, was negative in his attitude toward the research. This attitude could easily be conveyed to teachers and pupils, thus contaminating the experimental treatment and methods. In short, significant interactions must be handled with the same care as any other research results. They are interesting, even dramatic, as we have seen. Thus they can perhaps cause us to momentarily lose our customary caution. A precept that researchers should take seriously is: Whenever possible, *replicate* research studies. Replication should be routinely planned. It is especially necessary when complex relations are found. If an interaction is found in an original study and in a replication, it is probably not due to chance, though it could still be due to other causes. The word *replication* is used rather than *repetition* because in a replication, although the original relation is studied again, it might be studied with different kinds of participants, under somewhat different conditions, and even with fewer, more, or even different variables. The

▣ **TABLE 14.11**   *Example of Disproportion and Unequal Cell ns Arising from*
                    Nonexperimental Variables[a]

	Republican	Democrat	
Male	30	20	50
Female	20	30	50
	50	50	

[a]The cell entries are frequencies.

trend in the psychological research literature, happily, is to perform two or more related studies on the same basic problem. This trend is closely related to testing alternative hypotheses, whose virtue and necessity were discussed in an earlier chapter.

Two related difficulties of factorial analysis are unequal ns in the cells of a design and the experimental and nonexperimental use of the method. If the ns in the cells of a factorial design are not equal (and are disproportionate; that is, not in proportion from row to row or column to column), the orthogonality or independence of the independent variables is impaired. At times, one will even get negative sums-of-squares. While adjustments can be made, they are a bit awkward and not too satisfactory.[1] When doing experiments, the problem is not severe because participants can be assigned to the cells at random—except, of course, for attribute variables—and the ns kept equal or nearly equal. But in the nonexperimental use of factorial analysis, the ns in the cells get pretty much beyond the control of the researcher. Indeed, even in experiments, when more than one categorical variable is included (like Race and Sex), ns almost necessarily become unequal.

To understand this, take a simple example. Suppose we divided a group into two by Sex: 50 males and 50 females. A second variable is Political Preferences and we want to come up with two equal groups of Republicans and Democrats. But suppose that Sex is correlated with Political Preference. Then there may be, for example, more males who are Republican compared to females who are Republican, creating a disproportion. This is shown in Table 14.11. Add another independent variable and the difficulties increase exponentially.

What can we do, then, in nonexperimental research? Can't we use factorial analysis of variance? The answer is complex and is evidently not clearly understood. Factorial analysis of variance paradigms can and should be used, because they guide and clarify research. There are devices for surmounting the unequal n difficulty. One can make adjustments of the data, or equalize the groups by elimination of participants at random, but these are unwieldy devices. One analytic solution that has potential is multiple regression analysis. While the problems do not all disappear, many are minimized in the multiple regression framework. In general, factorial

---

[1]Computer programs such as SPSS makes these adjustments, but can be confusing since the adjusted sum of squares do not correspond to the actual sum-of-squares for independent variables.

analysis of variance is best suited to experimental research in which the participants can be assigned randomly to cells, the ns thus kept equal and the assumptions behind the method more or less satisfied. Nonexperimental research or experimental research that use a number of nonexperimental (attribute) variables might be better served with multiple regression analysis (see Keith, 1988). With equal ns and experimental variables, multiple regression analysis yields exactly the same sums-of-squares, mean squares, and F-ratios, including interaction F-ratios as the standard factorial analysis. Nonexperimental variables, which are a problem for factorial analysis, are less of a problem in multiple regression analysis. However, Simon (1975) and Lee (1995) have pointed out that multiple regression is no panacea for poorly designed research. We return to all this in a later chapter.

Interaction and Interpretation

We end this section on interaction with a complex and difficult problem: the interpretation of factorial analysis of variance results when interactions are significant. Suppose we have two variables, A and B. Both F-ratios are statistically significant and the interaction F-ratio is not significant. This is straightforward: there is no problem of interpretation. If, on the other hand, A, or B, or both are significant, and the interaction of A and B is also significant, there is reason for concern. Some writers say that the interpretation of significant main effects in the presence of interaction is not possible and, if done, can lead to incorrect conclusions. The reason is that when one says that a main effect is significant, one may imply that it is significant under all conditions, that M_{A_1} is greater than M_{A_2} with all kinds of individuals and in all kinds of places, for instance. If the interaction between A and B, however, is significant, the conclusion is empirically not valid. One has at least to qualify it: there is at least one condition, namely B that has to be taken into account. One must say, instead of the simple "If p, then q" statement, "If p, then q, under condition r," or, for example, M_{A_1} is greater than M_{A_2} under condition B_1 but not under condition B_2. A method of reinforcement, say Praise, is effective with middle-class children but not with working-class children.

Extended discussions of interactions can be found in: Edwards (1984). Although it is dated, a valuable and clear discussion of ordinal and disordinal interactions, and the virtue of graphing significant interactions is given in Lubin (1961). Pedhazur (1996) also discusses the interpretation of main effects when interactions are significant. Pedhauzer's discussion is particularly cogent when he attacks the difficulty of interpreting interactions in nonexperimental research.

A general rule is that when an interaction is significant, it may not be appropriate to try to interpret main effects, because the main effects are not constant but vary according to the variables that interact with them. This is especially true if the interaction is disordinal [see Figure 14.3 (d)], or if the main effect under study is weak. If a main effect is strong—the differences between means are large—and interaction is ordinal [see Figure 14.3 (e)], then one can perhaps interpret a main effect. Obviously, the interpretation of research data, when more than one independent variable is studied, is often complex and difficult. This is no reason to be discouraged, however.

Such complexity only reflects the multivariate and complex nature of psychological, sociological, and educational reality. The task of science is to understand this complexity. Such understanding can never be complete, of course, but substantial progress can be made with the help of modern methods of design and analysis. Factorial designs and analysis of variance are large achievements that substantially enhance our ability to understand complex psychological, sociological, and educational reality.

Factorial Analysis of Variance with Three or More Variables

Factorial analysis of variance works with more than two independent variables. Three, four, and more variables are possible and do appear in the literature. Designs with more than four variables, however, are uncommon. It is not so much because the statistics become complex and unwieldy. Rather, it is a matter of practicality and tradition. Using current research paradigms, it is very difficult just to get enough participants to fill the cells of complex designs. And it is even more difficult to manipulate four, five, or six independent variables at one time. For instance, take an experiment with four independent variables. The smallest arrangement possible is $2 \times 2 \times 2 \times 2$, which yields 16 cells into each of which some minimum number of participants must be placed. If 10 Ss are placed in each cell, it will be necessary to handle the total of 160 Ss in four different ways. Yet one should not be dogmatic about the number of variables. Perhaps in the next 10 years factorial designs with more than four variables will become common. Simon (1987) has argued for years for experiments to employ more independent variables. In fact, Simon and Roscoe (1984) have demonstrated the use of a new research paradigm that can be fruitful in terms of yielding good information. However, similar to the protest logged by Cohen (1994), academic psychology seems resistant to such changes. Indeed, when we later study multiple regression analysis, we will find that factorial analysis of variance can be done with multiple regression analysis, and that four and five factors are easily accommodated *analytically*. That is, the complexities of analysis of variance calculations with four or five independent variables are considerably simplified. Such analytic facilitation of calculations, however, in no way changes the *experimental* difficulties of managing several manipulated independent variables through more traditional approaches.

The simplest form of a three-variable factorial analysis of variance is a $2 \times 2 \times 2$ design. The study by Little, Sterling, and Tingstrom (1996) uses this design. Table 14.12 presents in tabular form the design of their study. Little, Sterling, and Tingstrom studied the effects of in-group biases on attribution. They wanted to determine if the match between the actor's origin and the participant's origin would result in a higher evaluation. The actor's location and the actor's race were varied to form four written vignettes. The vignettes described either a homogeneous in-group, homogeneous out-group, or one of two types of heterogeneous group membership

■ TABLE **14.12** *Three-variable Factorial Analysis of Variance Design* [a]

| | | Participant Location | | | |
| | | A_1 (Northeast USA) | | A_2 (Southeast USA) | |
	Mode	C_1 African American	C_2 White American	C_1 African American	C_2 White American
Actor's Location	B_1 (North USA)	$A_1B_1C_1$	$A_1B_1C_2$	$A_2B_1C_1$	$A_2B_1C_2$
	B_2 (South USA)	$A_1B_2C_1$	$A_1B_2C_2$	$A_2B_2C_1$	$A_2B_2C_2$

[a]From Little, Sterling, & Tingstrom (1996).

individual engaging in a negative behavior (fighting). Participants were recruited from two locations in the United States: Northeast and Southeast. Each participant was asked to read a short description of a behavior, and evaluate the person described. Evaluations were in the form of an attributional questionnaire, where high scores indicated high personal responsibility and low scores indicated low personal responsibility.

The researcher can now test seven hypotheses: the differences between A_1 and A_2 (participant location), between B_1 and B_2 (Actor Location), and between C_1 and C_2 (Actor Race). These are the main effects. Four interactions can also be tested: $A \times B$, $A \times C$, $B \times C$, and $A \times B \times C$. A final analysis of variance table would look like Table 14.13. It is evident that a great deal of information can be obtained from this one experiment. Contrast it with the one variable experiment in which only one hypothesis can be tested. The difference is not only great—it indicates a fundamentally different way of conceptualizing research problems.

Significant first-order interactions are reported more and more in published research studies. Some years ago they were considered to be rare phenomena. This is quite evidently not so anymore (see Gresham & Witt, 1997). Most of the methodological and substantive preoccupation with interaction in the literature is in education. It even has a name: ATI (Aptitude–Treatment Interaction) research. Evidently it has flourished because much or most educational research is preoccupied with improving instruction, and interactions of pupils' aptitudes and instructional methods are believed to be an important key to doing so. However, Gresham and Witt (1997) have pointed out that ATI research has not been fruitful.

Indeed, it is now apparent that interactions of variables are hypothesized on the basis of theory (see Tingstrom, 1989; Martin and Seneviratne, 1997). Part of the essence of scientific theory, of course, is specifying the conditions under which a phenomenon can and will occur. For example, Christenfeld (1997) was interested in the effect of distractions on coping with pain. Christenfeld felt that memory and possibly demand characteristics played a role in people's reported effectiveness of distraction on pain. This study tested the notion that the true effect of distraction may not be

▣ **TABLE 14.13** *Final Analysis of Variance Table for the 2 × 2 × 2 Design of Figure 14.4*

Source	df	ss	ms	F
Between Participant Location (A_1, A_2)	1			
Between Actor Location (B_1, B_2)	1			
Between Actor Race (C_1, C_2)	1			
Interaction: $A \times B$		1		
Interaction: $A \times C$		1		
Interaction: $B \times C$		1		
Interaction: $A \times B \times C$		1		
Within Groups		$N - 7$		
Total	$N - 1$			

detectable until after a delay. Pain was introduced to all participants by having each subject place a hand in an ice bath for 90 seconds. In Christenfeld's study, participants were assigned to either a low distraction or high distraction condition. Half of the participants in each group rated their pain immediately after the 90 seconds had elapsed. The other half filled out an identical form after performing an irrelevant cognitive task. Christenfeld found an interaction effect between distraction and time of pain ratings. The high distraction group who rated their pain immediately after removing their hand from the ice bath gave higher ratings than the low distraction group. For the group receiving a delay period before rating their pain, the pattern was reversed. Significant higher-order interactions, while not common, do occur. The trouble is that they are often hard to interpret. First- and second-order interactions can be handled, but third- and higher-order interactions make research life uncomfortable because one is at a loss as to what they mean. The literature does report some studies having a third-order interaction effect (see Bente, Feist, & Elder, 1996; Bjorck, Lee, & Cohen, 1997).

By now the reader no doubt realizes that in principle the breakdowns of the independent variables are not restricted to just two or three subpartitions. It is quite possible to have 2 × 4, 2 × 5, 4 × 6, 2 × 3 × 3, 2 × 5 × 4, 4 × 4 × 3 × 5. Blanton and Gerrard (1997) use a 2 × 2 × 3 × 3 design to study sexual motivation and risk perception of men. As always, the problem under investigation and the judgment of the researcher(s) are the criteria that determine what design and its concomitant analysis shall be.

Advantages and Virtues of Factorial Design and Analysis of Variance

Factorial analysis of variance, as we have seen, accomplishes several things, all of which are important advantages of this approach and method. First, it enables the researcher to manipulate and control two or more variables simultaneously. In educational research, not only is it possible to study the effects of teaching methods on achievement; we can also study the effects of both methods and, say, kinds of reinforcement. In psychological research, we can study the separate and combined effects of many kinds of independent variables, such as anxiety, guilt, reinforcement, prototypes, types of persuasion, race, and group atmosphere, on many kinds of dependent variables, such as compliance, conformity, learning, transfer, discrimination, perception, and attitude change. In addition, we can control variables such as sex, social class, and home environment.

A second advantage is that factorial analysis is more precise than one-way analysis. Here we see one of the virtues of combining research design and statistical considerations. It can be said that, other things being equal, factorial designs are "better" than one-way designs. This value judgment has been implicit in most of the preceding discussion. The precision argument adds weight to it and will be elaborated shortly.

A third advantage—and, from a large scientific viewpoint, perhaps the most important—is the study of the interactive effects of independent variables on dependent variables. This has already been discussed, but a highly important point must be added. Factorial analysis enables the research *to hypothesize interactions* because the interactive effects can be directly tested. If we go back to conditional statements and their qualification, we see the core of the importance of this statement. In a one-way analysis, we simply say: If p, then q; If such-and-such methods, then so-and-so outcomes. In factorial analysis, however, we utter richer conditional statements. We can say: If p, then q and If r, then q, which is tantamount to talking about the main effects in a factorial analysis. In the problem of Table 14.4, for instance, p is Methods (A) and r is Type of Motivation (B). We can also say, however: If p and r, then q, which is equivalent to the interaction of Methods and Type of Motivation. Interaction can also be expressed by: If p, then q, under condition r.

On the basis of theory, previous research, or hunch, researchers can hypothesize interactions. One hypothesizes that an independent variable will have a certain effect only in the presence of another independent variable. Christenfeld (1997), in the study of distraction and perceived pain, asked whether people who reported their pain immediately after the removal of the pain stimulus were more likely to report a higher level of pain than people who respond after a delay. Christenfeld found an interaction effect between the immediate–delayed condition and high–low distraction. Part of his results are given in Table 14.14. The means in the table reflect the amount of perceived pain. Neither main effect—time when the ratings were made or amount of distraction—was statistically significant, but the interaction between them was significant. When distraction was high, the immediate response condition

▣ TABLE 14.14 *Mean Pain Ratings Made Immediately After Ice Bath or After a Delay for Participants in Low- and High-Distraction Conditions (Christenfeld study)*[a]

	Immediate	Delayed
High Distraction	5.61	4.67
Low Distraction	5.44	5.67

[a]The higher the score the greater the pain.

produced higher pain ratings. However, when the distraction was low, the delayed responding condition produced higher pain ratings. The interaction hypothesis was supported—a finding of both theoretical and practical significance.

It has become common practice to partition a continuous variable into dichotomies or other polychotomies. In the Christenfeld study, for instance, a continuous measure—amount of distraction—was dichotomized. Note that we pointed out earlier that creating a categorical variable out of a continuous variable throws variance away, and thus should be avoided. Researchers should consider the power provided by multiple regression instead of analysis of variance. We will learn in a later chapter that factorial analysis of variance can be done with multiple regression analysis, and that with such analysis it is not necessary to sacrifice any variance by conversion of variables. Nevertheless, there are countervailing arguments: (1) If a difference is statistically significant and the relation is substantial, the variable conversion does not matter. The danger is in concealing a relation that in fact exists. (2) There are times when conversion of a variable may be wise—for example, for exploration of a new field or problem, and when measurement of a variable is at best rough and crude. In different words, although the rule is a good one, it is best not to be inflexible about using it. Good—even excellent—research has been performed using continuous variables that have been partitioned for one or another reason.

Factorial Analysis of Variance: Control

In a one-way analysis of variance, there are two *identifiable* sources of variance: that presumed to be due to the experimental effects, and that presumably due to error or chance variation. We now look at the latter more closely.

When participants have been assigned to the experimental groups at random, the only possible estimate of chance variation is the within-groups variance. But—and this is important—it is clear that the within-groups variance contains not only variance due to error, it also contains variance due to individual differences among the participants. Two simple examples are intelligence and sex; there are, of course, many others. If both girls and boys are used in an experiment, randomization can be used in order to balance the individual differences that are concomitant to sex. Then the number of girls and boys in each experimental group will be approximately equal. We can also arbitrarily assign girls and boys in equal numbers to the groups. This method, however, does not accomplish the overall purpose of randomization, which is to equalize the groups *on all* possible variables. *It does* equalize the groups as far as the sex variable is concerned, but we can have no assurance that other variables are equally distributed among the groups. Similarly for intelligence. Randomization, if successful, will equalize the groups such that the intelligence test means and standard deviations of the groups will be approximately equal. Here, again, it is possible to assign youngsters to the groups arbitrarily in a way to make the groups approximately equal, but then there is no assurance that other possible variables are similarly controlled, since randomization has been interfered with.

Let us now assume that randomization has been "successful." Then theoretically there will be no differences between the groups in intelligence and all other variables. But *there will still be individual differences in intelligence—and other variables— within each group.* With two groups, for instance, Group 1 might have intelligence scores ranging from, say, 88 to 145, and Group 2 might have intelligence scores ranging from 90 to 142. This range of scores in and of itself shows, just as the presence of boys and girls within the groups shows, that there are individual differences in intelligence *within* the groups. If this is true, how can we then say that the within-groups variance can be an estimate of error, of chance variation? The answer is that it is the best we can do under the design circumstances. If the design is of the simple one-way kind, there is no other measure of error obtainable. So we calculate the within-groups variance and treat it as though it were a "true" measure of error variance. It should be clear that the within-groups variance will be larger than the "true" error variance, since it contains variance due to individual differences as well as error variance. Therefore, an *F*-ratio may not be significant when in fact there is "really" a difference between the groups. Obviously, if the *F*-ratio is significant, there is not much to worry about because the between-groups variance is sufficiently large to overcome the overestimated error variance.

To summarize what has been said, let us rewrite an earlier theoretical equation:

$$V_t = V_b + V_w \qquad (14.3)$$

Since the within-groups variance contains more variance than error variance, the variance due to individual differences, in fact, we can write

$$V_w = V_i + V_e \qquad (14.4)$$

where V_i equals variance due to individual differences and V_e equals "true" error variance. If this is true, then we can substitute the right-hand side of Equation 14.4 for the V_w, in Equation 14.3 as follows:

$$V_t = V_b + V_i + V_e \qquad (14.5)$$

In other words, Equation 14.5 is a shorthand way to say what we have been saying above.

The practical research significance of Equation 14.5 is considerable. If we can find a way to control or measure V_i to separate it from V_w, then it follows that a more accurate measure of the "true" error variance is possible. Put differently, our ignorance of the variable situation is decreased because we identify and isolate more systematic variance. A portion of the variance that was attributed to error is identified. Consequently, the within-groups variance is reduced.

Many of the principles and much of the practice of research design is occupied with this problem, which is essentially a problem of control—the control of variance. When it was said earlier that factorial analysis of variance was more precise than simple one-way analysis of variance, we meant that, by setting up levels of an independent variable, say sex or social class, we decrease the estimate of error, the within-groups variance, and thus get closer to the "true" error variance. Instead of writing Equation 14.5, let us now write a more specific equation, substituting for V_i the variance of individual differences, V_{sc}, the variance for social class, and reintroducing V_w:

$$V_t = V_b + V_{sc} + V_w \qquad (14.6)$$

Compare this equation to Equation 14.3. More of the total variance, other than the between-groups variance, has been identified and labeled. This variance, V_{sc}, has in effect been taken out of the V_w of Equation 14.3.

Research Examples

A large number of interesting uses of factorial analysis of variance have been reported in recent years in the behavioral research literature. Indeed, one is confronted with an embarrassment of riches. A number of examples of different kinds have been selected to further illustrate the usefulness and strength of the method. We include more examples than usual because of the complexity of factorial analysis, its frequency of use, and its manifest importance.

Race, Sex, and College Admissions

In an ingenious, elegantly conceived and classical study, Walster, Cleary, and Clifford (1970) asked whether colleges in the United States discriminate against women and African American applicants. They used a $2 \times 2 \times 3$ factorial design in which race (white American, African American), sex (male, female), and ability (high, medium, low) were the independent variables; and Admission (scored on a five-point scale, with 1 equals rejection through 5 equals acceptance with encouragement) was the dependent variable. They selected 240 colleges randomly from a standard guide and sent specially prepared letters of application to the colleges from fictitious individuals who possessed, among other things, the race, sex, and ability levels mentioned above.

▣ TABLE 14.15 *Results of Walster, Cleary, and Clifford Study for Sex, Ability, and Admission (Means)*[a]

Sex	Ability High	Ability Medium	Low	
Male	3.75	3.48	3.00	3.41
Female	4.05	3.48	1.93	3.15
	3.90	3.48	2.47	

[a]Marginal means were calculated from cell means. The higher the mean the greater the acceptance.

For instance, the applicant might be an African American, male, with a medium level of ability. Note the clever manipulation of variables not usually amenable to experimental manipulation. Also note that the unit of analysis was Institutions.

Factorial analysis of variance showed that none of the three main effects was statistically significant. If this was all the information the researchers had, they could have concluded that there was no discrimination practiced. But one of the interactions—sex by ability—was statistically significant. The means for Sex and Ability are given in Table 14.15. (The variable Race is omitted because the race main effect and the interactions of race with the other variables were not significant.) An intriguing finding! It seems that females are discriminated against at the lower level of ability but not at the high and medium levels.

The Effect of Gender, Type of Rape, and Information on Perception

The perception of people toward a rape victim has received much media attention. Research has been done to determine the decision-making process by jurors in rape trials. Johnson (1994) conducted such a study using three independent variables and two dependent variables. Johnson wanted to determine the effect of gender (male versus female), type of rape (acquaintance versus stranger) and information admissibility (yes versus no) on perceived victim enjoyment and attribution of responsibility. A $2 \times 2 \times 2$ factorial design was used.

To reduce possible demand biases in the study, Johnson gave participants three passages to read and they answered various questions about the content in the passage. Participants were led to believe that the study was an impression formation study. Two of the passages were irrelevant to the study. In the experimental passage, a description was given of a female college student being raped. The passage was varied in the type of rape: acquaintance or stranger. The passage also gave the reactions of the victim's classmates. It was implied that the rape victim had a history of sexual promiscuity. Half of the participants were explicitly instructed to ignore classmate comments when making a perception of the victim (inadmissible); half were not

回 **TABLE 14.16** *Mean Perceptions by Type of Rape and Information Admissibility (Johnson study)*[a]

	Information Admissibility	
Type of Rape	Admissible	Inadmissible
Acquaintance	*4.0* **4.8**	*3.7* **3.9**
Stranger	*3.8* **3.5**	*1.6* **1.6**

[a]The numbers in italics record Perception of Enjoyment, the boldface values record Attribution of Responsibility.

given such instructions (admissible). Each subject was asked to respond to questions concerning the victim's enjoyment of the rape and the amount of responsibility attributed to the victim for the rape event.

Part of the summary data from the study are presented in Table 14.16. The values given are means. Higher values indicate higher probability of enjoyment and greater attribution of responsibility. Male participants perceived a higher probability of victim enjoyment of the rape than female participants. Participants who were not instructed to disregard the comments of the victim's classmates perceived a higher probability of victim enjoyment and attributed responsibility than those who were told not to consider the comments. Likewise, participants in the Acquaintance rape condition gave a higher probability of victim enjoyment and attribution of responsibility than Stranger rape. Note the suitability of factorial analysis of variance for the analytic problem and the applicability of the idea of interaction in this situation.

Student Essays and Teacher Evaluation

The above examples were limited to two or three independent variables. We now look briefly at a more complex example with more than three independent variables. The subject of the research has always been of great interest to educators: reading, scoring, and evaluating student essays. In what is probably an important study of the problem, Freedman (1979) manipulated the content, organization, mechanics, and sentence structure of essays. She rewrote eight student essays "of moderate quality" to be either stronger or weaker in the four characteristics just mentioned. (This was a difficult task, which Freedman did admirably.) The essays to be judged included both the original essays and the rewritten essays. The essays were then evaluated by 12 readers (another variable in the design). The dependent variable was quality, rated on a four-point scale. We have, then, a $2 \times 2 \times 2 \times 2 \times 12$ design (the 12 was the 12 readers). The factorial analysis of variance is summarized in Table 14.17.

These results are interesting and potentially important. First, the readers (R) did not differ, which is as it should be. Second, content and organization were both highly significant. (The author talks about "the largest main effect," which could have been better judged by, say, ω^2.) Mechanics (M) was also significant; Sentence

◨ **TABLE 14.17** *Factorial Analysis of Variance Results of Rewriting Effects (Freedman study of evaluation of essays)[a]*

Source	df	ms	F
Reader (R)	11	.448	
Content (C)	1	9.860	37.78**
Organization (O)	1	5.195	29.69**
Sentence Structure (SS)	1	1.500	2.54
Mechanics (M)	1	5.042	9.77**
$C \times SS$	1	1.960	6.30
$C \times M$	1	.990	3.18
$O \times SS$	1	3.767	12.11*
$O \times M$	1	6.155	19.79**
$SS \times M$	1	.001	

[a]Significant at .01 level; **significant at .001 level.

Structure (SS) was not. But the $O \times SS$ and the $O \times M$ significant interactions showed that the strength or weakness of mechanics and sentence structure mattered when essays had strong organization. This study and its essay assessment are certainly on another level of discourse from the more or less intuitive and loose methods that most use when judging student writing.

Computer Addendum

We saw how to use SPSS to analyze data with a *t*-test and a one-way ANOVA in the last chapter. To use SPSS for a factorial analysis of variance is very similar. Table 14.18 shows fictitious data presented in the traditional table form. Figure 14.4 shows

◨ **TABLE 14.18** *Factorial Design with Fictitious Data.*

		Difficulty		
		B_1 (Low)	B_2 (Medium)	B_3 (High)
Teaching Method	A_1 (Traditional)	18,17,17	17,16,15	11,12,10
	A_2 (Enhanced)	18,18,16	14,15,16	12,10,10

◙ FIGURE 14.4

	Type	Diffic	Score				
1	1	1	18				
2	1	1	17				
3	1	1	17				
4	1	2	17				
5	1	2	16				
6	1	2	15				
7	1	3	11				
8	1	3	12				
9	1	3	10				
10	2	1	18				
11	2	1	18				
12	2	1	16				
13	2	2	14				
14	2	2	15				
15	2	2	16				
16	2	3	12				
17	2	3	10				
18	2	3	10				

File Edit View Data Transform Statistics Graphs Utilities Windows Help

how those data were restructured into SPSS spreadsheet format. It is very important that the reader understand how to move from the data presentation in Table 14.18 to the data table used by SPSS. This fictitious study involved the effects of two independent variables on achievement. One independent variable (A) was the type of teaching method (traditional, enhanced). The second independent variable was difficulty of the test (low, medium, high). The dependent variable was the score on the test.

To perform the desired two-way analysis of variance, click "Statistics." This produces a menu of statistical analyses. Choose "ANOVA Models" (see Figure 14.5). When selected, another menu appears. From this second menu, choose "Simple Factorial." This is shown in Figure 14.5.

□ FIGURE 14.5

	Type	Diffic	Score				
1	1	1	18				
2	1	1	17				
3	1	1	17				
4	1	2	17				
5	1	2	16				
6	1	2	15				
7	1	3	11				
8	1	3	12				
9	1	3	10				
10	2	1	18				
11	2	1	18				
12	2	1	16				
13	2	2	14				
14	2	2	15				
15	2	2	16				
16	2	3	12				
17	2	3	10				
18	2	3	10				

File Edit View Data Transform Statistics Graphs Utilities Windows Help

Summarize ▶
Compare Means ▶
ANOVA Models ▶
Correlate ▶
Regression ▶
Log-linear ▶
Classify ▶
Data Reduction ▶
Scale ▶
Nonparametric Tests ▶

Simple Factorial
General Factorial
Multivariate
Repeated Measures

Choosing that option produces a new screen (see Figure 14.6) where you specify which of your variables are the dependent and independent variables. In the left-most box is a list of your three variables: "Diffic," "Score," and "Type." First, highlight "Score" and click the right-pointing arrow for the box labeled "Dependent." Next, highlight the variable name "Diffic." You want to enter "Diffic" into the box labeled "Factor(s)." To do this, click on the right-pointing arrow associated with the "Factor(s)" box (Figure 14.7 shows this).

After choosing the "Diffic" variable (Figure 14.7), you need to tell SPSS how many levels the "Diffic" variable has. Do this by clicking the "Define Range" button. When you do that, you get another screen (shown in Figure 14.8). Enter the

◙ FIGURE 14.6

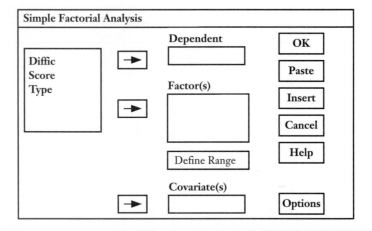

minimum and maximum values for the "Diffic" variable. There are three difficulty levels, so you can enter a "1" for the minimum value and a "3" for the maximum value. Then click on "Continue" when you are satisfied with your input. SPSS will now return you to the previous screen. There is one major change. Question marks no longer follow the Diffic variable name in the Factor(s) box. Instead you see "(1, 3)."

◙ FIGURE 14.7

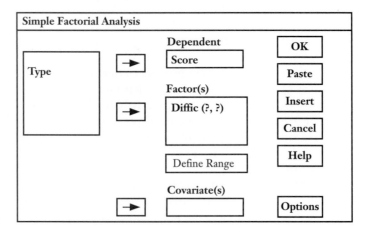

◉ FIGURE 14.8

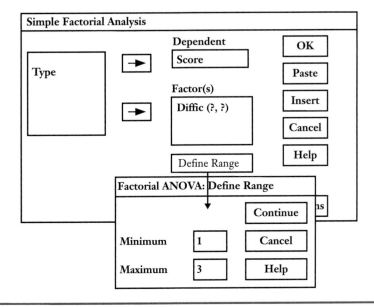

Your next task is to select the "Type" variable. Highlight it and click on the right-pointing arrow associated with the Factor(s) box. When this is done, the variable name "Type" appears in that box followed by question marks enclosed in parentheses (see Figure 14.9). Repeat previous steps by again clicking on the "Define Range" button to get a screen where you can enter the levels for the variable "Type."

◉ FIGURE 14.9

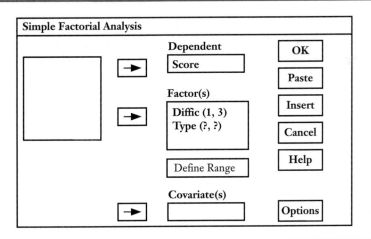

◙ FIGURE 14.10

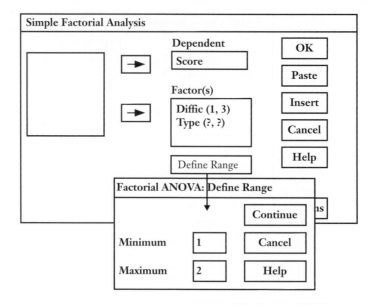

Since "Type" has only two levels, enter a "1" for the minimum value and a "2" for the maximum value (see Figure 14.10).

Figure 14.11 shows a screen where all of the variables have been defined. By clicking "OK," SPSS will perform the analysis. The results of the analysis are given in the shaded box on the opposite page.

◙ FIGURE 14.11

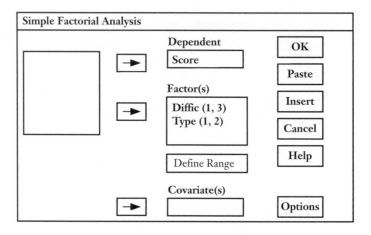

CELL MEANS

SCORE
by DIFFIC
TYPE

Total Population	14.56 (18)

DIFFIC

	1	2	3
	17.33	15.50	10.83
	(6)	(6)	(6)

TYPE

	1	2
	14.78	14.33
	(9)	(9)

TYPE
DIFFIC

	1	2
1	17.33	17.33
	(3)	(3)
2	16.00	15.00
	(3)	(3)
3	11.00	10.67
	(3)	(3)

ANALYSIS OF VARIANCE

SCORE
by DIFFIC
TYPE

EXPERIMENTAL sums of squares
Covariates entered FIRST

Source of Variation	Sum of Squares	DF	Mean Square	F	Sig of F
Main Effects	135.667	3	45.222	45.222	.000
DIFFIC	134.778	2	67.389	67.389	.000
TYPE	.889	1	.889	.889	.364
2-Way Interactions	.778	2	.389	.389	.686
DIFFIC TYPE	.778	2	.389	.389	.686
Explained	136.444	5	27.289	27.289	.000
Residual	12.000	12	1.000		
Total	**148.444**	**17**	**8.732**		

◙ FIGURE 14.12

```
┌─────────────────────────────────────────────────────────┐
│ Factorial ANOVA: Options                                 │
│                                                          │
│    Method              Statistics          ┌──────────┐ │
│    ○  Unique           ⊠  Means and counts  │ Continue │ │
│    ○  Hierarchical     □  Covariate coefficier└──────────┘ │
│    ⊗  Experimental     □  MCA               ┌──────────┐ │
│                                             │  Cancel  │ │
│    Enter Covariates    Maximum Interactions └──────────┘ │
│    □  Before           ⊗ 5 way    ○ 4 way   ┌──────────┐ │
│    □  With             ○ 3 way    ○ 2 way   │   Help   │ │
│    □  After            ○ none               └──────────┘ │
│                                                          │
│    ⊠  Display Labels                                     │
│                                                          │
└─────────────────────────────────────────────────────────┘
```

The output above shows the analysis of variance table and the appropriate cell means. The outputting of the cell means was accomplished by selecting the "Options" button in the screen shown in Figure 14.11. When the "Options" button is selected, the screen shown in Figure 14.12 appears. In order to get the means outputted with the Analysis of Variance, select "Experimental" as the Method and then choose "Means and counts."

CHAPTER SUMMARY

1. Factorial designs are frequently used in behavioral science research to analyze two or more independent variables simultaneously. The joint effect of the independent variables (interaction) on the dependent variable can be measured.
2. Every level of each independent variable is completely crossed with every level of the other independent variables.
3. Factorial designs are capable of handling complex designs.
4. Factorial designs are limited only by practicality.
5. These designs can deal with the differential effects of the variables and use conditional statements.
6. The *interaction* is defined as the combined influence of two or more independent variables on a dependent variable.
7. The interaction can occur in the absence of any separate effect of the independent variables.

8. The separate independent effects are called *main effects.*
9. In ANOVA for factorial designs, the total sums-of-squares is partitioned into the main effects, interaction effect(s), and the error (within-group) effect. The ANOVA summary table is a convenient way of presenting the analysis of the data.
10. There are two basic types of interaction effects: (i) ordinal—where one of the independent variables is significant along with a significant interaction effect; and (ii) disordinal—where there is a crisscross pattern when the cell means are plotted.
11. Factorial designs and the ANOVA for two independent variables is written as "*i* by *j*," where *i* is the number of levels of the first independent variable and *j* is the number of levels of the second independent variable.

STUDY SUGGESTIONS

1. Here are some varied and interesting psychological or educational studies that have used factorial analysis of variance in one way or another. Read and study two of them and ask yourself: Was factorial analysis the appropriate analysis? That is, might the researchers have used, say, a simpler form of analysis?

   Behling, D. (1995). Influence of dress on perception of intelligence and scholastic achievement in urban schools with minority populations. *Clothing and Textiles Research Journal, 13,* 11–16. This study examines the "halo" effect using a 6 × 2 × 2 × 3 × 3 (clothing style × sex of model × status × school × race) design. Results showed that teachers and students were influenced differently by clothing style.

   Cairns, E. (1990). Impact of television news exposure on children's perceptions of violence in Northern Ireland. *Journal of Social Psychology, 130,* 447–452. Assessed the impact of TV news exposure on Irish children's perceptions of the level of violence in their neighborhoods. A four-way ANOVA (area × sex × age × news exposure) was used. Results showed an effect for area and sex with respect to the high-violence area and boys. Two two-way interactions also reached statistical significance.

   Langer, E., & Imber, L. (1980). When practice makes imperfect: Debilitating effects of overlearning. *Journal of Personality and Social Psychology, 37,* 2014–2024. Uses a 3 × 3 and 3 × 2 factorial design; unusual findings.

   Many, J. E. (1991). The effects of stance and age level on children's literary responses. *Journal of Reading Behavior, 23,* 61–85. This study explored the effects of the use of aesthetic and efferent stances in response to literature. All participants read the same three short stories and gave free responses to each. Two-way ANOVA revealed significant effects for stance and grade level of understanding. The amount of understanding was found to increase with grade level. No interaction effects were found.

Wayne, S. J., Kaemar, K. M., & Ferris, G. R. (1995). Coworker responses to others' ingratiation attempts. *Journal of Management Issues, 7,* 277–289. This study uses a 2 × 2 × 2 × 2 (Ingratiation × Objective Performance × Reward × Time) factorial design to study coworker satisfaction and perception of fairness.

2. We are interested in testing the relative efficacies of different methods of teaching foreign languages (or any other subject). We believe that foreign language aptitude is possibly an influential variable. How might an experiment be set up to test the efficacies of the methods? Now add a third variable, Sex, and lay out the paradigms of both researches. Discuss the logic of each design from the point of view of statistics. What statistical tests of significance would you use? What part do they play in interpreting the results?

3. Write two problems and the hypotheses to go with them, using any three (or four) variables you wish. Scan the problems and hypotheses in Study Suggestions 2 and 3, Chapter 2, and the variables given in Chapter 3. Or use any of the variables of this chapter. Write at least one hypothesis that is an interaction hypothesis.

4. From the random numbers of Appendix C draw 40 numbers, 0 through 9, in groups of 10. Consider the four groups as A_1B_1, A_1B_2, A_2B_1, and A_2B_2.

    a. Do a factorial analysis of variance as outlined in the chapter. What should the A, B and $A \times B$ (interaction) F-ratios be like?

    b. Add 3 to each of the scores in the group with the highest mean. Which F-ratio or ratios should be affected? Why? Do the factorial analysis of variance. Are your expectations fulfilled?

5. Some students may wish to expand their reading and study of research design and factorial analysis of variance. Much has been written, and it is difficult to recommend books and articles. There are four books, however, that have rich resources and interesting chapters on design, statistical problems, assumptions and their testing, and the history of analysis of variance and related methods.

Collier, R., & Hummel, T. (1977). *Experimental Design and Interpretation.* Berkeley, CA.: McCutchan. This book was sponsored by the American Educational Research Association.

Harlow, L. L., Mulaik, S. A., & Steiger, J. H. (1997). *What if there were no significance tests?* Hillsdale, NJ: Lawrence Erlbaum.

Keren, G., & Lewis, C. (1993). *A handbook for data analysis in the behavioral sciences: Statistical issues.* Hillsdale, NJ: Lawrence Erlbaum.

Kirk, R. E. (1972). *Statistical issues: A reader for the behavioral sciences.* Monterey, CA.: Brooks/Cole.

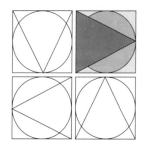

CHAPTER 15

ANALYSIS OF VARIANCE:
CORRELATED GROUPS

In the previous chapters, groups were independent on ANOVA. Participants who appeared in one group were not in any logical or meaningful way related to the participants in the other groups. In a 2×3 factorial, for example, there are six separate groups. Each group receives a different combination of treatments (independent variables) than the other groups. Generally, for independent groups, different participants are used in each treatment combination. In this chapter we will consider the situation where the participants are not independent. The term "correlated groups" is used because it best expresses the basic and distinctive nature of the kind of analysis of variance discussed in this chapter. Other more commonly used terms are "randomized blocks," "within subjects," and "repeated measures," but these are not completely general.

◫ TABLE 15.1 *Design of Marijuana, Alcohol, and Simulator Driving Experiment: Repeated Measures (Fictitious Scores)*[a]

Subjects	Marijuana (A_1)	Alcohol (A_2)	Control (A_3)	Sums, Rows
1	18	27	16	61
2	24	29	21	74
.	.	.	.	.
36	21	25	20	66
Sums	710	820	680	$\Sigma X_t = 2210$

[a]Although fictitious data were used, the design was taken from an actual research study by Crancer, Dille, Delay, Wallace, and Haykin (1969).

Suppose a research team wants to test the effects of marijuana and alcohol on driving. It can, of course, set up a one-way design or a factorial design. Instead, the investigators decide to use participants as their own controls. That is, each subject is to undergo three experimental treatments or conditions: marijuana (A_1), alcohol (A_2), and control (A_3). After each of these treatments, the participants will operate a driving simulator. The dependent variable measure is the Number of Driving Errors. A paradigm of the design of the experiment, with a few fictitious scores, is given in Table 15.1. Note that the sums of both columns and rows are given in the table. Note, too, that the design looks like that of one-way analysis of variance, with one exception: the sums of the rows. These are the sums of each subject's scores across the three treatments.

This is quite a different situation from the earlier models in which participants were assigned at random to experimental groups. Here, all participants undergo all treatments, making each subject his or her own control. More generally, instead of independence we now have dependence or correlation between groups. What does correlation between groups mean? It is not easy to answer this question with a simple statement.

Definition of the Problem

In one-way and factorial analysis of variance, the independence of groups, participants, and observations is a sine qua non of the designs. In both approaches participants are assigned to experimental groups at random. There is no question of correlation between groups—by definition. Except for variables specifically put into the design—like adding Sex to treatments—variance due to individual differences is distributed randomly among the experimental groups, and the groups are thus "equalized." Variance due to individual differences is known to be substantial if it can be isolated and extracted from the total variance. Then there should be a substantial increase in precision because this source of variation in the scores can be subtracted from the total variance. Thus a smaller error variance is created to use to evaluate the effects of the treatments.

In Chapter 14, one of the examples of factorial analysis of variance identified and subtracted variance due to social class from the total variance (see equations 14.3–14.6 and accompanying discussion), thus reducing the within-groups variance, the error term. The reasoning in this chapter is similar: isolate and extract variance in the dependent variable due to individual differences. To make this abstract discussion concrete, we use an easy example in which the idea of "matching" is introduced: Using the same participants in the different experimental groups, and matching participants on one, two, or more variables. This involves the same basic idea of correlation between groups. In the example that follows, matching is used to show the applicability of correlated groups analysis to a common research situation, because certain points about correlation and its effect can be made conveniently. Matching as a research device, however, is not generally advocated, for reasons that will be discussed in a later chapter.

A Fictitious Example

A school principal and members of the staff decided to introduce a program of education in intergroup relations as an addition to the school's curriculum. One of the problems that arose was in the use of motion pictures. Videos were shown in the initial phases of the program, but the results were not too encouraging. The staff hypothesized that the failure of the videos to have impact might have resulted from their not making any particular effort to bring out the possible applications of the video to intergroup relations. They decided to test the hypothesis that viewing the videos and then discussing them would improve the viewers' attitudes toward minority group members more than would just viewing the videos.

For a preliminary study, the staff selected a group of students randomly from the total student body, and paired the students on intelligence until 10 pairs were obtained, each pair being approximately equal in intelligence. The reasoning behind the experiment was that intelligence is related to attitudes toward minority groups, and needs to be controlled. Each member of each pair was assigned randomly to either an experimental or a control group, and then both groups were shown a video on intergroup relations. The A_1 (experimental) group had a discussion session after the video was shown; the A_2 (control) group had no such discussion after the video. Both groups were tested with a scale designed to measure attitudes toward minority groups. The attitude scores and the calculations for an analysis of variance procedure to be described are given in Table 15.2.

First we do a one-way analysis of variance as though the investigators had not matched the participants. We disregard the matching procedure and analyze the scores as though all the participants had been assigned to the two groups randomly,

◻ **TABLE 15.2** *Attitude Scores and Calculations of Analysis of Variance (Fictitious Example)*

	Groups		
Pairs	A_1 (*Experimental*)	A_2 (*Control*)	Σ
1	8	6	14
2	9	8	17
3	5	3	8
4	4	2	6
5	2	1	3
6	10	7	17
7	3	1	4
8	12	7	19
9	6	6	12
10	11	9	20
ΣX	70	50	$\Sigma X_t = 120$
M	7	5	$\Sigma X_t^2 = 930$

without regard to intelligence. The calculations are:

$$C = \frac{14{,}400}{20} = 720$$

$$Total = 930 - 720 = 210$$

$$Between\ Columns(A_1, A_2) = \left(\frac{70^2}{10} + \frac{50^2}{10} \right) - 720 = 20$$

The final analysis of variance table of this analysis is given in Table 15.3. Since the *F*-ratio of 1.89 is not significant, the two group means of 7 and 5 do not differ significantly. The interpretation of these data would lead the experimenters to believe that the video plus discussion had no effect. This conclusion would be wrong. The difference in this case is really significant at the 0.01 level. Let us assume that this statement is true; if it is true, then there must be something wrong with the analysis.

An Explanatory Digression

When subjects are matched on variables *significantly related* to the dependent variable, correlation is introduced into the statistical picture. In Chapter 14 we saw that it was

◉ **TABLE 15.3** *Final Analysis of Variance Table, One-Way Analysis of Fictitious Data from Table 15.2*

Source	df	ss	MS	F
Between groups (A_1, A_2)	1	20.00	20.0	1.89 (n.s.)
Within groups	18	190.00	10.56	
Total	19	210.00		

often possible to identify and control more of the total variance of an experimental situation by setting up levels of one or more variables presumably related to the dependent variable. The setting up of two or three levels of social class, for example, makes it possible to identify the variance in the dependent variable scores due to social class. Now, simply shift gears a bit. The matching of the present experiment has actually set up 10 levels, one for each pair. The members of the first pair had intelligence scores of say 130 and 132, the members of the second pair 124 and 125, and so on to the tenth pair, the members of which had scores of 89 and 92. Each pair (level) has a different mean. If intelligence is substantially and positively correlated with the dependent variable, then the dependent variable pairs of scores should reflect the matching on intelligence. That is, the dependent variable scores within each pair should be more like each other than they are like other dependent variable scores. So the matching on intelligence has "introduced" variance between pairs on the dependent variable, or *between-rows* variance.

Consider another hypothetical example to illustrate what happens when there is correlation between sets of scores. Suppose an investigator has matched three groups of subjects on intelligence, and that intelligence was perfectly correlated with the dependent variable, achievement of some kind. This is highly unlikely, but let's go along with it to get the idea. The first trio of subjects had intelligence scores of 141, 142, and 140; the second trio 130, 126, and 128; and so on through the fifth trio of 82, 85, and 82. If we check the rank orders in columns of the three sets of scores, they are exactly the same: 141, 130, . . . , 82; 142, 126, . . . , 85; 140, 128, . . . , 82. Since we assume that $r = 1.00$ between intelligence and achievement, then the rank orders of the achievement scores must be the same in the three groups. The assumed achievement-test scores are given on the left-hand side of Table 15.4. The rank orders of these fictitious scores, from high to low, are given in parentheses beside each achievement score. Note that the rank orders are the same in the three groups.

Now suppose that the correlation between intelligence and achievement was approximately zero. In such a case, no prediction could be made of the rank orders of the achievement scores or, to put it another way, the achievement scores would not be matched. To simulate such a condition of zero correlation, we broke up the rank orders of the scores on the left-hand side of Table 15.4 with the help of a table of random numbers. After drawing three sets of numbers 1 through 5, we rearranged the scores in columns according to the random numbers. (Before doing this, all the

回 **TABLE 15.4** *Correlated and Uncorrelated Scores (Fictitious Example)*

I. Correlated Groups				II. Uncorrelated Groups			
A_1	A_2	A_3	M	A_1	A_2	A_3	M
73 (1)	74 (1)	72 (1)	73	63 (2)	74 (1)	46 (5)	61.00
63 (2)	65 (2)	61 (2)	63	45 (5)	55 (3)	61 (2)	53.67
57 (3)	55 (3)	59 (3)	57	50 (4)	50 (4)	59 (3)	53.00
50 (4)	50 (4)	53 (4)	51	57 (3)	65 (2)	53 (4)	58.33
45 (5)	44 (5)	46 (5)	45	73 (1)	44 (5)	72 (1)	63.00
	$M_t = 57.80$				$M_t = 57.80$		

column rank orders were 1, 2, 3, 4, 5.) The first set of random numbers was 2, 5, 4, 3, and 1. The second number of column A_1 was put first. We next took the fifth number of A_1 and put it second. This process was continued until the former first number became the fifth number. The same procedure was used with the other two groups of numbers, with, of course, different sets of random numbers. The final results are given on the right-hand side of Table 15.4. The means of the rows are also given, as are the ranks of the column scores (in parentheses).

First, study the ranks of the two sets of scores. In the left-hand portion of the table, labeled I, are the correlated scores. Since the ranks are the same in each column, the average correlation between columns is 1.00. The numbers of the set labeled II, which are essentially random, present quite a different picture. The 15 numbers of both sets are exactly the same. So are the numbers in each column (and their means). Only the row numbers and, of course, the row means, are different. Look at the rank orders of II. No systematic relations can be found between them. The average correlation should be approximately zero, since the numbers were randomly shuffled. Actually it is 0.11.

Next, study the variability of the row means. Note that the variability of the means of I is considerably greater than that of II. If the numbers are random, the expectation for the mean of any row is the general mean. The means of the rows of II hover rather closely around the general mean of 57.80. The range is $63 - 53 = 10$. But the means of the rows of I do not hover closely around 57.80; their variability is much greater, as indicated by a range of $73 - 45 = 28$. Calculating the variances of these two sets of means (called *between-rows variance*), we obtain 351.60 for I and 58.27 for II. The variance of I is six times greater than the variance of II. This large difference is a direct effect of the correlation that is present in the scores of I but not in II. It may be said that the between-rows variance is a direct index of individual differences. The reader should pause here to review this example, especially the entries in Table 15.4, until the effect of correlation on variance is clear.

What is the effect of the estimate of the error variance of correlated scores? Clearly the variance due to the correlation is *systematic* variance, which must be removed from the total variance if a more accurate estimate of error variance is desired. Otherwise, the error variance estimate will include the variance due to individual differences, and the result will thus be too large. In the example of Table 15.4, we know that the shuffling procedure has concealed the systematic variance due to the correlation. By rearranging the scores the possibility of identifying this variance is removed. The variance is still in the scores of II, but it cannot be extracted. To show this, we calculate the variances of the error terms of I and II; that of I is 3.10, that of II, 149.77. By removing from the total variance the variance due to the correlation, it is possible to reduce the error term greatly, with the result that the error variance of I is 48 times smaller than the error variance of II. If there is substantial systematic variance in the sets of measures, and it is possible to isolate and identify this variance, then it is clearly worthwhile to do so.

Actual research data will not be as dramatic as the above example. Correlations are almost never 1. But they are often greater than .50 or .60. *The higher the correlation, the larger the systematic variance that can be extracted from the total variance, and the more the error term can be reduced.* This principle becomes very important not only in designing research, but also in measurement theory and practice. Sometimes it is possible to build correlation into the scores and then extract the variance due to the resulting correlated scores. For example, we can obtain a "pure" measure of individual differences by using the same participants on different trials. Obviously a participant's own scores will be more alike than they will be like the scores of others.

Reexamination of Table 15.2 Data

We return to the fictitious research data of Table 15.2—the effects of videos on attitudes toward minority groups. Earlier we calculated a between-columns (between-groups) sum-of-squares and variance, exactly as we did in one-way analysis of variance. We found that the difference between the means was not significant when this method was used. From the above discussion, we can surmise that if there is correlation between the two sets of scores, then the variance due to the correlation should be removed from the total variance and, of course, from the estimate of the error variance. If the correlation is substantial, this procedure should make quite a difference: the error term should get considerably smaller. The correlation between the sets of scores of A_1 and A_2 of Table 15.2 is .93. Since this is a high degree of correlation, the error term (when properly calculated) should be much lower than it was before.

The additional operation required is simple. Just add the scores in each row of Table 15.2 and calculate the between-rows sum-of-squares and the variance. Square the sum of each row and divide the result by the number of scores in the row; for example, in the first row: $8 + 6 = 14$; $(14)^2 \div 2 = 196 \div 2 = 98$. Repeat this procedure for each row, add the quotients, and then subtract the correction term C. This yields the between-rows sum-of-squares. (Since the number of scores in each row is always 2, it is easier, especially with a hand calculator, to add all the squared sums and then divide by 2.)

$$\text{Between rows (1, 2, 3, ...10)} = \left[\frac{(14)^2 + (17)^2 + \cdots + (20)^2}{2} \right] - 720$$

$$= 902 - 720 = 182$$

This between-rows sum-of-squares is a measure of the variability due to individual differences, as indicated earlier.

We have extracted from the total sum-of-squares the between-columns and the between-rows sums-of-squares. Now, set up the familiar equation used in one-way analysis of variance:

$$ss_t = ss_b + ss_w \tag{15.1}$$

The analysis of Table 15.3 is an example. We must alter this equation to suit the present circumstances. The former between-groups sum-of-squares, ss_b, is relabeled ss_c, which means the sum-of-squares of the columns. The sum-of-squares of the rows, ss_r, is added, and ss_w, must be relabeled since we now no longer have a within-groups variance. (Why?) We label it ss_{res}, meaning the sum-of-squares of the *residuals*. As the name indicates, the *residual* sum-of-squares means the sum-of-squares remaining after the sums-of-squares of columns and rows have been extracted from the total sum-of-squares. The equation then becomes

$$ss_t = ss_c + ss_r + ss_{res} \tag{15.2}$$

Briefly, the total variance has been broken down into two identifiable, or systematic, variances and one error variance. And this error variance is a more accurate estimate of error, or chance variation, of the scores than that of Table 15.3.

Rather than substitute in the equation, we set up the final analysis of variance table (Table 15.5). The F-ratio of the columns is now $20.00 \div .89 = 22.47$, which is significant at the .001 level. In Table 15.3 the F-ratio was not significant.

This is quite a difference. Since the between-columns variance is the same, the difference is due to the greatly decreased error term, now .89 when it was 10.56 before. By calculating the rows sum-of-squares and the variance, it has been possible to reduce the error term to about 1/12 of its former magnitude. In this situation, obviously, the former error variance of 10.56 was greatly overinflated. Some statistics texts (e.g., Kirk, 1990; Mendenhall & Beaver, 1997) refer to the columns as "treatments" and the rows as "blocks." Returning to the original problem, it is now possible to say that adding discussion after the video seems to have had a significant effect on attitudes toward minority groups.

Further Considerations

Before we leave this example, additional points need to be made. The first involves the error term and the within-groups and residual variances. When the variances of the columns and the rows are calculated, it is not possible to calculate a within-

☐ TABLE 15.5 *Complete Analysis of Variance Table: Data from Table 15.2*

Source	df	ss	MS	F
Between columns (A_1, A_2)	1	20	20.0	22.47 (0.001)
Between rows (1, 2, 3, . . . , 10)	9	182	20.22	22.72 (0.001)
Residual	9	8	0.89	
Totals	19	210		

groups variance, since there is in effect only one score per cell. Also bear in mind that both error variances, as calculated, *are only estimates of the error variance.* In the one-way situation, the only estimate possible is the within-groups variance. In the present situation, a better estimate is possible; "better" in the sense that there is more systematic variance. When it is possible to extract systematic variance we do so. It was possible to do so with the data from Table 15.2.

A second point is: Why not use the *t*-test? The answer is simple: Do so if you wish. If there is only one degree of freedom, that is, two groups, then *t* equals the square root of *F*, or $F = t^2$. The *t*-ratio of the data from Table 15.5 is simply: the square root of 22.47 = 4.74. But if there is more than one degree of freedom, the *t*-test must give way to the *F*-test. Moreover, the analysis of variance yields more information. The analysis of Table 15.5 tells us that the difference between the mean attitude scores of the experimental and control groups is significantly different. The *t*-test would have yielded the same information. But Table 15.5 also tells us—simply and clearly—that the matching was effective, or that the correlation between the dependent variable scores of the two groups is significant. Had the between-rows *F*-ratio not been significant, we would know that the matching had not been successful. Important information, indeed. Finally, the calculations of the analysis of variance, once understood, are easily remembered; whereas the equations used for estimating the standard error of the differences between the means seem to confuse the beginning student. (The simple formula given earlier has to be altered because of the correlation.)

Point three: post hoc tests of the significance of the differences between individual means can be made with, of course, more than two groups. The Scheffé, Tukey and other tests used for multiple comparisons are applicable. The Scheffé's test was covered in Chapter 13.

Finally, and most important, the principles discussed above are applicable to a variety of research situations. Their application to matching is perhaps the least important, though maybe the easiest to understand. Whenever the same subjects and repeated measures are used, the principles apply. When different classes or different schools are used in educational research, the principles apply: variance due to class and school differences can be extracted from the data. Indeed, the principles can be invoked for any research in which different experimental treatments are used in different units of a larger organization, institution, or even geographical area—provided these units differ in variables of significance to the research.

To see what is meant, imagine that the rows of the left side of Table 15.4 are different schools or classes in a school system, that the schools or classes differ significantly in achievement, as indicated by the row means, and that A_1, A_2, and A_3 are experimental treatments of an experiment done in each of the schools or classes (see Study Suggestion 2).

Two-way (two independent variables) analysis of variance is useful in the solution of certain measurement problems, particularly in psychology and education, as we will see in later chapters. Individual differences are a constant source of variance that needs to be identified and analyzed. A good example is seen in the study of raters and ratings. One can separate the variance of raters (judges) from the variance of the objects being rated. The reliability of measuring instruments can be studied because the variance of the items can be separated from the variance of the persons responding to the items. We return again and again to these important points and the principles behind them.

To illustrate the use of judges or raters as "blocks," consider the following example. Eight different judges evaluate four videos. Each video covers the same material. Each judge assigned a score between 0 and 20 to each video in terms of effectiveness of presentation. Each judge viewed the videos in random order. The table below gives the data, analysis, and summary. The analysis shows that the judges differ in their ratings of the videos. Hence, partitioning out their variance increases the effect between videos.

| | | | Videos | | |
Judges/Blocks	A	B	C	D	Row Totals
1	6	4	14	8	32
2	8	2	10	7	27
3	7	8	10	7	32
4	12	6	11	12	41
5	5	0	9	8	22
6	7	3	10	7	27
7	10	9	16	11	46
8	9	4	12	9	34
Column Totals	64	36	92	69	261

$$SS_{Total} = SD^2(N) = 3.3737^2(32) = 364.22$$

$$SS_{Video} = \left[\frac{64^2 + 36^2 + 92^2 + 69^2}{8} \right] - M^2(N) = 2327.13 - 8.15625(32) = 198.34$$

$$SS_{Judges} = \left[\frac{32^2 + 27^2 + ... + 34^2}{4} \right] - 2128.78125 = 106.97$$

$$SS_{Residual} = SS_{Total} - SS_{Video} - SS_{Judges} = 58/91$$

Source	df	ss	MS	F
Videos	3	198.34	66.11	23.53 (0.01)
Judges (Blocks)	7	106.97	15.28	5.44 (0.01)
Residual	21	58.91	2.81	
Total	31	364.22		

Extracting Variances by Subtraction

To be sure that the reader understands the points being made, previous examples are repeated here. In Table 15.6, two sets of numbers, labeled I and II, are given. The numbers in these sets are exactly the same, only their arrangements differ. In I, there is no correlation between the two columns of numbers; the coefficient of correlation

■ **TABLE 15.6** *Analyses of Variance of Randomized and Correlated Fictitious Data*

	I $r = 0.00$			II $r = 0.90$		
	A_1	A_2	Σ	A_1	A_2	Σ
	1	5	6	1	2	3
	2	2	4	2	4	6
	3	4	7	3	3	6
	4	6	10	4	5	9
	5	3	8	5	6	11
ΣX	15	20	$\Sigma X_t = 35$	15	20	$\Sigma X_t = 35$
M	3	4	$\Sigma X_t^2 = 145$	3	4	$\Sigma X_t^2 = 145$
			$M_t = 3.5$			$M_t = 3.5$

$$C = \frac{(35)^2}{10} = 122.50 \qquad\qquad C = \frac{(35)^2}{10} = 122.50$$

$$Total = 145 - 122.50 = 22.50 \qquad\qquad Total = 145 - 122.50 = 22.50$$

$$Between\ C = \left[\frac{15^2 + 20^2}{5}\right] - 122.50 = 2.50 \qquad Between\ C = \left[\frac{15^2 + 20^2}{5}\right] - 122.50 = 2.50$$

$$Between\ R = \left[\frac{6^2 + 4^2 + .. + 8^2}{2}\right] - 122.50 \qquad Between\ R = \left[\frac{3^2 + 6^2 + ... + 9^2}{2}\right] - 122.50$$

$$= 132.50 - 122.50 = 10 \qquad\qquad = 141.50 - 122.50 = 19$$

⊡ **TABLE 15.7** *Final Analysis of Variance Tables.*

		I (r = 0.00)			II (r = 0.90)		
Source	df	ss	MS	F	ss	MS	F
Between C	1	2.50	2.50	1.0	2.50	2.50	10.0 (0.05)
Between R	4	10.00	2.50	(n.s.)	19.00	4.75	
Residual C × R	4	10.00	2.50		1.00	0.25	
Totals	9	22.50			22.50		

is exactly zero. This is analogous to the assignment of participants to the two groups at random. One-way analysis of variance is applicable. In II, on the other hand, the A_2 numbers have been rearranged so that there is correlation between the A_1 and A_2 numbers. (Check the rank orders.) In fact, $r = 0.90$. One-way analysis of variance is not applicable here. If it is used with the numbers of II, the result will be exactly the same as it will be with the numbers of I, but we will then be disregarding the variance due to the correlation.

The calculations in Table 15.6 yield all the sums-of-squares except the residual sums-of-squares, which are obtained by subtraction. Since the calculations are so straightforward, we proceed directly to the final analysis of variance tables that are given in Table 15.7. The sums-of-squares for totals, columns, and rows are entered as indicated, with the appropriate degrees of freedom. The between-rows degrees of freedom are the number of rows minus one ($5 - 1 = 4$). The residual degrees of freedom, like the interaction degrees of freedom in factorial analysis of variance, are obtained by multiplying the between-columns and between-rows degrees of freedom: $1 \times 4 = 4$. Or simply subtract the between-columns and between-rows degrees of freedom from the total degrees of freedom: $9 - 1 - 4 = 4$. The residual sums-of-squares, similarly, are obtained by subtracting the between-columns and between-rows sums-of-squares from the total sums-of-squares. For I, $22.5 - 2.5 = 10.0 = 10$; for II, $22.5 - 2.5 - 19.0 = 1$.

These analyses need little elaboration. Note particularly that where there is correlation, the between-columns F-ratio is significant, but where the correlation is zero it is not significant. Note, too, the error term: for I ($r = .00$), it is 2.5: for II ($r = .90$), it is .25, which is 10 times smaller.

Removal of Systematic Sources of Variance

We now use the subtractive procedure of Chapter 6 to remove the two systematic sources of variance in the two sets of scores. First, remove the between-columns variance by correcting each mean so that it equals the general mean of 3.5. Then correct each score in each column similarly (as done for I and II in Table 15.8).

◉ TABLE 15.8 *Removal of Between-Columns Variance by Equalizing Column Means and Scores*

	I r = 0.00			II r = 0.90		
Correction	.5	−.5		.5	−.5	
	A_1	A_2	M	A_1	A_2	M
	1.5	4.5	3.0	1.5	1.5	1.5
	2.5	1.5	2.0	2.5	3.5	3.0
	3.5	3.5	3.7	3.5	2.5	3.0
	4.5	5.5	5.0	4.5	4.5	4.5
	5.5	2.5	4.0	5.5	5.5	5.5
M	3.5	3.5	$M_t = 3.5$	3.5	3.5	$M_t = 3.5$

If we now calculate the total sums-of-squares of I and II, in both cases we obtain 20. Compare this result to the former figure of 22.5. The correction procedure has reduced the total sums-of-squares by 2.5. These are, of course, the between-columns sums-of-squares. Note, again, that the correction procedure has had no effect whatever on the variance within each of the four groups of scores. Neither has it had any effect on the means of the rows.

◉ TABLE 15.9 *Removal of Between-Columns Variance by Equalizing Row Means and Scores*

	I r = 0.00				II r = 0.90		
Correction	A_1	A_2	M	Correction	A_1	A_2	M
+ 0.5	2.0	5.0	3.5	+ 2.0	3.5	3.5	3.5
+ 1.5	4.0	3.0	3.5	+ 0.5	3.0	4.0	3.5
0	3.5	3.5	3.5	+ 0.5	4.0	3.0	3.5
−1.5	3.0	4.0	3.5	−1.0	3.5	3.5	3.5
−0.5	5.0	2.0	3.5	−2.0	3.5	3.5	3.5
M	3.5	3.5	$M_t = 3.5$		3.5	3.5	$M_t = 3.5$

Next, remove the rows variance by letting each row mean equal 3.5, the general mean, and by correcting the row scores accordingly. This has been done in Table 15.9, which should be carefully studied. Note that the variability of both sets of scores has been reduced, but that the variability of the correlated set (II) has been sharply reduced. In fact, the scores of II have a range of only $4 - 3 = 1$, whereas the range of the I scores is $5 - 2 = 3$. The matching of the scores in II and its concomitant correlation enables us, via the corrective procedure, to reduce the error term sharply by "correcting out" the variance due to the correlation. The only variance now in the twice-corrected scores is the residual variance.

"Residual variance" is an apt term. It is the variance remaining after the two systematic variances have been removed. If we calculate the *total* sums-of-squares of I and II, we find them to be 10 and 1, respectively. If we calculate the sums-of-squares *within* the groups as with one-way analysis of variance, we find these also to be 10 and 1. Evidently there is no more systematic variance left in the scores—only error variance remains. The most important point to note is that the residual sum-of-squares of the uncorrelated scores is 10 times greater than the residual sum-of-squares of the correlated scores. Exactly the same operation was performed on both sets of scores. With the uncorrelated scores, however, it is not possible to extract as much variance as with the correlated scores.

Additional Correlated Analysis of Variance Designs

So far in our discussion concerning the analysis of variance we have seen three of the five basic designs. Chapter 13 covered the completely randomized design. This was a one-way ANOVA with independent groups. Independent groups are usually accomplished through random selection of participants and the random assignment of participants to treatment conditions. Chapter 14 introduced us to the randomized factorial design. Here we studied two or more independent or experimental variables at a time. Like the completely randomized design, the groups involved in the analyses were independent. With two independent variables, the analysis is referred to as a two-way ANOVA. In this chapter we have considered the randomized block design. This is a one-way ANOVA where the subjects are not independent. These designs involve the use of matching participants or using the same subject over a number of different treatment conditions. It is referred to as *randomized block* because the treatments are given to each subject in random order.

The two remaining basic ANOVA designs are variations of the randomized block design. One of these designs is called the split-plot or mixed factorial ANOVA. The other is the *n*-way within-participants design. Conceptually the simpler of the two is the *n*-way within-participants design. This design resembles the randomized factorial design. However, the participants are not assigned randomly to the treatments. In this design, one group of participants is exposed to all treatment combinations. You might remember that in the randomized factorial design, different groups of participants were used in each different treatment combination. With two independent variables, this would be called a two-way within-subjects ANOVA or a subjects-by-treatment-by-treatment ANOVA.

◨ **TABLE 15.10** *Layout of the Five ANOVA Designs*

(a) The completely randomized design (one-way ANOVA)

Independent Variable		
A₁	**A₂**	**A₃**
S_1	S_4	S_7
S_2	S_5	S_8
S_3	S_6	S_9
Group 1	Group 2	Group 3

(b) Randomized block design (one-way ANOVA)

Independent Variable		
A₁	**A₂**	**A₃**
S_1	S_1	S_1
S_2	S_2	S_2
S_3	S_3	S_3
S_4	S_4	S_4
S_5	S_5	S_5
Group 1	Group 1	Group 1

(c) Randomized factorial design (two-way ANOVA)

	Independent Variable 1		
Independent Variable 2	**A₁**	**A₂**	**A₃**
	S_1	S_7	S_{13}
	S_2	S_8	S_{14}
B_1	S_3	S_9	S_{15}
	Group 1	Group 3	Group 5
	S_4	S_{10}	S_{16}
B_2	S_5	S_{11}	S_{17}
	S_6	S_{12}	S_{18}
	Group 2	Group 4	Group 6

cont.

TABLE 15.10 *(continued)*

(d) Two-way within-subjects design (two-way ANOVA)

	Independent Variable 1		
Independent Variable 2	**A_1**	**A_2**	**A_3**
	S_1	S_1	S_1
	S_2	S_2	S_2
B_1	S_3	S_3	S_3
	Group 1	Group 1	Group 1
	S_1	S_1	S_1
B_2	S_2	S_2	S_2
	S_3	S_3	S_3
	Group 2	Group 2	Group 2

(e) Spilt-plot, mixed factorial design (two-way ANOVA)

	Independent Variable 1		
Independent Variable 2	**A_1**	**A_2**	**A_3**
	S_1	S_1	S_1
	S_2	S_2	S_2
B_1	S_3	S_3	S_3
	Group 1	Group 1	Group 1
	S_4	S_4	S_4
B_2	S_5	S_5	S_5
	S_6	S_6	S_6
	Group 2	Group 2	Group 2

With the mixed factorial ANOVA with two independent variables, each subject is exposed to all levels of one independent variable but only to one level of the second independent variable. The design is termed "mixed" because it has the features of both uncorrelated and correlated ANOVA. It can alternatively be described as a design having at least one between-subjects factor and at least one within-subjects factor. Table 15.10 (a), (b), (c), (d), and (e) shows the difference between the five ANOVA designs.

We have seen earlier in this chapter the procedure for partitioning the sum-of-squares in the completely randomized and randomized block ANOVAs. Similar logic toward partitioning is true for the mixed and within-subjects designs. Purdy, Avery, and Cross (1978) give a very good account of this as well as the layout of the data and the ANOVA summary table. Other excellent references are Hays (1994), Kirk (1995), Linton and Gallo (1975), McGuigan (1997), and Howell (1997).

Research Examples

Ironic Effects of Trying to Relax Under Stress

When we are in a stressful situation does it help to tell ourselves to relax and calm down? One would think that this is the best procedure to use in order to be healthier. Recently, a professional basketball player entered into a heated argument with the coach. After being separated, the player went to the locker room only to return 20 minutes later to attack the coach again. A number of researchers have documented the fact that telling ourselves to calm down and relax is not easy. In one such study, Wegner, Broome, and Blumberg (1997) demonstrated that conscious efforts to relax usually lead to a higher state of agitation. This study found that when participants were instructed to relax under high mental load they exhibited a higher level of agitation. On the other hand, participants who were under a low mental load or who were not told to relax tended to be less agitated. Wegner and associates used skin conductance level (SCL) as a measure of agitation. Higher values of SCL indicated higher the levels of agitation. While SCL served as the dependent variable for the study, the independent variables were load (high versus low), instruction (told to relax versus not told to relax), and period (Pre: first 5 minutes; Test: next 3 minutes; and Post: last 5 minutes). The last independent variable is the repeated measures. Each subject was exposed to all three levels of the period variable. The other two independent variables were between-subjects variables. Each subject was exposed to only one condition of high or low load and one of instructions. The design of this study can be classified as a mixed or split-plot ANOVA. The layout of the design with the means is given in Table 15.11. The analyses showed a significant effect for period, $F(2, 166) = 137.7, p < 0.001$.

Learning Sets of Isopods

In an interesting and effective demonstration of the use of participants as their own controls, in which two-way analysis of variance and the testing of learning theory with lower organisms were used, Morrow and Smithson (1969) showed that isopods (small crustaceans) can learn to learn. Many students, humanists, sociologists, educators, and even psychologists have criticized learning theorists and other psychological investigators for using animals in their research. While there can be legitimate criticism of psychological and other behavioral research, criticizing it because

▣ **TABLE 15.11** *Means for Load, Instructions, and Period (Wegner, Broome, & Blumberg study)[a]*

	Period		
Instruction/Load	**Pre**	**Test**	**Post**
None/Low	−0.51	4.27	1.58
None/High	−0.46	3.80	1.68
Relax/Low	0.38	3.50	1.80
Relax/High	0.10	5.70	2.58

[a]These values were estimated from examining Wegner, Broome and Blumberg's figure

animals are used is part of the frustrating, but apparently unavoidable, irrationality that plagues all human effort. Yet, it does have a certain charm, and can itself be the object of scientific investigation. Bugelski (1956) has written an excellent defense of the use of rats in learning research that should be read by students of behavioral research. Another excellent essay on a somewhat broader base is by Hebb and Thompson (1968). In any case, one of the reasons for testing similar hypotheses with different species is the same reason as why we replicate research in different parts of the United States and in other countries: generality. How much more powerful a theory is if it holds up with southerners, northerners, easterners, and westerners; with Germans, Japanese, Israelis, and Americans; and with rats, pigeons, horses, and dogs. Morrow and Smithson's (1969) study attempted to extend learning theory to little creatures whose learning one might believe governed by different laws than the learning of men and rats. They succeeded at least to some extent.

They trained eight isopods, through water deprivation and subsequent reinforcement for successful performance (wet blotting paper), to make reversals of their "preferences" for one or the other arm of a *T*-maze. When the *S*s had reached a specified criterion of correct turns in the maze, the training was reversed—that is,

▣ **TABLE 15.12** *Analysis of Variance of Morrow and Smithson Data*

Source	*df*	*ss*	*MS*	*F*
Reversal trials	9	3095.95	343.994	4.78 (0.01)
Isopods (blocks)	7	1587.40	226.771	3.15 (0.01)
Residual	63	4532.85	71.950	
Totals	79	9216.20		

turning in the direction of the other arm of the *T*-maze was reinforced until the criterion was reached. This was done with each isopod for nine reversals. The question is: Did the animals learn to make the reversals sooner as the trials progressed? Such learning should be exhibited by fewer and fewer errors.

Morrow and Smithson analyzed the data with two-way analysis of variance. The mean number of errors of the initial trial and the nine reversal trials consistently got smaller: 27.5, 23.6, 18.6, 14.3, 16.8, 13.9, 11.1, 8.5, 8.6, 8.6. The two-way analysis of variance table is given in Table 15.12. The analysis of variance was computed by the first author (FNK) from the original data given by Morrow and Smithson in their Table 1.

The ten means differ significantly, since the *F*-ratio for columns (reversal trials), 4.78, is significant at the .01 level. The *F* shows that there is correlation between the columns, and thus individual differences among the isopods, significant at the .01 level. It is a piquant note that even little crustaceans are individuals!

Business: Bidding Behavior

This example is taken from the marketing research literature. The study of behavior is prevalent in business research. A number of well-known businesses such as Proctor & Gamble hire a number of behavioral scientists to help conduct research on consumer products.

◫ **TABLE 15.13** *Bids from Three Contracting Companies (Reinmuth & Barnes data)*

Bid Trials	Company A	Company B	Company C	Σ
1	$45.00	42.50	$39.75	127.25
2	45.00	40.25	42.70	127.95
3	46.00	45.50	40.00	131.50
4	43.75	43.50	40.20	127.45
5	46.00	44.50	40.65	131.15
6	43.50	43.25	40.00	126.75
7	44.50	40.90	41.45	126.85
8	45.50	45.00	45.75	136.25
9	50.00	45.50	45.60	141.10
10	46.50	44.50	44.15	135.15
Σ	455.75	435.40	420.25	

▣ **TABLE 15.14** *Analysis of Variance of Reinmuth and Barnes Data*

Source	df	ss	MS	F
Contractors	2	63.463	31.7215	14.75(0.001)
Bid trials (blocks)	9	72.708	8.0787	3.76 (0.01)
Residual	18	38.7237	2.1513	
Totals	29	174.8947		

A study by Reinmuth and Barnes (1975) did not use the randomized block ANOVA to analyze their data. However, the data they collected in their study of the bidding behavior of three petroleum drilling companies fits the mode of randomized blocks. The study was actually a marketing problem involving the development of a mathematical model for competitive bidding. The data provided by Reinmuth and Barnes were 10 randomly selected bids out of 35 possible bids. The data are the cost estimates plus profit for using a drilling rig and a four-man crew on an hourly basis. Table 15.13 gives the data collected. The goal in using a randomized block analysis is to see if the three companies differ on bidding while accounting for the individual trial differences. The trials here are the 10 measurements taken on each company.

The analysis of variance summary table is given in Table 15.14. The ANOVA shows that the difference between contracting companies' bids are highly significant ($p < 0.001$). The blocks or the trial bids were also statistically significant. Company A was consistently the highest bidder whereas Company C was consistently the lowest bidder. Since the block source of variance was statistically significant, this tells us that the correlation between the contract companies and the bids contributed significantly to systematic variance. The η^2 for the data was .363. The correlations between the three contract companies were $r_{AB} = 0.55$, $r_{AC} = 0.64$ and $r_{BC} = 0.29$.

Computer Addendum

To show you how to use SPSS to perform an analysis of variance for correlated designs, we have chosen the data given for the Reinmuth and Barnes study. The data from Table 15.13 are converted to an SPSS spreadsheet and shown in Figure 15.1. Also shown in Figure 15.1 are the menus/screens that appear when "Statistics" and "ANOVA Models" are selected (highlighted).

From the menu of ANOVA models, select "Repeated Measures." After selecting the "Repeated Measures" option, a new screen is presented (shown in Figure 15.2). In the first box labeled "Within-Subject Factor Name," enter the label "Type" (to represent "type of company") In the box below it, enter the number "3." This tells

□ FIGURE 15.1

	compa	compb	compc				
File Edit View Data Transform Statistics Graphs Utilities Windows Help
1	45.00	42.50	39.75
2	45.00	40.25	42.70
3	46.00	45.50	40.00
4	43.75	43.50	40.20
5	46.00	44.50	40.65
6	43.50	43.25	40.00
7	44.50	40.90	41.45
8	45.50	45.00	45.75
9	50.00	45.50	45.60
10	46.50	44.50	44.15

Menu items shown: Summarize ▶, Compare Means ▶, ANOVA Models ▶, Correlate ▶, Regression ▶, Log-linear ▶, Classify ▶, Data Reduction ▶, Scale ▶, Nonparametric Tests ▶

Submenu: Simple Factorial, General Factorial, Multivariate, Repeated Measures

SPSS that there are three groups or blocks. After this is done, click the "ADD" button. You will then see "Type (3)" appear in the box next to the "ADD" button.

Next, click the "Define" button, which will produce a new panel (shown in Figure 15.3). In the left-most box, you will see the variable names of all three groups: "compa," "compb," and "compc." Highlight each of them, one at a time, and click on

□ FIGURE 15.2

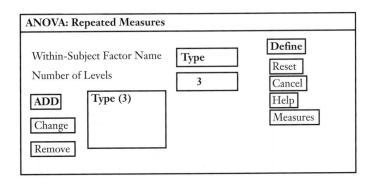

ANOVA: Repeated Measures

Within-Subject Factor Name — Type
Number of Levels — 3

ADD   Type (3)
Change
Remove

Define
Reset
Cancel
Help
Measures

▣ FIGURE 15.3

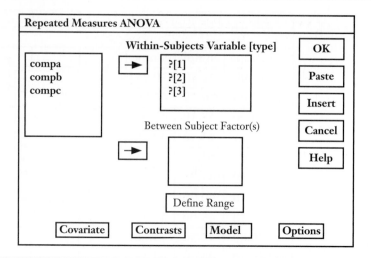

the right-point arrow associated with "Within-Subjects Variable" box. The result of this procedure is shown in Figure 15.4.

After you have done this for each group you are interested in, click the "OK" button and SPSS will execute and produce the output desired.

The abbreviated SPSS output is as shown in Figure 15.5. The blocking variable is represented as Within+Residual in the top half of the table. The Within+Resid-

▣ FIGURE 15.4

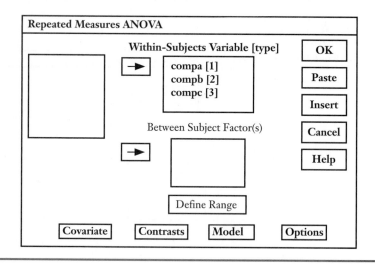

■ FIGURE 15.5

Source of Variation	SS	DF	MS	F Sig of F	
WITHIN+RESIDUAL	72.71	9	8.08		
CONSTANT	57325.67	1	57325.67	7095.93	000

Source of Variation	SS	DF	MS	F Sig of F	
WITHIN+RESIDUAL	38.72	18	2.15		
TYPE	63.46	2	31.73	14.75	000

ual in the bottom half is the error component. You will see that it corresponds to our hand-calculated summary in Table 15.14.

CHAPTER SUMMARY

1. Examines the analysis of variance for subjects who were not assigned randomly; that is, not independent (correlated) groups.
2. Subjects or groups are either matched or used in a repeated measures situation.
3. Demonstrates a one-way ANOVA with subjects matched across treatment conditions. When this occurs a significant difference may be masked by the correlation between treatment conditions and subjects.
4. Partitioning out the contribution of subjects or (correlation) blocks is another systematic source of variance.
5. With a high correlation between subjects and conditions, the amount of systematic variance removed from unaccounted for, or error, variance can be substantial.
6. Presents a summary of the types of ANOVAs covered in chapters 13, and 14: completely randomized design, the randomized block design, the randomized factorial design, the mixed factorial design, and the within-subjects design.
7. The mixed factorial design contains both independent and correlated groups.

STUDY SUGGESTIONS

1. Do two-way analysis of variance of the two sets of fictitious data from Table 15.6. Use the text as an aid. Interpret the results. Next, do two-way analysis of

variance for the two sets of Table 15.8; and Table 15.9. Lay out the final analysis of variance tables and compare. Carefully think through how the adjustive corrections have affected the original data.

2. Three sociologists were asked to judge the general effectiveness of the administrative offices of 10 elementary schools in a particular school district. One of their measures was Administrative Flexibility (the higher the score the greater the flexibility). The 10 ratings on this measure of the three sociologists are given below.

	S_1	S_2	S_3
1	9	7	5
2	9	9	6
3	7	5	4
4	6	5	3
5	3	4	2
6	5	6	4
7	5	3	1
8	4	2	1
9	5	4	4
10	7	5	5

a. Do a two-way analysis of variance as described in the chapter.
b. Do the three sociologists agree in their mean ratings? Does one of the sociologists appear to be severe in his ratings?
c. Are there substantial differences among the schools? Which school appears to have the greatest administrative flexibility? Which school has the least flexibility?
   [Answers: (a) F (columns) = 24.44 (.001); F (rows) = 14.89 (.001); (b) no, yes; (c) yes, no, 2, no, 8.]

3. Draw 30 digits, 0 through 9, from a table of random numbers (use Appendix C if you wish, or generate the numbers on a computer, microcomputer, or programmable calculator). Arbitrarily divide these drawn numbers into three groups of 10 digits each.
   a. Do a two-way analysis of variance. Assume that the numbers in each row are data from one individual.
   b. Now add constants to the three numbers of each row as follows: 20 to the first two rows, 15 to the second two rows, 10 to the third two rows, 5 to the fourth two rows, and 0 to the last two rows. Do a two-way analysis of variance of these "data."
   c. In effect, what have you done by "biasing" the row numbers in this fashion?
   d. Compare the sum-of-squares and the mean squares of (a) and (b). Why are the *total* sums-of-squares and mean squares different? Why are the *between-*

▣ TABLE 15.15 *Conditioning of Urine Secretion Data (Miller and DiCare Study)*[a]

(I) Two Samples Before Conditioning			(II) Sample Rewarded for Urine Increase	
Sample 1	Sample 2		Before	After
.023	.018	1	.023	.030
.014	.015	2	.014	.019
.016	.012	3	.016	.029
.018	.015	4	.018	.030
.007	.030	5	.007	.016
.026	.027	6	.026	.044
.012	.020	7	.012	.026

[a]The measures are millimeters per 100 grams of body weight. The data listed under I are those of two samples of rats assigned randomly to the two groups. The data listed under II are the before and after reward measures of Sample 1 of I. The data of I were analyzed with one-way analysis of variance; the data of II were analyzed with two-way, or repeated measures, analysis of variance.

       columns and the *residual* sums-of-squares and mean squares the same? Why are the *between-rows* sums-of-squares and mean squares different?

    e. Create a research problem out of all this and interpret the "results." Is the example realistic?

4. In an extraordinary series of studies, Miller (1969) has shown that, contrary to traditional belief, it is possible to learn to control autonomic responses like heartbeat, urine secretion, and intestinal contractions. In one of these studies, Miller and DiCara (1968) published all their data on the secretion of urine. Parts of the data are reproduced in Table 15.15. The data contained in II on the right are the increases in urine secretion of seven rats selected randomly from a group of 14 rats before and after "training." The training was instrumental conditioning: whenever a rat secreted urine it was rewarded. These data, then, are repeated measures. If the conditioning "worked," the means should be significantly different. The data of I (on the left) are the *before* measures of two randomly assigned groups (for another experimental purpose). Since these are urine secretion measures *before* the experimental manipulation, the means should not be significantly different. The analyses suggested above were not the analyses done by Miller and DiCara in their study.

    a. Do a one-way analysis of variance of the measures of I (use six decimal places).

    b. Do a two-way, or repeated measures, analysis of variance of the measures of II (use six decimal places). (Note: It might be easier to multiply each of the scores by 1,000 before doing the analyses; that is, move the decimal point three places to the right. Does this affect the F-ratios? If you do this, three decimal places are sufficient.)

    c. Interpret the results.

       [Answers: (a) $F = .73$(n.s.); (b) $F = 43.88$ ($p < 0.01$).]

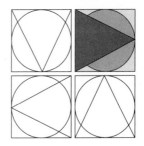

CHAPTER 16

NONPARAMETRIC ANALYSIS OF
VARIANCE AND RELATED STATISTICS

It is, of course, possible to analyze data and to draw inferences about relations among variables without statistics. Sometimes, for example, data are so obvious that a statistical test is not really necessary. If all the scores of an experimental group are greater than (or lesser than) those of a control group, then a statistical test is superfluous. It is also possible to have statistics of a quite different nature than those we have been studying, statistics that use properties of the data other than the strictly quantitative. We can infer an effect of X on Y if the scores of an experimental group are mostly of one kind, say high or low, as contrasted to the scores of a control group. This is because, on the basis of randomization and chance, we expect about the same numbers of different kinds of scores in both experimental and control groups. Similarly, if we arrange all the scores of experimental and control groups in rank order, from high to low, then on the basis of chance alone we can expect the sum or average of the

413

ranks in each group to be about the same. If they are not, if the higher or the lower ranks tend to be clustered in one of the groups, then we infer that "something" other than chance has operated.

Indeed, there are many ways to approach and analyze data other than comparing means and variances. But the basic principle is always the same if we continue to work in a probabilistic world: compare obtained results to chance or theoretical expectations. If, for example, we administer four treatments to participants and expect that one of the four will excel over the others, we can compare the mean of the favored group with the average of the other three groups in an analysis of variance and planned comparisons manner. But suppose our data are highly irregular in one or more ways, and we fear for the validity of the usual tests of significance. What can we do? We can rank order all the observations, for one thing. If none of the four treatments has any more influence than any other, we expect the ranks to disperse themselves among the four groups more or less evenly. If treatment A_2, however, has a preponderance of high (or low) ranks, then we conclude that the usual expectation is upset. Such reasoning is a good part of the basis of so-called nonparametric and distribution-free statistics. There is no single name for the statistics we are discussing. The two most appropriate names are "nonparametric statistics" and "distribution-free statistics." The latter, for instance, says that the statistical tests of significance make no assumptions about the precise form of the sampled population. In this book we will use "nonparametric statistics" to identify those statistical tests of significance not based on so-called classical statistical theory, which is based largely on the properties of means and variances, and the nature of distributions.

In this chapter, we examine certain interesting forms of nonparametric analysis of variance. Other forms of nonparametric statistics will be briefly mentioned. The chapter has two main purposes: to introduce the reader to the ideas behind nonparametric statistics, but especially nonparametric analysis of variance, and to bring out the essential similarity of most inference-aiding methods.

The student should be aware that careful study of nonparametric statistics gives depth of insight into statistics and statistical inference. The insight gained is probably due to the considerable loosening of thinking that seems to occur when working tangential to the usual statistical structure. One sees, so to speak, a broader perspective; one can even invent statistical tests, once the basic ideas are well understood. In short, statistical and inferential ideas are generalized on the basis of relatively simple fundamental ideas.

Parametric and Nonparametric Statistics

One of the more common questions posed to statisticians has been whether or not to use parametric and nonparametric statistical methods when analyzing data (see Allison, Gorman, & Primavera, 1993). A parametric statistical test, the kind of test we have studied to now, depends on a number of assumptions about the population from which the samples used in the test are drawn. The best-known assumption is that the population scores are normally distributed. A nonparametric or distribution-free statistical test depends on no assumptions as to the form of the sample population or the values of the population parameters. For example, nonparametric tests do not depend on the assumption of normality of the population scores. The problem of assumptions is difficult, thorny, and controversial. Some statisticians and researchers consider the violation of assumptions a serious matter that leads to invalidity of parametric statistical tests. Others believe that, in general, violation of the assumptions is not so serious because tests like the F- and t-tests are robust, which roughly means that they operate well even under assumption violations, provided the violations are not gross and multiple. But some have claimed that this view is tantamount to using a shoe as a hammer. Yes, a shoe can be used as a hammer in certain situations, but it really was designed to be worn to protect one's foot. Prokasy (1962) stated years ago that it may be fine to use parametric methods for questionable data in some situations, but the power of this analytical deduction is illusory if it is used to make inferences about psychological attributes. Brady (1988) states that social science data are generally imprecise. With such data, only the most conservative (nonparametric) statistical methods should be used on the data. Toothaker and Newman (1994), however, favor the use of parametric tests for nonnormal data. The argument goes back and forth concerning the use of robust parametric statistics for questionable data. Sawilowsky (1993) discusses the myths behind the argument between the use of parametric and nonparametric methods. The work of Zimmerman (see Zimmerman, 1995a,b; Zimmerman & Zumbo, 1993a,b, 1992) provides an alternative solution to this argument. Nevertheless, let's examine three important assumptions and the evidence for believing parametric methods to be robust. We also discuss a fourth assumption—independence of observations—because of its generality. It applies no matter what kind of statistical test is used. More important, its violation invalidates the results of most statistical tests of significance. Lix, Keselman, and Keselman (1996) present an analysis of all the literature on violations of the assumptions, and recommend which method to use under certain situations.

Assumption of Normality

The best-known assumption behind the use of many parametric statistics is the *assumption of normality*. It is assumed in using the t- and F-tests (and thus the analysis of variance), for example, that the samples with which we work have been drawn from populations that are normally distributed. It is said that if the populations from which samples are drawn are not normal, then statistical tests that depend on the normality assumption are vitiated. As a result, the conclusions drawn from sampled observations and their statistics will be in question. Supposedly, when in doubt about the normality of a population, or when one knows that the population is not normal, one should use a nonparametric test that does not make the normality assumption. Some teachers urge students of education and psychology to use only nonparametric tests on the questionable ground that most educational and psychological populations are not normal. But the issue is not that prosaic.

Homogeneity of Variance

The next most important assumption is that of *homogeneity of variance*. It is assumed, in analysis of variance, that variances within the groups are statistically the same. That is, variances are assumed to be homogeneous from group to group, within the bounds of random variation. If this is not true, the *F*-test is vitiated. There is good reason for this statement. We saw earlier that the within-groups variance was an average of the variances within the two, three, or more groups of measures. If the variances differ widely, then such averaging is questionable. The effect of widely differing variances is to inflate the within-groups variance. Consequently, an *F*-test may be not significant, when in reality there are significant differences between the means (Type II error).

Both of these assumptions have been examined rather thoroughly by empirical methods. Artificial populations have been set up, samples drawn from them, and *t*- and *F*-tests performed. The evidence to date is that the importance of normality and homogeneity is overrated, a view shared by the first author, but not necessarily by the second author. The paper by Zimmerman and Zumbo (1993b) shows situations where nonparametric methods fare better than parametric methods when certain assumptions were not met, and vice versa. If the populations are not too far off from normality, one could use parametric methods instead of nonparametric ones without too much concern. The reason for this is that parametric tests are almost always more powerful than nonparametric tests. (The power of a statistical test is the probability that the null hypothesis will be rejected when it is actually false.) There is one situation, or rather, combination of situations, that may be dangerous. Boneau (1960) found that when there was heterogeneity of variance and differences in the sample sizes of experimental groups, significance tests were adversely affected. Also, Zimmerman (1995b) has pointed out that outliers have a greater influence on parametric tests such as the *t*-test and *F*-test than nonparametric tests.

Continuity and Equal Intervals of Measures

A third assumption is that the measures to be analyzed are continuous measures with equal intervals. As we shall see in a later chapter, this assumption is behind the arithmetic operations of adding, subtracting, multiplying, and dividing. Parametric tests like the *F*- and *t*-tests depend on this assumption of course, but many nonparametric tests do not. This assumption's importance has also been overrated. Anderson (1972) has effectively disposed of it, and Lord (1972) has lampooned it in a well-known article on football numbers.

Despite these conclusions, one is well advised to bear these assumptions in mind. It is not wise to use statistical procedures—or, for that matter, any kind of research procedures—without due respect for the assumptions behind the procedures. If they are seriously violated, the conclusions drawn from research data may be in error. To the reader who has been alarmed by some statistics texts, the best advice probably is: Use parametric statistics, as well as the analysis of variance, routinely, but keep a sharp eye on data for gross departures from normality, homogeneity of variance, and equality of intervals. Be aware of measurement problems and their relation to statistical tests, and be familiar with the basic nonparametric statistics so that they can be used when necessary. Also bear in mind that nonparametric tests are often quick and easy to use and are excellent for preliminary, if not always definitive, tests.

Independence of Observations

Another assumption that is important in both measurement and statistics is that of independence of observations—also called statistical independence. We have already studied statistical independence in Chapter 7, where we examined independence, mutual exclusiveness, and exhaustiveness of events and their probabilities. (The reader is urged to review that section of Chapter 7.) We reexamine independence here, however, in the context of statistics because of the special importance of the principle involved. The independence assumption applies on both parametric and nonparametric statistics. That is, one cannot escape its implications by using a different statistical approach that does not involve the assumption.

The formal definition of statistical independence is: If two events, A_1 and A_2, are statistically independent, the probability of their intersection is: $p(A_1 \cap A_2) = p(A_1) \cup p(A_2)$. If, for example, a student takes a test of 10 items, the probability of getting any item to connect by chance (guessing) is 1/2. If the items and the responses to them are independent, then the probability of getting, say, items two, three, and seven to connect by chance is: $1/2 \times 1/2 \times 1/2 = .125$. And similarly for all 10 items: 0.001.

It is assumed in research that observations are independent, that making one observation does not influence the making of another observation. Example: If we are observing the cooperative behavior of children, and note that Anna seems to very cooperative, then we are likely to violate the independence assumption because we will *expect* her future behavior to be cooperative. If, indeed, the expectation operates, then our observations are not independent.

Statistical tests assume independence of the observations that yield the numbers that go into the statistical calculations. If the observations are not independent, arithmetic operations and statistical tests are vitiated. For example, if item 3 in the 10-item test really contained the correct answer to item 9, then the responses to the two items will not be independent. The probability of getting all 10 items correct by chance is altered. Instead of .001, the probability is some larger figure. The calculation of means and other statistics will be contaminated. Violation of this assumption seems to be fairly common, probably because it is easy to do.

In Chapter 7 we encountered an interesting and subtle example of violation of the assumption when we reproduced a table (Table 7.3) whose entries were aggressive acts rather than the numbers of animals who acted aggressively. Let's say we have a crossbreak tabulation of frequencies and calculate χ^2 to determine whether the cell entries depart significantly from chance expectation. The total N must be the total number of units in the sample. The units are individuals or some sort of aggregate (like groups), who have been independently observed. The Ns of statistical formulas assume that sample sizes are the numbers of units of the calculation, each unit being independently observed.

If, for example, one has a sample of 16 participants, then $N = 16$. Suppose one had observed varying acts of some of the participants and entered the frequencies of occurrence of these acts. Suppose, further, that a total of 54 such acts were observed and 54 was used as N. This would be a gross violation of the independence of observations assumption. In short, the entries in frequency tables must be the numbers of independent observations. One cannot count several occurrences of a kind of event from one person. If N is the number of persons, then it cannot become the number of occurrences of events of the persons. This is a subtle and dangerous point. The statistical analyses of a number of published studies suffer from violation of this principle. We have even seen a factorial analysis of variance table in which the tabled entries were numbers of occurrences of certain events and not the true units of analysis—the individuals of the sample. The difficulty is not so much that violation of independence is immoral; it is a research delinquency because it can lead to quite erroneous conclusions about the relation among variables.

Nonparametric Analysis of Variance

The nonparametric analysis of variance methods studied here, like so many other nonparametric methods, depend on ranking. We study basic forms: one-way and two-way analysis, or repeated measures analysis.

One-Way Analysis of Variance: The Kruskal–Wallis Test

An investigator interested in the differences in conservatism of three boards of education is unable to administer a measure of conservatism to the board members. The investigator therefore has an expert judge rank order all the members of the three boards on the basis of private discussions with them. The three boards have six, six, and five members, respectively. The ranks of all the board members are given in Table 16.1.

If there are no differences in conservatism between the three boards, then the ranks should be distributed randomly in the three columns; then the sums of the ranks (or their means) in the three columns should be approximately equal. On the other hand, if there are differences in conservatism between the three groups, then the ranks in one column should be higher than the ranks in another column—with a consequent higher sum or mean of ranks.

Kruskal and Wallis (1952) give a formula for assessing the significance of these differences. This formula and alternatives can be found in a number of statistics textbooks (see Comrey & Lee, 1995; Hays, 1994).

$$H = \frac{12}{N(N + 1)}\sum\frac{R_j^2}{n_j} - 3(N + 1) \qquad (16.1)$$

▣ **TABLE 16.1** *Ranks of 17 Members of Three Boards of Education on Judged Conservatism*

	Boards		
	I	**II**	**III**
	12	11	4
	14	16	3
	10	5	8
	17	7	1
	15	6	9
	13	2	
ΣRanks	81	47	25
M	13.5	7.83	5.00
	0		

where N equals total number of ranks; n_j equals number of ranks in group j; and R_j equals sum of the ranks in group j. Applying Equation 16.1 to the ranks of Table 16.1, we first calculate $\Sigma R_j^2/n_j$

$$\Sigma \frac{R_j^2}{n_j} = \frac{(81)^2}{6} + \frac{(47)^2}{6} + \frac{(25)^2}{5} = 1093.5 + 368.17 + 125.0 = 1586.67$$

Substituting in Equation 16.1, we find:

$$H = \frac{12}{17(17 + 1)} \cdot 1586.67 - 54 = 62.22 - 54 = 8.22$$

H is approximately distributed as χ^2. The degrees of freedom are $k - 1$, where k is the number of columns or groups, or $3 - 1 = 2$. Checking the χ^2 table, we find this to be significant at the .02 level. Thus the ranks are not random.

The Kruskal and Wallis method is analogous to one-way analysis of variance. It is simple and effective. Measurement is sometimes such that it is doubtful whether parametric analysis is legitimate. Of course, doubtful measures can also be transformed. The essence of the idea of transformations is to alter measures that are not respectable (these measures may lack normality or other reasons). They are transformed to respectability via a linear function of the sort $y = f(x)$, where y is a transformed score, x the original score, and f is some operation ("the square root of") on x (see Zimmerman, 1995a; Draper & Smith, 1981; Box, Hunter, & Hunter, 1978).

But in many cases it is easily possible to rank order the scores and do the analysis on the ranks. There are also research situations in which the only form of measurement possible is rank order, or ordinal measurement. The Kruskal and Wallis test is most useful in such situations. But it is also useful when data are irregular but amenable to ranking.

Two-Way Analysis of Variance: The Friedman Test

In situations in which participants are matched or the same participants are observed more than once, a form of rank-order analysis of variance, first devised by Friedman (1937), can be used. An ordinary two-way analysis of variance of the ranks can also be used.

An educational researcher, concerned with the relation between Role and Perception of Teaching Competence, asked groups of professors to rate each other on an instructor evaluation rating instrument. He also asked administrators and students to rate the same professors. Since the numbers of professors ("peers"), administrators, and students differed, he averaged the ratings of the members of each rating group. In effect, the hypothesis stated that the three groups of raters would differ significantly in their ratings. The researcher also wanted to know whether

▣ **TABLE 16.2** *Hypothetical Means of Ratings of Professors by Peers, Administrators, and Students, with Ranks of the Three Groups of Raters of the Mean Ratings*[a]

Professors	Peers		Administrators		Students	
A	28	(3)	19	(1)	22	(2)
B	22	(1)	23	(2)	36	(3)
C	26	(2)	24	(1)	29	(3)
D	44	(2)	34	(1)	48	(3)
E	35	(1)	39	(2)	40	(3)
F	40	(2)	38	(1)	45	(3)
ΣRanks	11		8		17	

[a]The numbers in the table are composite ratings. The numbers in parentheses are ranks: the higher the number (or rank), the greater the perceived competence. Note: The ratings of each *row* are ranked, reflecting the differences among the three groups of each professor.

there were significant differences among the professors. The data of one part of the study are given in Table 16.2.

There are a number of ways these data can be analyzed. First, of course, ordinary two-way analysis of variance can be used. If the numbers being analyzed seem to conform reasonably well to the assumptions discussed earlier, this would be the best analysis. In the analysis of variance, the F-ratio for columns (between raters) is 4.70, significant at the 0.05 level; and the F-ratio for rows is 12.72, significant at the 0.01 level. The hypothesis of the investigator is supported. This is indicated by the significant differences between the means of the three groups. The professors, too, differ significantly.

Now assume that the investigator is disturbed by the type of data collected and decides to use nonparametric analysis of variance. Clearly one should not use the Kruskal–Wallis method. The investigator decides to use the Friedman method, rank ordering the data by *rows*. In so doing he tests the differences between the columns. Obviously, if two or more raters are given the same ranking system, say 1, 2, 3, 4, 5, it is apparent that the sums and means of the ranks of the different raters will always be the same. In this analysis, then, the concentration is on the differences between the raters. One would ignore the differences between the professors (as rated). In what follows, then, we focus on the ranks in the parentheses to the right of each composite rating. We also focus on the sums of the ranks at the bottom of the table.

The formula given by Friedman is:

$$\chi_r^2 = \frac{12}{kn(n + 1)} \Sigma R_j^2 - 3k(n + 1) \tag{16.2}$$

where $\chi^2 = \chi^2$, ranks; k equals number of rankings; n equals number of objects being ranked; ΣR_j equals sum of the ranks in column (group) j; and ΣR_j^2 equals sum of the squared sums. First calculate ΣR_j^2

$$\Sigma R_j^2 = 11^2 + 8^2 + 17^2 = 474$$

Now determine k and n. The number of rankings is k, or the number of times that the rank-order system, whatever it is, is used. Here $k = 6$. The number of objects being ranked, n or the number of ranks, is 3. (Actually, the raters are not being ranked: 3 is the number of ranks in the rank-order system being used.) Now calculate χ_r^2.

$$\chi_r^2 = \frac{12}{(6)(3)(4)} \cdot 474 - (3)(6)(4) = 79 - 72 = 7$$

This value is checked against a χ^2 table, at $df = n - 1 = 3 - 1 = 2$. The value is significant at the 0.05 level. The reader should be warned that the level of significance is questionable since the n and k were relatively small.

The investigator was also interested in the significance of the differences among the professors as rated. He assigns ranks to the rating composites in columns

回 **TABLE 16.3** *Hypothetical Means of Ratings of Professors by Peers, Administrators, and Students, with Ranks*[a]

Professors	Peers		Administrators		Students		ΣR
A	28	(3)	19	(1)	22	(2)	5
B	22	(1)	23	(2)	36	(3)	6
C	26	(2)	24	(3)	29	(3)	7
D	44	(6)	34	(4)	48	(6)	16
E	35	(4)	39	(6)	40	(4)	14
F	40	(5)	38	(5)	45	(15)	

[a]The numbers in the table are composite ratings. The numbers in parentheses are ranks: the higher the number (or rank), the greater the perceived competence. Note: The ratings of each column are ranked, reflecting the differences among the six professors, as rated by each group.

(in parentheses in Table 16.3). These are the ranks that the rater groups assigned to the six professors. Professors who are rated high should get the higher ranks, which can be determined by adding their ranks across the rows (see ΣR column on the right-hand side of the table). This time $k = 3$ and $n = 6$. We calculate χ^2 again using Equation 16.2:

$$\chi_r^2 = \frac{12}{(3)(6)(7)} \cdot 787 - (3)(3)(7) = 11.95$$

Checking this value in a χ^2 table, at $df = n - 1 = 6 - 1 = 5$, we find it to be significant at the .05 level. The instructors, as rated, seem to be different.

Compare these results to the ordinary analysis of variance results. In the latter, the three groups were found to be significantly different at the .05 level. In the case of the significance of the differences between the professors, the analysis also showed significance. In general, the methods should agree fairly well.

Using another method of analysis of variance based on ranges rather than variances, the results of the Friedman test were confirmed. This method, called the *studentized range* test (see Pearson & Hartley, 1954) is useful. Ranges are good measures of variation for small samples but not for large samples. The principle of the studentized range test is similar to that of the *F*-test in that a within-groups range is used to evaluate the range of the means of the groups. Another useful method, that of Link and Wallace, is described in detail in Mosteller and Bush (1954). Both methods have the advantage that they can be used with one-way and two-way analyses. Still another method, which has the unique virtue of testing an *ordered* hypothesis of the ranks, is the *L*-test by Page (1963).

The Coefficient of Concordance, W

Perhaps using a measure of the association of the ranks provides a more direct-test of the investigator's hypothesis. Kendall (1948) has worked out such a measure, called the coefficient of concordance, W. We are now interested in the degree of agreement or association in the ranks of the columns of Table 16.2. Each rater group has virtually assigned a rank to each professor. If there was no association whatever between two of the rater groups, and a rank-order coefficient of correlation was computed between the ranks, it should be near zero. On the other hand, if there is agreement, the coefficient should be significantly different from zero.

The coefficient of concordance, W, expresses the average agreement, on a scale from .00 to 1.00, among the ranks. There are two ways to define W. The Kendall method will be presented first. According to this method, W can be expressed as the ratio between the *between-groups* (or ranks) sum-of-squares and the *total* sum-of-squares of a complete analysis of variance of the ranks. This ratio, then, is the correlation ratio squared, η^2, of ranked data.

Where there are k rankings of n individual objects, Kendall's coefficient of concordance is defined by

$$W = \frac{12S}{k^2(n^3 - n)} \tag{16.3}$$

S is the sum of the deviations squared of the totals of the n ranks from their mean. S is a between-groups sum-of-squares for ranks. It is like ss_b. (In fact, if we divide S by k, $S \div k$, we obtain the same between-groups sum-of-squares we would obtain in a complete analysis of variance of the ranks.)

$$S = (5^2 + 6^2 + \ldots + 15^2) - (63)^2/6 = 787 - 661.5 = 125.5$$

Since $k = 3$ and $n = 6$,

$$W = \frac{12 \times 125.50}{3^2(6^3 - 6)} = \frac{1506}{9(216 - 6)} = \frac{1506}{1890} = 0.797 = 0.80$$

The relation between the three sets of ranks is substantial. To assess the significance of W, the following formula can be used, provided that $k \geq 8$ and $n \geq 7$ (degrees of freedom are $n - 1$):

$$\chi^2 = k(n - 1)W \tag{16.4}$$

If k and n are small, appropriate tables of S can be used (see Bradley, 1968, pp. 323–325). F-ratios are also possible. One way is to do a two-way analysis of variance using the ranks as scores. Then $\eta^2 = W$, and the F-ratio tests both the statistical significance of η^2 and of W. $W = .80$ is statistically significant at the 0.01 level. The relation is high: evidently there is high agreement of the three groups in their rankings of the professors.

Properties of Nonparametric Methods

A large number of efficacious nonparametric methods are readily available, many or most of which are in Bradley's (1968) book or in Siegel and Castellan (1988). They are usually based on some property of data that can be tested against chance expectation. For example, the odds and evens of coin tossing are a dichotomous property that is conveniently tested with binomial statistics (see Chapter 7). Another data property is range. With small samples, the range is a good index of variability. A quick method of estimating the standard error of the mean, for instance is:

$$SE_{M(e)} = \frac{\text{Largest Observation} - \text{Smallest Observation}}{N}$$

A *t*-test of the difference between two means can be made with the following formula:

$$t_e = \frac{M_1 - M_2}{\frac{1}{2}(R_1 - R_2)}$$

where t_e equals estimated t; R_1 equals range of group 1, and R_2 equals range of Group 2.

Another property of data is what can be labeled *periodicity*. If there are different kinds of events (heads and tails, male and female, religious preference, etc.), and numerical data from different groups are combined and ranked, then by chance there should be no long runs of any particular event, like a long run of females in one experimental group. The runs test is based on this idea.

Still another property of data was discussed in Chapter 11: distribution. The distributions of different samples can be compared with each other or with a "criterion" group (like the normal distribution) for deviations. The Kolmogorov–Smirnov test analyzes goodness-of-fit of the distributions. It is a useful test, especially for small samples.

The most ubiquitous property of data, perhaps, is rank order. Whenever data can be ranked, they can be tested against chance expectation. Many, perhaps most, nonparametric tests are rank-order tests. The Kruskal–Wallis and the Friedman tests are, of course, both based on rank order. Rank-order coefficients of correlation are extremely useful. W is one of these. So are the Spearman rank-order coefficient of correlation and Kendall's tau.

Nonparametric methods are virtually inexhaustible. There seems to be no end to what can be done, given the relatively simple principles involved and the various properties of data that can be exploited: range, periodicity, distribution, and rank order. While means and variances have desirable statistical properties and advantages, we are in no way restricted to them. Medians and ranges, for example, are often appropriate ingredients of statistical tests. Much of the point of this chapter has been a covert repetition of the principle emphasized again and again—perhaps a bit tediously: Assess obtained results against chance expectation. There is no magic to nonparametric methods. No divine benison has been put on them. The same probabilistic principles apply.

Another point made earlier needs repetition and emphasis: Most analytic problems of behavioral research can be adequately handled with parametric methods. The F-test, t-test, and other parametric approaches are robust in the sense that they perform well even when the assumptions behind them are violated—unless, of course, the violations are gross or multiple. Nonparametric methods, then, are highly useful secondary or complementary techniques that can often be valuable in behavioral research. Perhaps most important, they again show the power, flexibility, and wide applicability of the basic precepts of probability and the phenomenon of randomness enunciated in earlier chapters.

Computer Addendum

The Kruskal–Wallis Test on SPSS

To show how to use SPSS to analyze data in the Kruskal–Wallis test, we created data for a fictitious study. In this study, three diet plans were compared on the percentage of weight loss. Table 16.4 shows the layout of the data. Note that for Plan A there were five participants, four participants for Plan B, and three participants for Plan C.

Figure 16.1 shows how the data are entered into the SPSS spreadsheet for analysis. People in Plan A were given a value of "1" on the "plan" variable; Plan B received a "2," and Plan C received a "3." In addition to the data layout, we also present the ensuing menus and screens when the "Statistics" option is selected.

Choose "Nonparametric Tests" from the first menu. This produces another menu. From this second menu select "K Independent Samples." After selecting "K Independent Samples" SPSS presents you with a screen where you define your variables (shown in Figure 16.2). This screen asks you to specify which variable is the dependent variable ("Test Variable List") and which one is the independent variable

▣ **TABLE 16.4** *Data from a Fictitious Study Comparing Diet Plans*

Plan A	23	41	42	36	30
Plan B	20	24	25	26	
Plan C	40	42	37		

▣ **FIGURE 16.1** *Related Data from Table 16.4*

	plan	weight				
1	1	23				
2	1	41				
3	1	42				
4	1	36				
5	1	30				
6	2	20				
7	2	24				
8	2	25				
9	2	26				
10	3	40				
11	3	42				
12	3	37				

File Edit View Data Transform Statistics Graphs Utilities Windows Help

Summarize ►
Compare Means ►
ANOVA Models ►
Correlate ►
Regression ►
Log-linear ►
Classify ►
Data Reduction ►
Scale ►
Nonparametric Tests ►

Chi-Square
Binomial
Runs
1 Sample K-S
2 independent samples
k independent sample
2 related samples
k related samples

▣ **FIGURE 1.2** *SPSS Panel for Variable Specification*

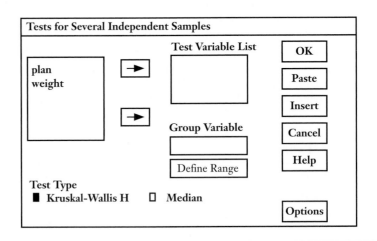

Tests for Several Independent Samples

plan
weight

Test Variable List

Group Variable

Define Range

Test Type
■ **Kruskal-Wallis H**   ☐ Median

OK

Paste

Insert

Cancel

Help

Options

FIGURE 16.3 *Moving the Variables "Weight" and "Plan" into Appropriate Boxes*

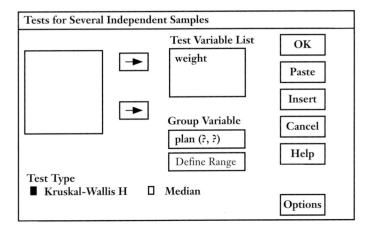

("Group Variable"). Highlight the variable "weight" (see Figure 16.3) and click the button associated with the "Test Variable List" box. Next, highlight the variable labeled "plan" and click the arrow button associated with the "Group Variable" box. You will need to define the range of values for the independent variable. Figure 16.3

FIGURE 16.4 *SPSS Screen to Define the Range of the Group Variable*

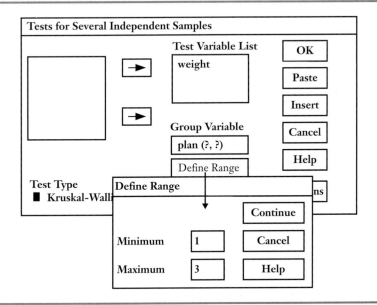

▣ **FIGURE 16.5** *SPSS Screen Before Requesting Analysis*

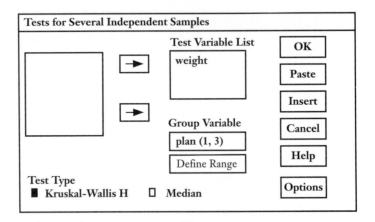

shows the resulting screen after you have specified the variables. Note that the independent variable "plan" has two question marks encased by parentheses. This says you have to tell SPSS the range of values you have assigned to levels of the independent variable.

▣ **FIGURE 16.6** *SPSS Output of Kruskal-Wallis Test*

```
- - - - Kruskal–Wallis One-Way ANOVA

WEIGHT by PLAN

Mean Rank Cases

   7.30    5  PLAN = 1
   3.25    4  PLAN = 2
   9.50    3  PLAN = 3
          12  Total

                 Corrected for ties
```

Chi-Square	D.F.	Significance	Chi-Square	D.F.	Significance
5.5731	2	.0616	5.5926	2	.0610

■ **FIGURE 16.7** *SPSS Spreadsheet for Data Given in Table 16.2*

	peers	admin	student	
				File Edit View Data Transform Statistics Graphs Utilities Windows Help
1	28	19	22	Summarize ▶
2	22	23	36	Compare Means ▶
3	26	24	29	ANOVA Models ▶ Correlate ▶
4	44	34	48	Regression ▶ Log-linear ▶
5	35	39	40	Classify ▶ Data Reduction ▶
6	40	38	45	Scale ▶ Nonparametric Tests ▶

File Edit View Data Transform Statistics Graphs Utilities Windows Help

	peers	admin	student
1	28	19	22
2	22	23	36
3	26	24	29
4	44	34	48
5	35	39	40
6	40	38	45

Summarize ▶
Compare Means ▶
ANOVA Models ▶
Correlate ▶
Regression ▶
Log-linear ▶
Classify ▶
Data Reduction ▶
Scale ▶
Nonparametric Tests ▶

Chi-Square
Binomial
Runs
1 Sample K-S
2 independent samples
k independent sample
2 related samples
k related samples

You have three independent groups (i.e., diet plans) and have numbered them "1, 2, and 3." When you click the "Define Range" button, you get another screen that allows you to define the range of discrete values assigned to your groups or levels of the independent variable (shown in Figure 16.4). Enter a "1" for the minimum value and a "3" for the maximum value. After you are finished, click the "OK" button. SPSS will now show the previous screen with the "plan" variable defined (shown in Figure 16.5). After you make sure that the "Kruskal–Wallis H" option is selected (the bullet is darkened), click the "OK" button and SPSS will perform the statistical analysis. An abbreviated version of the output is given in Figure 16.6.

■ **FIGURE 16.8** *SSPS Screen for Specifying Variables for Analysis*

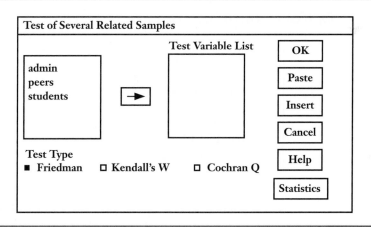

Test of Several Related Samples

Test Variable List

admin
peers
students

➡

OK
Paste
Insert
Cancel
Help
Statistics

Test Type
■ Friedman ☐ Kendall's W ☐ Cochran Q

FIGURE 16.9 *Resulting SPSS Screen Prior to Analysis*

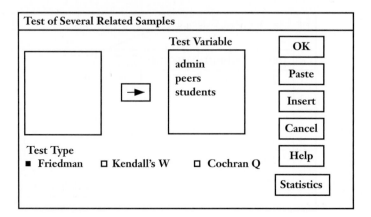

The Friedman Test on SPSS

The data from Table 16.2 was used to demonstrate the use of SPSS for the Friedman Test of *k*-related samples. Figure 16.7 shows the SPSS spreadsheet layout of the data. Figure 16.7 also shows the "Statistics" menu. From this menu, select "Nonparametric Tests," which leads to another menu. From this menu, choose "k related samples." When this is chosen, SPSS presents a new screen where you define the variables. Under "Test Type," choose "Friedman" test by clicking its bullet (shown in Figure 16.8). Next, highlight the three variables: "admin," "peers," "students" and move them to the "Test Variable" box by clicking the right arrow button. The result of this operation is shown in Figure 16.9. When you click the "OK" button, SPSS will perform the Friedman Test on the data. An edited version of the SPSS output is given in Figure 16.10.

FIGURE 16.10 *SPSS Output for Friedman Test*

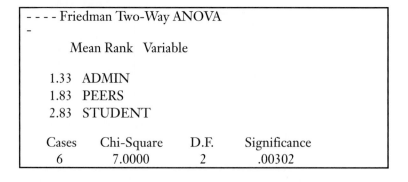

CHAPTER SUMMARY

1. Chapter considers analysis of variance for data that come from a questionable or unknown population.
2. Discusses the differences between parametric methods (e.g., t-test, F-test) and nonparametric methods (Wilcoxon, Mann–Whitney, Kruskal–Wallis)
3. There are four important assumptions which some feel must be met in order to use parametric methods:
   a. Assumption of normality
   b. Homogeneity of variance
   c. Continuity and equal intervals of measures
   d. Independence of observations
3. Research results on what happens in using parametric methods when these assumptions are violated have been equivocal.
4. There is still controversy as to which method is generally superior.
5. Coverage of nonparametric analysis of variance methods covers:
   a. Kruskal–Wallis nonparametric one-way ANOVA
   b. Friedman Test for two-way ANOVA
   c. Kendall's coefficient of concordance

STUDY SUGGESTIONS

1. A teacher interested in studying the effect of workbooks decides to conduct a small experiment with her class. She divides the class randomly into three groups of seven pupils each, calling these groups, A_1, A_2, and A_3. A_1 was taught without any workbooks, A_2 was taught with the occasional use of workbooks at the teacher's direction, and A_3 was taught with heavy dependence on workbooks. At the end of four months, the teacher tested the children in the subject matter. The scores she obtained were in percentage form, and she thought that it might be questionable to use parametric analysis of variance. She did not know that when scores are in percentage form, they can easily be transformed to scores amenable to parametric analysis. The appropriate transformation is called the *arc-sine* transformation. So she used the Kruskal–Wallis method. The data are as follows:

A_1	A_2	A_3
55	82	09
32	24	35
74	91	25
09	36	36
48	86	20
61	80	07
12	65	36

Convert the percentages into ranks (from 1 through 21) and calculate H. Interpret. (To be significant, H must be 5.99 or greater for the 0.05 level, and 9.21 for the 0.01 level. This is at $k - 1 = 2$ degrees of freedom, the χ^2 table.)

Note: Two cases of tied percentages and consequently tied ranks occur in these data. When ties occur, simply take the median (or mean) of the ties. For example, there are three 36s in the above table. The median (or mean) of the tenth, eleventh, and twelfth ranks, is 11. All three 36s, then, will be assigned the rank of 11. The next higher rank must then be 13, since 10, 11, and 12 have been "used up." Similarly there are two 09s, which occur at the second and third ranks. The median of 2 and 3 is 2.5. Both 09s are assigned 2.5 and the next higher rank, of course, is 4.)

[Answer: $H = 7.86$ (0.05).]

2. A social psychological researcher studied the relation between the discussion behavior of members of boards of education and their decisions. In this research, a particularly complex facet of discussion behavior, say Antagonistic Behavior, was to be measured. She wondered if this behavior could be reliably measured. She trained three observers and had them rank order the antagonistic behavior of the members of one board of education during a two-hour session. The ranks of the three observers are given below (high ranks show high antagonism):

Board Members	Observers O_1	O_2	O_3
1	3	2	2
2	2	4	1
3	6	6	7
4	1	1	3
5	7	7	6
6	4	3	5
7	5	5	4

a. What is the degree of agreement or concordance among the three observers (use W)?

b. Is W statistically significant? (Calculate χ^2 using Equation 16.4. If $\chi^2 = 12.59$, $df = 6$, it is significant at 0.05.)

c. Can the social psychologist say that she is reliably measuring "Antagonism" or "Antagonistic Behavior"?

[Answers: (a) $W = .86$; $\chi^2 = 15.43$ ($p < .05$); (b) Yes. (c) Yes.]

3. Using the "data" of Study Suggestion 2 above, do a one-way analysis of variance of the board members' Antagonism scores.

    a. What is the *F*-ratio? Is it statistically significant?

    b. Calculate η^2. (Recall that $\eta^2 = ss_b/ss_t$.) Compare to *W* calculated in Study Suggestion 2 above.

    c. Do the board of education members differ in antagonistic behavior? [Answers: (a) $F = 14.00$ ($p < .01$); (b) $\eta^2 = W = .86$; (c) Yes.]

4. Suppose you obtained the following scores on a complexity measure: 27, 21, 14, 12, 6. Do a rough and quick estimate of the standard error of the mean (see text).

    [Answer: $(27 - 6)/5 = 4.20$.]

5. Imagine that you are an analytic specialist and have been asked to invent and produce a method for assessing the statistical significance of runs. A run is a group of values or identifications connected with one population or sample. Suppose that you have a sample of men and women and are measuring some attribute but have no interest in Sex as a variable. Rank order the sample according to the sizes of the attribute scores. If Sex has no relation to the attribute, then when you rank-order the cases, the men and women should be mixed as though you had placed them throughout the sample at random. In this case, there would be many runs, for example, *MM, F, M, FF, M, F, MM, FF, M, F,* and thus little or no relation between Sex and the attribute. (Remember: the cases were ranked by the attribute.) There are 10 runs; they are italicized. This is relatively many runs in a sample of 15 cases. If, on the other hand, there were relatively few runs, for example: *MMMM, F, MM, F, M, FFFFFF,* or six runs, there could well be a relation between the attribute and Sex.

    a. How would you go about creating a test to assess the statistical significance of numbers of runs in a sample of *n* cases? (Hint: Think of using a random number generator on a computer or a table of random numbers. Don't try to find a formula. Just use brute force!)

    b. Make up two cases of samples of 20 each containing different numbers of runs and use your test to assess the significance of numbers of runs.

    c. Outline the basic principles of what you have done so that someone who does not know or understand statistics will understand you. Is your test a nonparametric test? Explain.

[Special note: This is probably a difficult exercise, but one well worth working at and discussing with others, especially in class.]

PART SIX
DESIGNS OF RESEARCH

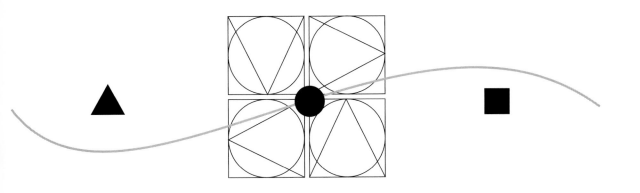

435

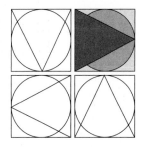

CHAPTER 17

ETHICAL CONSIDERATIONS IN CONDUCTING BEHAVIORAL SCIENCE RESEARCH

Fiction and Reality

In previous chapters we discussed science and the variables involved in social and behavioral sciences. We have also introduced some of the basic statistical methods used to analyze the data gathered from such research studies. In the chapters following this one, we will be discussing the actual conduct of the research process. Before doing this, we must present a very important topic. This topic involves the issue of research ethics. Some books have placed this topic in the latter part of the book after the research plan and designs have been discussed. We feel that this topic should be presented earlier. The student of research needs this information in order to design an ethically sound study using the methods given in the chapters that follow. It would be ideal if the researcher read this chapter, then read the chapters on research design and then return to reread the points made in this chapter.

What is "research ethics"? What is "research"? These two terms are difficult to define. Shrader-Frechette (1994) provides a definition by contrasting "research" from "practice." As we saw in an earlier chapter, research is an activity done to test theories, make inferences, and add or update information on a base of knowledge. Professional practice does not usually involve testing theories or hypotheses but rather enhances the welfare of clients using actions and information that have been demonstrated to be successful. Some of these actions were established through earlier scientific research. Even though both "research" and "practice" have ethics, the ethics involved with the research process are directed toward the individuals who do research and their conduct of the research process. Shrader-Frechette states that research ethics specifies the behavior researchers ought to show during the *entire* process of their investigation. Keith-Spiegel and Koocher (1985) discuss the ethics of psychological practice. Dawes (1994) gives a very critical view of the practice of psychology and psychotherapy. Part of Dawes's discussion concerns ethics of practice.

The discussion, emphasis, and practice of research ethics are relatively recent events. Before the twentieth century, those scientists who were caught experimenting on people without proper consent were punished. However, there were instances in history where the violations of research ethics yielded fruitful results. When one thinks about the ethics of doing research on humans or animals one cannot avoid mixed feelings. In examining history, there were those brave individuals like Edward Jenner who injected a child with a weaker form of the smallpox virus and in doing so developed a vaccine for smallpox. History has it that Edward Jenner did not get permission from anyone before doing this. Or consider Dr. Barry Marshall who, in order to show that peptic ulcers were caused by bacteria and not acids, swallowed the culture of bacteria himself and then successfully treated himself with doses of antibiotic drugs. Yet there are also documented cases of tragic consequences for researchers who failed to follow proper ethical principles of research, and those who committed scientific fraud. Some of these instances are noted and discussed in Shrader-Frechette (1994). This is an excellent book worth reading; we also recommend Miller and Hersen (1992) and Erwin, Gendin, and Kleiman (1994). Evidence of known or suspected fraud can be traced to research done in ancient Greece.

In conducting research, the sensitive researcher is often confronted with ethical dilemmas. Prior to the 1960s, researchers from all fields of science were left to their own consciences in terms of research ethics. Scholarly publications on the appropriate behavior of scientists provided some guidance, but none or few of the guidelines were mandated. The fictional story of Martin Arrowsmith, the protagonist in Sinclair Lewis's novel *Arrowsmith*, exemplifies an ethical dilemma. In this novel, Dr. Martin Arrowsmith in a laboratory study discovers by accident a principle that is effective in destroying bacteria. Arrowsmith calls it a "phage." When the bubonic plague breaks out in a third world country, Arrowsmith is sent to that country to help the afflicted and to test his phage. Arrowsmith had been taught that the true effectiveness of a phage can be determined by giving it to only half of the infected population. The other half would be given a placebo or no treatment at all. However, Arrowsmith upon seeing the alarming death rate (including the deaths of his wife and close friend) decides to give the phage to the entire population. If he followed his experimental plan and his phage was truly effective, the people receiving the phage would survive and those receiving the placebo would not. Arrowsmith's conscience would not allow him to deceive half of the population and let them die in the name of scientific research. He administered the phage to everyone. The plague did end after the natives were inoculated, but Arrowsmith never really knew whether or not his phage was effective. Although this is fiction, actual research scientists are at times faced with similar dilemmas.

A Beginning?

It was studies done in the 1960s and 1970s, where there was evidence of research fraud and deception of research participants, that led to a demand for specific mandated rules for the conduct of research. In 1974, the United States Congress called for the creation of institutional review boards. The purpose of these boards was to review the ethical conduct of those research studies that had received federal research grants. Later, in the 1980s, legislation passed which required federally funded research involving humans and animals to be reviewed for both ethical acceptability and research design. By the 1980s many of the major universities in the United States had guidelines for dealing with misconduct in research. Other countries also began to put forth guidelines and rules. The governments of Sweden and the Netherlands required that independent review committees evaluate all biomedical studies. Shrader-Frechette (1994) describes two broad categories in terms of ethical problems in scientific research: (1) processes, and (2) products. The research process is deemed harmful if participants do not give informed consent to the procedures used on them. The research process is also considered harmful if the participants are deceived or recruited using deceptive methods. The research product is harmful if the conduct of that research results in a harmful environment for anyone who comes into contact with it. Shrader-Frechette refers to this as "downwinders." The case of radiation poisoning due to scientific tests of nuclear weapons is an example of a research product that is harmful. Shrader-Frechette briefly describes this research and the consequences. Saffer and Kelly (1983) give a more complete account in an informative book titled *Countdown Zero*. Saffer and Kelly describe how the atmospheric tests of the atomic bomb in the desert of Nevada in the late 1940s carried over into other parts of the desert. The crew, staff, and actors in the movie *The Conqueror* were all exposed to radioactive sand during the filming of the movie in the desert. All of these people developed cancer and later died from cancer-related illnesses. Some of the well-known actors and actresses included John Wayne, Susan Hayward, and Dick Powell. Saffer and Kelly also describes how the United States military's research on how to fight a nuclear war in the 1950s led to the exposure of many military personnel to radiation fallout. Saffer himself was one of the soldiers who participated in such studies. Several years after leaving the service he noticed that fellow soldiers developed cancer.

One of the most infamous cases on the unethical use of deception was the *Tuskegee Study* (see Brandt, 1978). In 1932, the U.S. Public Health Service did an experiment on 399 poor, semiliterate, African American males who had contracted syphilis. One purpose of this study was to examine the effects of syphilis on untreated individuals. In order to get afflicted African American males to participate in the study, they were told they were being treated when in fact they were not. Symptoms of syphilis were measured and recorded periodically. Autopsies were performed on each individual after each death. It took 40 years for the public to become aware of this research tragedy. At the time of its disclosure, the study was still in progress. The research was clearly unethical; one reason was because treatment was still being withheld from the survivors as late as 1972. They could have been effectively treated with penicillin that became available in the 1940s. One of the major outcries of unethical research behavior has been focused on the use of deception.

Deception is still used in some research studies today. However, the research is critically evaluated before it can be done. All major universities in the United States have a research ethics and human usage committee that screens and evaluates studies for potential deceptions and harmful effects. It is their task to make sure no harm is inflicted on any of the participants.

One of the most noted studies in psychology that used deception was conducted by social psychologist Stanley Milgram, who recruited participants in a "learning" experiment (see Milgram, 1963). Those who volunteered were told that some would be teachers and the others would be learners. The teachers were in charge of teaching lists of words to the learners. The teachers were told to administer increasingly painful shocks each time the learners made an error. The real purpose of the experiment, however, was not to study learning but to study obedience to authority. Milgram was particularly interested in whether there was any truth to the claims of Nazi war criminals who said they did the atrocious acts because they were "ordered" to do so by their superiors. Unknown to the participants, all participants served as "teachers." That is, all participants were told that they were teachers. None of the participants served as "learners." The learners were confederates of the experimenter. They pretended to be participants who were chosen randomly to serve as learners. Furthermore, there were actually no shocks administered at any time. The teachers were tricked into believing that the learners' cries of pain and requests for assistance was real. When instructed to increase the severity of the shocks, some of the participants hesitated. However, when they were instructed by the experimenter to continue, they did so. They even continued "shocking" the learners beyond the point where the learners "begged" to be released from the experiment. The results were, to Milgram as well to others, almost beyond belief. A great many subjects (the "teachers") unhesitatingly obeyed the experimenter's "Please continue" or "You have no choice, you must go on" and continued to increase the level of the shocks, no matter how much the learner pleaded with the "teacher" to stop. What particularly surprised Milgram was that no one ever walked out of the laboratory in disgust or protest. This remarkable obedience was seen time and time again in several universities where the experiment was repeated. Public anger over this experiment centered on the deception that might have caused psychological discomfort and harm to the participants. More than that, some people overgeneralized and thought that many such psychological experiments were being conducted.

For years following this now-famous study, critics of his study repeatedly dogged Milgram. There was very little publicity surrounding the fact that Milgram did a number of follow-up studies on the participants and found that there were no negative effects. In fact, at the conclusion of each experimental session, the participants were debriefed and introduced to the "learner" to show that no dangerous electrical shocks were administered.

Another sensitive area has been one directed at fraud. This includes situations where the researcher altered data from a research study in order to show that a certain hypothesis or theory was true. Other cases of fraud involved the reporting of research findings for research studies that never took place. History shows that there have been a number of prominent individuals who have been involved in fraud (see Erwin, Gendin, & Kleiman, 1994). One of the more sensational cases of alleged fraud comes from psychology. The person involved was Sir Cyril Burt, a prominent British psychologist who received knighthood for his work on statistics and the heritability of intelligence. His work was marked by the use of identical twins whose genetic composition was the most alike. Burt supposedly demonstrated that there was a strong genetic component to intelligence by examining the intelligence of twins who were raised together versus those who were separated at birth and hence were reared apart. The intention was to determine how much influence the environment or heredity had on intelligence. In the mid 1970s after the death of Burt, Leon Kamin (1974) reported that a number of the correlations that Burt reported were identical to the third decimal place. By chance alone this was highly improbable. Later it was discovered that a few of Burt's co-authors on research articles published around the time of the Second World War could not be found. Many of Burt's critics felt that Burt created these co-authors in order to mislead the scientific community. Even Leslie Hearnshaw, who was commissioned by Burt's family to write a biography of Burt, claimed to have found evidence of fraud. This particular view of Burt's fraud is detailed in Gould (1981). However, Jensen (1992) presents a different sociohistorical view of Burt. Jensen states that the charges against Burt were never adequately proved. Jensen also gives information concerning Burt that was never mentioned in Gould's book or in other publications that were critical of Burt.

Such instances as Tuskegee, Milgram, and Burt brought about the creation of laws and regulations to restrict or stop unethical research behavior in the medical, behavioral, and social sciences. Professional organizations, such as the American Psychological Association and the American Physiological Society developed commissions to investigate and recommend action on reported cases of unethical research behavior. However, the reported incidence of unethical research by scientists has been minimal. Among the cases that have received the most negative publicity in behavioral science research involved Steven Breuning of the University of Pittsburgh. Breuning was convicted in 1988 of fabricating scientific data about drug tests (Ritalin and Dexedrine) on hyperactive children. Breuning's falsified results were widely cited and influenced several states to change their regulations on the treatment of these children. The Breuning case illustrates how dangerous the fraudulent behavior of a scientist can be.

In the physical sciences and medicine, Maurice Buchbinder, a cardiologist, was broached for research problems associated with his testing of the Rotablator. This device is a coronary vessel-cleaning device. Investigation revealed that the device was manufactured by a company in which Buchbinder had millions of dollars invested in stock. Among his ethical violations were (1) the failure to conduct follow-up examinations on about 280 patients, (2) the improper use of the device on patients with severe heart disease, and (3) not properly reporting some of the problems experienced by patients.

Douglas Richman was another research physician who received notoriety in his study of a new hepatitis treatment drug. Richman was cited for failing to report the death of the patients in the study, failing to inform the drug's manufacturer about the serious side effects, and failing to properly explain risks to patients in the study. Even though the reported incidence of fraud and unethical behavior by scientists is scarce, Shrader-Frechette (1994) has pointed out that many unethical behaviors go unnoticed or unreported. Even research journals do not mention anything about requiring an author to present information that a study was done ethically (e.g., with informed consent). It is possible that when a researcher studies the behavior of humans, that those humans are put at risk through coercion, deception, violation of privacy, breaches of confidentiality, stress, social injury, and failure to obtain free informed consent.

Some General Guidelines

The following guidelines are summaries taken from Shrader-Frechette's excellent book. Shrader-Frechette lays down the codes that should be followed by researchers in all areas of study where animals and humans are used as participants. One of the topics centers on situations where the researcher should not perform the research study. There are five general rules to follow when determining that the research should not be done.

- Scientists should not do research that puts people at risk.
- Scientists should not do research that violates the norms of free informed consent.
- Scientists should not do research that converts public resources to private gains.
- Scientists should not do research that could seriously damage the environment.
- Scientists ought not do biased research.

In the fifth and last point made by Shrader-Frechette, the implication is toward racial and sexual biases only. One should realize that in all research studies there are biases inherent in the research design itself.

However, one major criterion in deciding the execution of a research study is the consequences from that study. Shrader-Frechette states that there are studies that will put humans and animals at risk, but the nonexecution of that research may lead to even greater risks to humans and animals. In other words, not all potentially dangerous research should be condemned. Shrader-Frechette states:

> Just as scientists have a duty to do research but to avoid ethically questionable research, so also they have a responsibility not to become so ethically scrupulous about their work that they threaten the societal ends research should serve" (p. 37). . . .

Hence, the researcher must exercise some degree of common sense when deciding to do or not do the research study involving human and animal participants.

Guidelines from the American Psychological Association

In 1973, the American Psychological Association published ethical guidelines for psychologists. The original guidelines have gone through a number of revisions since then. The latest guidelines and principles were published in the March 1990 issue of *American Psychologist*. The *Ethical Principles of Psychologists and Code of Conduct* can be found in the 1994 edition of the *Publication Manual of the American Psychological Association*. The following section gives a brief overview of the ethical principles and codes that are relevant of behavioral science research. These guidelines are directed toward both human and animal research. All persons working on a research project are bounded by the codes of ethics regardless of whether or not they are professional psychologists or a member of the American Psychological Association.

General Considerations

The decision to undertake a research project lies solely with the researcher. Questions the researcher needs to ask himself or herself are: Is it worth doing? Will the information obtained from the study be valuable and useful for science and human welfare? Will it help improve the human health and welfare? If the researcher feels that the research is worthwhile, then the research must be conducted with respect and concern for the welfare and dignity of the participants.

The Participant at Minimal Risk

One of the major considerations on whether or not the study should be conducted is the decision concerning the well-being of the participant: Will there be a "subject at risk" or a "subject at minimal risk"? If there is the possibility of serious risk for the participant, the possible outcome of the research should indeed be of considerable value before proceeding. Researchers in this category should consult with colleagues before continuing. At most universities, there is a special committee that reviews research proposals to determine if the value of the research is worth placing participants at risk. At all times, the researcher must take steps to prevent harm befalling the participant. Student research projects should be conducted with the minimum amount of risk on the participants.

Fairness, Responsibility, and Informed Consent

Prior to participation, the researcher and the participant should enter into an agreement that clarifies the obligation and responsibilities. With certain studies this involves informed consent. Here the participant agrees to tolerate deception, discomfort, and boredom for the good of science. In return, the experimenter guarantees the safety and well-being of the participant. Psychological research differs from medical research in this regard. Medical research ethics requires the researcher to inform the participant what will be done to him or her and for what purpose. Most behavioral and social science research is not this restrictive. The behavioral science researcher needs to tell only those aspects of the study that may influence the participant's willingness to participate. Informed consent is not required in minimal-risk research. Still, it is a good idea for investigators in all fields of research to establish a clear and fair agreement with research participants prior to their participation.

Deception

Demand characteristics exist with many behavioral science studies. Participants volunteer with the belief that nothing harmful will be done to them. Their expectations and their desire to "do what the researcher wants" could influence the outcome of the study. Hence validity of the study would be compromised. The famous Hawthorne study is a case in point. In the Hawthorne study, factory workers were told ahead of time that some people will be coming to the factory to do a study on worker productivity. The workers, knowing that they would be studied for their productivity, behaved in ways they would not normally behave; that is, punctual, working harder, shorter breaks, and so on. As a result, the investigators were unable to get a true measure of worker productivity. This is where deception enters. Like a magic show, the participants' attentions are misdirected. If the investigators had entered the factory as "ordinary" workers, they could have obtained a clearer picture of worker productivity.

If the researcher can justify that deception is of value, and if alternative procedures are not available, then the participant must be provided with a sufficient explanation as soon as possible after the end of the experiment. This explanation is called *debriefing*. Any deceptive procedure that presents the participants with a negative perception of themselves must be avoided.

Debriefing

After collecting the data from the participant the nature of the research is carefully explained to the participant. Debriefing is an attempt to remove any misconceptions the participant may have about the study. This is an extremely important element in conducting a research study. Even the explanation of the study should not be aversive. It needs to be worded in a way such that those who have just been deceived will not feel foolish or stupid or embarrassed. In the event of student researchers, it would be beneficial for both the researcher and participant to review the data. The debriefing session could be used as a learning experience so that the student participant can become more knowledgeable about behavioral science research. Showing a student around the laboratory and explaining the apparatus is also advised if time permits.

For those studies where an immediate debriefing would compromise the validity of the study, the researcher may delay debriefing. However, the researcher must make all possible attempts to contact the participant once the entire study (data collection) is completed.

Freedom from Coercion

Participants must always be made to feel that they can withdraw from a study at any time without penalty or repercussions. Participants need to be informed of this prior to beginning the experimental session. The researcher at a university that uses introductory psychology students as participants should make it clear that their participation is voluntary. At some universities, the introductory psychology course has a graded research component. This component cannot be based solely on participation in research studies. For those who wish it, the research component can be satisfied through other means such as a research paper. Giving extra credit points for participation can be perceived as coercion.

Protection of Participants

The researcher must inform the participant of all risks and dangers inherent in the study. The researcher should realize that the participant is doing the researcher a favor by participating. Participation in any research may produce at least some degree of stress. Additionally, the researcher is obligated to remove any undesirable consequences of participation. This is relevant in cases where the participant is placed in a "do nothing" or control group. It would be unethical in a study that examines pain-management programs to place persons who are in chronic pain into a control group where they will receive no treatment.

Confidentiality

The issue of protecting the participant from harm includes confidentiality. The researcher must assure the participant that the data collected from them will be safeguarded. That is, the information collected from the participant will not be disclosed to the public in a way that could identify the participant. With sensitive data, the researcher must inform the participant how the data will be handled. In one study dealing with sexual behavior and AIDs, participants were asked to fill out a questionnaire, place the questionnaire in an unmarked envelope, and deposit the envelope in a sealed box. The researcher assured the participants that the questionnaires would only be seen by data-entry people who "won't know and cannot guess who they are." Smith and Garner (1976), for example, took extra precautions to assure the anonymity of participants in their study of homosexual behavior among male college athletes.

Ethics of Animal Research

To some people, the use of animals in research is inhumane and not necessary. However, research studies using animals have provided a number of worthwhile advancements for both animals and humans. Miller (1985) notes the major contributions that animal research has provided for society. Unlike human participants, animals do not volunteer. Contrary to the belief of animal right activists, very few studies today involve inflicting pain on animals. Experiments using animals as participants are generally permissible so long as the animals are treated humanely. APA provides guidelines on the use of animals for behavioral research and also logistical guidelines for their housing and care. There are eleven major points covered in APA's guidelines:

1. General: This involves the code behind the acquisition, maintenance, and disposal of animals. The emphasis is on the familiarity with the code.
2. Personnel: This point involves the people who will be caring for the animals and includes the availability of a veterinarian and supervisor of the facility.
3. Facilities: The housing of the animals must conform to the standard set by National Institute of Health (NIH) for the care and use of laboratory animals.
4. Acquisition of Animals: This point deals with how the animals are acquired. Covered are the rules for breeding and/or purchasing of animals.
5. Care and Housing of Animals: This deals with the condition of the facilities where the animals are kept.
6. Justification of Research: The purpose of the research using animals must be stated clearly.
7. Experimental Design: The research design of the study should include humane considerations. This would include the type of animal and how many animals.
8. Experimental Procedure: All experimental procedures must take into consideration the animal's well-being. Procedures must involve no inflicted pain. Any amount of induced pain must be justified by the value of the study. Any aversive stimuli should be set at the lowest level possible.
9. Field Research. Researchers doing field research should disturb the population as little as possible. There must be respect for property and privacy of inhabitants.
10. Educational Use of Animals: Alternative nonanimal studies should be considered. Classroom demonstrations using animals should be used only

when educational objectives cannot be made through the use of media. Psychologists need to include a presentation on the ethics of using animals in research.

11. **Disposition of Animals:** This point deals with what to do with the animal once the study is finished.

These guidelines (available from the American Psychological Association) should be made known to all personnel involved in the research and conspicuously posted wherever animals are maintained and used.

In assessing the research, the possibility of increasing knowledge about behavior, including benefit for health or welfare of humans and animals, should be sufficient to outweigh any harm or distress to the animals. Humane consideration for the well-being of the animals should thus always be kept uppermost in mind. If the animal is likely to be subjected to distress or pain, the experimental procedures specified in the guidelines of the American Psychological Association should be carefully followed, especially for surgical procedures. No animal should be discarded until its death is verified, and should be disposed of in a manner that is legal and consistent with health, environmental, and aesthetic concerns.

A recent book by Shapiro (1998) presents the history and current status on the use of animals in scientific research. This book contains articles that deal with ethics and situations when animal research is necessary and when it is not.

CHAPTER SUMMARY

1. The Tuskegee and Milgrim studies used a form of deception and are often cited as reasons why scientific research with humans and animals need to be regulated.
2. Fraud is also an issue of concern, since the work of individuals such as Burt and Breuning had a lot of influence on legislation and how people perceived themselves and others.
3. Organizations such as the American Psychological Association have set up guidelines on the ethics of doing research. They have also set up review boards to evaluate and take action on claims of ethical misconduct.
4. Researchers are obligated to do no physical or psychological harm to research participants.
5. Researchers must do research in a way that will produce useful information.
6. The ethical standards set up by the American Psychological Association include provisions for planning the research, protection of participants, confidentiality, debriefing, deception, informed consent, and freedom from coercion.
7. Guidelines are also provided for the use of animals in research on the care, feeding, and housing of animals; and what to do with animals after the end of the study.

STUDY SUGGESTIONS

1. Some feel that society has placed too many restrictions of scientists on how to conduct their research. List the strong and weak points behind these regulations.

2. What is the purpose of debriefing? Why is it necessary?

3. A student who is a fan of daytime talk shows wants to determine if the way a woman dresses influences men's behavior. She plans to attend two bars on a single night. In one bar she will dress provocatively and in the other she will dress in a business suit. Her dependent variable is the number of men who approach and talk to her. Do you see any ethical problems with this study design?

4. Visit the library and try to locate material pertaining to other incidences of fraud and unethical behavior by behavioral and medical scientists. How many of these can you find?

5. In the novel *Arrowsmith*, can you propose an alternative method that would have enabled Martin Arrowsmith to fully test his phage?

6. Locate and read at least one of the following articles:

   Braunwald, E. (1987). On analyzing scientific fraud. *Nature, 325,* 215–216.

   Broad, W. J., & Wade, N. (1982). *Betrayers of the truth.* New York: Touchstone.

   Brody, R. G., & Bowman, L. (1998). Accounting and psychology students' perceptions of whistle blowing. *College Student Journal. 32,* 162–166. (Does the college curriculum need to include ethics?)

   Fontes, L. A. (1998). Ethics in family violence research: Cross-cultural issues. *Family Relations: Interdisciplinary Journal of Applied Family Studies, 47,* 53–61.

   Herrmann, D., & Yoder, C. (1998). The potential effects of the implanted memory paradigm on child subjects. *Applied Cognitive Psychology, 12,* 198–206. (Discusses the danger of implanted memory.)

   Knight, J. A. (1984). Exploring the compromise of ethical principles in science. *Perspectives in Biology and Medicine, 27,* 432–442. (Explores the reasons for fraud and dishonesty in science.)

   Stark, C. (1998). Ethics in the research context: Misinterpretations and misplaced misgivings. *Canadian Psychology. 39,* 202–211. (A look at the ethics codes for the Canadian Psychological Association.)

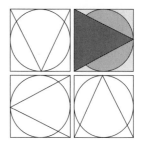

CHAPTER 18

RESEARCH DESIGN: PURPOSE AND PRINCIPLES

- ■ PURPOSES OF RESEARCH DESIGN
    An Example
    A Stronger Design
- ■ RESEARCH DESIGN AS VARIANCE CONTROL
    A Controversial Example
- ■ MAXIMIZATION OF EXPERIMENTAL VARIANCE
- ■ CONTROL OF EXTRANEOUS VARIABLES
- ■ MINIMIZATION OF ERROR VARIANCE

Research Design is the plan and structure of investigation, conceived so as to obtain answers to research questions. The plan is the overall scheme or program of the research. It includes an outline of what the investigator will do, from writing the hypotheses and their operational implications to the final analysis of data. The structure of research is harder to explain because the word *structure* is difficult to define clearly and unambiguously. Since it is a concept that becomes increasingly important as we continue our study, we here break off and attempt a definition and a brief explanation. The discourse will necessarily be somewhat abstract at this point. Later examples, however, will be more concrete. More important, we will find the concept powerful, useful, even indispensable, especially in our later study of multivariate analysis where "structure" is a key concept whose understanding is essential to understanding much contemporary research methodology.

A *structure* is the framework, organization, or configuration of elements of the structure related in specified ways. The best way to specify a structure is to write a mathematical equation that relates the parts of the structure to each other. Such a mathematical equation, since its terms are defined and specifically related by the equation (or set of equations), is unambiguous. In short, a structure is a paradigm or model of the relations among the variables of a study. The words *structure*, *model*, and *paradigm* are troublesome because they are hard to define clearly and unambiguously. A "paradigm" is a model, an example. Diagrams, graphs, and verbal outlines are paradigms. We use "paradigm" here rather than "model" because "model" has another important meaning in science—a meaning we return to in Chapter 37 when we discuss the testing of theory using multivariate procedure and "models" of aspects of theories.

A research design expresses both the structure of the research problem and the plan of investigation used to obtain empirical evidence on the relations of the problem. We will soon encounter examples of both design and structure that will perhaps enliven this abstract discussion.

Purposes of Research Design

Research design has two basic purposes: (1) *to provide answers to research questions* and (2) *to control variance*. Design helps investigators obtain answers to the questions of research and also to control the experimental, extraneous, and error variances of the particular research problem under study. Since all research activity can be said to have the purpose of providing answers to research questions, it is possible to omit this purpose from the discussion and to say that research design has one grand purpose: to control variance. Such a delimitation of the purpose of design, however, is dangerous. Without strong stress on the research questions and on the use of design to help provide answers to these questions, the study of design can degenerate into an interesting, but sterile, technical exercise.

Research designs are invented to enable researchers to answer research questions as validly, objectively, accurately, and economically as possible. Research plans are deliberately and specifically conceived and executed to bring empirical evidence to bear on the research problem. Research problems can be, and are, stated in the form of hypotheses. At some point in the research they are stated so that they can be empirically tested. Designs are carefully worked out to yield dependable and valid answers to the research questions epitomized by the hypotheses. We can make one observation and infer that the hypothesized relation exists on the basis of this one observation, but it is obvious that we cannot accept the inference so made. On the other hand, it is also possible to make hundreds of observations and to infer that the hypothesized relation exists on the basis of these many observations. In this case we may or may not accept the inference as valid. The result depends on how the observations and the inference were made. An adequately planned and executed design helps greatly in permitting us to rely on both our observations and our inferences.

How does design accomplish this? Research design sets up the framework for study of the relations among variables. Design tells us, in a sense, what observations to make, how to make them, and how to analyze the quantitative representations of the observations. Strictly speaking, design does not "tell" us precisely what to do, but rather "suggests" the direction of observation-making and analysis. An adequate design "suggests," for example, how many observations should be made, and which variables are active and which are attribute variables. We can then act to manipulate the active variables and to categorize and measure the attribute variables. A design tells us which type of statistical analysis to use. Finally, an adequate design outlines possible conclusions to be drawn from the statistical analysis.

An Example

It has been said that colleges and universities discriminate against women in hiring and in admissions. Suppose we wanted to test discrimination in admissions. The idea for this example came from the unusual and ingenious experiment cited earlier: Walster, Cleary, and Clifford (1970). We set up an experiment as follows. To a random sample of 200 colleges we send applications for admission, basing the applications on several model cases selected over a range of tested ability, with all details the same except for gender. Half the applications will be those from men and half from women. Other things being equal, we expect approximately equal numbers of acceptances and rejections. Acceptance, then, is the dependent variable. It is measured on a three-point scale: full acceptance, qualified acceptance, and rejection. Call male A_1 and female A_2. The paradigm of the design is given in Figure 18.1.

The design is the simplest possible, given minimum requirements of control. The two treatments will be assigned to the colleges at random. Each college, then, will receive one application, which will be either male or female. The difference between the means, M_{A_1} and M_{A_2} will be tested for statistical significance with a t- or F-test. The substantive hypothesis is: $M_{A_1} > M_{A_2}$, or more males than females will be accepted for admission. If there is no discrimination in admissions, then M_{A_1} is statistically equal to M_{A_2}. Suppose that an F-test indicates that the means are not significantly different. Can we then be sure that there is no discrimination practiced (on the average)? While the design of Figure 18.1 is satisfactory as far as it goes, perhaps it does not go far enough.

▣ FIGURE 18.1

Treatments	
A_1 (Male)	A_2 (Female)
Acceptance Scores	
M_{A_1}	M_{A_2}

⊡ FIGURE 18.2

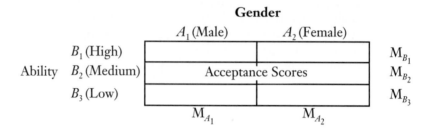

A Stronger Design

Walster and her colleagues used two other independent variables, Race and Ability, in a factorial design. We drop Race—it was neither statistically significant, nor did it interact significantly with the other variables—and concentrate on gender and ability. If a college bases its selection of incoming students strictly on ability, there is no discrimination (unless, of course, ability selection is called discrimination). Add Ability to the design of Figure 18.1; use three levels. That is, in addition to the applications being designated Male and Female, they are also designated as High Ability, Medium Ability, and Low Ability. For example, three of the applicants may be: male, medium ability; female, high ability; female, low ability. Now, if there is no significant difference between genders and the interaction between Gender and Ability is not significant, this would be considerably stronger evidence for no discrimination than that yielded by the design and statistical test of Figure 18.1. We now use the expanded design to explain this statement and to discuss a number of points about research design. The expanded design is given in Figure 18.2.

The design is a 2 × 3 factorial. One independent variable, A, is gender, the same as in Figure 18.1. The second independent variable, B, is ability, which is manipulated by indicating in several ways what the ability levels of the students are. It is important not to be confused by the names of the variables. Gender and Ability are ordinarily attribute variables and thus nonexperimental. In this case, however, they are manipulated. The students' records sent to the colleges were systematically adjusted to fit the six cells of Figure 18.2. A case in the A_1B_2 cell, for instance, would be the record of a male of medium ability. It is this record that the college judges for admission.

Let's assume that we believe discrimination against women takes a more subtle form than simply across-the-board exclusion: that it is the women of lower ability who are discriminated against (compared to men). This is an interaction hypothesis. At any rate, we use this problem and the paradigm of Figure 18.2 as a basis for discussing some elements of research design.

Research problems suggest research designs. Since the hypothesis just discussed is one of interaction, a factorial design is evidently appropriate. A is Gender; B is Ability. A is partitioned into A_1 and A_2, and B into B_1, B_2, and B_3.

The paradigm of Figure 18.2 suggests a number of things. First and most obvious, a fairly large number of participants is needed. Specifically, $6n$ participants are necessary (n equals number of Ss in each cell). If we decide that n should be 20, then we must have 120 Ss for the experiment. Note the "wisdom" of the design here. If we were only testing the treatments and ignoring ability, only $2n$ Ss would be needed. Please note that some, such as Simon (1976, 1987); Simon and Roscoe (1984); and Daniel (1976) disagree with this approach for all types of problems. They feel that many designs contains hidden replications and that one can do with a lot fewer participants than 20 per cell. Such designs do require a lot more careful planning, but the researcher can come out with a lot more useful information and study more independent variables than just two or three.

There are ways to determine how many participants are needed in a study. Such determination is part of the subject of "power," which refers to the ability of a test of statistical significance to detect differences in means (or other statistics) when such differences indeed exist. Chapter 8 discusses sample sizes and their relationship to research. Chapter 12, however, presents a method for estimating sample sizes to meet certain criteria. Power is a fractional value between 0 and 1.00 that is defined as $1 - \beta$, where β is the probability of committing a Type II error. The Type II error is failing to reject a false null hypothesis. If power is high (close to 1.00), this says that if the statistical test was not significant, the research can conclude that the null hypothesis is true. Power also tells you how sensitive the statistical test is in picking up real differences. If the statistical test is not sensitive enough to detect a real difference, the test is said to have low power. A highly sensitive test that can pick up true differences is said to have high power. In Chapter 16, we discussed the difference between parametric and nonparametric statistical tests. Nonparametric tests are generally less sensitive than parametric tests. As a result, nonparametric tests are said to have lower power than parametric tests. One of the most comprehensive books on the topic of power estimation is by Cohen (1988). Jaccard and Becker (1997) give an easy-to-follow introduction to power analysis.

Second, the design indicates that the "participants" (colleges, in this case) can be assigned randomly to both A and B because both are experimental variables. If Ability was a nonexperimental attribute variable, however, then the participants could be randomly assigned to A_1 and A_2, but not to B_1, B_2, and B_3.

Third, according to the design the observations made on the "participants" must be made independently. The score of one college must not affect the score of another college. Reducing a design to an outline like that shown in Figure 18.2 in effect prescribes the operations necessary for obtaining the measures that are appropriate for the statistical analysis. An F-test depends on the assumption of the independence of the measures of the dependent variable. If Ability here is an attribute variable and individuals are measured for intelligence, say, then the independence requirement is in greater jeopardy because of the possibility of one subject seeing another subject's paper, and because teachers may unknowingly (or knowingly) "help" students with answers, among other reasons. Researchers try to prevent such things—not on moral grounds but to satisfy the requirements of sound design and sound statistics.

A fourth point is quite obvious to us by now: Figure 18.2 suggests factorial analysis of variance, F-tests, measures of association and, perhaps, post hoc tests. If the research is well designed before the data are gathered—as it certainly was by Walster et al.—most statistical problems can be solved. In addition, certain troublesome problems can be avoided before they arise, or can even be prevented from arising at all. With an inadequate design, however, problems of appropriate statistical tests may be very troublesome. One reason for the strong emphasis in this book on treating design and statistical problems concomitantly is to point out ways to avoid these problems. If design and statistical analysis are planned simultaneously, the analytical work is usually straightforward and uncluttered.

A highly useful dividend of design is this: A clear design, like that in Figure 18.2, suggests the statistical tests that can be made. A simple one-variable randomized design with two partitions, for example, two treatments, A_1 and A_2, permit, only a statistical test of the difference between the two statistics yielded by the data. These statistics might be two means, two medians, two ranges, two variances, two percentages, and so forth. Only one statistical test is ordinarily possible. With the design of Figure 18.2, however, three statistical tests are possible: (1) between A_1 and A_2; (2) among B_1, B_2, and B_3, and (3) the interaction of A and B. In most investigations, all the statistical tests are not of equal importance. The important ones, naturally, are those directly related to the research problems and hypotheses.

In the present case the interaction hypothesis [or (3) above] is the important one, since the discrimination is supposed to depend on ability level. Colleges may practice discrimination at different levels of ability. As suggested above, females (A_2) may be accepted more than males (A_1) at the higher ability level (B_1), whereas they may be accepted less at the lower ability level (B_3).

It should be evident that research design is not static. A knowledge of design can help us to plan and do better research, and can also suggest the testing of hypotheses. Probably more important, we may be led to realize that the design of a study is not adequate to the demands we are making of it. What is meant by this somewhat peculiar statement?

Assume that we formulate the interaction hypothesis as outlined above without knowing anything about factorial design. We set up a design consisting, actually, of two experiments. In one of these experiments we test A_1 against A_2 under condition B_1. In the second experiment we test A_1 against A_2 under condition B_2. The paradigm would look like that shown in Figure 18.3. (To make matters simpler, we are only

▣ FIGURE 18.3

B_1, Condition Treatments		B_2, Condition Treatments	
A_1	A_2	A_1	A_2
M_{A_1}	M_{A_2}	M_{A_1}	M_{A_2}

using two levels of B_1, B_2, and B_3, but changing B_3 to B_2. The design is thus reduced to 2×2.)

The important point to note is that *no adequate* test of the hypothesis is possible with this design. A_1 can be tested against A_2 under both B_1 and B_2 conditions, to be sure. But it is not possible to know, clearly and unambiguously, whether there is a significant interaction between A and B. Even if $M_{A_1} > M_{A_2} \mid B_2$ (M_{A_1} is greater than M_{A_2}, under condition B_2), as hypothesized, the design cannot provide a clear possibility of confirming the hypothesized interaction, since we cannot obtain information about the differences between A_1 and A_2 at the two levels of B, B_1 and B_2. Remember that an interaction hypothesis implies, in this case, that the difference between A_1 and A_2 is different at B_1 from what it is at B_2. In other words, information of both A and B together *in one experiment* is needed to test an interaction hypothesis. If the statistical results of separate experiments showed a significant difference between A_1 and A_2 in one experiment under the B_1 condition, and no significant difference in another experiment under the B_2 condition, then there is good *presumptive* evidence that the interaction hypothesis is correct. But presumptive evidence is not good enough, especially when we know that it is possible to obtain better evidence.

In Figure 18.3, suppose the means of the cells were, from left to right: 30, 30, 40, 30. This result would seem to support the interaction hypothesis, since there is a significant difference between A_1 and A_2 at level B_2, but not at level B_1. But we could not know this to be certainly so, even though the difference between A_1 and A_2 is statistically significant. Figure 18.4 shows how this would look if a factorial design had been used. (The figures in the cells and on the margins are means.) Assuming that the main effects, A_1 and A_2; B_1 and B_2, were significant, it is still possible that the interaction is not significant. Unless the interaction hypothesis is specifically tested, the evidence for interaction is merely presumptive, because the planned statistical interaction test, that a factorial design provides, is lacking. It should be clear that a knowledge of design could have improved this experiment.

Research Design as Variance Control

The main technical function of research design is *to control variance*. A research design is, in a manner of speaking, a set of instructions to the investigator to gather and analyze data in certain ways. It is therefore a control mechanism. The statistical

▣ FIGURE 18.4

	A_1	A_2	
B_1	30	30	30
B_2	40	30	35
	35	30	

principle behind this mechanism, as stated earlier, is: *Maximize systematic variance, control extraneous systematic variance, and minimize error variance.* In other words, we must *control* variance.

According to this principle, by constructing an efficient research design the investigator attempts to: (1) maximize the variance of the variable or variables of the substantive research hypothesis, (2) control the variance of extraneous or "unwanted" variables that may have an effect on the experimental outcomes, and (3) minimize the error or random variance, including so-called errors of measurement. Let's look at an example.

A Controversial Example

Controversy is rich in all science. It seems to be especially rich and varied in behavioral science. Two such controversies have arisen from different theories of human behavior and learning. Reinforcement theorists have amply demonstrated that positive reinforcement can enhance learning. As usual, however, things are not so simple. The presumed beneficial effect of external rewards has been questioned; research has shown that extrinsic reward can have a deleterious influence on children's motivation, intrinsic interest, and learning. A number of articles and studies were published in the 1970s showing the possible detrimental effects of using reward. In one such study Amabile (1979) showed that external evaluation has a deleterious effect on artistic creativity. Others included Deci (1971), and Lepper and Greene (1978). At the time, even the seemingly straightforward principle of reinforcement is not so straightforward. However, in recent years a number of articles have appeared defending the positive effects of reward (see Eisenberger & Cameron, 1996; Sharpley, 1988; McCullers, Fabes, & Moran, 1987; Bates, 1979).

There is a substantial body of belief and research that indicates that college students learn well under a regime of what has been called *mastery learning*. Very briefly "mastery learning" means a system of pedagogy based on personalized instruction and requiring students to learn curriculum units to a mastery criterion (see Abbott & Falstrom, 1975; Ross & McBean, 1995; Senemoglu & Fogelman, 1995; Bergin, 1995). Although there appears to be some research supporting the efficacy of mastery learning, there is at least one study—and a fine study it is—by Thompson (1980) whose results indicate that students taught through the mastery learning approach do no better than students taught with a conventional approach of lecture, discussion, and recitation. This is an exemplary study, done with careful controls, over an extended time period. The example given below was inspired by the Thompson study. The design and controls in the example, however, are much simpler than Thompson's. Note, too, that Thompson had an enormous advantage: He did his experiment in a military establishment. This means, of course, that many control problems, usually recalcitrant in educational research, were easily resolved.

Controversy enters the picture because mastery learning adherents seem so strongly convinced of its virtues, while its doubters are almost equally skeptical. Will research decide the matter? Hardly. But let's see how one might approach a relatively modest study capable of yielding at least a partial *empirical* answer.

An educational investigator decides to test the hypothesis that achievement in science is enhanced more by a mastery learning method (*ML*) than by a traditional method (*T*). We ignore the details of the methods and concentrate on the design of the research. Call the mastery learning method A_1 and the traditional method A_2. As investigators we know that other possible independent variables influence achievement: intelligence, gender, social class background, previous experience with science, motivation, and so on. We would have reason to believe that the two methods work differently with different kinds of students. They may work differently, for example, with students of differing scholastic aptitudes. The traditional approach is effective, perhaps, with students of high aptitude, whereas mastery learning is more effective with students of low aptitude. Call aptitude *B:* high aptitude is B_1 and low aptitude B_2. In this example, the variable Aptitude was dichotomous into high and low groups. This is not the best way to handle the Aptitude variable. When a continuous measure is dichotomized or trichotomized, variance is lost. In a later chapter we will see that leaving a continuous measure and using multiple regression is a better method.

What kind of design should be set up? To answer this question it is important to label the variables and to know clearly what questions are being asked. The variables are:

Independent Variables		Dependent Variable
Methods	*Aptitude*	*Science Achievement*
Mastery Learning, A_1	High Aptitude, B_1	Test scores in science
Traditional, A_2	Low Aptitude, B_2	

We may as investigators also have included other variables in the design, especially variables potentially influential on achievement: general intelligence, social class, gender, high school average, for example. We also would use random assignment to take care of intelligence and other possible influential independent variables. The dependent variable measure is provided by a standardized science knowledge test.

The problem seems to call for a factorial design. There are two reasons for this choice: (1) There are two independent variables. (2) We have quite clearly an interaction hypothesis in mind, though we may not have stated it in so many words. We do have the belief that the methods will work differently with different kinds of students. We set up the design structure shown in Figure 18.5.

Note that all the marginal and cell means have been appropriately labeled. Note, too, that there is one *active variable*, Methods; and one *attribute variable*, Aptitude. You might remember from Chapter 3 that an *active variable* is an experimental or manipulated variable. An *attribute variable* is a measured variable or a variable that is a characteristic of people or groups; for example, intelligence, social class, and occupation (people); and cohesiveness, productivity, and restrictive–permissive atmosphere (organizations, groups, and the like). All we can do is to categorize the

◙ FIGURE 18.5

Methods

	A_1 (Mastery Learning)	A_2 (Traditional)	
B_1 (High Anxiety)	$M_{A_1B_1}$	$M_{A_2B_1}$	M_{B_1}
Aptitude	Science Knowledge Scores		
B_2 (Low Anxiety)	$M_{A_1B_1}$	$M_{A_1B_2}$	M_{B_2}
	M_{A_1}	M_{A_2}	

participants as high aptitude and low aptitude and assign them accordingly to B_1 and B_2. We can, however, assign the students randomly to A_1 and A_2, the Methods groups. This is done in two stages: (1) the B_1 (high aptitude) students are randomly assigned to A_1 and A_2 and (2) the B_2 (low aptitude) students are assigned randomly to A_1 and A_2. By so randomizing the participants we can assume that before the experiment begins, the students in A_1 are approximately equal to the students in A_2 in all possible characteristics.

Our present concern is with the different roles of variance in research design and the variance principle. Before going further, we name the variance principle for easy reference the "maxmincon" principle. The origin of this name is obvious: <u>max</u>imize the systematic variance under study; <u>con</u>trol extraneous systematic variance; and <u>min</u>imize error variance—with two of the syllables reversed for euphony.

Before tackling the application of the maxmincon principle in the present example, an important point should be discussed. Whenever we talk about variance, we must be sure to know which variance we are talking about. We speak of the variance of the methods, of intelligence, of gender, of type of home, and so on. This sounds as though we were talking about the independent variable variance. This is true and not true. We always mean the *variance of the dependent variable, and the variance of the dependent variable measures*, after the experiment has been done. This is not true in so-called correlational studies where, when we say "the variance of the independent variable," we mean just that. When correlating two variables, we study the variances of the independent and dependent variables "directly." Our way of saying "independent variable variance" stems from the fact that, by manipulation and control of independent variables, we influence, presumably, the variance of the dependent variable. Somewhat inaccurately put, we "make" the measures of the dependent variable behave or vary as a presumed result of our manipulation and control of the independent variables. In an experiment, it is the dependent variable measures that are analyzed. Then, from the analysis we infer that the variances present in the total variance of the dependent variable measures are due to the manipulation and control of the independent variables, and to error. Now, back to our principle.

Maximization of Experimental Variance

The experimenter's most obvious, but not necessarily most important, concern is to maximize what we will call the *experimental variance*. This term is introduced to facilitate subsequent discussions and, in general, simply refers to the variance of the dependent variable, influenced by the independent variable or variables of the substantive hypothesis. In this particular case, the experimental variance is the variance in the dependent variable, presumably due to methods, A_1 and A_2, and aptitude, B_1 and B_2. Although experimental variance can be taken to mean only the variance due to a manipulated or *active* variable, like methods, we shall also consider *attribute* variables, like intelligence, gender and, in this case, aptitude, experimental variables. One of the main tasks of an experimenter is to maximize this variance. The methods must be "pulled" apart as much as possible to make A_1 and A_2 (and A_3, A_4, and so on, if they are in the design) as unlike as possible.

If the independent variable does not vary substantially, there is little chance of separating its effect from the total variance of the dependent variable. It is necessary to give the variance of a relation a chance to show itself, to separate itself, so to speak, from the total variance, which is a composite of variances due to numerous sources and chance. Remembering this subprinciple of the maxmincon principle, we can write a research precept: *Design, plan, and conduct research so that the experimental conditions are as different as possible.* There are, of course, exceptions to this subprinciple, but they are probably rare. An investigator might want to study the effects of small gradations of, say, motivational incentives on the learning of some subject matter. Here one would not make the experimental conditions as different as possible. Still, they would have to be made to vary somewhat or there would be no discernible resulting variance in the dependent variable.

In the present research example, this subprinciple means that the investigator must take pains to make A_1 and A_2, the mastery learning and traditional methods, as different as possible. Next, B_1 and B_2 must also be made as different as possible on the aptitude dimension. This latter problem is essentially one of measurement, as we will see in a later chapter. In an experiment, the investigator is like a puppeteer making the independent variable puppets do what he or she wants. The strings of the A_1 and A_2 puppets are held in the right hand and the strings of the B_1 and B_2 puppets in the left hand. (We assume there is no influence of one hand on the other, that is, the hands must be independent.) The A_1 and A_2 puppets are made to dance apart just as the B_1 and B_2 puppets are made to dance apart. The investigator then watches the audience (the dependent variable) to see and measure the effect of the manipulations. If one is successful in making A_1 and A_2 dance apart, and if there is a relation between A and the dependent variable, the audience reaction—if separating A_1 and A_2 is funny, for instance—should be laughter. The investigator may even observe that he or she only gets laughter when A_1 and A_2 dance apart and, at the same time, B_1 or B_2 dance apart (interaction again).

Control of Extraneous Variables

The control of extraneous variables means that the influences of those independent variables extraneous to the purposes of the study are minimized, nullified, or isolated. There are three ways to control extraneous variables. The first is the easiest, if it is possible: to eliminate the variable as a variable. If we are worried about intelligence as a possible contributing factor in studies of achievement, its effect on the dependent variable can be virtually eliminated by using participants of only one intelligence level, say intelligence scores within the range of 90 to 110. If we are studying achievement, and racial membership is a possible contributing factor to the variance of achievement, it can be eliminated by using only members of one race. The principle is: *To eliminate the effect of a possible influential independent variable on a dependent variable, choose participants so that they are as homogeneous as possible on that independent variable.*

This method of controlling unwanted or extraneous variance is very effective. If we select only one gender for an experiment, then we can be sure that gender cannot be a contributing independent variable. But then we lose generalization power; for instance, we can say nothing about the relation under study with girls if we use only boys in the experiment. If the range of intelligence is restricted, then we can discuss only this restricted range. Is it possible that the relation, if discovered, is nonexistent or quite different with children of high intelligence or children of low intelligence? We simply do not know; we can only surmise or guess.

The second way to control extraneous variance is through randomization. This is the best way, in the sense that you can have your cake and eat some of it, too. Theoretically, randomization is the only method for controlling all possible extraneous variables. Another way to phrase it is: if proper randomization has been accomplished, then the experimental groups can be considered statistically equal in all possible ways. This does not mean, of course, that the groups are equal in all the possible variables. We already know that by chance the groups can be unequal, but the probability of their being equal is greater, with proper randomization, than the probability of their not being equal. For this reason, control of the extraneous variance by randomization is a powerful method of control. All other methods leave open many possibilities of inequality. If we match for intelligence, we may successfully achieve statistical equality in intelligence (at least in those aspects of intelligence measured), but we may suffer from inequality in other significantly influential independent variables like aptitude, motivation, and social class. A precept that springs from this equalizing power of randomization, then, is: *Whenever it is possible to do so, assign subjects to experimental groups and conditions randomly, and assign conditions and other factors to experimental groups randomly.*

The third method of controlling an extraneous variable is to build it right into the design as an independent variable. For example, assume that gender was to be controlled in the experiment discussed earlier and it was considered inexpedient or unwise to eliminate it. One could add a third independent variable, gender, to the design. Unless one were interested in the actual difference between the genders on the dependent variable or wanted to study the interaction between one or two of the other variables and gender, however, it is unlikely that this form of control would be used. One might want information of the kind just mentioned and also want to control gender, too. In such a case, adding it to the design as a variable might be desirable. The point is that building a variable into an experimental design "controls" the variable, since it then becomes possible to extract from the total variance of the dependent variable the variance due to the variable. (In the above case, this would be the "between-genders" variance.)

These considerations lead to another principle: *An extraneous variable can be controlled by building it into the research design as an attribute variable, thus achieving control and yielding additional research information about the effect of the variable on the dependent variable and about its possible interaction with other independent variables.*

The fourth way to control extraneous variance is to match participants. The control principle behind matching is the same as that for any other kind of control, the control of variance. Matching is similar—in fact, it might be called a corollary— to the principle of controlling the variance of an extraneous variable by building it into the design. The basic principle is to split a variable into two or more parts in a factorial design, say into high and low intelligence, and then randomize within each level as described above. Matching is a special case of this principle. Instead of splitting the participants into two, three, or four parts, however, they are split into *N*/2 parts, *N* being the number of participants used; thus the control of variance is built into the design.

In using the matching method several problems may be encountered. To begin with, the variable on which the participants are matched must be substantially related to the dependent variable or the matching is a waste of time. Even worse, it can be misleading. In addition, matching has severe limitations. If we try to match, say, on more than two variables, or even more than one, we lose participants. It is difficult to find matched participants on more than two variables. For instance, if one decides to match intelligence, gender, and social class, one may be fairly successful in matching the first two variables but not in finding pairs that are fairly equal on all three variables. Add a fourth variable and the problem becomes difficult, often impossible to solve.

Let us not throw out the baby with the bath water, however. When there is a substantial correlation between the matching variable or variables and the dependent variable (>.50 or .60), then matching reduces the error term and thus increases the precision of an experiment, a desirable outcome. If the same participants are used with different experimental treatments—called repeated measures or randomized block design—we have powerful control of variance. How can one match better on all possible variables than by matching a subject with oneself? Unfortunately, other negative considerations usually rule out this possibility. It should be forcefully emphasized that matching of any kind is no substitute for randomization. If participants are matched, *they should then be assigned to experimental groups at random.* Through a random procedure, like tossing a coin or using odd and even random numbers, the members of the matched pairs are assigned to experimental and control groups. If the same participants undergo all treatments, then the order of the treatments should be assigned randomly. This adds randomization control to the matching, or repeated measures control.

A principle suggested by this discussion is: *When a matching variable is substantially correlated with the dependent variable, matching as a form of variance control can be profitable and desirable.* Before using matching, however, carefully weigh its advantages and disadvantages in the particular research situation. Complete randomization or the analysis of covariance may be better methods of variance control.

Still another form of control, statistical control, was discussed at length in previous chapters, but one or two further remarks are in order here. Statistical methods are, so to speak, forms of control in the sense that they isolate and quantify variances. But statistical control is inseparable from other forms of design control. If matching is used, for example, an appropriate statistical test must be used, or the matching effect, and thus the control, will be lost.

Minimization of Error Variance

Error variance is the variability of measures due to random fluctuations whose basic characteristic is that they are self-compensating, varying now this way, now that way, now positive, now negative, now up, now down. Random errors tend to balance each other so that their mean is zero.

There are a number of determinants of error variance, for instance, factors associated with individual differences among participants. Ordinarily we call this variance due to individual differences "systematic variance." But when such variance cannot be, or is not identified and controlled, we have to lump it with the error variance. Because many determinants interact and tend to cancel each other out (or at least we assume that they do), the error variance has this random characteristic.

Another source of error variance is that associated with what are called errors of measurement: variation of responses from trial to trial, guessing, momentary inattention, slight temporary fatigue, lapses of memory, transient emotional states of participants, and so on.

Minimizing error variance has two principal aspects: (1) the reduction of errors of measurement through controlled conditions, and (2) an increase in the reliability of measures. The more uncontrolled the conditions of an experiment, the more the many determinants of error variance can operate. This is one of the reasons for carefully setting up controlled experimental conditions. In studies under field conditions, of course, such control is difficult; still, constant efforts must be made to lessen the effects of the many determinants of error variance. This can be done, in part, by specific and clear instructions to participants and by excluding from the experimental situation factors that are extraneous to the research purpose.

To increase the reliability of measures is to reduce the error variance. Pending fuller discussion later in the book, reliability can be taken to be the accuracy of a set of scores. To the extent that scores do not fluctuate randomly, they are reliable. Imagine a completely unreliable measurement instrument. This instrument does not allow us to predict the future performance of individuals. It gives a set of rank ordering values for a sample of participants at one time and a completely different set of rank ordering at another time. With such an instrument, it would not be possible to identify and extract systematic variances, since the scores yielded by the instrument would be like the numbers in a table of random numbers. This is the extreme case. Now, imagine differing amounts of reliability and unreliability in the measures of the dependent variable. The more reliable the measures, the better we can identify and extract systematic variances and the smaller the error variance in relation to the total variance.

Another reason for reducing error variance as much as possible is to give systematic variance a chance to show itself. We cannot do this if the error variance, and thus the error term, is too large. If a relation exists, we seek to discover it. One way to discover the relation is to find significant differences between means. But if the error variance is relatively large due to uncontrolled errors of measurement, the systematic variance—earlier called "between" variance—will not have a chance to appear. Thus, the relation, although it exists, will probably not be detected.

The problem of error variance can be put into a neat mathematical nutshell. Remember the equation:

$$V_t = V_b + V_e$$

where V_t is the total variance in a set of measures; V_b is the between-groups variance, the variance presumably due to the influence of the experimental variables; and V_e is the error variance (in analysis of variance, the within-groups variance and the residual variance). Obviously, the larger V_e is, the smaller V_b must be, with a given amount of V_t.

Consider the following equation: $F = V_b/V_e$. For the numerator of the fraction on the right to be accurately evaluated for significant departure from chance expectation, the denominator should be an accurate measure of random error.

A familiar example may make this clear. Recall that in the discussions of factorial analysis of variance and the analysis of variance of correlated groups, we talked about variance due to individual differences being present in experimental measures. We said that, while adequate randomization can effectively equalize experimental groups, there will be variance in the scores due to individual differences, for instance, differences due to intelligence, aptitude, and so on. Now, in some situations, these individual differences can be quite large. If they are, then the error variance and, consequently, the denominator of the F equation above, will be "too large" relative to the numerator; that is, the individual differences will have been randomly scattered among, say, two, three, or four experimental groups. Still they are sources of variance and, as such, will inflate the within-groups or residual variance, the denominator of the above equation.

CHAPTER SUMMARY

1. Research designs are plans and structures used to answer research questions.
2. Research designs have two basic purposes: (i) provide answers to research questions, and (ii) control variance.
3. Research designs work in conjunction with research hypotheses to yield a dependable and valid answer.
4. Research designs can also tell us what statistical test to use to analyze the data collected from that design.

5. When speaking of controlling variance, we can mean one or more of three things:

   - maximize systematic variance
   - control extraneous variance
   - minimize error variance

6. To maximize systematic variance, one should have an independent variable where the levels are very distinct from one another.

7. To control extraneous variance the researcher need to eliminate the effects of a potential independent variable on the dependent variable. This can be done by:

   - holding the independent variable constant; for example, if one knows gender has a possible effect, gender can be held constant by doing the study with only one gender (i.e., females).
   - randomization; meaning to choose participants randomly and then assigning each group of participants to treatment conditions randomly (levels of the independent variable).
   - build the extraneous variable into the design by making it an independent variable.
   - matching participants—this method of control might be difficult in certain situations; a researcher will never be quite sure that a successful match was made on all of the important variables.

8. Minimizing error variance involves measurement of the dependent variable. By reducing the measurement error one will have reduced error variance. The increase in the reliability of the measurement would also lead to a reduction of error variance.

STUDY SUGGESTIONS

1. We have noted that research design has the purpose of obtaining answers to research questions and controlling variance. Explain in detail what this statement means. How does a research design control variance? Why should a factorial design control more variance than a one-way design? How does a design that uses matched participants or repeated measures of the same participants control variance? What is the relation between the research questions and hypotheses and a research design? Invent a research problem to illustrate your answers to these questions (or use an example from the text).

2. Sir Ronald Fisher (1951), the inventor of analysis of variance, said in one of his books, it should be noted that the null hypothesis is never proved or established, but is possibly disproved, in the course of experimentation. Every experiment may be said to exist only in order to give the facts a chance of disproving the null hypothesis. Whether you agree or disagree with Fisher's statement, what do you think he meant by it? In framing your answer, remember the maxmincon principle and F-tests and t-tests.

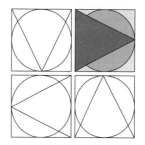

CHAPTER 19

INADEQUATE DESIGNS AND DESIGN CRITERIA

All disciplined creations of humans have form. Architecture, poetry, music, painting, mathematics, scientific research—all have form. People put great stress on the content of their creations, often not realizing that without strong structure, no matter how rich and how significant the content, the creations may be weak and sterile.

So it is with scientific research. The scientist needs viable and plastic form with which to express scientific aims. Without content—without good theory, good hypotheses, good problems—the design of research is empty. But without form, without structure adequately conceived and created for the research purpose, little of value can be accomplished. Indeed, it is no exaggeration to say that many of the failures of behavioral research have been failures of disciplined and imaginative form.

The principal focus of this chapter is on inadequate research designs. Such designs have been so common that they must be discussed. More important, the student should be able to recognize them and understand why they are inadequate.

This negative approach has a virtue: The study of deficiencies forces one to ask why something is deficient, which in turn centers attention on the criteria used to judge both adequacies and inadequacies. So the study of inadequate designs leads us to the study of the criteria of research design. We take the opportunity, too, to describe the symbolic system to be used, and to identify an important distinction between experimental and nonexperimental research.

Experimental and Nonexperimental Approaches

Discussion of design must be prefaced by an important distinction: that between experimental and nonexperimental approaches to research. Indeed, this distinction is so important that a separate chapter (Chapter 23) will be devoted to it later. An *experiment* is a scientific investigation in which an investigator manipulates and controls one or more independent variables and observes the dependent variable or variables for variation concomitant to the manipulation of the independent variables. An *experimental design*, then, is one in which the investigator *manipulates* at least one independent variable. In an earlier chapter we briefly discussed Hurlock's classic study (1925). Hurlock manipulated incentives to produce different amounts of retention. In the Walster, Cleary, and Clifford (1970) study (discussed in Chapter 18), sex, race, and ability levels were manipulated to study their effects on college acceptance: the application forms submitted to colleges differed in descriptions of applicants as male–female; white–black; and high, medium, or low ability levels.

In nonexperimental research one cannot manipulate variables or assign participants or treatments at random because the nature of the variables is such as to preclude manipulation. Participants come to us with their differing characteristics intact, so to speak. They come to us with their sex, intelligence, occupational status, creativity, or aptitude "already there." Wilson (1996) used a nonexperimental design to study the readability, ethnic content, and cultural sensitivity of patient education material used by nurses at local health department and community health centers. Here, the material preexisted. There was no random assignment or selection. Edmondson (1996) also used a nonexperimental design to compare the number of medication errors by nurses, physicians, and pharmacists in eight hospital units at two urban teaching hospitals. Edmondson did not choose these units or hospitals at random, neither were the medical professionals chosen at random. In many areas of research, likewise, random assignment is unfortunately not possible, as we will see later. Although experimental and nonexperimental research differ in these crucial respects, they share structural and design features that will be pointed out in this and subsequent chapters. In addition, their basic purpose is the same: to study relations among phenomena. Their scientific logic is also the same: to bring empirical evidence to bear on conditional statements of the form If p, then q. In some fields of behavioral and social sciences the nonexperimental framework is unavoidable. Keith (1988) states that a lot of studies conducted by school psychologists are of the nonexperimental nature. School psychology researchers as well as many in educational psychology must work within a practical framework. Many times, schools, classrooms, or even students are given to the researcher "as-is." Stone-Romero, Weaver, and Glenar (1995) have summarized nearly 20 years of articles from the *Journal of Applied Psychology*, concerning the use of experimental and nonexperimental research designs.

The ideal of science is the controlled experiment. Except, perhaps, in taxonomic research—research with the purpose of discovering, classifying, and measuring natural phenomena and the factors behind such phenomena—the controlled experiment is the desired model of science. It may be difficult for many students to accept this rather categorical statement since its logic is not readily apparent. Earlier it was said that the main goal of science was to discover relations among phenomena. Why then assign a priority to the controlled experiment? Do not other methods of discovering relations exist? Yes, of course they do. The main reason for the preeminence of the controlled experiment, however, is that researchers can have more confidence that the relations they study are the relations they think they are. The reason is not hard to see: They study the relations under the most carefully controlled conditions of inquiry known. The unique and overwhelmingly important virtue of experimental inquiry, then, is control. In a perfectly controlled experimental study, the experimenter can be confident that the manipulation of the independent variable affected the dependent variable and nothing else. In short, a perfectly conducted experimental study is more trustworthy than a perfectly conducted nonexperimental study. Why this is so should become more apparent as we advance in our study of research design.

Symbolism and Definitions

Before discussing inadequate designs, explanation of the symbolism to be used in these chapters is necessary. X is used to define an *experimentally manipulated* independent variable (or variables). X_1, X_2, X_3, and so on represent independent variables 1, 2, 3, and so on, though we usually use X alone, even when it can mean more than one independent variable. (We also use X_1, X_2, etc., to represent partitions of an independent variable, but the difference will always be clear.) The symbol (X) indicates that the independent variable is not *manipulated*—is not under the direct control of the investigator, but is *measured* or *imagined*. The dependent variable is Y: Y_b is the dependent variable *before* the manipulation of X, and Y_a the dependent variable *after* the manipulation of X. With $\sim X$, we borrow the negation sign of set theory: $\sim X$ ("not-X") to indicate that the experimental variable (the independent variable X) is *not* manipulated. [Note: (X) is a nonmanipulable variable and $\sim X$ is a manipulable variable that is not manipulated.] The symbol (R) will be used for the random assignment of participants to experimental groups and the random assignment of experimental treatments to experimental groups.

The explanation of $\sim X$ just given is not quite accurate because in some cases $\sim X$ can represent a different aspect of the treatment X, rather than merely the absence of treatment. In an older language, the experimental group was the group that was given the so-called experimental treatment, X; while the control group did not receive it, $\sim X$. For our purposes, however, $\sim X$ will do well enough, especially if we understand the generalized meaning of *control* discussed below. An *experimental group*, then, is a group of participants receiving some aspect or treatment of *X*. In testing the frustration–aggression hypothesis, the experimental group is the group whose participants are systematically frustrated. In contrast, the control group is one that is given "no" treatment.

In modern multivariate research, it is necessary to expand these notions. They are not changed basically; they are only expanded. It is quite possible to have more than one experimental group, as we have seen. Different degrees of manipulation of the independent variable are not only possible, they are often also desirable or even imperative. Further, it is possible to have more than one control group, a statement that at first seems like nonsense. How can one have different degrees of "no" experimental treatment? This occurs because the notion of *control* is generalized. When there are more than two groups, and when any two of them are treated differently, one or more groups serve as "controls" on the others. Recall that control is always control of variance. With two or more groups treated differently, variance is engendered by the experimental manipulation. So the traditional notion of *X* and ~*X* (treatment and no treatment) is generalized to $X_1, X_2, X_3, \ldots, X_k$, different forms or degrees of treatment.

If *X* is encased inside parentheses (*X*), this means that the investigator "imagines" the manipulation of *X*, or assumes that *X* occurred and that it is the *X* of the hypothesis. It may also mean that *X* is measured and not manipulated. Actually, we are saying the same thing here in different ways. The context of the discussion should make the distinction clear. Suppose a sociologist is studying delinquency and the frustration–aggression hypothesis. The sociologist observes delinquency, *Y*, and imagines that the delinquent participants were frustrated in their earlier years, or (*X*). All nonexperimental designs will have (*X*). Generally, then, (*X*) represents an independent variable *not under the experimental control of the investigator.*

One more point—each design in this chapter will ordinarily have an *a* and a *b* form. The *a* form will be the experimental form, or that in which *X* is manipulated. The *b* form will be the nonexperimental form, that in which *X* is not under the control of the investigator, or (*X*). Obviously, (~*X*) is also possible.

Faulty Designs

There are four (or more) inadequate designs of research that have often been used—and are occasionally still used—in behavioral research. The inadequacies of the designs lead to poor control of independent variables. We number each such design, give it a name, sketch its structure, and then discuss it.

Design 19.1: One Group		
(*a*) *X*	*Y*	(Experimental)
(*b*) (*X*)	*Y*	(Nonexperimental)

Design 19.1(a) has been called the "One-Shot Case Study," an apropos name given by Campbell and Stanley (1963). The (a) form is experimental, the (b) form nonexperimental. An example of the (a) form: a school faculty institutes a new curriculum and wishes to evaluate its effects. After one year, Y, student achievement, is measured. It is concluded, say, that achievement has improved under the new program. With such a design the conclusion is weak. Design 19.1(b) is the non-experimental form of the one-group design. Y, the outcome, is studied, and X is assumed or imagined. An example would be to study delinquency by searching the past of a group of juvenile delinquents for factors that may have led to their antisocial behavior. The method is problematic because the factors (variables) may be confounded. When the effect of two or more factors (variables) cannot be separated, the results are difficult to interpret. Any number of possible explanations might be plausible.

Scientifically, Design 19.1 is worthless. There is virtually no control of other possible influences on outcome. As Campbell (1957) pointed out, the minimum of useful scientific information requires at least one formal comparison. The curriculum example requires, *at the least*, comparison of the group that experienced the new curriculum with a group that did not experience it. The presumed effect of the new curriculum, say such-and-such achievement, might well have been about the same under any kind of curriculum. The point is not that the new curriculum did or did not have an effect. It was that without any formal, controlled comparison of the performance of the members of the "experimental" group with the performance of the members of some other group not experiencing the new curriculum, little can be said about its effect.

An important distinction should be made. It is not that the method is entirely worthless, but that it is *scientifically* worthless. In everyday life, of course, we depend on such scientifically questionable evidence; we have to. We act, we say, on the basis of our experience. We hope that we use our experience rationally. The everyday-thinking paradigm implied by Design 19.1 is not being criticized. Only when such a paradigm is used and said or believed to be scientific do difficulties arise. Even in high intellectual pursuits, the thinking implied by this design is used. Freud's careful observations and brilliant and creative analysis of neurotic behavior seem to fall into this category. The quarrel is not with Freud, then, but rather with assertions that his conclusions are "scientifically established."

Design 19.2: One Group, Before–After (Pretest, Posttest)

(a) Y_b	X	Y_a	(Experimental)
(b) Y_b	(X)	Y_a	(Nonexperimental)

Design 19.2 is only a small improvement on Design 19.1. The essential characteristic of this mode of research is that a group is compared to itself. Theoretically, there is no better choice, since all possible independent variables associated with the participants' characteristics are controlled. The procedure dictated by such a design is as follows. A group is measured on the dependent variable, Y, before experimental manipulation. This is usually called a *pretest*. Assume that the attitudes toward women of a group of participants are measured. An experimental manipulation designed to change these attitudes is used. An experimenter might expose the group to expert opinion on women's rights, for example. After the interposition of this X, the attitudes of the participants are again measured. The difference scores, or $Y_a - Y_b$, are examined for change in attitudes.

At face value, this would seem a good way to accomplish the experimental purpose. After all, if the difference scores are statistically significant, does this not indicate a change in attitudes? The situation is not so prosaic. There are a number of other factors that may have contributed to the change in scores. Hence, the factors are confounded. Campbell (1957) gives an excellent detailed discussion of these factors, only a brief outline of which can be given here.

Measurement, History, Maturation

First is the possible effect of the measurement procedure: measuring participants changes them. Can it be that the post-X measures were influenced not by the manipulation of X but by increased sensitization due to the pretest? Campbell (1957) calls such measures *reactive* measures, because they themselves cause the subject to react. Controversial attitudes, for example, seem to be especially susceptible to such sensitization. Achievement measures, though probably less reactive, are still affected. Measures involving memory are susceptible. If you take a test now, you are more likely to remember later things that were included in the test. In short, observed changes may be due to reactive effects.

Two other important sources of extraneous variance are *history* and *maturation*. Between the Y_b and Y_a testings, many things can occur other than X. The longer the period of time, the greater the chance of extraneous variables affecting the participants, and thus the Y_a measures. This is what Campbell (1957) calls *history*. These variables or events are *specific* to the particular experimental situation. *Maturation*, on the other hand, covers events that are *general*—not specific to any particular situation. They reflect change or growth in the organism studied. Mental age increases with time, an increase that can easily affect achievement, memory, and attitudes. People can learn in any given time interval, and the learning may affect dependent variable measures. This is one of the exasperating difficulties of research that extends over considerable time periods. The longer the time interval, the greater the possibility that extraneous, unwanted sources of systematic variance will influence dependent variable measures.

The Regression Effect

A statistical phenomenon that has misled researchers is the so-called *regression effect*. Test scores change as a statistical fact of life: on retest, on the average, they regress toward the mean. The regression effect operates because of the imperfect correlation between the pretest and posttest scores. If $r_{ab} = 1.00$, then there is no regression effect; if $r_{ab} = .00$, the effect is at a maximum in the sense that the best prediction of any posttest score from pretest score is the mean. With the correlations found in practice, the net effect is that lower scores on the pretest tend to be higher, and higher scores lower on the posttest—when, in fact, no real change has taken place in the dependent variable. Thus, if low-scoring participants are used in a study, their scores on the posttest will probably be higher than on the pretest due to the regression effect. This can deceive the researcher into believing that the experimental intervention has been effective when it really has not. Similarly, one may erroneously conclude that an experimental variable has had a depressing effect on high pretest scorers. Not necessarily so. The higher and lower scores of the two groups may be due to the regression effect. How does this work? There are many chance factors at work in any set of scores. Two excellent references on the discussion of the regression effect are Anastasi (1958) and Thorndike (1963). For a more statistically sophisticated presentation, see Nesselroade, Stigler, and Baltes (1980). On the pretest some high scores are higher than "they should be" due to chance, and similarly with some low scores. On the posttest it is unlikely that the high scores will be maintained, because the factors that made them high were chance factors—which are uncorrelated on the pretest and posttest. Thus the high scorer will tend to drop on the posttest. A similar argument applies to the low scorer—but in reverse.

Research designs have to be constructed with the regression effect in mind. There is no way in Design 19.2 to control it. If there was a control group, then one could "control" the regression effect, since both experimental and control groups have pretest and posttest. If the experimental manipulation has had a "real" effect, then it should be apparent over and above the regression effect. That is, the scores of both groups, other things being equal, are affected the same by regression and other influences. So if the groups differ in the posttest, it should be due to the experimental manipulation.

Design 19.2 is inadequate, not so much because extraneous variables and the regression effect can operate (the extraneous variables operate whenever there is a time interval between pretest and posttest), but *because we do not know whether they have operated, whether they have affected the dependent variable measures*. The design affords no opportunity to control or to test such possible influences.

Design 19.3: Simulated Before–After

	X	Y_a
Y_b		

The peculiar title of Design 19.3 stems in part from its very nature. Like Design 19.2 it is a before–after design. Instead of using the before and after (or pretest–posttest) measures of one group, we use as pretest measures the measures of another group, which are chosen to be as similar as possible to the experimental group, and thus a control group of a sort. (The line between the two levels above indicates separate groups.) This design satisfies the condition of having a control group, and is thus a gesture toward the comparison that is necessary to scientific investigation. Unfortunately, the controls are weak, a result of our inability to know that the two groups were equivalent before X, the experimental manipulation.

Design 19.4: Two Groups, No Control

(a)	X	Y	(Experimental)
	$\sim X$	$\sim Y$	
(b)	(X)	Y	(Nonexperimental)
	$(\sim X)$	$\sim Y$	

Design 19.4 is common. In (*a*) the experimental group is administered treatment X. The "control" group, taken to be, or assumed to be, similar to the experimental group, is not given X. The Y measures are compared to ascertain the effect of X. Groups or participants are taken "as they are," or they may be matched. The nonexperimental version of the same design is labeled (*b*). An effect, Y, is observed to occur in one group (top line) but not in another group, or to occur in the other group to a lesser extent (indicated by the $\sim Y$ in the bottom line). The first group is found to have experienced X, the second group not to have experienced X.

This design has a basic weakness: The two groups are *assumed* to be equal in independent variables other than X. It is sometimes possible to check the equality of the groups roughly by comparing them on different pertinent variables, for example, age, sex, income, intelligence, ability, and so on. This should be done if it is at all possible, but, as Stouffer (1950, p. 522) says, "there is all too often a wide-open gate through which other uncontrolled variables can march." Because randomization is not used—that is, the participants are not assigned to the groups at random—it is not possible to assume that the groups are equal. Both versions of the design suffer seriously from lack of control of independent variables due to lack of randomization.

Criteria of Research Design

After examining some of the main weaknesses of inadequate research designs, we are in a good position to discuss what can be called *criteria* of research design. Along with the criteria, we will enunciate certain principles that should guide researchers. Finally, the criteria and principles will be related to Campbell's (1957) notions of internal and external validity, which, in a sense, express the criteria another way.

Answer Research Questions?

The main criterion or desideratum of a research design can be expressed in a question: *Does the design answer the research questions?* or *Does the design adequately test the hypotheses?* Perhaps the most serious weakness of designs often proposed by the neophyte is that they are not capable of answering the research questions adequately. A common example of this lack of congruence between the research questions and hypothesis, on the one hand, and the research design, on the other, is matching participants for reasons irrelevant to the research and then using an experimental group—control group type of design. For instance, students often assume that because they match pupils on intelligence and sex that their experimental groups are equal. They have heard that one should match participants for "control" and that one should have an experimental group and a control group. Frequently, however, the matching variables may be irrelevant to the research purposes. That is, if there is no relation between, say, sex and the dependent variable, then matching on sex is irrelevant.

Another example of this weakness is the case where three or four experimental groups are needed. For example, three experimental groups and one control group, or four groups with different amounts or aspects of *X*, the experimental treatment is required. However, the investigator uses only two because he or she has heard that an experimental group and a control group are necessary and desirable.

The example discussed in Chapter 18 of testing an interaction hypothesis by performing, in effect, two separate experiments is another example. The hypothesis to be tested was that discrimination in college admissions is a function of both sex and ability level, that it is women of low ability who are excluded (in contrast to men of low ability). This is an interaction hypothesis and probably calls for a factorial-type design. To set up two experiments, one for college applicants of high ability and another for applicants of low ability, is poor practice because such a design, as shown earlier, cannot decisively test the stated hypothesis. Similarly, to match participants on ability and then set up a two-group design would miss the research question entirely. These considerations lead to a general and seemingly obvious precept:

Design research to answer research questions.

Control of Extraneous Independent Variables

The second criterion is *control*, which refers to control of independent variables: the independent variables of the research study and extraneous independent variables. Extraneous independent variables are, of course, variables that may influence the dependent variable but that are not part of the study. Such variables are confounded with the independent variable under study. In the admissions study of Chapter 18, for example, geographical location (of the colleges) may be a potentially influential extraneous variable that can cloud the results of the study. If colleges in the east, for example, exclude more women than colleges in the west, then geographical location is an extraneous source of variance in the admissions measures—which should somehow be controlled. The criterion also refers to control of the variables of the study. Since this problem has already been discussed and will continue to be discussed, no more need be said here. But the question must be asked: *Does this design adequately control independent variables?*

The best single way to answer this question satisfactorily is expressed in the following principle:

Randomize whenever possible: select participants at random; assign participants to groups at random; assign experimental treatments to groups at random.

While it may not be possible to select participants at random, it may be possible to assign them to groups at random; thus "equalizing" the groups in the statistical sense discussed in earlier chapters. If such random assignment of participants to groups is not possible, then every effort should be made to assign experimental treatments to experimental groups at random. And, if experimental treatments are administered at different times with different experimenters, times and experimenters should be assigned at random.

The principle that makes randomization pertinent is complex and difficult to implement:

Control the independent variables so that extraneous and unwanted sources of systematic variance have minimal opportunity to operate.

As we have seen earlier (Chapter 8), randomization theoretically satisfies this principle. When we test the empirical validity of an If p, then q proposition, we manipulate p and observe that q covaries with the manipulation of p. But how confident can we be that our If p, then q statement is really "true"? Our confidence is directly related to the completeness and adequacy of the controls. If we use a design similar to designs 19.1 through 19.4, we cannot have too much confidence in the empirical validity of the If p, then q statement, since our control of extraneous independent variables is weak or nonexistent. Because such control is not always possible in much psychological, sociological, and educational research, should we then give up research entirely? By no means. But we must be aware of the weaknesses of intrinsically poor design.

Generalizability

The third criterion, *generalizability*, is independent of other criteria because it is different in kind. This is an important point that will shortly become clear. It means simply: *Can we generalize the results of a study to other participants, other groups, and other conditions?* Perhaps the question is better put: *How much* can we generalize the results of the study? This is probably the most complex and difficult question that can be asked of research data because it touches not only on technical matters (like sampling and research design), but also on larger problems of basic and applied research. In basic research, for example, generalizability is not the first consideration, because the central interest is the relations among variables and why the variables are related as they are. This emphasizes the internal rather than the external aspects of the study. These studies are often designed to examine theoretical issues such as motivation or learning. The goal of basic research is to add information and knowledge to a field of study, but usually without a specific practical purpose. Its results are generalizable, but not in the same realm as results found in applied research studies. In applied research, on the other hand, the central interest forces more concern for generalizability, because one certainly wishes to apply the results to other persons and to other situations. Applied research studies usually have their foundations in basic research studies. Using information found in a basic research study, applied research studies apply those findings to determine if it can solve a practical problem. Take the work of B. F. Skinner for example. His early research is generally considered as basic research. It was from his research that schedules of reinforcement were established. However, later, Skinner and others (Skinner, 1968; Garfinkle, Kline, & Stancer, 1973) applied the schedules of reinforcement to military problems, educational problems, and behavioral problems. Those who do research on the modification of behavior are applying many of the theories and ideas tested and established by B. F. Skinner. If the reader will ponder the following two examples of basic and applied research, he or she can get closer to this distinction.

In Chapter 14 we examined a study by Johnson (1994) on rape type, information admissibility and perception of rape victims. This is clearly basic research: the central interest was in the relations among rape type, information admissibility, and perception. While no one would be foolish enough to say that Johnson was not concerned with rape type, information admissibility, and perception in general, the emphasis was on the relations among the variables of the study. Contrast this study with the effort of Walster et al. (1970) to determine whether colleges discriminate against women. Naturally, Walster and her colleagues were particular about the internal aspects of their study. But they perforce had to have another interest: Is discrimination practiced among colleges in general? Their study is clearly applied research, though one cannot say that basic research interest was absent. The considerations of the next section may help to clarify generalizability.

Internal and External Validity

Two general criteria of research design have been discussed at length by Campbell (1957) and by Campbell and Stanley (1963). These notions constitute one of the most significant, important, and enlightening contributions to research methodology in the past three or four decades.

Internal validity asks the question: Did *X*, the experimental manipulation, really make a significant difference? The three criteria of Chapter 18 are actually aspects of internal validity. Indeed, anything affecting the *controls* of a design becomes a problem of internal validity. If a design is such that one can have little or no confidence in the relations, as shown by significant differences between experimental groups, this is a problem of internal validity.

Earlier in this chapter we presented four possible threats to internal validity. Some textbook authors have referred to these as "alternative explanations" (see Dane, 1990) or "rival hypotheses" (see Graziano & Raulin, 1993). These were listed as measurement, history, maturation, and statistical regression. Campbell and Stanley (1963) also list four other threats. They are instrumentation, selection, attrition, and the interaction between one of more of those previously listed (total of eight).

Instrumentation is a problem if the device used to measure the dependent variable changes over time. This is particularly true in studies using a human observer. Human observers or judges can be affected by previous events or fatigue. Observers may become more efficient over time, and thus the later measurements are more accurate than earlier ones. On the other hand, with fatigue, the human observer would become less accurate in the later trials than the earlier ones. When this happens, the values of the dependent variable will change and that change will not be due solely to the manipulation of the independent variable.

With selection, Campbell and Stanley (1963) are talking about the type of participants the experimenter selects for the study. This is especially likely if the researcher is not careful in studies that do not use random selection or assignment. The researcher could have selected participants in each group that are very different on some characteristic, and as such could account for a difference in the dependent variable. It is important for the researcher to have the groups equal prior to the administration of treatment. If the groups are the same before treatment, then logic follows that if they are different following treatment then it was the treatment (independent variable) that caused the difference and not something else. However, if the groups are different to begin with and different after treatment it is very difficult to make a statement that the difference was due to treatment. Later when discussing quasi-experimental designs, we will see how we can strengthen the situation.

Attrition or experimental mortality deals with the drop out of participants. If too many participants in one treatment condition leave the study, the unbalance is a possible reason for the change in the dependent variable. Attrition also includes the departure of participants with certain characteristics.

Any of the previous seven threats to internal validity could also interact with one another. Selection could interact with maturation. This threat is especially possible when using participants who are volunteers. If the researcher is comparing two groups—one group consists are volunteers (self-selected), the other group consists of nonvolunteers—the performance between these two on the dependent variable may be due to the fact that volunteers are more motivated. Student researchers sometimes use the volunteer subject pool and members of their own family or social circle as participants. There may be a problem of internal validity if volunteers are placed in one treatment group and their friends are put into another.

A difficult criterion to satisfy—*external validity*—defines *representativeness* or *generalizability*. When an experiment has been completed and a relation found, to what populations could it be generalized? Can we say that *A* is related to *B* for all schoolchildren? All eighth-grade children? All eighth-grade children in this school system? or All eighth-grade children of only this school? Or must the findings be limited to the eighth-grade children with whom we worked? These very important scientific questions should always be *asked and answered*.

Not only must sample generalizability be questioned, it is also necessary to ask questions about the ecological and variable representativeness of studies. If the social setting in which the experiment was conducted is changed, will the relation of *A* and

B still hold? Will *A* be related to *B* if the study is replicated in a lower-class school? In a western school? In a southern school? These are questions of *ecological representativeness*.

Variable representativeness is more subtle. A question not often asked, but that should be asked, is: Are the variables of this research representative? When an investigator works with psychological and sociological variables, one assumes that the variables are "constant." If the investigator finds a difference in achievement between boys and girls, one can assume that sex as a variable is "constant."

In the case of variables like achievement, aggression, aptitude, and anxiety, can the investigator assume that the "aggression" of the suburban participants is the same "aggression" to be found in city slums? Is the variable the same in a European suburb? The representativeness of "anxiety" is more difficult to ascertain. When we talk of "anxiety," what kind of anxiety do we mean? Are all kinds of anxiety the same? If anxiety is manipulated in one situation by verbal instructions and in another situation by electric shock, are the two induced anxieties the same? If anxiety is manipulated by, say, experimental instruction, is this the same anxiety as that measured by an anxiety scale? Variable representativeness, then, is another aspect of the larger problem of external validity, and thus of generalizability.

Unless special precautions are taken and special efforts made, the results of research are frequently not representative, and hence not generalizable. Campbell and Stanley (1963) say that internal validity is the sine qua non of research design, but that the ideal design should be strong in both internal validity and external validity, even though they are frequently contradictory. This point is well taken. In these chapters, the main emphasis is on internal validity, with a vigilant eye on external validity.

Campbell and Stanley (1963) present four threats to external validity. They are reactive or interaction effects of testing, the interaction effects of selection biases and the independent variable, reactive effects of experimental arrangements and multiple-treatment interference.

In the reactive or interaction effect of testing, the reference is to the use of a pretest prior to administering treatment. Pretesting may decrease or increase the sensitivity of the participant to the independent variable. This would make the results for the pretested population unrepresentative of the treatment effect for the nonpretested population. The likelihood of an interaction between treatment and pretesting seems first to have been pointed out by Solomon (1949).

The interaction effects of selection bias and the independent variable indicates that selection of participants can very well affect generalization of the results. A researcher using only participants from the subject pool at a particular university, which usually consists of freshmen and sophomores, will find it difficult to generalize the findings of the study to other students in the university or at other universities.

The mere participation in a research study can be a problem in terms of external validity. The presence of observers, instrumentation, or laboratory environment could have an effect on the participant that would not occur if the participant was in a natural setting. The fact that one is participating in an experimental study may alter one's normal behavior. Whether the experimenter is male or female, African American or white American could also have an effect.

If participants are exposed to more than one treatment condition, performance on later trials is affected by performance on earlier trials. Hence, the results can only be generalized to people who have had multiple exposures given in the same order.

The negative approach of this chapter was taken in the belief that an exposure to poor but commonly used and *accepted* procedures, together with a discussion of their major weaknesses, would provide a good starting point for the study of research design. Other inadequate designs are possible, but all such designs are inadequate on structural principles alone. This point should be emphasized because in Chapter 20 we will find that a perfectly good design structure can be poorly used. Thus it is necessary to learn and understand the two sources of research weakness: intrinsically poor designs and intrinsically good designs poorly used.

CHAPTER SUMMARY

1. Studying faulty designs helps researchers design better studies by knowing what pitfalls to avoid.
2. Nonexperimental designs are those with nonmanipulated independent variables, absence of random assignment or selection.
3. Faulty designs include the "one-shot case study," the one group before–after design, simulated before–after design, and the two group no-control design.
4. Faulty designs are discussed in terms of internal validity.
5. Internal validity is concerned with how strongly the experimenter can state the effect of the independent variable on the dependent variable. The more confidence the experimenter has about the manipulated independent variable, the stronger the internal validity.
6. Nonexperimental studies are weaker in internal validity than experimental studies.
7. There are eight basic classes of extraneous variables which, if not controlled, may be confounded with the independent variable. These eight basic classes are called threats to internal validity.
8. Campbell's threats to internal validity can be outlined as follows:

   - History
   - Maturation
   - Testing or Measurement
   - Instrumentation
   - Statistical Regression
   - Selection
   - Experimental Mortality or Attrition
   - Selection–Maturation Interaction

9. External validity is concerned with how strong a statement the experimenter can make about the generalizability of the results of the study.
10. Campbell and Stanley give four possible sources of threats to external validity:

- Reactive or interaction effect of testing
- Interaction effects of selection biases and the independent variable
- Reactive effects of experimental arrangements
- Multiple-treatment interference

STUDY SUGGESTIONS

1. Suppose a liberal arts college decides to begin a new curriculum for all undergraduates. It asks the faculty to form a research group to study the program's effectiveness for two years. The research group, wanting to have a group with which to compare the new curriculum group, requests that the present program be continued for two years and that students be allowed to volunteer for the present or the new program. The research group believes that it will then have an experimental group and a control group.
Discuss the research group's proposal critically. How much faith would you have in the findings at the end of two years? Give reasons for your positive or negative reactions to the proposal.
2. Imagine that you are a graduate school professor and have been asked to judge the worth of a proposed doctoral thesis. The doctoral student is a school superintendent who is instituting a new type of administration into her school system. She plans to study the effects of the new administration for a three-year period and then write her thesis. She says that she will not study any other school situation during the period so as not to bias the results.
Discuss the proposal. When doing so, ask yourself: Is the proposal suitable for doctoral work?
3. In your opinion should all research be held rather strictly to the criterion of generalizability? Explain why or why not. Which field is likely to have more basic research: psychology or education? Why? What implications do your conclusions have for generalizability?
4. What does replication of research have to do with generalizability? Explain. If it were possible, should all research be replicated? Explain why or why not. What does replication have to, do with external and internal validity?

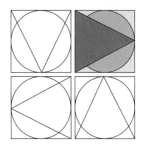

CHAPTER 20

GENERAL DESIGNS OF RESEARCH

Design is data discipline. The implicit purpose of all research design is to impose controlled restrictions on observations of natural phenomena. The research design tells the investigator, in effect: Do this and this; don't do that or that; be careful with this; ignore that; and so on. It is the blueprint of the research architect and engineer. If the design is poorly conceived structurally, the final product will be faulty. If it is at least well conceived structurally, the final product has a greater chance of being worthy of serious scientific attention. In this chapter, our main preoccupation is with several "good" basic designs of research. We also discuss certain conceptual foundations of research and some problems related to design—for instance, the rationale of control groups and the pros and cons of matching.

Conceptual Foundations of Research Design

The conceptual foundation for understanding research design was laid in Chapter 4 and Chapter 5, where sets and relations were defined and discussed. Recall that a *relation* is a set of ordered pairs. Recall, too, that a *Cartesian product* is all the possible ordered pairs of two sets. A *partition* breaks down a universal set *U* into subsets that are *disjoint* and *exhaustive*. A *cross partition* is a new partitioning that arises from successively partitioning *U* by forming all subsets of the form $A \cap B$. These definitions were elaborated in Chapter 5 and Chapter 6. We now apply them to design and analysis ideas.

Take two sets, *A* and *B*, partitioned into A_1 and A_2, B_1 and B_2. The Cartesian product of the two sets is:

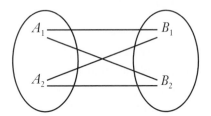

The ordered pairs, then, are: A_1B_1, A_1B_2, A_2B_1, A_2B_2. Since we have a set of ordered pairs, this is a relation. It is also a cross partition. The reader should look back at Figure 4.7 and Figure 4.8 of Chapter 4 to help clarify these ideas and to see the application of the Cartesian product and relation ideas to research design. For instance, A_1 and A_2 can be two aspects of any independent variable: experimental–control, two methods, male and female, and so on.

A *design* is some subset of the Cartesian product of the independent variables and the dependent variable. It is possible to pair each dependent variable measure, which we call *Y* in this discussion, with some aspect or partition of an independent variable. The simplest possible cases occur with one independent variable and one dependent variable. In Chapter 10, an independent variable, *A*, and a dependent variable, *B*, were partitioned into $[A_1, A_2]$ and $[B_1, B_2]$ and then cross partitioned to form the by-now familiar 2 × 2 crosstab, with frequencies or percentages in the cells. We concentrate, however, on similar cross partitions of *A* and *B*, but with continuous measures in the cells.

Take *A* alone, using a one-way analysis of variance design. Suppose we have three experimental treatments, A_1, A_2 and A_3, and, for simplicity, two *Y* scores in each cell. This is shown on the left of Figure 20.1, labeled (a). Say that six participants have been assigned at random to the three treatments, and that the scores of the six individuals after the experimental treatments are those given in the figure.

The right side of Figure 20.1, labeled (b), shows the same idea in ordered-pair or relation form. The ordered pairs are A_1Y_1, A_1Y_2, A_2Y_3, . . . , A_3Y_6. This is not, of course, a Cartesian product, which would pair A_1 with all the *Y*s, A_2 with all the *Y*s, and A_3 with all the *Y*s, a total of 3 × 6 = 18 pairs. Rather, Figure 20.1(b) is a subset of the Cartesian product, $A \times B$. Research designs are subsets of $A \times B$, and the design and the research problem define or specify how the subsets are set up. The

▣ FIGURE 20.1

(a)

A_1	A_2	A_3
7	7	3
9	5	3

(b)

A_1 〈 $Y_1 = 7$ / $Y_2 = 9$

A_2 〈 $Y_3 = 7$ / $Y_4 = 5$

A_3 〈 $Y_5 = 3$ / $Y_6 = 3$

subsets of the design of Figure 20.1 are presumably dictated by the research problem.

When there is more than one independent variable, the situation is more complex. Take two independent variables, A and B, partitioned into $[A_1, A_2]$ and $[B_1, B_2]$. The reader should not confuse this with the earlier AB frequency paradigm, in which A was the independent variable and B the dependent variable.

We must now have ordered triples (or two sets of ordered pairs): ABY. Study Figure 20.2. On the left side of the figure, labeled (a), the 2×2 factorial analysis of variance design and example used in Chapter 14 (see Figure 14.2 and Table 14.3 and Table 14.4) is given, with the measures of the dependent variable, Y, inserted in the cells. That is, eight participants were assigned at random to the four cells. Their scores, after the experiment, are $Y_1, Y_2, \ldots, Y_8$. The right side of the figure, labeled (b), shows the ordered triples, ABY, as a tree. Obviously these are subsets of $A \times B \times Y$ and are relations. The same reasoning can be extended to larger and more complex

▣ FIGURE 20.2

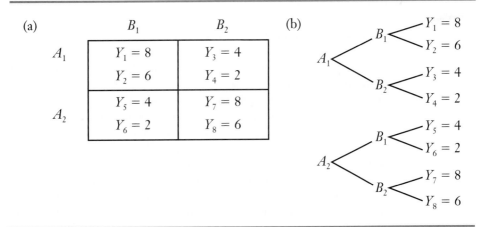

(a)

	B_1	B_2
A_1	$Y_1 = 8$ $Y_2 = 6$	$Y_3 = 4$ $Y_4 = 2$
A_2	$Y_5 = 4$ $Y_6 = 2$	$Y_7 = 8$ $Y_8 = 6$

(b)

A_1 〈 B_1 〈 $Y_1 = 8$ / $Y_2 = 6$; B_2 〈 $Y_3 = 4$ / $Y_4 = 2$

A_2 〈 B_1 〈 $Y_5 = 4$ / $Y_6 = 2$; B_2 〈 $Y_7 = 8$ / $Y_8 = 6$

designs, like a $2 \times 2 \times 3$ factorial (*ABCY*) or a $4 \times 3 \times 2 \times 2$ (*ABCDY*). (In these designations, *Y* is usually omitted because it is implied.) Other kinds of designs can be similarly conceptualized, though their depiction in trees can be laborious.

In sum, a research design is some subset of the Cartesian product of the independent and the dependent variables. With only one independent variable, the single variable is partitioned; with more than one independent variable, the independent variables are cross partitioned. With three or more independent variables, the conceptualization is the same; only the dimensions differ, for example, $A \times B \times C$ and $A \times B \times C \times D$ and the cross partitions thereof. Whenever possible, it is desirable to have "complete" designs—a complete design is a cross partition of the independent variables—and to observe the two basic conditions of disjointedness and exhaustiveness. That is, the design must not have a case (a participant's score) in more than one cell of a partition or cross partition, and all the cases must be used up. Moreover, the basic minimum of any design is at least a partition of the independent variable into two subsets, for example, *A* into A_1 and A_2. There are also "incomplete" designs, but "complete" designs are emphasized more in this book. See Kirk (1995) for a more complete treatment of incomplete designs.

The term "general designs" states that the designs given in the chapter are symbolized or expressed in their most general and abstract form. Where a simple *X* (representing an independent variable) is given, it must be taken to indicate more than one *X*—that is, *X* is partitioned into two or more experimental groups. For instance, Design 20.1, to be studied shortly, has *X* and ~*X*, meaning experimental and control groups, and thus is a partition of *X*. But *X* can be partitioned into a number of *X*s, perhaps changing the design from a simple one-variable design to, say, a factorial design. The basic symbolism associated with Design 20.1, however, remains the same. These complexities will, we hope, be clarified in this and succeeding chapters.

A Preliminary Note: Experimental Designs and Analysis of Variance

Before taking up the designs of this chapter, we need to clarify one or two confusing and potentially controversial points not usually considered in the literature. Most of the designs we consider are experimental. As usually conceived, the rationale of research design is based on experimental ideas and conditions. They are also intimately linked to analysis of variance paradigms. This is, of course, no accident. Modern conceptions of design, especially factorial designs, were born when analysis of variance was invented. Although there is no hard law that says that analysis of variance is applicable only in experimental situations—indeed, it has been used many times in nonexperimental research—it is generally true that it is most appropriate for the data of experiments. This is especially so for factorial designs where there are equal numbers of cases in the design paradigm cells, and where the participants are assigned to the experimental conditions (or cells) at random.

When it is not possible to assign participants at random, and when, for one reason or another, there are unequal numbers of cases in the cells of a factorial design, the use of analysis of variance is questionable, even inappropriate. It can also be clumsy and inelegant. This is because the use of analysis of variance assumes that the correlations between or among the independent variables of a factorial design are zero. Random assignment makes this assumption tenable since such assignment presumably apportions sources of variance equally among the cells. But random assignment can only be accomplished in experiments. In nonexperimental research, the independent variables are more or less fixed characteristics of the participants (e.g., intelligence, sex, social class, and the like). They are usually systematically correlated. Take two independent manipulated variables, say, reinforcement and anxiety. Because participants with varying amounts of characteristics correlated with these variables are distributed randomly in the cells, the correlations between aspects of reinforcement and anxiety are assumed to be zero. If, on the other hand, the two independent variables are intelligence and social class, both ordinarily nonmanipulable and correlated, the assumption of zero correlation between them necessary for analysis of variance cannot be made. Some method of analysis that takes account of the correlation between them should be used. We will see later in the book that such a method is readily available: multiple regression.

We have not yet reached a state of research maturity to appreciate the profound difference between the two situations. For now, however, let us accept the difference and the statement that analysis of variance is basically an experimental conception and form of analysis. Strictly speaking, if our independent variables are nonexperimental, then analysis of variance is not the appropriate mode of analysis. However, there are exceptions to this statement. For instance, if one independent variable is experimental and one nonexperimental, analysis of variance is appropriate. In one-way analysis of variance, moreover, since there is only one independent variable, analysis of variance can be used with a nonexperimental independent variable, though regression analysis would probably be more appropriate. In Study Suggestion 3, an interesting use of analysis of variance with nonexperimental data is cited.

Similarly, if for some reason the numbers of cases in the cells are unequal (and disproportionate), then there will be correlation between the independent variables, and the assumption of zero correlation is not tenable. This rather abstract and abstruse digression from our main design theme may seem a bit confusing at this stage of our study. The problems involved should become clear after we have studied experimental and nonexperimental research and, later in the book, that fascinating and powerful approach known as multiple regression.

The Designs

In the remainder of this chapter we discuss several basic designs of research. Remember that a design is a plan, an outline for conceptualizing the structure of the relations among the variables of a research study. A design not only lays out the relations of the study, it also implies how the research situation is controlled and how the data are to be analyzed. A design, in the sense of this chapter, is the skeleton on which we put the variable-and-relation flesh of our research. The sketches given in Designs

20.1–20.8, are the bare and abstract structure of the research. Sometimes analytic tables, such as Figure 20.2 (on the left) and the figures of Chapter 18 (e.g., figures 18.2, 18.3, and 18.5), are called *designs*. While calling them designs does no great harm, they are, strictly speaking, analytic paradigms. We will not be fussy, however. We will call both kinds of representations "designs."

Design 20.1: Experimental Group–Control Group: Randomized Participants

[R]	X	Y	(Experimental)
	~X	Y	(Control)

Design 20.1, with two groups as above, and its variants with more than two groups, are probably the "best" designs for many experimental purposes in behavioral research. Campbell and Stanley (1963) call this design the *posttest only control group design*, whereas Isaac and Michael (1987) refer to it as the *randomized control group posttest only design*. The [R] before the paradigm indicates that participants are assigned randomly to the Experimental Group (top line) and the Control Group (bottom line). This randomization removes the objections to Design 19.4 mentioned in Chapter 19. Theoretically, all possible independent variables are controlled. Practically, of course, this may not be so. If enough participants are included in the experiment to give the randomization a chance to "operate," then we have strong control, and the claims of internal validity are rather well satisfied. This design controls for the effects of history, maturation and pretesting but does not measure these effects.

If extended to more than two groups and if it is capable of answering the research questions asked, Design 20.1 has a number of advantages: (1) it has the best built-in theoretical control system of any design, with one or two possible exceptions in special cases; (2) it is flexible, being theoretically capable of extension to any number of groups with any number of variables; (3) if extended to more than one variable, it can test several hypotheses at one time; and (4) it is statistically and structurally elegant.

Before taking up other designs, we need to examine the notion of the control group, one of the creative inventions of the past hundred years, and certain extensions of Design 20.1. The two topics go nicely together.

The Notion of the Control Group and Extensions of Design 20.1

Evidently the word *control* and the expression "control group" did not appear in the scientific literature before the late nineteenth century. This is documented by Boring (1954). The notion of controlled experimentation, however, is much older. Boring says that Pascal used it as early as 1648. Solomon (1949) searched the psychological literature and could not find a single case of the use of a control group before 1901. Perhaps the notion of the control group was used in other fields, though it is doubtful that the idea was well developed. Solomon (p. 175) also says that the Peterson and

Thurstone study of attitudes in 1933 was the first serious attempt to use control groups in the evaluation of the effects of educational procedures. One cannot find the expression "control group" in the famous eleventh edition (1911) of the *Encyclopedia Britannica*, even though experimental method is discussed. Solomon also says that control group design apparently had to await statistical developments and the development of statistical sophistication among psychologists.

Perhaps the first use of control groups in psychology and education occurred in 1901 with the publication of Thorndike and Woodworth (1901). One of the two men who did this research, Thorndike, extended the basic and revolutionary ideas of this first research series to education (Thorndike, 1924). Thorndike's controls, in this gigantic study of 8,564 pupils in many schools in a number of cities, were independent educational groups. Among other comparisons, he contrasted the gains in intelligence test scores presumably engendered by the study of English, history, geometry, and Latin, with the gains presumably engendered by the study of English, history, geometry, and shopwork. He tried, in effect, to compare the influence of Latin and shopwork. He also made other comparisons of a similar nature. Despite the weaknesses of design and control, Thorndike's experiments and those he stimulated others to perform were remarkable for their insight. Thorndike even berated colleagues for not admitting students of stenography and typing who had not studied Latin, because he claimed to have shown that the influence of various participants on intelligence was similar. It is interesting that he thought huge numbers of participants were necessary—he called for 18,000 more cases. He was also quite aware, in 1924, of the need for random samples.

The notion of the control group needs generalization. Assume that in an educational experiment we have four experimental groups as follows. A_1 is reinforcement of every response, A_2 reinforcement at regular time intervals, A_3 reinforcement at random intervals, and A_4 no reinforcement. Technically, there are three experimental groups and one control group, in the traditional sense of the control group. However, A_4 might be another "experimental treatment"; it might be some kind of minimal reinforcement. Then, in the traditional sense, there would be no control group. The traditional sense of the term "control group" lacks generality. If the notion of control is generalized, the difficulty disappears. Whenever there is more than one experimental group and any two groups are given different treatments, control is present in the sense of comparison previously mentioned. As long as there is an attempt to make two groups systematically different on a dependent variable, a comparison is possible. Thus the traditional notion that an experimental group should receive the treatment not given to a control group is a special case of the more general rule that comparison groups are necessary for the internal validity of scientific research.

If this reasoning is correct, we can set up designs such as the following:

	X_1	Y
[R]	X_2	Y
	X_3	Y

or

	X_{1a}	Y
[R]	X_{1b}	Y
	X_{2a}	Y
	X_{2b}	Y

These designs will be more easily recognizable if they are set up in the manner of analysis of variance, as in Figure 20.3. The design on the left is a simple one-way analysis of variance design and the one on the right a 2 × 3 × 2 factorial design. In the right-hand design, X_{1a} might be experimental and X_{1b} control, with X_{2a} and X_{2b} either a manipulated variable or a dichotomous attribute variable. It is, of course, the same design as that shown in Figure 20.2(a).

The structure of Design 20.2 is the same as that of Design 20.1. The only difference is that participants are matched on one or more attributes. For the design to take its place as an "adequate" design, however, randomization must enter the picture, as noted by the small r attached to the M (for "matched"). It is not enough that matched participants are used. The members of each pair must be assigned to the two groups at random. Ideally, too, whether a group is to be an experimental or a control group is also decided at random. In either case, each decision can be made by flipping a coin or by using a table of random numbers. Odd numbers are used for one group and even numbers for the other group. If there are more than two groups, naturally, a random number system must be used.

Design 20.2: Experimental Group–Group: Matched Participants

	X	Y	(Experimental)
$[M_r]$			
	$\sim X$	Y	(Control)

As in Design 20.1, it is possible, though often not easy, to use more than two groups. (The difficulty of matching more than two groups was discussed earlier.) There are times, however, when a matching design is an inherent element of the research

◉ **FIGURE 20.3**

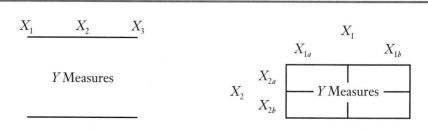

▣ FIGURE 20.4

Schools	X_{e1} **Experimental 1**	X_{e2} **Experimental 2**	X_c **Control**
1			
2			
3		Y Measures	
4			
5			

situation. When the same participants are used for two or more experimental treatments, or when participants are given more than one trial, matching is inherent in the situation. In educational research, when schools or classes are in effect variables when, say, two or more schools or classes are used and the experimental treatments are administered in each school or class then Design 20.2 is the basis of the design logic. Study the paradigm of a schools design in Figure 20.4. It is seen that variance due to the differences between schools, and such variance can be substantial, can be readily estimated.

Matching versus Randomization

Although randomization, which includes random selection and random assignment, is the preferred method for controlling extraneous variance, there is merit to the use of matching. In a number of situations outside academic circles, the behavioral scientist will not be able to use randomization in achieving constancy between groups prior to the administration of treatment. Usually in a university a participant pool is available from which to draw. Researchers in this situation can afford to use randomization procedures. In business research, however, this may not be the case. Popular among market researchers is the controlled store test. The controlled store test is an experiment that is done in the field. The second author has conducted such studies for a number of market research firms and a grocery chain in Southern California. One of the goals of the controlled store test is to be very discreet. If a manufacturer of soap products wants to determine the effects of a cents-off coupon on consumer purchasing behavior, that manufacturer does not want the competing manufacturer of a similar product to know about it. Why? Because if a competitor knew that a research study was going on in a store, they could go in and buy up their own product and hence contaminate the study.

To return to our discussion of randomization versus matching, often times a grocery chain or a chain of department stores has a finite number of stores to use in a study. Location and clientele exert a lot of influence on sales. Sales are usually the dependent variable in such studies. With a limited number of stores to choose from in order to perform the research, random assignment does not often work in equating groups of stores. One store in the chain might do three to four times the volume of business as another. If it is chosen at random, it will create a great deal of unbalance toward the group it falls into, especially if the other group does not have a similar store to balance it. In short, the groups will no longer be equal. Hence, the solution here is to match the stores on an individual basis. One-half of the matched pair is assigned randomly to one experimental condition and the other half receives the other condition. With more than two conditions, more stores would have to be matched and then assigned to treatment conditions.

In some human factors engineering studies using simulators, the use of randomization is sometimes not economically or practically feasible. Consider the testing of two configurations for a simulator. A researcher may want to know which one leads to fewer perceptual errors. Processes of randomization would say that the researcher should assign participants randomly to conditions as they enter the study. However, when it requires three to six months to change the configuration of the simulator, it is no longer feasible to proceed the "usual" way.

An important point to remember is that randomization—when it can be done correctly and appropriately—is generally considered better than matching. It is perhaps the only method for controlling unknown sources of variances. One of the major shortcomings of matching is that one can never be sure that an exact match has been made. Without that exactness, the inexactness can be an alternative explanation of why the dependent variable is different between the treatment conditions following experimental manipulation.

Matching by Equating Participants

The most common method of matching is to equate participants on one or more variables to be controlled. Christensen (1996) refers to this method as the *precision control method*; and Matheson, Bruce, and Beauchamp (1978) call it the *matched-by-correlated criterion design*. To control for the influence of intelligence on the dependent variable, for example, the researcher must be sure that the participants in each of the treatment groups are of the same intelligence level. The goal here is to create equivalent groups of participants. Using our example of intelligence, if we had only two treatment conditions, we would select pairs of participants with identical or near identical intelligence test scores. Half of each pair would be assigned at random to one treatment condition and the other half assigned to the other treatment condition. In a controlled store test, where location is an important variable to be controlled, we would find two stores of similar locale and call them a match. After we have built up, let's say 10 of such pairs, we can then take one-half of each pair and assign them to one test environment and one-half to the other. If we had required matching for three conditions, we would then have to find three people with the same intelligence score.

The major advantage in using this method is that it is able to detect small differences (increase in sensitivity) by ensuring that the participants in the various groups are equal on at least the paired variables. However, an important requirement is that the variables on which participants are matched must be correlated significantly with the dependent variable. We had shown in an earlier chapter that matching is most useful when the variables on which participants are matched correlate greater than 0.5 or 0.6 with the dependent variable.

This method of matching has two major flaws or disadvantages. First, it is difficult to know which are the most important variables to match. In most instances, there are many potentially relevant variables. In a study the researcher might match on age, sex, race, marital status, and intelligence. However, the researcher could have selected many other variables. The researcher should select those variables that show the lowest correlation with each other, but the highest correlation with the dependent variable.

A second problem is the decrease in finding eligible matched participants as the number of variables used for matching increases. To choose three or four variables to match on and then find enough participants that meet the matching criteria requires a lot of participants to choose from. The researcher would need a large pool of available participants in order to obtain just a few that are matched on all of the relevant variables. Matching affects the generalizability of the study. The researcher can only generalize the results to other individuals having the same characteristics as the matched sample.

The Frequency Distribution Matching Method

The individual-by-individual matching technique presented above is very good for developing equal groups, but many participants must be eliminated because they cannot be matched. The frequency distribution method attempts to overcome this disadvantage while retaining some of the advantages of matching. This technique, as its name implies, matches groups of participants in terms of overall distribution of the selected variable or variables, rather than on an individual-by-individual basis. Let's say that we want to have two or more groups matched on intelligence. Let's further say we want to use the frequency distribution method of matching. First we will need an intelligence test score on each child. We then need to create the two or more groups in a way such that the groups will have to have the same average intelligence test score, as well as the same standard deviation and skewness of the scores. Each group would be statistically equal—the mean, standard deviation, and skewness between each group would be statistically equivalent. A statistical test of hypotheses could be utilized, but the researcher needs to be aware that both types of errors should be considered. If more than one variable was considered to be relevant on which to match participants, each group of participants would be required to have the same statistical measures on all of these variables. The number of participants lost using this technique would not be as great as the number lost using the individual-by-individual method, because each additional participant would merely have to contribute to producing the appropriate statistical measures, rather than be identical to another participant on the relevant variables. Hence, this technique is more flexible in terms of being able to use a particular participant.

The major disadvantage of matching using the frequency distribution method occurs only when there is matching on more than one variable. Here the combinations of variables may be mismatched in the various groups. If age and reaction time were to be matched, one group might include older participants with slower reaction times and younger participants with quicker reaction times, whereas the other group would have the opposite combination. The mean and distribution of the two variables would be equivalent but the participants in each group would be completely different. This difference may affect the dependent variable.

Matching by Holding Variables Constant

Holding the adventitious variable constant for all experimental groups is another technique that can be used to create equal groups of participants. All participants in each experimental group will have the same degree or type of extraneous variable. If we need to control the variation caused by gender differences, we can hold sex constant by using only males or only females in the study. This has the effect of matching all participants in terms of the sex variable. This matching procedure creates a more homogeneous participant sample, because only participants with a certain type or amount of the fortuitous variable are used. A number of student research projects at universities use this method, especially when the participant pool has a majority of male or female participants. This technique of holding variables constant has at least two problems that could affect the validity of the study. The severity of the problem increases if too many variables are held constant. The first disadvantage is that the technique restricts the size of the participant population. Consequently, in some cases, it may be difficult to find enough participants to participate in the study. The early split-brain research of Roger Sperry has often been criticized by the restriction of the participants used in the study. His early studies used only epileptic patients. So a study using this method could be criticized on the basis of a selection bias.

The second drawback is more critical in that the results of the study are only generalizable to the type of participant used in the study. The results obtained from the epileptic patients study could only be generalized to other epileptic patients. If someone wanted to know whether non-epileptic patients would experience the same perceptual changes, the researcher would have to conduct a similar study using non-epileptic patients. Conclusions from such a study might indeed be the same as those obtained from the epileptic patient study, but separate studies must be conducted. The only way we can find out if the results of one study can be generalized to the population is to replicate the study using participants with different characteristics.

Matching by Incorporating the Nuisance Variable Into the Research Design

Another way of attempting to develop equal groups is to use the nuisance or extraneous variable as an independent variable in the research design. Assume that we were conducting a learning experiment on rats and wanted to control for the effects of weight. The thought here is that the animal with the greater weight will need to consume more food after a period of deprivation, and hence is more motivated. If we had used the method of holding weight constant, we would have far fewer participants. By using weight as an independent variable, we can use a lot more participants in the study. In statistical terms, the increase in the number of participants means an increase in power and sensitivity. By using an extraneous variable as an independent variable in the design, we can isolate a source of systematic variance and also determine if the extraneous variable has an effect on the dependent variable.

Building an extraneous variable into the design should not, however, be done indiscriminantly. Making the extraneous variable a part of the research design seems like an excellent control method, but this method is best used when there is an interest in the differences produced by the extraneous variable, or in the interaction between the extraneous variable and other independent variables. For a variable measured on a continuous scale, a researcher can still incorporate it into the design. The difference between a discrete and continuous extraneous variable would lie in the data analysis part of the research process. Using multiple regression or analysis of covariance would be preferable over analysis of variance.

Participant as Own Control

Since each individual is unique, it is difficult if not impossible to find another individual who would be a perfect match. However, a single person is always a perfect match to himself or herself. One of the more powerful techniques for achieving equality or constancy of experimental groups prior to the administration of treatment is to use that person in every condition of the experiment. Some refer to this as using the participants as their own control. Other than the reactivity of the experiment itself, the possibility of extraneous variation due to individual-to-individual differences is drastically minimized. This method of achieving constancy is common in some areas of the behavioral sciences. In psychology, the study of the interface of humans and machines (human factors or human engineering) utilizes this method. Simon (1976) presents a number of interesting experimental designs that use the same participant over many treatment conditions. However, this method does not fit all applications. Some studies involved with learning are not suitable, because a person cannot unlearn a problem so that he or she can now apply a different method. The use of this method also requires far more planning and more precise execution than others.

Additional Design Extensions:
Design 20.3 Using a Pretest

Design 20.3 has many advantages and is used frequently. Its structure is similar to that of Design 19.2, with two important differences: Design 19.2 lacks a control group and randomization. Design 20.3 is similar to designs 20.1 and 20.2, except that the "before" or pretest feature has been added. It is used frequently to study change. Like designs 20.1 and 20.2, Design 20.3 can be expanded to more than two groups.

Design 20.3: Before and After Control Group (Pretest–Posttest)

(a)		Y_b	X	Y_a	(Experimental)
	[R]	Y_b	~X	Y_a	(Control)

(b)		Y_b	X	Y_a	(Experimental)
	$[M_r]$	Y_b	~X	Y_a	(Control)

In Design 20.3(a), participants are assigned to the experimental group (top line) and the control group (bottom line) at random, and are pretested on a measure of Y, the dependent variable. The investigator can then check the equality of the two groups on Y. The experimental manipulation X is performed, after which the groups are again measured on Y. The difference between the two groups is tested statistically. An interesting and difficult characteristic of this design is the nature of the scores usually analyzed: difference, or change scores, $Y_a - Y_b = D$. Unless the effect of the experimental manipulation is strong, the analysis of difference scores is not advisable. Difference scores are considerably less reliable than the scores from which they are calculated. A clear explanation of why this is so is given by Friedenberg (1995) and Sax (1997). Although there are other problems, we discuss only the main strengths and weaknesses (see Campbell & Stanley, 1963, for a more complete discussion of this). At the end of the discussion, the analytic difficulties of difference or change scores will be examined.

Probably most important, Design 20.3 overcomes the great weakness of Design 19.2, because it supplies a comparison control group against which the difference, $Y_a - Y_b$, can be checked. With only one group, we can never know whether history, maturation (or both), or the experimental manipulation X produced the change in Y. When a control group is added, the situation is radically altered. After all, if the groups are equated (through randomization), the effects of history and maturation, if present, should be present in both groups. If the mental ages of the children of the experimental group increase, so should the mental ages of the children of the control group. Then, if there is still a difference between the Y measures of the two groups, it should not be due to history or maturation. That is, if something happens to affect the experimental participants between the pretest and the posttest, this something should also affect the participants of the control group. Similarly, the effect of testing—Campbell's reactive measures—should be controlled because, if the testing affects the members of the experimental group, it should similarly affect the members of the control group. (There is, however, a concealed weakness here, which will be discussed later.) This is the main strength of the well-planned, well-executed, before–after, experimental control group design.

On the other hand, before–after designs have a troublesome aspect, which decreases both internal and external validity of the experiment. This source of difficulty is the pretest. A pretest can have a sensitizing effect on participants. On internal validity, for example, the participants may possibly be alerted to certain events in their environment that they might not have ordinarily noticed. If the pretest is an attitude scale, it can sensitize participants to the issues or problems mentioned in the scale. Then, when the X treatment is administered to the experimental group, the participants of this group may be responding not so much to the attempted influence (the communication, or whatever method is used to change attitudes), as to a combination of their increased sensitivity to the issues and the experimental manipulation.

Since such interaction effects are not immediately obvious, and since they contain a threat to the external validity of experiments, it is worthwhile to consider them a bit further. One would think that, since both the experimental and the control groups are pretested, the effect of pretesting, if any, would ensure the validity of the experiment. Let us assume that no pretesting was done; that is, that Design 20.2 was used. Other things being equal, a difference between the experimental and the control groups after experimental manipulation of X can be assumed to be due to X. There is no reason to suppose that one group is more sensitive or more alert than the other, since they both face the testing situation after X. But when a pretest is used, the situation changes. While the pretest sensitizes both groups, it can make the experimental participants respond to X, wholly or partially, because of the sensitivity.

What we also have is a lack of generalizability or external validity, in that it may be possible to generalize to pretested groups but not to unpretested groups. Clearly, such a situation is disturbing to the researcher, since who wants to generalize to pretested groups?

If this weakness is important, why is this a good design? While the possible interaction effect described above may be serious in some research, it is doubtful that it strongly affects much behavioral research, provided researchers are aware of its potential and take adequate precautions. Testing is an accepted and normal part of many situations, especially in education. It is doubtful, therefore, that research participants will be unduly sensitized in such situations. Still, there may be times when they can be affected. The rule given by Campbell and Stanley (1963) is a good one: When unusual testing procedures are to be used, use designs with no pretests.

Difference Scores

Look at Design 20.3 again, particularly at changes between Y_b and Y_a. One of the most difficult problems that has plagued—and intrigued—researchers, measurement specialists, and statisticians is how to study and analyze such difference, or change, scores. In a book of the scope of this one, it is impossible to go into the problems in detail. The interested reader can read two excellently edited books: Harris (1963), and Collins and Horn (1991). General precepts and cautions, however, can be outlined. One would think that the application of analysis of variance to difference scores yielded by Design 20.3 and similar designs would be effective. Such analysis can be done if the experimental effects are substantial. But difference scores, as mentioned earlier, are usually less reliable than the scores from which they are calculated. Real differences between experimental and control groups may be undetectable simply because of the unreliability of the difference scores. To detect differences between experimental and control groups, the scores analyzed must be reliable enough to reflect the differences and thus to be detectable by statistical tests. Because of this difficulty, some researchers such as Cronbach and Furby (1970) say that difference or change scores should not be used. So what can be done?

The generally recommended procedure is to use so-called residualized or regressed gain scores. These scores are calculated by predicting the posttest scores from the pretest scores on the basis of the correlation between pretest and posttest, and then subtracting these predicted scores from the posttest scores to obtain the residual gain scores. (The reader should not be concerned if this procedure is not too clear at this stage. Later, after we study regression and analysis of covariance, it should become clearer.) The effect of the pretest scores is removed from the posttest scores; that is, the residual scores are posttest scores purged of the pretest influence. Then the significance of the difference between the means of these scores is tested. All this can be accomplished by using both the procedure just described and a regression equation, or by analysis of covariance.

Even the use of residual gain scores and analysis of covariance is not perfect, however. If participants have not been assigned at random to the experimental and control groups, the procedure will not save the situation. Cronbach and Furby (1970) point out that when groups differ systematically before experimental treatment in other characteristics pertinent to the dependent variable, statistical manipulation does not correct such differences. If, however, a pretest is used, use random assignment and analysis of covariance, remembering that the results must always be treated with special care. Finally, multiple regression analysis may provide the best solution of the problem, as we shall see later. It is unfortunate that the complexities of design and statistical analysis may discourage the student of research, sometimes even to the point of feeling helpless. But that is the nature of behavioral research: it merely reflects the exceedingly complex character of psychological, sociological, and educational reality. This is at one and the same time frustrating and exciting. Like marriage, behavioral research is difficult and often unsuccessful—but not impossible. Moreover, it is one of the best ways to acquire reliable understanding of our behavioral world. The point of view of this book is that we should learn and understand as much as we can about what we are doing, use reasonable care with design and analysis, and then do the research without fussing too much about analytic matters. The main thing is always the research problem and our interest in it. This does not mean a cavalier disregard of analysis. It simply means reasonable understanding and care, and healthy measures of both optimism and skepticism.

Design 20.4: Simulated Before–After, Randomized

		X	Y_a
[R]			
	Y_b		

The value of Design 20.4 is doubtful, even though it is considered to among the adequate designs. The scientific demand for a comparison is satisfied: there is a comparison group (lower line). A major weakness of Design 19.3 (a pallid version of Design 20.4) is remedied by the randomization. Recall that with Design 19.3 we were unable to assume beforehand that the experimental and control groups were equivalent. Design 20.4 calls for participants to be assigned to the two groups at random. It can thus be assumed that they are statistically equal. Such a design might be used when one is worried about the reactive effect of pretesting, or when, due to the exigencies of practical situations, one has no other choice. Such a situation occurs when one has the opportunity to try a method or some innovation only once. To test the method's efficacy, one provides a baseline for judging the effect of X on Y by pretesting a group similar to the experimental group. Then Y_a is tested against Y_b.

This design's validity breaks down if the two groups are not selected randomly from the same population, or if the participants are not assigned to the two groups at random. Further, even if randomization is used, there is no real guarantee that it worked in equating the two groups prior to treatment. It has the weaknesses mentioned in connection with other similar designs; namely, other possible variables may be influential in the interval between Y_b and Y_a. In other words, Design 20.4 is superior to Design 19.3, but should not be used if a better design is available.

Design 20.5: Three Group, Before–After

	Y_b	X	Y_a	(Experimental)
[R]	Y_b	$\sim X$	Y_a	(Control 1)
		X	Y_a	(Control 2)

Design 20.5 is better than Design 20.4. In addition to the assets of Design 20.3 it provides a way to possibly avoid confounding due to the interactive effects of the pretest. This is achieved by the second control group (third line). (It seems a bit strange to have a control group with an X, but the group of the third line is really a control group.) With the Y_a measures of this group available, it is possible to check the interaction effect. Suppose the mean of the Experimental group is significantly greater than the mean of Control Group 1. We may doubt whether this difference was really due to X. It might have been produced by increased sensitization of the participants after the pretest and the interaction of their sensitization and X. We now look at the mean of Y_a of Control Group 2. It, too, should be significantly greater than the mean of Control Group 1. If it is, we can assume that the pretest has not unduly sensitized the participants, or that X is sufficiently strong to override a sensitization—X interaction effect.

Design 20.6: Four Group, Before–After (Solomon)

	Y_b	X	Y_a	(Experimental)
	Y_b	$\sim X$	Y_a	(Control 1)
[R]		X	Y_a	(Control 2)
		$\sim X$	Y_a	(Control 3)

This design, proposed by Solomon (1949) is strong and aesthetically satisfying. It has potent controls. Actually, if we change the designation of Control 2 to Experimental 2, we have a combination of designs 20.3 and 20.1, our two best designs, where the former design forms the first two lines and the latter the second two lines. The virtues of both are combined in one design. Although this design can have a matching form, it is neither discussed here nor is it recommended. Campbell (1957) states that this design has become the new ideal for social scientists. While this is a strong statement, probably a bit too strong, it indicates the high esteem in which the design is held.

Among the reasons why it is a strong design is that the demand for comparison is well satisfied with the first two lines and the second two lines. The randomization enhances the probability of statistical equivalence of the groups, and history and maturation are controlled by the first two lines of the design. The interaction effect due to possible pretest participant sensitization is controlled by the first three lines. By adding the fourth line, temporary contemporaneous effects that may have occurred between Y_a and Y_b can be controlled. Because Design 20.1 and Design 20.3 are combined, we have the power of each test separately, and the power of replication because, in effect, there are two experiments. If Y_a of Experimental is significantly greater than Control 1, and Control 2 is significantly greater than Control 3, together with a consistency of results between the two experiments, this is strong evidence, indeed, of the validity of our research hypothesis.

What is wrong with this paragon of designs? It certainly looks fine on paper. There appear to be only two sources of weakness. One is practicability—it is harder to run two simultaneous experiments than one, and the researcher encounters the difficulty of locating more participants of the same kind.

The other difficulty is statistical. Note that there is a lack of balance of groups. There are four actual groups, but not four complete sets of measures. Using the first two lines, that is, with Design 20.3, one can subtract Y_b from Y_a or do an analysis of covariance. With the two lines, one can test the Y_as against each other with a t-test or F-test, but the problem is how to obtain one overall statistical approach. One solution is to test the Y_as of Control 2 and Control 3 against the average of the two Y_bs (the first two lines), as well as to test the significance of the difference of the Y_as of the first two lines. In addition, Solomon originally suggested a 2×2 factorial analysis of variance, using the four Y_a sets of measures. Solomon's suggestion is outlined in Figure 20.5. A careful study will reveal that this is a fine example of

◨ **FIGURE 20.5**

	X	$\sim X$
Pretested	X_a, Experimental 1	Y_a, Control 1
Not Pretested	Y_a, Control 2	Y_a, Control 3

research thinking, a nice blending of design and analysis. With this analysis we can study the main effects, X and $\sim X$, and Pretested and Not Pretested. What is more interesting, we can test the interaction of pretesting and X and get a clear answer to the previous problem.

While this and other complex designs have decided strengths, it is doubtful that they can be used routinely. In fact, they should probably be saved for very important experiments in which, perhaps, hypotheses already tested with simpler designs are again tested with greater rigor and control. Indeed, it is recommended that designs like 20.5 and 20.6 and certain variants of Design 20.6 (to be discussed later) be reserved for definitive tests of research hypotheses, after a certain amount of preliminary experimentation has been done.

CHAPTER SUMMARY

1. The design of a study is its blueprint or plan for the investigation.
2. A design is a subset of a Cartesian cross-product of levels of the independent variable.
3. The experimental design is where at least one of the independent variables used in the study is manipulated.
4. Nonexperimental designs are those designs where there is no randomization to equate the groups prior to administering treatment.
5. For experimental designs, usually the most appropriate statistical method to use is analysis of variance.
6. The assumptions of the analysis of variance are usually violated for nonexperimental designs. Multiple regression may be a more appropriate method of analyzing data from nonexperimental designs.
7. The experimental group–control group design with randomized participants (Design 20.1) is the best design for many experimental behavioral research studies.
8. The Solomon four group design (Design 20.6) handles many of the concerns of behavioral research. However, it uses the resources of two studies and may not be economically efficient.
9. Design 20.2 is like Design 20.1 except it uses matched participants.
10. The use of matched participants is useful in situations where randomization will not work properly.
11. There are several ways of matching participants. The most popular is the individual-by-individual method.
12. Matching has problems in that the researcher is never sure that all the important variables have been used in the match. Additionally, if too many variables are used to match, it becomes more difficult to find participants that match.
13. Design 20.3 uses a pretest. Pretesting is one way of determining if groups are equal or whether randomization has worked. However, pretesting also sensitizes participants to the experiment.

14. Difference scores are often used in designs that include a pretest. However, there are some problems with difference scores—they can be unreliable.
15. Design 20.4 is a simulated before–after design using randomized participants. The second (control) group is only measured on a pretest. The experimental group receives treatment and the posttest.
16. Design 20.5 is a three group before–after design. It is like Design 20.3 except for the introduction of a third group receiving treatment and no pretest is used.

STUDY SUGGESTIONS

1. The first sentence of this chapter is "Design is data discipline." What does this sentence mean? Justify it.
2. Suppose you are an educational psychologist and plan to test the hypothesis that feeding back psychological information to teachers effectively enhances the children's learning by increasing the teachers' understanding of the children. Outline an ideal research design to test this hypothesis, assuming that you have complete command of the situation and plenty of money and help. (These are important conditions, which are included to free the reader from the practical constraints that so often compromise good research designs.) Set up two designs, each with complete randomization, both following the paradigm of Design 20.1. In one of these use only one independent variable and one-way analysis of variance. In the second, use two independent variables and a simple factorial design. How do these two designs compare in their control powers and in the information they yield? Which one tests the hypothesis better? Explain why.
3. The advice in the text not to use analysis of variance in nonexperimental research does not apply so much to one-way analysis of variance as it does to factorial analysis. Neither does the problem of equal numbers of cases in the cells apply (within reason). In a number of nonexperimental studies, in fact, one-way analysis of variance has been profitably used. One such study is: Jones and Cook (1975). The independent variable was attitude toward African Americans, obviously not manipulated. The dependent variable was preference for social policy affecting African Americans.

   It is suggested that students read and digest this study. You may also want to do an analysis of variance of the data of the authors' Table 1, using the method outlined earlier of analysis of variance using ns, means, and standard deviations (see Addendum, Chapter 13).

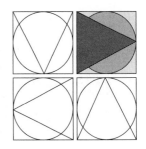

CHAPTER 21

RESEARCH DESIGN APPLICATIONS:
RANDOMIZED GROUPS AND
CORRELATED GROUPS

It is difficult to tell anyone how to do research. Perhaps the best thing to do is to make sure that the beginner has a grasp of principles and possibilities. In addition, approaches and tactics can be suggested. In tackling a research problem, the investigator should let the mind roam, speculate about possibilities, even guess the pattern of results. Once the possibilities are known, intuitions can be followed and explored. Intuition and imagination, however, are not much help if we know little or nothing of technical resources. On the other hand, good research is not just methodology and technique. Intuitive thinking is essential because it helps researchers arrive at solutions that are not merely conventional and routine. It should never be forgotten, however, that analytic thinking and creative intuitive thinking both depend on knowledge, understanding, and experience.

The main purposes of this chapter are to enrich and illustrate our design and statistical discussion with actual research examples, and to suggest basic possibilities for designing research so that the student can ultimately solve research problems. Our summary purpose, then, is to supplement and enrich earlier, more abstract design and statistical discussions.

Simple Randomized Subjects Design

In chapters 13 and 14 the statistics of simple one-way and factorial analysis of variance were discussed and illustrated. The design behind the earlier discussions is called *randomized subjects design*. The general design paradigm (designated as Design 20.1) is shown below.

$$[R] \quad \frac{X \qquad Y}{\sim\!X \qquad Y} \qquad \begin{matrix} \text{(Experimental)} \\ \text{(Control)} \end{matrix}$$

Research Example

The simplest form of Design 20.1 is a one-way analysis of variance paradigm, in which k groups are given k experimental treatments, and the k means are compared to analysis of variance or separate tests of significance. A glance at the left side of Figure 20.3 shows this simple form of Design 20.1 with $k = 3$. Strange to say, it is not used too often. Researchers more often prefer the factorial form of Design 20.1. An one-way example is given below. Random assignment is used. Unfortunately, some researchers do not report how participants were assigned to groups or treatments. The need to report the method of participant selection and assignment to experimental groups should by now be obvious.

Dolinski and Nawrat: Fear-then-Relief and Compliance

Studies on compliance have been of great interest to social psychologists. In Chapter 17 where we discussed the ethics of doing behavioral science research we mentioned the influence of the Milgrim study on how we now do behavioral research. Milgrim, if you recall was interested in why the Nazis during World War II complied to commit unspeakable acts of brutality to other humans. In a study by Dolinski and Nawrat (1998), another method that was used to induce compliance was explored. This was a method used by Nazis and Stalinists to get Polish prisoners to testify against themselves, their friends, and/or their families. Dolinski and Nawrat call this method "fear-then-relief." It involves putting a prisoner in a high state of anxiety, by jailers yelling, screaming, and threatening the prisoner. After achieving the desired level of fear, the anxiety-producing stimuli are abruptly removed. The prisoner is then treated kindly. The usual result of this procedure is the intensification of compliance behavior. Dolinski and Nawrat claim that compliance is due to the reduction of fear and not the fear itself. Although Dolinski and Nawrat use a very extreme example to illustrate their point, they also explain that the method is often used in some shape and form by dyads in everyday life. It can occur between parent and child, teacher and student, and employer and employee. Police use similar tactics with their "good cop–bad cop" routine, which usually involves one police officer ("bad cop") berating, screaming, and threatening a suspect. When the suspect reaches a level of high anxiety, another police officer ("good cop") removes the "bad cop" and talks kindly and sweetly to the prisoner. Terrorists also use this method on hostages.

Dolinski and Nawrat designed and conducted four experiments to test the "fear-then-relief" method's ability to induce compliance. We will describe one of those experiments here. In this experiment, 120 volunteer high school students from Opole, Poland, were assigned randomly to one of three experimental conditions. All participants were told that they were to partake in a study on the effects of punishment on learning. Group 1 experienced anxiety; they were told they would be given mild, not painful, electrical shock for each error they made. Group 2 participants experienced anxiety that was then reduced. They were initially given the same description as Group 1, but were later told that they would participate in a different study instead. This other study involved visual-motor coordination and no shock given. Group 3 was the control condition. These participants were told that they would be participating in a visual-motor coordination study. During the waiting period before the start of the experiment, each participant was asked to complete an anxiety questionnaire. After completing the questionnaire, a female student who was a confederate of the experimenter, but who appeared to be totally unattached from the experiment, introduced herself and asked each participant to join a charity action for an orphanage. Those who complied were asked how many hours they were willing to work for this action.

The manipulated independent variable in this study was the level of induced anxiety and relief. The dependent variables were compliance, amount of anxiety, and the number of hours of time donated for a good cause. Using a one-way analysis of variance, Dolinski and Nawrat obtained a significant F-value. Group 2, the group that felt anxiety and then had it reduced, had the highest rate of compliance and were willing to donate the greatest number of days. The level of anxiety for each group was in the expected direction. Group 1 experienced the highest degree of anxiety, followed by Group 2, and then Group 3. Table 21.1 presents the summary data for the study.

▣ **TABLE 21.1** *Anxiety Levels, Compliance, Number of Days Willing to Volunteer by Induced Anxiety and F-values (Dolinski & Nawrat study)*

Condition Group	Mean Anxiety Reported	Percentage Complying	Mean Number of Volunteered Days
Electrical Shock study	53.25	37.5	0.625
Electrical shock study changed to visual-motor coordination study	43.05	75.0	1.150
Visual-motor coordination study	34.45	52.5	1.025
F-value	108.9	6.13	2.11
	$(p < .00001)$	$(p < .003)$	$(p > .05)$

The results of the study upheld the Dolinski and Nawrat hypothesis that it was the "fear-then-relief," and not the emotion of anxiety itself, that led to a higher degree of compliance. Simply creating a state of anxiety in people is not enough to create compliance. In fact, this study found that the participants in Group 1 (induced anxiety), who felt the greatest amount of anxiety, complied less than the participants in Group 3 (control-low or no anxiety).

Factorial Designs

The basic general design is still Design 20.1, though the variation of the basic experimental group–control group pattern is drastically altered by the addition of other experimental factors or independent variables. Following an earlier definition of factorial analysis of variance, *factorial design is the structure of research in which two or more independent variables are juxtaposed in order to study their independent and interactive effects on a dependent variable.*

The reader may at first find it a bit difficult to fit the factorial framework into the general experimental group–control group paradigm of Design 20.1. The discussion of the generalization of the control group idea in Chapter 20, however, should have clarified the relations between Design 20.1 and factorial designs. The discussion is now continued. We have the independent variables A and B and the dependent variable Y. The simplest factorial design, the 2 × 2, has three possibilities: both A and B active; A active, B attribute (or vice versa); and both A and B attribute. (The last possibility, both independent variables attributes, is the nonexperimental case. As indicated earlier, however, it is probably not appropriate to use analysis of variance with nonexperimental independent variables.) Returning to the experimental group–control group notion, A, as usual, can be divided into A_1 and A_2, experimental and control with the additional independent variable B partitioned into B_1

and B_2. Since this structure is familiar to us by now, we need only discuss one or two procedural details.

The ideal participant assignment procedure is to assign participants to the four cells at random. If both A and B are active variables, this is possible and easy. Simply give the participants numbers arbitrarily from 1 through N (N being the total number of participants). Then, using a table of random numbers, write down numbers 1 through N as they turn up in the table. Place the numbers into four groups as they turn up, and then assign the four groups of participants to the four cells. To be safe, also assign the groups of participants randomly to the experimental treatments (the four cells). Label the groups 1, 2, 3, and 4, and then draw these numbers from a table of random numbers. Assume that the table yielded the numbers in this order: 3, 4, 1, and 2. Assign Group 3 participants to the upper-left cell, Group 4 participants to the upper-right cell, and so on.

Often, B will be an attribute variable, like gender, intelligence, achievement, anxiety, self-perception, race, and so on. The participant assignment must be altered. First, since B is an attribute variable, there is no possibility of assigning participants to B_1 and B_2 at random. If B is the variable gender, the best we can do is to assign males first at random to the cells A_1B_1 and A_2B_1, and then females to the cells A_1B_2 and A_2B_2.

Factorial Designs with More than Two Variables

We can often improve the design and increase the information obtained from a study by adding groups. Rather than A_1 and A_2, and B_1 and B_2, an experiment may profit from using A_1, A_2, A_3, and A_4; and B_1, B_2, and B_3. Practical and statistical problems increase and sometimes become quite difficult as variables are added. Suppose we have a $3 \times 2 \times 2$ design that has $3 \times 2 \times 2 = 12$ cells, each of which must have at least two participants, and preferably many more. (It is possible, but not very sensible, to have only one participant per cell if one can have more. Of course, there are designs that have only one participant per cell. This is covered in Chapter 22.) If we decide that 10 participants per cell are necessary, $12 \times 10 = 120$ participants will have to be obtained and assigned at random. The problem is more acute with one more variable, and the practical manipulation of the research situation is also more difficult. But the successful handling of such an experiment allows us to test a number of hypotheses and yields a great deal of information. The combinations of three-, four-, and five-variable designs give a wide variety of possible designs: $2 \times 5 \times 3$, $4 \times 4 \times 2$, $3 \times 2 \times 4 \times 2$, $4 \times 3 \times 2 \times 2$, and so on.

Research Examples of Factorial Designs

Examples of two- and three-dimensional factorial designs were described in Chapter 14. (A review of these examples is recommended because the reasoning behind the essential design can now be more easily grasped.) Since a number of examples of factorial designs were given in Chapter 14, we confine the examples given here to studies with unusual features or interesting results.

Sigall and Ostrove: Attractiveness and Crime

It has often been said that attractive women are treated differently than men and less attractive women. In most cases, perhaps, the reactions are "favorable": attractive women are perhaps more likely than less attractive women to receive the attention and favors of the world. Is it possible, however, that their attractiveness may in some situations be disadvantageous? Sigall and Ostrove (1975) asked the question: How is the physical attractiveness of a criminal defendant related to juridic sentences, and does the nature of the crime interact with attractiveness? They had their participants assign sentences, in years, to swindle and burglary offenses of attractive, unattractive, and control defendants. The factorial paradigm of the experiment, together with the results, is given in Table 21.2. (We forego describing many of the experimental details; they were well handled.)

In the burglary case, the defendant stole $2,200 in a high-rise building. In the swindle case, the defendant ingratiated herself with, and swindled, a middle-aged bachelor of $2,200. Note that the Unattractive and Control conditions did not differ much from each other. Both Attractive–Swindle (5.45) and Attractive–Burglary (2.80) differed from the other two conditions—but in opposite directions! Attractive–Swindle received the heaviest mean sentence: 5.45 years, whereas Attractive–Burglary received the lowest mean sentence: 2.80 years. The statistics support the preceding verbal summary—the interaction was statistically significant: The Attractiveness–Offense F, at 2 and 106 degrees of freedom, was 4.55, $p < .025$. In words, attractive defendants have an advantage over unattractive defendants, except when their crimes are attractiveness-related (Swindle).

Quilici and Mayer: Examples, Schema, and Learning

Do examples help students learn statistics? This was the basic question posed by cognitive scientists Quilici and Mayer (1996). In their study on analytic problem-solving, Quilici and Mayer examined only one of three processes that define analogical thinking. These researchers were concerned only with the recogni-

▣ **Table 21.2** *Mean Sentences in Years of Attractive, Unattractive, and Control Defendants for Swindle and Burglary (Sigall & Ostrove study)*[a]

	Defendant Condition		
	Attractive	**Unattractive**	**Control**
Swindle	5.45	4.35	4.35
Burglary	2.80	5.20	5.10

[a]$N = 120$, 20 per cell; F (interaction) = 4.55; ($p < .025$).

tion process that involves two techniques: (1) focus on the surface similarities between the example and actual problem to be solved, or (2) focus on the structural similarities.

Surface similarities deal with the shared attributes of objects in the problem cover story. With structural similarity, the concern is with the shared relations between objects in both example and problem. To study this phenomena, Quilici and Mayer used learning how to solve word problems in statistics. Quilici and Mayer felt that students who learn the structure of statistical word problems will be better able to solve other problems they encounter in the future by properly classifying them into the correct statistical method of analysis (e.g., *t*-test, correlation, etc). Four examples are given below to illustrate the difference between surface and structural similarities.

Example 1

A personnel expert wishes to determine whether experienced typists are able to type faster than inexperienced typists. Twenty experienced typists and 20 inexperienced typists are given a typing test. Each typist's average number of words typed per minute is recorded.

Example 2

A personnel expert wishes to determine whether typing experience goes with faster typing speeds. Forty typists are asked to report how many years they have worked as typists and are given a typing test to determine their average number of words typed per minute.

Example 3

After examining weather data for the past 50 years, a meteorologist claims that the annual precipitation varies with average temperature. For each of 50 years, she notes the annual rainfall and average temperature.

Example 4

A college dean claims that good readers earn better grades than poor readers. The grade point average is recorded for 50 first-year students who scored high on the reading comprehension test and for 50 first-year students who scored low on a reading comprehension test.

In examining these four problems taken from Quilici and Mayer (1996, p. 146), Example 1 and Example 2 would have the same surface features. Both deal with typists and typing. To solve Example 1 a *t*-test would be used to compare experienced with inexperienced typists. However, to solve Example 2, one would use a correlation since the question asks for a relation between typing experience and average number of words typed per minute. Hence Example 1 and Example 2 would be different structurally. Example 3 also looks at the relation between two variables: amount of rainfall and temperature. It would have the same structure as Example 2, but a different surface. They have the same structure because both require the use of correlation to solve the problem. Example 4 and Example 1 have the same structure, but a different surface.

Quilici and Mayer designed a study to determine if experience with examples foster structural schema construction. They hypothesize that statistical word problem exposure will cause students to be more sensitive to structural features of future word problems than to surface features. Students who are not exposed to statistical word problem examples will not exhibit such behavior. They also hypothesized that those exposed to three examples will be able to exhibit the behavior to a higher degree than those exposed to only one example. These researchers used a 3×4 factorial design. The first independent variable was structural characteristics (t-test, chi-square, and correlation). The second independent variable was surface characteristics (typing, weather, mental fatigue, and reading). There were two dependent variables: a structure usage score and a surface usage score. Participants were assigned randomly to treatment conditions. A two-way analysis of variance confirmed their hypothesis that those exposed to example would use a structure-based schema, whereas those not exposed to examples would not. However, there was no statistical difference between those that were exposed to three examples and those who received one example.

Hoyt: Teacher Knowledge and Pupil Achievement

We now outline an educational study done many years ago, because it was planned to answer an important theoretical and practical question, and because it clearly illustrates a complex factorial design. The research question was: What are the effects on the achievement and attitudes of pupils if teachers are given knowledge of the characteristics of their pupils? Hoyt's (1955) study explored several aspects of the basic question and used factorial design to enhance the internal and external validity of the investigation. The first design was used three times for each of three school participants and the second and third was used twice, once in each of two school systems.

The paradigm for the first design is shown in Figure 21.1. The independent variables were treatments, ability, sex, and schools. The three self-explanatory treatments were no information (N), test scores (T), and test scores plus other information (TO). Ability levels were High, Medium, and Low IQ. The variables Gender and Schools are obvious. Eighth-grade students were assigned at random within gender and ability levels. It will help us understand the design if we examine what a final analysis of variance table of the design looks like. Before doing so, however, it should be noted that the Achievement results were mostly indeterminant (or negative). The

◙ FIGURE 21.1

	N		T		TO	
	Male	**Female**	**Male**	**Female**	**Male**	**Female**
School *A* High IQ Medium IQ Low IQ						
School *B* High IQ Medium IQ Low IQ			Dependent Variable Measures			

F-ratios, with one exception, were not significant. Pupils' attitudes toward teachers, on the other hand, seemed to improve with increased teacher knowledge of pupils, an interesting and potentially important finding. The analysis of variance table is given in Table 21.3. One experiment yields 14 tests! Naturally, a number of these tests are not important and can be ignored. The tests of greatest importance (marked

◙ TABLE 21.3 *Sources of Variance and Degrees of Freedom for a 3 × 3 × 2 × 2 Factorial Design with Variables Treatments, Ability, Sex, and School (Total and Within Degrees of Freedom are Omitted)*

Source	*df*
Main Effects	
Between Treatments*	2
Between Ability Levels	2
Between Gender	1
Between Schools	1
First-Order Interactions	
Interaction: Treatments × Ability	4
Interaction: Treatments × Gender*	2
Interaction: Treatments × School*	2
Interaction: Ability × Gender	2
Interaction: Ability × School	2
Interaction: Gender × School	1
Second-Order Interactions:	
Interaction: Treatments × Ability × Gender*	4
Interaction: Treatments × Ability × School	4
Interaction: Ability × Gender × School	2
Third-Order Interactions:	
Interaction: Treatments × Ability × Gender × School	4

with asterisks in the table) are those involving the treatment variable. The most important test is between treatments, the first of the main effects. Perhaps equally important are the interactions involving treatments. Take the interaction treatment × sex. If this is significant, it means that the amount of information a teacher possesses about students has an influence on student achievement, but boys are influenced differently than girls. Boys with teachers who possess information about their pupils may do better than boys whose teachers do not have such information, whereas it may be the opposite with girls, or it may make no difference one way or the other.

Second-order or triple interactions are more difficult to interpret. They seem to be rarely significant. If they are significant, however, they require special study. Cross-tabulation tables of the means are perhaps the best way, but graphic methods, as discussed earlier, are often enlightening. The student will find guidance in Edwards's (1984) book or Simon's (1976) manuscript.

Evaluation of Randomized Subjects Designs

Randomized subjects designs are all variants or extensions of Design 20.1, the basic experimental group–control group design in which participants are assigned to the experimental and control groups at random. As such they have the strengths of the basic design, the most important of which is the randomization feature, and the consequent ability to assume the preexperimental approximate equality of the experimental groups in all possible independent variables. History and maturation are controlled because very little time elapses between the manipulation of X and the observation and measurement of Y. There is no possible contamination due to pretesting.

Two other strengths of these designs, springing from the many variations possible, are flexibility and applicability. These can be used to help solve many behavioral research problems, since they seem to be peculiarly well suited to the types of design problems that arise from social scientific and educational problems and hypotheses. The one-way designs, for example, can incorporate any number of methods, and the testing of methods is a major educational need. The variables that constantly need control in behavioral research—gender, intelligence, aptitude, social class, schools, and many others—can be incorporated into factorial designs, and thus are controlled. Also, with factorial designs it is possible to have mixtures of active and attribute variables—another important need. But there are also weaknesses.

One criticism has been that randomized subjects designs do not permit tests of the equality of groups, as do before–after (pretest–post test) designs. Actually, this is not a valid criticism for two reasons: (1) with enough participants and randomization, it can be assumed that the groups are equal, as we have seen; and (2) it is possible to check the groups for equality on variables other than Y, the dependent variable. For educational research, data on intelligence, aptitude, and achievement, for example, are available in school records. Pertinent data for sociology and political science studies can often be found in county and election district records.

Another weakness is statistical. One should have equal numbers of cases in the cells of factorial designs. It is possible to work with unequal ns, but it is both clumsy and a threat to interpretation. Dropping out cases at random or the use of missing data methods can cure small discrepancies (see Dear, 1959; Gleason & Staelin, 1975 for two excellent references on estimating missing data). This imposes a limitation on the use of such designs because it is often not possible to have equal numbers in each cell. One-way randomized designs are not so delicate: unequal numbers are not a difficult problem. How to adjust and analyze data for unequal ns is a complex, thorny, and much-argued problem. For a discussion in the context mostly of analysis of variance, see Snedecor and Cochran (1989). Discussion in the context of multiple regression, which is actually a better solution of the problem, can be found in Kerlinger and Pedhazur (1973) and Pedhazur (1996). Pedhazur's discussions are detailed and authoritative. He reviews the issues and suggests solutions.

Compared to matched groups designs, randomized subjects designs are usually less precise; that is, the error term is ordinarily larger, other things being equal. It is doubtful, however, whether this is cause for concern. In some cases it certainly is— for example, where a very sensitive test of a hypothesis is needed. In much behavioral research, though, it is probably desirable to consider as nonsignificant any effect that is insufficiently powerful to make itself felt over and above the random noise of a randomized subjects design.

All in all, then, these are powerful, flexible, useful, and widely applicable designs. In the opinion of the authors they are the best all-round designs, perhaps the first to be considered when planning the design of a research study.

Correlated Groups

A basic principle is behind all correlated groups designs: there is systematic variance in the dependent variable measures due to the correlation between the groups *on some variable related to the dependent variable.* This correlation and its concomitant variance can be introduced into the measures, and the design, in three ways:

1. use the same units, for example, participants, in each of the experimental groups,
2. match units on one or more independent variables that are related to the dependent variable, and
3. use more than one group of units, like classes or schools, in the design.

Despite the seeming differences among these three ways of introducing correlation into the dependent variable measures, they are basically the same. We now examine the design implications of this basic principle and discuss ways of implementing the principle.

The General Paradigm

With the exception of correlated factorial designs and so-called nested designs, all analysis of variance paradigms of correlated groups designs can be easily outlined. The word *group* should be taken to indicate set of scores. Then there is no confusion when repeated trials experiment is classified as a multigroup design. The general paradigm is given in Figure 21.2. To emphasize the sources of variance, means of columns and rows have been indicated. The individual dependent variable measures (Ys) have also been inserted.

It is useful to know the system of subscripts to symbols used in mathematics and statistics. A rectangular table of numbers is called a *matrix*. The entries of a matrix are letters and/or numbers. When letters are used, it is common to identify any particular matrix entry with two (sometimes more) subscripts. The first of these indicates the positional number of the row, the second the positional number of the column. Y_{32}, for instance, indicates the Y measure in the third row and the second column. Y_{52} indicates the Y measure of the fifth row and the second column. It is also customary to generalize this system by adding the letter subscripts. In this book, i symbolizes any row number and j any column number. Any number of the matrix is represented by Y_{ij}. Any number of the third row is Y_{3j}; and any number of the second column is Y_{i2}.

It can be seen that there are two sources of systematic variance: that due to columns, or treatments, and that due to rows (individual or unit differences). Analysis of variance must be of the two-way variety.

The reader who has studied the correlation variance argument of Chapter 15, where the statistics and some of the problems of correlated groups designs were presented, will have no difficulty with the variance reasoning of Figure 21.2. The intent of the design is to maximize the between-treatments variance, identify the between-units variance, and the error (residual) variance. The maxmincon principle

▣ Figure 21.2

| | | | Treatments | | | | |
Units	X_1	X_2	X_3	.	.	.	X_k	Row
1	Y_{11}	Y_{12}	Y_{13}	.	.	.	Y_{1k}	M_1
2	Y_{21}	Y_{22}	Y_{23}	.	.	.	Y_{2k}	M_2
	Y_{31}	Y_{32}	Y_{33}	.	.	.	Y_{3k}	M_3
.	.	.	.	.	.	.	.	.
.	.	.	.	.	.	.	.	.
n	Y_{n1}	Y_{n2}	Y_{n3}	.	.	.	Y_{nk}	M_n
	M_{x_1}	M_{x_2}	M_{x_3}	.	.	.	M_{x_k}	(M_t)

applies here as elsewhere. The only difference, really, between designs of correlated groups and randomized subjects is the rows or units variance.

Units

The units used do not alter the variance principle. The word *unit* is deliberately used to emphasize that units can be persons or participants, classes, schools, districts, cities, even nations. In other words, "unit" is a generalized rubric that can represent many kinds of entities. The important consideration is whether or not the units—whatever they are—differ from each other. If they do, *variance between units* is introduced. In this sense, talking about correlated groups or participants is the same as talking about variance between groups or participants. The notion of individual differences is extended to unit *differences.*

The real value of correlated groups design, beyond allowing the investigator to isolate and estimate the variance due correlation, is in guiding the investigator to design research to capitalize on the differences that frequently exist between units. If a research study involves different classes in the same school, these classes are a possible source of variance. It may thus be wise to use "classes" as units in the design. The well-known differences between schools are very important sources of variance in behavioral research. They may be handled as a factorial design, or they may be handled in the manner of the designs in this chapter. Indeed, if one looks carefully at a factorial design with two independent variables, one of them *schools*, and at a correlated groups design with units *Schools*, one finds, in essence, the same design. Study Figure 21.3. On the left is a factorial design and on the right a correlated groups design, but they look the same! They are the same, in variance principle. (The only differences might be numbers of scores in the cells and statistical treatment.)

One Group, Repeated Trials Design

In the one group, repeated trials design, as the name indicates, one group is given different treatments at different times. In a learning experiment, the same group of participants may be given several tasks of different complexity, or the experimental

▣ FIGURE 21.3

	Treatments			Treatments	
Schools	A_1	A_2	Schools	A_1	A_2
B_1			1		
B_2			2		
B_3			3		
Factorial Designs			Correlated Groups Design		

manipulation may be to present learning principles in different orders, say from simple to complex, from complex to simple, from whole to part, from part to whole.

It was said earlier that the best possible matching of participants is to match the participant with himself or herself. The difficulties in using this solution of the control problem have also been mentioned. One of these difficulties resembles pretest sensitization, which may produce an interaction between the pretest and the experimentally manipulated variable. Another is that participants mature and learn over time. A participant who has experienced one or two trials of an experimental manipulation and is facing a third trial, is now a different person from the one who faced trial one. Experimental situations differ a great deal, of course. In some situations, repeated trials may not unduly affect the performances of participants on later trials; in other situations, they may. The problem of how individuals learn, or become unduly sensitized during an experiment, is difficult to solve. In short, *history*, *maturation*, and *sensitization* are possible weaknesses of repeated trials. The regression effect can also be a weakness because, as we saw in an earlier chapter, low scorers tend to get higher scores and high scorers lower scores on retesting, simply due to the imperfect correlation between the groups. A control group is, of course, needed.

Despite the basic time difficulties, there may be occasions when a one group repeated trials design is useful. Certainly, in analyses of "time" data, this is the implicit design. If we have a series of growth measurements of children, for instance, the different times at which the measurements were made correspond to treatments. The paradigm of the design is the same as that shown in Figure 21.2. Simply substitute "participants" for "units" and label $X_1, X_2, \ldots$ as "trials."

From this general paradigm special cases can be derived. The simplest case is the one group, Before–After design, Design 19.2 (a), where one group of participants was given an experimental treatment preceded by a pretest and followed by a posttest. Since the weaknesses of this design have already been mentioned, further discussion is not necessary. It should be noted, though, that this design, especially in its nonexperimental form, closely approximates much commonsense observation and thinking. A person may observe educational practices today and decide that they are no good. In order to make this judgment, one implicitly or explicitly compares today's educational practices with educational practices of the past. From a number of possible causes, depending on the particular bias, the researcher will select one or more reasons for what he or she believes to be the sorry state of educational affairs: "progressive education," "educationists," "moral degeneration," "lack of firm religious principles," and so on.

Two Groups, Experimental Group–Control Group Designs

This design has two forms, the better of which (repeated here) was described in Chapter 20 as Design 20.2:

$[M_r]$	X	Y	(Experimental)
	$\sim X$	Y	(Control)

◉ FIGURE 21.4

	Treatments		
Pairs	X_e	X_c	
1	Y_{1e}	Y_{1c}	M_1
2	Y_{2e}	Y_{2c}	M_2
3	Y_{3e}	Y_{3c}	M_3
.	.	.	.
.	.	.	.
n	Y_{ne}	Y_{nc}	M_n
	M_e	M_c	

In this design, participants are first matched, and then assigned to experimental and control groups at random. In the other form, participants are matched, but not assigned to experimental and control groups at random. The latter design can be indicated by simply dropping the subscript r from M_r (described in Chapter 19 as Design 19.4, one of the less-adequate designs).

The design-statistical paradigm of this war-horse of designs is shown in Figure 21.4. The insertion of the symbols for the means shows the two sources of systematic variance: *Treatments* and *Pairs*, columns and rows. This is in clear contrast to the randomized designs in an earlier section of this chapter, where the only systematic variance was *Treatments* or columns.

The most common variant of the two group, experimental group–control group design is the Before–After, two group design [see Design 20.3 (b)]. The design-statistical paradigm and its rationale are discussed later.

Research Examples of Correlated Group Designs

Hundreds of studies of the correlated groups kind have been published. The most frequent designs have used matched participants, or the same participants with pre- and posttests. Correlated groups designs, however, are not limited to two groups; the same participants, for example, may be given more than two experimental treatments. The studies described below have been chosen not only because they illustrate correlated groups design, matching, and control problems, but also because they are historically, psychologically, or educationally important.

Thorndike's Transfer of Training Study

In 1924, E. L. Thorndike published a remarkable study of the presumed effect on intelligence of certain school participants. Students were matched according to scores on Form A of the measure of the dependent variable, Intelligence. This test also served as a pretest. The independent variable was One Year's Study of Participants, in subjects such as history, mathematics, and Latin. A posttest, Form B of the intelligence test, was given at the end of the year. Thorndike (1924) used an ingenious device to separate the differential effect of each school subject. He did this by matching on Form A of the intelligence test those pupils who studied, for instance, English, history, geometry, and *Latin*, with those pupils who studied English, history, geometry, and *shopwork*. Thus, for these two groups, he was comparing the differential effects of *Latin* and *shopwork*. Gains in final intelligence scores were considered a joint effect of growth plus the academic subjects studied.

Despite its weaknesses, this was a colossal study. Thorndike was aware of the lack of adequate controls, as revealed in the following passage on the effects of selection.

> The chief reason why good thinkers seem superficially to have been made such by having taken certain school studies, is that good thinkers have taken such studies. . . . When the good thinkers studied Greek and Latin, these studies seemed to make good thinkers. Now that the good thinkers study Physics and Trigonometry, these seem to make good thinkers. If the abler pupils should all study Physical Education and Dramatic Art these subjects would seem to make good thinkers (p. 98).

Thorndike pointed the way to controlled educational research, which has led to the decrease of metaphysical and dogmatic explanations in education. His work struck a blow against the razor-strop theory of mental training; the theory that likened the mind to a razor that could be sharpened by stropping it on "hard" subjects.

It is not easy to evaluate a study such as this, the scope and ingenuity of which is impressive. One wonders, however, about the adequacy of the dependent variable, Intelligence or Intellectual Ability. Can school subjects studied for one year have much effect on intelligence? Moreover, the study was not experimental. Thorndike measured the intelligence of students and let the independent variables, School Subjects, operate. No randomization, of course, was possible. As mentioned above, he was aware of this control weakness in his study, which is still a classic that deserves respect and careful study despite its weaknesses in history and selection (maturation was controlled).

Miller and DiCara: Learning of Autonomic Functions

In a previous chapter we presented data from one of the set of remarkable studies of the learning of autonomic functioning done by Miller and his colleagues (Miller, 1971; Miller & DiCara, 1968). Experts and nonexperts alike believe that it is not possible to learn and control responses of the autonomic nervous system. That is, glandular and visceral responses—heartbeat, urine secretion, and blood pressure, for example—were supposed to be beyond the "control" of the individual. Miller believed otherwise. He demonstrated experimentally that such responses are subject to instrumental learning. The crucial part of his method consisted of rewarding visceral responses when they occurred. In the study (data were cited in an earlier chapter of this book) rats were rewarded when they increased or decreased the secretion of

◙ TABLE 21.4 *Secretion of Urine Data, Increase Rats and Decrease Rats, Before and After Training (Miller & DiCara study)*

	Increase Rats[a]				Decrease Rats[b]		
Rats	Before	After	Σ	Rats	Before	After	Σ
1	.023	.030	.053	1	.018	.007	.025
2	.014	.019	.033	2	.015	.003	.018
3	.016	.029	.045	3	.012	.005	.017
4	.018	.030	.048	4	.015	.006	.021
5	.007	.016	.023	5	.030	.009	.039
6	.026	.044	.070	6	.027	.008	.035
7	.012	.026	.038	7	.020	.003	.023
Means	.017	.028			020	.006	.023

[a]Increase Before–After: $F = 43.875$ ($p < .001$); $\omega^2 = .357$. The measures in the table are milliliters per minute per 100 grams of weight.
[b]Decrease, Before–After: $F = 46.624$ ($p < .001$); $\omega^2 = .663$.

urine. Fourteen rats were assigned at random to two groups called "Increase Rats" and "Decrease Rats." The rats of the former group were rewarded with brain stimulation (which was shown to be effective for *increases* in urine secretion), whereas the rats of the latter group were rewarded for *decreases in* urine secretion during a "training" period of 220 trials in approximately three hours.

To show part of the experimental and analytic paradigms of this experiment, the data before and after the training periods for the Increase Rats and the Decrease Rats are given in Table 21.4 (extracted from the Miller & DiCara's Table 1). The measures in the table are the milliliters of urine secretion per minute per 100 grams of body weight. Note that they are very small quantities. The research design is a variant of Design 20.3 (a):

$$[R] \quad \frac{Y_b \quad X \quad Y_a}{Y_b \quad {\sim}X \quad Y_a} \quad \begin{matrix} \text{(Experimental)} \\ \text{(Control)} \end{matrix}$$

The difference is that $\sim X$, which in the design means absence of experimental treatment for the control group, now means reward for decrease of urine secretion. The usual analysis of the after-training measures of the two groups is therefore altered.

We can better understand the analysis if we analyze the data of Table 21.9 somewhat differently than Miller and DiCara did. (They used *t*-tests.) We did a two-way (repeated measures) analysis of variance of the Increase Rats data, Before and After, and the Decrease Rats data, Before and After. The Increase Before and After means were .017 and .028, and the Decrease means were .020 and .006. The Increase *F*-ratio was 43.875 (*df* = 1.6); the Decrease Rats *F* was 46.624. Both were highly significant. The two Before means of .017 and .020 were not significantly different, however. In this case, comparison of the means of the two After groups, the usual comparison with this design, is probably not appropriate because one was for increase and the other for decrease in urine secretion.

This entire study, with its highly controlled experimental manipulations and its "control" analyses, is an example of imaginative conceptualization and disciplined competent analysis. The above analysis is one example. But the study's authors did much more. For example, to be more sure that the reinforcement affected only urine secretion, they compared the Before and After heartrates (beats per minute) of both the Increase and the Decrease rats. The means were 367 and 412 for Increase rats, and 373 and 390 for the Decrease rats. Neither difference was statistically significant. Similar comparisons of blood pressure and other bodily functions were also not significant.

Students will do well to study this fine example of laboratory research until they clearly understand what was done and why. It will help students learn more about controlled experiments, research design, and statistical analysis, than most textbook exercises. It is a splendid achievement!

Tipper, Eissenberg, and Weaver: Effects of Practice on Selective Attention

When speaking about selective attention, one may recall the classic study by Stroop (1935) who demonstrated the role of interference on selective attention. Irrelevant stimulus can compete with the target stimulus for control of perceptual action. For those unfamiliar with this study, one memorable part was presenting participants with words such as *green* and *blue* that were printed in red or yellow. Participants were asked to name the colors in which the word was written but would instead read the words. People find it very difficult to suppress the habit of reading words even when they are asked not to. In order to do the task correctly, the participant must slow down and consciously suppress reading the words. This interference was called the Stroop effect. A large number of studies have been performed on selective attention since Stroop's famous study. Tipper, Eissenberg, and Weaver (1992) is one of them. This study is different in that they take issue with a number of studies that have been performed on selective attention. For one, Tipper et al. hypothesize that any selective attention experiment that uses a participant for one hour or so may be tapping into a different perceptual mechanism than those used in everyday life. Laboratory experiments usually require the participant to be present for about an hour. Within an hour the entire experimental experience is still novel. It may be that attentional selectivity is achieved by a different mechanism as the familiarity with the stimuli increases.

Tipper et al. designed a study to test their hypotheses concerning selective attention using a completely within-subjects design. All of the participants experienced all of the treatment conditions. They looked at the effect of interference on reaction time and errors. They had each participant experience both levels of interference: negative priming and response inhibition across 11 blocks or trials taken over 4 days (practice effect). Their results showed that there was an interference effect ($F = 35.15$, $p < .001$) when using reaction time as the dependent variable. The reaction times were longer when the distraction was present. They also found a practice effect (blocks) {$F = 9.62$, $p < .0001$) and no interaction effect. The practice effect indicated that the reaction time of participants becomes faster with the increase in practice. The fact that the interaction effect was not significant indicates that the interfering effects of the irrelevant stimulus remained constant even after extended practice. The findings of Tipper et al. do suggest that other mechanisms for selective attention exist and operate with different levels of experience.

Multigroup Correlated Groups Designs

Units Variance

While it is difficult to match three and four sets of participants, and while it is ordinarily not feasible or desirable in behavioral research to use the same participants in each of the groups, there are natural situations in which correlated groups do exist. These situations are particularly important in educational research. Until recently, the variances due to differences between classes, schools, school systems, and other "natural" units have not been well controlled or often used in the analysis of data. Perhaps the first indication of the importance of this kind of variance was given in Lindquist's (1940) fine book on statistical analysis in educational research. In this book, Lindquist placed considerable emphasis on schools variance. Schools, classes, and other educational units tend to differ significantly in achievement, intelligence, aptitudes, and other variables. The educational investigator has to be alert to these *unit differences*, as well as to *individual differences*.

Consider an obvious example. Suppose an investigator chooses a sample of five schools for their variety and homogeneity. The goal of course is external validity: representativeness. The investigator uses pupils from all five schools and combines the measures from the five schools to test the mean differences in some dependent variable. In so doing, the investigator is ignoring the variance due to the differences among schools. It is understandable that the means do not differ significantly; the schools variance is mixed in with the error variance.

Gross errors can arise from ignoring the variance of units such as schools and classes. One such error is to select a number of schools and to designate certain schools as experimental schools and others as control schools. Here the between-schools variance gets entangled with the variance of the experimental variable. Similarly, classes, school districts, and other educational units differ and thus engender variance. The variances must be identified and controlled, whether it be by experimental or statistical control, or both.

Factorial Correlated Groups

Factorial models can be combined with the units notion to yield a valuable design: *factorial correlated groups* design. Such a design is appropriate when units are a natural part of a research situation. For instance, the research may require the comparison of a variable before and after an experimental intervention, or before and after an important event. Obviously, there will be correlation between the before and after dependent variable measures. Another useful example is shown in Figure 21.5. This is a 3 × 2 factorial design with five units (classes, school, and so forth) in each level, B_1 and B_2.

The strengths and weaknesses of the factorial correlated groups design are similar to those of the more complex factorial designs. The main strengths are the ability to isolate and measure variances and to test interactions. Note that the two main sources of variance, Treatments (*A*) and Levels (*B*), and the units variance can be evaluated; that is, the differences between the *A*, *B*, and units means can be tested for significance. In addition, three interactions can be tested: treatments by levels, treatments by units, and levels by units. If individual scores are used in the cells instead of means, the triple interaction, too, can be tested. Note how important such interaction can be, both theoretically and practically. For example, questions like the following can be answered: Do treatments work differently in differ units? Do certain methods work differently at differing intelligence levels? with differing sexes? with children from differing socioeconomic levels? The advanced student will want to know how to handle units (schools, classes, etc.) and units variance in factorial

■ FIGURE 21.5

		Units	**Methods (Treatment)**		
			A_1	A_2	A_3
	B_1	1			
		2			
		3			
		4			
		5			
Levels (Devices, Types, etc.)				*Y* Means or Measures	
	B_2	1			
		2			
		3			
		4			
		5			

designs. Detailed guidance is given in Edwards (1984) and in Kirk (1995). The subject is difficult. Even the names of the designs become complex: randomized blocks, nested treatments, split-plot designs. Such designs are powerful, however: they combine virtues of factorial designs and correlated groups designs. When needed, Edwards and Kirk are good guides. Additionally, it is suggested that help be solicited from someone who understands both statistics and behavioral research. It is unwise to use computer programs just because their names seem appropriate or because they are available. It is equally unwise to seek analytic help from computer personnel. One cannot expect such people to know and understand, say, factorial analysis of variance. That is not their job. More will be said about computer analysis in later chapters.

Suedfeld and Rank: Revolutionary Leaders and Conceptual Complexity

Suedfeld and Rank (1976), in a study mentioned earlier in another context, tested the intriguing notion that successful revolutionary leaders—Lenin, Cromwell, Jefferson, for example—are conceptually simple in their public communications *before* revolution, and conceptually complex *after* revolution. Unsuccessful revolutionary leaders, on the other hand, do not differ in conceptual complexity before and after revolution. The problem lends itself to a factorial design and to repeated measures analysis. The design and the data on conceptual complexity are shown in Table 21.5. It can be seen that the successful leaders became conceptually more complex—from 1.67 to 3.65—but unsuccessful leaders did not change very much—2.37 and 2.21. The interaction F-ratio was 12.37, significant at the .005 level. The hypothesis was supported.

A few points should be made here. First, note the effective combining of factorial design and repeated measures. When appropriate, as in this case, the combination is highly useful mainly because it sets aside, so to speak, the variance in the dependent variable measures due to individual (or group or block) differences. The error term is thus smaller and better able to assess the statistical significance of mean differences. Second, this study was nonexperimental: no experimental variable was manipulated. Third, and most important, the intrinsic interest and significance of the research problem and its theory, and the ingenuity of measuring and using conceptual complexity as a variable to "explain" the success of revolutionary leaders

▣ **TABLE 21.5** *Factorial Design with Repeated Measures: Revolutionary Leaders (Suedfeld & Rank study)*[a]

	Pretakeover	Posttakeover	
Success	1.67	3.65	2.66
Failure	2.37	2.22	2.30
	1.96	3.05	

[a]Tabled measures are means of conceptual complexity measures. Interaction $F = 12.37$ ($p < .005$).

overshadow possible questionable methodological points. The above sentence, for instance, may be incongruent with the use of variables in this study. Suedfeld and Rank analyzed measures of the independent variable, conceptual complexity. But the hypothesis under study was actually: If conceptual complexity (after revolution), then successful leadership. But with a research problem of such compelling interest and a variable of such importance (conceptual complexity) imaginatively and competently measured, who wants to quibble?

Perrine, Lisle, and Tucker: Offer of Help and Willingness to Seek Support

Teachers at all levels of education use a course syllabus to introduce the course to students. How much and what features in the syllabus have the greatest impact on students even before classroom instruction starts? Perrine, Lisle, and Tucker (1995) developed a study to see if the offer of help on an instructor's syllabus encourages college students of differing ages to seek help from their instructors. According to Perrine et al., to their best knowledge this is the first study to explore the use of social support by college and university instructors to benefit students. Perrine et al. also studied the effect of class size on the student's willingness to seek help. The study used 104 undergraduate students of whom 82 were female and 22 were male. Each participant was asked to read a description of two psychology classes. The descriptions included statements made by the instructor of each class on the course syllabus. In the description, class size was manipulated. It was set either to 15, 45, or 150 students. The course was described as demanding with a lot of work, but enjoyable. It also encouraged the student not to fall behind in the readings and assignments. The two separate statements from the instructors consisted of one that was supportive and one that was neutral. In the supportive statement, the student was encouraged to approach the instructor for help if the student ever encountered problems in the class. The neutral one did not include such a statement. Each participant read both descriptions. After reading the descriptions, the participant responded to questions about his or her willingness to seek help from the instructor for six possible academic problems encountered in the class: (1) trouble understanding textbook, (2) low grade on first exam, (3) hard to hear instructor's lectures, (4) study skills ineffective for course, (5) thinking of dropping the course, and (6) trouble understanding major topic. The participant used a 6-point rating scale: $0 = $ definitely no to $6 = $ definitely yes.

The design was a $3 \times 2 \times 2$ (class size $\times$ syllabus statement $\times$ student age) factorial design. The design contained one manipulated (active) independent variable, one measured (attribute) independent variable and one within-subjects (correlated) independent variable. Class size was the randomized and manipulated dependent variable. Student Age was the measured independent variable, and Syllabus Statement was the correlated independent variable. Using the appropriate analysis of variance (usually referred to as mixed ANOVA when at least one independent variable is between-subjects and at least one other is within-subjects) participants expressed significantly more willingness to seek help from the instructor when the supportive statement appeared on the course syllabus, than when only the neutral statement appeared. Younger students (under age 25) expressed less willingness than older students. There was also an Age $\times$ Syllabus interaction ($F = 4.85$, $p < .05$) that

🔲 **TABLE 21.6** *Means and F-Values for Syllabus Statement Differences and Age Differences (Perrine, Lisle, & Tucker study)*

Academic Problem	Syllabus			Age		
	Supportive	Neutral	F	Older	Younger	F
Trouble understanding textbook	4.7	3.7	76.08**	4.8	4.1	5.48*
Low grade on first exam	4.8	4.0	49.89**	5.2	4.3	7.64*
Hard to hear instructor's lectures	4.4	3.8	36.05**	4.4	4.0	1.01
Study skills ineffective for course	4.7	3.6	79.57**	4.8	4.0	6.32*
Thinking about dropping the course	4.9	3.8	61.80**	4.8	4.3	2.18
Trouble understanding major topic	5.3	4.2	82.97**	5.3	4.6	7.69*

* $p < .05$
** $p < .01$

was significant. The response to the offer of help was different between age groups. The statements affected younger students less than older students. Class size did not appear to be a significant factor on whether or not students were willing to seek help. Table 21.6 presents the summary statistics for the study.

Analysis of Covariance

The invention of the analysis of covariance by Ronald Fisher was an important event in behavioral research methodology. Here is a creative use of the variance principles common to experimental design and to correlation and regression theory—which we study later in the book—to help solve a long-standing control problem.

Analysis of covariance is a form of analysis of variance that tests the significance of the differences among means of experimental groups after taking into account initial differences among the groups, and the correlation of the initial measures and the dependent variable measures. That is, analysis of covariance analyzes the differences between experimental groups on *Y*, the dependent variable, after taking into account either initial differences between the groups on *Y* (pretest), or differences between the groups in some potential independent variable or variables, *X*, substantially correlated with *Y*, the dependent variable. The measure used as a control variable—the pretest or pertinent variable—is called a *covariate*.

The reader should be cautious when using analysis of covariance. It is particularly sensitive to violations of its assumptions. The potential misuse of this method was of such concern that the journal *Biometrics* in 1957 devoted an entire issue to it. Elashoff (1969) wrote an important article for educational researchers on the use of this method. The consensus is that it is generally not a good idea to use this method for nonexperimental research designs.

Clark and Walberg: Massive Reinforcement and Reading Achievement

There is little point to describing the statistical procedures and calculations of analysis of covariance. First, in their conventional form, they are complex and difficult to follow. Second, we wish here only to convey the meaning and purpose of the approach. Third, and most important, there is a much easier way to do what analysis of covariance does. Later in the book we shall see that analysis of covariance is a special case of multiple regression and is much easier to do with multiple regression techniques. To give the reader a feeling for what analysis of covariance accomplishes, let us look at an effective use of the procedure in educational and psychological studies.

Clark and Walberg (1968) thought that their participants, potential school dropouts doing poorly in school, needed far more reinforcement (encouragement, reward, etc.) than participants doing well in school. They therefore used massive reinforcement with their experimental group participants and moderate reinforcement with their control group participants. Since their dependent variable, Reading Achievement, is substantially correlated with Intelligence, they also needed to control Intelligence. A one-way analysis of variance of the reading achievement means of the experimental and control groups yielded an F of 9.52, significant at the .01 level, supporting their belief. It is conceivable, however, that the difference between the experimental and control groups was due to intelligence rather than to reinforcement. That is, even though the Ss were assigned at random to the experimental groups, an initial difference in intelligence in favor of the experimental group may have been enough to make the experimental group reading mean significantly greater than the control group reading mean, since intelligence is substantially correlated with reading. With random assignment, it is unlikely to happen, but it can happen. To control this possibility, Clark and Walberg used analysis of covariance.

Study Table 21.7 which shows in outline the design and analysis. The means of the X and Y scores, as reported by Clark and Walberg, are given at the bottom of the table. The Y means are the main concern. They were significantly different. Although it is doubtful that the analysis of covariance will change this result, it is possible that the difference between the X means, 92.05 and 90.73, may have tipped the statistical scales, in the test of the difference between the Y means, in favor of the experimental group. The analysis of covariance F-test, which uses Y sums of squares

▣ **TABLE 21.7** *Analysis of Covariance Paradigm (Clark & Walberg study)*

	Experimental (Massive Reinforcement)		Control (Moderate Reinforcement)	
	X (Intelligence)	*Y* (Reading)	*X* (Intelligence)	*Y* (Reading)
Means	92.05	31.62	90.73	26.86

and mean squares purged of the influence of X, was significant at the .01 level: $F = 7.90$. Thus, the mean reading scores of the experimental and control groups differed significantly, after adjusting or controlling for intelligence.

Research Design and Analysis: Concluding Remarks

Four major objectives have dominated the organization and preparation of Part Six. The first was to acquaint the student with the principal designs of research. By so doing, it was hoped that narrowly circumscribed notions of doing research with, say, only one experimental group and one control group; or with matched participants; or with one group, before and after, may be widened. The second objective was to convey a sense of the balanced structure of good research designs, to develop sensitive feeling for the architecture of design. Design must be formally as well as functional (y fitted to the research problems we seek to solve). The third objective was to help the reader understand the logic of experimental inquiry and the logic of the various designs. Research designs are alternative routes to the same destination: reliable and valid statements of the relations among variables. Some designs, if practicable, yield stronger relational statements then other designs.

In a certain sense, the fourth objective of Part Six—to help the student understand the relation between the research design and statistics—has been the most difficult to achieve. Statistics is, in one sense, the technical discipline of handling variance. And, as we have seen, one of the basic purposes of design is to provide control of systematic and error variances. This is the rationale used for treating statistics in such detail in Part Four and Part Five, before considering design in Part Six. Fisher (1951, p. 3) expresses this idea succinctly when he says, "Statistical procedure and experimental design are only two different aspects of the same whole, and that whole comprises all the logical requirements of the complete process of adding to natural knowledge by experimentation."

A well-conceived design is no guarantee of the validity of research findings. Elegant designs nicely tailored to research problems can still result in wrong or distorted conclusions. Nevertheless, the chances of arriving at accurate and valid conclusions are better with sound designs than with unsound ones. This much is relatively sure: if a design is faulty, one cannot arrive at clear conclusions. If, for instance, one uses a two group, matched subjects design when the research problem logically demands a factorial design, or if one uses a factorial design when the nature of the research situation calls for a correlated groups design, no amount of interpretative or statistical manipulation can increase confidence in the conclusions of such research.

It is fitting that Fisher (1951) should have the last word on this subject. In the first chapter of his book, *The Design of Experiments*, he says:

> If the design of an experiment is faulty, any method of interpretation that makes it out to be decisive must be faulty, too. It is true that there are a great many experimental procedures which are well designed that may lead to decisive conclusions? but, on other occasions they may fail to do so; in such cases, if decisive conclusions are in fact drawn when they are unjustified, we may say that the fault

is wholly in the interpretation, not in the design. But the fault of interpretation . . . lies in overlooking the characteristic features of the design which lead to the result being sometimes inconclusive, or conclusive on some questions but not on all. To understand correctly the one aspect of the problem is to understand the other (p. 3).

Computer Addendum

Randomized designs can be analyzed with independent samples *t*-test or analysis of variance. The SPSS setup and discussions are given in Chapter 13 and Chapter 14. Here, we will discuss how to use SPSS to perform statistical analyses of data from a correlated groups design (repeated measures). For our discussion we will use the data from Miller and Dicara (1968) presented in Table 21.9.

Following our previously established data entry instructions, you would enter the data into SPSS so that the resulting SPSS spreadsheet would look like that shown in Figure 21.6.

Remember from our earlier discussion, the goal was to compare rats that had an increase in urine output to rats that had a decrease in urine output. The urine outputs of those rats that showed an increase in urine output are "before1" and "after1." The variables "before2" and "after2" are used to represent the before and after outputs of the rats that showed a decrease.

To instruct SPSS to perform the appropriate analysis for the data given in Table 21.9 and in Figure 21.6, point and click the "Statistics" option. This action will present a menu from which you choose "Compare Means." After clicking "Compare Means," another menu appears from which you choose "Paired Samples T-Test." After this has been chosen, a new screen is reached (see Figure 21.7).

FIGURE 21.6 *Miller and DiCara's Data in SPSS*

File Edit View Data Transform Statistics Graphs Utilities Windows Help

	before1	after1	before2	after2
1	.023	.030	.018	.007
2	.014	.019	.015	.003
3	.016	.029	.012	.005
4	.018	.030	.015	.006
5	.007	.016	.030	.009
6	.026	.044	.027	.008
7	.012	.026	.020	.003

Summarize ►
Compare Means ►
ANOVA Models ►
Correlate ►
Regression ►
Log-linear ►
Classify ►
Data Reduction ►
Scale ►
Nonparametric Tests ►

Means
One-Sample T-Test
Independent Samples T-Test
Paired Samples T-Test
One Way ANOVA

◙ **FIGURE 21.7** *SPSS Screen Used to Specify Variables for Analysis*

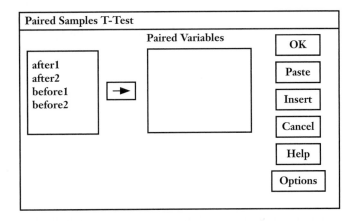

Two dependent samples *t*-tests can be tested simultaneously here by taking the following steps:

1. Highlight the "after1" variable (point and click on it).
2. Highlight the "before1" variable.
3. Click the arrow button.
4. Highlight the "after2" variable.
5. Highlight the "before2" variable.
6. Click the arrow button.

At this point you will see that SPSS has formed two difference equations displayed on the right side box. This is shown in Figure 21.8. When you click the "OK"

◙ **FIGURE 21.8** *Preparing for SPSS Analysis*

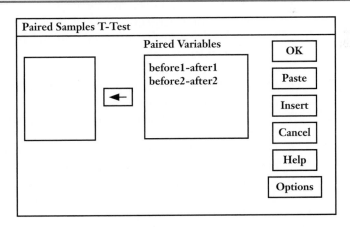

◨ FIGURE 21.9 *SPSS Output*

		Paired Differences Mean	Std. Deviation	t	df	Sig. (2-tailed)
Pair 1 Increase	BEFORE1- AFTER1	−.00111	.00445	−6.624	6	.001
Pair 2 Decrease	BEFORE2- AFTER2	.00137	.00531	6.828	6	.000

button, SPSS will perform the analysis and output it. An abbreviated version of the output is given in Figure 21.9.

The analysis just completed was done using SPSS's *t*-test. You can also perform the same analysis by using SPSS's "General Linear Model."

CHAPTER SUMMARY

1. Randomized subjects designs are the preferred designs of behavioral research.
2. Randomized subjects designs are true experiments with active, manipulated independent variables.
3. The statistical method usually used to analyze data from randomized subjects designs is analysis of variance.
4. Randomized subject designs usually require a large number (N) of participants to achieve the desired precision.
5. Correlated subjects designs usually involve
   a. using the same participants in each treatment condition
   b. matching participants on one or more independent variables related to the dependent variable
   c. using more than one group of participants (e.g., classrooms)
6. Units can be different kinds of entities. In psychological research, units are usually people or animals.
7. Correlated subjects designs include the one group repeated trials (measures) design.
8. Design 20.2 is the design to use when participants are matched and randomly assigned to treatment groups.
9. A covariate is a potential independent variable used to adjust the individual differences between groups that are *not* due to the treatment. Pretests are the most common covariates.

10. Analysis of covariance is a correlated subjects method of statistical analysis. A covariate adjusts the dependent variable, then the adjusted values are used in an analysis of variance. Multiple regression is another statistical method that can used for this purpose.

STUDY SUGGESTIONS

1. In studying research design, it is useful to do analyses of variance—as many as possible: simple one-way analyses and two-variable factorial analyses, perhaps even a three-variable analysis. By means of this statistical practice, you will gain a better understanding of the designs. You may well attach variable names to your "data" rather than working with numbers alone. Some useful suggestions for projects with random numbers follow.

   a. Draw three groups of random numbers 0 through 9. Name the independent and dependent variables. Express a hypothesis and translate it into design-statistical language. Do a one-way analysis of variance. Interpret.

   b. Repeat 1 (a) using five groups of numbers.

   c. Now, increase the numbers of one of your groups by 2, and decrease those of another group by 2. Repeat the statistical analysis.

   d. Draw four groups of random numbers, 10 in each group. Set them up, at random, in a 2 × 2 factorial design. Do a factorial analysis of variance.

   e. Bias the numbers of the two right-hand cells by adding 3 to each number. Repeat the analysis. Compare the results to (d).

   f. Bias the numbers of the data of (d) as follows: add 2 to each of the numbers in the upper-left and lower-right cells. Repeat the analysis. Interpret.

2. Return to Chapter 14, study suggestions 2 and 3. Work through both examples again. Are they easier for you now?

3. Suppose you are the principal of an elementary school. Some of the fourth- and fifth-grade teachers want to dispense with workbooks. The superintendent does not like the idea, but is willing to let you test the notion that workbooks do not make much difference. (One of the teachers has even suggested that workbooks may have bad effects on both teachers and pupils.) To test the efficacy of the workbooks, set up two research plans and designs: a one-way design and a factorial design. Consider the variables Achievement, Intelligence, and Gender. You might also consider the possibility of teacher attitude toward workbooks as an independent variable.

4. Suppose an investigation using Methods and Gender as the independent variables, and achievement as the dependent variable, has been done with the results reported in Table 21.8. The numbers in the cells are fictitious means. The F-ratios of Methods and Gender are not significant. The interaction F-ratio is significant at the .01 level. Interpret these results statistically and substantively. To do the latter, give names to each of the three methods.

TABLE 21.8 *Hypothetical Data (Means) of a Fictitious Factorial Experiment*

	Methods			
	A₁	A₂	A₃	
Male	45	45	36	42
Female	35	39	40	38
	40	42	38	

5. Although difficult and sometimes frustrating, there is no substitute for reading and studying original research studies. A number of studies using factorial design and analysis of variance have been cited and summarized in this chapter and in earlier chapters. Select and read two of these studies. Try summarizing one of them. Critique both studies for adequacy of design and execution of the research (to the best of your present knowledge and ability). Focus particularly on the adequacy of the design to answer the research question or questions.

6. We did a two-way (repeated measure) analysis of variance of the Miller and DiCara Increase Rats data in Table 21.9, with some of the results reported in the table: ω^2 (Hays omega-squared) was .357; ω^2 for the Decrease Rats data was .663. What do these coefficients mean? Why calculate them?

7. Kolb (1965), basing his work on the outstanding work of McClelland on achievement motivation, did a fascinating experiment with underachieving high school boys of high intelligence. Of 57 boys, he assigned 20 at random to a training program in which, through various means, the boys were "taught" achievement motivation (an attempt to build a need to achieve into the boys). The boys were given a pretest of achievement motivation in the summer, and given the test again six months later. The mean change *scores* were, for experimental and control groups, 6.72 and −.34, respectively. These were significant at the .005 level.

   a. Comment on the use of change scores. Does their use lessen your faith in the statistical significance of the results?

   b. Might factors other than the experimental training have induced the change? If so, which factors?

8. Lest the student believe that only continuous measures are analyzed and that analysis of variance alone is used in psychological and educational experiments, read the study by Freedman, Wallington, and Bless (1967) on guilt and compliance. There was an experimental group (Ss induced to lie) and a control group. The dependent variable was measured by whether a participant did or did not comply with a request for help. The results were reported in cross-tabulation frequency tables. Read the study and, after study-

ing the authors' design and results, design one of the three experiments another way. Bring in another independent variable, for instance. Suppose that it was known that there were wide individual differences in compliance. How can this be controlled? Name and describe two kinds of design to do it.

9. In a study in which training on the complexities of art stimuli affected attitude toward music, among other things, Renner (1970) used analysis of covariance, with the covariate being measures from a scale designed to measure attitude toward music. This was a pretest. There were three experimental groups. Sketch the design from this brief description. Why did Renner use the music attitude scale as a pretest? Why did she use analysis of covariance? (Note: The original report is well worth reading. The study, in part a study of creativity, is itself creative.)

10. In a significant study on the effect of a liberal arts education on complex concept formation, Winter and McClelland (1978) found the difference between seniors and freshmen attending a liberal arts college on measure of complex concept formation to be statistically significant ($M_s = 2.00$, $M_f = 1.22$; $t = 3.76$; ($p < .001$). Realizing that a comparison was needed, they also tested similar mean differences at a teachers college and a community college. Neither of these differences was statistically significant. Why did Winter and McClelland test the relation at the teachers college and the community college? It is suggested that students find and read the original report—it is well worth study—and do an analysis of variance from the reported ns, means, and standard deviations, using the method outlined in Chapter 13 (Addendum).

11. One virtue of analysis of covariance, seldom mentioned in texts, is that three estimates of the correlation between X and Y can be calculated. The three are: (i) the total r over all the scores; (ii) the between-groups r, which is the r between the X and Y means; (iii) and the within-groups r, the r calculated from an average of the rs between X and Y within the k groups. The within-groups r is the "best" estimate of the "true" r between X and Y. Why is this so?

[Hint: Can a total r, the one usually calculated in practice, be inflated or deflated by between-groups variance?]

PART SEVEN
TYPES OF RESEARCH

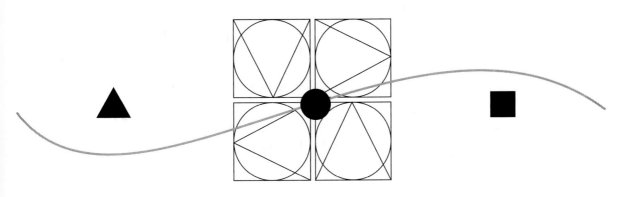

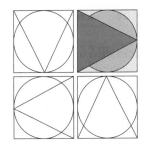

QUASI-EXPERIMENTAL AND $N = 1$ DESIGNS OF RESEARCH

In earlier chapters we stated and emphasized that one of the major goals of science is to find causal relations. In the behavioral sciences, the true experiment is the strongest approach used to meet this goal. When the true experiment is arranged and executed correctly, it can provide the researcher with a *cause-and-effect* statement concerning the relation between X (independent variable) and Y (dependent variable). This is generally considered the highest form of experimentation. However, there are research problems in the behavioral sciences and especially educational research that cannot be studied using a true experimental design. That is, Designs 20.1 through 20.6 and some of its variants covered in Chapters 20 and 21 cannot be used. One or more of the components of a true experiment is missing or has been weakened by the nature of the study, or poor planning. The weakening of the components of the true experiment is what we will discuss in this chapter. We will examine two research designs where one or more of the components of the true experiment have been compromised. The first is called *quasi experimental* designs and the second is called *single subject* or *N = 1* designs.

Compromise Designs a.k.a. Quasi-Experimental Designs

It is possible, indeed necessary, to use designs that are compromises with true experimentation. Recall that true experimentation requires at least two groups, one receiving an experimental treatment and one not receiving the treatment, or receiving it in different form. The true experiment requires the manipulation of at least one independent variable, the random assignment of participants to groups, and the random assignment of treatments to groups. When one or more of these prerequisites is missing for one reason or another, we have a *compromise design*. Compromise designs are popularly known as quasi-experimental designs. They are called quasi because quasi means "almost" or "sort of." Cook and Campbell (1979) present two major classifications of quasi-experimental design. The first is called the "nonequivalent control group designs," the second is the "interrupted time series designs." A number of research studies performed outside the laboratory could fall into one of these categories. Many marketing research studies are in the form of quasi-experimental designs. Often a researcher is asked to "design" and analyze the data from a study that was unplanned. For example, a grocery buyer decides to stock a different brand of baby food. Her superiors later ask if such a move was profitable. This buyer then consults with a market researcher to determine what can be done to show whether or not her decision was a profitable one. Such analyses would not have the niceties of random selection and assignment and would consist of data taken over time. Additionally, other ads or the season of the year could influence the baby food sales. The only component resembling a true experiment is the fact that the independent variable was manipulated. Not all stores received the different baby food product. With such problems, the researcher would turn to the use of quasi-experimental or compromise research designs.

Nonequivalent Control Group Design

Perhaps the most commonly used quasi-experimental design is the experimental group–control group pattern in which one has no clear assurance that the experimental and control groups are equivalent. Some such as Cook and Campbell (1979), Christensen (1997), Ray (1997), and Graziano and Raulin (1993) refer to it as the nonequivalent control group design. Cook and Campbell present eight variations of this design that they state are "interpretable":

no-treatment control group designs

nonequivalent dependent variables designs

removed treatment group designs

repeated treatment designs

reversed treatment nonequivalent control group designs

cohort designs

posttest only designs

regression continuity designs

In this book we will discuss in detail only one of these. It is the one most likely to occur in some shape and form in the research literature. For a thorough discussion of these eight types of nonequivalent control group designs, read Cook and Campbell (1979).

No-Treatment Control Group Design

The structure of the no-treatment control group design has already been considered in Design 20.3. Cook and Campbell (1979) refer to this design as the untreated control group design with pretest and posttest. The compromise form is as follows:

Design 22.1: No-Treatment Control Group Design

Y_b	X	Y_a	(Experimental)
Y_b	$\sim X$	Y_a	(Control)

The difference between Design 20.3 and Design 22.1 is sharp. In Design 22.1, there is no randomized assignment of participants to groups as in 20.3(a), and no matching of participants and then random assignment as in 20.3(b). Design 22.1, therefore, is subject to the weaknesses due to the possible lack of equivalence between the groups in variables other than X. Researchers commonly take pains to establish equivalence by other means, and, to the extent they are successful in doing so, the design is valid. This is done in ways discussed below.

It is sometimes difficult or impossible to equate groups by random selection or random assignment, or by matching. Should one then give up doing the research? By no means. Every effort should be made to (1) select and (2) to assign at random. If both of these are not possible, perhaps matching and random assignment can be accomplished. If matching and random assignment are not possible, an effort should be made to at least use samples from the same population, or samples that are as alike as possible. The experimental treatments should be assigned at random. Then the similarity of the groups should be checked using any information available (sex, age, social class, and so on). The equivalence of the groups could be verified using the means and standard deviations of the pretests: t-tests and F-tests will do. The distributions should also be checked. Although one cannot have the assurance afforded by randomization, if all these items check out satisfactorily, one can go ahead with a study knowing at least that there is no known evidence against the equivalence assumption.

These precautions increase the possibilities of attaining internal validity. There are still difficulties, all of which are subordinate to one main difficulty—*selection*. These other difficulties will not be discussed here. For detailed discussion, see Campbell and Stanley (1963), or Cook and Campbell (1979).

Selection is one of the difficult and troublesome problems of behavioral research. Since its aspects will be discussed in detail in Chapter 23 on nonexperimental research, only a brief description will be given here. One of the important reasons for the emphasis on random selection and assignment is to avoid the difficulties of selection. When participants are selected into groups on bases extraneous to the research purposes, we call this "selection," or alternatively, "self-selection." Take a common example: let us assume that volunteers are used in the experimental group and other participants are used as controls. If the volunteers differ in a characteristic related to Y, the dependent variable, the ultimate difference between the experimental and control groups may be due to this characteristic rather than to X, the independent variable (treatment). Volunteers may be more intelligent (or less intelligent) than nonvolunteers. If we were doing an experiment with some type of learning as the dependent variable, obviously the volunteers might perform better on Y because of superior intelligence, despite the initial likeness of the two groups on the pretest. Note that if we had used only volunteers and had assigned them to experimental and control groups at random, the selection difficulty is lessened. External validity or representativeness, however, would be decreased.

Cook and Campbell (1979) claim that even in very extreme cases, it is still possible to draw strong conclusions if all the threats to validity are considered and accounted for. Without the benefit of random assignment, attempts should be made through other means to eliminate rival hypotheses. We consider only the design that uses the pretest because the pretest could provide useful information concerning the effectiveness of the independent variable on the dependent variable. The pretest could provide data on how equal the groups are to each other prior to administering treatment to the experimental group.

Another more frequent example in educational research is to take some school classes for the experimental group and others for the control group. If a fairly large number of classes are selected and assigned at random to experimental and control groups, there is no great problem. But if they are not assigned at random, certain ones may select themselves into the experimental groups, and these classes may have characteristics that predispose them to have higher mean Y scores than the other classes. For example, their teachers may be more alert, more intelligent, and more aggressive. These characteristics interact with the selection to produce, irrespective of X, scores that are higher for the experimental group than for control group Y. In other words, something that influences the selection processes (e.g., volunteer participants), also influences the dependent variable measures. This occurs even though the pretest may show the groups to be the same (alike) on the dependent variable. The X manipulation is "effective" because of selection, or self-selection, but it is not effective in and of itself. Additionally, an educational researcher may have to receive the school district's approval for research. At times, the district will assign the school and the classroom that a researcher may use.

A classic study by Sanford and Hemphill (1952) reported in Campbell and Stanley (1963) used this design. This study was conducted at the U.S. Naval Academy at Annapolis. This study was done to see if a psychology course in the curriculum increased the students' (midshipmen) confidence in social situations. The second-year midshipmen were the first group of students to take the psychology course. The comparison or control group was the third-year class. The third-year students had not taken the course in their second year. A social situation questionnaire was administered to both classes at the beginning of the academic year and at the end of the year. The results showed an increase in confidence scores for the second-year class from 43.26 to 51.42. The third-year class also showed an increase, but this increase was considerably smaller changing from 55.80 to 56.78. One might conclude from these data that taking the psychology course did have an effect of increasing confidence in social situations. However, other explanations are also possible. One could explain that the greater gains made by the second-year class were the result of some maturational development that has its largest growth in the second year, with a smaller growth in the third year. If such a process exists, the larger score increase for the second-year class would have occurred even if the midshipmen had not taken the psychology class. The fact that the second-year class started with a lower score than the third-year class might indicate that these students had not yet reached a level equivalent to the third-year class. Also, the end-of-year scores of the second-year class were not equivalent to the beginning scores for the third-year class. A better and stronger design would be to create two equivalent groups from the second-year class through random selection and give at random the psychology class to only one group.

Possible outcomes from this design are given in Figure 22.1. There is the possibility of a different interpretation on causality depending on which outcome the researcher obtains. In almost all of the cases the most likely threat to internal validity would be the selection–maturation interaction. You might recall that this interaction occurs when (1) two groups are different to begin with as measured by the pretest; then (2) one of the groups experience greater differential changes, such as getting more experienced, more accurate, more tired, and so on, than the other group. The after-treatment difference, as observed in the posttest, can not exactly be attributed to the treatment itself.

In Figure 22.1(a), there are three possible threats to internal validity. As mentioned above, the most prevalent threat is the selection–maturation interaction. With the outcome in Figure 22.1a, Cook and Campbell (1979) state that there are four alternative explanations.

The first is selection–maturation interaction. Let's say the study involves comparing two strategies or methods of problem-solving. Group E has higher

◩ **FIGURE 22.1** *Five Possible Outcomes for the Nonequivalent Control Group Design*[a]

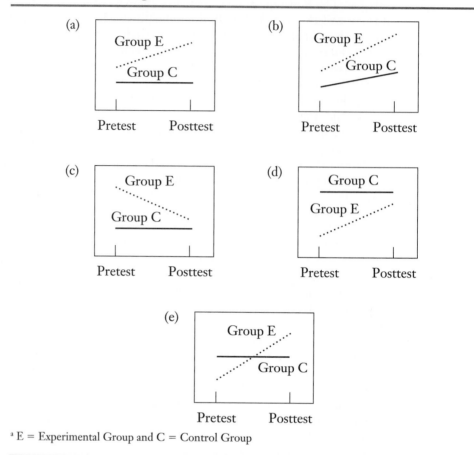

[a] E = Experimental Group and C = Control Group

intelligence than Group C. Group E scores higher on the pretest than Group C. Group E sees an increase in the posttest scores after treatment. Group C sees little or no change. One might feel that the treatment that Group E receives is superior to the treatment received by Group C. However, with selection–maturation interaction, Group E's increase may be due to their higher level of intelligence. With a higher level of intelligence, these participants can process more, or grow faster, than Group C.

A second explanation is one of instrumentation. The scale used to measure the dependent variable may be more sensitive at certain levels than others. Take percentiles for example. Percentiles have an advantage over raw scores in that they convey direct meaning without other pieces of information. However, percentiles are nonlinear transformations of the raw scores. In a normal distribution, changes in raw scores near the center of the distribution reflect bigger percentile changes than at the tails. A change of only 2 or 3 points on the raw score scale can reflect a 10 percentile point change near the center of the distribution. This would not be the case when considering the tails of the normal distribution. A change of 15 raw score points might be necessary to see a 10 percentile point increase at the tail of distribution. Hence, Group C's percentile measurements may not change much because the measurements are not sensitive enough to detect the changes [at the tails]. However, Group E will show a greater amount of change because its percentile happens to be in the more sensitive part of the measurement scale.

The third explanation is statistical regression. Let's say that the two groups, E and C, actually come from different populations, and Group C is the group of interest. The researcher wants to introduce an educational plan to help increase the intellectual functioning of these participants. These participants are selected because they generally score low on intelligence tests. The researcher creates a comparison or control group from normal scoring students. This group is depicted as Group E in Figure 22.1a. These students would be at the low end of the test score scale, but not as low as Group C. If this is the setup, then statistical regression is a viable alternative explanation. The increase in scores by Group E would be due to their selection on the basis of extreme scores. On the posttest, their scores would go up because they would be approaching the population baseline.

The fourth explanation centers on the interaction between history and selection. Cook and Campbell (1979) refer to this as the local history effect. In this situation, something other than the independent variable will affect one of the groups (Group E) and not the other (Group C). Let's say a market researcher wanted to determine the effectiveness of an ad for soup starters. Sales data are gathered before and after introducing the ad. Two groups are used from different regions of the country: one group is from Southern California and the other is from the Midwest. In this case, the growth in sales seen by one of the groups (E) may not necessarily be due to the ad. Both groups may have similar purchasing behavior during the spring and summer; that is, not a high need for soup starters. However, as the fall season approaches, the sale of soup starters may increase for the group in the Midwest. In Southern California, where the temperatures are considerably warmer all year around, the demand for soup starters would remain fairly constant. So here the explanation for increased sales in the Midwest would be the season of the year and not the ad.

All of the threats mentioned for Figure 22.1(a) are also true for Figure 22.1(b). While in Figure 22.1(a) one of the groups (Group C) remains constant, in Figure 22.1(b), both groups experience an increase from pretest to posttest. Selection– maturation is still a possibility, since by definition the groups are growing (or declining) at a different rate where the lower-scoring group (Group C) progresses at a lower rate than the high-scoring group (Group E). To determine if selection–maturation is playing a main role in the results, Cook and Campbell (1979) recommend two methods. The first method involves looking only at the data for the experimental group (Group E). If the within-group variance for the posttest is considerably greater than the within-group variance of the pretest, then there is evidence of a

🔳 **FIGURE 22.2** *Comparison of Experimental Group and Control Group*

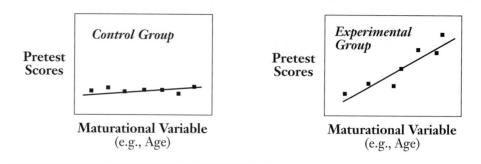

selection–maturation explanation. The second method is to develop two plots and the regression line associated with each plot. One plot is for the experimental group (Group E). The pretest scores are plotted against the maturational variable. The maturation variable can be age or experience. The second plot would be the same, except it would be for the control group (Group C). If the regression line slopes for each plot differ from each other, then there is evidence of a differential average growth rate, meaning that there is the likelihood of a selection–maturation interaction (see Figure 22.2).

The outcome shown in Figure 22.1(c) is more commonly found in clinical psychology studies. The treatment is intended to lead to a decline of an undesired behavior. Like the previous two outcomes, this one is also susceptible to selection–maturation interaction, statistical regression, instrumentation, and local history effects. In this outcome, the difference between the experimental and control groups is very dramatic on the pretest, but after the treatment the groups get closer to one another.

The fourth outcome is shown in Figure 22.1(d). This differs from the previous three in that the control group (Group C) starts out higher than the experimental group (Group E) and remains higher even at posttest. However Group E, showed a greater gain from pretest to posttest. Statistical regression would be a threat if the participants in Group E were selected on the basis of their extremely low score. Cook and Campbell (1979) state, however, that the selection–maturation threat can be ruled out since this effect usually results in a slower growth rate for low scores and a faster growth rate for high scorers. Here, the low scorers show the greater growth in scores than the high scorers. This evidence lends support to the effectiveness of the treatment condition received by Group E. What cannot be easily ruled out are the threats from instrumentation and local history that we saw in the previous three outcomes of nonequivalent control group designs.

With the final outcome shown in Figure 22.1(e), the means of the experimental (Group E) and control (Group C) groups are significantly different from one another at both pretest and posttest. However, the differences are in the reverse direction in the posttest than in the pretest. The trend lines cross over one another. Group E initially starts low but then overtakes Group C who initially scored high. Cook and Campbell (1979) found this outcome to be more interpretable than the previous four. Instrumentation or scaling is ruled out because no transformation of the scores could remove or reduce this crossover or interaction effect. Statistical regression becomes untenable because it is extremely rare that a low score can regress enough to overtake an initially high score. Other than a very complicated selection–maturation interaction effect, this pattern is not akin to selection–maturation threats. Maturation, for example, does not generally start off different, meet, and then grow apart in opposite directions. Hence, the outcome in Figure 22.1(e) seems to be the strongest one and should enable the researcher to make a causal statement concerning treatment. Cook and Campbell, however, warn that researchers should not plan on developing quasi-experimental research with the expectation of obtaining this outcome. Definitely, the designing of a nonequivalent control group study should be done with care and caution.

Research Examples

Nelson, Hall, and Walsh-Bowers: Nonequivalent Control Group Design

The research study by Nelson, Hall, and Walsh-Bowers (1997) specifically states that they *used a nonequivalent control group design* to compare the long-term effects of supportive apartments (SA), group homes (GH), and board-and-care homes (BCH) for psychiatric residents. Supportive apartments and group homes are run by nonprofit organizations; board-and-care homes are run for profit. The main goal was to compare the two intervention groups: supportive apartments and group homes. They were unable to assign participants to different housing settings randomly. Nelson et al. tried their best to match the residents, but there were some significant differences in the composition of the groups that led them to use the nonequivalent control group design. With this design they decided to use BCH residents as the comparison group. They could not correct through matching the following variables that could have an effect on the dependent variables: (1) The SA and GH groups tended to be younger than the BCH group (33 years versus 45), and had spent less time in residence (2.5 years versus 39 years). (2) The SA and GH residents had a higher level of education than those in the BCH group. Nelson et al. found a significant difference between these groups on these variables. Even though gender was not significant, there were more men than women in the SA and GH groups; and more women than men in the BCH group.

Nelson et al. state that the difference they found between these three groups on posttest measures could have been due to the selection problem, and not the type of care facility.

Chapman and McCauley: Quasi-Experiment

In this study, Chapman and McCauley (1993) examined the career growth of graduate students who applied for a National Science Foundation (NSF) Graduate Fellowship Award. Although one can perhaps think of this study as a nonexperimental one, Chapman and McCauley felt that it came under the classification of quasi-experimental. We shall see why. In comparing the award winners and non-winners, the choice of winners was not exactly done at random. The study did not look at the Quality Group 1 applicants. The Group 1 applicants were in the top 5% and all received awards. The Quality Group 2 NSF applicants made up of the next 10% and were considered a highly homogeneous group. Awards were given to approximately half of a homogeneous group of applicants in a procedure that Chapman and McCauley say approximates random assignment to either fellowship or honorable mention. The students were assigned with regard to academic promise. Chapman and McCauley assumed that differences in performance between Quality Group 2 applicants, who were and were not awarded an NSF fellowship, could reveal the effect of positive expectations associated with this prestigious award.

The results showed that those receiving an NSF award were more likely to finish the Ph.D. However, Chapman and McCauley found no reliable fellowship effect on achieving faculty status, achieving top faculty status, or submitting or receiving an NSF or a National Institutes of Health research grant. It seems that the positive expectancies associated with this prestigious award have some influence in graduate school, but no effect on accomplishments after graduate school.

Time Designs

Important variants of the basic quasi-experimental design are time designs. The form of Design 20.6 can be altered to include a span of time:

Y_b	X	Y_a	
Y_b	$\sim X$	Y_a	
	X		Y_a
	$\sim X$		Y_a

The Y_as of the third and fourth lines are observations of the dependent variable at any specified later date. Such an alteration, of course, changes the purpose of the design, and may cause some of the virtues of Design 20.6 to be lost. We might, if we had the time, the patience, and the resources, retain all the former benefits and still extend in time by adding two more groups to Design 20.6 itself.

A common research problem, especially in studies of the development and growth of children, involves the study of individuals and groups using time as a variable. Such studies are longitudinal studies of participants, often children, at different points in time. One such design among many might be:

Design 22.2: A Longitudinal Time Design (a.k.a. Interrupted Time Series Design)

Y_1	Y_2	Y_3	Y_4	X	Y_5	Y_6	Y_7	Y_8

Note the similarity to Design 19.2, where a group is compared to itself. The use of Design 22.2 allows us to avoid one of the difficulties of Design 19.2. Its use makes it possible to separate reactive measurement effects from the effect, of X. It enables us to determine, if the measurements have a reactive effect, and whether X was strong enough to overcome that effect. The reactive effect should show itself by comparing Y_3 to Y_4; this can be contrasted with Y_5. If there is an increase at Y_5 over and above the increase at Y_4 from Y_3, it can be attributed to X. A similar argument applies for maturation and history.

One difficulty with longitudinal or time studies, especially with children, is the growth or learning that occurs naturally over time: Children do not stop growing and learning for research convenience. The longer the time period, the greater the problem. In other words, time itself is a variable. With a design like Design 20.2, $Y_b X Y_a$, the time variable can confound X, the experimental independent variable. If there is a significant difference between Y_b and Y_a, one cannot tell whether X or a time "variable" caused the change. But with Design 22.2, one has other measures of Y, and thus a baseline against which to compare the change in Y presumably due to X.

One method of determining whether the experimental treatment had an effect is to look at a plot of the data over time. Caporaso (1973) presents a number of additional possible patterns of behavior that could be obtained from time-series data. Whether or not a significant change in behavior followed the introduction of the treatment condition, is determined by tests of significance. The most widely used statistical test is ARIMA (autoregressive, integrated, moving average) developed by Box and Jenkins, (1970) (see also Gottman, 1981). This method consists of determining whether or not the pattern of postresponse measures differs from the pattern of preresponse measures. The use of such a statistical analysis requires the availability of many data points.

The statistical analysis of time measures is a special and troublesome problem: The usual tests of significance applied to time measures can yield spurious results. One reason is that such data tend to be highly variable, and it is as easy to misinterpret changes not due to X as due to X. That is, in time data, individual and mean scores tend to move around a good bit. It is easy to fall into the trap of seeing one of these shifts as "significant," especially if it accords with our hypothesis. If we can legitimately assume that influences other than X—both random and systematic—are uniform over the whole series of Ys, the statistical problem can be solved. But such an assumption may be, and probably often is, unwarranted.

The researcher who explores time studies should make a special study of the statistical problems and consult a statistician. For the practitioner, this statistical complexity is unfortunate in that it may discourage needed practical studies. Since longitudinal single-group designs are particularly well suited to individual class research, it is recommended that in longitudinal studies of methods or studies of children in educational situations analysis be confined to drawing graphs of results and interpreting them qualitatively. Crucial tests, especially those for published studies, however, must be buttressed with statistical tests.

Multiple Time Series Design

The multiple time series design is an extension of the interrupted time series design. With the interrupted time series design, only one group of participants was used. As a result, alternative explanations can come from a history effect. The multiple time series design has the advantage of eliminating the history effect by including a control group comprised of an equivalent—or at least comparable—group of participants who do not receive the treatment condition. This is shown in Design 22.3 where one experimental group receives the treatment condition and the control group does not. Consequently, the design offers a greater degree of control over sources of alternative explanations or rival hypotheses. The history effects, for example, are controlled because they would influence the experimental and control groups equally.

Design 22.3: A Multiple Time Series Design

Y_1	Y_2	Y_3	Y_4	X	Y_5	Y_6	Y_7	Y_8	(Experimental)
Y_1	Y_2	Y_3	Y_4		Y_5	Y_6	Y_7	Y_8	(Control)

Naturally, there are other possible variations of Design 22.2 beside Design 22.3. One important variation is to add one or more control groups; another is to add more time observations. Still another is to add more Xs, more experimental interventions (see Gottman, 1981; Gottman, McFall, & Barnett, 1969; Campbell & Stanley, 1963).

Single Subject Experimental Designs

The majority of today's behavioral research involves using groups of participants. However, there are other approaches. In this section we deal with strategies for achieving control in experiments using one or only a few participants. These single-subject designs are sometimes referred to as the $N = 1$ design. Single-subject designs are an extension of the interrupted time series design. Where the interrupted time series generally looks at a group of individuals over time; for example, children, the single-subject study uses only one participant or at most a few participants. Even when a few participants are used, each is studied individually and extensively. These will also be called single-subject designs or studies. Although they have different names, they all share the following characteristics:

- Only one or a few participants are used in the study.
- Each subject participates in a number of trials (repeated measures). This is similar to the within-participants designs described in Chapter 21.
- Randomization (i.e., random assignment and/or random selection) procedures are hardly ever used. The repeated measurements or time intervals are instead assigned at random to the different treatment conditions.

These designs observe the organism's behavior before the experimental treatment and use the observations as a baseline measure. Observations taken after the treatment are then compared to the baseline observations. The participant serves as his or her own control. These designs are usually applied in school, clinical, and counseling research. They are used to evaluate the effects of behavioral interventions over time. This mode of research is popular among those who do operant learning experiments or behavior modification.

Research using single participants is not new, as the following illustrates. Gustav Fechner, who developed the discipline of psychophysics in the 1860s, used only two participants: himself and his brother-in-law. Fechner is credited with inventing the basic psychophysical methods that are still used today to measure sensory thresholds. Fechner heavily influenced Hermann Ebbinghaus, who is known for his experimental work on memory. Ebbinghaus also used himself as his own subject. Wilhelm Wundt, who is credited with founding the first psychological laboratory in 1879, conducted experiments measuring various psychological and behavioral responses in individual participants. I. P. Pavlov did his pioneering work on instrumental conditioning using individual dogs. The list of psychologists using single participants is extensive, with most of them occurring before 1930 and the advent of R. A. Fisher's and William Sealy Gossett's work in modern statistics.

Behavioral scientists doing research before the development of modern statistics attempted to solve the problem of reliability and validity by making extensive observations and frequent replication of results. This is a traditional procedure used by researchers doing single-subject experiments. The assumption is that individual participants are essentially equivalent and that one should study additional participants only to make certain that the original subject was within the norm.

The popularity of Fisher's work on analysis of variance and Gossett's work on the Student's t-test led the way for group-oriented research methodology. Some claim that these works were so popular that the single-subject tradition nearly became extinct. In fact, even in today's world, there are hiring practices at major universities that depend on whether the candidate is a group-oriented research scientist or a single-participants design-oriented researcher. Despite the popularity of Fisher's methods and group-oriented research, certain psychologists continued to work in the single-subject tradition The most notable of these was Burrus Frederick Skinner. Skinner refrains from using inferential statistics. He does not advocate the use of complex inferential statistics. Skinner feels that one can adequately demonstrate the effectiveness of the treatment by plotting the actions of the organism's behavior over time. Skinner called this the cumulative record. Some, such as E. L. Thorndike, call it a "learning curve." Skinner feels that it is more useful to study one animal for 1,000 hours than to study 1,000 animals for one hour. Sidman (1960) in his classic book describes Skinner's philosophy of research, and makes a clear distinction between the single-subject approach and the group approach to research. The single-subject approach assumes that the variance in the subject's behavior is dictated by the situation. As a result, this variance can be removed through careful experimental control. The group difference research attitude assumes that the bulk of the variability is inherent and can be controlled and analyzed statistically.

Some Advantages of Doing Single-Subject Studies

Group-oriented research usually involves the computation of the mean or some other measure of average or central tendency, but averages can be misleading. Look at (a) and (b) in Figure 22.3 — both have exactly the same values. If we were to compute the mean for the data in each figure, we would find that they are exactly equal. Even if we computed the standard deviation or variance, we would find that the two measures of variability are exactly the same. However, visual inspection for the data shows that the graph, Figure 22.3(a) exhibits a trend whereas Figure 22.3(b) does not. In fact, Figure 22.3(b) shows what appears to be a random pattern. The single-subject approach does not have this problem, because a participant is studied extensively over time. The cumulative record for that participant shows the actual performance of the participant.

One of the major problems in using large samples is that statistical significance can be achieved for differences that are very small. With inferential statistics a large sample will tend to reduce the amount of error variance. Take the t-test as an example. Even if the mean difference remains the same, the increase in sample size will tend to lower the standard error. With a reduction of the standard error, the t-value gets larger, hence increasing its chance of statistical significance. However, statistical significance and practical significance are two different things. The experiment may have little practical significance even if it has plenty of statistical significance. Simon (1987) has criticized the indiscriminant use of large groups of participants. He finds them wasteful and unable to produce useful information. Simon advocates the use of screening experiments to find the independent variables that have the greatest effect on the dependent variable. These would be the powerful variables that produce large effects. Simon doesn't exactly endorse single-subject designs. He advocates using well-constructed designs with the number of participants necessary to find the strongest effects. Simon (1976) refers to these as "Economical Multifactor Designs." Single-subject researchers, on the other hand, favor increasing the size of the effect rather than attempting to lower error variance. They feel that this can be done through tighter control over the experiment.

In this same vein, single-subject designs have the advantage over group-oriented designs in that with only a few participants researchers can test different treatments. In

▣ **FIGURE 22.3** *Comparison of Experimental Group and Control Group*

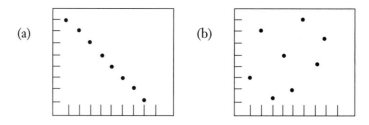

other words, they can determine the effectiveness or the ineffectiveness of a treatment intervention without employing a large number of participants, which can be costly.

With single-subject studies, the researcher can avoid some of the ethical problems that face group-oriented researchers. One such ethical problem concerns the control group. In some situations, the control group does not receive any real treatment. Although in most of the studies done today the participants in the control group are not harmed in any way, there are still some ethical questions. Take for example the study by Gould and Clum (1995) to determine if self-help with minimal therapist contact is effective in the treatment of panic disorder. All participants in this study were sufferers of panic attacks. The participants were assigned randomly to either an experimental or control group. The experimental group received self-help material. The control "did not receive treatment during the course of the experiment" (p. 536). Instead, the control group was told that they were on the waiting list for treatment.

In the study of certain type of individuals, the size of the population is small and hence it would be difficult to do adequate sampling or to obtain enough participants for the study. In fact, the study by Strube (1991) shows that even random sampling tends to fail when using small samples. If there are not enough participants of a certain characteristic available for study, the researcher can consider single-subject designs instead of abandoning the study. Simon (1987) cites the attempted study by Adelson and Williams in 1954 concerning the important training parameters in pilot education. The study was abandoned because there were too many variables to consider and not enough participants. Simon pointed out that the study could have been done, but not using the traditional group-oriented methodology.

Some Disadvantages of Using Single-Subject Designs

Single-subject studies are not without problems and limitations. Some of these will become more apparent when we actually discuss the types of single-subject designs. One of the more general problems with the single-subject paradigm is external validity. Some find it difficult to believe that the findings from one study using one subject (or maybe three of four) can be generalized to an entire population.

With repeated trials on one participant, one can question whether the treatment would be equally effective for a participant who has not experienced previous treatments. If we are talking about a therapeutic treatment, it may be the accumulation of sessions that is effective instead of one single session. The person going through the *n*-th trial can be a very different person from the one in the first trial. It is here that group-oriented research can eliminate this problem. Each person is given the treatment only once.

Single-subject studies are perhaps even more sensitive to aberrations on the part of the experimenter and participant. These studies are effective only if the researcher can avoid biases and the participant is motivated and cooperative. The researcher can be prone to look only for certain effects and ignore others. We discussed Blondlot earlier in this book. He was the only scientist able to see "N-rays." It wasn't so much that he was a fraud, but that he was biased toward seeing something that was not there. A researcher doing single-subject research could be affected more so than the group-oriented researcher and needs to develop a system of checks and balances to avoid this pitfall.

A number of research studies are by nature required to follow group-oriented methods and as such would be ill-suited for single-subject designs. For example, to study the behavior of jury members would require the use of groups and the influence of group dynamics. In a previous chapter, we discussed the research surrounding Janis's Groupthink. The study of this important phenomenon was best done with groups, since it was the group as a whole that displayed this phenomenon.

Some Single-Subject Research Paradigms

The Stable Baseline: An Important Goal

In a group-oriented design, one group of participants is compared to another. Or a group of participants receiving one condition is compared to the same set of participants receiving a different condition. We assume that the groups are equal prior to giving treatment so that, if the dependent variable differs after treatment, we can associate that difference to the treatment. The determination of an effective treatment is done by comparing the difference between the two groups statistically on some outcome variable. When we use only one subject, however, a different tactic must be employed. In this one-subject situation we need to compare the behavior that occurs before, to the behavior that occurs after, the introduction of the experimental intervention. The behavior before the treatment intervention must be measured over a long enough time period so that a stable baseline can be obtained. This baseline, or operant level, is important because it is compared to later behavior. If the baseline varies considerably, it could be more difficult to assess any reliable change in behavior following intervention. The baseline problem with single-subject designs is an important one. For a complete description of the problems and possible solutions, one should consult Barlow and Hersen (1984). Another excellent reference is Kazdin (1982).

An example when baseline measures are very important is in the use of a polygraph (lie detector). Here, the operator gets physiological measurements of the person (suspect). The operator asks the suspect a number of questions the answer to which are known to be true (name, eye color, place of birth, etc.). The responses emitted are recorded and used as the baseline measure for truthful responses. Another baseline is taken for responses known to be untrue: the suspect is told to deliberately lie to the questions asked. After establishing these two baselines, the question of importance (i.e., did you commit the crime?) is asked and compared to the two baselines. If the physiological response resembles the lie baseline, the suspect is considered to have lied.

Designs that Use the Withdrawal of Treatment

The ABA Design

The ABA design involves three major steps. The first step is to establish a stable baseline (A). The experimental intervention is applied to the participant in the second step (B). If the treatment is effective, there will be a response difference from the baseline. In order to determine if the treatment intervention caused the change in behavior, the researcher exercises step three: a return to baseline (A). The third step is required because we don't know what the response rate would have been if the participant received no treatment. We also need to know whether the response change was due to the treatment intervention or something else.

A major problem with the ABA design is that the effect of the intervention may not be fully reversible. If the treatment involved surgery, where the hypothalamus is removed or the corpus callosum is severed, it would be impossible to reverse these procedures. A learning method that causes some permanent change in a participant's behavior would not be reversible.

There are also some ethical concerns about reverting the organism back to the original state if that state was an undesirable behavior (Tingstrom, 1996). Experiments in behavior modification seldom return the participant back to baseline. This return to baseline is called the withdrawal condition. To benefit the participant, the treatment is reintroduced. The ABAB design does this.

Repeating Treatments (ABAB Designs)

There are two versions of the ABAB design. The first was briefly described in the above section. ABAB is the same as the ABA design except that treatment is reintroduced to the participant, and the participant leaves the study having achieved some beneficial level. Repeating the treatment also provides the experimenter with additional information about the strength of the treatment intervention. By demonstrating that the treatment intervention can bring the participant back to the beneficial level after taking that person back to baseline, lends strength to the statement that treatment caused the change in behavior; that is, evidence of internal validity. The ABAB design essentially produces the experimental effect twice.

The second variation of the ABAB design is called the *alternating treatments* design. In this variation there is no baseline taken. The A and B in this design are two different treatments that are alternated at random. The goal of this design is to evaluate the relative effectiveness of the two treatment interventions. The A and B may be two different methods of controlling overeating. The participant is given each treatment at different times. Over a period of time, one method might emerge as being more effective than the other. The advantage this design has over the first ABAB design is that there is no baseline to be taken, and the participant is not subjected to withdrawal procedures. Since this method involves comparing two sets of series of data, some have called it the between-series design.

There are some other interesting variations of the ABAB design where withdrawal of the treatment is not done. McGuigan (1996) calls it the ABCB design where in the third phase, the organism is given a "placebo" condition. This placebo condition is essentially a different method.

Single-subject designs are unlike group designs in that they only permit the researcher to vary one variable at a time. The researcher would not be able to determine which variable or which combination of variables caused the response changes, if two or more variables are altered simultaneously. The best that anyone can do is to make a statement that the combination of variables led to the change. However, the researcher won't be able to tell which one or how much of each. If there are two variables, called B and C, and the baseline is A, then a possible presentation sequence of the conditions would be A-B-A-B-BC-B-BC. In this sequence every condition was preceded and proceeded by the same condition at least once, with only one variable changing at a time.

The A-B-A-B-BC-B-BC design is often called an interaction design. All possible combinations of B and C, however, are not presented. Condition C is never presented alone (A represents the absence of B and C). The interaction here differs from the interaction discussed in the chapter on factorial designs. What is tested by this procedure is whether or not C adds to the effect of B.

In a learning experiment using this design, we could examine the effect of praising a student for giving the correct answer (C) to a question on geography along with a merit point (B). If we find that praise plus merit point has a greater effect than a merit point alone, we have information that is useful in designing a learning situation for this and other students; but we will not know the singular effect of praise. Praise used by itself may have been just as effective as the merit point plus praise; or praise by itself, may have little or no effect. We can, however, assess praise by lengthening the single-subject design: the A-B-A-B-BC-B-BC-C-BC sequence. But lengthening a single-subject experiment of this kind comes with other problems; for example, a subject may become fatigued or disinterested. As a result, too long of a session may not produce useful information even though the design looks sound.

A Research Example

Powell and Nelson: Example of an ABAB Design

This study by Powell and Nelson (1997) involved one participant, Evan, a 7-year-old boy, who had been diagnosed with attention deficit hyperactivity disorder (ADHD). Evan was receiving 15 mg of Ritalin® per day. Most of Evan's classroom behavior was described as undesirable. Evan also had poor peer relations and did not understand his schoolwork. The undesirable behaviors included noncompliance, leaving his desk, disturbing others, staring off into space, and not doing the work. Data were collected on the occurrence of interactions between Evan and his teacher.

The treatment intervention was letting Evan choose the class assignments he wanted to work on. There were two conditions: choice and no-choice. Baseline data were collected during the no-choice phase. Evan was given the same assignment as the rest of the class. During the choice phases, the teacher presented Evan with three different assignments and he chose one to complete. The assignment choices were identical in length and difficulty and varied only in content. Evan was not given the same choice of assignments twice.

Powell and Nelson used an ABAB design to evaluate the effects of choice-making on Evan's undesirable behavior. The results showed that during the choice condition, the number of undesirable behaviors decreased. This study supported the efficacy of choice-making as an antecedent control technique. These results suggest that educators attempting to manage the behaviors of students in classrooms may use choice procedures.

Using Multiple Baselines

There is a form of single-subject research that uses more than one baseline. Several different baselines are established before treatment is given to the participant. These types of studies are called *multiple baseline studies*. There are three classes of multiple baseline research designs: across behaviors, across participants, and across environments.

The use of multiple baselines is another approach to demonstrate the effectiveness of a treatment on behavior change. There is a common pattern for implementing all three classes of this design. That pattern is shown in Figure 22.4.

With the multiple baselines *across behaviors*, the treatment intervention for each different behavior is introduced at different times. In Figure 22.4, each baseline would be a baseline of a different behavior. In the case of an autistic child, Baseline 1 might be banging his or her head against the wall. Baseline 2 would be talking constantly in different tones and adding noises. Baseline 3 would be hitting others. The three baselines are established to see if the change in behavior coincides with the treatment intervention. If one of the behavior changes, while the other behaviors remain constant or stable at the baseline, the researcher could state that the treatment was effective for that specific behavior. After a certain period of time has passed, the same treatment is applied to the second undesirable behavior (Baseline 2). Every following behavior is subjected to the treatment in the same step-wise procedure. If the treatment intervention is effective in changing the response rate of each behavior, one can state that the treatment is effective.

An important consideration with this particular class of multiple baseline design is that one assumes the responses for each behavior are independent of the responses for the other behaviors. The intervention can be considered effective if this independence exists. If the responses are in some way correlated, then the interpretation of the results becomes more difficult.

■ **FIGURE 22.4** *General Format of Multiple Baseline Design*

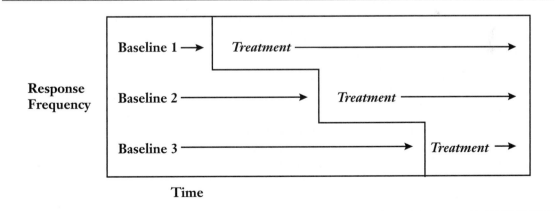

In the multiple baseline design *across participants*, the same treatment is applied in series to the same behavior of different individuals in the *same environment*. In Figure 22.4, each baseline represents a different participant. Each participant will receive the same treatment for the same behavior in the same environment. The study by Tingstrom, Marlow, Edwards, Kelshaw, and Olmi (1997) is an example of a multiple baseline study across participants. Their compliance training package is the treatment intervention. This intervention uses time-in (physical touch and verbal praise) and time-out (a coercive procedure) to increase the rate of student compliance to teachers' instructions. The behavior of interest here is compliance to teachers' instructions. The environment is the classroom. The participants of this study were three students—A, B and C—who have demonstrated noncompliance behavior. All three students have articulation and language disorders. The design of the study adhered to the following intervention phases: baseline, time-in only, time-in/time-out combined, and follow-up. Students B and C remained in the baseline phase, while the time-in only phase was implemented for student A. When A showed a change in compliance, the time-in only phase was implemented for B, while C remained in baseline. When B showed a change in compliance, time-in only was implemented for C. Tingstrom et al were able to demonstrate the effectiveness of the combined time-in and time-out intervention in increasing compliance.

In the multiple baseline design *across environments*, the same treatment is given to different participants who are in *different environments*. In Figure 22.4, each baseline represents a different participant in a different environment. The treatment and behavior under study would be the same. Here we may have three different patients where each is a resident in a different type of psychiatric care facility such as those studied by Nelson et al. discussed earlier in this chapter. In this study Nelson, Hall and Walsh-Bowers (1997) compared the long-term effects of supportive apartments (SA), group homes (GH) and board-and-care homes (BCH).

CHAPTER SUMMARY

1. True experiments are those where the experimenter can select the participants randomly, assign the participants to treatment conditions randomly, and control the manipulation of the independent variable. The quasi-experimental design lacks one or more of these features.

2. Cook and Campbell (1979) cover eight variations of the nonequivalent control group design. The one covered in this book is the no-treatment control group design. Five different results are discussed in terms of internal validity.

3. Time series designs are longitudinal designs that involve repeated measurements of the same dependent variables at different fixed intervals of time. Usually, at some point, treatment intervention is introduced.

4. Selection and selection–maturation interactions are two alternative explanations that plague the results obtained from quasi-experimental designs.

5. Experiments using single participants are not new. The early researchers in experimental psychology used single-subject designs.

6. In single-subject designs, researchers feel that with proper experimental control, variability of the situation can be removed.
7. Group-oriented researchers feel variability can be statistically analyzed.
8. Single-subject research has several advantages over group research in terms of flexibility and ethics. However, it suffers from external validity credibility.
9. Small but statistically significant effects found in group research may have little clinical or practical significance, and may have been artificially induced by large sample sizes. When this happens, the effect size is small. Single-subject research concentrates on effect size and not sample size.
10. The establishment of a stable baseline is one of the most important tasks in single-subject research.
11. The establishment of a baseline, followed by administration of treatment, followed by a withdrawal of the treatment, is called the ABA design.
12. A major problem with the ABA design is that the treatment may be irreversible—leaving the participant in the improved state, rather than returning that person to the original undesirable state.
13. A variation of the ABA design is the ABAB design wherein the participant is restored to the improved state.
14. In a single-subject study only one independent variable can be varied at a time.
15. The so-called interaction design does not permit testing for an interaction as defined earlier in factorial designs. It merely examines two variables jointly.
16. There are three types of multiple baseline designs. In each case, the intervention is introduced at different times for different behaviors, participants, or environments. If behavior changes coincide with the introduction of treatment, this gives evidence that the treatment is effective.

STUDY SUGGESTIONS

1. Look up each of the following studies and determine which are quasi-experimental, nonequivalent control group, and single-subject designs.

   Adkins, V. K., & Matthews, R. M. (1997). Prompted voiding to reduce incontinence in community-dwelling older adults. *Journal of Applied Behavior Analysis, 30*, 153–156.
   Lee, M. J., & Tingstrom, D. H. (1994). A group math intervention: The modification of cover, copy, and compare for group application. *Psychology in the Schools, 31*, 133–145.
   Streufert, S., Satish, U., Pogash, R., Roache, J., & Severs, W. (1997). Excess coffee consumption in simulated complex work settings: Detriment or facilitation of performance? *Journal of Applied Psychology, 82*, 774–782.

2. Why is a baseline measure necessary in single-subject designs?
3. Should the data from single-subject designs be analyzed statistically? Explain why or why not.

4. Give an example of when a single-subject design should be used. Also, cite a research situation in which group design is more appropriate.
5. A university student wants to do a time series study on the effects of the full moon on psychiatric patients. What dependent variable should this student use? Where should this person look to locate data for such a study?
6. Are single-subject studies applicable to medical research? Should medical school students be taught single-subject designs? Read the following article:

Bryson-Brockmann, W., and Roll, D. (1996). Single-case experimental designs in medical education: An innovative research method. *Academic Medicine, 71,* 78–85.

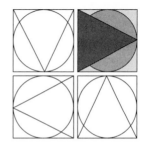

NONEXPERIMENTAL RESEARCH

Among prevalent fallacies, one of the most dangerous to science is that known as *post hoc, ergo propter hoc:* after this, therefore caused by this. We may joke, with a tinge of seriousness, "If I take an umbrella, it won't rain." We may even seriously say that delinquents are delinquent because of a lack of discipline in the schools, or that religious education makes children more virtuous. It is easy to assume that one thing causes another simply because it occurs before the other, and because one has such a wide choice of possible "causes." Then, too, many explanations often seem plausible. It is easy to believe, for instance, that the learning of children improves because we institute a new educational practice or teach in a certain way. We assume that the improvement in their learning was due to the new spelling method, to the institution of group processes into the classroom situation, to stern discipline and more home-work (or little discipline and less homework). We rarely realize that children will usually learn something if they are given the opportunity to learn.

The social scientist and the educational scientist constantly face the problem of the post hoc fallacy. The sociologist who seeks the causes of delinquency knows that extreme care must be used in studying the problem. Slum conditions, broken homes, amount of lead in water pipes, lack of love—each or all of these conditions are possible causes of delinquency. The psychologist seeking the roots of adult personality faces an even subtler problem: hereditary traits, child-rearing practices, educational influences, parental personality, and environmental circumstances are all plausible explanations. The educational scientist, with the goal of understanding the basis of successful school achievement, also faces a large number of reasonable possibilities: intelligence, aptitude, motivation, home environment, teacher personality, pupil personality, and teaching methods.

The danger of the post hoc assumption is that it can, and often does, lead to erroneous and misleading interpretations of research data, the effect being particularly serious when scientists have little or no control over time and independent variables. When they seek to explain a phenomenon that has already occurred, scientists are confronted with the unpleasant fact that they do not have real control of the possible causes. Hence, they must pursue a course of research action, different in execution and interpretation, from that of scientists who experiment.

Definition

Nonexperimental research is systematic empirical inquiry in which the scientist does not have direct control of independent variables because their manifestations have already occurred or because they are inherently not manipulable. Inferences about relations among variables are made, without direct intervention, from concomitant variation of independent and dependent variables.

Assume that an investigator is interested in the relation between sex and creativity in children. The investigator measures the creativity of a sample of boys and girls and tests the significance of the difference between the means of the two sexes. The mean of boys is significantly higher than the mean of girls. One conclusion is that boys are more creative than girls. This may or may not be a valid conclusion. The relation exists, true. With only this evidence, however, the conclusion is doubtful. We would ask the question: Is the demonstrated relation really between sex and creativity? Since other variables are correlated with sex, it might have been one or more of these other variables that produced the difference between the creativity scores of the two sexes.

Basic Difference Between Experimental and Nonexperimental Research

The basis of the structure in which experimental science operates is simple. One hypothesizes: If x, then y; if frustration, then aggression. Depending on circumstances and personal predilection in research design, one uses some method to manipulate or measure x. One then observes y to see if concomitant variation, the variation expected or predicted from the variation in x, occurs. If it does, this is evidence for the validity of the proposition, $x \rightarrow y$, "If x then y." Note that we here predict from a controlled x to y. To help us achieve control, we can use the principle of randomization and active manipulation of x and can assume, other things being equal, that y is varying as a result of the manipulation of x.

In nonexperimental research, on the other hand, y is observed, and an x, or several xs, are also observed. They are observed either before, after, or concomitant to the observation of y. There is no difference in the basic logic. It can be shown that the argument structure and its *logical* validity are the same in experimental and non-experimental research. Also, the basic purpose of both is the same: to establish the *empirical* validity of so-called conditional statements of the form: If p, then q. The essential difference is direct control of p, the independent variable. In experimental research, p can be manipulated, which is rather direct "control." When Clark and Walberg (1968) had teachers give one group of participants massive reinforcement and other teachers give another group moderate reinforcement, they were directly manipulating or controlling the variable reinforcement. Similarly, when Dolinski and Nawrat (1998) put one group under stress (anxiety), another under stress that was subsequently reduced, and a third group with little or no stress, they were directly manipulating the variable anxiety. In addition, participants can be assigned at random to the experimental groups.

In nonexperimental research, *direct* control is not possible: neither experimental manipulation nor random assignment can be used. These are two essential differences between experimental and nonexperimental approaches. Owing to lack of relative control of x and other possible xs, the "truth" of the hypothesized relation between x and y cannot be asserted with the confidence of the experimental situation. Basically, nonexperimental research has, so to speak, an inherent weakness: lack of control of independent variables.

The most important difference between experimental research and nonexperimental research, then, is *control*. In experiments, investigators at least have manipulative control: they have at least one active variable. If an experiment is a "true" experiment, they can also exercise control by randomization. They can assign participants to groups at random, or assign treatments to groups at random. In the nonexperimental research situation, this kind of control of the independent variables is not possible. Investigators must take things as they are and try to disentangle them.

Take a well-known case. When we paint the skins of rats with carcinogenic substances (x), adequately control other variables, and the rats ultimately develop carcinoma (y), the argument is compelling because x (and other possible xs, theoretically) is controlled and y is predicted. But when we find cases of lung cancer (y) and then go back among the possible multiplicity of causes (x_1, x_2, . . ., x_n) and pick cigarette smoking (say x_3) as the culprit, we are in a more difficult and ambiguous situation. Neither situation is sure, of course; both are probabilistic. But in the experimental case we can be considerably more sure if we have adequately made "other things being equal"—that the statement, If x, then y, is empirically valid. In the nonexperimental case, however, we are always on shakier ground because we cannot say, with nearly as much assurance, "other things being equal." We cannot control the independent variables by manipulation or by randomization. In short, the probability that x is "really" related to y is greater in the experimental situation than it is in the nonexperimental situation because the control of x is greater.

Self-Selection and Nonexperimental Research

In an ideal behavioral research world, the drawing of random samples of participants, and the random assignment of participants and treatments to groups, would always be possible. In the real world, however, one, two, or even all three of these possibilities do not exist. It is possible to draw participants at random in both experimental and nonexperimental research. But it is not possible, in nonexperimental research, to assign participants to groups at random or to assign treatments to groups at random. Participants can "assign themselves" to groups. They can "select themselves" into the groups on the basis of characteristics other than those that interest the investigator. The participants and the treatments come, as it were, already assigned to the groups.

Self-selection occurs when the members of the groups being studied are in the groups, in part, because they differentially possess traits or characteristics extraneous to the research problem; characteristics that possibly influence or are otherwise related to the variables of the research problem. Examples of self-selection may aid understanding.

In the well-known research on cigarette smoking and cancer, the smoking habits of a large number of people were studied. This large group was divided into those who had lung cancer—or who had died of it—and those who did not have it. The dependent variable was thus the presence or absence of cancer. Investigators probed the participants' backgrounds to determine whether they smoked cigarettes, and if so, how many. Cigarette smoking was the independent variable. The investigators found that the incidence of lung cancer rose with the number of cigarettes smoked daily. They also found that the incidence was lower in the cases of light smokers and nonsmokers. They came to the conclusion that cigarette smoking "causes" lung cancer. This conclusion may or may not be true. But the investigators cannot come to this conclusion, although they can say that there is a statistically significant relation between the variables. Note that careful scientific investigators will usually not use the word *cause* unless the study was performed under the strictest conditions. The word *cause* is used here to illustrate how the media often interprets scientific findings that suggest causality.

Scientific investigators also cannot state a causal connection because there are a number of other variables, any one of which, or any combination of which, may have caused lung cancer. And they have not controlled other possible independent variables. They *cannot* control them, except by testing alternative hypotheses, a procedure to be explained later. Even when they also study "control groups" of people who have no cancer, self-selection may be operating. Perhaps, for example, tense, anxious men are doomed to have lung cancer if they marry tall women. It may just happen that this type of man also smokes cigarettes heavily. The cigarette smoking is not what kills him—he kills himself by being tense and anxious—and possibly by marrying a tall woman. Such men are selected into the sample by investigators only because they smoke cigarettes. But such men select themselves into the sample because they commonly possess a temperament that happens to have cigarette smoking as a concomitant.

Self-selection can be a subtle business. There are two types: (1) self-selection into *samples* and (2) self-selection into *comparison groups*. The latter occurs when participants are selected because they are in one group or another: cancer and no cancer, college and no college, underachievement and no underachievement. That is, they are selected *because* they possess the dependent variable in greater or lesser degree. Self-selection into samples occurs when participants are selected in a nonrandom fashion into a sample.

The crux of the matter is that when *assignment* is not random, there is always a loophole for other variables to crawl through. When we put participants into groups, in the above case and in similar cases, or they "put themselves" into groups, on the basis of one variable, it is possible that another variable (or variables) correlated with this variable is the "real" basis of the relation. The usual nonexperimental study uses groups that exhibit differences in the dependent variable. In some longitudinal-type studies the groups are differentiated first on the basis of the independent variable. But the two cases are basically the same, since group membership on the basis of a *variable* always brings selection into the picture.

For example, we may select college freshmen at random and then follow them to determine the relation between intelligence and success in college. The students selected themselves into college, so to speak. One or more of the characteristics they bring with them to college, other than intelligence—socioeconomic level, motivation, family background—may be the principal determinants of college success. Starting with the independent variable, in this case intelligence, does not change the self-selective nature of the research situation. In the sampling sense, the students selected themselves into college, which would be an important factor if we were studying college students and noncollege students. But if we are interested only in the success and nonsuccess of *college* students, self-selection into college is irrelevant, whereas self-selection into success and nonsuccess groups is crucial. That we measure the intelligence of the students when they enter college and follow them through to success and nonsuccess does not change either the selection problem or the nonexperimental character of the research. In sum, the students selected themselves into college and selected themselves to succeed or not to succeed in college.

Large-Scale Nonexperimental Research

Research examples will, as usual, help us to understand the nature of nonexperimental research. Instead of summarizing only individual studies, as we have up to now, we describe both individual studies and sets of studies centered on some phenomenon or variable of interest. Nonexperimental behavioral research often focuses on large problems of social and human importance: social class, political processes, segregation and desegregation, public attitudes, school achievement, for example. The importance—*relevance* is the fashionable word—of the subject of these studies should not obscure our understanding of their nonexperimental character. Because nonexperimental research has inherent weaknesses, however, does not mean that experimental research is more important. As said earlier, the experiment is one of the great inventions of all time, an ideal of control toward which we aspire. This does not mean that experiments are necessarily "better" than nonexperimental studies. On the other hand, nonexperimental research is not necessarily "better" than experimental research because its content and variables seem to be socially important. This would be like saying that psychological research is "better" than sociological research because psychologists more often use an experimental approach and sociologists a nonexperimental approach!

Determinants of School Achievement

A large preoccupation of educational researchers has been a search for the determinants of school achievement. What factors lead to successful achievement in school? Intelligence is an important factor, of course. While measured intelligence, especially verbal ability, accounts for a large proportion of the variance of achievement, there are many other variables, psychological and sociological: sex, race, social class, aptitude, environmental characteristics, school and teacher characteristics, family background, teaching methods. The study of achievement is characterized by both experimental and nonexperimental approaches. We are here concerned only with the latter since it clearly illustrates problems of nonexperimental research.

In 1966 the now-famous Coleman report was published (Coleman, Campbell, Hobson, McPartland, Mood, Weinfeld, & York, 1966). As its title (*Equality of Educational Opportunity*) indicates, it was a large-scale attempt to answer the question: Do American schools offer equal educational opportunity to all children? Equally important, however, was the question of the relation between student achievement and the kinds of schools students attend. This study was a massive and admirable effort to answer these questions (and others). Its most famous and controversial finding was that the differences among schools account for only a small fraction of the differences in school achievement. Most achievement variance was accounted for by what the children brought with them to school. There was much to question about the study's methodology and conclusions. Indeed, its reverberations are still with us. Some major school districts across the United States used the report as justification for implementing certain controversial educational policies such as the bussing of children.

The principal dependent variable in this study was verbal achievement. There were, however, more than 100 independent variables. The authors used relatively sophisticated multivariate procedures to analyze the data. Much of the core of the analytic problems, the interpretations of the findings, and the subsequent critiques inhere in the nonexperimental nature of the research.

The controversial conclusion mentioned above of the relative importance of home background variables and school variables depends on a completely reliable and valid method for assessing relative impacts of different variables. In experimental research, one is safer drawing comparative conclusions because the independent variables are not correlated. In the real educational world, however, the variables are correlated, making their unique contributions to achievement difficult to determine. While there are statistical methods to handle such problems, no method can tell us unambiguously that X_1 influences Y to this or that extent, because the real influence may be X_2, which influences both X_1 and Y. The "correct" interpretation of the findings of *Equality*, and studies like it, is always unattainable. While there are powerful analytic methods to use with nonexperimental data, unequivocal answers to questions of the determinants of achievement are forever beyond reach.

Response Style Differences between East Asian and North American Students

This study by Chen, Lee, and Stevenson (1995) was a large-scale study that spanned four countries, four cultures and two continents. The major concern in this study centered on the use of rating scales. Rating scales are one of the staples in behavioral science research. However, are there cultural differences in how certain ethnic groups answer questions that use a rating scale? Chen et al. wanted to determine whether or not there existed a response style difference between East Asians and North Americans. These researchers collected data from 944 Japanese students, 1,357 Taiwanese students, 687 Canadian students, and 2,174 Midwestern and East Coast United States students. The comparisons in this study involved the differences between two cultures (East Asian versus North American) and the difference between the two representative groups within each culture (United States versus Canada, and Japan versus Taiwan). The questionnaire administered to these students included items on ideas, values, attitudes, beliefs, and self-evaluations related to school and daily life. A 7-point Likert scale was used, where a 7 usually indicated "more" or "strongly agreed"; a 1 was used for "not at all important," "less," or "strongly disagree." The results showed that in the area of individualism and collectivism there were highly significant differences between the two cultures. They also found a relation between endorsement of individualism and the use of extreme values on rating scales.

This study is also classified as nonexperimental because there is no manipulated independent variable. The independent variable in this study was culture and it was not manipulated. This study did shed light on a response style difference between different cultures. Regardless of the sampling in this study, the study is nonexperimental. Hence, one cannot really state explicitly that if you are from this culture, you will respond on rating scales in such-and-such way.

Smaller Scale Nonexperimental Research

To illustrate nonexperimental behavioral research studies or series of studies is not easy—there are too many of them; but a few satisfy the authors' personal criteria of methodological soundness and substantive interest. We have chosen the following studies for three reasons: (1) We felt each represents a unique, original, and interesting approach to an important sociological, psychological, or educational problem. (2) Each contributes significantly to scientific knowledge. (3) Each is nonexperimental.

Cochran and Mays: Sex, Lies, and HIV

This is the classic, often-cited, often-mentioned study concerning the difference in sexual behavior between men and women. Cochran and Mays (1990) found that advising young adults and teenagers about the precautions they should take to protect himself or herself from the human immunodeficiency virus (HIV) might be wasted. For example, one advice is for the person to ask his or her date about their risk history before deciding whether or not to engage in sexual intercourse. Cochran and Mays, however, found that young people tend to lie about their sexual history. In a sample of 665 students (age 18–25) in Southern California, 196 sexually experienced men and 226 sexually experienced women reported that they told a lie in order to have sex. That means over 63% of the sample stated that they have lied in the past in order to have sex with their date. Men were found to tell lies significantly more often than women. In addition, both men and women indicated that they would deceive their dating partner again. Men were found to be more willing to do this than women. A brief summary of Cochran and Mays's analysis of their 18-page questionnaire on sexual behavior, HIV-risk reduction, and deception in dating is given in Table 23.1. The comparison between men and women involves the measured or attributive independent variable, sex. This study has great significance when advising young people about safe-sex practices. The implication is that you

▣ TABLE 23.1 *Percent Responses to Sex and Dishonesty Questions by Men and Women (Cochran & Mays study)*

Question	Men	Women
Has told a lie in order to have sex	34	10
Lied about ejaculatory control or likelihood of pregnancy	38	14
Would lie about having negative HIV-antibody test	20	4
Would lie about ejaculatory control or likelihood of pregnancy	29	2
Would underestimate number of previous partners	47	42

cannot trust the word of your date. Even though the data points strongly toward men's willingness to lie in order to obtain sexual favors, one cannot automatically assume that all men will lie about their sexual history.

Elbert: Impaired Reading and Written Language in Attention Deficit Children

The phenomenon known as Attention Deficit Hyperactivity Disorder (ADHD) is currently a popular area of psychological and educational research. One of the major concerns is directed toward children who are afflicted with this disorder. Those children afflicted generally exhibit poor self-regulation of behaviors and poor academic performance (usually 1 to 1.5 standard deviation units below the scores of normal children). As research in this area matured, researchers turned their emphasis to more specific questions than a comparision of ADHD children to normal children. One area of interest is on the subclasses or subgroups within ADHD, specifically, Attention Deficit Disorder (ADD). These studies usually compared children with attention deficit and hyperactivity (ADD+H) to children with attention deficit and no hyperactivity (ADD-H).

One of those studies was done by Elbert (1993). Elbert wanted to determine if these two subgroups of ADHD (ADD+H and ADD-H) were different in achievement. Achievement was measured by standardized reading, spelling, and written language tests. Elbert also sought to determine if an interaction existed between gender (male and female), age (6-0 to 7-11, 8-0 to 9-11, and 10-0 to 12-11) and subgroup type (ADD+H and ADD-H). The study used data from 115 children between the ages of 6 through 12. Each child was classified as either ADD+H or ADD-H, using objective teacher evaluations and the guidelines set by Barkley (1990). Note that there is no manipulated independent variable here. Group membership was not done through random process. The nonexperimental nature of this study resulted in very different-sized groups. The ADD+H group had 83 children and the ADD-H group had 32 children. There was also more males (86) than females (29). Elbert did however, perform numerous analyses to check on the equality of the groups on the variables age, grade level, mother's level of education, and IQ. Statistical tests between ADD+H and ADD-H on these variables were not significant.

The results on reading scores showed a poorer performance by children in the ADD+H (97) group than the ADD-H (90) group. Elbert also found a significant gender-by-age interaction on reading scores. Post hoc tests showed the female children in the middle age group doing much worse than males. Statistical tests performed on spelling and written language scores showed no effect between age groups, gender or subgroup types. However, Elbert found a significant gender-by-age interaction effect. Again it was the middle age group females who had the poorest performance. Elbert also found than one subtest of spelling and written language (Written Spelling to Diction) was the most impaired skill in both ADD subgroups. Note the nonexperimental nature of Elbert's study. No manipulated independent variable and no randomization.

With these nonexperimental studies behind us, we can discuss and evaluate nonexperimental research in general. We precede evaluative discussion, however, with a more systematic inquiry into the testing of alternative hypotheses, one of the highly important features of scientific research.

Testing Alternative Hypotheses

Most investigations begin with hypotheses; the empirical implications of these hypotheses are then tested. Although we "confirm" hypotheses in the manner described in earlier chapters, we can also "confirm" and "disconfirm" hypotheses under study by trying to show that alternative plausible hypotheses are, or are not, supported. First, consider alternative independent variables as antecedents of a dependent variable. The reasoning is the same. If we say "alternative independent variables," for example, we are in effect stating alternative hypotheses or explanations of a dependent variable.

In nonexperimental studies, although one cannot have the confidence in the "truth" of an "If x, then y" statement that one can have in true experiments, it is possible to set up and test alternative or "control" hypotheses. (Of course, alternative hypotheses can also be and are tested in experimental studies.) This procedure has been formalized and explained by Platt (1964) who was influenced by Chamberlin (1890; 1965). Platt calls it "strong inference." Chamberlin aptly calls the procedure the "method of working multiple hypotheses," and outlines how the investigator's own "intellectual affections" can be guarded against. Chamberlin (p. 756) says:

> The effort is to bring up into view every rational explanation of new phenomena, and to develop every tenable hypothesis respecting their cause and history. The investigator thus becomes the parent of a family of hypotheses; and, by the parental relation to all, the investigator is forbidden to fasten his affections unduly upon any one.

For a historical development of the alternative hypothesis, see Cowles (1989).

Let x_1, x_2, and x_3 be three alternative independent variables, and let y be the dependent variable, the phenomenon to be "explained" with a statement of the form: "If x, then y." Assume that x_1, x_2, and x_3 exhaust the possibilities. This assumption cannot actually be made in scientific research, because it is practically impossible to exhaust all the possibilities. Still, here we will assume it for pedagogical reasons.

An investigator has evidence that x_1 and y are substantially related; having reason to believe that x_1 is the determinative factor, x_2 and x_3 are held constant. The working assumption is that one of the three factors x_1 or x_2 or x_3 is *the* "true" independent variable. Again, note the assumption. It may be none, or some combination of all three. Suppose that the investigator succeeds in eliminating x_2; that is, x_2 is shown that it is not related to y. If the investigator also succeeds in eliminating x_3, then the conclusion is that x_1 is the influential independent variable. Since the alternative or "control" hypotheses have not been substantiated, the original hypothesis is strengthened.

Similarly, we can test alternative *dependent* variables, which also imply alternative hypotheses. We shift the alternatives to the dependent variable. Alper, Blane, and Abrams (1955) illustrate this in a study of the different reactions of middle- and lower-class children to fingerpaints as a consequence of different child-rearing practices. The general question asked was: Do social class differences in child-training practices result in class differences in personality? The theory invoked required that there be differences in reactions to fingerpaints. Alper et al. reasoned that middle-class children would react differently than lower-class children to 16 different variables *when fingerpaints were used:* acceptance of task, washing, and so on. The reactions were significantly different on most of the variables. In a "control experiment," the same procedure was followed *using crayons instead of fingerpaints.* The two groups did not differ significantly on any of the 11 variables measured. This was a surprising contrast to the fingerpaint results. The study was nonexperimental because it was not possible to manipulate the independent variable, and because the children came to the study with their reactions ready-made. This use of a control study was ingenious and crucial. Imagine the researchers' consternation if the differences between the two groups on the crayon task had been significant!

Now, consider Sarnoff, Lighthall, Waite, Davidson, and Sarason's (1958) classic study that predicted that English and American children would differ significantly in test anxiety but not in general anxiety. The hypothesis was carefully delineated: If eleven-plus examinations are taken, then test anxiety results. (The eleven-plus examinations are given to English schoolchildren at age 11 to help determine their educational futures.) Since it was possible that there might be other independent variables causing the difference between the English and American children on test anxiety, the investigators evidently wished to rule out at least some of the major contenders. This they accomplished by carefully matching the samples: they probably reasoned that the difference in test anxiety might be due to a difference in general anxiety, since the measure of test anxiety obviously must reflect some general anxiety. If this was found to be so, the major hypothesis would not be supported. Therefore, Sarnoff et al., in addition to testing the relation between examination and test anxiety, also tested the relation between examination and general anxiety. The hypothesis that English children would have higher test anxiety scores than American children was supported by the data. They also found no significant difference between the two countries on general anxiety and that girls had a higher level of test anxiety than boys in both countries. Test anxiety was found to be positively correlated with grade level.

The method of testing alternative hypotheses, though important in all research, is particularly important in nonexperimental studies, because it is one of the only ways to control the independent variables of such research. Lacking the possibility of randomization and manipulation, nonexperimental researchers, perhaps more so than experimentalists, must be very sensitive to alternative hypothesis-testing possibilities.

Evaluation of Nonexperimental Research

The reader may feel from the preceding discussion that nonexperimental research is inferior to experimental research, but this conclusion would be unwarranted. It is easy to say that experimental research is "better" than nonexperimental research, or that experimental research tends to be "trivial," or that nonexperimental research is "merely correlational." Such statements, in and of themselves, are oversimplifications. What the student of research needs is a balanced understanding of the strengths and weaknesses of both kinds of research. To be committed unequivocally to experimentation or to nonexperimental research may be shortsighted.

The Limitations of Nonexperimental Interpretation

Nonexperimental research has three major weaknesses, two of which have already been discussed in detail: (1) the inability to manipulate independent variables, (2) the lack of power to randomize, and (3) the risk of improper interpretation. In other words, compared to experimental research, other things being equal, nonexperimental research lacks control; this lack is the basis of the third weakness: the risk of improper interpretation.

The danger of improper and erroneous interpretations in nonexperimental research stems in part from the plausibility of many explanations of complex events. It is easy to accept the first and most obvious interpretation of an established relation, especially if one works without hypotheses to guide investigation. Research unguided by hypotheses, or research "to find out things," is most often nonexperimental. Experimental research is more likely to be based on carefully stated hypotheses.

Hypotheses are if–then predictions. In a research experiment the prediction is from a well-controlled x to a y. If the prediction holds true, we are relatively safe in stating the conditional: "If x, then y." In a nonexperimental study under the same conditions, however, we are considerably less safe in stating the conditional, for reasons discussed earlier. Careful safeguards are more essential in the latter case, especially in the selection and testing of alternative hypotheses, such as the predicted lack of relation between the eleven-plus examination and general anxiety in the Sarnoff study. A predicted (or unpredicted) relation in nonexperimental research may be quite spurious, but its plausibility and conformity to preconception may make it easy to accept. This is a danger in experimental research, but it is less of a danger than it is in nonexperimental research because an experimental situation is so much easier to control.

Nonexperimental research that is conducted without hypotheses, without predictions, research in which data are just collected and then interpreted, is even more dangerous in its power to mislead. Significant differences or correlations are located if possible, and then interpreted. The second author of this book has witnessed graduate students collecting a large amount of data without hypotheses, and then using a computer program to perform every analysis possible with the hope of finding statistical significance somewhere. After one or more significant differences are found, hypotheses are then developed to fit the analysis. To illustrate the problem with this, assume that an educator decides to study the factors leading to underachievement. Selected are a group of underachievers and a group of normal achievers. Each group takes a battery of tests. Next, the means of the two groups on the tests are computed, and the mean differences are analyzed with t-tests. Among, say, 12 such differences, three are significant. The investigator concludes, then, that underachievers and normal achievers differ on the variables measured by these three tests. Armed with these analyses, the investigator now feels willing to tell others what characterizes underachievers. Since all three tests seem to measure insecurity, the cause of under-achievement is therefore insecurity.

When guided by hypotheses the credibility of the results of studies like the one just cited may be enhanced, but the results remain weak because they capitalize on chance: by chance alone one or two results of many statistical tests may be significant. Above all, plausibility can be misleading. A plausible explanation often seems compelling—even though quite wrong! It seems so obvious, for example, that conservatives and liberals are opposites. The research evidence, however, seems to indicate that they are not opposites (see Kerlinger, 1967, 1980, 1984). Another difficulty is that plausible explanations, once found and believed, are often hard to test. According to Merton (1949), post factum explanations do not lend themselves to nullifiability because they are so flexible. Whatever the observations, he says, new interpretations can be found to "fit the facts" (pp. 90–91).

The Value of Nonexperimental Research

Despite its weaknesses, much nonexperimental research must be done in psychology, sociology, and education simply because many research problems do not lend themselves to experimental inquiry. A little reflection on some of the important variables in behavioral research—intelligence, aptitude, home background, achievement, social class, rigidity, ethnocentrism—will show that they are not manipulable. Controlled inquiry is possible, of course, but true experimentation is not.

It can even be said that nonexperimental research is more important than experimental research. This is, of course, not a methodological observation. It means, rather, that most social scientific and educational research problems do not lend themselves to experimentation, although many do lend themselves to controlled inquiry of the nonexperimental kind. Consider Piaget's studies of children's thinking; the authoritarianism studies of Adorno, Frenkel-Brunswik, Levinson, and Sanford; the highly important study *Equality of Educational Opportunity*; and Cochran and Mays's study of lies and safe-sex practices. Consider further the influence of the nonexperimental study concerning cigarette smoking and health problems. It led to specific legislation to have warnings printed on the product itself. If a tally of sound and important studies in the behavioral sciences and education were made, it is possible that nonexperimental studies would outnumber and outrank experimental studies.

Conclusions

Students of research differ widely in their views of the relative values of experimental and nonexperimental research. There are those who exalt experimental research and decry nonexperimental research. There are those who criticize the alleged narrowness and lack of "reality" of experiments, especially laboratory experiments. These critics, especially in education, emphasize the value and relevance of nonexperimental research in "real life," "natural" situations (for a review, see Keith, 1988). A rational position seems obvious. If it is possible, use experimentation because, *other things being equal*, one can interpret the results of most experiments with greater confidence that statements of the "If p, then q" kind are what we say they are. It would also seem desirable to test the "If p, then q" propositions in other settings. One should also look for nonexperimental evidence of the empirical validity of one's hypotheses. So, if it is possible, conditional statements should be studied using both experimental and nonexperimental approaches. Some nonexperimental research studies are impressive and convincing. But how much more impressive and convincing it would be if similar conclusions arose from well-conducted experiments! Conversely, how much more convincing experimental conclusions are if substantiated by well-conducted nonexperimental research.

Replication is always desirable, even necessary. An important point being made is that replication of research does not only mean repetition of the same studies in the same settings. It can and should mean testing empirical implications of theory—interpreting "theory" broadly—in similar and dissimilar situations and experimentally and nonexperimentally. It is easier to ask for extensions of research from the laboratory to the field. But researchers should also try to conceive of experimental testing of propositions arrived at nonexperimentally. Of course, this is more difficult and is seldom done. The point made here is that it *should* be conceived and, when possible, done.

To adopt a firm position that experimental or nonexperimental research is the only road to research heaven is dogmatic guruism. It may be very difficult, perhaps impossible in many cases, to do both experimental and nonexperimental research on the same problem. Can one experimentally manipulate Cochran and Mays's gender variable or Chen, Lee, and Stevenson's cultural variable, for example? Difficult does not mean impossible, of course. Our point is that experimental and nonexperimental possibilities should be explored and exploited if it is possible to do so. Moreover, it should not immediately be assumed that it is not possible to do research differently from the way it has been done. There is no one methodological road to scientific validity; there are many roads. And we should choose our roads for their appropriateness to the problems we study. This does not mean, however, that we cannot exploit an approach that is different from what we are used to.

For some strange reason, perhaps the spurious belief in the alleged certitude of science, when people, including scientists, think of science and scientific research, they mistakenly believe there is only one "right" way to approach and do research. Rarely is such a mistake made in music, or art, or building a house. Science, too, has many roads, and experimental and nonexperimental approaches are two such broad roads. Neither is right or wrong. But they are different. Our task has been to try to understand the differences and their consequences. We are far from finished with the subject, however. Maybe we will even attain a fair degree of understanding before we are through. When thinking about the different viewpoints on experimental and nonexperimental methods, we should consider the Chinese maxim that states, "There are many paths to the top of the mountain, but the view there is always the same."

CHAPTER SUMMARY

1. Nonexperimental studies are just as valuable as experimental studies when they are conducted correctly.
2. One ingredient for a good nonexperimental study is the development of hypotheses before the start of the study.
3. Replication is used to increase the credibility of results obtained from nonexperimental studies.
4. Nonexperimental research is defined as that which does not have an active independent variable.
5. The most important difference between experimental and nonexperimental methods is control.
6. Self-selection of participants is a major problem with nonexperimental studies.
7. There are a large number of nonexperimental studies performed and published in the behavioral sciences.
8. Some nonexperimental studies—such as the one relating cigarette smoking to health problems—have been highly influential.
9. There are three major weaknesses in nonexperimental research: (i) independent variables cannot be manipulated, (ii) lack of randomization, and (iii) risk of improper interpretation.
10. The stepwise elimination of alternative hypotheses is one way at arriving at a possible variable that "causes" changes in the dependent variable.
11. Relatively new developments in nonexperimental studies have included the mathematical modeling of "cause-and-effect." These models do not really imply cause-and-effect.

STUDY SUGGESTIONS

1. A social psychologist plans to investigate factors behind anti-Semitism. He believes that people who have had authoritarian parents and authoritarian upbringing tend to be anti-Semitic. Would a research project designed to test this hypothesis be experimental or nonexperimental? Explain.

2. An educational psychologist decides to test the hypothesis that intelligence and motivation are the principal determinants of success in school. Would his research most likely be experimental or nonexperimental? Explain.

3. An investigator is interested in the relation between role perception and social values.
   a. Which is the independent variable? the dependent variable?
   b. Whatever judgment you have made, can you justifiably reverse the variables?
   c. Do you believe that a research project designed to investigate this problem would be basically experimental or nonexperimental?
   d. Can the investigator do two researches, one experimental and one nonexperimental, both designed to test the same hypothesis?
   e. If your answer to (d) was "Yes," will the variables of the two problems be the same? Assuming that the relations in both researches were significant, will the conclusions be substantially the same?

4. In the study suggestions of Chapter 2, a number of problems and hypotheses were given. Take each of these problems and hypotheses and decide whether research designed to explore the problems and test the hypotheses would be basically experimental or nonexperimental. Can any of the problems and hypotheses be tackled both ways?

5. McClelland (1961) presents data on the electrical production during 1952–1958 of countries high in n Achievement and low in n Achievement. Counting the number of countries in each of the four cells we obtain the results shown in Table 23.2.

▣ **TABLE 23.2** *Countries High and Low in Achievement Motivation Whose Electrical Production Was Above or Below Expectation (McClelland study)*[a]

	Above Expectation	**Below Expectation**
High Achievement Motivation	13 (65%)	7 (35%)
Low Achievement Motivation	5 (26%)	14 (70%)

[a]The cell entries are number of countries that, for example, had high Achievement Motivation and whose electrical output was above expectation (13). The indices in the parentheses are the percentages.

Do these results support McClelland's hypothesis? (Hint: Calculate χ^2 and C, as in Chapter 10. Use the percentages to help interpret the table.)

[Answer: $\chi^2 = 5.87$, $df = 1$ ($p < .05$); C = .36. Yes, the hypothesis is supported.]

6. The venturesome student may wish to take a plunge into stimulating, provocative, controversial, and important thinking. The famous Club of Rome report by Meadows, Meadows, Randers, and Behrens (1974) has outraged some observers, startled almost anyone who has read it, and disturbed everyone. Using important societal variables—natural resources, pollution, population, for example—and their complex interactions, ultimate disaster to cities and the world has been predicted. The research on which the conclusions are based is entirely nonexperimental. Read this report. Do you think that the research's nonexperimental character lowers its credibility?

7. Read one (or all) of the following studies. They all are nonexperimental. Write down the reasons why you think they are nonexperimental based on the points made in this chapter.

Goodman, S. H., & Emory, E. K. (1992). Perinatal complications in births to low socioeconomic status schizophrenic and depressed women. *Journal of Abnormal Psychology, 101,* 225–229.

Koniak-Griffin, D., & Brecht, M. (1995). Linkages between sexual risk taking, substance use, and AIDS knowledge among pregnant adolescents and young mothers. *Nursing Research, 44,* 340–346.

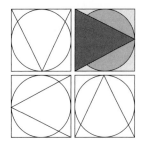

CHAPTER 24

LABORATORY EXPERIMENTS, FIELD EXPERIMENTS, AND FIELD STUDIES

Social scientific research can be divided into four major categories: laboratory experiments, field experiments, field studies, and survey research. This breakdown stems from two sources: the distinction between experimental and nonexperimental research and that between laboratory and field research. This chapter owes much to the material from three books: (1) Festinger and Katz (1953), (2) Taylor and Bodgan (1998), and (3) Padgett (1998). Although the Festinger and Katz publication is over forty-five years old, it remains a valuable source on many aspects of behavioral research methodology. We begin this chapter by presenting examples of the laboratory experiment, two field experiments, and a field study. We do this so that the reader can see the major components of each method and the differences between each method.

A Laboratory Experiment: Miller's Studies of the Learning of Visceral Responses

A brilliant series of experiments by Miller (1969, 1971) has upset a long-held and cherished belief: that learning occurs only with voluntary responses, and that the involuntary autonomic system is subject only to classical conditioning. This, in effect, says that responses like moving the hand and talking can be brought under control and thus taught; but that involuntary responses, like heartrate, intestinal contractions, and blood pressure, cannot be brought under instrumental control, and thus not "taught." To understand Miller's studies, we must define certain psychological terms. In *classical conditioning* a neutral stimulus, inherently unable to produce a certain response, becomes able to by being associated repeatedly with a stimulus inherently capable of doing so. The most famous example is Pavlov's dog salivating at the clicking of a metronome, which had been repeatedly associated with meat powder. In *instrumental* or *operant conditioning*, a reinforcement given to an organism immediately after it has made a response produces an increment in the response. Reward a response and it will be repeated. Voluntary responses or behavior are thought to be superior, presumably because they are under the control of the individual, whereas involuntary responses are inferior because they are not controlled. It has been believed that involuntary responses can be modified only by classical conditioning and not by instrumental conditioning. In other words, the possibility of "teaching" the heart, stomach, and blood is remote, since classical conditioning situations are difficult to come by. If the organs are subject to instrumental conditioning, however, they can be brought under experimental control, and can be "taught"; and they can "learn."

Miller's work has shown that, through instrumental conditioning, the heartrate can be changed, stomach contractions can be altered, and even urine formation can be increased or decreased! This discovery is of enormous theoretical and practical importance. To show the nature of laboratory experiments, we take one of Miller's interesting and creative experiments.

The idea of the experiment is simple: reward one group of rats when their heartrates go up, and reward another group when their heartrates go down. This is a straightforward example of the two-group design discussed earlier. Miller's big problem was control. There are a number of other causes of changed heartrate—for example, muscular exertion. To control such extraneous variables, Miller and a colleague (Trowill) paralyzed the rats with curare. But if the rats were paralyzed, what could be used as reward? They decided to use direct electrical stimulation of the brain. The dependent variable, heartrate, was continuously recorded with the electrocardiograph. When a small change in heartrate occurred (in the "right" way: up for one group, down for the other), an animal was given an electrical impulse to a reward center of its brain (see also, Olds & Fobes, 1981, brain research demonstrating that mild electrical stimulation of a certain part of the brain acts as a reward). This was continued until the animals were "trained."

The increases and decreases of heartrate were statistically reliable but small: only 5% in each direction. So Miller and another colleague (DiCara) used the technique known as shaping which, in this case, means rewarding first small changes and then requiring increasing changes in rate to obtain the rewards. This increased the heartrate changes to an average of 20% in either direction. Moreover, further research, using escape from mild shock as reinforcement, showed that the animals remembered what they had learned and "differentiated" the heart responses from other responses.

Miller has been successful in "training" a number of other involuntary responses: intestinal contraction, urine formation, and blood pressure, for example. In short, visceral responses *can be learned* and *can be shaped*. But can the method be used with people? Miller says that he believes people are as smart as rats, but that it has not yet been completely proved. Although the use of curare might present difficulty, people can be hypnotized, says Miller.

A Field Experiment: Rind and Bordia's Study on the Effects of a Server's "Thank You" and Personalization on Restaurant Tipping

Does the common practice among servers to write "thank you" on the back of the dining bill and deliver it in such a way that the diners will see the server's gratitude produce increased tips? If this does produce increased tips, then at an extremely low cost the server stands to benefit by this action. Rind and Bordia (1995) conducted this field experiment to determine the effectiveness of using this technique; namely, writing "thank you" and personalizing the server–diner interaction by adding the server's name. This study was conducted at an upscale restaurant in Philadelphia during the lunch period for five days. Fifty-one diners participated in the study. All the servers were female. The independent variable was Impression and consisted of three levels: (1) the back of the diner's bill either contained nothing, (2) the handwritten words "thank you," or (3) the words "thank you" plus the server's first name. Rind and Bordia hypothesized using impression management theory that the addition of written gratitude and personalization would lead to higher tips than if the server wrote nothing on the back of the bill. They also hypothesized that the personalization of the bill would lead to higher amounts of tips than no personalization. Each level or condition of the independent variable was determined randomly for each dining party. Prior to delivering the bill to the diners, the server picked one of three pennies (dated 1981, 1982, and 1983) from her pocket randomly. If she picked the 1981 coin, the server wrote nothing on the backside of the bill. If she selected the 1982 coin, the server wrote "thank you" on the back of the bill. If the coin chosen was 1983, the server wrote "thank you" on the back of the bill and also added her name. For each group of diners, the size of the tip, the size of the bill, the size of the dining party, and the method of payment were recorded. The results of this study showed that adding the words "thank you" to the bill resulted in significantly higher tips than if nothing was written on the bill (18% of the bill versus 16.3%). There was no significant differences between the written gratitude and the written gratitude plus personalization. Rind and Bordia mention that there are competing theories on why they got this result. However, from their results, it appears that this practice is a beneficial one for the server. These researchers also note the limitations of their experiment. For one, their choice of conducting the study at an upscale restaurant may produce different results than a study done at a typical restaurant. The use of only female servers leaves open the possibility that customers may treat male servers differently.

A Field Study: Newcomb's Bennington College Study

Newcomb (1943) conducted one of the most important classical studies concerning the influence of a college environment on students. In this study, Newcomb studied the entire student body of Bennington College (about 600 young women) from 1935 to 1939. An unusual facet of the study was Newcomb's attempt to explain both social and personality factors in influencing attitude changes in the students. Although other hypotheses were tested, the principal hypothesis of the Bennington study was that new students would converge on the norms of the college group, and that the more the students assimilated to the college community, the greater would be the change in their social attitudes.

Newcomb used a number of paper-and-pencil attitude scales, written reports on students, and individual interviews. The study was longitudinal and nonexperimental. The independent variable, while not easy to categorize, can be said to be the social norms of Bennington College. The dependent variables were social attitudes and certain behaviors of the students.

Newcomb found significant changes in attitudes between freshmen, on the one hand, and juniors and seniors, on the other. The changes were toward less conservatism on a variety of social issues. For example, the political preferences of juniors and seniors in the 1936 presidential election were much less conservative than those of freshmen and sophomores. Of 52 juniors and seniors, 15% preferred Landon (Republican); whereas of 52 freshmen, 62% preferred Landon. The percentages of preferences for Roosevelt (Democrat) were 54% and 29%. The mean scores of all students for four years on a scale designed to measure political and economic conservatism were freshmen, 74.2; sophomores, 69.4; juniors, 65.9, and seniors, 62.4. Evidently the college had affected the students' attitudes.

Newcomb asked a "control" question: Would these attitudes have changed in other colleges? To answer this question, Newcomb administered his conservatism measures to students of Williams College and Skidmore College. The comparable mean scores of Skidmore students—freshmen through seniors—were 79.9, 78.1, 77.0, and 74.1. It seems that Skidmore (and Williams) students did not change as much, and as consistently over time, as did the Bennington students.

Newcomb, Koenig, Flacks, and Warwick (1967) reported a follow-up study on the students at Bennington College after 25 years. They found that the changes had lasted and that the Bennington influence was persistent.

Characteristics and Criteria of Laboratory Experiments, Field Experiments, and Field Studies

A *laboratory experiment* is a research study in which the variance of all, or nearly all, of the possible influential independent variables not pertinent to the immediate problem of the investigation is kept at a minimum. This is accomplished by isolating the research in a physical situation apart from the routine of ordinary living, and by manipulating one or more independent variables under rigorously specified, operationalized, and controlled conditions.

Strengths and Weaknesses of Laboratory Experiments

The laboratory experiment has the inherent virtue of the possibility of relatively complete control. The laboratory experimenter can, and often does, isolate the research situation from the life around the laboratory by eliminating the many extraneous influences that may affect the independent and dependent variables.

In addition to situation control, laboratory experimenters can ordinarily use random assignment and can manipulate one or more independent variables. There are other aspects to laboratory control: the experimenter in most cases can achieve a high degree of specificity in the operational definitions of variables. The relatively crude operational definitions of field situations, such as many of those associated with the measurement of values, attitudes, aptitudes, and personality traits, do not plague the experimentalist, though the definitional problem is never simple. The Miller (1969, 1971) experiment is a good example. The operational definitions of reinforcement and heartrate change are precise and highly objective.

Closely allied to operational strength is the precision of laboratory experiments. Precise means accurate, definite, and unambiguous. Precise measurements are made with precision instruments. In variance terms, the more precise an experimental procedure is, the less the error variance. The more accurate or precise a measuring instrument is, the more certain we can be that the measures obtained do not vary much from their "true" values.

Precise laboratory results are achieved mainly by controlled manipulation and measurement in an environment from which possible "contaminating" conditions have been eliminated. Research reports of laboratory experiments usually specify in detail how the manipulations were done and the means taken to control the environmental conditions under which they were done. By specifying the conditions of the experiment exactly, we reduce the risk that participants may respond equivocally and thus introduce random variance into the experimental situation. Miller's experiment is a model of laboratory experimental precision.

The greatest weakness of the laboratory experiment is probably the lack of strength of independent variables. Since laboratory situations are, after all, situations that are created for special purposes, it can be said that the effects of experimental manipulations are usually weak. Increases and decreases in heartrate by electrical brain reinforcement, while striking, were relatively small. Compare this to the relatively large effects of independent variables in realistic situations. In the Bennington study, for example, the college community apparently had a massive effect. In laboratory research on conformity, only small effects are usually produced by group pressure on individuals. Compare this to the relatively strong effect of a large group majority on an individual group member in a real-life situation. The board of education member who knows that a desired action goes against the wishes of the majority of his or her colleagues, and perhaps the majority of the community, is under heavy pressure to converge on the norm.

One reason for the preoccupation with laboratory precision and refined statistics is the weakness of laboratory effects. To detect a significant difference in the laboratory requires situations and measures with a minimum of random noise, and accurate and sensitive statistical tests that will show relations and significant differences when they exist.

Another weakness is a product of the first: the artificiality of the experimental research situation. Actually, it is difficult to know if artificiality is a weakness or simply a neutral characteristic of laboratory experimental situations. When a research situation is deliberately contrived to exclude the many distractions of the environment, it is perhaps illogical to label the situation with a term that expresses in part the result being sought. The criticism of artificiality does not come from experimenters who know that experimental situations are artificial; it comes from individuals lacking an understanding of the purposes of laboratory experiments.

The temptation to interpret the results of laboratory experiments incorrectly is great. While Miller's results are believed by social scientists to be highly significant, they can only be tentatively extrapolated beyond the laboratory. Similar results may be obtained in real-life situations, and there is evidence that they do in some cases. But this is not necessarily so. The relations must always be tested anew under non-laboratory conditions. Miller's research, for instance, will have to be carefully and cautiously done with human beings in hospitals and even in schools.

Although laboratory experiments have relatively high internal validity, they lack external validity. Earlier we asked the question: Did *X*, the experimental manipulation, really make a significant difference? The stronger our confidence in the "truth" of the relations discovered in a research study, the greater the internal validity of the study. When a relation is discovered in a well-executed laboratory experiment, we generally can have considerable confidence in it, since we have exercised the maximum possible control of the independent variable and other possible extraneous independent variables. When Miller "discovered" that visceral responses could be learned and shaped, he could be relatively sure of the "truth" of the relation between reinforcement and visceral response in the laboratory. He had achieved a high degree of control and of internal validity.

One can say: If I study this problem using field experiments, *maybe* I will find the same relation. This is an empirical, not a speculative, matter; we must put the relation to test in the situation to which we wish to generalize. If a researcher finds that individuals converge on group norms in the laboratory, does the same or similar phenomenon occur in community groups, faculties, and legislative bodies? This lack of external validity is the basis of the objections of many educators to the animal studies of learning theory. Their objections are only valid if an experimenter generalizes from the behavior and learning of laboratory animals to the behavior and learning of children. Capable experimentalists, however, rarely blunder in this fashion—they know that the laboratory is a contrived environment.

Purposes of the Laboratory Experiment

Laboratory experiments have three related purposes. First, they are a means of studying relations under "pure" and uncontaminated conditions. Experimenters ask: Is x related to y? How is it related to y? How strong is the relation? Under what conditions does the relation change? They seek to write equations of the form $y = f(x)$, make predictions on the basis of the function, and see how well and under what conditions the function performs.

A second purpose should be mentioned in conjunction with the first purpose: the testing of predictions derived from theory, primarily, and other research, secondarily.

A third purpose of laboratory experiments is to refine theories and hypotheses, to formulate hypotheses related to other experimentally or nonexperimentally tested hypotheses and, perhaps most important, to help build theoretical systems. This was one of Miller's major purposes. Although some laboratory experiments are conducted without this purpose most laboratory experiments are, of course, theory-oriented.

The aim of laboratory experiments, then, is to test hypotheses derived from theory, to study the precise interrelations of variables and their operation, and to control variance under research conditions that are uncontaminated by the operation of extraneous variables. As such, the laboratory experiment is one of the great inventions of all time. Although weaknesses exist, they are weaknesses only in a sense that is really irrelevant. Conceding the lack of representativeness (external validity) the well-done laboratory experiment still has the fundamental prerequisite of any research: internal validity.

The Field Experiment

A field experiment is a research study conducted in a realistic situation in which one or more independent variables are manipulated by the experimenter under conditions as carefully controlled as the situation will permit. The contrast between the laboratory experiment and the field experiment is not sharp: the differences are mostly matters of degree. Sometimes it is hard to label a particular study "laboratory experiment" or "field experiment." Where the laboratory experiment has a maximum of control, most field experiments must operate with less control, a factor that is often a severe handicap.

Strengths and Weaknesses of Field Experiments

Field experiments have values that especially recommend them to social psychologists, sociologists, and educators because they are admirably suited to many of the social and educational problems of interest to social psychology, sociology, and education. Because independent variables are manipulated, and randomization is used, the criterion of control can be satisfied—at least theoretically.

The control of the experimental field situation, however, is rarely as tight as that of the laboratory. We have here both a strength and a weakness. The investigator in a field experiment, though having the power of manipulation, is always faced with the unpleasant possibility that the independent variables are contaminated by uncontrolled environmental variables. We stress this point because the necessity of controlling extraneous independent variables is particularly critical in field experiments. The laboratory experiment is conducted in a tightly controlled situation, whereas the field experiment takes place in a natural, often loose, situation. One of the main preoccupations of the field experimenter, then, is to try to make the research situation more closely approximate the conditions of the laboratory experiment. Of course this is often a difficult goal to reach, but if the research situation can be kept tight, the field experiment is powerful because one can, in general, have greater confidence that relations are indeed what one says they are.

As compensation for dilution of control, the field experiment has two or three unique virtues. The variables in a field experiment usually have a stronger effect than those of laboratory experiments. The effects of field experiments are often strong enough to penetrate the distractions of experimental situations. The principle is: The more realistic the research situation, the stronger the variables. This is one advantage of doing research in educational settings. For the most part, research in school settings is similar to routine educational activities, and thus need not necessarily be viewed as something special and apart from school life. Despite the pleas of many educators for more realistic educational research, there is no special virtue in realism as realism. Realism simply increases the strength of the variables. It also contributes to external validity, since the more realistic the situation, the more valid are generalizations to other situations likely to be.

Another virtue of field experiments is their appropriateness for studying complex social and psychological influences, processes, and changes in lifelike situations. Glick, DeMorest, and Hotze (1988), for example, studied the effects of group membership, personal space, and requests for help on people's interpersonal anxiety and compliance. These researchers did their research at a shopping mall using actual shoppers as participants. Schmitt, Dube, and Leclerc (1992) studied a similar problem on personal space by examining intrusions into waiting lines. These researchers conducted three laboratory experiments and a field experiment, in an attempt to determine whether behavioral reactions to the intrusions are based on personal or social interests. Jaffe (1991) did a field experiment on advertising targeted at women. In this research participants evaluated print advertisement that contained different positioning of women. The position used was either the traditional woman (nurturing, family-oriented) or the modern woman (successful in career and family). Rabinowitz, Colmar, Elgie, Hale, Niss, Sharp, and Sinclito (1993) studied the complex behavior of cashiers at souvenir shops that cater to tourists. These researchers wanted to know whether the mishandling of money was due to dishonesty, indifference, or carelessness. The Wogalter and Young (1991) study on the effectiveness of voice and printed warnings in handling hazardous substances, or a slippery floor in a shopping mall, can be very useful for those concerned with safety issues in an industrial or consumer setting. Wogalter and Young did two laboratory studies and one field experiment to demonstrate that the combination of printed and voice warnings were the most effective in producing behavioral compliance of people. All of these studies used experimental manipulation on participants from the real world in real-world settings.

Laboratory experiments are suited mainly for testing aspects of theories, whereas field experiments are suited both to testing hypotheses derived from theories and to finding answers to practical problems. Methods experiments in education, usually practical in purpose, often seeks to determine which method among two or more methods is best for a certain purpose. Industrial research and consumer research depend heavily on field experiments. Much social psychological research, on the other hand, is basically theoretical. The Schmitt et al. (1992) study mentioned above tested two theories about the behavioral reactions of people waiting in line who have experienced an intrusion. The two theories tested were the moral outrage theory and the individual cost theory. The Glick et al. (1988) and Jaffe (1991) field experiments were also theory-oriented.

Flexibility and applicability to a wide variety of problems are important characteristics of field experiments. The only two limitations are whether one or more independent variables can be manipulated, and whether the practical exigencies of the research situation are such that a field experiment can be done on the particular problem under study. Surmounting these two limitations is not easy. When it can be done, a wide range of theoretical and practical problems is open to experimentation.

As indicated earlier, the main weaknesses of field experiments are practical. Manipulation of independent variables and randomization are perhaps the two most important problems. They are particularly acute in research in school settings. Manipulation, although quite possible, may often not be practicable because, say, parents object when their children, who happen to have been assigned randomly to a control group, will not get a desirable experimental treatment. Or there may be objection to an experimental treatment because it deprives children of some gratification, or places them into conflict situations.

There is no real reason why randomization cannot be used in field experiments. Nevertheless, difficulties are frequently met. Unwillingness to break up class groups or to allow children to be assigned to experimental groups at random are examples. Even if random assignment is possible and permitted, the independent variable may be seriously blurred, because the effects of the treatments cannot be isolated from other effects. Teachers and children, for example, may discuss what is happening during the course of the experiment. To prevent such muddying of the variables, the experimenter should explain to administrators and teachers the necessity for random assignment and careful control.

An experimental field characteristic of a different nature is to some experimenters a weakness, and to others a strength. Field investigators have to be, at least to some extent, socially skilled operators. They should be able to work with, talk to, and convince people of the importance and necessity of their research. They should be prepared to spend many hours, even days and weeks, of patient discussion with people responsible for the institutional or community situation in which they are to work. For example, if they are to work in a rural school system, they should have knowledge of rural, as well as general, educational problems, and of the particular rural system they wish to study. Some researchers become impatient with these preliminaries because they are anxious to get the research job done. They find it difficult to spend the time and effort necessary in most practical situations. Others enjoy the inevitable socializing that accompanies field research. Good advice on handling this aspect of field situations is given by French (1953).

An important obstacle to good design, an obstacle that seems ordinarily to be overlooked, is the attitude of the researcher. For example, the planning of educational research often seems to be characterized by a negative attitude epitomized by such statements as, "That can't be done in schools," "The administrators and teachers won't allow that," and "Experiments can't be done on this problem in that situation." Starting with attitudes like these compromises any good research design before the research even begins. If a research design calls for the random assignment of teachers to classes, and if the lack of such assignment seriously jeopardizes the internal validity of the proposed study, every effort should be made to assign teachers at random. Educators planning research seem to assume that the administrators or the teachers will not permit random assignment. This assumption is not necessarily correct, however.

The consent and cooperation of teachers and administrators can often be obtained if a proper approach, with adequate and accurate orientation, is used, and if explanations of the reasons for the use of specific experimental methods are given. The points being emphasized are these: Design research to obtain valid answers to the research questions. Then, if it is necessary to make the experiment possible, modify the "ideal" design. With imagination, patience, and courtesy, many of the practical problems of implementation of research design can be solved satisfactorily.

One other weakness inherent in field experimental situations is lack of precision. In the laboratory experiment it is possible to achieve a high degree of precision or accuracy, so that laboratory measurement and control problems are usually simpler than those in field experiments. In realistic situations, there is always a great deal of systematic and random noise. In order to measure the effect of an independent variable on a dependent variable in a field experiment, it is not only necessary to maximize the variance of the manipulated variable and any assigned variables, but also to measure the dependent variable as precisely as possible. But in realistic situations, such as in schools and community groups, extraneous independent variables abound. And measures of dependent variables, unfortunately, are sometimes not sensitive enough to pick up the messages of our independent variables. In other words, the dependent variable measures are often so inadequate they cannot pick up all the variance that has been engendered by the independent variables.

Field Studies

Field studies are nonexperimental scientific inquiries aimed at discovering the relations and interactions among sociological, psychological, and educational variables in real social structures. In this book any scientific studies (large or small), that systematically pursue relations and test hypotheses, that are nonexperimental, and that are done in life situations (e.g., communities, schools, factories, organizations, and institutions) will be considered field studies.

The investigator in a field study first looks at a social or institutional situation, and then studies the relations among the attitudes, values, perceptions, and behaviors of individuals and groups in the situation. The field study investigator ordinarily manipulates no independent variables. Before we discuss and appraise the various types of field studies, it will be helpful to consider examples. We have already examined field studies in earlier chapters and in this chapter: the Newcomb Bennington study. We now briefly examine two smaller field studies.

Anderson, Warner, and Spencer (1984), studied the inflation bias of job applicants. The participants in this study were actual applicants for positions with the state of Colorado. Job applicants usually claim they have more experience and more knowledge than they really do. To measure the degree of this inflation, Anderson et al. created nonexistent tasks and asked the applicants how much experience they had with these tasks. The results showed that nearly half of the applicants claimed experience in one or more nonexistent tasks. Those applicants that claimed to have a great amount of experience at nonexistent tasks also overinflated their ability on real tasks. This field study yields important information for those involved in making hiring decisions. This was a field study because there was no manipulated independent variable. Real and bogus tasks were listed on a questionnaire and participants were asked to indicate the amount of experience they had on each task using a 4-point scale. Note that this study was not done in the laboratory, and used unsuspecting participants.

The field study by Tom and Lucey (1997) studied waiting time in checkout stations in supermarkets and customer satisfaction with the checker and the store. These researchers studied both fast and slow checkers during busy and nonbusy periods of store operations. The researchers recorded the waiting times for each customer, and also interviewed the customer as he or she departed from the store. The results showed that customers were generally more satisfied with the store and cashier when the perceived waiting time was short. However, Tom and Lucey noted that this is not always the case. In one of the two stores used in the study, they found some customers reporting higher satisfaction with slow cashiers. Further inquiries revealed that cashiers were slower because they took the time to give the customer more personal attention.

Note that the problems of these field studies were attacked nonexperimentally: neither randomization nor experimental manipulation was possible. In the Jones and

Cook study, data were collected directly from students at two universities. In the Tom and Lucey study only two grocery stores were used. Neither of these studies had randomization or an active independent variable, yet both were able to provide useful information.

Types of Field Studies

Katz (1953) has divided field studies into two broad types: *exploratory* and hypothesis testing. The exploratory type, says Katz, *seeks what is* rather than *predicts relations to be found*. The massive *Equality of Educational Opportunity*, cited in Chapter 23, exemplifies this type of field study. Exploratory studies have three purposes: to discover significant variables in the field situation, to discover relations among variables, and to lay the groundwork for later, more systematic and rigorous testing of hypotheses.

Throughout our book to this point, the use and testing of hypotheses have been emphasized. It is well to recognize, though, that there are activities preliminary to hypothesis testing in scientific research. In order to achieve the desirable aim of hypothesis testing, preliminary methodological and measurement investigation must often be done. Some of the finest work of the twentieth century has been in this area. An example is that done by the factor analyst who is preoccupied with the discovery, isolation, specification, and measurement of underlying dimensions of achievement, intelligence, aptitudes, attitudes, situations, and personality traits.

The second subtype of exploratory field studies—research aimed at discovering or uncovering relations—is indispensable to scientific advance in the social sciences. It is necessary to know, for instance, the correlates of variables. Indeed, the scientific meaning of a construct springs from the relations it has with other constructs. Assume that we have no scientific knowledge of the construct "intelligence"; we know nothing of its causes or concomitants. For example, suppose that we know nothing whatsoever about the relationship of intelligence to achievement. It is conceivable that we might do a field study in school situations. We might carefully observe a number of boys and girls who are said to be intelligent or nonintelligent by teachers (though here we introduce contamination because teachers must obviously judge intelligence, at least in part, by achievement). We may notice that a larger number of "more intelligent" children come from homes of higher socioeconomic levels; they solve problems in class more quickly than other children; have a broader vocabulary, and so on. We now have some clues to the nature of intelligence, so that we can attempt to construct a simple measure of intelligence. Note that our "definition" of intelligence springs from what presumably intelligent and nonintelligent children do. A similar procedure can be followed with the variable "achievement."

Strengths and Weaknesses of Field Studies

Field studies are strong in realism, significance, strength of variables, theory orientation, and heuristic quality. The variance of many variables in actual field settings is large, especially when compared to the variance of the variables of laboratory experiments. Consider the contrast between the impact of social norms in a laboratory experiment like Sherif's (1963), and the impact of these norms in a community where, say, certain actions of teachers are frowned upon and others approved. Consider also the difference between studying cohesiveness in the laboratory where participants are asked, for example, whether they would like to remain in a group (measure of cohesiveness), and studying the cohesiveness of a school faculty where staying in the group is an essential part of one's professional future. Compare the group atmosphere in the Bennington College Study and that in a field experiment where college instructors playing different roles engender different atmospheres. Variables such as social class, prejudice, conservatism, cohesiveness, and social climate can have strong effects in these studies. The strength of variables is not an unalloyed blessing, however. In a field situation there is usually so much noise in the channel that even though the effects may be strong and the variance great, it is not easy for the experimenter to separate the variables.

The realism of field studies is obvious. Of all types of studies, they most closely resemble real life. There can be no complaint of artificiality here. (The remarks about realism in field experiments apply, *a fortiori*, to the realism of field studies.)

Field studies are highly heuristic and ad hoc. One of the research difficulties of a field study is to keep it contained within the limits of the problem. Hypotheses frequently fling themselves at one because the field is rich in discovery potential. For example, one may wish to test the hypothesis that the social attitudes of board of education members is a determinant of board of education policy decisions. After starting to gather data, however, many interesting notions arise that can deflect the course of the investigation.

Despite these strengths, the field study is a scientifically weak cousin of laboratory and field experiments. Its most serious weakness, of course, is its nonexperimental character. Thus statements of relations are weaker than they are in experimental research. To complicate matters, the field situation almost always has a plethora of variables and variance. Think of the many possible independent variables that we can choose as determinants of delinquency or of school achievement. In an experimental study, these variables can be controlled to a large extent, but in a field study they must somehow be controlled by more indirect and less satisfactory means.

Another methodological weakness is the lack of precision in the measurement of field variables. In field studies the problem of precision is more acute, naturally, than in field experiments. The difficulty encountered by Astin (1968) in measuring college environment is one of many similar examples. Administrative environment, for example, was measured by students' perceptions of aspects of the environment. Much of the lack of precision is due to the greater complexity of field situations.

Studies of organizations, for example, are mostly field studies, and the measurement of organizational variables well illustrates the difficulties. "Organizational Effectiveness" appears to be as complex as "Teacher Effectiveness." For a thorough and enlightening discussion see Katz and Kahn (Chapter 8, 1978). This superb book well repays careful reading and study.

Other weaknesses of field studies are practical problems: feasibility, cost, sampling, and time. These difficulties are really *potential* weaknesses—none need be a real weakness. The most obvious questions that can be asked are: Can the study be done with the facilities at the investigator's disposal? Can the variables be measured? Will it cost too much? Will it take too much time and effort? Will the participants be cooperative? Is random sampling possible? Anyone contemplating a field study has to ask and answer such questions. In designing research it is important not to underestimate the large amounts of time, energy, and skill necessary for the successful completion of most field studies. The field researcher needs to be a salesperson, administrator, and entrepreneur, as well as investigator.

Qualitative Research

One area within field studies is qualitative research. Up until now, we have pretty much talked exclusively about quantitative research. Field studies with a quantitative emphasis have the problems mentioned in the last section. However, qualitative research is different since it does not rely on the use of numbers or measurements. This area of qualitative research has been growing in interest mainly because researchers have come to realize that not all studies can, or should be, quantified. There are areas for research where quantitative approaches cannot adequately capture the appropriate information. For example, quantitative research would be unable to capture valuable information that could be used to understand the life experiences of kidney patients who are on dialysis. Quantitative research can provide doctors and nurses with information on the relation between clinical factors (such as nutrition), and outcome measures (such as survival rates), but cannot tell us what the dialysis patient experiences. It is through a description of these experiences that could allow the development of better rehabilitation programs. The term "qualitative research" is used here to refer to social and behavioral research based on unobtrusive field observations that can be analyzed without using numbers or statistics. We mentioned earlier that those involved with operant learning or Skinnerian research also are not interested in using inferential statistics. However, they depart from qualitative research in that they do use numbers and measurements. The participants in the qualitative research studies may not be aware that they are being observed or studied. How much the participant is actively involved in the research process varies. Unlike single-subject or time-series research, the participant is unaware that any measurements are taken at all. Dooley (1995) presents an outstanding example of qualitative research with the study of cognitive dissonance theory. Dooley sites the research of Festinger (1956) that studied people who predict the end of the world but do not see their prediction come true. This type of research requires a research methodology that is nonquantitative and unobtrusive. It would be very difficult to have these people who belong to a sect come into a laboratory at a university to be studied. The researcher really cannot effectively study these people who have just experienced cognitive dissonance, by having them complete a questionnaire or participate in a structured interview. Instead, the researcher must be as unobtrusive as possible. The researcher would pose as someone who is curious or concerned, or might even join the sect as an observer and find the required information in a nonthreatening way. The participants are studied without them noticing that they are being studied. However, Festinger did the research a long time ago (1956). In today's environment, it would be extremely dangerous for researchers to join a sect for the purpose of studying them. Why? In recent years, especially in 1997, all members of a sect called Heaven's Gate committed suicide with the coming of the Hale-Bopp comet. The male members of this sect were subjected to severe physical/surgical alterations. There are also a number of powerful sects that utilized strong programming methods and hypnotic drugs on their members to keep them under control. So, although Dooley's example is a good illustration of qualitative research, the authors of this textbook do not recommend to anyone interested in doing qualitative research on sects to join or become a member of the sect.

It may be somewhat safer to consider a study done by Rosenhan (1973). Rosenhan was interested in the how psychiatric hospitals made psychiatric diagnoses, and what the experiences of a mental patient would be like. Rosenhan had eight of his confederates pose as psychiatric patients suffering from hallucinations. Each of these pseudopatients were admitted to different hospitals. During their stay, the pseudopatients never exhibited any symptoms. Rosenhan's confederates made observations of the hospital conditions, how they were treated, and the behavior of the staff and other patients. Rosenhan reported that the hospital staff never knew that the pseudopatients were not ill.

There are also, however, qualitative research studies where the participant knows that he or she is participating in a study. In such cases, the research needs to develop a high level of rapport with the participants. For example, Jones (1998) used the qualitative approach to study a unique culture (teenage and adolescent gangs) in American society. Little has been reported on gangs except statistics. Little is known about the dynamics within gangs and the difference between some types of gangs. Jones had to spend an enormous amount of time in prisons and detention centers interviewing gang members. The experiences of being in a gang, the dynamics between gang members, their value systems, and how these members of American society assign meaning to their lives, fit the goal of qualitative research methodology. Qualitative research such as the study by Jones is suited for studying complex life experiences.

Qualitative research is a field study because it is conducted in the field where the participants are behaving naturally. Heppner, Kivlighan, and Wampold (1992) refer to qualitative research as naturalistic–ethnographic or phenomenological. Heppner et al. present four differences between quantitative and qualitative research (summarized in Table 24.1).

Qualitative research has several advantages over quantitative research. Qualitative research uses direct observation and semistructured interviewing in real-world settings. The researcher looks for social transactions and interactions between people and events. The data collection process is less structured than quantitative research. The researcher may make a number of adjustments during the observations. The researcher may even develop new hypotheses during the research process. Qualitative research is naturalistic, participatory, and interpretive.

▣ TABLE 24.1   *Four Differences between Quantitative and Qualitative Research (Heppner, Kivlighan, & Wampold)*

Quantitative	Qualitative
Emanates from post-positivistic tradition; major constituents are physical objects and processes	Emanates from phenomenological perspective; emphasizes internal, mental events as the basic unit of existence
Assumes knowledge comes from observations of the physical world	Knowledge is actively constructed and comes from examining the internal constructs of people
Investigator makes inferences based on direct observations or derivatives of the direct observations	Investigator relies on outside observational schemes and tries to keep intact the participants perspective
Goal is to describe cause and effect	Attempts to describe the ways that people assign meaning to behavior

Quantitative research seldom deviates from the research plan. Qualitative research, on the other hand, is very flexible. This has led to some criticism of qualitative research. Some feel that qualitative research suffers from some of the same validity problems inherent in single-subject designs. Another area of vulnerability is experimenter bias. The qualitative researcher must be extra careful in guarding against viewing situations with a personal bias. However, qualitative researchers state that the unobtrusive involvement and natural blending of the observer into the environment reduces the amount of disruption in the setting and group under study. After a short period of time, participants return to their normal mode of behavior and no longer show a façade. The well-trained observer can acquire perceptions of the participants' behavior from different points of view. If done properly, the data collected from qualitative research can yield more information and less spurious variability than other research methods. Perhaps the two views of science presented by Sampson (1991) in Chapter 1 of this book encompass the differences between quantitative and qualitative research. In qualitative research, the determination of sample size can be done near the end of the study instead of at the beginning. Sample size determination isn't as important to the qualitative researcher. A rule in qualitative research is that the greater the number of interviews with each participant, the less the need for more participants.

The design of qualitative research usually uses an unobtrusive observer or a participant observer. As an unobtrusive observer the researcher makes passive observations and tries to avoid responding to the participant in any way. No variables are manipulated; the researcher just lets natural events occur. If the researcher wanted to see if the presence of another person in the restroom affects the willingness to wash one's hand, the researcher must wait and observe how people behave when there is another person in the restroom and when there is no other person. In quantitative research, the researcher would use a confederate to alter the situation (see Pedersen, Keithly, & Brady, 1986). In the participant-observer situation, the researcher becomes a part of the environment being studied. One feature of the participant-observer form is that the researcher can see the effect of manipulating his or her own behavior. Hence, occasionally, qualitative designs can resemble a natural experiment.

One of the more famous qualitative research studies is the work of Margaret Mead, who studied the Samoan culture. Such studies not only rely on personal observation but also often require the recruitment of informants. Studies such as those conducted to see what life was like for first-generation immigrants who came to the United States in the early part of the twentieth century can be a qualitative study. Interviewers can interview a number of first-generation immigrants and develop life histories. With enough life histories showing similar patterns of behavior a picture can be developed as to what life was like for those who lived in that era. For the best results, the interviews are tape recorded. The interview process is conducted in such a way and at such a length to enable the informant to adjust to the interviewer and the recording device. It is part of the plan of qualitative research to carefully choose the interviewer in order to have the best match to the informant.

Since diaries, recordings, and descriptions are taken from the people under study in their natural environment, ethical issues are very important. In particular, the confidentiality of records and information needs to be kept strictly secure. Hertz and Imber (1993) have stated that social science research tends to concentrate on the powerless (e.g., animals, college students) since they are easily accessible whereas the powerful are not (e.g., politicians, corporate executives, school administrators). It is doubtful that a student would be allowed to do a case study on the president of the university. Hence, some qualitative research studies involve deception. Deception is an issue that requires a case-by-case review and justification.

An excellent reference on qualitative research is Taylor and Bogdan, (1998). This book is in its third edition and provides clear details from designing, data collection, and final write up of qualitative research. Another very good reference on qualitative research is by Creswell (1998) who notes that there are five different traditions within qualitative research. He compares and critiques biography, phenomenology, ground theory, ethnography, and case study. Taylor and Bogdan, and Cresswell provide detailed examples of qualitative research. An excellent reference on the use of qualitative research methodology in studying renal failure patients is *the Renal Rehabilitation Report*[1] published by the Life Options Rehabilitation Advisory Council. In the July/August 1998 issue of this publication, there is a comparison of the traditional approach to the qualitative approach. This article gives reasons why qualitative

---

[1] A copy of this report is available from the Life Options Rehabilitation Resource Center at (800) 468–7777. The authors wish to thank Dr. Abdul Abukurah for providing us with a copy of this publication.

methods are good science. Where Creswell compares five different traditions within qualitative research, the article provides descriptions of seven different areas. Among the categories are Feminist Research, Action Research, and Qualitative Evaluation Research. With Feminist Research the focus is on the improvement of women's needs, interests, experiences, and aims. Action Research involves the joint effort of the researcher and participant in bringing about a change. Qualitative Evaluation Research deals with stories and cases studies.

Although we have given a positive view of qualitative research methods, not all individuals hold the same opinion. The bulk of the behavioral sciences—especially psychology—have been in favor of the quantitative approach. There have been a few, such as Sampson (1991) and Phillips (1973), who have stated that quantification is not the appropriate method for all research situations. Earlier we briefly discussed the benefits of quantitative methods; however, at the same time, we mentioned that they are unable to answer certain questions dealing with culture or certain ways of life. This conflict between the qualitative research methodology and the quantitative methodology is well documented in the literature (see Cook & Reichardt, 1979; Padgett, 1998). There have been staunch proponents for both sides. However, quantitative researchers, such as Cook and Reichardt, have discussed the issues and presented some thoughts on combining the two instead of separating them. They talk about the possibility of a research study that could have both qualitative and quantitative elements. In fact, Padgett (1998) lays out three forms for doing both quantitative and qualitative research in one study. The combination of the two methods—qualitative and quantitative—is called *multimethod research.*

According to Padgett, the first of the three ways of doing multimethod research is to start the research as qualitative and finish it as quantitative. The qualitative method is used to explore and identify the ideas, hypotheses, and variables, of interest to the researcher. This would be done through direct observation, interviewing, or focus groups. The concepts derived from the qualitative portion of the study can then be studied through the use of quantitative methods and hypothesis testing. The generalizability of the concepts and hypotheses tested through quantitative research can gain more credibility by obtaining a better link to the real world. Qualitative methods would have provide that link.

The second way of doing multimethod research is to use the quantitative method first, followed by the qualitative method. The results from the quantitative portion of the study are used as the starting point for the qualitative portion. Padgett feels that many quantitative studies could benefit from a qualitative analysis of the results. Qualitative methods could help provide insight and information concerning questions that were unanswered or unanswerable by the quantitative study. For example in quantitative studies that use multiple regression analysis (covered in a later chapter of this book), the researcher is more often than not, left with a certain percentage of unaccountable variance. For example, a research study that reports a correlation coefficient of 0.48 between Graduate Record Examination scores and Success in Graduate School is telling us that only 23% of the total variance of graduate school success is accounted for by GRE scores. This also says that 77% is unaccounted for. At this point, through the use of qualitative methods, we can begin the process of determining what other variables may be involved. This can in turn lead to another quantitative study which includes those variables found by the qualitative portion of the study.

The third mode discusssed by Padgett differs slightly from the first two, which have a more definite temporal division. That is, after completing one method, the other followed. In the third mode of multimethod research, both qualitative and quantitative approaches are used simultaneously. Such studies can have one method more dominant than the other. When this happens, one method—the less dominant one—is "nested" within the other—the dominant one. Padgett reports that there are more studies of this "nested" nature than a true integration of the two methods in the study. In the case where researchers follow a quantitative result with a qualitative finding, qualitative methods are said to supplement but not alter the quantitative approach to the study. In the opposite case where the qualitative method is the dominant one, the researcher conducts a survey or interview but uses standardized measurement scales and instruments in the process. This includes the use of Likert scales and census data to supplement the data obtained from intensive interviews. Here the quantitative data does not intrude into the inductive and holistic nature of qualitative methods.

Although the joint use of qualitative and quantitative methods is promising, there are still some doubts in the minds of many. Cook and Reichardt (1979), for example, state some of the obstacles facing multimethod research. The obstacles they state deal primarily with economics and training. A study with the joint efforts of qualitative and quantitative methods can be costly in terms of time and money. Even if multimethod research requires faith and vigilance, Padgett (1998) feels multimethod research is worth the cost and effort.

Addendum

The Holistic Experimental Paradigm

The Holistic experimental paradigm provides an economical means of empirically quantifying the complex relationships among critical factors affecting human performance on individual operational tasks. The approach produces an equation of required order for most of the potentially critical factors related to the task, people, equipment, environment, and time across their effective operational ranges. When combined with various bias-reduction techniques, the Holistic approach materially improves the predictive accuracy of the experimental results and produces more generalizable information than is possible with the few-factors-at-a-time approach.

Contrary to allegations made in many of today's behavioral science textbooks regarding large factorial experiments, the approach is extremely economical. In fact, by using fractional designs in a sequential manner it is far less expensive to do megafactor[2] experiments than it would be to obtain the same information about the same

---

[2]Dr. Charles Simon coined this term to avoid confusion with the word "multifactor" which textbook writers often refer to 2-, 3- and 4-factor experiments. The first definition of "mega" is "large," and "Megafactor" implies a much larger number of factors than have been used traditionally.

number of factors in a series of small experiments. Nor are large megafator experiments merely extensions of smaller experiments; they are done differently. They require fewer assumptions of the types present in the few-factor experiments and in the Holistic paradigm, the few assumptions that are made are tentative and will be eventually tested as the experiment progresses and modified as necessary. While the methodology is primarily suited to problems involving quantitative factors and the ANOVA model, many of its principles can be used across the board in behavioral science research. The approach is heuristic, pragmatic, and empirical.

The Holistic experimental paradigm is a complete methodology, one that integrates a set of principles, a strategy, and a body of techniques to provide minimum-biased quantitative answers to complex behavioral questions. Bias is defined as the difference between performance estimates based on the experimental results and performance obtained under operational conditions. The basic strategy in this Holistic approach was taken from G.E.P. Box's response surface methodology (Box, 1954), modified to fit the special problems encountered in behavioral experiments. However, the Holistic approach does not depend on a specific experimental design or statistical technique; to the contrary, statistical devices play a much smaller role than they do in traditional experiments.

The Holistic approach emphasizes a pre-experimental planning and exploration stage as a time to check for conditions that might adversely affect the conduct of the experiment and the operator's performance. At that time, relevant experimental factors are selected on the basis of the investigator's current knowledge and preliminary tests. Then, following Box's strategy of using a sequence of fractional factorial designs, those factors are studied at the lowest level of resolution, a first-order equation. Then, if it is found that this model does not adequately fit the empirical data, another block of data is collected to expand the order of the equation, and another test is made. Because most human performance can be adequately approximated by not more than a third order polynomial, one can usually conclude this iterative approach after taking considerably less data than would be required to fill the factorial design.

The more important techniques employed in this approach were developed mainly in the 1930s and 1960s. New techniques were developed to make the sequential data collection of hundreds of experimental conditions robust to trends and intraserial transfer, or "carryover" effects, without wasteful counterbalancing or randomizing. Other techniques employed in the Holistic approach include graphical transformations and graphical data analysis.

A critical analysis of the traditional approach to behavioral experimentation reveals that many of its rites have become sacrosanct, deified into something they are not. As this book goes to press, one of the icons of behavioral science, the test of statistical significance, is being challenged again (see Harlow, Mulaik & Steiger, 1997), as it frequently has been for more than thirty years (see Chapter 1 of Bakan, 1973).

Other so-called rules of scientific inquiry have dictated experiments that produce results of little or no enduring value and sometimes with totally incorrect conclusions. This can happen, for example, when critical factors not included in the experiment are held constant. The choice of the constant values at which such factors are held can alter the level of difficulty of the task and markedly alter the overall results. Randomization does not guarantee freedom from bias or "internal validity" and should only be used after all known systematic controls have been exhausted.

A procedure frequently recommended by traditionalist to improve the "external validity" or generalizability of the experimental results is to perform a few studies with modestly different parameters after a main experiment has been completed. This is an expensive hit or miss approach.

Generalization is achieved most accurately and economically in the Holistic approach by including all identifiably relevant factors in the original experimental plan.

The Holistic experimental paradigm was developed by Charles W. Simon over the past thirty years, supported primarily by research branches of the United States Air Force, Navy, and Army. In the 1970s, seminars were given to military and industrial research groups. To date, no consolidated report is available, only numerous reports of the various techniques, often isolated from one another and not necessarily up to date with recent developments. A book is currently in preparation.[3]

CHAPTER SUMMARY

1. Laboratory experiments, field experiments, and field studies are compared and contrasted.
2. The laboratory experiment has the greatest internal validity, but suffers from external validity.
3. Laboratory experiments generally show variables with a small effect, whereas field studies and field experiments show variables with large effects.
4. Even though field experiments have variables showing a large effect, it is often masked by other variables and difficult to sort out.
5. Laboratory experiments are heavily theory-oriented and are designed to test a general theory.
6. Field experiments and field studies are more applied-oriented, attempting to answer a specific question on observable phenomena.
7. Field experiments differ from laboratory experiments, in that field experiments do not have the strict controls found in laboratory research.
8. Field experiments attempt to conduct a laboratory-type study in a real-world environment using real-world participants. There is generally an active independent variable.
9. Field studies are nonexperimental studies performed in the real world. There is generally no active independent variable.
10. The goal of field studies is to discover the relations and interactions among a number of behavioral and social variables.

---

[3]Dr. Charles W. Simon prepared this description of the Holistic approach.

11. A majority of behavioral and social science research is oriented quantitatively. A quantitatively oriented field study is usually called a survey or epidemiological research. A qualitative-oriented field study is called qualitative or naturalistic-ethnographic research.

12. Qualitative research usually involves unobtrusive-observer or participant-observer approaches.

13. In the unobtrusive-observer approach, the observer blends into the environment and makes no contact with the participants. The participant-observer approach requires that the observer becomes a member of the group being studied.

14. Qualitative methods are well suited for studying little-known or complex human experiences. Qualitative research supplements quantitative research and does not attempt to supplant it.

STUDY SUGGESTIONS

1. Is factorial analysis of variance more likely to be used in laboratory experiments, field experiments, or field studies? Explain.

2. In Chapter 15, a study of the comparative effects of marijuana and alcohol was outlined. Suppose such a study is a laboratory experiment. Does that limit its usefulness and generalizability? Would such an experiment differ in generalizability from, a laboratory experiment of frustration and aggression?

3. Following is a list of studies. Some were summarized in earlier chapters, others were not. Look up these studies and then classify each as a laboratory experiment, a field experiment, or a field study. Explain why you categorize each study as you do.

Henemann, H. G. (1977). Impact of test information and applicant sex on applicant evaluation in a selection simulation. *Journal of Applied Psychology*, *62*, 524–526.

Johnson, C. B., Stockdale, M. S., & Saal, F. E. (1991). Persistence of men's misperceptions of friendly cues across a variety of interpersonal encounters. *Psychology of Women Quarterly*, *15*, 463–475.

McKay, J. R., Alterman, A. I., McLellan, T., Snider, E. C., & O'Brien, C. P. (1995). Effect of random versus nonrandom assignment in a comparison of inpatient and day hospital rehabilitation for male alcoholics. *Journal of Consulting and Clinical Psychology*, *63*, 70–78.

Reinholtz, R. K., & Muehlenhard, C. L. (1995). Genital perceptions and sexual activity in a college population. *Journal of Sex Research*, *32*, 155–165.

Wansink, B., Kent, R. J., & Hoch, S. J. (1998). An anchoring and adjustment model of purchase quantity decisions. *Journal of Marketing Research*, *35*, 71–81.

Wilson, F. L. (1996). Patient education materials nurses use in community health. *Western Journal of Nursing Research*, *18*, 195–205.

4. "The experiment is one of the great inventions of the last century." Do you agree with this statement? If so, give reasons for your agreement: Why is the statement correct (if, indeed, it is correct)? If you do not agree, explain why you don't. Before making snap judgments, read and ponder the references given in Study Suggestion 9, below.

5. Unfortunately, there has been much uninformed criticism of experiments. Before pronouncing rational judgments on any complex phenomenon one should first know what one's talking about and, second, one should know the nature and purpose of the phenomenon being criticized. To help you reach rational conclusions about the experiment and experimentation, the following references are offered as background reading.

Berkowitz L., & Donnerstein, E. (1982). External validity is more than skin deep: Some answers to criticisms of experiments. *American Psychologist, 3*, 245–257. (A penetrating answer to the criticism of experiments as lacking external validity.)

Kaplan, A. (1964). *The conduct of inquiry.* San Francisco, CA: Chandler. (Chapter IV, called "Experiment" seems to include most controlled observation.)

6. Those of you who wish to know more about the Holistic experimental paradigm might consult some of Charles W. Simon's early publications that give the philosophy behind the approach. Be aware that since they were written the approach has been refined and new techniques added.

Simon, C. W. (1976). Analysis of human factors engineering experiments: Characteristics, results and applications. Westlake Village, CA: Canyon Research Group, Inc., Tech. Rep. No. CWS-02-767, 104 pp. (AD A038-184).

Simon, C. W. (1978). New research paradigm for applied experimental psychology: A system approach. Westlake Village, CA: Canyon Research Group, Inc., Tech. Rep. No. CWS-04-77A, 123 pp. (AD A056-984).

Simon, C. W. (1987). Will egg-sucking ever become a science? *Human Factors Society Bulletin, 30*, 1-4.

Simon, C. W. & Roscoe, S. N. (1984). Application of a multifactor approach to transfer of learning research. *Human Factors, 26*, 591-612.

Westra, D. P., Simon, C. W., Collyer, S. C. & Chambers, W. S. (1982). *(Simulator design features for carrier landings: I. Performance experiments.* NAVTRAEQUIPCEN. (78-C-0060-7): 64 pp. (AD A122-064)

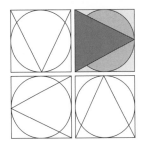

SURVEY RESEARCH

Survey research studies large and small populations (or universes) by selecting and studying samples chosen from the population to discover the relative incidence, distribution, and interrelations of sociological and psychological variables. As such, survey research can be classified as field studies with a quantitative orientation. Some consider it a variation of the correlational research design. This chapter concentrates on the use of survey research in scientific research and neglects so-called status surveys. Status surveys have a goal different from survey research. Its aim is to learn the status quo rather than to study the relations among variables; to examine the current status of some population characteristic. Status surveys were used as early as the 1830s in Great Britain to study the working conditions of children and adults during the Industrial Revolution. The development of survey research in the social and behavioral sciences is more modern—it is a twentieth-century development.

    There is no intention of derogating status surveys; they are useful, even indispensable. The intention is to emphasize the importance and usefulness of survey research in the scientific study of socially and educationally significant problems. The work of public opinion pollsters, such as Gallup and Roper, will not be examined. For a good account of polls and other surveys, see Parten (1950) in Chapter 1.

(Though dated, this book is still valuable.) A slightly newer book on how polls are used to sway public opinion in the United States is by Wheeler (1976). The standard text for many years, until it recently went out of print, is by Warwick and Lininger (1975); it has the advantage of having been guided by the thinking and practice of the Survey Research Center, University of Michigan. It also has the advantage of having a cross-cultural emphasis. Orlich (1978) presents the method and procedure of survey research in a very straightforward manner. Orlich even explains how to design and sequence the items of a survey. A few of the more recent publications on survey research methods are Alreck (1994), Babbie (1990), Suskie (1996), and Weisberg (1996).

Surveys covered by the above definition are often called *sample surveys*, probably because survey research developed as a separate research activity along with the development and improvement of sampling procedures. Survey research is considered to be a branch of social scientific research, which immediately distinguishes it from the status survey. Its procedures and methods have been developed mostly by psychologists, sociologists, economists, political scientists, and statisticians (see Campbell and Katona, 1953). These individuals have put a rigorous scientific stamp on survey research and, in the process, have profoundly influenced the social sciences.

The definition also links populations and samples. Survey researchers are interested in the accurate assessment of the characteristics of whole populations of people. They want to know, for example, how many persons in the United States voted for a Republican candidate and the relation between such voting and variables like sex, race, religious preference, and the like. They want to know the relation between attitudes toward education and public support of school budgets.

Only rarely, however, do survey researchers study whole populations; they study *samples* drawn from populations. From these samples they infer the characteristics of the defined population or universe. The study of samples from which inferences about populations can be drawn is needed because of the difficulties of studying whole populations. Random samples can often furnish the same information as a census (an enumeration and study of an entire population) at much less cost, with greater efficiency, and sometimes greater accuracy!

Sample surveys attempt to determine the incidence, distribution, and interrelations among sociological and psychological variables, and, in so doing, usually focus on people, the vital facts of people, and their beliefs, opinions, attitudes, motivations, and behavior. The social scientific nature of survey research is revealed by the nature of its variables, which can be classified as sociological facts, opinions, and attitudes. *Sociological facts* are attributes of individuals that spring from their membership in social groups: sex, income, political and religious affiliation, socioeconomic status, education, age, living expenses, occupation, race, and so on. The second type of variable is psychological and includes *opinions* and *attitudes* on the one hand, and *behavior* on the other. Survey researchers are interested not only in relations among sociological variables; they are more likely to be interested in what people think and do, and the relations between sociological and psychological variables. The study of the quality of American life done by the Survey Research Center of the University of Michigan, for instance, reports depressing data on the relation between race and feelings of trust in people, a sociological and a psychological variable (data are given

▣ **TABLE 25.1** *Relation between Race and Trust in People (in percentages)*
(Campbell et al. study).[a]

	Low Trust	High Trust
African Americans	72	28
White Americans	38	62

[a] *N* = 2070

in Table 25.1). The relation is substantial. Evidently, African American people feel less trustful of people than whites. As Campbell, Converse, and Rodgers (1976) say (p. 455), "those people who have been least successful in their encounters with society have the least reason to feel trustful of it."

Survey researchers, of course, also study the relations among psychological variables. But most relations of survey research are those between sociological and psychological variables: between education and tolerance, between race and self-esteem, and between education and sense of political efficacy.

Types of Surveys

Surveys can be conveniently classified by the following methods of obtaining information: personal interview, mail questionnaire, panel, and telephone. Of these, the personal interview far overshadows the others as perhaps the most powerful and useful tool of social scientific survey research. These survey types will be described here briefly; in later chapters, when reviewing methods of data collection, we will study the personal interview in depth.

Interviews and Schedules

The best survey research uses the personal interview as the principal method of gathering information. This is accomplished in part by the careful and laborious construction of a schedule or questionnaire. The term "schedule" will be used. It has a clear meaning: the instrument used to gather survey information through personal interview. "Questionnaire" has been used to label personal interview instruments and attitudinal or personality instruments. The latter are called "scales" in this book. Schedule information includes factual information, opinions and attitudes, and reasons for behavior, opinions, and attitudes. Interview schedules are difficult to construct; they are time consuming and relatively costly; but no other method yields the information they do.

The *factual information* gathered in surveys includes the so-called sociological data mentioned previously: gender, marital status, education, income, political preference, religious preference, and the like. Such information is indispensable, since it is used in studying the relations among variables and in checking the adequacy of samples. These data, which are entered on a "face sheet," are called "face sheet information." Such information, at least part of it, is ordinarily obtained at the beginning of the interview. Much of it is neutral in character and helps the interviewer establish rapport with the respondent. Questions of a more personal nature, such as those about income and personal habits, and questions that are more difficult to answer, such as the extent of the knowledge or ability of the respondent, can be reserved for later questioning, perhaps at the end of the schedule. The timing must necessarily be a matter of judgment and experience (see Warwick & Lininger, 1975).

Other kinds of factual information include what respondents know about the subject under investigation, what respondents did in the past, are doing now, and intend to do in the future. After all, unless we observe directly, all data about respondents' behavior must come from them or from other people. In this special sense, past, present, and future behavior can all be classified under the "fact" of behavior, even if the behavior is only an intention. A major point of such factual questions is that the respondent presumably knows a good deal about personal actions and behavior. If the respondent says he or she voted for a school bond issue, we can believe the statement is true—unless there is compelling evidence to the contrary. Similarly, we can believe the respondent, perhaps with more reservation (since the event has not happened yet), if the person voices intention to vote for a school bond issue.

Just as important, maybe even more important from a social scientific standpoint, are the beliefs, opinions, attitudes, and feelings that respondents have about cognitive objects. *Cognitive object* is an expression indicating the object of an attitude. Almost anything can be the object of an attitude, but the term is ordinarily reserved for important social "objects," for example, groups (religious, racial, and educational) and institutions (education, marriage, and political parties). A more general and probably better term, though one not in general use, is *referent*. Many of the cognitive objects of survey research may not be of interest to the researcher: investments, certain commercial products, political candidates, and the like. Other cognitive objects are more interesting: the United Nations, the Supreme Court, educational practices, integration, sexual behavior, federal aid to education, college students, and the feminist movement.

The personal interview can be helpful in learning respondents' reasons for doing or believing something. When asked reasons for actions, intentions, or beliefs, people may say they have done something, intend to do something, or feel certain ways about something. They may say that group affiliations or loyalties or certain events have influenced them. Or they may have heard about issues under investigation via the media. For example, a male respondent may say that he was formerly opposed to federal aid to education because he and his political party have always opposed governmental interference. However, he now supports federal aid because he has read a great deal about the problem in news-papers and magazines and has come to the conclusion that federal aid will benefit American education.

A respondent's desires, values, and needs may influence his or her attitudes and actions. When saying why one favors federal aid to education the respondent may indicate that his or her own educational aspirations were thwarted and that there has always been the yearning for more education. Or this person may indicate that one's own religious group has, as a part of its value structure, a deep commitment to the education of children. If the individual under study has accurately sounded his or her own desires, values, and needs—and can express them verbally—the personal interview can be very valuable.

Other Types of Survey Research

The next important type of survey research is the *panel*. A sample of respondents is selected and interviewed, and then reinterviewed and studied at a later time. The panel technique enables the researcher to study changes in behaviors and attitudes. Panels are used frequently in marketing research. It enables the researcher to see the impact of certain advertising changes on consumer purchasing behavior. A book on marketing research edited by Robert Ferber (1974) provides some excellent examples, procedures, and methods of survey research in marketing and advertising; those interested in doing behavioral and social science research in the business environment should read this book.

Telephone surveys have little to recommend them beyond speed and low cost. This is especially true when the interviewer is unknown to the respondent. The interviewer then is limited by possible nonresponse, uncooperativeness, and by reluctance to answer more than simple, superficial questions. Yet, telephoning can sometimes be useful in obtaining information essential to a study. Its principal defect, obviously, is the inability to obtain detailed information.

The *mail questionnaire* has serious drawbacks unless it is used in conjunction with other techniques. Two of these defects are possible lack of response and the inability to verify the responses given. These defects, especially the first, are serious enough to make the mail questionnaire worse than useless, except in highly sophisticated hands. Responses to mail questionnaires are generally poor. Returns of less than 40% are common. Higher percentages are rare. At best, the researcher must be content with returns as low as 50% or 60%.

Because mail questionnaires produce low returns, valid generalizations cannot be made. Although there are means of securing larger returns and reducing deficiencies—follow-up questionnaires, enclosing money, interviewing a random sample of nonrespondents, and analyzing nonrespondent data—these methods are costly, time-consuming, and often ineffectual. As Parten (1950) says, "Most mail questionnaires bring so few returns, and these from such a highly selected population, that the findings of such surveys are almost invariably open to question." The best advice would seem to be not to use mail questionnaires if a better method can possibly be used. If mail questionnaires are used, every effort should be made to obtain returns of better than 80–90%, and lacking such returns, to learn something of the characteristics of the nonrespondents. Sheatsley (1974) states that some respondents may misinterpret questions or ask other people for the answer. So not only is there a like-lihood of a poor response rate, there are issues concerning the accuracy of the responses given by those who do return the survey. Erdos (1974) and Warwick and Lininger (1975) provide techniques for increasing the response rate of mail surveys.

When compared with mail surveys, telephone surveys have the advantage of a higher return rate. However, they are limited to who one can obtain by phone and the brevity of the interview.

The Methodology of Survey Research

Survey research has contributed much to the methodology of the social sciences. Its most important contributions, perhaps, have been in rigorous sampling procedures, the overall design and the implementation of the design of studies, the unambiguous definition and specification of the research problem, and the analysis and interpretation of data.

In the limited space of a section of one chapter, it is obviously impossible to discuss adequately the methodology of survey research. Only those parts of the methodology germane to the purposes of this book, therefore, will be outlined: the survey or study design, the so-called flow plan or chart of survey researchers, the check of the reliability and validity of the sample, and the data-gathering methods. (Both sampling and analysis were discussed in earlier chapters.)

Survey researchers use a *flow plan* or *chart* to outline the design and subsequent implementation of a survey. The flow plan starts with the objectives of the survey, lists each step to be taken, and ends with the final report. First, the general and specific problems that are to be solved are as carefully and as completely stated as possible. Since, in principle, there is nothing very different here from the discussion for problems and hypotheses of Chapter 2, we can omit detailed discussion and give one simple hypothetical example. An educational investigator has been commissioned by a board of education to study the attitudes of community members toward the school system. On discussing the general problem with the board and the administrators of the school system, the investigator notes a number of more specific problems such as: Is the attitude of the members of the community affected by their having children in school? Does their educational level affect their attitudes?

One of the investigator's most important jobs is to specify and clarify the problem. To do this well, the investigator should not expect merely to ask people what they think of the schools, although this may be a good way to begin if one does not know much about the subject. Specific questions need to be asked that are aimed at various facets of the problem. Each of these questions should be built into the interview schedule. Some survey researchers design tables for the analysis of the data at this point in order to clarify the research problem and to guide the construction of interview questions. Since this procedure is recommended, let us design a table to show how it can be used to specify survey objectives and questions.

Take the question: Is attitude related to educational level? This question requires that "attitude" and "educational level" be defined operationally. Positive and negative

◻ FIGURE 25.1

	Positive Attitude	Negative Attitude
Some College		
High School Graduate		
Non-High School Graduate		

attitudes will be inferred from responses to schedule questions and items. If, in response to a broad question like, "In general, what do you think of the school system here?" a respondent says, "It is one of the best in this area," it can be inferred that he or she has a positive attitude toward the schools. Naturally, one question will not be enough. Related questions should also be used. A definition of "educational level" is quite easy to obtain. It is decided to use three levels: (1) Some College, (2) High School Graduate, and (3) Non-High School Graduate. The analysis paradigm might look like that shown in Figure 25.1.

The virtue of paradigms like this is that the researcher can immediately tell whether the specific problem has been stated clearly and whether the specific problem is related to the general problem. It will also give some notion as to how many respondents will be needed to fill the table cells adequately, as well as providing guidelines for coding and analysis. In addition, as Katz (1953, pp. 80–81) says,

> By actually going through the mechanics of setting out such tables, the investigators are bound to discover complexities of a variable that need more detailed measurement and qualifications of hypotheses in relation to special conditions.

The next step in the flow plan is the sample and the sampling plan. Sampling is much too complex to be discussed here in detail, so we outline only the main ideas. See Chapter 8 and Chapter 12 in this book, and Chapter 5 of Warwick and Lininger (1975) for a more detailed treatment of this topic. Warwick and Lininger's detailed example of multistage area sampling is especially helpful. *Area sampling* is the type most used in survey research. We must first define large areas to be sampled at random. This amounts to partitioning of the universe and random sampling of the cells of the partition. The partition cells may be areas delineated by grids on maps or aerial photographs of counties, school districts, or city blocks. Then further subarea samples may be drawn at random from the large areas already drawn. Finally, all individuals or families or random samples of individuals and families may be drawn.

First, the universe to be sampled and studied must be defined. Are all citizens living in the community included: community leaders? those citizens paying school taxes? those with children of school age? Once the universe is defined, a decision is made as to how the sample is to be drawn and how many cases will be drawn. In the best survey research, random samples are used. *Quota* samples are sometimes used instead of random samples, because random samples are high in cost and more difficult to execute. In a quota (or quota control) sample, "representativeness" is presumably achieved by assigning quotas to interviewers—so many men and women, so many white Americans and African Americans, and so on. Although quota sampling may achieve representativeness, it lacks the virtues of random sampling—and should therefore be avoided.

The next large step in a survey is the construction of the interview schedule and other measuring instruments to be used. This is a laborious and difficult business bearing virtually no resemblance to the questionnaires often hastily put together by neophytes. The main task is to translate the research question into an interview instrument and into any other instruments constructed for the survey. One of the problems of the study, for instance, may be: How are permissive and restrictive attitudes toward the discipline of children related to perceptions of the local school system? Among the questions to assess permissive and restrictive attitudes, one might be: How do you believe children should be disciplined? After drafts of the interview schedule and other instruments are completed, they are pretested on a small representative sample of the universe. They are then revised and put in final form.

The steps outlined above constitute the first large part of any survey. After the researcher has developed the survey instrument and determined which population is to be measured, the researcher also needs to decide whether the data will be collected using a cross-sectional design or a longitudinal design. The longitudinal design involves administering the survey many different times to the same group of participants. Surveys conducted in this way are able to assess the actual changes experienced by participants over time. Essentially these participants are tracked over time and measured periodically with the same measurement instrument. With the longitudinal design, the researcher can determine the impact that certain events will have on the person and future behavior. The attrition rate with a longitudinal study can be large, depending on the length of time over which the study is conducted. Also, it is dependent upon how willing the participants are to be available for each measurement. The cross-sectional design seems to have the advantage when it comes to participant attrition. Here, one group of people at different ages are all measured at the same time. Comparisons can be made between age groups as to the difference in responses given on the survey instrument. Although this sounds good, the cross-sectional method has its own problems. It is often difficult to assess developmental changes by comparing groups. For example, when comparing 10-year-olds with 15-year-olds, one needs to realize that the 15-year-old may have had an entirely different experience at ten than the typical 10-year-old of today.

Data collection is the second large part of survey research. Interviewers are oriented, trained, and sent out with complete instructions as to whom to interview and how the interview is to be handled. In the best surveys, interviewers are allowed no latitude as to whom to interview. They must interview those individuals and only those individuals designated, generally by random devices. Some latitude may be allowed in the actual interviewing and use of the schedule, but not much.

The work of interviewers is also systematically checked in some manner. For example, every tenth interview may be checked by sending another interviewer to the same respondent. Interview schedules are also studied for signs of spurious answering and reporting.

The third large part of the flow plan is analytical. The responses to questions are coded and tabulated. *Coding* is the term used to describe the translation of question responses and respondent information to specific categories for purposes of analysis. Take the example of Figure 25.1. All respondents must be assigned to one of the three educational level categories and a number (or other symbol) assigned to each level. Then each person must also be assigned to a "positive attitude" or "negative attitude" category. To aid in the coding, content analysis may be used. *Content analysis* is an objective and quantitative method for assigning types of verbal and other data to categories. Some marketing research companies have a specific department whose task is to do content analysis of responses to open-ended questions on a survey. Coding can also mean the analysis of factual response data and the subsequent assignment of individuals to classes or categories, or the assigning of categories to individuals; especially if one is preparing data entry for computer analysis. Such data entry consists of a large number of columns with a number of cells in each column. The fifth column may be assigned, say, to gender, with the numbers 0 and 1 used to designate female and male. Babbie (1995) gives instructions on developing code categories, codebook construction, and computer data-entry operations.

Tabulation is the recording of the numbers of types of responses in the appropriate categories, after which statistical analysis follows: percentages, averages, relational indices, and appropriate tests of significance. The analyses of the data are studied, collated, assimilated, and interpreted. Finally, the results of this interpretative process are reported.

Checking Survey Data

Survey research has a unique advantage among social scientific methods: it is often possible to check the validity of survey data. Some of the respondents can be interviewed again, and the results of both interviews checked against each other. It has been found that the reliability of personal factual items, like age and income, is high. The reliability of attitude responses is harder to determine because a changed response can mean a changed attitude. The reliability of average responses is higher than the reliability of individual responses. Fortunately, the researcher is usually more interested in averages, or group measures, than in individual responses.

One way of checking the validity of a measuring instrument is to use an outside criterion. One compares the results to some outside, presumably valid, criterion. For instance, a respondent claims to have voted in the last election of school board members. We can find out whether this is true or not by checking the registration and voting records. Ordinarily, individual behavior is not checked because information about individuals is difficult to obtain, but group information is often available. This information can be used to test to some extent the validity of the survey sample and the responses.

A good example of an outside check on survey data is the use of information from the last census. This is particularly useful in large-scale surveys, but may also help in smaller ones. Proportions of men and women, races, educational levels, age, and so on, in the sample and in the U.S. Census are compared. In the Verba and Nie (1972) study of political participation, for example, the authors report a number of such comparisons. Their sample estimates are accurate: only one of them, Age 20–34, deviates from the census estimates by more than 2%, which is reassuring evidence of the adequacy of the sample. To be sure, the sample was large (> 2,500), but smaller samples have also been found to be quite accurate. In one study of Detroit done by the University of Michigan in 1952, the sample was only 735, but the sample estimates were close to those of the 1950 census. Campbell and Katona (1953) discuss methods of checking sample validity and reliability. Warwick and Lininger (1975) give tables of sampling errors, with an explanation of their statistical meaning and use. We learn, for instance, that reported percentages between 20 and 80 from a sample of 700 have a standard error of 4. To reduce the standard error to 2 requires a sample of 3,000!

AIDS researchers Dr. Vickie Mays and Dr. Susan Cochran at the University of California, Los Angeles, have an ingenious way of checking some of the responses on their surveys. They put items in the questionnaires that are specific for certain groups of people. For example, they would include some questions that pertain only to gay men and other questions that pertain only to straight men. Later, after the data are collected, coded, and put into computer readable form, a statistical computer software program is used to perform a series of cross-tabulations of questions with the sexual preference variable. Those gay men who have answered straight-men-only questions or those straight men who have answered gay-men questions are flagged as data that were either miscoded or entered incorrectly into the computer. The actual response form can then be retrieved from the files, reexamined, and the data corrected. Since conducting a meaningful survey is expensive, each questionnaire from participants is important. Unlike some other areas of research where some would recommend dropping participant's data, survey research cannot do this and still expect to get the most accurate information.

Three Studies

Many surveys have been done, both good and bad. Most would probably not interest the student because they are little more than refined attempts to obtain simple information: studies of presidential voting, industrial plants, and so on. There are, however, surveys of considerable—even great—interest and significance to behavioral scientists. We have summarized three of these studies here.

Verba and Nie: Political Participation in America

Verba and Nie (1972) asked, among other things, how the political participation of citizens of a democracy influences governmental processes. They interviewed more than 2,500 residents of the United States in 200 locales in 1967, selected by an area probability sampling procedure. (Their census–sample comparisons showed generally high agreement.) The main finding was that citizen participation does indeed influence political leaders, but it is the more affluent, better-educated, and generally higher status citizens whose participation is influential. The authors point out that although Americans are not noted for class–based ideology, social status does relate to participation. The study was especially characterized by sophisticated measurement and analytical methodology, and by a major disconcerting finding. We will return to it and its methodology in later chapters.

Docter and Prince: A Survey of Male Cross-Dressers

Docter and Prince (1997) reports that one of the last major published survey of male-to-female transvestites occurred in 1972. The study by Docter and Prince (1997) used the same survey instrument as the one used in 1972 to measure cross-dressers in 1992. These researchers added some additional questions concerning cross-dressing and sexual excitement. One of the goals was to assess if any changes have taken place since the 1972 survey. The reason why these researchers felt that there may have been some changes centers around the decriminalization of cross-dressing in some areas of the United States, the larger media exposure that transvestites and transsexuals have been receiving, and the growth of support groups and national organizations. Docter and Prince compared the two samples surveyed on at least six dimensions: (1) demographic, childhood and family factors, (2) sexual orientation and sexual behavior, (3) cross-gender identity, (4) cross-gender role behavior, (5) future plans to live entirely as a woman, and (6) reliance on counseling or mental health services. Docter and Prince use the terms "transvestite" and "cross-dresser" interchangeably; defined as biological males who occasionally dress in women's clothes. They, however, do not seek sexual reassignment. A transgenderist is one who lives continuously in the gender role opposite of his or her biological sex without sexual reassignment procedures; a transsexual is one who has had sexual reassignment. Docter and Prince surveyed 1,032 self-defined periodic cross-dressers, age 20–80. All were biological males. The sample population were volunteers from all over the United States who responded to the request for research participants at club meetings, conventions, and in publications for cross-dressers. The 1992 sample represented a much broader base of cross-dressers than the 1972 sample: The 1972 sample consisted of mostly readers of one transvestite publication; the 1992 sample was composed of readers of a number of different publications and members of cross-dressing clubs. The comparison between the two samples showed that there were some changes between the cross-dressers in 1972 and those in 1992. In particular, there were more in 1992 sample that were interested in living full-time as a woman. There were more in the 1992 sample who had a preferred gender identity that was equally male and female than in the 1972 sample. Docter and Prince (1997) document the differences in the sampling method between the two samples and note the shortcomings of the more recent sample when compared to the earlier sample. This is the nature of survey research. Certain things change over time that make it difficult to obtain the exact same research environment from one time period to another.

Sue, Fujino, Hu, Takeuchi, and Zane: Community Health Services for Ethnic Minorities

This study (1991) may not exactly fit what some would term as survey research. These researchers did not design the survey for the study, neither did they collect the data for the study. Instead, they used the data supplied from the Automated Information System (AIS) maintained by the Los Angeles County Department of Mental Health. These data were used by the government agency for the purpose of system management, revenue collection, clinical management, and research. The clients were all outpatient service recipients. This study qualifies as survey research because the study was a field study—quantitative and epidemiological—which gathered information that described the relations between variables within the dataset. This type of survey research is based on the search of records (Isaac & Michael 1987). Sue et al. used the data to answer some questions concerning mental health services for four ethnic groups: African Americans, Asian Americans, Latino Americans, and white Americans. The AIS sample consisted of 7,136 Asian Americans, 47,220 African Americans, 58,844 Latino Americans, and 99,036 white Americans. The original dataset covered a 15-year period. Sue, et al. used only the latest five-year period. In a personal communication, Sue informed the second author (HBL) that he and his staff spent a great deal of time, effort, and money in reorganizing the data so that it would be amenable to their research. The hypothesis that these researchers tested was that those clients who were matched both ethnically and by gender with a therapist would show greater mental health improvement. The measure of mental health was the Global Assessment Scale (GAS). The dependent variables for this study were dropout from treatment, mean number of treatment sessions, and treatment outcomes. The results of the study showed for all groups, except African Americans, lower odds of dropping out of treatment when clients were matched in ethnicity with the therapist. When matched on gender, only Asian Americans and white Americans showed a lower chance of dropping out of treatment. This finding points to an important ingredient in preventing client dropout at public mental health facilities. Sue et al. found in analyzing the AIS data that only one-third of the ethnic clients were treated by same-ethnicity therapists, whereas 75% of the white Americans were treated by white therapists. For the mean number of treatment sessions, all groups with an ethnic client–therapist match produced a higher number of mean treatment sessions. However, on the gender match variable, only Mexican Americans and white Americans showed a higher number of treatment sessions. The GAS was used to measure treatment outcome. There was no gender match effect. With ethnic match, only Mexican Americans showed higher GAS scores at the time of treatment termination.

Hall, Kaplan, and Lee (1994), using the same database but looking only at children clients, found similar patterns. They found that younger children showed greatest improvement when matched with similar therapists in the areas of ethnicity and language. This could be attributed to the fact that language in younger bilingual children is not as well developed, resulting in the need for a therapist who can meet their language or cultural needs. Another study based on this important database is Russell, Fujino, Sue, Cheung, and Snowden (1996).

Applications of Survey Research to Education

These studies clearly show the applicability of survey research and its methodology in sociology, social psychology, social work, clinical psychology, and political science. Survey research's strong emphases on representative samples, overall design, plan of research, and expert interviewing using carefully and competently constructed interview schedules have had, and will continue to have, beneficial influence on behavioral research. Despite its evident potential value in all behavioral research fields, survey research has not been used to as great an extent where it would seem to have large theoretical and practical value: in education. Its distinctive usefulness in education and educational research seems to have been slower in realization. However, a review of the current literature shows that this may be changing. This section is therefore devoted to application of survey research to education and educational problems.

Obviously, survey research is a useful fact-finding tool for education. An administrator, board of education, or staff of teachers can learn a great deal about a school system or a community without contacting every child, every teacher, and every citizen. In short, the sampling methods developed in survey research can be very useful. It is unsatisfactory to depend on relatively hit-or-miss, so-called representative samples based on "expert" judgments. Neither is it necessary to gather data on whole populations; samples are sufficient for many purposes.

Most research in education is conducted using relatively small nonrandom samples. If hypotheses are supported, they can later be tested with random samples of populations and, if again supported, the results can be generalized to populations of schools, children, and laypeople. In other words, survey research can be used to test hypotheses already tested in more limited situations, with the result that external validity is increased.

Survey research seems ideally suited to some of the large controversial issues of education. For example, its ability to handle "difficult" problems like integration and school closings through careful and circumspect interviewing puts it high on the list of research approaches to such problems. Interviews of random samples of citizens and teachers of school districts just starting a gifted or special education program or experiencing the probable closure of certain elementary schools because of declining enrollment, can provide valuable information on the concerns and fears of citizens, so that appropriate measures can be taken to inform them and lessen their fears. The effect of these measures can, of course, also be studied.

Survey research is probably best adapted to obtaining personal and social facts, beliefs, and attitudes. It is significant that, although hundreds of thousands of words are spoken and written about education and about what people presumably think about education, there is little dependable information on the subject. We simply do not know what people's attitudes toward education are. We have to depend on feature writers and so-called experts for this information. Boards of education frequently depend on administrators and local leaders to tell them what the people think. Some of the questions that can be asked, and possibly answered, using survey research are: Will the community support an expanded budget next year? What will they think about dividing school districts? How will parents react to bussing children to achieve desegregation? What is the current curriculum? What is the attrition rate of graduate students? To what extent do medical students cheat in medical school? Do children from different cultural backgrounds who live in Israel differ in their fears? An early outstanding example of survey research in education is by Gross, Mason, and McEachern (1958). This study should be read by educational administrators and board of education members.

It is encouraging that in the past twelve years more studies are being done on the educational environment. Take, for example, the study by Stile, Kitano, Kelley, and Lecrone (1993). These researchers did a national survey of what is happening in preschool and kindergarten programs for gifted children. Their survey examined schools in all 50 states, five U.S. territories, and the District of Columbia. They reported that only 29 out of the 50 states (58%) and one territory had programs for gifted children. These programs totaled over 2,655 school districts. Only 16 states show that they have programs at the kindergarten level for gifted children that come from disadvantaged families. Although the Stile et al. study seems somewhat like a status survey, it does point out what the "big picture" looks like for gifted education programs in the United States and its territories. It also points out the type of funding used for gifted programs.

The study by Cooke, Sims, and Peyrefitte (1995) provides information not previously published on graduate student dropout. Much is known about undergraduate student dropout rates, but little is known about graduate students. Generally, sampling of graduate students is not as plentiful as it is for undergraduate students. In this study, the researchers gathered data from 230 graduate students enrolled in business, engineering, public administration, and education programs. These programs were chosen because of the higher numbers of ethnic minority students enrolled. The survey instrument was mailed to participants in early 1992, and a follow-up survey was mailed 18 months later. The two surveys were used to determine whether attrition could be predicted after 18 months. The results showed that ethnic minorities had a higher intention of quitting graduate school and were less satisfied with graduate school than non ethnic minorities. However, even though these difference, existed, they were not found to be related to attrition. Attrition was more closely related to the variables—need for achievement, affective commitment, and whether or not the graduate program met one's expectations.

Little and Lee (1995) conducted a survey of all graduate school psychology programs across the United States. Their purpose was to determine the amount of training graduate students were receiving in the areas of statistics and research methods. Among their numerous comparisons was the comparison of programs that awarded doctorates to those that did not. Little and Lee were not only interested in the quantity of courses, but also in the content of the courses and in the use of computer statistical software. A total of 181 surveys were mailed out to National Association of School Psychologists (NASP) and American Psychological Association (APA) certified programs as well as those listed in *Petersen's Guide to Graduate Education*. Of these, 101 usable surveys were obtained. The results showed no significant differences within subdoctoral and doctoral programs in the quantity of statistics and research design courses. However, differences were found when comparing subdoctoral programs to doctoral programs. Doctoral programs generally required twice as many statistics and research design courses than subdoctoral programs. Little and Lee provide valuable information that can be used by existing and new graduate programs in school psychology to adjust or develop their curriculum.

Baldwin, Daugherty, Rowley, and Schwarz (1996) sent a survey to 3,975 second-year medical students attending 31 medical schools; 2,459 (62%) completed the survey questionnaire. The survey was conducted to determine the extent of cheating behavior and attitude. Thirty-nine percent of the respondents stated that they had seen at least one incident of cheating. Nearly two-thirds of the sample claim that they have heard of other students cheating. Cheating was divided into categories: (1) obtaining prior information about the test, (2) copying another student's answers during the test, and (3) exchanging answers during the test. Eighty-two percent of the students who claimed they had cheated in medical school also stated that they had cheated in school prior to entering medical school. Nearly 5% of the students reported they had cheated sometime during the first two years of medical school. More men than women stated that they had cheated on exams.

Advantages and Disadvantages of Survey Research

Survey research has the advantage of wide scope: a great deal of information can be obtained from a large population. A large population or a large school system can be studied with much less expense than that incurred by a census. While surveys tend to be more expensive than laboratory and field experiments and field studies, for the amount and quality of information they yield, they are economical. Further, existing educational facilities and personnel can be used to reduce the costs of the research.

Survey research information is accurate—within sampling error, of course. The accuracy of properly drawn samples is frequently surprising, even to experts in the field. A sample of 600 to 700 individuals or families can give a remarkably accurate portrait of a community—its values, attitudes, and beliefs.

Coupled with these advantages are the inevitable weaknesses and disadvantages. A first disadvantage is that survey information does not ordinarily penetrate very deeply below the surface. The scope of the information sought is usually emphasized at the expense of depth. This seems to be a weakness, however, that is not necessarily inherent in the method. The Verba and Nie (1972), and Smith and Garner (1976; see also Garner & Smith, 1977) studies show that it is possible to go considerably below surface opinions. Smith and Garner designed a procedure to accompany a well-designed questionnaire that allowed them to tap into the homosexual behavior of college athletes. Instead of giving a survey instrument once, they gave it at least three times to check the consistency of responses. They also developed other means of checking the responses of athletes on a very sensitive subject and took extra nonthreatening means of collecting their data. By doing so, Smith and Garner were able to obtain useful information on a highly emotional topic. Despite these examples of the depth of information from survey research, the survey seems best adapted to extensive rather than intensive research. Other types of research are perhaps better adapted to deeper exploration of relations.

A second disadvantage is a practical one. Survey research is demanding of time, energy, and money. In a large survey, it may be months before a single hypothesis can be tested. Sampling and the development of good schedules are major operations. Interviews require skill, time, and money. Surveys on a smaller scale can avoid these problems to some extent.

Any research that uses sampling is naturally subject to sampling error. While it is true that survey information has been found to be relatively accurate, there is always that one chance in 20 or 100 that an error—more serious than might be caused by minor fluctuations of chance—may occur. The probability of such an error can be diminished by building safety checks into a study—by including comparison with census data or other outside information and by independent sampling of the same population.

A potential, rather than an actual, weakness of this method is that the survey interview can temporarily lift the respondent out of his or her own social context, which may make the results of the survey invalid. The interview is a special event in the ordinary life of the respondent. This apartness may make the respondent talk and interact with the interviewer in an unnatural manner. For example, a mother, when queried about her child-rearing practices, may give answers that reveal methods she would like to use, rather than those she actually uses. It is possible for interviewers to limit the effects of lifting respondents out of social context by skilled handling, especially by one's manner and by careful phrasing and asking of questions (see Cannell and Kahn, 1968).

Survey research also requires a good deal of research knowledge and sophistication. The competent survey investigator must know sampling, question and schedule construction, interviewing, the analysis of data, and other technical aspects of the survey. Such knowledge is difficult to come by. Few investigators get this kind and amount of experience. As the value of survey research, both large- and small-scale, becomes appreciated, it can be anticipated that such knowledge and experience will be considered, at least in a minimal way, to be necessary for researchers.

Meta-Analysis

At the time of this writing, the number of reported research studies using meta-analysis is on the rise. The student perusing through the literature is bound to come across a study that uses meta-analysis. What is *meta-analysis* and why is it covered under survey research? Well, many writers of research textbooks have had a difficult time in placing this method within specific topic chapters. Robert Rosenthal, one of the leading authorities on this subject, placed the topic of meta-analysis in the appendix of his book with Ralph Rosnow on behavioral research (Rosnow & Rosenthal, 1996). Some authors have integrated it within chapters on statistics. We are no different. We perceive this method as one that belongs under survey research. Although no questionnaire is designed and no sample is planned, it does involve looking at previously collected data. These data come from the research literature itself. One might say that it is a kind of a survey of the literature. Meta-analysis is quantitative and nonexperimental in nature. Some, such as Mann (1990), have referred to it as a natural experiment. The purpose of meta-analysis is to look through the literature on a specific topic that contains a large number of studies. Some of these studies may agree with one another in some way. If they do, they produce a convergence of knowledge and that knowledge, is useful in making decisions. For example, if there is an effect of coaching on the Scholastic Aptitude Test (SAT), all studies conducted on this topic should have similar basic findings. Meta-analysis involves taking all of these studies collectively to determine if a similar finding is found again and again under differing situations. The goal is to be able to state some kind of general behavioral law. Unlike "regular" research studies that have the individual participant or groups of participants as the unit of measurement, meta-analysis uses the individual studies themselves as the unit of measurement. The results of these individual research studies are summarized using measures of effect size similar to the ETA-squared (η^2) or omega-squared (ω^2) discussed in an earlier chapter, used for individual research studies. In meta-analysis, the effect size is measured using a d-statistic. Much of the meta-analytic research done today reports in tabular form the various studies, the sample size, and the effect size. Table 25.2 shows a table adapted from Scogin and McElreath's (1994) study on the effectiveness of psychosocial intervention on depression for older adults.

To determine the overall effect for the phenomenon under study, Rosenthal (1978) gives a statistical procedure for computing the combined effect size.

▣ **TABLE 25.2** *Meta-Analytic Table of Sample Size and Effect Size (from Scogin & McElreath)*

Study	Sample Size	Effect Size
1	31	.41
2	36	.00
3	84	.97
4	61	.70
5	28	.82
6	20	.28

Rosenthal essentially takes the p-values[1] for each study, finds the standard score for each p-value and uses it in the formula:

$$Z_{overall} = \frac{\sum_{i=1}^{n} Z_i}{\sqrt{n}}$$

The probability for this Z-value is then determined through the use of a normal distribution table (see Appendix B). This will tell the researcher whether or not the overall combined effect of the studies is statistically significant. Hence, in a meta-analysis, the researcher can find a large number of studies for a particular phenomenon that were not statistically significant. However, when they are combined, statistical significance can be achieved; for example, if a researcher found four studies that had the following p-values: .25, .32, .04, .19 for a one-tailed test. Their corresponding Z-values are .69, .47, 1.75, and .50 respectively. Note that only one of these studies was statistically significant. The overall Z-value for this example would be

$$Z_{overall} = \frac{0.69 + 0.47 + 1.75 + 0.50}{\sqrt{4}} = \frac{3.41}{2} = 1.72$$

This overall Z-value is significant at the 0.0427 level. Rosenthal (1978) shows nine ways of pooling results from studies to create an overall statistic.

Meta-analysis should not be confused with two other similar approaches: replication and analysis with different models or methods. With replication, the same methodology and same data collected are used from a different sample. The goal of replication studies is to establish the reliability of the results in the same situation. With the different methods approach, the same data are collected from a different sample, or the original data are used; however, with this approach, different methods are used. The objective here is to find out how robust the original findings were. Effort is taken to find the best-fitting model for prediction or decision-making. This might be construed as a form of "data mining," or multiple methods research. Meta-analysis essentially combines these two, looking at different methods *and* different data. The objective with meta-analysis is to generalize the results to new situations.

The development of meta-analysis is credited to Glass (1976). Smith and Glass (1977) demonstrated meta-analysis by searching the psychological literature in an effort to determine the effectiveness of psychotherapy. They found nearly 400 studies giving information on psychotherapy relevant to their goal. Smith and Glass were

---

[1]The p-value is another way of expressing the probability of a type I error. Generally, studies report the results as either $p < .05$ (statistically significant) or $p > .05$ (not statistically significant). However, in recent years, with the availability of high-speed computers and computer programs, the p-value is directly computed.

able to synthesize the results from each of these studies to state a general conclusion about the effectiveness of psychotherapy. In addition, they were able to compare the relative effectiveness of several different methods of treatment within psychotherapy. Hence, meta-analysis is able to answer a number of research and practical questions that individual research studies cannot. For example, Blumenthal (1998) uses a meta-analysis to answer questions surrounding gender differences in the perception of sexual harassment. This study has great significance in the area of court and legislative cases or legal policies. Most studies on sexual harassment have involved participants who are presented with one or two brief scenarios on an incident and then asked a series of questions concerning the situation. While most studies present results that men and women differ in perception of sexual harassment, the magnitude of the findings have varied. There are even some studies that have found no significant differences. Blumenthal's study examines the literature on this topic and determines in a systematic way what the general picture is like on this topic. Blumenthal's study utilizes computer searches for studies with keywords such as "sexual harassment," "perception," and "gender differences." The advent of computerized searches has facilitated the growth of meta-analytic studies.

Prior to the development of meta-analysis, researchers relied on articles that appeared in review publications such as *Psychological Review, American Psychologist, Psychological Bulletin, Harvard Educational Review,* and the *Annual Review of Psychology* for summaries of research that had been done in a certain area. Writers of reviews were generally chosen because they were considered experts in that area. Although these reviewers made great efforts to present the data objectively, some level of subjectivity was unavoidable. Mann (1990) presents a few examples of subjective reviews done with the traditional approach in medical science. Mann states that there is always the likelihood that certain important elements may be overlooked when doing one of these traditional reviews. Meta-analysis provides a methodology that supplements these reviews and fills a critical need in science. That need is the resolution of conflicting research findings. Simon (1987) feels that meta-analysis will not be able to completely resolve the conflict. He bases his argument on the premise that meta-analytic studies do not consider enough independent variables. In considering the problem posed by Adelson and Williams reported in Simon (1987), meta-analysis would not be able to answer the question as to which of 34 possible independent variables have the greatest effect on pilot performance.

To illustrate some of the areas addressable by meta-analysis, we will cite some of the studies that have been done. Scogin and McElreath (1994) did a meta-analysis of 17 studies concerned with the efficacy of psychosocial treatments for depression of older adults. These 17 studies met their criterion of studies that had a control condition. These researchers searched the literature for articles that pertained to the topic from the years 1975 to 1990. The average effect size found by these researchers was statistically significant and indicated that those who received psychosocial treatment were healthier than those who did not receive the treatment. Verhaeghan and DeMeersman (1998) did a meta-analysis of studies that compared younger and older adults on the Stroop interference effect. We mentioned the Stroop effect in an earlier chapter. Research participants were found to name the color of the ink the word was printed in, rather than the word itself. That is, with the word *yellow* printed in green-colored ink, participants tended to say "green" when asked to read the word. Verhaeghan and DeMeersman were able to find 20 such studies in a computer search of the literature. Verhaeghan and DeMeersman's finding showed that the Stroop effect was unaffected by age. Hellman (1997) used a meta-analysis to study the relation between job satisfaction and intent to leave the job. Hellman identified 38 studies within a 13-year period search of the literature. The relation between these two variables were consistently found to be statistically significant and in the negative direction. That is, the higher the satisfaction the less likely to leave, or the lower the satisfaction the higher the intent to leave.

Meta-analysis is a method that can summarize the results of many studies conducted on the same or similar topic area. It does not require that studies be exactly replicated. Additionally, it has the support of at least one quantitative index—average effect size—to help in the evaluation. Plus, effect size indices can also be compared to each other statistically. There is, however, at least one problem that has been associated with meta-analysis—the "file drawer problem." It arises from the fact that journal editors generally do not accept for publication articles that have "nonsignificant" results. That is, studies where the null hypothesis is not rejected, or studies that are not statistically significant at the mystical $\alpha = .05$ level. Barber (1976) calls it the "negative effect." Such studies are deemed "unpublishable." So meta-analysis, which is usually done by surveying the research literature for published articles in the area of interest, will contain only the analyses and conclusions drawn from studies that are "statistically significant." Meanwhile, researchers may have stored in their "file drawers" research studies that failed to yield a significant result. If such a file drawer exists with a large number of nonsignificant findings, the meta-analysis reported by researchers may be overly optimistic. To counteract this problem, a number of researchers have developed tables and methods to give the researcher some idea as to the amount of tolerance or distortion that may be present (see Bradley & Gupta, 1997; Sharpe, 1997). However, Rosenthal and Rubin (1978) have developed a statistical formula to determine how many negative studies would be needed to overturn the conclusion drawn from using the positive studies in a meta-analysis. Rosenthal and Rubin have shown that for 345 published studies, 65,123 unpublished studies showing a negative effect would be needed. However, as Light and Pillemer (1984) have pointed out, there is a major difference between 50 unpublished no-effect studies and 50,000 unpublished no-effect studies, even though both are below the 65,123 stated by Rosenthal and Rubin.

The statistical analysis of meta-analysis can be quite complex. We mentioned briefly about computing effect sizes. However, the analysis goes beyond this. A number of computer programs are available to handle the computations (see Johnson, 1993; Mullen, 1993).

CHAPTER SUMMARY

1. Survey research is a type of quantitative field study.
2. Survey research attempts to find relations between sociological and psychological variables.

3. Survey research is a development of the twentieth century.

4. The general focus of survey research is on people.

5. Interviews, schedules, panels, telephone and mail surveys are different types of surveys.

6. The type of survey that yields the best information is the interview. Mail surveys contain the greatest amounts of problems.

7. Survey research can obtain a wide range of information, but cannot provide in-depth information. It is more extensive than intensive.

8. The methodology of survey research includes a "flow plan." This plan outlines the design and implementation of a survey.

9. The construction of the questionnaire or survey is one of the important parts of the plan. Another part is the sampling plan (i.e., who to sample and how will the sampling be done?).

10. Data collection can be a laborious task. If interviews are used, then interviewers need to be trained properly.

11. Getting the data into machine-readable form is another big task in survey research. This would also include the analysis of the data.

12. Survey research can be expensive in terms of time, money, and labor. In a large survey, findings are not quickly accessible before the end of the study.

13. Meta-analysis is a form of survey research. Experimental research usually uses an individual participant as a unit of measurement. In meta-analysis, the individual studies are themselves the unit of measurement.

14. Meta-analysis involves collecting a number of studies on a similar topic and summarizing the findings. The goal is to define some general law of behavior.

STUDY SUGGESTIONS

1. Following are several good examples of survey research; some are books and others are articles. Choose one of them. If you choose a book, read the first chapter to learn the problem of the study. Then go to the technical section (if one exists) to see how the sampling and interviewing was done. (Most published survey research studies contain such a section.) Try to determine the main variables and their relations. Overviews of content are included in brackets.

Cai, D., & You, M. (1998). An ergonomic approach to public squatting-type toilet design. *Applied Ergonomics, 29,* 147–153. [A study on the public squatting type toilet design.]

Glock, C., & Stark, R. (1966). *Christian beliefs and anti-Semitism.* New York: Harper & Row. [Religion and prejudice.]

Lortie, D. (1975). *Schoolteacher: A sociological study.* Chicago: University of Chicago Press. [A valuable and insightful study of teachers.]

MacDonald, S., Wells, S., & Lothian, S. (1998). Comparison of lifestyle and substance use factors related to accidental injuries at work, home, and recreational events. *Accident Analysis and Prevention, 30,* 21–27.

Miller, W., & Levitin, T (1976). *Leadership and change: The new politics and the American electorate.* Cambridge, MA.: Winthrop. [The "New Left" and the "Silent Minority." Based on Survey Research Center data of 25 years.]

Murray, A. (1998). The home and school background of young drivers involved in traffic accidents. *Accident Analysis and Prevention, 30,* 169–182. [Investigates the relation between home and school backgrounds and accident data of over 4,000 male and female drivers, age 16–22.]

Oates, G. L. (1997). Self-esteem enhancement through fertility? Socioeconomic prospects, gender, and mutual influence. *American Sociological Review, 62,* 965–973. [Determines whether or not having children influences one's self-esteem.]

2. Rensis Likert was an outstanding social scientist, a methodological pioneer of survey research, and the founder of the Institute for Social Research of the University of Michigan (of which the Survey Research Center is a part). Two of his colleagues, Seashore and Katz (1982) wrote an obituary in which they described Likert's contributions. It is suggested that students read the obituary, which is virtually an account of the birth and growth of important methodological aspects of survey research, as well as an interesting description of the contributions of this creative and competent individual.

3. Read one the following references on the method of meta-analysis.

Light, R. J., & Pillemer, D. B. (1984). *Summing up: The science of reviewing research.* Cambridge, MA: Harvard University Press.

Farley, J. U., & Lehmann, D. R. (1986). *Meta-analysis in marketing: Generalization of response models.* Lexington, MA: Lexington Books.

Plucker, J. A. (1997). Debunking the myth of the "highly significant" result: Effect sizes in gifted education research. *Roeper Review, 20,* 122–126.

Rosenthal, R. (1984). *Meta-analytic procedures for social research.* Thousand Oaks, CA: Sage.

Sharpe, D. (1997). Of apples and oranges, file drawers and garbage: Why validity issues in meta-analysis will not go away. *Clinical Psychology Review, 17,* 881–901.

4. Ever have a headache? You may find the following article of interest.

McCrory, D. C., & Hasselblad, V. (1997). Cranial electrostimulation for headache: Meta-analysis. *Journal of Nervous and Mental Disease, 185,* 766–767.

PART EIGHT
MEASUREMENT

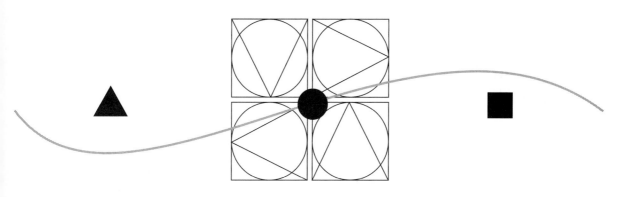

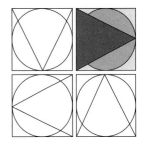

FOUNDATIONS OF MEASUREMENT

Measurement is one of the key building blocks for research. Any quantification of events, objects, places, and things involves measurement. Janda (1998) puts it aptly in the preface of his book that measurement is critical to all areas of psychology and the social sciences. All of the statistical procedures described in this book depend on measurement. Most data collection methods that eventually require some kind of quantification rely on measurement. Stevens (1951, 1968) states, "In its broadest sense, measurement is the assignment of numerals to objects or events according to rules." Stevens's definition succinctly expresses the basic nature of measurement. To understand it, however, requires the definition and explanation of each important term—a task to which this chapter is devoted.

Suppose we ask a judge to stand seven feet away from a group of students, to look at the students, and then to estimate the degree to which each of them possess five attributes: niceness, strength of character, personality, musical ability, and intelligence. The estimates are to be given numerically with a scale of numbers from 1 to

5, 1 indicating a very small amount of the characteristic in question and 5 indicating a great deal. In other words, the judge, just by looking at the students, is to assess how "nice" they are, how "strong" their characters are, and so on, using the numbers 1, 2, 3, 4, and 5 to indicate the amounts of each characteristic they possess.

This example may seem a little ridiculous, but most of us go through much the same procedure all our lives. We often judge how "nice," how "strong," how "intelligent" people are simply by looking at them and talking to them. It only seems silly when it is given as a serious example of measurement. Silly or serious, it *is* an example of measurement, since it satisfies the definition. The judge assigned numerals to "objects" according to rules. The objects, the numerals, and the rules for the assignment of the numerals to the objects were all specified. The numerals were 1, 2, 3, 4, and 5; the objects were the students; the rules for the assignment of the numerals to the objects were contained in the instructions to the judge. The end product of the work—the numerals—might then be used to calculate measures of relation, analyses of variance, and the like.

The definition of measurement includes no statement about the quality of the measurement procedure. It simply says that, somehow, numerals are assigned to objects or to events. The "somehow" is naturally important—but not to the definition. Measurement is a game we play with objects and numerals. Games have rules. It is, of course, important for other reasons that the rules be "good" rules, but whether the rules are "good" or "bad," the procedure is still measurement. Why this emphasis on the definition of measurement and on its "rule" quality? There are three reasons.

First, measurement, especially psychological and educational measurement, is misunderstood. It is not difficult to understand certain measurements used in the natural sciences—length, weight, and volume, for example. Even measures more removed from common sense can be understood without wrenching elementary intuitive notions too much. But to understand that the measurement of characteristics of individuals and groups, such as intelligence, aggressiveness, cohesiveness, and anxiety, involves *basically* and *essentially* the same thinking and general procedure is more difficult. Indeed, many say it cannot be done. Knowing and understanding that measurement is the assignment of numerals to objects or events by rule, then, helps to erase erroneous and misleading conceptions of psychological and educational measurement.

Second, the definition tells us that, if rules can be set up on some rational or empirical basis, measurement of anything is *theoretically* possible. This greatly widens the scientist's measurement horizons. The scientist will not reject the possibility of measuring some property because the property is complex and elusive. It is understood that measurement is a game that may or may not be playable with this or that property at a given time. Playing the game of measurement is never rejected even though the scientist understands the difficulties involved with it.

Third, the definition alerts us to the essential neutral core of measurement and measurement procedures and to the necessity for setting up "good" rules; rules whose virtue can be empirically tested. A measurement procedure is no better than its rules. The rules given in the example above were poor. The procedure was a measurement procedure; the definition was satisfied. But it was a poor procedure for reasons that should become apparent later.

Definition of Measurement

To repeat our definition, "measurement is the assignment of numerals to objects or events according to rules." A *numeral* is a symbol in the form: 1, 2, 3, . . . , or I, II, III. It has no quantitative meaning unless we give it such a meaning; it is simply a symbol of a special kind. It can be used to label objects, such as baseball players, billiard balls, or individuals, drawn in a sample from a universe. We could just as well use the word *symbol* in the definition. It is quite possible, even necessary, to assign symbols to objects or sets of objects according to rules. *Numeral* is used because measurement ordinarily uses numerals, which, after being assigned quantitative meaning, become numbers. A *number*, then, is a numeral that has been assigned quantitative meaning.

The term "assigned" in the definition means *mapping*. Recall that earlier we talked about mapping the objects of one set onto the objects of another set. A function, *f*, is a rule of *correspondence*. It is a rule that assigns to each member of one set some one member of another set. The members of the two sets can consist of *any* objects. In mathematics, the members are generally numbers and algebraic symbols. In research, the members of one set can be individuals, or symbols representing the individuals, and the members of the other set can be numerals or numbers. In most psychological and educational measurement, numerals and numbers are mapped onto, or assigned to, individuals. Usually, in mapping, the members of the domain are said to be mapped onto members of the range. In order to preserve consistency with the definition of measurement given above and to be able to always conceive of the measurement procedure as a function, the mapping has been turned around. This conception of mapping is also consistent with the earlier definition of a function as a rule that assigns to each member of the domain of a set some one member of the range. The rule describes how the pairs are to be ordered.

The most interesting—and difficult—work of measurement is the rule. A rule is a guide, a method, a command that tells us what to do. A mathematical rule is *f*, a function; *f* is a rule for assigning the objects of one set to the objects of another set. In measurement a rule might say: "Assign the numerals 1 through 5 to individuals according to how nice they are. If an individual is very, very nice, let the number 5 be assigned to him or her. If an individual is not at all nice, let the number 1 be assigned. Assign to individuals between these limits numbers between the limits." Another rule is one we have already met a number of times: "If an individual is male, assign him a 0. If an individual is female, assign her a 1." Of course, we would have to have a prior rule or set of rules defining male and female.

Assume that we have a set, *A*, of five persons, three women and two men: a_1, a_3, and a_4 are women; a_2 and a_5 are men. We wish to measure the variable, Sex. Assuming we have a prior rule that allows us unambiguously to determine sex, we use the rule given in the preceding paragraph: "If a person is a woman, assign 0; if a man,

◉ FIGURE 26.1

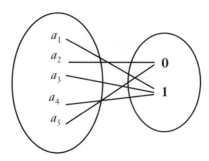

assign 1." Let 0 and 1 be a set. Call it B. Then $B = \{0, 1\}$. The measurement diagram is shown in Figure 26.1.

This procedure is the same as the one we used in Chapter 5 when discussing relations and functions. Evidently, measurement is a relation. Since to each member of A, the domain, one and only one object of B, the range, is assigned, the relation is a function. Does this mean then, that all measurement procedures are functions? Yes, they are, provided the objects being measured are considered the domain and the numerals being assigned to, or mapped onto them, are considered the range.

Here is another way to bring set, relation, function, and measurement ideas together. Recall that a relation is a set of ordered pairs. So is a function. Any measurement procedure, then, sets up a set of ordered pairs, the first member of each pair being the object measured, and the second member the numeral assigned to the object according to the measurement rule, whatever it is. We can thus write a general equation for any measurement procedure:

$$f = \{(x, y); x = \text{any object, and } y = \text{a numeral}\}$$

This is read: "The function, f, or the rule of correspondence, is equal to the set of ordered pairs (x, y) such that x is an object and each corresponding y is a numeral." This is a general rule and will fit any case of measurement.

Let us cite another example to make this discussion more concrete. The events to be measured, the xs, are five children. The numerals are the ranks 1, 2, 3, 4, and 5. Assume that f is a rule that instructs a teacher as follows: "Give the rank 1 to the child who has the greatest motivation to do schoolwork. Give the rank 2 to the child who has the next greatest motivation to do schoolwork, and so on to the rank 5, which you should give to the child with the least motivation to do schoolwork." The measurement or the function is shown in Figure 26.2.

Note that f, the rule of correspondence, might have been: "If a child has high motivation for schoolwork, give him or her a 1, but if a child has low motivation for schoolwork give him or her a 0." Then the range becomes $\{0,1\}$. This simply means

◉ FIGURE 26.2

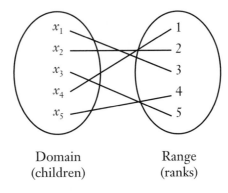

Domain
(children)

Range
(ranks)

that the set of five children has been partitioned into two subsets. Each of which will be assigned, by means of f, the numerals 0 and 1. A diagram of this resembles Figure 26.1 with the set A being the domain and the set B the range.

Returning to the rules, here is where evaluation comes into the picture. Rules may be "good" or "bad." With "good" rules we have "good," or sound, measurement, other things being equal. With "bad" rules we have "bad," or poor measurement. Many things are easy to measure because the rules are easy to draw up and follow. To measure sex is easy, for example, since several simple and fairly clear criteria can be used to determine sex and to tell the investigator when to assign 1 and when to assign 0. It is also easy to measure certain other human characteristics: hair color, eye color, height, weight. Unfortunately, most human characteristics are far more difficult to measure, mainly because it is difficult to devise clear rules that are "good." Notwithstanding, we must always have rules of some kind in order to measure anything.

Measurement and "Reality" Isomorphism

Measurement can be a meaningless business, as we have seen. How can this be avoided? The definition of sets of objects being measured, the definition of the numerical sets from which we assign numerals to the objects being measured, and the rules of assignment or correspondence have to be tied to "reality." When the hardness of objects is measured, there is little difficulty. If a substance a can scratch b (and not vice versa), then a is harder than b. Similarly, if a can scratch b, and b can scratch c, then (probably) a can scratch c. These are empirical matters that are easily tested, so that we can find a rank order of hardness. A set of objects can be measured for its hardness by a few scratch tests, and numerals can be assigned to indicate degrees of hardness. It is said that the measurement procedure and the number system are *isomorphic* to reality.

Isomorphism means identity or similarity of form. The questions asked are: Is this set of objects isomorphic to that set of objects? Are the two sets the same or similar in some formal aspect? Do the measurement procedures being used have some rational and empirical correspondence with "reality"?

To show the nature of isomorphism, we can again use the idea of the correspondence of sets of objects. We may wish to measure the *persistence* of seven individuals. Suppose, also, that there is an omniscient being. This being knows the exact amount of persistence each individual possesses; that is, it knows the "true" persistence values of each individual. (Assume that *persistence* has been adequately defined.) But *you*, the measurer, do not know these "true" values. It is necessary for you to *assess* the persistence of the individuals in some fallible way, and you think you have found such a way. For instance, you might assess persistence by giving the individuals tasks to perform and noting the total time each individual requires to complete a task, or you might note the total number of times he or she tries to do a task before turning to some other activity (Feather, 1962). You use your method and measure the persistence of the individuals. You come out with, say, the seven values 6, 6, 4, 3, 3, 2, 1. Now the omniscient being knows the "true" values. They are 8, 5, 2, 4, 3, 3, 1. This set of values is "reality." The correspondence of your set to "reality" is shown in Figure 26.3.

In two cases, you have assessed the "true" values exactly. You have "missed" all the others. Only one of these "misses," however, is serious, and there is a fair correspondence between the two rank orders of values. Note, too, that the omniscient being knew that the "true" values of persistence run from 0 through 8, whereas your measurement system only encompasses 1 through 7.

While this example is a bit fanciful, it does show in a crude way the nature of the isomorphism problem. The ultimate question to be asked of any measurement procedure is: "Is the measurement procedure isomorphic to reality?" You were not too far off in measuring persistence. The only trouble is that we rarely discover as simply as this the degree of correspondence to "reality" of our measurements. In fact, we often do not even know whether we are measuring what we are trying to measure! Despite this difficulty, scientists must test, in some manner, the isomorphism with "reality" of the measurement numbers games they play.

▣ **FIGURE 26.3**

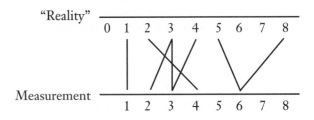

Properties, Constructs, and Indicants of Objects

We say we measure objects, but this is not quite true. We measure the properties, or the characteristics, of these objects. Even this qualification is not quite true, however. We actually measure *indicants* of the properties of objects, so that when we say we measure objects we are really saying that we measure indicants of the properties of objects. This is generally true of all science, though the properties of some natural objects are much closer to direct observation than others. For instance, the property of sex associated with animal objects is closely tied to direct observation. As soon as relatively simple physical properties are left behind for more complex and elusive properties—which are of much greater interest to social scientists and educators—direct observation of properties is impossible. Hostility cannot be directly observed, neither can morale, anxiety, intelligence, creativeness, and talent. We must always *infer* these properties or characteristics from observation of presumed indicants of the properties.

Indicant is merely a convenient word used to mean something that points to something else. If a boy continually strikes other boys, we may say his behavior is an indicant of his underlying hostility. If someone's hands sweat excessively, we may say that the person is anxious. A female child plays a Schubert impromptu beautifully; we say she has "talent." If a male child marks a certain number of objective-type items in an achievement test correctly, we say he has a certain level of achievement. In each of these cases, some identifiable behavior is an indicant of an underlying property. Obviously, we are on much shakier ground when drawing such inferences from observed behavior than when directly observing properties like hair color, size, and sex. To measure a child's cooperativeness, dependency, and imaginativeness is very different from measuring that child's height, weight, or wrist-bone development. The fundamental process of measurement is the same, but the rules are far more difficult to prescribe. Moreover, the observations of the psychological properties are much further removed from the actual properties than are those of the physical properties. This is perhaps the single greatest difficulty of psychological and educational measurement.

The indicants from which properties are inferred are specified by operational definitions, definitions that specify the activities or "operations" necessary to measure variables or constructs. A *construct* is an invented name for a property. Many constructs have been used in previous chapters: authoritarianism, achievement, social class, intelligence, persistence, and so on. The concepts or constructs under discussion are also called "latent variables." This is an important expression that is being fruitfully used in what has been called analysis of covariance structures, or so-called causal analysis. A *latent variable* is a construct, an unobserved variable, that is presumed to underlie varied behaviors, and that is used to "explain" these behaviors. "Verbal ability," "conservatism," and "anxiety," for example, are latent variables. Their use will be explained later in the book when we study factor analysis and analysis of covariance structures.

Constructs, commonly and somewhat inaccurately called variables, are defined in two general ways in science: by other constructs, and by experimental and measurement procedures. These were earlier called *constitutive* and *operational defini-tions.* An operational definition is necessary in order to measure a property or a construct. This is done by specifying the observations of the behavioral indicants of the properties.

Numerals are assigned to the behavioral indicants of properties. Then, after making observations of the indicants, the numbers (numerals) are substituted for the indicants and analyzed statistically. As an example, consider investigators who are working on the relation between intelligence and honesty. They define *intelligence* operationally as scores on an intelligence test. *Honesty* is defined operationally as observations in a contrived situation permitting pupils to cheat or not to cheat. The intelligence numerals assigned to pupils can be the total number of items correct on the test, or some other form of score. The honesty numerals assigned to pupils are the number of times they did not cheat when they could have cheated. The two sets of numbers may be correlated or otherwise analyzed. The coefficient of correlation, say, is .55, significant at the .01 level. All this is fairly straightforward and quite familiar. What is not so straightforward and familiar is this: If the investigators draw the conclusion that there is a significant positive relation between intelligence and honesty, they are taking a large inferential leap from behavior indicants in the form of marks on paper and observations of "cheating" behavior to psychological properties. That they may be mistaken should be quite obvious.

Levels of Measurement and Scaling

Levels of measurement, the scales associated with the levels, and the statistics appropriate to the levels are complex, even controversial, problems. The difficulties arise mainly from disagreement over the statistics that can be used legitimately at the different levels of measurement. The Stevens's position and definition of measurement cited earlier is a broad view that, with liberal relaxation, is followed in this text. A more restrictive—yet defensible—position requires that differences between measures be interpretable as quantitative *differences in the property measured.* "Quantitative," in the view of some experts, means that a difference in magnitude between two attribute values represents a corresponding quantitative difference in the attributes (see Jones, 1971, pp. 335–355). This view, strictly speaking, rules out, as *measurement*, nominal and ordinal scales, which we will define in the next section of this chapter. We believe that actual measurement experience in the behavioral sciences and education justifies a more relaxed position. Again, it does not matter terribly, provided the student *understands* the general ideas being presented. We recommend that the more advanced student read chapters 1 and 2 of Torgerson (1958) and Chapter 1 of Nunnally (1978). Both references give fine presentations. Comrey (1950, 1976) and Michell (1990) heavily influenced the second author's orientation to this chapter. Comrey (1976) presents an insightful essay on the fundamental measurement problem in the social and behavioral sciences. An older, outstanding treatise that has strongly influenced this text is by Guilford (1954). The curious student will enjoy the collection of articles on the controversy published in Chapter 2 of a book edited by Kirk (1972). Readers who intend doing research and who will always be faced with measurement problems should carefully and repeatedly read Nunnally's (1978) or Nunnally and Bernstein's (1994) excellent presentations of the problems and their solution.

In the ensuing discussion, we first consider the fundamental scientific and measurement problem of classification and enumeration.

Classification and Enumeration

The first and most elementary step in any measurement procedure is to define the objects of the universe of discourse. Suppose U, the universal set, is defined as all tenth-grade pupils in a certain high school. Next, the properties of the objects of U must be defined. All measurement requires that U be broken down into at least two subsets. The most elementary form of measurement would be to classify or categorize all the objects as possessing or not possessing some characteristic. Say this characteristic is maleness. We break U down into males and nonmales, or males and females. These are, of course, two *subsets* of U, or a *partitioning* of U. (Recall that partitioning a set consists of breaking it down into subsets that are *mutually exclusive* and *exhaustive*. That is, each set object must be assigned to one subset and one subset only, and all set objects in U must be so assigned.)

What we have done is to classify the objects of interest to us. We have put them into categories—we have partitioned them. The obvious simplicity of this procedure seems to cause difficulty for students. People spend much of their lives categorizing things, events, and people. Life could not go on without such categorizing, yet to associate the process with measurement seems difficult.

After a method of classification has been found, we have in effect a rule for telling which objects of U go into which classes or subsets or partitions. This rule is used and the set objects are put into the subsets. Here are the boys; here are the girls. Easy. Here are the middle-class children; here are the working-class children. Not as easy, but not too hard. Here are the delinquents; here are the nondelinquents. Harder. Here are the bright ones; here are the average ones; here are the dull ones. Much harder. Here are the creative ones: here are the noncreative ones. Very much harder.

After the objects of the universe have been classified into designated subsets, the members of the sets can be counted. In the dichotomous case, the rule for counting was given in Chapter 4. If a member of U has the characteristic in question, say *maleness*, then assign a 1. If the member does not have the characteristic, then assign a 0 (see Figure 26.1). When set members are counted in this fashion, all objects of a subset are considered to be equal to each other and unequal to the members of other subsets.

There are four general levels of measurement: nominal, ordinal, interval, and ratio. These four levels lead to four kinds of scales. Some writers on the subject admit only ordinal, interval, and ratio measurement, whereas others say that all four belong to the measurement family. Comrey and Lee (1995) feel that the nominal scale is measurement. However, it is not so much quantitative as it is in ordinal, interval, and ratio. That is, the numbers used in nominal measurement are just numeral labels attached to predefined categories. We need not be too fussy about this as long as we understand the characteristics of the different scales and levels.

Nominal Measurement

The rules used to assign numerals to objects define the kind of scale and the level of measurement. The lowest level of measurement is *nominal* measurement (see earlier discussion of categorization). The numbers assigned to objects are numerical without having a number meaning; they cannot be ordered or added. They are *labels* much like the letters used to label sets. If individuals or groups are assigned 1, 2, 3, these numerals are merely names. For example, baseball and football players are assigned such numbers. Telephones are assigned such numbers. Groups may be given the labels I, II, and III, or A_1, A_2, and A_3. We use nominal measurement in our everyday thinking and living. We identify others as "men," "women," "Protestants," "Australians," and so on. At any rate, the symbols assigned to objects, or rather, to the sets of objects, constitute nominal scales. Some experts do not believe that this is measurement, as indicated previously. But, such exclusion of nominal measurement would prevent much social scientific research procedure from being called measurement. Since the definition of measurement is satisfied, and since the members of labeled sets can be counted and compared, it would appear that nominal procedures *are* measurement.

The requirements of nominal measurement are simple. All the members of a set are assigned the same numeral, and no two sets are assigned the same numeral. Nominal measurement—at least in one simple form—was expressed in Figure 26.1, where the objects of the range, {0, 1}, were mapped onto the as, the objects of U, the five people, by the rule: "If x is male, assign 0; if x is female, assign 1." This is how nominal measurement is quantified when only a dichotomy is involved. When the partition contains more than two categories, some other method must be used. Basically, nominal measurement quantification amounts to counting the objects in the cells of the subsets or partitions.

Ordinal Measurement

Ordinal measurement requires that the objects of a set can be rank ordered on an operationally defined characteristic or property. The so-called transitivity postulate must be satisfied: If a is greater than b, and b is greater than c, then a is greater than c. Other symbols or words can be substituted for "greater than," for example, "less than," "precedes," "dominates," and so on. Most measurement in behavioral research depends on this postulate. It must be possible to assert ordinal or rank order statements like the one just used. That is, suppose we have three objects, a, b, and c, and a is greater than b, and b is greater than c. If we can also justifiably say that a is greater than c, then the main condition for ordinal measurement is satisfied. Be wary, however. A relation may seem to satisfy the transitivity postulate but may not actually do so. For example, can we always say *a* dominates *b*, and *b* dominates *c*; therefore *a* dominates *c*? Think of husband, wife, and child. Think, too, of the relations "loves," "likes," "is friendly to," or "accepts." In such cases, the researcher should demonstrate transitivity. The procedure can be generalized in three ways.

First, any number of objects of any kind can be measured ordinally simply by extension to *a*, *b*, *c*, . . . , *n*. (Even though two objects may sometimes be equal, ordinal measurement is still possible.) We simply need to be able to say $a > b > c > \ldots > n$ on some property.

The second extension consists of using combined properties or combined criteria. Instead of using only one property, we can use two or more. For example, instead of ranking a group of college students on academic achievement by grade-point averages, we may wish to rank them on the combined criteria of grade-point average and test scores. (Grade-point averages, too, are composite scores.)

The third extension is accomplished by using criteria other than "greater than." "Less than" occurs to us immediately. "Precedes," "is above," and "is superior to" may be useful criteria. In fact, we might substitute symbols other than ">" or "<." One such symbol is "*O*." It can be used to mean any operation, such as those just named, in which the transitivity postulate is satisfied: *a O b* might mean "*a* precedes *b*," or "*a* is subordinate to *b*," and *a O b O c* might mean "*a* is superior to *b*, *b* is superior to *c*, and *a* is superior to *c*."

The numerals assigned to ranked objects are called *rank values*. Let *R* equal the set of *ranked objects*: $R = \{a > b > \ldots > n\}$. Let R^* equal the set of *rank values*: $R^* = \{1, 2, \ldots, n\}$. We assign the objects of R^* to the objects of *R* as follows: the largest object is assigned 1, the next in size 2, and so on to the smallest object which is assigned the last numeral in the particular series. If this procedure is used, the rank values assigned are in the reverse order. If, for instance, there are five objects, with *a* the largest, *b* the next, through *e*, the smallest, then:

Objects	R	R*
a	1	5
b	2	4
c	3	3
d	4	2
e	5	1

Of course, one step can be skipped by assigning R^* directly: by assigning 5 to *a*, 4 to *b*, through 1 to *e*.

Ordinal numbers indicate rank order and nothing more. The numbers neither indicate absolute quantities, nor do they indicate that the intervals between the numbers are equal. For instance, it cannot be assumed that because the *numerals* are equally spaced the underlying properties they represent are also equally spaced. If two participants have the ranks 8 and 5 and two other participants the ranks 6 and 3, we cannot say that the differences between the first and second pairs are equal. There is also no way to know that any individual has none of the property being measured. Rank order scales are not equal interval scales, neither do they have absolute zero points.

Interval Measurement (Scales)

Interval or *equal interval scales* possess the characteristics of nominal and ordinal scales, especially the rank order characteristic. In addition, numerically equal distances on interval scales represent equal distances in the property being measured. Thus, suppose we had measured four objects on an interval scale and gotten the values 8, 6, 5, and 3. We can then legitimately say that the difference between the first and third objects in the property measured, $8 - 5 = 3$, is equal to the difference between the second and fourth objects, $6 - 3 = 3$. Another way to express the equal interval idea is to say that the *intervals* can be added and subtracted. An interval scale is assumed as follows:

a	b	c	d	e
1	2	3	4	5

The interval from *a* to *c* is $3 - 1 = 2$. The interval from *c* to *d* is $4 - 3 = 1$. We can add these two intervals $(3 - 1) + (4 - 3) = 2 + 1 = 3$. Now note that the interval from *a* to *d* is $4 - 1 = 3$, or expressed in an equation, $(d - a) = (c - a) + (d - c)$. If these intervals were five pupils measured on an interval scale of achievement, then the differences in achievement between pupils *a* and *c* and between *b* and *d* would be equal. We could not say, however, that the achievement of *d* was twice as great as that of pupil *b*. (Such a statement would require one higher level of measurement.) Note that it is not *quantities* or *amounts* that are added and subtracted; it is *intervals* or *distances*.

One of the best-known examples of the interval scale is the centigrade or Celsius temperature scale. This scale has an arbitrary zero point where water freezes and arbitrary number of 100 where water boils. The points in between can be divided equally using the expansion of mercury in a thermometer. Equal units along the scale represent equal amounts of expansion of mercury. Since we do not have an absolute zero point, we are unable to make the statement that 100° centigrade is twice as hot as 50° centigrade. We can say, however, that the difference or distance between 100° and 75° is the same as the difference between 50° and 25°

As Comrey (1976) mentioned, the social and behavioral sciences have a more difficult time proving equal units of measurement than the physical or natural sciences. The data collected in the social and behavioral sciences are not quite as clear cut as the data provided with temperature. What the social and behavioral sciences attempt to do is to obtain measurements that follow a normal distribution ("bell-shaped" curve). If the measuring instrument can do this, it is considered a good one from a measurement (scaling) point of view. The conversion of these measurements to standard or Z-scores will result in units that may be considered quantitatively equal. Scaling methods that use the normal curve to obtain measurements on the interval scale can at best be treated as approximations with unknown accuracy. Comrey and Lee (1995) present such a method in Chapter 5 of their book.

Ratio Measurement (Scales)

The highest level of measurement is ratio measurement, and the measurement ideal of the scientist is the ratio scale. A *ratio scale*, in addition to possessing the characteristics of nominal, ordinal, and interval scales, has an absolute or natural zero that has empirical meaning. If a measurement is zero on a ratio scale, then there is a basis for saying that some object has none of the property being measured. Since there is an absolute or natural zero, all arithmetic operations are possible, including multiplication and division. Numbers on the scale indicate the actual amounts of the property being measured. If a ratio scale of Achievement existed, then it would be possible to say that a pupil with a scale score of 8 has an Achievement twice as great as a pupil with a scale score of 4.

One of the major problems in the behavioral and social sciences is that the operation of addition cannot be defined (Comrey, 1950). Also, there are no really satisfactory substitutes for the addition operator in the social and behavioral sciences that will enable the researcher to obtain a ratio scale of measurement. There have been some scaling procedures that are complex and partially successful, but in general, the data that behavioral and social scientists work with are not even approximately ratio scale data.

Comparisons of Scales: Practical Considerations and Statistics

The basic characteristics of the four types of measurement and their accompanying scales have been discussed. What kinds of scales are used in behavioral and educational research? Mostly nominal and ordinal are used, though the probability is high that many scales and tests used in psychological and educational measurement approximate interval measurement well enough for practical purposes, as we shall see.

First, consider nominal measurement. When objects are partitioned into two, three, or more categories on the basis of group membership—sex, ethnic identification, married–single, Protestant–Catholic–Jew, and so forth—measurement is nominal. When continuous variables are converted to attributes, as when objects are divided into high–low and old–young, we have what can be called quasi-nominal measurement: although capable of at least rank order, the values are in effect collapsed to 1 and 0.

It is instructive to study the numerical operations that are, in a strict sense, legitimate with each type of measurement. With nominal measurement the counting of numbers of cases in each category and subcategory is, of course, permissible. Frequency statistics like χ^2 percentages, and certain coefficients of correlation (contingency coefficients) can be used. This sounds thin. Actually, it is a good deal. A good principle to remember is this: If one cannot use any other method, one can almost always partition or cross partition participants. If we are studying the relation between two variables and do not have any way to measure them in an ordinal or interval fashion adequately, some way can probably be found to divide the objects of study into at least two groups. For example, in studying the relation between the motivation of board of education members to become board members and their religion, as Gross, Mason, and McEachern (1958) did, we may be able to have knowledgeable judges divide the sample of board members into those with "good" motivation and those with "poor" motivation. Then we can cross partition religion with the motivation dichotomy and thus study the relation.

Intelligence, aptitude, and personality test scores are, *basically and strictly speaking,* ordinal. They indicate with more or less accuracy not the *amounts* of intelligence, aptitude, and personality traits of individuals, but rather the *rank order positions* of the individuals. To see this, we must realize that ordinal scales do not possess the desirable characteristics of equal intervals or absolute zeroes. Intelligence test scores are examples. An individual with a zero score on an intelligence measure does not necessarily have no intelligence, because there is no absolute zero on an intelligence test scale. The zero is arbitrary, and without an absolute zero, addition of *amounts* of intelligence has little meaning, since arbitrary zero points can lead to different sums. Adding two people together where each has an intelligence score of 70 is not equivalent to one person with an IQ of 140. On a scale with an absolute zero point the following addition is performed: $2 + 3 = 5$. Then the sum is 5 scale units above zero. But if the arbitrary zero point is inaccurate and the "real" zero point is at the scale position 4 scale points lower than the arbitrary zero position, then the former 2 and 3 should really be 6 and 7, and $6 + 7 = 13$!

The lack of a real zero in ordinal scales is not as serious as the lack of equal intervals. Even without a real zero, *distances* within a scale can be added, provided that these distances are equal (empirically). The situation might be somewhat as indicated in Figure 26.4. The scale on the top ("true" scale) indicates the "true" values of a variable. The bottom scale (ordinal scale) indicates the rank order scale used by an investigator. In other words, an investigator has rank ordered seven persons quite well, but his ordinal numerals, which look equal in interval, are not "true," although they may be fairly accurate representations of the empirical facts.

Strictly speaking, the statistics that can be used with ordinal scales include rank order measures such as the rank order coefficient of correlation, *r*, Kendall's *W,* and rank order analysis of variance, medians, and percentiles. If only these statistics (and others like them) are legitimate, how can statistics like *r*, *t*, and *F* be used with what are in effect ordinal measures? And they are so used, without a qualm by most researchers. One of the exceptions is Cliff (1996), who feels that social and behavioral

⊡ FIGURE 26.4

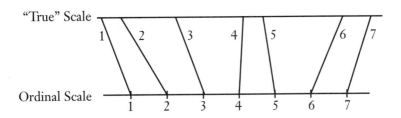

science data are ordinal at best, and as such only ordinal methods of data analysis should be used.

Although this is a moot point to some, the situation is not as difficult as it seems. As Torgerson (1958) points out, some types of natural origin have been devised for certain types of measurement. In measuring preferences and attitudes, for example, the neutral points (on either side of which are degrees of positive and negative favoring, approving, liking, and preferring) can be considered natural origins. Besides, ratio scales, while desirable, are not absolutely necessary because most of what we need to do in psychological measurement can be done with equal interval scales.

The lack of equal intervals is more serious since distances *within* a scale cannot theoretically be added without interval equality. Yet, though most psychological scales are basically ordinal, we can with considerable assurance often assume equality of interval. The argument is evidential. If we have, say, two or three measures of the same variable, and these measures are all substantially and linearly related, then equal intervals can be assumed. This assumption is valid because the more nearly a relation approaches linearity, the more nearly equal are the intervals of the scales. This also applies, at least to some extent, to certain psychological measures like intelligence, achievement, and attitude tests and scales.

A related argument is that many of the methods of analysis we use work quite well with most psychological scales. That is, the results we get from using scales and assuming equal intervals are quite satisfactory. The point of view adopted in this book is, then, a pragmatic one: that the assumption of interval equality works. Still, we are faced with a dilemma: If we use ordinal measures as though they were interval or ratio measures, we can err in interpreting data and the relations inferred from data, though the danger is probably not as grave as it has been made out to be. There is no trouble with the numbers, as numbers. They do not know the difference between ρ and r or between parametric and nonparametric statistics, neither do they know the assumptions behind their use. But we do, or should, know the differences and the consequences of ignoring the differences. On the other hand, if we abide strictly by the rules, we cut off powerful modes of measurement and analyses and are left with tools inadequate to cope with the problems we want to solve (see Nunnally, 1978; Comrey & Lee, 1995).

What is the answer, the resolution of the conflict? Part of the answer was given above: it is probable that most psychological and educational scales approximate interval equality fairly well. In those situations in which there is serious doubt as to interval equality, there are technical means for coping with some of the problems. The competent research worker should know something of scaling methods and certain transformations that change ordinal scales into interval scales (see Barlett, 1947; Guilford, 1954, chap. 8; and Li, 1957). The subject of transformations and their purposes and uses is an important one, but has not been given the attention it deserves by social and behavioral scientists. Most of the recent references on transformations have come from applied statisticians: Mosteller and Tukey (1977); Box, Hunter, and Hunter (1978); Draper and Smith (1981); Box and Draper (1987); and Jennrich (1995). Among the behavioral sciences, the following references cover this topic: Cohen and Cohen (1983), Gorsuch (1983), and Howell (1997).

In the state of measurement at present, we cannot be sure that our measurement instruments have equal intervals. It is important to ask the question: How serious are the distortions and errors introduced by treating ordinal measurements as though they were interval measurements? With care in the construction of measuring instruments, and especially with care in the interpretation of the results, the consequences are evidently not serious. The more powerful statistical methods are less dependent on the underlying scale of measurement than on the distributional properties of the data.

The best procedure would seem to be to treat ordinal measurements as though they were interval measurements, but to be constantly alert to the possibility of gross inequality of intervals. As much as possible about the characteristics of the measuring tools should be learned. Through the appropriate refinement of measurement methods and scaling procedures, data that are approximately normal in shape can be obtained. With such data, the more powerful parametric methods of statistical analysis can be used. The researcher needs to be aware that it is still incorrect to ignore the scaling properties of data. For example, it would be inappropriate for a researcher to interpret a group with a mean of 50 to be twice as big as a group that had a mean of 25. Much useful information has been obtained by treating ordinal data as interval, with resulting scientific advances in psychology, sociology, and education. In short, it is unlikely that researchers will be led seriously astray by heeding this advice, if they are careful in applying it. For a useful review of the literature on the problem of scales of measurement and statistics, read Gardner (1975) or Michell (1990).

CHAPTER SUMMARY

1. Measurement is an important component of research.
2. Without measurement or quantification of information, many methods of statistical analysis cannot be used.
3. Stevens defines measurement as the process of assigning numbers to objects and events according to some rule.
4. Stevens defines four sets of rules: nominal, ordinal, interval, and ratio.

5. Most behavioral and social science data are ordinal. However, through certain scaling methods and assumptions, it can be considered as interval scaled data.

6. Comrey states that an important consideration is that behavioral science data can be considered as interval if the measurement process produces data that follow a normal distribution.

7. Measurement involves an isomorphism between numbers and reality.

8. The argument continues as to which is the better way to handle social and behavioral science data.

STUDY SUGGESTIONS

1. What is the first step in measurement?

2. According to Stevens, what are the rules that are a part of the measurement process?

3. Give an example from science or everyday life that illustrates ordinal measurement.

4. An interesting paper written many years ago by Prokasy (1962) is still relevant with today's argument about using parametric methods on ordinal data. Read Prokasy's article and then read Cliff's (1996) Chapter 1.

5. Read F. M. Lord's article on the statistical treatment of football numbers (in Kirk, 1972). This article humorously describes how some people view and use numbers. Can numbers from a nominal scale be added together?

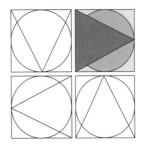

After assigning numerals to objects or events according to rules, we must face two major problems of measurement: reliability and validity. We have devised a measurement system and have administered the measuring instruments to a group of participants. We must now ask and answer the questions: What is the reliability of the measuring instrument? What is its validity?

If one does not know the reliability and validity of one's data, little faith can be put in the results obtained and the conclusions drawn from the results. These are two key psychometric properties that must be satisfied in order to answer the many criticisms leveled at social and behavioral science data and measuring methods. The data of the social sciences and education, derived from human behavior and human products, are, as we saw in Chapter 26, some steps removed from the properties of scientific interest. Thus their validity can be questioned. Concern for reliability comes from the necessity for dependability in measurement. The data of all psychological and educational measurement instruments contain errors of measurement. To the extent that they do so, the data they yield will not be dependable.

641

Definitions of Reliability

Synonyms for reliability are *dependability*, *stability*, *consistency*, *reproducibility*, *predictability* and *lack of distortion*. Reliable people, for instance, are those whose behavior is consistent, dependable, predictable—what they do tomorrow and next week will be consistent with what they do today and what they have done last week. They are stable, we say. Unreliable people, on the other hand, are those whose behavior is much more variable. They are unpredictably variable. Sometimes they do this, sometimes that. They lack stability. We say they are inconsistent.

So it is with psychological and educational measurements: they are more or less variable from occasion to occasion. They are stable and relatively predictable or they are unstable and relatively unpredictable; they are consistent or not consistent. If they are reliable, we can depend on them. If they are unreliable, we cannot depend on them.

It is possible to approach the definition of reliability in three ways. One approach is epitomized by the question: If we measure the same set of objects again and again with the same or comparable measuring instrument, will we get the same or similar results? This question implies a definition of reliability in *stability*, *dependability*, and *predictability* terms. It is the definition most often given in elementary discussions of the subject.

A second approach is epitomized by the question: Are the measures obtained from a measuring instrument the "true" measures of the property measured? This is a *lack of distortion* definition. Compared to the first definition, it is further removed from common sense and intuition, but it is also more fundamental. These two approaches or definitions can be summarized in the words *stability* and *lack-of-distortion*. As we will see later, however, the lack of distortion definition implies the stability definition. By reliability we mean the degree to which the measurement agrees with itself. In Chapter 28 we will be dealing with validity. The terms "reliability" and "validity" are often confused, but there is a clear distinction between them. Reliability has nothing to do with the truthfulness of the measurement. Some authors have referred to reliability as accuracy (see Magnusson, 1967; Tuckman, 1975). This is true, but it is often confused with what is meant as accuracy in terms of validity. Validity also deals with accuracy but in a way that differs from reliability. Reliability is concerned with the accuracy with which a measuring instrument measures whatever it measures. The keyword here is "whatever." If we have a test that we feel measures math ability, we really don't know if the test really measures math ability. If the test is highly reliable, we only know that it is measuring "something" accurately. To be sure that the math ability test actually measures math ability, we would be dealing with validity issues.

There is a third approach to the definition of reliability, an approach that not only helps us better define and solve both theoretical and practical problems, but also implies other approaches and definitions. We can inquire how much *error of measurement* there is in a measuring instrument. Recall that there are two general types of variance: systematic and random. *Systematic variance* leans in one direction—scores tend to be all positive or all negative or all high or all low. Error in this case is constant or biased. *Random* or *error variance* is self-compensating—scores tend now to lean this way, now that way. Errors of measurement are random errors. They are the sum of a number of causes. Among the causes are the ordinary random or chance elements present in all measures due to unknown causes, temporary or momentary fatigue, fortuitous conditions at a particular time that temporarily affect the object measured or the measuring instrument, fluctuations of memory or mood, and other factors that are temporary and shifting. To the extent that errors of measurement are present in a measuring instrument, the instrument is unreliable. In other words, reliability can be defined as the relative absence of errors of measurement in a measuring instrument.

Reliability is the *lack of distortion* or *precision* of a measuring instrument. Remember, a highly reliable measure only tells us that it is measuring something precisely or consistently. It may not be measuring what we think it is measuring. An example to illustrate this is the weight scale we have in our homes. Let's say this weight scale always overestimates a person's weight by 10 pounds. If you got on this scale 50 times over a period of 1 hour, you will find very little fluctuation in the weight registered on the scale. This weight scale is precise in the sense that it consistently gives you the same weight. However, it is inaccurate in that it always gives the wrong weight by 10 pounds. This weight scale would be deemed reliable but not valid.

Suppose a sportsman wishes to compare the precision of two guns. One is an old piece made a century ago but still in good condition. The other is a modern weapon made by an expert gunsmith. Both pieces are solidly fixed in granite bases and aimed and zeroed in by a sharpshooter. Equal numbers of rounds are fired with each gun. In Figure 27.1, the hypothetical pattern of shots on a target for each gun is shown. The target on the left represents the pattern of shots produced by the older gun. Observe that the shots are considerably scattered. Now observe that the pattern of shots on the target on the right is more closely packed. The shots are closely clustered around the bull's-eye.

Let us assume that numbers have been assigned to the circles of the targets: 3 to the bull's-eye, 2 to the next circle, 1 to the outside circle, and 0 to any shot outside the target. It is obvious that if we calculated measures of variability, say a standard deviation, from the two shot patterns, the old rifle would have a much larger measure of variability than the newer rifle. These measures can be considered reliability indices. The smaller variability measure of the new rifle indicates much less error, and thus much greater accuracy. The new rifle is reliable; the old rifle is less reliable.

Now, consider Figure 27.2. Here we have the same pattern of shots from both rifles but they are not centered on the target as in Figure 27.1. The new rifle would still be considered more reliable than the old rifle. But since both are off target the aim is not accurate. Here, the precision of the rifles' shot patterns measures reliability while the accuracy of the aim of the rifles measures validity. Figure 27.1 is a crude way of demonstrating reliability with validity; Figure 27.2 demonstrates reliability with low or no validity. It is possible to have reliability without validity, but not the other way around. Reliability by itself is of little use in evaluating most measurements. As seen above, a measurement can be consistently wrong. It is no guarantee

回 FIGURE 27.1

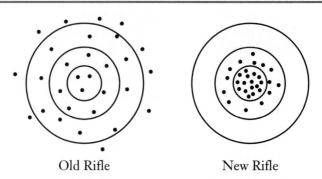

Old Rifle   New Rifle

that the measurement instrument is any good. However, the absence of high reliability does indicate the measurement instrument is a poor one.

Similarly, psychological and educational measurements have greater and lesser reliabilities. A measuring instrument, say an arithmetic achievement test, is given to a group of children—usually only once. Our goal, of course, is a multiple one: we seek to hit the "true" score of each child. To the extent that we miss the "true" scores, our measuring instrument, our test, is unreliable. The "true," the "real," arithmetic scores of five children, say, are 35, 31, 29, 22, 14. Another researcher does not know these "true" scores. The obtained results are 37, 30, 26, 24, 15. While not a single case hit the "true" score, they all have the same rank order. This researcher's reliability and precision are surprisingly high.

回 FIGURE 27.2

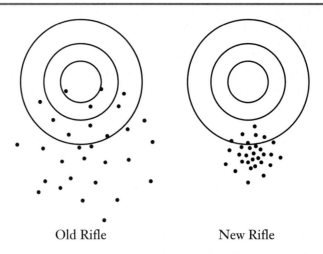

Old Rifle   New Rifle

▣ TABLE 27.1 *"True," Reliable, and Unreliable Obtained Test Scores and Rank Orders of Five Children*

(1) "True" Scores	(Rank)	(2) Scores from Reliable Test	(Rank)	(3) Scores from Unreliable Test	(Rank)
35	(1)	37	(1)	24	(4)
31	(2)	30	(2)	37	(1)
29	(3)	26	(3)	26	(3)
22	(4)	24	(4)	15	(5)
14	(5)	15	(5)	30	(2)

Suppose that the five scores had been 24, 37, 26, 15, 30. These are the same five scores, but they have a very different rank order. In this case, the test would be unreliable because of its lack of precision. To demonstrate this more compactly, the three sets of scores, with their rank orders, have been set beside each other in Table 27.1. The rank orders of the first and second columns covary exactly. The rank order coefficient of correlation is 1.00. Even though the test scores of the second column are not the exact scores, they are in the same rank order. On this basis, using a rank order coefficient of correlation, the test is reliable. The rank order coefficient of correlation between the ranks of the first and third columns, however, is zero, so that the latter test is completely unreliable.

Theory of Reliability

The example given in Table 27.1 epitomizes what we need to know about reliability. The treatment of reliability in this chapter is based on classical test theory. There is a much more advanced treatment of reliability by Cronbach, Gleser, Nanda, and Rajaratnam (1972) called generalizability theory. In this chapter we will deal with the more traditional approach to reliability. To do this, it is necessary to formalize the intuitive notions and to outline a theory of reliability. This theory is not only conceptually elegant, it is also practically powerful. It helps to unify measurement ideas and supplies a foundation for understanding various analytic techniques. The theory also ties in nicely with the variance approach emphasized in earlier discussions.

Any set of measures has a total variance; that is, after administering an instrument to a set of objects and obtaining a set of numbers (scores), we can calculate a mean, a standard deviation, and a variance. Let us be concerned here only with the variance. The variance, as seen earlier, is a total obtained variance, since it includes variances due to several causes. In general, any *total obtained variance* (or sum of squares) includes systematic and error variances.

Each person has an obtained score, X_t. (The "t" represents "total.") Some authors would refer to this as the observed score. It is sometimes just written as "O" or X_o. This would be the measurement we take on an object, person, thing, or event. This observed score has two components: a "true" component, and an error component. We assume that each person has a "true" score, X_∞. (The "∞" is the infinity sign, and is used to signify "true.") An alternative symbol that the reader may see in the literature is T or X_T. This score would be known only to an omniscient being because the measurement system is imperfect. Also note what was stated previously. The true score may include properties other than the property we want to measure. The problem of measuring that property is one of validity. The other component is the error score, X_e or E; error, in this case, does not mean a mistake has been made. Rather, the error score is some increment or decrement resulting from several of the factors responsible for not being able to measure the true score. For example, a student may have an obtained score less than the "true" score because that person was ill the day of the examination. Hence, one can state that the difference between the true and obtained score is error. Some errors are accountable, others are not.

This reasoning leads to a simple equation basic to the theory:

$$X_t = X_\infty + X_e$$

or

$$X_o = X_T + X_e$$

or

$$O = T + E$$

This states, succinctly, that any obtained score is made of two components: a "true" component, and an error component. The only part of this definition that gives any real trouble is X_∞, which can be conceived to be the score an individual would obtain if all internal and external conditions were "perfect" and the measuring instrument was "perfect." A bit more realistically, it can be considered to be the mean of a large number of administrations of the test to the same person. Symbolically, $X_\infty = (X_1 + X_2 + \ldots + X_n)/n$. Lord and Novick (1968) call the "true" score the expected value of an observed score, which can be interpreted as the average score an individual would obtain if an infinite number of independent repeated measurements are taken on an individual. Consider the following. If we wanted to know our height, we can measure ourselves one time. Will this give us our "true" height? Unlikely, since the measurement device is fallible. Hence we would be better off if we took multiple measurements of our height and then computed the mean of the heights. This mean would be closer to our true height than any of the measurements taken alone. If the number of measurements approach infinity, the mean will get closer and closer to the true height.

With a little simple algebra, Equation 27.1 can be extended to yield a more useful equation in variance terms:

$$V_T = V_\infty + V_E \qquad\qquad \textbf{(27.2)}$$

or

$$V_O = V_T + V_e$$

Equation 27.2 shows that the total obtained variance of a test is made up of two variance components: a "true" component, and an "error" component. If, for example, it were possible to administer the same instrument to the same group 4,367,929 times, and then to calculate the means of each person's 4,367,929 scores, we would have a set of "nearly true" measures of the group. In other words, these means are the X_∞s of the group. We could then calculate the variance of the X_∞s yielding V_∞. This value must always be less than V_t or V_o, the variance calculated from the obtained set of original scores, (the X_ts or Os), because the original scores contain error. However, the "true," or "nearly true," scores have no error, the error having been washed out by the averaging process. Put differently, if there were no errors of measurement in the X_ts or Os, then $V_t = V_\infty$ or $V_o = V_T$. But, there are always errors of measurement, and we assume that if we knew the error scores and subtracted them from the obtained scores we would obtain the "true" scores.

We never know the "true" scores, neither do we really ever know the error scores. Nevertheless, it is possible to estimate the error variance. By so doing, we can, in effect, substitute in Equation 27.2 and solve the equation. This is the essence of the idea, even though certain assumptions and steps have been omitted from the discussion. A diagram may show the ideas more clearly. Let the total variances of two tests be represented by two bars. One test is highly reliable; the other test only moderately so, as shown in Figure 27.3. Tests A and B have the same total variance, but 90% of Test A is "true" variance and 10% is error variance. Only 60% of Test B is "true" variance and 40% is error variance. Test A is thus much more reliable than Test B.

🔲 **FIGURE 27.3**

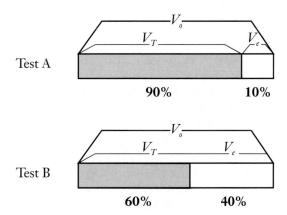

Reliability is defined, so to speak, through error: the more error, the greater the unreliability; the less error, the greater the reliability. Practically speaking, this means that if we can estimate the error variance of a measure we can also estimate the measure's reliability. This brings us to two equivalent definitions of reliability:

1. Reliability is the proportion of the "true" variance to the total obtained variance of the data yielded by a measuring instrument.
2. Reliability is the proportion of error variance to the total variance yielded by a measuring instrument subtracted from 1.00, the index 1.00 indicating perfect reliability.

It is easier to write these definitions in equation form:

$$r_{tt} = \frac{V_{\infty}}{V_t} = \frac{V_T}{V_o} \tag{27.3}$$

$$r_{tt} = 1 - \frac{V_e}{V_t} = 1 - \frac{V_e}{V_o} \tag{27.4}$$

where r_{tt} is the reliability coefficient and the other symbols are as defined before. Equation 27.3 is theoretical and cannot be used for calculation. Equation 27.4 is both theoretical and practical. It can be used both to conceptualize the idea of reliability and to estimate the reliability of an instrument. An alternate equation to (27.4) is:

$$r_{tt} = \frac{V_t - V_e}{V_t} = \frac{V_o - V_e}{V_o} \tag{27.5}$$

This alternate definition of reliability will be useful in helping us to understand what reliability is.

Two Computational Examples

To show the nature of reliability, two examples are given in Table 27.2. One, labeled I in the table, is an example of high reliability; the other, labeled II, is an example of low reliability. Note carefully that exactly the same numbers are used in both cases. The only difference is that they are arranged differently. The situation in both cases is this: five individuals have been administered a test of four items. (This is unrealistic, of course, but will do to illustrate several points.) The data of the five individuals are given in the rows; the sums of the individuals are given to the right of the rows (Σ_t). The sums of the items are given at the bottom of each table (Σ_{tt}). In addition, the sums of the individuals on the odd items (Σ_{odd}) and the sums of the individuals on the even items (Σ_{eve}) are given on the extreme right of each subtable. The calculations necessary for two-way analyses of variance are given below the data tables.

To make the examples more realistic, imagine that the data are scores on a 6-point scale, say attitudes toward school. A high score means a high favorable attitude, a low score a low favorable (or unfavorable) attitude. (It makes no difference, however, what the scores are. They can even be 1s and 0s resulting from marking items of an achievement test: right equals 1, and wrong equals 0.) In I, Individual 1 has a high favorable attitude toward school, whereas Individual 5 has a low favorable attitude toward school. These are readily indicated by the sums of the individuals (or the means): 21 and 5. These sums (Σ_t) are the usual scores yielded by tests. For instance, if we wanted to know the mean of the group, we would calculate it as $(21 + 18 + 14 + 10 + 5)/5 = 13.60$.

The variance of these sums provides one of the terms of equations 27.4 and 27.5, but not the other: V_t, but not V_e. By using the analysis of variance it is possible to calculate both V_t and V_e. The analyses of variance of I and II show how this is done. These calculations need not occupy us long, since they are subsidiary to the main issue.

The analysis of variance yields the variances: Between Items, Between Individuals, and Residual or Error. The F-ratios for Items are not significant in I or II. (Note that both mean squares are 2.27. Obviously they must be equal, since they are calculated from the same sums at the bottoms of the two subtables.) Actually, we are not interested in these variances—we only want to remove the variance due to items from the total variance. Our interest lies in the Individual variances and in the Error variances, which are circled in the subtables. The total variance of equations 27.3, 27.4, and 27.5 is interesting because it is an index of differences between individuals. It is a measure of individual differences. Instead of writing V_t, then, let us write V_{ind}, meaning the variance resulting from individual differences. By using either (27.4) or (27.5), we obtain reliability coefficients of .92 for the data of I, and .45 for the data of II. The hypothetical data of I are reliable; those of II are not as reliable.

By Equation 27.4:

$$r_{tt} = 1 - \frac{V_e}{V_{ind}} = 1 - \frac{.81}{10.08} = .92 \quad r_{tt} = 1 - \frac{2.60}{4.70} = .45$$

By Equation 27.5:

$$r_{tt} = \frac{V_{ind} - V_e}{V_{ind}} = \frac{10.08 - 0.81}{10.08} = .92 \quad r_{tt} = \frac{4.70 - 2.60}{4.70} = .45$$

Odd–Even:

$$r_{tt} = .91 \qquad r_{tt} = .32$$

Perhaps the best way to understand this is to return to Equation 27.3. Now we write $r_{tt} = V_\infty/V_{ind}$. If we had a direct way to calculate V_∞, we could quickly calculate r_{tt}, but as we saw before, we do not have a direct way. There is a way to estimate it, however. If we can find a way to estimate V_e the error variance, the problem is solved

▣ **TABLE 27.2** *Demonstration of Reliability and Computation of Reliability Coefficients (hypothetical examples)*

	I: $r_{tt} = .92$							II: $r_{tt} = .45$						
	Items								**Items**					
Individuals	**a**	**b**	**c**	**d**	Σ_t	Σ_{odd}	Σ_{eve}	**Individuals**	**a**	**b**	**c**	**d**	Σ_t	Σ_{odd}	Σ_{eve}
1	6	6	5	4	21	11	10	1	6	4	5	1	16	11	5
2	4	6	5	3	18	9	9	2	4	1	5	4	14	9	5
3	4	4	4	2	14	8	6	3	4	6	4	2	16	8	8
4	3	1	4	2	10	7	3	4	3	6	4	3	16	7	9
5	1	2	1	1	5	2	3	5	1	2	1	2	6	2	4
Σ_{tt}	18	19	19	12	$\Sigma X_t = 68$			Σ_{tt}	18	19	19	12	$\Sigma X_t = 68$		
					$(\Sigma X_t)^2 = 4624$								$(\Sigma X_t)^2 = 4624$		
					$\Sigma X_t^2 = 288$								$\Sigma X_t^2 = 288$		

$$C = \frac{(68)^2}{20} = 231.20 \qquad\qquad\qquad C = \frac{(68)^2}{20} = 231.20$$

Total = $288 - 231.20 = 56.80$ $\qquad\qquad$ Total = 56.80

Between Items = $\dfrac{1190}{5} - 231.20 = 6.80$ $\qquad\qquad$ Between Items = 6.80

Between Individuals = $\dfrac{1086}{4} - 231.2$ $\qquad\qquad$ Between Individuals = $\dfrac{1000}{4} - 231.20$

$\qquad\qquad\qquad\qquad = 40.30$ $\qquad\qquad\qquad\qquad\qquad\qquad = 18.80$

Source	df	ss	ms	F	Source	df	ss	ms	F
Items	3	6.80	2.27	2.80 (n.s.)	Items	3	6.80	2.27	1 (n.s.)
Individual	4	40.30	(10.08)	12.44 (.001)	Individuals	4	18.80	(4.70)	1.81 (n.s.)
Residual	12	9.70	(0.81)		Residual	12	31.20	(2.60)	
Total	19	56.80			Total	19	56.80		

because V_e can be subtracted from V_{ind} to yield an estimate of V_∞. Obviously, we can ignore V_∞ and subtract the proportion V_e/V_{ind} from 1 and get r_{tt}. This is a perfectly acceptable way to calculate r_{tt} and to conceptualize reliability. Reasoning from $V_{ind} - V_e$ is perhaps more fruitful and ties in nicely with our earlier discussion of components of variance.

We stated in Chapter 13 that each statistical problem has a total amount of variance and each variance source contributes to this total variance. We translate the reasoning of Chapter 13 to the present problem. In random samples of the same population, V_e and V_w should be statistically equal. But, if V_b, the between-groups variance, is significantly greater than V_w, the within-groups (error) variance, then there is something in V_e over and above chance. That is, V_e includes the variance of V_w and, in addition, some systematic variance.

Similarly, we can say that if V_{ind} is significantly greater than V_e, then there is something in V_{ind} over and above error variance. This excess of variance would seem to be due to individual differences in whatever is being measured. Measurement aims at the "true" scores of individuals. When we say that reliability is the precision of a measuring instrument, we mean that a reliable instrument more or less measures the "true" scores of individuals, the "more or less" depending on the reliability of the instrument. That "true" scores are measured can be inferred only from the "true" *differences* between individuals, although neither of these can of course, be directly measured. What we do is to infer the "true" differences from the fallible, empirical, measured differences, which are always to some extent corrupted by errors of measurement.

Now, if there is some way to remove from V_{ind} the effect of errors of measurement, some way to free V_{ind} of error, we can solve the problem easily. We simply subtract V_e from V_{ind} to get an estimate of V_∞. Then the proportion of the "pure" variance to all the variance, "pure" and "impure," is the estimate of the reliability of the measuring instrument. To summarize symbolically:

$$r_{tt} = \frac{V_\infty}{V_{ind}} = \frac{V_{ind} - V_e}{V_{ind}} = 1 - \frac{V_e}{V_{ind}}$$

The actual calculations are given at the bottom of Table 27.2.

Returning to the data of Table 27.2, let us see if we can "see" the reliability of I and the unreliability of II. Look first at the columns where the totals of the individuals are recorded (Σ_t). Note that the sums of I have a greater range than those of II: $21 - 5 = 16$ and $16 - 6 = 10$. Given the same individuals, the more reliable a measure the greater the range of the sums of the individuals. Think of the extreme: A completely unreliable instrument would yield sums that are like the sums yielded by random numbers and, of course, the reliability of random numbers is approximately zero. (The nonsignificant F-ratio for Individuals, 1.81, in II indicates that $r_{tt} = .45$ is not statistically significant.)

Now examine the rank orders of the values under the items, *a*, *b*, *c*, and *d*. In I, all four rank orders are about the same. Apparently, each item of the attitude scale is measuring the same thing. To the extent that the individual items yield the same rank orders of individuals, the test is reliable. The items hang together, so to speak. They are internally consistent. Also, note that the rank orders of the items of I are about the same as the rank order of the sums.

The rank orders of the item values of II are quite different. The rank orders of *a* and *c* agree very well; they are the same as those of I. The rank orders of *a* and *b*, *a* and d, b and d, and c and d, however, do not agree very well. Either the items are measuring different things, or they are not measuring very consistently. This lack of congruence of rank orders is reflected in the totals of the individuals. Although the rank order of these totals is similar to the rank order of the totals of I, the range or variance is considerably less, and there is lack of spread between the sums (for example, the three 16s).

We conclude our consideration of these two examples by considering certain figures in Table 27.2 not considered before. On the right-hand side of both I and II the sums of the odd items (Σ_{odd}) and the sums of the even items (Σ_{eve}) are given. Simply add the values of odd items across the rows: $a+c$: $6 + 5 = 11$, $4 + 5 = 9$, $4 + 4 = 8$, and so forth, in I. Then also add the values of the even items in I: $b + d$: $6 + 4 = 10$, $6 + 3 = 9$, and so forth. If there were more items, for example, a, b, c, d, e, f, g, then we would add: $a + c + e + g$ for the odd sums, and $b + d + f$ for the even sums. To calculate the reliability coefficient, calculate the product-moment correlation between the odd sums and the even sums, and then correct the resulting coefficient with the Spearman–Brown formula. The sums of both the odd and the even items are, of course, the sums of only half the items in a test. They are therefore less reliable than the sums of all the items. The Spearman–Brown formula corrects the odd–even coefficient (and other part coefficients) for the lesser number of items used in calculating the coefficient. (More on this in a latter section of this chapter. One can also consult a number of good test and measurement books such as Anastasi & Urbina, 1997; Brown, 1983; Friedenberg, 1995; or Sax, 1997). The odd–even r_{tt}s for I and II are .91 and .32, respectively; fairly close to the analysis of variance results of .92 and .45. (With more participants and more items, the estimates will ordinarily be close.)

This simple operation may seem mystifying. To see that this is a variation of the same variance and rank order theme, let us first note the rank order of the sums of the two examples. The rank orders of Σ_{odd} and Σ_{eve} are almost the same in I, but quite different in II. The reasoning is the same as before. Evidently, the items are measuring the same thing in I, but in II the two sets of items are not consistent. To reconstruct the variance argument, remember that by adding the sum of the odd items to the sum of the even items for each person the total sum, or $\Sigma_{odd} + \Sigma_{eve} = \Sigma_{t}$, is obtained.

The Interpretation of the Reliability Coefficient

If r, the coefficient of correlation, is squared, it becomes a coefficient of determination. It gives us the proportion or percentage of the variance shared by two variables. If $r = .90$, then the two variables share $(.90)^2 = 81\%$ of the total variance of the two variables in common. The reliability coefficient is also a coefficient of determination. Theoretically, it tells how much variance of the total variance of a measured variable is "true" variance. If we had the "true" scores and could correlate them with the scores of the measured variable, and square the resulting coefficient of correlation, we would obtain the reliability coefficient.

Symbolic representation may make this clear. Let $r_{t\infty}$ be the coefficient of correlation between the obtained scores and the "true" scores, X_∞. The reliability coefficient is defined:

$$r_{tt} = (r_{t\infty})^2 \tag{27.6}$$

Although it is not possible to calculate $r_{t\infty}$ directly, it is helpful to understand the rationale of the reliability coefficient in these theoretical terms. The correlation of the true score with the observed score is often referred to as the *index of reliability*.

Since a true score is something that exists but cannot be measured, obviously the index of reliability cannot be computed directly. As a result, the reliability coefficient cannot be obtained directly, at least through this approach. However, there are several ways that the reliability of measurements can be computed. Magnusson (1967) refers to these as practical methods for estimating reliability. The first of these involves administering the same measurement instrument to the same group of people on two different occasions. The time spread between occasions depends on the type of measurement and the purpose of the measurements. Usually, the time interval between occasions is chosen so that sufficient decay of memory for the responses occurs. The proper execution of this procedure leads to two measurements per person. These measurements, which occur in pairs, are used in a formula to compute the correlation. This correlation between scores on occasion 1 and occasion 2 is called the *test–retest reliability*. Its use is to measure the stability over time. This is not a good way of computing the reliability coefficient if attrition is high or the organisms being measured will be going through a dramatic developmental change between time period 1 and time period 2. If the measuring instrument is a vocabulary test, test–retest reliability may not be fruitful if the test is given to children on two or more occasions that are exposed to an educational environment where their vocabulary grows rapidly. Another theoretical interpretation is to conceive that each X_∞ can be the mean of a large number of X_ts derived from administering the test to an individual a large number of times, other things being equal. The idea behind this notion has been explained before. The first administration of the test yields, say, a certain rank order of individuals. If the second, third, and further measurings all tend to yield approximately the same rank order, then the test is reliable. This is a stability or test–retest interpretation of reliability.

Another method one can use to compute the reliability coefficient is to develop two *equivalent* or *parallel forms* of the measurement instrument. In testing, this would be creating two forms of the test. These two forms would be equivalent but not identical. They would be composed of similar items possibly from the same pool of items. Each person would be subjected to measurements by both instruments. As a result, each person would then have two scores and, again, the pairs of scores would be used in a correlation formula to compute the correlation. This correlation would be referred to as a parallel or equivalent form of reliability. This method has the advantage of minimizing attrition. Also, we won't have to worry too much about whether the people being measured will remember their responses. However, parallel forms do have some problems. For one it requires the researcher to create two forms of the test. These two tests would need to have mean and standard deviation scores that are statistically equivalent. Also, the desired procedure would require that the people being measured would have to be subjected to measurements for a longer period of time and as such could suffer from fatigue and boredom. If so, this would affect their performance on the later items and could contribute to lowering the reliability coefficient.

The third category for computing the reliability coefficient is called *internal consistency*. There are several approaches to internal consistency. Each approach depends on certain assumptions that can be made about the measurements. The first is called *split-half reliability*; the second is called *coefficient alpha*, and the third is called the *Kuder–Richardson formulas 20 and 21* (KR-20, KR-21). Although we will use the word *test* in the following discussion to designate the measurement instrument, it doesn't necessarily have to be a test per se. As we briefly mentioned and demonstrated earlier, the split-half reliability involves dividing the test into two halves. The goal is to obtain two equal or equivalent halves. This can be accomplished by either summing together all the responses on the items in the first half or summing all the item responses in the second half. If the items are all homogeneous, the two halves would be equal. If our test starts with easier items and progresses to more difficult ones, then the method previously mentioned will not be effective in producing equal halves. The recommended method here would be to sum all of the responses for the odd-numbered items to create one total, and then to sum all of the responses for the even-numbered items for the other total. In either case above, each person will have two half-sum scores. These scores are correlated using our standard formula. The resulting correlation would be termed "split-half reliability." As demonstrated in Magnusson (1967), Allen and Yen (1979), and the classical work by Gullikson (1950) with homogeneous items, the longer the test (more items) the higher the reliability; the shorter the test (fewer items) the lower the reliability. With the split-half reliability method, we are no longer talking about a full-length test reliability: the split-half reliability will underestimate the true reliability since it is now the correlation of two halves of the test. When using the split-half reliability, we need to use one of three formulas to estimate the full-length reliability of the test based on half-length values.

One such formula is the Spearman–Brown Prophecy formula. The Spearman–Brown Prophecy formula has other uses besides split-half. Using this formula along with the assumption that the halves are equal, an estimate of the full-length reliability can be computed. The formula for the Spearman–Brown is

$$r'_{tt} = \frac{nr_{tt}}{1 + (n - 1)r_{tt}}$$

For the split-half, n is set equal to 2. The r_{tt} is the split-half reliability and r'_{tt} is the estimated full-length reliability.

The other two formulas are different in appearance but both have the same goal. Before describing them, let us reiterate that the Spearman–Brown formula can be applied to other reliability situations (see Anastasi & Urbina, 1997). Also, it could be used when the researcher is relatively sure that the two halves are equal. If there is any doubt about the homogeneity of the halves, Spearman–Brown should not be used since it will overestimate the full-length reliability. Instead, one should either use the Rulon formula or the Guttman formula (Magnusson, 1967). Both of these take into account the differences between the halves. Both the Rulon and Guttman formulas estimate the full-length reliability without the use of the split-half reliability.

The Rulon formula is

$$r_{tt} = 1 - \frac{V_d}{V_t} = 1 - \frac{V_{(a-b)}}{V_t}$$

and the Guttman formula is

$$r_{tt} = 2\left[1 - \frac{(V_a + V_b)}{V_t}\right]$$

where a is for the first half-total scores and b is the second half-total scores. V_d is the variance of the difference scores ($d = a - b$), V_t is the variance of the total scores ($t = a + b$). V_a is the variance of one of the half-total scores and V_b is the variance of the other half-total scores.

To summarize, the test items are considered homogeneous. This interpretation in effect boils down to the same idea as other interpretations: precision. Take any random sample of items from the test, and any other random and different sample of items for the test. Treat each sample as a separate subtest. Each individual will then have two scores: one X_t for one subsample and another X_t for the other subsample. Correlate the two sets, continuing the process indefinitely. The average intercorrelation of the subsamples (corrected by the Spearman–Brown formula) shows the test's internal consistency. But this really means that each subsample—if the test is reliable—succeeds in producing approximately the same rank order of individuals. If it does not, the test is not reliable.

The split-half reliability is based on two halves that are usually considered as equivalent or parallel. If we develop this concept further by considering each item as a separate parallel test, we can derive some of the measures of reliability that are commonly found in the psychological and educational research literature. In 1937, Kuder and Richardson developed this idea, which resulted in two of the most often used reliability formulas for internal consistency: KR-20 and KR-21. They are numbered as such because the KR-20 was the twentieth equation in their paper and the KR-21 was the twenty-first equation. Both equations assume that every item has the same mean and variance. The Kuder–Richardson formulas are applicable to measuring instruments (e.g., tests) with a dichotomous or binary or answering scoring system. An example of dichotomous scoring is items that are scored as either correct (1) or incorrect (0). Tests with true–false responses are also considered a dichotomous scoring system. If we let p_i stand for the proportion of test takers who answer item-i

correctly (or answer item as "true") then q_i is the proportion that answer item i incorrectly (or answered "false"). k is the number of items on the test. With this information, the KR-20 formula looks like:

$$r_{tt} = \frac{k}{k-1}\left(\frac{V_t - \sum p_i q_i}{V_t}\right)$$

If we assume that every item has the same p_i and q_i then the $\sum p_i q_i$ can be replaced by $kp_i q_i$. In doing this we arrive at KR-21.

$$r_{tt} = \frac{k}{k-1}\left(\frac{V_t - kp_i q_i}{V_t}\right)$$

which can be further simplified to:

$$r_{tt} = \frac{k}{k-1}\left(1 - \frac{Mk - M^2}{kV_t}\right)$$

where k is the number of items and M is the mean of the total scores. Essentially, KR-21 is a special case of KR-20 where the $p_i q_i$ (also known as item difficulties or endorsement) are equal. If a researcher wants to obtain the most conservative estimate of reliability for an instrument with items using binary scoring this formula is recommended. Note that this coefficient will underestimate KR-20 if the item difficulties or endorsement have a wide range.

As a reminder, the KR-20 and KR-21 formulas are applicable where items within the measuring instrument (e.g., test) have binary scoring or the response scale is dichotomous. If the scoring or answering format is not binary this formula cannot be used. From the time period between the Kuder–Richardson development in 1937 until Cronbach's development of coefficient alpha in 1951, many psychological tests were developed with a binary response system. With Cronbach's (1951) creation, researchers were able to assess the internal consistency reliability of their instrument that had different scoring and response scales. In fact, through a mathematical proof, it can be demonstrated that the Kuder–Richardson formulas are special cases of Cronbach's coefficient alpha or Cronbach's alpha. Of this class of reliability coefficients, coefficient alpha is the most general. With coefficient alpha, it is now possible for a researcher to find the reliability of the instrument that used Likert scales. Cronbach's alpha formula looks like:

$$r_{tt} = \alpha = \frac{k}{k-1}\left(1 - \frac{\sum V_i}{V_t}\right)$$

An alternative method of writing coefficient alpha using the intercorrelations between items is

$$r_{tt} = \frac{n\bar{r}_{tt}}{1 + (n-1)\bar{r}_{tt}}$$

where $\bar{r}_{tt}$ is the mean of the interitem correlations. What this essentially says is that if we correlated each item with every other item in the instrument, found the mean of those correlations, and then plugged into the Spearman–Brown formula the mean of the interitem correlations, we would come up with coefficient alpha or the Kuder–Richardson formula.

Let us also point out that our computational example done earlier in this chapter is an example where we can use the analysis of variance to determine the reliability coefficient, and should be equivalent to coefficient alpha.

The Stanadard Error of the Mean and the Standard Error of Measurement

Two important aspects of reliability are the reliability of means and the reliability of individual measures. These are tied to the standard error of the mean and the standard error of measurement. In research studies, ordinarily, the standard error of the mean and related statistics—like the standard error of the differences between means and the standard error of a correlation coefficient—is the more important of these. Since the standard error of the mean was discussed in considerable detail in an earlier chapter, it is only necessary to say here that the reliability of specific statistics is another aspect of the general problem of reliability. The standard error of measurement, or its square, the standard variance of measurement, needs to be defined and identified, if only briefly. This will be done through use of a simple example.

An investigator measures the attitudes of five individuals and obtains the scores given under the column labeled X_t in Table 27.3. Assume, further, that the "true" attitude scores of the five individuals are those given under the column labeled X_∞. (Remember, however, that in reality we can never know these scores.) It can be seen that the instrument is reliable. While only one of the five obtained scores is exactly the same as its companion "true" score, the differences, between those obtained scores that are not the same and the "true" scores, are all small. These differences are shown under the column labeled "X_e": they are "error scores." The instrument is evidently fairly accurate. The calculation of r_{tt} confirms this impression: .71.

A rather direct measure of the reliability of the instrument can be obtained by calculating the variance or the standard deviation of the error scores (X_e). The variance of the error scores and the variances of the X_t and X_∞ scores have been calculated and entered in Table 27.3. The variance of the error scores we now label, justifiably, the *standard variance of measurement*, which might more accurately be called "the standard variance of errors of measurement." The square root of this statistic is called the *standard error of measurement*. The standard variance of measurement is defined:

$$SV_{meas} = V_t (1 - r_{tt})$$ (27.7)

This statistic can only be calculated, obviously, if we know the reliability coefficient. Note that if there is some way to estimate SV_{meas}, then it is possible to calculate the reliability coefficient. This bears further investigation.

■ TABLE 27.3   *Reliablility and Standard Error of Measurement (hypothetical example)*

	X_t	X_∞	X_e
	2	1	1
	1	2	−1
	3	3	0
	3	4	−1
	6	5	1
Σ:	15	15	0
M:	3	3	0
V:	2.8	2.0	.80

$$r_{tt} = 1 - \frac{V_e}{V_t} = 1 - \frac{V_e}{V_O} = 1 - \frac{.80}{2.80} = 0.71 \qquad r_{t\infty} = 0.845$$

$$r_{tt} = \frac{V_\infty}{V_t} = \frac{2.00}{2.80} = 0.71 \qquad\qquad r_{tt} = r_{t\infty}^2 = (.845)^2 = 0.71$$

$$SV_{meas} = V_t(1 - r_{tt}) = 2.80 \, (1 - 0.71) = 0.81$$

$$SE_{meas} = SD_t\sqrt{1 - r_{tt}} = \sqrt{SV_{meas}}\sqrt{0.81} = 0.90$$

We start with the definition of reliability given earlier: $r_{tt} = V_\infty / V_t = 1 - V_e/V_t$. A slight algebraic manipulation yields the standard variance of measurement:

$$r_{tt} = 1 - \frac{V_e}{V_t}$$

$$r_{tt}V_t = V_t - V_e$$

$$V_e = V_t - r_{tt}V_t$$

$$V_e = V_t(1 - r_{tt})$$

The right side of the equation is the same as the right side of Equation 27.7. Therefore $V_e = SV_{meas}$, or the error variance used earlier in the analysis of variance, is the standard variance of measurement. The standard variance of measurement and the standard error of measurement of the example have been calculated in Table 27.3. They are .81 and .90, respectively. As textbooks of measurement (e.g., Anastasi

& Urbina, 1997) show, they can be used to interpret individual test scores. Such interpretation will not be discussed here; these statistics have been included only to show the connection between the original theory and ways of determining reliability.

One more calculation in Table 27.3 needs explanation. If we correlate the X_t, and the X_∞ scores, we obtain a coefficient of correlation of .845. Now we obtain this coefficient, $r_{t\infty}$, directly, and square it to obtain the reliability coefficient (see Equation 27.6). The latter, of course, is the same as before: .71.

The Improvement of Reliability

The principle behind the improvement of reliability is the one previously called the *maxmincon* principle—in a slightly different form: "Maximize the variance of the individual differences and minimize the error variance." Equation 27.4 clearly indicates this principle. The general procedure follows.

First, write the items of psychological and educational measuring instruments unambiguously. An ambiguous event can be interpreted in more than one way. An ambiguous item permits error variance to creep in because individuals can interpret the item differently. Such interpretations tend to be random and hence increase error variance and decrease reliability.

Second, if an instrument is not reliable enough, add more items of equal kind and quality. This will usually, though not necessarily, increase reliability by a predictable amount. Adding more items increases the probability that any individual's X_t is close to his or her X_∞. This is a matter of the sampling of the property or the item space. With few items, a chance error looms large. With more items, it looms less large. The probability of its being balanced by another random error the other way is greater when there are more items. Summarily, more items increase the probability of accurate measurement. (Remember that each X_t is the sum of the item values for an individual.)

Third, clear and standard instructions tend to reduce errors of measurement. Great care must always be taken when writing the instructions, to state them clearly. Ambiguous instructions increase error variance. Further, measuring instruments should always be administered under standard, well-controlled, and similar conditions. If the situations of administration differ, error variance can again intrude. In the psychological and education fields, a test that has uniformity in administration and scoring is called a *standardized test*. Hence, standardized tests are those that have been subjected to the rigor of error variance reduction.

So how do we know that we have written ambiguous or unambiguous items? How do we know that the items we have added in an attempt to increase reliability are of the equal kind and quality? There exists a set of statistical procedures called *item analysis*, which helps us answer these questions. Item analysis is used to increase both the reliability and validity of a test. It does this by evaluating each item separately to determine if the item is good or poor. Whether the item measures what we want it to measure is a validity issue. Validity is discussed in Chapter 28. In tests where answers are evaluated as either being correct or incorrect (such as cognitive tests), items can be evaluated in terms of their level of difficulty. For tests where there are no right or wrong answers (such as those found in affective tests), the index of endorsement would be used instead of difficulty. The difficulty index is a simple ratio of the number of people answering the item correctly and the total number of people who took the test. The index of endorsement is computed as the ratio of the number of people selecting an answer to the total number of people who responded to the test. So essentially the difficulty index and endorsement index is similar computationally.

$$\text{Item Difficulty} = \frac{number\ of\ people\ answering\ item\ correctly}{total\ number\ of\ people\ taking\ test}$$

$$\text{Index of Endorsement} = \frac{number\ of\ people\ selecting\ answer}{total\ number\ of\ people\ taking\ test}$$

For the difficulty index, the larger the value the easier the item. This says more people are getting the item correct. Items with indices of 0.0 or 1.00 contribute very little to the test in terms of informing us about the differences among people. When every student gets almost all the items correct on an easy math test, this tells us very little about the difference between people in math ability. On the other hand, a test consisting of overly difficult items also cannot tell us how individuals differ. No matter what their abilities are, everyone will get those items incorrect. As a rule, most test creators agree that the best items in terms of difficulty and endorsement are those with values between .5 and .7. Some recommend combining items of different levels of difficulty but with an overall index between .5 and .7.

After difficulty or endorsement, the next index for item analysis is the *item discrimination index*. It is this statistic that will (on cognitive tests) tell the researcher how effectively the item was able to discriminate between high scorers and low scorers. A good item is thought of as one where the high scorers get the item correct and all low scorers answer it incorrectly. When this occurs, the item will have the maximum discriminability. The item discrimination index is best suited for cognitive tests. These are tests that have right and wrong answers. For tests such as affective tests (e.g., personality) where there are no right or wrong answers, the item-to-total-score correlation is used. The item-to-total-score correlation can also be used for cognitive tests.

With the item discrimination index, the researcher would first determine the top-scoring group and the bottom-scoring group. The total scores are used to do this. It is highly recommended that the two groups are equal in terms of the number of people in each. The number in each group varies depending on the number of people who took the test. Then the number of people within each group who got the item correct are counted. A difference score is computed between the number in the top-scoring group who got the item correct and the number in the low-scoring group who got the same item correct. The item discrimination index is the ratio of the difference and the number of people in the top-scoring group. We could have used in the denominator of this computation the number of people in the low-scoring group, but the number should be the same:

$$\text{Discrimination index for item } i = \frac{P_T - P_B}{\text{\# of people in Top group}}$$

where P_T is the number of people in the Top group that got the item correct and P_B is the number of people in the Bottom group that got the item correct.

Values of 0.0, 1.0, and -1.0 are rare. If the index is negative the item has reverse discrimination. This would tell the researcher that there is definitely something wrong with this item. Good items are expected to have positive values. The higher the value, the greater the discrimination.

In the case of the item-to-total score correlation, the researcher would essentially correlate each item score or response to the total score. The idea here is that if the item is part of a whole—a whole that measures something we want—it should have a high correlational value with the total. Remember, since we expect the items to be homogeneous, the correlation of each item with the total score should be high. An item that correlates low with the total is interpreted as an item that is measuring something that differs from what the other items are measuring. The item is not homogenous with the other items. With the high-speed computer and available statistical software, a researcher can get these correlations very easily. Friedenberg (1995) gives a very good presentation on how to compute these indices.

Item analysis using these more traditional approaches works relatively well. However, there is a new development which features clear improvements over the traditional approaches. This "new-kid-on-the block" in item analysis is called *Item Response Theory* or *IRT*. IRT involves a lot more mathematics than the traditional approach. Its major goal is to scale the difficulty or endorsement of the items. Due to its mathematical complexity, it is best done via computer programs. A company named Assessment Systems Corporation distributes several of these programs through Lawrence Erlbaum Associates. This method essentially involves the use of the *item-characteristic curve* with *latent-trait* theory. In latent-trait theory one assumes that test performance can be accounted for by the test taker's position on a hypothetical and unobservable characteristic (i.e., trait). There is no implication that the trait causes behavior nor does it imply that such a trait exists physically or physiologically. Latent traits are merely statistical constructs created from empirical data. The basic measurement used in IRT is a probability. It is the probability that a person with a specified ability or latent trait answers an item correctly with a specified difficulty level. With items that are not scored correct or incorrect, IRT can still produce a probability that a person of a certain characteristic will give a specific answer based on the endorsements of that item.

The item-characteristic curve is a graph of the relation between the test taker's test score and the performance on a particular item. The test score, of course, measures how much of the attribute or trait the test taker has. Performance on a particular item is usually in the form of a probability or proportion. The better items will tend to exhibit a pattern where high scorers tend to get the item correct while low scores tend to get the item incorrect. The steeper the curve going from low scores to high scores (positive slope), the better the discrimination power of that item. Items with negative discrimination have a negative slope. These items have a problem that requires further analysis. The item-characteristic curve can also give a measure of item difficulty. By taking the .50 level of probability or proportion and finding the corresponding total test score for that level, this total score can be used as a measure of difficulty. This total tests score would correspond to that point where 50% of the test takers got the item correct. This differs slightly from that the item difficulty index discussed earlier, but, it is just as useful. Through the use of mathematical and statistical curve fitting, a researcher can obtain indices of discrimination and difficulty from the item-characteristic curves. The nonlinear curve fitting used in these procedures is beyond the scope of this book. The reader is referred to several good references that treat this topic: Allen and Yen (1979), Baker (1992), Crocker and Algina (1986), and Wright and Stone (1979).

The Value of Reliability

To be interpretable, a test must be reliable. Unless one can depend on the results of the measurement of one's variables, one cannot with any confidence determine the relations between the variables. Since unreliable measurement is measurement overloaded with error, the determination of relations becomes a difficult and tenuous task. Is an obtained coefficient of correlation between two variables low because one or both measures are unreliable? Is an analysis of variance F-ratio not significant because the hypothesized relation does not exist, or because the measure of the dependent variable is unreliable?

Reliability, while not the most important facet of measurement, is still extremely important. In a way, this is like the money problem: the lack of it is the real problem. High reliability is no guarantee of good scientific results, but there can be no good scientific results without reliability. In brief, reliability is a necessary but not sufficient condition of the value of research results and their interpretation.

At this point, we need to ask the question: How high a reliability coefficient do we need? There is no hard and fast answer to this question. For some reason, a number of researchers have declared .7 as the cutoff for acceptable and unacceptable reliabilities. There is no evidence to support this arbitrary rule. In fact, most authors of measurement textbooks do not set such a value. Anastasi and Urbina (1997), for example, make no mention of such a rule. Nunnally (1978) states that a satisfactory level of reliability is dependent upon how the measure is used. In some cases a reliability value of .5 or .6 is acceptable, whereas in others a value of .9 is barely acceptable. A low reliability value may be acceptable if the measuring instrument has high validity. Gronlund (1985) states that most teacher-made tests have reliabilities between .60 and .85, and yet they are useful in instructional decisions. Gronlund also gives the considerations that should go into deciding whether a reliability value is acceptable. The considerations all center on what type of decision is made using the test or measuring instrument. If the decision made by the test is important, final, irreversible, unconfirmable, concerned with individuals, and/or has lasting consequences, a high level of reliability is necessary. If the decision is of minor importance, made at an early stage, is reversible, confirmable by other data, concerns groups, and/or has temporary effects, a low value of reliability is acceptable.

CHAPTER SUMMARY

1. This chapter primarily examines the classical theory of reliability. It also looks at some of the "newer" developments in this area.
2. Reliability is defined as the consistency or stability of the measuring instrument.
3. Classical test theory composed the equation: $X_t = X_\infty + X_e$ where X_t is the observed score, X_∞ is the true score, and X_e is the error score.
4. Reliability and validity are often confused because both deal with the accuracy of measurements. However, reliability is less concerned with whether or not the instrument actually measures what we want it to measure. Its accuracy issue concerns measurement of the "true" score.
5. A measurement can be both reliable and invalid at the same time. The measurement instrument can measure something inaccurately all the time.
6. Of interest is the index of reliability; it is the correlation between true scores and observed scores. However, true scores are unobservable.
7. The reliability coefficient is the square of the index of reliability.
8. Practical methods of obtaining the reliability coefficient is through

   test–retest, parallel forms, internal consistency

9. Internal consistency can be obtained through one of the following methods: split-half, Kuder–Richardson formulas 20 and 21, coefficient alpha

10. The standard error of measurement tells us how much error is in our reliability coefficient.
11. To improve reliability, we can write better items, add more similar items, and standardize the administration and scoring of the measuring instrument and responses.
12. Item analysis gives us information on how good or how poor our items are within the measuring instrument.
13. How high the reliability coefficient has to be in order to be acceptable depends on the type of decision to be made and the conditions under which the coefficient was determined.

STUDY SUGGESTIONS

1. How does generalizability theory differ from classical test theory?
2. Of the following, which do you think is more useful for researchers: (a) validity, or (b) reliability? Justify your choice.
3. Outline some of the problems with (a) test–retest reliability, and (b) parallel forms reliability. Give an example where you would and would not use each of these.
4. Given the following situations listed below, indicate which reliability coefficient would be the most appropriate?
   a. A typing test given to a word-processing class
   b. A psychological problem checklist used by therapists
   c. A cognitive achievement test
   d. A spelling test on four-letter words
   e. The number of "aggressive" acts by a male monkey in a zoo during the same 10-minute time period each day
   f. After a group of students completed a test, the test was divided into two parts and separate scores were computed for each student; the correlation of the two scores was .79
5. How many different components can you arrive at that would be part of the error term in the classical test theory equation: $X_t = X_\infty + X_e$?
6. Give an explanation as to why a "true" score or measurement can never be attained.
7. A split-half reliability is .7. What is the estimated full-length reliability?
8. If a test–retest reliability of a 50-item test is .65, what would be the estimated reliability if an additional 50 similar items were added to the test?

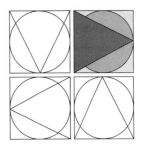

CHAPTER 28

VALIDITY

The subject of validity is complex, controversial, and peculiarly important in behavioral research. Here, perhaps more than anywhere else, the nature of reality is questioned. It is possible to study reliability without inquiring into the meaning of variables. It is not possible to study validity, however, without sooner or later inquiring into the nature and meaning of one's variables.

When measuring certain physical properties and relatively simple attributes of persons, validity is no great problem. There is often rather direct and close congruence between the nature of the object measured and the measuring instrument. The length of an object, for example, can be measured by laying sticks marked in a standard numbering system (feet or meters) on the object. Weight is more indirect, but not difficult: An object placed in a container displaces the container downward. The downward movement of the container is registered on a calibrated index (pounds or ounces). With some physical attributes, then, there is little doubt of what is being measured.

On the other hand, suppose an educational scientist wishes to study the relation between intelligence and school achievement or the relation between authoritarianism and teaching style. Now there are no rulers to use, no scales with which to weigh the degree of authoritarianism, no clear-cut physical or behavioral attributes that point unmistakably to teaching style. In such cases it is necessary to invent indirect means to measure psychological and educational properties. These means are often so indirect that the validity of the measurement and its products is doubtful.

Types of Validity

The most common definition of validity is epitomized by the question: Are we measuring what we think we are measuring? The emphasis in this question is on what is being measured. For example, a teacher has constructed a test to measure *understanding* of scientific procedures and has included in the test only *factual* items about scientific procedures. The test is not valid because, while it may reliably measure the pupils' *factual knowledge* of scientific procedures, it does not measure their *understanding* of such procedures. In other words, it may measure what it measures quite well, but it does not measure what the teacher intended it to measure.

Although the most common definition of validity was given above, it must immediately be emphasized that there is no one validity. A test or scale is valid for the scientific or practical purpose of its user. Educators may be interested in the *nature* of high school pupils' achievement in mathematics. They would then be interested in *what* a mathematics achievement or aptitude test measures. They might, for example, want to know the factors that enter into mathematics test performance and their relative contributions to this performance. On the other hand, they may be primarily interested in knowing the pupils who will probably be successful, and those who will probably be unsuccessful in high school mathematics. They may have little interest in *what* a mathematics aptitude test measures. They are interested mainly in successful *prediction*. Implied by these two uses of tests are different kinds of validity. We now examine an extremely important development in test theory: the analysis and study of different kinds of validity. Although there are different types, the researcher should design the validation study with only one type in mind. Some researchers compute all validity coefficients only to discover that each gives a different value.

The most important classification of types of validity is that prepared by a joint committee of the American Psychological Association, the American Educational Research Association, and the National Council on Measurements used in Education. Three types of validity are discussed: *content*, *criterion-related*, and *construct*. Each of these will be examined briefly, though we put the greatest emphasis on construct validity, since it is probably the most important form of validity from the scientific research point of view.

Content Validity and Content Validation

A university psychology professor has given a course to seniors in which she has emphasized the understanding of principles of human development. She prepares an objective-type test. Wanting to know something of its validity, she critically examines each of the test's items for its relevance to understanding principles of human development. She also asks two colleagues to evaluate the content of the test. Naturally, she tells the colleagues what it is she is trying to measure. She is investigating the *content validity* of the test.

Content validity is the *representativeness* or *sampling adequacy* of the content—the substance, the matter, the topic—of a measuring instrument. *Content validation* is guided by the question: Is the substance or content of this measure representative of the content or the universe of content of the property being measured? Any psychological or educational property has a theoretical universe of content consisting of all the things that can possibly be said or observed about the property. The members of this universe, U, can be called "items." The property might be "arithmetic achievement," to take a relatively easy example. U has an infinite number of members: all possible items using numbers, arithmetic operations, and concepts. A test high in content validity would theoretically be a representative sample of U. If it was possible to draw items from U at random in sufficient numbers, then any such sample of items would presumably form a test high in content validity. If U consists of subsets A, B, and C, which are arithmetic operations, arithmetic concepts, and number manipulations, respectively, then any sufficiently large sample of U would represent A, B, and C approximately equally. The test's content validity would be satisfactory.

Ordinarily, and unfortunately, it is not possible to draw random samples of items from a universe of content. Such universes exist only theoretically. True, it is possible and desirable to assemble large collections of items, especially in the achievement area, and to draw random samples from the collections for testing purposes. But the content validity of such collections, no matter how large and how "good" the items, is always in question.

If it is not possible to satisfy the definition of content validity, how can a reasonable degree of content validity be achieved? Content validation consists essentially in judgment. Alone or with others, one judges the representativeness of the items. One may ask: Does this item measure Property M? To express it more fully, one might ask: Is this item representative of the universe of content of M? If U has subsets, such as those indicated above, then one has to ask additional questions; for example: Is this item a member of the subset M_1 or the subset M_2?

Some universes of content are more obvious and much easier to judge than others; the content of many achievement tests, for instance, would seem to be obvious. The content validity of these tests, it is said, can be assumed. While this statement seems reasonable, and while the content of most achievement tests is "self-validated" in the sense that the individual writing the test, to a degree, defines the property being measured (for example, a teacher writing a classroom test of spelling or arithmetic), it is dangerous to assume the adequacy of content validity without systematic efforts to check the assumption. For example, an educational investigator, testing hypotheses about the relations between social studies achievement and other variables, may assume the content validity of a social studies test. The theory from which the hypotheses were derived, however, may require *understanding* and *application* of social studies ideas, whereas the test used may be almost purely factual in content. The test lacks content validity for the purpose. In fact, the investigator is not really testing the stated hypotheses.

Content validation, then, is basically judgmental. The items of a test must be studied, each item being weighed for its presumed representativeness of the universe. This means that each item must be judged for its presumed relevance to the property being measured, which is no easy task. Usually other "competent" judges should judge the content of the items. The universe of content must, if possible, be clearly defined; that is, the judges must be furnished with specific directions for making judgments, as well as with specification of what they are judging. Then, some method for pooling independent judgments can be used. An excellent guide to the content validity of achievement tests is Bloom (1956). This is a comprehensive attempt to outline and discuss educational goals in relation to measurement. Bloom's work has been termed "Bloom's Taxonomy."

There is another type of validity that is very similar to content validity. It is called *face validity*. Face validity is not validity in the technical sense. It refers to what the test appears to measure. Trained or untrained individuals would look at the test and decide whether or not the test measures what it was supposed to measure. There is no quantification of the judgment or any index of agreement that is computed between judges. Content validity is quantifiable through the use of agreement indices of judges' evaluations. One such index is Cohen's *Kappa* (Cohen, 1960).

Criterion-Related Validity and Validation

As the unfortunately clumsy name indicates, *criterion-related validity* is studied by comparing test or scale scores with one or more external variables, or criteria, known or believed to measure the attribute under study. One type of criterion-related validity is called *predictive validity*. The other type is called *concurrent validity*, which differs from predictive validity in the time dimension. Predictive validity involves the use of future performance of the criterion, whereas concurrent validity measures the criterion at about the same time. In this sense, the test serves to assess the present status of individuals.

Concurrent validity is often used to validate a new test. At least two concurrent measures are taken on each examinee. One of these would be the new test and the other would be some existing test or measure. Concurrent validity would be found by correlating the two sets of scores. In the intelligence testing area, the new tests, and even revisions of older tests, generally use the Stanford–Binet or the Wechsler test as the concurrent criterion.

When one predicts success or failure of students from academic aptitude measures, one is concerned with predictive criterion-related validity. How well does the test (or tests) predict graduation or grade-point average? One does not focus so much on what the test measures, but rather on its predictive ability. In fact, in criterion-related validation, which is often practical and applied research, the basic interest is usually more in the criterion, some practical outcome, than in the predictors. (In basic research this is not so.) The higher the correlation between a measure or measures of academic aptitude and the criterion, say grade point average, the better the validity. In short and again, the emphasis is on the criterion and its prediction. Thorndike (1996) gives a discussion of what constitutes a good criterion.

The word *prediction* is usually associated with the future. This is unfortunate because, in science, prediction does not necessarily mean forecast. One "predicts" from an independent variable to a dependent variable. One "predicts" the existence or nonexistence of a relation; one even "predicts" something that happened in the past! This broad meaning of prediction is the one intended here. In any case, criterion-related validity is characterized by prediction to an *outside* criterion and by checking a measuring instrument, either now or in the future, against some outcome or measure. In a sense, all tests are predictive; they "predict" a certain kind of outcome, some present or future state of affairs. Aptitude tests predict future achievement; achievement tests predict present and future achievement and competence; and intelligence tests predict present and future ability to learn and to solve problems. Even if we measure self-concept, we predict that if the self-concept score is so-and-so, then the individual will be such-and-such now or in the future.

The single greatest difficulty of criterion-related validation is the criterion. Obtaining criteria may even be difficult. Which criterion can be used to validate a measure of teacher effectiveness? Who is to judge teacher effectiveness? Which criterion can be used to test the predictive validity of a musical aptitude test?

Decision Aspects of Validity

Criterion-related validity, as indicated earlier, is ordinarily associated with practical problems and outcomes. Interest is not so much in what is behind test performance as it is in helping to solve practical problems and to make decisions. Tests are used by the hundreds for the predictive purposes of screening and selecting potentially successful candidates in education, business, and other occupations. Does a test, or a set of tests, materially aid in deciding on the assignment of individuals to jobs, classes, schools, and the like? Any decision is a choice among treatments, assignments, or programs. Cronbach (1971) points out that to make a decision, one predicts the person's success under each treatment and then use, some rule to translate the prediction into an assignment. A test high in criterion-related validity is one that helps investigators make successful decisions in assigning people to treatments, conceiving *treatments* broadly. An admissions committee or administrator decides to admit or not admit an applicant to college on the basis of a test of academic aptitude. Obviously, such use of tests is highly important, and the tests' predictive validity is also highly important. The reader is referred to Cronbach's essay for a good exposition of the decision aspects of tests and validity.

A major contribution in this area is by Taylor and Russell (1939). These researchers demonstrated that tests with low validity can still be effectively used for decision purposes. They developed the Taylor–Russell Table, which utilizes three pieces of information: validity coefficient, selection ratio, and base rate. The selection ratio pertains to the number of people (applicants) who will be selected out of the total number of people. If there were only 10 positions and 100 people applying, the selection ratio would be 0.10 or 10%. The base rate is that proportion of people in the population with a certain characteristic. This figure is generally reported in the press. The base rate for women, for example, is .52 or 52% of the population in the United States. Without using a test, if we gathered randomly 100 persons in a room, 52 of them would be women. Any of these three components can be varied and in so doing has an effect on the accuracy of selection. That is, it can help make a better decision. Anastasi and Urbina (1997) give a good account of how this method works. The interested reader would need to consult the original Taylor and Russell article to see the complete range of tables. Essentially better prediction can be made using a low validity test if the selection ratio is small. Since 1939, there have been a few modification, and additions to this method. These include Abrahams, Alf, and Wolfe (1971); Pritchard and Kazar (1979); and Thomas, Owen, and Gunst (1977).

Multiple Predictors and Criteria

Both multiple predictors and multiple criteria can be and are used. Later, when we study multiple regression, we will focus on multiple predictors and how to handle them statistically. Multiple criteria can be handled separately or together, though it is not easy to do the latter. In practical research, a decision must usually be made. If there is more than one criterion, how can we best combine them for decision-making? The relative importance of the criteria, of course, must be considered. Do we want an administrator high in problem-solving ability, high in public-relations ability, or both? Which is more important in the particular job? It is highly likely that the use of both multiple predictors and multiple criteria will become common, as multivariate methods become better understood and the computer is used routinely in prediction research.

Construct Validity and Construct Validation

Construct validity is one of the most significant scientific advances of modern measurement theory and practice. It is a significant advance because it links psychometric notions and practices to theoretical notions. The classic work in this area is Cronbach and Meehl (1955). Measurement experts, when they inquire into the construct validity of tests, usually want to know which psychological or other property or properties can "explain" the variance of tests. They wish to know the "meaning" of tests. If a test is an intelligence test, they want to know which factors lie behind test performance. They ask: Which factors or constructs account for variance in test performance? Does this test measure verbal ability and abstract reasoning ability? Does it also "measure" social class membership? They ask, for example, what proportion of the total test variance is accounted for by each of the constructs—verbal ability, abstract reasoning ability, and social class membership. In short, they seek to explain individual differences in test scores. Their interest is usually more in the properties being measured, than in the tests used to accomplish the measurement.

Researchers generally start with the constructs or variables entering into relations. Suppose that a researcher has discovered a positive correlation between two measures, one a measure of educational traditionalism and the other a measure of the perception of the characteristics associated with a "good" teacher. Individuals high on the traditionalism measure see the "good" teacher as efficient, moral, thorough, industrious, conscientious, and reliable. Individuals low on the traditionalism measure may see the "good" teacher in a different way. The researcher now wants to know *why* this relation exists, what is behind it. To accomplish this, the meaning of the constructs entering the relation, "perception of the 'good' teacher" and "traditionalism" must be studied. How to study these meanings is a construct validity problem. This example was extracted from Kerlinger and Pedhazur (1968).

One can see that construct validation and empirical scientific inquiry are closely allied. It is not simply a question of validating a test. One must try to validate the theory behind the test. Cronbach (1990) says that there are three parts to construct validation: suggesting which constructs possibly account for test performance, deriving hypotheses from the theory involving the construct, and testing the hypotheses empirically. This formulation is but a précis of the general scientific approach discussed in earlier chapters.

The significant point about construct validity that sets it apart from other types of validity, is its preoccupation with theory, theoretical constructs, and scientific empirical inquiry, involving the testing of hypothesized relations. Construct validation in measurement contrasts sharply with approaches that define the validity of a measure, primarily by its success in predicting a criterion. For example, a purely empirical tester might say that a test is valid if it efficiently distinguishes individuals high and low in a trait. *Why* the test succeeds in separating the subsets of a group is of no great concern. It is enough that it does.

Convergence and Discriminability

Note that the testing of alternative hypotheses is particularly important in construct validation, because both convergence and discriminability are required. *Convergence* means that evidence from different sources gathered in different ways all indicate the same or similar meaning of the construct. Different methods of measurement should converge on the construct. The evidence yielded by administering the measuring instrument to different groups in different places should yield similar meanings or, if not, should account for differences. A measure of the self-concept of children, for instance, should be capable of similar interpretation in different parts of the country. If it is not capable of such interpretation in some locality, the theory should be able to explain why—indeed, it should predict such a difference.

Discriminability means that one can empirically differentiate the construct from other constructs that may be similar, and that one can point out what is *unrelated* to the construct. We point out, in other words, what other variables are correlated with the construct and how they are so correlated. But we also indicate which variables should be uncorrelated with the construct. We point out, for example, that a scale to measure Conservatism should and does correlate substantially with measures of Authoritarianism and Rigidity—the theory predicts this—but not with measures of Social Desirability (see Kerlinger, 1970). Let us illustrate these ideas.

A Hypothetical Example of Construct Validation

Let us assume that an investigator is interested in the determinants of creativity and the relation of creativity to school achievement. The investigator notes that the most sociable persons, who exhibit affection for others, also seem to be less creative than those who are less sociable and affectionate. The goal is to test the implied relation in a controlled fashion. One of the first tasks is to obtain or construct a measure of the sociable–affectionate characteristic. The investigator, surmising that this combination of traits may be a reflection of a deeper concern of love for others, calls it *amorism*. An assumption is made about individual differences in amorism; that is, some people have a great deal of it, others a moderate amount, and still others very little.

The first step is to construct an instrument to measure amorism. The literature gives little help, since scientific psychologists have rarely investigated the fundamental nature of love. Sociability, however, has been measured. The investigator must construct a new instrument, basing its content on intuitive and reasoned notions of what amorism is. The reliability of the test, tried out with large groups, runs between .75 and .85.

The question now is whether or not the test is valid. The investigator correlates the instrument, calling it the *A*-scale, with independent measures of sociability. The correlations are moderately substantial, but additional evidence is needed to claim that the test has construct validity. Certain relations are deduced that should and should not exist between amorism and other variables. If amorism is a general tendency to love others, then it should correlate with characteristics like cooperativeness and friendliness. Persons high in amorism will approach problems in an ego-oriented manner as contrasted to persons low in amorism, who will approach problems in a task-oriented manner.

Acting on this reasoning, the investigator administers the *A*-scale and a scale to measure subjectivity to a number of tenth-grade students. To measure cooperativeness, an observation of the classroom behavior of the same group of students is made. The correlations between the three measures are positive and significant. Note that we would not expect high correlation between the measures. If the correlations were too high, we would then suspect the validity of the *A*-scale. It would be measuring, perhaps, subjectivity or cooperativeness, but not amorism.

Knowing the pitfalls of psychological measurement, the investigator is not satisfied. These positive correlations may be due to a factor common to all three tests, but irrelevant to amorism; for example, the tendency to give "right" answers. (This would probably be ruled out, however, because the observation measure of cooperativeness correlates positively with amorism and subjectivity.) So, taking a new group of participants, the investigator administers the amorism and subjectivity scales, has the participants' behavior rated for cooperativeness, and, in addition, administers a creativity test that has been found in other research to be reliable.

The investigator states the relation between amorism and creativity in hypothesis form: The relation between the *A*-scale and the creativity measure will be negative and significant. The correlations between amorism and cooperativeness and between amorism and subjectivity will be positive and significant. "Check" hypotheses are also formulated: The correlation between cooperativeness and creativity will not be significant, it will be near zero; but the correlation between subjectivity and creativity will be positive and significant. This last relation is predicted on the basis of previous research findings. The six correlation coefficients are given in the correlation matrix of Table 28.1. The four measures are labeled as follows: A, amorism; B, cooperativeness; C, subjectivity; and D, creativity.

The evidence for the construct validity of the *A*-scale is good. All the *r*s are as predicted; especially important are the *r*s between D (creativity) and the other variables. Note that there are three different kinds of prediction: positive, negative, and zero. All three kinds are as predicted. This illustrates what might be called *differential prediction* or *differential validity*—or discriminability. It is not enough to predict, for instance, that the measure presumably reflecting the target property be positively correlated with one theoretically relevant variable. One should, through deduction from the theory, predict more than one such positive relation. In addition, one should predict zero relations between the principal variable and variables "irrelevant" to the theory. In the example above, although cooperativeness was expected to correlate with amorism, there was no theoretical reason to expect it to correlate at all with creativity.

An example of a different kind is the investigator who deliberately introduces a measure that would, if it correlates with the variable whose validity is under study,

▣ **TABLE 28.1** *Intercorrelations of Four Hypothetical Measures (N = 90)*[a]

	B	C	D
A	.50	.60	−.30
B		.40	.05
C			.50

[a] A = Amorism; B = Cooperativeness; C = Subjectivity; D = Creativity. Correlation coefficients .25 or greater are significant at the .01 level.

invalidate other positive relations. One bugaboo of personality and attitude scales is the social desirability phenomenon mentioned earlier. The correlation between the target variable and a theoretically related variable may be due to both instruments measuring social desirability, rather than the variables they were designed to measure. One can partly check against this tendency by including a measure of social desirability along with the other measures.

Despite all the evidence leading the investigator to believe that the A-scale has construct validity, there may still be doubt. So a study is developed in which pupils who are high and low in amorism solve problems. The prediction is that pupils low in amorism will solve problems more successfully than those high in amorism. If the data support the prediction, this is further evidence of the construct validity of the amorism measure. It is, of course, a significant finding in and of itself. Such a procedure, however, is probably more appropriate with achievement and attitude measures. One can manipulate communications, for example, in order to change attitudes. If attitude scores change according to theoretical prediction, this would be evidence of the construct validity of the attitude measure, since the scores would probably not change according to prediction if the measure were not measuring the construct.

The Multitrait–Multimethod Matrix Method

A significant and influential contribution to testing validity is Campbell and Fiske's (1959) use of the ideas of convergence and discriminability and correlation matrices to bring evidence to bear on validity. To explain the method, we use some data from a study of social attitudes by Kerlinger (1967, 1984). It has been found that there are two basic dimensions of social attitudes, which correspond to philosophical, sociological, and political descriptions of liberalism and conservatism. Two different kinds of scales were administered to graduate students of education and groups outside the universities in New York, Texas, and North Carolina. One instrument, Social Attitudes Scale, had the usual attitude *statements*, 13 liberal and 13 conservative items. The second instrument, Referents-I, or REF-I, used attitude *referents* (single words and short phrases: *private property*, *religion*, and *civil rights*, for example) as items, 25 liberal referents and 25 conservative referents. The samples, the scales, and some of the results are described in Kerlinger (1972). The data reported in Table 28.2 were obtained from a Texas sample, $N = 227$ graduate students.

We have, then, two completely different kinds of attitude instruments, one with referent items and the other with statement items, or Method 1 and Method 2. The two basic dimensions being measured were liberalism (L) and conservatism (C). Do the L and C subscales of the two scales measure liberalism and conservatism? Part of the evidence is given in Table 28.2, which presents the correlations among the four subscales of the two instruments, as well as the subscale reliability coefficients, calculated from the responses to the two scales.

In a multitrait–multimethod analysis, more than one attribute and more than one method are used in the validation process. The results of correlating variables within and between methods can be presented in a so-called multitrait–multimethod matrix. The matrix (matrices) given in Table 28.2 is the simplest possible form of

TABLE 28.2 *Correlations between Social Attitude Dimensions across Two Measurement Methods, Multitrait-Multimethod Approach, Texas Sample (N = 227)*[a]

		Method 1 (Referents)		Method 2 (Referents)	
		L_1	C_1	L_2	C_2
Method 1	L_1	(.85)			
(Referents)	C_1	−.07	(.88)		
Method 2	L_2	.53	−.15	(.81)	
(Referents)	C_2	−.37	.54	−.09	(.82)

[a]Method 1: Referents; Method 2: Statements; L = Liberalism; C = Conservatism. The diagonal parenthesized entries are internal consistency reliabilities; the italicized entries (.53 and .54) are cross-method L–L and C–C correlations (validities).

such an analysis: two variables and two methods. Ordinarily one would want to use more variables.

The most important part of the matrix is the diagonal of the cross-method correlations. In Table 28.2, this is the Method 1–Method 2 matrix in the lower-left section of the table. The diagonal values should be substantial, since they reflect the magnitudes of the correlations between the same variables measured differently. These values, italicized in the table (.53 and .54), are fairly substantial.

In this example, the theory calls for near-zero or low negative correlations between L and C (see Kerlinger, 1967 for a more complete development of this). The correlation between L_1 and C_1 is −.07 and between L_2 and C_2 is −.09, both in accord with the theory. The cross-correlation between L and C, that is, the correlation between L of Method 1 and C of Method 2, or between L_1 and C_2, is −.37, higher than the theory predicts (an upper limit of −.30 was adopted). With the exception of the cross-correlation of −.37 between L_1 and C_2, then, the construct validity of the social attitudes scale is supported. One will, of course, want more evidence than the results obtained with one sample. And one will also want an explanation of the substantial cross-method negative correlation between L_1 and C_2. The example, however, illustrates the basic ideas of the multitrait-multimethod approach to validity.

Campbell and Fiske (1959) used specific terminology to describe each correlation in the table. The *monomethod–monotrait* are the reliabilities. These are found in the main diagonal of the matrix. In Table 28.2, these are the values .85, .88, .81, and .82, enclosed in parentheses. The *heteromethod–monotrait* are the validities which we discussed above. They are .53 and .54 in Table 28.2. There are two other types of correlation: the *monomethod–heterotrait* (the values −.07 and −.09), and the *heteromethod–heterotrait* (these were −.37 and −.15). Campbell and Fiske state that in order to have complete evidence of construct validity, the correlations must follow a set pattern. Failure to meet the requirements weakens validity concerns. There have been some articles trying to resolve this problem by relaxing some of the requirements. These articles claim a partial degree of success.

The model of the multitrait–multimethod procedure is an ideal. If possible, it should be followed. Certainly the investigation and measurement of important constructs, like conservatism, aggressiveness, teacher warmth, need for achievement, honesty, and so on, ultimately require it. In many research situations, however, it is difficult or impossible to administer two or more measures of two or more variables to relatively large samples. Though efforts to study validity must always be made, research should not be abandoned just because the full method is not feasible.

Research Examples of Concurrent Validation

Wood (1994) gives a good example of how to validate a test that uses medical and physiological data. Here the criterion is an actual physical measurement. Wood developed an instrument called the Breast Self-Examination Proficiency Rating Instrument (BSEPRI). This test measured how knowledgeable the test taker was about breast self-examination. The participants in the study were nursing students. Half of them were given instructions on self-examination and the other half were not. A t-test showed that those receiving instructions scored significantly higher than those that did not. Wood obtained concurrent validity by correlating the palpation scores of the instrument with the students' ability to detect lumps in a silicon model.

Iverson, Guirguis, and Green (1998) examined the concurrent validity of a short form of Wechsler Adult Intelligence Scale–Revised (WAIS–R). This short form consisted of seven subscales. The short form was developed for assessing patients with a diagnosis of a schizophrenia spectrum disorder. IQ scores estimated by this short form have a high correlation with full-form IQ scores. The verbal IQs, performance IQs, and full scale IQs estimated by the short form were highly correlated with the full form IQs. The correlations (validity coefficient) ranged from 0.95 to 0.98. In general, the seven subtest short form was shown to have adequate concurrent validity and is suitable for assessing intellectual functioning in persons with psychotic disorders. Iverson et al. correlated the new test (short form) with the established test (full scale) to obtain a measure of concurrent validity. Comrey (1993) used a similar procedure to create the short form of the Comrey Personality Scales (CPS). Using existing data, Comrey extracted the "best" items for each scale (discussed below) and computed two total scores: one on the short form, and the other on the original form. Correlating the two scores yielded a value for concurrent validity.

Research Examples of Construct Validation

In a sense, any type of validation is construct validation. Loevinger (1957) argues that construct validity, from a scientific point of view, is the whole of validity. At the other extreme, Bechtoldt (1959) argues that construct validity has no place in psychology. Horst (1966) says that it is very difficult to apply the Cronbach and Meehl ideas within the logical and practical theory of psychometrics. However, when hypotheses are tested, when relations are empirically studied, construct validity is involved. Because of its importance, we now examine two research examples of construct validation.

A Measure of Anti-Semitism

In an unusual attempt to validate their measure of anti-Semitism, Glock and Stark (1966) used responses to two incomplete sentences about Jews: "It's a shame that Jews . . ." and "I can't understand why Jews . . ." Coders considered what each subject had written and characterized the responses as negative, neutral, or positive images of Jews. Each subject, then, was characterized individually as having one of the three different perceptions of Jews. When the responses to the Index of Anti-Semitic Beliefs, the measure being validated, were divided into None, Medium, Medium High, and High Anti-Semitism, the percentages of negative responses to the two open-ended questions were, respectively: 28, 41, 61, 75. This is good evidence of validity because the individuals categorized None to High Anti-Semitism by the measure to be validated, the Index of Anti-Semitic Beliefs, responded to an entirely different measure of anti-Semitism, the two open-ended questions, in a manner congruent with their categorization by the index.

A Measure of Personality

In a later chapter we will be discussing an important analytic tool called *factor analysis*. However, it is necessary to mention this method in light of construct validation. In recent years, factor analysis seems to be the method of choice for many involved with construct validity. Factor analysis is essentially a method of finding those variables that have something in common. If some items of a personality test are designed to measure extraversion, then in a factor analysis, those items should have high loadings on one factor and low on the others.

In the mid-1950s Professor Andrew L. Comrey at University of California, Los Angeles, undertook a task to examine all of the existing well-known, published personality tests. His initial goal was to try to determine who had the correct (valid) measure of personality. To do this, Dr. Comrey used factor analysis. Contrary to his initial expectations, a new personality test of its own unique character emerged. Comrey's personality test, now called the Comrey Personality Scales (CPS) was among the first to be developed using factor analysis. In 1970, after approximately 15 years of research and test construction, the Comrey Personality Scale was published (see Comrey & Lee, 1992 for a summary and procedure). Comrey's construct for personality consists of eight major dimensions:

Trust versus Defensiveness

Orderliness versus Lack of Compulsion

Social Conformity versus Rebelliousness

Activity versus Lack of Energy

Emotional Stability versus Neuroticism

Extraversion versus Introversion

Masculinity versus Femininity (renamed as Mental Toughness versus Sensitivity)

Empathy versus Egocentrism

Since 1970, Comrey has published a number of articles supporting the validity of the Comrey Personality Scales. This was done by first administering the CPS, or a translated form of the CPS, to different groups of people. After obtaining the data, each set of data was factor analyzed. In each case, the same eight factors emerged. Although this does not say exclusively there are eight factors of personality, the data support it. In recent research by Brief, Comrey, and Collins (1994), the CPS was translated into Russian and administered to 287 male and 170 female Russian participants. The data supported six of the eight subscales. The only subscales that did not receive enough support were Empathy versus Egocentrism and Activity versus Lack of Energy.

In a short article, Comrey, Wong, and Backer (1978) present a simple procedure for validating the Social Conformity versus Rebelliousness scale. In one study, Comrey et al. recruited two groups of participants: Asians and non-Asians. The traditional view of Asians is that they are more socially conforming than non-Asians. There is some evidence to support this claim, such as strong parental influence, strong traditional values, and so on. [Scattone and Saetermoe (1997) is one research study that demonstrated this.] Hence in this study by Comrey and others, the established notion concerning the difference between Asians and non-Asians on social conformity was used as the criterion or "outside measure." The participants all took the Comrey Personality Scales; however, only the Social Conformity versus Rebelliousness was of interest for this study. Using a *t*-test, these researchers showed a statistically significant difference between Asians and non-Asians on the Social Conformity versus Rebelliousness scale. This study could be used as an example illustrating discriminant validity.

The second study in this article demonstrated convergent validity. One expects that Social Conformity is related to political affiliation and philosophy. It is generally thought that Conservatives are more socially conforming than Liberals, who are considered more rebellious. In this study, persons completed the Comrey Personality Scales and answered questions about political affiliation. Comrey et al. found a statistically significant correlation between political affiliation and scores on the Social Conformity versus Rebelliousness scale. This provided additional information as to the validity of that scale. Even though this article is short, it is well presented. The student learn a great deal from reading this article.

The Measurement of Democracy

What do we mean by *democracy?* The word is used constantly, but what do we mean when we use it? Even more difficult, how is it measured? Bollen (1980) defined and measured "democracy," used it as a variable, and demonstrated the construct validity of his Index of Political Democracy. He examined previous uses and definitions carefully, explained the theory behind the construct, and extracted from earlier measures important facets of political democracy to construct his measure. It has two large aspects—political liberty, and popular sovereignty—which can be called latent variables. Each aspect has three facets: *press freedom, freedom of group opposition*, and *government sanctions* (absence of) for political liberties; and *fairness of elections, executive selection*, and *legislative selection* for popular sovereignty. It is these six "indicators" that are used to measure the political democracy of countries. Each indicator is defined operationally and a 4-point scale used to apply to any country. Popular sovereignty, for instance, is measured by assessing to what extent the elite of a country are accountable to the people: wide franchise, equal weighting of votes, and fair electoral processes. The six indicators are combined into a single index or score (see Bollen, 1979, for a detailed description of the index and its scoring). Note that "Indicator," or "Social Indicator," is an important term in contemporary social research. Unfortunately, there is little agreement on just what indicators are. They have been variously defined as indices of social conditions, statistics, and even variables. In Bollen's paper, they are variables. For a discussion of definitions, see Jaeger (1978).

Through factor analysis and other procedures, Bollen brought empirical evidence to bear on the reliability and construct validity of the index. He showed, for example, that the six indicators are manifestations of an underlying latent variable, which is "political democracy." He also showed that the index is highly correlated with other measures of democracy. Finally, index values were calculated for a large number of countries. These values seem to agree with the extent of democracy (on a scale of 0–100) in the countries, for example, U.S., 92.4; Canada, 99.5; Cuba, 5.2; United Arab Republic, 38.7; Sweden, 99.9; Soviet Union, 18.2; Israel, 96.8. Bollen has evidently successfully measured a highly complex and difficult construct.

Other Methods of Construct Validation

In addition to the multitrait–multimethod approach and the methods used in the above studies, there are other methods of construct validation. Any tester is familiar with the technique of correlating items with total scores. In using the technique, the total score is assumed to be valid. To the extent that an item measures the same thing as the total score does, the item is valid (see Chapter 27, or Friedenberg, 1995, for discussion on item analysis).

In order to study the construct validity of any measure, it is always helpful to correlate the measure with other measures. The amorism example discussed earlier illustrated the method and the ideas behind it. But, would it not be more valuable to correlate a measure with a large number of other measures? Is there any better way to learn about a construct than to know its correlates? Factor analysis is a refined method of doing this. It tells us, in effect, what measures measure the same thing and to what extent they measure what they measure.

Factor analysis is a powerful and indispensable method of construct validation. Bollen (1980) used it in his validation of the Index of Political Democracy and Comrey used it to develop an entire personality test. Although it has been briefly characterized earlier and will be discussed in detail in a later chapter, its great importance in validating measures warrants characterization here. It is a method for reducing a large number of measures to a smaller number, called *factors*, by discovering which ones "go together" (i.e., which measures measure the same thing) and the relations between the clusters of measures that go together. For example, we may give a group of individuals 20 tests, each presumed to measure something different. We may find, however, that these 20 tests have enough redundancy that they can be explained with only five measures or factors.

A Variance Definition of Validity: The Variance Relation of Reliability and Validity

The variance treatment of validity presented here is an extension of the treatment of reliability presented in Chapter 27. Both treatments follow Guilford's presentation of validity.

In the last chapter, reliability was defined as

$$r_{tt} = \frac{V_\infty}{V_t} \tag{28.1}$$

the proportion of "true" variance to total variance. It is theoretically and empirically useful to define validity similarly:

$$Val = \frac{V_{co}}{V_t} \tag{28.2}$$

where *Val* is the validity, V_{co} the common factor variance, and V_t the total variance of a measure. Validity is thus seen as the proportion of the total variance of a measure that is common factor variance.

Unfortunately, we are not yet in a position to present the full meaning of this definition. An understanding of so-called factor theory is required, but factor theory will not be discussed until later in the book. Despite this difficulty, we must attempt an explanation of validity in variance terms if we are to have a well-rounded view of the subject. Besides, expressing validity and reliability mathematically will unify and clarify both subjects. Indeed, reliability and validity will be seen to be parts of one unified whole.

Common factor variance is the variance of a measure that is shared with other measures. In other words, common factor variance is the variance that two or more tests have in common.

In contrast to the common factor variance of a measure is its *specific variance, V_{sp},* the systematic variance of a measure that is not shared by any other measure. If a test measures skills that other tests measure, we have common factor variance; if it also measures a skill that no other test measures, we have specific variance. Figure 28.1 expresses these ideas and also adds the notion of error variance. The *A* and *B* circles represent the variances of Tests *A* and *B*. The intersection of *A* and *B*, $A \cap B$, is the relation of the two sets. Similarly, $V(A \cap B)$ is common factor variance. The specific variances and the error variances of both tests are also indicated.

From this viewpoint, then, and following the variance reasoning outlined in the last chapter, any measure's total variance has several components: common *factor*

🔲 FIGURE 28.1

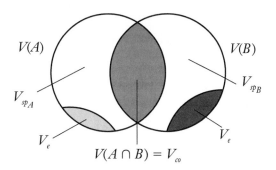

$$V(A \cap B) = V_{co}$$

variance, specific variance, and *error variance.* This is expressed by the equation:

$$V_t = V_{co} + V_{sp} + V_e \tag{28.3}$$

To be able to talk of proportions of the total variance, we divide the terms of Equation 28.3 by the total variance:

$$\frac{V_t}{V_t} = \frac{V_{co}}{V_t} + \frac{V_{sp}}{V_t} + \frac{V_e}{V_t} \tag{28.4}$$

How do Equations 28.1 and 28.2 fit into this picture? The first term on the right of the equal sign, V_{co}/V_t, is the right-hand member of (28.2). Therefore validity can be viewed as that part of the total variance of a measure that is not specific variance and not error variance. This is easily seen algebraically:

$$\frac{V_{co}}{V_t} = \frac{V_t}{V_t} - \frac{V_{sp}}{V_t} - \frac{V_e}{V_t} \tag{28.5}$$

By a definition of the previous chapter, reliability can be defined as

$$r_{tt} = 1 - \frac{V_e}{V_t} \tag{28.6}$$

This can be written:

$$r_{tt} = \frac{V_t}{V_t} - \frac{V_e}{V_t} \tag{28.7}$$

The right-hand side of the equations, however, is part of the right-hand side of (28.5). If we rewrite (28.5) slightly, we obtain

$$\frac{V_{co}}{V_t} = \frac{V_t}{V_t} - \frac{V_e}{V_t} - \frac{V_{sp}}{V_t} \qquad (28.8)$$

This must mean, then, that validity and reliability are close variance relations. Reliability is equal to the first two right-hand members of (28.8). So, bringing in (28.1):

$$r_{tt} = \frac{V_t}{V_t} - \frac{V_e}{V_t} = \frac{V_\infty}{V_t} \qquad (28.9)$$

If we substitute in (28.8), we get

$$\frac{V_{co}}{V_t} = \frac{V_\infty}{V_t} - \frac{V_{sp}}{V_t} \qquad (28.10)$$

Thus we see that the proportion of the total variance of a measure is equal to the proportion of the total variance that is "true" variance minus the proportion that is specific variance. Or, the validity of a measure is that portion of the total variance of the measure that shares variance with other measures. Theoretically, valid variance includes no variance due to error, neither does it include variance that is specific to this measure and this measure only.

This can all be summed up in two ways. First, we sum it up in an equation or two. Let us assume that we have a method of determining the common factor variance (or variances) of a test. (Later we shall see that factor analysis is such a method.) For simplicity, suppose that there are two sources of common factor variance in a test—and no others. Call these factors A and B. They might be verbal ability and arithmetic ability, or they might be liberal attitudes and conservative attitudes. If we add the variance of A to the variance of B, we obtain the common factor variance of the test, which is expressed by the equations,

$$V_{co} = V_A + V_B \qquad (28.11)$$

$$\frac{V_{co}}{V_t} = \frac{V_A}{V_t} + \frac{V_B}{V_t} \qquad (28.12)$$

Then, using (28.2) and substituting in (28.12), we obtain

$$Val = \frac{V_A}{V_t} + \frac{V_B}{V_t} \qquad (28.13)$$

The total variance of a test, as we said before, includes the common factor variance, the variance specific to the test and to no other test (at least as far as present information goes), and error variance. Equations 28.3 and 28.4 express this. By substituting in (28.4) the equality of (28.12), we obtain

$$\frac{V_t}{V_t} = \overbrace{\frac{V_A}{V_t} + \frac{V_B}{V_t}}^{h_2} + \underbrace{\frac{V_{sp}}{V_t} + \frac{V_e}{V_t}}_{r_{tt}} \tag{28.14}$$

The first two terms on the right-hand side of (28.14) are associated with the validity of the measure, and the first three terms on the right are associated with the reliability of the measure. These relations have been indicated. Common factor variance, or the validity component of the measure, is labeled h^2 (*communality*), a symbol customarily used to indicate the common factor variance of a test. Reliability, as usual, is labeled r_{tt}.

To discuss all the implications of this formulation of validity and reliability would take us too far astray at this time. All that is needed now is to try to clarify the formulation with a diagram and a brief discussion.

Figure 28.2 is an attempt to express Equation 28.14 diagrammatically. The figure represents the contributions of the different variances to the total variance (taken to be equal to 100%). Four variances, three systematic variances and one error variance, comprise the total variance in this theoretical model. Naturally, practical outcomes never look this neat. It is remarkable, however, how well the model works. The variance thinking, too, is valuable in conceptualizing and discussing measurement outcomes.

The contribution of each source of variance is indicated. Of the total variance, 80% is reliable variance. Of the reliable variance, Factor A contributes 30% and Factor B contributes 25%, and 25% is specific to this test. The remaining 20% of the total variance is error variance. The test may be interpreted as quite reliable, since a

■ FIGURE 28.2

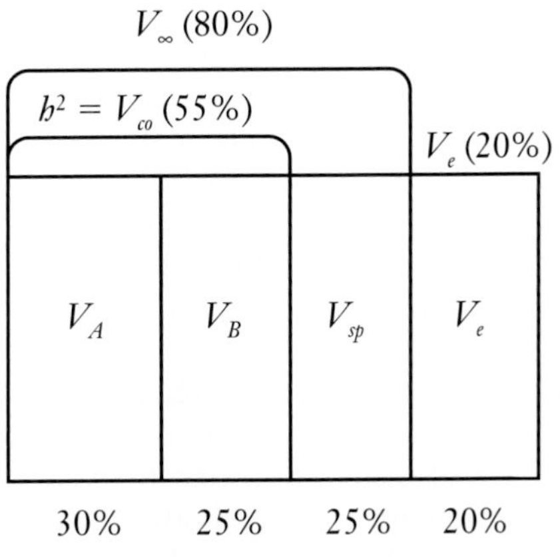

sizable proportion of the total variance is reliable or "true" variance. The interpretation of validity is more difficult. If there were only one factor, say A, and it contributed 55% of the total variance, then we could say that a considerable proportion of the total variance was valid variance. We would know that a good bit of the reliable measurement would be the measurement of the property known as A. This would be a construct validity statement. Practically speaking, individuals measured with the test would be rank-ordered on A with adequate reliability.

With the above hypothetical example, however, the situation is more complex. The test measures two factors, A and B. There could be three sets of rank orders, one resulting from A, one from B, and one from *specific*. While repeat reliability might be high, if we thought we were measuring only A, to the extent we thought so, the test would not be valid. We might, however, have a score for each individual one on A and one on B. In this case the test would be valid. Note that even if we thought the test was measuring only A, predictions to a criterion might well be successful, especially if the criterion had a lot of both A and B in it. The test could have predictive validity even though its construct validity was questionable.

Indeed, modern developments in measurement indicate that such multiple scores have become more and more a part of accepted procedure.

Statistical Relation between Reliability and Validity

Although they appear in different chapters, the topics of reliability and validity are not separate—both deal with the level of excellence of a measuring instrument. We have seen in past discussions that we can have a reliable measure that is not valid. However, a measuring instrument without reliability would automatically designate it to the "poor" stack. Also, we had briefly mentioned that if we have a valid measure then we also have a reliable one. In Chapter 27 we discussed what happens to the reliability coefficient when we increase the length of the test. What happens to validity with an increase in length? Is it equally affected by the increase in length as reliability? The answer is "no." Gullikson (1950) classical work present formulas to show the relationship. If enough items are added to the test to double the reliability coefficient, the validity coefficient only increases by 41%. The prophetic formulas for validity usually involve the reliability coefficient in some shape and form. For example, there is a formula to predict the maximum validity coefficient based on the reliability coefficient. Using this formula it may be possible to obtain a validity coefficient higher than the reliability. However, in practice it is very difficult to obtain a validity coefficient that is larger than the reliability. The thinking here is that one would expect that a test correlated with itself should be higher than the same test correlated with an outside measure or criterion.

If it was possible to eliminate measurement errors of the test and the criterion, we would essentially have a correlation between the true scores of both measures. We have seen that measurement errors tend to lower the coefficient values. We can, in a hypothetical realm, find what the validity coefficient might be if measurement error could be eliminated in (i) both criterion and test, (ii) criterion only, and (iii) test only. Such corrections are referred to as *corrections for attenuation*. If we let r_{xy} be the correlation between criterion x and test, y, the formula to correct for attenuation in both is

$$Corrected\ r_{xy} = \frac{r_{xy}}{\sqrt{r_{xx}r_{yy}}}$$

The formula to determine what the validity might be if we had a *perfect criterion* is

$$r_{\infty y} = \frac{r_{xy}}{\sqrt{r_{xx}}}$$

The formula to determine the validity coefficient if we had a *perfect test* is

$$r_{x\infty} = \frac{r_{xy}}{\sqrt{r_{yy}}}$$

These formulas should not be used to make decisions about individuals, but are useful in determining if making a test or criterion more reliable is worth the effort. These formulas show what would happen to validity as changes are made in reliability.

The Validity and Reliability of Psychological and Eduational Measurement Instruments

Poor measurement can invalidate any scientific investigation. Most of the criticisms of psychological and educational measurement, by professionals and laypeople alike, center on validity. This is as it should be. Achieving reliability is to a large extent a technical matter. Validity, however, is much more than technique. It bores into the essence of science itself. It also bores into philosophy. Construct validity, particularly, since it is concerned with the nature of "reality" and the nature of the properties being measured, is heavily philosophical.

Despite the difficulties of achieving reliable and valid psychological, sociological, and educational measurements, great progress has been made in this century. There is growing understanding that all measuring instruments must be critically and empirically examined for their reliability and validity. The day of tolerance of inadequate measurement has ended. The demands imposed by professionals, the theoretical and statistical tools available and those being rapidly developed, and the increasing sophistication of graduate students of psychology, sociology, and education have set new high standards that should be healthy stimulants to the imaginations of both research workers and developers of scientific measurement.

CHAPTER SUMMARY

1. Validity deals with accuracy. Does the instrument measure what it is supposed to measure?

2. There are three types of validity

- content
- criterion-related
- construct

3. Content validity is concerned with the representativeness or sampling adequacy of the test's content.
4. Face validity is similar to content validity, but it is nonquantitative and involves merely a visual inspection of the test by sophisticated or unsophisticated reviewers.
5. Under criterion-related validity there are two methods: concurrent and predictive.
6. The distinguishing characteristic between concurrent and predictive validities is the temporal relationship between the instrument and the criterion.
7. An instrument high in criterion-related validity helps test users make better decisions in terms of placement, classification, selection, and assessment.
8. Construct validity seeks to explain individual differences in test scores. It deals with abstract concepts that may contain two or more dimensions.
9. Construct validity requires both convergence and discriminability.
10. Convergence states that instruments purporting to measure the same thing should be highly correlated.
11. Discriminability is shown when instruments that supposedly measure different things have a low correlation.
12. A method used to show both convergence and discriminability is Campbell and Fiske's (1959) multitrait–multimethod matrix.
13. We can show the relationship between validity and reliability mathematically.
14. Knowledge on how measurements are interpreted is important to research studies.
15. Two less traditional topics concerning interpretation and validity are: criterion-referenced testing and information referenced testing (or admissible probability measurement).

STUDY SUGGESTIONS

1. The measurement literature is vast. The following references have been chosen for their particular excellence or their relevance to important measurement topics. Some of the discussions, however, are technical and difficult. The student will find elementary discussions of reliability and validity in most measurement texts.

Allen, M. J., & Yen, W. M. (1979). *Introduction to measurement theory*. Belmont, CA: Brooks/Cole.

Cronbach, L. J., & Meehl, P. (1955). Construct validity in psychological tests. *Psychological Bulletin, 52,* 281–302. [A most important contribution to modern measurement and behavioral research.]

Cureton, E. (1969). Measurement theory. In R. Ebel, V. Noll, & R. Bauer, Eds., *Encyclopedia of educational research* (4th ed.), pp. 785–804. New York: Macmillan. [A broad and firm overview of measurement, with an emphasis on educational measurement.]

Horst, P. (1966). *Psychological measurement and prediction.* Belmont, CA: Wadsworth.

Tryon, R. (1957). Reliability and behavior domain validity: A reformulation and historical critique. *Psychological Bulletin, 54,* 229–249. [This is an excellent and important article on reliability. It contains a good worked example.]

The following anthologies of measurement articles are valuable sources of the classics in the field. This is especially true of the Mehrens and Ebel and the Jackson and Messick volumes.

Anastasi, A. (Ed.). (1966) *Testing problems in perspective.* Washington, DC: American Council on Education.

Barnette, W. L. (Ed.). (1976). *Reading in psychological tests and measurement* (3rd ed.). Baltimore, MD: Williams & Wilkins.

Chase, C., & Ludlow G. (Eds.). (1966). *Readings in educational and psychological measurement.* Boston: Houghton Mifflin.

Jackson, D., & Messick, S. (Eds.). (1967). *Problems in human assessment.* New York: McGraw-Hill.

Mehrens W., & Ebel, R. (Eds.). (1967). *Principles of educational and psychological measurement.* Skokie, IL: Rand McNally.

2. An important method in validity studies is cross-validation. Advanced students can profit from Mosier's essay in the Chase and Ludlow book listed above. A brief summary of Mosier's essay can be found in Guilford (1954, p. 406).
3. The more advanced student will also want to know something about response sets—a threat to validity, particularly to the validity of personality, attitude, and value items and instruments. *Response sets* are tendencies to respond to items in certain ways—high, low, approve, disapprove, extreme, and so on—regardless of the content of the items. The resulting scores are therefore systematically biased. The literature is extensive and cannot be cited here. An excellent exposition, however, can be found in Nunnally, (1978), chap. 16, especially pp. 655ff. Advocates of the effects of response sets on measurement instruments are quite strong in their statements. Rorer (1965), has thrown a considerable dash of salt on the response-set tail.

   The position taken in this book is that response sets certainly operate and sometimes have considerable effect, but that the strong claims of advocates are exaggerated. Most of the variance in well-constructed measures seems to be due to variables being measured, and relatively little to response sets. Investigators must be aware of response sets and their possible deleterious effects on measurement instruments, but should not be afraid to use the instruments. If one were to take too seriously the schools of thought on response sets and on what has been called the experimenter effect (in education, the Pygmalion effect) discussed earlier, one would have to abandon behavioral research except, perhaps, research that can be done with so-called unobtrusive measures.

4. Imagine that you have given a test of six items to six persons. The scores of each person on each item are given below. Say that you have also given another test of six items to six persons. These scores are also given below. The scores of the first test, I, are given on the left; the scores of the second test, II, are given on the right.

I							II						
			Items							*Items*			
Persons	*a*	*b*	*c*	*d*	*e*	*f*	Persons	*a*	*b*	*c*	*d*	*e*	*f*
1	6	6	7	5	6	5	1	6	4	5	6	6	3
2	6	4	5	5	4	5	2	6	2	7	4	4	4
3	5	4	7	6	4	3	3	5	6	5	3	4	2
4	3	2	5	3	4	4	4	3	4	4	5	4	5
5	2	3	4	4	3	2	5	2	1	7	1	3	5
6	2	1	3	1	0	2	6	2	3	3	5	0	2

The scores in II are the same as those in I, except that the orders of the scores of Items (*b*), (*c*), (*d*), and (*f*) have been changed.

a. Do a two-way analysis of variance of each set of scores. Compare and interpret the *F*-ratios. Pay special attention to the *F*-ratio for Persons (Individuals).

b. Compute $r_{tt} = (V_{ind} - V_e)/V_{ind}$ for I and II. Interpret the two r_{tt}s. Why are they so different?

c. Add the odd items across the rows; add the even items. Compare the rank orders and the ranges of the odd totals, the even totals, and the totals of all six items. The coefficients of correlation between odd and even items, corrected, are .98 and .30. Explain why they are so different. What do they mean?

d. Assume that there were 100 persons and 60 items. Would this have changed the procedures and the reasoning behind them? Would the effect of changing the orders of, say, five to 10 items have affected the r_{tt}s as much as in these examples? If not, why not?
   [Answers: (a) I: $F_{items} = 3.79$ (.05); $F_{persons} = 20.44$ (.001). II: $F_{items} = 1.03$ (n.s); $F_{persons} = 1.91$ (n.s). (b) I: $r_{tt} = .95$; II: $r_{tt} = .48$.]

PART NINE
METHODS OF OBSERVATION AND DATA COLLECTION

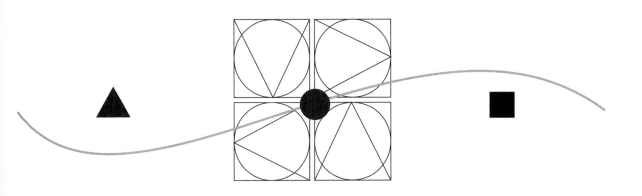

Chapter 29
INTERVIEWS AND INTERVIEW SCHEDULES

Chapter 30
OBJECTIVE TESTS AND SCALES

Chapter 31
OBSERVATIONS OF BEHAVIOR AND SOCIOMETRY

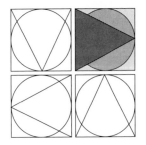

INTERVIEWS AND INTERVIEW SCHEDULES

The interview is perhaps the most ubiquitous method of obtaining information from people. It has been and still is used in all kinds of practical situations: the lawyer obtains information from a client; the physician learns about a patient; the admissions officer or professor determines the suitability of students for schools, departments, and curricula. Only recently, however, has the interview been used systematically for scientific purposes, both in the laboratory and in the field.

Data-collection methods can be categorized by the degree of their directness. If we wish to know something about people, we can ask them about it directly. They may or may not give us an answer. On the other hand, we may not ask a direct question. We may use an ambiguous stimulus, like a blurred picture, a blot of ink, or a vague question; and then ask for impressions of the stimulus, on the assumption that the respondents will give the needed information without knowing they are giving it. This method is highly indirect. Most of the data-collection methods used in psychological and sociological research are relatively direct or moderately indirect. Rarely are highly indirect means used.

Interviews and schedules (questionnaires) are ordinarily quite direct. This is both a strength and a weakness. It is a strength because a great deal of the information needed in social scientific research can be obtained from respondents by direct questions. Though the questions may have to be carefully handled, respondents can, and usually will, give much information directly. There is information, however, of a more difficult nature that respondents may be unwilling, reluctant, or unable to give readily and directly—for example, information on income, sexual relations, and attitudes toward religion and minority groups. In such cases, direct questions may yield data that are invalid. Yet, properly handled, even personal or controversial material can be successfully obtained through interviews and schedules.

The interview is probably one of the oldest and most often used devices for obtaining information. It has important qualities that objective tests and scales and behavioral observations do not possess. When used with a well-conceived schedule, an interview can obtain a great deal of information. It is flexible and adaptable to individual situations, and can often be used when no other method is possible or adequate. These qualities make it especially suitable for research with children. Methods and considerations for interviewing children are given in Aldridge and Wood (1998) and in Poole and Lamb (1998). Minkes, Robinson, and Weston (1994) provide explanations on how to interview children who have disabilities. Ellis (1989) describes how to conduct an interview with gifted Canadian children. An interviewer can know whether the respondent, especially a child, does not understand a question and can, within limits, repeat or rephrase the question. Questions about hopes, aspirations, and anxieties can be asked in such a way as to elicit accurate information. Most important, perhaps, the interview permits probing into the context and reasons for answers to questions. McReynolds (1989) summarizes the status of clinical measurement instruments, one of which is the *interview schedule*.

The major shortcoming of the interview and its accompanying schedule is practical. Interviews take a lot of time. Getting information from one individual may take as long as an hour or even two hours. This large time investment costs effort and money. Andrews (1974) gives the requirements in terms of recruiting, training, selecting, and supervising of a well-conducted research study using the interview method. One of the important components of the interview is supervision. Andrews lists at least nine responsibilities a supervisor should have. So, whenever a more economical method answers the research purposes, interviews should not be used. Emory (1976) cites research that has been done on interviewer characteristics. These studies found evidence that trivial characteristics could influence the results of the interview. For example, Emory cites the fact that women are better interviewers than men and that married men are better than single women. Emory also cites a study done by the National Opinion Research Center (NORC) relating characteristics to the quality of the interview. Training interviewers so that they produce the same level of quality requires time, resources, and perhaps even prior experience.

Interviews and Schedules as Tools of Science

For the most part, interviews and schedules have been used simply for gathering so-called facts. The most important use of interviews should be to study relations and to test hypotheses. The interview, in other words, is a psychological and sociological measuring instrument. Perhaps more accurately, the products of interviews—respondents' answers to carefully contrived questions—can be translated into measures of variables. Interviews and interview schedules are therefore subject to the same criteria of reliability, validity, and objectivity as other measuring instruments.

An interview can be used for three main purposes:

1. It can be an exploratory device to help identify variables and relations, to suggest hypotheses, and to guide other phases of the research.
2. It can be the main instrument of the research. In this case, questions designed to measure the variables of the research will be included in the interview schedule. These questions are then to be considered as items in a measurement instrument, rather than as mere information-gathering devices.
3. The interview can supplement other methods: follow up unexpected results, validate other methods, and go deeper into the motivations of respondents and their reasons for responding as they do.

In using interviews as tools of scientific research, we must ask the questions: Can data on the research problem be obtained in an easier or better way? To achieve reliability, for example, is not a small problem. Interviewers must be trained; questions must be pretested and revised to eliminate ambiguities and inadequate wording. Is it worth the effort? Validity, too, is no small problem. Special pains must be taken to eliminate interviewer bias; questions must be tested for unknown biases. The particular research problem and the nature of the information sought must, in the final analysis, dictate whether the interview will be used. Cannell and Kahn (1968, chapter 15) and Warwick and Lininger (1975, chapter 7) provide detailed guidance on whether an interview should or should not be used.

The Interview

The *interview* is a face-to-face interpersonal role situation in which one person (the interviewer) asks a person being interviewed (the respondent) questions designed to obtain answers pertinent to the research problem. There are two broad types of interview: *structured* and *unstructured*, or *standardized* and *unstandardized* (see Cannell & Kahn, 1968). In the standardized interview, the questions, their sequence, and their wording are fixed. An interviewer may be allowed some liberty in asking questions, but relatively little. The *Interviewer's Manual* (1976) produced by the Institute for Social Research at the University of Michigan states that the view toward the interview is evolving from the traditional view. The interview is seen as an interaction, an active role relation between interviewer and interviewee, in which the interviewer is even a teacher. Cannell and Kahn (1968), and Dohrenwend and Richardson (1963) provide additional information on this topic. This liberty is specified in advance. Standardized interviews use interview schedules that have been carefully prepared to obtain information pertinent to the research problem.

Unstandardized interviews are more flexible and open. Although the research purposes govern the questions asked, their content, their sequence, and their wording are in the hands of the interviewer. Ordinarily no schedule is used. In other words, the unstandardized, nonstructured interview is an open situation in contrast to the standardized, structured interview, which is a closed situation. This does not mean that an unstandardized interview is casual. It should be just as carefully planned as the standardized one. Green and Tull (1988) state that unstructured interviews can obtain information that structured interviews cannot. With the informal approach of the unstructured interview, the researcher can get ideas concerning the interviewee's motives. Such unstructured interviews are at times called *depth interviews*. They are especially useful for doing exploratory studies. Our concern here is mainly with the standardized interview. It is recognized, however, that many research problems may, and often do, require a compromise type of interview in which the interviewer is permitted to use alternate questions that fit for particular respondents and particular questions. The actual procedure of conducting an interview is not discussed in this book. The reader will find guidance in the Study Suggestions for this chapter.

The Interview Schedule

Interviewing itself is an art, but the planning and writing of an interview schedule is even more so. It is unusual for a novice to produce a good schedule, at least without considerable prior study and practice. There are several reasons for this, the main ones probably being the multiple meaning and ambiguity of words, the lack of sharp and constant focus on the problems and hypotheses being studied, a lack of appreciation of the schedule as a measurement instrument, and a lack of necessary background and experience.

Kinds of Schedule Information and Items

Three kinds of information are included in most schedules: face sheet (identification) information, census-type (or sociological) information, and problem information. Except for identification, these types of information were discussed in an earlier chapter. The importance of identifying each schedule accurately and completely, however, needs to be mentioned. The careful researcher should learn to identify with letters, numbers, or other symbols, every schedule and every scale. In addition, identifying information for each individual must be recorded systematically. Two types of schedule items are in common use: *fixed-alternative* (or closed) and *open-ended* (or open). A third type of item, having fixed alternatives, is also used: *scale* items.

Fixed-Alternative Items

Fixed-alternative items, as the name indicates, offer the respondent a choice among two or more alternatives. These items are also called *closed* or *poll* questions. The commonest kind of fixed-alternative item is dichotomous: it asks for Yes–No, Agree–Disagree, and other two-alternative answers. A third alternative, Don't Know or Undecided, is also often added.

An example of a fixed-alternative item is

Do you feel that the U.S. government has found a cure for AIDS but is withholding it?

Yes . . . . [ ]
No . . . .[ ]
Don't know . . . .[ ]

Although fixed-alternative items have the decided advantages of achieving greater uniformity of measurement and thus greater reliability, of forcing the respondent to answer in a way that fits the response categories previously set up, and of being easily coded, they have certain disadvantages. The major disadvantage is their superficiality: Without probes they do not ordinarily get beneath the response surface. They may also irritate a respondent who finds none of the alternatives suitable. Worse, they can force responses. A respondent may choose an alternative to conceal ignorance or choose alternatives that do not accurately represent facts or opinions. These difficulties do not mean that fixed-alternative items are bad and useless. On the contrary, they can be used to good purpose if they are judiciously written, used with probes, and mixed with open items. A *probe* is a device used to find out respondents' information on a subject, their frames of reference, or, more usually, to clarify and ascertain reasons for responses given. Probing increases the "response-getting" power of questions without changing their content. Examples of probes are: "Tell me more about that." "How is that?" "Can you explain that?" (see Warwick & Lininger, 1975, pp. 210–215).

Open-Ended Items

Open or open-ended items are an extremely important development in the technique of interviewing. *Open-ended* questions are those that supply a frame of reference for respondents' answers, but put a minimum of restraint on the answers and their expression. While their content is dictated by the research problem, they impose no other restrictions on the content and manner of respondent answers. Examples will be given later.

Open-ended questions have important advantages, but they have disadvantages, too. If properly written and used, however, these disadvantages can be minimized.

Open-ended questions are flexible; they have possibilities of depth; they enable the interviewer to clear up misunderstandings (through probing), to ascertain a respondent's lack of knowledge, to detect ambiguity, to encourage cooperation and achieve rapport, and to make better estimates of respondents' true intentions, beliefs, and attitudes. Their use also has another advantage: the responses to open-ended questions can *suggest* possibilities of relations and hypotheses. Respondents will sometimes give unexpected answers that may indicate the existence of relations not originally anticipated.

A special type of open-ended question is the *funnel.* Actually, this is a set of questions directed toward getting information on a single important topic or a single set of related topics. The funnel starts with a broad question and narrows down progressively to the important specific point or points. Warwick and Lininger (1975) point out that the merits of the funnel is that it allows free response in the earlier questions, narrows down to specific questions and responses, and also facilitates the discovery of respondents' frames of reference. Another form of funnel starts with an open general question and follows up with specific closed items. The best way to get a feeling for good open-ended questions and funnels is to study examples.

To obtain information on child-rearing practices, Sears, Maccoby, and Levin (1957) used a number of good open-ended and funnel questions. One of them, with the authors' comments in brackets, is:

Example

> All babies cry, of course. [Note that the interviewer puts the parent at ease about her child's crying.] Some mothers feel that if you pick up a baby every time it cries, you will spoil it. Others think you should never let a baby cry for very long. [The frame of reference has been clearly given. The mother is also put at ease no matter how she handles her baby's crying.] How do you feel about this?
>
> > (a) What did you do about this with X?
> >
> > (b) How about in the middle of the night?

This funnel question set not only reaches attitudes, it also probes specific practices.

Scale Items

A third type of schedule item is the scale item. A *scale* is a set of verbal items to each of which an individual responds by expressing degrees of agreement or disagreement, or some other mode of response. Scale items have fixed alternatives and place the responding individual at some point on the scale. (They will be discussed at greater length in Chapter 30). The use of scale items in interview schedules is a development of great promise, since the benefits of scales are combined with those of interviews. We can include, for example, a scale to measure attitudes toward education in an interview schedule on the same topic. Scale scores can be obtained in this way for each respondent and can be checked against open-ended question data. One can measure the *tolerance of nonconformity*, as Stouffer (1955) did, by having a scale to measure this variable embedded in the interview schedule.

Criteria of Question-Writing

Criteria or precepts of question-writing have been developed through experience and research. Some of the most important of these are given below in the form of questions. Brief comments are appended to the questions. When confronted with the actual necessity of drafting a schedule, the student should consult more extended treatments, since the ensuing discussion, in keeping with the discussion of the rest of the chapter, is intended only as an introduction to the subject. For practical guidance, see Emory (1976, chapter 8), which provides a good summary and key points in creating the schedule; Noelle-Neuman (1970), and Warwick and Lininger (1975). Emory emphasizes how to test the instrument before its actual use, how to sequence the items or questions, and what to do under certain situations. Other references are Atkinson (1971), Beed and Stimson (1985), and Mishler (1986).

1. *Is the question related to the research problem and the research objectives?* Except for factual and sociological information questions, all the items of a schedule should have some research problem function. This means that the purpose of each question is to elicit information that can be used to test the hypotheses of the research.
2. *Is the type of question appropriate?* Some information can best be obtained with the open-ended questions—reasons for behavior, intentions, and attitudes. Certain other information, on the other hand, can be obtained more expeditiously with closed questions. If all that is required of a respondent is the preferred choice of two or more alternatives, and these alternatives can be clearly specified, it would be wasteful to use an open-ended question (see Dohrenwend & Richardson, 1963; Schuman & Presser, 1979; Warwick & Lininger, 1975).
3. *Is the item clear and unambiguous?* An ambiguous statement or item is one that permits or invites alternative interpretations, and differing responses resulting from the alternative interpretations. So-called double-barreled questions are ambiguous, for example, because they provide two or more frames of reference rather than only one. Respondents, even if not baffled by the complexity and alternatives offered by the following question, can hardly respond using a common frame of reference and understanding of what is wanted. "How are you and your family getting along this year?" Does the questioner mean finances, marital happiness, health status, or what?

   A great deal of work has been done on item-writing. Certain precepts, if followed, help the item writer avoid ambiguity. First, questions that contain more than one idea to which a respondent can react should be avoided. An item like "Do you believe that the educational aims of the modern high school and the teaching methods used to attain these aims are educationally sound?" is an ambiguous question, because the respondent is asked about both educational aims and teaching methods in the same question. Second, avoid ambiguous words and expressions. A respondent might be asked the question, "Do you think the teachers in your school get fair treatment?" This is an ambiguous item because "fair treatment" might refer to several different areas of treatment. The word *fair*, too, can mean "just," "equitable," "not too good," "impartial," and "objective." The question needs a clear context, an explicit frame of reference. (Sometimes, however, ambiguous questions are deliberately used to elicit different frames of reference.)

4. *Is the question a leading question?* Leading questions suggest answers. As such, they threaten validity. If you ask a person "Have you read about the local school situation?" you may get a disproportionately large number of "yes" responses because the question may imply that it is bad not to have read about the local school situation.

5. *Does the question demand knowledge and information that the respondent does not have?* To counter the invalidity of response due to lack of information, it is wise to use information-filter questions. Before asking a person what he or she thinks of UNESCO, first find out whether he or she knows what UNESCO is and means. Another approach is possible. You can explain UNESCO briefly, and then ask the respondent what he or she thinks of it.

6. *Does the question demand personal or delicate material that the respondent may resist?* Special techniques are needed to obtain information of a personal, delicate, or controversial nature. Ask income and other personal matters late in the interview after rapport has been built up. When asking about something that is socially disapproved, show that some people believe one way and others believe another way. Don't make the respondent, in effect, disapprove of himself or herself. The respondent needs to be reassured that all answers and responses will remain confidential.

7. *Is the question loaded with social desirability?* People tend to give responses that are socially desirable; responses that indicate or imply approval of actions or things that are generally considered to be good. We may ask a person about his or her feelings toward children. Everyone is supposed to love children. Unless we are careful, we will get a stereotyped response about children and love. Also, when we ask if a person votes, we must be careful since everyone is supposed to vote. If we ask respondents their reactions to minority groups, we again run the risk of getting invalid responses. Most educated persons, no matter what their "true" attitudes, are aware that prejudice is disapproved. A good question, then, is one in which respondents are not led to express merely socially desirable sentiments. At the same time, one should not question respondents so that they are faced with the necessity of giving socially undesirable responses.

The Value of Interviews and Interview Schedules

The interview, when coupled with an adequate schedule of pretested worth, is a potent and indispensable research tool, yielding data that no other research tool can yield. It is adaptable, capable of being used with all kinds of respondents in many kinds of research, and uniquely suited to exploration in depth. But do its strengths balance its weaknesses? And what is its value in behavioral research when compared to other methods of data collection?

The most natural tool with which to compare the interview is the so-called questionnaire. As noted earlier, "questionnaire" is a term used for almost any kind of instrument that has questions or items to which individuals respond. Although the term is used interchangeably with "schedule," it seems to be associated more with self-administered instruments that have items of the closed- or fixed-alternative type.

The *self-administered instrument* has certain advantages. With most or all of its items of the closed type, greater uniformity of stimulus, and thus greater reliability, can be achieved. In this respect, it has the advantages of objective-type, written tests and scales, if they are adequately constructed and pretested. A second advantage is that, if anonymous or confidential, honesty and frankness may be encouraged. This kind of instrument can also be administered to large numbers relatively easily. A somewhat dubious advantage is that it can be mailed to respondents. Further, it is economical. Its cost is ordinarily a fraction of that of interviews.

The disadvantages of the self-administered instrument (when mailed) seem to outweigh its advantages. The principal disadvantage is low percentage of returns. A second disadvantage is that it may not be as uniform as its seems. Experience has shown that the same question frequently has different meanings for different people. As we saw, this can be handled in the interview. But we are powerless to do anything about it when the instrument is self-administered. Third, if only closed items are used, the instrument displays the same weaknesses of closed items discussed earlier. On the other hand, if open items are used, the respondent may object to writing the answers, which reduces the sample of adequate responses. Many people cannot express themselves adequately in writing, and many who can express themselves dislike doing so.

Because of these disadvantages, the interview is probably superior to the self-administered questionnaire. (This objection does not, of course, include carefully constructed personality and attitude scales.) The best instrument available for sounding people's behavior, future intentions, feelings, attitudes, and reasons for behavior would seem to be the structured interview coupled with an interview schedule that includes open-ended, closed, and scale items. Of course, the structured interview must be carefully constructed and pretested, and administered only by skilled interviewers. The cost in time, energy, and money, and the very high degree of skill necessary for its construction, are its main drawbacks. Once these disadvantages are surmounted, the structured interview is a powerful tool.

The Focus Group and Group Interviewing:
Another Interviewing Method

Perhaps this topic belongs in an earlier chapter when we were discussing qualitative methods. Some researchers equate the focus group method as qualitative research (Calder, 1977). Some have referred to this method as Group Interviews (Wells, 1974). Basch (1987) reports that this method was discussed by Bogardus in 1926 but only used occasionally from that time until the 1980s. The primary users of the focus group until recently were market and business researchers. Basch (1987) feels that the focus group method has promise in areas other than marketing. He feels that it could be a research technique for improving health education research, practice, and theory. The method provides an in-depth view of people. Sudman, Bradburn, and Schwarz (1996) believe the focus group methodology is useful in determining how respondents retrieve and process information.

The focus group technique involves interviewing two or more people at the same time. The size of the focus group should be large enough to generate diverse viewpoints, but small enough to be manageable. Krueger (1994) recommends seven to ten people per focus group. This will allow each person the opportunity to participate in the discussion. There is a moderator who leads the discussion in a free and open manner. This moderator or facilitator must be well trained. It is the moderator's function to keep the discussion from straying too far from the topic of interest. The topic under discussion can be any subject. The respondent's answers are not actively solicited. There is no direct prompting. In marketing or consumer research the topic would concern a product or service. In psychology, one might be interested in the language used by African American gay men (Mays, Cochran, Bellinger, Smith, Henley, et al., 1992). In health, one would use a focus group to determine fears about seatbelts or airbags. One of the goals is to examine people's attitudes and behaviors. The other goal is to find out what each participant thinks about the topic under discussion. The opinions and descriptions are elicited from the respondents. Through the discussions, the researcher hopes to be able to discover important insights that can be used later to solve problems. Calder (1977) states that the focus group method is useful in discovering information that can be used to design a quantitative research study. Some have used the focus group as a means of developing questionnaires. Focus group research can also help researchers develop constructs to be used in future studies. Calder calls this "prescientific knowledge."

One of the advantages of focus groups is in their cost. It costs very little to do a focus group. The major costs would be the recruiting and pay for the moderator. Also, the participants may receive a token payment for their time. The focus group is also quick to do. The ideas of the respondents are available very quickly and videotaping of the sessions can be done for further analysis at a later date. The focus group is very good at generating hypotheses for further research. In marketing research, the focus group allows the client (manufacturer) who commissioned the study to be an active participant in the focus group. In this way, that person can get the information firsthand. This is possible because groups are kept to a manageable size. The interaction between respondents can provide stimulating exchanges that result in useful information, unobtainable with other research methods. And, as mentioned previously, focus groups are very flexible. An experienced moderator can direct, but yet let promising ideas flow.

The focus group, however, is not very good in producing concrete information. One should not base a decision solely from information gathered from a focus group. It has been criticized by quantitative researchers as "unscientific" and not trustworthy. Questions are not standardized and may vary from group to group. With the use of very small groups, the focus group data suffers from generalizability. Unlike structured survey research, the focus group does not expend a great deal of effort in making certain the group is representative. As with any group dynamics, there will be a few individuals who will dominate the conversation. The moderator needs to have sufficient experience to minimize this without shutting down the flow of communication. Focus group interviewing takes a lot of patience and skill. Berger (1991) gives some valuable suggestions for the moderator. Berger also gives an outline as to what a write-up should contain for a focus group. Some participants take the focus group as an opportunity to vent their emotions. Hence, topics that are sensitive should not be explored using focus groups. Some very good references on focus groups are given in the Study Suggestions. Focus groups are a qualitative method of research. As such they are capable of producing rich information untapped by quantitative methods. They are best suited for learning what clients may want, or what people think about certain policies and rules. Focus groups have been shown to be effective when studying organizations.

Some Examples of Focus Group Research

Audience Studies Incorporated (ASI) is a marketing research firm that has operated out of Hollywood, California for many years. Consumers are invited to a showing, which presents a television show and commercials. For their participation, there are drawings for prizes such as shampoo, toothpaste, analgesics, and so on. During the showing of the program and commercials, the participants use an electronic rating device to communicate their thoughts about what they are viewing. These responses are recorded. The participants also complete questionnaires after each commercial or program. From this group, several persons are chosen to participate in focus groups. Manufacturers of consumer products usually commission ASI to conduct these focus groups to get ideas about how their product fares against the competition. On several occasions, representatives of the manufacturer participate in the focus group so that they can get information directly. For example, if a manufacturer is looking to develop a new product, the information coming from focus groups could give insights as to what should go into that product in terms of manufacturing and marketing.

Mays et al. (1992) used a focus group involving African American gay males. The topic under discussion was sexual behavior and HIV. Using this method, Mays et al. were able to create a gay vernacular list for African American males. These results are useful in comparing African American and white American gay males, and also in the construction of questionnaires designed to tap sexual behavior of African American gay males. The knowledge obtained from this study could also serve to educate counselors and health professionals that deal with the African American gay male. Mays et al. (1992, p. 432) state

> In using the terminology presented here for the conduct of HIV-related research, it is important to remember that linguistic and cognitive processes are [e]mbedded in a context. In assessing the sexual behavior of Black gay men, the asking of questions that embody their vernacular must also be asked from a framework of their experience.

Sussman, Burton, Dent, Stacy, and Flay (1991) issued a caution in using focus groups. They feel that focus groups may induce certain *group effects* that might bias responses. Their study explored the extended focus group procedure, which includes a pregroup questionnaire. The questionnaire includes material that will be covered during the focus group session, and may affect group members by having them commit to a position before group discussion begins. These researchers feel that people rely on the responses of other people, converging to a collective norm. That is, some respondents will become more extreme in their judgments following group discussions.

One of the collective norm effects is the *group polarization effect.* The involvement in a group may bias participants to respond in more extreme ways. Specifically, Sussman et al. (1991) looked for a polarization of attitudes (a group-influence bias effect). The discussion in the focus group was directed at how to recruit adolescent tobacco users into a cessation clinic. There were 31 focus groups. Each group was administered pretest and posttest questionnaires. The data collected supported a group polarization effect. After participating in a focus group, the respondents had a higher evaluation of the self-generated recruitment strategies. They also reported that if they were smokers, these strategies would induce them to join the program themselves. This study showed that focus groups might not extract the reporting of new strategies. However, they do appear to be effective in injecting into the participants a more favorable attitude toward self-generated solutions to problems.

CHAPTER SUMMARY

1. The interview is the oldest and most universal method of extracting large amounts of information from people.
2. The data collection methods used in an interview can be classified by the amount of directness in the questions and questioning.
3. Interviews require a lot of time. Hence, data collection is expensive in terms of time, effort and money.
4. Interviews require well-trained interviewers and a well-developed questionnaire.
5. The interview can be used for three main purposes: as an exploratory device

to generate ideas and hypotheses, as the the main instrument used in a study, and as a supplement to other methods and/or used as a follow-up.

6. The interview is a face-to-face interpersonal role situation. It can be structured or unstructured.

7. One type of unstructured interview is the group interview or focus groups.

8. There are three kinds of information sought in interview schedules: Identification, Census-type (sociological), and Problem.

9. The type of items used in an interview schedule are: fixed-alternative items, open-ended items, and scale items.

10. There are seven criteria for writing items/questions in the schedule.

11. The focus group method is an unstructured interview using a small number of participants. These are low in cost and quick to do.

12. Focus group research is qualitative research.

13. Focus groups have a problem in generalization.

STUDY SUGGESTIONS

1. Several valuable references on the interview and the interview schedule a few are listed and annotated below.

Classical Works

Cannell, C., & Kahn, R. (1968). Interviewing. In G. Lindzey & E. Aronson, Eds., *The handbook of social psychology*, vol. II (2nd ed.). Reading, MA: Addison-Wesley. 526–595.

Survey Research Center. (1976). *Interviewer's manual* (rev. ed.). Ann Arbor, MI: Institute for Social Research, University of Michigan. [An excellent guide to the practical aspects of interviewing.]

Warwick, D., & Lininger, C. (1975). *The sample survey: Theory and practice.* New York: McGraw-Hill.

More Recent Works

Beed, T. W., & Stimson, R. J. (1985). *Survey interviewing: Theory and techniques.* New York: Routledge, Chapman, and Hall.

Bowden, J. C. (1995). *An investigator's guide to interviewing and interrogation.* Orlando, FL: Bowden.

Knale, S. (1996). *Interviews: An introduction to qualitative research interviewing.* Thousand Oaks, CA: Sage.

Lukas, S. (1993). *Where to start and what to ask: The assessment handbook.* New York: Norton.

Mollica, R. F., & Caspi-Yavin, Y. (1991). Measuring torture and torture-related symptoms. *Psychological Assessment, 3,* 581–587. [Discusses why current interviewing instruments and techniques are inaccurate when interviewing people who have been tortured.]

Myers, J. (1996). *Interviewing young children about body touch and handling.* Chicago, IL: University of Chicago Press.

2. Good interview schedules are fortunately plentiful. The reader should study two or three of them carefully. The suggested schedules that follow are both well constructed and substantively interesting. Note that published schedules usually have extensive methodological discussions accompanying them. The student can learn a good deal about interview scale construction from study of these discussions.

Campbell A., Converse, P., & Rodgers, W. (1976). *The quality of American life.* New York: Russell Sage Foundation, app. B. [A long schedule with many scale items and careful interviewer instructions. Also a substantively important study.]

Free L., & Cantril, H. (1967). *The political beliefs of Americans.* New Brunswick, NJ: Rutgers University Press, app. B. [Presents good questions, probes, and fixed-alternative items.]

Glock, C., & Stark, R. (1966). *Christian beliefs and anti-Semitism.* New York: Harper & Row. [The complete schedule, mostly with fixed-alternative items, is given at the end of the book.]

3. The examples given in 2 above, are all survey research, the field of research in which the art and technique of interviewing were developed and first used. Interviews, however, can be and have been used in what can be called "normal" studies, studies whose only, or main, interest is in pursuing relations among variables. The Burt (1980) study of attitudes toward rape is a good example, other examples follow.

"Normal" Studies

Beckman, L. J., & Mays, V. M. (1985). Educating community gatekeepers about alcohol abuse in women: Changing attitudes, knowledge and referral practices. *Journal of Drug Education, 15,* 289–309. [Used a phone interview to assess the effect of two workshops on knowledge, attitudes, and referral practices toward women suffering from alcohol abuse.]

Campbell, A., & Schuman, H. (1968). *Racial attitudes in fifteen cities.* Ann Arbor, MI: Institute for Social Research, University of Michigan. [A combination of "survey" and attitudinal questions aimed at understanding racial attitudes and their change.]

Doob, A., & MacDonald, G. (1979). Television viewing and fear of victimization: Is the relationship causal? *Journal of Personality and Social Psychology, 37,* 170–179. [Conducted a door-to-door interview to determine if people who watch more television have more fears than people who watch less television. A comparison was made between those that live in a low crime rate area and those living in a high crime rate area.]

Gersch, I. S., & Nolan, A. (1994). Exclusion: What the children think. *Educational Psychology in Practice, 10*, 35–45. [Designed, administered, and analyzed a interview schedule to measure children's attitudes and experiences about school. This instrument was used to assess students who were excluded.]

Jones, S. L. (1996). The association between objective and subjective caregiver burden. *Archives of Psychiatric Nursing, 10*, 77–84. [In three waves of data collection, telephone interviews were used to develop associations between objective and subjective burdens of caregivers.]

4. The following are books and articles dealing with the theory and practice of focus groups in the social and behavioral science. Focus groups often serve as idea-generators and for testing hypotheses in an informal setting. Find one of these and read the chapters on methodology.

Berger, A. A. (1991). *Media research techniques.* Newbury Park, CA: Sage.

Greenbaum, T. L. (1993). *The handbook for focus group research.* New York: Lexington Books.

Morgan, D. L. (1988). *Focus groups as qualitative research.* Newbury Park, CA: Sage.

Templeton, J. F. (1994). *The focus group: A strategic guide to organizing, conducting, and analyzing the focus group interview.* Chicago, IL: Probus Publishing.

Vaughn, S. (1996). *Focus group interviews in education and psychology.* Thousand Oaks, CA: Sage.

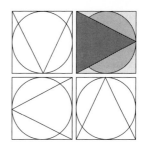

OBJECTIVE TESTS AND SCALES

In the behavioral sciences, the most used method of observation and data collection is the test or scale. The considerable time researchers spend in constructing or finding measures of variables is well spent because adequate measurement of research variables is at the core of behavioral scientific work. In general, too little attention has been paid to the measurement of the variables of research studies. What good are intriguing and important research problems, sophisticated research design, and intricate statistical analysis if the variables of research studies are poorly measured? Fortunately, great

707

progress has been made in understanding psychological and educational measurement theory and in improving measurement practice. In this chapter we examine some of the technology behind objective measurement procedures.

Objectivity and Objective Methods of Observation

Objectivity, a central and essential characteristic of scientific methodology, is easy to define but evidently hard to understand. It is also controversial. Objectivity is agreement among expert judges on what is observed. Objective methods of observation are those in which anyone following the prescribed rules will assign the same numerals to objects and sets of objects as anyone else. An objective procedure is one in which agreement among observers is at a maximum. In variance terms, observer variance is at a minimum. This means that judgmental variance, the variance due to differences in judges' assignment of numerals to objects, approaches zero. An extended discussion of objectivity is in Kerlinger (1979, pp. 9–13 and 262–264). The importance of understanding objectivity in science cannot be overemphasized. It is especially important to understand that scientific objectivity is methodological and has little or nothing to do with objectivity as a presumed characteristic of scientists. Whether a scientist as a person is or is not objective is not the point. The point is that scientific objectivity inheres in methodological procedures characterized by agreement among expert judges—and nothing more.

All methods of observation are inferential: Inferences about properties of the members of sets are made on the basis of the numerals assigned to the set members with interviews, tests, scales, and direct observations of behavior. The methods differ in their directness or indirectness, in the degree to which inferences are made from the raw observations. The inferences made by using objective methods of observations are usually lengthy, despite their seeming directness. Most such methods permit a high degree of interobserver agreement, because participants make marks on paper, the marks being restricted to two or more choices among alternatives supplied by the observer. From these marks on paper the observer infers the characteristics of the individuals and sets of individuals making the marks. In one class of objective methods, the marks on paper are made by the observer (or judge) who looks at the object or objects of measurement and chooses between given alternatives. In this case, too, inferences about the properties of the observed object or objects are made from the marks on paper. The main difference lies in who makes the marks.

It should be recognized that all methods of observation have some objectivity. There is no sharp dichotomy; in other words, between so-called objective methods and other methods of observation. There is, rather, a difference in the degree of objectivity. Again, if we think of degrees of objectivity as degrees of agreement among observers, the ambiguity and confusion often associated with the problem disappear.

We will agree, then, that what are here called objective methods of observation and measurement have no monopoly on objectivity or on inference, but that they are more objective and no less inferential than any other method of observation and measurement. The methods to be discussed in this chapter will by no means exhaust possible methods, since the subject is large and varied. They are considered only as measures of variables, to be viewed and assessed the same as all other measures of variables.

Tests and Scales: Definitions

A *test* is a systematic procedure in which individuals are presented with a set of constructed stimuli to which they respond. The responses enable the tester to assign the testees numerals or sets of numerals from which inferences can be made about the testees' possession of whatever the test is supposed to measure. This definition says little more than that a test is a measurement instrument.

A *scale* is a set of symbols or numerals so constructed that the symbols or numerals can be assigned by rule to the individuals (or their behaviors) to whom the scale is applied, the assignment being indicated by the individual's possession of whatever the scale is supposed to measure. Like a test, a scale is a measuring instrument. Indeed, except for the excess meaning associated with test, we can see that test and scale are similarly defined. Strictly speaking, however, scale is used in two ways: to indicate a measuring instrument and to indicate the systematized numerals of the measuring instrument. We use it in both senses without worrying too much about distinctions. Remember this, however: tests are scales, but scales are not necessarily tests. This can be said because scales do not ordinarily have the meanings of competition and success or failure that tests do. Significantly, we say "achievement testing," not "achievement scaling"; "intelligence testing" and not "intelligence scaling."

Types of Objective Measures

Most of the hundreds, perhaps thousands, of tests and scales can be divided into the following classes: intelligence and aptitude tests, achievement tests, personality measures, attitude and value scales, and miscellaneous objective measures. We discuss each of these types of measure from a research point of view.

Intelligence and Aptitude Tests

In psychological and educational research, a measure of intelligence or aptitude is often needed, either as an independent variable or as a dependent variable. In assessing the effects of educational programs of one kind or another on educational achievement, for instance, it is usually necessary to control intelligence so that the differences found between experimental treatment groups cannot be attributed to differences in intelligence rather than to the treatments. There are a number of good group intelligence tests that researchers can use, perhaps a so-called omnibus test. (An *omnibus test* is one that has items of different types—verbal, numerical, spatial, and others—in one instrument.) These tests are ordinarily highly verbal and correlate substantially with school achievement. Buros's (1998) handbooks are useful guides to such tests. Anastasi (1988) gives a classified list of representative tests in her book, and breaks down the test into separate classifications such as intelligence, personality, and so on.

Aptitude is the potential ability for achievement. Aptitude tests are used mainly for guidance and counseling. They can also be used in research, particularly as control variables. A *control variable* is one whose effect on a dependent variable may need to be nullified. For example, in studying the effect of a remedial reading program on reading achievement, verbal aptitude may need to be attributed to possible group differences in verbal ability. Similarly, other possible influential variables— numerical and spatial abilities, for instance—may need to be controlled. Aptitude tests can be useful in such cases.

Achievement Tests

Achievement tests measure present proficiency, mastery, and understanding of general and specific areas of knowledge. For the most part, they are measures of the effectiveness of instruction and learning and, of course, are enormously important in education and educational research. Indeed, in research involving instructional methods, achievement, as we have seen, is often the dependent variable.

Achievement tests can be classified in several ways. For our purposes, we break them down into, first, standardized and specially constructed tests. *Standardized tests* are published group tests that are based on general educational content common to a large number of educational systems. They are the products of a high degree of professional competence and skill in test-writing and, as such, are usually quite reliable and generally valid. They are also endowed with elaborate tables of norms (averages) that can be used for comparative purposes. *Specially constructed tests* are ordinarily teacher-made tests to measure more limited and specific achievements. They may, of course, also be constructed by educational researchers for measuring limited areas of achievement or proficiency.

Second, standardized achievement tests can be further classified into general and special tests. *General tests* are typically batteries of tests that measure the most important areas of school achievement: language usage, vocabulary, reading, arithmetic, and social studies. Special achievement tests, as the name indicates, are tests in individual subjects, such as history, science, and English.

Researchers often have no choice of achievement tests because school systems have already selected them. When given choice, however, researchers must carefully assess the kind of achievement test that their research problems require. Suppose the research variable in a study is "achievement in understanding concepts." Many, perhaps most, tests used in schools will not be adequate for measuring this variable. In such cases, researchers can choose a test specifically designed to measure the understanding of concepts, or can devise such tests themselves. The construction of an achievement test is a formidable job, the details of which cannot be discussed here. The student is referred to specialized texts. Unfortunately, there are few texts on the construction of tests and scales for research purposes. The many texts and other discussions of measurement focus for the most part on the construction and use of instruments for applied purposes. Researchers who need to construct achievement measures of one kind or another, however, will find excellent guidance in Adkins

(1974); Cangelosi (1990); Gronlund (1988); Haladyna (1997); Hopkins (1989); and Osterlind (1989). Researchers who need to construct attitude scales will find Edwards's (1957) book invaluable. Dawes (1972) covers some methods that Edwards did not cover.

Personality Measures

The measurement of personality traits is the most complex problem of psychological measurement. The reason is simple: Human personality is extremely complex. For the purposes of measurement, personality can be viewed as the organization of the traits of the individual. A *trait* is a characteristic of an individual revealed through recurring behaviors in different situations. We say an individual is compulsive, or has the trait of compulsivity because that person is observed to be overly neat in dress and speech, to be always punctual, to want everything to be very orderly, and to dislike and avoid irregularities.

The major problem in personality measurement is validity. To measure personality traits validly requires knowledge of what these traits are, how they interact and change, and how they relate to each other—a formidable, even forbidding, requirement. The wonder is not, as naive critics love to point out, that personality cannot be measured because it is too elusive, too complex, too existential, or that measurement efforts have not been too successful, but rather that some measure of success in so difficult a task has been achieved. Nevertheless, the problem of validity is considerable.

There are two general approaches to the construction and validation of personality measures: the a priori method, and the construct or theoretical method. In the *a priori method*, items are constructed to reflect the personality dimension to be measured. Since the introvert is frequently a retiring person, we might write items about the preference to be alone. This might, for instance, include items indicating one's preference to shun parties in order to measure introversion. Since the anxious person will probably be nervous and disorganized under stress, we might write items suggesting these conditions in order to measure anxiety. In the a priori method, then, the scale writer collects or writes items that ostensibly measure personality traits.

This approach is essentially that of early personality test-writers. While there is nothing inherently wrong with the method—indeed, it will have to be used, especially in the early stages of test and scale construction—the results can be misleading. Items do not always measure what we think they measure. Sometimes we even find that an item we thought would measure, say, social responsibility, actually measures a tendency to agree with socially desirable statements. For this reason, the a priori method, used alone, is insufficient. As such, personality tests generally lack content validity.

The method of validation often used with a priori personality scales is the *known group method*. To validate a scale of social responsibility, one might find a group of individuals known to be high in social responsibility, and another known to be low in social responsibility. If the scale differentiates the groups successfully, it is said to have validity.

A priori personality and other measures will continue to be used in behavioral research. Their blind and naive use, however, should be discouraged. Their construct and criterion-related validities must be checked, especially through factor analysis and other empirical means. Measures of personality, as well as other measures, have too often been used merely because users think they measure whatever they are said to measure.

The *construct* or *theoretical method* of personality measure construction emphasizes the relations of the variable being measured to other variables, the relations prompted by the theory underlying the research. While scale construction must always to some extent be a priori, the more personality measures are subjected to the tests of construct validity the more faith we can have in them. It is not enough simply to accept the validity of a personality scale, or even to accept its validity because it has successfully differentiated, say, artists from scientists, teachers from non-teachers, normal persons from neurotic persons. Ultimately, its construct validity, its successful use in a wide variety of theoretically predicted relations, must be established.

Attitude Scales

Attitudes, while treated separately here and in most textbook discussions, are really an integral part of personality. Modern theorists, too, consider intelligence and aptitude as parts of personality. Personality measurement, however, is mostly of traits. A *trait*, as mentioned in the previous section, is a relatively enduring characteristic of the individual to respond in a certain manner in all situations. If one is dominant, one exhibits dominant behavior in most situations. If one is anxious, anxious behavior permeates most of one's activities. An *attitude*, on the other hand, is an organized predisposition to think, feel, perceive, and behave toward a referent or cognitive object. It is an enduring structure of beliefs that predisposes the individual to behave selectively toward attitude referents.

A *referent* is a category, class, or set of phenomena: physical objects, events, behaviors, and even constructs (see Brown, 1958). People have attitudes toward many different things: ethnic groups, institutions, religion, educational issues and practices, the Supreme Court, civil rights, private property, and so on. One has, in other words, an attitude toward something "out there." A trait has subjective reference; an attitude has objective reference. One who has a hostile attitude toward foreigners may be hostile only to foreigners, but one who has the trait hostility is hostile toward everyone (at least, potentially).

There are three major types of attitude scales: summated rating scales, equal-appearing interval scales, and cumulative (or Guttman) scales. A summated rating scale (one type of which is called a Likert-type scale) is a set of attitude items, all of which are considered of approximately equal "attitude value," and to each of which participants respond with degrees of agreement or disagreement (intensity). The scores of the items of such a scale are summed, or summed and averaged, to yield an individual's attitude score. As in all attitude scales, the purpose of the summated rating scale is to place an individual somewhere on an agreement continuum of the attitude in question.

It is important to note two or three characteristics of summated rating scales, since many scales share these characteristics. First, U, the universe of items, is conceived to be a set of items of equal "attitude value," as indicated in the definition given above. This means that there is no scale of items, as such. One item is the same as any other item in attitude value. The individuals responding to items are "scaled." This scaling comes about through the sums (or averages) of the individuals' responses. Any subset of U is theoretically the same as any other subset of U: a set of individuals would be rank ordered the same using U_2 or U_1.

Second, summated rating scales allow for the intensity of attitude expression. Participants can agree or they can agree strongly. There are advantages to this, as well as disadvantages. The main advantage is that greater variance results. When there are five or seven possible categories of response, it is obvious that the response variance should be greater than with only two or three categories (for example, agree, disagree, no opinion). The variance of summated rating scales, unfortunately, often seems to contain response set variance. Individuals have differential tendencies to use certain types of responses: extreme responses, neutral responses, agree responses, disagree responses. This response variance confounds the attitude (and personality trait) variance. The individual differences yielded by summated rating attitude scales (and similarly scored trait measures) have been shown to be due in part to response set and other similar extraneous sources of variance. The response set literature is large and cannot be cited in detail. Nunnally's (1978) discussion is well balanced. While response set can be considered a mild threat to valid measurement, its importance has been overrated and the available evidence does not justify the strong negative assertions made by response set enthusiasts. In other words, while one must be conscious of the possibilities and threats, one should certainly not be paralyzed by the somewhat blown-up danger (see Rorer, 1965 for more on this).

Following are two summated rating items from a scale constructed by Burt (1980, p. 222) for her study of attitudes toward rape. They were written to measure sex–role stereotyping. A 7-point scale ranging from strongly agree (7) to strongly disagree (1) was used. The values in parentheses (and the values in between) are assigned to the responses indicated.

> There is something wrong with a woman who doesn't want to marry and raise a family.
> A woman should be a virgin when she marries.

Thurstone's equal-appearing interval scales are built upon different principles. While the ultimate product, a set of attitude items, can be used for the same purpose of assigning individuals attitude scores, equal-appearing interval scales also accomplish the important purpose of scaling the attitude items. Each item is assigned a scale value, which indicates the strength of attitude of an agreement response to the item. The universe of items is considered to be an ordered set; that is, items differ in scale value. The scaling procedure finds these scale values. In addition, the items of the final scale to be used are so selected that the intervals between them are equal, an important and desirable psychometric feature.

The following equal-appearing interval items, with the scale values of the items, are from Thurstone and Chave's (1929, p. 61–63, 78) scale, Attitude toward the Church:

I believe the church is the greatest institution in America today. (Scale value: 0.2)

I believe in religion, but I seldom go to church. (Scale value: 5.4)

I think the church is a hindrance to religion for it still depends upon magic, superstition, and myth. (Scale value: 9.6)

In the Thurstone and Chave scale, the lower the scale value, the more positive the attitude toward the church. The first and third items were the lowest and highest in the scale. The second item, of course, had an intermediate value. The total scale contained 45 items with scale values ranging over the whole continuum. Usually, however, equal-appearing interval scales contain considerably fewer items.

The third type of scale, the *cumulative* or *Guttman scale*, consists of a relatively small set of homogeneous items that are unidimensional (or supposed to be). A unidimensional scale measures one variable, and one variable only. The scale gets its name from the cumulative relation between items and the total scores of individuals. For example, we ask four children three arithmetic questions: (a) $28/7 = ?$, (b) $8 \times 4 =$, and (c) $12 + 9 = ?$ Child 1 who gets (a) correct is very likely to get the other two (b and c) correct. Child 2 who misses (a), but gets (b) correct, is also likely to get (c) correct. Child 3 who gets only (c) correct is unlikely to get (a) and (b) correct. The situation can be summarized as follows (the table includes the score of the fourth child, who gets none correct):

	(a)	(b)	(c)	Total Score
Child 1	1	1	1	3
Child 2	0	1	1	2
Child 3	0	0	1	1
Child 4	0	0	0	0

(1= Correct; 0 = Incorrect)

Note the relation between the pattern of item responses and total scores. If we know a child's total score, we can predict that child's pattern, if the scale is cumulative, just as knowledge of correct responses to the harder items are predictive of the responses to the easier items. Note, too, that both items and persons are scaled.

Similarly, people can be asked various questions about an attitudinal object. If upon analysis the patterns of responses arrange themselves in the manner indicated above (at least fairly closely), then the questions or items are said to be unidimensional. Therefore, people can be ranked according to their scale responses (see Edwards, 1957, chapter 7, for a discussion on the cumulative unidimensional scales).

It is obvious that these three methods of constructing attitude scales are very different. Note that the same or similar methods can be used with other kinds of personality and other scales. The summated rating scale concentrates on the participants and their places on the scale. The equal-appearing interval scale concentrates on the items and their places on the scale. Interestingly, both types of scales yield about the same results as far as reliability and the placing of individuals in attitudinal rank orders are concerned. Cumulative scales concentrate on the scalability of sets of items and on the scale positions of individuals.

Of the three types of scales, the summated rating scale seems to be the most useful in behavioral research. It is easier to develop and, as indicated above, yields about the same results as the more laboriously constructed equal-appearing interval scale. Used with care and knowledge of its weaknesses, summated rating scales can be adapted to many needs of behavioral researchers. Cumulative scales would seem to be less useful and less generally applicable. If one clear-cut cognitive object is used, a short, well-constructed cumulative scale may yield reliable measures of a number of psychological variables: tolerance, conformity, group identification, acceptance of authority, permissiveness, and so on. It should be noted, too, that the method could be improved and altered in various ways. Dawes (1972) and Edwards (1957) describe how to construct and evaluate cumulative scales as well as summated rating and equal-appearing interval scales

Value Scales

Values are culturally weighted preferences for things, ideas, people, institutions, and behaviors (Kluckhohn, 1951, pp. 388–433). Whereas attitudes are organizations of beliefs about things "out there," predispositions to behave toward the objects or referents of attitudes, values express preferences for modes of conduct and end-states of existence (Rokeach, 1968). Words like *equality, religion, free enterprise, civil rights,* and *obedience* express values. Simply put, values express the "good," the "bad," the "shoulds," and the "oughts" of human behavior. Values put ideas, things, and behaviors on Approval–Disapproval continua. They imply choices among courses of action and thinking.

To give the reader some flavor of values, here are three items. Individuals can be asked to express their approval or disapproval of the first and second items, perhaps in summated rating form, and to choose from the three alternatives of the third item.

> For one's own good and for the good of society, a person must be held in restraint by tradition and authority.
> Now more than ever we should strengthen the family, the natural stabilizer of society.
> Which of the following is the most important in living the full life: education, achievement, or friendship?

Unfortunately, values have received little scientific study, even though they and attitudes are a large part of our verbal output, and are probably influential determinants of behavior. The measurement of values has thus suffered. Social and educational values will probably become the focus of much more theoretical and empirical work in the future, however, since social scientists have become increasingly aware that values are important influences on individual and group behavior (see Dukes, 1955; Haddock & Zanna, 1998; Hendrick, Hendrick, & Dicke, 1998; Hogan, 1973; Lubinski, Schmidt, & Benbow, 1996; Pittel & Mendelsohn, 1966; Robinson, 1996). A source of values scales is Levitin (1969). A highly suggestive and valuable essay appeared over 45 years ago is by Kluckhohn, (1951). Thurstone's (1959) essay on values measurement is still important.

Types of Objective Scales and Items

Two broad types of items in general use are those in which responses are independent and those in which they are not independent. *Independence* here means that a person's response to an item is unrelated to a response to another item. True–False, Yes–No, Agree–Disagree, and Likert items all belong to the independent type. The subject responds to each item freely with a range of two or more possible responses from which one can choose one. Nonindependent items, on the other hand, force the respondent to choose one item or alternative that precludes the choice of other items or alternatives. These forms of scales and items are called forced-choice scales and items. The subject is faced with two or more items or subitems and asked to choose one or more of them according to some criterion, or even criteria.

Two simple examples will show the difference between independent and nonindependent items. First, a set of instructions that allows independence of response might be given to the respondent. Second, a contrasting set of instructions, with more limited choices (nonindependent):

Examples

> Indicate beside each of the following statements how much you approve them, using a scale from 1 through 5, 1 meaning "Do not approve at all" and 5 meaning "Approve very much."

> Forty pairs of statements are given below. From each pair, choose the one you approve more. Mark it with a check.

Advantages of independent items are economy and the applicability of most statistical analyses to responses to them. Also, when each item is responded to, a maximum of information is obtained, each item contributing to the variance. Less time is taken to administer independent scales, too, but they may suffer from response set bias. Individuals can give the same or similar response to each item: they can endorse them all enthusiastically or indifferently depending on their particular response predilections. The substantive variance of a variable, then, can be confounded by response set.

The forced-choice type of scale avoids, at least to some extent, response bias. At the same time, though, it suffers from a lack of independence, a lack of economy and over complexity. However, there are some researchers, such as Comrey (1970), who have built into the personality test a response bias scale. Forced-choice scales can also strain the subject's endurance and patience, resulting in less cooperation. Still, many experts believe that forced-choice instruments hold great promise for psychological and educational measurement. Other experts are skeptical.

Scales and items, then, can be divided into three types: Agreement–Disagreement (or Approve–Disapprove, or True–False, and the like) rank order, and forced-choice. We discuss each of these briefly. Lengthier discussions can be found in the literature (see Edwards, 1957; Guilford, 1954).

Agreement–Disagreement Items

There are three general forms of Agreement–Disagreement items:

1. Those permitting one of two possible responses.
2. Those permitting one of three or more possible responses.
3. Those permitting more than one choice of three or more possible responses.

The first two of these forms supply alternatives like "Agree–Disagree"; "Yes–No"; "Yes–?–No"; "Approve–No Opinion–Disapprove"; "Approve Strongly–Approve–Disapprove–Disapprove Strongly"; "1, 2, 3, 4, 5." Participants choose one of the supplied responses to report their reactions to the items. In so doing they give reports of themselves or indicate their reactions to items. Most personality and attitude scales use such items. If a person is constructing an instrument using this approach, how the scale is worded is very important. Let's say for example, we have developed the following 5-point Likert scale:

1 = Disagree

2 = Somewhat Disagree

3 = Neutral

4 = Somewhat Agree

5 = Agree

The problem here centers on how the reader interprets the meaning of each scale point. One responder may choose a "2" and another responder chooses "4." They both may have had the same interpretation. If one somewhat agrees, then that person may also somewhat disagree. Hence, the confusion.

The third type of scale in this group presents a number of items: participants are instructed to indicate those items that describe them, items with which they agree, or simply items that they choose. The adjective check list is a good example. The subject is presented with a list of adjectives, some indicating desirable traits, like thoughtful, generous, and considerate; and others indicating undesirable traits, like cruel, selfish, and mean. They are asked to check those adjectives that characterize them. (Of course, this type of instrument can also be used to characterize other persons.) A better form, perhaps, would be a list with all positive adjectives of known scale values from which participants are asked to select a specific number of their own personal characteristics. The equal-appearing interval scale and its response system of checking those attitude items with which one agrees is, of course, the same idea. The idea is a useful one, especially with the development of factor scales, scaling methods, and the increasing use of choice methods.

The scoring of Agreement–Disagreement types of items can be troublesome since not all the items, or the components of the items, receive responses. (With a summated rating scale or an ordinary rating scale, participants usually respond to all items.) In general, however, simple systems of assigning numerals to the various choices can be used. For instance, Agree–Disagree can be 1 and 0; Yes–No can be 1,

0, −1, or, avoiding minus signs: 2, 1, 0. The responses to the summated rating items described earlier are simply assigned 1 through 5 or 1 through 7.

The main thing researchers have to keep in mind is that the scoring system has to yield interpretable data congruent with the scoring system. If scores of 1, 0, −1 are used, the data must be capable of a scaled interpretation; that is, 1 is "high" or "most," −1 is "low" or "least," and 0 is in between. A system of 1, 0 can mean high and low or simply presence or absence of an attribute. Such a system can be useful and powerful, as we saw earlier when discussing variables like sex, race, social class, and so on. In sum, the data yielded by scoring systems have to have clearly interpretable meanings in some sort of quantitative sense. The student is referred to Ghiselli's (1964, pp. 44–49) discussion of the meaningfulness of scores. Some experts however have been critical of using 0–1 or binary scoring systems. Comrey, during his development of the Comrey Personality Scales discovered that items that use a binary response scheme are subjected to problems and distortions that one would not necessarily get if the scale was 3 points or more. The results of Comrey's study on scales are summarized in Comrey (1978) and Comrey and Lee (1992).

Various systems for weighting items have been devised, but the evidence indicates that weighted and unweighted scores give much the same results. Students seem to find it hard to believe this. (Note that we are talking about the weighting of responses to items.) Although the matter is not completely settled, the evidence is strong that, in tests and measures of sufficient numbers of items—say 20 or more—weighting items differentially does not make much difference in final outcomes. Neither does the different weighting of responses make much difference (see Guilford, 1954; Nunnally, 1978). It also makes no difference at all, in variance terms, if you transform scoring weights linearly. You may have participants use a system, +1, 0, −1, and of course, these scores can be used in analysis. But you can add a constant of 1 to each score, yielding 2, 1, 0. The transformed scores are easier to work with, since they have no minus signs.

Rank Order Items and Scales

The second group of scale and item types is ordinal or rank order, which is a simple and most useful form of scale or item. A whole scale can be rank ordered; that is, participants can be asked to rank all the items according to some specified criterion. We might wish to compare the educational values of administrators, teachers, and parents, for instance. A number of items presumed to measure educational values can be presented to the members of each group with instructions to rank order them according to their preferences.

In her study of attitudes toward women's liberation, Taleporos (1977) developed a rank order scale of social problems. Participants were asked to rank order the following social problems: Drug Addiction, Environmental Pollution, Race Discrimination, Sex Discrimination, Violent Crime, and Welfare. Taleporos expected that the two groups she was studying would rank the social issues similarly except for the issue Sex Discrimination. Her hypothesis was supported. This was a productive use of rank order scaling.

Rank order scales have three convenient analytic advantages:

1. The scales of individuals can easily be intercorrelated and analyzed. Composite rank orders of groups of individuals can also easily be correlated.
2. Scale values of a set of stimuli can be calculated using one of the rank order methods of scaling (see Guilford, 1954).
3. The scales partially escape response set and the tendency to agree with socially desirable items.

Forced-Choice Items and Scales

The essence of a forced-choice method is that the subject must choose among alternatives that on the surface appear about equally favorable (or unfavorable). Strictly speaking, the method is not new. Pair comparisons and rank order scales are forced-choice methods. What is different about the forced-choice method, as such, is that the discrimination and preference values of items are determined, and items approximately equal in both are paired. In this way, response set and "item desirability" are to some extent controlled. (*Item desirability* means that one item may be chosen over another simply because it expresses a commonly recognized desirable idea. If a man is asked if he is careless or efficient, he is likely to say he is efficient, even though he is careless.)

The method of paired comparisons (or pair comparisons) has a long and respectable psychometric past. It has, however, been used mostly for purposes of determining scale values (Guilford, 1954). Here we look at paired comparisons as a method of measurement. The essence of the method is that sets of pairs of stimuli, or items of different values on a single continuum or on two different continua or factors, are presented to the subject with instructions to choose one member from each pair on the basis of some stated criterion. The criterion might be: which one better characterizes the subject, or which does the subject prefer. The items of the pairs can be single words, phrases, sentences, or even paragraphs. For example, in his Personal Preference Schedule, Edwards (1953) effectively paired statements that expressed different needs. One item measuring the need for autonomy, for instance, is paired with another item measuring the need for change. The subject is asked to choose one of these items. It is assumed that the person will choose the item that fits his or her own needs. A unique feature of the scale is that the social desirability values of the paired members were determined empirically and the pairs matched accordingly. The instrument yields profiles of need scores for each individual.

In some ways, the two types of paired comparisons technique, (1) the determining of scale values of stimuli, and (2) the direct measurement of variables, are the most satisfying of psychometric methods. They are simple and economical because there are only two alternatives. Further, a good deal of information can be obtained with a limited amount of material. If, for example, an investigator has only 10 items, say five of Variable *A* and five of Variable *B*, a scale of 5 × 5 or 25 items can be constructed, since each *A* item can be systematically paired with each *B* item. (The scoring is simple: assign a "1" to *A* or *B* in each item, depending on which alternative the subject chooses.) Most important, paired comparison items force the participants to choose. Although this may irk some participants, especially if they believe that neither item represents what they would choose (that is, choosing between coward and weakling to categorize oneself), it is really a customary human activity. We must make choices every day of our lives. It can even be argued that Agreement–Disagreement items are artificial and that choice items are "natural." In a study of Adler's concept of social interest (valuing things other than self), Crandall (1980) used paired comparisons to develop his Social Interest Scale. Judges rated 90 traits for their relevance to social interest. Forty-eight pairs were then used, one member of each pair having relevance for social interest, the other member not having such relevance. Then, after item analysis to determine the most discriminating items, a 15-item scale was developed. Unfortunately, Crandall does not report the form of the scale. The idea, however, is a good one: He used the strength of paired comparisons to find good items for a final scale.

Forced-choice items of more than two parts can assume a number of forms with three, four, or five parts, the parts being homogeneous or heterogeneous in favorableness or unfavorableness. We discuss and illustrate only one of these types to demonstrate the principles behind such items. By factor analysis, a procedure known as the *critical incidents technique*, or some other method, items are gathered and selected. It is usually found that some items discriminate between criterion groups and others do not. Both kinds of items—call them discriminators and irrelevants— are included in each item set. In addition, preference values are determined for each item.

A typical forced-choice item is a *tetrad*. One useful form of tetrad consists of two pairs of items, one pair high in preference value, the other pair low in preference value, one member of each pair being a discriminator (valid), and the other member being irrelevant (not valid). A scheme of such a forced-choice item is

high preference–discriminator
high preference–irrelevant
low preference–discriminator
low preference–irrelevant

A subject is directed to choose the item of the tetrad that he or she most prefers, or that is the best description of himself or herself (or someone else), and so on. This person is also directed to select the item that is least preferred or least descriptive of himself or herself.

The basic idea behind this rather complex type of item is, as indicated earlier, that response set and social desirability are controlled. The subject cannot tell, at least not theoretically, which are the discriminator items and which the irrelevant items; neither can items be picked on the basis of preference values. Thus the tendency to evaluate oneself (or others) too high or too low is counteracted, and validity is therefore presumably increased (see Guilford, 1954).

A forced-choice item of a somewhat different type, constructed by the first author of this text for illustrative purposes using items from actual research is:

conscientious

agreeable

responsive

sensitive

One of the items (sensitive) is an *A* item, and one (conscientious) a *B* item. (*A* and *B* refer to adjectival factors.) The other two items are presumably irrelevant. Participants can be asked to choose the one or two items that are most important for a teacher to have.

Forced-choice methods seem to have great promise. Yet there are technical and psychological difficulties, among which the most important seem to be the lack of independence of items, the perhaps too complex nature of some items, and the resistance of participants to difficult choices. The reader is referred to Guilford's (1954) or Bock and Jones's (1968) discussions of the subject: these are authoritative, objective, and brief; and to the reviews by Scott (1968) and Zavala (1965). (For some more recent references on forced-choice items and scaling, see Borg, 1988; Bownas and Bernardin, 1991; Closs, 1978; Deaton, Glasnapp and Poggio, 1980; Hyman and Sharp, 1983; May and Forsyth, 1980; Presser and Schuman, 1980; Ray, 1990; and Stanley, Wandzilak, Ansorge, and Potter, 1987.)

Ipsative and Normative Measures

A distinction that has become important and that is generally misunderstood in research and measurement is that between normative and ipsative measures. *Normative measures* are the usual kind of measures obtained with tests and scales: they can vary independently; that is, they are relatively unaffected by other measures, and are referred for interpretation to the mean of the measures of a group, individuals' sets of measures having different means and standard deviations. *Ipsative measures*, on the other hand, are systematically affected by other measures and are referred for interpretation to the same mean, each individual's set of measures having the same mean and standard deviation. To cut through this rather opaque verbiage, just think of a set of ranks, 1 through 5, 1 indicating the "first," "highest," or "most," and 5 indicating "last," "lowest," and "least," with 2, 3, and 4 indicating positions in between. No matter who uses these ranks, the sum and mean of the ranks is always the same, 15 and 3, and the standard deviation is also always the same, 1.414. Ranks, then, are ipsative measures.

If the values 1, 2, 3, 4, and 5 were available for use to rate, say, five objects, and four people rated the five objects, we might obtain something like the following:

	People			
	1	2	2	3
	2	2	1	2
Objects	3	4	5	3
	4	3	5	3
	5	5	4	2
Sum:	15	16	17	13
Mean:	3.0	3.2	3.4	2.6

Note that the sums and means (and standard deviations, too) are different. These are normative measures. Theoretically, with normative measures there are no constraints on the value that individual A can give to object C—except, of course, the numbers 1 through 5.

With ipsative measures, however, the procedure—in this case of ranking—has built-in systematic restraints. Each individual must use each of 1, 2, 3, 4, and 5 once and once only, and all of them must be used. This says that when five objects are being ranked and one is given, say, Rank 1, there are only four ranks remaining to assign. After the next object is assigned 2, there are only three remaining, and so on until the last object to which 5 must be assigned. Similar reasoning applies to other kinds of ipsative procedures and measures: paired comparisons, forced-choice tetrads or pentads, Q methodology.

The important limitation on ipsative procedures is that, strictly speaking, the usual statistics are not applicable, since such statistics depend on assumptions that ipsative procedures systematically violate. Moreover, the ipsative procedure produces spurious negative correlation between items. In a paired comparisons instrument, for instance, the selection of one member of a pair automatically excludes the selection of the other member. This means lack of independence and negative correlation among items as a function of the instrumental procedure. Most statistical tests, however, are based on the assumption of independence of the elements entering statistical formulas. And analysis of correlations, as in factor analysis, can be seriously distorted by the negative correlations. Unfortunately, these limitations have not been understood, or have been overlooked by investigators who, for example, have treated ipsative data normatively (Hicks, 1970). The reader is encouraged to demonstrate the behavior of ipsative scales by setting up a small matrix of ipsative numbers generated hypothetically by responses to a paired comparisons scale. Use 1s and 0s and calculate the rs between items over individuals.

Choice and Construction of Objective Measures

One of the most difficult tasks for the behavioral researcher when faced with the necessity of measuring variables is to find a way through a mass of already existing measures. If a good measure of a particular variable exists, there seems to be little point in constructing a new measure. The question is, however: Does a good measure exist? The answer to this question may require much search and study. The student should first know which type of variable is to be measured. Some guidance has been attempted within the structure just provided. One must know clearly whether the variable is an aptitude, achievement, personality, attitude, or some other kind of variable. The second step is to consult one or two texts that discuss psychological tests and measures. Next, consult Buros's justly well-known guides. While Buros gives excellent guidance to published tests, many good measures have not been published commercially. Thus the periodical literature may need to be searched. Although many scales are not available commercially, they can be reproduced (with permission) and used for research purposes. Other valuable sources are Andrulis (1977); Comrey, Backer, and Glaser (1973); Fischer and Corcoran (1994); Goldman, Saunders, and Busch (1996); Keyser and Sweetland (1987); and Taulbee (1983).

Valuable sources of information on tests and scales are the journals *Psychological Bulletin, Journal of Psychoeducational Assessment, Applied Psychological Measurement, Educational and Psychological Measurement, Journal of Educational Measurement, Psychological Assessment,* and *Journal of Experimental Education.*

An investigator may find that no measure exists for measuring the desired attributes. Or, if a measure exists, it may be unsatisfactory for the purpose intended. Therefore, the investigator must construct a new measure or instrument, or abandon the variable. The construction of objective tests and scales is a long and arduous task. There are no shortcuts. A poorly constructed instrument may do more harm than good because it may lead the investigator to erroneous conclusions. The investigator who must construct a new instrument, then, has to follow certain well-recognized procedures and be governed by accepted psychometric criteria.

Tremendous progress has been made in the objective measurement of intelligence, aptitudes, achievement, personality, and attitudes. Opinion is divided, often sharply, on the value of objective measurement, however. The most impressive gain has been made in the objective measurement of intelligence, aptitudes, and achievement. Gains in personality and attitude measurement have not been as impressive. The problem, of course, is validity, especially the validity of personality measures.

Two or three recent developments are most encouraging. One is the increasing realization of the complexity of measuring any personality and attitude variable. A second is the technical advances made in doing so. Another closely allied development is the use of factor analysis to help identify variables and to guide the construction of measures. A third development (discussed in an earlier chapter) is the increasing knowledge, understanding, and mastery of the validity problem itself, and especially the realization that validity and psychological theory are intertwined.

CHAPTER SUMMARY

1. The test or scale is the most utilized method in the behavioral sciences for collecting data.
2. A goal is to develop and use tests that are objective. However, objectivity is not easy to understand.
3. Scientific objectivity does not depend on the characteristics of the scientist.
4. Scientific objectivity involves agreement between expert judges. Methods of observation and data collection have different degrees of objectivity.
5. A test is a systematic procedure to determine the behavior of individuals.
6. A scale is a set of symbols or numerals constructed in a way such that these numerals or symbols can be assigned to individuals using some rule.
7. Aptitude tests measure a person's potential for achievement. They are used primarily for guidance and counseling.
8. Achievement tests measure present proficiency, mastery, and understanding of general and specific areas of knowledge. Teacher-made tests are considered to be achievement tests.
9. Measuring personality traits is the most complex problem of psychological measurement. Personality is very complex with problems of validity.
10. There are two methods for constructing and validating personality measures: a priori, and construct method.
11. Attitude scales measure the predisposition of an individual to think, feel, perceive, and behave toward another person, idea, or object.
12. There are three types of attitude scales: summated rating scale, equal-appearing interval scales, and cumulative or Guttman scales.
13. The summated rating scale is the most often used scale in the behavioral sciences.
14. Value scales measure a person's expressed preference for modes of conduct. These include religion and free enterprise.
15. There are two types of objective scales: independent and nonindependent.
16. With independent objective scales, a person's response to one item is not related to his or her response on another item. With nonindependent items, a certain response to an item could lead the respondent to more in-depth questions.
17. Scales and items can be divided into three types: Agreement–Disagreement, rank order, and forced-choice.
18. Normative measures are not affected by other measures. However, ipsative measures are affected by other measures.
19. The researcher should take the time to determine if a test already exists for the study. There are a number of published and unpublished sources for tests. A new test should be created only if no test exists for the researcher's purpose.

STUDY SUGGESTIONS

1. The following annotated references may help students find their way in the large, difficult, but highly important field of objective tests and scales—especially in education.

Adkins, D. (1974). *Test construction: Development and interpretation of achievement tests* (2nd ed.). Columbus, OH: Charles E. Merrill. [An invaluable book for practitioners and researchers.]

Bloom, B. (Ed.). (1976). *Taxonomy of educational objectives. The classification of educational goals: Handbook 1, cognitive domain.* New York: David McKay. [This basic and unusual book attempts to lay a foundation for cognitive measurement by classifying educational objectives and by giving numerous precepts and examples. Pages 201–207, which outline the book, are useful to test constructors and educational researchers.]

Impara, J. C., & Plake, B. S. (Eds.). (1998). *Buros 13th mental measurements yearbook.* Lincoln, NE: Buros Institute. [Descriptions and reviews of published tests and measures of all kinds. See, also, earlier editions.]

Mehrens, W., & Ebel, R. (Eds.). (1967). *Principles of educational and psychological measurement.* Chicago: Rand McNally. [A valuable collection of many of the classic contributions to measurement and test theory and practice.]

2. To gain insight into the rationale and construction of psychological measuring instruments, it is helpful to study relatively complete accounts of their development. The following annotated references describe the development of interesting and important measurement instruments and items.

Allport, G., Vernon, P., & Lindzey, G. (1951). *Study of values. Manual of directions* (rev. ed.). Boston: Houghton Mifflin.

Comrey, A. L. (1961). Factored homogeneous item dimensions in personality research. *Educational and Psychological Measurement, 21,* 417–431.

Comrey, A. L., & Lee, H. B. (1992). *A first course in factor analysis* (2nd ed.). Hillsdale, NJ: Lawrence Erlbaum.

Edwards, A. (1953). *Personal preference schedule, manual.* New York: Psychological Corp. [Measures needs in a forced-choice format (pair comparisons).]

Likert, R. (1932). A technique for the measurement of attitudes. *Archives of Psychology, No. 140.* [Likert's original monograph describing his technique, an important landmark in attitude measurement.]

Thurstone L., & Chave, E. (1929). *The measurement of attitude.* Chicago: University of Chicago Press. [This classic describes the construction of the equal-appearing interval scale to measure attitudes toward the church.]

Woodmansee, J., & Cook, S. (1967). Dimensions of verbal racial attitudes: Their identification and measurement. *Journal of Personality and Social*

Psychology, 7, 240–250. [Probably the best measure of attitudes toward blacks. The inventory is given in the Robinson, Rusk, and Head volume cited in Study Suggestion 3.]

3. The following are three useful anthologies of attitude, value, and other scales. Their usefulness inheres not only in the many scales they contain, but also in perspicacious critiques that focus on reliability, validity, and other characteristics of the scales.

Robinson J., Rusk J., & Head, K. (1968). *Measures of political attitudes.* Ann Arbor: Institute for Social Research, University of Michigan.

Robinson, J., & Shaver P. (1969). *Measures of social psychological attitudes.* Ann Arbor: Institute for Social Research, University of Michigan.

Shaw M., & Wright, J. (1967). *Scales for the measurement of attitudes.* New York: McGraw-Hill.

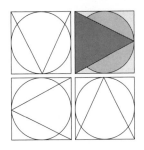

CHAPTER 31

OBSERVATIONS OF BEHAVIOR AND SOCIOMETRY

Everyone observes the actions of others. We look at other persons and listen to them talk. We infer what others mean when they say something; and we infer the characteristics, motivations, feelings, and intentions of others on the basis of these observations. We say, "She is a shrewd judge of people," meaning that her

727

observations of behavior are keen and that we think her inferences of what lies behind the behavior are valid. This day-to-day kind of observation of most people, however, is unsatisfactory for science. Social scientists must also observe human behavior, but they are dissatisfied with uncontrolled observations. They seek reliable and objective observations from which they can draw valid inferences. They treat the observation of behavior as part of a measurement procedure: they assign numerals to objects according to rules, in this case human behavioral acts or sequences of acts.

Although this may seem simple and straightforward, evidently it is not: There is much controversy and debate about observation and methods of observation. Critics of the point of view that observations of behavior must be rigorously controlled—the point of view espoused in this chapter and elsewhere in this book—claim that it is too narrow and artificial. Instead, say the critics, observations must be naturalistic: Observers must be immersed in ongoing realistic and natural situations and must observe behavior as it occurs in the raw, so to speak. As we will see, however, observation of behavior is extremely complex and difficult.

Basically, there are two modes of observation: we can watch people do and say things, and we can ask people about their own actions and the behavior of others. The principal ways of getting information are either by experiencing something directly, or by having someone tell us what happened. In this chapter we are concerned mainly with seeing and hearing events and observing behavior, and solving the scientific problems that spring from such observation. We also examine, if briefly, a method for assessing the interactions and interrelations of group members: sociometry. Sociometry is a special and valuable form of observation: Group members observe each other and record their reactions to each other so that researchers can assess the sociometric status of groups.

Problems in Observing Behavior

The Observer

The major problem of behavioral observation is with the observer. One of the difficulties with the interviews is that the interviewer is part of the measuring instrument. This problem is almost nonexistent in objective tests and scales. In behavioral observation, the observer is both a crucial strength and a crucial weakness. This is because the observer must digest the information derived from observations and then draw inferences about constructs. The observer looks at a certain behavior—say a child striking another child—and somehow must process this observation and make an inference that the behavior is a manifestation of the construct "aggression" or "aggressive behavior," or even "hostility." The strength and the weakness of the procedure is the observer's powers of inference. If it were not for inference, a machinated observer would be better than a human observer. The strength is that the observer can relate the observed behavior to the constructs or variables of a study by bringing together the behavior and construct. One of the recurring difficulties of measurement is to bridge the gap between behavior and construct.

The basic weakness of the observer is that incorrect inferences can be made from observations. Take two extreme cases. Suppose, on the one hand, that an observer who is strongly hostile to parochial school education observes parochial school classes. It is clear that this person's bias may well invalidate the observation. The observer can easily rate an adaptable teacher as somewhat inflexible because of an existing bias or perception that parochial school teaching is inflexible. Or this observer may judge the actually stimulating behavior of a parochial school teacher to be dull. On the other hand, assume that an observer can be completely objective and knows nothing whatever about public or parochial education. In a sense any observations made will not be biased, but they will be inadequate. Observation of human behavior requires competent knowledge of that behavior, and even of the meaning of the behavior.

There is, however, another problem: The observer can affect the objects of observation simply by being part of the observational situation. Actually and fortunately, this is not a severe problem. Indeed, it is more of a problem to the uninitiated, who seem to believe that people will act differently, even artificially, when observed. Observers appear to have little effect on the situations they observe. Individuals and groups seem to adapt rather quickly to an observer's presence and to act as they would usually act. This does not mean that the observer cannot have an effect. It means that if the observer takes care to be unobtrusive and not to give the persons being observed the feeling that judgments are being made, then the observer as an influential stimulus is mostly nullified. Babbie (1995) states there that is no complete protection from the observer effect. However, knowledge and sensitivity to this problem will help provide partial protection.

Validity and Reliability

On the surface, nothing seems more natural when observing behavior than to believe that we are measuring what we say we are measuring. When an interpretative burden is placed on the observer, however, validity may suffer (as well as reliability). The greater the burden of interpretation, the greater the validity problem. This does not mean, however, that no burden of interpretation should be placed on the observer.

A simple aspect of the validity of observation measures is their predictive power. Do they predict relevant criteria dependably? The trouble, as usual, is in the criteria. Independent measures of the same variables are rare. Can we say that an observational measure of teacher behavior is valid because it correlates positively with superiors' ratings? We might have an independent measure of self-oriented needs, but would this measure be an adequate criterion for observations of such needs?

An important clue to the study of the validity of behavioral observation measures would seem to be construct validity. If the variables being measured by an observational procedure are embedded in a theoretical framework, then certain relations should exist. Do they indeed exist? Suppose our research involves Bandura's (1982) self-efficacy theory and that we have constructed an observation system whose purpose is to measure performance competence. The theory says, in effect, that perceived self-efficacy, or the self-perception of competence, affects the competence of a person's actual performance: the higher one's self-efficacy, the higher the performance competence. If we find that self-perception of competence and measures of actual observed competence of doing certain prescribed tasks is positive and substantial, then the hypothesis derived from the theory is supported. But this is also evidence of the construct validity of the observation system.

The reliability of observation systems is a simpler matter, though by no means an easy one. It is often defined as agreement among observers. From this viewpoint, film, videotape, and audiotape records can help to achieve very high reliability. Agreement among observers, however, has potential defects. For example, the magnitude of an index of agreement is partly due to chance agreement, and thus needs correction. Perhaps the safest course to follow is to use different methods of assessing reliability just as we would with any measures used in behavioral research: agreement of observers, repeat reliability, and the analysis of variance approach. Assessing reliability and agreement among observers are especially difficult problems of direct observation, because the usual statistics depend on the assumption that measures are independent—and they are often not independent. Most of the work done in this area has come from or based on the work of Cohen and Fleiss on coefficient kappa (Fleiss, 1986; Fleiss & Cohen, 1973). The use of generalizability theory holds promise in the measurement of reliability for nominal data (Li & Lautenschlager, 1997). Some developments have come from the health sciences where observation and agreement plays a heavy role in analyses and decisions (see Dunn, 1989, 1992). Medley and Mitzel (1963) give a thorough but technically complex exposition of the reliability of ratings in an analysis of variance framework. Hollenbeck (1978) and Rowley (1976) discuss reliability of observations when measures are nominal. More recent reviews on reliability of observations and interrater reliability are Dewey (1989), McDermott (1988), Perreault and Leigh (1989), Schouten (1986), Topf (1986), Zegers (1991), and Zwick (1988). The Perreault and Leigh article discusses the topic from the marketing research point of view. Topf reviews the use of the nominal reliability measures in nursing research, and McDermott discusses its application in school psychology. Chan (1987), Oud and Sattler (1984), and Powers (1985) have written computer programs to help researchers compute observer agreement statistics.

It is necessary, then, to define fairly precisely and unambiguously what is to be observed. If we are measuring Curiosity, we must tell the observer what curious behavior is. If Cooperativeness is being measured, we must somehow tell the observer how cooperative behavior is distinguished from other kinds of behavior. This means that we must provide the observer with some form of operational definition of the variable being measured; we must define the variable behaviorally.

Categories

The fundamental task of the observer is to assign behaviors to categories. From our earlier work on partitioning, recall that categories must be exhaustive and mutually exclusive. To satisfy the exhaustiveness condition, one must first define U, the universe of behaviors to be observed. In some observation systems, this is not hard to do. McGee and Snyder (1975), testing the hypothesis that people who salt their food before they taste it perceive control of behavior as being more from within the individual (dispositional control) than from the environment (situational control), simply observed participants' salting of food in restaurants. In other observation systems it is more difficult. Many or most of the observation systems cited in Simon and Boyer's (1970) huge anthology of observation instruments, *Mirrors for Behavior*, are complex and hardly easy to use. This work consists of 14 volumes of behavior observation instruments! Most of these instruments, 67 of 79, are used for educational observations. Readers who intend to use behavior observation in their research should consult these volumes, especially volume 1, which contains a general discussion on pages 1–24.

In keeping with the emphasis of this book—that the purpose of most observation is to measure variables—we cite a classroom observation system from the highly interesting, even creative, work of Kounin and his colleagues (Kounin & Doyle, 1975; Kounin & Gump, 1974). The system reported is more complex than the salt-tasting observation system, but much less complex than many classroom observation systems. The variable observed was task-involvement, which was observed by videotaping 596 lessons and then observing playbacks of the tapes to obtain the involvement measures. These measures were categorized as high task involvement and low task involvement. The authors also measured continuity in lessons by creating categories that reflected greater or lesser continuity in the lessons. When the children's behavior was observed, they used the categories to record the pertinent observed behaviors.

Units of Behavior

Deciding which units to use in measuring human behavior is still an unsettled problem. Here one is often faced with a conflict between reliability and validity demands. Theoretically, one can attain a high degree of reliability by using small and easily observed and recorded units. One can attempt to define behavior quite operationally by listing a large number of behavioral acts, and can thus ordinarily attain a high degree of precision and reliability. Yet in so doing one may also have so reduced the behavior that it no longer bears much resemblance to the behavior one intended to observe. Thus validity may be lost.

On the other hand, one can use broad "natural" definitions and perhaps achieve a high degree of validity. One might instruct observers to observe Cooperation and define Cooperative Behavior *as* "accepting other persons' approaches, suggestions, and ideas; working harmoniously with others toward goals," or some such rather broad definition. If observers have had group experience and understand group processes, then it might be expected that they could validly assess behavior as cooperative and uncooperative by using this definition. Such a broad, even vague, definition enables the observer to capture, if he or she can, the full flavor of cooperative behavior. But its considerable ambiguity allows differences of interpretation, thus probably lowering reliability.

Some researchers who are strongly operational in their approach insist on highly specific definitions of the variables observed. They may list a number of specific behaviors for the observer to note. No others would be observed and recorded. Extreme approaches like this may produce high reliability, but they may also miss part of the essential core of the variables observed. Suppose 10 specific types of behavior are listed for Cooperativeness. Suppose, too, that the universe of possible behaviors consists of 40 or 50 types. Clearly, important aspects of cooperativeness will be neglected. While what is measured may be reliably measured, it may be quite trivial or partly irrelevant to the variable

Cooperativeness

This is the molar–molecular problem of any measurement procedure in the social sciences. The *molar approach* takes larger behavioral wholes as units of observation. Complete interaction units may be specified as observational targets. Verbal behavior may be broken down into complete interchanges between two or more individuals, or into whole paragraphs or sentences. The *molecular approach*, by contrast, takes smaller segments of behavior as units of observation. Each interchange or partial interchange may be recorded. Units of verbal behavior may be words or short phrases. Molar observers start with a general broadly defined variable, as given earlier, and observe and record a variety of behaviors under the one rubric. They depend on experience and knowledge to interpret the meaning of the behavior they observe. Molecular observers, on the other hand, seek to push their own experience, knowledge, and interpretation out of the observational picture. They record what they see—and no more.

Observer Inference

Observation systems differ on another important dimension: the *amount of inference* required of the observer. Molecular systems require relatively little inference. The observer simply notes that an individual does or says something. For example, a system may require the observer to note each interaction unit, which may be defined as any verbal interchange between two individuals. If an interchange occurs, it is noted; if it does not occur, it is not noted. Or a category may be "Strikes another child." Every time one child strikes another it is noted. No inferences are made in such systems—if, of course, it is ever possible to escape inferences (for example, "strikes"). Pure behavior is recorded as nearly as possible.

Observer systems with such low degrees of observer inference are rare. Most systems require some degree of inference. An investigator may be doing research on board-of-education behavior, and may decide that a low inference analysis is suited to the problem, and use observation items like "Suggests a course of action," "Interrupts another board member," "Asks a question," "Gives an order to superintendent," and the like. Since such items are comparatively unambiguous, the reliability of the observation system should be substantial.

Systems with higher degrees of inference required of the observer are more common and probably more useful in most research. The high inference observation system gives the observer labeled categories that require greater or lesser interpretation of the observed behavior. For example, suppose that dominance is to be measured. It can be defined as attempts by an individual to show intellectual (or other) superiority over other individuals, with little recognition of group goals and the contributions of others. This will, of course, require a high degree of observer inference, and observers will have to be trained so that there is agreement on what constitutes dominant behavior. Without such training and agreement—and probably observer expertise in group processes—reliability can be endangered. A sophisticated discussion concerning inference in observation is given in Weick (1968). Weick also discusses biases in observation and suggests methodological solutions for minimizing the effects of bias. Similar remarks are pertinent when we try to measure many psychological and sociological variables: cooperation, competition, aggressiveness, democracy, verbal aptitude, achievement, and social class, for example. For recent discussions of observation and inference in these areas one can read Alexander, Newell, Robbins, and Turner (1995); Borich and Klinzing (1984); Chavez (1984); Hartmann and Wood (1990); Jaffe (1997); Nurius and Gibson (1990); and Timberlake and Silva (1994). Borich and Klinzing and Chavez's articles apply to classroom observations. Hartmann and Wood deal with behavioral observation systems used in behavior modification. Nurius and Gibson deal with clinical observation and inference found in social work. Closely related are the Jaffe and the Alexander et al. papers that deal with clinical observations. Timberlake and Silva deal with the observation and inference obtained from watching the behavior of animals.

It is not possible to make flat generalizations on the relative virtues of systems with differing degrees of inference. Probably the best advice to the neophyte is to aim at a medium degree of inference. Too vague categories with too little specification of what to observe put an excessive burden on the observer. Different observers can too easily put different interpretations on the same behavior. Too specific categories, while they reduce ambiguity and uncertainty, may tend to be too rigid and inflexible, even trivial. Better than anything else, the student should study various successful systems, paying special attention to the behavior categories and the definitions (instructions) attached to the categories for the guidance of the observer.

Generality or Applicability

Observation systems differ considerably in their *generality*, or degree of *applicability* to research situations other than those for which they were originally designed. Some systems are quite general: they are designed for use with many different research problems. The well-known Bales (1951) group interaction analysis is one such general system. This is a low inference system in which all verbal and nonverbal behavior, presumably in any group, can be categorized into one of 12 categories: "shows solidarity," "agrees," "asks for opinion," and so on. The 12 categories are grouped into three larger sets: social–emotional–positive, social–emotional–negative, and task–neutral.

Some systems, however, were constructed for particular research situations to measure particular variables. The salting food example, above, is quite specific, hardly applicable to other situations. The Kounin and Doyle (1975) system, while specifically constructed for Kounin's research, can be applied in many classroom situations. Indeed, most systems devised for specific research problems can probably be used, often with modification, for other research problems.

We want to emphasize that "small" observation systems can be used to measure specific variables. Suppose, for instance, that the attentiveness of elementary school pupils is a key variable in a theory of school achievement. Attentiveness (as a trait or habit) in and of itself has little effect on achievement: let's say the correlation is zero. It is a key variable because, with a certain method of teaching, it interacts with the method and has a pronounced indirect effect on achievement. Assuming that this is so, we must measure attentiveness. It seems clear that we will have to observe pupil behavior, while the method in question and a "control" method are being used. In such a case, we will have to find or devise an observation system that focuses on attentiveness. In assessing the influence of classroom environment, for example, Keeves (1972) found it necessary to measure attentiveness. He did this by observing students who were required to attend to tasks prescribed by the teacher. Scores that indicated attentiveness or the lack of it were assigned. This "small" observation system was reliable and apparently valid. It is likely that such targeted systems will be used increasingly in behavioral research, especially in education.

Sampling of Behavior

The last characteristic of observations, sampling, is, strictly speaking, not a characteristic. It is a way of obtaining observations. Before using an observation system in actual research, when and how the system will be applied must be decided. If classroom behaviors of teachers are to be observed, how will the behaviors be sampled? Will all the specific behaviors in one class period be observed, or will examples of specified behaviors be sampled systematically or randomly? In other words, a sampling plan of some kind must be devised and used.

There are two aspects of behavior sampling: event sampling and time sampling. *Event sampling* is the selection for observation of integral behavioral occurrences or events of a given class. Examples of integral events are temper tantrums, fights and quarrels, games, verbal interchanges on specific topics, classroom interactions between teachers and pupils, and so on. The investigator who is pursuing events must either know when the events are going to occur and be present when they occur, as with classroom events, or wait until they occur, as with quarrels.

Event sampling has three virtues: (1) The events are natural lifelike situations and thus possess an inherent validity not ordinarily possessed by time samples. (2) An integral event possesses a continuity of behavior that the more piecemeal behavioral acts of time samples do not possess. If one observes a problem-solving situation from beginning to end, one is witnessing a natural and complete unit of individual and group behavior. By so doing, one achieves a whole and realistic larger unit of individual or social behavior. As we saw in an earlier chapter, when field experiments and field studies were discussed, naturalistic situations have an impact and a closeness to psychological and social reality that experiments do not usually have. (3) The third virtue of event sampling inheres in an important characteristic of many behavioral events: they are sometimes infrequent and rare. For example, one may be interested in decisions made in administrative or legislative meetings. Or one may be interested in the ultimate step in problem-solving. Teachers' disciplinary methods may be a variable. Such events and many others are relatively infrequent. As such, they can easily be missed by time sampling; they therefore require event sampling. If one takes the more active view of observation advocated by Weick (1968), however, one can arrange situations to ensure more frequent occurrence of rare events.

Time sampling is the selection of behavioral units for observation at different points in time. They can be selected in systematic or random ways to obtain samples of behaviors. A good example is teacher behavior. Suppose the relations between certain variables like teacher alertness, fairness, and initiative, on the one hand; and pupil initiative and cooperativeness, on the other hand, are studied. We may select random samples of teachers and then take time samples of their behavioral acts. These time samples can be systematic: three 5-minute observations at specified times during each of, say, five class hours, the class hours being the first, third, and fifth periods one day, and the second and fourth periods the next day. Or they can be random: five 5-minute observation periods selected at random from a specified universe of 5-minute periods. Obviously, there are many ways that time samples can be set up and selected. As usual, the way such samples are chosen, their length, and their number must be influenced by the research problem. In a fascinating study of leadership and the power of group influence with small children, Merei (1949) points out that time sampling would show only leaders giving orders and the group obeying, whereas prolonged observations would show the inner workings of ordering and obeying.

Time samples have the important advantage of increasing the probability of obtaining representative samples of behavior. This is true, however, only of behaviors that occur fairly frequently. Behaviors that occur infrequently have a high probability of escaping the sampling net, unless huge samples are drawn. Creative behavior, sympathetic behavior, and hostile behavior, for example, may be quite infrequent. Still, time sampling is a positive contribution to the scientific study of human behavior.

Time samples, as implied earlier, suffer from lack of continuity, lack of adequate context, and perhaps naturalness. This is particularly true when small units of time and behavior are used. Still, there is no reason why event sampling and time sampling cannot sometimes be combined. If one is studying classroom recitations, one can draw a random sample of the class periods of one teacher at differing times, and observe all recitations during the sampled periods in their entirety.

Some very good references on event sampling and time sampling are Arrington (1943), Martin and Bateson (1993), Wright (1960), and Zeren and Makosky (1986). The Zeren and Makosky article is noteworthy because it describes a classroom exercise to teach students how to make systematic observation of spontaneous human behavior. Three observational techniques (time sampling, event sampling, and trait rating) are also described and compared through their use on simulated behavior presented on television. The classroom activity included a lecture about observational methods, an exercise utilizing one of the three methods, and a class discussion. The article discusses how to teach the scientific approach to gathering observational data, the importance of precise operational definitions on interrater agreement, and the calculation of reliability coefficients.

Rating Scales

To this point, we have been talking only about the observation of *actual behavior*. Observers look at and listen to the objects of regard directly. They sit in the classroom and observes teacher–pupil and pupil–pupil interactions. Or they may watch and listen to a group of children solving a problem behind a two-way mirror.

There is another class of behavioral observation, however, that needs to be mentioned. This type of observation will be called *remembered behavior* or *perceived behavior*. It is conveniently classified under the topic of rating scales. In measuring remembered or perceived behavior, we ordinarily present observers with an observation system in the form of a scale of some kind, and ask them to assess an object on one or more characteristics, the object not being present. In order to do this, they must make assessments on the basis of past observations, or on the basis of perceptions of what the observed object is like, and how it will behave. A convenient way to measure both actual behavior and perceived or remembered behavior is with rating scales.

A *rating scale* is a measuring instrument that requires the rater or observer to assign the rated object to categories or continua that have numerals assigned to them. Rating scales are perhaps the most ubiquitous of measuring instruments, probably because they are seemingly easy to construct and, more important, easy and quick to use. Unfortunately, the apparent ease of construction is deceptive, and the ease of use carries a heavy price: lack of validity due to a number of sources of bias that enter into rating measures. Still, with knowledge, skill, and care, ratings can be valuable.

For an excellent discussion of rating scales, see Guilford (1954), Nunnally (1978), Nunnally and Bernstein (1993) and Torgeson (1958). For a relatively nontechnical presentation of rating scales, one can read Selltiz, Jahoda, Deutsch, and Cook (1961). Although rating scales were mentioned earlier in this book, they were not systematically discussed. In reading what follows, the student should bear in mind that rating scales are really objective scales. As such, they might have been included in Chapter 30. Their discussion was reserved for this chapter because the discussion of Chapter 30 focused mainly on measures responded to by the subject being measured. Rating scales, on the other hand, are measures of individuals and their reactions, characteristics, and behaviors by observers. The contrast, then, is between how the subject sees himself or herself and how others perceive the subject. Rating scales are also used to measure psychological objects, products, and stimuli, such as handwriting, concepts, essays, interview protocols, and projective test materials.

Types of Rating Scales

There are four or five types of rating scales. Two of these types were discussed in Chapter 30. They were the checklists and forced-choice instruments. We consider now only three types and their characteristics: the category rating scale, the numerical rating scale, and the graphic rating scale. They are quite similar, differing mainly in details.

The *category rating scale* presents observers or judges with several categories from which they pick the one that best characterizes the behavior or characteristic of the object being rated. Suppose a teacher's classroom behavior is being rated. One of the characteristics rated, say, is Alertness. A category item might be as shown in the first example. A different form uses condensed descriptions, such an item might look like that shown in the second example.

Examples

> How alert is she? (Check one)
> Very alert
> Alert
> Not alert
> Not at all alert

> Is she resourceful? (Check one)
> Always resourceful; never lacking in ideas
> Resources are good
> Sometimes flounders for ideas
> Unresourceful; rarely has ideas

Numerical rating scales are perhaps the easiest to construct and use. They also yield numbers that can be used directly in statistical analysis. In addition, because the numbers may represent equal intervals in the mind of the observer, they may approach interval measurement (see Guilford, 1954, p. 264). Any of the above category scales can be quickly and easily converted to numerical rating scales simply by affixing numbers before each of the categories. The numbers 3, 2, 1, 0, or 4, 3, 2, 1 can be affixed to the Alertness item above. A convenient method of numerical rating is to use the same numerical system, say 4, 3, 2, 1, 0 with each item. This is, of course, the system used in summated-rating attitude scales. In rating scales, it is probably better, however, to give both the verbal description and the numerals.

In *graphic rating scales* lines or bars are combined with descriptive phrases. The alertness item, just discussed, could look like this in graphic form:

Very Alert   Alert   Not Alert   Not at all Alert

Such scales have many varieties: vertical segmented lines, continuous lines, unmarked lines, lines broken into marked equal intervals (as above), and others. These are probably the best of the usual forms of rating scales. They fix a continuum in the mind of the observer. They suggest equal intervals. They are clear and easy to understand and use. Guilford (1954, p. 268) overpraises them a bit when he says, "The virtues of graphic rating scales are many; their faults are few," but his point is well taken.

Weaknesses of Rating Scales

Ratings have two serious weaknesses, one is extrinsic, the other is intrinsic. The extrinsic defect is that they are seemingly so easy to construct and use that they are used indiscriminately, frequently without knowledge of their intrinsic defects. We will not pause to mention the errors that can creep into the unskillful construction and use of rating scales. Rather, we warn the reader against seizing them for any and all measurement needs. One should first ask the question: Is there a better way to measure my variables? If so, use it. If not, then study the characteristics of good rating scales, work with painstaking care, and put the rating results to empirical test and adequate statistical analysis.

The intrinsic defect of rating scales is their proneness to constant or biased error. This is not new to us, of course. We met this problem when considering response set. With ratings, however, it is particularly threatening to validity. Constant rating error takes several forms, the most pervasive of which is the famous *halo effect.* This is the tendency to rate an object in the constant direction of a general impression of the object. Everyday cases of halo are believing a man to be virtuous because we like him; and/or giving high praise to Republican presidents and damning Democratic ones.

Halo manifests itself frequently in measurement, especially with ratings. Professors assess the quality of essay test questions higher than they should be because they like the testee. Or they may rate the second, third, and fourth questions higher (or lower) than they should because the fittest question was well answered (or poorly answered). Teacher evaluation of children's achievement that is influenced by the children's docility or lack of docility is another case of halo. In rating individuals on rating scales, there is a tendency for the rating of one characteristic to influence the ratings of other characteristics. Halo is difficult to avoid. It seems to be particularly strong in traits that are not clearly defined, not easily observable, and that are morally important (see Guilford, 1954, p. 279).

Two important sources of constant error are the error of severity and the error of leniency. The *error of severity* is a general tendency to rate all individuals too low on all characteristics. This is the tough marker: "Nobody gets an A in my classes." The *error of leniency* is the opposite general tendency to rate too high. This is the good fellow who loves everybody—and the love is reflected in the ratings.

An exasperating source of invalidity in ratings is the *error of central tendency*, the general tendency to avoid all extreme judgments and rate right down the middle of a rating scale. It manifests itself particularly when raters are unfamiliar with the objects being rated.

There are other less important types of error that will not be considered here. More important is how to cope with the types listed above. This is a complex matter that cannot be discussed here. The reader is referred to Guilford (1954, pp. 280–288, 383, 395–397), where many devices for coping with error are discussed in detail. Systematic errors can be dealt with to some extent by statistical means. Guilford has worked out an ingenious method using analysis of variance. The basic idea is that variances due to participants, judges, and characteristics are extracted from the total variance of ratings. The ratings are then corrected. An easier method when rating individuals on only one characteristic is two-way (correlated groups) analysis of variance. Reliability can also be easily calculated. The use of analysis of variance to estimate reliability, as we learned earlier, was Hoyt's (1941) contribution. Ebel (1951) applied analysis of variance to reliability of ratings.

Rating scales can and should be used in behavioral research. Their unwarranted, expedient, and unsophisticated use has been rightly condemned. But this should not mean general condemnation. They have virtues that make them valuable tools of scientific research: they require less time than other methods; they are generally interesting and easy for observers to use; they have a very wide range of application; they can be used with a large number of characteristics. It might be added that they can be used as adjuncts to other methods. That is, they can be used as instruments to aid behavioral observations, and they can be used in conjunction with other objective instruments, with interviews, and even with projective measures.

Examples of Observation Systems

Other behavioral observation systems (not mentioned earlier) are summarized below to help the student get a feeling for the variety of systems that are possible and the ways in which such systems are constructed and used. In addition, the student may gain further understanding of when behavioral observation is appropriate.

Time Sampling of Play Behavior of Hearing-Impaired Children

Play behavior is considered an important component of normal child development. However, hearing-impaired children have communication deficits that interfere with normal play development. Hearing-impaired children have been found to be involved in less complex and less social play than normal children. In their study of the play behavior of hearing-impaired children, Esposito and Koorland (1989) used a momentary time sampling technique to record the behavior of two children in different play settings (a 3.5-year-old and a 5-year-old). The goal was to use the data to compare the behavior of hearing-impaired children when integrated and not integrated with nonimpaired children. This involved observing and recording the behavior of each child during 10-second intervals for two 10-minute sessions per day for four days per week for two weeks during indoors free play. One setting was integrated and the other was not integrated. Free-play behavior of each child was coded according to the play categories defined by Higginbotham, Baker, and Neill (1980). There are eight major categories of play that can be further categorized as Social Play, Cognitive Play, and Nonplay. These researchers found differences in play behavior between the two types of settings. If peer interaction during play contributes to normal child development, then these results suggest that integrated environments are better suited for hearing-impaired children.

Observation and Evaluation of College Teaching

In one of the relatively few—and better—studies of college teachers and teaching, Isaacson, McKeachie, Milholland, and Lin (1964), after considerable preliminary work on items and their dimensions or factors, had college students rate and evaluate their teachers, based on their remembered observations and impressions. A number of similar studies have been published since this study appeared, but it is still one of the best. The observation system presented was not devised deliberately to measure variables, but rather to help evaluate teaching performance. Neverthe-less, its two basic dimensions can, of course, be used as variables in research. A remarkable aspect of studies to evaluate college teachers is that researchers seem not to be aware that the purpose of such observation systems should be the improvement of instruction (or to use their dimensions as research variables), and not for administrative purposes (see Kerlinger, 1971).

Isaacson et al. used a 46-item rating scale and instructed the students to respond according to the frequency of the occurrence of certain behavioral acts, and not according to whether the behaviors were desirable or undesirable. Their basic interest was in the dimensions or underlying variables behind the items. They found six such dimensions (factors). The first dimension was related to general teaching skill.

Although the six factors are important because they seem to show various aspects of teaching (for example, Structure, which is the instructor's organization of the course and its activities, and Rapport, which is the more interactive aspects of teaching and friendliness), we concentrate on the first. Here are three of the items:

> He put his material across in an interesting way. He stimulated the intellectual curiosity of his students. He explained clearly and his explanations were to the point (p. 347).

The most effective item, however, was even more general:

How would you rate your instructor in general (all-around) teaching ability?
a. An outstanding and stimulating instructor
b. A very good instructor
c. A good instructor
d. An adequate, but not stimulating instructor
e. A poor and inadequate instructor

While we may question calling this study and others like it observation studies, there is certainly observation, though it is quite different in being remembered and indirect, global and highly inferential, and, finally, much less systematic in actual observation. We ask students to remember and rate behaviors that they may not have paid particular attention to. Nevertheless, the Isaacson et al. study, along with other studies, have shown that this form of observation can be used in instructor and course evaluation reliably.

Assessment of Behavioral Observation

There is no doubt whatever that objective observation of human behavior has advanced beyond the rudimentary stage. The advances, like other methodological and measurement advances made in the past 10 to 20 years, have been striking. The growth of psychometric and statistical mastery and sophistication has been felt in the observation and assessment of actual and remembered behavior. Social scientific research can and will profit from these advances. Many educational research problems, for example, strongly demand behavior observations: children in classrooms interacting with each other and with teachers, administrators and teachers discussing school problems in staff meetings, boards of education working toward policy decisions. Both basic and applied research, especially research involving group processes and group decisions, can profit from direct observation. And it can be used in field studies, field experiments, and laboratory experiments. Here is a methodological approach that is essentially the same in field and laboratory situations.

The difficulty in using full-scale systems, has undoubtedly discouraged the use of observation in behavioral research. But observations must be used when the variables of research studies are interactive and interpersonal in nature, and when we wish to study the relations between actual behavior, like class management techniques or group interaction, and other behaviors or attribute variables. Important as is asking about behavior, there is no substitute for seeing, as directly as possible, what people actually do when confronted with different circumstances and different people. Moreover, in much, perhaps most, behavioral research, it is probably not necessary to use the larger observation systems. As shown earlier, smaller systems can be devised for special research purposes. Keeves's (1972) limited system was highly appropriate for his purpose. In any case, scientific behavioral research requires direct and indirect observations of behavior, and the technical means of making such observations are becoming increasingly adequate and available. The next century should see considerable understanding and improvement of methods of observation, as well as their increased meaningful use.

Sociometry

We constantly assess the people with whom we work, go to school, and live at home. We judge them for their suitability to work, play, and live with us. And we base our judgments on our observations of their behavior in different situations. We judge, we say, on the basis of our "experience." The form of measurement we now consider sociometry, is based on these many informal observations. Again, the method is based on remembered observations and the inevitable judgments we make of people after observing them.

Sociometry and Sociometric Choice

Sociometry is a broad term indicating a number of methods of gathering and analyzing data on the choice, communication, and interaction patterns of individuals in groups. One might say that sociometry is the study and measurement of social choice. It has also been called a means of studying the attractions and repulsions of members of groups.

A person is asked to choose one or more other persons according to one or more criteria supplied by the researcher: With whom would you like to work? With whom would you like to play? The person then makes one, two, three, or more choices from among the members of one's own group (usually) or from other groups. What could be simpler and more natural? The method works well for kindergartners and for atomic scientists.

Sociometric choice should be rather broadly understood: it not only means "choice of people," it may also mean "choice of lines of communication," "choice of lines of influence," or "choice of minority groups." The choices depend on the instructions and questions given to individuals. A sample list of sociometric questions and instructions follows:

Example

With whom would you like to work (play, sit next to, and so on)?
Which two members of this group (age group, class, club, for instance) do you like the most (the least)?
Who are the three best (worst) pupils in your class?
Whom would you choose to represent you on a committee to improve faculty welfare?
Which four individuals have the greatest prestige in your organization (class, company, team)?
Which two groups of people are the most acceptable (least acceptable) to you as neighbors (friends, business associates, professional associates)?

Obviously, there are many possibilities. Some of these possibilities are discussed in Lindzey and Byrne (1968). In addition, these possibilities can be multiplied simply by asking: Who do you think would choose you to . . . ? and Whom do you think the group would choose to . . . ? Participants can also be asked to rank others using sociometric criteria, providing there are not too many to rank. Or rating scales can be used.

Members of a group or organization can be asked to rate each other using one or more criteria. We can phrase the sociometric instructions something like the following:

Example

> Here is a list of the members of your group. Rate each according to whether you would like to work with him/her on a committee to draft a set of bylaws. Use the numbers 4, 3, 2, 1, and 0, where 4 means you would like to work with him/her very much, 0 you would not want to work with him/her at all, and the other numbers representing intermediate degrees of liking to work with him/her.

Clearly, other methods of measurement can be used. The main difference is that sociometry always has such ideas as social choice, interaction, communication, and influence behind it.

Methods of Sociometric Analysis

There are three basic forms of sociometric analysis: sociometric matrices, sociograms or directed graphs, and sociometric indices. Of all the methods of sociometric analysis, *sociometric matrices*, to be defined presently, perhaps contain the most important possibilities and implications for the behavioral researcher. *Sociograms* are diagrams or charts of the choices made in groups. We shall discuss sociograms or directed graphs very little, since they are used more for practical than for research purposes and their analysis is mathematically difficult, requiring more space than we can spare. The reader who requires more detail and explanation is directed to Fienberg and Wasserman (1981), and Ove (1981). *Sociometric indices* are single numbers calculated from two or more numbers yielded by sociometric data. They indicate sociometric characteristics of individuals and groups.

Sociometric Matrices

We learned earlier that a *matrix* is a rectangular array or table of numbers or other symbols. For those who are unfamiliar with matrices we recommend reading Lindzey and Byrne (1968, pp. 470–473) for a good review of matrix analysis.

Explanation of elementary matrix operations and sociometric matrices can be found in Kemeny, Snell, and Thompson (1966, pp. 217–250, 384–406). A good elementary presentation of matrices can be found in Davis (1973). An older but still valuable review of mathematical and statistical methods for analyzing group structure and communication is presented by Glanzer and Glaser (1959).

In sociometry we are usually concerned mainly with square, or $n \times n$ matrices, n being equal to the number of persons in a group. Rows of the matrix are labeled i; columns are labeled j; i and j, of course, can stand for any number and any person in the group. If we write a_{ij}, this means the entry in the i-th row and j-th column of the matrix, or, more simply, any entry in the matrix. It is convenient to write *sociometric matrices*. These are matrices of numbers expressing all the choices of group members in any group.

Suppose a group of five members has responded to the sociometric question, "With whom would you like to work on such-and-such a project during the next two months? Choose two individuals." The responses to the sociometric question are, of course, *choices*. If a group member chooses another group member, the choice is represented by a 1. If a group member does not choose another, the lack of choice is represented by 0. (If rejection had been called for, -1 could have been used.) The sociometric matrix of choices, C, of this hypothetical group situation is given in Table 31.1.

It is possible to analyze the matrix in a number of ways. But first let us be sure we know how to read the matrix. It is probably easier to read from left to right, from i to j. Member i chooses (or does not choose) member j. For example, a chooses b and e; c chooses d and e. Sometimes it is convenient to speak passively, "b was chosen by a, d, and e," or "c was chosen by no one."

◨ **TABLE 31.1** *Sociometric Choice Matrix: Five-Member Group, Two-Choice Question*[a]

		a	b	c	d	e
				j		
	a	0	1	0	0	1
	b	1	0	0	0	1
i	c	0	0	0	1	1
	d	0	1	0	0	1
	e	1	1	0	0	0
	Σ	2	3	0	1	4

[a] Individual i chooses individual j. That is, the table can be read by rows: b chooses a and e. It can also be read by columns: b is chosen by a, d, and e. The sums at the bottom indicate the number of choices each individual receives.

The analysis of a matrix usually begins by studying it to see who chose whom. With a simple matrix this is easy. There are three kinds of choices: simple or one-way, mutual or two-way, and no choice. We look first at simple choices. (This was discussed in the preceding paragraph.) A *simple* one-way choice is where i chooses j, but j does not choose i. In Table 31.1, c chose d, but d did not choose c. We write: $i \rightarrow j$, or $c \rightarrow d$. A *mutual* choice is where i chooses j and j also chooses i. In the table, a chose b and b chose a. We write: $i \leftrightarrow j$, or $a \leftrightarrow b$. We might count mutual choices in Table 31.1: $a \leftrightarrow b$, $a \leftrightarrow e$, $b \leftrightarrow e$.

The extent to which any member is chosen is seen easily by adding the columns of the matrix. Obviously, e is "popular": this person was chosen by all the other group members; a and b received two and three choices, respectively. Evidently, c is not at all popular: no one chose this person; d is not popular either, receiving only one choice. If individuals are allowed unlimited choices, that is, if they are instructed to choose any number of other individuals, then the row sums take on meaning. Participants can be told to choose one, two, three, or more other persons. Three seems to be a common number of choices. The number allowed should be dictated by the research purposes. We might call these sums indices of, say, Gregariousness.

There are other methods of matrix analysis that are potentially useful to researchers. For example, by relatively simple matrix operations one can determine cliques and chains of influence in small and large groups. These matters, however, are beyond the scope of this book.

Sociograms or Directed Graphs

The simplest analyses are like those just discussed. But with a matrix larger than the one in Table 31.1 it is almost impossible to digest the complexities of the choice relations. Here *sociograms* are helpful, provided the group is not too large. We now change the name "sociogram" to "directed graph." This is a more general mathematical term that can be applied to any situation in which i and j are in some relation R. Instead of saying "i chooses j," it is quite possible to say "i influences j," or "i communicates to j," or "i is a friend of j," or "i dominates j." In symbolic shorthand, we can write, generally: iRj. Specifically, we can write for the examples just given: iCj (i chooses j), iIj (i influences j), iCj (i communicates to j), iFj (i is a friend of j), iDj (i dominates j). Any of these interpretations can be depicted by a matrix such as that of Table 31.1 and by a directed graph. A directed graph is given in Figure 31.1.

We see at a glance that e is the center of choice. We might call this person a leader. Or we might say this person is either a likable or competent person. More important, note that a, b, and e choose each other. This is a clique. We define a *clique* as three or more individuals who mutually choose each other. Festinger, Schachter, and Back (1950) present a valuable method for identifying cliques within groups. Looking for more double-headed arrows, we find none. Now we might look for individuals with no arrowheads pointing at them: c is one such individual. We can say that c is not chosen, or neglected. For more information on cliques and their identification one can consult Glanzer and Glaser (1959, pp. 326–327). Glanzer and

▣ FIGURE 31.1

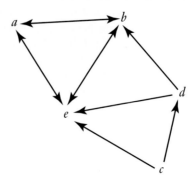

Glaser succinctly outline methods of the multiplication of binary matrices (1, 0), whose application yields useful insights into group structure.

Note that directed graphs and matrices say the same thing. We look at the number of choices *a* receives by adding the 1s in the a column of the matrix. We get the same information by adding the number of arrowheads pointing at *a* in the graph. For small and medium-size groups and for descriptive purposes, graphs are excellent means of summarizing group relations. For larger groups (larger than 20 members) and more analytic purposes, they are not as suitable. They become difficult to construct and to interpret. Moreover, different individuals can draw different graphs using the same data. Matrices are general and, if handled properly, not too difficult to interpret. Different individuals must, with the same data, write exactly the same matrices.

Sociometric Indices

In sociometry many indices are possible. Three are given below. The student will find others in the literature. The discussion of this section is for the most part based on Proctor and Loomis (1951).

A simple but useful index is:

$$CS_j = \frac{\Sigma c_j}{n-1} \qquad (31.1)$$

where CS_j = the choice status of Person j; Σc_j = the sum of choices in Column j; and n = the number of individuals in the group ($n-1$ is used because one cannot count the individual himself or herself). For C of Table 31.1, $CS_e = 4/4 = 1.00$ and $CS_a = 2/4 = .50$. How well or how poorly chosen an individual is, is revealed by CS. It is, in short, the *choice status*. It is, of course, possible to have a choice rejection index. Simply put, the number of 0s in any column in the numerator of Equation 31.1.

Group sociometric measures are perhaps more interesting. A measure of the cohesiveness of a group is:

$$Co = \frac{\Sigma(i \leftrightarrow j)}{\left[\dfrac{n(n-1)}{2}\right]} \qquad\qquad (31.2)$$

Group cohesiveness is represented by Co and $\Sigma(i \leftrightarrow j)$ equals sum of mutual choices (or mutual pairs). This useful index is the proportion of mutual choices to the total number of possible pairs. In a five-member group, the total number of possible pairs is five things taken two at a time:

$$\left|\frac{5}{2}\right| = \frac{5(5-1)}{2}$$

If, in an unlimited choice situation, there were two mutual choices, then $Co = 2/10 = .20$, a rather low degree of cohesiveness. In the case of limited choice, the formula is:

$$Co = \frac{\Sigma(i \leftrightarrow j)}{\left[\dfrac{dn}{2}\right]} \qquad\qquad (31.3)$$

where d equals the number of choices each individual is permitted. For C of Table 31.1 $Co = 3/(2 \times 5/2) = 3/5 = .60$, a substantial degree of cohesiveness.

Research Uses of Sociometry

Since the data of sociometry seem so different from other kinds of data, students may find it difficult to think of sociometric measurement as measurement. No doubt sociometric data are different, but they are the result of observation, and *they are measures*. Since they are measures, they also have the basic measurement concerns, such as reliability and validity. Lindzey and Byrne (1968) discuss these measurement issues. Sociometric measurements are useful, for example, in classifying individuals and groups. In the classic Bennington College study, Newcomb (1943) measured individual prestige by asking students to name five students they would choose as most worthy to represent Bennington College at an important gathering of students from all types of American colleges. He then grouped students by frequency of choice and related this measure of *sociometric prestige* to political and economic conservatism. In reading the examples of this section, the student should clearly realize that sociometry is a method of observation and data collection that, like any other method of observation, obtains measures of variables.

Prejudice in Schools

Rooney-Rebeck and Jason (1986) investigated the effects of cooperative group peer tutoring on the interethnic relations of black American, white American and Latino American first- and third-grade children. These researchers made direct observations of social interactions on the playground before and after an eight-week intervention program. Sociometric indices were computed to measure the interethnic associations. Rooney-Rebeck and Jason found an increase in interethnic interactions and sociometric choices for first-graders. These first-graders also showed improvement in their arithmetic and reading grades. However, no significant changes were found among the third-grade students in either interethnic associations or academic performance. It appears from these findings that a cooperative peer tutoring classroom structure may be beneficial to first-grade children, but not necessarily for third-grade children. The researchers suggest that this may be due to limited experience with academic competition and overt ethnic prejudices of first-grade children.

Sociometry and Stereotypes

Gross, Green, Storck, and Vanyur (1980) used a combination of sociometric and stereotypic ratings to study the attitudes of people. Participants of both sexes viewed a videotape of either a male or a female homosexual stimulus person. The participants were divided into three groups. One group of participants was informed that the stimulus person was a homosexual before viewing the tape. The second group was informed after the viewing, and the third group was never informed. Results revealed that trait ratings were more stereotypical and sociometric ratings less favorable for the stimulus person in both disclosure conditions: immediate or delayed. Those stimulus persons who were identified as homosexuals were judged more stereotypically by participants of their own sex. Men generally rated the stimulus person more harshly in the delayed condition than in the immediate disclosure conditions.

Sociometry and Social Status

A number of studies have been conducted using sociometry to measure social status. One of these studies follow, which involve social status among school-aged children.

Inderbitzen, Walters, and Bukowski (1997) studied the relation between sociometric status groups and social anxiety in adolescent peer relations. The participants consisted of 973 students in grades 6 through 9. The number of boys and girls was almost equal. These participants completed the Social Anxiety Scale for Adolescents and a sociometric nomination task. The sociometric nomination task included behavioral descriptors such as liked most, liked least, starts fights the most, best sense of humor, class leader, easiest to push around, and most cooperative. These sociometric nominations were then used to classify students into standard sociometric status groups such as popular, average, rejected, neglected, and controversial; as well as into rejected subgroups: aggressive rejected and submissive rejected. Results indicated that students classified as rejected and neglected reported more social anxiety than those classified as average, popular, or controversial. In addition, submissive rejected students reported significantly more social anxiety than did aggressive rejected or average students. Through the use of sociometry, one can discover the existence of adolescents' peer problems.

Race, Belief, and Sociometric Choice

Graham and Cohen (1997) studied the relation between race and sex in children's peer relationships. These relationships were measured by sociometric ratings and observed friendships. This study observed every student in a single elementary school. This included grades 1 to 6. This school was chosen because it had nearly an even number of black American to white American children in each class. The students were also divided into two age groups: grades 1 to 3 and grades 4 to 6. Regardless of age, race, or sex, and relationship measures, children favored same-sex peers over same-race peers. This says that boys preferred social interactions with other boys regardless of race and girls preferred to interact with other girls regardless of race. Although older black American children had more same-race than cross-race mutual friends, black American children were more accepting of white American children than the reverse. Despite some same-race preferences, cross-race evaluations were generally quite positive on both peer relationship measures.

Sociometry is a simple, economical, and naturalistic method of observation and data collection. Whenever human actions such as choosing, influencing, dominating, and communicating—especially in group situations—are involved, sociometric methods can usually be used. They have considerable flexibility. If defined broadly, they can be adapted to a wide variety of research in the laboratory and in the field. Their quantification and analysis possibilities, though not generally realized in the literature, are rewarding. The ability to use the simple assignment of 1s and 0s is particularly fortunate, because powerful mathematical methods can be applied to the data with uniquely interpretable and meaningful results. Matrix methods are the outstanding example. With these methods, one can discover cliques in groups, communication and influence channels, patterns of cohesiveness, connectedness, hierarchism, and so on.

As mentioned earlier, sociometrics like other measurement methods, are not without shortcomings. Longshore (1982), for example, advocates the use of other unobtrusive methods rather than sociometrics when studying delicate problems such as desegregation. Longshore points out that social scientists have not found consistent findings on desegregation, because researchers were more concerned with the outcomes of desegregation instead of the wide range of conditions under which desegregation occurs. Longshore says that the assessment of short-term outcomes should be assessed through measures such as unobtrusive observation of playgroups or classes instead of sociometrics.

CHAPTER SUMMARY

1. There is a lot of controversy and debate about observation and methods of observation.

2. Two basic modes of observation

- We can watch peoples' overt actions (i.e., what they do and what they say)
- We can ask people about their own actions and the behavior of others

3. The observer could be a major problem in the study. The observer could make incorrect inferences about the observed behavior.

4. The observer can affect the objects of observation by being part of the observational system.

5. Observed measurements are subject to reliability and validity requirements. By having the observer interpret the observation, validity may be reduced.

6. Reliability for observations is in the form of agreement between judges or observers. The behavior to be measured through direct observation must be stated clearly with good operational definitions.

7. A fundamental task for the observer is to categorize the observed data. Categories are created, and as certain behaviors are observed, a tally or note is made in that category.

8. Units of behavior are sometimes vague or broad. Some researchers use very strict operational definitions.

9. All observation requires some level of interpretation from the observer.

10. Different observation systems vary in the amount of generalizability. Some are very general, others are quite specific.

11. Behaviors can be sampled using event sampling or time sampling techniques. Each has advantages and disadvantages.

12. One type of observation involves observers presented with an observation system in the form of a rating scale. They are asked to assess an object in terms of one or more characteristics.

13. There are five types of rating scales:

- checklist
- forced-choice instruments
- category rating scale
- numerical rating scale
- graphic rating scale

14. Ratings have two serious weaknesses:
   a. Because ratings are easy to construct and use, they may be created without knowledge of their intrinsic defects.
   b. Ratings are prone to constant or bias error.

15. Sociometry is a broad term indicating the number of methods of gathering and analyzing data on choice, communication, and interaction patterns of individuals in groups.

16. There are three basic forms of sociometric analysis: sociometric matrices, sociograms or directed graphs, and sociometric indices.

STUDY SUGGESTIONS

1. The student should study one or two behavior observation systems in detail. For students of education, the Medley and Mitzel (1963) system will yield high returns. Other students will want to study one or two other systems. It is authoritative and clear with many examples. The two best general references are the Heyns and Lippitt (1954), and Weick (1968) in the first and second editions of the *Handbook of Social Psychology*. An anthology of 79 observation systems has been published by Simon and Boyer (1970) in cooperation with Research for Better Schools, Inc., a regional education laboratory. The researcher who intends using observations should consult this huge collection of systems. The student of education will find excellent summaries and discussions of educational observation systems in Dunkin and Biddle (1974). The following articles are valuable. Boice points out the lack of training for making observations of behavior and makes suggestions for such training. Herbert and Attridge provide criteria for observation systems. They also point out that knowledge of such systems is limited.

   Boice, R. (1983). Observational Skills. *Psychological Bulletin, 93*, 3–29.
   Herbert, J., & Attridge, C. (1975). A guide for developers and users of observation systems and manuals. *American Educational Research Journal, 12*, 1–20.

2. An investigator, studying the influence patterns of boards of education, obtained the following matrix from one board of education. (Note that this is like an unlimited choice situation because each individual can influence all or none of the members of the group.) Read the matrix: *i* influences *j*.

		j				
		a	*b*	*c*	*d*	*e*
	a	0	0	1	1	0
	b	0	0	0	0	1
i	*c*	1	0	0	1	0
	d	1	0	1	0	0
	e	0	1	0	0	0

   a. What conclusions can you reach from study of this matrix? Is the board divided? Is there likely to be conflict?
   b. Draw a graph of the influence situation. Interpret the graph.

    c. Is there a clique on the board? (Define clique as given in the test.) If so, who are its members?

    d. What members have the least number of influence channels? Are they, then, much less influential than the other members, other things being equal?

    [Answers: (c) Yes: a, c, d; (d) b and e.]

3. For the situation in Study Suggestion 2, calculate the cohesiveness of the group using Equation 32.2.

    [Answer: $Co = .40$.]

4. Read one of the following articles, which apply sociometrics. Pay close attention to how it was done.

> Ray, G. E., Cohen, R., Secrist, M.E., & Duncan, M. K. (1997). Relating aggressive and victimization behaviors to children's sociometric status and friendships. *Journal of Social and Personal Relationships, 14,* 95–108. [This study focused on the relation between peer nominations of 9- to 12-year-old students for aggressive and victimization behaviors and peer group sociometric status: popular, average, rejected, and the number of mutual friends.]

> Schwendinger, H., & Schwendinger, J. R. (1997). Charting subcultures at a frontier of knowledge. *British Journal of Sociology, 48,* 71–94. [This article describes a research program for studying adolescent subcultures using graphs of large subcultural networks. These graphs and networks are produced by social-type and sociometric methods in order to understand adolescents and delinquency.]

5. Read one of the following studies on time sampling or event sampling. Make a note on how the authors execute each of these procedures.

> Bass, R. F., & Aserlind, L. (1984). Interval and time-sample data collection procedures. Methodological issues. *Advances in Learning and Behavioral Disabilities, 3,* 1–39. [Time sampling]

> Brown, K. W., & Moskowitz, D. S. (1998). Dynamic stability of behavior: The rhythms of our interpersonal lives. *Journal of Personality, 66,* 105–134. [Event sampling]

> Childs, G. H. (1997). A concurrent validity study of teachers' ratings for nominated "problem" children. *British Journal of Educational Psychology, 67,* 457–474. [Time sampling]

> Peregrine, P. N., Drews, D. R., North, M., & Slupe, A. (1993). Sampling techniques and sampling error in naturalistic observation: An empirical evaluation with implications for cross-cultural research. *Cross-Cultural Research: Journal of Comparative Social Science, 27,* 232–246. [Compares event, time, and cluster sampling]

PART TEN
MULTIVARIATE APPROACHES

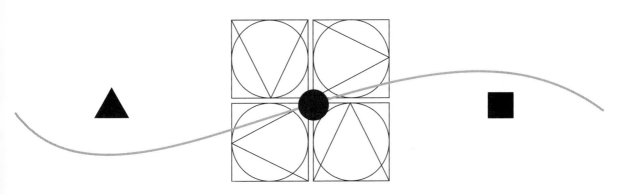

PART TEN

MULTIVARIATE APPROACHES

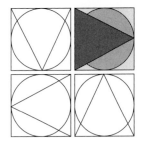

MULTIPLE REGRESSION ANALYSIS: FOUNDATIONS

Multiple regression analysis is a method for studying the effects and the magnitudes of the effects of more than one independent variable on one dependent variable, using principles of correlation and regression. We turn immediately to research and defer explanation until later.

Three Research Examples

How are air pollution and socioeconomic status related to mortality from respiratory ailments? Lave and Seskin (1970) in their study of English and American data, used multiple regression analysis to answer the question. In their studies in English boroughs, they assessed the presumed effects of air pollution and socioeconomic status, as independent variables, on mortality rates of lung cancer, bronchitis, and pneumonia, as dependent variables.

The overall effect of the two independent variables on the dependent variable is expressed by the square of a correlation coefficient called the coefficient of multiple correlation, or R^2. This coefficient's interpretation is similar to that of r^2, which we discussed much earlier. Recall that squaring a correlation coefficient yields an estimate of the amount of variance shared by two variables. This notion is used a great deal in regression analysis.

It is the proportion of the variance of the dependent variable, in this case mortality, accounted for by the two independent variables. The R^2s between mortality due to bronchitis on the one hand, and air pollution and socioeconomic status on the other hand, ranged from .30 to .78 in different samples in England and Wales, indicating substantial relations. The R^2s for the dependent variables, lung cancer and pneumonia mortalities, were similar. Multiple regression also enables the researcher to learn something of the relative influences of independent variables. In most of the samples, air pollution was more important than socioeconomic status. As a "control" analysis, Lave and Seskin (1970) studied other cancers that would presumably not be affected by air pollution. The R^2s were consistently lower, as expected. Extension of the research to metropolitan areas in the United States yielded similar results. Students should bear in mind our earlier discussions of the difficulty in interpreting nonexperimental results. Lave and Seskin, however, have built a strong case, even though some of their interpretation was questionable. At this point, it would be wise for readers to return to the discussion "Multivariate Relations and Regression" in Chapter 5.

How are dietary restraint, energy intake, and physical activity related to body weight? Klesges, Isbell, and Klesges (1992) used multiple regression analysis to try answering this question. This study is of interest because of the number of health problems associated with obesity. These researchers collected one year of data on 287 adults. The dependent variable was the weight change from baseline to the one-year follow-up. The independent variables were weight at baseline, body mass index, restraint score, age, total energy intake, percentage of fat intake, percentage of carbohydrates and physical activity levels. The height and weight measurements of these participants were used to estimate body mass. The dietary intake measures were taken each week. Physical activity was measured through a physical activity questionnaire containing 16 items representing physical activities. Restraint was measured through a restraint scale. Two separate regression analyses were done. One was for men and the other was for women.

The R^2 between the dependent variable, weight change, and a linear combination of the independent variables was .13 for men and .21 for women. This says that the independent variables studied by Klesges et al. accounted only for 13% of the variability observed in weight change for men and 21% for women. The figure for the men was not statistically significant at the $\alpha = .05$ level. However, the regression equation for women was significant at the $\alpha = .01$ level. Through the use of regression, however, these researchers were able to determine that for men, initial body weight and body mass were the two strongest variables in accounting for weight change. For women, the most important variables were initial body weight and restraint.

In a study of the prediction of high school GPA (grade point average), Holtzman and Brown (1968) used two independent variable measures: study habits and attitudes (Habits) and scholastic aptitude (Aptitude). The correlations between high school GPA (the dependent variable) and Habits and Aptitude in grade 7 ($N = 1,684$) were .55 and .61. The correlation between Habits and Aptitudes was .32. How much more variance was accounted for by adding the scholastic aptitude measure to the study habits measure? If we combine Habits and Aptitudes optimally to predict GPA, we obtain a correlation of .72. The answer to the question, then, is $.72^2 - .55^2 = .52 - .30 = .22$, or 22% more of the variance of GPA is accounted for by adding Aptitudes to Habits.

These are examples of multiple regression analysis. The basic idea is the same as simple correlation except that k, where k is greater than 1, independent variables are used to predict the dependent variable. In simple regression analysis, a variable, X, is used to predict another variable, Y. In multiple regression analysis, variables $X_1, X_2, \ldots, X_k$ are used to predict Y. The method and the calculations are done in a manner to give the "best" prediction possible, given the correlations among all the variables. In other words, instead of saying "If X, then Y," we say "If $X_1, X_2, \ldots, X_k$, then Y," and the results of the calculations tell us how "good" the prediction is and approximately how much of the variance of Y is accounted for by the "best" linear combination of the independent variables.

Simple Regression Analysis

We say that we study the regression of Y scores on X scores. We wish to study how the Y scores "go back to," how they "depend on," the X scores. Galton (see Cowles, 1989), who first worked out the notion of correlation, got the idea from the notion of "regression toward mediocrity," a phenomenon observed in studies of inheritance. (The symbol r used for the coefficient of correlation originally meant "regression.") Tall men will tend to have shorter sons, and short men taller sons. The sons' heights, then, tend to "regress to," or "go back to," the mean of the population. Statistically, if we want to predict Y from X and the correlation between X and Y is zero, then our best prediction is to the mean. That is, for any given X, say X_7, we can only predict the mean of Y. The higher the correlation, however, the better the prediction. If $r = 1.00$, then prediction is perfect. To the extent that the correlation departs from 1.00, to that extent predictions from X to Y are less than perfect. If we plot the X and Y values when $r = 1.00$, they will all lie on a straight line. The higher the correlation, the closer the plotted values will be to the regression line (see Chapter 5).

To illustrate and explain the notion of statistical regression, we use two fictitious examples with simple numbers. The numbers used in the two examples are the same except that they are arranged differently. These examples are taken from Chapter 15,

🔲 **TABLE 32.1** *Regression Analysis of Two Sets of Scores*

A. $r = .90$					B. $r = .00$				
Y	X	XY	Y'	d	Y	X	XY	Y'	d
1	2	2	1.2	−.2	1	5	5	3	−2
2	4	8	3.0	−1.0	2	2	4	3	−1
3	3	9	2.1	.9	3	4	12	3	0
4	5	20	3.9	.1	4	6	24	3	1
5	6	30	4.8	.2	5	3	15	3	2
Σ:	15	20	69	0	15	20	60		0
M:	3	4	$\Sigma d^2 = 1.90$			3	4	$\Sigma d^2 = 10.00$	
Σ²:	55	90				55	90		

$$\Sigma y^2 = 55 - \frac{(15)^2}{5} = 10 \qquad\qquad \Sigma y^2 = 55 - \frac{(15)^2}{5} = 10$$

$$\Sigma x^2 = 90 - \frac{(20)^2}{5} = 10 \qquad\qquad \Sigma x^2 = 90 - \frac{(20)^2}{5} = 10$$

$$\Sigma xy = 69 - \frac{(15)(20)}{5} = 9 \qquad\qquad \Sigma xy = 60 - \frac{(15)(20)}{5} = 0$$

$$b = \frac{\Sigma xy}{\Sigma x^2} = \frac{9}{10} = .90 \qquad\qquad b = \frac{0}{10} = 0$$

$$a = \bar{Y} - b\bar{X} = 3 - (.90)(4) = -.60 \qquad\qquad a = 3 - (0)(4) = 3$$

$$Y' = a + bX = -.60 + .90X \qquad\qquad Y' = 3 + (0)X$$

where in considering the analysis of variance, we studied the effect on the F-test of the correlation between experimental groups. The examples are given in Table 32.1. In the example on the left, labeled A, the correlation between the X and Y values is .90, whereas in the example on the right, labeled B, the correlation is 0. Certain calculations necessary for regression analysis are also given in the table: the sums and means, the deviation sums-of-squares of X and Y ($\Sigma x^2 = \Sigma X^2 - (\Sigma X)^2/n$), the deviation cross products ($\Sigma xy = \Sigma XY - (\Sigma X)(\Sigma Y)/n$), and certain regression values to be explained shortly.

🔲 FIGURE 32.1

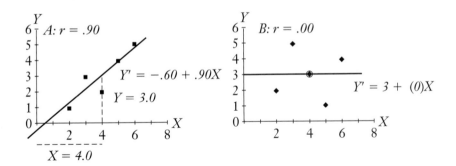

First, note the difference between the scores in sets A and B. They differ only in the order of the scores of the second or X columns. The two different orders produce very different correlations between the X and Y scores. In the A set, $r = .90$, and in the B set, $r = .00$. Second, note the statistics at the bottom of the table. Σx^2 and Σy^2 are the same in both A and B, but Σxy is 9 in A and 0 in B. Let us concentrate on the A set of scores. The basic equation of simple linear regression is:

$$Y' = a + bX \qquad (32.1)$$

where $X =$ the scores of the independent variable, $a =$ intercept constant, $b =$ regression coefficient, and $Y' =$ predicted scores of the dependent variable. A regression equation is a prediction formula: Y values are predicted from X values. The correlation between the observed X and Y values in effect determines how the prediction equation "works." The intercept constant, a, and the regression coefficient, b, will be explained shortly.

The two sets of X and Y values of Table 32.1 are plotted in Figure 32.1. Lines have been drawn in each plot to "run through" the plotted points. If we had a way of placing these lines so that they would simultaneously be as close to all the points as possible, then the lines should express the regression of Y on X. The line in the left plot, where $r = .90$, runs close to the plotted XY points. In the right plot, however, where $r = .00$, it is not possible to run the line close to all the points. The points are, in effect, placed randomly, since $r = .00$.

The correlations between X and Y, $r = .90$ and $r = .00$, determine the slopes of the regression lines (when the standard deviations of X and Y are equal, as they are in this case). The *slope* indicates the change in Y with a change of one unit of X. In the $r = .90$ example, with a change of 1 in X, we predict a change of .90 in Y. This is expressed trigonometrically as the length of the line opposite the angle made by the regression line divided by the length of the line adjacent to the angle. In Figure 32.1, if we drop a perpendicular from the regression line—the point where the X and Y means intersect, for example—to a line drawn horizontally from the point where the regression line intersects the Y axis, or at $Y = -.60$, then $3.6/4.0 = .90$. A change of 1 in X means a change of .90 in Y. Raw scores have been used for most of the examples in this chapter because they better fit our purposes. A thorough treatment of regression, however, requires discussions using deviation scores and standard scores. The emphasis here, as elsewhere in the book, is on research uses of the methods and techniques, and not on statistics as such. The student should supplement his or her study, therefore, with good basic discussions of simple and multiple regression. See the references in the study suggestions at the end Chapter 33.

The plot of the X and Y values of Example B (right part of Figure 32.1) is quite different. In Example A, one can rather easily and visually draw a line through the points and achieve a fairly accurate approximation to the regression line. But in Example B this is hardly possible. We can draw the line only by using other guidelines, which we get to shortly. Another important thing to note is the scatter or dispersion of the plotted points around the two regression lines. In Example A, they cling rather closely to the line. If $r = 1.00$, they would all be on the line. When $r = .00$, on the other hand, they scatter widely about the line. *The lower the correlation, the greater the scatter.*

In order to calculate the regression statistics of the two examples, we must calculate the deviation sums-of-squares and cross products. This has been done at the bottom of Table 32.1. The formula for the *slope*, or *regression coefficient*, b, is:

$$b = \frac{\Sigma xy}{\Sigma x^2} \tag{32.2}$$

The two b's are .90 and .00. The *intercept constant*, a, is calculated with the formula:

$$a = \bar{Y} - b\bar{X} \tag{32.3}$$

The as for the two examples are $-.60$ and 3; for Example A, $a = 3 - (.90)(4) = -.60$. The intercept constant is the point where the regression line intercepts the Y-axis. To draw the regression line, lay a ruler between the intercept constant on the Y-axis and the point where the mean of Y and the mean of X meet. (In Figure 32.1, these points are indicated with small squares in Example A and diamonds in Example B.)

The final steps in the process, at least as far as it will be taken here, are to write regression equations and then, using the equations, calculate the predicted values of Y, or Y', given the X values. The two equations are given in the last line of Table 32.1. First look at the regression equation for $r = .00$: $Y' = 3 + (0)X$. This means, of course, that all the predicted Ys are 3, the mean of Y. When $r = 0$, the best prediction is the mean, as indicated earlier. When $r = 1.00$, at the other extreme, the reader can see that one can predict exactly: one simply adds a, the constant, to the X scores. When $r = .90$, prediction is less than perfect and one predicts Y' values calculated with the regression equation. For example, to predict the first Y' score, we calculate:

$$Y'_1 = -.60 + (.90)(2) = 1.20$$

The predicted scores of the A and B sets have been given in Table 32.1. (See columns labeled Y'.) Note an important point: If for Example A we plot the X and the predicted Y or Y' values, the plotted points all lie on the regression line. That is, the regression line of the figure represents the set of predicted Y values, given the X values and the correlation between the X and the observed Y values.

We can now calculate the predicted values of Y. The higher the correlation, the more accurate the prediction. The accuracy of the predictions of the two sets of scores can be clearly shown by calculating the differences between the original Y values and the predicted Y values, or $Y - Y' = d$, and then calculating the sums-of-squares of these differences. Such differences are called *residuals*. In Table 32.1, the two sets of residuals and their sums-of-squares have been calculated (see columns labeled d). The two values of Σd^2, 1.90 for A and 10.00 for B, are quite different, just as the plots in Figure 32.1 are quite different: The values of the B set, $r = .00$, is much greater than that of the A, or $r = .90$, set. That is, the higher the correlation, the smaller the deviations from prediction and thus the more accurate the prediction.

In the next section, we will examine an extension of the simplest model of regression. The extended method called multiple regression has a far wider utility in research than the simple model presented here. However, one should not think that the simplest model is without value or use. The simple regression model can indeed provide valuable research and practical information. For example, Erlich and Lee (1978) showed how this simple regression model with some additional statistics (confidence band or interval) can be used to determine accountability of educational instruction and policy.

Multiple Linear Regression

The method of multiple linear regression extends the ideas presented in the preceding section to more than one independent variable. From knowledge of the values of two or more independent variables, $X_1, X_2, \ldots, X_k$, we want to predict to a dependent variable, Y. Earlier in the book we talked about the great need to assess the influence of several variables on a dependent variable. We can, of course, predict from verbal aptitude, say, to reading achievement, or from conservatism to ethnic attitudes. But how much more powerful it would be if we could predict from verbal aptitude together with other variables known or thought to influence reading—for example, achievement motivation and attitude toward school work. Theoretically, there is no limit to the number of variables we can use, but there are practical limits. Although only two independent variables are used in the example that follows, the principles apply to any number of independent variables.

An Example

Take one of the problems just mentioned. Suppose we had reading achievement (RA), verbal aptitude (VA), and achievement motivation (AM) scores on 20 eighth-grade pupils. We want to predict to reading achievement, Y, from verbal aptitude, X_1,

回 **TABLE 32.2** *Fictitious Example: Reading Achievement (Y), Verbal Aptitude (X_1), and Achievement Motivation (X_2) Scores*

Y	X_1	X_2	Y'	Y − Y' = d
2	2	4	3.0305	−1.0305
1	2	4	3.0305	−2.0305
1	1	4	2.3534	−1.3534
1	1	3	1.9600	−.9600
5	3	6	4.4944	.5056
4	4	6	5.1715	−1.1715
7	5	3	4.6684	2.3316
6	5	4	5.0618	.9382
7	7	3	6.0226	.9774
8	6	3	5.3455	2.6545
3	4	5	4.7781	−1.7781
3	3	5	4.1010	−1.1010
6	6	9	7.7059	−1.7059
6	6	8	7.3125	−1.3125
10	8	6	7.8799	2.1201
9	9	7	8.9504	.0496
6	10	5	8.8407	−2.8407
6	9	5	8.1636	−2.1636
9	4	7	5.5649	3.4351
10	4	7	5.5649	4.4351
Σ: 110	99	104		0
M: 5.50	4.95	5.20		
Σ^2: 770.0	625.0	600.0		81.6091

and achievement motivation, X_2. Or, we want to calculate the regression of reading achievement on *both* verbal aptitude and achievement motivation. If the scores on verbal aptitude and achievement motivation were standard scores, we might average them, treat the averages as one composite independent variable, and calculate the regression statistics as we did earlier. We might not do too badly either. But there is a better way.

Suppose the X_1 (verbal aptitude), X_2 (achievement motivation), and Y (reading achievement), scores of the 20 subjects and the sums, means, and raw score sums-of-squares are those of Table 32.2 (Disregard the Y' and d columns for the moment.) We need to calculate the *deviation* sums-of-squares, the deviation cross products, the standard deviations and the correlations among the three variables. These are the basic statistics that are calculated for almost any set of data. They are given in Table 32.3. The calculations are not done here because their mechanics were covered in earlier chapters. The student should do them and note that the obtained results will probably be slightly different from those reported above. Such differences are due to rounding errors—an ever-present problem in multivariate analysis. In fact, the results of this problem, obtained on a desk calculator, are slightly different from those obtained by computer. The sums-of-squares and cross products are given in the diagonal (from upper left to lower right) and above it, and the correlations are given below the diagonal. The rs of prime interest are those of the two independent variables with the dependent variable, r_{y1} and r_{y2}, .6735 and .3946 respectively. With these routine calculations out of the way, we can concentrate on the basic notions of multiple regression. The fundamental regression equation is:

$$Y' = a + b_1 X_1 + \cdots + b_k X_k \qquad (32.4)$$

▣ **TABLE 32.3** *Deviation Sums-of-Squares and Cross Products, Correlation Coefficients, and Standard Deviations (Data from Table 34.2)*[a]

	y	x_1	x_2
y	165.00	100.50	39.00
x_1	.6735	134.95	23.20
x_2	.3946	.2596	59.20
s	2.9469	2.6651	1.7652

[a]The tabled entries are as follows. The first line gives, successively, Σy^2, the sum-of-squares of the deviation scores for Y, the cross product of the deviations of X_1 and Y, or $\Sigma x_1 y$ and finally $\Sigma x_2 y$. The entries in the second and third lines, on the diagonal or above, are Σx_1^2, $\Sigma x_1 x_2$, and (in the lower right corner) Σx_2^2. The italicized entries *below* the diagonal are the correlation coefficients. The standard deviations are given in the last line.

The symbols have the same meaning as those of the simple regression equation, except that there are k independent variables and k regression coefficients. Somehow, the a and bs must be calculated from knowledge of the Xs and Y. These calculations are the most complex of multiple regression analysis. For only two independent variables, algebraic formulas given in statistics books can be used (see Cohen & Cohen, 1983; Draper & Smith, 1981; Neter, Wasserman & Kutner, 1983; or Pedhazur, 1996). The calculation of a, once the bs are found, is straightforward. The problem is the calculation of the bs when there are more than two independent variables. Only the general ideas behind the calculations will be explained, since the details would take us too far from our central concern. The reader is asked to consult any and or all of the following: Pedhazur (1996); Draper and Smith (1981); Neter, Wasserman, and Kutner (1983); Kerlinger and Pedhazur (1973); Cohen and Cohen (1983).

What we have, in effect, is a set of linear equations, one equation for each independent variable. The objective of the determination of the bs of Equation 32.4 is to find those b values that will minimize the sums-of-squares of the residuals. This is the *principle of least squares*. The calculus provides the method of differentiation for doing this. If used, it yields a set of simultaneous linear equations called *normal* equations (no relation to normal distribution). A convenient form of these equations contains the coefficients of correlation among all the independent variables and between the independent variables and the dependent variable and a set of weights called *beta weights*, β_j, that will be explained later (they are like the b weights). The normal equations for the above problem are:

$$r_{11}\beta_1 + r_{12}\beta_2 = r_{y1}$$
$$r_{12}\beta_1 + r_{22}\beta_2 = r_{y2}$$

(32.5)

where β_j equals beta weights; r_{12} equals the correlations among the independent variables; and r_{yj} the correlations between the independent variables and the dependent variable, Y. (Note that $r_{12} = r_{21}$, and that $r_{11} = r_{22} = 1.00$. Note, too, that Equation 32.5 can be extended to any number of independent variables.)

Probably the best way—certainly the most elegant way—to solve the equations for the β_j is to use matrix algebra. Unfortunately, knowledge of matrix algebra cannot be assumed. So the actual solution of the equations using matrix algebra must be omitted but the solution for two independent variables can be obtained algebraically without using matrices. However, any size greater than this would certainly require the use of a computer program because the amount of computations increase exponentially. We will show how the solution can be obtained with a little algebra. To use the normal equations given above, we will need to compute r_{12}, r_{y1} and r_{y2}. Remember, r_{11} and r_{22} are both equal to 1.00. From examining Table 32.3, we obtain $r_{12} = .259562$, $r_{y1} = .6735$ and $r_{y2} = .394604$. Putting these values into the normal equations, we get:

$$1.000000\beta_1 + .259562\beta_2 = .6735$$

$$.259562\beta_1 + 1.00000\beta_2 = .394604$$

Take each normal equation and rearrange them so that β_1 is on one side of the equal sign and everything else is on the other side:

$$\beta_1 = .6735 - .259562\beta_2$$

$$\beta_1 = 1.5202688 - 3.8526441\beta_2$$

Now set the β_1s equal to each other and solve for β_2.

$$.6735 - .259562\beta_2 = 1.5202688 - 3.8526441\beta_2$$

$$3.5930821\beta_2 = .8467688$$

$$\beta_2 = \frac{.8467688}{3.5930821} = .235666 \approx .2357$$

Solving for β_1 we substitute the value of β_2 back into the equation: $\beta_1 = .6735 - .259562\beta_2$. So,

$$\beta_1 = .6735 - .259562 \times .235666 = .6123$$

The solution for our two variable situation given above, yields the following beta weights: $\beta_1 = .6123$ *and* $\beta_2 = .2357$. The *b* weights or unstandardized regression weights are then obtained from the following formula:

$$b_j = \beta_j \frac{s_y}{s_j} \tag{32.6}$$

where s_j equals standard deviations of variables one and two (see Table 32.3) and s_y equals standard deviation of Y. Substituting in Equation 32.6 we obtain:

$$b_1 = (.6123)\left(\frac{2.9469}{2.6651}\right) = .6771$$

$$b_2 = (.2357)\left(\frac{2.9469}{1.7652}\right) = .3934$$

To obtain the intercept constant, extend Equation 32.3 to two independent variables:

$$a = \overline{Y} - b_1\overline{X_1} - b_2\overline{X_2}$$

$$a = 5.50 - (.6771)(4.95) - (.3934)(5.20) = .1027$$

An alternative method of finding the unstandardized regression coefficients is by using the normal equations. Note here, these normal equations will directly give the regression weights. The normal equations given above would be used to obtain the regression coefficients.

$$nb_0 + \Sigma x_1 b_1 + \Sigma x_2 b_2 = \Sigma y$$

$$\Sigma x_1 b_0 + \Sigma x_1^2 b_1 + \Sigma x_1 x_2 b_2 = \Sigma x_1 y$$

$$\Sigma x_2 b_0 + \Sigma x_1 x_2 b_1 + \Sigma x_2^2 b_2 = \Sigma x_2 y$$

Note that for two independent variables, there are three normal equations and that sometimes b_0 is used to represent the intercept or constant term. There are three equations given above with three unknown parameters to be estimated: b_0, b_1 and b_2. The computations to solve for the regression weights are too laborious to be done by hand and so no computations will be presented here.

Finally, we write the complete regression equation:

$$Y' = a + b_1 X_1 + b_2 X_2$$

$$Y' = .1027 + .6771 X_1 + .3934 X_2$$

Substituting the observed values of X_1 and X_2 of Table 34.2, the predicted values of Y are obtained. For example, calculate the predicted Ys for the fifth and twentieth subjects:

$$Y'_5 = .1027 + (.6771)(3) + (.3934)(6) = 4.4944$$

$$Y'_{20} = .1027 + (.6771)(4) + (.3934)(7) = 5.5649$$

These values and the other 18 values are given in the fourth column of Table 32.2. The fifth column of the table gives the deviations from regression, or the residuals, $Y_i - Y'_i = d_i$. For example, the residuals for Y_5 and Y_{20} are

$$d_5 = Y_5 - Y'_5 = 5 - 4.4944 = .5056$$

$$d_{20} = Y_{20} - Y'_{20} = 10 - 5.5649 = 4.4351$$

Note that one deviation is small and the other large. The residuals are given in the last column of Table 32.2. Most of them are relatively small; about half are positive and half are negative.

The sum-of-squares due to regression can now be calculated, but the regression of Y on X_1 and X_2 must be considered. Square each of the Y' values of the fourth column of Table 32.2 and sum:

$$(3.0305)^2 + \ldots + (5.5649)^2 = 688.3969$$

Now use the usual formula for the deviation sum-of-squares (see Chapter 13):

$$\Sigma y^2 = 688.3969 - \frac{(110)^2}{20} = 83.3969$$

Similarly, calculate the sum-of-squares of the residuals:

$$\sum d^2 = (-1.0305)^2 + \cdot \cdot \cdot + (4.4351)^2 = 81.6091$$

Note that this is a "good" example of the errors that accumulate through rounding. The actual regression sum-of-squares, calculated by computer, is 83.3909, an error of .006. Also note, however, that even though the residuals were calculated from the hand-calculated predicted Ys, the sum-of-squares of the residuals is exactly that produced by the computer, 81.6091.

As a check, calculate:

$$ss_{reg} + ss_{res} = ss_t$$

$$83.3969 + 81.6091 = 165.0060$$

The regression and residual sums-of-squares are not usually calculated in this way. They were calculated here just to show what these quantities are. Had the formulas that are ordinarily employed been used, we might not have seen clearly that the regression sum-of-squares is the sum-of-squares of the Y' values calculated by using the regression equation. We also might not have seen clearly that the residual sum-of-squares is the sum-of-squares calculated with the ds of the fifth column of Table 32.2. Recall, too, that the a and the bs (or βs) of the regression equation were calculated to satisfy the least-squares principle; that is, to minimize the ds, or errors of prediction—or, rather, to minimize the sum-of-squares of the errors of prediction. To summarize, the regression sum-of-squares expresses that portion of the total sum-of-squares of Y due to the regression of Y, the dependent variable, on X_1 and X_2, the independent variables. The residual sum-of-squares expresses that portion of the total sum-of-squares of Y that is *not* due to the regression.

The reader may wonder: Why bother with this complicated procedure of determining the regression weights? Is it necessary to invoke a least-squares procedure? Why not just average the X_1 and X_2 values and call the means of the individual X_1 and X_2 values the predicted Ys? The answer is that it might work quite well. Indeed, in this case it would work very well, almost as well, in fact, as the full regression procedure. But it might *not* work too well. The trouble is that you do not really know when it will work well and when it will not. The regression procedure always "works," other things being equal. It always minimizes the squared errors of prediction. Note that in both cases linear equations are used and that only the coefficients differ:

Regression equation: $Y' = a + b_1X_1 + b_2X_2$

Mean equation: $Y' = \dfrac{1}{2}X_1 + \dfrac{1}{2}X_2$

Of the innumerable possible ways of weighting X_1 and X_2, which should be chosen if the least-squares principle is not used? It is conceivable, of course, that one has prior knowledge or some reason for X_1 and X_2. X_1 may be the scores on some test that has been found to be highly successful in prediction. X_2 may be a successful predictor, too, but not as successful as X_1. Therefore one may decide to weight X_1 very heavily, say four times as much as X_2. The equation would be: $Y' = 4X_1 + X_2$. And this might work well. The trouble is that seldom do we have prior knowledge, and even when we do, it is rather imprecise. How can the decision be reached to weight X_1 four times as much as X_2? An educated guess can be made. The regression method is not a guess, however. It is a precise method based on the data and on a powerful mathematical principle. It is in this sense that the calculated regression weights are "best."

The regression and residual sums-of-squares can be calculated more readily than indicated above. The formulas are:

$$ss_{reg} = b_1 \Sigma x_1 y + \ldots + b_k \Sigma x_k y \tag{32.7}$$

$$ss_{res} = ss_t - ss_{reg} \tag{32.8}$$

In the present case, (32.7) becomes:

$$ss_{reg} = b_1 \Sigma x_1 y + b_2 \Sigma x_2 y$$

This is easily calculated by substituting the two b values calculated above and the cross products given in Table 32.3.

$$ss_{reg} = (.6771)(100.50) + (.3934)(39.00) = 83.3912$$

$$ss_{res} = 165.0 - 83.3912 = 81.6088$$

Within errors of rounding, these are the values calculated directly from the fourth and fifth columns of Table 32.2. (Note the "most accurate" values given by a computer: $ss_{reg} = 83.3909$ and $ss_{res} = 81.6091$, which of course total $ss_t = \Sigma y^2 = 165.0$.)

The Multiple Correlation Coefficient

If the ordinary product-moment coefficient of correlation between the predicted values Y' and the observed values of Y is calculated, we obtain an index of the magnitude of the relation between, on the one hand, a least-squares composite of X_1 and X_2 and, on the other hand, Y. This index is called the *multiple correlation coefficient*, R. Although in this chapter it is usually written as R for the sake of brevity, a more satisfactory way to write it is with subscripts: $R_{y.12\ldots k}$, or, in this case, $R_{y.12}$. The theory of multiple regression seems to be especially elegant when we consider the multiple correlation coefficient. It is one of the links that bind together the various aspects of multiple regression and analysis of variance. The formula for R that expresses the first sentence of this paragraph is:

$$R = \frac{\Sigma yy'}{\sqrt{\Sigma y^2 \Sigma y'^2}} \tag{32.9}$$

Its square is calculated:

$$R^2 = \frac{(\Sigma yy')^2}{\Sigma y^2 \Sigma y'^2} \tag{32.10}$$

Using the Y and Y' values of Table 32.2, we obtain: $R^2 = .5054$ and $R = \sqrt{.5054} = .7109$. Calculating these values is a good exercise. We already have $\Sigma y^2 = 165$. Then calculate:

$$\Sigma y'^2 = \Sigma Y'^2 - \frac{(\Sigma Y')^2}{N} = 688.3969 - \frac{(110)^2}{20} = 83.3969$$

and

$$\Sigma yy' = \Sigma YY' - \frac{(\Sigma Y)(\Sigma Y')}{N} = 688.3939 - \frac{(110)(110)}{20} = 83.3939$$

It can be shown algebraically that $\Sigma y'^2$ equals $\Sigma yy'$. The difference of .003 is due to rounding errors.

R, then, is the highest possible correlation between a least-squares linear composite of the independent variables and the observed dependent variable. R^2, analogous to r^2, indicates that portion of the variance of the dependent variable, Y, due to the independent variables in concert. R, unlike r, varies only from 0 to 1.00; it does not have negative values.

Two other important conclusions can be reached by calculating the correlations of the residuals, d_i, of Table 32.2, with X_1 and X_2, on the one hand, and with Y, on the other hand. The correlations of the residuals with X_1 and X_2 are both zero. This is not surprising when it is realized that, by definition, the residuals are that part of Y not accounted for by X_1 and X_2. That is, when the Y' values are subtracted from the Y values, that portion due to the regression of Y on X_1 and X_2 is taken from them. Whatever is left over, then, is unrelated to either X_1 or X_2. If the student will take the trouble to calculate the correlation between the d vector—a vector is a single set of measures, either in a column or a row—and either the X_1 or the X_2 vector, one will see that this is true. Don't underestimate the importance of doing such calculations and pondering their meaning. This is especially important in helping to understand multiple regression and other multivariate techniques. It can be a serious mistake to let the computer do everything for us, especially with package programs. For the simpler statistics, like r and the various sums-of-squares, write relatively simple programs for a microcomputer, store them on floppy disks, and use them when needed. An important research implication of this generalization will also be discussed later when actual research examples are summarized and discussed.

The correlation of the residuals, d_i, of Table 32.2 with the original Y values also helps to clarify matters. This correlation is: $r_{dy} = .7033$, and its square is: $r_{dy}^2 = (.7033)^2 = .4946$. If this latter value is added to the R^2 calculated earlier, the result is interesting: $R^2 + r_{dy}^2 = .5054 + .4946 = 1.0000$. And this will always be true: "1.0000" represents the total variance of Y. The variance of Y due to Ys regression on X_1 and X_2 is .5054. The variance of Y not due to the regression of Y on X_1 and X_2 can be calculated: $1.0000 - .5054 = .4946$, which is, of course, the value of r_{dy}^2 just calculated directly. The meaning of r_{dy}^2 can be seen in two ways. The direct calculation of the correlation shows that the residuals constitute that part of the variance of Y not due to the regression of Y on X_1 and X_2. In the present case, 51% ($R_2 = .51$) of the variance of the reading achievement (Y) of the 20 pupils is accounted for by a least-squares linear combination of verbal aptitude (X_1) and achievement motivation (X_2). But 49% of the variance is due to other variables and to error. After discussing more usual ways to calculate R and R^2, we will again consider the proportion or percentage interpretation of R^2.

In sum, R^2 is an estimate of the proportion of the variance of the dependent variable Y, accounted for by the independent variables X_j. R, the multiple correlation coefficient, is the product-moment correlation between the dependent variable and another variable produced by a least-squares combination of the independent variables. Its square is interpreted analogously to the square of an ordinary correlation coefficient. It differs from the ordinary coefficient, however, in taking values only from 0 to 1. R is not as useful and interpretable as R^2, and henceforth R^2 will be used almost exclusively in subsequent discussions.

The proportion or percentage interpretation of R^2 becomes clearer if a sum-of-squares formula is used:

$$R^2 = \frac{ss_{reg}}{ss_t} \tag{32.11}$$

where ss_t is, as usual, the total sum-of-squares of Y, or Σyt^2. Substituting the regression sum-of-squares calculated earlier by Formula 34.7, and the total sum-of-squares from Table 32.3, we obtain:

$$R^2 = \frac{83.3912}{165.000} = .5054$$

And R^2 is seen to be that part of the Y sum-of-squares associated with the regression of Y on the independent variables. As with all proportions, multiplying it by 100 converts it to a percentage.

Formula 32.11 provides another link to the analysis of variance. In Chapter 13 on the foundations of analysis of variance, a formula for calculating η, the *correlation ratio*, was given (Formula 13.4). Square that formula:

$$\eta^2 = \frac{ss_b}{ss_t}$$

where ss_b equals the between-groups sum-of-squares, and ss_t equals total sum-of-squares. ss_b is the sum-of-squares due to the independent variable. ss_{reg} is the sum-of-squares due to regression. Both terms refer to the sum-of-squares of a dependent variable due to an independent variable or to independent variables.

R and R^2 can be and are often inflated. Therefore, R^2 should be interpreted conservatively. If the sample is large, say over 200, there is little cause for concern. If the sample is small, however, it is wise to reduce the calculated R^2 by a few points. A *shrinkage formula* can be used to do:

$$R_c^2 = 1 - (1 - R^2)\left(\frac{N - 1}{N - n - 1}\right)$$

where R_c^2 equals shrunken or corrected R^2; N equals size of sample; n equals total number of variables in the analysis. Using this formula, the R^2 in the example reduces to .45. When comparing R_c^2 to R^2, we can see how much R^2 was inflated by chance error. From this formula we can also see the effect a small sample size has on the value of R_c^2. Small samples tend to yield unstable R^2 values and this can be determined by using the shrinkage formula given above.

Tests of Statistical Significance

Earlier we studied the simple regression of Y on X. To test the statistical significance of simple regression, we can assess the significance of the correlation coefficient between X and Y, r_{xy}, by referring to an appropriate table. Some well-known books containing tables used in statistical analyses are Beyer (1990), and Burlington and May (1970). With the advances in statistical computer programs and their high accessibility, table lookups are being used less and less by researchers. Computer programs can now compute and output the probability of a Type I error along with the test statistic, making it unnecessary for table look up. However, from an educational point of view students need to know about table lookups so that they can understand the computer output. Tests of statistical significance in multiple regression, though more complex, are based on the relatively simple idea of comparing variances (or mean squares) as in analysis of variance. The same questions asked many times before must be asked again: Can this R^2 have arisen by chance? Does it depart sufficiently from chance expectation that it can be said to be "significant"? Similar questions can be asked about individual regression coefficients. In this chapter and the next, F-tests will be used almost exclusively. They fit in nicely with both regression analysis and analysis of variance, and are both conceptually and computationally simple. Analyses can be performed on each regression coefficient. A t-test of a regression coefficient, if significant, indicates that the regression weight differs significantly from zero, which means that the variable with which it is associated contributes significantly to the regression. The t-test for individual regression coefficients are given in the next section. First we are going to use the F-test to determine if the complete regression model is statistically significant.

One is expressed by Equations 34.12a and 34.12b:

$$F = \frac{ss_{reg}/df_1}{ss_{res}/df_2} \tag{32.12a}$$

$$F = \frac{ss_{reg}/k}{ss_{res}/(N - k - 1)} \tag{32.12b}$$

where ss_{reg} sum-of-squares due to regression; ss_{res} equals residual or error sum-of-squares; k equals number of independent variables; N equals sample size. If df_1 and df_2, the degrees of freedom for the numerator and denominator of the F-ratio in Equation 32.12a, are defined, we get Equation 32.12b. These formulas are important because they are used to test the significance of any multiple regression problem. Using the values calculated earlier for the example of Table 32.2, now calculate:

$$F = \frac{83.3912/2}{81.6091/(20 - 2 - 1)} = \frac{41.6956}{4.8005} = 8.686$$

Note that the idea expressed by this formula is in the same family of ideas as analysis of variance. The numerator is the mean square due to the regression, analogous to the between-groups mean square, and the denominator is the mean square *not* due to regression, which is used as an error term, analogous to the within-groups mean square, or error variance. The basic principle, again, is always the same: variance due to the regression of Y on $X_1, X_2, \ldots X_k$, or, in analysis of variance, due to the experimental effects, is evaluated against variance presumably due to error or chance. This basic notion, elaborated at length in earlier chapters, can be expressed:

$$\frac{\text{regression variance}}{\text{error variance}} : \frac{\text{experimental variance}}{\text{error variance}}$$

Another formula for F is:

$$F = \frac{R^2/k}{(1 - R^2)/(N - k - 1)} \tag{32.13}$$

where k and N are the same as above. For the same example:

$$F = \frac{.5054/2}{(1 - .5054)/(20 - 2 - 1)} = \frac{.2527}{.0291} = 8.684$$

which is the same as the F-value obtained with Equation 32.12, within errors of rounding. At 2 and 17 degrees of freedom, it is significant at the .01 level. This formula is particularly useful when our research data are only in the form of correlation coefficients. In such a case, the sums-of-squares required by Equation 32.12 may not be known. Much regression analysis can be done using only the matrix of correlations among all the variables, independent and dependent. Such analysis is beyond the scope of this book. Nevertheless, the student of research should be aware of the possibility (see Pedhazur, 1996).

Significance Tests of Individual Regression Weights

Significance of the individual regression coefficients are of interest to many researchers because they tell the researcher which independent variables, in a statistical sense, make the greatest contribution in explaining the dependent variable. For example, the admissions officer for a major university would have available a number of variables that may be pertinent to predicting or explaining success in college. However, with actual analysis, some of those variables would make considerably less contribution than others. For example McWhirter (1997) was able to identify which variables predicted intimate loneliness and social loneliness of college students.

The formula to test for significance of individual regression weights or coefficients is

$$t_i = \frac{b_i}{s_{bi}}$$

where b_i is the regression coefficient and s_{bi} is the standard error for the variable i. This formula looks simple enough; however, the computation of the standard error is complex. The best way to obtain the standard error is through a computer program or if necessary, matrix algebra. This t-test is conducted with a degrees of freedom equal to $n -$ (number of regression coefficients in the regression equation).

Interpretation of Multiple Regression Statistics

The interpretation of multiple regression statistics can be complex and difficult. Indeed, the interpretation of multivariate analysis statistics is in general considerably more difficult than the interpretation of the univariate statistics studied earlier. We therefore go into the interpretation of the statistics of our example in some depth.

Statistical Significance of the Regression and R^2

The F-ratio of 8.684 calculated above tells us that the regression of Y on X_1 and X_2, expressed by $R^2_{y.12}$, is statistically significant. The probability that an F-ratio this large will occur by chance is less than .01 (it is actually about .003), which means that the relation between Y and a least-squares combination of X_1 and X_2 could probably not have occurred by chance.

$R = .71$ can be interpreted much like an ordinary coefficient of correlation, except that the values of R range from 0 to 1.00, unlike r, which ranges from -1.00 through 0 to 1.00. $R^2 = .71^2 = .51$ is more meaningful and useful, however. It means that 51% of the variance of Y is accounted for, or "determined," by X_1 and X_2 in combination. It is accordingly called a *coefficient of determination*. An alternative labeling of this statistic is *SMC*, which represents for "squared multiple correlation."

Relative Contributions to Y of the Xs

Let us ask, somewhat diffidently, a more difficult question: What are the relative contributions of X_1 and X_2, of verbal aptitude and achievement motivation, to Y, reading achievement? The restricted scope of this book does not permit an examination of the answers to this question in the detail it deserves. The problem of the relative contribution of independent variables to a dependent variable or variables is one of the most complex and difficult of regression analyses. It seems that no really satisfactory solution exists, at least not when the independent variables are correlated. Nevertheless, the problem cannot be neglected. The reader should bear in mind, however, that considerable reservation must be attached to the above and later discussions. The technical and substantive problems of interpretation of multiple regression analysis are discussed in two or three of the references given in study suggestion 1 in Chapter 33.

One would think that the regression weights, b or β, would provide us with a ready means of identifying the relative contributions of independent variables to a dependent variable. And they do, but only roughly and sometimes misleadingly. Earlier it was said that the regression coefficient b is called the *slope*. The slope of the regression line is at the rate of b units of Y for one unit of X. In the little problem A of Table 32.1, for instance, $b = .90$. Thus, as said earlier, with a change of 1 unit in X we predict a change of .90 in Y. In multiple regression, however, straightforward interpretation like this is not so easy, because there is more than one b. Nevertheless, we can say, *for present pedagogical purposes*, that if X_1 and X_2 have about the same scale of values—in the example of Table 32.2, the values of X_1 and X_2 are in the approximate range of 1 to 10—the bs are weights that show roughly the relative importance of X_1 and X_2. In the present case, the regression formula is:

$$Y' = .1027 + .6771X_1 + .3934X_2$$

We can say that X_1, verbal aptitude, is weighted more heavily than X_2, achievement motivation. This happens to be true in this case, but it may not always be true, especially with more independent variables.

Regression coefficients, unfortunately for interpretative purposes, are not stable. They change with different samples and with addition or subtraction of independent variables to the analysis (see Dillon & Goldstein, 1984; Howell, 1997; Pedhazur, 1996). There is no absolute way to interpret them. If the correlations among the

🔳 **TABLE 32.4** *Multiple Regression Examples With and Without Correlations between Independent Variables*

	A				B		
1	**2**	**Y**		**1**	**2**	**Y**
1.00	.50	.87		1.00	0	.87
.50	1.00	.43		0	1.00	.43
.87	.43	1.00		.87	.43	1.00

$R^2_{y.12} = .76$ $\qquad\qquad\qquad\qquad\qquad\qquad\qquad\qquad\qquad R^2_{y.12} = .94$

independent variables are all zero or near zero, interpretation is greatly simplified. But many or most variables that are correlated with a dependent variable are also correlated among themselves. The example of Table 32.3 shows this: the correlation between X_1 and X_2 is .26, a modest correlation, to be sure. Such intercorrelations are often higher, however. And the higher they are (up to a certain point), the more unstable the interpretation situation.

The ideal predictive situation is when the correlations between the independent variables and the dependent variable are high, and the correlations among the independent variables are low. This principle is important. The more the independent variables are intercorrelated, the more difficult the interpretation. Among other things, one has greater difficulty telling the relative influence on the dependent variable of the independent variables. Examine the two fictitious correlation matrices of Table 32.4 and the accompanying R^2s. In the two matrices, the independent variables, X_1 and X_2, are correlated .87 and .43, respectively, with the dependent variable, Y. But the correlations between the independent variables differ in the two cases. In matrix A, $r_{12} = .50$, a substantial correlation. In matrix B, however, $r_{12} = 0$.

The contrast between the R^2s is dramatic: .76 for A and .94 for B. Since, in B, X_1 and X_2 are not correlated, any correlations they have with Y contribute directly to the prediction and the R^2. When the correlations between the independent variables are exactly zero, as in matrix B, then R^2 is easy to calculate. It is simply the sum-of-squares of the rs between each independent variable and the dependent variable: $(.87)^2 + (43)^2 = .94$. When the independent variables are correlated, as in matrix A ($r_{12} = .50$), some of the common variance of Y and X_1 is also shared with X_2. In short, X_1 and X_2 are to some extent redundant in predicting Y. In matrix B there is no such redundancy.

The situation is clarified, perhaps, by Figure 32.2. Let the circles stand for the total variance of Y, and let this total variance be 1.00. Then the portions of the variance of Y accounted for by X_1 and X_2 can be depicted. In both circles, the light gray shading indicates the variance accounted for by X_1, or V_{X_1} and the dark gray shading X_2, or V_{X_2}. (The variances remaining after V_{X_1} and V_{X_2} are the residual variances, labeled in the figure.) In B, V_{X_1} and V_{X_2} do not overlap. In A, however, V_{X_1} and V_{X_2}

◉ **FIGURE 32.2**

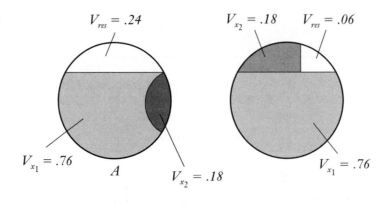

$$R_{y\cdot12}^2 = .76$$
$$R_{y\cdot12}^2 = V_{x_1} + V_{x_2}$$
$$= .76 + 0 = .76$$

$$R_{y\cdot12}^2 = .94$$
$$R_{y\cdot12}^2 = V_{x_1} + V_{x_2}$$
$$= .76 + .18 = .94$$

overlap. Simply because $r_{12} = 0$ in B and $r_{12} = .50$ in A, the predictive power of the independent variables is much greater in B than in A. This is, of course, reflected by the R^2s: .76 in A and .94 in B.

While this is a contrived and artificial example, it has the virtue of showing the effect of correlation between the independent variables and thus illustrates the principle enunciated above. It also reflects the difficulty of interpreting the results of most regression analysis, since in much research the independent variables are correlated. And when more independent variables are added, interpretation becomes still more complex and difficult. A central problem is: How does one sort out the relative effects of the different Xs on Y? The answer is also complex. There are ways of doing so, some more satisfying than others, but none completely satisfactory. Perhaps the most satisfactory way, at least in the authors' opinion and experience, is to calculate *squared semipartial correlations* (also called *part correlations*). These are calculated with the formula:

$$SP^2 = R_{y.12\cdots k}^2 - R_{y.12\cdots(k-1)}^2$$

or in the present case, for B:

$$SP^2 = R_{y.12}^2 - R_{y.1}^2 - .94 - .76 = .18$$

which indicates the contribution to the variance of Y of X_2 *after X_1 has been taken into account.* The same calculation for A yields: $.76 - .76 = 0$, which indicates that X_2

contributes nothing to the variance of Y, after X_1 has been taken into account. (Actually, there is a slight increase that emerges only with a large number of decimal places.)

The student is referred to Howell (1997), Dillon and Goldstein (1984), and Pedhazur (1996) for discussions of the problems involved. Kerlinger and Pedhazur (1973) also discuss the problem in considerable detail and relate it to research examples.

Other Analytic and Interpretative Problems

A number of problems in multiple regression analysis cannot be discussed in this book in the detail they deserve. Some, however, must be mentioned because of the increasing importance of multiple regression in behavioral research. One, mentioned earlier, is the problem of regression weights. In this chapter and the next, the discussion has been confined to b weights because in most research uses of regression, we predict with raw or deviation scores, and bs are used with such scores. Beta, or β weights, on the other hand, are used with standard scores. They are called *standard partial regression coefficients*. "Standard" means that they would be used if all variables were in standard score form. "Partial" means that the effects of variables other than the one to which the weight applies are held constant. For example, $\beta_{y.123}$ or β_1 in a three-variable (independent variable) problem, is the standard partial regression weight, which expresses the change in Y due to change in X_1, with variables two and three held constant. A second meaning, used in theoretical work, is that b is the population regression weight that β estimates. We omit this meaning. βs can be translated into bs with the formula:

$$b_j = \beta_j \frac{s_y}{s_j}$$

where s_y equals standard deviation of Y and s_j standard deviation of variable j. The b weights, too, are partial regression coefficients, but are not in standard form.

Another problem is that in any given regression, R, R^2, and the regression weights will be the same no matter what the order of the variables. If one or more variables are added or subtracted from the regression, however, these values will change. And regression weights can change from sample to sample. In other words, there is no absolute quality about them. One cannot say, for instance, that because verbal and numerical aptitudes have, say, regression weights of .60 and .50 in one set of data, they will have the same values in another set.

Earlier in this book it was said, "Design is data discipline." The design of research and the analysis of data spring from the demands of research problems. Again, the order of entry of independent variables into the regression equation is determined by the research problem and the design of the research, which is itself determined by the research problem.

Although the order of entry of variables and the changes in regression weights that can occur with differing samples are difficult problems, one must remember that the final regression weights do not change with differing orders of entry. This is a real compensation, especially useful in prediction. In many research problems, for example, the relative contribution of variables is not a major consideration. In such cases, one wants the total regression equation and its regression weights mainly for prediction and for assessing the general nature of the regression situation.

However, when the researcher wants to find the contribution of each independent variable, the Beta weights (standardized regression weights) should be used. These Beta weights have been scaled so that they can be compared to each other directly. The unstandardized regression weights reflect the measurement scale used to measure that variable. Hence, the unstandardized regression weights cannot be directly compared. Further, the significance of the Beta weights is equal to the significance of the change in R^2 when an independent variable is entered last into the regression equation.

Another important point is that there usually is limited usefulness to adding new variables to a regression equation. Because many variables of behavioral research are correlated, the principle illustrated by the data of Table 32.4, and discussed earlier, operates so as to decrease the usefulness of additional variables. If one finds three or four independent variables that are substantially correlated with a dependent variable and not highly correlated with each other, one is lucky. But it becomes more and more difficult to find other independent variables that are not in effect redundant with the first three or four. If $R^2_{y.123} = .50$, then it is unlikely that $R^2_{y.1234}$ will be much more than .55, and $R^2_{y.12345}$ will probably be no more than .56 or .57. We have a regression law of diminishing returns. When independent variables are added, one notes how much they add to R^2 and tests their statistical significance. The formula for doing so, much like formula 34.13, is:

$$ F = \frac{(R^2_{y.12.k_1} - R^2_{y.12.k_2})/(k_1 - k_2)}{(1 - R^2_{y.12.k1})/(N - k_1 - 1)} $$

where k_1 is the number of independent variables of the larger R^2, k_2 number of independent variables of the smaller R^2, and N equals number of cases. This formula will be used later. Although an F calculated like this may be statistically significant, especially with a large sample, the actual increase in R^2 may be quite small. In a study by Layton and Swanson, (1958) the addition of a sixth independent variable yielded a statistically significant F-ratio, but the actual increase in R^2 was .0147! The difference between the R^2s in the numerator is the squared semipartial correlation coefficient earlier.

It was said above that R, R^2, and the regression coefficients remain the same, if the same variables are entered in different orders. This should not be taken to mean, however, that the order in which variables enter the regression equation does not matter. On the contrary, order of entry can be very important. When the independent variables are correlated, the relative amount of variance of the dependent variable that each independent variable accounts for or contributes can change drastically with different orders of entry of the variables. With the A data of Table 32.4, for example, if we reverse the order of X_1 and X_2, their relative contributions change rather markedly. With the original order, X_2 contributed nothing to R^2, whereas with the order reversed X_2 becomes X_1 and contributes 19% $[r^2 = (.43)^2 = .19)]$ to the total R^2, and the original X_1, which becomes X_2, contributes 57% (.19 + .57 = .76). The order of variables, while making no difference in the final R^2 and thus in overall prediction, is a major research problem.

However, multicolinearity or correlated independent variables is not always undesirable. In some cases when multiple regression is used to establish the validity of a measure or scale, correlated independent variables can be most useful. Independent variables, that have zero or near-zero correlation with the dependent variable but a high correlation with another independent variable, can actually improve the amount of variance shared by the dependent and independent variables. This type of independent variable is called a *suppressor variable*. Some researchers such as Dr. Leonard Helmers of New Orleans[1] refer to them as "trim" variables. These variables have the effect of eliminating, suppressing, or trimming irrelevant variance in the other independent variables. Suppose we wanted to develop a regression equation to predict mechanical skills. We might use as our dependent variable the person score on a performance test of mechanical skills. We may select a written mechanical aptitude test as an independent (predictor) variable. We may want to include a suppressor variable, such as reading comprehension. Reading comprehension would be a candidate for a suppressor variable, since it is most likely uncorrelated with mechanical skills, but related to the written Mechanical Aptitude Test, because this test requires reading. So the two independent variables—Mechanical Aptitude and Reading Comprehension—may be correlated, and Mechanical Performance Test may be correlated with the Mechanical Aptitude Test, but the Reading Comprehension Test would not be correlated with the Mechanical Performance Test.

In other situations, a researcher may not be aware that a suppressor variable was used in the analysis. So how can one tell if he or she has a suppressor variable in this case? Well, if we have a computer program like SPSS or Statistical Analysis System (SAS), the output generated by these computer programs can, under careful scrutiny, be used to detect the presence of a suppressor variable. The first step is to determine which independent variables have a non-zero beta weight. If we find one and the absolute value of the simple correlation between the dependent variable and this independent variable is considerably smaller than the beta weight associated with that independent variable, we may have a suppressor variable. Also, if the beta weight for that independent variable is non-zero and the simple correlation between the dependent variable and the independent variable has the opposite sign of the beta

---

[1]Personal communication. Dr. Helmers is the former Research Director at ASI Marketing, Inc., Hollywood, California.

weight, this is a signal that the independent variable may be a suppressor variable. In some research analysis like those found in marketing research, these suppressor variables are dropped from the analysis and the regression equation is recomputed.

Examples of suppressor variables can be found in the literature. Hadfield, Littleton, Steiner, and Woods (1998) used multiple regression to analyze the pedological skills of students and to test the hypothesis that mathematics content knowledge would be the most significant correlate to microteaching effectiveness. [Videotape ratings were used to measure teaching effectiveness. The independent variables were pedagogical content knowledge, math content knowledge, math anxiety, and spatial ability.] They found mathematics content knowledge and mathematics anxiety scores acted like suppressor variables. With these variables in the regression equation, there was a 25% increase in the variance accounted for. However, both of these variables had a low correlation with the dependent variable, teaching effectiveness, but correlated with the other independent variables.

Leichtman and Erickson's (1979) study of cognitive, demographic, and interactional determinants of role-taking skills in fourth-grade children, developed a regression equation where five variables predicted 36% of the variance of the role-taking scores. These variables were the WISC Vocabulary score, Matching Familiar Figures Test errors, sex, neighborhood, and handedness. The WISC Vocabulary score was found to be a suppressor variable. The WISC Vocabulary score was correlated with the other independent variables, but it was not correlated with the dependent variable: Role-taking scores.

Research Examples

DDT and Bald Eagles

One of the several controversies over despoliation of the environment by commercial interests and the opposition and protests of environmentalist groups has focused on the use of DDT. One effect of DDT spraying has been the decimation of bird species. For example, reproduction of the bald eagle population was seriously affected. In December 1972, the Environmental Protection Agency banned DDT spraying. Grier (1982) in a study of the effect of the ban on bald eagle reproduction, reported the average number of young eagles per geographical area for the years 1966 through 1981. His regression (and other) analyses of the reproduction averages (means) before and after the ban showed that the two slopes, or b coefficients, differed significantly. From 1966 to 1974, $b = -.07$, indicating a decrease in reproduction over the years, but from 1973 to 1981 $b = .07$, indicating an increase. (Both bs were statistically significant.) The method of comparing slopes statistically is given in Pedhazur (1996), Howell (1997), and Lee and Little (1996). The simple regressions are calculated using years as the independent variable and reproduction rates as the dependent variable. The correlation before the DDT ban was $-.74$, but after the ban it was .80 (by our calculations). The two regressions have been plotted in Figure 32.3. The plot portrays the regression of mean eagle young per geographical area on

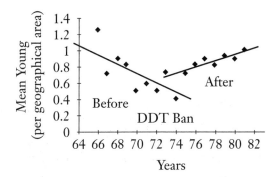

the years 1966 through 1974 (before the DDT ban) and the years 1975–1981 (after the ban). The regression before the ban was calculated through 1974 because the effect of the ban could not have been expected to manifest itself for about a year. Grier did his calculation through 1973. The sharp difference between the two relations or slopes is dramatic.

Inflation Bias in Self-Assessment Examinations

Do job applicants often tell the truth about their capabilities? Employers are becoming increasingly concerned over whether or not the credentials presented by a job applicant are truthful. Anderson, Warner, and Spencer (1984) used multiple regression to help answer this question. The participants for this study were 351 job applicants for positions with the state of Colorado. These applicants were asked to indicate their degree of experience with certain job tasks. Some of the job tasks presented to the applicant were bogus. An inflation bias scale was created by the researchers to determine the extent the applicants overrepresented himself or herself. Multiple regression analysis was used to help determine the validity of this measurement scale. Applicants for a clerical position were asked to indicate how many words per minute they could type in addition to completing the inflation bias scale. These applicants were then given an actual typing performance test. The researchers then used the typing test as the dependent variable in a multiple regression with the inflation bias scale and the self-assessment exam. The results of this investigation are given in Table 32.7. The correlation between the typing test and the self-assessment exam was .27 ($r^2 = .073$) and .41 ($r^2 = .168$) for the inflation scale. As far as explaining the variation in the typing test scores, the inflation scale increased the predictability. Although Anderson et al. did not use a suppressor variable to increase the R^2 for their study, they could have. A likely candidate for the job of suppressor variable might be reading comprehension. Since reading comprehension is needed in order to read the

◫ **TABLE 34.7** *Amount of Variance Explained by Self-assessment Exam and Inflation Scale on Typing Performance*

Independent Variable	R^2	ΔR^2	
Self-assessment	.07	.07	$p < .05$
Inflation Scale	.23	.16	$p < .05$
Interaction	.25	.02	$p > .05$

questionnaire on self-assessment and it is probably uncorrelated with actual typing performance it might be a suppressor variable.

Multiple Regression Analysis and Scientific Research

Multiple regression is close to the heart of scientific investigation. It is also fundamental in statistics and inference, and is tightly tied to basic and powerful mathematical methods. From the researcher's point of view, moreover, it is useful and practical: It performs its analytic job successfully and efficiently. In explaining these strong and sweeping statements, it may be possible to clarify what we have already learned.

The scientist is concerned, basically, with propositions of the "If p, then q" kind. Such propositions "explain" phenomena. When we say, "If positive incentive, then higher achievement," we are to some extent "explaining" achievement. But this is hardly enough. Even if supported by a good deal of empirical evidence, it does not go very far in explaining achievement. In addition to other If–then statements of a similar kind, the scientist must ask more complex questions. The scientist may ask, for example, under what conditions the statement, "If positive incentive, then higher achievement," is valid. Is it true of black American children as well as white American children? Is it true of children of both lower and higher intelligence? To test such questions and to advance knowledge, scientists in effect write statements of the kind, If p, then q, under conditions r, s, and t, where p is an independent variable; q a dependent variable; and r, s, and t other independent variables. Other kinds of statements can, of course, be written—for example, If p and r; then q. In such a case p and r are two independent variables, both of which are required for q.

The point of all this is that multiple regression can handle such cases successfully. In most behavioral research there is usually one dependent variable, though we are theoretically not restricted to only one. Consequently, multiple regression is a general method of analyzing much behavioral research data. Certain other methods of analysis can be considered special cases of multiple regression. The most prominent is analysis of variance, all types of which can be conceptualized and accomplished with multiple regression analysis.

It was said earlier that all control is control of variance. Multiple regression analysis can be conceived as a refined and powerful method of "controlling" variance. It accomplishes this the same way analysis of variance does: by estimating the magnitudes of different sources of influence on Y, different sources of variance of Y, through analysis of the interrelations of all the variables. It tells how much of Y is presumably due to $X_1, X_2 \ldots X_k$. It gives some idea of the relative amounts of influence of the Xs. And it furnishes tests of the statistical significance of combined influences of Xs on Y and of the separate influence of each X. In short, multiple regression analysis is an efficient and powerful hypothesis-testing and inference-making technique. It is so because it helps scientists study, with relative precision, complex interrelations between independent variables and a dependent variable, and thus helps them "explain" the presumed phenomenon represented by the dependent variable.

CHAPTER SUMMARY

1. Multiple regression is a method for studying the effects, and the magnitude of the effects, of more than one independent variable on one dependent variable.

2. Simple regression involves one independent variable and one dependent variable.

3. Through the method of least-squares, multiple regression involves finding the best regression weights that maximize the relation between a linear combination of the independent variables and the dependent variable.

4. R is the multiple correlation. It is the correlation between the actual dependent variable values and the predicted dependent variable values.

5. The multiple correlation squared, R^2, is a statistic used to determine the quality of the regression equation found through empirical data.

6. Computations for multiple regression are intensive. Using a computer program is recommended.

7. The multiple correlation squared, or coefficient of determination, is used in statistical tests to determine if the regression equation is explaining a significant amount of the variance.

8. A problem with multiple regression is that the independent variables may be correlated. As such, they lead to unstable estimates of the regression coefficients and interpretation difficulties.

9. The entire regression equation can be tested for statistical significance and so can each individual regression weight.

◉ **FIGURE 32.4**

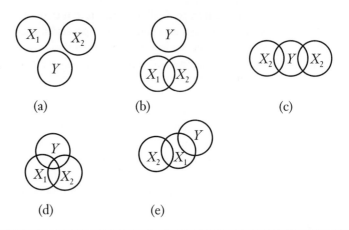

(a)   (b)   (c)

(d)   (e)

10. Tests on the individual regression weights will inform the researcher as to which variable is contributing toward the explanation of the dependent variable.

STUDY SUGGESTIONS

1. Read one or more of the following studies that used multiple regression. Make note of the variables used, the computer program(s) used, and the conclusions drawn from the results.

   Abel, M. H. (1998). Interaction of humor and gender in moderating relationships between stress and outcomes. *Journal of Psychology, 132,* 267–276.

   Connelly, C. D. (1998). Hopefulness, self-esteem, and perceived social support among pregnant and nonpregnant adolescents. *Western Journal of Nursing Research, 20,* 195–209.

   Ho, R. (1998). The intention to give up smoking: Disease versus social dimensions. *Journal of Social Psychology, 138,* 368–380.

   Stalenheim, E. G., Eriksson, E., von Knorring, L., & Wide, L. (1998). Testosterone as a biological marker in psychopathy and alcoholism. *Psychiatry Research, 77,* 79–88.

2. Given the Venn diagrams shown in Figure 32.4 one dependent variable, Y, and two independent variables: X_1 and X_2.

a. Determine which has a suppressor variable.
b. Which is ideal for multiple regression?
c. Indicate which one(s) exhibit multicollinearity.
d. Which would produce an unusable regression equation?
e. Which would most likely yield nonsignificant statistical tests on the regression equation?
f. Which would most likely yield nonsignificant statistical tests on the individual regression coefficients?

a. Determine which lines slope over variable.
b. ...
c. Indicate which ... model in this table are ...
d. ...
e. We should omit ... would simplify ... and ... the ...
   the equation.
f. ...

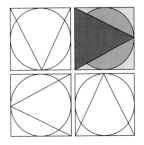

CHAPTER 33

MULTIPLE REGRESSION, ANALYSIS OF VARIANCE, AND OTHER MULTIVARIATE METHODS

- ONE-WAY ANALYSIS OF VARIANCE AND MULTIPLE REGRESSION ANALYSIS
- CODING AND DATA ANALYSIS
- FACTORIAL ANALYSIS OF VARIANCE, ANALYSIS OF COVARIANCE, AND RELATED ANALYSIS
    Discriminant Analysis, Canonical Correlation, Multivariate Analysis of Variance, and Path Analysis
- RIDGE REGRESSION, LOGISTIC REGRESSION, AND LOG-LINEAR ANALYSIS
    Logistic Regression
    Multiway Contingency Tables and Log-Linear Analysis
- MULTIVARIATE ANALYSIS AND BEHAVIORAL RESEARCH.

Close examination shows the conceptual bases underlying different approaches to data analysis to be the same or similar. The symmetry of the fundamental ideas has great aesthetic appeal, and is nowhere more interesting and appealing than in multiple regression and analysis of variance. Earlier, in discussing the foundations of analysis of variance, the similarity of the principles and structures of analysis of variance and so-called correlational methods was brought out. We now link the two approaches and, in the process, show that analysis of variance can be done using multiple regression. In addition, the linking of the two approaches will happily yield unexpected bonuses. We will see, for example, that certain analytic problems that are intractable with analysis of variance—or at least difficult and certainly inappropriate—are quite easily conceptualized and accomplished by the judicious and flexible use of multiple regression and its variants. Because of space constraints and because the book's purpose is not to teach the mechanics of statistical methods and approaches, the discussion will be quite limited: Some of what is said must be taken on faith. Nevertheless, even at a somewhat limited level of discourse we will find that certain difficult problems associated with analysis of variance are naturally and easily handled with multiple regression type analysis. Some of these associated problems include analysis of covariance, pretest and posttest data, unequal numbers of cases in cells (of factorial designs), categorical dependent variables, multiway contingency tables, and the handling of both experimental and nonexperimental data.

One-Way Analysis of Variance and Multiple Regression Analysis

Suppose an experiment has been done with three methods of presenting verbal materials to ninth-grade children. The dependent variable is comprehension measured by an objective test of the materials. Suppose, also that the results were those given in Table 33.1. Obviously, an analysis of variance can be and should be done. The analysis of variance results are given at the bottom of the table. Students are urged to do the calculations of the examples of this chapter. This is urgently necessary for full understanding of important points to be made in the chapter. For example, do the analysis of variance calculations of Table 33.1 and the multiple regression calculations of the problem in Table 33.2, study and ponder the results of both analyses. Do not leave it to a computer program, which you may not understand. Work through the examples whenever possible. If you do succumb to the temptation to use one of the large computer or microcomputer packages, be wary. The quality of statistical software for microcomputers (and large computers) is sometimes questionable. The F-ratio in Table 33.1 is 18, which, at 2 and 12 degrees of freedom, is significant at the .01 level. The effect of the experimental treatment is clearly significant: $\eta^2 = ss_b/ss_t = 90/120 = .75$. The relation between the experimental treatment and comprehension is strong.

Now, transfer your thinking from an analysis of variance framework to a multiple regression framework. Can we obtain $\eta^2 = .75$ "directly"? The independent variable, Methods, can be conceived as membership in the three experimental groups, A_1, A_2, and A_3. This membership can be expressed by 1s and 0s: if a subject is a member of A_1, assign a 1; if a member of A_2 or of A_3, assign a 0. Or, we can assign 1s to A_2 membership and 0s to the members of the other two groups. The results will be basically the same. Indeed, use any two different numbers, for instance—1 and 10 or 31 and 5, or any two random numbers, and the basic results will be the same. The as-

◨ TABLE 33.1 *Fictitious Data and One-way Analysis of Variance Results, Three Experimental Groups*

A_1	A_2	A_3
4	7	1
5	8	2
6	9	3
7	10	4
8	11	5

Source	df	ss	ms	F
Between Groups	2	90.0	45.0	18.0 $(p < .01)$
Within Groups	12	30.0	2.5	
Total	14	120		

signment of 1s and 0s, however, has interpretative advantages that will be mentioned later (see Cohen & Cohen, 1983), and generally works better with computer statistical software. The regression analysis layout of the data of Table 33.1 is given in Table 33.2. Treat the 15 dependent variable measures in the column labeled Y as a single set of scores. Treat the "scores" of X_1 and X_2 similarly, except that the 1s and 0s indicate group membership. The members of A_1 have been assigned 1s in the column X_1, while the members of A_2 and A_3 have been assigned 0 (second column). The members of A_2 have been assigned 1s in the third column, X_2, while the members of A_1 and A_3 have been assigned 0s. One may ask: Where is A_3 in the table? When coding experimental groups, there are only $k - 1$ coded vectors (columns), where k equals the number of experimental treatments (in this case $k = 3$). Expressed differently, there is one coded vector (columns) for each degree of freedom. Recall from our earlier discussion of analysis of variance that the between-groups degrees of freedom was $k - 1$. In this case, there are three treatments, A_1, A_2, and A_3 and $k = 3$. Therefore, there are $k - 1 = 2$ coded vectors. These vectors of 1s and 0s are called *dummy variables* (see Suits, 1967, for more detail on dummy variables). For full discussions of coding variables for multiple regression analysis, see chapter 6 and 7 of Kerlinger and Pedhazur (1973) or Pedhazur (1996). They fully express the three experimental treatments.

Now do a multiple regression analysis of the data in Table 33.3 just as in Chapter 32. The sums-of-squares and cross products necessary for the analysis are given in Table 33.3. For example:

$$\Sigma x_1^2 = (1^2 + 1^2 \ldots + 0^2) - \frac{5^2}{15} = 5 - 1.6667 = 3.3333$$

$$\Sigma x_2 y = (0)(4) + (0)(5) + \ldots + (0)(5) - \frac{(5)(90)}{15} = 45 - 30 = 15$$

$$\Sigma x_1 x_2 = (1)(0) + (1)(0) + \ldots + (0)(0) - \frac{(5)(5)}{15} = 0 - 1.6667 = -1.6667$$

To calculate the regression and residual sums-of-squares, use Formulas 32.7 and 32.8 of Chapter 32 (given here with the numbering of this chapter):

◻ **TABLE 33.2** *Regression Layout and Calculations (Data from Table 33.1)*

	Y	X_1	X_2
	4	1	0
A_1	5	1	0
	6	1	0
	7	1	0
	8	1	0
A_2	7	0	1
	8	0	1
	9	0	1
	10	0	1
	11	0	1
A_3	1	0	0
	2	0	0
	3	0	0
	4	0	0
	5	0	0
Σ:	90	5	5
M:	6	.3333	.3333
Σ^2:	660	5	5

$$ss_{reg} = b_1 \Sigma x_1 y - b_2 \Sigma x_2 y \qquad (33.1)$$

$$ss_{res} = ss_t - ss_{reg} \qquad (33.2)$$

We have in Table 33.3 all the above values except b_1 and b_2, the regression coefficients, and a, the intercept. There are several ways to calculate the bs, but they are beyond the scope of our treatment. So we accept them on faith: $b_1 = 3$ and $b_2 = 6$. The intercept a is calculated

$$a = \overline{Y} - b_1 \overline{X}_1 - b_2 \overline{X}_2 \qquad (33.3)$$
$$= 6 - (3)(.3333) - (6)(.3333) = 3.$$

The sums of cross products are given in Table 33.3: $\Sigma x_1 y = 0$ and $\Sigma x_2 y = 15$. Substituting in 33.1 and 33.2, we obtain:

$$ss_{reg} = (3)(0) + (6)(15) = 90.$$

$$ss_{res} = 120 - 90 = 30.$$

To calculate R^2, use Formula 32.11 of Chapter 32 (with a new number):

$$R^2 = \frac{ss_{reg}}{ss_t} = \frac{90}{120} = .75$$

$$R = \sqrt{.75} = .8660 \qquad (33.4)$$

Finally, calculate the F-ratio using Formula 34.13, again with a new number:

$$F = \frac{R^2/k}{(1 - R^2)/(N - k - 1)} \qquad (33.5)$$

where k equals number of independent variables and N equals number of cases.

□ **TABLE 33.3** *Sums-of-Squares and Cross Products (Data from Table 35.2)*[a]

	x_1	x_2	y
x_1	3.3333	−1.6667	0
x_2		3.3333	15.0000
y			120.0000

[a]The values on the diagonal are the deviation sums-of-squares: $\Sigma x_1{}^2$, $\Sigma x_2{}^2$, and $\Sigma y_t{}^2$. The remaining three values above the diagonal are the deviation cross products: $\Sigma x_1 x_2$, $\Sigma x_1 y$, and $\Sigma x_2 y$.

Substituting:

$$F = \frac{.75/2}{(1 - .75)/(15 - 2 - 1)} = \frac{.375000}{.020833} = 18.$$

Another formula for F can be borrowed from the previous chapter:

$$F = \frac{ss_{reg}/df_1}{ss_{reg}/df_2} = \frac{ss_{reg}/k}{ss_{res}/(N - k - 1)} = \frac{90/2}{30/(15 - 2 - 1)} = \frac{45}{2.5} = 18.$$

This F-ratio is then checked in an F-table (see Kerlinger & Pedhazur, 1973, App. D or Appendix C of this book), at $df = 2, 12$. The entry at $p = .05$ is 3.88, and at $p = .01$ it is 6.93. Since F of 18 calculated above is greater than 6.93, the regression is statistically significant, and R^2 is statistically significant. Note that even though A_3 was not coded—it had no coded vector of its own—its mean is easily recovered by substituting 0's for X_1 and X_2.

While it has been shown that multiple regression analysis accomplishes what one-way analysis of variance does, can it be said that there is any real advantage to using the regression method? Actually, the calculations are more involved. Why do it, then? The answer is that with the kinds of data of the example above there is no practical advantage beyond aesthetic nicety and conceptual clarification. But when research problems are more complex—when, for example, interactions, covariates (intelligence test scores), nominal variables (sex, social class), continuous variables and nonlinear components (X^2, X^3) are involved—the regression procedure has decided advantages. Indeed, many research analytic problems that analysis of variance cannot handle readily or at all can be fairly readily accomplished with multiple regression analysis. Factorial analysis of variance, analysis of covariance, and, indeed, all forms of analysis of variance can also be done with regression analysis. Since it is not our purpose to teach statistics and the mechanics of analysis, we refer the reader to appropriate discussions like those cited earlier in this chapter. We will explain in the next section, however, the nature of highly important methods of coding variables and their use in analysis.

Coding and Data Analysis

Before enlarging the discussion of multiple regression and analysis of variance, we need to know something about different ways of coding experimental treatments for multiple regression analysis. A code is a set of symbols assigned to a set of objects for various reasons. In multiple regression analysis, coding is the assignment of numbers to the members of a population or sample to indicate group or subset membership according to a rule determined by an independent means. When some characteristic or aspect of the members of a population or sample is objectively defined, it is then possible to create a set of ordered pairs, the first members of which constitute the dependent variable, Y, and the second members numerical indicators of subset or group membership.

In the preceding discussion of the coding of experimental treatments in the multiple regression analogue of one-way analysis of variance, 1s and 0s were used. Vectors of 1s and 0s are correlated. In Table 33.3, for instance, the sum of the cross products, $\Sigma x_1 x_2$, is -1.6667, and $r_{12} = -.50$. Such 1 and 0, or *dummy*, coding works quite well. It is also possible to use other forms of coding. One of these, effects coding, consists of assigning $\{1, 0, -1\}$ or $\{1, -1\}$ to experimental treatments. Although a useful method, it will be discussed only briefly.

To clarify matters, the coding of the data of Table 33.2, a multiple regression analogue of the one-way analysis of variance of the data of Table 33.1, with three experimental groups or treatments, is laid out in Table 33.4. Under the heading "Dummy" is given the dummy coding of Table 33.4, using only two subjects per experimental group. Since there are two degrees of freedom, or $k - 1 = 3 - 1 = 2$, there are two column vectors labeled X_1 and X_2. The dummy coding assignment has already been explained: A "1" indicates that a subject is a member of the experimental group against which the 1 is placed, and a 0 that the subject is not a member of the experimental group.

Under the Effects column, the coding is seen to be $\{1, 0, -1\}$. Effects coding is virtually the same as dummy coding—indeed, it has been called dummy coding—except that one experimental group, usually the last, is always assigned -1s. If the ns of the experimental groups are equal, the sums of the columns of the codes equal zero. The vectors, however, are not systematically uncorrelated. The correlation between the two columns under Effects in Table 33.4, for example, is .50. (Contrast this with the correlation between the Dummy code columns: $r = -.50$.)

☐ **TABLE 33.4** *Examples of Dummy, Effects, and Orthogonal Coding of Experimental Treatments*[a]

Groups	Dummy		Effects		Orthogonal	
	X_1	X_2	X_1	X_2	X_1	X_2
A_1	1	0	1	0	0	2
	1	0	1	0	0	2
A_2	0	1	0	1	-1	-1
	0	1	0	1	-1	-1
A_3	0	0	-1	-1	1	-1
	0	0	-1	-1	1	-1
	$r_{12} = -.50$		$r_{12} = .50$		$r_{12} = .00$	

[a]In the dummy coding, A_3 is a control group. In the orthogonal coding, A_2 is compared to A_3, and A_1 is compared to A_2 and A_3, or $(A_2 + A_3)/2$.

Each of these two systems of coding has its own characteristics. Two of the characteristics of dummy coding were discussed in the previous section. One of the characteristics of effects coding, on the other hand, is that the intercept constant a, yielded by the multiple regression analysis, will equal the grand mean, or M_1, of Y. For the data of Table 33.2, the intercept constant is 6.00, which is the mean of all the Y scores.

The third form of coding is orthogonal coding; it is also called "contrasts" coding, but some contrasts coding can be nonorthogonal. As its name indicates, the coded vectors are orthogonal or uncorrelated. If an investigator's main interest is in specific contrasts between means rather than the overall F-test, orthogonal coding can provide the needed contrasts. In any set of data, a number of contrasts can be made. This is, of course, particularly useful in analysis of variance. The rule is that only contrasts that are orthogonal to each other, or independent, are made. For example, in Table 33.4, the coding of the last set of vectors is orthogonal: each of the vectors totals to zero and the sum of their products is zero, or

$$(0 \times 2) + (0 \times 2) + (-1)(-1) + \ldots + (1)(-1) = 0$$

r_{12} is also equal to zero.

Instead of the dummy coding of Table 33.2, suppose we now use orthogonal coding. Suppose we also decide to test A_2 against A_3, or $M_{A_2} - M_{A_3}$, and also test A_1 against A_2 and A_3, or $M_{A_1} - (M_{A_2} + M_{A_3})/2$. X_1 is then coded $(0, -1, 1)$ and X_2 is coded $(2, -1, -1)$, as shown by the orthogonal coding of Table 33.5. The interested reader grounded in analysis of variance can follow up such possibilities by reading Cohen and Cohen (1983) or Kerlinger and Pedhazur, (1973).

No matter what kind of coding is used, R^2, F, the sums-of-squares, the standard errors of estimate, and the predicted Ys will be the same (the means of the experimental groups). The intercept constant, the regression weights, and the t-tests of b weights will be different. Strictly speaking, it is not possible to recommend one method over another; each has its purposes. At first, it is probably wise for the student to use the simplest method, dummy coding, or 1s and 0s. One should fairly soon use effects coding, however. Finally, orthogonal coding can be tried and mastered. Before using orthogonal coding to any extent, the student should study the topic of comparisons of means (see Hays, 1994).

The simplest use of coding is to indicate nominal variables, particularly dichotomies. Some variables are "natural" dichotomies: sex, public school–parochial school, conviction–no conviction, vote for–vote against. All these can be scored (1, 0) and the resulting vectors analyzed as though they were continuous score vectors. Most variables are continuous, or potentially so, however, even though they can always be treated as dichotomous. In any case, the use of (1, 0) vectors for dichotomous variables in multiple regression is highly useful.

With nominal variables that are not dichotomies we can still use (1, 0) vectors. One simply creates a (1, 0) vector for each subset but only one of a category or partition. Suppose the category A is partitioned into A_1, A_2, A_3, say Protestant,

Catholic, Jew. Then a vector is created for Protestants, each of which is assigned a 1, the Catholics and Jews are assigned 0. Another vector is created for Catholics: each Catholic is assigned 1; Protestants and Jews are assigned 0. It would, of course, be redundant to create a third vector for Jews. The number of vectors is $k - 1$, where k equals the number of subsets of the partition or category.

While sometimes convenient or necessary, partitioning a continuous variable into a dichotomy or trichotomy discards information. If, for example, an investigator dichotomizes intelligence, ethnocentrism, cohesiveness of groups, or any other variable that can be measured with a scale that even approximates equality of intervals, possible valuable information is being discarded. To reduce a set of values with a relatively wide range to a dichotomy is to reduce its variance and thus its possible correlation with other variables. A good rule of research data analysis, therefore, is: Do not reduce continuous variables to partitioned variables (dichotomies, trichotomies, etc.) unless compelled to do so by circumstances or the nature of the data (seriously skewed, bimodal, etc.).

Factorial Analysis of Variance, Analysis of Covariance, and Related Analyses

It is with factorial analysis of variance, analysis of covariance, and nominal variables that we begin to appreciate the advantages of multiple regression analysis. We do little more here than comment on the use of coded vectors in factorial analysis of variance. Exceptionally full discussions can be found in Pedhazur's (1996) exhaustive work. We will, however, explain the basic reason why multiple regression analysis is often better than factorial analysis of variance.

The underlying difficulty in research and analysis is that the independent variables in which we are interested are correlated. Analysis of variance, however, assumes that they are uncorrelated. If we have, say, two experimental independent variables and subjects are assigned at random to the cells of a factorial design, we can assume that the two independent variables are not correlated—by definition. And factorial analysis of variance is appropriate. But if we have two nonexperimental variables and the two experimental variables, we cannot assume that all four independent variables are uncorrelated. Although there are ways to analyze such data with analysis of variance, they are cumbersome and "unnatural." Moreover, if there are unequal ns in the groups, analysis of variance becomes still more inappropriate because unequal ns also introduce correlations between independent variables. The analytic procedure of multiple regression, on the other hand, takes cognizance, so to speak, of the correlations among the independent variables as well as between the independent variables and the dependent variable. This means that multiple regression can analyze—separately or together—both experimental and nonexperimental data effectively. Moreover, continuous and categorical variables can be used together.

When subjects have been assigned at random to the cells of a factorial design and other things are equal, there isn't much benefit derived from using multiple regression. But when the *n*s of the cells are unequal, and one wants to include one, two, or more control variables—like intelligence, sex, and social class—or the analysis involves using continuous variables, then multiple regression should be used. This point is most important. In analysis of variance, the addition of control variables is difficult and clumsy. With multiple regression, however, the inclusion of such variables is easy and natural: each is merely another vector of scores, another X_j!

Analysis of Covariance

Analysis of covariance (not analysis of covariance structures, which we study later) is a particularly good example of the value of a multiple regression approach, because it is hard and cumbersome in the analysis of variance framework, and easily and readily grasped and done in a regression framework. What analysis of covariance does in its traditional application (see Hays, 1994) is to test the significance of the differences among means after taking into account or controlling initial individual differences on a *covariate*, a variable that is correlated with the dependent variable. (This correlation is taken into account.) In the multiple regression approach, however, the covariate's influence is controlled just as though it were any independent variable whose influence on the dependent variable has to be controlled. The covariate can be a pretest or a variable whose influence must be "removed" statistically.

Large-scale studies by Prothro and Grigg (1960) and McClosky (1964) found people's agreement with social issues became greater when the issue became more abstract. Suppose a political scientist believes that authoritarianism has a good deal to do with this relation, that the more authoritarian the person, the more that person agrees with abstract social assertions. In order to study the relation between abstractness and agreement, the researcher will have to control Authoritarianism. In other words, the political scientist is interested in studying the relation between abstractness of issues and statements on the one hand, and agreement with such issues and statements on the other. At this point there is no interest in authoritarianism and agreement. The interest is *to control the influence of authoritarianism on agreement. Authoritarianism is the covariate.*

The political scientist devises three experimental treatments, A_1, A_2, and A_3, different levels of abstractness of materials. Responses are obtained from 15 subjects who have been assigned randomly to the three experimental groups, five in each group. Before the experiment begins, the investigator administers the F (Authoritarianism) scale to the 15 subjects and uses these measures as a covariate. The goal is to control the possible influence of authoritarianism on agreement. This is a fairly straightforward analysis of covariance problem in which we test the significance of the differences among the three agreement means after correcting the means for the influence of authoritarianism and taking into account the correlation between authoritarianism and agreement. We now do the analysis of covariance using multiple regression analysis.

◉ **TABLE 33.5** *Fictitious Analysis of Covariance Problem, Three Experimental Groups and One Covariate*

		Treatments			
A_1		A_2		A_3	
X	Y	X	Y	X	Y
12	12	6	9	12	15
11	12	9	9	10	12
10	11	11	13	4	9
12	10	14	14	4	8
10	12	2	5	8	11

First, the data are presented in the usual analysis of covariance way in Table 33.5. In analysis of covariance one does separate analyses of variance on the X scores, the Y scores, and the cross products of the X and Y scores, XY. Then, using regression analysis, one calculates sums-of-squares and mean squares of the errors of estimate of the total and the within-groups and, finally, the adjusted between-groups. Since the concern here is not with the usual analysis of covariance procedure, we do not do these calculations. Instead, we proceed immediately to a multiple regression approach to the analysis.

The data of Table 33.5, arranged for multiple regression analysis, are given in Table 33.6. As usual, there is one vector for the dependent variable, Y. A second vector, X_1, is the covariate. The remaining two vectors, X_2 and X_3, represent the experimental treatments A_1 and A_2. (It is not necessary to have a vector for A_3, since there is only one vector for each degree of freedom, and there are only two degrees of freedom.)

A regression analysis yields: $R^2_{y.123} = .8612$ and $R^2_{y.1} = .7502$. To test the significance of the differences among the means of A_1, A_2, and A_3, after adjusting for the effect of X_1, the variance in Y due to the covariate is subtracted from the total variance accounted for by the regression of Y on variables X_1, X_2 and X: $R^2_{y.123} - R^2_{y.1}$. This remainder is then tested:

$$F = \frac{(R^2_{y.123} - R^2_{y.1})/(k_1 - k_2)}{(1 - R^2_{y.123})/(N - k_1 - 1)} \quad \text{(33.6)}$$

where k_1 equals the number of independent variables associated with $R^2_{y.123}$ the larger R^2, and equals the number of independent variables associated with $R^2_{y.1}$, the smaller R^2. Thus by substituting the values we get:

$$F = \frac{(.8612 - .7502)/(3 - 1)}{(1 - .8612)/(15 - 3 - 1)} = \frac{.0555}{.0126} = 4.405$$

which, at 2 and 11 degrees of freedom, is significant at the .05 level. (Note that an ordinary one-way analysis of variance of the three groups, without taking the covariate into account, yields a nonsignificant F-ratio.) $R^2_{y.23}$ or the variance of Y accounted for by the regression on variables two and three (the experimental treatments), after allowing for the correlation of variable 1 and Y, is .1110. While this is not a strong relation, especially compared to the massive correlation between the covariate, authoritarianism, and Y ($r^2_{1y} = .75$), it is not inconsequential. Evidently, abstractness of issues influences agreement responses: the more abstract the issues, the greater the agreement. Authoritarianism is unlikely to have a correlation with Y of .87. The example was deliberately contrived to show how a strong influence like the covariate X can be controlled and the influence of the remaining variables (in this case experi-

▣ **TABLE 33.6** *Fictitious Analysis of Covariance Data of Table 35.6 Arranged for Multiple Regression Analysis*[a]

	Y	X_1	X_2	X_3
A_1	12	12	1	0
	12	11	1	0
	11	10	1	0
	10	12	1	0
	12	10	1	0
A_2	9	6	0	1
	9	9	0	1
	13	11	0	1
	14	14	0	1
	5	2	0	1
A_3	15	12	0	0
	12	10	0	0
	9	4	0	0
	8	4	0	0
	11	8	0	0

[a] Y = dependent variable; X_1 = covariate; X_2 = treatment A_1; X_3 treatment A_2.

mental treatments) evaluated. Note that Formula 33.6 can be used in any multiple regression analysis; it is not limited to analysis of covariance or other experimental methods.

The analysis of covariance, then, is seen to be simply a variation on the theme of multiple regression analysis. And in this case it happens to be easier to conceptualize than the rather elaborate analysis of covariance procedure—especially if there is more than one covariate (see Bruning and Kinte, 1987 or Li, 1957). The covariate is nothing more than an independent variable. Moreover, a variable considered as a covariate in one study can easily be considered as an independent variable in another study.

Discriminant Analysis, Canonical Correlation, Multivariate Analysis of Variance, and Path Analysis

Canonical correlation and discriminant analysis address themselves to two important research questions: What is the relation between two sets of data with several independent variables and several dependent variables? How can individuals best be assigned to groups on the basis of several variables? Canonical correlation analysis addresses itself to the first question, and discriminant analysis to the second. As one would expect from the name, multivariate analysis of variance is the multivariate counterpart of analysis of variance: the influence of k independent experimental variables on m dependent variables is assessed. Path analysis is more a graphic and heuristic aid than a multivariate method. As such, it has great usefulness, especially for helping to clarify and conceptualize multivariate problems.

Discriminant Analysis

A *discriminant* function is similar to a regression equation with a categorical dependent variable. Each, however, has a different purpose. This dependent variable is usually represented in the form of group membership. In multiple regression, however, the linear combination of the predictor or independent variables is used to estimate the dependent variable. The dependent variable in regression is a continuous measure. Most researchers use multiple regression to estimate the values of the dependent variable for the purpose of selection. That is, if a predicted value for a set of independent variable values exceeds a certain cutoff, a decision is made. Discriminant analysis is involved with classification and not necessarily selection. Given a profile of scores on the independent variables, discriminant analysis can help a researcher determine to which group that individual belongs. Some natural scientists have applied the method to help classify anthropological findings of bones or animals. Like multiple regression, the independent variables are assumed to be continuous but the dependent variable is categorical. In the most elementary situations, the discrete or categorical dependent variable has only two categories. The problem that discriminant function attempts to resolve is finding a set of coefficients or weights, u_i, for the independent variables (also called discriminating variables). We want to find these weights so that we can test whether a particular combination of the independent variables resembles those members in Category 1 or more closely resembles those in Category 2. The major goal is to weight and linearly combine the independent variables so that the categories are forced to be as different statistically as possible.

Discriminant analysis answers two major questions. First, it will tell us whether or not the set of independent variables is any good in distinguishing between the two groups or categories. The second question is only important if the answer to the first question is "yes" The second deals with classification. It will tell us which group or category a single individual should belong to. In other words, the discriminant function separates the members of the group maximally. It tells us to which group each member probably belongs. Additionally, it can also test to determine which of the independent variables account for the difference between the groups. In short, if we have two or more independent variables and the members of, say, two groups, the discriminant function gives the "best" prediction, in the least-squares sense, of the "correct" group membership of each member of the sample.

Some researchers have stated that two-group discriminant analysis is the same as multiple regression except that the dependent variable, Y, is dichotomous instead of continuous. Some have gone as far as to say that any binary coding of the dependent variable (dummy coding) can be used. However, this is not exactly true. Lindeman, Merenda, and Gold (1980) have shown that the regression weights from multiple regression, b_is, are proportional to the discriminant function weights, u_is, if the dependent variable is coded as $n_2/(n_1 + n_2)$ for members of group 1 and $- n_1/(n_1 + n_2)$ for members in Group 2.

The linear discriminant analysis as formulated by Fisher (1936), is an appropriate method when the dependent variable is categorical. The independent or predictor variables should be measured on an interval scale. In order to test whether there is a statistically significant difference between the groups, the independent variables must be distributed normally with equal variances and covariances. In order to use discriminant analysis properly for classification, other assumptions about the data are made. One assumption is that one must believe that each individual profile has an equal probability of being in each group or category. One must also assume that the cost of misclassification for each individual is the same. These assumptions necessary for discriminant function are not always satisfied. As a result, in recent years, many researchers have turned away from discriminant analysis in favor of logistic regression.

Canonical Correlation

It is not too large a conceptual step from multiple regression analysis with one dependent variable to multiple regression analysis with more than one dependent variable. Computationally, however, it is a considerable step. We will not, therefore, supply the actual calculations. The regression analysis of data with k independent variables and m dependent variables is called *canonical correlation analysis*. This method was developed by Hotelling (1935, 1936). The basic idea is that, through least-squares analysis, two linear composites are formed: one for the independent variables X_i, and one for the dependent variables Y_j. The correlation between these two composites is the canonical correlation. And, like R, it will be the maximum correlation possible given the particular sets of data. It should be clear that what has been called until now multiple regression analysis is a special case of canonical analysis. In view of practical limitations on canonical analysis, it might be better to say that canonical analysis is a generalization of multiple regression analysis.

Canonical correlation can have one or more of the following objectives.

1. Testing whether two sets of variables are correlated or not correlated.
2. Finding two sets of weights or coefficients so that the correlation between the two sets is at a maximum.
3. Finding the variables in each set that make the greatest contribution in the correlation between the sets.
4. Predicting values in one set of variables using values entered into the other set.

Of these perhaps the third point is the most interesting and useful. For example, we may want to determine which achievement-based variables would have the greatest relation with a set of performance measures. Canonical correlation can provide that information. After all, if we have a set of achievement-based variables, such as a battery of achievement tests, not every test is the same. Also, one cannot reasonably expect them to make the same contribution. Hence, it is logical for us to think of canonical correlation as a step-by-step method that selects two variables, one from each set of variables that have the strongest relation over any other pair. After that, it will then continue to find the next best pair.

As far as the assumptions we need to make when applying canonical correlation to our data, they are not as important if we do not make inferences about the canonical statistic. If we use it only for descriptive purposes, we do not have to assume that the data come from a multinormal distribution or that the data come from a population with a common variances and covariance. However, if we are to make inferences, as in a test of statistical significance, then these assumptions must be met. Additionally, both the independent and dependent variables must be measured on an interval scale, or that one set is measured on an interval scale and the other is on a dichotomous scale.

Similar to multiple regression and discriminant analysis, the goal here for canonical correlation to find weights or coefficients. The difference is that there are two sets instead of one: one set for the independent variable (also called *predictors*), and another set for the dependent variables (also called *criterion*). The weights for both sets of variables are found so that they would maximize the correlation between the two sets. So, unlike multiple regression and discriminant analysis, canonical correlation is capable of producing more than one set of weights for the independent and dependent variables. However, the first set of weights would be the set that accounts for the greatest amount of variance. Each linear combination of variables (there is one for each set of variables) is often called a *canonical variate* (see Lindeman, Merenda, and Gold, 1980).

Research Example

Bedini, Williams, and Thompson (1995) used canonical correlation to study the relation between employment burnout and therapeutic role stress. This study dealt only with therapeutic recreation specialists. The burnout measures: Emotional Exhaustion, Depersonalization, and Personal Accomplishment were used as the dependent variables, whereas role stress measures: Role Ambiguity, and Role Conflict were used as the independent variables. The researchers found one function that explained the relation between the two sets of variables. This function accounted for almost 36% of the explained variance between the two sets. Additional analyses determined that approximately 53% of the variance for burnout is accounted for by the role stress variables. The results suggest that people who are experiencing role stress are more likely to be burned out, for example, experience emotional exhaustion, depersonalization, and a sense of low personal accomplishment.

Multivariate Analysis of Variance

As one might suspect, analysis of variance has its multivariate counterpart, *multivariate analysis of variance*, which enables researchers to assess the effects of *k* independent variables on *m* dependent variables. Like its univariate companion, which we examined in some detail earlier, it is or should be used for experimental data. The multivariate analysis of variance, or MANOVA, is a method closely related to discriminant analysis with multiple groups. This similarity is only on its structure and not necessarily where it should be used and what the assumptions are. Like the univariate version of analysis of variance presented in an earlier chapter, the designs used for univariate (one dependent variable) can be used for multiple dependent variables. In other words, each participant of the study is measured more than once, so that the person has at least two dependent measures. In some cases, it can be two or more different dependent variables. In others it could be the same variable measured at different times. The latter is often called *repeated measures analysis of variance*. Some researchers have inappropriately called and analyzed the data from their study as a repeated-measures ANOVA. They should have called and analyzed the data using a MANOVA. The reasons for this is that one would need to meet the requirement that the error component of the scores are independent. This is the homogeneity of variance assumptions, which often times is difficult to meet especially if the dependent variables are not truly repeated measures. There are statistical tests available to test this assumption (see Kirk, 1995).

MANOVA, however, has a few assumptions of its own that could be questioned. The within-group variances measured for the dependent variables for each of the groups in the analysis must be equal. Also, we would need to assume that the dependent variables are distributed as a multivariate normal distribution. Tests for multivariate normality are not sufficiently advanced. The determination is usually done in a piecemeal series of tests.

The multivariate analysis of variance is at its best when the assumptions are met and also when there is a substantial correlation between the dependent variables. If the correlation between the dependent variables is low or near zero, the researcher would make no gain by using a MANOVA. In this case, separate ANOVAs can be computed with each dependent variable serving as a single outcome measure. If this is the case, the researcher will need to adjust the level of the Type I error to compensate for the family-rate or family-wise error. With the other extreme, if the correlation between the dependent variables is at or near 1.00, we know that the two are measuring essentially the same thing and are redundant. With that, only a single ANOVA need be computed for one of those dependent variables.

We forgo further discussion here except to say that, as in all or most multivariate analysis, the results of multivariate analysis of variance are sometimes difficult to interpret. This is because the difficulties mentioned earlier of assessing the relative importance of variables in this influence on one dependent variable, as in multiple regression analysis, are often compounded in multivariate analysis of variance, canonical correlation, and discriminant analysis. If an interaction effect is statistically significant, the process of sorting out which variables are involved in the interaction effect can be unwieldy. Bray and Maxwell (1982) and Pedhazur (1996) provide very good discussions of multivariate analysis of variance. Note also that if there are covariates involved, we would have MANCOVA.

Nemeroff's (1995) study on disease and perception of contagion used a design where the collected data can be analyzed by MANOVA. This study was done to examine how people react to individuals who have a contagious disease. In this study, participants were given crayons and four sheets of blank paper. They were each told to draw the flu germ for different target people: self, friend, lover, stranger, and disliked person. These drawings were scored on several dimensions by trained judges. These evaluation scores served as the dependent variables. The dimensions Active, Big, and Complex were combined into a single measure—Intensity. Active was scored on how active or passive the germ appeared. Complex was concerned with the amount of detail the participant put into the drawings. The remaining three individual variables were Abstraction, Reaching, and Happy. Abstraction referred to how personified the drawing appeared. Reaching referred to how contained the germ appeared, and Happy measured the judges perception of how nice or happy the germ appeared. The independent variable for this study was the source individuals, for example, lover, self, stranger, and so on.

Through the use of MANOVA, Nemeroff found that people do perceive the flu germ differently when it comes from a different source of contagion. For example, self-germs differed from stranger germs on intensity. Lover germs were perceived as being less angry in color than disliked-person germs, which were found to be the most threatening. The lover germ was found to be the least threatening.

Path Analysis

The development of path analysis is credited to Wright (1921). The goal was to develop a causal model for genetics and biology using correlations. As we have discussed earlier, correlations do not imply causality. However, Wright was able to use them as such because his studies were done under very tight controls. Wright distinguished between direct and indirect effects using correlations and regression. A variable X may have a direct effect on the variable Y but an indirect effect on the variable Z. This effect is established by examining the standardized regression weights (correlations) between X and Y, X and Z, and Y and Z. If the correlation between 'X and Y' and 'Y and Z' are substantial, but the correlation between X and Z is minimal we have a direct effect between X and Y and between Y and Z, and an indirect one between X and Z. Wright's contribution also included a way to use tracing rules in path diagrams to perform the necessary computations.

A rediscovery of Wright's work occurred in sociology in the mid-1960s to early 1970s. These methods then became popular with psychological and educational researchers in the 1970s and 1980s. Bentler (1986) gives a good historical perspective of this transition. However, the behavioral and social science data are not quite like the data Wright collected and used. As such, to call it a "causal" model is misleading. Wright, as mentioned, had very tight controls on the genetic and breeding variables, but the level of control in the social and behavioral science studies is much lower. Blalock (1972) mentions the requirements for doing a path analysis where the results would be useful. Today, path analysis still serves as a useful research tool in developing a conceptual model that can be tested empirically. Although the term "causal modeling" lingers, it is not really causal. This will be true also when we consider the later chapter on structural equation modeling. A book that gives good coverage of path analysis is Loehlin (1998).

Path analysis is a form of applied multiple regression analysis that uses path diagrams to guide problem conceptualization or to test complex hypotheses. Through its use one can calculate the direct and indirect influences of independent variables on a dependent variable. These influences are reflected in so-called path coefficients, which are actually regression coefficients (beta, β or b). Moreover, one can test different path models for their congruence with observed data (see Pedhazur, 1996). While path analysis has been and is an important analytic and heuristic method, it is doubtful that it will continue to be used to help test models for their congruence with obtained data. Rather, its value will be as a heuristic method to aid conceptualization and the formation of complex hypotheses. The testing of such hypotheses, however, will probably be done with analytic tools more powerful and more appropriate for such testing. The method covered in Chapter 35 is currently the best method to use in analyzing and testing hypotheses from path analytic models. Let us look at an example to give a general idea of the approach.

Consider the two models, a and b, of Figure 33.1 Suppose we are trying to "explain" achievement, x_4, in the figure, or GPA. We believe that model a is "correct"; you believe, however, that model b is "correct." Model a says, in effect, that SES and intelligence both influence x_3, n achievement, or need for achievement (n-Ach), and that x_3 influences x_4, GPA or achievement. Well and good! We believe, in other words, that model a best expresses the relations among the four variables. On the other hand, you believe that model b is a better representation. It adds a direct influ-

■ **FIGURE 33.1** x_1 = Socioeconomic Status (SES); x_2 = Intelligence; x_3 = *n*-Ach, or Need for Achievement; x_4 = GPA, Grade Point Average (GPA), (Achievement)

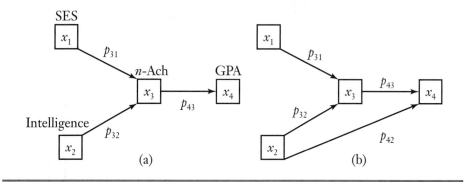

ence of x_2, intelligence, on x_4, achievement (note the paths from x_2 to x_4 and from x_2 to x_3 to x_4). Which model is "correct"? It is possible in path analysis to test the two models using the method in Chapter 35.

Ridge Regression, Logistic Regression, and Log-linear Analysis

Ridge Regression

Ridge regression is a method well-known to applied statisticians and engineering science researchers. However, it has not been popular in psychological or behavioral science research. The inventors of the method, Arthur Hoerl and Robert Kennard, published their monumental paper in 1970. Despite psychology's attitude toward this method, the impact of Hoerl and Kennard's paper has been so great, the Institute for Scientific Information has designated it a "Citation Classic" (Hoerl, 1995).

Psychology usually associates the paper by Price (1977) as psychology's introduction to ridge regression. However, Simon's (1975) well-written and informative manuscript on the topic preceded Price's by two years. Also, Bolding and Houston (1974) wrote a computer program to perform ridge regression. Simon (1975) demonstrated how the method could be used in human factor studies where all the requirements of a true experiment were not met. These studies involved one or more predictor variables that were *highly* correlated. These correlated variables were due to the failure of completing a true experiment or to the investigator's inability to select or control relevant experimental conditions. Simon refers to these types of studies as "undesigned" studies. Keith (1988) and Price (1977) call them "nonexperimental research." Hoerl and Kennard (1970) call them "non-orthogonal studies."

Ridge regression's disfavor in psychological research may be due in part to the criticisms leveled at the method by Rosenboom (1979). Most Bayesian methods or biased-estimation techniques require human intervention and judgment instead of a strictly mathematical analytical method such as least squares. Ridge regression is one of these methods. As such, it has been considered dishonest. Even authors of well-known statistics textbooks such as Draper and Smith (1981) have stated that the method was very controversial in the 1970s. However, as stated in an article by Frank and Friedman (1993), ridge regression is clearly the better method of regression analysis under many nonexperimental conditions. Many researchers agree with Keith (1988) that multiple regression is the method of choice when it comes to nonexperimental studies. However, multiple regression breaks down swiftly when the predictor variables are highly correlated or collinear. This is due to the fact that multiple regression as it currently stands in most statistical computer packages uses the method of least-squares. The reader should note that the second author of this book is taking a rather extreme position on this topic. For research studies where the predictor variables are correlated slightly or moderately (around .5 or less) the need for using a method such as ridge regression may not be necessary. In fact, Keith (1999) has pointed out that multiple regression yields fairly stable estimates of the regression coefficients when the level of collinearity is moderate.

The Problem with Ordinary-Least-Squares (OLS)

A purpose of multiple regression analysis is to obtain a set of unbiased coefficients or weights that will have a minimum amount of variable error and a reasonable fit to an existing set of data. A popular method for doing this is the method of ordinary-least-squares (OLS). This method is covered in every elementary statistics textbook as well as in an earlier chapter of this book. It is straightforward, mathematically determined, and requires no human judgment. This method involves estimating the regression coefficients with the constraint that the sum-of-squares of the difference between the predicted and the observed outcome measure is at a minimum:

$$\Sigma(Y_i' - Y_i)^2 = \text{minimum for the equation } Y = \beta_0 + \beta_1 x_1 + \beta_2 x_2 \ldots + \beta_n x_n + e.$$

In this equation the Xs are the predictor variables and the Y is the dependent or criterion variable. When the predictor variables are mathematically independent (i.e., the correlations between the Xs are equal to *zero*), the estimated regression coefficients are reasonable representations of the true regression coefficients within the limits of sampling fluctuations. When the predictor variables are highly correlated, the individual regression coefficients calculated using the OLS method are often unsatisfactory. The matrix of highly intercorrelated predictor variables is called *ill-conditioned*. The predictive qualities of this equation generated by least-squares are reasonably accurate for the data used to generate the equation. However, for a new set of data applied to the same regression equation results in poor predicted values for the outcome measure. That is, cross-validation of the regression equation is extremely poor. Also, the relative effects of the individual regression coefficients cannot be evaluated. In other words, the regression coefficients obtained from using least-squares on correlated predictor variables may not make sense when evaluated in real-world terms. Hoerl and Kennard (1970) and resummarized by Simon (1975) stated that one or more of the following characteristics could occur in a least squares fit of correlated predictor variables:

1. regression coefficients become too large in absolute value,
2. some coefficients may have the wrong sign,
3. the coefficients are unstable; another set of data for the same variables will produce different outcome values, and
4. individual regression weights are over- or underestimating the effect of a particular variable.

Two variables highly correlated will result in coefficients where one variable receives a large weight and the other receives a small insignificant weight. A more complete discussion on the dangers of ordinary OLS is given by Newman (1976).

Hoerl and Kennard (1970) developed an alternative to the conventional multiple regression approach with correlated predictor variables. This method was created to allow researchers to assess variables in chemical engineering problems where it would be impractical to drop variables or create composite ones. This method, called *ridge regression*, yields a better prediction equation than one would get from using least-squares. It is better because the estimated coefficients are closer to the true coefficients on the average. The signs on the coefficients are more accurate; the coefficients are more stable, with a higher likelihood of being repeated for a new set of data, and the estimated outcome measure can be made with a smaller mean square error. Through ridge regression the eigenvalues will become less discrepant.

Essentially, ridge regression analysis is identical to OLS regression except that a small number, k, has been added to the diagonal of the correlation matrix of predictor variables. The addition of this number k to the diagonal makes the matrix less ill-conditioned. It also has the effect of lowering the mean square error when compared to least-squares. The best k value is the one where the regression coefficients have stabilized and the residual sums-of-squares is low. To find this value, the researcher must try several values of k. A number of researchers have objected to this ad hoc method of selecting k. As demonstrated by Simon (1975) the k value can be directly added to the diagonal of the correlation matrix and then submitted to a regression computer program, or the researcher can add dummy cases to the original data (augmented data) and selecting the zero intercept option of the computer program. BMDP (Dixon, 1990) has a subprogram in their statistical package for performing ridge regression. Lee (1980) shows how one can do this with regression programs that do not have a zero intercept option. Several studies have been done to develop a more analytical way of determining *k*. The discussion of those studies would consume too much space for this book. The reader is asked to consult Simon's paper or Draper and Smith (1981).

The price that one pays in using ridge regression is that the regression coefficients are no longer unbiased and the RSS is not a minimum. However, the benefits of a properly executed ridge regression may outweigh these negatives. However, like all statistical methods, ridge regression must be used correctly. Draper and Smith (1981, p. 322) put it most directly with their statement:

> The ridge regression selection is not a miraculous panacea. It is a least squares solution restricted by the addition of some external information about the parameters. The blind use of ridge regression without this realization is dangerous and misleading. If the external information is sensible and is not contradicted by the data, then ridge regression is also sensible.

Research Example

Bee and Beronja (1986) used ridge regression in a study of college students with an undetermined major. These researchers collected ACT test results along with collegiate academic performance and personality measures, such as motivation and work habits. The goal was to develop a regression equation that could predict college academic performance (grade point average) using personality variables, program experience variables (e.g., level of difficulty of courses in major area) and precollege test scores (ACT). These explanatory or independent variables were collinear. When Bee and Beronja fitted the data by the ordinary regression method, they found none of the explanatory variables to be related significantly to academic performance. The ridge regression estimates, however, provided a very different result. Ridge regression found the variables, ACT–Math, work habits, motivation to succeed, and difficulty of math courses to be significantly related to academic performance. Bee and Beronja found that $k = .4$ yield the best results in the ridge regression. All of the regression weights found using ordinary-least-squares were not statistically significant ($p > .05$). However, four of the regression weights determined by ridge regression were significant.

Logistic Regression

We discussed earlier in the book multiple regression and discriminant function analysis. Generally, if one has a categorical dependent variable, the recommendation was to do a discriminant function analysis. However, a discriminant function analysis is only effective if the variables meet certain assumptions. In some studies within the social and behavioral science, the independent or predictor variables are categorical or nominal. When this occurs, the discriminant function analysis begins to lose its effectiveness in terms of its goodness-of-fit to the data. If one uses multiple regression, the equation of best fit may be way off and yield an equation that may not yield useful information. After all, the traditional multiple regression assumes the data are measured on an interval scale (or something close to that) and follows a normal distribution.

A method that has been gaining much popularity in recent years is logistic regression. This development seems rather new to researchers in the field of psychology, sociology, and education. The life and medical sciences have been using it for a much longer period. The social sciences' lag on the use of this method is ironic. Back in the late 1960s psychologists and social researchers at the University of Michigan's Institute for Social Research (ISR) had developed the methods called *multiple classification analysis* (MCA) and *Multivariate Nominal Scale Analysis* (MNA), which is now referred to as *logistic regression.* Psychology actually had an early introduction to the method that lay latent for years except for those who were affiliated with or knowledgeable of ISR.

Andrews, Morgan, Sonquist, and Klem (1973) describe a technique for examining the relations between independent variables and a dependent variable that resembles multiple regression. They point out the problem involved when the independent or predictor variables are measured on a nominal scale and offer a solution. Multiple Classification Analysis, MCA as they call it, can take nominal or non-nominal data for the predictor variables. For the dependent or criterion variable, the data can be measured on an interval scale or dichotomous scale. The *multivariate nominal scale analysis* (Andrews & Messenger, 1973) is an expansion of MCA. It allows for nominally scaled dependent variables with more than two categories. By today's labeling, MCA is called *logistic regression,* and MNA is called *polychotomous logistic regression* (see Dixon, 1990). We will use the more popular terms in our discussion of this method.

Logistic regression, therefore, is a technique for fitting a regression surface to data in which the dependent variable is a dichotomy. In educational psychology we might classify students as High or Low mental functioning. Or, if we are referring to therapy, it would be Improved or Not Improved; Successful or Not Successful. For every study that uses a dichotomous dependent variable, logistic regression is a viable candidate as the method of analysis. However, one may ask, "Which should I use—discriminant analysis or logistic regression?" There is a controversy surrounding the comparison of discriminant analysis and logistic regression. Press and Wilson (1978) reported the situations in which discriminant analysis does quite well; that is, the data meets the assumptions. However, when the assumptions are not met, logistic regression yields a superior form of analysis. Logistic regression has fewer assumptions to satisfy but is no panacea for data collected under questionable research designs. Discriminant analysis can easily produce a probability of success that lies outside the range of 0 and 1, which is not acceptable. Logistic regression, on the other hand, does not produce probabilities beyond 0 and 1. Both will yield regression estimates and both are capable of classifying individuals. In logistic regression, a researcher gets an added bonus: The regression coefficient or weights can be transformed into *odds ratios,* a useful statistic that we described in Chapter 10. It is useful in giving the researcher ideas as to what is going on within the data.

In a direct comparison between discriminant analysis and logistic regression, logistic regression fares much better when variables are non-normal. Also, logistic regression is not as strongly affected as discriminant analysis when meaningless variables are included in the analysis. This includes variables that are dichotomous or have been subjected to dummy coding. The use of dichotomous variables is very common in the behavioral science research. So if one's research data contains categorical or nominally scaled variables or there is some reasonable doubt about some of the variables, it is probably best to use logistic regression instead of discriminant analysis.

A similar comparison could be made between logistic regression and ordinary multiple regression using dichotomous independent and dependent variables. With multiple regression, predicted values can fall outside the 0, 1 range. Also, if the calculated variances of the dependent variable were to fluctuate for values of the independent variables, such as having more 1s than 0s for one level and equal 0s and 1s in another, the analysis will produce a large variance. As a result, the assumption of homogeneity of variance and normality will be violated. However, there are situations where multiple regression with a dichotomous dependent variable would give good results (see Cox & Wermuth, 1992).

A Research Example

The data for this example comes as a courtesy of Dorothy Scattone at the University of Southern Mississippi. Her study dealt with the perceptions of two different groups of Asians toward physical and mental disabilities. One group of Asians was born and raised in an Asiatic country and the other group consisted of American-born Asians. The participants were 215 college students who answered a number of questions concerning certain disabilities such as Down Syndrome or their level of acceptance of people with asthma or facial scars, and so on. These variables are measured on a 5-point rating scale where 5 equals high acceptance and 1 equals low acceptance.

The results of this analysis show us which variables discriminated between American-born and foreign-born Asians, and tells us the probabilities. For the Stutter variable participants are asked to indicate the level of acceptance for a person who has a speech problem, namely, stuttering, where 1 equals no acceptance to 5 equals full acceptance. With full acceptance, the respondent agrees that he or she is willing to have the person as a member of the family through marriage. Since this variable was significant it tells us that U.S.-born and foreign-born Asians differ in their response. The odds ratio for the variables is a different way of talking about probabilities. The advantage that the odds ratio has over the test of significance is that the odds-ratio is relatively unaffected by sample size. For Stuttering, the odds ratio was .4516. This says foreign-born Asians are .4516 times less likely to accept a person with stuttering than U.S.-born Asians or, in other words, U.S.-born Asians are 2.2 times more likely to accept a person with these disabilities than foreign-born Asians (1/.4516).

In addition to this information, the logistic regression analysis also provides a measure of how accurate the regression equation is in terms of classification. With the data we have here, the logistic regression equation was able to correctly classify

76.74% of the cases. The equation was generally more accurate in predicting for-eign-born Asians (92.02%) than U.S.-born Asians (28.85%). There are other statis-tics, such as the Wald Test, that are associated with a logistic regression output. We will not be discussing them here. Rather, we will refer the reader to such books as Hosmer and Lemeshow (1989) or Shoukri and Edge (1996).

Multiway Contingency Tables and Log-Linear Analysis

It is fitting that we introduce this section following logistic regression because the topic we are about to undertake deals exclusively with categorical data. In logistic regression, we have a dichotomous dependent variable and categorical and interval independent variables. With multiway contingency tables, we deal only with categor-ical data. The analyses of multiway contingency tables are important because a lot of the data used by behavioral and social scientists are categorical. The use of traditional analysis of variance and multiple regression approaches toward analyzing categorical data does not work well in many cases.

We studied the one- and two-dimensional contingency table in Chapter 10. At that time, we briefly introduced the notion of multiway tables. Traditionally, many researchers studied multiway contingency tables by looking at a series of two-way tables. The computations are relatively straightforward and the researcher can usu-ally arrive at some reasonable conclusion about the data. Also, they are more unlikely to have sparse or empty cells. One of the most likely events that will occur in large tables is sparse cells or empty cells, which can affect the results of the analysis. Hence, many researchers would collapse categories to eliminate this problem. However, the series of two-way contingency tables in analyzing multiway contin-gency tables is not able to capture the existence of higher order interaction effects between the dimensions. Glick, DeMorest, and Hotze (1988) give a good example of how to analyze a three-way contingency table correctly with a series of two-way analyses. They were also able through a progression of logical statements and analy-ses to arrive at a conclusion about the three-way interaction term. We will see later in this section a reanalyses of their data in light of multiway contingency tables or log-linear analysis. Also, the associations between variables are different under two-way analysis than under multiway since the multiway takes into consideration the other variables involved. Further, the use of only two-way tables does not allow for the simultaneous comparison of all pairwise associations.

Remember in the categorical data analysis of Chapter 10, we stated the difference between observed values and expected values. Both of these represent fre-quencies within each cell of a contingency table. If the expected frequencies fit the observed frequencies, we would say that there was no relation between the two categorical variables. This is so because the expected frequencies are computed under conditions of what we might expect if there was no relation between the two variables. Hence, if the observed frequencies fit the expected frequencies, we can conclude that our collected data found no relation. Subsequently, if there was a lack of fit, then we say that the two variables are related. The analysis of multiway contingency tables operates pretty much the same way. The researcher specifies a model involving the variables, such as no three-way interactions or only specific two-way interactions. After the model is specified, expected frequencies are generated. If the observed frequencies fit the expected frequencies, then we know that the chosen model fits the observed data and the elements of the model account for the observed values. In multiway tables, one of the goals is to find the variables that are related to other variables. Finding the expected values so that we can test to see if the observed values fit is more computationally demanding than for the simple two-way tables. Although we will not go through the actual computations, we can direct the reader to useful references that clearly show the operation. One of the more popular algorithms for finding the expected values was developed by Deming and Stephan (1940). A description of this method can be found in their original article. It can also be found in the 1964 Dover republication of Deming's 1943 book or in Dillon and Goldstein (1984). Dillon and Goldstein give a very clear and easy to follow computational example. Sometimes the Deming and Stephan method is called *iterative proportional fitting*. True to its name, iterative proportional fitting requires an initial estimate of the expected frequencies, and then through a number of steps they are adjusted. In the first iteration, estimates are obtained to be used in the next iteration. Just as in logistic regression, the iterations cease once two successive iterations produce estimates that are very close to one another.

A benefit produced by the log-linear approach is one of parsimony. That is, with the log-linear approach, the researcher specifies a model of terms to be fitted very much like what is done in analysis of variance or multiple regression. The researcher attempts to obtain the best-fit possible with the fewest terms. Let us say we let m_{ij} represent the expected frequency in cell (i, j) of a two-way contingency table. Let us label one of the variables as A and the other as B. A would have i categories and B would have j categories. We can express the model for this contingency table as

$$\log_e(m_{ij}) = \mu + \mu_{A(i)} + \mu_{B(j)} + \mu_{AB(i,j)}.$$

Sometimes, this equation is written without the subscripts i and j. These subscripts are used to indicate the number of categories in each variable. If the equation is written without the subscripts, the categories are implied. For the sake of simplicity, we will write our equations without direct reference to the number of categories in each variable. One will note that this equation resembles the one used in analysis of variance. However, among the differences, the reader needs to remember that with multiple regression or analysis of variance, the equation is developed to predict or account for the variation from individual to individual. In different words, analysis of variance and multiple regression make an estimate of the dependent variable for each case or individual. In log-linear or contingency tables, the prediction is to the cell frequency or category and not to the individual. Although a number of writers (Bakeman & Robinson, 1994; Fienberg, 1980; Howell, 1997; Kennedy, 1992) of multiway contingency tables and log linear analysis make analogies to multiple regression and analysis of variance, they emphasize this one major difference.

In log-linear analysis, if we had three categorical variables we would write it as

$$\log_e(m_{ij}) = \mu + \mu_A + \mu_B + \mu_C + \mu_{AB} + \mu_{AC} + \mu_{BC} + \mu_{ABC}$$

Note that in each model, there are main terms and the interactions. When all possible combinations of the terms are accounted for in the equation, the model is referred to as *saturated*. The goodness-of-fit statistic will be a perfect zero telling us the model fits the observed data; that is, the observed values fit the expected values. However, a researcher can with this method of analysis fit different models. Guidance dictated by theory or previous information can be used to eliminate some of the terms. If the observed data are found to fit the expected values generated by the new model, we have successfully fit a more parsimonious model. These more parsimonious models are often referred to as *reduced models* or *unsaturated models*. What a good-fitting unsaturated model tells us is that we didn't need all of the terms of the saturated model in order to get a decent fit of the observed values to the expected values.

The interaction terms of the log-linear model are referred to as *higher order terms*. The more terms in the interaction, the higher the term. In the three-way model presented above, the μ_{ABC} term is the highest order term, whereas μ is the lowest order term. This brief specification is important when discussing the difference between hierarchical and nonhierarchical models. Some experts on log-linear analysis for contingency tables have stated that the hierarchical model is the most useful and the results from non-hierarchical models are questionable (Bakeman & Robinson, 1994; Howell, 1997). We will restrict our discussion here to hierarchical models only. In hierarchical models we view the higher order terms as a composite of lower order terms. In order to compute μ_{AB} we would need to also compute μ, μ_A, and μ_B, which are all the lower order terms. Thus, in hierarchical models, higher order terms are included only if the lower order terms are also included in the model. Nonhierarchical models don't have this restriction and as such can obtain results that are difficult to interpret.

There can be a large number of unsaturated models. As the number of categorical variables increase, the number of models also increase. In some cases it becomes very difficult to test all of the models. In fact, the researcher should not try to test all models in the hope of finding one that fits the data. The model should be based on theory or a combination of theory and previous findings. Take for example the study by Glick, DeMorest, and Hotze (1988). They found a three-way interaction without the use of what we call log-linear analysis. This three-way interaction term, μ_{ABC}, in log-linear terms would be the highest order term for the data. Hence we would specify the model with the three-way term. Or, if we wanted to expand on their analysis and include a fourth categorical variable, we would definitely include in the model a term for the three-way interaction. Deciding which terms to include in the model for testing is called *specification*.

Specifying the model for a log-linear analysis on contingency tables uses a special notation. Capital letters of the alphabet surrounded by brackets are used to represent the effect of each variable separately. For example, when we refer to the *A* effect in a three-way table we would write [A]. With a hierarchical model if we state [AB], we are referring to the model:

$$\log_e(m_{ij}) = \mu + \mu_A + \mu_B + \mu_C + \mu_{AB}$$

If we write [A][BC] we are referring to the model

$$\log_e(m_{ij}) = \mu + \mu_A + \mu_B + \mu_C + \mu_{BC}$$

If we write [ABC], we would be talking about the saturated model:

$$\log_e(m_{ij}) = \mu + \mu_A + \mu_B + \mu_C + \mu_{AB} + \mu_{AC} + \mu_{BC} + \mu_{ABC}$$

Bakeman and Robinson (1994) use a notation system that slightly differs from this. The computer program that accompanies their book is very easy to use and appears to be as well written as some of the commercially available programs. However, their computer program does not print out the brackets "[ ]."

The goodness-of-fit statistic that we saw in Chapter 10 has a formal name which we did not mention. This name is necessary for this chapter mainly because we will introduce another goodness-of-fit statistic. The one we saw in Chapter 10 is called the Pearson Chi-Square. Its formula is

$$\chi^2 = \Sigma\left[\frac{(f_o - f_e)^2}{f_e}\right]$$

Another statistic that is almost identical to the Pearson χ^2 is the likelihood ratio χ^2. To distinguish between the two, the likelihood ratio chi-square is usually written as G^2. As discussed by Wickens (1989), the two are nearly identical in their approximation of a chi-square distribution. The choice of which one is used is a matter of preference. Wickens does mention that the Pearson χ^2 is more familiar and is intuitively clearer than the likelihood ratio. Some computer programs give both. The advantage that the likelihood ratio chi-square (G^2) has over the Pearson chi-square is computational. The likelihood ratio formula does not use the expected frequencies in a direct way. The likelihood ratio chi-square for a two-way table is given as

$$G^2 = 2\left(\Sigma f_{0_{ij}}\log f_{0_{ij}} - \Sigma R_i \log R_i - \Sigma C_j \log C_j + N \log N\right)$$

where

$$\Sigma f_{0_{ij}} \log f_{0_{ij}}$$

is the sum of the observed values times the log of the observed value in each cell of the contingency table.

$$\Sigma R_i \log R_i$$

▣ **TABLE 33.7** *Marginals and Cell Frequency*

	C_1	C_2	C_3	
R_1	$x_{11} = 34$	$x_{12} = 26$	$x_{13} = 75$	$x_{1+} = 135$
R_2	$x_{21} = 20$	$x_{22} = 30$	$x_{23} = 82$	$x_{2+} = 132$
	$x_{+1} = 54$	$x_{+2} = 56$	$x_{+3} = 157$	$x_{++} = 267$

is the sum of the row total times the log of the row totals,

$$\Sigma C_j \log C_j$$

is the sum of the column totals times the log of the column totals. The "N" in $N \log N$ is the total frequency count. The use of these symbols is only effective when talking about two-dimensional tables. With three-way or multiway tables, researchers would use a different notation. The observed cell values for a three-way table would be written as x_{ijk}. What we would designate as row total and column totals in a two-way table are now called *marginal totals*. For a three-way table, they would be written as x_{+jk}, x_{i+k}, x_{ij+}. The grand total, or the total number of counts is x_{+++}. These notations can also be used for a two-way contingency table. Table 33.7 shows the relation of contingency components and notation.

We can then rewrite the goodness-of-fit equation for a two-way contingency table as

$$G^2 = 2(\Sigma x_{ij} \log x_{ij} - \Sigma x_{i+} \log x_{i+} - \Sigma x_{+j} \log x_{+j} + x_{++} \log x_{++})$$

For our sample data in Table 33.7,

$$
\begin{aligned}
G^2 &= 2 \,(34 \log 34 + 26 \log 26 + 75 \log 75 + 20 \log 20 + 30 \log 30 \\
&\quad + 82 \log 82 - 135 \log 135 - 132 \log 132 - 54 \log 54 - 56 \log 56 \\
&\quad - 157 \log 157 + 267 \log 267) \\
&= 2 \,(119.8996 + 84.7105 + 323.8116 + 59.9147 + 102.0359 + 361.3510 \\
&\quad - 662.2121 - 644.5299 - 215.4051 - 225.4197 - 793.8306 + 1491.7954) \\
&= 2 \,(2.1213) = 4.2426
\end{aligned}
$$

Had we computed χ^2 instead of G^2, the χ^2 value would be 4.1943. The computation of this value required the additional calculation for the expected values, fe_{ij}. For this example they would be $fe_{11} = 27.3$, $fe_{12} = 28.31$, $fe_{13} = 79.38$, $fe_{21} = 26.7$, $fe_{22} = 27.69$, and $fe_{23} = 77.62$. As we can see, G^2 and χ^2 do not produce the same value. Both values, however, are evaluated with the same number of degrees of freedom and also with the same chi-square table.

Research Example

Since Glick et al. (1988) give their data in their article, we will use their data to illustrate the log-linear approach to multiway contingency tables. Glick et al. studied three variables: Compliance, Distance, and Group Membership. The variable compliance had two categories: Complied or Refused. Group Membership involved whether or not the requester of a favor was a member of the same group as the participant. That is, did the requester have a similar physical appearance as the participant? If the answer was "yes," then he or she was considered as an In Group confederate; if "no," he or she was an Out Group confederate. The distance variable measured three distances of near, medium, or far. These researchers hypothesized that people would be willing to comply if the Out Group confederate was further away from them than In Group confederates. The researchers were essentially hypothesizing a three-way interaction. We can write the Glick et al. log-linear model as:

$$\log_e(m_{ij}) = \mu + \mu_C + \mu_D + \mu_G + \mu_{CD} + \mu_{CG} + \mu_{DG} + \mu_{CDG}$$

If we can obtain an adequate fit between expected values and observed values *without* the three-way interaction term, it would tell us that the data couldn't justify the three-way interaction. As such, the data would not uphold the researchers' hypothesis. This might mean that the effect of interpersonal distance on compliance is not different between In Group and Out Group members.

In using Bakeman and Robinson's (1994) computer program, *ILOG*, that accompanies their textbook, we obtained the following result given in Table 33.8.

Here we can see what happens to G^2 when we fit the saturated model. The saturated model fits the observed data perfectly. Next we remove the three-way interaction term from the model; that is, we test the model:

$$\log_e(m_{ij}) = \mu + \mu_C + \mu_D + \mu_G + \mu_{CD} + \mu_{CG} + \mu_{DG}$$

If the G^2 statistic is not significant, we know that we have found at least one model that fits the observed data well. When we fit the model, the G^2 that we obtain is 12.4

◙ **TABLE 33.8** *Analysis of Glick, et. al. data*

Model	G^2	df	Sig.	Term Deleted	ΔG^2	Δdf
[CDG] (saturated)	0.0	0	$p > 0.05$	—		
[DG][CD][CG]	12.4	2	$p < 0.005$	CDG	12.4	2
[CD][CG]	13.0	4	$p < 0.05$	DG	0.6	2
[CG][D]	20.2	6	$p < 0.005$	CD	7.2	2
[DG][C]	26.8	7	$p < 0.001$	CG	6.6	1

with 2 degrees of freedom. If we consult a χ^2 table for $\alpha = .05$ and $df = 2$ the critical value is 5.99. Since 12.4 exceeds 5.99 we have a statistically significant χ^2 test and this tells us the model does not fit. In looking at Table 33.8 we have listed the results of the statistical test for each model. All of the reduced models tested are statistically significant. This tells us that the models we tested do not fit the observed data. Since the only model that fits the data is the saturated model, we reach the same conclusion that Glick et al. had found. There is a three-way interaction between the variables.

Multivariate Analysis and Behavioral Research

Although our study of multivariate methods has been rather superficial, we must still stop to place them into the research scheme of things and to evaluate them. Should we abandon analysis of variance, for example, simply because multiple regression can accomplish all that analysis of variance can—and more? Some such implication has perhaps been picked up by the reader. Isn't multiple regression analysis really unsuited to experimental data because it is a so-called correlational method (which it is only in part)? Other important questions can and should be asked and answered, especially at this time in the development of behavioral science research. We are at the point, perhaps, of an important transition. Since Fisher invented and expounded on the analysis of variance in the 1920s and 1930s, the method, or rather, approach, has had great influence on behavioral research, particularly in psychology. Are we now about to leave this stage? Have we entered a "multivariate stage"? If so, it can have an enormously important influence on the kind and quality of research done by psychologists, sociologists, and educators in the next century. Obviously, we can't handle all such questions in a textbook. But we should at least try to open the door to the student.

Should the analysis of variance approach be supplanted by multiple regression analysis? We don't think it should. But is this merely a sentimental clinging to something we have found interesting and satisfying? Perhaps. But there is more to it than that. There is little point to using multiple regression in the ordinary analysis of variance problem situation: random assignment of subjects to experimental treatments; equal or proportional ns in the cells; one, two, or three independent variables. Another argument for analysis of variance is its usefulness in teaching. Multiple regression analysis, while elegant and powerful, lacks the structural heuristic quality of analysis of variance. There is nothing quite so effective in teaching and learning research as drawing paradigms of the designs using analysis of variance analytic partitioning.

The answer is that both methods should be taught and learned. The additional demands on both teacher and student are inevitable, just as the development, growth, and use of inferential statistics earlier in the century made their teaching and learning inevitable. Multiple regression and other multivariate methods, however, will no doubt suffer some of the lack of understanding, even opposition, that inferential statistics has suffered. Even today there are psychologists, sociologists, and educators who know little about inferential statistics or modern analysis, and who even oppose their learning and use. This is part of the social psychology and pathology of the subject, however. While there will no doubt be cultural lag, the ultimate acceptance of these powerful tools of analysis is probably assured.

Multivariate methods, as we have seen, are not easy to use and to interpret as univariate methods. This is due not only to their complexity; it is due more so to the complexity of the phenomena that behavioral scientists work with. One of the drawbacks of educational research, for instance, has been that the enormous complexity of a school or a classroom could not adequately be handled by the too-simple methods used. Some scientists feel that they can never mirror the "real" world with their methods of observation and analysis. They are individuals bound to simplifications of the situations and problems they study. They can never "see things whole," just as no human being can see and understand the whole of anything. But multivariate methods mirror psychological, sociological, and educational reality better than simpler methods, and they enable researchers to handle larger portions of their research problems. In educational research, the days of the simple methods experiment with an experimental group and a control group are almost over. In sociological research, the reduction of much valuable data to frequency and percentage crossbreaks will decrease relative to the whole body of sociological research.

Most important of all, the healthy future of behavioral research depends on the healthy development of psychological, sociological, and other theories to help explain the relations among behavioral phenomena. By definition, theories are interrelated sets of constructs or variables. Obviously, multivariate methods are well adapted to testing fairly complex theoretical formulations, since their very nature is the analysis of several variables simultaneously. Indeed, the development of behavioral theory must go hand in hand, even depend on, the assimilation, mastery, and intelligent use of multivariate methods. We will see in the last two chapters of this book a different multivariate view on doing research in the social and behavioral sciences.

CHAPTER SUMMARY

1. This chapter examines the differences and similarities between analysis of variance and multiple regression.
2. Multiple regression can essentially do all of the analyses that ANOVA is capable of and more.
3. Analysis of variance has a structure that is intuitively appealing to researchers.
4. This chapter discusses the differences between different types of coding: Dummy, Effects, and Orthogonal. Each would produce the same R^2, but individual variable coefficients will be different.
5. The difference between analysis of variance and analysis of covariance is that in ANOVA, the independent variables are uncorrelated. In analysis of

covariance, at least one variable is correlated with the other independent variables.

6. This correlated variable is called a *covariate*. It is used to remove its variance from the dependent variable before the independent variables are tested.

7. Analysis of covariance is handled easily by multiple regression.

8. Discriminant analysis is similar to multiple regression with a few exceptions. The dependent variable is categorical in discriminant analysis. Plus it gives a statistic that tells you how well the discriminant function classifies observations.

9. With canonical correlation, instead of one dependent variable, as in multiple regression and discriminant analysis, it has more. The goal is to find two sets of coefficients that maximize the variance between the two sets of variables.

10. Multivariate analysis of variance or MANOVA is the multivariate equivalent to analysis of variance. In univariate ANOVA the analysis is done for one dependent variable at a time. With the multivariate analysis of variance, multiple dependent variables are considered at the same time.

11. MANOVAs, as with all multivariate methods, can lead to results that are difficult to interpret.

12. Path analysis uses standardized regression weights to study the direct and indirect effects of variables on other variables. It is best used as a conceptual model to be tested.

13. Path analysis involves drawing a path diagram that shows how the variables are related.

14. Ridge regression was first used in chemical engineering by Arthur Hoerl. It was later expanded into a tool for other areas.

15. Ordinary-least-squares is the statistical method used by most multiple regression computer programs However, when the independent variables are highly correlated with each other, least-squares runs into problems in terms of estimation.

16. Ridge regression adds a bias into the equation and as such will stabilize the regression coefficients. Ridge regression is a controversial topic in the behavioral sciences.

17. Logistic regression is the popular and alternative approach to discriminant analysis. It does not have quite the restrictions placed on discriminant analysis.

18. With less restrictions, logistic regression can handle a variety of problems. Like discriminant analysis, logistic regression has a categorical dependent variable.

19. Multiway contingency tables are handled using log-linear analysis.

20. The major idea behind log-linear analysis for multiway contingency tables is to find the proper model that will account for the variation in the observed values.

21. There are hierarchical and nonhierarchical models in log-linear analysis. The hierarchical is the most useful. Nonhierarchical models are subject to problems in interpretation.

STUDY SUGGESTIONS

1. Unfortunately, completely satisfactory elementary treatments of multiple regression are scarce, especially if one expects concomitant regression treatment of analysis of variance. Perhaps satisfactory elementary treatment of such a complex subject is not possible. The following annotated references on multiple regression and other multivariate methods may be helpful. Some of these are also listed in the Reference section because they have been cited in this chapter.

Kerlinger, F., & Pedhazur, E. (1973). *Multiple regression in behavioral research.* New York: Holt, Rinehart and Winston. [A text that attempts to enhance understanding of multiple regression and its research uses by providing as simple an exposition as possible and many examples with simple numbers. Also has a complete multiple regression computer program in the appendix.]

Pedhazur, E. (1996). *Multiple regression in behavioral research: Explanation and prediction* (3rd ed.). Orlando, FL: Harcourt Brace. [The revision of the Kerlinger and Pedhazur text. It is, however, much more detailed and thorough. Highly recommended.]

Stevens, J. P. (1996). *Applied multivariate statistics for the social sciences* (3rd ed.) Mahwah, NJ: Lawrence Erlbaum. [A very readable book on multivariate statistics. Annotated with computer output from popular statistical programs.]

Tabachnick, B., & Fidell, L. (1996). *Using multivariate statistics* (3rd ed.). New York: HarperCollins. [Shows multivariate statistics from a computer output point of view. Very useful for those who want to know about multivariate statistics and also the computer programs used to do the analyses.]

After the student and researcher have mastered the elements of multiple regression analysis and have had some experience with actual problems, the following references provide sophisticated guidance in the use of multiple regression analysis and, more important, the interpretation of data.

Cohen, J., & Cohen, P. (1983). *Applied multiple regression/correlation analysis for the behavioral sciences* (2nd ed.). Mahwah, NJ: Lawrence Erlbaum. [An excellent treatment of multiple regression. Shows how many problems where analysis of variance was used could have been analyzed with multiple regression. Also shows how multiple regression can be used to study causality.]

Daniel, C., Wood, F. S., & Gorman, J. W. (1980). *Fitting equations to data: Computer analysis of multifactor data.* (2nd ed.). New York: Wiley. [Summary through examples of how these staticians approached the analysis of research data where researchers did not follow the standard requirements of statistical design of experiments. Uses a lot of computer-generated analysis and explanations.]

Draper, N., & Smith, H. (1981). *Applied regression analysis* (2nd ed.). New York: John Wiley & Sons. [A classic in the field of regression analysis. Requires some sophistication mathematically, but it is an often cited and useful book.]

Kleinbaum, D. G., Kupper, L. L., Muller, K. E. & Nizam, A. (1997). *Applied regession analysis and other multivariable methods.* (3rd ed.). Belmont, CA: Duxbury. [This book clarifies the confusion between multivariate and multivariable. This book was briefly mentioned in Chapter 2. It is worthwhile reading.]

Mendenhall, W. (1968). *An introduction to linear models and the design and analysis of experiments.* Belmont, CA: Wadsworth. [Undoubtedly one of the best books written that introduces the unsophisticated to the use of multiple regression (general linear model) in place of analysis of variance. It requires knowledge of matrix algebra. This book is now out of print.]

Neter, J., Wasserman,W. & Kutner, M. H. (1996). *Applied linear regression models* (3rd ed.). Burr Ridge, IL: Irwin. [A book similar to Woodward, Bonett, and Brecht listed below. Good coverage of the use of regression. Requires knowledge of matrix algebra.]

The following books are fundamental: they emphasize the theoretical and mathematical bases of multivariate methods.

Carroll, J. D., & Green, P. (1997). *Mathematical tools for applied multivariate analysis* (3rd. ed.). New York: Academic Press. [An outstanding book on the mathematical basis of multivariate analysis. Highly recommended.]

Kenny, D. (1979). *Correlation and causality.* New York: John Wiley & Sons. [Worth many hours of study.]

Wickens, T. D. (1994). *The geometry of multivariate statistics.* Mahwah, NJ: Lawrence Erlbaum. [Introduces the procedures of multivariate statistics in a geometric way. It helps the student conceptualize multivariate relationships.]

2. Suppose that a social psychologist has two correlation matrices:

	X_1	X_2	Y		X_1	X_2	Y
X_1	1.00	0	.70	X_1	1.00	.40	.70
X_2	0	1.00	.60	X_2	.40	1.00	.60
Y	.70	.60	1.00	Y	.70	.60	1.00
		A				B	

a. Which matrix, A or B, will yield the higher R^2? Why?
b. Calculate the R^2 of matrix A.
[Answers: (a) Matrix A; (b) $R^2 = .85$]

3. Here are three sets of simple fictitious data, laid out for an analysis of variance. Lay out the data for multiple regression analysis, and calculate as much of the regression analysis as possible. Use dummy coding (1, 0), as in Table 33.2. The b coefficients are: $b_1 = 3$: $b_2 = 6$.

A_1	A_2	A_3
7	12	5
6	9	2
5	10	6
9	8	3
8	11	4

Imagine that A_1, A_2, and A_3 are three methods of changing racial attitudes and that the dependent variable is a measure of change with higher scores indicating more change. Interpret the results. [Answers: a = 4; R^2 =.75; F = 18, with df = 2, 12; ss_{reg} = 90; ss_t = 120. Note that these fictitious data are really the scores of Table 33.2 with 1 added to each score. Compare the various regression and analysis of variance statistics, above, with those calculated with the data of Table 33.2]

4. Using the data of Table 34.2 in Chapter 34, calculate the sums of each X_1 and X_2 pair. Correlate these sums with the Y scores. Compare the square of this correlation with $R^2_{y.12} = .51$ ($r^2 = .70^2 = .49$). Since the two values are quite close, why shouldn't we simply use the averages of the independent variables and not bother with the complexity of multiple regression analysis?

5. The following lists several interesting studies that have used multiple regression, path analysis, and discriminant analysis effectively. Read one or two of them carefully. Those marked with an asterisk are perhaps easier than the others.

Abel, M. H. (1998). Interaction of humor and gender in moderating relationships between stress and outcomes. *Journal of Psychology, 132,* 267–276. [Uses multiple regression to study the moderating effects of humor on stress and anxiety.]

Bachman, I., & O'Malley, P. (1977). Self-esteem in young men: A longitudinal analysis of the impact of educational and occupational attainment. *Journal of Personality and Social Psychology, 35,* 365–380. [An outstanding educational study that used path analysis. Results contrary to expectation.]

Fischer, C. (1975). The city and political psychology. *American Political Science Review, 69,* 559–571. [Uses path analysis to study sense of political efficacy.]

Frederick, C. M., & Morrison, C. S. (1998). A mediational model of social physique anxiety and eating disordered behaviors. *Perceptual and Motor Skills, 86,* 139–145. [Develops a very simple and easy to understand path model relating physique anxiety, eating disorder traits, and eating disorder behavior.]

Leith, K. P., & Baumeister, R. F. (1998). Empathy, shame, guilt and narratives of interpersonal conflicts: Guilt prone people are better at perspective taking. *Journal of Personality, 66,* 11–39. [Uses multivariate analysis of variance, analysis of covariance, and path analysis to study guilt-prone people.]

Marjoribanks, K. (1972). Ethnic and environmental influences on mental abilities. *American Journal of Sociology, 78,* 323–337. [An interesting use of the addition and subtraction of R_2s to assess the relative influence of variables, especially of the environment and ethnicity.]

Onwuegbuzie, A. J. (1997). The teacher as researcher: The relationship between research anxiety and learning style in a research methodology course. *College Student Journal, 31,* 496–506. [This study uses multiple regression to determine some of the characteristics of research-anxious teachers in terms of what kind of learning style.]

Ronis, D. L., Antonakos, C. L., & Lang, W. P. (1996). [Usefulness of multiple equations for predicting preventive oral health behaviors. *Health Education Quarterly, 23,* 512–527. [Discusses the results of a study using canonical correlation. They found three functions to account for three oral health behaviors.]

Vincke, J., & Bolton, R. (1997). Beyond the sexual model: Combining complementary cognitions to explain and predict unsafe sex among gay men. *Human Organization, 56,* 38–46. [Uses both multivariate analysis of variance and discriminant analysis to assess the pleasures and dangers of unprotected sexual practices.]

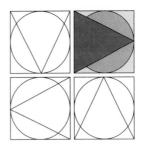

FACTOR ANALYSIS

Factor analysis is referred to by many researchers as the queen of analytic methods. This is due to its power, elegance, and closeness to the core of scientific purpose. It is, however, a method that is not free of controversy. Even though it is a powerful method, it is not a panacea for badly designed or undesigned studies. Comrey (1978) pointed out that factor analysis has been a topic of much discussion and criticism. However, despite the criticisms, its growth in usage continues. In this chapter we explore what factor analysis is and why and how it is done. We will also look at the pitfalls that a researcher may encounter if he or she is not careful when using this powerful method. In the exploration we will also examine past and current research in which factor analysis has been a central methodology.

Factor analysis serves the cause of scientific parsimony. It reduces the multiplicity of tests and measures to greater simplicity. It tells us, in effect, what tests or measures belong together—which ones virtually measure the same thing—and how much they do so. It thus reduces the number of variables with which the scientist must cope. It also helps the scientist locate and identify unities or fundamental properties underlying tests and measures. Let us say that a researcher has measured a group of people on 20 variables. Correlations between the variables are computed and summarized in the form of a correlation matrix. When a researcher examines a table of correlations between variables, it is very difficult to interpret what is really going on. It is usually difficult to find an interpretable pattern of correlations. Factor analysis is designed to take those correlations and find some order within them. The method is designed to find what the variables have in common. Even though our discussion of factor analysis in this chapter will center on the use of correlation coefficients, factor analysis is not limited to just correlational matrices. In the social, behavioral, and educational sciences, however, the correlation is the most often used index in a factor analysis.

A *factor* is a construct, a hypothetical entity, a latent variable that is assumed to underlie tests, scales, items, and, indeed, measures of almost any kind. For those behavioral science researchers who are developing scales or tests, factor analysis can be used to provide evidence as to the absence or presence of validity. A number of factors have been found to underlie intelligence, for example: verbal ability, numerical ability, abstract reasoning, spatial reasoning, memory, and so on. Similarly, aptitude, attitude, and personality factors have been isolated and identified. Even nations and people have been factored!

Foundations

A Brief History

The development of the method called factor analysis is attributed to Charles Spearman. In 1904, Spearman published a 93-page article covering his theory of intelligence and the development of the method to confirm his theory that one common factor accounted for all of human intelligence. This single factor is called *g*, or general factor. Spearman analyzed tables of correlations between psychological tests and showed that there was one factor common to all of the tests. The leftover variances were attributed to the specific tests. Sometimes Spearman's theory is referred to as the two-factor theory. Spearman also linked his theory to neurophysiology by claiming that the *g* factor served the entire human cortex or nervous system. Many researchers did much work on Spearman's theory. Some of the more notable names are mentioned in Ferguson (1971) or Carroll (1993). The concept of *g* is controversial. Even though many have developed empirical studies to show that it does not exist, its usage and reference remains. One of the main antagonists of Spearman's theory was L. L. Thurstone (1947) who provided initial evidence that there were factors of intelligence and called these "Primary Mental Abilities." Although Thurstone provided ammunition against Spearman, his theory of intelligence was also shown later to be questionable.

Despite these roots, beginnings, and initial intentions of factor analysis, the methods created as a result of Spearman and Thurstone's work remain important. In their efforts to "prove" each other wrong, modern and creative methods of factor analysis emerged. Researchers are still using these methods today. Thurstone's contribution to the field is monumental. Most of modern factor analysis is the direct result of his work. Professor Andrew Comrey of UCLA once told the second author of this textbook that Thurstone (1947) laid the groundwork for about 90% of modern factor analysis. Researchers since that time have been attempting to define the last 10%. Thurstone effectively took Spearman's method of factor analysis and improved upon it. Thurstone was responsible for the development of the centroid method. Prior to the advent of the high-speed computer, factor analyses were done by hand. The centroid method provided a very good approximation to the more powerful method developed by Hotelling (1933). Hotelling's principal factor method was better suited for computers, but was extremely laborious for hand computations. For the purpose of easing interpretation of factor analytic results, Thurstone also developed the method of rotation and the concept of simple structure. Simple structure is one of the key developments within the factor analytic methodology.

In this chapter and in the next, we will try to make as few references as possible to matrix algebra. However, the discussion of factor analysis requires reference to matrices. Some explanations become easier using them. This is especially true when we discuss confirmatory factor analysis and structural equation modeling.

A Hypothetical Example

Suppose we administer six tests to a large number of seventh-grade pupils. We suspect that the six tests are measuring not six but some smaller number of variables. The tests are *vocabulary, reading, synonyms, numbers, arithmetic* (standardized test), *arithmetic* (teacher-made test). The names of these tests indicate their nature. We label them, respectively, *V, R, S, N, AS, ATM.* (The last two tests, though both arithmetic, contain different content. We assume a good reason for including both of them in our little test battery.) After the tests are administered and scored, coefficients of correlation are calculated between each test and every other test. We lay out the *r*s in a correlation matrix (usually called **R** matrix). The matrix is given in Table 34.1.

Recall that a matrix is any rectangular array of numbers (or symbols). Correlation matrices are always square and symmetric. This is because the lower half of the matrix below the main diagonal (from upper left to lower right) is the same as the upper half of the matrix. That is, the coefficients in the lower half are identical to those in the upper half, except for their arrangement. (Note that the top row is the same as the first column, the second row the same as the second column, and so on.). If we interchange the rows and the columns of the correlation matrix the resulting matrix will look identical to the original matrix. When this happens we know that the matrix is symmetrical. Also, when we interchange rows with the columns, the

◻ **TABLE 34.1** *R Matrix: Correlation Coefficients among Six Tests*

		V	R	S	N	AS	ATM
	V		.72	.63	.09	.09	.00
Cluster I	R	.72		.57	.15	.16	.09
	S	.63	.57		.14	.15	.09
	N	.09	.15	.14		.57	.63
	AS	.09	.16	.15	.57		.72
	ATM	.00	.09	.09	.63	.72	

Cluster II

resulting matrix is called a *transpose*. If we have a matrix labeled **A**, the transpose is labeled $\mathbf{A}^T$. We will make use of this concept later.

The problem before us is expressed in two questions: How many underlying variables, or factors, are there? What are the factors? They are presumed to be underlying unities behind the test performances reflected in the correlation coefficients. If two or more tests are substantially correlated, then the tests share variance. They have common factor variance. They are measuring something in common.

The first question in this case is easy to answer. There are two factors. This is indicated by the two clusters of *r*s, circled and labeled Cluster I and Cluster II in Table 36.1. Note that *V* correlates with *R*, .72; *V* with *S*, .63; and *R* with *S*, .57. *V, R,* and *S* appear to be measuring something in common. Similarly, *N* correlates with *AS*, .57, and with *ATM*, .63; and *AS* correlates with *ATM*, .72. *N, AS,* and *ATM* are measuring something in common. The tests in Cluster I, though themselves intercorrelated, are not to any great extent correlated with the tests in Cluster II. Likewise, *N, AS,* and *ATM*, though themselves intercorrelated, are not substantially correlated with the tests *V, R,* and *S*. What is measured in common by the tests in Cluster I is evidently not the same as what is measured in common by the tests of Cluster II. There appear to be two clusters or factors in the matrix. The reader should note that in this presentation, occasional oversimplifications and somewhat unrealistic examples are used. The **R** matrix of Table 34.1 is unrealistic. All the tests would be positively correlated, and the two factors would probably emerge. In addition, clusters, while similar to factors, are *not* factors. For simplicity and pedagogy, however, we risk these oversimplifications.

By inspecting the **R** matrix, we have determined that there are two factors underlying these tests. The second question (What are the factors?) is almost always more difficult. When we ask what the factors are, we seek to name them. We want *constructs* that explain the underlying unities or common factor variances of the factors. We ask what is common to the tests *V, R,* and *S,* on the one hand; and to the tests *N, AS,* and *ATM,* on the other hand. *V, R,* and *S* are vocabulary, reading, and synonym tests. All three involve words, to a large extent. Perhaps the underlying factor is *verbal ability.* We name the factor *Verbal,* or *V. N, AS,* and *ATM* all involve numerical or arithmetic operations. Suppose we named this factor *Arithmetic*. A friend points out to us that test N does not really involve arithmetic operations, since it consists mostly of manipulating numbers nonarithmetically. We overlooked this in our eagerness to name the underlying unity. Anyway, we now name the factor *Numerical*, or *Number*, or *N*. There is no inconsistency: all three tests involve numbers and numerical manipulation and operation.

Both questions have been answered: there are two factors, and they are named *Verbal, V*, and *Numerical, N*. It must be hastily and urgently pointed out, however, that neither question is ever finally answered in actual factor analytic research. This is especially true in early investigations of a field. The number of factors can change in subsequent investigations using the same tests. One of the V tests may also have some variance in common with another factor, say K. If a test measuring K is added to the matrix, a third factor may emerge. Perhaps more important, the name of a factor may be incorrect. Subsequent investigation using these V tests and other tests may show that V is not now common to all the tests. The investigator must then find another construct, another source of common factor variance. In short, factor names are tentative; they are hypotheses to be tested in further factor analyses and other kinds of research.

Factor Matrices and Factor Loadings

If a test measures only one factor, it is said to be *factorially pure*. To the extent that a test measures a factor, it is said to be *loaded* on the factor, or *saturated* with the factor. Factor analysis is not really complete unless we know whether a test is factorially pure and how saturated it is with a factor. If a measure is not factorially pure, we usually want to know what other factors pervade it. Some measures are so complex that it is difficult to tell just what they measure. A good example is teacher grades, or grade-point averages, that could consist of a number of dimensions of student performance. If a test contains more than one factor, it is said to be *factorially complex*.

Some tests and measures are factorially quite complex. The Stanford–Binet Intelligence Test, the Otis intelligence tests, and the F (authoritarianism) scale are examples. A desideratum of scientific investigation is to have pure measures of variables. If a measure of numerical ability is not factorially pure, how can we have confidence that a relation between numerical ability and school achievement, say, is really the relation we think it is? If the test measures both numerical ability and verbal reasoning, doubt is thrown upon relations studied with its help.

To solve these and other problems, we need an objective method to determine the number of factors, the tests loaded on the various factors, and the magnitude of the loadings. There are several factor analytic methods to accomplish these purposes. We discuss one of these later.

One of the final outcomes of a factor analysis is called a *factor matrix*, a table of coefficients that expresses the relations between the tests and the underlying factors. The factor matrix yielded by factor analyzing the data of Table 34.1 with the principal factor method, one of the several methods available, and subsequent factor rotation (discussed later), is given in Table 34.2. The entries in the table are called *factor loadings.* They can be written a_{ij}, meaning the loading *a* of *test i* on *factor j.* In the second line, .79 is the factor loading of test *R* on factor *A.* Some factor analysts label final solution factors I, II, . . . or I', II', and so on. In this chapter we label unrotated factors I, II, . . . and rotated (final solution) factors *A, B* ... In the fourth line, .70 is the factor loading of test *N* on factor *B.* Test *AS* has the following loadings: .10 on factor *A* and .79 on factor *B.*

Factor loadings are not difficult to interpret. They range from −1.00 through 0 to +1.00, like correlation coefficients. They are interpreted similarly. In fact, they express the correlations *between the tests and the factors.* For example, test *V* has the following correlations with factors *A* and *B*, respectively: .83 and .01. Evidently, test *V* is highly loaded on *A*, but not at all on *B.* Tests *V, R,* and *S* are loaded on *A* but not on *B.* Tests *N, AS,* and *ATM* are loaded on *B* but not on *A.* All the tests appear to be "pure."

The entries in the last column are called *communalities,* or h^2s. They are the sums-of-squares of the factor loadings of a test or variable. For example, the communality of test *R* is $(.79)^2 + (.10)^2 = .63$. The communality of a test or variable is its common factor variance. This will be explained later when we discuss factor theory.

Before going further, we should again note that this example is unrealistic. Factor matrices rarely present such a clear-cut picture. Indeed, the factor matrix of Table 34.2 was "known." The author first wrote the matrix given in Table 34.3. If this matrix is multiplied by itself, the **R** matrix of Table 34.1 (with diagonal values) will be obtained. In this case, all that is necessary to obtain **R** is to multiply each row by every other row. For example, multiply row *V* by row *R*: $(.90)(.80) + (.00)(.10) = .72$; row *V* by row *S*: $(.90)(.70) + (.00)(.10) = .63$; row *S* by row *AS*: $(.70)(.10) + (.10)(.80) = .15$; and so on. The resulting **R** matrix was then factor analyzed. This matrix multiplication operation springs from what is called the *basic equation of factor analysis:* $\mathbf{R} = \mathbf{FF^T}$, which says succinctly in matrix symbols what

▣ **TABLE 34.2** *Factor Matrix of Data from Table 34.1, Rotated Solution*[a]

Tests	A	B	h^2
V	.83	.01	.70
R	.79	.10	.63
S	.70	.10	.50
N	.10	.70	.50
AS	.10	.79	.63
ATM	.01	.83	.70

[a]See text for identification of the tests. "Significant" loadings are italicized. See also, footnotes to Table 34.5.

◙ **TABLE 34.3** *Original Factor Matrix from which the **R** Matrix of Table 36.1 was Derived*

Tests	*A*	*B*	*h²*
V	.90	.00	.81
R	.80	.10	.65
S	.70	.10	.50
N	.10	.70	.50
AS	.10	.80	.65
ATM	.00	.90	.81

was said more laboriously above. Sometimes this fundamental equation is written as $\mathbf{R} = \mathbf{AA}^\mathsf{T}$ or $\mathbf{R} = \mathbf{P\Phi P}^T + \mathbf{U}$. The last equation is the most general of the three. A thorough understanding of factor analysis requires a good understanding of matrix algebra.

It is instructive to compare Table 34.2 and Table 34.3. Note the discrepancies, which are small. That is, the fallible factor analytic method cannot perfectly reproduce the "true" factor matrix. It estimates it. In this case the fit is close because of the deliberate simplicity of the problem. Real data are not so obliging. Moreover, we never know the "true" factor matrix. If we did, there would be no need for factor analysis. We usually estimate the factor matrix from the correlation matrix. The complexity and fallibility of research data frequently make this estimation a difficult business.

Some Factor Theory

In Chapter 28 we wrote an equation that expresses sources of variance in a measure (or test):

$$V_t = V_{co} + V_{sp} + V_e \tag{34.1}$$

where V_t equals total variance of a measure; V_{co} equals common factor variance, or the variance that two or more measures share in common; V_{sp} equals specific variance, or the variance of the measure that is not shared with any other measure, that is, variance of that measure and no other; V_e equals error variance.

The common factor variance V_{co} was broken down into two sources of variance, *A* and *B*, two factors (see Equation 28.11):

$$V_{co} = V_A + V_B \tag{34.2}$$

V_A might be verbal ability variance, and V_B might be numerical ability variance. This is reasonable if we think of the sums-of-squares of factor loadings of any test:

$$b_i^2 = a_i^2 + b_i^2 + \ldots + k_i^2 \tag{34.3}$$

where $a_i^2, b_i^2, \ldots$ are the squares of the factor loadings of test i, and b_i^2 is the communality of test i. But $b_i^2 = V_{co}$. Therefore, $V(A) = a^2$ and $V(B) = b^2$, and Equation 34.2 is tied to real factor analytic operations.

But there may, of course, be more than two factors. The generalized equation is

$$V_{co} = V_A + V_B + \ldots + V_k \tag{34.4}$$

Substituting in Equation 34.1, we obtain

$$V_t = V_A + V_B + \ldots + V_k + V_{sp} + V_e \tag{34.5}$$

Dividing through by V_t we find a proportional representation:

$$\frac{V_t}{V_t} = 1.00 = \overbrace{\frac{V_A}{V_t} + \frac{V_B}{V_t} + \ldots + \frac{V_k}{V_t}}^{b^2} + \frac{V_{sp}}{V_t} + \frac{V_e}{V_t} \tag{34.6}$$

$$\underbrace{\phantom{\frac{V_A}{V_t} + \frac{V_B}{V_t} + \ldots + \frac{V_k}{V_t} + \frac{V_{sp}}{V_t}}}_{r_{tt}}$$

The b^2 and r_{tt} parts of the equation have been labeled as they were in Chapter 28. This equation has beauty. It ties tightly together measurement theory and factor theory. b^2 is the proportion of the total variance that is common factor variance. r_{tt} is the proportion of the total variance that is reliable variance. V_e/V_t is the proportion of the total variance that is error variance. In Chapter 28 an equation like this enabled us to tie reliability and validity together. Now it shows us the relation between factor theory and measurement theory. We see, in brief, that the *main problem of factor analysis is to determine the variance components of the total common factor variance.*

Take test V in Table 34.2. A glance at Equation 34.6 shows us, among other things, that the reliability of a measure is always greater than, or equal to, its communality. Test V's reliability, then, is at least .70. Suppose $r_{tt} = .80$. Since $V_t/V_t = 1.00$, we can fill in all the terms:

$$\frac{V_t}{V_t} = 1.00 = \overbrace{(.83)^2 + (.01)^2}^{b^2 = .69} + \overbrace{.11}^{V_{sp}} + \overbrace{.20}^{V_e}$$

$$\underbrace{}_{r_{tt} = .80}$$

Test V, then, has a high proportion of common factor variance and a low proportion of specific variance.

◙ FIGURE 34.1

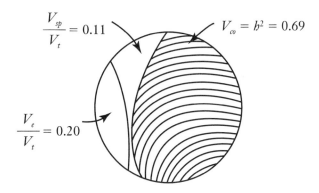

$\dfrac{V_{sp}}{V_t} = 0.11$ $V_{co} = h^2 = 0.69$

$\dfrac{V_e}{V_t} = 0.20$

The proportions can be seen clearly in a circle diagram. Let the area of the circle equal the total variance, or 1.00 (100% of the area), in Figure 34.1. The three variances have been indicated by blocking out areas of the circle. V_{co} or h^2, for example, is 69%, V_{sp} is 11%, and V_e is 20% of the total variance.

A factor analytic investigation including test V would tell us mainly about V_{co}, the common factor variance. It would tell us the proportion of the test's total variance that is common factor variance and would give us clues to its nature by telling us which other tests share the same common factor variance and which do not.

Graphical Representation of Factors and Factor Loadings

The student of factor analysis must learn to think spatially and geometrically in order to grasp the essential nature of the factor approach. There are several good ways to do this. A table of correlations can be represented by the use of vectors and the angles between them. Here we use a more common method. We treat the row entries of a factor matrix as coordinates and plot them in geometric space. In Figure 34.2 the factor matrix entries of Table 34.2 have been plotted.

The two factors, A and B, are laid out at right angles to each other. These are called *reference axes*. Appropriate factor-loading values are indicated on each of the axes. Then each test's loadings are treated as coordinates and plotted. For example, test Rs loadings are (.79, .10). Go out .79 on A and up .10 on B. This point has been indicated in Figure 34.2 by a circled letter indicating the test. Plot the coordinates of the other five tests similarly.

The factor structure can now be clearly seen. Each test is highly loaded on one factor but not on the other. They are all relatively "pure" measures of their respective factors. A seventh point has been indicated in Figure 34.2 by a circled *cross* in order to illustrate a presumed test that measures both factors. Its coordinates are (.60, .50). This means that the test is loaded on both factors: .60 on A and .50 on B. It is

⊡ **FIGURE 34.2**

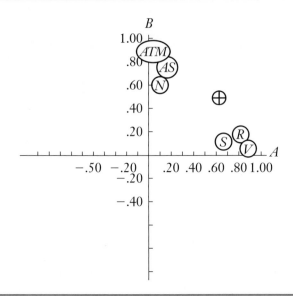

not "pure." Note that factor structures of this simplicity and clarity, where (1) the factors are orthogonal (the axes at right angles to each other), (2) the test loadings are substantial and "pure," (almost no tests loaded on two or more factors), and (3) only two factors, are not common. Again, the reader should be aware that our example is not with real data.

Most published factor analytic studies report more than two factors. Four, five, even nine, ten, and more factors have been reported. Graphical representation of such factor structures in one graph is, of course, not possible. Factor analysts customarily plot factors two at a time, though it is possible to plot three at a time. It must be admitted, however, that it is difficult to visualize or keep in mind complex *n*-dimensional structures. One therefore visualizes two-dimensional structures and generalizes to *n* dimensions algebraically. A fortunate aspect of computer factor analysis programs is that such factor plotting is easily possible. Comrey (see Comrey & Lee, 1992) has written a graphical computer program that allows the user to plot factors two at a time.

Extraction and Rotation of Factors, Factor Scores, and Second-Order Factor Analysis

Modern factor analysis as defined by Thurstone (1947) involves a number of steps. The first step is factor extraction. Many of the methods yield factors that are uninterpretable. Hence these "unrotated" factors are rotated for purposes of interpretation.

There are a number of methods of extracting factors from a correlation matrix including: principal factor, centroid, maximum likelihood, minimum residual, image, power vectored, and alpha. We cannot discuss all these methods here. Our purpose is elementary basic understanding. We therefore limit our discussion to one of the methods. The method that is used the most at present and widely available at computer installations is the principal factor method.

The reader may ask: Why not use a comparatively simple cluster method like the inspection approach used earlier, instead of a complex method like the principal factor method? Cluster methods can be used (see Lee & MacQueen, 1980) and have been recommended. They depend on our identifying clusters and presumed factors by finding interrelated groups of correlation coefficients or other measures of relation. In Table 34.1, the clusters are easy to locate. In most **R** matrices, however, the clusters cannot be so easily identified. More objective and precise methods are needed.

In this section we examine the major steps involved in factor analysis. We will be unable to present all the necessary details to be complete. Instead, we hope to give the reader the essence of factor analysis and refer the details to very good texts. We will give brief reviews of these texts in the Study Suggestions.

The major steps in studies using factor analysis are summarized as follows:

Data → Correlation → Factor Extraction → Factor Rotation

The Communality and Number of Factors Problems

Prior to choosing which method to use in extracting the factors, the researcher must decide on what to put in the diagonal cells of the correlation matrix as communality estimates and how many factors to extract. Comrey (1978) points out that these are the two most difficult decisions a researcher must make when doing a factor analysis. What one uses as communality estimates and how many factors to extract, can have a major impact on the final solution (see Comrey & Lee, 1992; Lee & Comrey, 1979; Lee, 1979). If the correct communalities are known and used in the factor analysis, the correct number of factors will be obtained using the principal factor method described in the next section. Hence, when a researcher uses the principal factor method, the communality estimates play an important role in determining the obtained factor solution and should be chosen carefully. Computer programs have definitely made computing factor solutions easier. However, one of their major drawbacks is that there are default settings for the programs in terms of how the factor extraction is done. Hubbard and Allen (1989) have compared the factor solutions obtained from two popular computer programs using the default values. They found very different solutions. Some programs use the eigenvalue-one rule where unities are placed in the diagonal as communality estimates and all factors are extracted that have an eigenvalue equal to or greater than 1.00. Sometimes this method is referred to as *truncated principal components*. This has both intuitive and mathematical appeal since it seems to present a solution to both problems. However, Comrey and Lee (1992) have warned against the use of this method indiscriminantly. It tends to over-inflate the communalities and the factor loadings. The distortions are then further amplified by factor rotation. Yet it is still one of the most heavily used procedures. Psychological and educational tests that were developed using this method, such as the Social Skills Rating Scale (Gresham & Elliot, 1990), should be interpreted with caution. Comrey and Lee (1992) as well as Gorsuch (1983) have warned against doing "blind" factor analysis and then interpreting the results as truth. Another popular communality estimate is the squared multiple correlation, R^2. Research by Guttman (1956) has shown that this statistic is the lower bound for the communality estimates and as such could underestimate the true communality values. Others have recommended the use of the largest correlation for the variable with other variables as the initial communality estimate.

The Principal Factor Method

The principal factor method is mathematically satisfying because it yields a mathematically unique solution of a factor problem. Perhaps its major solution feature is that it extracts a maximum amount of variance as each factor is calculated. In other words, the first factor extracts the most variance, the second the next most variance, and so on. The first factor consists of weights or coefficients that will maximize the squared correlations between the variables and the factor. The contribution of the first factor is then removed from the correlation matrix. This "new" correlation matrix is then used to find coefficients of a factor that maximizes the squared correlations between the variables and the second factor. Each subsequent extracted factor will have less and less variance than the one before it. The extraction of factors ceases when the variance becomes negligible, or when the extraction process reaches the number of factors set by the researcher. Every factor extracted will consist of coefficients that are uncorrelated with the coefficients of the other factors. In other words, each factor is independent of the other factors.

To show the logic of the principal factor method without considerable mathematics is difficult. One can achieve a certain intuitive understanding of the method, however, by approaching it geometrically. Conceive tests or variables as points in *m*-dimensional space. Variables that are highly and positively correlated should be near each other and away from variables with which they do not correlate. If this reasoning is correct, there should be swarms of points in space. Each of these points can be located in the space if suitable axes are inserted into the space, one axis for each dimension of the *m* dimensions. Then any point's location is its multiple identification obtained by reading its coordinates on the *m* axes. The factor problem is to project axes through neighboring swarms of points and to so locate these axes that they "account for" as much of the variances of the variables as possible.

We can demonstrate these ideas with a simple two-dimensional example, Suppose we have five tests. These tests are situated in two-dimensional space as indicated in Figure 34.3. The closer two points are, the more they are related. The

■ FIGURE 34.3

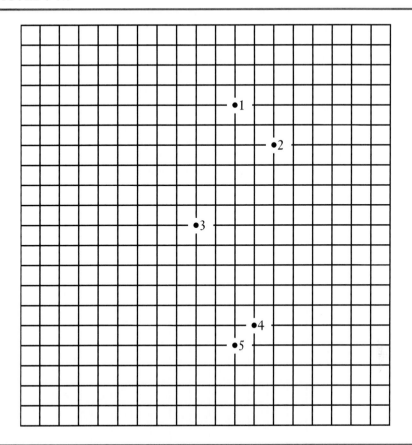

problem is to determine: (1) how many factors there are; (2) which tests are loaded on which factors; and (3) the magnitudes of the test loadings.

The problem will now be solved in two different ways, each interesting as well as instructive. First, we solve directly from the points themselves. Follow these directions. Draw a vertical line three units to the left of point 3. Draw a horizontal line one unit below point 3. Label these reference axes I and II. Now read off the coordinates of each point, for instance, point 2 is (.70, .50), point 4 is (.60, − .40). Write a "factor matrix" with these five pairs of values.

Rotate the axes orthogonally and clockwise so that axis I goes between points 4 and 5. Axis II, of course, will go between points 1 and 2. (The use of a protractor is recommended: the rotation should be approximately 40°.) Label these "new" rotated axes *A* and *B*. Cut a strip of four-to-the-inch graph paper. (The points are plotted on this size graph paper.) Count the base of each square as .10 (.10 = 1/4 inch; 10 units, of course, equal 1.00). Using the strip as a measuring device, measure the distances of the points on the new axes. For example, point 2 should be close to (.22, .83), and point 5 should be close to (.71, −.06). (It does not make much difference if there are small discrepancies.) The original (I and II) and rotated (*A* and *B*) axes and the five points are shown in Figure 34.4.

Now write both factor matrices, unrotated and rotated. They are given in Table 34.4. The problem is solved: There are two factors. Points (tests) 1 and 2 are high on factor *B*, points 4 and 5 are high on factor *A*, and point 3 has low loadings on both factors. The three questions originally asked have been answered.

This procedure is analogous to psychological factor problems. Tests are conceived as points in factor *m*-dimensional space. The factor loadings are the coordinates. The problem is to introduce appropriate reference frames or axes and then to "read off" the factor loadings. Unfortunately, in actual problems we do not know the number of factors (the dimensionality of the factor space and thus the number of axes) or the location of the points in space. These must be determined from data.

◉ **FIGURE 34.4**

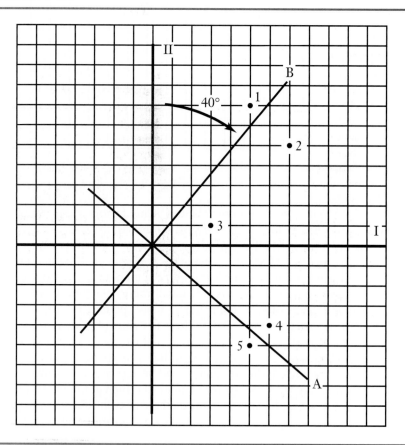

⊡ **TABLE 34.4** *Unrotated and Rotated Matrices, Point-Distance Problem*[a]

Points	Unrotated		Points	Rotated	
	I	II		A	B
1	.50	.70	1	−.07	*.86*
2	.70	.50	2	.22	*.83*
3	.30	.10	3	.17	.27
4	.60	−.40	4	*.72*	.08
5	.50	−.50	5	*.71*	−.06

[a] The substantial rotated loadings are in italics.

The above description is figurative. One does not "read off" factor loadings from reference axes; one calculates them using rather complex methods. The principal factor method actually involves the solution of simultaneous linear equations. The roots obtained from the solution are called *eigenvalues. Eigenvectors* are also obtained; after suitable transformation, they become the factor loadings. The fictitious **R** matrix of Table 34.1 was solved in this manner, yielding the factor matrix to be given later in Table 34.5. Most computer analysis programs use principal factor solutions. The student who expects to use factor analysis to any extent should study the method carefully and at least understand what it does. There is nothing quite so dangerous and self-defeating as using computer programs blindly. This is especially true in factor analysis.

Rotation and Simple Structure

Most factor extraction methods produce results in a form that is difficult or impossible to interpret. If we look at the unrotated factors in Table 34.4 we can see this. Thurstone (1947, pp. 508–509) argued that it was necessary to rotate factor matrices if one wanted to interpret them adequately. He pointed out that original factor matrices are arbitrary in the sense that an infinite number of reference frames (axes) can be found to reproduce any given **R** matrix (see Thurstone, 1947, p. 93). A principal factor matrix and its loadings account for the common factor variance of the test scores, but do not in general provide scientifically meaningful structures. It is the configurations of tests or variables in factor space that are of fundamental concern. In order to discover these configurations adequately, the arbitrary reference axes must be rotated. In other words, we assume that there are unique and "best" positions for the axes, "best" ways to view the variables in *n*-dimensional space.

There is no intention here of reifying constructs, variables, or factors. Factors are merely structures or patterns produced by covariances of measures. What is meant by "best way to view the variables" is the most parsimonious, the simplest way.

A "best" way can be predicted from theory and hypotheses. Or a "best" way may be discovered from a structure so clear and strong as to almost compel belief in its validity and "reality."

Among Thurstone's important contributions, his invention of the ideas of simple structure and factor axes rotation are perhaps the most important. With them he laid down relatively clear guidelines for achieving psychologically meaningful and interpretable factor analytic solutions. In Table 34.2 we reported a factor matrix obtained from the **R** matrix of Table 34.1. This was the final *rotated* matrix and not the matrix originally produced by the factor analysis. The *unrotated* matrix originally produced by the principal factor method is given on the left side of Table 34.5. The rotated factors are reproduced on the right side of the table. The communalities (h^2) are also given. They are the same for both matrices.

If we try to interpret the unrotated matrix on the left of the table, we run into trouble. It can be said that all the tests load substantially on a general factor I; and the second factor, II, is bipolar. (A *bipolar factor* is one that has substantial positive and negative loadings.) This amounts to saying that all the tests measure the same thing (factor I), but that the first three measure the negative aspect of whatever the second three measure (factor II). But aside from the ambiguous nature of such an interpretation, we know that the reference axes, I and II, and consequently the factor loadings, are arbitrary. Look at the factor plot of Figure 34.2. There are two clearly defined clusters of tests clinging closely to the axes A and B. There is *no* general factor here, neither is there a bipolar factor. The second major problem of factor analysis, therefore, is to discover a unique and compelling solution or position of the reference axes.

Plot the loadings of I and II, and we "see" the original unrotated structure. This has been done in Figure 34.5. Now swing the axes so that I goes as near as possible to the V, R, and S points and, at the same time, II goes as near as possible to the N, AS, and ATM points. A rotation of 45° will do nicely. We then obtain essentially the

⊡ **TABLE 34.5** *Unrotated and Rotated Factor Matrices,* **R** *Matrix from Table 36.1*[a]

	Unrotated		Rotated		
Tests	I	II	*A*	*B*	*h²*
V	.60	−.58	*.83*	.01	.70
R	.63	−.49	*.79*	.10	.63
S	.56	−.43	*.70*	.10	.50
N	.56	.43	.10	*.70*	.50
AS	.63	.49	.10	*.79*	.63
ATM	.60	.58	.01	*.83*	.70

[a] Significant loadings > 2.30 are italicized

◉ FIGURE 34.5

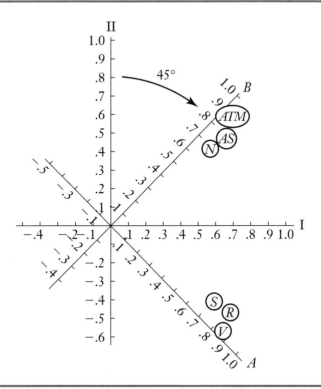

structure of Figure 34.2. That is, the new rotated positions of the axes and the positions of the six tests are the same as the positions of the axes and tests of Figure 34.2. The structure simply leans to the right. Turn the figure so that the *B* of the *B* axis points directly up and this becomes clear. It is now possible to read off the new rotated factor loadings on the rotated axes. Since the axes are kept at a 90° angle, this is called an *orthogonal* rotation.

This example, though unrealistic, may help the reader understand that factor analysts search for the unities that presumably underlie test performances. Spatially conceived, they search out the relations among variables "out there" in multidimensional factor space. Through knowledge of the empirical relations among tests or other measures, they probe in factor space with reference axes until they find the unities or relations among relations—if they exist.

Significant loadings ($\geq$ .30) are italicized. Note that the *A* and *B* vectors are reversed in this table. The h^2s calculated from the unrotated and rotated values are differ slightly, owing to errors of rounding, For example, $.60^2 + .58^2 = .70$ and $.83^2 + .01^2 = .69$. The correct computer values have been used in the table (and in Table 34.2).

To guide rotations, Thurstone laid down five principles or rules of simple structure. The rules are applicable to both orthogonal and oblique rotations, although Thurstone emphasized the oblique case. (Oblique rotations are those in which the angles between axes are acute or obtuse.) The simple structure principles are as follows:

1. Each row of the factor matrix should have at least one loading close to zero.
2. For each column of the factor matrix there should be at least as many variables with zero or near-zero loadings as there are factors.
3. For every pair of factors (columns) there should be several variables with loadings in one factor (column) but not in the other.
4. When there are four or more factors, a large proportion of the variables should have negligible (close to zero) loadings on any pair of factors.
5. For every pair of factors (columns) of the factor matrix there should be only a small number of variables with appreciable (non-zero) loadings in both columns.

In effect, these criteria call for as "pure" variables as possible; that is, each variable loaded on as few factors as possible, and *as many zeros as possible in the rotated factor matrix*. In this way, the simplest possible interpretation of the factors can be achieved. In other words, rotation to achieve simple structure is a fairly objective way to achieve variable simplicity or to reduce variable complexity.

To understand this, imagine an ideal solution in which simple structure is "perfect." It might look like this, say, in a three-factor solution:

Tests	A	B	C
1	X	0	0
2	X	0	0
3	X	0	0
4	0	X	0
5	0	X	0
6	0	X	0
7	0	0	X
8	0	0	X
9	0	0	X

The Xs indicate substantial factor loadings, 0s near-zero loadings. Of course, such "perfect" factor structures are rare. It is more likely that some of the tests have loadings on more than one factor. Still, good approximations to simple structure have been achieved, especially in well-planned and executed factor analytic studies. Comrey (1978) points out that simple structure will work well if the study is well-designed with several well-defined factors each measured by several pure factor measures that are normally distributed and with high reliability. However, Comrey also states that undesigned or poorly designed studies will have complex variables. And as a result the solution will not fit simple structure very well.

Before leaving the subject of factor rotations it must be pointed out that there are a number of rotational methods. The two main types of rotation are called "orthogonal" and "oblique." *Orthogonal* rotations maintain the independence of factors; that is, the angles between the axes are kept at 90°. If we rotate factors I and II orthogonally, for instance, we swing both axes together, maintaining the right angle between them. This means that the correlation between the factors is zero. The rotation just performed in Figure 34.5 was orthogonal. If we had four factors, we would rotate I and II, I and III, I and IV, II and III, and so on, maintaining right angles between each pair of axes. Some researchers prefer to rotate orthogonally. Others insist that orthogonal rotation is unrealistic, that actual factors are not usually uncorrelated, and that rotations should conform to psychological "reality."

Rotations in which the factor axes are allowed to form acute or obtuse angles are called *oblique*. Obliqueness, of course, means that factors are correlated. There is no doubt that factor structures can be better fitted with oblique axes and the simple structure criteria better satisfied. Some researchers might object to oblique factors because of the possible difficulty of comparing factor structures from one study to another. We leave this controversial subject with two remarks. First, the type of rotation seems to be a matter of taste. Second, the reader should understand both types of rotation to the extent that he or she can interpret both kinds of factors, and be particularly careful when confronted with the results of oblique solutions. They contain peculiarities and subtleties not present in orthogonal solutions.

The factor rotation that we have seen so far is the graphic approach. Before high-speed digital computers, researchers who did factor analyses used this graphical or hand method of rotation. The imprecise nature of graphical rotations through visual approximation was one of the major criticisms of the method. However, when computers became more accurate and reliable in the mid-1950s, a number of analytic rotational methods emerged where the rotations were performed using a mathematical formula. The most popular of these was the one developed by Henry Kaiser (1958) called Varimax. Virtually every computer package that performs factor analyses today uses this method of rotation. Many of those programs have Varimax as the default rotational method. In Kaiser's obituary, Jensen and Wilson (1994) stated that Kaiser's 1958 article is the third most cited article in the psychological literature. Varimax works very well in approximating simple structure in well-designed factor analytic studies. If a researcher is looking for a general factor, Varimax does not fare as well. The goal of Varimax is to disperse the maximum amount of variance across the factors while simultaneously trying to obtain simple structure. If the researcher includes too many factors for Varimax, then a possible result is the artificial inflation of some small factors. Hence, Varimax is sensitive to the number of factors used in rotation.

If a researcher is interested in finding a general factor, the best orthogonal method available is Comrey's (1967) Tandem Criteria. The Tandem Criteria consists of two steps and each step is based on a different principle.

Principle 1: If two variables are correlated, they should appear on the same factor. (Criterion 1)

Principle 2. If two variables are not correlated, they should not appear on the same factor. (Criterion 2)

It is Criterion 1, or Principle 1, that is of interest to us if we seek a general factor. Criterion 1 attempts to spread out the variance from the larger factors to the smaller ones, while satisfying Principle 1 at the same time. If a general factor exists, the variables that are correlated with one another will be retained as much as possible on the same factor rather than being spread around.

Just as there are many factor extraction methods, there are many rotational methods in addition to the ones we have mentioned thus far. There are different methods for orthogonal rotation as well as oblique. The reader can consult Gorsuch (1983) and Comrey and Lee (1992) for a list.

Second-Order Factor Analysis

Second-order factor analysis is a highly important but neglected approach to complex data analysis and hypothesis testing. When factors are rotated obliquely, there are correlations between factors. Earlier in this chapter we mentioned the fundamental equation of factor analysis. One version of it was $R = P\Phi P^T + U$. The Φ matrix contains the correlations between factors. In orthogonal rotations, the Φ matrix is not used since the factors are uncorrelated. In doing second-order factor analysis in the traditional manner, this Φ matrix is factor analyzed. For the sake of completeness, the P matrix is the factor pattern matrix. It contains the factor loadings. P^T is its transpose and U is the matrix containing the uniqueness of each variable.

In a provocative factor analytic and canonical correlation study of the redundancy present in student test scores, Lohnes and Marshall (1965) extracted two factors from 21 ability and achievement tests. The unrotated factor loadings of eight of their measures, four ability tests and four grades (English, arithmetic, social studies, science), have been plotted in Figure 34.6. The axes have been rotated obliquely so that they will go through the two clusters of loadings. There is an acute angle of about 39° between the rotated axes, now labeled I′ and II′. Any angle other than 90° between axes means correlation between factors. In this case, the correlation is approximately .78, quite high.

Imagine this situation multiplied over six, eight, or 10 factors: there would be a set of correlations among the factors. Factor analyze these correlations and we have second-order factor analysis, which is a method of finding the factors behind the factors. The famous g of intelligence testing is evidently a second-order factor or higher. Whenever large numbers of ability tests are factor analyzed, the correlations among the tests are usually positive. Factor analyze them and some such pattern, as in Figure 34.6, though more complex, emerges. Calculate the correlations between the factors and again factor analyze and a single factor, perhaps g, may emerge.

Additional information on second-order and higher-order factor analysis can be found in Gorsuch (1983). The researcher can go through the process of finding

◨ FIGURE 34.6

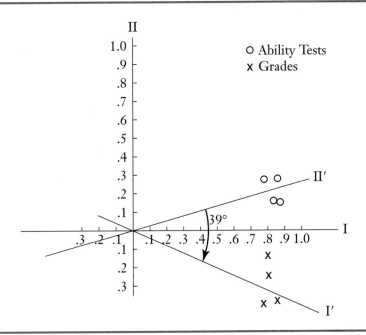

first-order oblique factors and then factor analyzing the correlation matrix of factors, but there is an alternative approach. With the availability of computer programs such as LISREL, EQS, and AMOS, the researcher can perform a higher-order factor analysis rather easily and in one step. Comrey and Lee (1992) show how to do a second-order factor analysis using EQS.

Factor Scores

While second-order factor analysis is more oriented toward basic and theoretical research, another technique of factor analysis, so-called factor scores or measures, is eminently practical, though not without theoretical significance. *Factor scores* are measures of individuals on factors. Suppose, like Lohnes and Marshall (1965), we found two factors underlying 21 ability and grade measures. Instead of using all 21 scores of groups of children in research, why not use just two scores calculated from the factors? Lohnes and Marshall recommend just this, pointing out the redundancy in the usual scores of pupils. These factor scores are, in effect, weighted averages, weighted according to the factor loadings.

Here is an oversimplified example. Suppose the factor matrix of Table 34.2 were actual data and that we want to calculate the A and B factor scores of an individual. The raw scores of one individual on the six tests, say, are: 7, 5, 5, 3, 4, and 2. We multiply these scores by the related factor loadings, first for factor A and then for factor B, as follows:

A: $FA = (.83)(7) + (.79)(5) + (.70)(5) + (.10)(3) + (.10)(4) + (.01)(2) = 13.98$

B: $FB = (.01)(7) + (.10)(5) + (.10)(5) + (.70)(3) + (.79)(4) + (.83)(2) = 7.99$

The individual's "factor scores" are $FA = 13.98$ and $FB = 7.99$. We can, of course, calculate other individuals' "factor scores" similarly.

This is not the best way to calculate factor scores. Comrey and Lee (1992), Gorsuch (1983), and Harman (1976) present alternative methods for computing factor scores. They also discuss the pros and cons of each method. However, the example presented here was invented just to convey the idea of such scores as weighted sums or averages, the weights being the factor loadings. In any case, the method, though not extensively used in the past, has great potential for complex behavioral research. Instead of using many separate test scores, fewer factor scores can be used. An excellent real example is described by Mayeske (1970) who participated in the reanalysis of the data from the highly influential Coleman, Campbell, Hobson, et al. (1966) report, *Equality of Educational Opportunity.*

Research Examples

Most factor analytic studies have factored intelligence, aptitude, and personality tests and scales, the tests or scales themselves being intercorrelated and factor analyzed. The Thurstone example discussed below is an excellent example; indeed, it is a classic. Persons, or the responses of persons, can also be factored. The variables entered into the correlation and factor matrices, in fact, can be tests, scales, persons, items, concepts, or whatever can be intercorrelated. The studies outlined below have been selected not to represent factor analytic investigations in general, but rather to familiarize the student with different uses of factor analysis.

The Comrey Personality Scales

Comrey's (1970) work on personality research can serve as one of the best examples on the use of factor analysis. The Comrey Personality Scales, also known as the CPS, is an inventory of factored personality traits. This taxonomy of personality traits was developed over a period of 15 years. It was originally inspired by the discrepancies between well-known authors of personality tests and personality theorists. What began as an endeavor to resolve the differences between the personality theorists ended with the emergence of the Comrey Personality Scales. The CPS shared some of the characteristics of the other tests but it is distinct from them.

In order to obtain a stable factor solution and control of the factor hierarchy, Comrey developed a unit of measurement called the "Factored Homogeneous Item Dimension" (FHID), which was developed to alleviate some of the problems experienced in factoring items. One problem concerns the unreliability associated with single items. The other deals with the extraction of item factors that are low-level factors consisting of items that may be similar in wording or other distinguishing feature. These low-level, item-factors don't usually give the researcher much information on the underlying personality trait. The FHID is no more than a sum of the scores for items that define the FHID. Since the FHID is a sum, it is more reliable than any single item.

A factor analysis of the FHIDs yields eight factors. The names of these factors are T—Trust versus Defensiveness; O—Orderliness versus Lack of Compulsion; C—Social Conformity versus Rebelliousness; A—Activity versus Lack of Energy; S—Emotional Stability versus Neuroticism; E—Extraversion versus Introversion; M—Mental Toughness versus Sensitivity; and P—Empathy versus Egocentrism.

Additional information on the steps and procedures on developing the CPS can be found in Comrey and Lee (1992), Comrey (1980), and in Comrey (1988). Comrey and his associates have over the years from the 1970s to the 1990s validated this eight-factor structure in a number of different cultures and different countries. Comrey's ongoing research on the CPS demonstrates all the right steps a researcher takes in doing a factor analytic study.

Thurstone Factorial Study of Intelligence

Thurstone and Thurstone (1941), in their monumental work on intelligence factors and their measurement, factor analyzed 60 tests plus the three variables Chronological Age, Mental Age, and Sex. The analysis was based on the test responses of 710 eighth-grade pupils to the 60 tests. It revealed essentially the same set of so-called primary factors that had been found in previous studies.

The Thurstones chose the three best tests for each of seven of the 10 primary factors. Six of these tests seemed to have stability at differing age levels sufficient for practical school use. They then revised and administered these tests to 437 eighth-grade schoolchildren. The main purpose of the study was to check the factor structure of the tests. In other words, they predicted that the same primary factors of intelligence put into the 21 tests would emerge from a new factor analysis on a new sample of children.

Fluid and Crystallized Intelligence

One of the most active, important, and controversial problems of behavioral scientific and practical interest is the nature of mental abilities. Different theories with differing amounts and kinds of evidence to support them have been propounded by some of the ablest psychologists of the century: Spearman, Thurstone, Burt, Thorndike, Guilford, Cattell, and others. There can be no doubt whatever of the high scientific and practical importance of the problem. We have alluded, if only briefly, to the work and thinking of Thurstone and Guilford. We now describe, also briefly, one among the many factor analytic studies of Cattell (1963).

The famous general factor of intelligence, *g*, can be shown to be a second-order factor that runs through most tests of mental ability. Cattell believes, in effect, that there are two *g*s, or two aspects of *g*: crystallized and fluid. *Crystallized intelligence* is exhibited by cognitive performances in which "skilled judgment habits" have become fixed or crystallized owing to the earlier application of general learning ability to such performances. The well-known verbal and number factors are examples. *Fluid* *intelligence*, on the other hand, is exhibited by performances characterized more by adaptation to new situations, the "fluid" application of general ability, so to speak. Such ability is more characteristic of creative behavior than is crystallized intelligence. If tests are factor analyzed and the correlations among the factors found are themselves factored (second-order factor analysis), then both crystallized and fluid intelligence should emerge as second-order factors.

Cattell administered Thurstone's primary abilities tests and a number of his own mental ability and personality tests to 277 eighth-grade children, factor analyzed the 44 variables, and rotated the obtained 22 factors (probably too many) to simple structure. The correlations among these factors were themselves factored, yielding eight second-order factors. (Recall that oblique rotations yield factors that are correlated.) Although Cattell included a number of personality variables, we concentrate only on the first two factors: fluid intelligence and crystallized intelligence. He reasoned that Thurstone's tests, since they measure crystallized cognitive abilities, should load on one general factor, and that his own culture-fair tests, since they measure fluid ability, should load on another factor. They did. The two sets of factor loadings are given in Table 34.6, together with the names of the tests. The two factors were also correlated positively ($r = .47$), as predicted.

TABLE 34.6 *Part of Second-Order Factor Matrix (Cattell Fluid and Crystallized Intelligence Study)*[a]

	$F_1(gf)$	$F_2(gc)$
Thurstone Tests:		
Verbal	.15	.46
Spatial	.32	.14
Reasoning	.08	.50
Number	.05	.59
Fluency	.07	.09
Cattell Tests:		
Series	.35	.43
Classification	.63	−.02
Matrices	.50	.10
Topology	.51	.09

[a]*gf* = general factor, fluid; *gc* = general factor, crystallized. Italics supplied by the author (FNK). These are only two of Cattell's eight factors.

This study demonstrates the power of an astute combination of theory, test construction, and factor analysis. Similar to Guilford's equally astute conceptualization and analysis of convergent, divergent, and other factors mentioned earlier, it is a significant contribution to psychological knowledge of an extremely complex and important subject. However, in order to get a complete view, one should also read Humphreys's (1967) article that critiques Cattell's theory.

Confirmatory Factor Analysis

The methods of factor analysis described up to this point represent traditional procedures that are now commonly referred to as "exploratory factor analysis," or EFA. Newer methods with a stronger base in statistical hypothesis testing theory have been developed. These newer methods are referred to as "confirmatory factor analysis." However, there are a few variations of confirmatory factor analysis. There are the earlier ones based on EFA and the newer ones based on a stricter statistical theory. We will refer to the newer approaches as CFA.

Earlier in this chapter, it was emphasized that exploratory factor analytic methods are most powerful when employed in a hypothesis-testing manner. That is, hypotheses are developed about the factors to be found in a given domain and which variables measure them. Several variables are chosen for each hypothesized factor that should provide relatively pure factor measures of that factor. Data are collected for a large sample and factor analyzed to see how well the obtained factors and the variables loaded on them correspond to the originally hypothesized factor structure. On the basis of the first analysis, revisions are made in the hypothesis and in the variables designed to measure each factor, and the study is repeated. This process is continued programmatically until the factor structure that emerges corresponds reasonably well to the factor structure hypothesized in advance.

This approach represents the earlier type of confirmatory factor analysis in which the number of factors that emerges from the analysis is not restricted to a preconceived number. If the "correct" number happens to be what was hypothesized, fine, but it is not prespecified. Further, the loadings are allowed to fall where they may, rather than being forced to conform as much as possible to a prespecified pattern. In particular, large numbers of parameters are not forced to zero. The proportion of variance attributed to unique factors for each variable emerges as an end result of the analysis rather than being a parameter to be estimated, per se. Thus, in EFA, one can evaluate how well the obtained solution fits a preconceived factor pattern but without using powerful optimization techniques to force a fit that may hold up poorly with new data.

Some of these earlier EFA confirmatory factor analysis approaches are called *Procrustean* solutions. (see Comrey & Lee, 1992). This approach can take various forms. One can rotate a given unrotated matrix as closely as possible to a target matrix, either orthogonal or oblique. The target matrix could be a hypothesized matrix based on theory or on expectations developed from previous research. Least-squares methods are typically employed to find the transformation matrix that will accomplish the desired rotations. The Verba and Nie (1972) study is an example of a confirmatory factor analysis done using this approach.

These earlier methods of confirmatory factor analysis probably will become less popular, now that the newer methods can perform the same kind of task in most cases and also provide a statistical test of goodness-of-fit, along with indications on how to improve the model.

These newer methods, which we refer to as CFA, are based on the work of Lawley (1940). Lawley introduced the method of maximum likelihood to factor analysis and later expanded it (see Lawley & Maxwell, 1971). Gorsuch (1983) points out that CFA has its roots in the Maxwell–Lawley Maximum Likelihood factor analysis method. These newer methods are generally noted by the absence of factor rotation. CFA is actually a special case of a more general set of statistical analysis methods that are called *covariance structure analysis*. This section provides an introduction to CFA and shows how it differs from EFA.

In its present form, CFA is attributed by many to Joreskog and his associates (Joreskog, 1967, 1969, 1970; Joreskog & Goldberger, 1972) although Bock and Bargmann (1966) suggested something similar at an earlier date. The Bock and Bargmann procedure requires the researcher to specify all of the parameters in the factor-loading matrix, the matrix of correlations among the factors, and the unique variance matrix. Using these a priori specified matrices, an estimated correlation or covariance matrix is created. This matrix is then compared to the sample correlation or covariance matrix via a goodness-of-fit statistic such as the Bartlett test (see Morrison, 1967). This procedure is generally difficult to carry out unless the researcher knows what initial matrix values would be appropriate. Bernstein (1988) refers to this as the "weak constraint solution."

Joreskog (1969) recognized that only some, but not all, of the parameters could be estimated. Joreskog's development allows the researcher to specify some of the parameters and allow the others to be estimated from the data. These modifications made Joreskog's method an important improvement over previous procedures. The actual computational work for doing a confirmatory factor analysis is done via a computer program. Currently the programs of choice are LISREL, EQS, and AMOS. All three of these computer programs are used for covariance structure analysis. Each uses a slightly different algorithm for the computations. With each new program release, it gets easier to use.

As with EFA, however, proper use of such CFA methods as LISREL, EQS, and AMOS require the researcher to have a thorough knowledge of the area being studied and what represents a "good" hypothesis concerning the underlying factor structure. It is not a method that can be applied successfully to a large body of data with many variables where the investigator has no idea about what the underlying factor structure might be.

Earlier in this chapter we discussed the correlation matrix. This matrix or table contains the correlation coefficient of every variable with every other variable. In matrix notation this is written as **R**. In order to understand CFA, we need to reexamine the fundamental equation of factor analysis that we presented earlier. This equation was

$$\mathbf{R} = \mathbf{P}\Phi\mathbf{P}^\mathrm{T} + \mathbf{U}$$

The **P** matrix or table contains the factor loadings. It is also referred to as the factor pattern matrix. If we rewrite this matrix so that the rows of the matrix are interchanged with the columns of the matrix, that transformed matrix is called the transpose of **P** and is written as **P**ᵀ. The Φ matrix tells us how much the factors are correlated with one another. **U** represents the amount of uniqueness within each variable.

The goal is to find the values for **P**, Φ, and **U** that best reproduces the correlation matrix **R**. The reproduced correlation matrix is denoted as **R′**. Hence we have our factor analysis equation:

$$\mathbf{R'} = \mathbf{P}\,\Phi\,\mathbf{P}^\mathrm{T} + \mathbf{U}$$

An acceptable solution for **P**, Φ, and **U** will be one where **R′** and **R** differ by a very small amount. In other words, the values within these matrices are found so that **R** and **R′** have a good fit. One of the more popular goodness-of-fit indices is the normed fit index by Bentler & Bonnet (1980). There are a number of goodness-of-fit statistics that are generally employed (see Comrey & Lee, 1992, chapter 12).

In developing the CFA model, the researcher must choose which values within the **P**, Φ, and **U** matrices are to be fixed and those which are to be estimated. Constraints can be imposed on certain values, such as by specifying a range of values within which they must fall. These values are also called *parameters.*

Structural equation approaches to confirmatory factor analysis as implemented through LISREL and EQS are powerful new factor analytic procedures that often may represent the method of choice in a given situation. They are not the only approaches, however, that could be employed; and in many cases, other methods may be preferred.

Whatever method researchers may find to be the most appropriate for their data, it is clear that factor analysis has undergone a major revolution in recent years. Powerful new methods are now available that dramatically expand research workers' capacity to examine the implications of their data. It must be emphasized, however, that these newer methods should be viewed as complementing rather than supplanting older EFA methods that may continue to be the most effective procedures for dealing with many data analysis situations. For the foreseeable future, therefore, students of factor analysis will need to become familiar with both EFA and CFA methods.

Research Example Using Confirmatory Factor Analysis

The article by Keith (1997) provides a number of research examples where CFA is applied to problems within school psychology. This outstanding article is easy to read, well written, and highly recommended to those looking for good examples of where confirmatory factor analysis can be used. Keith tests the structure of a number of psychological tests to determine if their claims are true using confirmatory factor analysis. He gives a complete explanation of the model to be tested and the goodness-of-fit statistics provided by confirmatory factor analysis.

◉ **TABLE 34.7** *Theoretical Structure of the KAIT*

Fluid Intelligence	Crystallized Intelligence	Delayed Recall
Rebus Learning	Definitions	Rebus Delayed Recall
Logical Steps	Auditory Comprehension	Auditory Delayed Recall
Mystery Codes	Double Meanings	
Memory for Block Designs	Famous Faces	

In one such demonstration, Keith tested the claims of the Kaufman Adult Intelligence Test (KAIT). The KAIT consists of 10 subtests. Four of the subtests are designed to measure the fluid part of intelligence (gf), another four measures the crystallized part of intelligence (gc) and two tests are designed to measure Delayed Recall. The fluid and crystallized components of intelligence were mentioned earlier when we discussed Cattell's theory of intelligence. That theory was later modified by John Horn (See Cattell, 1987; Horn & Cattell, 1966) and is now called the Horn–Cattell theory of intelligence. The fluid and crystallized parts of intelligence are only two parts of the complete theory. Delayed recall measures the test-taker's memory of material learned in the early parts of the test. Table 34.7 presents the theoretical structure or construct of the KAIT.

Using the fundamental equation of factor analysis $\mathbf{R} = \mathbf{P}\mathbf{\Phi}\mathbf{P}^T + \mathbf{U}$, the parameters within these matrices can be designated as the following:

$$
\Phi = \begin{array}{c} \\ F1 \\ F2 \\ F3 \end{array}
\begin{array}{ccc} F1 & F2 & F3 \\ \end{array}
\left[\begin{array}{ccc}
1.00 & & \\
* & 1.00 & \\
* & * & 1.00
\end{array} \right]
$$

$$
\mathbf{P} = \begin{array}{c} \\ X_1 \\ X_2 \\ X_3 \\ X_4 \\ X_5 \\ X_6 \\ X_7 \\ X_8 \\ X_9 \\ X_{10} \end{array}
\begin{array}{ccc} F1 & F2 & F3 \\ \end{array}
\left[\begin{array}{ccc}
* & 0 & 0 \\
* & 0 & 0 \\
* & 0 & 0 \\
* & 0 & 0 \\
0 & * & 0 \\
0 & * & 0 \\
0 & * & 0 \\
0 & * & 0 \\
0 & 0 & * \\
0 & 0 & *
\end{array} \right]
$$

$$
\mathbf{U} = \begin{array}{c}
\begin{array}{cccccccccc}
X_1 & X_2 & X_3 & X_4 & X_5 & X_6 & X_7 & X_8 & X_9 & X_{10}
\end{array} \\
\begin{array}{c}
X_1 \\ X_2 \\ X_3 \\ X_4 \\ X_5 \\ X_6 \\ X_7 \\ X_8 \\ X_9 \\ X_{10}
\end{array}
\left[\begin{array}{cccccccccc}
* & & & & & & & & & \\
0 & * & & & & & & & & \\
0 & 0 & * & & & & & & & \\
0 & 0 & 0 & * & & & & & & \\
0 & 0 & 0 & 0 & * & & & & & \\
0 & 0 & 0 & 0 & 0 & * & & & & \\
0 & 0 & 0 & 0 & 0 & 0 & * & & & \\
0 & 0 & 0 & 0 & 0 & 0 & 0 & * & & \\
* & 0 & 0 & 0 & 0 & 0 & 0 & 0 & * & \\
0 & 0 & 0 & 0 & 0 & * & 0 & 0 & 0 & *
\end{array}\right]
\end{array}
$$

The asterisks in every matrix indicate the parameters to be estimated by the data. In the Φ matrix, the asterisks are the correlations between the factors. In the $\mathbf{P}$ matrix, the asterisks are the factor loadings; and in the $\mathbf{U}$ matrix, the asterisks are for the correlations between the variables. In the Φ matrix, the diagonal values are fixed at 1.00. In the $\mathbf{P}$ matrix, the desired solution would have simple structure. The nonmarker variables are forced to have values of zero. In the $\mathbf{U}$ matrix, there is a unique variance for each of the 10 variables. They receive asterisks also because they will be estimated by the data. In this particular model, Keith states that Rebus Learning (Variable 1) may be correlated with Rebus Delayed Recall (Variable 9) and that Auditory Delayed Recall (Variable 10) would be related to Auditory Comprehension (Variable 6). These correlations can also be estimated from the data and as such receive asterisks in the $\mathbf{U}$ matrix for those values. When we refer to the "data," we are talking about the scores from participants on the 10 variables and the matrix of intercorrelations for those 10 variables.

Once we have set up our model and what parameters are to be estimated, we can write the proper control commands for computer programs such as EQS, LISREL, and AMOS. Problems of this nature are far too laborious to be done by hand.

Keith (1997) presents the model and the estimates in the form of a path diagram. Path diagrams, as we saw earlier, are useful conceptual and visual models for problems in confirmatory factor analysis and structural equation modeling.[1]

Keith found that the goodness-of-fit statistics indicate that the KAIT model fits the observed data. Keith presents six such statistics for goodness-of-fit and gives an explanation of them. The chi-square test that we have seen in past chapters can be used as a goodness-of-fit statistic; however, it is affected by changes in sample sizes. There are others that are more suitable.

This is only one such model demonstrated by Keith. His paper goes on to show several different variations of models that can be tested. Keith states that there

---

[1]Structured equation modeling is an alternative set of terms for analysis of covariance structure.

are many more models and problems that CFA can perform. Just as Comrey and Lee (1992) show how to test a hypothesized factor structure in two separate samples simultaneously, Keith shows how one can test the similarities of factors across different intelligence tests (e.g., Wechsler Intelligence Scale for Children or WISC and the Kaufman Assessment Battery for Children or K-ABC).

Factor Analysis and Scientific Research

Factor analysis has two basic purposes: to explore variable areas in order to identify the factors presumably underlying the variables; and, as in all scientific work, to test hypotheses about the relations among variables. The first purpose is well-known and fairly well accepted. The second purpose is not so well-known or so well accepted.

In conceptualizing the first purpose—the exploratory or reductive purpose—one should keep construct validity and constitutive definitions in mind. Factor analysis can be conceived of as a construct validity tool. Recall that validity was defined in Chapter 28 as common-factor variance. Since the main preoccupation of factor analysis is common factor variance, by definition it is firmly tied to measurement theory. Indeed, this tie was expressed earlier in the section headed "Some Factor Theory," where equations were written to clarify factor analytic theory. (See, especially, Equation 34.6.)

Recall, too, that construct validity seeks the "meaning" of a construct through the relations between the construct and other constructs. In early chapters of this book when types of definitions were discussed, we learned that constructs could be defined in two ways: by operational definitions, and by constitutive definitions. Constitutive definitions are definitions that define constructs with other constructs. Essentially, this is what factor analysis does. It may be called a constitutive meaning method, since it enables the researcher to study the constitutive meanings of constructs—and thus their construct validity.

The measures of three variables, say, may share something in common. This something itself is a variable, presumably a more basic entity than the variables used to isolate and identify it. We give this new variable a name; in other words, we construct a hypothetical entity. Then, to inquire into the "reality" of the variable, we may systematically devise a measure of it and test its "reality" by correlating data obtained with the measure with data from other measures theoretically related to it. Factor analysis helps us check our theoretical expectations.

Part of the basic life-stuff of any science is its constructs. Old constructs continue to be used; new ones are constantly being invented. Note some of the general constructs directly pertinent to behavioral and educational research: achievement, intelligence, learning, aptitude, attitude, problem-solving ability, needs, interests, creativity, conformity. Note some of the more specific variables important in behavioral research: test anxiety, verbal ability, traditionalism, convergent thinking, arithmetic reasoning, political participation, and social class. Clearly, a large portion of scientific behavioral research effort has to be devoted to what might be called *construct investigation* or *construct validation*. This requires factor analysis.

When we talk about relations we talk about the relations between constructs: intelligence and achievement, authoritarianism and ethnocentrism, reinforcement and learning, organizational climate and administrative performance—all these are relations between highly abstract constructs or latent variables. Such constructs usually have to be defined operationally to be studied. Factors are latent variables, of course, and the major scientific factor analytic effort in the past has been to identify the factors and occasionally use the factors in measuring variables in research. Rarely have deliberate attempts been made to assess the effects of latent variables on other variables. With recent advances and developments in multivariate thinking and methodology, however, it is clear that it is now possible to assess the influence of latent variables on each other. This important development will be discussed and illustrated in Chapter 35 on analysis of covariance structures. We will find there that the scientist can obtain indices of the magnitudes and statistical significance of the effects of latent variables on other latent variables. If this is so, then factor analysis becomes even more important in identifying the latent variables or factors, and the scientist has to exercise great care in the interpretation of data in which the influences of latent variables are assessed.

Many research areas, then, can well be preceded by factor analytic explorations of the variables of the area. This does not mean that a number of tests are thrown together and given to any samples that happen to be available. Factor analytic investigations, both exploratory and hypothesis testing, have to be painstakingly planned. Variables that may be influential have to be controlled—sex, education, social class, intelligence, and so on. Variables are not put into a factor analysis just to put them in. They must have legitimate purpose. If, for instance, one cannot control intelligence by sample selection, one can include a measure of intelligence (verbal, perhaps) in the battery of measures. By identifying intelligence variance, one has in a sense controlled intelligence. One can learn whether one's measures are contaminated by response biases, by including response-bias measures in factor analyses.

The second major purpose of factor analysis is to test hypotheses. One aspect of hypothesis testing has already been hinted at: one can put tests or measures into factor analytic batteries deliberately to test the identification and nature of factors. The design of such studies has been well outlined by Comrey, Thurstone, Cattell, Guilford, and others. First, factors are "discovered." Their nature is inferred from the tests that are loaded on them. This "nature" is set up as a hypothesis. New tests are constructed and given to new samples of subjects. The data are factor analyzed. If the factors emerge *as predicted*, the hypothesis is to this extent confirmed, the factors would seem to have "reality." But this certainly does not end the matter. One still has to test, among other things, the factors' relations to other factors. One still has to place the factors, as constructs, in a nomological network of constructs.

A less well-known use of factor analysis, described by Fruchter (1966), involves using factor analysis in testing experimental hypotheses. For example, one may hypothesize that a certain method of teaching reading changes the ability patterns of pupils, so that verbal intelligence is not as potent an influence as it is with other teaching methods. An experimental study can be planned to test this hypothesis. The effects of the teaching methods can be assessed by factor analyses of a set of tests given before and after the different methods were used. Woodrow (1938) tested a similar hypothesis when he gave a set of tests before and after practice in seven tests: adding, subtracting, anagrams, and so on. He found that factor loading patterns *did* change after practice.

In considering the scientific value of factor analysis, the reader must be cautioned against attributing "reality" and uniqueness to factors. The danger of reification is great. It is easy to name a factor and then to believe there is a reality behind the name. But giving a factor a name does not give it reality. Factor names are merely attempts to epitomize the essence of factors. They are always tentative, subject to later confirmation or disconfirmation. Then, too, many things can produce factors. Anything that introduces correlation between variables "creates" a factor. Differences in sex, education, social and cultural background, and intelligence can cause factors to appear. Factors also differ—at least to some extent—with different samples. Response sets or test forms may cause factors to appear. Despite these cautions, it must be said that factors do emerge repeatedly with different tests, different samples, and different conditions. When this happens, we have fair assurance that there is an underlying variable that we are measuring successfully.

As we mentioned at the beginning of this chapter, there are serious criticisms of factor analysis. The major valid criticisms center around the indeterminancy of how many factors to extract from a correlation matrix, and the problem of how to rotate factors. Another difficulty that bothers critics and devotees alike is what can be called the "communality problem," or what quantities to put into the diagonal of the **R** matrix before factoring. In an introductory chapter, these problems cannot be discussed in detail. The reader is referred to the discussions of Cattell (1978), Comrey and Lee (1992), Cureton and D'Agostino (1983), Gorsuch (1983), Guilford (1954), Harman (1976), and Thurstone (1947). A criticism of a different order seems to bother educators and sociologists and some psychologists. This takes two or three forms that seem to boil down to distrust, sometimes profound, combined with antipathy toward the method, due to its complexity and, strangely enough, its objectivity.

The argument runs something like this. Factor analysts throw a lot of tests together into a statistical machine and spit out factors that have little psychological or sociological meaning. The factors are merely artifacts of the method. They are averages that correspond to no psychological reality, especially the psychological reality of the individual, other than that in the mind of the factor analyst. Besides, you can't get any more out of factor analysis than you put into it.

The argument is basically irrelevant. To say that factors have no psychological meaning and that they are averages is both true and untrue. If the argument were valid, no scientific constructs would have any meaning. They are all, in a sense, averages. They are all inventions of the scientist. This is simply the lot of science. The basic criterion of the "reality" of any construct, any factor, is its empirical, scientific "reality." If, after uncovering a factor, we can successfully predict relations from theoretical presuppositions and hypotheses, then the factor has "reality." There is no more reality to a factor than this, just as there is no more reality to an atom than its empirical manifestations.

The argument about only getting out what is put into a factor analysis is meaningless as well as irrelevant. No competent factor analytic investigator would ever claim more than this. But this does not mean that nothing is discovered in factor analysis. Quite the contrary. The answer is, of course, that we get nothing more out of factor analysis than we put into it, but that we do not know *all* we put into it. Neither do we know which tests or measures share common factor variance; nor do we know the relations between factors. Only study and analysis can tell us these things. We may write an attitude scale that we believe measures a single attitude. A factor analysis of the attitude items, naturally, cannot produce factors that are not in the items. But it can show us, for example, that there are two or three sources of common variance in a scale that we thought to be unidimensional. Similarly, a scale that we believe measures Authoritarianism may be shown by factor analysis to measure Intelligence, Dogmatism, and other variables.

If we examine empirical evidence rather than opinion, we must conclude that factor analysis is one of the most powerful tools yet devised for the study of complex areas of behavioral scientific concern. Indeed, factor analysis is one of the creative inventions of the 20th century, just as are intelligence testing, conditioning, reinforcement theory, the operational definition, the notion of randomness, measurement theory, research design, multivariate analysis, the computer, and theories of learning, personality, development, organizations, and society.

It is fitting that this chapter conclude with some words of a great psychological scientist, teacher, and factor analyst, Louis Leon Thurstone (1959, p.8):

> As scientists, we have the faith that the abilities and personalities of people are not so complex as the total enumeration of attributes that can be listed. We believe that these traits are made up of a smaller number of primary factors or elements that combine in various ways to make a long list of traits. It is our ambition to find some of these elementary abilities and traits.

All scientific work has this in common, that we try to comprehend nature in the most parsimonious manner. An explanation of a set of phenomena or of a set of experimental observations gains acceptance only insofar as it gives us intellectual control or comprehension of a relatively wide variety of phenomena in terms of a limited number of concepts. The principle of parsimony is intuitive for anyone who has even slight aptitude for science. The fundamental motivation of science is the craving for the simplest possible comprehension of nature, and it finds satisfaction in the discovery of the simplifying uniformities that we call scientific laws.

CHAPTER SUMMARY

1. Factor analysis examines a set of variables and determines which ones belong together. The variables that are grouped together are called a *factor*.
2. A factor is a construct, a hypothetical entity, or a latent variable that underlies measurements of any kind.

3. Charles Spearman developed factor analysis, but it was Louis Thurstone who expanded and enhanced it. Thurstone is called the "father of modern factor analysis."

4. Some of Thurstone's contributions include the centroid method of extraction, factor rotation, and simple structure. Both rotation and simple structure are used to make factors more interpretable.

5. The fundamental equation of factor analysis is $\mathbf{R} = \mathbf{P}\Phi\mathbf{P}^\mathrm{T} + \mathbf{U}$.

6. The fundamental equation shows how the correlation matrix $\mathbf{R}$ is partitioned into a factor loading matrix $\mathbf{P}$, correlation between factors, Φ and uniqueness, $\mathbf{U}$. $\mathbf{R}$ is the observed data. All the others are estimated from the data.

7. There are a number of different factor extraction methods. The most popular has been the principal factor method.

8. The principal factor method requires the researcher to supply communality estimates and state the number of factors to extract.

9. The communality estimates and the number of problems have been difficult problems to solve in factor analysis. There is no clear-cut set of rules for either. Comrey has, however, developed a method that does not use communality estimates.

10. Communality refers to the proportion of total variance that is common factor variance. A goal of factor analysis is to find the variance components of the total common factor variance.

11. Factor scores involve combining the values of those variables that defined the factor. It is a new transformed score. If a battery of 10 tests yield three factors, then each test-taker would have three factor scores.

12. Factor analysis currently has two methodologies. The traditional method is now called Exploratory Factor Analysis or EFA, and the newer method is called Confirmatory Factor Analysis or CFA.

13. Exploratory factor analysis is usually used to learn or to discover which factors underlie the data. Some researchers that are experienced users of this method know how to test hypotheses about the factors.

14. Confirmatory Factor Analysis is used to test hypotheses about the factor structure. In CFA a model is developed, based on theory or past findings, and then tested against empirical data.

15. Confirmatory factor analysis is just a special case of a group of analyses called *covariance structure analysis*.

STUDY SUGGESTIONS

1. The more advanced student will find the following selected articles valuable:

Comrey, A. L. (1978). Common methodological problems in factor analytic studies. *Journal of Consulting and Clinical Psychology, 46*, 648–659. [A nonmathematical review of the problems found in factor analytic studies.]

Comrey, A. L. (1985). A method for removing outliers to improve factor analytic results. *Multivariate Behavioral Research, 20,* 273–281. [Shows how to detect and remove outliers that have a negative effect on a factor analysis solution.]

Comrey, A. L., & Montag, I. (1982). Comparison of factor analytic results with two-choice and seven-choice personality item formats. *Applied Psychological Measurement, 6,* 285–289. [Compared two results of a factor analysis on the Comrey Personality Scales, one analysis with a two-choice response format, and another with a seven-choice format. Results indicate a superiority for the seven-choice over the two-choice item format for personality inventories.]

Dunlap, W. P., & Cornwell, J. M. (1994). Factor analysis of ipsative measures. *Multivariate Behavioral Research, 29,* 115–126. [Discusses factor analysis with ipsative measures. The authors show analytically the fundamental problems that ipsative measures impose for factor analysis. These researchers recommend that factor analysis should not be done on data that are known to be ipsative.]

Fleming, J. S. (1981). The use and misuse of factor scores in multiple regression analysis. *Educational and Psychological Measurement, 41,* 1017–1025. [Discusses when and where factor analysis may be used along with multiple regression for prediction purposes.]

Lee, H. B., & Comrey, A. L. (1979). Distortions in a commonly used factor analytic procedure. *Multivariate Behavioral Research, 14,* 301–321. [A study comparing the most popular method of factor extraction and rotation with other methods. It shows how distorted some solutions can get using the most popular methods.]

Montanelli, R., & Humphreys, L. (1976). Latent roots of random data correlation matrices with squared multiple correlations on the diagonal: A Monte Carlo study. *Psychometrika, 41,* 341–348. [Excellent random correlation and regression method on the number-of-factors problem.]

Overall, J. (1965). Note on the scientific status of factors. *Psychological Bulletin, 61,* 270–276. [Excellent, even brilliant, analysis of basic factor analytic notions.]

Peterson, D. (1965). Scope and generality of verbally defined personality factors. *Psychological Review, 72,* 48–59. [Very convincing on the number-of-factors problem.]

2. As usual, there is no substitute for the study of actual research uses of methods. The student should, therefore, read two or three good factor analytic studies. Select from those cited in the chapter or from the following:

Carroll, J. B. (1993). *Human cognitive abilities: A survey of factor-analytic studies.* New York: Cambridge University Press. [An analysis and reanalysis of intelligence studies that used factor analysis. Gives a very good history of the psychology of individual differences.]

Daniel, L. G., & Siders, J. A. (1994). Validation of teacher assessment instruments: A confirmatory factor analytic approach. *Journal of Personnel Evaluation in Education, 8,* 29–40. [Examined construct validity of the Mississippi Teacher Assessment Instrument used for certification of beginning teachers. An exploratory factor analysis found four factors, however, confirmatory factor analyses failed to yield an acceptable structural model.]

Fleming, J. S., & Whalen, D. J. (1990). The personal and academic self-concept inventory: Factor structure and gender differences in high school and college samples. *Educational and Psychological Measurement, 50,* 957–967. [Applied confirmatory factor analysis to several competing structural models of the Personal and Academic Self-Concept Inventory, an expansion of the Self-Rating Scales.]

Isaacson, R. L., McKeachie, W. J., Milholland, J. E., & Lin, Y. G. (1964). Dimensions of student evaluations of teaching. *Journal of Educational Psychology, 55,* 344–351. [A competent study of the factors behind student evaluations of instructors. The first factor is important.]

Mitrushina, M., & Satz, P. (1991). Changes in cognitive functioning associated with normal aging. *Archives of Clinical Neuropsychology, 6,* 49–60. [Used factor analysis on memory and psychomotor tests to find cognitive functioning factors in elderly participants. Factor scores were computed and used in analysis of variance.]

Thurstone, L. L. (1944). *A factorial study of perception.* Psychometric Monographs, no. 4. Chicago: University of Chicago Press. [Another Thurstone pioneering and classic study.]

3. Here is a small fictitious correlation matrix, with the tests labeled.

		1	2	3	4	5	6
1.	Vocabulary	.70	.22	.20	*.15*	*.25*	
2.	Analogies	.70		.15	.26	.12	.30
3.	Addition	.22	.15		.81	.21	.10
4.	Multiplication	.20	.26	.81		.31	.29
5.	Recall First Names	.15	.12	.21	.31		.72
6.	Recognize Figures	.25	.30	.10	.29	.72	

a. Do an "armchair" factor analysis. That is, by inspection of the matrix determine how many factors there probably are and which tests are on which factors.

b. Name the factors. How sure are you of your names? What can you do to be more sure of your conclusions?

4. Some excellent books on factor analysis that one may want to read for more information:

Cattell, R. B. (1978). *The scientific use of factor analysis in the behavioral and life sciences.* New York: Plenum. [This is an outstanding book covering all that had happened in factor analysis since Cattell's publication of his 1952 book. It is composed of two parts and introduces mathematical concepts gradually.]

Comrey, A. L., & Lee, H. B. (1992). *A first course in factor analysis* (2nd ed.). Hillsdale, NJ: Lawrence Erlbaum. [Instead of introducing the student to matrix mathematics within a chapter, this book gradually introduces matrices and their use in factor analysis. The topics within this book supplement the coverage given in other factor analysis books. Chapter 11 is especially valuable because it shows the reader how the Comrey Personality Scales were developed using factor analysis. This book presents valuable methods not normally found in other textbooks.]

Cureton, E. E., & D'Agostino, R. B. (1983). *Factor analysis: An applied approach.* Hillsdale, NJ: Lawrence Erlbaum. [A book that present models and theories of exploratory factor analysis without the use of advanced mathematics such as calculus. It contains a good chapter on matrix algebra and gives good coverage on using principle-axis methods for common factor analysis. Also provides some comparisons between different methods of factor extraction and rotation.]

Gorsuch, R. (1983). *Factor analysis* (2nd ed.). Hillsdale, NJ: Lawrence Erlbaum. [This book is scholarly, authoritative, informative. One of its great virtues is that it thoroughly explores the most difficult and troublesome problems of factor analysis. Gorsuch not only explains the technical ideas but also cites theoretical contributions and empirical investigations of the problems. *Highly recommended* as a reference work for behavioral researchers.]

Mulaik, S. A. (1972). *The foundations of factor analysis.* New York: McGraw-Hill. [A mathematically sophisticated treatment of factor analysis. Definitely not for those without extensive mathematical training such as multivariable calculus. This book is now out of print but may be available though Books-on-Demand.]

Rummel, R. J. (1970). *Applied factor analysis.* Evanston, IL: Northwestern University Press. [A comprehensive book on exploratory factor analysis with a political science emphasis. It requires some knowledge of mathematics. Contains some good chapters on matrix algebra and its use in explaining factor analysis. A good explanation is provided for the various factor models. However, it does not discuss extensively the issues involved in using and interpreting factor analytic solutions.]

Thurstone, L. L. (1947). *Multiple factor analysis.* Chicago: University of Chicago Press. [This is a classic work by the creator of modern factor analysis. Although this book is over 50 years old, the material covered is still relevant.]

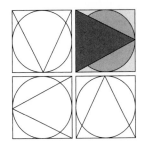

CHAPTER 35

ANALYSIS OF COVARIANCE STRUCTURES

- COVARIANCE STRUCTURES, LATENT VARIABLES, AND TESTING THEORY
- TESTING ALTERNATIVE FACTOR HYPOTHESES: DUALITY VERSUS BIPOLARITY OF SOCIAL ATTITUDES
- LATENT VARIABLE INFLUENCES: THE FULL EQS SYSTEM
- SETTING UP THE EQS STRUCTURE
- RESEARCH STUDIES
- CONCLUSIONS—AND RESERVATIONS

In this long and involved dissertation on the foundations of behavioral research, we have often talked of the importance of theory and the testing of theory. We have from time to time stressed the purpose of scientific research as formulating explanations of natural phenomena and submitting implications of the explanations to empirical test. In this chapter, we study and try to understand a highly developed and sophisticated conceptual and analytic system to model and test scientific behavioral theories: *analysis of covariance structures*. Analysis of covariance structure also has another name; it is sometimes called *structural equation modeling* (SEM). In order to understand this methodology, we focus largely on some powerful mathematical-statistical systems and computer programs. There are at least three well-known ones that exist at this time. In the mid-1970s, LISREL (*Linear Structural Relations*) was conceived and developed by Joreskog and his colleagues (Joreskog & Sorbom, 1993) to set up and analyze covariance structures. The early versions of this computer program required setup statements that were difficult. However, later generations became much easier. Until recently it was a part of the statistical package called SPSS and is still the method of choice for some modelers. In the late 1970s and early 1980s, the computer program called EQS by Bentler (1986) was developed. Researchers interested in covariance structure analysis found Bentler's program much easier to use. The program statements and the modeling symbols were easier to understand than those in LISREL. However, LISREL has improved its user interface tremendously with the release of LISREL version 8. Although somewhat dated now, Brown (1986) compared LISREL and EQS in terms of parameter estimation for confirmatory factor analysis. We will use EQS because many have found it easier to understand. It uses standard labeling whereas LISREL modeling uses a lot of Greek letters. However, once a researcher is familiar with covariance structure or structural equation modeling, the differences are less important.

Researchers now have a third computer program and system to contend with. It is called Analysis of Moment Structures (AMOS) published by SmallWaters Corporation (Arbuckle, 1995). They have a demo version of their program on their Internet Website. The most current version allows the user to specify, view, and modify the structural model *graphically*, using drawing tools. Each of these programs and approaches has consistently made it easier for researchers to capitalize on using structural equation modeling or analysis of covariance structure.

Unfortunately, even with improved computing programs and numerous books and manuals on the subject (see Schumacker & Lomax, 1996), analysis of covariance structures or structural equation modeling is still not easy to learn for those without a mathematics background. The difficulty, it must be confessed, is to explain the system in language comprehensible to nonmathematical readers and, at the same time, to stay within the purposes and confines of this book. So the discussion is limited to presenting and explaining the bare mathematical skeleton of the system and how and why it is used. Fortunately, our subject is closely related to the discussions of multiple regression analysis and factor analysis of chapters 32, 33, and 34.

Covariance Structures, Latent Variables, and Testing Theory

Analysis of covariance structures can be viewed as a combination of factor analysis and multiple regression analysis. In fact, Lee and Jennrich (1984) have shown how one can use nonlinear regression analysis to analyze covariance structure data. Its most important strength is that the effects of latent variables on each other and on observed variables can be assessed. A *latent variable*, recall, is a construct or hypothetical "entity": intelligence, verbal ability, spatial ability, prejudice, anxiety, achievement. Latent variables are, of course, unobserved variables whose "reality" we assume or infer from observed variables or indicators. Factors are latent variables, constructs we invent to help explain observed behavior.

We introduced confirmatory factor analysis in Chapter 34, and this is one form of covariance structures. The reader may remember that a path diagram was most useful in conceptualizing what the model looked like. In the analysis of covariance structures, we will use path models a lot. Once the path model is laid out correctly, EQS, LISREL or AMOS can be used. Throughout this chapter, path models will be used to describe the covariance structure model.

There are 10 key points that a modeler must consider when writing a path diagram that will be analyzed using EQS. By following these points, the path analysis diagram will fit the program statements of EQS. We will list these points and then discuss each one. These 10 points are relevant for the simplest covariance structure to the most complex.

1. There is a one-way arrow from each independent variable pointing toward the dependent variable.
2. Every variable that has a one-way arrow pointing toward it generates one linear regression equation in the covariance or structural equation model.
3. There is an asterisk (*) embedded in each arrow from the independent variables to the dependent variable. These tell us that there are free parameters to be estimated for these paths.
4. The asterisk identifies a free parameter in the model.
5. All covariances (correlation) between independent variables are also free parameters in the model. Free covariance parameters are indicated by two-way arrows with an asterisk in the middle.
6. Variances of the measured independent variables are also free parameters. These variables are underlined in their boxes with an asterisk next to their symbol.
7. All independent variables have variances as parameters in the model.
8. Dependent variables do not have variances as parameters in the model.
9. All latent (unmeasured) independent variables in the model must have their scale fixed in one of two ways:
   a. Set the regression coefficient to a fixed value. It is usually set to 1.0.
   b. Fix its variance at some known value, usually 1.0.
10. In most cases, E values (measurement error) have their regression coefficients fixed at 1.0, and so no asterisk appears in the arrow pointing to the dependent variable.

In EQS, modeling calls for independent and dependent variables. Either one or both can be measured or latent. Occasionally, latent variables are also called *unmeasured variables*. For dependent variables that are measured, an "E" symbol is used to represent its measurement error. A "D" symbol is used to represent the measurement error for latent dependent variables. Depending on the numbering of the dependent variables, a number is attached to the "E" or "D."

The simplest covariance structure is regression analysis. If we let x_1 be the dependent variable, and x_2, x_3, and x_4 be the independent variables, we can write the model equation as:

$$x_1 = B_2x_2 + B_3x_3 + B_4x_4 + e \qquad (35.1)$$

The scores in this equation are in deviation score form. This makes it unnecessary to have the intercept term. The B values are the standardized regression

◉ **FIGURE 35.1**

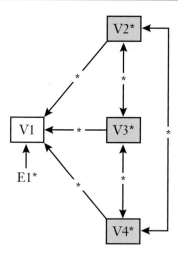

weights. The single equation regression model shown in Equation 37.1 can be represented by the path diagram in Figure 35.1.

Measured data variables are represented in boxes or rectangles and contain within them identifying numbers, such as Vl, V2, V3, V4, or more, as required. That is, squares or rectangles are used to enclose a variable that is observed and not latent. In the case of linear regression analysis, all of the variables are considered observed or measured. As we mentioned in the previous chapter in discussing confirmatory factor analysis, circles or ellipses are used to enclose variables that are latent or unmeasured. In our regression example there are four variables in the equation: x_1, x_2, x_3, x_4. Hence, EQS requires that we call them V1, V2, V3, and V4. There is a one-way arrow from each of the independent variables V2, V3, and V4 pointing toward variable V1. From point two given above, every variable that has a one-way arrow pointing to it generates one linear regression equation in the model. There is only one such variable here, V1, and hence only one equation.

There is an asterisk or star (*) embedded in each of the arrows from V2, V3, and V4 to V1 indicating that there are free parameters to be estimated in connection with these paths, one for each star. There is also a one-way arrow pointing from E1 toward V1, indicating that the regression equation contains an error variable, E1, which is also an independent variable in the model. The star (*) notifies the program that the preceding value is an estimate and not a fixed value. The star also identifies a free parameter in the model. Counting the number of stars enables the researcher to determine the total number of free parameters being estimated for the model. E1 is presumed to be uncorrelated with V2, V3, and V4; hence, no two-way arrows appear between these variables in the path diagram. Also note that the coefficient for E1 has been set to 1.0. We have put the 1.0 in to be consistent with key point #10. The 1.0 is usually implied (not written).

Other free parameters in the model include all the covariances among the independent measured variables, V2, V3, and V4. Two-way arrows with a star in the middle indicate free covariance parameters. This adds three more free parameters.

Additional free parameters include the variances of the independent measured variables: V2, V3, and V4. The fact that these variances are free parameters is indicated in the model by shading V2, V3, and V4 in their boxes and placing stars (*) next to their symbols. It is easy to lose sight of the fact that the variances of these independent variables are parameters in the model. The shading makes it easier to remember that the EQS program setup must contain either estimates or fixed values for these variance parameters. This adds three more free parameters (indicated by the *s).

One more variance must be estimated in the model because the general rule is that all independent variables have variances as parameters in the model, which includes all the *error* variables as well as the independent *measured* variables. Dependent variables, however, do not have variances as parameters in the model. A star (*) is placed beside E1 in the path diagram in Figure 35.1 to show that its variance is a free parameter in the model. This now gives a total of 10 stars in the path diagram, indicating that there are 10 free parameters to be estimated.

There is one additional parameter in the model that is fixed at 1.0—the regression coefficient for E1. To be redundant with key point #9, all independent unmeasured variables in the model must have their scale fixed in one of two ways: (a) set a regression coefficient at a fixed value, usually 1.0, which was done here for E1; or (b) fix its variance at some known value, usually 1.0. In most cases, the E values have their regression coefficients fixed at 1.0 and consequently in the path diagram no star (*) appears within the arrow pointing to the dependent variable with which that error variable is associated.

It is not possible to fix both the regression weight *and* the variance for an E variable because the product of these two numbers must be free to accommodate the amount of error in predicting the dependent variable correctly. Thus, one or the other is fixed, but not both.

There are 10 free parameters to be estimated for the regression model in Figure 37.1 from a total of 10 data points. The data points consist of the variances and covariances of the measured variables, V1, V2, V3, and V4, or $(n(n + 1))/2$ where n is the number of variables. That is, there are six covariances and four variances. The number of degrees of freedom for estimating the model is given by the number of data points minus the number of free parameters in the system, which in this case is $10 - 10$ or zero.

When there are no degrees of freedom, the model is said to be "saturated"; that is, values can be obtained for the free parameters that will reproduce the input data exactly. Thus, there is no question about the model fitting the data, and no chi-square test or other statistical test needed to see how good the fit is because the fit is perfect. For this reason, regression models are not considered to be of much interest in covariance structure analysis. In general, those who choose to use covariance structure analysis wish to develop a model that has considerably more data points than free parameters to be estimated. In such cases, it is a challenge to find an unsaturated model and a set of parameters that will reproduce the data reasonably well, that is, give a good fit. Only this type of model (one with a number of degrees of freedom greater than zero), will be able to convey any scientific information of theoretical significance.

If all of this is still too abstract, let's examine an example from actual research. This research was conducted by Kerlinger (1972). It has the virtues of familiarity and relative simplicity.

Testing Alternative Factor Hypotheses: Duality Versus Bipolarity of Social Attitudes

Recall that there are two general views of the social attitudes we generally associate with liberalism and conservatism. One view—the much more commonly held one among both scientists and laypeople—is that liberal and conservative issues and people are opposed to each other: What the liberal is for, the conservative is against, and vice versa. This was earlier expressed as a *bipolar theory*. It implies one dimension of attitudes, with liberal issues and people at one end and conservative issues and people at the other end:

Liberalism   Conservatism

The contrasting theory, hypothesis, or conception, of social attitudes says, in effect, that liberal issues and ideas are in general different and virtually independent of conservative issues and ideas. Liberalism and Conservatism, to use the abstract names of the latent variables, are not necessarily opposed to each other: They are two separate and independent ideologies or sets of related beliefs that can be expressed as orthogonal dimensions:

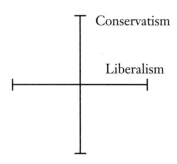

This conception of the structure of social attitudes is a *dualistic* one.

The two contrasting "theories" of the structure of social attitudes can be expressed by the two factor matrices, *A* and *B*, given in Table 35.1. These can be called "target" matrices because they are set up to express contrasting analyses. Suppose we have administered six social attitude scales to a large heterogeneous sample of individuals. Scales 1, 2, and 3 are Conservative scales; and scales 4, 5, and 6 are Liberal scales. The responses of the sample to the six scales were correlated and factor analyzed, say. The results of the factor analysis that the duality and bipolarity theories imply are given in the table. The +s indicate substantial and positive loadings, the −s indicate substantial and negative loadings, and the 0s indicate near-zero loadings. The dualistic theory (*A*) implies, of course, two orthogonal factors, and the bipolarity theory (*B*) implies one factor with substantial positive and negative loadings. *A* and *B* of the table succinctly express the two models implied by the two theories. If we plotted the "loadings" of the duality theory, they would look like those of Figure 34.7 in Chapter 34. The plot of the bipolarity theory loadings can be plotted on a single axis, with the positive loadings at one end of the axis and the negative loadings at the other end.

As we mentioned before and reiterate here, researchers who use analysis of covariance structures like to develop models in path diagrams. The path diagrams for the two factor models are given in Figure 35.2. (See Chapter 33 for a discussion of path diagrams.) At this time only we will write the path model in terms of EQS notation. The beginner will find EQS notation much easier to understand than LISREL's. EQS modeling uses only four symbols: V for measured variables, F for latent variables, E for errors, and D for disturbances. E is used to represent measurement error for the V variables and D is used to represent measurement error for the latent variables. LISREL is more complicated.

In light of the nature of this book, it makes better sense for the uninitiated to use the modeling notation given by EQS. LISREL modeling uses a lot of Greek letters

▣ **TABLE 35.1** *Factor Analytic Structures Implied by the Dualistic Hypothesis (A) and the Bipolar Hypothesis (B)*[a]

(A) Dualistic Scales	I	II	Type	(B) Bipolar Scales	I	Type
1	+	0	*C*	1	+	*C*
2	+	0	*C*	2	+	*C*
3	+	0	*C*	3	+	*C*
4	0	+	*L*	4	−	*L*
5	0	+	*L*	5	−	*L*
6	0	1	*L*	6	2	*L*

[a]+ = indicates positive factor loadings; − = indicates negative factor loadings; 0 = zero loadings. *L* = Liberal scales; *C* = Conservative scales.

◉ **FIGURE 35.2**   *$x_1, x_2, \ldots, x_6$, observed measures (scales); ξ_1, ξ_2: Xsi 1: Conservatism (C); Xsi 2: Liberalism (L); $\lambda_{11}, \lambda_{21}, \lambda_{31}, \ldots$: lambda's, factor loadings; $\delta_1, \delta_2, \ldots$: delta 1, delta 2, . . : error terms*

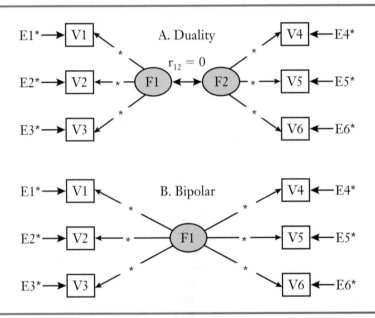

for certain component or parameter designation. This can terrify some students and prevent them from learning about an outstanding research methodology and analysis.

For our example, $x_1, x_2, \ldots, x_6$ are the observed variables; x_1, x_2, and x_3 measures of Conservatism; and x_4, x_5, and x_6 measures of Liberalism. These would be written as V1, V2, V3, V4, V5, V6 in EQS, where V1, V2, and V3 measure Conservatism and V4, V5, and V6 measure Liberalism. In both notations, observed variables are indicated by boxes (i.e., squares or rectangles); unobserved, latent variables, or factors by circles or ellipses. In the duality model F_1 and F_2 are used to represent conservatism and liberalism. The error terms in EQS are written E1, E2, E3, E4, E5, and E6. In the path model given in Figure 35.3, an asterisk is placed next to each E value. This says that the errors or unique values will be estimated by the data. The correlation between the latent variables is to be estimated, so it is also specified with an asterisk. Since the theory says that conservatism and liberalism are separate and distinct factors, we predict $r_{12} = 0$.

The bipolarity theory diagram is easier to explain. We have, of course, the same six xs, or observed variables and the same six error terms. We also have six factor loadings. There is only one factor, or F_1. In the duality model, there are twelve factor loadings, but six of them are predicted to be positive and substantial and the rest are constrained to be zero. "Constrained," or "fixed" values are maintained during the computations. In the bipolarity model, there are six factor loadings: three positive (the path arrows are marked +) and three negative (marked −). In other words, we predict the two factor matrices of Table 35.1, except that in the table we only use +s and −s rather than factor loadings.

To determine which of the two models is closer to empirical "reality," we must test each separately and then test one against the other. This is done using the information or the data we have: the correlations among the observed variables x_1, x_2, . . . , x_6. This matrix of correlations, **R**, is a covariance matrix. Variables (or attitude scales) 1, 2, and 3 are measures of Conservatism; variables 4, 5, and 6 are measures of Liberalism. The duality hypothesis predicts substantial and positive correlations among 1, 2, and 3; and substantial and positive correlations among 4, 5, and 6. The duality hypothesis also predicts zero or near-zero rs between the C variables (1, 2, and 3) and the L variables (4, 5, and 6). We call these *cross-correlations*.

The method actually used in analysis of covariance structures is as follows. The data are analyzed according to the model setup, in this case the duality model: two orthogonal factors (see Figure 35.2a). From the parameters estimated by the data analysis, factor analysis in this case, an **R** matrix is calculated by using the estimated parameters of the theoretical model. This is done by writing equations for each of the Vs.

To help us clearly understand what is done and why, we first set up the two theories in path diagrams. The reader may find the following explanation to be redundant, but we have found this to be helpful in learning and understanding this method. Behavioral researchers who use "modeling" or "causal modeling," as it is called, use path diagrams to help conceptualize the research problems they are studying and, almost more important, to learn the empirical implications of theories under test. We strongly recommend that students try to set up any research problem under study in a path diagram. It forces one to conceptualize and bring out the basic structures of problems. In any case, the duality and bipolarity "theories" of social attitudes have been set up in the two path diagrams, *A* and *B*, of Figure 35.3. It is customary in such path diagrams to use squares for observed variables and circles for unobserved or latent variables. Single-headed arrows are used to indicate influences, double-headed arrows to indicate correlations. If we do a principal factor factor analysis of the present problem, for instance, 12 factor loadings would be estimated: a_{11}, a_{12}, a_{21}, a_{22}, . . . , a_{61}, a_{62}. The problem in the EQS or covariance structure framework, however, is different because we have specified that six factor loadings, or as, are to be estimated; the remaining loadings are constrained to be 0s under the duality hypothesis. To be sure we see and understand the difference, we set out the two factor matrices in Table 35.2. Note that there are 12 factor loadings to be calculated in A, ordinary factor analysis, and only six loadings to be calculated in B, the covariance structure solution constrained by the 0s because of the duality hypothesis.

The difference between the two approaches is striking—and very important. In ordinary factor analysis all the factor loadings are estimated, but in analysis of covariance structures only those factor loadings germane to the hypothesis are estimated. All the rest are constrained to be zero—a perfect simple structure. To

🔲 **TABLE 35.2** *Factor Matrices of (a) Ordinary Factor Analysis and (b) EQS Constrained Factor Analysis*[a]

Variables	a. Ordinary Factor Analysis		Variables	b. EQS Constrained Factor Analysis		Type[a]
	I	II		I	II	
1	a_{11}	a_{12}	1	a_{11}	0	C
2	a_{21}	a_{22}	2	a_{21}	0	C
3	a_{31}	a_{32}	3	a_{31}	0	C
4	a_{41}	a_{42}	4	0	a_{42}	L
5	a_{51}	a_{52}	5	0	a_{52}	L
6	a_{61}	a_{62}	6	0	a_{62}	L

[a]C = Conservative; L = Liberal.

emphasize the points being made, the actual estimated parameters are given in Table 35.4. The final rotated factors of an ordinary factor analysis are given in *a*, and the covariance structure constrained solution is given in *b*. You may well ask: What happens to the factor loadings where the 0s are in *b*? The point is that *b* expresses the "pure" form of the duality hypothesis. As said earlier, the computer is instructed to do the calculations keeping the 0s of Table 35.2 and Table 35.3 intact. But how about the fairly large negative loadings, −.44 and −.36 in *a*, the conventional factor

🔲 **TABLE 35.3** *Obtained Factor Matrices (a) Conventional (Rotated) and (b) EQS Constrained Factors*[a]

Variables	a. Conventional Factor		Variables	b. EQS Constrained Factors		Type
	I	II		I	II	
1	.69	.19	1	.65	0	C
2	.70	.33	2	.87	0	C
3	.68	.14	3	.63	0	C
4	−.44	.51	4	0	.71	L
5	−.05	.64	5	0	.54	L
6	−.36	.55	6	0	.63	L

[a]The conventional factor analysis was the principal factor method with varimax rotation; the EQS method was maximum likelihood. All loadings of *b* are statistically significant. The correlation between the two factors was −.15, not statistically significant.

analysis? Both are substantial, negative, and statistically significant, contrary to the duality hypothesis. They are deviations from the duality model. The key question, then, is: Are the deviations large enough to invalidate the hypothesis, which specifies 0s? We will return to this point shortly.

The model of Figure 35.2 A requires calculation of the error terms, E. The six error terms were calculated, but we are not interested in the method of calculation. Much more interesting and relevant to the duality hypothesis is the estimation of variances and covariances, because it expresses the relations between the F1 and F2 factors. Remember that the duality hypothesis included the correlation between the two factors: it will be zero or close to zero. Look back at Figure 35.2 A, and note that, in accordance with the duality hypothesis $r_{12} = 0$. While r_{12} can be constrained to be zero, we chose, instead, to let EQS estimate the correlation between factors for reasons to be given later. To reflect this in Figure 35.2 A, we would change the r_{12} to an asterisk. The variances of F1 and F2 are set equal to 1.00, the variances of E1, E2, ... , E6 are to be estimated and r_{12} is specified as "free." (Remember, when a parameter is "free," the program estimates its value.)

In the analysis, $r_{12} = -.157$ is not statistically significant. So, in effect, the two factors are orthogonal, which is consistent with the duality hypothesis. Recall that the theory says that Conservatism and Liberalism are separate and independent dimensions of social attitudes. This means, of course, that the correlation between them is zero (or close to zero).

The crucial question, however, is: Is the whole model congruent with the data? The whole model of the duality hypothesis is expressed by Figure 35.2 A. Following the rules of EQS, we instruct the computer to estimate the six factor loadings, a_{11}, a_{21}, a_{31}, a_{42}, a_{52}, a_{62} while maintaining the zero constraints in the matrix. We also specify that the error terms of the six equations be calculated. We must also specify what the relations between the two factors will be. We must therefore tell EQS what to do with the variances of the factors, F1 and F2. We do this by instructing EQS to estimate r_{12}, the correlation between F1 and F2. In traditional factor analysis this would involve estimating the values in the Φ matrix (see Chapter 34). Following an iterative procedure, the computer program estimates the 13 values we have specified to be estimated, using the correlations among the six variables (Table 35.2) as input data. It also constrains the zeroes of Table 35.2 and sets the latent variables (or factors) variances equal to 1.00. The factor loadings are given in Table 35.3 B, and $r_{12} = -.157$. The six error terms are .76, .50, .78, .71, .84, and .77. Are these values congruent with the data, or alternatively, does the duality model "fit" the data? Before we answer these questions we need to mention that there are a number of other important methodological points we are not discussing here, like the assumptions behind the analysis. One of the assumptions is that the distribution of the observed or measured variables is multivariate normal. Another assumption or requirement is identification: The covariance structure problem must be set up so that all estimated parameters can be identified. There are research problems where these assumptions may not be true. The core idea behind the assessment of the "goodness of fit" of a theoretical model is simple and powerful. Use the estimated parameter values and the constrained values to calculate a predicted or reproduced or fitted correlation matrix, $\mathbf{R}^*$. The matrix $\mathbf{R}^*$ can in this case be generated by multiplying the rows of Table 37.4: $r_{12}^* = (.65)(.87) + (0)(0) = .57$; $r_{13} = (.65)(.63) + (0)(0) = .41$; $r_{23} = (.57)(.41) + (0)(0) = .55$; and so on. This $\mathbf{R}^*$ is then compared to the obtained or observed correlation matrix, $\mathbf{R}$, which can be done by subtracting $\mathbf{R}^*$ from $\mathbf{R}$, or $\mathbf{R} - \mathbf{R}^*$. This matrix of differences is called a *residual matrix*. In covariance structure analysis the residuals are usually analyzed with one of three models or fitting functions:

1. Unweighted least-squares
2. Generalized or weighted least-squares
3. Maximum likelihood

As we saw in Chapter 34, there are a number of different goodness-of-fit statistics. The oldest of these—chi-square—is sometimes reported but not used as the only statistic because its evaluation is based on sample size. As the sample size gets larger, small differences will become statistically significant, indicating a lack-of-fit. Bentler (1980) gives an excellent review of goodness-of-fit statistics and suggests the use of statistics that do not depend on sample size. The program EQS, developed by Bentler (1986), originally used such a fit statistic called the Bentler–Bonett *normed fit index* or NFI. The NFI is now obsolete. The current fit index of choice is the Comparative Fit Index (CFI), and a value of 0.95 or higher is representative of a good fit between model and data. Values of CFI less than 0.95 tell the researcher that there is room for improvement in how the model is specified. It essentially says the model does not fit the data very well. If one gets values around 0.95 or higher, the fit of the data to the model is quite good and it is unlikely that any further respecification of the model will alter the index very much. LISREL, developed by Joreskog and Sorbom (1993) originally used a different goodness-of-fit statistic called the Root Mean Square Residual or RMR. However, all popular programs now have all of the common fit statistics such as the Goodness-of-Fit Index or GFI and the Adjusted Goodness-of-Fit Index (AGFI) (see Comrey & Lee, 1992; or Keith, 1999, for further explanations of these indices).

From the EQS results, the chi-square statistic for duality model is 121.253 based on 8 degrees of freedom. The probability value for the chi-square statistic is less than 0.001. This tells us that the data did not fit our model. The Bentler–Bonett Normed Fit Index was .840, telling us that improvements can be made for a better fit.

We are after the ideas behind the method. The principle is: *The smaller the residuals, the better the fit; the larger the residuals, the poorer the fit.* If the hypothesis or model is valid empirically, the less the model-generated covariance (correlation) matrix, $\mathbf{R}^*$ will differ from the observed correlation matrix $\mathbf{R}$. Both situations are reflected in the matrix of residuals, $\mathbf{R} - \mathbf{R}^*$, and in measures, like NFI that reflect the magnitudes of the residuals. Again, the larger the residuals, the poorer the fit. (All three covariance structure computer programs obligingly print the residual matrix.)

The empirical implications of the bipolarity hypothesis are depicted in Figure 35.2 B. There is, of course, only one factor: F1. The conservatism measures V1, V2, and V3 (or x_1, x_2, and x_3) are marked "+"; and those for V4, V5, and V6 (or x_4, x_5, and x_6) are marked "−," which is consistent with the bipolarity hypothesis. That is, we expect one bipolar factor with the Conservative measures having positive signs and the Liberal measures negative signs (or vice versa). The six EQS estimated factor loadings on *one* factor were .67, .83, .65, −.25, .12, and −.15. $\chi^2 = 313.143$ based on 9 degrees of freedom. The probability value for the chi-square statistic is less than 0.001. The Bentler–Bonett NFI = .586. These values indicate that the goodness-of-fit for the bipolar model was considerably worse than the one for the duality model.

The factor loadings are interesting and informative. Those of the three Conservative measures, V1, V2, and V3, are positive and substantial; those of the Liberal measures are all low. Evidently, the one-factor model is inadequate: the three liberal measures are "lost." The χ^2 is also significant, indicating a lack of fit. Now look at the residuals in the top half of Table 35.5. Note carefully that the residuals for r_{45}, r_{46}, and r_{56} are substantial: .416, .393, and .389. The correlations among the liberal measures, V4, V5, and V6, were "missed" by the one-factor solution, the model for the bipolarity hypothesis. It appears that the bipolarity model has not succeeded very well. The duality model, on the other hand, performed better on all counts.

We now make a final test: we directly compare the two models. This is done through the χ^2 tests. The χ for the bipolarity model was 313.143, at 9 degrees of freedom, whereas the χ^2 for the duality model was 121.253, at 8 degrees of freedom. Recall that earlier we had the computer estimate r_{12}, , even though, strictly speaking, we should have "fixed" it at zero, or $r_{21} = 0$. This is because the pure duality model predicts orthogonal factors. One of the main reasons for doing this was to "use up" one degree of freedom so that the χ^2s of the two models could be compared. The direct test is $\chi^2_{bip} − \chi^2_{du} = 191.89$. The degrees of freedom are also subtracted: $9 − 8 = 1$. Had we not estimated r_{12}, the degrees of freedom for both models would have been the same, making a χ^2 comparison impossible. $\chi^2 = 191.89$, at $df = 1$, is evaluated. It is highly significant. This indicates the superiority of the duality hypothesis (since the bipolarity model χ^2 is significantly larger than the duality model χ^2). If there is no significant difference between the χ^2s of the two models, then the bipolarity hypothesis is as "good" (or as "poor") as the duality hypothesis. One cannot then infer that one hypothesis is more satisfactory than another. Remember, a model that is congruent with the data will have a χ^2 that is not statistically significant. If, however, the difference between the χ^2s is significant, one can then infer that the model with the larger χ^2 is *less* satisfactory than the model with the smaller χ^2. Another way of putting it is that the difference χ^2s, if significant, tests the importance of the parameters that differentiate the models.

This is difficult to show and explain the way the problem has been done. A more elegant approach is as follows. Set up the duality model as has been done above. Then set up the bipolarity model exactly the same except for the r_{12} term. For the duality model, estimate r_{12}, as above. This will yield a χ^2 with $df = 8$. Now set up the bipolarity model fixing $r_{12} = 1.00$, with $df = 9$. This will yield exactly the same parameter estimates as if the program had been told that there was only one factor, except that the one-factor loadings will appear on two factors. Since the correlation between the two factors is 1.00, the net effect is the same as with one factor. The test of the alternative hypotheses, $\chi_{bip}^2 - \chi_{dual}^2$ will be the same as that given above. However, it is now clear that the two models differ only in the one parameter: ϕ_{21}. This is one of the reasons for estimating ϕ_{21}, or r_{12}, in the duality model: For a test of alternative hypotheses, there must be a difference in degrees of freedom. Moreover, one model must be a subset of the other model. This means that both models estimate the same parameters except (in this case) for one parameter.

Latent Variable Influences: The Full EQS System

In the above attitude example only one part of the covariance structure or structural equations modeling system was used. If ordinary first-order factor analysis was the intended solution, then what was performed is all that was necessary. The most interesting problems, however, study the relations between independent variables and dependent variables. Before discussing the formal properties of the system, let's examine a simple fictitious example. We lay out the path diagram of the example to have something concrete to refer to. It is given in Figure 35.3. The example is a small model of Ability and Achievement. We say, in effect: Verbal Ability and Numerical Ability influence Achievement positively. Although perhaps not very interesting, the example has the virtue of being obvious and easily understood. No attempt is made to test alternative hypotheses here even though there are a number of possibilities. We seek only to convey the essence of the system.

▣ **FIGURE 35.3** *Influence of Ability on Achievement: (fictitious example)*

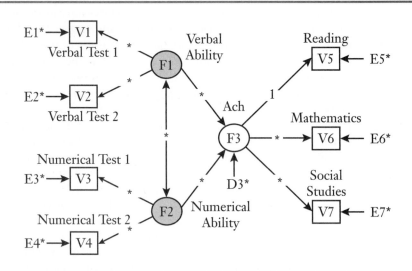

Look at this system and its function from a regression point of view. First, regard the left side of Figure 35.3. We have four tests: Verbal Test 1, Verbal Test 2, Numerical Test 1, and Numerical Test 2, V1, V2, V3, and V4 using EQS notation. They are measured dependent variables. We calculate the 4×4 correlation matrix, factor analyze it, and obtain the two factors, F1 and F2, as in Figure 35.3. The arrows with asterisks pointing toward the dependent variables from F1 and F2, contains the factor loadings: a_{11}, a_{21}, a_{32}, and a_{42}. The other loadings will be set at zero as we did earlier with the attitude duality hypothesis:

Tests	I	II
1	a_{11}	0
2	a_{21}	0
3	0	a_{32}
4	0	a_{42}

We can perceive the as as regression coefficients. The regression equation for V1 is:

$$V1 = a_{11}F1 + E1$$

We seek the regression of V1 on F1, just as we sought the regression of y on x, or y on x_1, x_2, . . . We can think of the factor loadings, a, as serving the same function as the regression coefficients, b or β, of Chapter 32. The same reasoning applies to the right side of Figure 35.4: we can write the regression of V5 on F3 as:

$$V5 = a_1F3 + E5$$

There are in this covariance structure two separate factor analyses or regression systems: one is on the left side, and one on the right side. Either side can be used for confirmatory or hypothesis testing factor analysis, as when we tested the duality and bipolarity hypotheses. What is more interesting and innovative, however, is to ask and answer research questions about the regression of the latent variable on other latent variable(s). We ask, in effect, about the relations between and F1, F2, and F3, or the regression of F3 on F1 and F2, considering F1 and F2 as independent variables and F3 as dependent variables. This is what the structural equation or analysis of covariance structure does.

The research problem of Figure 35.3 can be expressed as the multivariate relation between the independent variables and the dependent variables. It might be approached, for instance, using canonical correlation, which would express the overall relation between the Vs on the left side (i.e., V1, V2, V3, and V4); and the Vs on the right side (V5, V6, and V7). But canonical correlation is not capable of refining the relations. It pursues the relation between two sets of variables using *all* of the variables. Ordinarily, it is not concerned, with the latent variables. The model and hypotheses implied by Figure 35.3 say, in effect, that the left side measured dependent variables reflect two factors, Verbal Ability (V1 = Verbal Test 1, and V2 = Verbal Test 2) and Numerical Ability (V3 = Numerical Test 1, and V4 = Numerical Test 2). The latent variables are Verbal Ability, F1, and Numerical Ability, F2. The three Achievement variables are Reading, V5; Mathematics, V6; and Social Studies, V7. They are presumed to measure one factor, Achievement—in other words, a one-factor hypothesis. Note carefully that hypotheses that are not satisfactory, in the sense that they are not congruent with the data, can be stated easily, invalidating the entire model. For example, the variables V5, V6, and V7, which we said measured reflections of *one* factor or latent variable, might be incorrect. Perhaps two factors are necessary. That is, Figure 35.3 has one factor, F3, for Achievement. But there may really be two factors, F3 and F4. After all, V5 is a reading test and V6 is a mathematics test, and we know that these are usually two different factors. If so, then the model of Figure 35.3 is deficient in this regard.

Setting Up the EQS Structure

We finally arrive at the crucial relation: that between and F1 and F2, the latent independent variables; and F3, the latent dependent variable. Our substantive hypothesis may state that Verbal Ability F1, and Numerical Ability F2, both influence Achievement F3.

This hypothesis is not too fascinating but one amenable to example and explanation. In order to test it, we must set up the problem and model of Figure 35.3 in EQS structure and statements. This is a crucial and difficult step in EQS. At the risk of provoking boredom, let us pursue the ideas and set them up in equations and matrix equations, after spelling out the individual variable equations. First, the equations for the left side of Figure 35.3:

$$
\begin{aligned}
V1 &= .3^*F1 && + E1 \\
V2 &= .3^*F1 && + E2 \qquad\qquad (35.2) \\
V3 &= + .3^*F2 && + E3 \\
V4 &= + .3^*F2 && + E4
\end{aligned}
$$

The ".3*" says that there are coefficients that will be estimated from the data. These will be the factor loadings. The value ".3" is an arbitrary "best guess" starting value for estimating.

For EQS specification, we write the same equations in matrix form:

$$
\begin{bmatrix} V_1 \\ V_2 \\ V_3 \\ V_4 \end{bmatrix} = \begin{bmatrix} a_{11} & 0 \\ a_{21} & 0 \\ 0 & a_{32} \\ 0 & a_{42} \end{bmatrix} \begin{bmatrix} F_1 \\ F_2 \end{bmatrix} + \begin{bmatrix} E_1 \\ E_2 \\ E_3 \\ E_4 \end{bmatrix} \qquad (35.3)
$$

Where the *as* are estimated from the data. (Students should pause here, study Figure 35.4 and Equations 35.2 and 35.3, and try to understand their meaning.)

The right side is a bit easier:

$$V5 = 3*F3 + E5$$

$$V6 = 3*F3 + E6 \qquad (35.4)$$

$$V7 = 3*F3 + E7$$

In matrix form:

$$\begin{bmatrix} V_5 \\ V_6 \\ V_7 \end{bmatrix} = \begin{bmatrix} a_1 \\ a_2 \\ a_3 \end{bmatrix} F_3 + \begin{bmatrix} E_5 \\ E_6 \\ E_7 \end{bmatrix} \qquad (35.5)$$

A fictitious correlation matrix was synthesized so that the EQS solution would support the model of the path diagram of Figure 35.3 and the equations written on the basis of the diagram. The results were satisfactory. The chi-square statistic was statistically significant. This indicates a possible lack-of-fit. However, as we mentioned earlier in this chapter, there are other indices that may be better indicators of fit. The Bentler–Bonett Normed Fit Index (NFI) was .94. This is a very good value. It is generally considered that any value 0.9 or above indicates a good-fitting model. Other indices calculated by EQS such as the comparative fit index (CFI = .95) supports the conclusion that the model was satisfactory.

Although the parameters of the factor analyses (or regression analyses) for the left side and right side of Figure 35.3 are also satisfactory, they are not reported. This is because our interest is in testing the model for congruence with the data, in this case a correlation matrix. Plus we are also interested in assessing the relations between the latent variables Verbal Ability and Numerical Ability, on the one hand, and Achievement, on the other hand. The values expressing these influences are presented in Figure 35.4. This is the same as Figure 35.3 except the estimated parameters are shown.

It was said earlier that analysis of covariance structures and the computer program used to do the necessary complex computations, are not easy to learn. Even using the simpler approach of EQS, it can be difficult for the inexperienced. The 10 points mentioned earlier are important for those who want to use this extremely powerful method. However, even they are not easy to understand. So then why bother with it? Can't the factor analyses and the regression analyses be done separately with far less wear and tear on the behavioral scientist? Yes and no. The separate factor analyses of the left side and right side variables of Figure 35.3 can indeed be done separately. In fact, psychometric and factor analytic studies should be done before EQS or structural equation modeling is used. But the general regression analysis just described obviously cannot be done for research problems that are complex, involving latent variables, indirect and direct measures. One may, of course, try various approaches to the analysis of the data. But there appears to be no simple way to study sets of complex relations and to test the congruence of theoretical models with observed data. The ideas of analysis of covariance structures are mathematically

◫ **FIGURE 35.4** *Same Path Diagram as Figure 35.3 with Parameter Estimates*

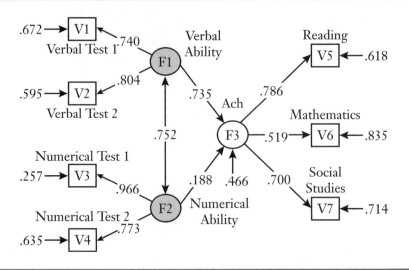

and statistically powerful, conceptually penetrating, and aesthetically satisfying. The conception of EQS, LISREL, AMOS and other similar computer programs are highly ingenious, productive, and creative achievements. They are, at the present writing, the highest development of behavioral scientific and analytic thinking, a development that brings psychological and sociological theory and multivariate mathematical and statistical analysis together into a unique and powerful synthesis that will probably revolutionize behavioral research. It is in this sense that analysis of covariance structures is said to be the culmination of contemporary methodology.

Research Studies

In the relatively short time that analysis of covariance structures and computer programs for doing covariance structure analysis have been functional and available—since the early and middle 1970s—the approach has been used in a number of fields fruitfully. Some of these studies are reanalyses of existing data; others are studies that were conceived with analysis of covariance structures in mind (see Study Suggestion 2). The first study of attitude structure discussed in this chapter was only one of 12 sets of attitude data that were reanalyzed using structural equation models or covariance structure analysis. Most of the evidence supported the duality hypothesis (see Kerlinger, 1980). Joreskog and his colleagues have reanalyzed the data of a number of psychological and sociological studies (see Magidson, 1979). The first study described in detail below is a covariance structure reanalysis of the data of a large study of political participation in America.

Bentler and Woodward (1978) used covariance structure analysis to reanalyze Head Start data—with depressing results. They found that the Head Start program had no significant effects on the Head Start children's cognitive abilities. Judd and Millburn (1980) studied the attitude structure of the general public of the United States. Using panel data from surveys done in 1972, 1974, and 1976, they investigated the Campbell, Converse, Miller, and Stokes (1960) contention that the general public does not have meaningful and stable social attitudes. They found that the noneducated public *does* have consistent ideological predispositions.

Verba and Nie: Political Participation in America

In a study of political participation, Verba and Nie (1972) reasoned from political theory that there should be four factors behind 13 variables of political participation. These factors and variables are given in Figure 35.5. This study was confirmatory factor analysis. It seemed that they were correct in their structural hypothesis, and we applauded their careful and competent work. But factor analysis has been criticized for, among other things, its lack of rigor. Can we put Verba and Nie's structural hypothesis to a more rigorous test? Let's use EQS on the problem. Note, however, that Verba and Nie did not use structural equations. Hence, the results we present here are from our reanalysis of their data.

The path analytic diagram model that follows from the theoretical discussion of Verba and Nie is given in Figure 35.5. V1, V2, V3, . . . , V13 are the measured dependent variables. The error component, associated with each dependent variable are E1, E2, E3, . . . , E13. There are four hypothesized factors. F1, F2, F3, and F4. These are the latent independent variables. All four factors are hypothesized to be correlated with one another. Remember that when the factors are correlated, the solution is oblique. Verba and Nie found the following factors: A—Campaign Activity (variables 1—5); B—Voting (variables 6, 7, and 8); C—Cooperative Activity (variables 9–11); D—Contacting (variables 12 and 13).

EQS was instructed to calculate the estimates of the parameters of Figure 35.5 and then to use the parameters to calculate a predicted correlation matrix $\mathbf{R}^*$. Finally, to assess the adequacy of the fit of the model of the four oblique factors of Figure 35.5, $\mathbf{R} - \mathbf{R}^*$, the differences or residuals, and various "fit" statistics were calculated.

The overall results support Verba and Nie's model of four oblique factors, even though the $\chi^2 = 406.648$, at $df = 59$, is highly significant. The large χ^2 is clearly due to the very large N of 3,000, and is thus not a good measure of fit. (An identical solution with a reduced N of 300 produced a $\chi^2 = 40.54$, which is not significant.) The root mean square residual (RMS) was 0.03. This small index merely reflected the generally small residuals. A Bentler–Bonnet Normed Fit Index (NFI) calculated by EQS was .961, which is very high. The Comparative Fit Index (CFI) was a very high .966. These indices point to a very good fit. In short, the fit of the model of Figure 35.5 is good. Verba and Nie's theoretical reasoning and measurement procedure appears to have been sound. They have contributed to understanding of the political process and to the nature and meaning of participation in the political process significantly.

▣ **FIGURE 35.5** *Path Diagram (Verba & Nie Study).*

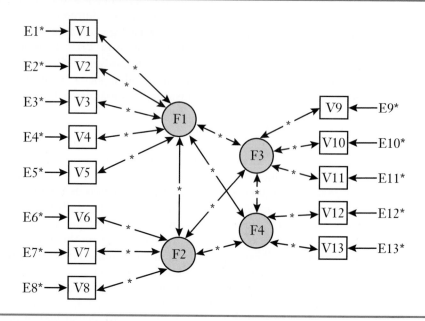

[a]1. Persuade others how to vote; 2. Actively work for party or candidate; 3. Attend political meeting or rally; 4. Contribute money to party or candidate; 5. Membership in political clubs; 6. Voted in 1964 presidential election; 7. Voted in 1960 presidential election; 8. Frequency of voting in local elections; 9. Work with others on local problems; 10. Form a group to work on local problems; 11. Active membership in community problem-solving organizations; 12. Contact local officials; 13. Contact state and national officials.

[b]Factor I: Campaign Activity (Variables 1–5); Factor II; Voting (Variable 6–8); Factor III: Cooperative Activity (Variables 9–11); Factor IV: Contracting (Variables 12–13).

Brecht, Dracup, Moser, and Riegel: Relationship of Marital Quality and Psychosocial Adjustment

In a past chapter we discussed nonexperimental research, which includes those studies with no manipulation of the independent variables. Generally, the variation between existing variables is studied and in some cases a causal inference is implied weakly. Such studies are prevalent in research done in applied settings. Researchers doing studies in applied settings do not usually have the luxury of random assignment or random selection. Keith (1999) states specifically that a large number of research studies done in school psychology are nonexperimental in nature. Another area where nonexperimental research is the dominant methodology is in the health sciences. We refer particularly to nursing research. Nursing databases are large but complex and nonexperimental. However, key information can be obtained from such data and research.

One fruitful method of analyzing nursing's nonexperimental data is covariance structure analysis or structural equation modeling (SEM). One such study that properly and successfully used this method and as such demonstrated the value of such a method was by Brecht, Dracup, Moser, and Riegel (1994).

Here the researchers studied the psychosocial adjustment of patients suffering from heart disease. Past research on this topic had been suggestive of relations between certain variables and psychosocial adjustment, but the precise nature of the relationship of variables and adjustment has not been defined. Brecht et al. attempted to define this by addressing the finding that some patients recover faster from cardiac surgery than others and experience less emotional distress.

Brecht et al. hypothesized that the quality of the marital relationship, dysphoria (anxiety, depression and hostility), age, and time since surgery have possible indirect and direct effects on psychosocial adjustment. The sample consisted of 198 male cardiac patients. Measurements on the variables were taken at two different times. The first was at the beginning of the study (Time 1), and the second (Time 2) was done three months later. The primary dependent variable was Psychosocial Adjustment. It was measured using the Psychosocial Adjustment to Illness Scale (PAIS). High scores on this scale indicated poorer adjustment. The quality of marital relationship was measured using the Spanier Dyadic Adjustment Scale, and dysphoria was measured using the Multiple Affect Adjective Checklist (MAACL).

The original complete Brecht, et al. model was not given in the article. This is common practice for published articles where the model is extensive and space is limited. What is generally reported is the final model. During the model testing process, statistically nonsignificant paths were eliminated using the Wald test, which is one of two popular tests for finding which parameters are not necessary in the model (for more details, see Bentler, 1995; Ullman, 1996). The final Brecht, et al. model is given in Figure 35.6. It demonstrates some of the things that covariance structure analysis can do. For one, the structure of the model can be tested over time. In other words, it is capable of analyzing complex data collected longitudinally. The data or model at Time 1 can be considered a baseline measure of the relations. Also, these researchers allowed for the correlation between error measured across time.

The final structural model was supported by the data. The goodness-of-fit statistic, χ^2 was 109.41, with 90 degrees of freedom. This chi-square value was not significant. Also the Bentler–Bonnet NFI was 0.95. Both statistics point to a good fit of the empirical data to the hypothesized model. All of the coefficients shown in Figure 35.6 were estimated from the EQS program and were statistically significant.

Brecht et al.'s findings imply that developing a better marital relationship would promote healthier psychosocial adjustment to illness, if we can accept the notion that we are dealing with "causal" modeling. With this information, cardiac nurses or counselors can focus on supporting a healthy marital relationship between male heart patients and their wives. They can teach the dyad strategies for achieving a positive marital relation. By doing so, it gives the patient the chance of significant improvement in emotional stress.

■ **FIGURE 35.6** *Covariance Structural Model (Brecht et al. data)*

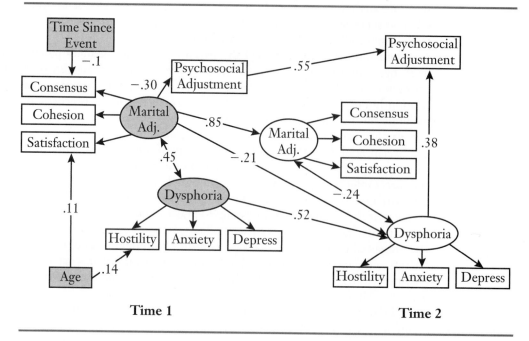

Conclusions — and Reservations

It would be wrong to create an impression in the reader's mind that all problems attacked with analysis of covariance structures or structural equation modeling work out as well as those described in this chapter, or that it should be used with all multivariate research problems. Quite the contrary. The purpose of this final section of the chapter is to try to put the subject into reasonable perspective.

Let's ask the most difficult question first: When should this procedure be used? As usual with such questions, it is hard to say clearly and unambiguously when it should be used. One fairly safe precept is that it should *not* be used routinely or for ordinary statistical analysis and calculations. For instance, it should not be used to factor analyze a set of data to "discover" the factors behind the variables of the set. It is simply not as well suited to exploratory factor analysis and may be an "overkill" in testing mean differences between groups or subgroups of data. If it is possible to use a simpler procedure—like multiple regression, logistic regression, multiway contingency tables, or analysis of variance—and obtain answers to research questions, then using structural equation modeling is pointless. That inappropriate use will be attempted is obvious. LISREL, EQS, and AMOS computer programs have been made easier and easier for researchers to use. Many state in their advertisement that "no experience is necessary to do structural equation modeling." What this means, among other things, is that structural equation modeling will be used more often. Unlike many other procedures, using analysis of covariance structure requires rather difficult conceptualization, technical understanding of measurement theory, multiple regression, and factor analysis. The ready availability of "easy-to-use" computer programs could lead to the inappropriate use of analysis of covariance structure. The same was true, if to a lesser extent, of the use of factor analysis. Yet, factor analysis has been integrated "successfully" into the body of behavioral research methodology, but too often poorly used (see Comrey, 1978). The nature of computer packages almost makes this inevitable. One of their purposes is to make easy what is essentially not easy. So we will be seeing the publication of many studies that have used LISREL, EQS, AMOS and other similar programs inadequately. In short, these covariance structure programs should only be used at a relatively late stage of a research program when "crucial" tests of complex hypotheses are needed.

Analysis of covariance structures are most suited to the study and analysis of complex structural theoretical models in which complex chains of reasoning are used to tie theory to empirical research. Under certain conditions and limitations, the system is a powerful means of testing alternative explanations of behavioral phenomena. To solve a covariance structures' problem adequately usually requires a good deal of preliminary thought and analysis—away from the computer and its programs.

Another use to which covariance structure computer programs can be well put is checking on complex results from other analyses. In the past, for example, path analysis has been used to analyze the data of many research problems. While path analysis is a useful approach to research problems—it is particularly helpful in conceptualizing the problems—it cannot accomplish what computer programs like LISREL can. Maruyama and Miller (1979) made this point when they discussed why they used LISREL to reanalyze the desegregation data of Lewis and St. John (1974). Structural equation modeling programs like EQS and LISREL often have the capability of neatly settling research hypotheses issues when other methods cannot. Yet it is not a generally applicable methodology. It is definitely not a panacea for badly designed studies.

There are often technical difficulties in using these methods. We have already discussed large and significant χ^2s with large numbers of subjects, and have suggested remedies, especially study of residuals and the use of other goodness-of-fit indices, like the Bentler NFI or the CFI, that do not depend on sample size. Another remedy is the testing of alternative hypotheses when the problem permits such testing.

One of the most difficult problems is that of *identification*. A model being tested must be overidentified. This means that there must be more data points, usually variances and covariances, than parameters estimated. If there are n measured dependent variables then there can be no more than t parameters estimated from the data, where $t = n(n + 1)/2$. If $n = 5$, then $t = 5(5 + 1)/2 = 15$, and no more than 15 parameters can be estimated in a model. There are other conditions that can make a model not identifiable, but it is extremely difficult to specify them in advance.

The most common technical difficulty is closely related to identification. For any one or combination of reasons, the computer program may not run and may announce that "something" is wrong. But what? On the other hand, the computer run may be completed, but some of the parameters may not make sense. For example, negative variances may be reported. Why? Anyone who has used "canned" computer programs to any extent is familiar with the lugubrious messages the computer announces. When an expert is consulted, the answer is invariably: "There is something wrong with the model." Yes, of course! But what? And, naturally, theoretical models often do not fit: "There is something wrong with the model!" And, too, there is the frequent occurrence of the computer analysis that works beautifully, but the statistics indicate that the researcher's model doesn't fit. Is the theory wrong? If one is strongly committed to a theoretical position, it may be difficult to admit this. In any case, one has to check several possibilities. First, the model doesn't fit because it was poorly or incorrectly conceptualized. Second, it doesn't fit because the user of the computer programs made a mistake (or two, or three) in using the system. Third, the computer analysis won't work because there are flaws in the data (strong multi-collinearity in a correlation matrix, for example). And fourth, the model doesn't fit because the theory from which it was derived is wrong or inapplicable.

Inadequate measurement is a limitation of much behavioral research. The technical difficulty of measuring psychological and sociological variables is still not appreciated by researchers in psychology, sociology, and education. It is not easy to devise tests and scales to measure psychological and sociological constructs. It is also not easy to do the psychometric research necessary to establish the reliability and validity of the measures used. It is even more difficult, evidently, to admit that one's measures are deficient. Refer back to Comrey's research on personality in Chapter 34. The development of the Comrey Personality Scale required 15 years of work. Too often in behavioral research, measures in common use are accepted and used without question. And rarely are assumptions about study variables questioned. If we are measuring, say, Authoritarianism, we assume that part of the latent variable Authoritarianism is Antiauthoritarianism (whatever that is). Early in this chapter and in Chapter 34 we studied research that sprang from questioning the commonly held assumption that Conservatism and Liberalism are logical and empirical opposites. Unfortunately, a number of studies have been done—and marred—by measurement of social attitudes based on this asumption (see Kerlinger, 1984). Similarly, other studies have been marred, perhaps ruined, both by incorrect assumptions and inadequate measurement.

An analytic methodology, no matter how well conceived and powerful, cannot make up for measures whose reliability and validity are unsatisfactory. Validity by assumption is a particularly severe threat to scientific conclusions, because measurement procedures are not questioned or tested: Their reliability and validity are assumed. It is a poor factor analysis that emerges from factoring what is in effect sloppy choice or construction of tests and scales. Similarly, it is poor use of analysis of covariance structures when some or all of the measures used have little sound technical basis in psychometric theory and empirical research. The point being made should be strongly emphasized: Elegant procedures applied to poor data, gathered without regard to theory and logical analysis, cannot produce anything of scientific value.

Another difficulty for users of analysis of covariance structure is that modern multivariate structural analysis is quite different from most earlier statistical analysis. The preoccupation of classical statistics was assessing whether observed mean differences (in an analysis of variance) or the joint and separate contributions of independent variables (in a multiple regression analysis) were statistically significant. With structural modeling, however, implications of a theory are built into a model that reflects the theory and its implications: latent variables are included, their relations and effects assessed, and the whole structure of relations subjected to simultaneous testing. The test or tests are based on the congruence of the hypothesized model with the obtained data. It is not surprising that researchers experience logical, technical, and theoretical failures. Indeed, it is surprising that models can be and are successfully tested, given the complexity and even delicacy of the undertaking.

There seems to be no reasonable alternative, however. Science requires the formulation of theories *and* their empirical testing. Behavioral science and research deal with psychological and sociological explanations of complex human and social phenomena. They therefore require both complex theories in which sets of observed and latent variables are related to each other *and* complex methods of conceptualizing and analyzing the data that are produced by controlled observation and measurement of the sets of variables. To date, multivariate analysis and analysis of covariance structures seem to be the most promising ways to accomplish the goals of behavioral science. That they will pose many difficult, even intractable, methodological problems is obvious. That they will yield both theoretical and practical advances and benefits has already been demonstrated in this chapter.

Despite the difficulties and reservations mentioned above, there can be little doubt that analysis of covariance structures and the computer programs that implement it are outstanding, highly valuable, and useful contributions to scientific behavioral research. We conclude this chapter by saying that their use and influence will have strong and salutary effects on the development of psychological and sociological theory and its testing, and on the material advance of scientific behavioral research in general.

CHAPTER SUMMARY

1. Analysis of covariance structure is also called structural equation modeling (SEM). At one time it was called causal modeling, but that term was later dropped since causality cannot be inferred from correlations.
2. Modern covariance structure analysis was introduced by Bock and Bargmann and developed by Joreskog.
3. Analysis of covariance structure is considered to be the highest form of analysis for social and behavioral science data. It is a complex combination of multiple regression and factor analysis.

4. Path diagrams are often used to develop pictorially the structural model to be tested. There are certain rules to follow when developing path diagrams in order to ease the translation into computer program analyses.

5. There are essentially three different types of variables in covariance structure analysis:

  • Independent variables (measured or latent)
  • Dependent variables (measured or latent)
  • Error measurements

6. Latent variables are often called factors or unmeasured variables.

7. The computer program used by the authors to perform analysis of covariance structure is Bentler's EQS.

8. EQS is (in the opinion of the second author) an easier method for beginners to understand.

9. LISREL by Joreskog is also used in many studies reported in journals. AMOS is another program which many claim is easy to use.

10. Analysis of covariance structure computer programs are capable of doing confirmatory factor analysis.

11. Identification is among the problems encountered in structural modeling covariance structures. The model needs to be overidentified.

12. There need to be more data points than parameters estimated, in order for the model to work properly.

13. Analysis of covariance structure is best used in later stages of research where the researcher has gathered sufficient information on the relations between variables.

14. The availability of computer programs, such as EQS, LISREL, and AMOS, and their growing ease in use, bring with them the possibility of bad research studies.

15. Regardless of the statistical methodology employed by the researcher, validity remains an important goal in research studies.

STUDY SUGGESTIONS

1. The subject of covariance structure analysis presupposes knowledge of matrix algebra, factor analysis, and multiple regression analysis. Almost all of Joreskog's papers are difficult to read. His earlier works are contained in the book by Magidson (1979). Here is a list of references that discuss analysis of covariance structure. Some are quite readable.

Bentler, P. M. (1980). Causal modeling. *Annual Review of Psychology, 31,* 419–456. [One of the early clearly written discussions on analysis of covariance structures. Bentler and others doing research in this area at that time used the word *causal*. This was later criticized by Freedman (1987) (see Freedman citation below).]

Cliff, N. (1987). Comments on Professor Freedman's paper. *Journal of Educational Statistics, 12*, 158–160. [An update of his 1983 paper with some information provided by Freedman's paper.]

Freedman, D. A. (1987). As others see us. A case study of causal modeling methods. *Journal of Educational Statistics, 12*, 101–128. [This article pointed out that causal inferences cannot be made from the use of correlations. This led many to avoid using the word causal when dealing with covariance structure analysis. Freedman also states that there are a number of assumptions that are difficult to check and may be false in specific applications.]

Hayduk, L. A. (1987). Structural equation modeling with LISREL: Essentials and advances. Baltimore: Johns Hopkins University Press. [A well-written book with excellent explanations of the LISREL model for analyzing structural equations. It is, however, not for the beginner because it requires knowledge of matrix algebra.]

Loehlin, J. C. (1998). *Latent variable models: An introduction to factor, path, and structural analysis* (3rd ed.). Mahwah, NJ: Lawrence Erlbaum. [Provides a good definition of path analysis and latent trait analysis. Points out the caution that a researcher should take in analysis of covariance structures. A heavy emphasis on path diagrams in discussing structural equations. Topics discussed can be applied to any of the many computer programs for covariance structure analysis.]

Ullman, J. B. (1996). Structural equation modeling. In B. G. Tabachnick & L. S. Fidell, Eds., *Using multivariate statistics* (3rd ed.). New York: Harper & Row, pp. 709–811. [A popular book; Chapter 14 is well written covering the "nuts-and-bolts" of structural equation modeling. Provides a good comparison of the computer programs that perform covariance structure analysis. The material in this book with the exception of Chapter 14 was written entirely by Tabachnick and Fidell; Ullman is the only contributor.]

2. Six research studies that have profitably used analysis of covariance structures follow.

Holahan, C. J., Moos, R. H., Holahan, C. K., & Brennen, P. L. (1995). Social support, coping, depressive symptoms in a late-middle-aged sample of patients reporting cardiac illness. *Health Psychology, 14*, 152–163. [Using LISREL, developed a predictive model of depressive symptoms. The article contains the correlation matrix of nine observable variables. It is ideal for students who want to try out EQS, LISREL, or AMOS programs.]

Keith, T. Z. (1999). Structural equation modeling in school psychology. In C. R. Reynolds & T. B. Gutkin, Eds. *Handbook of school psychology* (3rd. Ed.). New York: Willey, pp. 78–107. [An outstanding chapter written by one of the leading research methodologists in school psychology. Keith provides an overview of how covariance structure analysis or structural equation modeling is used to handle complex non-experimental studies in school psychology. Easy to read. Highly recommended.]

Musil, C. M., Jones, S. L., & Warner, C. D. (1998). Structural equation modeling and its relationship to multiple regression and factor analysis. *Research in Nursing and Health, 21,* 271–281. [Uses a conceptual and nontechnical approach to explain how structural equations can be used in nursing research. The authors show how the method was used to study the relationships among stresses, strains, and physical health in elder adults.]

Nyamathi, A., Stein, J. A., & Brecht, M.-L. (1995). Psychosocial predictors of AIDS risk behavior and drug use behavior in homeless and drug addicted women of color. *Health Psychology, 14,* 265–273. [Developed a structural model relating personal and social resources, coping styles, risk reduction and AIDS risk. These researchers obtained a set of factors (latent variables) and then modeled the factors.]

Wolfle, L., & Robertshaw, D. (1982). Effects of college attendance on locus of control. *Journal of Personality and Social Psychology, 43,* 802–810. [Interesting and well-done study of data from a national longitudinal study of the high school class of 1972.]

Wyllie, A., Zhang, J. F., & Casswell, S. (1998). Positive responses to televised beer advertisements associated with drinking and problems reported by 18- to 29-year-olds. *Addiction, 93,* 749–760. [Used structural equation modeling to study the relation between responses to alcohol advertisements and drinking behavior and alcohol-related problems. Researchers hypothesized that positive responses to televised beer advertisements attributed to the quantity of alcohol consumed on drinking occasions, which in turn contributed to the level of alcohol-related problems. The model was consistent with the hypothesis.]

APPENDIXES

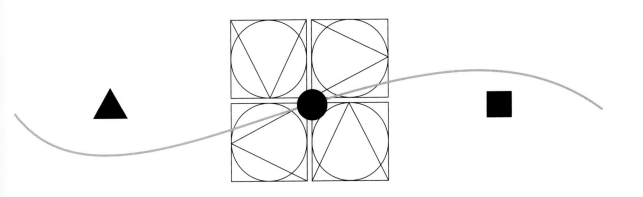

APPENDIX A

APPENDIX B

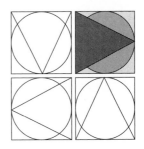

GUIDE FOR WRITING RESEARCH REPORTS

The principal means of scientific communication is the research paper. Over the years, the format of such reports has become standardized in a way to best meet the requirements of scientific communication. The conventions for writing a scientific report are concerned with the organization of the report and the style of presentation. Report writing must be both brief and clear. Typographical errors, strikeovers, cross–outs, and badly written statements detract from the presentation of the report.

When writing the report of an experiment, it is necessary that the experimenter include everything relevant to the problem under study. The theoretical basis of the study must be emphasized. The reader of the report must be able to understand how prediction follows from theory. The report must be clear in every detail concerning the manner in which the study was carried out. The report must show precisely how conditions were set up to permit manipulation or the study of the variables in the order demanded by the hypothesis. The report must be sufficiently detailed to permit the exact duplication of the study by another independent researcher. Finally, the report must state what results were obtained and what interpretation of these can be made within the context of the theory. An experimental report is a complete cycle beginning with theory and ending with theory.

There are a number of popular styles for writing research reports. They are all similar as far as what the researcher should put into the paper. However, the details within the styles themselves differ. Among one of the more popular and "easier" styles is the one by the American Psychological Association. This style is often referred to as "APA Style." Although it was originally developed for psychology journals published by the American Psychological Association, it has made its way into non-APA journals and also non-psychology journals.

It is this style that we will present here since it is the most often used style of writing found in the social and behavioral sciences. Even many education journals have adopted this style. However, our descriptions are brief and one of the goals is to give the reader a general idea of how research papers are organized. This is no substitute for the actual Manual of the American Psychological Association (1994). From its origin as a brief size manual, the manual has grown considerably in size and detail. The most current edition published in 1994 consists of 368 pages. Obviously, a brief section in a textbook cannot possibly capture all of the details contained in the current full-sized manual. The brief presentation here will be enough to give the reader some information that will help that person when consulting the actual manual itself. Also, there are several publications geared toward helping the beginner learn and understand this style of presentation (see Gelfand & Walker, 1990; Hubbach, 1995; Parrott, 1994; Pyrczak & Bruce, 1992). The Hubbach (1996) book includes special sections on scientific papers, APA style and excellent examples.[1]

The outline of the research paper for APA style is:

1. Title Page
2. Abstract
3. Introduction
4. Method
    a. Participants
    b. Apparatus/Materials
    c. Procedure
5. Results
6. Discussion
7. References
8. Tables
9. Figures

Title Page

The title page is a separate page that contains the title of the study. It also contains the running head and the name of the author or authors with their institutional affiliation. The running head is a one to two key word description of the study and appears on every page of the manuscript. If your manuscript is submitted for publication, it serves as a useful identification tool for the editor.

The purpose of a title is to provide a miniature description of your study. To convey the most information, titles typically include the independent and the dependent variables of the experiment. A simple model of a title is as follows: THE DEPENDENT VARIABLES AS A FUNCTION OF THE INDEPENDENT VARIABLES. To write a title for your experiment you could simply substitute the dependent variable(s) and independent variable(s) into the simple model. This might give you something like, Sexual Stimulation as a Function of Caffeine or Reduction

---

[1]The authors thank Roberta J. Landi for calling our attention to the Hubbach book.

of Anxiety by Use of Filmed Modeling. Titles such as "Psychology Experiment" or "Course Project" are NOT acceptable. The title should generally be 15 words or less.

Abstract

The purpose of an abstract is to provide a summary of the research paper. It must contain enough information to tell the reader the purpose and results of the research. It must contain the major points from each section of the paper:

- a statement of the problem
- a very brief description of the method
- a definition of all abbreviations and acronyms
- the most important results, and
- the conclusions.

The abstract is typed as a single paragraph with no paragraph indentation. Like the title page, the abstract appears on a page by itself. It should not exceed 15 single-spaced type-written lines or 200 words. It must not include any data or extensive interpretation. This section is labeled "Abstract" and the label is centered on the page.

Introduction

a. The introduction must begin with the *background* of the experiment or study. This is an account of the theory and previous research relevant to your study. The introduction tells the reader the importance of the study by giving a brief review of the literature of papers that are relevant to this research study. Using APA style, this is the only section of the paper that does not receive a label. In different words, *no* label such as "Introduction" is to appear in the paper written in APA style. One must be accurate in reporting of previous work that was relevant to the research study. All direct copying must be encased in quotation marks, and proper reference to the source must be made. Be sure the studies cited are relevant to the experiment. Referrals to articles done by other researchers in the introduction (or any section of the paper) are done by giving the last name of each author and the year of publication. The year of publication is encased in parentheses. The complete reference for any citation must be given in the Reference section that is at the end of the paper.

Example

Smith and Martin (1953) reported that the performance of their participants improved under these conditions, while a decrement in performance was observed by other investigators (Burns, 1950; Stevens & White, 1943).

Specific references to information in a book or journal article is indicated as follows:

Thomas (1983, p. 304) reported that . . . .
The results of an earlier study (Carter, 1992, pp. 279–285) led to . . .

A researcher should never list a reference that has not been read personally. In reporting information obtained from a secondary source, cite the secondary source in the text and list it in the references.

Example

An experiment by Jones as reported by McGeoch (1982), found that . . .

b. After the reader has been given the background for the study, the introduction proceeds with the purpose or theoretical base for your experiment. The specific problem under study is stated along with a theoretical or literary statement of the hypothesis to be tested and general predictions and expectations of the outcome of the research.

Example

Dysphoria may serve as a significant confounding variable. . . . Therefore, we conducted a study to examine the relationships among . . .

c. The hypothesis must then be translated into operational terms. The researcher must specify what variables are to be manipulated (independent), if any, and which are to be observed (dependent). The independent and dependent variables should be made clear *without* using a sentence that says: "The independent variable was_____ and the dependent variable was _____." Rather, one might say something like: "In this experiment (study), the number of correct answers to test questions was investigated as a function of the rate of presentation of the questions," or "We hypothesized that the indirect effects of marital relationship on psychosocial adjustment are mediated through. . . ."

d. Finally, use the Introduction to define any terms that are used for the first time. If the researcher wants to refer to the Comrey Personality Scales as the CPS, a sentence such as:

The Comrey Personality Scales (Comrey, 1970), hereafter referred to as the CPS was used to . . .

A word like *learning* is probably too general to use in exact technical writing. Say exactly which learning paradigm is meant. This would be the same for words like *personality* or *anxiety*.

There is a tendency to write too much detail in the Introduction. The details of the experiment or study are not to be presented in the introduction section of the paper. The details of the experiment or study are presented in the Method section. It is allowable to have an outline or the general methodology to be followed in the introduction, but no details given. The results of the study should not appear in the Introduction. There is a separate section for that.

Method

The Method section has three subheadings: Participants, Apparatus/Materials, and Procedure. Each are described separately below. The Method section as a whole, describes the experimentation or the conduct of the study. It must be written in sufficient detail so that other investigators could take the description and repeat what has been done *exactly*.

Participants

The Participants section constitutes a description of the characteristics of the participants used in the study or experiment. It tells who the participants were, how many there were, and any details that might be relevant. It also includes how the participants were selected. Among the description of the participants, most studies describe the participants in terms of gender, age, education level, ethnicity, and any other such relevant descriptors.

Example

> The participants (Ss) were 48 people chosen from a sample of those seated by the fountain in front of City Hall at 10 to 11 AM on a Monday in the month of July 1998. The 18 males and 30 females, ranging in age from 15 to 35, represented every third person that stopped at the fountain for a period of at least 5 minutes. Ten other people who were contacted refused to fill out the questionnaire.

When groups of participants are used, a description must be provided telling the reader how the participants were assigned to the various groups or treatment conditions.

Apparatus and Materials (Instrumentation)

All nontrivial materials and apparatus used in the experiment must be described in sufficient detail for someone to set up the identical situation. If the experiment required pencils, they need not be defined here unless they were unusual pencils that have a specific effect on the study. If you are using standardized materials or apparatus, such as a personality test, they are not usually referenced here unless they had some special features that were most important in your experiment. Standard existing instruments such as the Comrey Personality Scales is referenced in the procedure section. If you construct or use new materials or apparatus, such as those of your own creation, you must describe them fully. Include information about materials used to time and/or record responses. If certain special equipment was used in the experiment such as "the Smith-Johnson Oscillator Coil Model 9" the reader should be informed as to where such a device can be obtained.

Procedure

The Procedure section is a description or account of the sequence of events that took place during the execution of the study or experiment. In short, this tells what was done by the experimenter(s) and to the participant(s). You should describe what was done, in what order, for how long, et cetera.

Example

> The data were collected on each participant using a drug frequency questionnaire during the fourth period in a school day. The participants were asked to indicate the amount of alcohol they consumed.

The statistical methods used to analyze the data collected from the study and/or the design of the research study may be presented in the procedure section.

It is possible that at some time you will discover you have deviated from the procedure that you should have followed. If this happens, describe the procedure exactly as it was conducted—not as it should have been conducted. This is usually carelessness, but it is ultimately excusable.

Dishonesty is not excusable. Procedure sections may tend to get too complicated in experiments where there are several phases or conditions. In this case, it is frequently helpful to adopt labels for the phases or conditions. For example, with a teaching machine you might divide a trial into the "study phase" and the "test phase" for purposes of distinctive and simplified reference later.

Results

The data obtained in the study or experiment and the analysis performed on them are reported in the Results section.

a. It begins with a description of the dependent variable measures that were recorded during the experimental session. With a teaching machine example, you would record the number of errors and the length of time to answer the questions.

b. Next, describe the data from the experiment. The data you report will generally be some type of summary of the raw data. For example, perhaps you are going to report the results in terms of the means and standard deviations of the raw data recorded during the session. You might say, "The mean and standard deviation of the number of errors were calculated for each series of 20 questions."

c. Then refer to the place where these data can be found. Data can be presented in either tables or figures (graphs). They are labeled using numbers and referred to by number. As an example, you might say, "The mean errors for each series of 20 questions is shown in Table 1 (or Figure 1)." If you have several dependent variables, the results for each variable may require a separate table or figure. Rules for the preparation of tables and figures are given in a later section of this appendix.

d. After you refer to a table or figure, you should describe the important features of the data shown in the figure or table. There is much information presented in a table or figure and it is your job to aid the reader in comprehending it. You must point out the important features, the general trends, and any inversions or peculiarities that seem to you to be important; that is, which seem to be more than chance occurrences.

You should support your analysis of the information in a table or figure by giving some appropriate data values to illustrate your point. Do not, however, attempt to cite all of the data. That is what tables and figures are for. If you have 25 pages of a computer output, this output must be summarized and put into a table or figure. If the output is to be included, it will only be an attachment to the paper. Large attachments are generally unacceptable if the manuscript is submitted for publication.

Example

As shown in Figure 1, the functions for reward and non-reward conditions begin at the same level. The mean number of errors on the first trial was approximately 4.5 for both conditions. After the first trial, the errors for the reward condition began to drop at a fairly steady rate, while the errors for the non-reward condition remained relatively constant. For instance, on the second trial, .50 fewer errors were made in the reward condition, but by the sixth trial this difference had increased until 3.39 fewer errors were made in the reward condition. Overall, the mean number of errors decreases as a function of trials in the reward condition, but not in the non-reward condition.

One final rule for writing the Results section is that there must be *no discussion* in the Results section. That is, there is no personal opinion or interpretation of the data summaries. Only the facts of the findings are presented in the Results section of the paper. This is more fully explained in the next section.

Discussion

The purpose of the Discussion section is to interpret the results and to explain the conclusions to which they led. It is here that the contribution or value of your experiment or study is made clear.

    a. The discussion generally begins with a concise statement of the important results.

Example

The results of the present study are in agreement with other studies comparing alcohol to drug abuse in Latin American youths.

    b. Next is the interpretation of the results. An inference is made from the particular dependent measures of the experiment to the psychological process of interest.

Example

Asian youths have consistently reported lower drug use because they may feel more threatened by the perceived consequences of their acknowledged drug use.

Apparently there is a difficult distinction between Results and Discussion sections involved here. In the Results section you adhere strictly to the particular dependent variables of the study. All inferences, interpretations, extrapolations, and reasonable opinion belong in the Discussion section.

For example, in the Results section, the research study talks about a decrease in errors as a function of trials in the reward condition, while errors remain constant in the non-reward condition. In the Discussion section, this might be interpreted to mean that acquisition (or learning) took place in the reward condition, but not in the non-reward condition. The interpretation that learning has been affected differentially involves and inference made from the error data, and therefore belongs in the Discussion and not in the Results section.

    c. The results of your experiment or study should then be related to the results of other studies on the same or similar problems, and/or to any relevant theories with which you are familiar and can document. Point out how your results agree or disagree with previous work, how they extend the body of knowledge, support or disagree with theory, and so on. The relation of your results to other results or theories must also be rationalized. If there is agreement, it is sufficient to simply state exactly what the agreement is. In the case of disagreement, you should offer some possible reasons for the discrepancy. Typically, the first explanation that will occur to you is that there was something wrong with your experiment. This may or may not be true. If it is true, point out exactly what the weakness was and *why*.

d. Any weaknesses or flaws in your experiment that limit the usefulness or generality of the conclusions that can be drawn should be discussed. When you report a weakness, also explain why it is a weakness, and indicate how it can be corrected. Do not create a lengthy list of criticisms, this will only create a bad impression to the reader/reviewer.

e. A good way to end a discussion is to suggest what the next experiment on the same topic might be. If you attempt to do this, be sure to explain the experiment in enough detail for it to be meaningful, and explain the reasoning that makes it the logical step. Statements like the following examples must be avoided because they waste space and time.

Examples

Bigger rewards should be used in the next experiment.
Better participants should have been used.

You would need to explain why the current set of participants were deficient and how the newer participants would be different.

References

Only references cited in the body of the paper must be given in the reference list. *All citations must appear in the reference list.* The listing is in alphabetical order by first author's last name. The author's first and middle initials follow the last name. *The names of journals are written out in full.*

For journal articles, page numbers for the entire article are cited. Do not cite the total number of pages in a book. In an edited book, list only the page numbers that pertain to that part of the book (chapter) written by the author(s) you are citing. Examples of the style to be used for the most frequent types of references are given below. The type of publication is noted inside brackets only to help you to identify each—you would not do this in your paper's reference section.

Note that American Psychological Association style of writing references has the year of publication encased in parentheses, following the authors' names. The article title follows the date. Only the first letter of the first word in each sentence of the article title is capitalized. The first letter of the first word following a colon is also capitalized. The name of the journal, volume number of journal and page numbers of the article within that journal are listed next. The name of the journal and the volume number is either underlined or set in *italics*. The beginning letters of the journal title are capitalized (initial capitalization).

For books, the author's name is followed by the date of publication encased in parentheses. The title of the book is given next. Note that only the first letter of the first word in each sentence of the book title is capitalized. The title of the book is also <u>underlined</u> or set *italics*. The title of the book is followed either by the edition number of the book (2nd edition [no italics]), or by the volume number (vol. 3 [no italics]). If no special edition or volume number is needed, then follow the title with a period. The city followed by a colon (:), and the name of the publisher followed by a period (.) concludes the entry.

Examples

Erlich, O., & Lee, H. B. (1978). Use of regression analysis in reporting test results for accountability. *Perceptual and Motor Skills, 47,* 879–882. [Journal article, two authors]

Hollenbeck, A. (1978). Problems of reliability in observational research. In G. Sackett, Ed., *Observing behavior: Vol. 2. Data collection and analysis methods* (pp. 79–98). Baltimore: University Park Press. [Chapter in an edited volume, with volume also having a special title]

Jeffrey, W. E. (1969). Early stimulation and cognitive development. In J.P. Hill, Ed., <u>Minnesota Symposia on Child Development (vol. 3)</u> (pp. 46–61). Minneapolis: University of Minnesota Press. [Chapter in an edited volume]

Kerlinger, F. N. (1986). *Foundations of behavioral research* (3rd ed.). Fort Worth, TX: Harcourt Brace. [Book]

Stevens, S. S. (Ed.). (1951). <u>Handbook of experimental psychology.</u> New York: JohnWiley & Sons. [Book with editor as author]

Yi, S. (1977). Some implications of Jeffrey's serial habituation hypothesis: A theoretical basis of resolving one-look versus multiple-look attentional account of discrimination learning. *Journal of General Psychology, 97,* 89–99. [Journal article, one author]

The Preparation of Figures

Figures must contain the basic information necessary for comprehension without detailed reference to the text. This requires careful labeling of coordinates and a complete caption (title). When more than one curve is shown on the same set of coordinates, you must use a legend as in Figure A.1, or label the curve directly. *The figure caption appears below the art* and consists of a very brief summary of what is plotted on the graph. Avoid captions like "Graph of the Results" or "A Graph of . . ." Only the first word in the caption is capitalized and a period is placed at the end. Number the figures successively with Arabic numerals. Use a ruler to connect the data points. Do not smooth the curve by drawing it freehand. If possible, use one of the many computer programs for generating graphs. Microsoft Excel, for example, is capable of producing some very nice-looking graphs suitable for presentation in an article. Some word-processing programs such as Microsoft Word are also capable of producing graphs. There are, of course, other very elaborate programs for constructing graphs.

The Preparation of Tables

As with figures, tables must contain sufficient information to be understood largely independent of the text. The title must state concisely what is contained in the table. Make the title as specific as possible. Avoid titles like: "Data Table," "Table of

Example

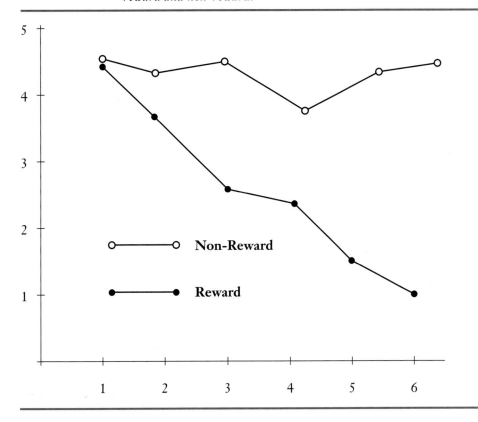

🔲 **FIGURE A.1** *Mean number of errors as a function of trials under conditions of reward and non-reward.*

Results," or "Table showing . . ." In general, avoid uncommon abbreviations. If they are necessary, they should be explained in a footnote to the table.

Arrange the table in a form that is easy for the reader to interpret. If necessary, more than one table should be used. *The title is centered above the table.* Headings, capitalization, and other important features of a table can be derived from a study of Table A.1 (page A14) in this document. Note that computer word-processing programs such as Microsoft Word have built-in capabilities for generating tables. Be sure the data included in your table is aligned properly; that is, percent signs, decimals, and columns. This makes it easier for the reader to view and follow the data.

Although no exact limitation is set for the number of figures and tables, many journals will have limited space for articles and as such request that only the most necessary tables and figures be included in the actual paper. A researcher with a large number of tables, figures, computer output, and such can make them available to

Example

■ **TABLE A.1** *Mean Errors as a Function of Trials under Conditions of Reward and Non-reward.*

	Mean Errors	
Trials	*Reward*	*Non-reward*
1	4.49	4.51
2	3.80	4.30
3	2.62	4.45
4	2.31	3.87
5	1.46	4.37
6	1.12	4.51

interested readers. There is an organization that will accept these materials and for a nominal fee make them available to any one interested in seeing the additional data. If the researcher chooses to use this service, a reference or a footnote should be made in the actual paper. That footnote might look like the following.

Example

[1]The correlation matrices on which this study was based have been deposited with the National Auxiliary Publications Service. See NAPS Document No. _____ for ____ pages of supplementary material from NAPS, c/o Microfiche Publications, 248 Hempstead Turnpike, West Hempstead, NY 11552. Remit in advance, in U.S. funds only, $ _____ for photocopy or $ _____ for microfiche. Outside of U.S. and Canada add postage of $ ____ or $ _____ for microfiche postage.

This material would be prepared and submitted with the article for publication. The material would be labeled for deposit with NAPS. If the manuscript is accepted for publication, the additional information is sent to NAPS. NAPS will return to the author and journal editor the document number and charge amounts.

The Use of Abbreviations

When a word or term is used very frequently in a report, it may be abbreviated. Abbreviations for participant(s) and experimenter(s) are standard and are almost always used:

Examples:

> participant = S   participants = S s   participant's = S's   participants' = Ss'
> experimenter = E experimenters = E s experimenter's = E's experimenters' = Es'

Other abbreviations are not standard and must be defined the first time they are used.

Example

> The apparatus was a visual test module (VTM). The VTM was programmed to
> . . . The test instrument was the Comrey Personality Scales, hereafter referred
> to as the CPS, consisted of eight scales.

Style, Tenses, Et Cetera

The activity described in the research report took place in the past and is described in the past tense. Personal pronouns are very rarely used, and so are statements about E's desires, wishes, conclusions, and so on.

Examples

> Poor: The E wanted to find out . . .
> Better: The purpose of the study was . . .
> Poor: We decided that the experiment showed . . .
> Better: The conclusion of the study was . . .

Avoid excessive use of parenthetical expressions. There is a tendency to refer to figures and tables parenthetically, which should be avoided. For example, avoid saying: "The mean errors decreased as a function of trials (Table 1)." For long sentences, however, readability may be improved through the use of parenthetical expressionsm keep in mind that you must write for the general reader. This means that you must explain things. However, you should not take on the task of teaching the reader about certain areas of basic understanding. For example, it is fine to refer to Skinner's theory of learning without going into the details of Skinner's theory. However, DO NOT ASSUME THE READER knows the study to which you are referring.

References

American Psychological Association (1994). *Publication manual for the American Psychological Association.* Washington, DC: Author.

Gelfand, H., & Walker, C. J. (1990). *Mastering APA style: Student's workbook and training guide.* Washington, DC: American Psychological Association.

Hubbach, S.M. (1995). *Writing research papers across the curriculum*(4th ed.) Fort Worth, TX: Harcourt Brace.

Parrott, L. (1994). *How to write psychology papers.* New York: Harper-Collins.

Pyrczak, F., & Bruce, R. R. (1992). *Writing empirical research reports.* Los Angeles, CA: Pyrczak Publishing.

Touching, Psychological Gender, and Helping

Sample Student Report

Karen Siegel who is currently a doctoral student at California School of Professional Psychology, San Diego, wrote the following report as an undergraduate at California State University, Northridge. It clearly illustrates how a paper is written using APA style. The report is reproduced with permission from Karen Siegel.

Prosocial Behavior as Affected by Touch and Psychological Gender

Karen Siegel
California State University Northridge

Abstract

This study predicted that prosocial (helping) behavior between female participants and experimenter would be enhanced by a casual, intentional touch of short duration. Also investigated was the effect of the participants' psychological gender (androgynous feminine or masculine) on their helping behavior. Forty volunteer female student participants filled out a questionnaire (the Bem Sex-Role Inventory) which measured their psychological gender, and were then either touched or not touched in a 2 × 3 combined, between-subjects design. The measured variable was whether the subject helped retrieve "accidentally" dropped pencils. Results showed that participants who were touched displayed more helping behavior than those who were not touched, but that their psychological gender had no effect.

Prosocial Behavior as Affected by Touch and Psychological Gender

There exists a large body of literature regarding the effect of various forms of touch on human behavior and health. Touch is considered by many researchers to be one of the most basic and earliest forms of communication (Frank, 1957; Montagu, 1971) and to be crucial for healthy emotional, social, and physical development (Harlow, 1958). Another facet of this atavistic manifestation of nonverbal communication is its manipulative property. Touch in the service of social control (defined by Edinger & Patterson, 1983, as "a more deliberate, purposeful response designed to promote a change in the other person's behavior") has been examined in a number of studies employing many modalities. In an influential 1973 study, Henley (1973) argued that touch communicates a message of power and status. She reported an asymmetry in the touches exchanged between the sexes (men touched women more than vice versa in public). Nguyen, Heslin, and Nguyen (1975) reported that types of touch are associated with the same meanings by men and women, but feelings differ, and accurate decoding of a tactile message depends not only on how it is transmitted, but also on where it is applied.

A later analysis examining the generality of asymmetry between the sexes in the use of intentional touch revealed complexities precluding a simplistic understanding of this issue. Certain of Hall and Veccia's (1990) findings differed from Henley's, and they asserted that it is not clear what different touches mean to the sexes and whether dominance/status can explain the sex effects. Major, Schmidlin, and Williams (1990) explored another of the many variations on the asymmetry theme. They found that gender patterns in touch vary markedly by setting and age, which underscores the situational specificity of gender-linked behaviors.

In a less complex context, other studies have been done relating touch (nonverbal intimacy) and increased compliance to requests made (Kleinke, 1976). Willis and Hamm (1980) found that touch is particularly important in obtaining same-sex compliance. Paulsell and Goldman (1984) examined the influence of touching different body locations (shoulder, upper and lower arm, and hand) in helping behavior. They learned that female confederates obtained varying helping responses, while for the male confederates little variation in help occurred, whether the participants were or were not touched.

High levels of nurturing and supportive behaviors are arguably a function of what is considered in American culture to be stereotypically feminine behavior. According to Bem (1975) an individual's psychological gender dictates his or her style and range of behavior. A narrowly masculine self-concept may inhibit so-called feminine behavior (such as being affectionate or gentle) and vice versa, whereas an androgynous self-concept, incorporating but not excluding masculine and feminine attributes, widens the range of behaviors that may be chosen from situation to situation.

In this experiment, the basic manipulative quality of touch in a limited interaction was studied. The effect of an innocuous, casual touch, within the context of a verbal interaction, on the helping behavior of female college student volunteers were tested. In addition, the participants were measured for psychological androgyny, femininity or masculinity with Bem's Sex-Role Inventory (1974).

It was conjectured that the condition leading to the most consistent helping response would be the touched subject with a feminine and/or androgynous profile. Conversely, it was predicted that those with a masculine profile who did not receive the touch treatment would proffer the least assistance.

Method

A 2 × 3 combined, between-subjects design was used with touch/no touch serving as one independent variable and the participants' psychological gender serving as the other independent variable. The helping behavior that was recorded was whether the participants helped retrieve pencils dropped by the experimenter immediately after instigating the touch/no touch variable.

Participants

Forty female California State University Northridge students, ranging in age from approximately 18 to 28 years, served as volunteers. In an attempt to eliminate any extraneous, possibly confounding variables concerning cultural dissimilarities in attitude toward touch and personal body space, only participants raised in the United States were used.

Procedure

This experiment employed a touch condition and a no-touch control situation, with the "touch" consisting of a light pat to the upper arm (the area that obtained the highest level of helping behavior in Paulsell & Goldman's [1984] study).

Each subject was given the Bem Sex-Role Inventory on an individual basis after being told they would be filling out a questionnaire. The experimenter supplied a pencil from a box of 20, which later served as a prop. Most participants completed the inventory, consisting of 60 adjectives and phrases printed on a single sheet, in 10 minutes or less. They were also instructed to ask for the definition of any unfamiliar phrase or word. After the subject had completed the questionnaire, the experimenter—who remained in the room the entire time—walked over to the seated subject, picked up the form and thanked the subject for participating, during which time the touch to the upper arm was or was not introduced. Immediately subsequent to this the experimenter dropped pencils from the box and quickly bent over to pick them up. The subject either got up to help (and was given a score of 1) or did not (and was given a score of 0). Prior to filling out the Bem Inventory, the subject was advised to keep seated after she was done to make helping a less accessible choice, in an attempt to render more effective the touch/no touch variable.

Results

The proportion of participants who helped and were touched (.708) was significantly greater than those who were not touched (.438), as determined by a one-tailed z-test for proportions ($z = 1.71$, $p < .05$). The significance of psychological gender was also analyzed in this manner comparing the helping behavior scores of androgynous with feminine, androgynous with masculine and feminine with masculine participants separately, as well as comparing the touch/no touch variable in each psychological gender, with no significant difference between proportions found.

A chi-square comparing the effects of the touch/no touch variable with the psychological gender of each subject on her helping behavior was not significant [$\chi_2(2) = 0.97$, $p > .05$].

Discussion

As predicted, the results of this study indicated that the helping behavior of female participants toward a same-sex experimenter was increased by an intentional, casual touch, of short duration, to the upper arm.

Female participants were used for two reasons. First, there was no male confederate, and it was highly likely that almost all male participants would help a female experimenter. (Paulsell and Goldman [1984] reported that 90% of male participants touched on the upper arm by female confederates helped pick up items dropped by those confederates.) Second, utilizing female participants controlled for any possible asymmetry in perceived gender-related status (Henley, 1973).

Though care was taken to eliminate any other explanations for this significant finding, any future investigations of this nature might be better designed as a double-blind study, since researcher expectations can be transmitted in nonverbal manners such as directness of gaze (Kleinke, 1977) or tone of voice (Goldman & Fordyce). (Similarity in communication involving these particular expressions were maintained as much as was controllable by this experimenter.)

The recent popularity of the topic of prosocial behavior has spawned a number of combinations of manipulations for the prediction of helping behavior, with significant results. Major, Schmidlin, and Williams (1990) studied the impact of age of the participants, along with the setting in which the touch occurred, on gender patterns of intentional touch. Another study by Hewitt and Feltham (1982) combined location of touch (six spots from hand to back) with gender of experimenter and subject Nguyen, Heslin, and Nguyen (1975) looked at the interpretations of different types of touch and body locations by men and women.

This study was conducted in light of the focus on the modern paradigm of the (preferable) condition of psychological androgyny. Psychological androgyny is the individual's ability, as defined by Bem (1974), to be not dichotomous in sex role, but both masculine and feminine, both assertive and yielding, both instrumental and expressive, in order to have access to an entire range of behaviors that include "masculine" and "feminine." Though no significant relationship was found between prosocial behavior and psychological gender in this particular study, this could still be a variable of interest in future experiments specifically designed to measure behaviors as affected by a subject's psychological gender. One variation might be a female experimenter with male participants measured in the same manner as this study, but using a different measurable variable, one that ideally would not involve courtly behavior. Other combinations of gender of experimenter and subject would merit examination, as well as combining the effect of psychological gender with other variables. In any case, further study does seem warranted.

References

Bem, S. L. (1974). The measurement of psychological androgyny. *Journal of Consulting and Clinical Psychology, 42*, 155–162.

Bem, S. L (1975). Sex role adaptability: One consequence of psychological androgyny. *Journal of Personality and Social Psychology, 31*, 634–643.

Edinger, E.. A., & Patterson, M. L. (1983). Nonverbal involvement and social control. *Psychological Bulletin, 93*, 30–56.

Frank, L. K. (1957). Tactile communication *Genetic Psychology Monographs, 56*, 219–225.

Goldman, M. & Fordyce, J. (1983). Prosocial behavior as affected by eye contact, touch, and voice expression. *Journal of Social Psychology, 121*, 125–129.

Hall, J. A., & Veccia, E. M. (1990). More "touching" observations; new insights on men women and interpersonal touch. *Journal of Personality and Social Psychology, 59*, 1155–1162.

Harlow, H. F. (1958). The nature of love. *American Psychologist, 13*, 673–685.

Henley, N. M. (1973). Status and sex: Some touching observations. *Bulletin of the Psychonomic Society, 2*, 91–93.

Hewitt, J. & Feltham, D. (1982). Differential reaction to touch by men and women. *Perceptual & Motor Skills, 55*, 1291–1294.

Kleinke, C. L. (1977). Compliance to requests made by gazing and touching experimenters in field settings. *Journal of Experimental Social Psychology, 13*, 218–223.

Major, B., Schmidlin, A M., & Williams, L. (1990). Gender patterns in social touch: The impact of setting and age. *Journal of Personality and Social Psychology, 58*, 634–643.

Montagu, A. (1971). *Touching: The human significance of the skin*. New York: Columbia University Press.

Nguyen, T. D., Heslin, R., & Nguyen, M. L. (1975). The meaning of touch: Sex differences. *Journal of Communications, 25*, 92–103.

Paulsell, S., & Goldman, M. (1984). The effect of touching different body areas on prosocial behavior. *The Journal of Social Psychology, 122*, 269–273.

Willis, F. N., & Hamm, H. K. (1980). The use of interpersonal touch in securing compliance. *Journal of Nonverbal Behavior, 5*, 49–55.

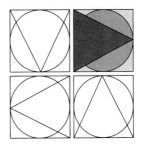

APPENDIX B[1]

▣ TABLE A   *Table of Random Numbers*

1	53	95	67	80	79	93	28	69	25	78	13	24	100	62	62	21	11	4	54	44	59	90	78	83	4	97	61	52	75	91
2	62	12	27	41	5	4	19	34	84	78	71	45	73	79	33	57	29	58	75	20	79	78	68	31	25	30	97	31	82	51
3	90	16	47	72	20	60	70	71	2	67	21	65	7	39	58	81	64	11	70	4	79	44	47	7	74	34	55	28	90	19
4	10	59	4	76	80	6	82	20	60	92	33	61	76	83	73	12	84	43	90	71	82	28	21	61	31	92	100	75	22	31
5	32	17	36	64	8	30	80	95	61	33	65	5	39	88	36	44	42	43	5	88	81	13	63	15	47	92	20	62	5	60
6	54	71	27	89	41	53	60	10	2	91	76	95	98	91	64	65	23	57	16	0	90	52	26	90	49	31	68	29	58	10
7	10	60	18	77	34	59	28	99	15	11	70	34	27	78	67	19	97	30	23	60	0	22	11	12	54	50	93	25	69	54
8	42	20	24	36	78	58	82	81	49	91	35	53	30	92	57	19	97	40	58	13	39	42	25	3	97	64	100	55	24	7
9	73	55	87	48	49	97	60	92	27	78	2	55	29	76	99	21	45	72	56	24	16	33	50	84	12	65	4	30	48	56
10	21	56	41	23	58	57	49	49	70	33	6	79	95	3	70	38	26	26	5	89	49	0	68	57	53	91	66	81	53	83
11	9	60	37	99	6	41	69	97	18	44	100	18	46	3	90	57	22	82	15	38	73	97	74	9	35	82	66	34	84	14
12	63	26	41	8	21	38	15	63	38	100	68	89	24	39	19	29	93	97	40	91	70	41	95	83	33	25	33	94	44	39
13	98	72	9	45	69	50	7	86	5	80	0	8	28	96	45	0	0	13	95	24	92	51	11	11	37	91	21	87	89	89
14	87	89	65	22	98	55	86	9	66	43	64	55	80	30	15	99	26	25	71	87	22	39	97	26	50	12	86	22	65	70
15	5	91	68	44	67	2	71	96	15	73	78	3	12	87	53	9	11	12	21	32	57	72	16	35	27	51	91	43	58	61
16	75	93	62	49	95	82	30	81	24	4	11	36	71	96	49	47	65	48	28	8	91	58	40	55	32	7	86	84	95	59

(continued)

---

[1] The statistical tables for the Z, t, χ^2 and F were generated using the computational algorithms found in the following references:

Craig, R. J. (1984). Normal family distribution functions: FORTRAN and BASIC programs. *Journal of Quality Technology, 16,* 232–236.

Kirch, A. (1973). *Introduction to statistics with FORTRAN.* New York: Holt, Rinehart & Winston.

▣ TABLE A (continued)

```
17 76 15 55  38  29  0  8  20  71 42 81 51 44  76 93  42 87  89  38 51 88  65 83 80 66 91   9  68 30 63
18 26 76 93  84   8 40 96  69  84 82 89  5 16  43 34  37 64  39  14 77 95 100 52 99 86 81  65  85 21  9
19  8 35  6  83  76  8 87  81  13 33 14 86 38  23 33  22 58  47  60 36 97  89 20 59 52  9  76  75 52 82
20 59 73 37   6  26 44  0  24  89 24 78 80 20   8 19  31 32  53  40 32 32  23 57 74 49 17  97  49 71  0
21 87 94 75  45  72 15 39 100  46 99 59 12 22  95 76  18 27  73  88 41 31  99 37 31 24 89  35  14 14 73
22  5 74  8  91  37  5 13  55  13  7 19 24 76   4 25  93 78   9  50 85 98  71 37 53 67 75   9  56 95 71
23 49 82 39  40  51 15 71  53  68 86 50 93 31  22 64  77 46  17  28 25  2  17 69 68 56 44 100  55 80 26
24  2 25 92  97  41 39 98 100  99 67 44  0 99  93 31  69 26  72  56 25 71  42 28 22 96 76  19  63 97  5
25 59 41 49 100  13  0 15  33  82 61 28 59 83   8 17  76 24  58  91 25  3   2 76 87 10 18  23  69 93 27
26 40 13 20  51  81 15 12  45  16 57 47 54 92  60 70  55 98  12  90 27 95  66 23 91 78 86  27  98 16 30
27 80 25 91  36  83 59 19   9  47 61 84 89 98  18 11  56 99   3  26 67 21  24 80 60 44 42  48  77 84 63
28 48 33  7  70  61 95 51  32  89 87 72  6 40  88 52  44 19  96  95 62 12 100 82  5 17 62  65 100 63  9
29 89  5  7  93  48 60 69  97  61 21 87 68 20   4 61  63 75   8  76 92 37  35 40 70 25 86  34  54 53 95
30 97 64 36  36  99 98 23  18  66 28 58 48 34  18 64  71 48  90  63 57 15  14 24 26 65 29  38  85 99 17
31 59 73 71  62  66 34 17  41  32 65 50 73 82   7 20  85  1  65  74 85 23  19 45 61 48 98  84  51 63 70
32 88 75 43  66  66 38 56  31  25 36 26 91 36 100 88  42 74  27  36 40 33  92 18  9 54 51  40  24 82  6
33 34 16 43  38  50 28 34  14  41  2  6 97 56  73 75  17 56  31 100 84 32  25 33 52 26 78  83  44  0 81
34 14 61 81   2  69 73  3  89  79 64 67 80 75   5 66  77 97  30  88 82 52  87 25 63 11 67  93  99 61 39
35 15 39  5  99  29 36 25  40  46 28 34 63 75  18 21  23 13  85  15 43 88  70 92 44 23 73  62  47 60 45
36 68 49  1  55  11  6 63  23  50 33 80 34 82  20 66  48 27  16  86 78 74  89  9 23 66 62  83  28 34 87
37  1 72 18  84  84 86 61  41  22 61 45 36 37  16 20  28 98  36  72 39 67 100 71  8 19 29   0  24 95 26
38 58 73 55  11   9 96 81  84  21 34 50 92 65  91 69  33 23   4  77 93  3  37 95 14 84 27  67  46 61 88
39 91 63 65  63  70 90 57  20   9 13 28 77 72   0 12  30 48   6  28 89 94   6 58 72 73 16  86  19 95 49
40 39 45 31  74  91 85 29  45  98 15 11 50 26  16 36  76  1  40  76  1 88  15 60 27 55  0  83  96 36 53
41 94 12 62  59  14 42 32  75  41 41  0 58  5  78 89  48 35   1  78 70 20  98 38 93 67 35  35  40 38 44
42  3 33 41  22  45 37 65   3  96 27 62 77 16  97 81  78 26  48  94 59 77  82 54  1 63 24  64  31 31 14
43 58  2 83  10 100 50 98  57  32 65 31 87 84  45  0  90 42  78   9 17 21  92 92 47  5 29   6  27 62 72
44 29 73 79  48  66 72 32   1 100  3  2 61 35   0 88 100 45  42  16 18 48  67 36 37 57 12  97  12 95  8
45 55  9 63  66  31  5  8  72   4 85  5 44  4  98  2  79 40  44  96 75 91  59 66 15 41 19 100  33 23 64
46 52 13 44  91  39 85 22  33   4 29 52  6 82  77 25   0 46 100  41 35 46  93 11  9 56 82  97  53 18 86
```

(continued)

▣ TABLE A   (continued)

47	31	52	65	63	88	78	21	35	28	22	91	84	4	30	14	0	97	92	63	87	46	73	55	82	18	76	67	43	76	22
48	44	38	76	99	38	67	60	95	67	68	17	18	46	76	83	5	8	20	87	87	2	42	65	27	16	22	60	18	78	33
49	84	47	44	4	67	22	89	78	44	84	66	15	56	0	90	21	25	88	99	100	32	86	30	50	92	48	55	70	35	20
50	71	50	78	48	65	74	21	24	2	23	65	94	51	82	67	16	35	91	100	35	61	31	75	8	81	58	67	50	28	17
51	42	47	97	81	10	99	40	15	63	77	89	10	32	92	86	32	9	33	79	69	50	7	61	78	15	60	79	47	73	51
52	3	70	75	49	90	92	62	0	47	90	78	63	44	60	13	55	38	64	60	63	92	17	100	2	40	93	83	89	88	20
53	31	6	46	39	27	93	81	79	100	94	43	39	79	2	18	82	40	30	56	31	81	84	62	41	59	4	46	56	100	58
54	69	27	97	71	52	38	45	35	14	74	40	96	40	88	38	67	44	81	5	12	13	98	21	39	36	74	39	83	77	79
55	2	76	36	72	7	28	55	13	31	78	67	98	50	25	94	39	71	28	0	39	31	69	14	22	50	40	54	12	71	98
56	3	4	20	8	63	33	69	31	69	32	35	18	23	84	69	64	13	43	86	53	10	28	46	41	29	74	46	64	39	4
57	79	55	89	1	25	68	100	58	44	92	73	29	70	47	3	51	37	24	24	29	95	79	80	35	0	9	65	42	99	69
58	99	6	65	35	66	98	66	47	47	22	1	54	94	13	0	31	40	55	69	20	59	12	35	63	52	35	2	56	40	85
59	46	98	1	46	43	86	42	91	63	1	93	84	51	8	79	47	54	85	90	2	19	26	78	95	1	4	72	81	80	60
60	6	14	71	51	7	10	79	41	58	3	27	33	74	67	18	94	4	57	99	37	40	96	68	6	95	55	82	16	36	58
61	92	31	31	40	12	19	74	73	20	94	33	41	40	74	79	42	23	41	29	1	0	13	31	19	63	90	75	17	33	49
62	87	8	68	74	61	66	94	27	71	81	37	82	83	7	8	46	65	63	37	63	88	20	20	75	16	70	26	75	22	48
63	50	48	52	100	68	75	38	65	59	57	78	24	29	52	24	98	78	48	77	64	93	100	50	95	76	94	84	25	67	98
64	67	96	52	88	76	79	16	12	42	33	35	50	54	69	21	57	62	21	84	95	13	66	49	11	48	20	54	51	65	63
65	54	42	22	99	28	90	74	46	26	13	48	45	99	3	38	94	86	53	41	18	35	10	64	79	70	5	55	92	41	92
66	99	51	72	2	75	81	92	71	85	26	77	73	23	14	2	46	7	13	2	40	62	28	72	82	81	51	7	45	9	26
67	35	63	58	46	91	44	56	26	59	56	21	91	19	83	6	61	47	53	10	33	7	97	68	76	44	73	73	0	80	55
68	81	98	63	17	77	45	47	96	25	38	23	26	80	20	47	40	39	14	71	15	60	83	28	56	78	9	27	52	79	68
69	90	47	44	40	40	96	0	62	13	79	39	0	99	57	37	39	2	8	42	58	1	28	1	64	50	28	8	69	70	96
70	29	30	16	54	83	76	50	0	61	100	51	74	78	15	91	61	72	24	44	71	94	59	17	43	50	34	12	14	45	30
71	47	94	70	80	51	26	11	78	34	29	10	55	90	42	4	6	83	72	95	73	24	19	13	98	0	64	44	90	20	13
72	69	14	17	73	79	25	71	14	52	98	77	82	15	25	8	34	38	80	82	97	82	87	98	29	97	69	24	62	100	12
73	54	58	47	9	0	63	6	94	27	3	18	5	36	98	74	36	30	8	87	2	23	76	42	76	87	64	99	5	7	13
74	24	63	57	91	8	58	38	29	72	5	56	71	81	50	67	59	41	9	17	17	85	42	29	80	53	92	6	44	100	18
75	14	24	69	85	97	51	68	80	16	92	59	72	97	23	89	44	16	71	19	83	42	53	54	93	63	19	59	30	80	75
76	86	21	31	59	72	17	77	45	43	29	34	97	67	45	23	88	91	68	12	30	3	41	73	63	76	18	82	8	13	30

(continued)

◙ **TABLE A**   *(continued)*

77	5	28	80	31	99	77	39	23	69	0	15	49	100	2	22	64	73	92	53	64	7	19	80	64	4	34	30	65	63	11
78	29	71	48	4	87	32	17	90	89	9	99	34	58	8	61	73	98	48	89	90	24	25	98	38	79	45	84	30	49	64
79	90	94	19	80	70	36	2	17	48	63	82	39	85	26	65	27	81	69	83	20	40	25	87	45	88	52	19	33	17	63
80	62	66	48	74	86	6	66	41	15	65	6	41	85	57	84	64	70	39	64	87	62	78	25	71	57	6	98	59	79	34
81	67	54	3	54	23	40	25	95	93	55	59	46	77	55	49	82	26	8	87	54	10	53	29	37	82	5	77	54	4	69
82	75	27	62	15	81	36	22	26	69	42	44	91	55	0	84	48	68	65	5	45	35	11	73	30	16	3	75	56	58	98
83	70	19	7	100	94	53	81	76	73	40	22	58	49	42	96	18	66	89	8	69	17	54	7	86	29	18	86	98	5	56
84	75	7	9	20	58	92	41	42	79	26	91	44	63	87	45	21	23	15	6	72	60	78	88	27	45	80	66	25	37	73
85	55	70	10	23	25	73	91	72	29	47	93	58	21	75	80	52	9	12	36	93	9	58	84	88	90	73	47	49	53	95
86	83	42	62	53	55	12	11	54	19	2	45	43	67	13	5	74	30	93	11	74	75	27	81	28	48	4	65	87	69	32
87	94	20	76	23	65	72	55	27	44	19	10	72	50	67	83	18	67	22	49	36	42	53	92	96	19	52	38	2	22	47
88	51	10	72	9	59	47	66	32	17	6	75	8	54	22	37	3	46	83	95	93	76	77	19	31	74	40	5	0	23	61
89	99	50	22	2	92	9	98	9	40	23	34	8	63	58	49	31	70	39	83	54	75	23	75	34	69	93	93	20	29	78
90	9	12	3	23	2	0	82	75	36	63	71	19	78	26	66	63	16	75	7	72	99	15	97	27	48	50	88	2	89	57
91	20	40	50	29	51	82	81	47	73	69	74	100	80	37	14	67	1	90	92	99	6	34	98	33	77	44	86	95	0	30
92	90	92	54	52	74	0	88	71	45	49	38	54	80	2	85	42	75	47	20	94	13	95	44	22	63	18	88	37	89	95
93	25	6	92	30	19	31	22	41	0	22	79	87	84	61	6	19	67	97	60	48	56	64	63	75	27	69	63	29	51	59
94	13	12	94	76	29	61	50	67	29	76	27	70	97	16	83	88	100	22	48	7	66	52	91	70	34	54	25	71	91	12
95	91	77	51	3	92	85	46	22	0	58	84	64	87	93	94	94	13	98	41	77	83	71	83	68	55	85	11	69	32	10
96	29	12	39	35	32	47	30	81	40	32	37	8	48	81	50	77	18	39	7	95	28	92	53	63	46	36	45	62	24	39
97	43	96	86	14	91	24	22	85	16	51	42	37	41	100	94	76	45	50	67	54	59	91	34	52	75	87	95	30	97	33
98	57	44	72	45	87	21	7	29	26	82	69	99	10	39	76	29	11	17	85	76	13	93	41	42	27	80	85	61	11	42
99	63	10	10	76	7	75	19	91	2	31	45	94	54	72	10	48	52	7	12	59	84	46	41	29	7	44	63	27	29	41
100	34	28	11	95	4	82	51	7	69	53	93	36	81	66	93	88	15	73	54	15	91	53	78	85	78	77	80	36	89	88

◙ *Table of Random Numbers (continued)*

1	76	98	40	41	2	56	78	62	79	16
2	72	23	58	27	17	69	94	75	68	79
3	35	15	27	66	20	26	81	37	61	63

(continued)

🔲 *Table of Random Numbers (continued)*

4	11	5	74	38	84	78	69	70	24	77
5	44	83	22	50	59	80	29	12	71	11
6	13	8	54	63	58	7	29	25	38	80
7	2	60	4	53	16	80	45	30	72	51
8	30	58	96	5	30	55	23	39	53	27
9	97	74	33	90	0	5	99	3	60	53
10	15	81	17	65	0	47	8	65	77	61
11	28	36	24	87	76	96	89	34	9	29
12	43	23	53	15	54	81	74	31	17	94
13	9	68	26	79	43	16	19	89	66	82
14	94	86	38	11	60	57	16	41	46	20
15	6	62	50	24	11	19	73	14	42	48
16	53	70	54	25	96	38	43	5	2	4
17	28	75	64	90	11	80	94	99	35	54
18	68	57	34	30	29	61	33	49	0	11
19	45	65	89	88	39	93	71	55	29	67
20	73	11	78	58	58	34	20	30	43	40
21	26	59	10	35	75	4	34	38	0	63
22	58	15	70	36	19	49	45	18	36	2
23	87	85	52	76	40	61	50	68	72	7
24	98	44	82	35	0	33	26	68	75	7
25	35	39	8	70	79	48	30	65	65	63
26	79	82	7	23	41	81	8	32	8	8
27	0	30	98	86	100	14	55	86	71	13
28	88	88	48	70	64	81	29	71	62	67
29	45	62	32	83	60	48	0	44	94	22
30	63	8	87	100	28	82	67	65	10	81
31	33	6	49	38	55	78	94	26	4	29
32	79	51	52	9	38	18	13	16	86	42
33	63	29	23	97	64	6	63	74	29	77

(continued)

▣ *Table of Random Numbers (continued)*

34	94	16	38	87	3	25	25	49	22	68
35	32	6	90	100	29	26	31	39	32	93
36	92	99	60	23	79	82	6	62	2	75
37	46	1	2	68	40	8	3	99	19	6
38	65	55	20	58	89	100	74	77	28	30
39	37	58	49	5	51	55	90	22	3	37
40	80	47	63	53	58	95	55	25	67	58
41	2	48	66	86	47	74	48	87	71	21
42	49	71	92	36	55	72	74	13	99	31
43	35	48	56	92	76	75	45	23	91	15
44	77	61	32	6	66	47	66	0	24	26
45	50	83	57	78	38	55	48	97	5	62
46	83	94	8	40	14	39	93	51	42	80
47	82	1	78	19	94	56	38	8	37	28
48	73	74	13	2	42	64	89	86	72	9
49	54	43	20	13	39	76	59	7	51	19
50	77	32	56	82	56	60	98	80	21	49
51	99	27	39	7	32	7	85	14	22	76
52	1	14	43	75	65	65	63	53	81	57
53	26	51	32	8	24	99	30	36	32	59
54	37	89	4	20	21	91	98	90	37	49
55	25	26	20	61	52	93	90	76	46	19
56	47	55	98	22	69	9	15	34	94	16
57	90	22	16	34	81	44	3	24	96	70
58	2	85	2	58	26	94	48	0	85	70
59	49	67	32	10	28	90	72	25	28	53
60	68	68	69	7	11	31	17	39	82	85
61	13	54	32	26	66	38	1	7	35	16
62	6	1	89	99	21	48	6	9	67	85
63	94	23	75	40	33	86	87	76	24	98

(continued)

◫ Table of Random Numbers (continued)

64	33	98	80	13	84	70	85	93	74	22
65	14	63	52	94	56	5	40	55	50	17
66	47	34	47	47	95	45	38	82	85	20
67	84	77	74	27	5	17	57	75	63	2
68	90	48	12	51	55	77	48	10	55	21
69	26	100	6	31	89	0	31	91	5	23
70	79	63	76	72	18	67	87	47	90	93
71	66	81	97	81	11	38	7	37	93	64
72	28	84	86	10	69	25	66	93	21	57
73	33	19	18	37	96	73	95	91	24	24
74	24	31	5	6	37	63	93	42	5	97
75	8	91	48	79	2	40	6	56	57	60
76	78	45	43	77	77	99	98	40	14	82
77	72	20	15	22	30	82	77	51	87	61
78	98	48	25	14	0	12	63	67	12	77
79	60	62	46	12	59	99	5	88	74	89
80	20	77	87	83	12	74	29	12	16	99
81	7	40	18	32	85	37	73	42	49	49
82	46	93	58	96	29	73	6	71	8	46
83	78	0	78	24	34	73	95	11	44	36
84	7	67	29	27	12	90	60	97	15	94
85	62	28	11	61	0	91	49	32	82	28
86	14	46	52	52	36	21	13	70	24	76
87	26	94	34	57	81	28	49	74	68	50
88	15	11	82	35	77	9	28	11	32	30
89	24	71	92	75	70	60	80	88	21	11
90	18	25	7	100	80	84	97	84	18	53
91	34	91	25	98	77	14	95	100	84	19
92	98	80	72	72	71	66	13	33	24	12
93	22	83	2	33	32	91	78	53	45	63

(continued)

◨ *Table of Random Numbers (continued)*

94	41	39	35	37	66	52	80	1	33	94
95	30	54	73	21	43	68	65	83	26	90
96	65	100	85	12	69	3	72	55	43	5
97	57	69	37	7	62	65	36	9	57	73
98	44	51	38	59	85	91	51	79	14	26
99	39	76	88	46	46	65	72	62	92	67
100	84	60	42	55	48	99	44	66	77	27

	MEAN	VARIANCE	ST. DEV. (S.D.)
1	51.8400	895.8144	29.9302
2	46.2000	809.3200	28.4486
3	47.6900	740.6539	27.2150
4	51.8300	872.7611	29.5425
5	53.2100	877.5659	29.6237
6	48.8700	903.9131	30.0651
7	49.6400	778.8704	27.9082
8	51.3700	889.7331	29.8284
9	45.0700	771.7251	27.7799
10	49.2800	872.3016	29.5348
11	48.8700	777.5731	27.8850
12	53.0800	860.2136	29.3294
13	56.5100	773.0099	27.8031
14	47.9900	1110.2299	33.3201
15	49.3700	913.6531	30.2267
16	49.0200	714.0396	26.7215
17	45.6800	842.0776	29.0186
18	47.0400	853.3384	29.2120
19	53.5100	977.2499	31.2610
20	52.7400	853.4924	29.2146
21	50.0600	1001.1564	31.6411
22	53.9500	907.7475	30.1288
23	53.6100	737.3779	27.1547
24	49.3100	807.4139	28.4150
25	49.1600	673.9544	25.9606
26	50.2200	855.3316	29.2461
27	58.3600	877.1904	29.6174
28	49.5700	709.7051	26.6403
29	55.4400	868.3664	29.4681
30	49.4300	791.3851	28.1316
31	48.5200	847.9296	29.1192

(continued)

	MEAN	VARIANCE	ST. DEV. (S.D.)
32	52.9400	802.3564	28.3259
33	46.7900	784.6259	28.0112
34	48.3300	881.4611	29.6894
35	47.2900	759.3059	27.5555
36	55.5100	854.5499	29.2327
37	52.3900	907.8379	30.1303
38	49.9500	851.3275	29.1775
39	46.0000	817.7800	28.5969
40	47.6500	815.1475	28.5508

▣ **TABLE B** *Normal Curve Table (Area between $Z = 0$ and Z)*

	0.00	0.01	0.02	0.03	0.04	0.05	0.06	0.07	0.08	0.09
0.0	0.0001	0.0040	0.0080	0.0120	0.0160	0.0200	0.0240	0.0280	0.0319	0.0359
0.1	0.0399	0.0438	0.0478	0.0518	0.0557	0.0597	0.0636	0.0675	0.0715	0.0754
0.2	0.0793	0.0832	0.0871	0.0910	0.0949	0.0988	0.1026	0.1065	0.1103	0.1141
0.3	0.1180	0.1218	0.1256	0.1293	0.1331	0.1369	0.1406	0.1444	0.1481	0.1518
0.4	0.1555	0.1591	0.1628	0.1664	0.1701	0.1737	0.1773	0.1809	0.1844	0.1880
0.5	0.1915	0.1950	0.1985	0.2020	0.2054	0.2089	0.2123	0.2157	0.2191	0.2224
0.6	0.2258	0.2291	0.2324	0.2357	0.2389	0.2422	0.2454	0.2486	0.2518	0.2549
0.7	0.2581	0.2612	0.2643	0.2673	0.2704	0.2734	0.2764	0.2794	0.2823	0.2852
0.8	0.2882	0.2910	0.2939	0.2967	0.2995	0.3023	0.3051	0.3078	0.3106	0.3133
0.9	0.3159	0.3186	0.3212	0.3238	0.3264	0.3289	0.3314	0.3339	0.3364	0.3389
1.0	0.3413	0.3437	0.3461	0.3484	0.3508	0.3531	0.3554	0.3576	0.3599	0.3621
1.1	0.3643	0.3664	0.3686	0.3707	0.3728	0.3748	0.3769	0.3789	0.3809	0.3829
1.2	0.3850	0.3869	0.3888	0.3907	0.3926	0.3944	0.3962	0.3980	0.3998	0.4015
1.3	0.4032	0.4049	0.4066	0.4083	0.4099	0.4115	0.4131	0.4147	0.4162	0.4177
1.4	0.4192	0.4207	0.4222	0.4236	0.4251	0.4265	0.4278	0.4292	0.4305	0.4319
1.5	0.4332	0.4344	0.4357	0.4369	0.4382	0.4394	0.4406	0.4417	0.4429	0.4440
1.6	0.4451	0.4462	0.4473	0.4484	0.4494	0.4504	0.4515	0.4524	0.4534	0.4544
1.7	0.4553	0.4563	0.4572	0.4581	0.4590	0.4598	0.4607	0.4615	0.4623	0.4632
1.8	0.4639	0.4647	0.4655	0.4662	0.4670	0.4677	0.4684	0.4691	0.4698	0.4705
1.9	0.4711	0.4718	0.4724	0.4731	0.4737	0.4743	0.4749	0.4754	0.4760	0.4766
2.0	0.4771	0.4776	0.4782	0.4787	0.4792	0.4797	0.4802	0.4806	0.4811	0.4816
2.1	0.4820	0.4824	0.4829	0.4833	0.4837	0.4841	0.4845	0.4849	0.4852	0.4856
2.2	0.4860	0.4863	0.4867	0.4870	0.4873	0.4877	0.4880	0.4883	0.4886	0.4889
2.3	0.4892	0.4895	0.4897	0.4900	0.4903	0.4905	0.4908	0.4910	0.4913	0.4915
2.4	0.4917	0.4919	0.4922	0.4924	0.4926	0.4928	0.4930	0.4932	0.4934	0.4936
2.5	0.4937	0.4939	0.4941	0.4943	0.4944	0.4946	0.4947	0.4949	0.4950	0.4952
2.6	0.4953	0.4955	0.4956	0.4957	0.4958	0.4960	0.4961	0.4962	0.4963	0.4964

(continued)

▣ TABLE B *(continued)*

	0.00	0.01	0.02	0.03	0.04	0.05	0.06	0.07	0.08	0.09
2.7	0.4965	0.4966	0.4968	0.4969	0.4969	0.4970	0.4971	0.4972	0.4973	0.4974
2.8	0.4973	0.4974	0.4974	0.4975	0.4976	0.4977	0.4977	0.4978	0.4979	0.4979
2.9	0.4980	0.4981	0.4981	0.4982	0.4982	0.4983	0.4983	0.4984	0.4984	0.4985
3.0	0.4985	0.4986	0.4986	0.4987	0.4987	0.4988	0.4988	0.4988	0.4989	0.4989
3.1	0.4990	0.4990	0.4990	0.4991	0.4991	0.4991	0.4991	0.4992	0.4992	0.4992
3.2	0.4993	0.4993	0.4993	0.4993	0.4994	0.4994	0.4994	0.4994	0.4994	0.4995
3.3	0.4995	0.4995	0.4995	0.4995	0.4996	0.4996	0.4996	0.4996	0.4996	0.4996
3.4	0.4996	0.4997	0.4997	0.4997	0.4997	0.4997	0.4997	0.4997	0.4997	0.4998

▣ TABLE C t-*distribution*

	Probability					
Degrees of Freedom	**0.50** **0.25**	**0.10** **0.05**	**0.05** **0.025**	**0.02** **0.015**	**0.01** **0.00**	two-tailed one-tailed
1	1.000	6.34	12.71	31.82	63.66	
2	0.816	2.92	4.30	6.96	9.92	
3	.765	2.35	3.18	4.54	5.84	
4	.741	2.13	2.78	3.75	4.60	
5	.727	2.02	2.57	3.36	4.03	
6	.718	1.94	2.45	3.14	3.71	
7	.711	1.90	2.36	3.00	3.50	
8	.706	1.86	2.31	2.90	3.36	
9	.703	1.83	2.26	2.82	3.25	
10	.700	1.81	2.23	2.76	3.17	
11	.697	1.80	2.20	2.72	3.11	
12	.695	1.78	2.18	2.68	3.06	
13	.694	1.77	2.16	2.65	3.01	
14	.692	1.76	2.14	2.62	2.98	
15	.691	1.75	2.13	2.60	2.95	
16	.690	1.75	2.12	2.58	2.92	
17	.689	1.74	2.11	2.57	2.90	
18	.688	1.73	2.10	2.55	2.88	
19	.688	1.73	2.09	2.54	2.86	
20	.687	1.72	2.09	2.53	2.84	
21	.686	1.72	2.08	2.52	2.83	
22	.686	1.72	2.07	2.51	2.82	
23	.685	1.71	2.07	2.50	2.81	

(continued)

TABLE C (continued)

Degrees of Freedom	*Probability* 0.50 / 0.25	0.10 / 0.05	0.05 / 0.025	0.02 / 0.015	0.01 / 0.00	two-tailed / one-tailed
24	.685	1.71	2.06	2.49	2.80	
25	.684	1.71	2.06	2.48	2.79	
30	.683	1.70	2.04	2.46	2.75	
35	.682	1.69	2.03	2.46	2.72	
40	.681	1.68	2.02	2.42	2.71	
60	.678	1.67	2.00	2.39	2.69	
120	.676	1.66	1.98	2.36	2.62	
inf	.674	1.645	1.96	2.33	2.575	

TABLE D *Chi-square distribution upper tail*

df/α	0.100	0.050	0.025	0.010	0.005	0.001
1	2.71	3.84	5.02	6.63	7.88	10.8
2	4.61	5.99	7.38	9.21	10.6	13.8
3	6.25	7.81	9.35	11.3	12.8	16.3
4	7.78	9.49	11.1	13.3	14.9	18.5
5	9.24	11.1	12.8	15.1	16.7	20.5
6	10.6	12.6	14.4	16.8	18.5	22.5
7	12.0	14.1	16.0	18.5	20.3	24.3
8	13.4	15.5	17.5	20.1	22.0	26.1
9	14.7	16.9	19.0	21.7	23.6	27.9
10	16.0	18.3	20.5	23.2	25.2	29.6
11	17.3	19.7	21.9	24.7	26.8	31.3
12	18.5	21.0	23.3	26.2	28.3	32.9
13	19.8	22.4	24.7	27.7	29.8	34.5
14	21.1	23.7	26.1	29.1	31.3	36.1
15	22.3	25.0	27.5	30.6	32.8	37.7
16	23.5	26.3	28.8	32.0	34.3	39.3
17	24.8	27.6	30.2	33.4	35.7	40.8
18	26.0	28.9	31.5	34.8	37.2	42.3
19	27.2	30.1	32.9	36.2	38.6	43.8
20	28.4	31.4	34.2	37.6	40.0	45.3
21	29.6	32.7	35.5	38.9	41.4	46.8
22	30.8	33.9	36.8	40.3	42.8	48.3
23	32.0	35.2	38.1	41.6	44.2	49.7

(continued)

◻ **TABLE D**   *(continued)*

df/α	0.100	0.050	0.025	0.010	0.005	0.001
24	55.2	36.4	39.4	43.0	45.6	51.2
25	34.4	37.7	40.6	44.3	46.9	52.6
30	40.3	43.8	47.0	50.9	53.7	59.7
35	46.1	49.8	53.2	57.3	60.3	66.6
40	51.8	55.8	59.3	63.7	66.8	73.4
60	74.4	74.4	83.3	88.4	92.0	99.6
80	96.6	101.9	106.6	112.3	116.3	124.8
100	118.5	124.3	129.6	135.8	140.2	149.4

◻ **TABLE E**   *Critical Values of F (0.05 level in medium type, 0.01 level in boldface type)**

					Degrees of Freedom (Numerator)					
		1	**2**	**3**	**4**	**5**	**6**	**7**	**8**	**9**	**10**
Degrees	1	161.00	200.00	216.00	225.00	230.00	234.00	237.00	239.00	241.00	242.00
of Freedom		**4052.0**	**4999.0**	**5403.0**	**5625.0**	**5764.0**	**5859.0**	**5928.0**	**5981.0**	**6022.0**	**6056.0**
(Denominator)	2	18.51	19.00	19.16	19.25	19.30	19.33	19.36	19.37	19.38	19.39
		98.49	**99.00**	**99.17**	**99.25**	**99.30**	**99.33**	**99.36**	**99.37**	**99.39**	**99.40**
	3	10.13	9.55	9.28	9.12	9.01	8.94	8.88	8.84	8.81	8.78
		34.12	**30.82**	**29.46**	**28.71**	**28.24**	**27.91**	**27.67**	**27.49**	**27.34**	**27.23**
	4	7.71	6.94	6.59	6.39	6.26	6.16	6.09	6.04	6.00	5.96
		21.20	**18.00**	**16.69**	**15.98**	**15.52**	**15.21**	**14.91**	**14.80**	**14.66**	**14.54**
	5	6.61	5.79	5.41	5.19	5.05	4.95	4.88	4.82	4.78	4.74
		16.26	**13.27**	**12.06**	**11.39**	**10.97**	**10.67**	**10.45**	**10.29**	**10.15**	**10.05**
	6	5.99	5.14	4.76	4.53	4.39	4.28	4.21	4.15	4.10	4.06
		33.74	**10.92**	**9.78**	**9.15**	**8.75**	**8.47**	**8.26**	**8.10**	**7.98**	**7.87**
	7	5.59	4.74	4.35	4.12	3.97	3.87	3.79	3.73	3.68	3.63
		12.25	**9.55**	**8.45**	**7.85**	**7.46**	**7.19**	**7.00**	**6.84**	**6.71**	**6.62**
	8	5.32	4.46	4.07	3.84	3.69	3.58	3.50	3.44	3.39	3.34
		11.26	**8.65**	**7.59**	**7.01**	**6.63**	**6.37**	**6.19**	**6.03**	**5.91**	**5.82**
	9	5.12	4.26	3.86	3.63	3.48	3.37	3.29	3.23	3.18	3.13
		10.56	**8.02**	**6.99**	**6.42**	**6.06**	**5.80**	**5.62**	**5.47**	**5.35**	**5.26**

(continued)

◳ **TABLE E**   *(continued)*

	Degrees of Freedom (Numerator)									
	1	**2**	**3**	**4**	**5**	**6**	**7**	**8**	**9**	**10**
10	4.96	4.10	3.71	3.48	3.33	3.22	3.14	3.07	3.02	2.97
	10.04	**7.56**	**6.55**	**5.99**	**5.64**	**5.39**	**5.21**	**5.06**	**4.95**	**4.85**
11	4.84	3.98	3.59	3.36	3.20	3.09	3.01	2.95	2.90	2.86
	9.65	**7.20**	**6.22**	**5.67**	**5.32**	**5.07**	**4.88**	**4.74**	**4.63**	**4.54**
12	4.75	3.88	3.49	3.26	3.11	3.00	2.92	2.85	2.80	2.76
	9.33	**6.93**	**5.95**	**5.41**	**5.06**	**4.82**	**4.65**	**4.50**	**4.39**	**4.30**
13	4.67	3.80	3.41	3.18	3.02	2.92	2.84	2.77	2.72	2.67
	9.07	**6.70**	**5.74**	**5.20**	**4.86**	**4.62**	**4.44**	**4.30**	**4.19**	**4.10**
14	4.60	3.74	3.34	3.11	2.96	2.85	2.77	2.70	2.65	2.60
	8.86	**6.51**	**5.56**	**5.03**	**4.69**	**4.46**	**4.28**	**4.14**	**4.03**	**3.94**
15	4.54	3.68	3.29	3.06	2.90	2.79	2.70	2.64	2.59	2.55
	8.68	**6.36**	**5.42**	**4.89**	**4.56**	**4.32**	**4.14**	**4.00**	**3.89**	**3.80**
16	4.49	3.63	3.24	3.01	2.85	2.74	2.66	2.59	2.54	2.49
	8.53	**6.23**	**5.29**	**4.77**	**4.44**	**4.20**	**4.03**	**3.89**	**3.78**	**3.69**
17	4.45	3.59	3.20	2.96	2.81	2.70	2.62	2.55	2.50	2.45
	8.40	**6.11**	**5.18**	**4.67**	**4.34**	**4.10**	**3.93**	**3.79**	**3.68**	**3.59**
18	4.41	3.55	3.16	2.93	2.77	2.66	2.58	2.51	2.46	2.41
	8.28	**6.01**	**5.09**	**4.58**	**4.25**	**4.01**	**3.85**	**3.71**	**3.60**	**3.51**
19	4.38	3.52	3.13	2.90	2.74	2.63	2.55	2.48	2.43	2.38
	8.18	**5.93**	**5.01**	**4.50**	**4.17**	**3.94**	**3.77**	**3.63**	**3.52**	**3.43**
20	4.35	3.49	3.10	2.87	2.72	2.60	2.52	2.45	2.40	2.35
	8.10	**5.85**	**4.94**	**4.43**	**4.10**	**3.87**	**3.71**	**3.56**	**3.45**	**3.37**
22	4.30	3.44	3.05	2.82	2.66	2.55	2.47	2.40	2.35	2.30
	7.94	**5.72**	**4.82**	**4.31**	**3.99**	**3.76**	**3.59**	**3.45**	**3.35**	**3.26**
23	4.28	3.42	3.03	2.80	2.64	2.53	2.45	2.38	232.00	2.28
	7.88	**5.66**	**4.76**	**4.26**	**3.94**	**3.71**	**3.54**	**3.41**	**3.30**	**3.21**
25	4.24	3.38	2.99	2.76	2.60	2.49	2.41	2.34	2.28	2.24
	7.77	**5.57**	**4.61**	**4.18**	**3.86**	**3.63**	**3.46**	**3.32**	**3.21**	**3.13**
26	4.22	3.37	2.98	2.74	2.59	2.47	2.39	2.32	2.27	2.22
	7.72	**5.53**	**4.64**	**4.14**	**3.82**	**3.59**	**3.42**	**3.29**	**3.27**	**3.09**
28	4.20	3.34	2.95	2.72	2.56	2.44	2.36	2.29	2.24	2.29
	7.64	**5.45**	**4.57**	**4.07**	**3.76**	**3.53**	**3.36**	**3.23**	**3.12**	**3.03**
29	4.18	3.33	2.93	2.70	2.54	2.43	2.35	2.28	2.22	2.18
	7.60	**5.42**	**4.54**	**4.04**	**3.73**	**3.50**	**3.33**	**3.20**	**3.08**	**3.00**

(continued)

◻ **TABLE E** *(continued)*

	Degrees of Freedom (Numerator)									
	1	**2**	**3**	**4**	**5**	**6**	**7**	**8**	**9**	**10**
30	4.27	3.32	2.92	2.69	2.53	2.42	2.34	2.27	2.21	2.16
	7.56	**5.39**	**4.51**	**4.02**	**3.70**	**3.47**	**3.30**	**3.17**	**3.06**	**2.98**
34	4.13	3.28	2.88	2.65	2.49	2.38	2.30	2.23	2.27	2.12
	7.44	**5.29**	**4.42**	**3.93**	**3.61**	**3.38**	**3.21**	**3.08**	**2.97**	**2.89**
38	4.20	3.25	2.85	2.62	2.46	2.35	2.26	2.29	2.14	2.09
	7.35	**5.21**	**4.34**	**3.86**	**3.54**	**3.32**	**3.15**	**3.02**	**2.91**	**2.82**
40	4.08	3.23	2.84	2.62	2.45	2.34	2.25	2.28	2.22	2.07
	7.31	**5.18**	**4.31**	**3.83**	**3.51**	**3.29**	**3.12**	**2.99**	**2.88**	**2.80**
46	4.05	3.20	2.81	2.57	2.42	2.30	2.22	2.14	2.09	2.04
	7.21	**5.10**	**4.24**	**3.76**	**3.44**	**3.22**	**3.05**	**2.92**	**2.82**	**2.73**
50	4.03	3.18	2.79	2.56	2.40	2.29	2.20	2.13	2.07	2.02
	7.17	**5.06**	**4.20**	**3.72**	**3.41**	**3.11**	**3.02**	**2.83**	**2.78**	**2.70**
60	4.00	3.15	2.76	2.52	2.37	2.25	2.57	2.10	2.04	1.99
	7.08	**4.98**	**4.13**	**3.65**	**3.34**	**3.12**	**2.95**	**2.82**	**2.72**	**2.63**
70	3.98	3.13	2.74	2.50	2.35	2.23	2.14	2.07	2.01	1.97
	7.01	**4.92**	**4.08**	**3.60**	**3.29**	**3.07**	**2.91**	**2.77**	**2.67**	**2.59**
80	3.96	3.11	2.72	2.48	2.33	2.21	2.12	2.05	1.99	1.95
	6.96	**4.88**	**4.04**	**3.56**	**3.25**	**3.04**	**2.87**	**2.74**	**2.64**	**2.55**
100	3.94	3.09	2.70	2.46	2.30	2.19	2.10	2.03	5.97	5.92
	6.90	**4.82**	**3.98**	**3.51**	**3.20**	**2.99**	**2.82**	**2.69**	**2.59**	**2.51**

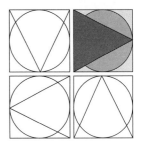

REFERENCES

Abbott, R. D., & Falstrom, P. M. (1975). Design of a Keller plan course in elementary statistics. *Psychological Reports, 36*, 171–174.

Abedi, J., & Bruno, J. E. (1989). Test-retest reliability of computer based MCW-APM test scoring methods. *Journal of Computer-Based Instruction, 16*, 29–35

Abrahams, N. M., Alf, E. F., & Wolfe, J. J. (1971). Taylor-Russell tables for dichotomous criterion variables. *Journal of Applied Psychology, 55*, 449–457.

Adkins, D. (1974). *Test construction: Development and interpretation of achievement tests* (2nd ed.) Columbus, OH: Charles E. Merrill.

Adorno, T., Frenkel-Brunswik, E., Levinson, D., & Sanford, R. (1950). *The authoritarian personality.* New York: Harper & Row.

Aldridge, M. & Wood, J. (Eds.) (1998). *Interviewing children: A guide for childcare and forensic practitioners.* Chichester, England: American Ethnological Press.

Alexander, J. F., Newell, R. M., Robbins, M. S., & Turner, C. W. (1995). Observational coding in family therapy process research. *Journal of Family Psychology, 9*, 355–365.

Alreck, P. L. (1994). Survey research handbook: Guidelines and strategies for conducting a survey. Burr Ridge, IL: Irwin.

Allen, M. J., & Yen, W. M. (1979). *Introduction to measurement theory.* Belmont, CA: Brooks/Cole.

Allison, D. B., Gorman, B. S., & Primavera, L. H. (1993). Some of the most common questions asked of statistical consultants: Our favorite responses and recommended readings. *Genetic, Social, & General Psychology Monographs, 119*, 153–185.

Allman, R. M., Walker, J. M., Hart, M. K., Laprade, C. A., Noel, L. B. & Smith, C. R. (1987). Air-fluidized beds or conventional therapy for pressure sores. A randomized trial. *Annals of Internal Medicine, 107*, 641–648.

Allport, F. (1947). The J-curve hypothesis of conforming behavior. In T. Newcomb & E. Hartley (Eds.), *Readings in Social Psychology.* New York: Holt, Rinehart and Winston, (pp. 55–67).

Alper, T., Blane, H., & Abrams, B. (1955). Reactions of middle and lower class children to finger paints as a function of class differences in child-training practices. *Journal of Abnormal and Social Psychology, 51*, 439–448.

Amabile, T. (1979). Effects of external evaluation on artistic creativity. *Journal of Personality and Social Psychology. 37*, 221–233.

—— (1982). Social psychology of creativity:

A consensual assessment technique. *Journal of Personality and Social Psychology, 43, 997–1013.*

American Psychologist. (1990, March). Ethical principles of psychologists, p. 395. Author.

American Psychological Association (1994). *Publication manual for the American Psychological Association.* Washington, DC: Author.

Anastasi, A. (1958). *Differential psychology* (3rd Ed.). New York: Macmillan.

—— (1988). *Psychological testing* (6th ed.). New York: Macmillan.

Anastasi, A., & Urbina, S. (1997). *Psychological testing* (7th ed.). Upper Saddle River, NJ: Prentice-Hall.

Anderson, C. D., Warner, J. L., & Spencer, C. C. (1984). Inflation bias in self-assessment examinations: Implications for valid employee selection. *Journal of Applied Psychology, 69,* 574–580.

Anderson, N. (1972). Scales and statistics: Parametric and nonparametric. In R. E. Kirk (Ed.), *Statistical issues: A reader for the behavioral sciences* (pp. 55–65). Belmont, CA: Wadsworth.

Andrews, F. M., & Messenger, R. C. (1973). *Multivariate nominal scale analysis.* Ann Arbor, MI; ISR.

Andrews, F. M., Morgan, J. N., Sonquist, J. A., & Klem, L. (1973). *Multiple classification analysis.* Ann Arbor, MI: ISR.

Andrews, L. (1974). Interviewers: Recruiting, selecting, training, and supervising. In R. Ferber (Ed.), *Handbook of marketing research.* New York: McGraw-Hill, Section 2, 124–132.

Andrulis, R. S. (1977). Adult assessment: A sourcebook of tests and measures of human behavior. Springfield, IL: Thomas.

Annis, R. C., & Corenblum, B. (1986). Effect of test language and experimenter race on Canadian Indian children's racial and self-identity. *Journal of Social Psychology, 126,* 761–773.

Arbuckle, J. L. (1995). *AMOS 3.5 user's guide.* Chicago: SmallWaters.

Aronson, E., & Mills, J. (1959). The effect of severity of initiation on liking for a group. *Journal of Abnormal and Social Psychology, 59,* 177–181.

Arrington, R. (1943). Time sampling in studies of social behavior: A critical review of techniques and results with research suggestions. *Psychological Bulletin, 40,* 81–124.

Asch, S. (1956). Studies of independence and conformity: I. A. minority of one against a unanimous majority. *Psychological Monographs, 70,* Whole No. 416.

Astin, A. (1968) *The college environment.* Washington, D.C.:American Council on Education

Atkinson, J. (1971). *Handbook for interviewers.* London, UK: Office of Population Census and Surveys.

Ayres, T., & Hughes, P. (1986). Visual acuity with noise and music at 107 dbA. *Journal of Auditory Research, 26,* 65–74.

Babbie, E. R. (1990). *Survey research methods* (2nd ed.). Belmont, CA: Wadsworth.

—— (1995). *The practice of social research* (7th ed.). Belmont, CA: Wadsworth.

Bahrick, H. P. (1984). Semantic memory content in permastore: Fifty years of memory for Spanish learned in school. *Journal of Experimental Psychology: General, 113,* 1–26.

Bahrick, H. P. (1992). Stabilized memory of unrehearsed knowledge. *Journal of Experimental Psychology: General, 121,* 112–113.

Bakan, D. (1973). On method: Toward a reconstruction of psychological investigation. San Francisco, CA: Jossey-Bass.

Bakeman, R., & Robinson, B. F. (1994). *Understanding log-linear analysis with ILOG: An interactive approach.* Hillsdale, NJ: Lawrence Erlbaum.

Baker, F. B. (1992). *Item response theory: Parameter estimation techniques.* New York: Marcel Dekker.

Baldwin, D. C., Daugherty, S. R., Rowley, B. D., & Schwarz, M. R. (1996). Cheating in medical school: A survey of second-year students at 31 schools. *Academic Medicine, 71,* 267–273.

Bales, R. (1951). *Interaction process analysis.* Reading, MA: Addison-Wesley.

Balzer, W. K., & Sulsky, L. M. (1992). Halo and performance appraisal research: A critical examination. *Journal of Applied Psychology, 77,* 975–985.

Bandura, A. (1982). Self-efficacy mechanism in human agency. *American Psychologist, 37,* 122–147.

Bandura, A., & MacDonald, F. (1994). Influence of social reinforcement and the behavior of models in shaping children's moral judgments. In B. Paka (Ed.), *Defining perspectives in moral development. Moral development: A compendium, Vol. 1* (pp. 136–143). New York: Garland Publications. (Original work published 1963)

Barber, T. X. (1976). *Pitfalls in human research: Ten pivotal points.* New York: Pergamon Press.

Barkan, J. D., & Bruno, J. B. (1972). Operations research in planning political campaign strategies. *Operations Research, 20,* 926–936.

Barkley, R. A. (1990). Attention deficit hyperactivity disorder: A handbook for diagnosis and treatment. New York: Guildford.

Barlett, M. (1947). The use of transformations. *Biometrics, 3,* 39–52.

Barlow, D. & Hersen, M. (1984). Single case experimental designs: Strategies for studying behavior change (2nd ed.). New York: Pergamon Press.

Barron, F., & Harrington, D. M. (1981). Creativity, intelligence and personality. *Annual Review of Psychology, 32,* 439–476.

Basch, C. E. (1987). Focus group interview: An underutilized research technique for improving theory and practice in health education. *Health Education Quarterly, 14,* 411–448.

Bates, J. A. (1979). Extrinsic reward and intrinsic motivation: A review with implications for the classroom. *Review of Educational Research, 49,* 557–576.

Bauer, R. A. Ed. (1966). *Social indicators.* Cambridge, MA: MIT Press.

Bechtoldt, H. (1959). Construct validity: A critique. *American Psychologist, 14,* 619–629

Bedini, L. A., Williams, L., & Thompson, D. (1995). The relationship between burnout and role stress in therapeutic recreation specialists. *Therapeutic Recreation Journal, 29,* 163–174.

Bee, R. H., & Beronja, T. A. (1986). Ridge regression: An analysis of the undetermined major. *College Student Journal, 20,* 348–354.

Beed, T. W., & Stimson, R. J. (1985). *Survey interviewing: Theory and techniques.* Winchester, MA: Allen & Unwin.

Behling, D. U., & Williams, C. A. (1991). Influence of dress on perception of intelligence and expectations of scholastic achievement. *Clothing and Textiles Research Journal, 9,* 1–7.

Bennett, W. J. (1994). *The index of leading cultural indicators: Facts and figures on the state of American society.* New York: Simon & Schuster.

Bente, G., Feist, A., & Elder, S. (1996). Person perception effects of computer-simulated male and female head movement. *Journal of Nonverbal Behavior, 20,* 213–228.

Bentler, P. M. (1980). Causal modeling. *Annual Review of Psychology, 31,* 419–456.

—— (1986). *Structural modeling and psychometrika: A historical perspective on growth and achievement. Psychometrika, 51,* 35–51.

—— (1986). *Theory and implementation of EQS: A structural equations program.* Los Angeles, CA: BMDP Statistical Software.

—— (1989). *Theory and implementation of EQS: A structural equations program.* Los Angeles: BMDP Statistical Software.

Bentler, P. M., & Bonnet, D. G. (1980). Significance tests and goodness-of-fit in the analysis of covariance structures. *Psychological Bulletin, 88,* 588–606.

Bentler, P. M., & Woodward, J. A. (1978). A Head Start re-evaluation: Positive effects are not demonstrable. *Evaluation Quarterly, 2,* 493–510.

Bernstein, J. H. (1988). *Applied multivariate analysis*. New York: Springer.

Bock, R. D., & Bargmann, R. E. (1966). Analysis of covariance structures. *Psychometrika, 31*, 507–534.

Berger, A. A. (1991). *Media research techniques*. Newbury Park, CA: Sage.

Bergin, D. A. (1995). Effects of a mastery versus competitive motivation situation on learning. *Journal of Experimental Education, 63*, 303–314.

Berk, R., Ed. (1982). *Handbook of methods for detecting test bias*. Baltimore: Johns Hopkins University Press.

Berkowitz, L. (1983). Aversively stimulated aggression: Some parallels and differences in research with humans and animals. *American Psychologist, 38*, 1135–1144.

Berquier, A., & Ashton, R. (1992). Characteristics of the frequent nightmare sufferer. *Journal of Abnormal Psychology, 101*, 246–250.

Beyer, W. H. (1971). *Basic statistical tables*. Cleveland, OH: The Chemical Rubber Company.

—— (1990). Standard probability and statistical tables and formulas. Boca Raton, FL: CRC Press.

Bierman, H., Bonini, C. P., & Hausman, W. H. (1991). *Quantitative analysis for business decisions* (8th ed.). Burr Ridge, IL: Richard Irwin.

Bishop, Y. M. M., Fienberg, S. R., & Holland, P. W. (1975). *Discrete multivariate analysis: Theory and practice*. Cambridge, MA: MIT Press.

Bishop, Y., Fienberg, S., & Holland, P. (1976). *Discrete multivariate analysis*. Cambridge, MA: MIT Press.

Bjorck, J. P., Lee, Y. S., & Cohen, L. H. (1997). Control beliefs and faith as stress moderators for Korean Americans versus Caucasian American Protestants. *American Journal of Community Psychology, 25*, 61–72.

Blanton, H., & Gerrard, M. (1997). Effect of sexual motivation on men's risk perception for sexually transmitted disease: There must be 50 ways to justify a lover. *Health Psychology, 16*, 374–379.

Blaser, M. J. (1996). The bacteria behind ulcers. *Scientific American, 274*, 104–107.

Blalock, H. M. (1971). *Causal models in the social sciences*. New York: Norton.

—— (1972). Causal inferences in nonexperimental research. New York: Norton.

Block, N. & Dworkin, G., Eds. (1976). *The IQ controversy*. New York: Pantheon. Valuable readings by leaders in the controversy.

Bloom, B. (1956). *Taxonomy of educational objectives, Handbook l: Cognitive domain*. New York: David McKay.

Blumenthal, J. A. (1998). The reasonable woman standard: A meta-analytic review of gender differences in perceptions of sexual harassment. *Law and Human Behavior, 22*, 33–57.

Bock, R. D., & Jones, L. V. (1968). *The measurement and prediction of judgment and choice*. San Francisco, CA: Holden-Day.

Bogardus, E. S. (1926). The group interview. *Journal of Applied Sociology, 10*, 372–382.

Bolding, J. T., & Houston, S. R. (1974). A FORTRAN computer program for computation of ridge regression coefficients. *Educational and Psychological Measurement, 34*, 151–152.

Bollen, K. (1979). Political democracy and the timing of development. *American Sociological Review, 44*, 572–587.

—— (1980). Issues in the comparative measurement of political democracy. *American Sociological Review, 45*, 370–390.

Bolman, W. M. (1995). The place of behavioral science in medical education and practice. *Academic Medicine, 70*, 873–878.

Boneau, C. (1960). The effects of violations of assumptions underlying the *t*-test. *Psychological Bulletin, 57*, 49–64.

Borack, J. I. (1997). A technique for estimating the probability of detecting a nongaming drug user. *The American Statistician, 51*, 134–137.

Borenstein, M., Cohen, J., & Rothstein, H. (1997). *Statistical power analysis, power and precision!* Mahwah, NJ: LawrenceErlbaum.

Borg, I. (1988). Revisiting Thurstone and Coombs' scales on the seriousness of crimes and offences. *European Journal of Social Psychology, 18,* 53–61.

Borgatta, E. F. (1963). A new systematic observation system: Behavior Scores System (BSs system), *Journal of Psychological Studies, 14,* 24–44.

Borich, G., & Klinzing, G. (1984). Some assumptions in the observation of classroom process with suggestions for improving low inference measurement. *Journal of Classroom Interaction, 20,* 36–44.

Boring E. (1954). The nature and history of experimental control. *American Journal of Psychology, 67,* 573–589.

Borrowman, M. (1960). History of education. In C. Harris, Ed., *Encyclopedia of educational research* (3rd ed.) (pp. 661–668). New York: Macmillan.

Bownas, D. A., & Bernardin, H. J. (1991). Suppressing illusory halo with forced-choice items. *Journal of Applied Psychology, 76,* 592–594.

Box, G. E. P. (1954). The exploration and exploitation of response surfaces: Some general considerations and examples. *Biometrics, 10,* 16–60.

Box, G. E. P., & Jenkins, G. M. (1970). *Time-series analysis: forecasting and control.* San Francisco: Holden-Day.

Box, G. E. P., & Draper, N. R. (1987). *Empirical model-building and response surfaces.* New York: John Wiley & Sons.

Box, G. E. P., Hunter, W. G., & Hunter, J. S. (1978). Statistics for experimenters: An introduction to design, data analysis, and model building. New York: John Wiley & Sons.

Bradley, J. (1968). *Distribution-free statistical tests.* Englewood Cliffs, NJ: Prentice-Hall.

Bradley, M. T., & Gupta, R. D. (1997). Estimating the effect of the file drawer problem in meta-analysis. *Perceptual and Motor Skills, 85,* 719–722.

Brady, M. E. (1988). J. M. Keynes' position on the general applicability of mathematical, logical and statistical methods in economics and social sciences. *Synthese, 76,* 1–24.

Brady, M. E., & Lee, H. B. (1989a). Dynamics of choice behavior: The logical relation between linear objective probability and nonlinear subjective probability. *Psychological Reports, 64,* 91–97.

Brady, M. E., & Lee, H. B. (1989b). Is there an Allais paradox: A note on its resolution? *Psychological Reports, 64,* 1223–1230.

Brady, M. E., & Lee, H. B. (1991). Theoretical comparison of decision theories of J. M. Keynes, Kahneman and Tversky, and Einhorn-Hogarth. *Psychological Reports, 69,* 243–251.

Braithwaite, R. (1996). *Scientific explanation.* Herndon, VA: Books International. (Original work published 1953).

Brandt, A. M. (1978). Racism and research: The case of the Tuskegee syphilis study. *Hastings Center Report, 8,* 21–29.

Braud, L., & Braud, W. (1972) Biochemical transfer of relational responding. *Science, 176,* 942–944.

Bray, I., & Maxwell, S. (1982). Analyzing and interpreting significant MANOVAs. *Review of Educational Research, 52,* 340–367.

Brecht, M. L., Dracup, K., Moser, D. K., & Riegel, B. (1994). The relationship of marital quality and psychosocial adjustment to heart disease. *Journal of Cardiovascular Nursing, 9,* 74–85.

Brief, A. P., Butcher, A. H., & Roberson, L. (1995). Cookies, disposition and job attitudes: The effect of positive mood-inducing events and negative affectivity on job satisfaction in a field experiment. *Organizational Behavior and Human Decision Processes, 62,* 55–62.

Brief, D. E., Comrey, A. L., & Collins, B. E. (1994). The Comrey Personality Scales in Russian: A study of concurrent, predictive and external validity. *Personality and Individual Differences, 16,* 113–122.

Bross, I. (1953). *Design for decision.* New York: Macmillan.

Brown, F. G. (1983). *Principles of educational and psychological testing* (3rd ed.). New York: Holt, Rinehart & Winston.

Brown, R. (1958). *Words and things.* New York: Free Press.

Brown, R. L. (1986). A comparison of LISREL and EQS programs for obtaining parameter estimates in confirmatory factor analysis studies. *Behavior Research Methods, Instruments and Computers, 18,* 382–388.

Bruning, J.L. & Kinte, B. L. (1987). *Computational handbook of statistics.* (3rd. ed.). Glenville, IL: Harper Collins.

Bruno, J. E. (Ed.). (1972). Emerging issues in education: Policy implications for the schools. Lexington, MA: Heath

—— (1986). Assessing the knowledge base of students with admissible probability measurement (APM): A microcomputer-based information theoretic approach to testing. *Measurement and Evaluation in Counseling and Development, 19,* 116–130.

Bruno, J. E. (1989). Monitoring the academic progress of low achieving students: An analysis of right–wrong (R–W) versus information referenced (MCW–APM) formative and summative evaluation procedures. *Journal of Research and Development in Education, 23,* 51–61.

Bruno, J. E., & Dirkzwager, A. (1995). Determining the optimal number of alternatives to a multiple-choice test item: An information theoretic perspective. *Educational and Psychological Measurement, 55,* 959–966.

Buchler, J. (1955). *Philosophical writings of Peirce.* New York: Dover.

Bugelski, B. (1956). *The psychology of learning.* New York: Holt, Rinehart and Winston.

Bureau of the Census. (1978). *Social and economic characteristics of the metropolitan and nonmetropolitan population; 1977 and 1970.* Washington, DC: U.S. Bureau of the Census.

Burnam, T. (1975). *The dictionary of misinformation.* New York: Ballantine.

Burlington, R., & May, D. (1970). *Handbook of probability and statistics with tables* (2nd ed.). New York: McGraw-Hill.

Buros, O. K., Ed. (1998). *The 13th mental measurements yearbook.* Highland Park, NJ: Gryphon Press.

Burt, M. (1980). Cultural myths and support for rape. *Journal of Personality and Social Psychology, 38,* 217–230.

Calder, B. J. (1977). Focus groups and the nature of qualitative market research. *Journal of Marketing Research, 14,* 353–364.

Camel, J. E., Withers, G. S., & Greenough, W. T. (1986). Persistence of visual cortex dendritic alterations induced by post weaning exposure to a "superenriched" environment in rats. *Behavioral Neuroscience, 100,* 810–813.

Cameron, J., & Pierce, W. D. (1994). Reinforcement, reward and intrinsic motivation: A meta-analysis. *Review of Educational Research, 64,* 363–423.

Cameron, J., & Pierce, W. D. (1996). The debate about rewards and intrinsic motivation: Protests and accusations do not alter the results. *Review of Educational Research, 66,* 39–51.

Camilli, G. (1994). *Methods for identifying biased test items.* Thousand Oaks, CA: Sage.

Campbell, A. (1976). Subjective measures of well being. *American Psychologist, 31,* 117–124.

—— (1981). The sense of well-being in America: Recent patterns and trends. New York: McGraw-Hill.

Campbell, A., Converse, P.E., Miller W.E., & Stokes, D.E. (1960). *The American voter.* New York: Wiley.

Campbell, A., Converse, P., & Rodgers, W. (1976). *The quality of American life: Perceptions, evaluations, satisfactions.* New York: Russell Sage Foundation.

Campbell, A., & Katona, G. (1953). The sample survey: A technique for social-science research. In L. Festinger & D. Katz, (Eds.), *Research methods in the behavioral sciences* (Chapter 1). New York: Holt, Rinehart and Winston.

Campbell, D. (1957). Factors relevant to the validity of experiments in social settings. *Psychological Bulletin, 54*, 297–312.

Campbell, D., & Stanley, J. (1963). *Experimental and quasi-experimental designs for research.* Chicago: Rand McNally.

Campbell, D. T., & Fiske, D.W. (1959). Convergent and discriminant validation by the multitrait–multimethod matrix *Psychological Bulletin, 54*, 81–105.

Cangelosi, J. S. (1990). *Designing tests for evaluating student achievement.* White Plains, NY: Longman.

Cannell, C., & Kahn, R. (1968). Interviewing. In G. Lindzey and E. Aronson (Eds.), *The handbook of social psychology* (2nd ed.). Reading, MA: Addison-Wesley, 526–595.

Capaldi, D. H., Crosby, L., & Stoolmiller, M. (1996). Predicting the timing of first sexual intercourse for at-risk adolescent males. *Child Development, 67*, 344–359.

Caporaso, J. A. (1973). Quasi-experimental approaches to social sciences. In J. A. Caporaso & L. L. Ross (Eds.), *Quasi-experimental approaches.* Evanston, IL: Northwestern University Press.

Carroll, J. B. (1993). *Human cognitive abilities: A survey of factor-analytic studies.* Cambridge: Cambridge University Press.

Carroll, J. D., & Green, P. (1997). *Mathematical tools for applied multivariate analysis* (3rd ed.). New York: Academic Press.

Carroll, L., Hoenigmann-Stovall, N., & Whitehead, G. I. (1996). Interpersonal consequences of narcissism. *Psychological Reports, 79*, 1267–1272.

Cason, H. (1930). Common annoyances: A psychological study of everyday aversions and irritations. *Psychological Monographs, 40*, 1–218.

Cattell, R.B. (1963). Theory of fluid and crystallized intelligence: A critical experiment. *Journal of Educational Psychology, 54*, 1–22.

—— (1978). *The scientific use of factor analysis in the behavioral and life sciences.* New York: Plenum Press.

—— (1987). *Intelligence: Its structure, growth and action.* Amsterdam: North Holland.

Cervone, D. (1987). Chi-square analyses of self-efficacy data: A cautionary note. *Cognitive Theory and Research, 11*, 709–714.

Chamberlin, T. (1965). The method of multiple working hypotheses. *Science, 147*, 754–759. (Originally published in *Science*, 1890, vol. 15).

Chambers, B., & Abrami, P. C. (1991). The relationship between student team learning outcomes and achievement, causal attributions and affect. *Journal of Educational Psychology, 83*, 140–146.

Chan, T. S. (1987). A DBASE III program that performs significance testing for the kappa coefficient. *Behavior Research Methods, Instruments, and Computers, 19*, 53–54.

Chapman, G. B., & McCauley, C. (1993). Early career achievements of National Science Foundation (NSF) graduate applicants: Looking for Pygmalion and Galatea effects on NSF winners. *Journal of Applied Psychology, 78*, 815–820.

Chavez, R. C. (1984). The use of high-inference measures to study classroom climates: A review. *Review of Educational Research, 54*, 237–261.

Chen, C., Lee, S., & Stevenson, H. W. (1995). Response style and cross-cultural comparisons of rating scales among East Asian and North American students. *Psychological Science, 6*, 170–175.

Child, I., Potter, E., & Levine, E. (1946). Children's textbooks and personality development: An exploration in the social psychology of education. *Psychological Monographs, 60*.

Christenfeld, N. (1997). Memory for pain and the delayed effects of distraction. *Health Psychology, 16*, 327–330.

Christensen, L. B. (1996). *Experimental methodology* (6th ed.). Needham Heights, MA: Allyn & Bacon.

Christensen, L.B. (1997) *Experimental methodology*. (7th ed.). Boston: Allyn & Bacon.

Clark, C., & Walberg, H. (1968). The influence of massive rewards on reading achievement in potential school dropouts. *American Educational Research Journal, 5,* 305–310.

Cliff, N. (1996). *Ordinal methods for behavioral data analysis.* Mahwah, NJ: Lawrence Erlbaum.

Clogg, C. C. (1979). Some latent structure models for the analysis of Likert-type data. *Social Science Research, 8,* 287–301.

Closs, S. J. (1978). An algorithm for integrating preference and like–dislike responses to the same test items. *Journal of Occupational Psychology, 51,* 147–154.

Cochran, S. D., & Mays, V. M. (1990). Sex, lies and HIV. *New England Journal of Medicine, 322,* 774–775.

Cochran, S. D., & Mays, V. M. (1994). Depressive distress among homosexually active African-American men and women. *American Journal of Psychiatry, 15,* 524–529.

Cochran, S. D., DeLeeuw, J., & Mays, V. M. (1995). Optimal scaling of HIV-related sexual risk behaviors in ethnically diverse homosexually active men. *Journal of Clinical and Consulting Psychology, 63,* 270–279.

Cohen, J. (1960). A coefficient of agreement for nominal scales. *Educational and Psychological Measurement, 20,* 37–46.

—— (1988). *Statistical power analysis for the behavioral sciences* (2nd. ed.). Hillsdale, NJ: Lawrence Erlbaum.

—— (1994) The earth is round (p < .05). *American Psychologist, 49,* 997–1003.

Cohen, J., & Cohen, P. (1983). *Applied multiple regression/correlation analysis for the behavioral sciences* (2nd ed.). Mahwah, NJ: Lawrence Erlbaum.

Cohen, M. R. (1997). *A Preface to logic.*

New York: Meridian. (Original work published 1956).

Coleman, J., Campbell, E., Hobson, C., McPartland, J., Mood, A., Weinfeld, F., & York, R. (1966). *Equality of educational opportunity.* Washington, DC: U.S. Government Printing Office.

Collins, L. M., & Horn, J. L. (Eds.). (1991). *Best methods for the analysis of change: Recent advances, unanswered questions, future directions.* Washington, DC: American Psychological Association.

Colwell, J. C., Foreman, M. D., & Trotter, J. P. (1993). A comparison of the efficacy and cost-effectiveness of two methods of managing pressure ulcers. *Debubitus, 6(4),* 28–36.

Comrey, A. L. (1950). An operational approach to some problems in psychological measurement. *Psychological Review, 57,* 217–228.

—— (1962). The minimum residual method of factor analysis. *Psychological Reports, 11,* 15–18.

—— (1967). Tandem criteria for analytic rotation in factor analysis. *Psychometrika, 32,* 143–154.

—— (1970). *Comrey personality scales.* San Diego, CA: EdITS.

—— (1976). Mental testing and the logic of measurement. In W. L. Barnette (Ed.), *Readings in psychological tests and measurements* (3rd ed.). Baltimore, MD: Williams and Wilkins, 1–10.

—— (1978). Common methodological problems in factor analysis. *Journal of Consulting and Clinical Psychology, 46,* 648–659

—— (1980). *Handbook of interpretations for the Comrey Personality Scales.* San Diego, CA: EDITS.

—— (1988). Factor analytic methods of scale development in personality and clinical psychology. *Journal of Consulting and Clinical Psychology, 56,* 754–761.

—— (1993). *EdITS Manual for the Comrey Personality Scales.* San Diego, CA: Educational and Industrial Testing Service.

—— (1993). *EdITS Manual for the Comrey Personality Scales.* San Diego, CA: Educational and Industrial Testing Service.

Comrey, A. L., Backer, T. C., & Glaser, E. M. (1973). *A sourcebook for mental health measures.* Los Angeles, CA: Human Interaction Research Institute.

Comrey, A. L., & Lee, H. B. (1995). *Elementary statistics: A problem-solving approach* (3rd ed.). Dubuque, IA: Kendall-Hunt.

Comrey, A. L., & Lee, H. B. (1992). *A first course in factor analysis* (2nd. ed.). Hillsdale, NJ: Lawrence Erlbaum.

Comrey, A. L., Wong, C., & Backer, T. E. (1978). Further validation of the Social Conformity scale of the Comrey Personality Scales. *Psychological Reports, 43,* 165–166.

Conant, J. B. (1951). *Science and common sense.* New Haven: Yale University Press.

Conger, A. J. (1974). A revised definition for suppressor variables: A guide to their identification and interpretation. *Educational and Psychological Measurement, 34,* 35–46.

Congressional Quarterly. (December 18, 1993), 51, 3496.

Congressional Quarterly. (January 20, 1996), 54 (January, 20), 169.

Congressional Quarterly. (1993). Volume 51, pp. 3497 (No. 266) and (No. 290).

Cook, T.D. & Campbell, D.T. (1979). *Quasi-experimentation: Design and anlysis issues for field settings.* Chicago: Rand Mc-Nally.

Cook, T. D., & Reichardt, C. S. (Eds.). (1979). *Qualitative and quantitative methods in evaluation research.* Beverly Hills, CA: Sage.

Cooke, D. K., Sims, R. L., & Peyrefitte, J. (1995). The relationship between graduate student attitudes and attrition. *Journal of Psychology, 129,* 677–688.

Cooley, W., & Lohnes, P. (1985). *Multivariate data analysis.* Melbourne, FL: Krieger. (Reprint of 1971 book originally published by Wiley)

Coren, S., Ward, L. M., & Enns, J. T.

(1994). *Sensation and perception* (4th ed.). Fort Worth, TX: Harcourt Brace.

Cornwall, T. (1996). Too dangerous for words. *The Times Higher Education Supplement,* no. 1245.

Cowles, M. (1989). *Statistics in psychology: An historical perspective.* Hillsdale, NJ: Lawrence Erlbaum.

Cox, D. R., & Wermuth, N. (1992). A comment on the coefficient of determination for binary responses. The *American Statistician, 46,* 1–4.

Crancer, A., Dille, J. M., Delay, J. C., Wallace, J. E., & Haykin, M.D. (1969). Comparison of the effects of marijuana and alcohol on simulated driving performance. *Science, 164,* 851–854.

Crandall, J. (1980). Adler's concept of social interest: Theory, measurement, and implications for adjustment. *Journal of Personality and Social Psychology, 39,* 481–495.

Creswell, J. W. (1998). *Qualitative inquiry and research design: Choosing among five traditions.* Thousand Oaks, CA: Sage Publications.

Crocker, L., & Algina, J. (1986). *Classical and modern test theory.* Fort Worth, TX: Harcourt Brace.

Cronbach, L. (1951). Coefficient alpha and the internal structure of tests. *Psychometrika, 16,* 297–334.

Cronbach, L., & Furby, L. (1970). How should we measure "change"—or should we? *Psychological Bulletin, 74,* 68–80.

Cronbach, L. J., & Gleser, G. (1953). Assessing similarity between profiles. *Psychological Bulletin, 50,* 456–473.

Cronbach, L. Gleser, G., Nanda, H., & Rajaratnam, N. (1972). *The dependability of behavioral measurement: Theory of generalizability for scores and profiles.* New York: John Wiley & Sons.

Cronbach, L. J. (1970). *Essentials of psychological testing* (3rd ed.). New York: Harper & Row.

—— (1971). Test validation. In R. Thorndike, Ed., *Educational measurement*

(2nd ed.) Washington, DC: American Council on Education.

—— (1990). *Essentials of psychological testing* (5th ed.). Reading, MA: Addison-Wesley.

Cronbach, L. J., & Meehl, P. (1955). Construct validity in psychological tests. *Psychological Bulletin, 52,* 281–302.

Cureton, E. E., & D'Agostino, R. B. (1983). *Factor analysis: An applied approach.* Hillsdale, NJ: Lawrence Erlbaum.

Curtis, E. W. (1985). Variance components: Partialed vs. common. *Educational and Psychological Measurement, 45,* 577–591.

Cutler, W. B., Preti, G., Krieger, A., & Huggins, G. R. (1986). Human axilliary secretions influence women's menstrual cycles: The role of donor extract from men. *Hormones and Behavior, 20,* 463–473.

Cutright, P. (1963). National political development: Measurement and analysis. *American Sociological Review, 27,* 229–245.

Dane, F. C. (1990). *Research methods.* Pacific Grove, CA: Brooks-Cole.

Daniel, C. (1976). Applications of statistics to industrial experimentation. New York: Wiley.

Dawes, R. M. (1994). House of cards: Psychology and psychotherapy built on myth. New York: The Free Press.

Davis, P. J. (1973). *The mathematics of matrices: A first book of matrix theory and linear algebra* (2nd ed.). Lexington, MA: Xerox. York: The Free Press.

—— (1972). *Fundamentals of attitude measurement.* New York: John Wiley & Sons.

Day, N. E., & Schoenrade, P. (1997). Staying in the closet versus coming out: Relationship between communication about sexual orientation and work attitudes. *Personnel Psychology, 50,* 147–163.

Dayton, G. C. (1976). Perceptual creativity: Where inner and outer reality come together. *Journal of Creative Behavior, 10,* 256–264.

DeCorte, E., and Verschaffel, L. (1981). Children's solution processes in elementary arithmetic problems: Analysis and improvement. *Journal of Educational Psychology, 73,* 765–779.

de Weerth, C., & Kalma, A. F. (1993). Female aggression as a response to sexual jealousy: A sex role reversal? *Aggressive Behavior, 19,* 265–279.

Dear, R. E. (1959). *A principal-component missing data method for multiple regression models.* Technical Report SP-86. Santa Monica, CA: Systems Development Corporation.

Deaton, W. L., Glasnapp, D. R., & Poggio, J. P. (1980). Effects of item characteristics on psychometric properties of forced-choice scales. *Educational & Psychological Measurement, 40,* 599–610.

Deci, E. (1971). Effects of externally mediated rewards on intrinsic motivation. *Journal of Personality and Social Psychology, 18,* 105–115.

Deming, W. E. (1964). Statistical adjustment of data. New York: Dover. (Reprint of 1943 edition)

Deming, W. E., & Stephan, F. F. (1940). On a least-squares adjustment of sample frequency table when the expected marginal totals are known. *Annals of Mathematical Statistics, 11,* 427–444.

Dewey, J. (1982). *Logic: The theory of inquiry.* New York: Irvington Publishers. (Original work published 1938)

—— (1991). *How we think.* Amherst: Prometheus. (Original work published 1933)

Dewey, M. E. (1989). A note on the computation of Cohen's kappa. *British Journal of Mathematical and Statistical Psychology, 42,* 191–195.

Dill, J. C., & Anderson, C. A. (1995). Effects of frustration justification in hostile aggression. *Aggressive-Behavior, 21(5),* 359–369.

Dillon, W. R., & Goldstein, M. (1984). *Multivariate analysis: Methods and applications.* New York: John Wiley & Sons.

Dion, K. L., & Cota, A. A. (1991). The Ms. stereotype: Its domain and its role of explicitness in title preference. *Psychology of Women Quarterly, 15,* 403–410.

Dixon, W.J. (1990). *BMDP statistical software.* Berkeley, CA: University of California Press.

Docter, R. F., & Prince, V. (1997). Transvestitism: A survey of 1,032 cross-dressers. *Archives of Sexual Behavior, 26,* 589–605.

Doctor, R. S., Cutris, D., & Isaacs, G. (1994). Psychiatric morbidity in policemen and the effect of brief psychotherapeutic intervention: A pilot study. *Stress Medicine,* 10, 151–157.

Dohrenwend, B., & Richardson, S. (1963). Directiveness and nondirectiveness in research interviewing: A reformulation of the problem. *Psychological Bulletin, 60,* 475–485.

Dollard, J., Doob, L., Miller, N., Mowrer, O., & Sears, R. (1939). *Frustration and aggression.* New Haven: Yale University Press.

Dolinski, D., & Nawrat, R. (1998). "Fear-then-relief" procedure for producing compliance: Beware when the danger is over. *Journal of Experimental Social Psychology, 34,* 27–50.

Doob, A. N., & McLaughlin, D. S. (1989). Ask and you shall be given: Request size and donations to a good cause. *Journal of Applied Social Psychology, 19,* 1049–1056.

Dooley, D. (1995). *Social research methods* (3rd ed.). Englewood Cliffs, NJ: Prentice-Hall.

Doscher, M-L., & Bruno, J. E. (1981). Simulation of inner-city standardized testing behavior: Implications for instructional evaluation. *American Educational Research Journal, 18,* 475–489.

Draper, N., & Smith, H. (1981). *Applied regression analysis* (2nd ed.). New York: John Wiley & Sons.

Dukes, W. (1955). Psychological studies of values. *Psychological Bulletin, 52,* 24–50.

Duncan, O. D. (1966). Path analysis: Socio-logical examples. *American Journal of Sociology, 72,* 1–16.

Duncan, O. D., Featherman, D., & Duncan, B. (1972). *Socioeconomic background and achievement.* New York: Seminar Press.

Dunkin, M., & Biddle, B. (1974). *The study of teaching.* New York: Holt, Rinehart & Winston.

Dunn, G. (1989). *Design and analysis of reliability studies: The statistical evaluation of measurement errors.* Oxford, England: Oxford University Press.

—— (1992). Design and analysis of reliability studies. *Statistical Methods in Medical Research, 1,* 123–157.

Dutton, D., & Lake, R. (1973). Threat of own prejudice and reverse discrimination. *Journal of Personality and Social Psychology, 28,* 94–100.

Ebel, R. (1951). Estimation of the reliability of ratings. *Psychometrika, 16,* 407–424.

Elbedour, S., Shulman, S., & Kedem, P. (1997). Children's fears: Cultural and developmental perspectives. *Behaviour Research and Therapy, 35,* 491–496.

Edgington, E. S. (1980). *Randomization tests.* New York: Marcel Dekker.

Edgington, E. S. (1996). Randomized single-subject experimental designs. *Behaviour Research and Therapy, 34,* 567–574.

Edmondson, A. C. (1996). Learning from mistakes is easier said than done: Group and organizational influences on the detection and correction of human error. *Journal of Applied Behavioral Science, 32,* 5–28.

Edwards, A. (1953). *Personal preference schedule, manual.* New York: Psychological Corporation.

—— (1957). *Techniques of attitude scale construction.* New York: Appleton-Century-Crofts.

Edwards, A. L. (1984). *Experimental Design in Psychological Research* (5th ed.). Reading, MA: Addison-Wesley.

Eisenberger, R., & Cameron, J. (1996). Detrimental effects of reward:

Reality or myth? *American Psychologist, 51,* 1153–1166.

Elashoff, J. (1969). Analysis of covariance: A delicate instrument. *American Educational Research Journal, 6,* 383–401.

Elbert, J. C. (1993). Occurrence and pattern of impaired reading and written language in children with ADDS. *Annals of Dyslexia, 43,* 26–43.

Elias, F. G. (1989). Task-focused self-disclosure: Effects on group cohesiveness, commitment to task and productivity. *Small Group Behavior, 20,* 87–96.

Eliopoulos, C. (1993). *Gerontological nursing* (3rd. Ed.). Philadelphia: J. B. Lippincott.

Ellis, J. L. (1989). Evaluating idiosyncratic programs in education for the gifted. Special issue: The education of the gifted child in Canada. *Canadian Journal of Education, 14,* 93–101.

Emory, C. W. (1976). *Business research methods.* Homewood, IL: Irwin.

Enslein, K., Ralston, A., & Wilf, H. (Eds.) (1977). *Statistical methods for digital computers. Volume 3 of mathematical methods for digital computers.* New York: John Wiley & Sons.

Erdos, P. L. (1974). Data collection methods: Mail surveys. In R. Ferber (Ed.), *Handbook of marketing research.* New York: McGraw-Hill.

Erlich, O., & Lee, H. B. (1978). Use of regression analysis in reporting test results for accountability. *Perceptual and Motor Skills, 47,* 879–882.

Erwin, E., Gendin, S., & Kleiman, L. (1994). *Ethical issues in scientific research: An anthology.* New York: Garland.

Esposito, B. G., & Koorland, M. A. (1989). Play behavior of hearing-impaired children: Integrated and segregated settings. *Exceptional Children, 55,* 412–419.

Estes, W. K. (1991). *Statistical models in behavioral research.* Hillsdale, NJ: Lawrence Erlbaum.

Evans, R. I., Turner, S. H., Ghee, K. L., & Getz, J. G. (1990). Is androgynous sex role related to cigarette smoking in adolescents? *Journal of Applied Social Psychology, 20,* 494–505.

Ezekiel, M., & Fox, K. A. (1959). *Methods of correlation and regression analysis* (3rd ed.). New York: Wiley.

Fallon, A., & Rozin, P. (1985). Sex differences in perception of desirable body shape. *Journal of Abnormal Psychology, 94,* 102–105.

Farlow, S. I. (1988). *Finite mathematics and its applications.* New York: Random House.

Feather, N. (1962). The study of persistence. *Psychological Bulletin, 59,* 94.

Feldman, R. S., Coats, E. J., & Spielman, D. A. (1996). Television exposure and children's decoding of nonverbal behavior. *Journal of Applied Social Psychology, 26,* 1718–1733.

Feller, W. (1967). An introduction to probability theory and its applications (3rd ed.). New York: Wiley.

Ferber, R., (Ed.) (1974). *Handbook of marketing research.* New York: McGraw-Hill

Ferguson, G. A. (1971). *Statistical analysis in psychology and education* (3rd ed.). New York: McGraw-Hill.

Festinger, L., & Katz, D. (1953). *Research methods in the behavioral sciences.* New York: Holt, Rinehart and Winston.

Festinger, L., Schachter, S., & Back, K (1950). *Social pressures in informal groups.* New York: Harper & Row.

Fienberg, S. R. (1980). *The analysis of cross-classified categorical data* (2nd ed.). Cambridge, MA: MIT Press.

Fienberg, S., & Wasserman, S. (1981). Categorical data analysis of single sociometric relations. In S. Leinhardt, Ed., *Sociological Methodology 1981* (pp. 156–192). San Francisco: Jossey-Bass.

Firkowska, A., Ostrowska, A., Sokolowska, M., Stein, Z., Susser, M., & Wald, I. (1978). Cognitive development and social policy. *Science, 200,* 1357–1362.

Fisher, R.A. (1936). The use of multiple measurements in taxonomic problems. *Annals of Eugenics, 7,* 179–188.

—— *Statistical methods for research workers* (11th ed.). New York: Hafner.

—— (1950). *The design of experiments* (6th ed.). New York: Hafner.

Fischer, J., & Corcoran, K. J. (1994). *Measures for clinical practice: A sourcebook* (2nd ed.). New York: Free Press.

Fleiss, J. L. (1986). *The design and analysis of clinical experiments.* New York: John Wiley & Sons.

Fleiss, J. L., & Cohen, J. (1973). The equivalence of weighted kappa and the intraclass correlation coefficient as measures of reliability. *Educational and Psychological Measurement, 33,* 613–619.

Flowers, M. (1977). A laboratory test of some implications of Janis' groupthink hypothesis. *Journal of Personality and Social Psychology, 35,* 888–896.

Foster, N., Dingman, S., Muscolino, J., & Jankowski, M. A. (1996). Gender in mock hiring decisions. *Psychological Reports, 79,* 275–278.

Francis-Felsen, L. C., Coward, R. T., Hogan, T. L., & Duncan, R. P. (1996). Factors influencing intentions of nursing personnel to leave employment in long-term care settings. *Journal of Applied Gerontology, 15,* 450–470.

Frank, I.E., & Friedman, J. H. (1993). A statistical view of some chemometrics regression tools. *Technometrics, 35,*109–135.

Freedman, D. A. (1987). As others see us. A case study of causal modeling methods. *Journal of Educational Statistics, 12,* 101–128.

Freedman, J., Wallington, S., & Bless, E. (1967). Compliance without pressure: The effect of guilt. *Journal of Personality and Social Psychology, 7,* 117–124.

Freedman, S. (1979). How characteristics of student essays influence teachers' evaluations. *Journal of Educational Psychology, 71,* 328–338.

French, J. (1953). Experiments in field settings. In L. Festinger & D. Katz (Eds.), *Research methods in the behavioral sciences* (pp. 118–129). New York: Holt, Rinehart and Winston.

Frentz, C., Gresham, F. M., & Elliot, S. N. (1991). Popular, controversial, neglected and rejected adolescents: Contrasts of social competence and achievement differences. *Journal of School Psychology, 29,* 109–120.

Friedman, M. (1937). The use of ranks to avoid the assumption of normality implicit in the analysis of variance. *Journal of the American Statistical Association, 32,* 675–701.

Friedenberg, L. (1995). *Psychological testing: Design, analysis and use.* Boston, MA: Allyn & Bacon.

Fruchter, B. (1966). Manipulative and hypothesis-testing factor-analytic experimental designs. In R. Cattell, Ed., *Handbook of multivariate experimental psychology.* Skokie, IL: Rand McNally, pp. 330–354.

Fukada, H., Fukada, S., & Hicks, J. (1997). The relationship between leadership and sociometric status among preschool children. *Journal of Genetic Psychology, 158,* 481–486.

Garfinkle, P. E., Kline, S. A., & Stancer, H. C. (1973). Treatment of anorexia nervosa using operant conditioning techniques. *Journal of Nervous and Mental Disease, 157,* 428–433.

Gardner, P. (1975). Scales and statistics. *Review of Educational Research, 45,* 43–57.

Garner, B., & Smith, R. W. (1977). Are there really any gay male athletes? An empirical survey. *Journal of Sex Research, 13, 22*–34.

Gates, A., & Taylor, G. (1925). An experimental study of the nature of improvement resulting from practice in a mental function. *Journal of Educational Psychology, 16,* 583–592.

Gelfand, H., & Walker, C. J. (1990). *Mastering APA style: Student's workbook and training guide.* Washington, DC: American Psychological Association.

Ghiselli, E. (1964). *Theory of psychological measurement.* New York: McGraw-Hill.

Giere, R. (1979). *Understanding scientific reasoning*. New York: Holt, Rinehart and Winston.

Gillings, V., & Joseph, S. (1996). Religiosity and social desirability: Impression management and self-deceptive positivity. *Personality and Individual Differences, 21,* 1047–1050.

Glanzer, M., & Glaser, R. (1959). Techniques for the study of group structure and behavior: Analysis of structure. *Psychological Bulletin, 56,* 317–332.

Glass, G. V. (1976). Primary, secondary and meta-analysis of research. *Educational Researcher, 6,* 3–8.

Gleason, T. L., & Staelin, R. (1975). A proposal for handling missing data. *Psychometrika, 40,* 229–252.

Glick, P., DeMorest, J. A., & Hotze, C.A. (1988). Keeping your distance. Group membership, personal space and request for small favors. *Journal of Applied Social Psychology, 18,* 315–330.

Glock, C., & Stark, R. (1966). *Christian beliefs and anti-Semitism*. New York: Harper & Row.

Gnanadesikan, R. (1997). *Methods for statistical data analysis of multivariate observations* (2nd ed.). New York: John Wiley & Sons.

Goldman, R. A., Saunders, J., & Busch, J. (1996). *Directory of unpublished experimental mental measures*, Vol. 1–3. Washington, DC: APA Books.

Goldstein, H., & Lewis, T. (1996). *Assessment: Problems, developments, and statistical issues; a volume of expert contributions*. New York: John Wiley & Sons.

Goodman, L. A. (1971). The analysis of multidimensional contingency tables: Stepwise procedures and direct estimation methods for building models for multiple classifications. *Technometrics, 13,* 33–61.

Gordon, R. A. (1996). Impact of ingratiation on judgment and evaluations: A meta-analytic investigation. *Journal of Personality and Social Psychology, 71,* 54–70.

Gorsuch, R. L. (1983). *Factor analysis (2nd ed.)*. Hillsdale, NJ: Lawrence Erlbaum.

Gottman, J. M. (1981). *Time-series analysis: A comprehensive introduction for social scientists*. New York: Cambridge University Press.

Gottman, J. M., McFall, R., & Barnett, J. (1969). Design and analysis of research using time series. *Psychological Bulletin, 72,* 299–306.

Gould, R. A., & Clum, G. A. (1995). Self-help plus minimum therapist contact in the treatment of panic disorder: A replication and extension. *Behavior Therapy, 26,* 533–546.

Gould, S. J. (1981) *The mismeasure of man*. New York: Norton.

Graham, J. A., & Cohen, R. (1997). Race and sex as factors in children's sociometric ratings and friendship choices. *Social Development, 6,* 355–372.

Graziano, A. M., & Raulin, M. L. (1993). *Research methods: A process of inquiry* (2nd ed.). New York: HarperCollins.

Green, P. E., & Tull, D. S. (1988). *Research for marketing decisions* (5th ed.). Englewood Cliffs, NJ: Prentice-Hall.

Gregory, R. J. (1996). *Psychological testing: History, principles and applications* (2nd ed.). Boston, MA: Allyn & Bacon.

Gresham, F. M., & Elliot, S. N. (1990). *Social skills rating system manual*. Circle Pines, MN: American Guidance Service.

Gresham, F. M., & Witt, J. C. (1997). Utility of intelligence tests for treatment planning, classification, and placement decisions: Recent empirical findings and future directions. *School Psychology Quarterly, 12,* 249–267.

Grier. J. (1982). Ban of DDT and subsequent recovery of reproduction in bald eagles. *Science, 218,* 1232–1234.

Griffiths, M. J., Bevil, C. A., O'Connor, P. C., & Wieland, D. M. (1995). Anatomy and physiology as a predictor of success in baccalaureate nursing students. *Journal of Nursing Education, 34,* 61–62.

Grizzle, J. E., Starmer, C. F., & Koch, G.

G. (1969). Analysis of categorical data by linear models. *Biometrics, 25*, 489–504.

Gronlund, N. E. (1985). *Measurement and evaluation in teaching* (5th ed.). New York: Macmillan.

Gross, A. E., Green, S. K, Storck, J. T., & Vanyur, J. M. (1980). Disclosure of sexual orientation and impressions of male and female homosexuals. *Personality and Social Psychology Bulletin, 6*, 307–314.

Gross, N., Mason, W., & McEachern, A. (1958). Explorations in role analysis: Studies of the school superintendency role. New York: John Wiley & Sons.

Guida, F. V., & Ludlow, L. H. (1989). A cross-cultural study of test anxiety. *Journal of Cross-Cultural Psychology, 20*, 178–190.

Guilford, J.P. (1952). When not to factor analyze. *Psychological Bulletin, 49*, 26–37.

—— (1954). *Psychometric methods* (2nd ed.). New York: McGraw-Hill.

Guilford, J. P., & Fruchter, B. (1978). *Fundamental statistics in psychology and education* (6th ed.). New York: McGraw-Hill.

—— (1967). *The nature of human intelligence.* New York: McGraw-Hill.

Gulliksen, H. (1950). *Theory of mental tests.* New York: John Wiley & Sons.

Guttman, L. (1956). Best possible systematic estimates of communalities. *Psychometrika, 21*, 273–285.

Haddock, G., & Zanna, M. P. (1998). Authoritarianism, values, and the favorability and structure of antigay attitudes. In G. M. Herek, Ed., *Stigma and sexual orientation: Understanding prejudice against lesbians, gay men, and bisexuals.* Thousand Oaks, CA: Sage, 82–107.

Hadfield, O. D., Littleton, C. E. , Steiner, R. L., & Woods, E. S. (1998). Predictors of preservice elementary teacher effectiveness in the microteaching of mathematics lessons. *Journal of Instructional Psychology, 25*, 34–47.

Haladyna, T. M. (1997). *Writing test items to evaluate higher order thinking.* Boston, MA: Allyn & Bacon.

Hall, J., Kaplan, D., & Lee, H. B. (1994, October). Counselor–client matching on ethnic, gender and language: Implications for school psychology. Paper presented at the Annual Convention for the Association for the Advancement of Behavioral Therapy, San Diego, CA.

Hardy, K. (1974). Social origins of American scientists and scholars. *Science, 185*, 497–506.

Harlow, L. L., Mulaik, S. A., & Steiger, J. H. (Eds.). (1997). *What if there were no significance tests?* Mahwah, NJ: Lawrence Erlbaum. [This book is a collection of articles debating the usefulness of significance testing and the recommendation of other methods to be used.]

Harman, H. H. (1976). *Modern factor analysis* (3rd ed.). Chicago: University of Chicago Press.

Harman, H. H., & Jones, W. H. (1966). Factor analysis by minimizing residuals (Minres). *Psychometrika, 31*, 351–368.

Harris, C. W. (Ed.). (1963). *Problems in measuring change.* Madison: University of Wisconsin Press.

Hart, S. D., Forth, A. E., & Hare, R. D. (1990). Performance of criminal psychopaths on selected neuropsychological tests. *Journal of Abnormal Psychology, 99*, 374–379.

Hartmann, D. P., & Wood, D. D. (1990). Observational methods. In A. S. Bellack, M. Hersen, & A. E. Kazdin, Eds., *International handbook of behavior modification and therapy* (2nd ed.) (pp. 107–138). New York: Plenum Press.

Hauser, R. M. (1997). *Indicators of children's well-being.* New York: Russell Sage.

Hays, W. L. (1994). *Statistics* (5th ed.). Fort Worth, TX; Harcourt Brace Jovanovich.

Hebb, D., & Thompson, W. (1968). The social significance of animal studies. In G. Lindzey & E. Aronson, Eds., *The handbook of social psychology*, vol. 2. (2nd ed.). New York: Random House, pp. 729–774.

Hellman, C. M. (1997). Job satisfaction and intent to leave. *Journal of Social Psychology, 137*, 677–689.

Hendrick, C., Hendrick, S. S., & Dicke, A. (1998). The love attitudes scale: Short form. *Journal of Social & Personal Relationships, 15,* 147–159.

Hendrickson, A., & White, P. (1964). PRO-MAX: A quick method for rotation to oblique simple structure. *British Journal of Statistical Psychology, 17,* 65–70.

Heppner, P. P., Kivlighan, D. M., & Wampold, B. E. (1992). *Research design in counseling.* Pacific Grove, CA: Brooks-Cole.

Hergenhahn, B. R. (1996). *Introduction to theories of learning* (5th ed.). Paramus, NJ: Prentice-Hall

Herrnstein, R. J., & Murray, C. (1996). *The bell curve: Intelligence and class structure in American life.* New York: The Free Press.

Hertz, R., & Imber, J. B. (1993). Fieldwork in elite settings: Introduction. *Journal of Contemporary Ethnography, 22,* 3–6.

Heyns, R., & Lippitt, R. (1954). Systematic observation techniques. In G. Lindzey, Ed., *Handbook of social psychology* (pp. 374–404). Cambridge, MA: Addison-Wesley.

Hicks, L. (1970). Some properties of ipsative, normative, and forced-choice normative measures. *Psychological Bulletin, 74,* 167–184.

Hilliard, S., Nguyen, M., & Domjan, M. (1997). One-trial appetitive conditioning in the sexual behavior system. *Psychonomic Bulletin & Review, 4,* 237–241.

Higginbotham, D. J., Baker, B. M., & Neill, R. D. (1980). Assessing the social participation and cognitive play abilities of hearing-impaired preschoolers. *The Volta Review, 82,* 261–270.

Hoch, S. J. (1986). Counterfactual reasoning and accuracy in predicting personal events. *Journal of Experimental Psychology: Learning, Memory, Cognition, 11,* 719–731.

Hoaglin, D.C., Mosteller, F., & Tukey, J. W. (1985). *Exploring data tables, trends and shapes.* New York: Wiley.

Hodson, R. (1989). Gender differences in job satisfaction: Why women aren't more dissatisfied. *Sociological Quarterly, 30,* 385–399.

Hoerl, A.E. & Kennard, R.W. (1970). Ridge regression: Applications to non-orthogonal problems. *Technometrics, 12,* 69–82.

Hoerl, R.W. (1995). Arthur E. Hoerl, developer of ridge regression, dies. *Amstat News, 216,* 51.

Hogan, J., & Hogan, R. (1989). How to measure employee reliability. *Journal of Applied Psychology, 74,* 273–279.

Hogan, R. (1973). Moral conduct and moral character. *Psychological Bulletin, 79,* 217–232.

Holden, C. (1996). Wiley declines to publish Jensen book. *Science, 293,* 877.

Holtgraves, T. (1997). Politeness and memory for wording of remarks. *Memory and Cognition, 25,* 106–116.

Holtzman, W., & Brown, W. (1968). Evaluating the study habits and attitudes of high school students. *Journal of Educational Psychology, 59,* 404–409.

Hollenbeck, A. (1978). Problems of reliability in observational research. In G. Sackett, Ed., *Observing behavior: Vol. 2. Data collection and analysis methods* (pp. 79–98). Baltimore: University Park Press.

Hom, H. L., Berger, M., Duncan, M. K., Miller, A., & Belvin, A. (1994). The effects of cooperative and individualistic reward on intrinsic motivation. *Journal of Genetic Psychology, 155,* 87–97.

Hopkins, C. D. (1989). *Classroom testing: Construction.* Itasca, IL: F. E. Peacock Publishers.

Horn, J. L. & Cattell, R. B. (1966). Refinement and test of the theory of fluid and crystallized general intelligence. *Journal of Educational Psychology, 57,* 253–270.

Hosmer, D., & Lemeshow, S. (1989) *Applied logistic regression.* New York: John Wiley & Sons.

Horst, P. (1961). Relations among sets of measures. *Psychometrika, 26,* 129–149.

—— (1966). *Psychological measurement and prediction.* Belmont, CA: Wadsworth.

Hotelling, H. (1935). The most predictive

criterion. *Journal of Educational Psychology, 26,* 139–142.

—— (1936). Relations between two sets of variates. *Biometrika, 28,* 321–377.

—— (1933). Analysis of a complex of statistical variables into principal components. *Journal of Educational Psychology, 24,* 417–441.

House, J. D. (1983). Effects of restriction of range on predictive validity for the Graduate Record Examination. *Psychological Reports, 53,* 710.

Howell, D. C. (1997). *Statistical methods for psychology* (4th ed.). Belmont, CA: Duxbury Press.

Hoyt, C. (1941). Test reliability obtained by analysis of variance. *Psychometrika, 6,* 155–160.

Hoyt, K. (1955). A study of the effects of teacher knowledge of pupil characteristics on pupil achievement and attitudes towards classwork. *Journal of Educational Psychology, 46,* 302–310.

Hubbach, S.M. (1995). *Writing research papers across the curriculum* (4th ed.) Fort Worth, TX: Harcourt Brace.

Hubbard, R. & Allen, S.J. (1989). On the number and nature of common factors extracted by the eigen value-one rule using BMDP vs. SPSS. *Psychological Reports, 65,* 155–160.

Hurlock, E. (1925). An evaluation of certain incentives used in schoolwork, *Journal of Educational Psychology. 16,* 145–149.

Hutchinson, S. J., & Turner, J. A. (1988). Developing a multidimensional turnover prevention program. *Archives of Psychiatric Nursing, 2,* 373–378.

Humphreys, L. (1967). Critique of Cattell's theory of fluid and crystallized intelligence: A critical experiment. *Journal of Educational Psychology. 58,*129–136.

Hyatt, S. P., & Tingstrom, D. H. (1993). Consultant's use of jargon during intervention presentation: An evaluation of presentation modality and type of intervention. *School Psychology Quarterly, 8,* 99–109.

Inderbitzen, H.M., Walters, K. S., &

Bukowski, A. L. (1997). The role of social anxiety in adolescent peer relations: Differences among sociometric status groups and rejected subgroups. *Journal of Clinical Child Psychology, 26,* 338–348.

Isaac, S., & Michael, W. B. (1987). *Handbook in research and evaluation* (2nd ed.). San Diego, CA: EDITS.

Isaacson, R. L., McKeachie, W. J., Milholland, J.E., & Lin, Y. G. (1964). Dimensions of student evaluations of teaching. *Journal of Educational Psychology, 55,* 344–351.

Iverson, G. L., Guirguis, M., & Green, P. (1998). Assessing intellectual functioning in persons with schizophrenia spectrum disorders using a seven subtest short form of the WAIS-R. *Schizophrenia Research, 30,* 165–168.

Jaccard, J., & Becker, M. A. (1997). *Statistics for the behavioral sciences* (3rd ed.). Pacific Grove, CA: Brooks-Cole.

Jaeger, R. (1978). About educational indicators: Statistics on the conditions and trends in education. In L. Shulman (Ed.), *Review of research in education, vol. 6.* Itasca, IL : Peacock Publishers.

Jaffe, C. M. (1997, Spring). Inference and evidence in the clinical situation: The analyst's use of the self. *Journal of the American Psychoanalytic Association, 45,* 545–556.

Jaffe, L. J. (1991). Impact of positioning and sex-role identity on women's responses to advertising. *Journal of Advertising Research, 31,* 57–64.

James, W. (1890). *The principles of psychology.* New York: Holt.

Janda, L. H. (1998). *Psychological testing: Theory and applications.* Boston, MA: Allyn and Bacon.

Janis, I. (1971). Groupthink. *Psychology Today,* November, 43–46, 74–86.

Jensen, A. (1980). *Bias in mental testing.* New York: Free Press.

—— (1998). *The g-factor: The science of mental ability.* Westport, CT: Greenwood Press.

Jensen, A. R. (1992). Scientific fraud or false accusations? The case of Cyril Burt. In

D. J. Miller & M. Hersen (Eds.), *Research fraud in the behavioral and biomedical sciences* (pp. 97–124). New York: Wiley.

Jensen, A. R., & Wilson, M. (1994). Henry Felix Kaiser (1927–1992). *American Psychologist, 49,* 1085.

Jennrich, R. I. (1995). *An introduction to computational statistics: Regression analysis.* Englewood Cliffs, NJ: Prentice-Hall.

Johnson, B. T. (1993). Dstat: Version 1.10. Software for the meta-analytic review of research literature. Mahwah, NJ: Lawrence Erlbaum.

Johnson, J. D. (1994). The effect of rape type and information admissibility on perception of rape victims. *Sex Roles, 30,* 781–792. Also appears in Patten, M. L. (Ed.) (1997). *Educational and psychological research.* (2nd ed.). Los Angeles, CA: Pyrczak.

Jones, D. G. (1998). *A qualitative investigation into the dynamics of youth gangs.* Unpublished manuscript. University of Southern Mississippi.

Jones, J. S., Hoerle, D., & Rieske, R. (1995). Stethoscopes: A potential vector of infection? *Annals of Emergency Medicine, 26,* 296–299.

Jones, L. (1971). The nature of measurement. In R. Thorndike (Ed.), *Educational measurement* (2nd ed.). Washington, DC: American Council on Education, 335–355

Jones, S., & Cook, S. (1975). The influence of attitude on judgments of the effectiveness of alternative social policies. *Journal of Personality and Social Psychology, 32,* 767–773.

Jones, W. P. (1991). Bayesian ideal types: Integration of psychometric data for visually impaired persons. *Journal of Visual Impairment and Blindness, 85,* 408–410.

Joreskog, K. G. (1967). Some contributions to maximum likelihood factor analysis. *Psychometrika, 32,* 443–482.

—— (1969). A general approach in confirmatory maximum likelihood factor analysis. *Psychometrika, 34,* 183–202.

—— (1970). A general method for analysis of covariance structures. *Biometrika, 57,* 239–251

Joreskog, K. G., & Goldberger, A. S. (1972). Factor analysis by generalized least squares. *Psychometrika, 37,* 243–260

Joreskog, K. G., & Sorbom, D. (1993). *LISREL-8 Structural equation modeling with SIMPLIS command language.* Mahwah, NJ: Lawrence Erlbaum.

Judd, C., & Milburn, M. (1980). The structure of attitude systems in the general public: Comparisons of a structural equation model. *American Sociological Review, 45,* 627–643.

Kagan, J., & Zentner, M. (1996). Early childhood predictors of adult psychopathology. *Harvard Review of Psychiatry, 3,* 341–350.

Kaiser, H. F. (1958). The Varimax criterion for analytic rotation in factor analysis. *Psychometrika, 23,* 187–200.

Kamin, L. J. (1974). *The science and politics of IQ.* New York: Wiley.

Katz, D. (1953). Field studies. In L. Festinger & D. Katz (Eds.), *Research methods in the behavioral sciences, 9* (pp. 75–83). New York: Holt, Rinehart and Winston.

Katz, D., & Kahn, R. (1978). *The social psychology of organizations* (2nd ed.). New York: John Wiley & Sons, 1978.

Kazdin, A. E. (1982). *Single-case research designs: Methods for clinical and applied settings.* New York: Oxford University Press.

Keane, B. (1990). The effect of relatedness on reproductive success and mate choice in the white-footed mouse, peromyscus leucopus. *Animal Behaviour, 39,* 264–273.

Keeves, J. (1972). *Educational environment and student achievement.* Melbourne: Australian Council for Educational Research.

Keith, T. Z. (1988). Research methods in school psychology: An overview. *School Psychology Review, 17,* 502–520.

—— (1999). Structural equation modeling in school psychology. In C. R. Reynolds & T. B. Gutkin, Eds., *Handbook of school psychology* (3rd ed.). New York: John Wiley & Sons, pp. 78–107.

—— (1997). Using confirmatory factor analysis to aid in understanding the constructs measured by intelligence tests. In D. P. Flanagan, J. L. Genshaft, & P. L. Harrison, Eds. *Beyond traditional intellectual assessment: Contemporary and emerging theories, tests and issues.* New York: Guilford Press, 373–402.

Keith-Spiegel, P., & Koocher, G. P. (1985). *Ethics in psychology: Professional Standards in Cases.* Hillsdale, NJ: Lawrence Erlbaum.

Kemeny, J. (1959). *A philosopher looks at science.* New York: Van Nostrand Reinhold.

Kemeny, J., Snell, J., & Thompson, G. (1974). *Introduction to finite mathematics* (3rd ed.). Englewood Cliffs, NJ: Prentice-Hall.

Kendall, M. (1948). *Rank correlation methods.* London: Griffin.

Kendall, M.G. (1972). Hiawatha designs an experiment. In R.E. Kirk, Ed., *Statistical issues: A reader for the behavioral sciences.* Monterey, CA: Brooks/Cole, pp. 175–176.

Kennedy, J. J. (1992). *Analyzing qualitative data: Log-linear analysis for behavioral research* (2nd ed.). New York: Praeger.

Kenny, J. M. (1985). Hypothesis testing: An analogy with the criminal justice system. *Statistics Division Newsletter. American Society for Quality Control, 6,* 8–9.

Keren, G., & Lewis, C. (Eds.). (1993). *Handbook for data analysis in the behavioral sciences: Methodological issues.* Hillsdale, NJ: Lawrence Erlbaum. [A good book, collecting a number of previous and current contributions to research methodology.]

Kerlinger, F. N. (1967). Social attitudes and their criterial referents: A structural theory. *Psychological Review, 74,* 110–122.

—— (1969). Research in education. In R. Ebel, V. Noll, & R. Bauer (Eds.), *Encyclopedia of educational research* (4th ed.). New York: Macmillan.

—— (1970). A social attitude scale: Evidence on reliability and validity. *Psychological Reports, 26,* 379–383.

—— (1971). Student evaluation of university professors. *School and Society, 99,* 353–356.

—— (1972). The structure and content of social attitude referents: A preliminary study. *Educational and Psychological Measurement, 32,* 613–630.

—— (1977). The influence of research on educational practice. *Educational Researcher, 16,* 5–12.

—— (1979). *Behavioral research: A conceptual approach.* New York: Holt, Rinehart and Winston.

—— (1980). Analysis of covariance structure tests of a criterial referents theory of attitudes. *Multivariate Behavioral Research, 15,* 403–422.

—— (1984). *Liberalism and conservatism: The nature and structure of social attitudes.* Hillsdale, NJ: Lawrence Erlbaum.

—— (1986). *Foundations of behavioral research* (3rd ed.). Fort Worth, TX: Harcourt Brace

Kerlinger, F. N., Middendorp, C. & Amón, J. (1976). The structure of social attitudes in three countries: Tests of a criterial referents theory. *International Journal of Psychology, 11,* 265–279.

Kerlinger, F. N., & Pedhazur, E. (1968). Educational attitudes and perceptions of desirable traits of teachers. *American Educational Research Journal, 5,* 543–560.

—— (1973). *Multiple regression analysis in behavioral research.* New York: Holt, Rinehart and Winston.

Kerlinger, F. N., & Rokeach, M. (1966). The factorial nature of the *F* and *D* scales. *Journal of Personality and Social Psychology, 4,* 391–399.

Kershner, R., & Wilcox, L. (1974). *The anatomy of mathematics* (2nd ed.). New York: Ronald.

Keynes, J. M. (1979). *A treatise on probability.* New York: AMS Press. (Original work published 1921)

Keyser, D. J., & Sweetland, R. C. (1987). *Test critiques compendium: Reviews of major tests from the test critiques series.* Kansas City, MO: Test Corporation of America.

Kinder, D., & Sears, D. (1981). Prejudice and politics: symbolic racism versus racial threats to the good life. *Journal of Personality and Social Psychology, 40,* 414–431.

Kirk, R. E. (1972). *Statistical issues: A reader for the behavioral sciences.* Monterey, CA: Brooks/Cole.

—— (1990). *Statistics: An introduction* (3rd ed.). Fort Worth, TX: Holt, Rinehart and Winston.

—— (1995). *Experimental designs: Procedures for the behavioral sciences* (3rd ed.). Pacific Grove, CA: Brooks/Cole.

Kirscht, J., & Dillehay, R. (1967). *Dimensions of authoritarianism: A review of research and theory.* Lexington, KY: University of Kentucky Press.

Klayman, J., & Ha, Y.-W. (1987). Confirmation, disconfirmation and information in hypothesis testing. *Psychological Review, 94,* 21–28.

Kleinbaum, D. G., Kupper, L. L., Muller, K. E., & Nizam, A. (1997). *Applied regression analysis and other multivariable methods* (3rd ed.). Belmont, CA: Duxbury.

Klesges, R. C., Isbell, T. R., & Klesges, L. M. (1992). Relationship between dietary restraint, energy intake, physical activity and body weight: A prospective analysis. *Journal of Abnormal Psychology, 101,* 668–674.

Klonoff, E. A., & Landrine, H. (1994). Culture and gender diversity in commonsense beliefs about the causes of six illnesses. *Journal of Behavioral Medicine, 17,* 407–418.

Kluckhohn, C. (1951). Values and value-orientations in the theory of action. In T. Parsons and E. Shils, Eds., *Toward a general theory of action.* Cambridge, MA: Harvard University Press.

Kolb, D. (1965). Achievement motivation training for underachieving high-school boys. *Journal of Personality and Social Psychology, 2,* 783–792.

Kounin, J., & Doyle, P (1975). Degree of continuity of a lesson's signal system and the task involvement of children. *Journal of Educational Psychology, 67,* 159–164.

Kounin, J., & Gump, P. (1974). Signal systems of lesson settings and the task-related behavior of preschool children. *Journal of Educational Psychology, 66,* 554–562.

Kramer, M., & Schmidhammer, J. (1992). The chi-square statistic in ethology: Use and misuse. *Animal Behaviour, 44,* 833–841.

Krech, D., & Crutchfield, R. (1948). *Theory and problems of social psychology.* New York: McGraw-Hill.

Krueger, R.A. (1994). *Focus groups: A practical guide for applied research.* (2nd ed.) Thousand Oaks, CA: Sage.

Kruskal, W., & Wallis, W. (1952). Use of ranks in one-criterion variance analysis. *Journal of the American Statistical Association, 47,* 583–621.

Kubat, M. (1993). Flexible concept learning in real-time systems. *Journal of Intelligent and Robotic Systems, 8(2),* 155–171.

Kuder, G. F., & Richardson, M. W. (1937). The theory of the estimation of test reliability. *Psychometrika, 2,* 151–160.

Kumar, K., & Beyerlein, M. (1991). Construction and validation of an instrument for measuring ingratiatory behaviors in organizational settings. *Journal of Applied Psychology, 76,* 619–627.

Kumpfer, K. L., Turner, C., Hopkins, R., & Librett, J. (1993). Leadership and team effectiveness in community coalitions for the prevention of alcohol and other drug abuse. *Health Education Research, 8,* 359–374.

Lachenbruch, P. A. (1975). *Discriminant analysis.* New York: Hafner.

Lamb, K. (1997). IQ and PC (Intelligent quotient, political correctness). *National Review, 49,* 39–42.

Langer, E., & Imber, L. (1980). When practice makes imperfect: Debilitating effects of overlearning, *Journal of Personality and Social Psychology, 37,* 2014–2024.

Lane, D. S. (1986). Systematic investigation of critical variables within a conditional reasoning instructional system used with preadolescence. *Journal of Early Adolescence, 6,* 155–171.

Lariviere, N. A., & Spear, N. E. (1996). Early Pavlovian conditioning impairs later Pavlovian conditioning. *Developmental Psychobiology, 29,* 613–635.

Lave, L., & Seskin, E. (1970). Air pollution and human health. *Science, 169,* 723–733.

Lawley, D. N. (1940). The estimation of factor loadings by the method of maximum likelihood. *Proceedings of the Royal Society of Edinburgh, 60,* 64–82.

Lawley, D. N. & Maxwell, A. E. (1971). *Factor analysis as a statistical method* (2nd ed.). London: Butterworth.

Layton, W., & Swanson, E. (1958). Relationship of ninth-grade differential aptitude test scores to eleventh-grade test scores and high school rank. *Journal of Educational Psychology, 49,* 153–155.

Lee, H. B. (1979). *An empirical comparison of some factor analytic methods.* Unpublished doctoral dissertation, University of California, Los Angeles.

—— (1980). The estimation of ridge coefficients using regression programs without a zero intercept option. *Educational and Psychological Measurement, 40,* 745–750.

—— (1995). Ridge regression: A statistical method for school psychology research. *The School Psychologist, 49,* 107–109.

Lee, H. B., & Comrey, A. L. (1979). Distortions in a commonly used factor analytic procedure. *Multivariate Behavioral Research, 14,* 301–321.

Lee, H. B., & Little, S. G. (1996). Analyzing data from a regression-discontinuity study: A research note. Unpublished manuscript, California State University, Northridge, CA.

Lee, H. B., & MacQueen, J. B. (1980). A *k*-means cluster analysis computer program with cross-tabulations and next-nearest neighbor analysis. *Educational and Psychological Measurement, 40,* 133–138.

Lee, S. Y., & Jennrich, R. I. (1984). The analysis of structural equation models by means of derivative free nonlinear least squares. *Psychometrika. 49,* 521–528.

Leichtman, S.R., & Erickson, M. T. (1979). Cognitive, demographic and interactional determinants of role-taking skills in fourth grade children. *Perceptual and Motor Skills, 49,* 247–253.

Lepper, M., & Greene, D. (Eds.). (1978). *The hidden costs of reward.* Hillsdale, N.J: Lawrence Erlbaum.

Lepper, M., Greene, D., & Nisbett, R. (1973). Undermining children's intrinsic interest with extrinsic reward: A test of the overjustification hypothesis. *Journal or Personality and Social Psychology, 28,* 129–137.

Lester, D. (1989). Attitudes toward AIDS. *Personality and Individual Differences, 10,* 693–694.

Levitin, T. (1969) Values. In J. Robinson and P. Shaver, Eds., *Measures of psychological attitudes.* Ann Arbor: Institute for Social Research, University of Michigan.

Lewin, K. (1935). *A dynamic theory of personality.* New York: McGraw-Hill.

Lewis, R., & St. John, N. (1974). Contribution of cross-racial friendship to minority group achievement in desegregated classrooms. *Sociometry, 37,* 79–91.

Lewontin, R., Rose, S., & Kamin, L. (1984). *Not in our genes.* New York: Pantheon Books.

Li, J. C. R. (1957). *Introduction to statistical inference.* Ann Arbor, MI: Edwards Brothers.

Li, M. F., & Lautenschlager, G. (1997). Generalizability theory applied to categorical data. *Educational and Psychological Measurement, 57,* 813–822.

Life Options Rehabilitation Advisory Council. (1998, July/August). Using qualitative research to study renal rehabilitation. *Renal Rehabilitation Report, 6,* 1–5.

Light, R. J., & Pillemer, D. B. (1984). *Summing up: The science of reviewing research.* Cambridge, MA: Harvard University Press.

Lindeman, R. S., Merenda, P. F., & Gold, R. Z. (1980). *Introduction to bivariate and multivariate analysis.* Glenview, IL: Scott-Foresman.

Lindquist, E. (1940). *Statistical analysis in educational research.* Boston, MA: Houghton Mifflin.

Lindzey, G., & Byrne, D. (1968). Measurement of social choice and interpersonal attractiveness. In G. Lindzey & E. Aronson, Eds., *The handbook of social psychology* (2nd ed.) (pp. 425–525). Reading, MA: Addison-Wesley.

Linton, M., & Gallo, P. (1975). *The practical statistician: Simplified handbook of statistics.* Monterey, CA: Brooks/Cole.

Little, S. G. (1997). Graduate education of the top contributors to the school psychology literature: 1987–1995. *School Psychology International, 18,* 15–27.

Little, S. G., & Lee, H. B. (1995, August). *Education in statistics and research design in school psychology: A national survey.* Paper presented at the Annual Convention for the American Psychological Association, New York, NY.

Little, S. G., Sterling, R. C., & Tingstrom, D. H. (1996). The influence of geographic and racial cues on evaluation of blame. *Journal of Social Psychology, 136,* 373–379.

Lix, L. M., Keselman, J. C., & Keselman, H. J. (1996). Consequences of assumption violations revisited: A quantitative review of alternatives to the one-way analysis of variance F-test. *Review of Educational Research, 66,* 579–619.

Loehlin, J. C. (1992). Latent variable models: An introduction to factor, path and structural analysis (2nd ed.) Hillsdale, NJ: Lawrence Erlbaum

—— (1998). *Latent variable models: An introduction to factor, path and structural analysis* (3rd ed.). Hillsdale, NJ: Lawrence Erlbaum

Loehlin, J., Lindzey, G., & Spuhler, J. (1975). *Race differences in intelligence.* San Francisco: Freeman.

Loevinger, J. (1957). Objective tests as instruments of psychological theory. *Psychological Reports, 3,* 635–694. (Monograph Supplement 9.)

Lohnes, P., & Marshall, T. (1965). Redundancy in student records. *American Educational Research Journal, 2,* 19–23.

Longshore, D. (1982). Social psychological research on school desegregation: Toward a new agenda. *New Directions for Testing & Measurement, 14,* 39–52.

Lord, F. (1972). On the statistical treatment of football numbers. In R. E. Kirk (Ed.). *Statistical issues: A reader for the behavioral sciences* (pp. 52–54). Belmont, CA: Wadsworth.

Lord, F., & Novick, M. (1968). *Statistical theories of mental test scores.* Reading, MA: Addison-Wesley.

Lubin, A. (1961). The interpretation of significant interaction. *Educational and Psychological Measurement, 21,* 807–817.

Lubinski, D., Schmidt, D. B., & Benbow, C. P. (1996). A 20–year stability analysis of the study of values for intellectually gifted individuals from adolescence to adulthood. *Journal of Applied Psychology, 81,* 443–451.

Luhtanen, R., & Crocker, J. (1992). A collective self-esteem scale: Self-evaluation of ones' social identity. *Personality and Social Psychology Bulletin, 18,* 302–318.

Lynch, M. P., Short, L. B., & Chua, R. (1995). Contributions of experience to the development of musical processing in infancy. *Developmental Psychobiology, 28,* 377–398.

MacDonald, T. K., Zanna, M. P., & Fong, G. T. (1996). Why common sense goes out the window: Effects of alcohol on intentions to use condoms. *Personality and Social Psychology Bulletin, 22,* 763–775.

McClelland, D. (1961). *The achieving society.* Princeton, NJ: Van Nostrand.

McClosky, H. (1964). Consensus and ideology in American politics. *American Political Science Review, 58,* 361–382.

McCullers, J. C., Fabes, R. A., & Moran, J. D. (1987). Does intrinsic motivation theory explain the adverse effects of rewards on immediate task performance? *Journal of Personality & Social Psychology, 52,* 1027–1033.

McDermott, P. A. (1988). Agreement among diagnosticians or observers: Its importance and determination. *Professional School Psychology, 3,* 225–240.

McGee, M., & Snyder, M. (1975). Attribution and behavior: Two field studies. *Journal of Personality and Social Psychology, 32,* 185–190.

McGuigan, F. J. (1997). *Experimental psychology: Methods of research.* (7th ed.). Upper Saddle River, NJ: Prentice-Hall.

McKinney, C. H., Antoni, M. H., Kumar, M., Tims, F. C., & McCabe, P. M. (1997). Effects of guided imagery and music (GIM) therapy on mood and cortisol in healthy adults. *Health Psychology, 16,* 390–400.

McReynolds, P. (1989). Diagnosis and clinical assessment: Current status and major issues. *Annual Review of Psychology, 40,* 83–108.

McWhirter, B.T (1997). Loneliness, learned resourcefulness, and self-esteem in college students. *Journal of Counseling and Development, 75,* 460–469.

Magidson, J. (Ed.). (1979). *Advances in factor analysis and structural equation models.* Cambridge, MA: ABT Books.

Magnusson, D. (1967). *Test theory.* Reading, MA: Addison-Wesley.

Malone, J. C. (1991). *Theories of learning: A historical approach.* Pacific Grove: Brooks/Cole.

Mann, C. (1990). Meta-analysis in the breech. *Science, 249,* 476–480.

Marlow, A. G., Tingstrom, D. H., Olmi, D. J., & Edwards, R. P. (1997). The effects of classroom-based time-in/time-out on compliance rates in children with speech/language disabilities. *Child and Family Behavior Therapy, 19,* 1–15.

Margenau, H. (1977). *The nature of physical reality.* Woodbridge, CT: Ox Bow Press. (Original work published 1950).

Martens, B. K., Hiralall, A. S., & Bradley, T. A. (1997). Improving student behavior through goal setting and feedback. *School Psychology Quarterly, 12,* 33–41.

Matheson, D. W., Bruce, R. L., & Beauchamp, K. L. (1978). *Experimental psychology: Research design and analysis* (3rd ed.). New York: Holt, Rinehart & Winston.

Martin, P., & Bateson, P. P. G. (1993). *Measuring behaviour: An introductory guide* (2nd ed.). Cambridge, England: Cambridge University Press.

Martin, P. R., & Seneviratne, H. M. (1997). Effects of food deprivation and stressors on head pain. *Health Psychology, 15,* 310–318.

Maruyama, G., & Miller, N. (1979). Reexamination of normative influence processes in desegregated classrooms. *American Educational Research Journal, 16,* 273–283.

Mattson, D. E. (1986). *Statistics: Difficult concepts, understandable explanations.* Oak Park, IL: Bolchazy-Carducci Publishers.

May, R. B., & Forsyth, G. A. (1980). Age differences in forced and free choice dimensional responding. *Journal of General Psychology, 102,* 107–120.

Mayeske, G. (1970). Teacher attributes and school achievement. In *Do teachers make a difference?* (pp. 100–119). Washington, DC: U.S. Government Printing Office.

Mays, V. M., & Arrington, A. (1984, April). *Gender and ethnicity in shared space violation: Who acts like they own the space?* Paper presented at the Second International Interdisciplinary Congress on Women (April 17–21). The Netherlands: Groninger.

Mays, V. M., Cochran, S. D., Bellinger, G., Smith, R. G., Henley, N., Daniels, M., Tibbits, T., Victorianne, G. D., Osei, O. K., & Birt, D. K. (1992). The language of black gay men's sexual behavior: Implications for AIDS risk reduction. *Journal of Sex Research, 29*, 425–434.

Meadows, D. H., Meadows, D. L., Randers, J., & Behrens, W. (1974). *The limits to growth* (2nd ed.). New York: Universe Books.

Medley, D., & Mitzel, H. (1963). Measuring classroom behavior by systematic observation. In N. Gage Ed., *Handbook of research in teaching* (pp. 247–328). Skokie, IL: Rand-McNally.

Meiksins, P. F., & Watson, J. M. (1989). Professional autonomy and organizational constraint: The case of engineers. *Sociological Quarterly, 30*, 561–585.

Mendenhall, W., & Beaver, R. J. (1994). *Introduction to probability and statistics* (9th ed.). Belmont, CA: Wadsworth.

Merei, F. (1949). Group leadership and institutionalization. *Human Relations, 2*, 23–39.

Merton, R. (1949). *Social theory and social structure.* New York: Free Press.

Michell, J. (1990). *An introduction to the logic of psychological measurement.* Hillsdale, NJ: Lawrence Erlbaum.

Milgrim, S. (1963). Behavioral study of obedience. *Journal of Abnormal and Social Psychology, 67*, 371–378.

Miller, D., & Swanson, G. (1960). *Inner conflict and defense.* New York: Holt, Rinehart and Winston.

Miller, D. J. & Hersen, M. (1992) *Research fraud in the behavioral and biomedical sciences.* New York: Wiley.

Miller, L. C., Cooke, L. L., Tsang, J., & Morgan, F. (1992). Should I brag? Nature and impact of positive and boastful disclosures for women and men. *Human Communications Research, 18*, 364–399.

Miller, N. (1969). Learning of visceral and glandular responses. *Science, 163*, 434–445.

Miller, N. (1971). *Selected papers.* New York: Aldine.

Miller, N. E. (1985). The value of behavioral research on animals. *American Psychologist, 40*, 423–440.

Miller, N., & DiCara, L. (1968). Instru-

mental learning of urine formation by rats: Changes in renal blood flow. *American Journal of Physiology, 215*, 677–683.

Minkes, J., Robinson, C., & Weston, O. (1994). Consulting the children: Interviews with children using residential respite care services. *Disability and Society, 9*, 47–57.

Mishler, E. G. (1986). *Research interviewing: Context and narrative.* Cambridge, MA: Harvard University Press.

Moran, J. D., & McCullers, J. C. (1984). A comparison of achievement scores in physically attractive and unattractive students. *Home Economics Research Journal, 13*, 36–40.

Morrison, D. (1967). *Multivariate statistics.* New York: McGraw-Hill.

Morrison, T., & Morrison, M. (1995). A meta-analytic assessment of the predictive validity of the quantitative and verbal components of the Graduate Record Examination with graduate grade-point-average representing the criterion of graduate success. *Educational and Psychological Measurement, 55*, 309–316.

Morrow, J., & Smithson, B. (1969). Learning sets in an invertebrate. *Science, 164*, 850–851.

Mosteller, F., & Tukey, J. W. (1977). *Data analysis and regression: A second course in statistics.* Reading, MA: Addison-Wesley.

Mosteller, F., & Bush, R. (1954), Selected quantitative techniques. In G. Lindzey (Ed.), *Handbook of social psychology* (pp. 328–331), vol. I. Reading, MA: Addison-Wesley.

Mullen, B. (1993). *Advanced basic meta-analysis.* Mahwah, NJ: Lawrence Erlbaum.

Murphy, J. M., Olivier, D. C., Monson, R. R., & Sobol, A.M. (1991). Depression and anxiety in relation to social status: A prospective epidemiological study. *Archives of General Psychiatry, 48(3)*, 223–229.

Murray, C. (1997). Professor Jensen's opus. *National Review, 49*, 40.

Neisser, U. (1998). The rising curve: Long-term gains in IQ and related measures. Washington, DC: APA Books.

Nelson, G., Hall, G. B., & Walsh-Bowers, R. (1997). A comparative evaluation of supportive apartments, group homes and board-and-care homes for psychiatric consumer/survivors. *Journal of Community Psychology, 25,* 167–188.

Nemeroff, C. J. (1995). Magical thinking about illness virulence: Conceptions of germs from "safe" versus "dangerous" others. *Health Psychology, 14,* 147–151.

Nesselroade, J., Stigler, S., & Baltes, P. (1980). Regression toward the mean and the study of change. *Psychological Bulletin, 88,* 622–637.

Neter, J., Wasserman, W., & Kutner, M. H. (1983). *Applied linear regression models.* Homewood, IL: Irwin.

Newcomb, T. (1943). *Personality and social change.* New York: Holt, Rinehart & Winston.

—— (1950). *Social psychology.* New York: Holt, Rinehart & Winston.

—— (1978). The acquaintance process: Looking mostly backwards. *Journal of Personality and Social Psychology, 36,* 1075–1083.

Newcomb, T., Koenig, K., Flacks, R., & Warwick, D. (1967). *Persistence and change: Bennington College and its students after twenty-five years.* New York: John Wiley & Sons.

Newman, J. (1988). *The world of mathematics.* Redmond, WA: Microsoft Press.

Newman, J. R. (1976, August). *Comparison of least squares versus Bayes estimates of regression weights.* Paper presented to the American Psychological Association, San Francisco, CA.

Nisbett, R., & Ross, L. (1980). *Human inference: Strategies and shortcomings of social judgment.* Englewood-Cliffs, NJ: Prentice Hall.

Noelle-Neuman, E. (1970). Wanted: Rules for wording structured questionnaires, *Public Opinion Quarterly, 35,* 191–201.

Norman, D. (1976). *Memory and attention: An introduction to human information processing* (2nd ed.). New York: Wiley.

Northrop, F. (1983). *The logic of the sciences and the humanities.* Woodbridge, CT: Ox Bow Press. (Original work published 1947).

Norusis, M. J. (1992). SPSS/PC+ base system user's guide. Version 5.0. Chicago: SPSS, Inc.

Nunnally, J. (1978). *Psychometric theory* (2nd ed.). New York: McGraw-Hill.

Nunnally, J., & Bernstein, I. (1994). *Psychometric theory* (3rd ed.). New York: McGraw-Hill.

Nunnikhoven, T. S. (1992). A birthday problem solution from nonuniform birth frequencies. *The American Statistician, 46,* 270–274.

Nurius, P. S., & Gibson, J. W. (1990). Clinical observation, inference, reasoning, and judgment in social work: An update. *Social Work Research and Abstracts, 26,* 18–25.

O'Connell, R. H., Lee, H. B., & Bruno, J. E. (1992). *Assessment of student outcomes using information referenced testing.* Paper presented at the California State University Teaching and Learning Exchange, Los Angeles, California.

O'Donnell, T. S. (1991). *World quality of life indicators.* Santa Barbara, CA: ABC-CLIO.

Oldani, R. (1997). Causes of increases in achievement motivation: Is the personality influenced by prenatal environment? *Personality and Individual Differences, 22,* 403–410.

Olds, M., & Fobes, J. (1981). The central basis of motivation: Intracranial self-stimulation studies. *Annual Review of Psychology, 32,* 523–574.

Onwuegbuzie, A. J., & Seaman, M. A. (1995). The effect of two constraints and statistics test anxiety on test performance in a statistics course. *Journal of Experimental Education, 63,* 115–124.

Orlich, D. C. (1978). *Designing sensible surveys.* Pleasantville, NY: Redgrave Publishing

Orpen, C. (1996). Construct validation of a measure of ingratiatory behavior in organizational settings. *Current Psychology: Developmental, Learning, Personality, Social, 15(1)*, 38–41.

Osgood, D. W., Wilson, J. K., O'Malley, P. M., Bachman, J. G., & Johnston, L. D. (1996). Routine activities and individual deviant behavior. *American Sociological Review, 61*, 635–655.

Oshagan, H., & Allen, R. L. (1992). Three loneliness scales: An assessment of their measurement. *Journal of Personality Assessment, 59*, 380–409.

Osterlind, S. J. (1989). *Constructing test items.* Boston: Kluwer Academic Publishers.

Oud, J. H., & Sattler, J. M. (1984). Generalized kappa coefficient: A Microsoft BASIC program. *Behavior Research Methods, Instruments, and Computers, 16*, 40.

Ove, F. (1981). A survey of statistical methods for graph analysis. In S. Leinhardt, Ed., *Sociological Methodology 1981* (pp. 110–155). San Francisco: Jossey-Bass.

Padgett, D. K. (1998). *Qualitative methods in social work research: Challenges and rewards.* Thousand Oaks, CA: Sage.

Page, E. (1963). Ordered hypotheses for multiple treatments: A significance test for linear ranks. *Journal of the American Statistical Association, 58*, 216–230.

Parrott, L. (1994). *How to write psychology papers.* New York: Harper-Collins.

Parten, M. (1950). *Surveys, polls, and samples.* New York: Harper & Row.

Payette, K. A., & Clarizio, H. F. (1994). Discrepant team decisions: The effects of race, gender, achievement, and IQ on LD eligibility. *Psychology in the Schools, 31*, 40–48.

Pearson, E., & Hartley, H. O. (1954). *Biometrika tables for statisticians*, vol. I. Cambridge: Cambridge University Press.

Pedersen, D., Keithly, S., & Brady, M. (1986). Effects of an observer on conformity to handwashing norm. *Perceptual and Motor Skills, 62*, 169–170.

Pedhazur, E. (1996). *Multiple regression in behavioral research: Explanation and prediction.* (3rd ed.). Orlando: Harcourt Brace.

Peng, S. S., & Wright, D. (1994). Explanation of academic achievement of Asian-American students. *Journal of Educational Research, 87*, 346–352.

Perreault, W. D., & Leigh, L. E. (1989). Reliability of nominal data based on qualitative judgments. *Journal of Marketing Research, 26*, 135–148.

Perrine, R. M., Lisle, J., & Tucker, D. L. (1995). Effect of a syllabus offer of help, student age and class size on college students' willingness to seek support from faculty. *Journal of Experimental Education, 64*, 41–52.

Peterson's Guide to Graduate and Professional Programs (1994) 29th Edition. Princeton, NJ: Petersons' Guides.

Phillips, D. L. (1973). *Abandoning method.* San Francisco, CA: Jossey-Bass.

Piaget, J. (1957). *Logic and psychology.* New York: Basic Books.

Piaget, J., Garcia, R., Davidson, P. M., & Easley, J. (1991). *Toward a logic of meaning.* Hillsdale, NJ: Lawrence Erlbaum.

Pittel, S., & Mendelsohn, G. (1966). Measurement of moral values. *Psychological Bulletin, 66*, 22–35.

Platt, J. (1964). Strong inference. *Science, 146*, 347–353.

Poincare, H. (1996). *Science and method.* Herndon, VA: Books International. (Original work published 1952).

Polanyi, M. (1974). *Personal knowledge: Toward a post critical philosophy.* Chicago: University of Chicago Press. (Original work published 1958).

Poole, D.A. & Lamb, H.E. (eds.) (1998). *Investigative interviews of children: A guide for helping professionals.* Washington, D.C.: American Psychological Association.

Porch, A. M., Ross, T. P., Hanks, R., & Whitman, D. R. (1995). Ethnicity, socioeconomic background and psychosis-proneness in a diverse sample of college students. *Current Psychology: Developmental, Learning, Personality, Social, 13*, 365–370.

Powell, S., & Nelson, B. (1997). Effects of choosing academic assignments on a student with attention deficit hyperactivity disorder. *Journal of Applied Behavior Analysis, 30*, 181–183.

Powers, S. (1985). A Pascal program that assesses the interrater reliability of nominal scales. *Educational and Psychological Measurement, 45*, 613–614.

Press, S. J., & Wilson, S. (1978). Choosing between logistic regression and discriminant analysis. *Journal of the American Statistical Association, 73*, 699–705.

Presser, S., & Schuman, H. (1980). The measurement of a middle position in attitude surveys. *Public Opinion Quarterly, 44*, 70–85.

Price, B. (1977). Ridge regression: Applications to nonexperimental data. *Psychological Bulletin, 84*, 759–766.

Pritchard, D.A., & Kazar, D. (1979). Expanded Taylor-Russell tables. *Catalog of Selected Documents in Psychology*. Washington, DC: American Psychological Association.

Probst, A. L. (1988). The alpha-beta wars: Which risk are you willing to live with? *Statistics Division Newsletter. American Society for Quality Control, 8*, 7–9.

Proctor, C., & Loomis, C. (1951). Analysis of sociometric data. In M. Jahoda, M. Deutsch & S. Cook, Eds., *Research methods in social relations, part 2* (pp. 561–585). New York: Holt, Rinehart & Winston.

Prokasy, W. F. (1962). Inference from analysis of variance of ordinal data. *Psychological Reports, 10*, 35–39.

—— (1987). A perspective on the acquisition of skeletal responses employing the Pavlovian paradigm. In I. Gormezano, W. F. Prokasy, & R. Thompson (Eds.), *Classical conditioning* (3rd ed.). Hillsdale, NJ: Lawrence Erlbaum.

Prothro, J., & Grigg, C. (1960). Fundamental principles of democracy: Bases of agreement and disagreement. *Journal of Politics, 22*, 276–294.

Purdy, J. E., Avery, D. D., & Cross, H. A. (1978). *Supplement and laboratory manual for experimental methodology in psychology*. Monterey, CA: Brooks-Cole.

Pury, C. L. S., & Mineka, S. (1997). Covariation bias for blood-injury stimuli and aversive outcomes. *Behavior Research and Therapy, 35*, 35–47.

Pyrczak, F., & Bruce, R. R. (1992). *Writing empirical research reports*. Los Angeles, CA: Pyrczak Publishing.

Quilici, J. L., & Mayer, R. E. (1996). Role of examples in how students learn to categorize statistics word problems. *Journal of Educational Psychology, 88*, 144–161.

Rabinowitz, F. E., Colmar, C., Elgie, D., Hale, D., Niss, S., Sharp, B., & Sinclitco, J. (1993). Dishonesty, indifference or carelessness in souvenir shop transactions. *Journal of Social Psychology, 133*, 73–79.

Rand Corporation. (1955). A million random digits with 700,000 normal deviates. New York: Free Press.

Ray, J. J. (1990). Acquiescence and problems with forced-choice scales. *Journal of Social Psychology, 130*, 397–399.

Ray, W. J. (1997). *Methods: Toward a science of behavior and experience* (5th ed.) Pacific Grove, CA: Brooks-Cole.

Reinholtz, R. K. & Muehlenhard, C. L. (1995). Genital perceptions and sexual activity in a college population. *Journal of Sex Research, 32*, 155–165.

Reinmuth, J. E., & Barnes, J. D. (1975). A strategic competitive bidding approach to pricing decisions for petroleum industry drilling contractors. *Journal of Marketing Research, 12*, 362–365.

Renner, V. (1970). Effects of modification of cognitive style on creative behavior. *Journal of Personality and Social Psychology, 14(4)*, 257–262.

Reynolds, C. R., & Brown, R. T. (Eds.). (1984). *Perspectives on bias in mental testing*. New York: Plenum Press.

Richter, M. L., & Seay, M. B. (1987). Anova designs with subjects and stimuli as random effects: Application to prototype effects in recognition memory. *Journal of Personality and Social Psychology, 53,* 470–480.

Rind, B. (1997). Effects of interest arousal on compliance with a request for help. *Basic and Applied Social Psychology, 19,* 49–59.

Rind, B., & Bordia, P. (1995). Effect of server's "thank you" and personalization on restaurant tipping. *Journal of Applied Social Psychology, 25,* 745–751.

Robinson, W. P. (1996). *Deceit, delusion, and detection.* Thousand Oaks, CA: Sage.

Rokeach, M. (1968). *Beliefs, attitudes, and values.* San Francisco: Jossey-Bass

Rokeach, M., & Mezei, L. (1966). Race and shared belief as factors in social choice. *Science, 151,* 167–172.

Rooney-Rebeck, P., & Jason, L. (1986). Prevention of prejudice in elementary school students. *Journal of Primary Prevention, 7,* 63–73.

Rorer, L. (1965). The great response-style myth. *Psychological Bulletin, 63,* 129–156.

Ross, B. H., & Murphy, G. L. (1996). Category-based predictions: Influence of uncertainty and future associations. *Journal of Experimental Psychology: Learning, Memory & Cognition, 22,* 736–753.

Ross, L. L., & McBean, D. (1995). A comparison of pacing contingencies in class using a personalized system of instruction. *Journal of Applied Behavior Analysis, 28,* 87–88.

Rosch, E. (1973). Natural categories. *Cognitive Psychology, 4,* 328–350.

Rosch, E. H. (1973). On the internal structure of perceptual and semantic categories. In T. E. Moore (Ed.), *Cognitive development and the acquisition of language* (pp. 111–144). New York: Academic Press.

Rosenberg, M., & Simmons, R. (1971). *Black and white self-esteem: The urban child.* Washington, DC: American Sociological Association.

Rosenboom, W.W. (1979). Ridge regression: Bonanza or beguilement? *Psychological Bulletin, 82,* 242–249.

Rosenhan, D. L. (1973). On being sane in insane places. *Science, 179,* 250–258.

Rosenquist, P. B., Bodfish, J. W., & Thompson, R. (1997). Tourette syndrome associated with mental retardation: A single-subject treatment study with haloperidol. *American Journal of Mental Retardation, 101,* 497–504.

Rosenthal, R. (1978). Combining results of independent studies. *Psychological Bulletin, 85,* 185–193.

Rosenthal, R., & Rubin, D. B. (1978). Interpersonal expectancy effects: The first 345 studies. *Behavioral and Brain Sciences, 3,* 377–415.

Rosnow, R. L., & Rosenthal, R. (1996). *Beginning behavioral research* (2nd ed.). Englewood-Cliffs, NJ: Prentice-Hall.

Rowley, G. (1976). The reliability of observational measures. *American Educational Research Journal, 13,* 51–59.

Rozeboom, W. W. (1960). The fallacy of the null hypothesis significance test. *Psychological Bulletin, 57,* 416–428.

Rozin, P., Nemeroff, C., Wane, M., & Sherrod, A. (1989). Operation of the sympathetic magical law of contagion in interpersonal attitudes among Americans. *Bulletin of the Psychonomic Society, 27,* 367–370.

Russell, G. L., Fujino, D. C., Sue, S., Cheung, M-K., & Snowden, L. R. (1996). The effects of therapist–client ethnic match in the assessment of mental health functioning. *Journal of Cross-Cultural Psychology, 27,* 598–615.

Saal, F. K., Johnson, C. B., & Weber, N. (1989). Friendly or sexy: It may depend on whom you ask. *Psychology of Women Quarterly, 13,* 263–276.

Saal, F. K., & Moore, S. C. (1993). Perceptions of promotion fairness and promotion candidates' qualifications. *Journal of Applied Psychology, 78,* 105–110.

Sacher, J. A., & Fine, M. A. (1996). Predicting relationship status and satisfaction after six months among dating couples. *Journal of Marriage and the Family, 58,* 21–32.

Saffer, T. H., & Kelly, O. E. (1983). *Countdown zero*. New York: Putnam.

Sampson, E. E. (1991). *Social worlds. Personal lives: An introduction to social psychology*. Orlando: Harcourt Brace Jovanovich.

Sanford, F. H., & Hemphill, J. K. (1952). An evaluation of a brief course in psychology at the U.S. Naval Academy. *Educational and Psychological Measurement, 12*, 194–216.

Saris, W., & Stronkhorst, L. (1984). *Causal modeling in nonexperimental research*. Amsterdam: Sociometric Research Foundation.

Sarnoff, I., Lighthall, F., Waite R., Davidson, K., & Sarason, S. (1958). A cross-cultural study of anxiety among American and English school children. *Journal of Educational Psychology, 49*, 129–136.

Sawilowsky, S. S. (1993). Comments on using alternatives to normal theory statistics in social and behavioural science. *Canadian Psychology, 34*, 432–439.

Sax, G. (1997). Principles of educational and psychological measurement and evaluation (4th ed.). Belmont, CA: Wadsworth.

Scattone, D., & Saetermoe, C. L. (1997, April). *Asian views on disabilities*. Poster and paper presented at the Annual Convention, Western Psychological Association, Seattle, Washington.

Schacter, S., Ellertson, N., McBride, D., & Gregory, D. (1951). An experimental study of cohesiveness and productivity. *Human Relations, 4*, 229–238.

Schmitt, B. H., Dube, L., & Leclerc, F. (1992). Intrusions into waiting lines: Does the queue constitute a social system? *Journal of Personality and Social Psychology, 63*, 806–815.

Scheffe, H. (1959). *Analysis of variance*. New York: Wiley.

Schouten, H. J. (1986). Nominal scale agreement among observers. *Psychometrika, 51*, 453–466.

Schumacker, R. E., & Lomax, R. G. (1996). *A beginner's guide to structural equation modeling*. Mahwah, NJ: Lawrence Erlbaum.

Schuman, H., & Presser, S. (1979). The open and closed question. *American Sociological Review, 44*, 692–712.

Schunk, D. H. (1996). *Learning theories: An educational perspective*. Westerville, OH: Merrill.

Scott, K. S., Moore, K. S., & Miceli, M. P. (1997). An exploration of the meaning and consequences of workaholics. *Human Relations, 50*, 287–314.

Scott, W. (1968). Comparative validities of forced-choice and single-stimulus tests. *Psychological Bulletin, 70*, 231–244.

Scogin, F., & McElreath, L. (1994). Efficacy of psychosocial treatments for geriatric depression: A quantitative review. *Journal of Consulting and Clinical Psychology, 62*, 69–74.

Sears, R., Maccoby, E., & Levin, H. (1957). *Patterns of child-rearing*. New York: Harper & Row.

Seashore, S., & Katz, D. (1982). Obituary: Rensis Likert (1903–1981). *American Psychologist, 37*, 851–853.

Selltiz, C., Jahoda, M., Deutsch, M., & Cook, S. W. (1961). *Research methods in social relations*. New York: Holt, Rinehart & Winston.

Senemoglu, N., & Fogelman, K. (1995). Effects of enhancing behavior of students and use of feedback-corrective procedures. *Journal of Educational Research, 89*, 59–63.

Sharpley, C. F. (1988). Effects of varying contingency and directness of rewards upon children's performance under implicit reward conditions. *Journal of Experimental Child Psychology, 45*, 422–437.

Shapiro, K. J. (1998). Animal models of human psychology: Critique of science, ethics, and policy. Seattle, WA: Hogrefe & Huber.

Sharpe, D. (1997). Of apples and oranges, file drawers and garbage: Why validity issues in meta-analysis will not go away. *Clinical Psychology Review, 17*, 881–901.

Shaw, J. I., & Skolnick, P. (1995). Effects of prohibitive and informative judicial instructions on jury decision making. *Social Behavior and Personality, 23,* 319–325.

Shaw, J. I., Borough, H. W., & Fink, M. I. (1994). Perceived sexual orientation and helping behavior by males and females: The wrong number technique. *Journal of Psychology and Human Sexuality, 6,* 73–81.

Sheatsley, P. B. (1974). Survey design. In R. Ferber (Ed.), *Handbook of marketing research.* New York: McGraw-Hill.

Sheridan, S. M. (1997). Conceptual and empirical bases of conjoint behavioral consultation. *School Psychology Quarterly, 12,* 119–133.

Sherif, M. (1965). Formation of social norms: The experimental paradigm. In H. Proshansky & B. Seidenberg (Eds.), *Basic studies in social psychology* (pp. 461–471). New York: Holt, Rinehart and Winston.

Shoffner, L. B. (1990). The effects of home environment on achievement and attitudes toward computer literacy. *Educational Research Quarterly, 14(1),* 6–14.

Shoukri, M. M., & Edge, V. L. (1996). *Statistical methods for health sciences.* Boca Raton, FL: CRC Press.

Shrader-Frechette, K. (1994). *Ethics of scientific research.* New York: Rowman & Littlefield.

Sidman, M. (1960). *Tactics of scientific research.* New York: Basic Books.

Siegel, S., & Castellan, N.J. (1988). *Nonparametric Statistics* (2nd ed.). New York: McGraw-Hill.

Sigall, H., & Ostrove, N. (1975). Beautiful but dangerous: Effects of offender attractiveness and nature of the crime on juridic judgment. *Journal of Personality and Social Psychology, 31,* 410–414.

Silverman, S. (1993). Student characteristics, practice and achievement in physical education. *Journal of Educational Research, 87,* 54–61.

Simmons, R., & Rosenberg, M. (1971). Functions of children's perceptions of the stratification system. *American Sociological Review, 36,* 235–249.

Simon, A., & Boyer, E. (1970). *Mirrors for behavior.* Philadelphia, PA: Research for Better Schools.

Simon, C. W. (1975). Technical Report No. 75–287. *Methods for improving information from "undesigned" human factor experiments.* Culver City, CA: Hughes Aircraft Company.

—— *Methods for improving information from "undesigned" human factors experiments.* Hughes Aircraft Company. Technical Report.

—— (1976). *Economical multifactor designs for human factors engineering experiments.* Culver City, CA: Hughes Aircraft Company.

—— (1987). Will egg-sucking ever become a science? *Human Factors Society Bulletin, 30,* 1–4.

Simon, C. W., & Roscoe, S. N. (1984). Application of a multifactor approach to transfer of learning research. *Human Factors, 26,* 591–612.

Skinner, B. F. (1945). The operational analysis of psychological terms. *Psychological Review, 52,* 270–277.

Skinner, B. F. (1968). *The technology of teaching.* New York: Appleton-Century-Crofts.

Smeltzer, S. C., & Bare, B. G. (1992). *Brunner and Suddarth's textbook of medical surgical nursing* (7th ed.). Philadelphia: J. B. Lippincott.

Smith, B. C., Penrod, S. D., Otto, A. L., & Park, R. C. (1996). Jurors' use of probabilitisc evidence. *Law and Human Behavior, 20,* 49–82.

Smith, E. E. (1995). Concepts and categorization. In E. E. Smith & D. N. Osherson (Eds.), *Thinking: An invitation to cognitive science* (2nd ed.). Cambridge, MA: MIT Press.

Smith, K. J. (1992). *Finite mathematics* (3rd ed.). Pacific Grove, CA: Brooks/Cole.

Smith, M. (1969). The schools and prejudice: findings. In C. Glock and E. Siegelman, Eds., *Prejudice USA* (pp. 112–135). New York: Praeger.

Smith, M. L., & Glass, G. V. (1977). Meta-analysis of psychotherapy outcome studies. *American Psychologist, 32,* 752–760.

Smith, R. W., & Garner, B. (1976, June). *Are there really any gay male athletes?* Paper presented at the Society for the Scientific Study of Sex Convention, San Diego, California.

Snedecor, G., & Cochran, W. (1989). *Statistical Methods* (8th ed.). Ames: Iowa State University Press.

Social Science Research Council (1946). *Theory and practice in historical study: A report of the committee on historiography.* New York: Author.

Solomon, R. (1949). An extension of control group design. *Psychological Bulletin, 46*, 137–150.

Somers, M. J. (1996). Modeling employees withdrawal behavior over time: A study of turnover using survival analysis. *Journal of Occupational and Organizational Psychology, 69*, 315–326.

Sorenson, A., Husek, T., & Yu, C. (1963). Divergent concepts of teacher role: An approach to the measurement of teacher effectiveness, *Journal of Educational Psychology, 54*, 287–294.

Spearman, C. (1904). General intelligence, objectively determined and measured. *American Journal of Psychology, 15*, 201–293.

Spilich, G. J., June, L., & Remer, J. (1992). Cigarette smoking and cognitive performance. *British Journal of Addiction, 87*, 1313–1326.

Stanley, R. O., Hyman, G. J., & Sharp, C. S. (1983). Levenson's Locus of Control Scale: An alternative scaling format. *Psychological Reports, 52*, 824–826.

Steele, C. M., Spencer, S. J., & Lynch, M. (1993). Self-image resilience and dissonance: The role of affirmational resources. *Journal of Personality and Social Psychology, 64*, 885–896.

Stein, J. A., Newcomb, M. D., & Bentler, P. M. (1996). Initiation and maintenance of tobacco smoking: Changing personality correlates in adolescence and young adulthood. *Journal of Applied Social Psychology, 26*, 160–187.

Stevens, S. S. (1951). Mathematics, measurement, and psychophysics. In S. S. Stevens (Ed.), *Handbook of experimental psychology*. New York: John Wiley & Sons, 1–49.

—— (1968). Measurement, statistics, and the schemapiric view. *Science, 161*, 849–856.

Stile, S. W., Kitano, M., Kelley, P., & Lecrone, J. (1993). Early intervention with gifted children: A national survey. *Journal of Early Intervention, 17*, 30–35.

Stilson, D. W. (1966). *Probability and statistics in psychological research and theory*. San Francisco: Holden-Day.

Stone-Romero, E. F., Weaver, A. E., and Glenar, J. L. (1995). Trends in research design and data analytic strategies in organizational research. *Journal of Management, 21*, 141–157.

—— (1955). *Communism, conformity, and civil liberties*. New York: Doubleday.

Stoneberg, C., Pitcock, N., & Myton, C. (1986). Pressure sores in the homebound: One solution, alternating pressure pads. *American Journal of Nursing, 86*, 426–428.

Stouffer, S. (1950). Some observations on study design. *American Journal of Sociology, 55*, 355–361.

—— (1955). *Communism, conformity, and civil liberties*. Garden City, NY: Doubleday.

Strack, F., Martin, L. L. & Stepper, S. (1998). Inhibiting and facilitating conditions of the human smile" A nonobtrusive test of facial feedback hypothesis. *Journal of Personality and Social Psychology, 54*, 768–777.

Strom, B., Hocevar, D., & Zimmer, J. (1990). Satisfaction and achievement antagonists in ATI research on student-oriented instruction. *Educational Research Quarterly, 14(4)*, 15–21.

Stroop, J. R. (1935). Studies of interference in serial verbal reactions. *Journal of Experimental Psychology, 18*, 643–662.

Strube, M. J. (1991). Small sample failure of random assignment: A further examination. *Journal of Consulting and Clinical Psychology, 59*, 346–350.

Strutton, D., Pelton, L. E., & Lumpkin, J.

R. (1995). Sex differences in ingratiatory behavior: An investigation of influence tactics in the salesperson-customer dyad. *Journal of Business Research, 34,* 35–45.

Stuart, D. L., Gresham, F. M., & Elliot, S. N. (1991). Teacher rating of social skills in popular and rejected males and females. *School Psychology Quarterly, 6,* 16–26.

Sudman, S., Bradburn, N. M., & Schwarz, N. (1996). *Thinking about answers: The application of cognitive processes to survey methodology.* San Francisco, CA: Jossey-Bass.

Suedfeld, P., & Rank, A. (1976). Revolutionary leaders: Long-term success as a function of changes in conceptual complexity. *Journal of Personality and Social Psychology, 34,* 169–178.

Sue, S., Fujino, D. C., Hu, L., Takeuchi, D. T., & Zane, N. W. S. (1991). Community mental health services for ethnic minority groups: A test of the cultural responsiveness hypothesis. *Journal of Consulting and Clinical Psychology, 59,* 533–540.

Suen, H. K. (1990). *Principles of test theories.* Hillsdale, NJ: Lawrence Erlbaum.

Suits, D. (1967). Use of dummy variables in regression equations. *Journal of the American Statistical Association, 52,* 548–551.

Survey Research Center. (1976). *Interviewer's manual* (rev. ed.). Ann Arbor, MI: Institute for Social Research, University of Michigan.

Suskie, L. (1996). *Questionnaire survey research: What works.* Tallahassee, FL: Association for Instructional Research.

Sussman, S., Burton, D., Dent, C. W., Stacy, A. W., & Flay, B. R. (1991). Use of focus groups in developing an adolescent tobacco use cessation program. Collective norm effects. *Journal of Applied Social Psychology, 21,* 1772–1782.

Swanson, E. A., Maas, M. L., & Buckwalter, K. C. (1994). Alzheimer's residents' cognitive and functional measures: Special and traditional care unit comparison. *Clinical Nursing Research, 3,* 27–41.

Tabachnick, B.G., & Fidell, L. S, (1996). *Using multivariate statistics* (3rd ed.). New York: Harper & Row.

Talaga, J. A., & Beehr, T. A. (1995). Are there gender differences in predicting retirement decisions? *Journal of Applied Psychology, 80,* 16–28.

Taleporos, E. (1977). Motivational patterns in attitudes towards the women's liberation movement. *Journal of Personality, 45,* 484–500.

Tang, J. (1993). Whites, Asians and blacks in science and engineering: Reconsideration of their economic prospects. *Research in Social Stratification and Mobility, 12,* 289–291.

Taris, T. W. (1997). Reckless driving behaviour of youth: Does locus of control influence perceptions of situational characteristics and driving behavior? *Personality and Individual Differences, 23,* 987–995.

Tate, M. (1955). *Statistics in education.* New York: Macmillan.

Tatsuoka, M. (1987). *Multivariate analysis: Techniques for educational and psychological research* (2nd ed.). Paramus, NJ: Prentice-Hall.

Taulbee, C. S. (1983). *A comprehensive annotated bibliography of selected psychological tests.* Troy, NY: Waitson

Taylor, H.C., & Russell, J.T. (1939) The relationship of validity coefficients to the practical effectiveness of tests in selection. Discussion and tables. *Journal of Applied Psychology, 23,* 565–578.

Taylor, S. J., & Bogdan, R. (1998). *Introduction to qualitative research methods: A guidebook and resource* (3rd ed.) New York: John Wiley & Sons.

Tetenbaum, T. (1975). The role of student needs and teacher orientations in student ratings of teachers. *American Educational Research Journal. 12,* 417–433.

Thomas, J. G., Owen, D. B., & Gunst, R. F. (1977). Improving the use of educational tests as selection tools. *Journal of Educational Statistics, 2,* 55–77.

Thompson, S. (1980). Do individualized mastery and traditional instructional systems yield different course effects in college calculus? *American Educational Research Journal, 17,* 361–375.

Personality and Social Psychology, 53–1), 5–13.

Weick, K. E. (1968). Systematic observational methods. In G. Lindzey & E. Aronson, Eds. *The handbook of social psychology, Volume 2* (2nd ed.) (pp. 357–451). Reading, MA: Addison-Wesley

Weisberg, H. (1996). *An introduction to survey research, polling and data analysis* (3rd ed.). Thousand Oaks, CA: Sage.

Wells, W. D. (1974). Group interviewing. In R. Ferber, Ed., *Handbook of marketing research.* New York: McGraw-Hill, Section 2, Part B, Chapter 7, 2–133 to 2–146.

Wheeler, M. (1976). *Lies, damn lies, and statistics: The manipulation of public opinion in America.* New York: Dell.

Whitehead, A. N. (1992). *An introduction to mathematics.* New York: Oxford University Press. (Original work published 1911)

Wickens, T. D. (1989). *Multiway contingency table analysis for the social sciences.* Hillsdale, NJ: Erlbaum.

Williams, B. (1978). *A sampler on sampling.* New York: Wiley.

Wilson, A. B., Jensen, A. R., & Elliot, D. L. (1966). Education of disadvantaged children in California: A report to the California state committee on public education. State Department of Education, Sacramento, California.

Wilson, F. L. (1996). Patient education materials nurses use in community health. *Western Journal of Nursing Research, 18,* 195–205.

Wilson, G. D., & Reading, A. E. (1989). Pelvic shape, gender role conformity and sexual satisfaction. *Personality and Individual Differences, 10,* 577–579.

Winograd, E., & Soloway, R. (1986). On forgetting the locations of things stored in special places. *Journal of Experimental Psychology: General, 115,* 366–372.

Winter, D., & McClelland, D. (1978). Thematic analysis: An empirically derived measure of the effects of liberal arts education. *Journal of Educational Psychology, 70,* 8–16.

Wogalter, M. S., & Young, S. L. (1991). Behavioural compliance to voice and print warnings. *Ergonomics, 34,* 79–89.

Wolfe, M. (1992). *Where we stand: Can America make it in the global race for wealth, health and happiness?* New York: Bantam.

Wood, R. W. (1973). N rays. In R. L. Weber's (Ed.), *A random walk in science: An anthology.* London: Institute of Physics.

Wood, R. Y. (1994). Reliability and validity of a breast self-examination proficiency rating instrument. *Evaluation and the Health Professions, 4,* 418–435.

Woodrow, H. (1938). The relation between abilities and improvement with practice. *Journal of Educational Psychology, 29,* 215–230.

Woodward, J. A., Bonett, D. G., & Brecht, M-L. (1990). *Introduction to linear models and experimental design.* San Diego, CA: Harcourt Brace Jovanovich.

Wright, B. D., & Stone, M. H. (1979). *Best test designs.* Chicago, IL: Mess Press.

Wright, H. F. (1960). Observational child study. In P. Mussen, Ed., *Handbook of research methods in child development* (pp. 71–139). New York: John Wiley & Sons.

Wright, R. (1975). The affective and cognitive consequences of an open education elementary school. *American Educational Research Journal, 12,* 449–465.

Wright, S. (1921). Correlation and causation. *Journal of Agricultural Research, 20,* 557–585.

Wright, S. (1921). Correlation and causation. *Journal of Agricultural Research, 20,* 557–583.

Zajonc, R. (1980). Feeling and thinking: Preferences need no inferences. *American Psychologist, 35,* 151–175.

Zakay, D., Hayduk, L. A., & Tsal, Y. (1992). Personal space and distance misperception: Implications of a novel observation. *Bulletin of the Psychonomic Society, 30,* 33–35.

Zavala, A. (1965). Development of the forced-choice rating scale technique. *Psychological Bulletin, 63,* 117–124.

Zavala, K. J., Barnett, J. E., Smedi, K. J., Istvan, J. A., & Matarazzo, J. D. (1990). Concurrent use of cigarettes, alcohol and coffee. *Journal of Applied Social Psychology, 20,* 825–845.

Zegers, F. E. (1991). Coefficients for inter-rater agreement. *Applied Psychological Measurement, 15,* 321–333.

Zenderland, L. (1997). The bell-curve and the shape of history. *Journal of the History of the Behavioral Sciences, 35,* 135–139.

Zeren, A. S., & Makosky, V. P. (1986). Teaching observational methods: Time sampling, event sampling, and trait rating techniques. *Teaching of Psychology, 13,* 80–82.

Zimmerman, D. W. (1995a). Increasing the power of the ANOVA F-test for outlier prone distributions by modified ranking methods. *Journal of General Psychology, 122,* 83–94.

Zimmerman, D. W. (1995b). Increasing the power of nonparametric tests by detecting and downweighting outliers. *Journal of Experimental Education, 64,* 71–78.

Zimmerman, D. W., & Zumbo, B. D. (1992). Parametric alternatives to the student *t*-test under violation of normality and homogeneity of variance. *Perceptual & Motor Skills, 74,* 835–844.

Zimmerman, D. W., & Zumbo, B. D. (1993a). Relative power of the Wilcoxon test, the Friedman test, and repeated measures ANOVA on ranks. *Journal of Experimental Education, 62,* 75–86.

Zimmerman, D. W., & Zumbo, B. D. (1993b). The relative power of parametric and nonparametric statistical methods. In G. Keren & C. Lewis (Eds.), *A handbook for data analysis in the behavioral sciences: Methodological issues* (pp. 481–517). Hillsdale, NJ: Lawrence Erlbaum.

Zwick, R. (1988). Another look at interrater agreement. *Psychological Bulletin, 103,* 374–378.

—— (1993). Pairwise comparison procedures for one-way analysis of variance designs. In G. Keren & C. Lewis (Eds.), *A handbook for data analysis in the behavioral sciences.* Hillsdale, NJ: Lawrence Erlbaum.

NAME INDEX

SUBJECT INDEX